Sites and Pots: Settlement and Economy in Southern Tuscany (AD 300-900)

Emanuele Vaccaro

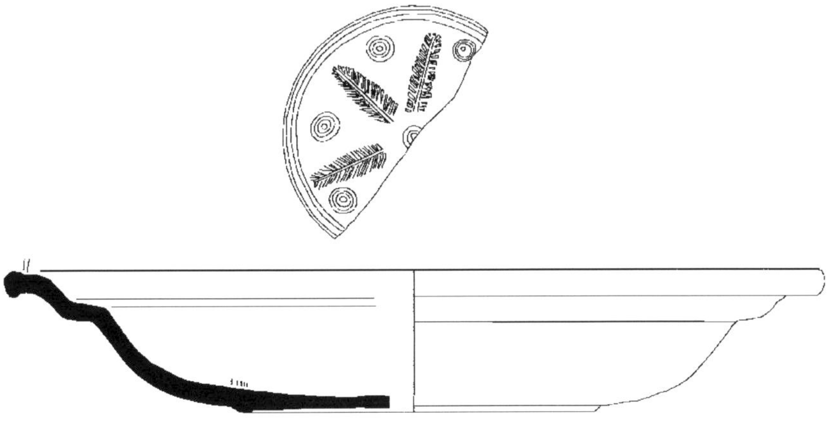

BAR International Series 2191
2011

Published by

Archaeopress
Publishers of British Archaeological Reports
Gordon House
276 Banbury Road
Oxford OX2 7ED
England
bar@archaeopress.com
www.archaeopress.com

BAR S2191

Sites and Pots: Settlement and Economy in Southern Tuscany (AD 300-900)

ISBN 978 1 4073 0746 6

Printed in England by 4edge Ltd, Hockley

All BAR titles are available from:

Hadrian Books Ltd
122 Banbury Road
Oxford
OX2 7BP
England
www.hadrianbooks.co.uk

The current BAR catalogue with details of all titles in print, prices and means of payment is available free from Hadrian Books or may be downloaded from www.archaeopress.com

This book is dedicated to Mareda and Rino, my marvellous parents

Preface and Acknowledgements

This book is based on my doctoral thesis in Medieval Archaeology, examined at the University of Siena in July 2007. The book is organized along similar lines to the original dissertation although both contents and structure have been significantly revised, expanded and sometimes modified in light of my subsequent research experience at the McDonald Institute for Archaeological Research and the Faculty of Classics at Cambridge University from late September 2009, where I currently hold a Marie Curie intra-European Fellowship funded by the European Union.[1] My research experience at Cambridge has given me a vital opportunity to review the data presented in my doctoral thesis thanks to the new and fruitful stimuli deriving from my collaboration with world class scholars and the opportunity to spend a crucial part of my research career in an academic environment where debate is both lively and constructively stimulating. During the composition of this volume I made some significant alterations to my doctoral thesis, removing some materials and adding others. However, time restrictions led me to consider November 2009 as the cut-off point for new bibliography (the text was completed in March 2010, six months after I took up my post-doctoral position at Cambridge). As such, this volume will not take into consideration the new data from the excavations conducted by the Soprintendenza per i Beni Archeologici della Toscana at the Roman and late antique site of Scoglietto (in the lower Ombrone valley). The same is true of the data from the 2009-2010 excavations in the Cinigiano area, immediately inland of the study area under consideration here, led by the Universities of Philadelphia, Cambridge and Siena and co-directed by the author, even though these are of fundamental importance for the study of the late antique economy and of settlement patterns. The available data will be comprehensively reviewed, with a comparison of Roman and late antique settlement systems in inland and coastal areas of southern Tuscany, in a forthcoming paper. Another methodological issue is the absolute dates for the record of African Red Slip ware and Tunisian amphorae documented in the territorial context discussed here. These dates are drawn mainly from Hayes 1972, Atlante I, Mackensen 1993, Mackensen 1998 and Tortorella 1998 and Keay 1984 (see bibliography). The new and influential study of Tunisian pottery in late Antiquity (including finewares, amphorae, coarsewares and other classes of ceramic materials) carried out by Michel Bonifay was published in 2004 and only became available in libraries at a later stage in 2005 when I had already catalogued the majority of the ARS and Tunisian amphorae. For reasons of consistency I have preferred the new Bonifay chronologies in cases where these differ significantly from others and particularly in the analysis of specific sites, such as the possible 4th-century AD shipwreck at Cala del Barbiere (Chapter 7). By contrast, these new dates were not used, again for reasons of consistency, in the analysis of the trends for ARS in rural areas and at those sites which were analysed separately. I intend to publish a new analysis of the all these data in light of the new chronologies in the near future, comparing and examining the results to determine if and how they differ and any economic implications of these differences.

[1] The research providing these results was funded by the [European Community's] Seventh Framework Programme [FP7/2007-2013] under *grant agreement* n°236093.

This book is divided in 10 chapters presenting and discussing the data on settlement patterns and ceramic production, trade and consumption in the Tuscan Maremma during the period AD 300-900. Chapter 1 introduces the research project and how it originated, defining the context and methodological approaches. I also present the state of the art before 2000, when I first started working in this area, and how the data gathered during previous field research was integrated and compared with that collected in 2000-2008, using a wider range of methodologies including field walking survey, excavation and a diachronic study of ceramics. Chapters 2 and 3 are devoted to a discussion of the transformation undergone by the settlement network between the 4th and 7th centuries AD; to provide the reader with a broader chronological overview I also provide a brief discussion of settlement patterns in the late Republican and early imperial periods, already presented in greater depth in a recent paper. [2] Chapters 4-7 focus on the analysis, at different levels, of the system of ceramic production and trade in late Antiquity. In Chapter 4 I analyse the evidence from some crucial ceramic assemblages covering the period AD 300-600 from the North Hill of the ancient town of Roselle. Chapter 5 focuses on the circulation of Mediterranean, interregional and regional ceramics in the study area from the 4th to the early 7th century AD. Special attention was paid to three settlements (the cave sites of Scoglietto and Spaccasasso and the villa of Paduline-Serrata Martini) as they exemplify the range of "pottery-connections" that the area continued to engage from the mid-5th to the very beginning of the 7th century AD. Chapter 6 discusses the data from the systematic analysis of underwater finds from the sea-port of *Portus Scabris* (modern Portiglioni) which sheds light on the system of trade during the period AD 400-700 and extending into the Middle Ages. Chapter 7 partly follows on from the previous chapter, investigating underwater finds and a possible 4th-century AD shipwreck at Cala del Barbiere near Punta Ala, just a few kilometres south of Portiglioni along the coast. Chapters 6 and 7 shed light on the system of ceramic exchange and redistribution using maritime *cabotage* routes and overland connections. Chapter 8 tackles the reconstruction of the 8th- and 9th-century AD settlement network, and re-assesses the importance of both nucleated and semi-centralized sites in the plains which have gone largely unidentified in southern Tuscany. Chapter 9 analyses the transformation of ceramic production and circulation between the late Lombard and Carolingian periods and the emergence of a localized but still dynamic system of trade. Finally, Chapter 10, the conclusion, attempts to place the late antique and early medieval settlement and economic patterns of southern Tuscany in a broader Mediterranean context.

I would like to thank the many people who, in different ways, have helped to develop and improve this research and to mature the ideas later transferred into this book. First, I should thank Riccardo Francovich, my late Professor, who promoted and actively supported my research in southern Tuscany and was always open to frank and illuminating discussions. I am particularly grateful to Mari Ghisleni, my wonderful wife and colleague, who has been standing by me since 2004 and supporting what she sometimes describes as my excessive passion for my job. I owe a huge debt of gratitude to Kim Bowes, a true friend more than just a colleague. She has always encouraged me even in the most difficult moments and contributed through her

[2] Vaccaro 2008.

collaboration to the development of my research in Tuscany and more recently in Sicily. The same debt of gratitude is due to Richard Hodges who has enthusiastically mentored my research and offered advice since 2007. In Cambridge I found a truly stimulating and gratifying academic environment. I am greatly indebted to Graeme Barker and Martin Millett for their enlightening insights and advice, and for inspiring my revision and re-visitation of this work thanks to our frequent meetings and discussions. At Cambridge University I would also like to thank James Barrett, Sara Harrop and Simon Stoddart for their support. I should not forget to acknowledge my debt to many people from the University of Siena. I am thankful to Stefano Campana for our long-standing collaboration and the methodological and technological experience I gained as a member of the Laboratory of Landscape Archaeology & Remote Sensing (LAP&T) from its inception. I am also grateful to Antonia Arnoldus Huyzendveld, Giovanna Bianchi, Federico Cantini, Carlo Citter, Roberto Farinelli, Giancarlo Macchi and Marco Valenti, who contributed, through a frank and positive exchange of opinions, to the development and improvement of my research. I thank Franco Cambi, Lucia Saguì and Giulio Volpe for their insights on the study of settlement patterns and ceramics. I owe a debt of gratitude to Chris Wickham, whose influential work on the late antique and early medieval Mediterranean has been a reference point for my research, and for encouraging the publication of this book. Nor can I forget the importance of my lively debates with Lisa Fentress, Maria Grazia Celuzza and Michelle Hobart, whose remarkable work in the *Ager Cosanus* represented a crucial point of comparison for my research. I am also grateful to Paul Reynolds for our collaboration in Butrint (Albania), which helped further my knowledge of Roman and late antique ceramics and to Michel Bonifay for his helpful comments on the underwater finds from *Portus Scabris* and Cala del Barbiere. Many people from the Soprintendenza per i Beni Archeologici della Toscana promoted and supported my research. Among them I am indebted to Biancamaria Aranguren, Mario Çygielman and Pamela Gambogi. A particular thanks to Erika Milburn, translator of this book, for her paintstaking and invaluable collaboration. Last, but not least, I will always be deeply grateful to the Italian and foreign students who have worked with me on field and lab research in southern Tuscany, without whose immense contribution this book would not exist.

Emanuele Vaccaro
December 2010
Cambridge

Contents

1. Definition, Methodologies and Objectives of the Archaeological Research in the Alma, Bruna, Ombrone and Osa Valleys (Province of Grosseto)

1.1 The "Birth" of a Research Project

The research presented in this volume derives from the combination of two different projects. The first was undertaken on commission by the Department of Archaeology and the History of Art of the University of Siena whilst the second was run directly by the Faculty of Medieval Archaeology of the same university. In the summer of 2003, SPEA Autostrade a company operating in the motorway infrastructure development sector engaged a team of researchers from the University of Siena[1] and the Archaeological cooperative ASTRA to evaluate the archaeological impact of a project to build the so-called "braccio tirrenico" between Rosignano Marittimo (province of Livorno) and Civitavecchia (province of Viterbo), intended to complete the A12 motorway along Italy's Tyrrhenian coast.

The team of archaeologists from Siena was given the task of studying the proposed routes between Pescia Romana and Rosignano, whilst those from the ASTRA cooperative undertook a similar study in Lazio. The long stretch between the Tuscany-Lazio border and Rosignano Marittimo was subdivided into different segments, each of which was then assigned to a single team.[2] One of the areas at greatest archaeological risk from the construction of this new motorway was the stretch between Talamone and Grosseto where very little archaeological research had previously been undertaken.[3] Essentially, whilst in other areas the systematic surface surveys organized by the University of Siena during over twenty years have led to the acquisition of a substantial archaeological record, allowing us to make a preliminary estimate of the potential risk, this was impossible for the aforementioned stretch.

The systematic surveys along SPEA's three proposed routes between Talamone and Grosseto were entrusted to the author as they represented a perfect complement to another project begun in the spring of 2003: the "Valutazione e Valorizzazione del Potenziale Archeologico del Parco Regionale della Maremma" (Evaluation and Enhancement of the Archaeological Potential of the Maremma Regional Park).[4] Two of the three proposed routes ran through the park area. Route no. 3 crossed the entire park lengthwise from Fattoria Fontenuova at Talamone to the Ombrone river. Route no. 2 followed route no. 1 along the upper Osa valley before descending towards Cupi and following route no. 3 (Figures 1 and 2).

It was immediately apparent that the need to understand and safeguard the archaeological heritage of this area was closely linked to the need to preserve the Park's natural landscape. Equally, while we had little previous knowledge of the archaeological potential of the lowlying belt between Grosseto and Talamone, between the Monti dell'Uccellina to the west and the proposed Park area to the east, the outlook for the area further inland between the upper Osa valley and the Rispescia stream, crossed by SPEA's proposed route no. 1, was even bleaker. This made it necessary to undertake further research in the field, both in the coastal belt and in subcoastal areas in order to improve the archaeological record and fill this gap in our knowledge. The possibility of systematically investigating areas not covered by earlier topographical surveys but potentially extremely rich in archaeology thanks to their proximity to the coast and the extremely varied natural landscape with an abundance of water resources[5], represented an extraordinary research opportunity. We were able to develop a research strategy *ex novo*, thus ensuring that the data acquired would be uniform.

Our research between the catchment basins of the Ombrone river to the north and the Osa river to the south also represented a natural extension towards the south of the archaeological studies conducted on several occasions in the plain of the ancient Lake Prile. Up to the late Middle Ages, this large brackish coastal lagoon was not only a fundamental economic resource but also the major landscape feature in the Maremma.

C. B. Curri's unsystematic studies, undertaken during the 1970s[6] in the area between Castiglione della Pescaia and Vetulonia along the north-west bank of Lake Prile, were followed in the second half of the 1980s by sample surface surveys in the *Ager Rusellanus* organized by the Faculty of Medieval

[1] The project was directed by Riccardo Francovich and Franco Cambi. Those in charge of the various studies (field surveys, analysis and processing of remote sensing data, research on existing bibliography, archive research) were: Maria Aprosio, Lucia Botarelli, Stefano Campana, Anna Caprasecca, Carlo Casi, Marcello Cosci, Marco Firmati and the author.

[2] The surface surveys were undertaken with the precious assistance of students and graduates from the University of Siena and other Italian universities whom I wish to thank.

[3] The sampling undertaken during the *Ager Cosanus*-Valle dell'Albegna Project covered the Gulf of Talamone but no systematic surveys were done in the areas to the north of the gulf. (Carandini-Cambi 2002, pp.44-45); the surface surveys in the *Ager Rusellanus* only partially covered areas south of the Ombrone with some fieldwalking undertaken in the Poggio Cavolo area (Citter 1988-1989).

[4] The project organized by the Faculty of Medieval Archaeology of the University of Siena, with Riccardo Francovich as the scientific director and the author, Stefano Campana and Carlo Citter as coordinators, took place between September 2003 and September 2005.

[5] The area lies between the catchment basins of the Ombrone to the north and the Osa to the south; the area between the two rivers is home to a network of smaller watercourses. There are also numerous natural springs in this area (see the *Carta Geologica d'Italia*, Sheet 128: Grosseto and Sheet 135: Orbetello, with the descriptive notes published in Motta 1969 and Signorini 1967 respectively).

[6] Curri 1978.

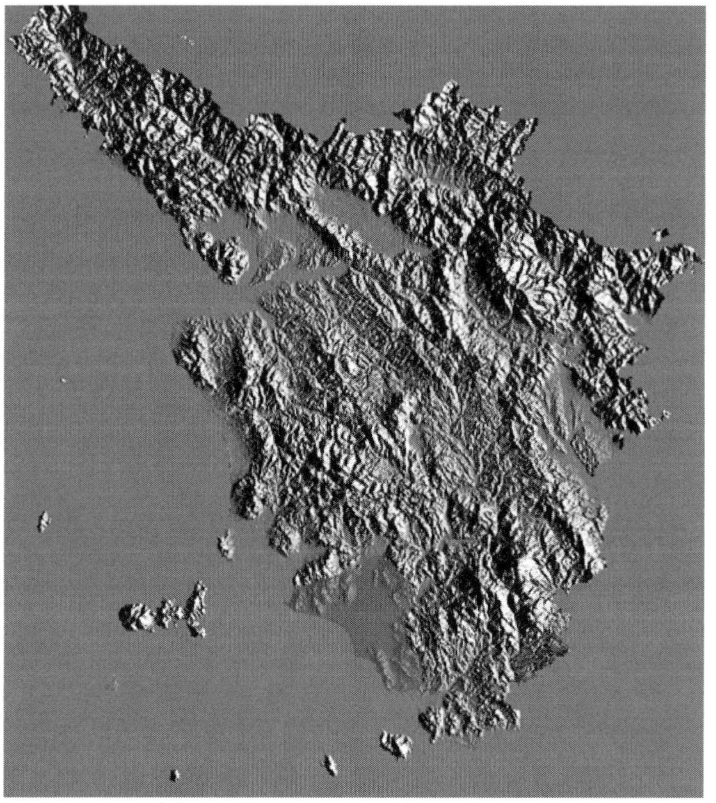

Fig.1_ Overview of the study area in southern Tuscany (light grey colour).

Archaeology of the University of Siena.[7] This research, conducted systematically using selected samples, was given a new impulse between 2000 and 2002 with a project aimed at analysing the formation process of the medieval landscape in the municipal territory of Castiglione della Pescaia.[8]

In light of this, it seemed appropriate to combine both new and earlier studies in a wide-ranging and ambitious programme of systematic research on settlement patterns and economic dynamics during the long period between the 4th and 11th centuries AD. Naturally, the surface surveys undertaken between 2003 and 2005 between the lower Ombrone river and the Osa river entailed the investigation and documentation of all the archaeological features identified, from the prehistoric period to the late Middle Ages, in order to respond effectively to the need to safeguard and enhance this heritage. During the analytical phase, however, we concentrated on those sites falling within the chronological range covered by this research project.

1.2 Historiographical Goals

The idea of undertaking an archaeological project of such vast scope responds to the need to gain a preliminary overview of an area, that of Grosseto, which has for many years been the focus of the research interests of the Faculty of Medieval Archaeology at the University of Siena.[9]

The main aim was to analyse settlement patterns over the long term. We chose to concentrate on the chronological horizon from the 4th to the 9th century AD, between the Constantinian and Carolingian periods, in an attempt to understand and analyse the transformations undergone by the late antique landscape and the formation of the early medieval landscape which led to the creation of a settlement network based around fortified villages between the 10th and 11th centuries. Although priority was given to this period, special attention was also devoted to the analysis of population patterns and economic structures from the late Republic onwards in order to identify any elements of continuity and discontinuity between the Roman period and late Antiquity. We think that the transformations taking place between the 4th and 7th centuries can only be fully understood by comprehensively studying settlement trends in the immediately preceding period. Above all, it was essential to determine the extent to which the "villa

[7] Research conducted by C. Citter for his undergraduate thesis. For a preliminary overview see Citter 1996b.

[8] Research conducted by the author for his undergraduate thesis in Medieval Archaeology examined in the academic year 2001-2002.

[9] To cite only the most important archaeological studies conducted within the chosen study area we should mention, alongside the surface surveys already listed: the excavation of the Cassero Senese fortress belonging to the Grosseto city walls (Francovich-Gelichi 1980), the urban archaeology campaign in the historic centre of Grosseto conducted between 1998 and 2005 (Francovich *et alii* 2000; Citter 2005 (ed.); Citter 2007c) and the topographical surveys in the Scarlino area which also covered that portion of the Alma valley in the municipal territory of Castiglione della Pescaia (Cucini 1989a; Cucini 1985).

schiavistica" model, well-documented further south in the *Ager Cosanus,*[10] had become established in this area and the space available for settlement types such as villages or isolated farmsteads in a villa-dominated landscape. This is important not only for the definition of settlement patterns but also of economic systems, in order to measure the resistance of small and medium-sized properties to the large *fundi* belonging to the villas.

In light of the data emerging from a comparison between the *Ager Cosanus*[11] (province of Grosseto) and the Volterra area[12] (provinces of Livorno and Pisa) it seems clear that the greater or lesser impact and the more or less radical nature of Romanization had a long-term effect on population patterns, to the extent that these factors heavily influenced the evolution of settlement networks in late Antiquity. In order to obtain a more uniform reading of these processes it was thus necessary to study the Roman period in depth, identifying the types of sites attested and the relations between them.

The choice of this area also raised the issue of the relations between the countryside and cities old and new. During the Middle Ages, Roselle gradually lost its central role and population to Grosseto, which became a true city in 1138 when the bishop's seat was moved here and the settlement was awarded the designation *civitas.*[13]

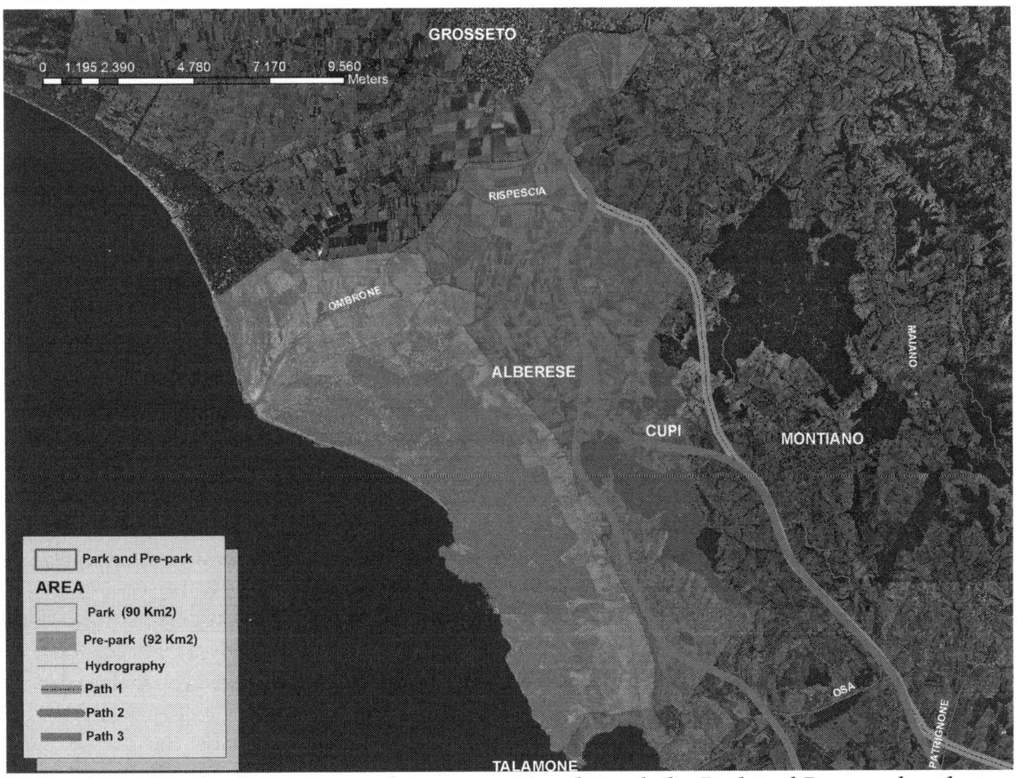

Fig.2_ Mapowing the three proposed routes running through the Park and Proposed park areas.

In fact, from late Antiquity onwards the area between the Alma and Osa rivers was shared between the two dioceses of Roselle-Grosseto and Sovana, whose borders are still disputed. According to the *Rationes Decimarum* of 1276 the border followed the course of the Ombrone river fairly closely[14]; however, during the Carolingian period it seems likely that the diocese of Roselle also comprised areas further south, reaching as far as Alberese.[15] This problem is of limited relevance to our study since only the large area beween the Alma valley and the catchment basin of the Ombrone river can have been in direct contact with the bishop's seat

[10] Regoli 2002a; Carandini 1989.

[11] The Roman conquest in this area must have been radical and brutal, with obvious consequences for social and settlement structures. During an initial phase it seems that the native Etruscans were forced to move to more marginal and outlying areas, leaving the best areas to the new colonists. Only later were the conditions for an integration between victors and the vanquished created. The significant development of the "villa schiavistica" in the *Ager Cosanus* seems to have led to an evident decrease in small and medium-sized peasant landholdings. See Celuzza 2002c, pp.103-113; Regoli 2002a, pp.145-154.

[12] In the Volterra area Romanization was a relatively slow and untraumatic process which did not lead to an upheaval in existing settlement patterns or the social marginalization of the Etruscan aristocracy. The "villa schiavistica" does not seem to have taken hold whilst the organization of farm work seems to have been based on the labour of the free local population. Medium and small landholdings were only partially affected by the multiplication of villas between the 2nd and 1st centuries BC, as clearly indicated by the farmstead at Podere San Mario, characterized by a continuity of life during the long period between the 4th century BC and the 6th century AD. See Terrenato 1998; Motta 1997; Motta *et alii* 1993.

[13] The bull of Pope Innocent III of April 1138 is published in Ughelli 1717-1722, X, coll.268-269.

[14] Guidi 1932.

[15] Citter 2006b.

(first Roselle and later Grosseto). The more southerly portions of our study area, between the Ombrone to the north and the catchment basin of the Osa to the south, were very marginal and decentralized with respect to the city of Sovana; this must have limited the extent to which the city influenced the surrounding areas. By contrast, Vetulonia, the area's other ancient city, lost its urban character early on; it was in a phase of stagnation already between the late Republic and early Empire when production and economic interests, and thus settlement solutions, turned towards the west bank of Lake Prile, leading to the gradual depopulation of the countryside around the city.[16]

We therefore decided to contextualize the long-term settlement dynamics in that part of the study area between the Alma and Ombrone valleys, taking into consideration the potential relations first with the city of Roselle and later with Grosseto. The possibility of studying the late antique ceramic contexts from the excavations conducted on the North Hill at Roselle represented an excellent opportunity to make a close comparison between material culture in the city and that of contemporary rural sites, thus ensuring that we understood the role played by the city in redistributing imported goods.

In a long-term perspective, it was essential to study the extent to which this coastal area was integrated into maritime trade circuits between the early imperial period and late Antiquity. The aim was to determine how far the area relied on other regions for its supply of foodstuffs or, alternatively, how far it had developed an agricultural production able to respond effectively to local demand.

It is fairly obvious that coastal areas have easier access to products imported from overseas but it is important to understand if all settlements had access to Mediterranean goods, regardless of their status, or if there was a hierarchy in the redistribution process which only touched upon privileged rural contexts, the residence of the rural elites, and cities. Additionally, a long-term analysis of transport amphorae may provide arguments *ex silentio* on the basis of which to formulate hypotheses on the area's productive specializations, applying the principle according to which imported goods were not easily available *in loco* or were so valuable as to trigger long-distance trade mechanisms.

The picture emerging from the study of the pottery materials yielded by the excavations on the North Hill in the city of Roselle and that provided by finds from surface surveys was completed by the systematic analysis of the pottery attested at three excavation contexts in direct contact with the sea: the Scoglietto cave inhabited in late Antiquity, the 6th/7th-century rubbish dump in a room of the imperial villa of Paduline at Castiglione della Pescaia and above all the underwater deposit at *Portus Scabris*. The study of the latter site, although it lies about 5.5 km north of the northern "boundary" of our study area, represented a unique opportunity to interpret the relations between the Maremman coastal belt and Mediterranean trade circuits. The harbour at Portiglioni, still in use in the late Middle Ages[17], also allowed us to investigate trends in the flow of goods which can be documented through archaeology (amphorae, fineware and coarseware) between late Antiquity and the Middle Ages.

Another cornerstone of this research was the definition of the degree of complexity of early medieval settlement typologies in an attempt to understand if the establishment of villages on hilltops[18] which, according to stratigraphic excavations in the provinces of Siena and Grosseto appear to be a key feature of rural population patterns, coexisted with other forms of settlement or not.

On the one hand, the excavations at Scarlino castle, the context closest to our study area to have been dug extensively, have shown that the village began to form during the late 6th century and reached full maturity well before the site was fortified.[19]

On the other hand, the surface surveys in the municipal territories of Roccastrada[20] and Gavorrano[21] suggested that between the 6th and 7th centuries settlement clusters tended to develop on the slopes near the hilltops where castles were later built. This tells us that there was probably an intermediate phase in the reconquest of the hilltops. Additionally, early medieval pottery indicators have been found inside the 10th/11th-century castles.[22]

The picture emerging from the existing literature is complicated still further by the proposed reconstruction of the 7th- to 9th-century population network in the lower Albegna valley. On the basis of a combination of some archaeological features and the few documentary sources available, a settlement network has been proposed for this area characterized by a mixture of centralized village-type clusters, some established on top of villas with phases dating up to late Antiquity and others established *ex novo*, and a "relatively high density" of scattered settlements.[23]

[16] On these issues see Vaccaro 2008.

[17] Ceccarelli Lemut 2004.
[18] See especially Francovich-Hodges 2003; Valenti 2004.
[19] Francovich-Hodges 2003, pp.68-70 and 79-80; Marasco 2002-2003.
[20] Guideri 2000a, pp.11-21; Guideri 2000b, pp.18-20.
[21] Dallai-Farinelli 1998.
[22] For example at Fornoli, S.Disdagio and Litiano, in Guideri 2000a, p.19.
[23] Fentress-Wickham 2002a, pp.259-261; Fentress-Wickham 2002b, pp.60-63.

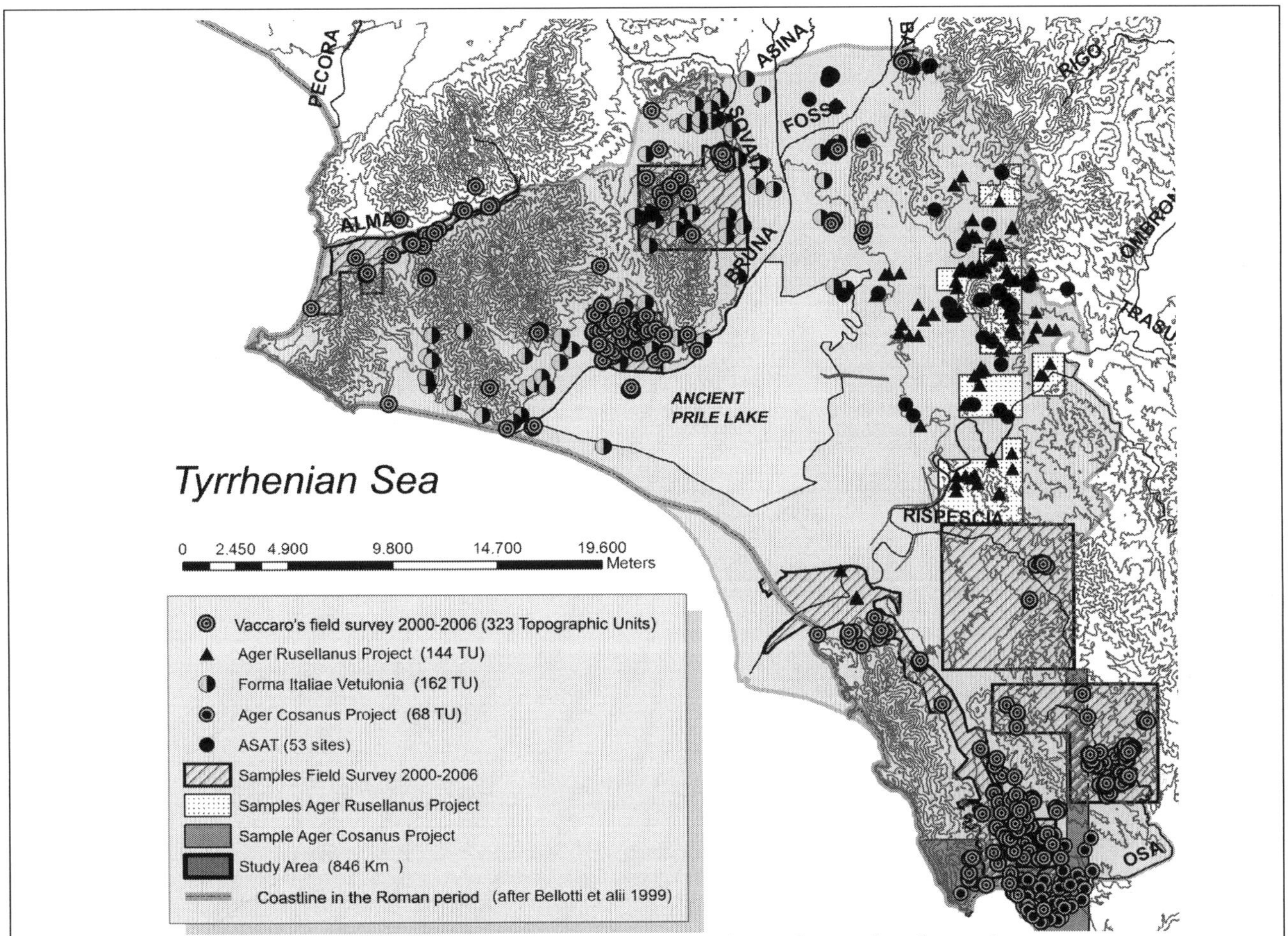

Fig.3_ Field walking surveys and the archaeological record in the study area.

Despite the large number of archaeological studies conducted in neighbouring areas, the early medieval settlement system has escaped precise definition. This made it necessary to analyse the area systematically in order to formulate a preliminary overview of rural population patterns between the 7th and 9th centuries.

Another important aspect of this project which overlaps with that described above was the accurate determination of pottery "fossil guides" for the early Middle Ages. These are fundamental both for the identification of contexts from this period and for the study of production systems and the circulation of commodities destined for mass consumption.

In much of the western Mediterranean, the High Middle Ages were characterized by a simplification and localization of production structures and trade[24]; this made it essential to study the ceramic classes produced *in loco* analytically in combination with systematic research on pottery fabrics in order to determine their range of circulation and the intensity of trade. This type of approach represents a perfect complement to research on the territorial scale since it allows us to identify any internal subdivisions and attempt a comprehensive interpretation of a complex picture. Similarly, we also attempted to define the relationship between the development of fortified sites and pre-existing early medieval settlements; in other words the frequency with which hilltop castles represented a further phase in the development and consolidation, very evident on the material level, of the long process of establishment of the local aristocracies whose presence is expressed through their control over the population resident in villages and the intensive exploitation of available resources.

1.3 The Distribution of Sample Areas and the Overall Results of the Territorial Study

1.3.1. New and Existing Sample Areas Between the Alma and Osa Valleys

The study area occupies a broad coastal and subcoastal strip in the province of Grosseto between the Alma valley to the north and the Osa valley to the south. The area runs along a stretch of coast about 60 km long, almost 28 km wide in the north along the river Bruna and gradually narrowing towards the south, where it comprises the whole Osa valley, a maximum of about 7.5 km from the coast.

The area covers a total of 846 km^2 including the entire municipal territories of Castiglione della Pescaia and Grosseto, part of the territory of Magliano in Toscana and Orbetello and a small portion of the municipalities of Roccastrada and Gavorrano (Figure 3).

[24] On this aspect see in general on Italy Wickham 2005, pp.728-741.

Within the study area the current coastline, from north to south, runs from the eastern end of the Gulf of Follonica, bounded by the mountains of Collacchie di Gavorrano on one side and Tirli on the other, with the sandbanks of Pian d'Alma area between them. At Punta Ala the cliffs turn eastwards to reach the Punta delle Rocchette di Capalbo, where the coast becomes sandy. At Castiglione della Pescaia, near the mouth of the Bruna, there is a clear gap between the beach and the coastal hills, which give way to a broad coastal plain in the Grosseto area. Here it is still possible to identify the last remains of Lake Prile in the swamp of Diaccia Botrona. The coastal sand bank forms an arc reaching the delta of the Ombrone and, beyond the river mouth, forms a series of dunes running up to the coastal range of the Monti dell'Uccellina.

This mountain range is over 13 km long and in its central and northern parts often over 300 m high, reaching 417 metres above sea level on Poggio Lecci. The hills become gradually lower towards the south and the Gulf of Talamone. Here a small, shallow bay surrounds the hill of Talamonaccio where the Osa river runs into the sea.[25] Further inland, the study area consists of a group of hills, mostly 100-200 m high and rarely reaching 300 m: Montepescali, Poggio Calvello, Roselle, Poggio Cavolo, the hills of the Regional Park and finally Poggio Civitella, overlooking the Gulf of Talamone.

This is thus an extremely complex natural landscape, comprising plains and coastal dunes, hills and inland plateaux within the space of only a few kilometres.

Since this research project aimed not only to recover and review the existing archaeological record but also to meet the new need to assess the archaeological potential of little known areas, we were forced to adopt a sampling strategy which was as uniform and extensive as possible[26], allowing us to obtain a coherent and comprehensive evaluation of long-term settlement dynamics in the context as a whole. As such, when deciding which new sample areas to survey we opted to position the transects in the various river valleys running through the study area in order to identify any affinities and/or differences between the coastal and subcoastal belt. This reasoned sampling process[27] applied to the study area necessarily had to tackle the problems of archaeological visibility[28] resulting from the presence of dense woodland which limited the accessibility of some areas, and the major transformations undergone by the natural landscape in historical times, especially between the Roman period and the Middle Ages. As concerns the former it should be noted that a significant portion of the study area, about 224 km^2, is impossible to study systematically using traditional field walking techniques due to the widespread presence of Mediterranean scrub, broad leafed trees and conifers. These types of plant cover were fairly evenly distributed within the study area, with a particularly high concentration in the northern segment and in the south-west, but were absent from the area between Roselle and Grosseto. It was more difficult to determine the true extent of those areas of land where field walking would be unable to provide useful information on the chronological period dealt with here due to changes in the natural landscape between Roman period and the Middle Ages.

[25] For an analytical description of the current coastline and in general on the processes of evolution of the Tuscan coast see Pardi 1993, especially p.14.

[26] In landscape archaeology studies, areas are sampled by choosing to investigate only some zones, considered sufficiently large and complex to be representative of the context as a whole. The results obtained from the samples are then used to reconstruct settlement dynamics in the area as a whole. To ensure that the sampling process is as detailed as possible, archaeologists attempt to subdivide the area into all its natural components (on the basis of geomorphological, pedological and hydrographic criteria) so that the sum of the samples is adequately representative of each of these. Criteria other than those relating to the natural landscape may also be applied, including historical and archaeological criteria, on the basis of information acquired prior to field work and depending on the aims of the research. Sampling therefore cannot follow fixed and universally valid rules, nor is there a single type of sampling; rather the sampling process varies depending on various factors relating both to the type of natural landscape, to visibility requirements and to the objectives of the archaeologists. See Cambi-Terenato 1994, pp.144-150; Terrenato 2000, pp.47-48.

[27] The sampling of an area using transects positioned on the basis of a clearly explained criterion is the most common practice in landscape archaeology. Since this approach is based on criteria established in advance by the archaeologists, it is possible to counterbalance and control any biases which may emerge. Reasoned sampling has been a feature of all the systematic surface surveys undertaken during major archaeological mapping projects in Tuscany. On the *Ager Cosanus*-Valle dell'Albegna Project see Cambi 1986, pp.527-544; on the *Cecina Survey* see Regoli 1992, 545-560; on the methodological criteria used to create the *Carta Archeologica della Provincia di Siena* see especially Valenti 1999; Campana 2002; Felici 2004.

[28] From the mid-1980s onwards landscape archaeology has made increasingly concerted efforts to evaluate and limit the conditioning imposed by archaeological visibility. Since then the awareness of the direct relationship between surface visibility and the potential, not only for identifying sites but also for reading and interpreting them correctly, has increased. Understanding the complex range of factors (vegetation, geopedological properties of the soils, anthropization processes affecting the countryside, agriculture, etc) which limit surface visibility makes it possible to evaluate their true impact on the sample of archaeological features identified and the extent to which they are representative of the study area as a whole. The mechanisms influencing visibility turn the study context into a sort of mosaic made up of areas which are easy to survey and others which are difficult to access or where it is impossible to evaluate the buried deposits. On these aspects see Francovich-Valenti 2001; Cambi 2000b; Terrenato-Ammermann 1996; Cambi-Terrenato 1994; Barker 1986. In this context it is worth noting the successful experiment conducted by the Faculty of Medieval Archaeology during the *Carta Archeologica della Provincia di Grosseto* Project which entailed the development of a holistic approach to the study of the landscape. This involved the use of both new and traditional technologies in order to obtain a uniform and complex analysis of the contexts, from a macro-territorial scale down to the detailed level of the individual site. Among the various research techniques used it is worth noting: surface surveys combined with mobile GIS systems loaded onto PDAs; aerial surveys; the use of satellite images; the photointerpretation of historic aerial photographs; extensive geophysics; digital photogrammetry; and, finally, the use of LiDAR. See Campana 2005, p.462.

A recent complex study has examined how the Ombrone river delta has advanced[29], with special emphasis on the long period between the 7th century BC and the 19th century AD. Examining the spatial and temporal succession of the various sandbars characterizing the delta plain made it possible to reconstruct the main stages in the evolution of the river delta.

For the purposes of this study, the most interesting fact is that the whole cone holding the last stretch of the Ombrone river is the outcome of a long-term phenomenon which accelerated rapidly from the 14th century AD onwards, due partly to human activities, such as the deforestation of the slopes, but especially to some major floods. In the 7th century BC the coastline ran roughly halfway between Vacchereccia and Scoglietto; subsequently, the progradation taking place between the Etruscan and Roman periods led to an advance of about 700 m. The 9th-century AD sandbank near Scoglietto, by contrast, was extremely close to the Roman sandbank; here, as we will see, the river port on the Ombrone which remained in use up to late Antiquity was identified. By the 13th century the coastline must have advanced further by another 700 m or so.

In light of this proposed reconstruction, we thought there was little point in surveying the river delta, covering over 20 km^2, since it formed almost exclusively in a period following that under investigation and would therefore not have contributed significantly to our research. The aforementioned geomorphological study was also fundamental in directing surface surveys towards the Scoglietto area, in the search for any surviving traces of harbour structures.

The second issue, in some ways even more complex, concerns the transformations undergone by Lake Prile, the brackish lagoon which occupied much of what is now a plain between Grosseto and Castiglione della Pescaia. Detailed and exhaustive studies of the lake, combining a geopedological approach with an analysis of the distribution of historical settlement features around its shores, are lacking. Today, all that remains of Lake Prile is a relict swamp in what was once its western end in the Diaccia Botrone area near Castiglione della Pescaia.

In light of the data currently available[30], we can say that the most recent separation of the Prile from the sea and the independent development of the inland salty lagoon, distinct from the Tyrrhenian Sea and the Ombrone river, dates to the early 1st millennium BC. In around the 7th century BC the Lake Prile basin must have been below the 5m contour line; this also marks the limit of the archaeological features of the Villanova and Etruscan periods.[31]

The lake was separated from the sea by a row of sand dunes between what was at the time the mouth of the Ombrone[32] and the Prile estuary. In the 1st century AD the area occupied by the lake must have fallen slightly due to climate changes which led to a decrease in rainfall, an increase in temperature and a slight drop in sea levels.[33] Curri and Banti proposed a reconstruction hypothesis for the hydrological situation in the 1st century AD which is confirmed by the distribution of Roman archaeological features around the probable shores of Lake Prile and by the information which can be gleaned from the historical cartography prior to the reclamation of the area under the Lorraine between the 1820s and the 1850s.[34]

Figure 3 shows the size of the brackish lagoon in the early imperial period on the basis of the information provided by Curri and Banti. The construction of a DTM using points of known height and contour lines within the area potentially occupied by Lake Prile during this period shows that it corresponds to a portion of the Grossetan plain which lies constantly beneath 4 m above sea level; much of the western area near Castiglione della Pescaia is below one metre above sea level.

This finding is in line with the theory according to which the deepest part of the lake was the north-western end, navigable throughout the Middle Ages as we know from a series of place names such as Porto a Colle and Porto alle Cavalle, which still exist in the area between Macchiascandona and Badiola.[35]

During the late Empire, a dry phase probably led the brackish lagoon to contract but this appears to have been followed immediately afterwards by a humid and rainy phase lasting until the 9th century AD, thus recreating the hydrographic conditions of the early Empire.[36] Different climate conditions emerged only after 800 AD, leading to a rise in sea levels and thus allowing coastal swamps to form along both the Tyrrhenian and Adriatic coasts.[37] Obviously it is

[29] This research project comprised field surveys, photointerpretation, historic cartography, land registry documents and an analysis of the distribution of known settlement features. For the phase between the 7th century BC and the 7th century AD we made use of earlier models, based partly on remote sensing data. See Bellotti *et alii* 1999 pp.141-147; Bellotti *et ali*i 2004, pp.71-90; on the transformations undergone by the delta between the 7th century BC and the 9th century AD see especially Bravetti-Pranzini 1993, pp.481-493 and Bravetti-Pranzini 1987, pp.85-92.

[30] Stea-Tenerini 1996; Bravetti-Pranzini 1987; Borghi 1978. See most recently Arnoldus Huyzendveld 2007.

[31] *Atlante Sedi Umane* 1970, Pl.CXXIX.

[32] See above Fig.IV for the coastline during the Etruscan period.

[33] Stea-Tenerini 1996, p.18.

[34] Curri 1978, pp.30-41; Banti 1978, pp.41-51.

[35] *Atlante Sedi Umane* 1970, Pl.CXXIX.

[36] Stea-Tenerini 1996, p.18.

[37] *Ibidem*, p.18.

difficult to reconstruct accurately the transformations undergone by the lake over the long term although the suggestion that it changed shape only slightly between the early Empire and the early Middle Ages seems acceptable.

As concerns our research, when choosing the areas to sample we took into consideration the hypothetical extension of the brackish lagoon between the Roman period and the early Middle Ages, thus excluding from our inquiries all areas which may have been underwater between the 1st and 9th centuries AD, a total of about 85 km^2.

On the basis of these premises (the size of Lake Prile, the late medieval and post-medieval development of the Ombrone delta, the presence of areas impossible to survey due to plant cover), only 517 km^2 out of a total of 846 km^2 in the study area could be studied systematically through surface surveys. Of the 329 km^2 not sampled, roughly 32% could in any case not have hosted permanent settlements in light of the formation and transformation of the natural landscape.

Preceding topographical surveys conducted during projects in the municipal territory of Castiglione della Pescaia[38] and in the area between Roselle and Grosseto had involved the distribution of transects covering much of the Alma, Bruna and Ombrone valleys, a total of about 76 km^2, of which 32.1 km^2 were intensively surveyed. It is also worth noting that we have no information on the true extent of the areas studied in the zone between Castiglione della Pescaia and Vetulonia covered by C.B. Curri's surface surveys, thanks to which a large number of surface features were identified.[39]

The new sample areas surveyed during this project were mainly located in the strip of land between the Ombrone and Osa catchment basins. We thus selected all the surveyable areas in the Parco Regionale della Maremma, part of the narrow Rispescia valley, the upper Osa valley and the area facing the Gulf of Talamone, covering a total of 115 km^2. Further north, our approach entailed a series of in-depth surveys at important sites mentioned in publications or in previous unpublished research and in areas where the documentary sources allowed us to identify settlement features of interest to the date range 4th-9th century AD.

The new studies between 2003 and 2005 thus covered an area of 35.8 km^2 intensively. If we add up the areas fieldwalked during earlier archaeological surveys and those surveyed during this research project we have a total of about 68 km^2 studied within the broader context between the Alma and Osa valleys.

[38] Vaccaro 2001/2002 and Vaccaro 2005c.

[39] The total number of TUs identified during the *Forma Italiae* – Vetulonia Project amount to 172 if we consider only those within our study area or immediately outside it.

Considering that at least 85 km^2 of our 846 km^2 study area were probably impassable because they were covered by Lake Prile and a further 20 km^2 were occupied by the later formation of the Ombrone river delta, the sample area surveyed represents just over 9% of the surface available between the 4th and 9th centuries AD.

The percentage surveyed increases still further if we exclude those areas where limited visibility at ground level would have made archaeological surveys pointless: on the basis of this argument the area surveyed covers over 13% of the potential study area. This proportion might rise again were we to have data of help in determining the sample area actually surveyed during the *Forma Italiae* and Albegna Valley projects.

When surveying wooded areas we applied a multi-scalar approach involving a careful verification of the anomalies visible on aerial photographs[40] and the sites mentioned in archive sources. On several occasions we systematically cleaned exposed sections in order to intercept the stratigraphies *in situ* and collect pottery materials of help for dating purposes.

The total area sampled measured 191 km^2, with systematically and intensively surveyed areas occupying 68 km^2;[41] to these we should add the areas studied during the *Ager Cosanus*-Albegna Valley Project and the Forma Italiae project at Vetulonia, for which we know the total number of sites found but not the area surveyed.

If we add up the new and preceding surveys, we have 750 Topographic Units ranging from Proto-history to the Middle Ages. The total number of off-site features is 114, with a particularly high concentration in the area between the lower Ombrone valley and the Osa valley where the new territorial research approach led us to record sporadic artefacts systematically.

1.3.2. Methods for Analysing Archaeological Features Identified During Earlier Studies

Bearing in mind the time-frame considered in this research project we thought it important to review all the pottery materials collected during the archaeological surveys carried out in the area between Roselle and Grosseto in the second half of the 1980s.[42] These were analysed systematically with the aim of identifying, among the coarsewares, indicators of help

[40] To this end we surveyed the features mentioned in the *Atlante dei Siti d'Altura della Toscana*, and then checked the anomalies relating to hilltop sites in the field.

[41] The new field surveys (2000-6) systematically investigated an area of 51.2 km^2; in the *Ager Rusellanus* project an area of 16.7 km^2 was surveyed.

[42] I would like to thank Carlo Citter for his generosity in supporting this further phase of processing of the pottery materials documented during his undergraduate thesis project.

in finding other settlement features of the late antique and early medieval periods hitherto unidentified due to our lesser understanding of this pottery class.[43] This approach turned out to be extremely fruitful, leading to the identification of as many as 6 new 5th/6th-century AD frequentations of contexts abandoned after the early Imperial period or even earlier, and of two settlements dating to between the late 9th and the 11th century established on top of sites abandoned after the 2nd/3rd century AD. However, new field work was undertaken only for a limited area in the territory between Grosseto and Roselle. The surface surveys and geophysical surveys were particularly intensive at Aiali, just north of Roselle, where this new research campaign has made a crucial contribution to the study of settlement dynamics in the city's hinterland between late Antiquity and the Middle Ages.[44]

Unfortunately it was impossible to apply the same research strategy to the materials collected during C. B. Curri's unsystematic surveys in the Vetulonia area. The potential for identifying late antique and early medieval phases was necessarily limited to an examination of the published pottery, represented almost exclusively by finewares, whilst very few references to amphorae and coarsewares were available.

This is a significant limitation considering that, in light of more recent studies, the late antique use of large and medium-small contexts in the area between the Alma and Osa valleys is not always attested by ARS. As we will see, this class declines in a fairly generalized way from the last quarter of the 5th century whilst coarseware, with or without a slip, made regionally and sub-regionally, continues to be present, sometimes exclusively. This obstacle could not always be overcome by checking the settlement features published by C. B. Curri in the field although this was done by the author during the surveys carried out in the municipal territory of Castiglione della Pescaia.

We should also take into consideration the gradual depletion of archaeological contexts and surface features due to normal farming activities between the 1970s and the present. Above all, we should stress that these have intensified with the planting of huge vineyards managed in entrepreneurial style in an area – between Badiola and Castiglione della Pescaia along the final stretch of the Bruna river – where Curri's studies had already noted that the network of Roman settlements was less dense.

The significant improvement in our knowledge which could have resulted from the systematic reexamination of the materials collected during the 1970s is clear from the results of the reassessment between 2000 and 2002 of some large villas in use at least up to the 5th century AD[45] near the west bank of the ancient Lake Prile. The surface readability of these features is now compromised and they have yielded only a few pottery finds of use for dating purposes.[46]

1.4 Research Methods and Techniques: Archaeological Surveys and Excavations

1.4.1. The concepts of site and off-site and their application to this study

From the earliest surface surveys there has been a tendency to label as a 'site' any scatter of archaeological materials, creating the conviction, not always accurate, that all areas of ceramic fragments indicate the existence of a buried deposit. It was only in the 1970s that the features identified during surveys began to be interpreted with greater caution, since the sample of materials visible on the surface is heavily influenced by various factors, including the type of land use, light conditions and the experience of the surveyor.[47] The anthropic and natural processes which determine the quality and quantity of finds present on the surface are difficult to ascribe to fixed and predetermined categories.[48] As such, it is objectively difficult to make a clear distinction between what is actually a site, understood as an anomalous concentration of artefacts in the field, and what is in fact an off-site, in other words a sporadic presence of materials. The methodological debate over the correct interpretation of off-site was particularly intense during the 1980s[49] and still continues today. The main aim was to reach an accurate interpretation of those areas characterized by the presence of sporadic materials, in

[43] This approach was inspired by the recent Tiber Valley Project conducted between 1997 and 2002 as part of the research on Roman archaeology at the British School at Rome. A team composed of different archaeological specialists reviewed the materials collected during the South Etruria Survey along the Tiber Valley: a total of about 90,000 fragments from 2500 sites of different dates. Particularly important were the new data acquired on the period between the 5th and 7th centuries AD: in the Farfa area the studies undertaken between the 1950s and 1970s had signalled the presence of 10 sites of the mid-5th/6th centuries and only 5 settlements of the mid-6th/7th centuries. The new studies of the materials, thanks to the improved chrono-typologies for coarsewares now available, led to the identification of a total of 21 features dating to the mid-5th/6th centuries and 16 to the mid-6th/7th century. Similar data have emerged for the Sabine area, where the reexamination of ceramic materials led to an increase in features dating to the mid-5th/6th century and the late 6th/7th century compared to those documented by the South Etruria Survey. See Patterson *et alii* 2004.

[44] These studies, run by the Landscape Archaeology and Remote Sensing Laboratory of the University of Siena at Grosseto and coordinated by S. Campana employed a multi-scalar research methodology (traditional surface surveys, collection of materials from virtual grids and geophysical surveys) in the area of a large villa identified near Aiali during the aerial survey of 2003. See Campana 2006b; Campana-Francovich-Felici 2005, Vaccaro-Ghisleni-Campana 2009 and Campana-Piro 2009. From 2005, intensive fieldwalking campaigns were also extended to the areas surrounding the large Roman and late antique settlement complex, reoccupied at the end of the High Middle Ages.

[45] This date is proposed on the basis of the ARS typologies recorded by Curri.

[46] I refer in particular to the large Roman villas Curri 1978, sites no.75, 88, 97.

[47] Barker 1995 (ed.), pp.45-46.

[48] Bintliff 2000, p.200.

[49] Bintliff-Snodgrass 1988, pp.506-513.

other words attested with lower than average densities for the study area[50] but which are nonetheless an indication of human activities in the area and thus of the intensity of its exploitation.[51] The potential for identifying and understanding such features is directly proportional to the intensity of surface surveys. For example, a survey entailing fieldwalking with walkers 15 m from one another is unlikely to lead to an identification of all the off-sites present and their true significance.[52] A series of studies undertaken over the past 20 years in the Mediterranean has shown that in some regions (France, Italy, Greece and the Middle East) there were brief periods during which farming activities intensified significantly, translating in material terms into complex operations to fertilize and manure the land. As a consequence, domestic organic waste, including fragments of pottery containers which had broken and were therefore useless, were scattered over the fields to increase their productivity.[53] As such, large cities can be linked to the large-scale manuring of the farmland in their hinterland but on a different scale this mechanism also holds true for other large rural contexts such as Roman and late antique villas or villages of different periods. It has been rightly noted that the most intensive manuring must have been carried out in vegetable gardens in the immediate vicinity of rural sites; genuine concentrations of materials thus formed in these areas rather than scatters with a low density of finds per m^2 .[54]

Whereas in the vicinity of large rural contexts or cities we can identify the signs of intensive manuring operations, signalled by the presence of sporadic ceramic fragments, it is equally true that fields at some distance from the rural site to which they belonged must have been manured simply by grazing animals rather than by scattering domestic waste. However, it would be simplistic and over-schematic to ascribe all the off-sites identified in the field to this common denominator, since other factors may also have led to the formation of these features. In the past, during periods when farming activities were at their most intense, in many parts of Italy peasants lived for more or less extended periods in shelters near the fields where they worked; they may have broken pottery vessels and then thrown the fragments into nearby fields. Similarly, the seasonal frequentation of some areas linked to transhumance may have created a scatter of sporadic materials.[55]

Finally, we should mention another order of factors which may lead to the presence of off-site materials in a given area. These features sometimes represent the last ephemeral traces of archaeological contexts which have been severely depleted by repeated farming activities.[56] Naturally, it is not at all easy to distinguish between off-sites resulting from manuring and those which actually signal the presence of buried deposits which have been irrevocably compromised. A valid strategy for attempting to resolve this problem may be the quantitative and qualitative study of the materials. For example, if the ratio of bricks to pottery in a given number of off-sites is identical to that characterizing true sites belonging to the same chronological horizon, it is possible that the sporadic materials in question belong to deposits severely damaged by ploughing.[57] This concept is easy to understand if we consider that pottery breaks easily during transport or when used by people working farmland and that it may end up among the organic waste used for manuring; the same is unlikely to occur for bricks.

Various projects have attempted to identify a density threshold of finds per m^2 making it possible to distinguish between sites and off-sites; however, the results are not always convincing.[58] There are too many factors, which cannot always be fully reconstructed, which may lead to the greater or lesser concentration of finds on the surface. The distribution of artefacts is heavily influenced by erosion and accumulation, land use, the depth of the buried deposit beneath the land surface; additionally the degree of fragmentation of the finds depends on the number of ploughings to which the field has been subjected.[59] The formation of the sample of materials visible on the surface is also influenced by cultural factors; for example, a farmstead of the imperial period generally yields a large number of ceramic finds, given the broad range of classes used (fineware, coarseware, transport amphorae), and bricks. The surface finds from a hut of the 8th/9th century AD are very different because such sites did not have access to the same variety of pottery types, generally represented only by coarsewares, nor do they usually yield bricks, with the exception of the odd reused fragment.

This study dealt with these issues through a strategy entailing, on the one hand, the systematic survey of all features identifiable either as Topographical Units[60] or as off-sites and, on the other, replicated collections at those contexts which, during initial fieldwalking, left some doubts as to their correct interpretation. In our

---

[50] *Ibidem*.

[51] Barker 1995 (ed.), p.46.

[52] Bintliff 2000, p.203.

[53] Stoddart-Whitehead 1991, pp.141-148.

[54] In the case of the villa at Settefinestre in the *Ager Cosanus*, manuring covered an area of vegetable gardens over 200 m wide starting from the kitchens; the broken pottery, initially next to the wall of the service wing of the main building, was mixed with the organic materials. Fentress 2000, p.46.

[55] Barker 1995 (ed.), pp.34-37.

[56] Experimental studies have been conducted to calculate the time required for the depletion of a buried deposit to reach levels such as to impede an effective understanding of the remaining traces. See Ammermann 1985, pp.33-40.

[57] Fentress 2000, pp.47-48.

[58] For example, in the Neothermal Dalmatia Project a site has a minimum density of 4 finds per 25 m^2 whilst in the Rieti Survey the threshold is 10 fragments per 100 m^2. See Cambi-Terrenato 1994, p.169.

[59] Bintliff 2000, p.206.

[60] For the traditional Site/TU data sheet used during this study see Ricci 1983, pp.495-506.

opinion it was essential to document all the features identified to obtain a picture which was as uniform and exhaustive as possible, not only of the settlement network but also of forms of land use and their intensity. We chose not to apply a fixed criterion for the density of finds per m^2 to distinguish between TUs and off-sites since the broad chronological range (4th - 9th century AD) covered by the features studied in depth would have raised those cultural problems mentioned above. In our opinion, a particularly fruitful approach was to assess the state of conservation of the finds yielded by off-site features, attempting to understand if the greater or lesser degree of wear resulted from the depletion of a potential deposit or from the genuinely sporadic nature of the find. Equally useful was the evaluation of the relationship between different classes of materials, stressing in particular the quantity ratio of pottery finds to bricks; these ratios were later compared with those for true settlements belonging to the same chronological phase.

1.4.2. Traditional Field Walking and the Contribution of New Technologies

As already noted, archaeological surveys played a crucial role in this research project. It is fairly obvious that any type of research which aims to examine a territorial context of greater or lesser size cannot do without the exhaustive fieldwalking of representative samples. Traditional fieldwalking, in accordance with what is now a consolidated practice in the archaeological mapping projects in the provinces of Siena and Grosseto, made systematic use of GPS technology.[61] The constant availability of hand-held DGPS devices[62] provided us with an excellent navigational tool on which to enter the necessary maps in both vectorial and raster formats, as well as speeding up the process of documenting and recording the features identified. GPS devices were used in motion mode for most operations in the field (recording concentrations of archaeological materials) whilst for documenting specific finds, the boundaries of wall structures or occasional sections we used the static method, positioning the device at the point or at the corners to be recorded for a sampling time of 60 seconds per measurement[63], thus increasing the accuracy of the data.

The stop and go recording mode turned out to be particularly useful for surveys in wooded areas where horizontal visibility falls to a distance of a few metres.[64] Another fundamental use of GPS in areas covered by woodland was navigation aimed at checking anomalies showing up on aerial photographs. In these contexts, we were able to load the reference maps, usually in the form of orthophotographs to a scale of 1:10,000 with the trace to be checked superimposed on them in vectorial format, onto hand-held devices. This was a highly effective and effortless method compared to walking through dense woodland with only a paper map. During surveys, GPS was always used for absolute positioning[65]: this is an acceptable compromise between the metrical accuracy of the recording of surface features, which are subject to constant transformations in their form, and the speed of the acquisition process which does not require further processing.

Topographical surveying was carried out using the traditional fieldwalking technique with equidistant parallel lines walked by individual surveyors. Fieldwalking was extremely intensive in order to document as many features as possible inside each site during the survey. The large number of fieldwalkers available, never less than ten, allowed us to make systematic use of a distance of 5 m between fieldwalkers. Considering that the surface surveys were carried out by students, for many of whom this was the first surveying experience, we decided to give each walker a notebook in which to write down every tiny feature noted during their walk. Every time we completed the survey of a field without finding concentrations of materials, this procedure allowed us to reconstruct all the tiny traces present accurately, from an individual brick fragment to isolated pottery sherds. At this point we were able to rewalk the line in question to find the fragment, which was collected after georeferencing it accurately.

[61] On the use of GPS and its possible applications, tested during the territorial research projects organized by the Medieval Archaeology Faculty at the University of Siena see Campana 2006b, pp.208-223; Campana 2002, pp.59-60 and p.68; more in general on the use of GPS in archaeology see Gabrielli 2001, pp.329-354.

[62] The GPS device used was Trimble's *Geo Explorer II*, with *ArcPad* software used for navigation and documentation in the field. The data acquired in the field were downloaded daily onto a GIS base created with ArcGis 8.2 developed specifically for this research project.

[63] On these aspects see Gabrielli 2001, pp.346-347.

[64] This type of use makes it possible to record only the station points making it possible to avoid the creation of the frequent spikes in the read out due to the lower quality of the signal, which thus require a longer processing time. See in particular Campana 2006b, pp.210-211.

[65] In this mode the device is used independently with metrical accuracy, sufficient for surveying operations. To obtain sub-metrical accuracy it would have been necessary to carry out a differential correction by correlating the systematic errors of a known reference base with the mobile roving device. This procedure is considered preferable for surveys which require greater accuracy, such as archaeological excavations or the grids used for geophysical surveys. On these aspects see Campana 2006b, pp.203-207; Gabrielli 2001, pp.336-338.

1.4.3. Excavations and the Choice of Contexts

This multi-scalar research project on the Maremma area was initially intended to include digging test pits at some of the sites of greatest interest for the study of settlement patterns between the 4th and 10th centuries AD emerging from surface surveys.

The definition of the formation process of the early medieval village was one of the main problems posed when setting out the goals of this study. The surveys carried out between 2003 and 2005 provided an extremely varied and complex picture of population structures between the 8th and 10th centuries, suggesting the need to undertake stratigraphic excavations at at least two different settlement clusters.

The intensive and detailed surveys and the geophysical studies undertaken at the fortified hilltop village of Poggio Cavolo, already subjected to specific research[66], made a crucial contribution to determining the site's topographical layout and above all its date.[67] This context lies in a privileged position, ensuring total control over the plain of Grosseto, over the final stretch of the Ombrone river and over inland areas of the Maremma. Thanks to new surface surveys and excavation, the site yielded a series of pottery indicators which allowed us to date its abandonment to no later than the late 12th or early 13th century and its stable use beginning at least by the (late?) 9th or early 10th century. This site thus corresponds to the model of the early medieval village, later fortified and then precociously abandoned. Stratigraphic excavations allowed us to investigate in depth a settlement whose urban structure was not monumentalized during the late Middle Ages. It thus thus allowed us to fully understand the formative phases of this hilltop village, any hierarchical organization of its internal spaces and the material culture of what appears to be a true central place in the coastal Maremma between the early and central Middle Ages.[68] It was also necessary to excavate stratigraphically one of the contexts in the plains identified during recent surveys and which, thanks to the analysis of the pottery repertoires, we were able to date to between the 7th and 9th century. It would have been particularly interesting to excavate the lowlying village of Podere Serratone, only 4.5 km from Poggio Cavolo and abandoned no later than the late 9th century; unfortunately this was impossible due to the objections of the landowners. However, the stratigraphic excavations at one of the farmsteads making up the early medieval dispersed settlement of Casa Andreoni, facing the Gulf of Talamone, turned out to be equally fruitful. Since this settlement type was essentially unknown in Tuscany, but finds close analogies in this area with another contemporary cluster in the upper Osa valley also identified during this research project, it was essential to excavate stratigraphically in order to define the topography of this type of context and attempt to understand its various phases and any relations with pre-existing sites. Finally, also important for our research was the brief excavation campaign between February and March 2008 at the long lasting site of San Martino *de plano* in the middle Bruna valley, undertaken in collaboration with the Soprintendenza per i Beni Archeologici della Toscana. The choice of this site reflected not only the need for a more in-depth understanding aimed at better safeguarding the archaeological potential of a context under threat from repeated deep ploughing but also the interest in investigating a site occupied, albeit intermittently, from the Etruscan period to the Middle Ages.

1.5. Methods Applied to the Analysis of Pottery from Surface Surveys

The study of the surface pottery deposits was conducted on two different levels: digital recording and systematic analysis of the objects belonging to the chronological range 4th-9th century AD. By contrast, in the case of multi-period sites, such as those contexts established in the late Republic or early Empire and frequented until late Antiquity, we undertook a preliminary quantification of the finds dating to before the 4th century AD in order to understand how the increase or decrease in pottery related to any transformations in settlement structure or the surface area occupied.

During infra-site surveys we tried to record accurately the distribution of materials belonging to different phases within multi-period deposits. Combining this research method with the careful examination of pottery and the quantification of ceramics in terms of the minimum number of forms in the shape of diagnostic fragments belonging to identifiable typologies (rims, bases and handles) in some of the cases discussed allowed us to reconstruct hypothetically how the site's topographical layout evolved over time.[69] We considered the most frequently used method, EVE, inapplicable.[70] This method is completely unsuitable for surface pottery since the fragmentation of ceramics is significantly affected by post-depositional activities and the measurement of all the rim and base percentages per type is unlikely to be representative of the number of

[66] Citter 1997; Citter 1995a.

[67] Campana-Francovich-Vaccaro 2005, and in particular the remarks by Frezza-Ghisleni, in the same article; see most recently Farinelli-Vaccaro,-Salvadori 2008.

[68] On the excavations at Poggio Cavolo between 2005 and 2007 see Farinelli-Vaccaro-Salvadori 2008. The excavation data are not provided here since they mainly refer to phases of the 10th-12th century and thus fall outside the chronological range of interest.

[69] For this method see Millett 2000, Campana-Francovich-Vaccaro 2005 and Cirelli 2006.

[70] On this method see Orton *et alii* 1993. The method involves estimating the sum of percentages of rims or bases belonging to each ceramic type with the same fabric identified in each excavated context and hence defining the minimum number of documented specimens per type in light of the percentages.

specimens per type documented in the ploughsoil. We think it is much more prudent and effective to rely on the number of diagnostic sherds per type.

The data acquired from the analysis of the late antique pottery contexts on the slopes of the north hill at Roselle, the frequent attestation of African red slip ware and the comparison with the late antique and early medieval ceramic sequences already available for Tuscany allowed us to subdivide the surface features into distinct phases, with the identification of at least three phases between the 4th and the early 7th century AD:

- 4th to mid-5th century AD;
- mid-5th to mid-6th century;
- second half of the 6th to early 7th century.

It was more difficult to define early medieval ceramic "fossil guides"; this was made possible by the identification of short-lived settlements founded *ex novo* between the late 6th and 7th centuries and developing particularly between the 8th and 9th centuries, as well as by the excavation of one of these (Casa Andreoni) and of the site of San Martino *de plano*.

However, the pottery dating to between the 4th and 10th centuries was not used simply as a chronological indicator but was employed systematically for the study of socio-economic systems.

For the late antique period we worked at two different levels of detail; a detailed level and a territorial level. At the detailed level we attempted to determine the quantity ratio of products imported from elsewhere in the Mediterranean and/or outside the region to commodities manufactured regionally or locally within individual contexts, both urban and rural, with the aim of identifying any differences in the social status of those living at different sites. In the infra-site studies of large settlements like villas and villages we opted to georeference imported goods in order to identify any internal distinctions and thus a possible spatial hierarchy depending on the wealth of the consumers.

On the territorial scale we studied the distribution over time of African red slip ware and transport amphorae in order to track general trends in the influx of imported commodities and relate these to major political events in Italy between the 4th and 6th centuries.[71]

For the early Middle Ages we systematically analysed all the surface deposits and those from the excavations at Casa Andreoni whilst at San Martino *de plano* we studied some representative contexts in order to identify the changes undergone by domestic pottery repertoires between the 4th and the early 10th century.

Special care was devoted to an examination of the local circulation of the pottery produced by the kiln at Podere Serratone and other types of materials whose production structures have not yet been found but whose manufacture *in loco* is suggested by an analysis of the fabrics.

The study of body clays, conducted systematically for all excavated contexts, some late antique surface features and all the surface features of the 8th-10th century[72] entailed an initial macroscopic examination[73], subsequently perfected with an optical reflected light microscopic analysis.[74]

The results obtained were highly encouraging from various points of view. Above all the creation of a large database of the body clays of the late antique amphorae from *Portus Scabris* provided us with an effective tool with which to analyse amphora fragments which could not be assigned to specific typologies from other surface and excavation contexts. A comparison of the fabrics allowed us to determine the provenance of non-diagnostic fragments; in some cases the close relations between fabrics and typologies allowed us to go further and suggest the typology from which the fragment came.

The optical microscope analysis of the fabrics attested at the late antique site in the Scoglietto cave led to the identification of some mineral phases associated with coarsewares not attested at other settlements in the study area. This allowed us to reconstruct the flow of coarsewares imported from Lazio through a comparison with contexts outside the region where the same relationships between form and fabric were recorded.

Also interesting were the applications to the distributive study of early medieval pottery. The relationship form/type/fabric was employed systematically to investigate the range of circulation of artefacts on a local scale, attempting to identify any differences within the study area.

71 We used the individual weighted means method; on this method see Fentress-Perkins 1988 and Terrenato-Ricci 1998.

72 We decided to study the pottery fabrics of the early and central Middle Ages systematically in order to attempt to determine the area of distribution of these artefacts which, as is known, during the High Middle Ages rarely exceeds a sub-regional scale.

73 The analysis of the fabrics of late antique ceramics from the excavations at Roselle was limited to a macroscopic reading.

74 The fabrics were analysed using an optical microscope Stemi 2000-C Zeiss model with magnifications ranging from x6.5 to x50.

2. Roman and Late Antique Settlement Patterns in Four River Valleys (Osa, Ombrone, Bruna and Alma)

2.1. Introduction

Part of this chapter has been already published as an article in JRA 2008.[1] However, I thought it worthwhile to re-print it here in similar form, though enriched and partly reworked with some new data acquired during fieldwork in 2007 and 2008. Though this book focuses on the period AD 300-900, a brief discussion of the period 200 BC-AD 200 is helpful for reconstructing settlement and economic patterns in the long term. This additional information provides readers with a more analytical set of data on the basis of which to understand changes over the *longue durée*. A more comprehensive analysis of settlement patterns in this area, especially between the late Republican and middle imperial periods can be found in my JRA paper.

2.2. Second Century BC-First Century AD: an Overview

The period between the 2nd century BC and the 1st century AD represents the point of maximum development of rural settlements, as we know from the large number of sites, 217 in total (Fig.1). Particularly noteworthy is the appearance of a large number of rural villas, with at least 30 sites founded between the late Republic and early Empire. Moving from south to north, villas were mainly located in the coastal plains, with a high density around the gulf of Talamone, and in the area between the town of Roselle and the ancient mouth of the Ombrone river.

A remarkable concentration of villas was found around the western shores of Lake Prile, where it seems that, from the late Republican period onwards, major economic interests focused on the exploitation of the salt lake's resources. In the hinterland of the town of Vetulonia, by contrast, the distribution of archaeological sites allows us to deduce a significant decline in the rural population which seems to have begun in the late Republican period. Further north in the Alma valley only one villa has been identified; it was apparently located in a landscape characterized by a network of small and medium-sized farms.

Interestingly, large villas with monumental architectural features are the exception rather than the rule[2]: most villas are rural rather than residential in nature.[3] These settlements are represented by fairly large scatters, generally covering between 5000 and 15,000 m^2; there are two exceptions: the Aiali villa (4 ha), in the hinterland of Roselle, and that of Santa Francesca near the gulf of Talamone (5 ha).[4] The most frequent villa size (5000 to 15,000 m^2) in our study area is identical to that of the medium-sized and small villas in the Albegna valley, where sixteen villas cover an area of 15,000 m^2 and fourteen are represented by scatters covering 2 to 4 ha.[5]

In the area between the Osa and Alma valleys, the scatters interpreted as villas present large quantities of fine and coarsewares in association with tiles, bricks for *opus spicatum*, *cocciopesto* and very few valuable architectural elements; there are often adjacent outbuildings and storage places whose existence is revealed by smaller assemblages with tiles, amphorae, *dolia* and coarseware a few metres from the central site. However, a peculiarity of these sites seems to be their scarce monumentality: only five villas seem to have had monumental features. The surveys of the villas in this area have only rarely identified valuable architectural elements, such as columns and mosaics; by contrast, these elements are well represented in many villas of the *Ager Cosanus*. Here about 56% of the villas built between the 2nd and the mid-1st century BC present a marked distinction between the *pars urbana* and the *pars rustica*, with sumptuous architectural features being present not only at the larger villas, but also at smaller ones.[6] On the basis of the survey evidence, we can assume that the villas in the area between the Osa and Alma rivers were production units aimed mostly at subsistence agriculture and perhaps in part at the accumulation of surpluses for a small-scale local trade which did not require the production of amphorae, used mainly for maritime trade. The absence of amphora kilns in this area may indicate the lack of specialized agriculture on these estates and the minimal or non-existent development of an intensive slave-based economy aimed at producing a surplus destined for larger markets, as was the case in the *Ager Cosanus*.

---

[1] Vaccaro 2008.

[2] Specifically, no more than five villas seem to play a central role in the settlement hierarchy from the Roman to the late antique period (Aiali, Casette di Mota, San Martino di Sterpeto, Paduline-Serrata Martini and Santa Francesca).

[3] This interpretation is currently based mainly on the analysis of ploughsoil assemblages. A villa recently excavated at Nomadelfia, in the hinterland of the town of Roselle, had two building phases: a first dated to the late Republican period and a second to the 1st c. AD. The floor plan is fairly simple and schematic: during the first phase some residential rooms were built, with an austere *pars urbana* being added later. On this site see Çygielman 2004 (ed.).

[4] On the villa near Talamone see in particular Corsi 2002.

[5] The *Ager Cosanus* is also home to smaller villas, covering an area of 2000-6000 m^2 (35 sites) and 8000-12,000 m^2 (27 sites). On these data see Regoli 2002a, 146.

[6] On the villas of the *Ager Cosanus* see Regoli 2002a, 145-154.

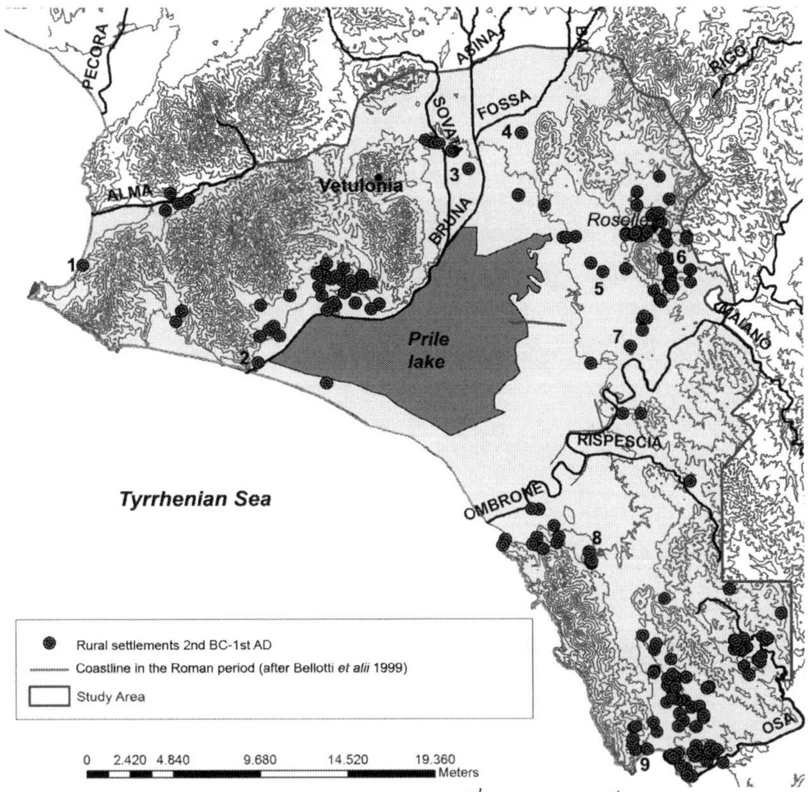

Fig.1_ Distribution of rural sites from the 2nd BC to the 1st AD (217 in total). The main sites and places mentioned in this chapter: 1.Val Piastrone; 2.Paduline-Serrata Martini; 3.Casa Guglielmini; 4.San Martino de plano; 5.Aiali; 6.Casette di Mota; 7.Sterpeto; 8.Hasta (Alberese); 9.Santa Francesca. (From Vaccaro 2008).

The process of Romanization in the study area may not have entailed radical changes to local economic systems; these seems to have been oriented mainly towards extensive agriculture, the exploitation of forest resources[7] and, in the vicinity of Lake Prile, salt production and fishing.

An analysis of the distribution of settlements during this period reveals the development of nucleated sites, which coexist with a network of small and medium-sized scattered sites. Between the 2nd century BC and the 1st century AD, there is evidence for the existence of at least 10 villages; 57 farms and 55 small houses indicate the presence of dispersed settlements. When calculating the total number of residential sites we should also consider 38 sites which could not be assigned to a specific category, some of which may have been small settlements, such as individual houses, severely disturbed by ploughing in the modern period.[8]

The Roman and late antique villages[9] in this area are characterized by clusters of surface scatters of varying sizes and shapes; these may belong to farmsteads and small houses but also to storage facilities and stables. These scatters are more or less evenly distributed within the area covered by the villages, which varies in size between 5000 m^2 and 40,000 m^2. Villages are documented around the gulf of Talamone, the most densely settled part of the study area during this period. In inland areas, nucleated settlements are found in the upper Osa valley and along the Rispescia stream; in both cases we are dealing with long-lived villages founded in the early imperial period and occupied until late Antiquity.

Further north, between the Ombrone valley and the Alma river, there is less evidence for the existence of villages, with only three sites: that of *San Martino de plano* occupied until the late 6th or early 7th century AD (on the middle Bruna river); another where we found evidence of iron working located near the gulf of Punta Ala and dating from the early to middle imperial period, which may have acted as a support for *cabotage* routes; and finally the village of Casa Guglielmini, in the hinterland of the town of Vetulonia,

[7] According to Livy, the town of Roselle supplied Rome with wheat and timber during the Second Punic War (Tit.Liv., *Ab Urbe condita*, XXVIII, XLV, 14). Forest exploitation probably included pasture for pig farming, perhaps to produce a surplus partly intended for consumption in Rome. See also Celuzza 1994, 552.

[8] Among the total number (217) of sites dating to between the 2nd BC and the 1st c. AD we should also consider some production facilities and tombs identified during the surveys.

[9] In this project we chose to use the more generic and neutral term village instead of *vicus*, as this distinction can be made only when written and epigraphic sources confirm the identification of a specific site. For this choice see in particular Cambi 2000, 175 .

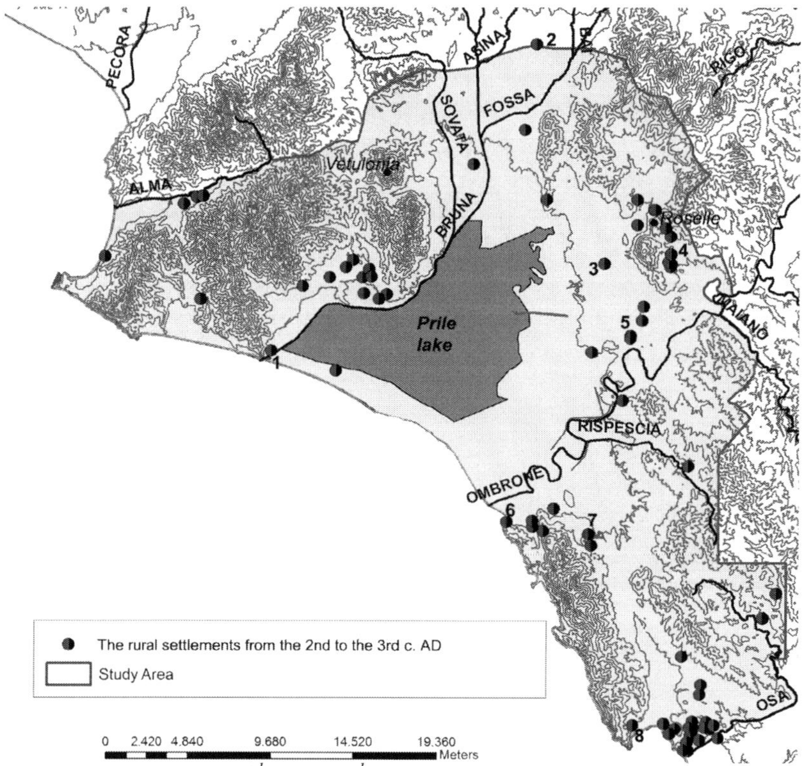

Fig.2_ Distribution of rural sites from the 2nd to the 3rd AD (78 in total). The main sites and places mentioned in this chapter: 1.Paduline-Serrata Martini; 2.Tabbiano; 3.Aiali; 4.Casette di Mota; 5.Sterpeto; 6.Scoglietto; 7.Hasta (Alberese); 8.Santa Francesca. (From Vaccaro 2008).

which seems to have been occupied only in the late Republican period.[10]

The most interesting feature of late Republican and early imperial settlement patterns is the marked increase in the number of small and medium-sized scattered sites; these are often found in the vicinity of the villas, thus creating an extremely varied settlement network. Attempting to interpret these types of surface evidence we could assume that the majority of the small houses close to the villas were inhabited by the dependent peasants who worked in the *fundi*. On the other hand, some farm sites found in parts of the countryside distant from villas may have been inhabited by small land-owners, evidence of the existence of small and medium-sized properties distinct from the larger villa estates.

The settlement patterns of this area during the period between the 2nd century BC and the 1st century AD are thus comparable to those of the *Ager Volaterranus*, where the presence of the free peasantry seems to have remained largely constant after Romanization and where villa owners, instead of using slave labour, employed free peasants living in small houses near the villas.[11] The economic framework of the study area seems to be different from that of the neighbouring *Ager Cosanus*, where the "villa schiavistica" system was better developed, as was intensive agriculture for commercial purposes.

2.3. Second and Third Centuries AD: the Decrease of Settlement Density in the Middle Imperial Period

The settlement density of the study area decreased markedly between the 2nd and 3rd centuries AD. A total of 78 sites date to this phase; 95% of these can be interpreted as residential sites. Compared to the settlement patterns of the late Republican and early imperial periods, when there were 194 residential sites, this represents a significant decrease (about 61.5%) in the total number of sites occupied (Fig.2).

During the middle imperial period, many parts of the Italian peninsula saw a decline in settlement density and a drop in agricultural and craft production, with fairly significant variations at the local level.[12] The study area appears to have been less severely affected by the economic and settlement crisis than the *Ager Cosanus*[13]; this may be explained by the more marked development of the slave villa system in the *Ager*

[10] On the village of Casa Guglielmini see Curri 1978.
[11] For settlement patterns in the *Ager Volaterranus* in the Roman period see Motta *et alii* 1993, 114-115; Motta 1997; Terrenato 1998, 94-114.

[12] See for example Vera 1998, 318.
[13] In the *Ager Cosanus*, during the middle imperial period, of 109 villas known to have been occupied in the previous phase only 92 survived; farms and houses decreased from 195 in the late Republican and early imperial periods to 92 sites in the middle Empire; the number of villages also declined with only 66% surviving. See Celuzza 2002, 196-209.

Cosanus, whose products, from the early to mid-2nd century AD, were less in demand on the local and Mediterranean markets due to an increasing influx of products from the Roman provinces, which were widely distributed.[14] However the main differences between these two areas can be better understood and evaluated in the long term, and are reflected in particular by the greater endurance of the settlements between the Osa and Alma valleys.

In the study area, villas and villages seem to have been less severely affected by the decline in settlement than farmsteads and individual houses. 63% of villas (19 sites) and 60% of villages (6 sites) survived; all the villas already existed in the late Republican and early imperial periods, whilst one of the six villages, at Podere Selvaccia in the middle Bruna valley, seems to have been founded *ex novo* in this period. A higher percentage of farms disappeared than of villas and villages. Of the 57 farm sites known to have been occupied during the late Republican and early imperial periods, only 23 (40%) were still in use during the middle Empire. Furthermore, there is no evidence for new foundations of this type of site.

The decline in the number of small houses was even more marked: of the 55 sites of the preceding period only 7 (12.7%) survived in the middle imperial age. Another interesting feature which underlines this notable decline in small sites is the decrease in undefined surface features which fall from 38 to 17 sites.

The disappearance of some villas can be explained as an effect of the development of the great estate system, whereby several villas and their *fundi* were grouped together under a single owner who managed the property principally through rental contracts.[15] However, archaeological field surveys in the study area did not uncover sufficient evidence to say that villas increased in size during this period, possibly due to the concentration of the population at a few large villas. Nevertheless, we cannot rule out that the two maritime villas of Santa Francesca near the gulf of Talamone and of Paduline-Serrata Martini near the Lake Prile estuary, which were founded between the 1st and 2nd century AD and continued to be occupied through to late Antiquity, may have attracted the population of the surrounding areas.

The villa of Aiali, in the plain between Grosseto and the Etruscan-medieval town of Roselle, is the only villa which seems to have increased in size during the middle imperial period. The aerial and geophysical surveys undertaken between 2001 and 2006[16] enabled us to identify a complex and varied Roman site that seems to have been continuously occupied from the late Republican period to late Antiquity (Fig.3). Using the data from the multi-methodological Aiali project (especially aerial and intensive geophysical surveys) we can now propose a preliminary reconstruction of the topographical layout of this site.[17] Several very interesting elements emerge from an analysis of the plan of both the main building complexes identified, which undoubtedly belong to two different construction periods as we can see from their different alignments. A large building, covering about 1800 m^2 (37 x 49 m) in total, was found in the northern part of the survey area. This complex was arranged around a rectangular courtyard orientated NE-SW: some rooms opened off the central courtyard (which possibly had a peristyle), mostly located in the north-eastern part, while no clearly visible trace of rooms was found in the south-western part. The plan of this building seems to be that of a small to medium-sized *villa rustica*; in light of the surface materials collected during some intensive fieldwalking surveys, the residential area seems to have lacked monumental features. Even more interesting is a second building complex, oriented E-W and located 120 m from the first. This complex has a very compact plan, characterized by a rectangular structure (38 x 10 m) at the centre and two symmetrical square rooms (about 16 x 16 m) on the short sides. Two long narrow corridors run along the sides of the rectangular structure, while four roughly square structures (about 10 x 10 m) are located at the corners. This complex, like the first complex, covers an area of about 1800 m^2. Three small buildings, located NW of this second site, have the same alignment and dimensions as the four corner structures. Obviously, the differing orientation of the complexes shows that they belong to two distinct building phases, but it is difficult to establish the relative chronology of the two sites on the basis of topographical data alone. A particularly interesting feature of complex 2 is the four corner structures, which could be identified as towers on the basis of comparisons with late antique "fortified" residential buildings in both Italy and Thrace.[18] In the

[14] See in particular Panella 1993.

[15] On the concentration of several villa estates in the hands of a few owners in various regions of Italy from the middle to late imperial period, see Vera 1983, Carandini 1985, Capogrossi Colognesi 1986, Vera 1986, Regoli 2002b, and Vera 2005.

[16] On the Aiali project see Francovich-Campana-Felici 2005, Campana-Piro-Felici-Ghisleni 2006, Campana-Piro 2009, Vaccaro-Ghisleni-Campana 2009.

[17] See in particular Vaccaro-Ghisleni-Campana 2009.

[18] See in particular the villa of Palazzolo, near Ravenna, which is believed to have belonged to a Gothic owner, and the villas of Orlandovtsi and Pernik in Thrace, Sfameni 2005, p.615, Figs 7-9.

Fig.3_ The Roman and late antique settlement complex at Aiali in light of geophysical surveys. (From Vaccaro-Ghisleni-Campana 2009).

case of Aiali the four structures, which with the rest of the villa may form part of a single building project, cannot be dated without archaeological excavation. It seems certain that these rooms/towers were built at the same time given their position and dimensions, but there is no clear evidence whether they belonged to the original plan or were added later. Villas with corner towers already existed in the early imperial period, although this architectural model became more common during late Antiquity, partly as an effect of the militarization of the countryside but also as a mark of socio-economical distinction for the owner.[19] Towers of this kind did not always play a military and defensive function but often served an aesthetic purpose, as in the case of the villa of La Olmeda in *Hispania*, monumentalized in the 4th century AD.[20] Complex 2 at Aiali, unique in Tuscany, seems to have reached its point of maximum development during the middle imperial period, at least on the basis of the analysis of surface pottery, and may have been similar to the seigniorial villas mentioned in the middle to late imperial written sources. Here they are described using the term *praetoria* because they consisted of isolated residential buildings surrounded by farm buildings, just as military *praetoria* were surrounded by barracks, stables and grain stores.[21] The topographical layout of complex 2 resembles that of late antique *villae-praetoria*, since it has a residential building at the centre surrounded by smaller structures. Perhaps this villa in the *Ager Rusellanus* was the residence of a *possessor* and an administrative centre where the agricultural resources of a large estate were managed. According to the pottery evidence, collected systematically using a system of virtual grids, the villa was founded in the early imperial period but we can assume the existence of an earlier late Republican site, perhaps a farmstead, which developed into a villa.[22] The surface collection, carried out in 2004 within two predefined grids[23] entailed the systematic collection of artefacts from an area of a hectare (25% of the entire villa scatter) and allows us to propose a preliminary reconstruction of the site and its expansion and contraction over the long term. An initial significant development of the site seems to have begun during the early imperial period, but it was between the 2nd and the first half of the 3rd century AD that the site reached its maximum size, as we can see from the broad distribution of African Red Slip A ware. The ceramic assemblages tell us that the villa survived into the late 6th and perhaps the early 7th century, but without extensive excavations it is hard to say what structural and economic changes took place during late Antiquity. However we should note the large quantity and broad distribution of *ingobbiata di rosso* ware and other coarseware dating from the 4th to 6th centuries throughout most of the site scatter. On the basis of this evidence it is possible that the site did not change significantly in size over the long term.

[19] *Ibidem*, p.613.
[20] Chavarrìa Arnau 2007, pp.216-219.
[21] Carandini 1989, p.102.

[22] Surface collections in the villa area led to the identification of a few late Republican artefacts, in particular fragments of Black glaze ware and Dressel 1 amphorae.
[23] We decided to apply an on-site total recovery by gridding, using two predefined grids with a sampling interval of 10 m. The grids were positioned over the residential area of the villa and the anomaly of two adjacent buildings not aligned with the main structures.

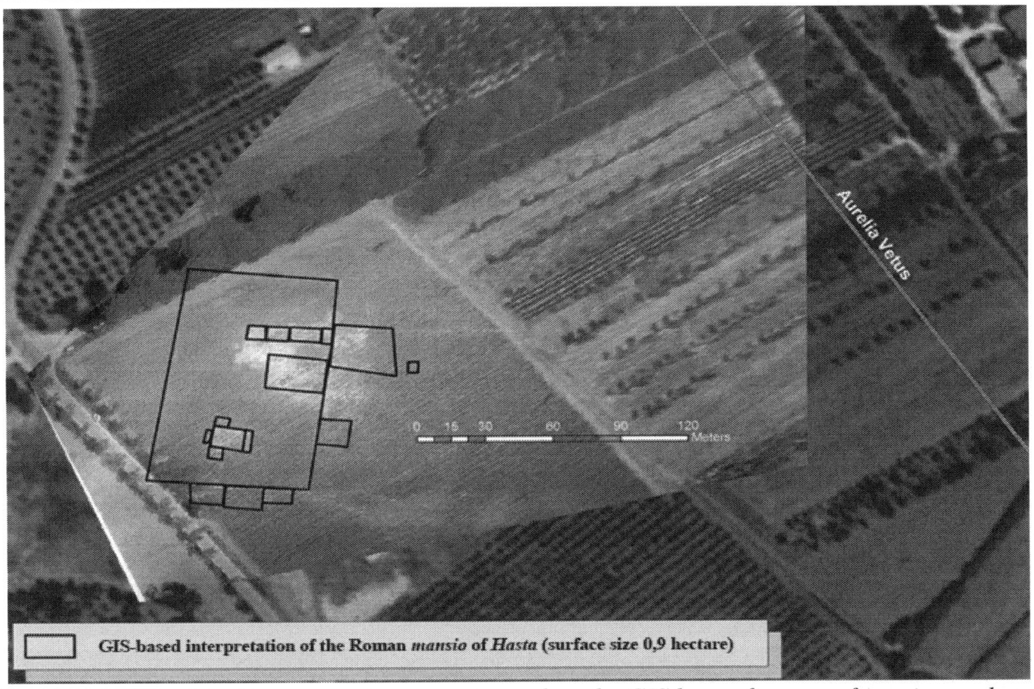

Fig.4_ The general plan of the Hasta mansio, reconstructed on the GIS base after georeferencing and rectifying the aerial photograph.

The other two important villas discovered in the hinterland of Roselle in the late 1980s, Casette di Mota and Sterpeto[24], ranging in size from 5000 m^2 to 20,000 m^2, were probably founded during the late Republican period and survived until the 6th century AD; however, these sites do not appear to have increased in size between the middle and late imperial periods, in line with the general trend for the study area.

A complex site in the lower Ombrone valley, near Alberese, is the *mansio* of *Hasta*[25], discovered by chance in the late 1980s and mentioned in the *Tabula Peutingeriana*. An oblique aerial photograph, taken immediately after very deep ploughing, made it possible to reconstruct the floor plan of the building, occupying an area of about 9000 m^2 (Fig.4). The site covers a chronological range from the early imperial period to the beginning of the 6th century AD. A preliminary re-examination of the materials collected in the late 1980s seems to indicate a considerable quantity of early imperial ceramics and a progressive decrease in diagnostic pottery from the 3rd century AD onwards. In this case, too, there is no evidence for an increase in the size of the villa between the middle imperial period and late Antiquity; on the contrary, the occupied area seems to have decreased progressively over the long term.

Some villages seem to have survived into the middle imperial period, with 5 (50%) of those existing during the previous phases remaining in use. Furthermore, there is evidence for a new foundation in this period; significantly, this site seems to have been the only one founded *ex novo* between the 2nd and 3rd centuries AD. The clustering settlement pattern already documented in this period may be an important forerunner of a trend which became more marked in later centuries and in particular during the late antique and early medieval phases.[26] Additionally, in terms of absolute rural population figures, the long-lasting presence of large villages and the foundation of at least one new nucleated site in the middle imperial period, in the Bruna valley, partly compensates for the marked decrease caused by the abandonment of several villa sites and farmsteads. The village of *Tabbiano*, in the middle Bruna valley, has a scatter size of about 6000 m^2; during the field survey a considerable quantity of ceramics dating from the 2nd to the 6th century AD was collected. According to the surface ceramic evidence this village was established only in the middle imperial period. However, a few fragments of Black Glaze ware and Aretine sigillata (both with only one specimen) may indicate the existence of a former small site that developed into a village.

Much caution is called for when using survey data to reconstruct social patterns at our sites, making it virtually impossible to determine the social composition of the villages surveyed. Using the survey data we can only surmise that middle to late imperial villages were inhabited by dependent peasants grouped together under an owner; alternatively, the residents of the village may have been free farmers who cultivated fields in the surrounding area, or a mixture of free and dependent peasants. It is probable that village society was fairly heterogeneous. An interesting factor

[24] Both villas were discovered during the *Ager Rusellanus* project in the 1980s. See Citter 1988-1989; Citter 1996b.

[25] On this site see also Vaccaro 2005d.

[26] On the development of the village from late Antiquity to the early Middle Ages see Francovich-Hodges 2003; Francovich 2004; Valenti 2004; Arthur 2005.

emerging from infra-site surveys at middle imperial to late antique villages is the systematic presence, among the pottery collected, of African red slip ware and Mediterranean amphorae dating from the 4th to the 6th century AD, perhaps evidence of an established system of trade connections and, speculatively, of a complex social structure comprising small and medium landowners with access to Mediterranean foodstuffs and craft products.

In the area between the Osa and Alma valleys, from the early 4th to the mid-6th century AD, along with signs of a progressively diminishing settlement density and the spread of the large estate system, some villages and a few medium-sized farmsteads survive in areas with fewer villas; in a few cases we even have evidence for new foundations and the expansion of inhabited areas.

2.4. Early Fourth to Mid-Fifth Century AD: the Survival of a Complex Settlement Network in the "First Phase" of Late Antiquity

The period, between the early 4th and the mid-5th century AD, is characterized by a further drop in the total number of rural sites: 59% of those formerly present were abandoned. Although the decrease in settlements is marked, it does not seem to have triggered a decline in the socio-economic complexity of the study area, where the presence of some medium to large sites indicates the survival of a well-structured and complex settlement network (Fig.5). In this period 57% of the villas known to have been occupied during the previous phase survived, while less than 17% of the villages disappeared. Small to medium sites, such as farmsteads, were more severely affected by the decline in rural settlements: only 10 farms (43.4%) and three houses (42.8%) survived. Nonetheless the foundation of a new farmstead in the lower Ombrone valley and the probable growth in size of another farm near Poggio Castellaccio, in the upper Osa valley, are evidence of the widespread persistence of small peasant sites.

The excavations in the city of Grosseto carried out between 1997 and 2005[27] revealed that a seasonal settlement was founded during this phase; the site may initially have been used periodically as a base for farming and salt production.

During this phase the ceramic evidence, and in particular African red slip C and D ware and amphorae, seems to suggest that a market economy survived and that the circulation of Mediterranean goods persisted at high levels. Interestingly, field surveys at about 60% of the sites documented in this phase yielded fragments of Tunisian amphorae dating from the 4th to the mid-5th century AD.[28] However we should stress a slight decrease in the total number of amphorae circulating in this phase compared with the previous period.

The survey data indicate some important differences in settlement patterns along the four valleys of the study area. The area near the gulf of Talamone seems to have seen a critical drop in the number of sites: only two survived during this period, the villa of Santa Francesca and the village of Podere Laschi, founded during the early imperial period and maintaining its size of 1.2 ha through to late Antiquity. During the 4th and 5th centuries, this site further developed its connections with Mediterranean markets, as revealed by the increase in African red slip D ware and Tunisian amphorae (particularly Keay XXV and *spatheia* Keay XXVI).

Along the Osa valley four sites seem to have survived; that near a bend in the vicinity of the mouth is characterized by significant transformations during the late 4th and early 5th AD. This site, probably a farmstead, was founded at the beginning of the 1st century AD and survived unaltered in form and size (about 600 m^2) until the early 4th century. Subsequently, the ceramic evidence suggests that the site may have been uninhabited for about a century. The farm was then reoccupied from the beginning of the 5th to the mid-6th century AD, albeit with some topographical changes: the site shifted partially southwards and it decreased in size (200 m^2). The shrinkage of the occupied area is not automatic proof of the impoverishment of its residents, perhaps a small group of free peasants, who had the economic capacity to purchase a wide range of regional and Mediterranean goods; these include *ingobbiata di rosso* ware and amphorae containing Tuscan wine ("Empoli" type), African red slip D ware and amphorae from Tunisia, the eastern Mediterranean area and southern Spain.[29] Interestingly, the late antique site received a continuous supply of Mediterranean goods whereas during the previous period the small number of imported amphorae suggests subsistence agriculture. Differences between the two site phases are also reflected by changes in building materials: from the use of tiles and stone to perishable materials, as indicated by a dark soil mark, possible evidence of the decay of structures built of perishable materials, matching the late antique ploughed site.[30]

---

[27] For the changes at the site of Grosseto from late Antiquity to the Middle Ages see Francovich *et alii* 2000, Citter 2005 (ed.) and Citter 2007 (ed.).

[28] Between the 4th to the mid-5th century AD the so-called "contenitori cilindrici della tarda età Imperiale" (Keay XXV) are widely documented in the study area, but we can also mention other types such as Keay VII, Keay XXVI and Keay XXXVA.

[29] On the site and its ceramics see Ciampoltrini-Rendini 1989.

[30] *Ibidem*. The spread of perishable housing in the Tuscan countryside seems to have begun from the 5th century AD onwards (for a summary of the problem in Tuscany see Valenti 2004, 65-77), due to the economic and cultural changes characteristic of the northern and central Italian peninsula between late Antiquity and the early Middle Ages. On the widespread appearance of simplified

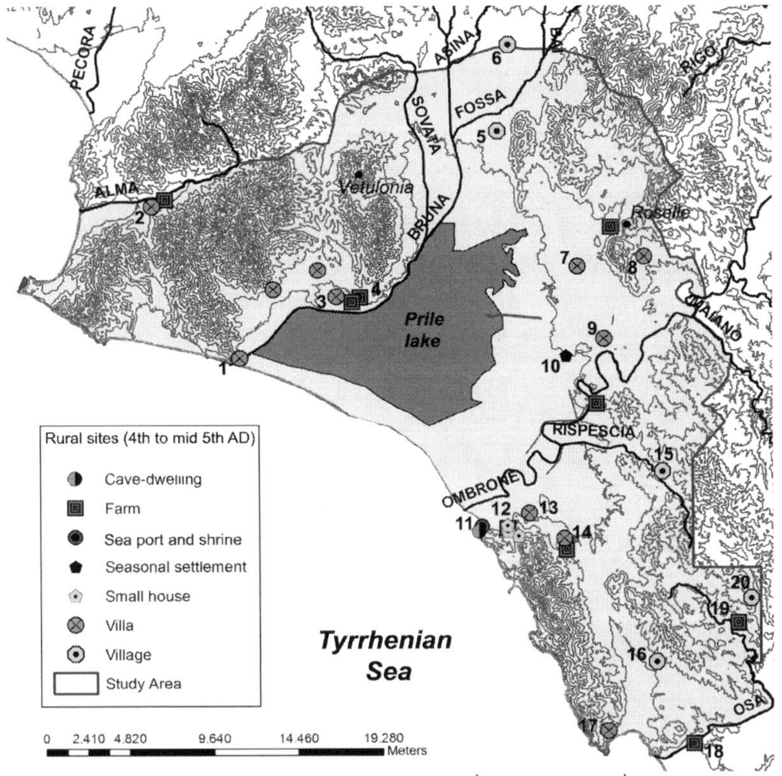

Fig.5_ Distribution of rural sites from the early 4th to the mid/5th c. A.D. (32 in total). The main sites and places mentioned in this chapter: 1.Paduline-Serrata Martini; 2.Alma; 3.Fosso Cortigliano; 4.Fattoria Badiola; 5.San Martino de plano; 6.Tabbiano; 7.Aiali; 8.Casette di Mota; 9.Sterpeto; 10.Grosseto; 11.Scoglietto; 12.Vacchereccia; 13.Podere Montesanto; 14.Hasta (Alberese); 15.Podere Serratone; 16.Podere Laschi; 17.Santa Francesca (Telamone); 18.Bend of the Osa river; 19.Poggio Castellaccio; 20.Poggio Querce Grossa. (From Vaccaro 2008).

Along the upper Osa stream, at the foot of Poggio Castellaccio, we still find two adjacent sites (each scatter measures about 1000 m^2), probably corresponding to a well-structured and complex farmstead, founded in the early imperial period and staying the same size until the 5th century AD. A few ceramics were collected about 140 metres east of the "twin farms" during the field survey, dating to between the 4th and the 6th century, together with a fragment of soapstone, perhaps indicating a more intensive use of the area for farming in late Antiquity. Further inland an important early imperial to 6th century AD village, with a surface size of 8000 m^2 which remained constant until the late 5th AD, is situated near Quercia Grossa.

The decline in rural settlements, which appears to be marked along the Osa river and around the gulf of Talamone, is less severe to the north, along the Ombrone valley, where villa sites and farmsteads continued to be well documented between the 4th and 5th centuries AD. In the hinterland of the town of Roselle, three large villas (Aiali, Sterpeto and Casette di Mota) continued to be in use in the late antique period. By contrast, two villas on the lower Ombrone river saw a significant decline in surface size: *Hasta* (*mansio*) and Podere Montesanto. The lack of excavated key sites means we must exercise great caution in interpreting the villas of late Antiquity; field surveys are insufficient even to tell us if the villas underwent structural and functional changes, and if a former villa had become a farm or a village.[31] However, intensive infra-site surveys can at least show whether there was a contraction in the occupied area over the long term. The three villas mentioned above seem to have stayed the same size.

The villa sites of *Hasta* and Podere Montesanto, probably founded in the early imperial period, continued to be inhabited until the late 5th or early 6th AD: however, an analysis of the pottery collected allows us to identify a progressive decline in the numbers of chronological indicators from the 4th to the early 6th century AD, after a peak in the early and middle imperial periods. This suggests a reduction in the occupied area and a decrease in the total number of

construction techniques from the 4th c. A.D. on, see also Brogiolo-Chavarría 2005, 53-66.

[31] For the changes undergone by late antique villas see Francovich Hodges 2003; Lewit 2003; Arthur 2004; Brogiolo, Chavarría, Valenti (edd) 2005; Lewit 2005; Wickham 2005.

residents.[32] 600 m south of the villa site of *Hasta*, along the main *Aurelia Vetus* road, the field survey discovered three small farms. It is unclear whether these sites were occupied by dependent peasants, the work-force of the villa/*mansio*, or by small landowners. Perhaps at least one of these farms[33], surviving well into the 5th century, may be related to a small property near the *fundus* of the villa. This site seems to have been continuously supplied with Mediterranean goods[34] during a period that sees a progressive decline in the quantities of imported pottery at the villa. About 2 km to the north, near the *Aurelia Vetus*, a second complex settlement was discovered, closely linked to the road network. The villa of Podere Montesanto covers over 15,000 m^2, quite similar to the dimensions of the *Hasta mansio*. The history of the occupation of the two sites also seems to have been similar, with an intensive phase of occupation between the 1st and the 3rd centuries AD and evidence of continuity through the 5th and probably up to the beginning of the 6th century, though with a substantial contraction in the settled area.

A possible market place in the lower Ombrone valley was the sea-port of Scoglietto on the Roman river mouth.[35] During the autumn of the 2002, an inscription dedicated to *Dianae Umbronensis*, generically dated to the early to middle imperial period, was discovered at this site: evidence of a small shrine dedicated to the goddess, whose epithet is closely related to the Ombrone river. The later field survey at the site, located in a wooded area, uncovered a few remains of a wall, fragments of marble architectural features and a ceramic and tile surface assemblage covering about 1700 m^2. On the basis of field data we may assume that a sea-port was founded here in the early imperial period, surviving until the 5th or perhaps the mid-6th century AD.[36] Probably the sea-port maintained a role in the redistribution of Mediterranean goods along the Ombrone river well into late Antiquity. This can be proved in part by the remarkable presence of African red slip D ware and Tunisian amphorae collected at the near-by farm. founded *ex novo* during this phase at Vacchereccia, only 1.4 km further east along the river.[37] Near this farm, 140 m to the south, a single house or perhaps a storeroom probably related to the farm dates to between the early 4th and the mid-5th century AD.[38] All this evidence indicates the persisting vitality of the settlement network in the lower Ombrone valley during the late Roman period. Although the foundation of new sites in late Antiquity is rare in the study area, it is worth noting that two new sites are located in close proximity to one another along the lower Ombrone river (Fig.6).

To the north, along the middle Bruna river, settlement patterns are characterized by the continuity of the two villages of *San Martino de plano* and *Tabbiano*. The first is an interesting example of a village that increased in size during the late antique period. The site was founded during the late Republic and survived, with no gap in the surface ceramics, until the late 6th or early 7th century AD. Infra-site surveys and the systematic analysis of the ceramics collected allow us to propose a hypothetical reconstruction of topographical changes over the long term. From the late Republican period to the early 4th century AD, this site took the form of a farmstead surrounded by a few small houses and/or outbuildings, with a total size of about 3000 m^2. During the 5th to 6th century, the site doubled in size (6000 m^2). The new village still comprised a central farm, larger than the earlier one, and a larger number of surrounding structures (perhaps houses and storehouses), located no more than 100 m from the centre (Fig.7). In late Antiquity the village, like the farm near a bend in the lower Osa river, may have intensified its connections with overseas markets as indicated by the increase in African red slip D ware (forms Hayes 61B, 67, 91B and 99) and the amount of Tunisian and eastern Mediterranean amphorae (particularly Keay LXII and *spatheia* Keay XXVI; the eastern Mediterranean amphorae have not been attributed to a specific late Roman type because we collected only a few fragments of ribbed walls). The late antique development of this site may have been a result of a nucleation trend among the population of the middle Bruna river. Perhaps this area, whose most important rural sites seem to have been the two villages of *San Martino de plano* and *Tabbiano*, specialized in cereal cultivation, carried out by the peasants living in the villages exploiting the broad plains with a low

[32] On settlement patterns in this area from the 4th to mid-6th c. AD see also Vaccaro 2005d.
[33] The farms mentioned above were surveyed in the autumn of 2004. Later, during the aerial surveys of the XIV Summer School in Archaeology in the summer of 2005, directed by Riccardo Francovich and Stefano Campana, we were able to identify a complex group of traces matching the surface scatters of the farms. The excellent results of the aerial photographs allow us to determine the floor plan of the building, a rectangle with internal partitions covering about 300 m^2.
[34] The later ceramics collected at this site are African red slip D ware (Hayes 61B and Hayes 67) and Tunisian amphorae (Keay XXV and XXXV A).
[35] The archaeological and geo-pedological data seem to agree in suggesting that Scoglietto was the sea-port on the Ombrone river. See also Chapter 1 for the changes in the Ombrone delta through the ages.
[36] The later archaeological materials are Tunisian (Keay XXV and Keay XXVI) and eastern Mediterranean (LR 2) amphorae. We must stress the scarcity of diagnostic pottery due to the low archaeological visibility of the wooded area.
[37] At this site African red slip ware is the best represented ceramic class (forms Hayes 61A and B, 67, 91A/B); also well attested are Tunisian amphorae (Keay XXV and Keay LXII).
[38] The diagnostic materials are a few fragments of Keay XXV amphorae and coarse ware dating from the 5th to the 6th c. AD.

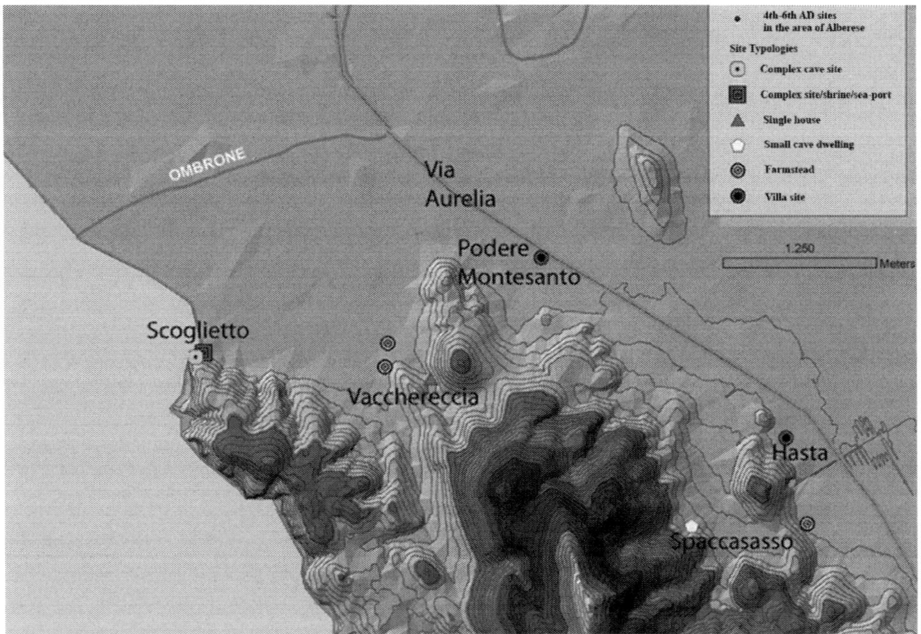

Fig.6_ The settlement network in the lower Ombrone valley (4th-mid-5th AD).

settlement density. We cannot rule out that the central farm in the *San Martino de plano* village, where the field survey collected most of the late antique imported pottery, such as African red slip D ware and Tunisian amphorae, may have been the residence of an owner.

In the middle Bruna valley, the Etruscan and Roman town of Vetulonia continued to be occupied but it underwent structural and functional changes between the late Republic and early Empire, which saw the onset of a progressive and significant shrinkage of the inhabited area. New excavations undertaken by the Soprintendenza per i Beni Archeologici della Toscana within the city-walls have shown that part of the ancient town was still occupied by a semicircular structure, perhaps an oven, related to a rubbish dump containing Tunisian and regional finewares and amphorae. This indicates continuing connections with overseas and regional markets during the period between the early 4th and mid-5th century AD.[39]

Around the western side of Lake Prile, between Badiola and the ancient estuary, we can note the survival of two medium-sized villas, two farmsteads and the monumental maritime villa of Serrata Martini-Paduline with its related village. The two surviving villas in this area, unlike the maritime villa near the estuary of the salt lake, show a marked shrinkage of the occupied area, as revealed by the drop in the number of late antique diagnostic ceramics. Obviously we cannot rule out that these sites survived not as villas but as some different form of settlement. Another villa, along the Cortigliano stream, seems to have been abandoned no later than the late 4th or early 5th century AD. Subsequently the villa was reused as a small burial ground, generically dated to between the 5th and the beginning of the 7th century. During this period the area around Fattoria Badiola still hosted a few sites, perhaps related to this cemetery. A brief and limited excavation at this villa, undertaken in 1974, discovered at least two graves: one was stone built and tile covered while the other was earth cut and slab covered (Fig.8). Two other graves were destroyed by mechanical ploughing before the excavation.[40] The graves contained no funerary equipment, although during the excavation a bronze hair pin was found, whose flat head was decorated with concentric circles, perhaps dating to between late Antiquity and the early Middle Ages.[41] Only a very small portion of the villa was excavated, so no evidence was recovered for a continuity of occupation by a small farming community that used part of the villa as a burial ground; however, more detailed excavations may identify evidence of a rural settlement still surviving on top of the villa or in its vicinity.[42]

[39] See Çygielman 2006a.

[40] On this site and the burial ground see Curri 1978, Site 75.

[41] A similar bronze hair pin comes from the Byzantine *castrum* of Sant'Antonino, in the Finale Ligure, dating from the late 6th to the 7th AD, see De Vingo-Fossati 2001, 501.

[42] For similar cases see in particular Christie 2004, 20-23.

To the north, along the Alma river, only two sites continued to be occupied in this period: a villa and a farmstead. On the basis of the ploughsoil ceramics, both sites saw a reduction in the occupied area: materials dating from the 4th to 5th centuries were collected only in an area of the villa equivalent to about 10 % of its former size (1.5 ha); while on the farm only three vessels of this period were recovered near the south-western corner of the scatter.[43]

2.5. Late Fifth to Mid-Sixth Century AD: Surviving Settlement Complexity in 'the Second Phase' of Late Antiquity

In the study area, the period between the late 5th and the mid-6th century AD did not see a further drop in rural settlement density. Some villages continued to be occupied until the Greek-Gothic war and for a brief period between the late 5th and the early decades of the 6th century AD the number of small dispersed sites actually increased. The phenomenon of the late antique re-occupation of deserted sites was particularly concentrated in the hinterland of the town of Roselle, but is also documented along the western side of Lake Prile, at Le Mortelle. These small dispersed sites testify to the reuse of Roman settlements deserted for a few centuries. An overview of the site distribution provides sufficient evidence of the continuity of a structured settlement network up until the Greek-Gothic war; we cannot interpret this as evidence of the reversal of the earlier trend but only as proof that socio-economic systems retained a degree of vitality [44] (Fig.9). We can see a drop in the total number of villas, from 11 sites to 8, and farms, from 10 to 5; villages seem to have undergone an interesting growth phase, going from 5 during the former phase to 7. A new phenomenon in the rural settlement patterns of this area is represented by two cave-dwelling sites along the lower Ombrone river, on the northern and eastern sides of the Monti dell'Uccellina, while the seasonal settlement of Grosseto persists.

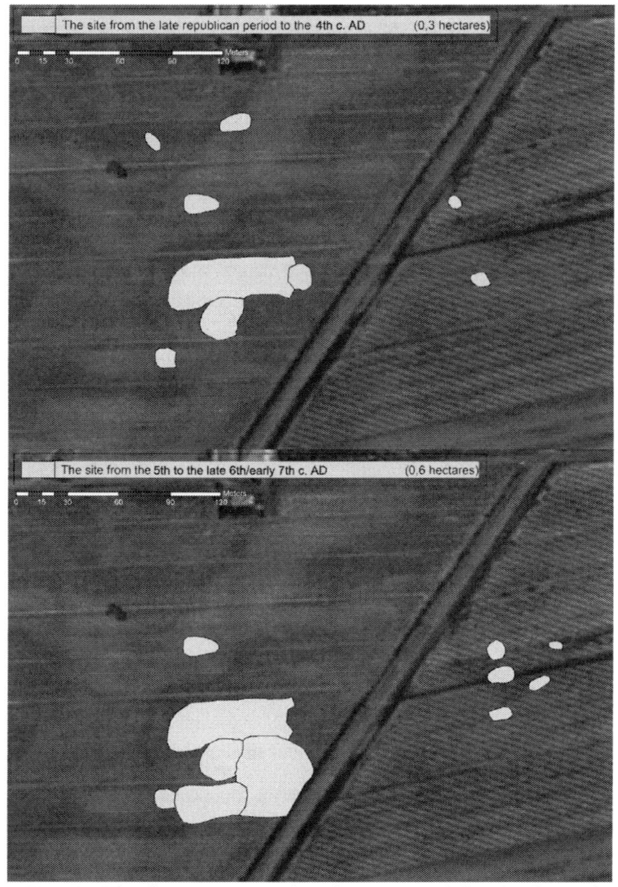

Fig.7_ The late antique development of the nucleated site of San Martino de plano on the middle Bruna river, in light of the infra-site survey (From Vaccaro 2008).

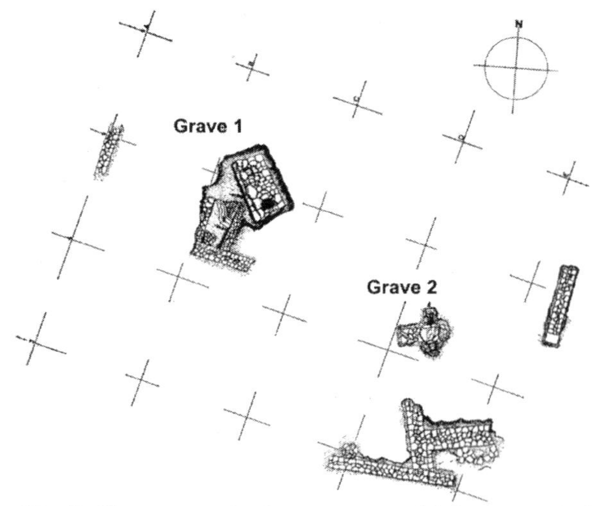

Fig.8_ Two graves in the cemetery which reoccupied the Roman villa on the Cortigliano stream (from Curri 1978).

[43] We can attribute to this phase only a form of African red slip D ware (Hayes 61B) and two types of bowl in *ingobbiata di rosso* ware.

[44] In *Apulia*, in south-eastern Italy, recent field surveys and excavations have shown a marked boom in rural settlements during late Antiquity. See in particular: Volpe 2005; Goffredo-Volpe 2005 and Romano-Volpe 2005.

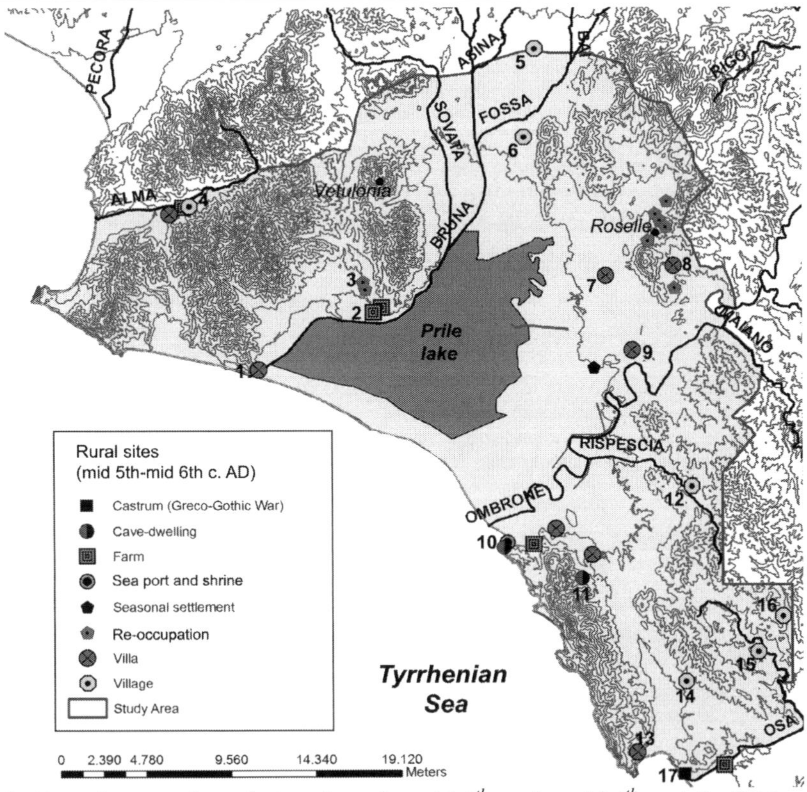

Fig.9_ Distribution of rural sites from the mid-5th to the mid-6th c. A.D. (33 in total). The main sites and localities mentioned in the text: 1.Paduline-Serrata Martini; 2.Fattoria Badiola; 3.Le Mortelle; 4.Val Molina; 5.Tabbiano; 6.San Martino de plano; 7.Aiali; 8.Casette di Mota; 9.Sterpeto; 10.Scoglietto; 11.Spaccasasso; 12.Podere Serratone; 13.Santa Francesca; 14.Podere Laschi; 15.Poggio Vicarina; 16.Poggio Querce Grossa; 17.Talamonaccio. (From Vaccaro 2008).

As concerns connections with Mediterranean markets, we must stress the slight decrease in the total number of sites with sufficient resources to purchase African red slip D ware, which still enjoyed a wide circulation.[45] Interestingly, during this phase, ARS and Mediterranean amphorae are almost exclusively documented at larger sites, such as villas and villages, and rarely at farmsteads. We cannot rule out that issues of supply and demand may explain the reduction in the total number of sites purchasing ARS and Mediterranean amphorae: perhaps the reason was the change in the value of imported goods, which became more expensive and restricted in their social distribution. ARS dating from the mid-5th to the 6th century was found only at 16 sites, while in the previous phase it was documented at 27 sites; Mediterranean amphorae of the 'second late antique phase' were collected at 11 sites, 31% less than before. This second phase seems to have been characterized by an exponential increase in regional ceramic productions, in the form of colour-coated wares and plain wares that gradually came to meet most of the local demand for fine and coarseware.

From the late 5th to the mid-6th century, 5 villas of the 8 still documented probably maintained a central role in the organization of rural settlements and in the exploitation of the countryside; the other three (*Hasta*, Podere Montesanto and the villa on the Alma river) show a marked reduction in the area occupied, probably losing complexity and falling to a lower rank in the settlement hierarchy. This is true of the only villa found in the Alma valley, which had already shrunk in size during the previous phase. According to the field survey data, the site was abandoned no later than the end of the 5th century AD, although a ditch dug for agricultural purposes yielded evidence of some limited and unsophisticated occupation in the 6th century AD. A clay layer, rich in charcoal and ceramics, was identified on top of a probable collapse layer about 40-50 cm below the land level. The ceramics collected, particularly *ingobbiata di rosso* and coarsewares, can be dated to the late 5th-6th century AD: possible evidence that the site was occupied at this period. Obviously this evidence demonstrates that the site survived, but the reduction in the occupied area, the probable building of structures in perishable materials on top of a collapse layer, and the absence of imports suggest significant socio-economic change. Probably these are signs not of a continuity of the villa, but perhaps of a different use or reoccupation of its structures, after a short interval, for quite different

[45] An analysis of the distribution of African red slip ware in this area over the long term shows a brief period of growth in the first quarter of the 6th century AD compared to the levels of the last quarter of the 5th AD.

purposes.[46] Without extensive excavations it is almost impossible to interpret this data correctly; therefore, we must ask whether the occupation represents a reuse of the site after a short period of desertion, perhaps as an effect of the possible transfer of this property to new owners, or whether the site was used by local farmers, who modified the settlement structure.[47] It seems fairly certain that this phase saw a further drop in rural population levels in the lower Alma valley as documented by the small amount of ceramic evidence collected at the farm[48] situated only 1 km east of the villa.

The apparent drop in rural population levels in this part of the Alma valley seems to have been partially counterbalanced by the foundation of what may be a new late antique small village at Val Molina. Along a country road, field surveys identified an occasional section with archaeological layers measuring 100 m in length. These dark layers yielded ceramic assemblages of coarse and kitchenwares, a few fragments of African red slip D ware (forms Hayes 91B and 99B), in association with a very small number of little stones and tiles. The same classes of materials were found, in smaller quantities, in the field next to the section. On the basis of the field survey evidence we can assume that this may have been a very small village or more accurately a hamlet, whose dwellings were completely built out of perishable materials or which at most had stone wall bases and perhaps tiled roofs. The numerous pieces of iron slag from the section and the field are evidence of iron working at this site, in accordance with a pattern typical of the sites along the Alma river from the Etruscan to medieval periods.

Along the lower Ombrone river, the decline of the last villas and farms does not seem to be due only to rural population decline, but probably results partially from the development of two cave-dwelling sites, perhaps as an effect of the shift of part of the local population and a fairly radical transformation in dwelling habits. Up to this phase, settlement patterns in this area were characterized by small to large farming sites, such as villas, farmsteads and houses, located along the *Aurelia Vetus* and near the market place of Scoglietto, which was probably one of the main gateways for the trade in overseas goods towards sub-coastal areas. Although the evidence for the development of coastal cave-dwelling sites in late Antiquity is scarce, this could tentatively be explained as the result of a change in the economic and production systems of the area. In the case of the late antique cave site of Scoglietto, 300 m west of the sea-port of the same name, the seaside location would tend to rule out a strategic and defensive function. Rather, it seems highly likely that the site was used to provide new support for the *cabotage* system making use of coastal routes; it was nearer the coast than the presumed port, located on the cape of the same name. The late antique cave site of Spaccasasso, on the eastern side of the Monti dell'Uccellina, was probably occupied by a single family group, specializing in the exploitation of woodland resources and perhaps in pig farming, certainly less labour-intensive than cultivating the alluvial plains along the Ombrone river. The development of the cave-dwelling sites of Scoglietto and Spaccasasso probably represented a turning point in the settlement trends of this area, which show a progressive decline in the number of farming sites during the 'second phase' of late Antiquity. There is no clear evidence for the continuing use of the sea-port of Scoglietto after the first half of the 6th century AD. However, the high percentage of Mediterranean and interregional ceramics from the two cave-dwelling sites indicates a continuity of connections between this area and the overseas trade circuits using the coastal routes of the central and northern Tyrrhenian sea. The economic resources of their inhabitants, who, at this late date, were still integrated into long-distance maritime trade systems, must also have remained considerable. A *sondage*, undertaken in 2005 at the cave site of Scoglietto, provided evidence of interest for an interpretation of the late antique settlement.[49] During this study, a heap of earth, produced by previous excavations in the 1930s[50] and 1940s[51] which aimed to investigate the prehistoric occupation of the cave, was re-excavated. An occasional use of the cave, possibly for a few burials dating to the early Roman period, is documented by a bowl in Arretine sigillata and 4 coins (two late Republican and two early imperial). Later, a further occasional use of the site is indicated by a Hayes 63 bowl in African red slip D ware, dating to the last quarter of the 4th century AD.[52] However, the most organized and complex occupation of the cave dates to between the mid-/late 5th and the mid-6th century AD. We can ascribe to this phase at least 59 ceramic forms including African red slip D ware (forms Fulford 65.2/Hayes 104A, Fulford 52.2/Hayes 93, Hayes 12/102 and Mackensen 24), colour-coated ware, Tunisian amphorae (Keay LXIIA type), Tunisian coarse ware and also locally and regionally produced kitchenware, the latter frequently presenting traces of fumigation suggesting domestic use.[53] Furthermore, the large number of coins, probably belonging to this late antique phase, appears crucial for its broader economic implications. During the excavations, 66 coins were collected, dated to between the second half of the 3rd and the beginning of the 5th

[46] On the relation between continuity of occupation and discontinuity of function during late Antiquity and the early Middle Ages, see in particular Carandini 1993b, 11-38.
[47] See in general Christie 2004, 8-12 and 20-23; Brogiolo 2005, 7-16; Wickham 2005, 477-481.
[48] During the previous phase this farm was still characterized by a marked reduction in size, but only two diagnostic vessels dating to this second phase were collected at the site, perhaps indicating periodic use.
[49] On this excavation see Cavanna-Cavanna 2006, 84-87; on the Roman and late antique pottery see Vaccaro 2007; on the coins see De Benetti 2007.
[50] See Sestini-Cardini 1935.
[51] Rittatore 1951, 27.
[52] See Hayes 1972, 109.
[53] See Chapter 5 for a detailed analysis of the ceramic assemblage from the cave-site.

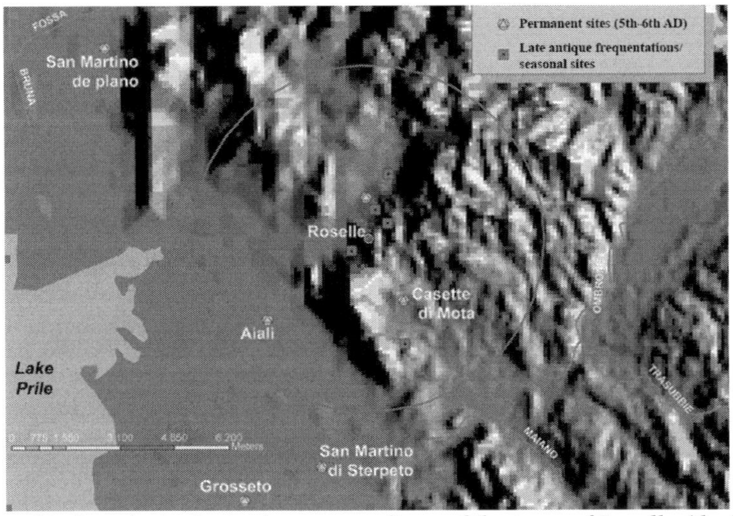

Fig.10_ Rural sites reused in late Antiquity in the surroundings of the town of Roselle (the buffer zone with a 5-km radius is centred on the town).

century AD, perhaps testifying to the continuing circulation of small bronze coins of the middle and late Empire during later periods, for minor commercial transactions. Another possible confirmation (along with the imported ceramics and coins) that activities related to overseas trade and exchange took place at this site is represented by two bronze coin weights whose weights are equivalent respectively to the *solidus aureus* and the *tremissis*.[54] All this evidence shows not only the strong connections of this site with Mediterranean and extra-regional markets, but also, speculatively, a probable role in the redistribution of imported goods towards the interior.

Settlement patterns in the hinterland of the town of Roselle and along the western side of Lake Prile seem to have been quite different. Both these areas see the occasional reuse from the late 5th to mid-6th century AD, with chronological and functional discontinuity, of sites abandoned no later than the middle imperial period. The new residents of these sites were probably single family groups who used the deserted structures on a seasonal rather than year-round basis. The re-examination of the ceramics collected during the *Ager Rusellanus* project in the late 1980s allowed us to identify some previously unknown cases of reuse during the late antique period (phase two).[55] It is important to note that 6 of these new sites were located around the town, within a 5 km radius from the city centre (Fig.10). Most of the reused sites were abandoned during the early or middle imperial periods, but two sites had already been deserted after the late Republic or as early as after the Etruscan archaic period; this is the case of a probable barrow, the area of which was partially reused in late Antiquity.

It is not easy to interpret this evidence, represented by a few late antique diagnostic ceramics from earlier sites[56]; we could suggest a short-term increase in dispersed settlements around the city as an effect of a new agricultural policy pursued by the local, probably urban, *élites*, or perhaps even by the bishop of Roselle himself[57], with the aim of intensifying the exploitation of agricultural resources and/or developing animal husbandry in the hinterland of the town. Probably the ruins of the original structures remained visible for some time and may have been used as seasonal dwellings or shelters by peasants. These sites were probably used on an occasional basis, perhaps during the times of the year when farming required the constant presence of the labourers. This phenomenon may date to the Gothic period, and in particular the reign of Theodoric, when the new political situation produced a period of peace and stability: an ideal situation in which to intensify the cultivation of the countryside. In fact, as some historians have pointed out[58], this long period of political and military stability not only ensured the potential for agricultural development without the danger of raids and the destruction of crops and livestock, but also led to an increase in the rural and urban population as a consequence of the greater availability of food. It seems certain, as is also confirmed by the ceramic evidence, that the increase in dispersed settlements around the town did not survive the Greek-Gothic war, when major changes took place in the settlement network.

[54] See De Benetti 2007.

[55] I was privileged to be able to re-examine the materials from Carlo Citter's *Ager Rusellanus* project (Citter 1988-1989) in 2002. I would like to thank Citter for this opportunity.

[56] This reuse is characterized by no more than 3 or 4 late antique ceramic forms in *ingobbiata di rosso* or coarse wares.

[57] The first mention of a *Vitalianus* or *Vitellianus*, *rusellanus* bishop, dates to AD 499. See Ughelli, 1718, III, 660.

[58] See in particular Forni 1993, 679-719, but also Vera 1993, 139-141. A passage from Cassiodorus' *Variae*, in which the author discusses the Gothic period in propagandistic fashion, is of great interest in this context: *'quia longa quies et culturam agris praestitit et populos ampliavit'* (see *Variae*, VIIII, X, 2, 276).

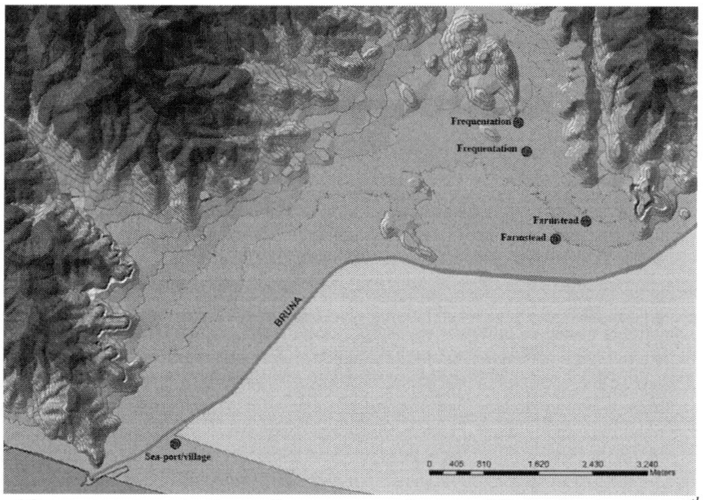

Fig.11_ The settlement network along the western shores of Lake Prile (mid-5th-mid-6th AD).

Two sites abandoned during the middle imperial period and reused in late Antiquity have also been identified in the Le Mortelle area, along the western side of Lake Prile. Here, a villa and a farmstead about one Km to the east of the two farms at Fattoria Badiola[59], occupied continuously from the late Republican period through to late Antiquity, were occasionally reused between the 5th and the mid-6th century AD.[60] This period saw the disappearance of the last remaining villas along the western side of the lake, with the sole central place being the site of Paduline-Serrata Martini near the Prile estuary (Fig.11). The area between Le Mortelle and Fattoria Badiola was thus totally lacking in villas, with only the two farms mentioned above surviving. Perhaps, in this context, the late antique reoccupation of abandoned sites may be evidence of an attempt to limit the progressive depopulation of this area through the reuse of the ruins of a few villas and farmsteads on the part of dependant or free peasants who maintained socio-economic links with the area's two late antique farmsteads. In this area, the rural population seems to have had a mainly subsistence economy, as shown by the lack of Mediterranean amphorae dating from the mid-5th to the late 6th/early 7th centuries AD and by the marked drop in the quantities of African red slip D ware dating from the mid- to late 5th to the 6th century AD.[61] By contrast, Mediterranean imports are still documented during this phase at the site of Paduline-Serrata Martini, only 7 km to the west. Apparently, after the late 5th or early 6th century AD, the site of Paduline-Serrata Martini did not play a constant role in redistributing overseas imports towards sub-coastal areas, while the ceramic profile of the few farmsteads along the western side of Lake Prile reveals closer links with the local and regional ceramic trade.

Villages continue to be well documented during this phase along each of the four valleys in the study area. Above we discussed the village of Val Molina, which may have absorbed part of the rural population of the Alma river. To the south, in the middle Bruna valley, the villages of *San Martino de plano* and *Tabbiano* survived well into the 6th century AD. In this context, the data from the rescue excavations conducted by the University of Siena in collaboration with the Soprintendenza per i Beni Archeologici della Toscana are of special interest.[62] The stratigraphic rescue excavations, which will be dealt with further later in this book, concentrated mainly on four excavation areas at some distance from one another. The aim was to determine the degree of conservation of the archaeological deposits and collect data on the topography of a site whose chronological and spatial complexity had already been noted during repeated infra-site surveys. As concerns the late antique period, which according to the surface data seemed to represent the site's period of maximum growth, the discoveries in Area 3000 turned out to be totally unexpected and of enormous interest. A test pit measuring about 4 x 4 m brought to light two burials in an earth grave cut into the clay deposit. The graves appeared to be bounded by low stone walls. That on the north side of T2 was well made with a poor-quality whitish mortar, whilst that bounding tomb T3 to the south was far more roughly built. Tomb T2, the earlier of the two, evidently belonged to a woman of high rank (Fig.12). The burial's valuable funerary equipment has

[59] During this phase one of the two farms seems to have seen a marked reduction in the occupied area from 1500 m^2 to only 100 m^2, while the other remained the same size (about 2500 m^2).

[60] The reuse of the villa and the farmstead in the Le Mortelle area is revealed by only three late antique ceramic forms from each site. An important diagnostic form is a type of flanged bowl in *ingobbiata di rosso* or *acroma depurata* ware, modelled on the African red slip type Hayes 91, variant C, and frequently attested in 6th -century AD stratified contexts of the town of Roselle.

[61] A fragment of a Hayes 104A large bowl was collected at a farm near Fattoria Badiola; a fragment of a Hayes 91B flanged bowl comes from the reuse of a villa at Le Mortelle.

[62] The excavations were directed jointly by Mario Çygielman (Soprintendenza per i Beni Archeologici della Toscana) and the author. A preliminary report on the excavations has already been published in Çygielman-Vaccaro-Agricoli-Ghisleni 2009, pp.259-277. Here I will summarize briefly the main data on the late antique occupation of the site.

Fig.12_ The late antique graves T2 and T3 discovered during the rescue excavations at San Martino in piano (photo by the author).

been dated by Çygielman[63] to between the 5th and 6th century AD. The deceased's personal ornaments comprised a pair of circular earrings made of solid gold with little globes attached to the lower edge, ending in a hook from which to hang a pendant (Figs.13-14); three bronze hairpins found next to and behind the skull, suggesting a complex hairstyle; a necklace from which at least seven amber necklace beads of ellipsoid shape survive; two spherical beads found at the sides of the burial, possibly from a bracelet. The clothing and/or a possible head covering must have been richly decorated, as we know from at least 100 glass beads (diameter between 0.1 and 0.3 cm) and as many as 70 pieces of gold thread with a hole running through the middle (length between 0.6 and 1 cm) (Figs.15-16).[64] It was clear from the excavations that tomb T2 was earlier than tomb T3, since the latter avoided cutting into the existing grave, but their exact dates are unknown. Since the two graves were close to one another they may have belonged to two members of the same family. The skeleton from T3, which was fairly poorly preserved, is still being studied, as is that from T3; given the absence of funerary equipment in the latter grave we have no information on the gender of the burial. Interestingly, the deposition of the burial in T3 suggests the use of a wooden litter as indicated by the two parallel grooves on the west side of the grave; these are probably the imprints of the wooden handles of a funerary bed. Both burials are characterized by an identical funerary ritual, similar to a *bustum,* with fires being lit near both tombs as indicated by the large quantities of charcoal mixed with sandy-clayey soil filling both graves and the reddened walls of the sides of the tombs. The extreme wealth of tomb T2, located in an area which was economically marginal, sheds new light on the possible existence of a local elite living in the most well-structured and flourishing sites in the countryside, such as *San Martino de plano*.

Another nucleated site, at Podere Serratone, along the Rispescia stream, was founded in the early imperial period and continued to be occupied at least until the 5th century AD. Near the gulf of Talamone the village of Podere Laschi still survived during the 6th century AD, as we know from the presence of Mediterranean goods such as African red slip D ware (Hayes 91C and 99B) and Tunisian amphorae (Keay LXII). The trend towards nucleation seems to have been more marked along the upper Osa valley where the long-lasting village of Querce Grossa, founded in the late Republican period, survived into the 6th century AD and where above all there is evidence for a new foundation on the south slope of Poggio Vicarina. This village, situated between 70 and 90 m above sea level, probably on an ancient terracing system, lies only 800 m west of the two farms at the foot of Poggio Castellaccio, which did not survive the late 5th century AD. Since the village was founded immediately after the desertion of the farms, and given the proximity of these sites to one another, we may be dealing with a population shift within the context of a nucleation trend[65], perhaps involving other as yet unidentified settlements. The ceramics collected at the village site

[63] *Ibidem*, particularly pp.309-311.

[64] *Ibidem*, pp.310-311.

[65] On the phenomenon of settlement shift in central and northern Europe during late Antiquity and the early Middle Ages see Hamerow 2002, 104-106.

Fig.13_ Position of the two gold earrings during the excavation (photo by the author).

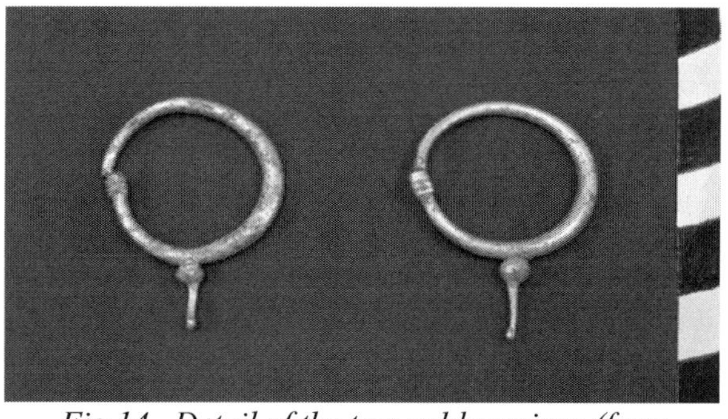

Fig.14_ Detail of the two gold earrings (from Çygielman-Vaccaro-Agricoli-Ghisleni 2009).

show that it was established in the 6th century AD and occupied for a fairly short period, perhaps until the early 7th century AD. Field surveys identified a scatter covering more than a hectare, presenting differences in the density of ceramics; within the scatter we recorded at least six clusters with distinct edges, probably corresponding to five small farms or houses and one storeroom, lying in the vicinity of one another but with no evidence of a planning process. However, some possible distinctions in the social structure of the site are reflected by the distribution of African red slip D ware (forms Hayes 80B/99 and 91C) and generic Tunisian and eastern Mediterranean amphorae which are concentrated in the uppermost house. The cluster measuring 6x5 m, situated some 50 m to the north of the house, can probably be identified as a small storeroom.[66] The ceramics from the other clusters consisted of traditional local coarse ware, with some items made in imitation of the Hayes 61B bowl and the Hayes 91C flanged bowl in ARS, and kitchenware, whilst African red slip D ware was completely absent. The ceramic associations may indicate that those resident in the uppermost house enjoyed a privileged position within the village.

To summarize, we can assume that during the second phase of late Antiquity the settlement network remained fairly varied and complex; the main evidence for this hypothesis is the survival of some villages and some new foundations, including cave-dwellings and small villages. In the hinterland of Roselle, the short term growth of a few small dispersed sites which reused ancient structures could be seen as an attempt to

Fig.15_ Glass beads decorating the clothing/head covering (from Çygielman-Vaccaro-Agricoli-Ghisleni 2009).

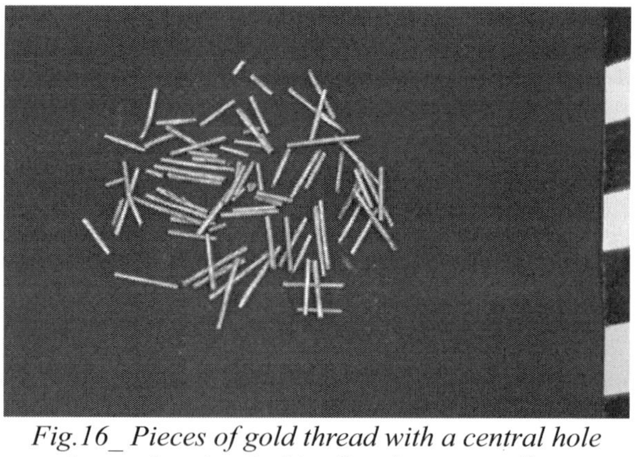

Fig.16_ Pieces of gold thread with a central hole decorating the clothing/head covering (from Çygielman-Vaccaro-Agricoli-Ghisleni 2009).

re-launch the cultivation of the countryside around the town; the same phenomenon, documented in the area of Le Mortelle, on the western shores of the salt lake, may have had a similar purpose. By this phase many of the former villas had disappeared, while at least three, surviving until the early decades of the 6th century AD, revealed a different use of the structures and above all a substantial reduction in the area occupied. Only 5 villas seem to have remained the same size and perhaps maintained an important role in managing the territory, though without extensive excavations it is impossible to say what sort of structural and social changes occurred at these sites.[67]

Field surveys are unable to identify social distinctions within the sites found; we must thus ask whether important components of the settlement network such

[66] Virtually only fragments of generic Tunisian amphorae and a few fragments of coarse ware were collected from this small cluster.

[67] On the same problem in the Tiber valley see Patterson *et alii* 2004, 18-20.

as villages and farms were inhabited by free peasants, or whether the social structure of these sites might be more complex, with both dependant and free peasants living here. An open problem is the identification of the main late antique central places in the study area. The town of Vetulonia lost its urban structure and its governing role fairly early on, probably between the early and middle imperial periods; by contrast, Roselle saw a reduction in the occupied area and important functional changes in some parts of the town, but maintained a central role in the area's settlement network from late Antiquity to the Middle Ages, becoming a bishop's seat by AD 499 and until 1138.[68] Perhaps Roselle continued to be home to an urban élite after the middle Empire and into the late antique and early medieval periods, though there is definitive proof of the existence of a privileged class only for a period after that considered here, when a burial ground, whose graves contained equipment dating to the mid-7th century, was established in the area around the city cathedral.[69] Probably, within the study area, the town of Roselle and the last surviving villas of Paduline-Serrata Martini, Aiali, Sterpeto, Casette di Mota and Santa Francesca were home to the local élites well into the late antique period. Only very few of the former rural sites seem to have survived the Greek-Gothic war.

2.6. Concluding Remarks on the Late Antique Period

The generalized survival of a sophisticated and well-structured rural settlement network at least up to the early-6th century AD, based on a system of villages and on the continuing occupation of some villas and farmsteads, thus suggests a more complex and varied population pattern than that described in some recent studies of settlement and economic systems in southern Tuscany.[70] The recent discovery of the rich grave of San Martino represents clear proof of the existence of a local élite which was still active between the 5th and 6th century and which still tended to occupy the largest and topographically most complex sites in this area and which represented itself in the funerary ritual through the richness of the funerary equipment. To this we should add the data on the production and circulation of pottery, which will be discussed in the following chapters, and which indicate this area's high degree of integration into overseas trade circuits at least until AD 520, and a large-scale circulation of the good quality pottery made on a regional scale. The discovery of numerous bronze coins and above all two coin weights at the Scoglietto cave context, which now increasingly appears to be a small centre for the redistribution of goods from the sea towards inland areas, suggests the existence of an exchange economy which still regularly used coinage of small denominations.

[68] On the town of Roselle during the long period between the Etruscan period and the Middle Ages see Nicosia-Poggesi 2004 (eds.).
[69] See Celuzza-Fentress 2004.
[70] On the marked loss of complexity of both settlement and economic systems in southern Tuscany as early as the 5th century AD see in particular Valenti 2004 and Francovich-Hodges 2003.

3. The Mid-Sixth and Seventh Centuries: the End of the Late Antique Landscape. Towards a New Rural Population Model

The picture of a still dynamic countryside during the early decades of the 6th century was destined to change radically in the second half of this century in the aftermath of the Greek-Gothic war. The disastrous effects on Italy's social/settlement and economic structures of this war are now widely recognized.[1] Not even the countryside of Apulia in southern Italy, which enjoyed a phase of significant demographic growth and booming construction between the 4th century and the early decades of the 6th century, seems to have been immune to the impact of this crisis.[2] The overall picture for Tuscany, by contrast, especially in the areas subjected to systematic and intensive surface surveys, shows signs of a significant population decline between the 4th and 6th centuries compared to the levels documented in the early and middle imperial period.[3]

The study area shows a higher degree of resistance to the supposed decline taking place between the 4th and early 6th century. This is indicated above all by a series of settlements founded *ex novo*, especially villages and medium-small sites, but also cave-dwellings which seem at least in part to counterbalance the high number of abandonments in terms of population levels. After mid-century, the data from studies in this area fall back into line with the overall picture; the 33 settlements attested between the mid-5th and the mid-6th centuries fall to 12 in use between the late 6th and early 7th century, a decrease of 275% (Fig.1). Villages are confirmed as the most successful form of settlement over the long term, with at least 3 previously attested sites surviving and the establishment of new contexts which saw their phase of maximum growth during the early Middle Ages (Graphs I-II). By contrast, only four villas continue to be frequented up to the early 7th century: Paduline at Castiglione della Pescaia, Aiali, San Martino di Sterpeto and Talamone.

Fig.1_ Distribution of mid-6th to early 7th AD rural sites in the study area.

However, the contexts which have yielded reliable data on the most recent frequentations suggest that these were highly precarious forms of settlement, probably no longer connected to the villa's function as an administrative centre. At Paduline, the last phase of use is marked by a layer of rubbish deposited in a room belonging to the bath area, while we know nothing of the structural transformations undergone by the complex. The materials from this rubbish dump, dating to between the mid-6th and early 7th century, indicate continuing commercial contacts with North Africa and probably with central and southern Italy, although most of the pottery found was made within the region. Although the continuing use of the bath structures for completely different purposes indicates that the site was undergoing a process of defunctionalization with significant alterations to its topographical layout, the

[1] See most recently Brogiolo 2005, Wickham 2005 and Ward-Perkins 2005, but also Wickham 2003, pp.390-393.

[2] Volpe makes a good case for the need to establish a chronology of late antique events in those areas of Apulia currently being studied, with a clear distinction between a 4th/5th and early 6th century phase of particular vitality and a late 6th/7th century phase when almost all the sites identified in the Celone and Ofanto valleys were abandoned (Volpe 2005, especially pp.305-309).

[3] The details provided in Valenti 2004, p.72 tell us that the various surveys conducted in the two provinces of Siena and Grosseto identified 2521 settlements existing between the 1st and 4th centuries AD, falling to 506 between the 4th and 6th centuries and to 201 between the 6th and 7th.

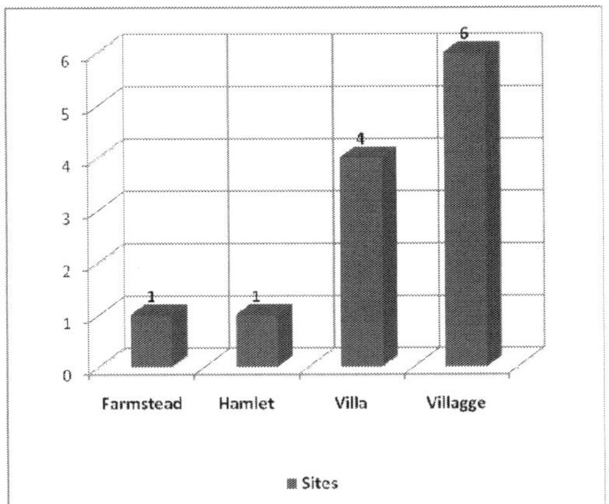

Graph I_ Types of sites dating from the mid-6th to the early 7th AD.

telling presence of products imported from elsewhere in the Mediterranean and from other regions of Italy may indicate the presence of an elite still sufficiently wealthy to access these commodities.

These few facts seem sufficient to suggest that the final phase of the villas was one of continuing settlement, not always associated with the continuing role of the site as an administrative centre. Some villas may have succeeded in maintaining an important role in the rural population hierarchy up to the late 6th century. However, this settlement and cultural model, already in decline (Graph II), gradually vanished after the Greek-Gothic war due to the marked weakening of the local aristocracies and the process of cultural change affecting the customs of the elites, less interested in expressing their status through monumental country residences.[6]

Chris Wickham has recently suggested that some villas may have maintained their role as the administrative centre of large estates during the Transition, despite having lost their monumental character.[7] However, it is difficult to shed light on this aspect through archaeological surface surveys.[8]

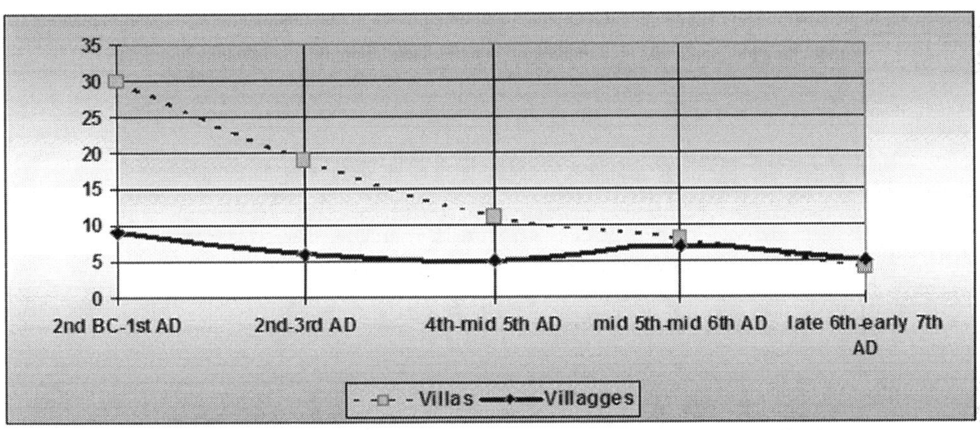

Graph II_ Comparison of villas and villages in the longue durée.

The villa at Aiali yielded very few pottery indicators dating to the late 6th century; these include a specimen of the *Atlante* I, Pl. XLVI, no. 7 dish, dating to between 580 and the 7th century, and a few specimens of flanged bowls made from purified fabrics. It is even more difficult to determine the purposes for which the villa at Talamone was used during this phase, on the basis of the data hitherto published.[4] An occupation of the site during the early Middle Ages has been suggested on the basis of pottery generically dated to the 7th-9th century, but whose definition and chronology remain fairly controversial in the absence of a systematic publication of the typologies found.[5]

By contrast, villages were successful settlement types, which not only responded effectively to their inhabitants' subsistence needs,[9] but also ensured control over the rural population on the part of the elites in those cases where the site's social composition comprised not only small peasant landowners but also dependent peasants. The success of villages over the *longue durée* is further confirmed by those instances where the population may have shifted from late antique settlements to centralized or dispersed early medieval villages placed within a circumscribed area of farmland.

[4] Fentress-Wickham 2002a, p.260.

[5] An initial attempt to define early medieval pottery indicators, in the form of jugs with a strap handle level with the edge and a grey core in the fracture (features which are too generic to date them with accuracy) can be found in Cambi-Fentress 1989, pp.74-86, with a tentative date of the 6th-7th century, later recalibrated to the central centuries of the High Middle Ages (Fentress-Wickham 2002b, especially p.61 note 4).

[6] On the latter aspect see Brogiolo-Chavarría 2005, p.67 and Wickham 2005, pp.478-479.

[7] Wickham 2005, p.477.

[8] This theory is valid in cases where structures can be identified next to the villas for the storage of foodstuffs produced by the *fundus* or where there are traces of craftworking activities connected with the processing of agricultural produce, dating to the final phases of life.

[9] On the role of the village as a form of settlement able to respond effectively to the subsistence needs of the rural population see Francovich 2004.

Two villages were founded *ex novo* between the late 6th and the 7th century: at Podere Serratone, along the Rispescia river, and at Casa Andreoni in the area overlooking the Gulf of Talamone. At Grosseto, after a period of at least two centuries characterized by the presence of a seasonal settlement linked to the exploitation of agricultural resources and above all to salt production and probably dependent on the nearby villa of San Martino di Sterpeto, the village proper began to form between the late 6th and the 7th century.[10] To these contexts we should add the small settlement near La Pescaia; this was a short-lived settlement abandoned before the central centuries of the High Middle Ages.

Detailed surveys carried out in this area[11] intercepted a settlement in the plains dated to between the late 6th and the 7th century on the basis of the ceramic evidence.[12] The materials of this date cover a total area of about 4500 m^2 and are in part superimposed on small quantities of evidence from the late Republican period. During the infra-site survey we identified at least 5 areas with a higher concentration of pottery, reused bricks and small pieces of limestone within the main scatter; these probably belonged to the same number of dwellings and cover a total of just over 1100 m^2.[13] Without extensive excavation, it is currently impossible to determine if this settlement cluster also comprised other dwellings; the settlement lies near the Rigo stream and has recently been covered by alluvial deposits, perhaps limiting our understanding of the site's topography (Fig.2). The settlement must have lain along a secondary road, probably of pre-Roman origin, linking the major road system with the inland part of the territory of Roselle, attested in the sources from the year 1298 with the name "via dei Muriccenghi".[14] The aggregated settlement of La Pescaia seems to have survived for no more than two or three generations during the 7th century. The dwellings were probably built using mixed materials, as indicated by the concentrations of stones and dark earth associated with pottery materials; the domestic pottery repertoires were extremely basic: cooking pots and *testi* for cooking, and jars/tankards for use at table and for storage.

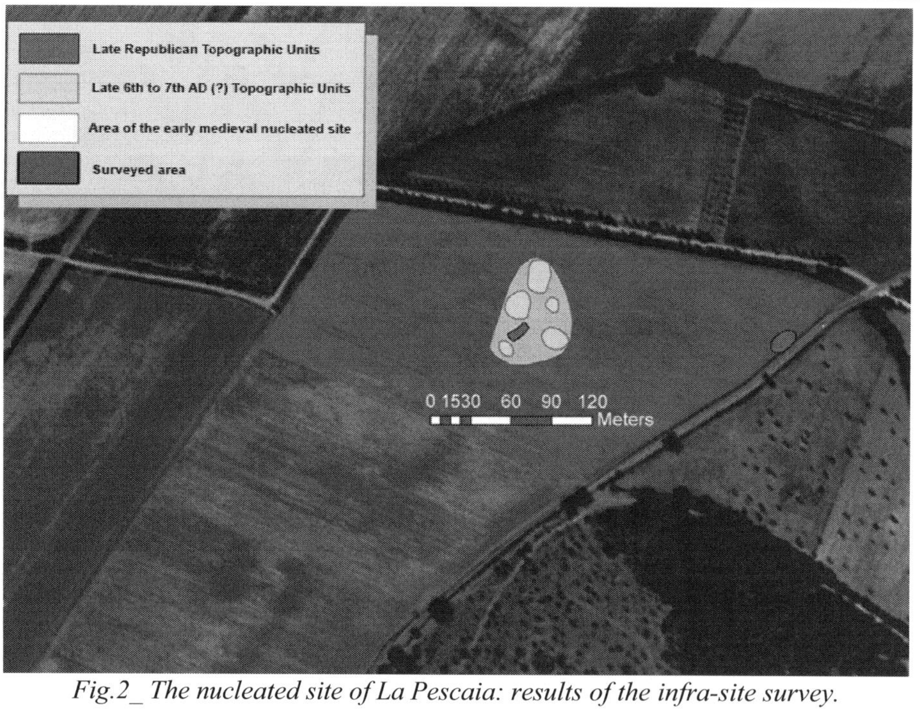

Fig.2_ The nucleated site of La Pescaia: results of the infra-site survey.

By the transition to the 7th century the late antique landscape had definitively vanished. With the exception of some sites established between the late 6th and the 7th century and destined for further development, the settlement system still surviving in the immediate aftermath of the Greek-Gothic war

[10] On Grosseto see Citter 2005 (ed.).
[11] The detailed study was undertaken to check the potential presence of traces belonging to a Lombard burial ground (to be discussed below), partially brought to light during the early 1930s during farm work (Cappelli 1934, pp.64-66).
[12] The pottery found at the site is extremely worn, considerably limiting the sample of specimens which can be assigned to specific typologies. An interesting fact is the absence of ARS and imitations of ARS, suggesting that the context was founded in the late 6th or more probably the 7th century. The materials of use for dating purposes include some specimens of a type of jug or tankard fairly common in Tuscan contexts of the 6th and 7th centuries. These are made from a semi-purified fabric and have thickened strap handles whose point of attachment is impossible to determine and barely everted and rounded rims. See Ciampoltrini 1998, pp. 289-304 and the specimen identified during the excavation of the earthen house of the 6th/7th century at San Quirico in the Chianti Senese in Valenti 1995a, pp.360-364, and especially on the artefact: p.147, Pl. LXVII, 8; p.363, Fig.90. A similar type is attested at the village of Poggio Vicarina, dating to between the 6th and early 7th century.
[13] T.U.'s La Pescaia 1.1 (318 m^2), La Pescaia 1.2 (361 m^2), La Pescaia 1.3 (86 m^2), La Pescaia 1.4 (244 m^2) and La Pescaia 1.6 (95 m^2).
[14] Prisco 1994, pp.312-313, Pl.6.

collapsed. The Lombard conquest of this area in the early 590s[15] thus affected a settlement network which was already heavily compromised and did not entail any significant changes. Even the pottery evidence shows clearly that contacts with the Mediterranean world had become progressively rarer from the mid-6th century and had in most cases ceased definitively by the third quarter of this century.

important role in the Byzantine authorities' control over the Ligurian coastal belt. But this is just one aspect of this change. A crucial factor, which in part led to the trade collapse, was the decrease in the economic power of the elites in much of Italy, and in particular in the centre and north of the peninsula.[16] This was accompanied by cultural changes affecting the aristocratic classes, due essentially to contacts with the new populations that had settled in Italy.[17] These cultural changes led, among other things, to a gradual loss of interest in those types of settlement, especially villas, which had been characteristic of the late antique rural nobility, now replaced by far more basic types of buildings. The identification of a clear break in the 7th century with respect to the late antique world, which continued to maintain a vibrant settlement pattern and complex economy, thus seems difficult to deny.

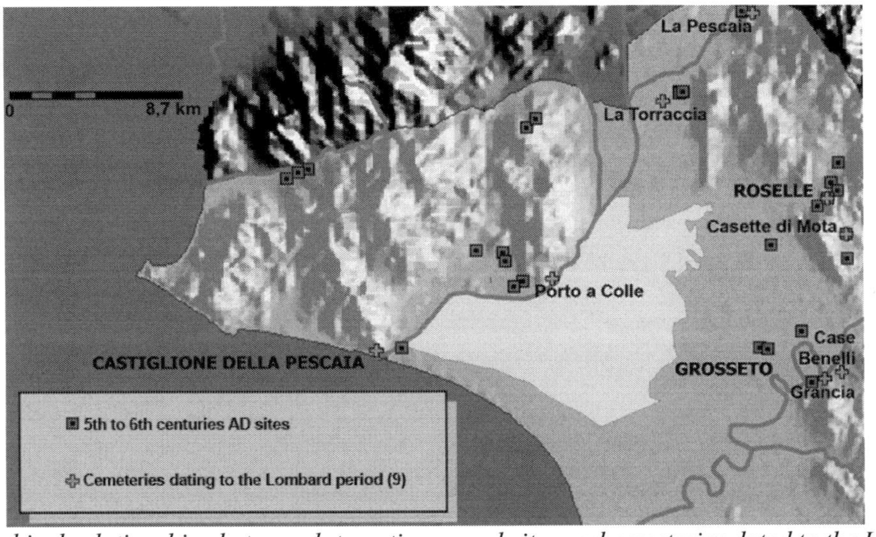

Fig.3_ Topographical relationships between late antique rural sites and cemeteries dated to the Lombard period.

Whilst for the central part of the early Middle Ages (mid-8th to 9th century) the territorial survey and the stratigraphic excavations at the sites of Casa Andreoni and *San Martino de plano* produced data of help in the study of settlement patterns, the population patterns of the mid-7th century, after the disappearance of the last late antique sites shortly after the year 600 are essentially impossible to interpret coherently given the lack of available data. This problem is in part linked to the difficulty of identifying diagnostic ceramics characteristic of this century. Whilst we now have a good understanding of late antique coarsewares and our knowledge of those of the central part of the High Middle Ages has been improved by some important publications we are still lacking an accurate definition of ceramic indicators of the 7th century. This problem is compounded by some more general structural considerations which require discussion.

The complicated events of the period between the last quarter of the 5th century and the third quarter of the 6th century, which saw the establishment of the Gothic kingdom and the disastrous impact of almost twenty years of war, in no way counterbalanced by the Byzantine reconquest which in much of central and northern Italy lasted only about fifteen years before the Lombard invasion, triggered a generalized decline.

As we will see, at the scale of our study area this translated into the collapse of long-range trade which continued to touch only on contexts which played an

[15] Kurze 2002a.

However, even within this profoundly different picture we can see clear signs of the continuing existence of a local elite, both urban and rural, which now tends to represent itself through funerary rites. In the area between the lower Ombrone river and the Bruna river,[18] with a particular concentration on the north-western banks of Lake Prile and in the hinterland of Roselle, we have clear evidence of funerary contexts ascribable, thanks to their funerary equipment of the second half of the 7th century, to the local aristocratic classes (Fig.3).[19] Unfortunately, with the lucky

[16] On this aspect see Wickham 2005, p.740.

[17] On this aspect see most recently Lewit 2005, pp.255-256, who dates the phenomenon to as early as the 4th/5th-early 6th century. See also Volpe 2005, p.305.

[18] Further south the only burials with grave goods of the second half of the 7th century were found in the Bengodi area near the Talamonaccio hill (Von Vacano 1985, pp.208-211).

[19] For the first mention of the various contexts see: von Hessen 1971 for the cemeteries of Grancia, Casette di Mota and the isolated find at Case Benelli; Celuzza 1994a for the necropolis of Roselle; Cappelli 1934 and von Hessen 1975 for the burial ground at La Pescaia; von Hessen 1975 for the isolated find at Grosseto; Curri 1978 for the male burial at La Torraccia; Vaccaro 2005c for the *scramasax* from Porto a Colle; Citter 1995a for the burial ground at Castiglione della Pescaia.

exception of the urban cemetery next to the cathedral church of Roselle,[20] none of these contexts has been subjected to extensive archaeological analysis aimed at determining their relations with nearby settlements. The important cemetery of Grancia, all of which has been excavated albeit not stratigraphically, nonetheless represents a fundamental context with its total of 80 tombs and subdivision into various phases.[21] Also important is the burial ground near Casette di Mota where at least 14 tombs have been identified,[22] established above the villa of the same name and with phases dating up to the 6th century. Of further interest in this context, thanks to the recent discovery of the late 6th-7th century settlement at La Pescaia, is the small cemetery studied between the 1920s and 1930s a few hundreds of metres west of the settlement site.[23] In other cases we are dealing with chance discoveries made during earthmoving work which have not led to extensive archaeological investigations.

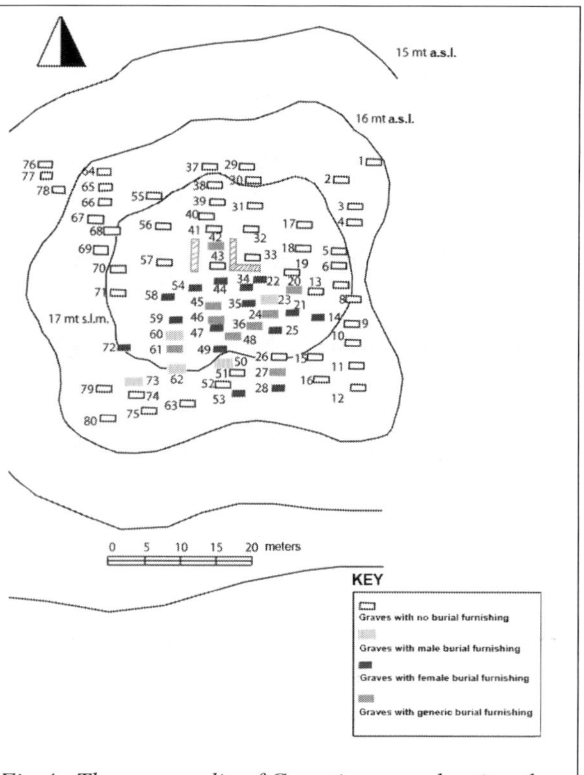

Fig.4_ The necropolis of Grancia: map showing the graves on the basis of the presence/absence of funerary equipment and gender (re-elaborated from von Hessen 1971).

It is important to note the date of these funerary features: the analysis of the funerary equipment has suggested a generic attribution to the second half of the 7th century.[24] The late date of the contexts compared to the various phases of the Lombard conquest, and the failure to undertake an anthropological study of the skeletons, makes an analysis aimed at determining the ethnicity of the burials impossible. More interesting are the socio-economic implications emerging from the analysis of markers of an internal hierarchy within individual cemeteries, and above the implications of their territorial distribution in relation to the 5th /6th-century settlement network. Whilst awaiting the publication of the city cemetery of Roselle, Grancia is the context most suited to an infra-site analysis since it has been fully excavated. This is not the time or the place to deal with aspects relating to the structure of this cemetery, already discussed in detail;[25] however, it is worth focusing on some important observations. Of the 80 excavated tombs, two of which may be double tombs, only 29 contained funerary equipment. Of these, 15 can be ascribed to women and 4 to men whilst in the remainder the funerary equipment was not indicative of gender (Fig.4). The tombs which yielded items of personal clothing were found mainly in the central and southern part of the hill. Around this cluster, clearly the oldest part of the cemetery, other phases of burials developed between the 7th and 8th century,[26] arranged in parallel oriented rows belonging to no more than a couple of generations. The tombs without funerary equipment were interspersed among those where grave goods were found, possibly indicating a composite structure which also included people of lower rank. Overall, the funerary equipment seems to reflect a degree of social uniformity in the most ancient nucleus at Grancia: the most commonly found objects are quintuple belt ornaments for men and convex disc brooches for women. There are at least three exceptions, represented by the male tombs nos 60 and 62 and the woman's grave no. 72: the former are the only tombs to have yielded a complete set of belt ornaments whilst the third contained a convex disc brooch made of silver rather than bronze. The picture emerging from the analysis of the funerary equipment from other cemeteries is identical, with no particularly valuable objects, whilst belt ornaments for men and convex disc brooches continue to be common. According to von Hessen, the latter are modelled on late antique and Byzantine typologies and represent a typical variant of the costume of this area.[27] The attestation of this type of funerary equipment, then,

[20] See Celuzza 1994a on the excavations conducted between the late 1980s and early 1990s.
[21] Von Hessen 1971, pp.66-67.
[22] *Ibidem*, pp.67-68.
[23] For a general reassessment of the published funerary equipment from La Pescaia see Vaccaro 2005c.

[24] On the date of the funerary equipment see veda von Hessen 1971, p.67.
[25] Von Hessen 1971; Citter 1997.
[26] Starting from the late 7th century, the "Christianization of death" led to the gradual abandonment of the practice of burying the dead with funerary equipment; the preservation of the memory of the dead was entrusted to the practice of donations to churches and monasteries which in return ensured the salvation of the soul, thus encouraging the consolidation of the properties belonging to the family of the deceased which controlled these church institutions; see Brogiolo 1999, pp.205-206, with bibliography.
[27] Von Hessen 1971, pp.58-59.

indicates the persistence of features typical of Roman and Byzantine tradition,[28] mixed with features more characteristic of Germanic dress in an acculturation process which involved an exchange of cultural features. The particularly elite burials include no. 2 at La Pescaia, whose grave goods are even more valuable than those found in tomb no. 72 at Grancia.[29] Among the funerary equipment found with the burial, alongside two earrings in the form of golden baskets dating to the mid-7th century,[30] were two disc brooches, one of which was made of silver and adorned with a central *omphalos* from which four pieces of silver leaf radiated out to form a Greek cross; the other, made of bronze has a red stone set at the centre[31]. The richness and variety of the funerary equipment makes this the richest female burial in the Prile area hitherto published (Fig.5). This woman was without doubt an important member of the local aristocracy which settled in the countryside around Lake Prile in the early Middle Ages.

Fig.5_ Funerary equipment from grave n.2 at La Pescaia (after Cappelli 1934).

A particularly important feature is the rarity with which weapons are attested and thus the number of members of the local aristocracies who represented themselves by borrowing features typical of the costume of the free men of Lombard tradition, in other words the *exercitales*[32]. In total only four *scramasax* of the second half of the 7th century are documented. One of these comes from the rural cemetery of Grancia (tomb 61), one with a gold damascening from the cemetery at Roselle and one each from the apparently isolated tombs of La Torraccia[33] and Porto a Colle[34] (Fig.6). The presence of these military features, though scarce, appears to characterize particularly important parts of the landscape. Whilst on the one hand the attestation at Roselle can easily be explained with the role which the city continued to play within the early medieval population network and thus with the existence of an urban ruling class, the find from Grancia may be linked to the strategic and economic importance of controlling the Ombrone river. This cemetery is located in a protected position on a modest hill overlooking the river and perhaps a ford, whilst the settlement from which the burials came, though not yet identified in the field, was probably in the immediate vicinity. Equally significant is the location of the tomb at Porto a Colle; on the basis of the placename this must have been a harbour on the brackish lagoon. Finally, the tomb at La Torraccia lies less than 900 m from the important village of San Martino *de plano*, inhabited up to the 6th/early 7th century and, more importantly, on the road built in Roman times running around the east side of Lake Prile.[35] The presence of tombs belonging to locally prominent individuals at key places in the Maremman countryside allows us to advance some considerations on land management during a period in which the markers of social distinction are difficult to document archaeologically. By this period, the process of acculturation of both Romans and Lombards was complete;[36] what the burial grounds tell us is that a local elite developed which exploited patterns of self-representation in part typical of Christianized Germanic customs – documented by the presence of little gold crosses and cross-shaped brooches[37] – and which used ceramic items of late Roman tradition[38]

[28] Von Hessen 1975, p.60.
[29] This tomb only yielded the silver convex disc brooch, with a gem that was originally set in its centre (von Hessen 1971, p.77).
[30] On the date of the basket earrings from La Pescaia see Possenti 1994, p.97, n.99.
[31] See Cappelli 1934 for the publication of the materials and Vaccaro 2005c for a discussion.

[32] On the social importance and military role of the *exercitales* see Gasparri 1990, pp.289-290.
[33] Curri 1978, p.105.
[34] Vaccaro 2005c.
[35] On the importance of this road in attracting the early and central medieval population see Chapter 8.
[36] On the process of acculturation of the Lombards and the local population in the *Tuscia* see Citter 1997.
[37] In the burial ground at La Pescaia, one tomb yielded three pieces of gold leaf with holes allowing them to be sewn onto fabric; these probably belonged to a little gold cross in fragmentary condition (Vaccaro 2005c); at Grancia a cross-shaped brooch was found in an unusual position, on the forehead of the burial. The function of this brooch must have been similar to that of the little gold crosses fixed to a veil placed over the face of the burial (Von Hessen 1971, pp.59-60).
[38] Pottery is documented in a tomb in the burial ground on the hill at Castiglione della Pescaia and above all in the small cemetery of La Pescaia. Here the association of coarseware with adornments belonging to clothing is a constant. One of the vessels from La Pescaia, which has since been lost, was probably a pitcher with a spiral decoration (Capelli 1934 describes the item, speaking of a one-handled clay pot with lengthwise undulating stripes); this form is fairly typical of residential and especially funerary contexts of the transitional period (Ciampoltrini 1998, pp.289-304). This specimen, like the flask with a combed decoration and a few red drips from the burial ground at Castiglione della Pescaia is modelled on late antique

probably manufactured by workshops scattered around different parts of *Tuscia*.

Whilst the discussions of ethno-genesis which have long attracted the attention of archaeologists take second place here during this late phase, it is essential to consider the relations between the funerary contexts of the mid-7th century and the distribution of late antique and early medieval settlements in order to determine if there was a hierarchical organization of the countryside, albeit weak and unstructured, even during the transitional period.

Moving in an arc starting from the south-eastern part of the Prile plain we can observe that only the cemetery at Grancia and the two tombs at Casa Benelli[39] do not appear to be directly related to a late antique settlement in their vicinity; however, this may be because the surveys undertaken in this area were less intensive. The only settlement identified at a distance of a few hundred metres is a farmstead; however, this was abandoned by the late 5th century AD and therefore cannot be the settlement inhabited by the population of Grancia. The theory advanced years ago[40] concerning the relations between a hypothetical late antique and early medieval *castrum* at Poggio Cavolo and the cemetery has not been confirmed by the 2005-2007 excavations at the hilltop site[41]. It seems more likely that the cemetery and the settlement coincided topographically at least in part, given the identification of wall structures in the central area of the flat summit of the low Grancia hill.[42] It is important to note that the nearby burials follow the line of these walls. Despite a rapid study of the cemetery[43] we found no other features belonging to the settlement; it therefore seems likely, given the favourable location of the site, that a late antique settlement context was reused for the establishment of a settlement with a cemetery, in accordance with a model that is archaeologically well attested in this and other areas.[44]

prototypes – especially *olpai* – enhanced and in part transformed with the addition of new formal and above all decorative elements. The frequent attestation of similar objects, often of high quality, in the Tuscan funerary contexts of the late 6th and 7th century is probably due to the presence of workshops operating at the sub-regional level for a clientele which was both local and otherwise, but which in any case identified this object as a typical element of its own customs.

[39] The two burials from Casa Benelli belong to the funerary contexts of the second half of the 7th century in this area on the basis of the characteristics of the funerary equipment (Maetzke 1959, p.82).

[40] See most recently Citter 1997.

[41] Excavations at this hilltop village showed that the most ancient phases hitherto identified belong to no earlier than the 9th-early 10th century, and above all demonstrated the absence of materials, including residual materials, belonging to a significant late antique and early medieval phase.

[42] Von Hessen 1971, p.57, Fig.9.

[43] *Ibidem*, p.55.

[44] On the reuse of late antique buildings for funerary and residential purposes between the late 6th and 7th century see in general Brogiolo-Chavarría 2005, pp.92-101.

The burial ground at Casette di Mota is a textbook example of a cemetery established on top of a large villa, with living phases still documented throughout the 6th century. This topographical overlap may indicate the existence of an area still used for residential purposes by the individuals who inherited control over the building and its *fundus*, probably still managed in accordance with traditional late antique models. The burial ground at La Pescaia, by contrast, does not seem to be directly related to a late Roman settlement; it may belong to the small late 6th/7th-century village already mentioned.

The isolated warrior's tomb at La Torraccia, a few km from the north-east bank of Lake Prile, lies in an area densely inhabited in Roman times;[45] particularly noteworthy is the village of San Martino *de plano* which, though founded during the late Republican period, underwent a phase of significant expansion between the 5th and the early 7th century AD, presenting continuity in its relations with Mediterranean trade.

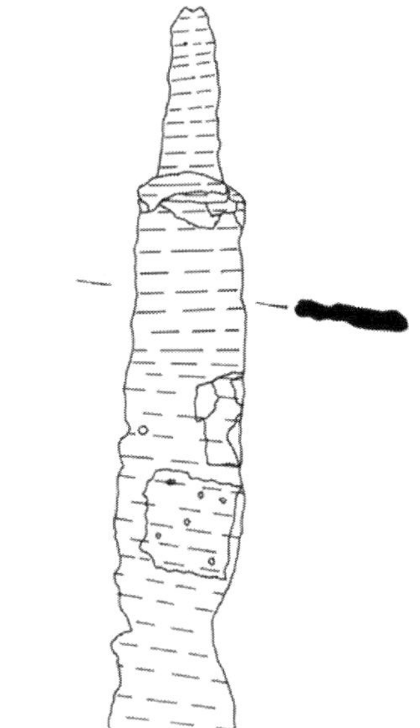

Fig.6 _ Scramasax found near Porto a Colle (Castiglione della Pescaia-GR). Drawn by the author, courtesy of the Director of the "Museo Archeologico e di Arte Sacra di Grosseto".

[45] See Curri 1978, especially pp.89-112.

The other warrior's tomb, at Porto a Colle, lies in a key strategic position for the control of economic activities on the west bank of Lake Prile and especially in the Fattoria Badiola area, which apparently continued to be inhabited throughout the 6th century.

Yet more complex is the case of Castiglione della Pescaia, where the establishment of a hilltop burial ground, later occupied by the medieval castle, coincides to a surprising extent with the abandonment, by the mid-7th century, of the harbour settlement of Paduline-Serrata Martini. The location of the tombs, which contained both male and female funerary equipment similar to those of the second half of the 7th century found at Grancia,[46] suggests that the settlement in the plains shifted to the hilltop, perhaps at the behest of the local aristocracy.

In general, the location of the funerary contexts of the second half of the 7th century seems to be determined by economic rather than strategic goals. They are found in areas which maintained a dynamic settlement network up to the late 6th century and were established at long-lasting villas and villages as well as in towns, indicating a tendency to maintain or recover part of the land management system inherited from late Antiquity, albeit with some evident changes in the location of settlements, as at Castiglione della Pescaia. The unusual "density" of funerary contexts of the second half of the 7th century in the Prile plain is probably no accident; this seems to be linked to the economic and property interests in this area of two major powers, the Duchies of Lucca and Chiusi, thanks to the Lombard conquest of the Grossetan Maremma. According to the reconstruction proposed by Kurze,[47] our study area fell under Lombard control in the early 590s following the combined invasion by Chiusi from the east and Lucca from the north. The presence of an enclave controlled by Chiusi on the west bank of Lake Prile which remained under the control of the public demesne of this city throughout the Lombard period, and the widespread presence of estates owned by Lucca in the plain of Grosseto even after the end of the early Middle Ages represent incontrovertible proof of this. What remains to be determined, then, is the social role played by the individuals buried in the cemeteries of the Prile area, who tend to represent themselves as an elite. The most plausible theory is that these were local groups whose prestige and economic power derived from their close ties to the far wealthier members of the urban aristocracies of Lucca and Chiusi. The latter probably delegated the management and supervision of the estates acquired about three quarters of a century early to the local ruling classes when they conquered the Maremma. Their local power thus derived from the ability of the individuals who represented themselves in the cemeteries to take on the role of *actores*, effectively controlling farming and animal husbandry[48] but above all the production and transportation of salt[49] on behalf of the two inland towns. In their funerary rites the elite of the Maremma modelled themselves on the far richer and more complex models of the aristocracy on which they depended, but without equalling the luxury and complexity of their funerary equipment.

[46] The surviving objects include a convex disc brooch and an ornament for a man's belt made of bronze. On these objects see also Citter 1995a, p.216.

[47] Kurze 2002a.

[48] As concerns the rent paid periodically by the tenants of the Bishop of Lucca we can mention three main lease contracts, dating to between the late Lombard and early Carolingian periods, all for estates in southern Tuscany (in the diocese of Sovana, south of the study area). According to these agreements the tenants were expected, in addition to some unpaid labour (*corvée*), to pay a periodic rent in kind (farm animals). This rent was taken to Roselle, leading us to assume the presence in the town or its environs of a collection site, possibly managed by the Bishop's trustee. For the documents, dated AD 762, 770 and 777 see respectively: *C.L.A.*, Lucca IV, n.973, pp.64-65; *C.L.A.*, Lucca VI, n.1011, pp.7-9; *C.L.A.*, Lucca VII, n.1061, pp.55-57. These documents may provide later evidence for a practice well-rooted in this territory since as early as the 7th century AD.

[49] On the two documents of AD 772 specifying a rent of ten and four *moggi* to be paid by the two tenants living near Giuncarico, in the Bruna valley, to the *exercitalis* of Chiusi *Guntifrido*, see *C.D.L.* I, nos. 263-264, pp.362-367.

4. Pottery Consumption in the City of Roselle in Light of the Sample Contexts on the North Hill

4.1 Methodological Foreword

The pottery analysed here forms part of the massive archaeological deposit from one sector of the city of Roselle, located on the north hill. The excavations were conducted by the Museo Archeologico e d'Arte della Maremma between 1987 and 1991, under the scientific directorship of M.G. Celuzza,[1] and covered the area hosting the partially excavated buildings of the Hadrianic bath complex, later reused as substructures for the cathedral church.[2] The pottery contexts studied in this chapter belong to the period between the abandonment of the bath complex, before the 4th century, and the construction of the cathedral which, on the basis of new data, can be dated to between the second half of the 6th and the early 7th century. The materials post-dating the early 7th century have not yet been examined given the presence of a large cemetery surrounding the church, used uninterruptedly between the 7th and 12th centuries. Under these circumstances, only a systematic analysis of the pottery from all the layers would have provided helpful information on the pottery repertoires in use over this long period. The use of this area as a cemetery between the 7th and 12th centuries has led to a modest increase in the anthropic

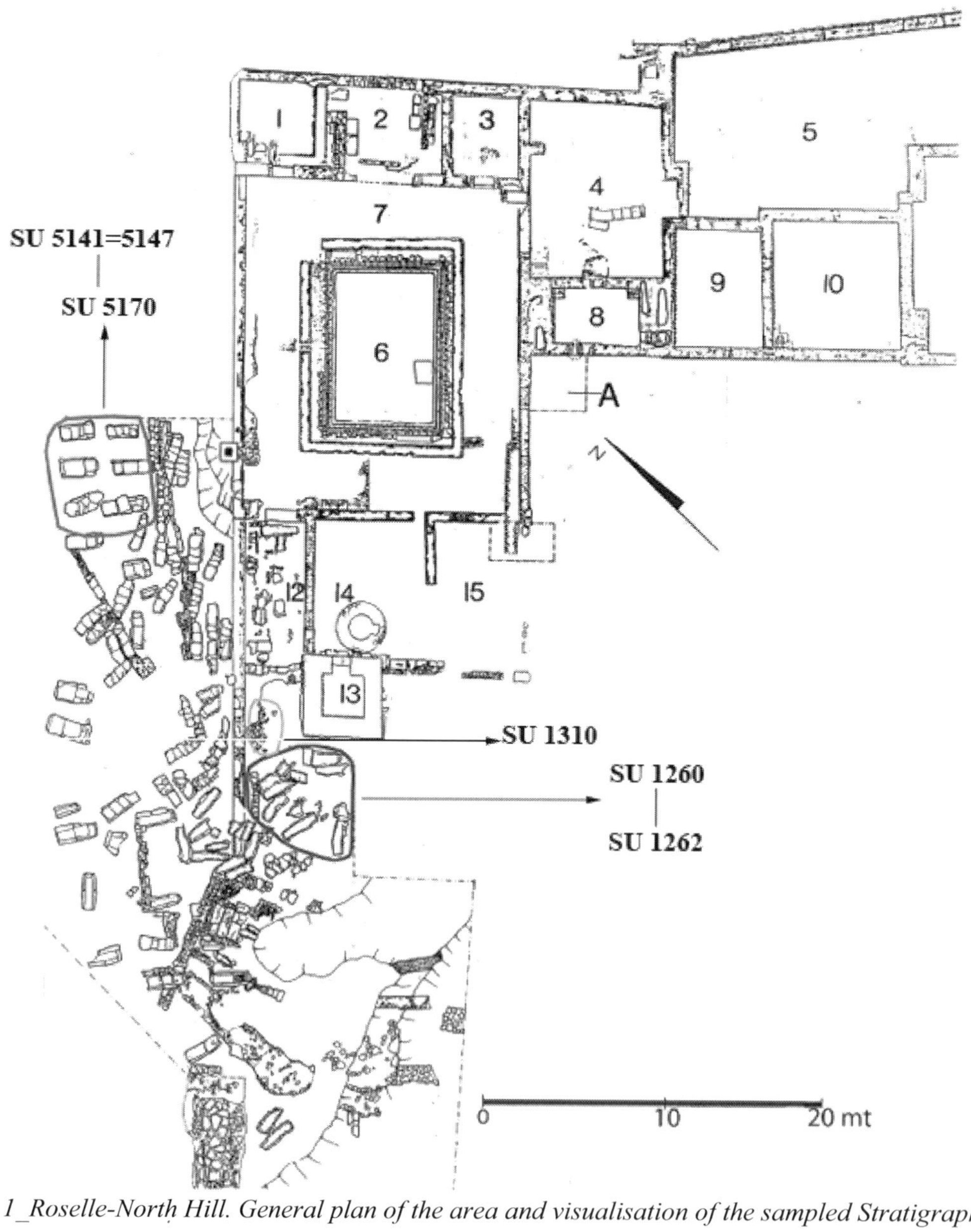

Fig.1_Roselle-North Hill. General plan of the area and visualisation of the sampled Stratigraphic Units.

[1] I would like to thank Mariagrazia Celuzza for allowing me to analyse the pottery excavated at the north hill of Roselle and for giving me access to the documentation on the excavations.

[2] On the transformation of the urban landscape of Roselle between the late Roman period and the early Middle Ages see Celuzza-Fentress 1994, Celuzza 1998b, pp.147-156.

layers and the scarce attestation of pottery materials from the early and middle part of the Middle Ages due to the constant mingling of the same layers of earth resulting in a high proportion of residual materials.

The pottery deposit was studied at differing degrees of resolution. For the period up to late Antiquity we tackled problems relating to the context's long-term economic history. This was followed by a more detailed and systematic analysis of the materials yielded by some layers of key importance for the study of pottery consumption during the period between the 4th and the 6th century AD.

The first, more general, level of analysis entailed the systematic study of the entire sample of African red slip ware yielded by the excavations on the north hill. This study was conducted in a highly analytical fashion by recording all the fragments belonging to the various productions. The aim was to reconstruct the history of relations between flows of Tunisian goods and socio-economic conditions in the urban context over the long term and to identify any changes which these relations might have undergone.

Thanks to their widespread distribution, Mediterranean slip wares and especially those from North Africa are valuable indicators for commercial traffic across the Mediterranean. This pottery class was not exported on its own but circulated mainly as a secondary product accompanying foodstuffs, of greater importance to centres of consumption. Thanks to the very narrow chronologies of the numerous types of fineware produced by the African potters, these allow us, to an even greater extent than amphorae, to track distribution trends within individual contexts, identifying periods of continuity or interruption which help to improve our understanding of a site's history.

The second, more detailed, level of analysis considered five contexts, selected for their wealth of pottery materials and chronology, covering the period between the 4th/early 5th century and the late 6th/early 7th century. The decision to study these sample contexts in depth was dictated by our objectives: to investigate the economy of late antique Roselle by evaluating the relations between pottery classes of local, regional, Italic and Mediterranean origin. This approach should allow us to advance some preliminary hypotheses on the economic history of an urban area which had become of central importance by the Hadrianic era and which rose to prominence once again between late Antiquity and the early Middle Ages when it was chosen for the construction of the cathedral church and the adjoining cemetery.

Contexts 5141, 5147=5170, 1260 and 1262 (Fig.1) belong to two different excavation areas: one (Area 5000) on the slopes of the north hill, immediately west of the Hadrianic baths; the other (Area 1000) in the area of the cathedral church and the early medieval cemetery. More specifically, context 5141 represents the definitive collapse of a structure which was still in partial use during late Antiquity, as indicated by the earth layer context 5147=5170; this layer presented several burnt patches, perhaps belonging to fireplaces, alongside ash, numerous miscellaneous metal fragments and a significant quantity of pottery. In all likelihood, this layer resulted from the abandonment of a production activity linked to the recovery and reuse of scrap metal. The room's reoccupation for this new purpose can be dated with certainty to a phase during which the baths, built in the Hadrianic period, had lost their original function. Given the context's properties, we can say that a workshop or a second-hand shop was established on the north slopes of the town in late Antiquity. A similar situation, again in Roselle, can be found in the final phase of use of the *Domus dei Mosaici* in the area south of the Forum.[3] Between the late 3rd and 4th centuries,[4] this prestigious building continued to be used but lost its original function when a metalworking shop or more probably a shop for the recycling and reworking of scrap metal was established here. The layers belonging to this late phase of reuse of the *Domus dei Mosaici* present similar characteristics to contexts 5147=5170, with the presence of ash, large quantities of charcoal and an abundance of metal. The chronology of the two contexts also appears to be roughly similar: the workshop inside the *domus* was dated by the excavator to between the late 3rd/early 4th and the late 4th century on the basis of numismatic evidence,[5] although other evidence suggests that the final chronology should be lowered to the early decades of the 5th century. The metalworking activities taking place in Area 5000 must have ended no later than the early 5th century, as clearly indicated by the pottery materials from the abandonment phase dating to between the 4th and early 5th centuries.

The frequent presence of joins between the few pottery fragments found in context 5141 (collapse of the building) and the more substantial finds from context 5147=5170 (abandonment of production activities) strongly suggests that we should not make a clear distinction between these two episodes; this material should be treated as belonging to a homogeneous and coherent context. There are in fact no chronological discrepancies between the pottery from the collapse layer and that from the abandonment layer.

[3] On the *Domus dei Mosaici* and a preliminary ceramic report see Michelucci 1985.
[4] The late Roman ceramics from the excavation of the *Domus dei Mosaici* are currently being studied for a project, directed by the author, aimed at reanalysing some key assemblages.
[5] Michelucci 1985, pp.115-116.

Fig.2_ Location of the North Hill area at Roselle.

Also of great importance is the study of contexts 1262 and 1260, interpreted respectively as the collapse of the bath building and the arrangement/levelling of this collapse layer with the addition of earth and other materials. These two contexts provide an extremely detailed picture of pottery consumption between the late 5th and mid-6th centuries (context 1262) and during the second half of the 6th century (context 1260). Although context 1260 is not directly related to the nearby church buildings, the stratigraphic sequence suggests that it is contemporary with or slightly earlier than the cathedral[6]. This is an extremely important piece of evidence which allows us to date the construction of the cathedral church to between the second half of the 6th and the early 7th century, a phase immediately predating the earliest phase of the cemetery, whose grave goods can be dated to the first half of the 7th century.

The construction of the cathedral in the early Lombard period and not, as previously thought, between the late 5th and early 6th centuries,[7] represents concrete proof of the economic power wielded by the city aristocracy and the bishop, its most important exponent, as late as the early 7th century.[8] This may also help to explain the origins and social destination of the first phase of the cemetery, laid out in an orderly fashion on terraces on the slope north of the cathedral facade and facing onto it:[9] the cemetery consists of tombs of regular shape, separate one from the other and oriented north-south; their grave goods date to no earlier than the first half of the 7th century. They clearly belonged to a local elite who chose this area as a privileged place for burial.

Fig.1 also shows the area hosting a circular hut built on top of the collapse of the Hadrianic bath complex. For this structure, we examined the pottery materials from the fill of a post hole (context 1310); this contained reliable chronological indicators allowing us to date the building's abandonment to between the mid-6th and the early 7th century, shortly before or during the construction of the cathedral. Initially, in the absence of evidence providing a precise date, this hut had prudently been assigned to the fairly broad period between the defunctionalization of the bath complex and the construction of the church.[10] However, its purpose remains open to interpretation: a residential hut or a functional structure, perhaps related to the construction of the cathedral.

4.2. Fineware Between the Second and Sixth Centuries AD: the Monopoly of ARS

Well-established and complex trade links connect Roselle with Tunisia for the supply of overseas fineware. Mediterranean slip wares from areas other than the various regions of Tunisia are completely absent from the context on the north slope between the 2nd and late 6th centuries AD. This appears to be in line with the findings from the surface surveys undertaken in the area between the Osa and Alma valleys, where the monopoly of African red slip ware appears to be absolute.

However, given the albeit tenuous and probably occasional connections that appear to exist between Roselle and various regions of the eastern Mediterranean as late as the 6th century we would also have expected to find some Phocaean red slip ware. This production is documented between the mid-5th and the 6th century, though in smaller percentages than

[6] Personal communication provided by Mariagrazia Celuzza (director of the excavations).
[7] The Lombard conquest of the territory of Roselle took place under King Agilulf, in about AD 593. See Kurze 2002a, p. 138 and pp.142-149.
[8] On the economic power of bishops in the late antique and early medieval period see Mor 1986, pp.7-15 and Volpe 2007.
[9] Celuzza 1994, p.609.
[10] *Ibidem*, p.608.

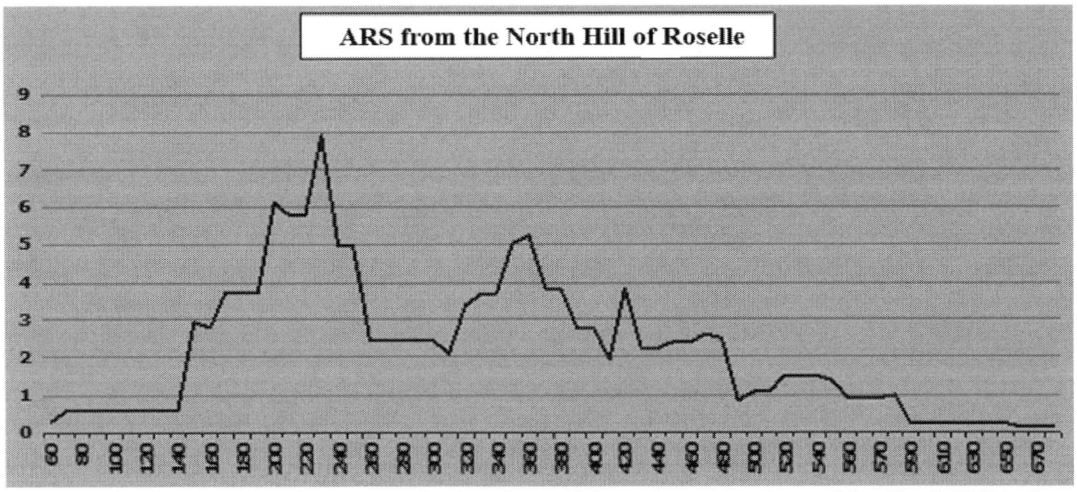

Graph I_ Individual weighted means applied to the ARS from the excavations of the North Hill in Roselle (value/years).

ARS, at various sites in the western Mediterranean.[11] Its absence is particularly surprising in light of the attestation of some specimens at Cosa;[12] however, this discrepancy can be explained not by confirming its absence from Roselle but by the failure to analyse other pottery contexts of the 5th and 6th centuries which might have yielded some specimens. As such, the generally low frequency of attestation of this class in Italy, with the exception of some specific contexts,[13] may indicate that its presence at Tyrrhenian coastal sites north of Rome was episodic and occasional, not indicative of a high and constant level of demand for these wares. The attestation of "fairly modest quantities"[14] of Phocaean red slip ware in contexts on the Ligurian coast such as Albenga and Ventimiglia can be explained by their privileged nature as large centres of consumption for imported Mediterranean products. Additionally, the Roman ports of Ostia and Portus appear to have played a fundamental role in organizing trade networks for the redistribution of Mediterranean goods to the smaller towns of the Tyrrhenian coast north of Rome. Given the small amounts of Phocaean slip ware found in Roman contexts,[15] it thus seems fairly natural that this class should be present in modest quantities or nonexistent in the settlements of the southern Tuscan coastal belt. Further confirmation of the absolute monopoly of Tunisian fineware over other Mediterranean slip wares comes from the finds at *Portus Scabris*, where a substantial influx of ARS is documented between the 4th and 6th centuries, with more limited quantities continuing to arrive into the 7th century; other classes of Mediterranean fineware are completely absent. Phocaean red slip ware therefore appears to have been unable to conquer large markets in the western Mediterranean and to challenge the primacy of African red slip ware.

The commercial success of Tunisian fineware can be explained in part by the fact that it could be sold completely or partially without incurring transport costs. ARS was a secondary product carried by the ships whose cargos consisted mainly of foodstuffs destined for the *annona*: grain and to a lesser extent oil from North Africa. As such, the *navicularii* who worked within this system of taxes in kind benefited from a series of incentives, including tax rebates, that allowed them to sell other goods not subject to taxation at a lower price after they had delivered the requisite foodstuffs to Rome; these goods included ARS.[16] The hierarchical control exercised by the state over the supply of taxes in kind thus triggered a mechanism by which the circulation of goods along the fiscal axis between Carthage and Rome was so well-structured and consolidated as to be immune to competition from trade flows from other Mediterranean regions, at least until the tax system was interrupted by the Vandal conquest of Carthage. Even after this, however, the consolidated primacy of Tunisian finewares was not challenged despite the new commercial opportunities opening up for the eastern markets thanks in part to the promotion by Constantinople of the wine produced here. Clearly, if the increase in the imports of transport containers from the eastern Mediterranean to Italian contexts[17] was not matched by a comparable increase

---

[11] On the production and distribution of Phocaean red slip ware see Martin 1998, pp.109-122 and also Reynolds 1995, pp.34-36.

[12] A specimen of a Hayes 3F dish is documented at Cosa; a few more fragments of Phocaean red slip ware were found during the excavations; see Fentress *et alii* 1991, p.216, and also Hayes 1972, p.416.

[13] An exceptional case is that of the late Roman villa of Agnuli at Mattinata, where Phocaean red slip ware is quantitatively predominant over African red slip ware. In general the distribution of this class of fineware mainly concerns the coastal sites of south-east Italy, more directly linked to the Aegean area, see Martin 1998, pp.115-118.

[14] Gandolfi 1998, p.254.

[15] The overview in Martin 1998, p.119, Fig.6, nos 32-34, provides a clear picture of the limited distribution of Phocaean red slip ware. This picture has now been confirmed and developed by new data from several Roman contexts where Phocaean red slip ware is quite rare. A good example is the north-east sector of the *Domus Tiberiana*, where African red slip ware is absolutely predominant, with Phocaean red slip being documented by only 2 fragments in Phase IV (first quarter of the 7th century AD) see Munzi *et alii* 2004, p.99.

[16] See McCormick 2001, pp.87-92.

[17] Arthur 1998, pp.157-179.

in Aegean and eastern slip wares, these were unable to compete with ARS even on the free market.

Moving on to discuss the ARS found at Roselle in detail, the context on the north slope yielded a total of 389 fragments belonging to a total minimum number of 190 individuals. Of these, 36% belong to production A, only 0.5% to production A/D, 17.9% to production C and the remaining c. 45.6% to production D. Of the minimum number of 190 specimens identified only some (63.7%), the majority, belong to an identifiable typology. On the basis of the typologies identified, a minimum number of 46 forms belong to production A, a minimum number of 1 to production A/D, 27 to production C and 51 to production D (Graphs II-III).

To investigate the distribution trend for ARS throughout its period of attestation at the context on the north slope and to evaluate any implications this might have for socio-economic and settlement patterns we analysed the individual weighted means.[18] The curve in Graph I highlights a first important fact allowing us to date the point at which production A ARS first began to be purchased in significant quantities at this context to the middle of the 2nd century. We identified only a single minimum individual dating to before this point: a Hayes 3A dish, produced in the second half of the 1st century AD. Some typologies which had already begun production at the turn of the 1st century continued to be widespread up to the second half of the 2nd century (Hayes 7A and 3B); most of the types that can be ascribed to production A belong to the period between the 2nd and the first half of the 3rd century (Hayes 9A, 9B, 14A, 14B, 14/17, 26, 27, 27 no. 7, 3C, 6C, 8A and 8B).[19] The supremacy of African red slip ware among the finewares reaches its maximum peak between the end of the 2nd and the early 3rd century, following what we could describe as a well-documented general trend which sees Tunisian fineware becoming dominant on the western Mediterranean markets thanks to a good price/quality ratio. This in turn was due to the favourable economic conditions created by state incentives for North African agricultural production, leading to an increase in manufacturing activities aimed at the export of secondary products to accompany the foodstuffs required by the Roman *annona*.[20]

The increasing quantities of imported ARS found at the context on the north slope at Roselle appear to be in line with the overall picture for the settlement. During this phase the urban topography remained sound, as also indicated by monumental building projects such as the Hadrianic bath complex on the north slope.

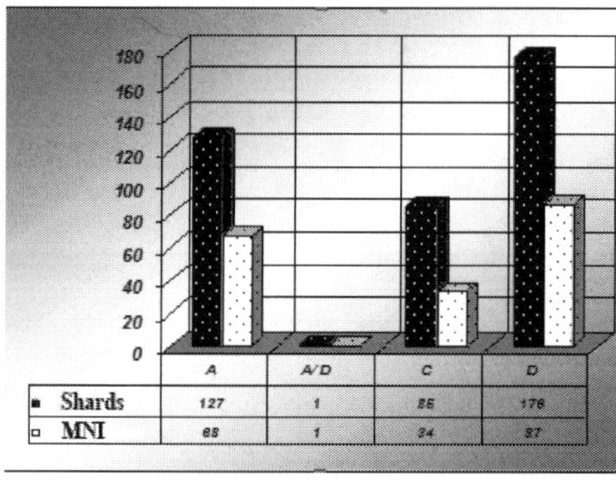

Graph II_ARS: productions, fragments and MNI.

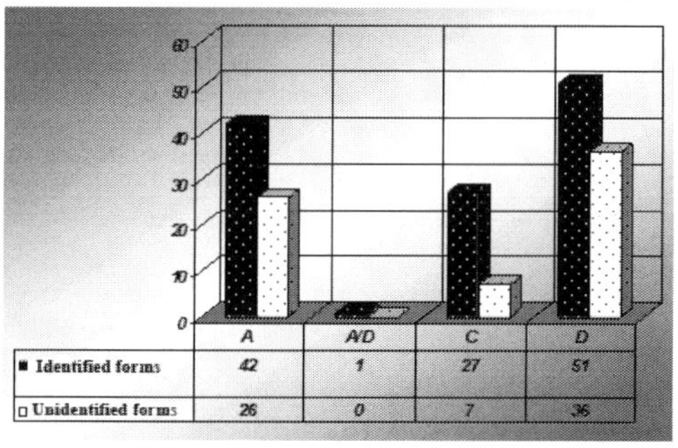

Graph III_ARS: productions, identified forms and unidentified forms.

After the early 3rd century, the trend for African red slip ware shows an obvious reversal lasting until the early 4th century, with a sudden and pronounced decline comparable to that later documented in the last quarter of the 5th century.

The contraction in the volumes of ARS at this time can be explained in part by the decommissioning of the production A workshops in the Carthage area. This was not compensated for by production A/D, which in our context is documented with only a single specimen from the first half of the 3rd century (Hayes 32).

Not even the establishment of workshops in Byzacaena from the early 3rd century and the export of the production C pottery manufactured here[21] seems to have succeeded, at least initially, in rebalancing the negative situation found at Roselle and other western Mediterranean contexts analysed using the same methodology, especially the Cosa area.[22]

[18] The first pioneering attempt to analyse the distribution of African red slip ware in the western Mediterranean using individual weighted means is Fentress-Perkins 1988, pp.205-214 and Fentress *et alii* 2004. See also the discussion in Wilson 2009, pp.237-242.

[19] The dates for African red slip ware are mainly those provided in Hayes 1972; *Atlante I*, pp.11-227; Tortorella 1998, pp.41-69 and Bonifay 2004.

[20] Panella 1993, pp.617-619.

[21] For production C African red slip ware see *Atlante I*, pp.58-60.

[22] The Albegna valley, during the 3rd century AD, presents a trend similar to that documented at Roselle during the same period; for the African red slip ware in the *Ager Cosanus* see Fentress-Perkins 1988, p.208, Fig.2.

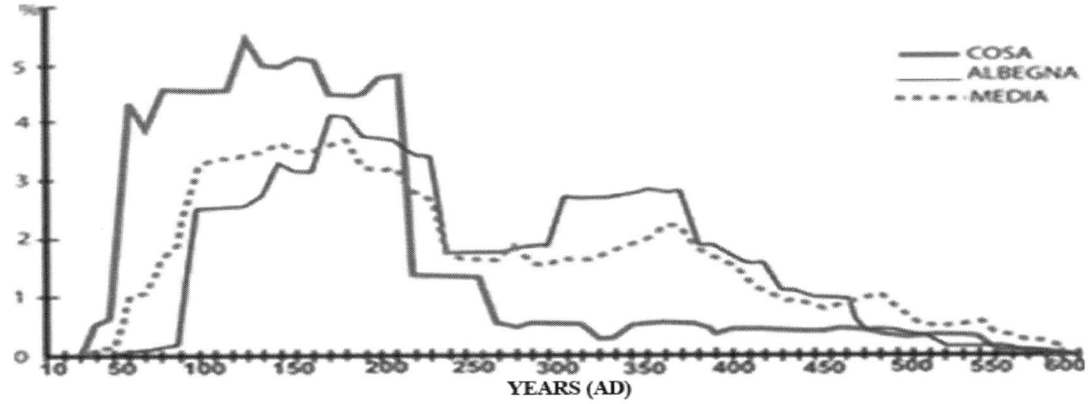

Graph IV_ IWM of the ARS from Cosa and the Albegna valley (re-elaborated after Fentress 2003, p.70).

The destinies of a town and its territory generally run parallel; this is true of the *Ager Rusellanus* and also appears to be so for the Cosa area.[23] Although it retained some public functions, the 3rd-century town continued to be a town only because its space bounded by walls gave it this status. From a topographical point of view, however, it had very little in common with the organic and complex city of the late Republic; the difference is all the more notable if we consider the public and administrative functions previously concentrated here.

At Cosa the drop in attestations of African red slip ware during the 3rd century coincides with a more general contraction in the size of the town, which appears to cover a surface area of just under 1.5 hectares, compared to a total area of 13.4 hectares within the city walls (Graph IV). At Cosa the only building projects of the Severan period are the reoccupation of four *insulae* and the construction of a *mithraeum* and the sanctuary of *Liber Pater*.[24]

No data is available on the shape of the town immediately following the Severan period, a time at which acquisitions of ARS in Cosa and its territory become progressively rarer.

At Roselle, although the data currently in our possession do not provide an equally clear picture of the transformations underway in the town during the Middle Empire, we can nonetheless note the absence of significant building projects during the 3rd century. A telling instance is the history of the *Domus dei Mosaici*,[25] the prestigious residential and official building south of the Forum constructed after the mid-1st century BC and restored and enlarged under Tiberius and Claudius. Despite the presumed continuity of settlement, the fate of this complex remains obscure between the mid-2nd century AD, when the building underwent radical restructuring work to render it yet more luxurious and opulent, and the late 3rd/early 4th century when its function changed radically.

Essentially, at Roselle as at Cosa the decline in the quantities of African red slip ware attested during the course of the 3rd century requires contextualization within a more general economic and settlement crisis. The effects of the economic decline in southern Etruria are clearly mirrored by the state of decadence affecting the towns in this area; of these, only Roselle seems to have enjoyed a slight recovery from the 4th century onwards.

The decrease in imported fineware thus coincided with a more general negative situation. On the one hand this was due to the reorganization of manufacturing activities in Tunisia, with the production C workshops in the centre of the country replacing the production A workshops in the Carthage area, but not immediately capable of inheriting their capacity for commercial penetration. On the other hand, the loss of economic power, especially of less central towns, led to a decrease in their capacity to access overseas goods. On the north slopes at Roselle 3 production C forms are documented with certainty, for a total minimum number of 27 identifiable individuals. The Hayes 50 deep dish, with variants A and B, is the most frequently attested type with about 85% of the total, followed by another type of deep dish, Hayes 45A, with about 11% of minimum individuals. The remaining 4% consists of flat-based Hayes 48 no. 13 dishes. Worth noting is the complete absence from this context of later production C forms. Productions C^4 and C^5 are not documented at all, though these are fairly widespread in other late antique settlements in the territory between the lower Bruna valley and the lower Ombrone valley; to these we should add the significant finds at the harbour site of *Portus Scabris*.

Roselle's economic and urban recovery in the early 4th century is reflected in the gradual increase in the "volume" of African red slip ware documented. This growth is rapid and progressive, reaching a peak in the

[23] On the long-term transformation of the urban landscape at Cosa see Fentress 2003 (ed.), especially pp.13-143 and also Vaccaro 2005b, pp.489-494.
[24] See Citter-Vaccaro 2003, p.310.
[25] See Michelucci 1985; Michelucci 1998, pp.122-137.

360s. This is an absolutely unexpected finding considering the context's history.

The baths built here during the Hadrianic period must have completely lost their original function given that, at precisely this time, the workshop of an artisan/second-hand dealer involved in the recovery of scrap metal became established here, in an area near the west side. Further proof that this area had lost its central status and that the bath complex no longer served its original function comes from the construction between AD 366 and 370 of a new bath complex, some distance from the Forum near the town gate accessed by the south-east road.[26] This building, dedicated by the *rector Tusciae et Umbriae*, suggests a new but probably short-lived interest on the part of central powers in revitalizing the urban fabric and relaunching the town as an economic and administrative centre. The superimposition of the maximum peak in attestations of ARS after the 2nd century and the construction of the new bath complex is probably coincidental, but it is nevertheless likely that this renewal of central interest in Roselle succeeded in triggering a fairly positive overall economic trend.

Although the urban structure of the town gradually collapsed, as indicated particularly by the Forum's probable loss of its civic and administrative functions and the appearance, from the late 4th century onwards, of the first burials on the central plateau,[27] its economy appears to have remained fairly vibrant. Further proof of this is the refurbishment and rehabilitation, between the 4th and 5th centuries, of the shops established in the early Empire along the *Decumanus maximus*.[28] The commercial and craftworking activities taking place here between the 4th and 5th centuries may be connected to the establishment of a market in the Forum.

During this period at Cosa, the marked decrease in African red slip ware faithfully reflects the town's general decline and the drop in population. Here, in contrast to Roselle, the significant and progressive decline in attestations was not followed by a recovery, except for a short interval in the first half of the 6th century. In the territory around Cosa, by contrast, the second half of the 4th century saw a significant intensification in the imports of ARS, coinciding with a phase of marked diffusion of production D wares (Graph IV).[29]

The town of Cosa saw the most severe crisis in its urban fabric between the 4th and 5th centuries: the inhabited area contracted so markedly that only just over 800 m² of the site, out of a total of 13.4 hectares, have yielded traces of frequentation.[30] The African red slip ware belonging to this phase – only 18 fragments – was found exclusively in the area of the Atrium Building I and the sanctuary of *Liber Pater*.[31]

By contrast, in light of the data examined here Roselle's economy experienced a period if not of growth then at least of recovery during the 4th century, immediately followed by signs of a crisis. In the 4th century, the high frequency of attestations of ARS suggests the consolidation and intensification of trade flows from Tunisia, destined mainly for the Roman *annona* (grain and oil), but with significant quantities of goods (African red slip ware) being traded commercially at other markets in the Mediterranean basin. The reestablishment of the fiscal axis between Rome and Carthage had positive effects seen in most centres of consumption in the western Mediterranean. Contacts between Carthage itself and major towns in the western Empire intensified, with the demand for foodstuffs (mainly grain and oil, but also fish sauces) and Tunisian finewares increasing significantly.

If we observe the relations between the increase in attestations of ARS at Roselle in the mid-4th century and the types documented from this phase onwards, it is apparent that this increase in quantity is directly correlated with the productive and typological renewal of the workshops in the Carthage area; these introduced the new production D in the early years of the 4th century. The close link between typological innovation and the increase in the amounts of pottery in circulation is a feature common to most of the sites in the western Mediterranean that have been subjected to quantitative analysis.[32] However, the underlying reasons for this connection are not entirely clear. One possible explanation is structural and not linked to changes in taste and fashions. According to this theory, a higher demand for pottery was met, not by increasing production at existing workshops but through recourse to a larger number of small production sites. This multiplied the potential for potters to try out new solutions with the aim of beating the competition from other workshops. A direct consequence of this was the introduction onto the markets of a multiplicity of new forms produced by numerous workshops.[33] The macroscopic examination of the fabrics associated with production D ARS provides some interesting information on the organization of production structures. At Roselle, at least four different fabrics are documented (Sig 2, Sig 3, Sig 6 and Sig 7).[34] Of these, the most common is Sig 2, associated with 57.1% of fragments and a minimum number of 64% of forms, followed by Sig 3, present in about 21% of specimens

[26] The foundation date of the bath complex near the south gate is based on a inscription mentioning a *Betitius Perpetuus Arzygius*, who was *rector Tusciae et Umbriae* between AD 366 and 370, see De Marinis 1998b, pp.162-164.
[27] Rizzitelli 1999, pp.108-109.
[28] Mangani 1998, pp.143-146.
[29] Fentress 2003 (ed.), p.70, Fig.25.
[30] Vaccaro 2005b.
[31] Fentress 2003 (ed.), p.69.
[32] On the distribution of African red slip ware between the 4th and 5th centuries AD see Reynolds 1995, pp.14-27.
[33] For this hypothesis see McCormick 2001, pp.58-59.
[34] See the catalogue of fabrics for details.

and 24.4% of fragments. Significantly less common is Sig 6 with 9% of specimens and 6.5% of fragments and finally Sig 7, found in only 6% of individuals and 12% of fragments (Graph V). An analysis of the relations between fabrics and typologies has supplied some interesting data (Table I).

First, it is worth noting that the workshop or workshops using fabric Sig 2 remained in operation for a considerable period. This workshop began production in the early decades of the 4th century and continued to operate continuously until the end of the 6th century, producing a large range of forms. A comparison with the massive production activity of the El Mahrine kilns,[35] in north-eastern Tunisia, which operated continuously between the first third of the 4th century and AD 640/660 provides some useful information on the provenance of some of the production D wares documented at Roselle. All the forms made using fabric Sig 2 from Roselle belong to the broad production repertoire of El Mahrine which, between the 4th and mid-7th centuries, numbered at least 64 different fineware forms. It would in any case be unsurprising if the production D ARS attested at Roselle, as at *Portus Scabris*, came mainly from El Mahrine, given the enormous importance of this production site. The analysis of the relations between production D fabrics and forms also supplies another interesting fact relating to fabric Sig 6. This fabric is associated with a specimen of an *Atlante I*, Pl. XLVI, nos 1-2 flat-based dish (Pl. I, no. 10), with 2 specimens of Hayes 104A deep dishes whose bases are decorated with parallel polished stripes (Pl. I, no. 8), and with

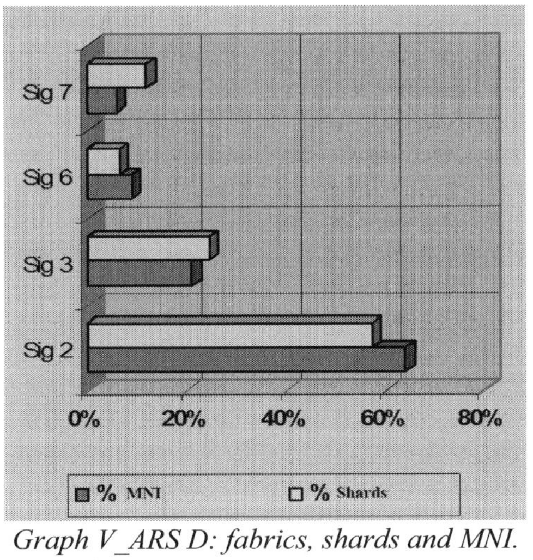

Graph V_ARS D: fabrics, shards and MNI.

another 2 base fragments of unidentifiable typology but presenting identical decorations. Since this fabric, fairly distinctive for its softness and uneven fracture, is not documented in association with forms made before the 6th century, it may have been used by a workshop which began production during the final phase of Vandal rule in North Africa or more probably just after

Fabrics	*Hayes and Atlante I forms*
Sig 2	H.58B, n.11; H.59; H.61A; H.61B; H.63; H.67; H.87A; H.91A/B; H.91B; H.91C; H.99A; H.99B; H.104A; H.104B
Sig. 3	H.50B; H.58B, n.11; H.59; H.91A/B; H.93B; H.99A
Sig. 6	H.104 A; *Atlante I*, Tav.XLVI, nn.1-2; bases characterised by ring foot and burnished pattern
Sig. 7	H.50B

Tab. I_ ARS D: types and fabrics

the Byzantine reconquest. One of the peculiarities of this workshop was the application of polished decorations, fairly typical of later productions such as the Hayes 105 and Hayes 109 flat-based dishes,[36] widespread during the 7th century.

TYPES AND FORMS ATTESTED BETWEEN THE FOURTH AND SIXTH CENTURIES

We will now consider the first phase of production D in greater detail. The context on the north slope yielded 3 types of dishes: Hayes 58B, no. 11, Hayes 59, Hayes 61A (Pl. I, nos 1-2) and the flat-based dishes Hayes 50B and 63. These forms were introduced in the first quarter or middle of the 4th century and circulated up to the first two decades of the 5th, with production ceasing definitively by the middle of this century. The Hayes 59 dish is the most frequently documented production D form in the Roselle context. This confirms a trend similar to that of the territory where it is also well documented, albeit to a lesser extent than another extremely popular deep dish, Hayes 67, which is not particularly well-represented at Roselle (Graph VI).

Other forms introduced at a later date, possibly between the last third of the 4th and early 5th century, like Hayes 61B (Pl. I, nos 3-4), which replaced the earlier variant A, circulated until the 470s. Among these we can note the presence of a single specimen of the Hayes 67 dish and 10 specimens of the Hayes 61B dish; the latter appears to have been significantly more popular than its earlier variant. At Roselle, the two variants Hayes 61A and Hayes 61B are attested in a ratio of 1 to 5, confirming the interesting data from *Portus Scabris* documenting the considerable success of the later variant.

[35] On the El Mahrine workshops and their ceramic repertoire see Mackensen 1993.

[36] For this surface decoration see types Hayes 105 and Hayes 109 from the late 7th-century AD context at the Crypta Balbi in Rome. Saguì *et alii* 2001, pp.268-269.

The significant quantitative increase in ARS during the mid-4th century is followed by a new reversal immediately afterwards, between the last quarter of the 4th and the early 5th century. This is fairly unexpected considering that the year AD 400 marked the point of maximum commercial penetration of production D African red slip ware in the markets of the western Mediterranean, coinciding with the phase of maximum expansion and development of the North African economy.[37]

One possible explanation for the decrease in ARS at this time is the gradual increase in the production of Italic finewares between the 4th and early 5th centuries; these were an acceptable and certainly less expensive substitute for African red slip ware. Among these, a formidable competitor was the so-called *sigillata chiara tarda* of central and northern Italy;[38] this pottery class is still difficult to classify and its widespread

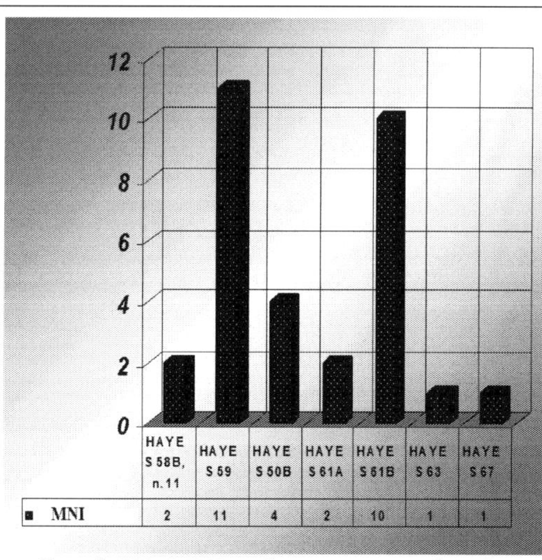

Graph VI_ MNI and main types of ARS D documented from the 4th to the 6th centuries AD.

distribution in central Italy[39] makes it necessary to re-evaluate the extent to which it represented a genuine commercial phenomenon. Another type of Italic fineware is *ingobbiata di rosso*, less prized but nonetheless produced in a well-organized way, which became extremely widespread in Tuscany between the 4th and early 5th centuries at both rural and urban sites.

On the north slope, contexts 5147=5170 and 5141 of the 4th/early 5th century indicate a clear prevalence of *sigillata chiara italica* and *ingobbiata di rosso* ware over African red slip ware. However, it is difficult to determine with certainty if the quantitative increase in Italic tableware caused the decrease in attestations of ARS or whether a structural decline in the influx of African red slip ware led to the reorganization and reinforcement of Italic workshops capable of meeting the demands of a market which remained large and complex and which could no longer be satisfied completely by Tunisian wares. In around the 420s attestations of ARS again recover slightly, probably thanks to the introduction of new variants, especially the Hayes 61B deep dish, whose success in the context on the north slope has already been noted.

To a more modest extent, the increase in Tunisian products on the Roselle market also depends on the appearance of a new variant, the Hayes 91B flanged bowl, whose production began in the early decades of the 5th century and continued until about the mid-6th century (Pl. I, no. 5). In the context on the north slope a minimum number of 2 forms certainly belonging to this type are attested; a further 2 are extremely fragmentary, making it difficult to determine with certainty if they belong to a variant A or B.[40] Before the Vandal conquest of North Africa, Roselle shows, albeit with values fairly distant from those of the mid-4th century, signs of a significant degree of integration into the economic system of the Mediterranean revolving largely around the fiscal and commercial axis between Tunisia and Rome. During this phase the Roselle market, in line with other large centres of consumption,[41] does not seem to be in any way adversely affected by the political and military turmoil occasioned by the various waves of Barbarians who crossed and devastated various regions in the West during the first decade of the 5th century.[42] There does, however, appear to have been a fairly significant decline during the 430s and 440s, coinciding with the Vandal conquest of North Africa and the interruption of the supply of taxes in kind to Rome.

---

[37] Wickham 2005, pp.720-728.

[38] The first attempt to define this ceramic class, produced mainly from the 2nd to the 5th centuries AD, was carried out by Luisa Brecciaroli Taborelli, see Brecciaroli Taborelli 1978, pp.1-38. For a recent overview of tableware manufacturing in late Roman Italy see Fontana 2005, pp.259-278.

[39] A preliminary analysis of the distribution of *sigillata chiara italica* can be found in Brecciaroli Taborelli 1978, p.5 Fig.1. According to Brecciaroli Taborelli, this ceramic class was widely documented at several sites along the Adriatic coast between Ravenna and Portorecanati, as well as inland at Gubbio and Arezzo. The large quantities of *sigillata chiara italica* found in the central Adriatic area led to it being described as *sigillata medio-adriatica*. This definition must now be reconsidered in light of the much broader distribution of the ceramic class in central and northern Italy and the identification of fabrics which can be macroscopically differentiated from those typical of the central Adriatic. The considerable quantities of *sigillata chiara italica* found at Fiesole, Florence and Roselle suggests the existence of various workshops located in the *Tuscia* and specializing in this production. For Roselle see also the preliminary data from the *Domus dei Mosaici* in Michelucci 1985, especially pp.109-111; for Florence-via de'Castellani see Cantini 2007; for Fiesole see Bianchi 1990, pp.158-168.

[40] The application of individual weighted means to these 2 specimens took into consideration the long period of production of both ARS variants Hayes 91A and Hayes 91B.

[41] For the general positive trend of Mediterranean trade between the late 4th and early 5th century AD see Panella 1993, pp.637-641.

[42] For an overview of the subsequent Barbarian invasions of Italy between AD 401 and 410 see Ward Perkins 2005, pp.1-62.

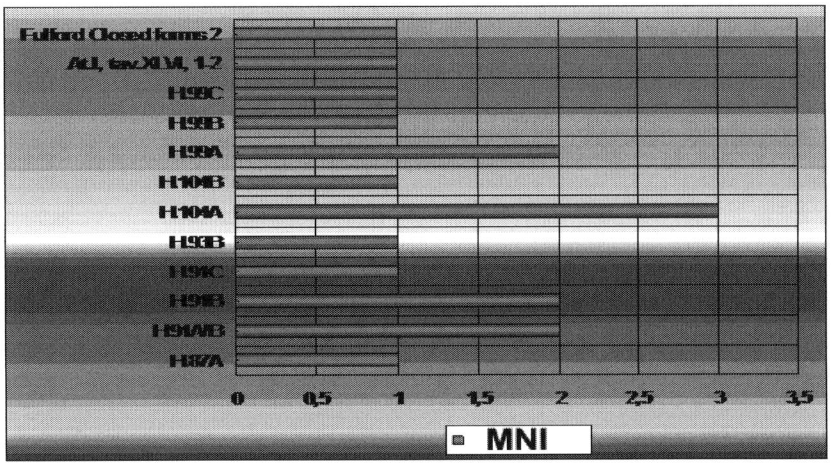

Graph VII_ ARS D: types documented between the 5th and early 7th AD.

Taxes in kind represented the major driving force that led large areas of Tunisia to specialize in the production of oil and grain; this was also the main channel for the absorption of any surplus production.[43] When this non-commercial trade axis between Rome and Carthage collapsed, the structural underpinning for a productive specialization that had its origins in the 2nd century AD also collapsed. Other significant trade flows of a purely commercial rather than fiscal nature left North Africa bound for the major towns of the Mediterranean. From these, a dense network of minor trade routes developed to reach less important settlements; these nonetheless guaranteed full integration into the complex and strongly hierarchical system of Mediterranean trade. In the immediate aftermath of the Vandal conquest of Carthage, most of these trade circuits were sufficiently well-established to survive the interruption of the fiscal axis between Rome and Tunisia with ease. In Italy, however, the collapse of the system of linked industries created by the *annona* naturally led to a decline in the volume of goods in circulation, although their level of penetration remained high, ensuring a capillary distribution.[44]

The generalized decline in North African imports to Italy during the early Vandal period (AD 439-475) suggests that most trade along the Rome-Carthage axis, even that which was not connected to the supply of taxes in kind to Rome, nonetheless benefited from this well-structured non-commercial trade system.

The Vandal conquest of Carthage led to a decline in Italy's economic power as the mainstay of the taxation system collapsed. Economic growth in Africa, which peaked in around AD 400, was closely linked to its role as the main production centre for foodstuffs subject to well-organized and regulated forms of "taxation". However, at least in the short term, the Vandal conquest did not lead to a decline in production in North Africa, whose economy remained dynamic.[45]

African red slip ware shows a further decline in the 470s after a phase of stagnation following the drop in attestations of the second quarter of the 5th century. This was followed by another phase of stagnation at very low levels lasting until the 530s.

Only small quantities of the ARS forms introduced by the Tunisian potters during the early Vandal period are present at Roselle (Graph VII). These include 1 specimen each of the deep dishes Hayes 87A and 93B and 2 of the Hayes 99A bowl, whose production began in around the mid-5th century and continued until the first half of the following century. To these we should add 1 flask of type Fulford Closed Forms 2 (Pl. I, no. 11).[46] The data from the excavations by the British Mission at Carthage have dated this type to between the second quarter of the 5th and the mid-6th century, although its production must have continued well beyond this, as indicated by the various specimens attested between the late 6th and the 7th century in the *castrum* of Sant'Antonino di Perti.[47] However, the Roselle context where our specimen was found – context 5506 –, dated to between the late 5th and early 6th century, makes it possible to ascribe it to the phase of highest frequency at Carthage.

It cannot be ruled out that the decrease in attestations of ARS recorded in around the 470s was related to the

[43] Wickham 2005, pp.720-728.

[44] On the circulation of ARS in the western Mediterranean during the first phase of the Vandal kingdom in North Africa see Reynolds 1995, pp.17-18. There is a marked difference between two macro-areas: Rome, with central and southern Italy, shows a decrease in ARS between AD 430 and 475; southern France, Liguria, Alicante, the Balearic Isles, north-western Sicily and the territory of *Tarraco* reveal an increase in ARS. It is highly likely that the trade in Tunisian foodstuffs and ARS towards the markets of *Baetica* and *Tarraconensis* was encouraged by good political relations between the Vandals who settled in North Africa and the Visigoths who settled in *Baetica* and *Tarraconensis*. See Panella 1993, p.651.

[45] Possible evidence for this is the introduction of new typologies in both productions C and D and the new amphora typologies introduced in the mid-5th century AD by the workshops which had shifted inland towards the management centres of the large estates. See Panella 1993, p.643 and also Peacock *et alii* 1989, pp.179-222, particularly p.203, Fig.2.

[46] See Fulford-Peacock 1984, p.84 and Pl.82, Fig.25, no.2.3.

[47] Mannoni-Murialdo (eds.) 2001, p.337, and p. 335, Pl.25 no.103.

immediate repercussions of the fall of the western Empire on economic systems and on the complex web of relations in the western Mediterranean. In Italy, the fall of Rome put an end to the commercial interdependence of the various regions of the Mediterranean basin. This seems to have led, at least in the short term, to a decrease in imports of fineware to less prosperous areas and towns which were politically and economically marginal[48] and thus to a further increase in the production of Italic tablewares such as *ingobbiata di rosso*.

The increase in the marginal costs of export[49] affecting the circulation of Tunisian products after the Vandal conquest may have led not to a systematic decrease in all commodities arriving from this area but rather to a drop in secondary products such as fineware. It is worth reflecting on the constant presence of North African transport containers at Roselle in contexts dated up to the late 5th century,[50] in contrast to the declining quantities of ARS. The most likely explanation is that, whilst overseas foodstuffs continued to be purchased despite rising prices because these were essential in the absence of a self-sufficient economy, the increasing costs of ARS drove people to turn to well-organized regional markets to meet their pottery needs. In light of the distribution trends for ARS in the study area, this would mean that in smaller towns from the late 5th century onwards ARS was no longer a product destined for mass consumption. Instead, it had become an elite product, which was redistributed from major markets like Rome only when there was a demand from members of the urban and rural elites.

As already noted, the period of stagnation following the decrease in ARS during the 470s lasted until the 520s. After this we see an interesting increase in attestations lasting at least until the mid-6th century, at which point there is another fairly marked decline. The recovery, beginning in the final decades of Vandal rule in North Africa and lasting until the Byzantine reconquest and the Greek-Gothic war is interesting. Worth noting first of all are the typological innovations promoted by the Tunisian workshops in the late Vandal period. In the early 6th century we see the introduction onto the markets of a new type of deep dish, Hayes 104, present at Roselle with the two variants most typical of the 6th century: A (Pl. I, no. 8) and B (Pl. I, no. 9). This form is accompanied by new variants of forms which had begun production earlier, such as the Hayes 99B bowl (Pl. 1, no. 6) and the Hayes 91C flanged bowl. All these forms continued to be manufactured at least until 570/580, making it impossible to determine whether they reached Roselle during the last phase of the Vandal domination of North Africa or after the Byzantine reconquest by Belisarius' troops between 533 and 534. It is certainly possible, as is frequently the case in the history of the circulation of ARS, that a phase characterized by typological innovations coincided with increasing demand, documented on an archaeological level by the presence of new forms and variants indicating an increase in attestations. However, another more complex hypothesis cannot be ruled out, although it is not easy to prove on the basis of the data currently available.

First, we should note one important fact: the "curve" for ARS at Roselle between the 520s and 550s is not wholly in line with that for ARS in the rural sites between the Alma and Osa valleys during the same period. Here the trend for ARS presents a significant and progressive decline after about 530, explained by the period of marked socio-political and economic instability triggered by the outbreak of the Greek-Gothic war.

At Roselle, by contrast, the positive trend continued throughout the second quarter of the 6th century, with a new decline in around the 560s. Events in the town during the 6th century may also provide an interesting lens through which to read the pottery data. On the basis of some still inconclusive evidence, it has been suggested that a *castrum* was built at Roselle during the 6th century, as at Cosa.[51] The site's good strategic position, on high ground and naturally protected, would have made it easy to defend. The construction of a few well-considered defensive structures would have sufficed to give the plateau a new military purpose, whilst the robust wall circuit would have done the rest. The substantial remains of structures belonging to fortifications, unfortunately impossible to date, have been found on the highest area of the site, occupied by the amphitheatre.[52] Another interesting but not

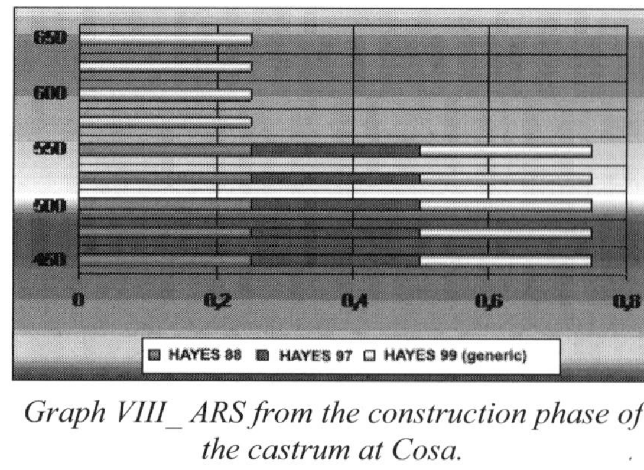

Graph VIII_ ARS from the construction phase of the castrum at Cosa.

[48] A negative trend in ARS distribution is documented in the *Ager Cosanus* between the late 5th and early 6th century AD, see Fentress-Perkins 1988, p.208, Fig.2. A similar trend is also documented in the study area between the Osa and Alma rivers.
[49] Wickham 2005, pp.709-713.
[50] This observation derives from an overview of the late Roman ceramic assemblages excavated on the north slopes at Roselle. The preliminary analysis was carried out by the author.

[51] Celuzza-Fentress 1994, pp.609-610.
[52] Celuzza 1998a, p.45.

necessarily defensive structure which can be ascribed to the 6th century[53] is the wall in *opus africanum* built above the road whose construction entailed the demolition of the entrances to some houses or shops. The small building with a rectangular base partially obstructing the south-east road, by contrast, had a purely military function: it can be identified as a *phylacterion*.[54] No definitive information is available on the period at which this structure was built; a *terminus post quem* of the early 5th century has been proposed. However this does not rule out a 6th-century date, perhaps in relation to the militarization of the town at the time of the Greek-Gothic war.

If Roselle, like Cosa,[55] took on a prevalently military and strategic function during the 6th century, this would help to explain why attestations of ARS in our context recovered significantly in the second half of this century. Cosa similarly regained importance thanks to the establishment of a farmstead for the storage of foodstuffs on the *arx* and later the construction of the *castrum*, also on the *arx*, in connection with the village which had developed in the Forum. At the same time we see an increase in attestations of ARS and to a lesser extent other Mediterranean slip wares; North African, Italic and Eastern transport containers[56] are also present. The recovery of attestations of ARS between the early and the third quarter of the 6th century at Cosa reflects the renewed interest in the settlement on the part of central powers thanks specifically to its role during the Greek-Gothic war. The chronology of the later forms in African red slip ware attested at Cosa and Roselle seems to suggest that relations with Mediterranean trade networks intensified especially in the first half of the 6th century. At Roselle only a single new form dating to after the mid-6th century is attested: a Hayes 99B/C (Pl. I, no. 7). An isolated specimen of the flat-based dish *Atlante I*, Pl. XLVI, 1-2 belongs to the late production phase of ARS, characterized by types produced between 580 and the 7th century (Pl. I, no. 10). However, its presence in a context stratigraphically predating the construction of the church (context 5006) allows us to date its "arrival" at Roselle to before the late 6th/early 7th century.

The data from Cosa do not differ significantly from the picture supplied by the sample from Roselle. The ARS from the construction phase of the *castrum* appears to date essentially to the long period between the mid-5th and the mid-6th century,[57] whilst any later dates can be explained by the long chronology of the generic Hayes 99 bowl, manufactured between the mid-5th century and 625/650 (Graph VIII). More detailed information comes from an analysis of the weighted means of non-

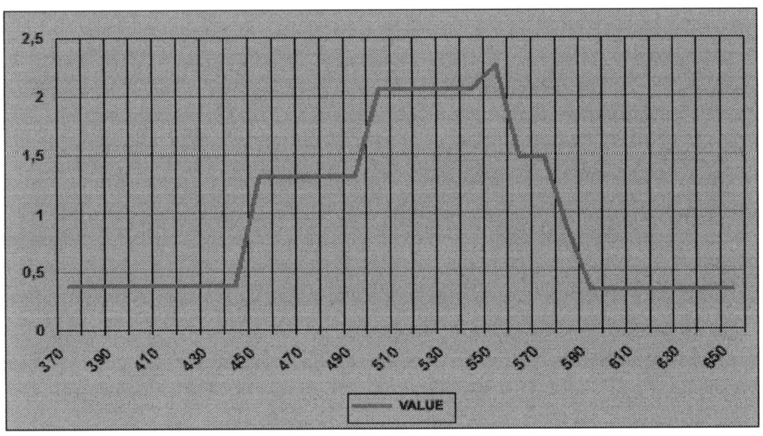

Graph IX_ The ARS trend over time (IWM) from Brown's excavation at the Byzantine castrum in Cosa.

[53] On this structure and its possible function as a terracing wall see *ibidem*, p.45. It is also worth noting the use of the same building technique for the defensive structures of two sites interpreted as 6th-century AD *castra*: Cosa and Talamonaccio. See Fentress *et alii* 1991, pp.208-209.

[54] On this structure see De Marinis 1998a, pp.159-160.

[55] At Cosa, the short-lived revival between the late 5th and the 6th century AD was probably linked to the site's strategic role rather than to a persisting urban role. Between the late 5th and late 6th century AD settlement patterns at Cosa were characterized by two main phases: the construction of a farmhouse with associated granary and stables and subsequently the building of a *castrum*, both located on the *Arx*. During the 6th century the Forum was briefly revitalized when a small village, a Christian church and a small cemetery were established there. The well-organized layout of this occupation is indicated by the development of a road connecting the village to the *Arx*. On the transformation taking place at Cosa during the 6th century AD see Fentress 2003 (ed.), pp.72-80 and also Vaccaro 2005b.

[56] I refer to the ceramics from the construction phase of the *castrum*, in Fentress *et alii* 1991, pp.215-216. The 6th-century AD ARS, found *in situ*, is represented by forms Hayes 88, 97 and 99, to which we must add a minimum vessel of *céramique derive de sigillée paléochrétienne* (DSP). Many non-stratified ceramics were also found: forms Hayes 91A-B, 91D, 93, 94, 99A-B, 99C, 103, 104 and Fulford 68.1 in ARS and 1 specimen of Hayes 3F dish in PRS. The amphora record is represented by a single specimen of Keay LXII from Tunisia and a generic eastern Mediterranean amphora with a ribbed wall. More data has recently been provided by reanalysing the Forum cistern dump, which dates to the first half of the 6th century AD. Forms Hayes 91C, 99A, 88, 103D and 104 are attested. Among the latest amphorae: 1 specimen of Keay LII, 2 local or regional wine amphorae, a Keay LXII and finally a LRA1. See Fontana 2003, pp.309-313.

[57] Fentress *et alii* 1991, p.215.

stratified materials from the *castrum* which present a similar peak in ARS attestations during the first half of the 6th century, with a further increase in around the 550s.[58] The interesting data from Roselle, confirmed by the more systematic ARS data from Cosa, offer fairly convincing support for the idea that the state played a role in supplying these two sites during the first half of the 6th century (Graph IX).

In both cases this phenomenon does not appear to have lasted much beyond mid-century, indicating that the sites played a strategic role during the Greek-Gothic war rather than during later military operations linked to the Lombard conquest. Had these two contexts fallen into the sphere of imperial political and military influence at this later point we would expect the presence of Mediterranean goods to remain constant up to the end of the 6th century with larger numbers of the ARS typologies introduced after the last quarter of the 6th century.[59] It is fairly likely that Roselle, like Cosa, was supplied by small vessels plying minor trade routes during the decades of the Greek-Gothic war: these routes departed from the Roman ports of Ostia and Portus, controlled by Byzantine garrisons during military operations.

The Byzantine reconquest of North Africa in 534 re-established favourable conditions for the resumption of supplies of taxes in kind and trade flows in general, although these remained[60] modest compared to a century earlier. During the initial phase of this recovery an important part was probably played by the military taxes in kind destined for the imperial troops engaged in the war against the Goths in Italy. The vital role of sites like Roselle and Cosa in Byzantine military strategy represented an opportunity for a temporary increase in the range of goods available. In this case, the war did not lead to a decline in pottery imports as it did in the surrounding countryside, but rather to a short-lived percentage increase in the fineware arriving here as an accompaniment to North African foodstuffs.

After the mid-6th century the picture for ARS imports at Roselle falls into line with that for the territory[61], presenting obvious symptoms of the marked decline which eventually led to the definitive interruption of imports between the 580s and 590s. Clearly the recovery in the second quarter of the century was closely linked to circumstances rather than being determined by structural economic growth. The drop in imports thus began well before the 590s; the Lombard conquest of the Roselle area in around 593 only dealt the final blow to the surviving weak links between the town of Roselle and the Mediterranean world.[62]

4.3. The Pottery From Contexts 5147=5170 and 5141: the Abandonment and Collapse of the Workshop (Fourth-Early Fifth Century AD)

FINEWARE AND COARSEWARE FOR USE AT TABLE

The abandonment layer context 5147=5170 yielded a broad range of tableware forms, both fineware and coarseware, in use before the mid-5th century (Graphs X-XI).

AFRICAN RED SLIP WARE

African red slip ware is documented with a total of 73 fragments belonging to a minimum number of 18 forms. Among these we can note the presence of forms produced before the deposit's supposed date of formation: these include 4 production C Hayes 50A and A/B dishes (AD 230/240-360) and an obviously residual production A Hayes 8A (mid-2nd/early 3rd century AD). The later pottery, by contrast, consists of 2 production D types, attested with 2 specimens each: the Hayes 50B flat-based dish and the Hayes 59 bowl (Graph XII).

The 2 production D^2 Hayes 50B flat-based dishes are characterized by their wide rim diameter: 36/37 cm in one case and 34 cm in the other. The lip is plain in the former and pointed in the latter; the base is flat (Pl.II, nos 2-3).

[58] I refer to the ARS found during Brown's excavation of the *Arx*. Unfortunately well-quantified data (MNI) are not available for these ceramic assemblages aside from a fairly generic number of fragments. To analyse these ARS finds using individual weighted means I had to use the total number of sherds for each type which does not necessarily correspond to the true minimum number of individuals. For the raw data see Fentress *et alii* 1991, p.215.

[59] For a comparison with a Byzantine *castrum* supplied directly by the State between the late 6th and mid-7th century AD see the case of Sant'Antonino di Perti, in the Finale Ligure, in Mannoni-Murialdo 2001 (eds.), especially pp.255-316.

[60] It is worth noting the increase of ships in circulation documented by shipwrecks and ARS in several sites of the western Mediterranean during the central decades of the 6th century AD, after the Byzantine conquest of North Africa. For a detailed analysis of these issues and their socio-economic implications see Zanini 1996, pp.677-688.

[61] In contrast to the territory, the context analysed on the north slope at Roselle yielded 2 minimum vessels in ARS whose production started after the mid-6th century AD (a Hayes 99C bowl and an *Atlante I*, Pl.XLVI, nos 1-2 dish). The redistribution of these late products to Roselle was nonetheless an ephemeral and possibly occasional phenomenon.

[62] The distribution of Mediterranean goods in Italy (especially ARS, LR1, LR4, LR5/6 and globular amphorae) between the 6th and 7th centuries AD, according to the recent enlightening analysis by Enrico Zanini, clearly reveals the close connection between the territories which continued to be ruled by the Byzantine Empire and the flow of imported foodstuffs and craft products, apart from rare exceptions such as Brescia and a few *castra* in northern Italy, see Zanini 2003, pp.381-394, in particular Figs 10-14.

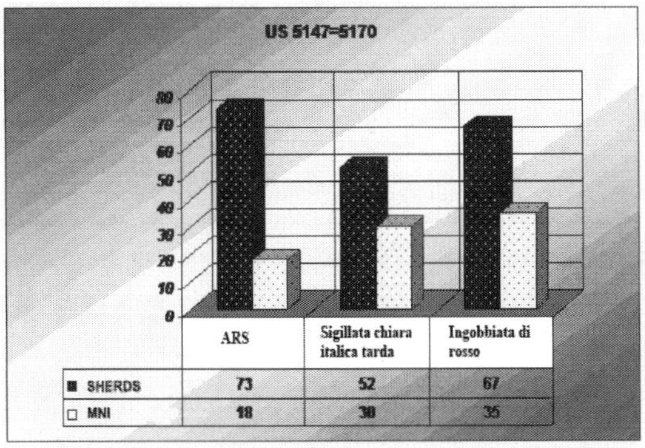

Graph X_ Finewares from SU 5147=5170.

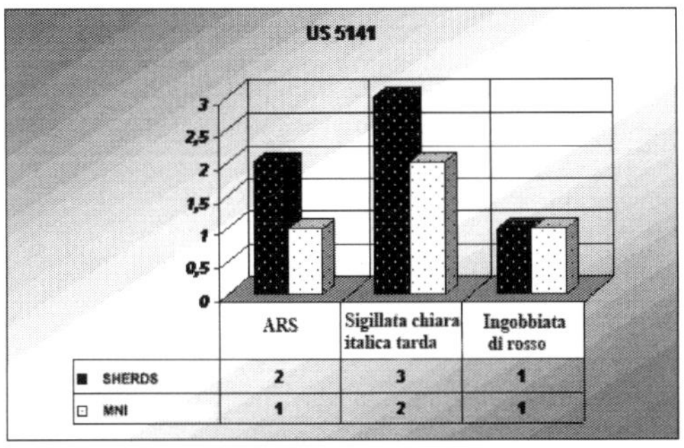

Graph XI_ Finewares from SU 5141.

The Hayes 59 large bowl has a flat rim measuring 31 cm in diameter and presenting two grooves; the base is slightly concave and the outer surface of the body is decorated with ridges. The base presents a decoration of palm leaves and rosettes, made using moulds of type *Atlante I*, Pl. LVII B, no. 59 and *Atlante I*, Pl. LVIII B, no. 61, belonging to Hayes styles A (i) and A (ii). The final chronology for these forms reaches the early decades of the 5th century (Pl. II, no. 3).

The presence of ARS in context 5141 (collapse of the structure) is of little interest; only a single minimum form in production C^1 or C^2 is documented.

SIGILLATA CHIARA TARDA DELL'ITALIA CENTRO-SETTENTRIONALE

The fineware assemblage is characterized by large quantities of *sigillata chiara tarda* from northern and central Italy. In total, context 5147=5170 yielded 52 fragments for a total minimum number of 32 forms, whilst context 5141 yielded 3 fragments belonging to a minimum number of 2 individuals. We were able to distinguish this pottery class among the numerous pieces of Italic tableware with a red slip thanks to some forms presenting the overpainted decorations typical of this class; this allowed us to select the two fabrics associated with this decoration. The next step was to analyse all the pottery fragments associated with these fabrics and compare the identifiable typologies with

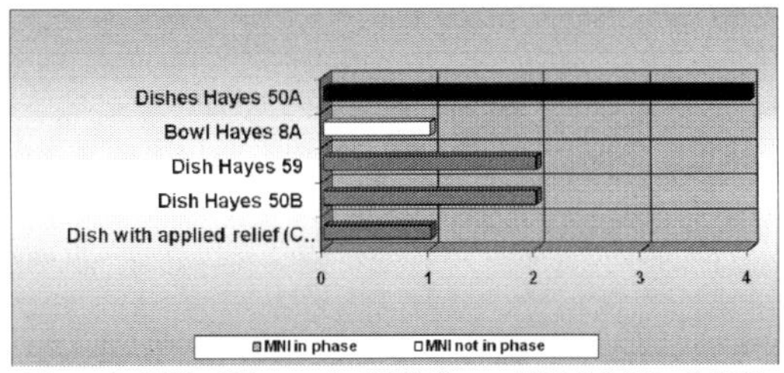

Graph XII_ Phased ARS from SU 5147=5170.

those already known for this pottery class.[63] At this point, using the detailed descriptions of the fabrics attested at Fiesole, we attempted to ascribe the specimens from Roselle to the production areas identified in earlier research projects.[64] However, it is important to note that there is an objective difficulty in distinguishing fragments and types belonging to Italic *sigillata chiara tarda* ware from the broader category of productions covered to a greater or lesser extent with a red slip in the many cases where these do not have overpainted decorations or are highly fragmentary. Generally speaking, the fabrics and slips of specimens belonging to this class are not of significantly higher quality than the numerous other types of red-slipped wares.

In some cases, morphological characteristics are not of much more assistance; as noted at Roselle, some forms such as the large deep dishes with slightly everted, plain or externally oblique rims seem to have been made both in *sigillata chiara tarda* and *ingobbiata di*

MNI	Fabrics
11	AD 45
19	AD 46

US 5147=5170

MNI	Fabrics
2	AD 46

US 5141

Tab. II_ Comparison of Minimum Number of Individuals (MNI) and fabrics in terra sigillata chiara tarda dell'Italia centro-settentrionale.

[63] A fundamental reference point is the first classification in Brecciaroli Taborelli 1978, pp.1-38. Other useful points of comparison are with specimens belonging to this ceramic class from the excavations at the Pionta Hill in Arezzo (Tortorella 1991, pp.103-114) at Fiesole (Bianchi-Palermo 1990a, pp.158-167) and finally at the *Domus dei Mosaici* in Roselle (Michelucci 1985).

[64] Three different sources were suggested for the specimens of *sigillata chiara italica* from Fiesole. One, which accounts for more specimens than the others, is the so-called *medio-adriatica*, documented by vessels whose decorations and fabrics are similar to those identified by Brecciaroli Taborelli at *Sentinum*, in the province of Ancona, and assigned to a production area located between the Marche and Romagna on the central Adriatic coast. A second group of finds was attributed to workshops in northern Italy, while the third group is more generic and includes typologies which apparently cannot be assigned to the first two sources. See Bianchi-Palermo 1990a, pp.158-159 and pp.166-167 for the macroscopic characterization of the fabrics.

rosso wares. As such the only true distinction between these two wares, which have more features in common than differences, seems to be the characteristic painted decorations in colours ranging from dark brown to black.

These decorations, applied using a brush and forming simple pairs of concentric circles (Pl.II, no. 5), sometimes connected by *tremoli a raggiera* (Pl. II, no. 4),[65] represented the initial indicator for the presence of this class at Roselle. However, the lack of intact specimens made it impossible to determine whether or not all the pottery forms of larger diameter had decorations. We did ascertain that a number of bases with low ring feet belonging to small bowls and ascribed to this class on the basis of their fabric did not have overpainted decorations.

For the purposes of comparison, Pl. III nos 1 and 2 shows two almost intact specimens of Italic *sigillata chiara tarda* with overpainted decorations from the *Domus dei Mosaici*. Both are modelled on ARS Tunisian prototypes: the flat-based dishes Hayes 50B and Hayes 63 respectively.

These painted forms suggest a significant decorative intent, perhaps indicating that this class was of some importance within the hierarchy of late antique Italic tableware. At the same time, however, the properties of the fabrics suggest that the clays chosen were too porous to ensure that the slip adhered well to the surface. The surface treatment is also frequently sloppy, as indicated by the wheel marks visible on both the inside and outside.

The data on the territorial distribution of these products confirms that they were of some value. In Tuscany these wares have been found prevalently in urban rather than rural contexts, as indicated by attestations at Roselle, Fiesole, Arezzo and Florence. In the territory between the Alma and Osa valleys, with the exception of Roselle itself, the only three contexts to have yielded a few specimens are the large villas occupied up to late Antiquity: San Martino, Casette di Mota and Aiali, all in the immediate vicinity of the town. As already mentioned, two fabrics are documented: AD 45 and AD 46;[66] these were used to make a minimum of 11 and 19 forms respectively from context 5147=5170. The 2 minimum forms from context 5141 are made using fabric AD 46 (Table II).

Among the most important types is a deep dish, made of fabric AD 46, characterized by a short flat rim with a diameter of 31 cm, which has no close morphological parallels with the typologies of *sigillata chiara tarda* hitherto identified (Pl. IV, no. 1). This form is fairly similar to the African production D[1] prototype Hayes 58B, dated mainly to the 4th century although it is well-documented at Ostia in contexts of the late 4th/early 5th century.[67] Another type of deep dish made of the same fabric has a rim flattened on the upper surface and measuring 28 cm in diameter (Pl. IV, no. 4). This form resembles another in Italic *sigillata chiara tarda* from a context of the late 4th/early 5th century in the *Domus dei Mosaici*.[68] A type of dish with a flat base, gently flaring walls and a thinned and flattened or externally oblique rim (Pl. IV, nos 5-7), with a diameter ranging from 22 to 23 cm, is documented in association with both fabrics. This typology seems to be identical to Brecciaroli Taborelli no. 22, although the specimens from *Sentinum* have larger rim diameters, between 30 and 32 cm.[69] A common type of bowl has a thinned plain rim generally presenting one and sometimes two grooves beneath it (Pl. IV, no. 2). This form, made from fabric AD 45, is also attested in the *Domus dei Mosaici* in association with materials from the late 4th/early 5th century.[70] Among the forms made using fabric AD 46 one common type is the carinated bowl with a rounded rim, often presenting grooves on the outside and in one case with an indented decoration underneath the grooves (Pl. IV, no. 3). This form, identical to Brecciaroli Taborelli 4, from which it differs for the indented decoration, is also documented at the *Domus dei Mosaici* in a layer where it is associated with the Hayes 67 deep dish.[71] Finally, it is worth mentioning a specimen of small pot with a shaped rim measuring 12 cm in diameter, presenting grooves on the outer surface and formally reminiscent of models characteristic of Ligurian kitchenware.[72] This type presents no affinities with the forms in Italic *sigillata chiara tarda* hitherto identified; however the fabric, AD 46, and the coral red slip allow us to assign it to this class (Pl. IV, no. 8).

As we have seen, the presence of very similar types made from different fabrics suggests the need for a degree of caution in determining provenance and in postulating schematic and oversimplified connections between a repertoire of forms and a given production area. In fact, in light of the data from Roselle and other sites, it appears fairly clear that the low degree of standardization of the forms in circulation and the fairly large number of fabrics attested reflect the existence of several workshops. The potters working here, whilst making reference to similar formal patterns, introduced new typologies and variants during their manufacturing activities. Additionally, the gradual

---

65 On this and other types of decoration see Brecciaroli Taborelli 1978. Tortorella proposed an interesting hypothesis regarding the relations between the feather-rouletting decorations typical of some forms in ARS, such as the Hayes 91 flanged bowl, and the *tremoli a raggera* which is a typical decoration of some vessels in *sigillata chiara italica*. For this hypothesis see Tortorella 1991, p.105.

66 For a description of the fabrics see the Catalogue.

67 *Atlante I*, p.82.

68 See Michelucci 1985, p.140, Pl.XVI, no.686.

69 Brecciaroli Taborelli 1978, p.34.

70 Michelucci 1985, p. 70, Pl.XV, no.625.

71 Michelucci 1985, p.43, Pl.XV, no.320.

72 Although the vessel mentioned above served for use at table and not for cooking foods, it is worth noting the presence of morphologically similar cooking pots in the early to mid-imperial contexts of *Albintimilium*, see Olcese 1993, p.197, Fig.34, nos 35-36.

increase in the number of Tuscan contexts yielding specimens belonging to this class, with forms that sometimes differ from one context to another, may reflect the existence of various small production centres active in the *Tuscia* during the 4th and 5th centuries.

INGOBBIATA DI ROSSO

The other important class of Italic tableware, attested in significant quantities in context 5147=5170, is *ingobbiata di rosso* ware.[73] This class is represented by a total of 67 fragments belonging to a minimum number of 35 forms. There is a perfect balance of open and closed forms, each documented with 42.8% of the total minimum individuals. The remaining 14.4% is too fragmentary to be identifiable. The open forms include basins, large bowls or bowls, deep dishes and a type of small vessel; most of the closed forms are juglets with 1 specimen of table jar. It is immediately apparent that the repertoire of closed tableware forms consists almost exclusively of *ingobbiata di rosso* ware; this class also comprises other functional forms not available in other pottery classes such as basins and small vessels.

Essentially, *ingobbiata di rosso* ware is characterized by a far broader and more complex range of shapes, comprising all the main forms required for use at table.

The picture that emerges of the production of this class is also extremely complex, as indicated by the analysis of fabrics and morphologies. Each individual functional form is present with a large variety of typologies, to the extent that it is impossible to identify constant morphological affinities between individual objects. The large number of fabrics documented (eight: seven purified and one selected), is also of considerable assistance in formulating a hypothesis as to how production was organized (Table III).

[73] I use this definition to refer to a heterogeneous ceramic class, whose main characteristics are: the use of a red to brown slip, generally fairly dilute; the use of porous fabrics; a very low degree of standardization; and finally some morphological relations with ceramic prototypes in ARS. A fairly typical characteristic is the distribution of the red slip: it is frequently distributed evenly all over the external surface and only on a thin strip below the rim of closed vessels; open vessels are frequently slipped all over the internal surface and only partially on the upper part of the external surface. Nonetheless some open forms with a more uniform slip on both inner and outer surfaces are documented. The procedure by which vessels in *ingobbiata di rosso* were slipped entailed dipping the vessel partially or completely into an iron-rich clay wash. Local productions belonging to this ceramic class are particularly widespread from the 4th century AD onwards in several areas of central and southern Italy. For a preliminary overview of its geographical distribution see Fontana 1998, pp.83-100. On the circulation of *ingobbiata di rosso* ware in Tuscany and the morphological repertoire see: for the Siena area, Cantini 2005a, pp.151-176 and Valenti 1996, pp.143-169; for Lucca, Ciampoltrini-Notini 1990, pp.561-592, Ciampoltrini *et alii* 1991, pp.699-715, Ciampoltrini-Notini 1993, pp.393-407; Ciampoltrini 1994, pp.597-627; for Volterra and its territory, Lupi 1998, pp.625-628. Finally for the Tuscan islands see: for the island of Gorgona, Gambogi-Firmati 1998, pp.635-638; for the island of Giglio, Rendini 1998, pp.639-643.

Considering the relations between forms and fabrics, we can note that five of the eight fabrics are used to produce both closed and open forms, whilst the remaining three are used exclusively to make either open forms (AD 42, SEL 9) or closed forms (AD 40). However, if we go on to analyse the continuity of use of the two purified fabrics in pottery found in 6th-century layers (contexts 1262 and 1260), we see that these are associated with both open and closed forms. This suggests that the differentiation noted in context 5147=5170 may result from the limited size of the sample rather than from a characteristic of production (Table IV). The fact that 62.5% of the fabrics were certainly used to make various poorly standardized forms of *ingobbiata di rosso* ware suggests the existence of several independent workshops. Each of these was probably able to supply local and regional markets with most if not all of the pottery forms needed for use at table or for storage, probably leading to strong competition between individual production centres.

The most frequently documented form in context 5147=5170 is the hemispherical bowl, present with at least two main versions. That with a rounded and internally thickened rim is attested both in a small version with a rim diameter of 15 cm and an external groove marking the transition between rim and wall (Pl. V, no. 1), and in a larger version with a rim diameter of 18 cm and a deep body (Pl. V, no. 2). Another type with a rim flattened on the upper surface and the same diameter as that described above is characterized by markedly flaring walls and a shallow body (Pl. V, no. 3). Whilst the first two types present close similarities with red-slipped Fiesolan wares of the second half of the 4th century,[74] the latter appears morphologically identical to Brecciaroli Taborelli 7 in Italic *sigillata chiara tarda*;[75] however, the slip, absent

MNI	Fabrics
2	AD 6
8	AD 7
13	AD 4
4	AD 43
2	AD 44
1	SEL 9
2	AD 40
3	AD 42

US 5147=5170

MNI	Fabrics
1	AD 7

US 5141

Tab. III_ Comparison of Minimum Number of Individuals (MNI) and fabrics in ingobbiata di rosso.

[74] Bianchi-Palermo 1990b, p.370, Pl.25, no.29.

[75] Brecciaroli Taborelli 1978.

Fabrics	Functional vessels
AD 6	Dish; generic closed form
AD 7	Dishes; basin; jug; generic closed forms
AD 4	Domestic jar; generic closed form; generic open form; basin
AD 43	Generic closed form; jug; small vessel
AD 44	Large bowl/dish; generic closed form
SEL 9	Large bowl/dish
AD 40	Jug; generic closed form
AD 42	Generic open form; large bowl/dish

US 5147=5170

Tab. IV_ Comparison of fabrics and functional vessels in ingobbiata di rosso.

from part of the outer surface of the body, and the fabric suggest that it does not belong to this class.

The morphological repertoire of *ingobbiata di rosso* ware is enriched by other functional forms including the flat-based dish with very flaring walls and a barely receding rim. This form is documented in a version whose rim measures 28 cm in diameter. Its shallow body and maximum wall height of about 4 cm suggest that it was used for the consumption of solid foods like meat or fish (Pl. V, no. 5). This form presents some fairly close analogies with the *Atlante I*, Pl. XXXVI, nos 3-4 dish, from which it differs for the slightly incurving rim. Although we can not say for sure that our dish was modelled on the North African prototype, dating to between the last quarter of the 4th and first half of the 5th century, it seems highly likely that the potter was familiar with the African form and that he later modified its characteristic shape. Another common open form is a type of basin with a more or less thickened rim and carinated wall (Pl. V, no. 6). This form is documented with several variants that differ mainly for the width and thickness of the rim. The basin with a conical body and carinated wall is one of the most frequently documented *ingobbiata di rosso* forms in the late antique contexts of the Prile area, whilst it is absent further north in the Alma valley and further south in the Osa valley. A long series of variants is documented at the two villas with late antique phases at Aiali and San Martino, in the *Ager Rusellanus*. The small vessel with a thickened ring foot, on the other hand, is attested by a single specimen; this form has an everted plain rim with a diameter of 6 cm (Pl. V, no. 4). Given its size and extremely limited volume it must have been used to serve sauces or spices at table.

The most common closed form is the jug, documented with a minimum of at least 3 identifiable forms and associated with three different fabrics. The rim is usually gently everted and plain; the fragmentary state of the sherds does not allow us to determine the shape of the handles (Pl. V, no. 7). A type of table jar is also attested; it has a fairly everted rim, measuring 16/17 cm in diameter, and a decoration of two thin raised strips on the neck (Pl. V, no. 8). The two most commonly documented closed forms, the jug and the table jar, complete the varied repertoire of open forms in *ingobbiata di rosso* ware. Whereas the latter were used essentially to consume semiliquid foods (bowls and basins) or solid foods (dishes and deep dishes), the former were used to hold and mix liquids, thus creating a set of tableware which was potentially independent of the contribution of other classes of fineware.

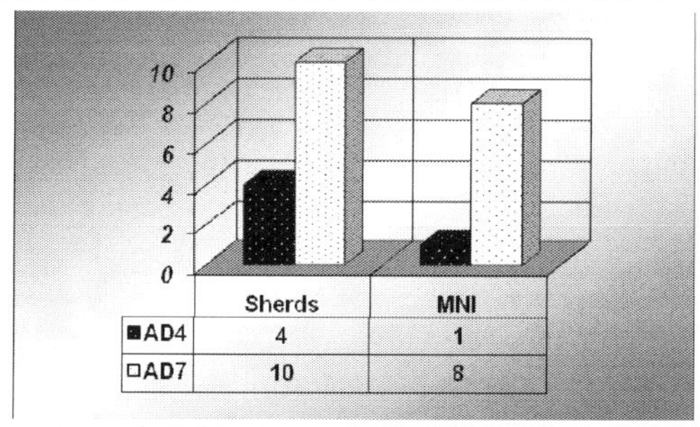

Graph XIII_ Acroma depurata from SU 5147=5170.

ACROMA DEPURATA

Further confirmation of the complex and varied repertoire of forms produced by the *ingobbiata di rosso* workshops and their versatility is the attestation in context 5147=5170 of a minimum of 9 unslipped forms made using two of the fabrics associated with red-slipped tableware. These 9 specimens are made from purified fabrics: 89% from fabric AD 7 and the remaining 11% from fabric AD 4 (Graph XIII). The Roselle context tells us that the production of *acroma depurata* ware was mainly aimed at closed forms for use at table and for storage, including some large forms, whilst open forms are represented by a single bowl.

The identifiable forms include a small one-handled jug with a vertical plain rim. The handle is pseudo-rectangular in section and is set directly on the rim, rising slightly above it at the point of contact (Pl. VI, no. 1). Another type with a similar rim diameter (about 8 cm) has a short vertical neck and a barely everted lip (Pl. VI, no. 2). The table jar with a rounded and slightly thickened rim set on a sub-vertical neck has an extremely wide mouth. Internally, at the junction between the neck and the shoulder, is a fairly pronounced ledge (Pl. VI, no. 3). Another table jar with a flat rim measuring 16 cm in diameter (Pl. VI, no. 4) completes the repertoire of closed forms.

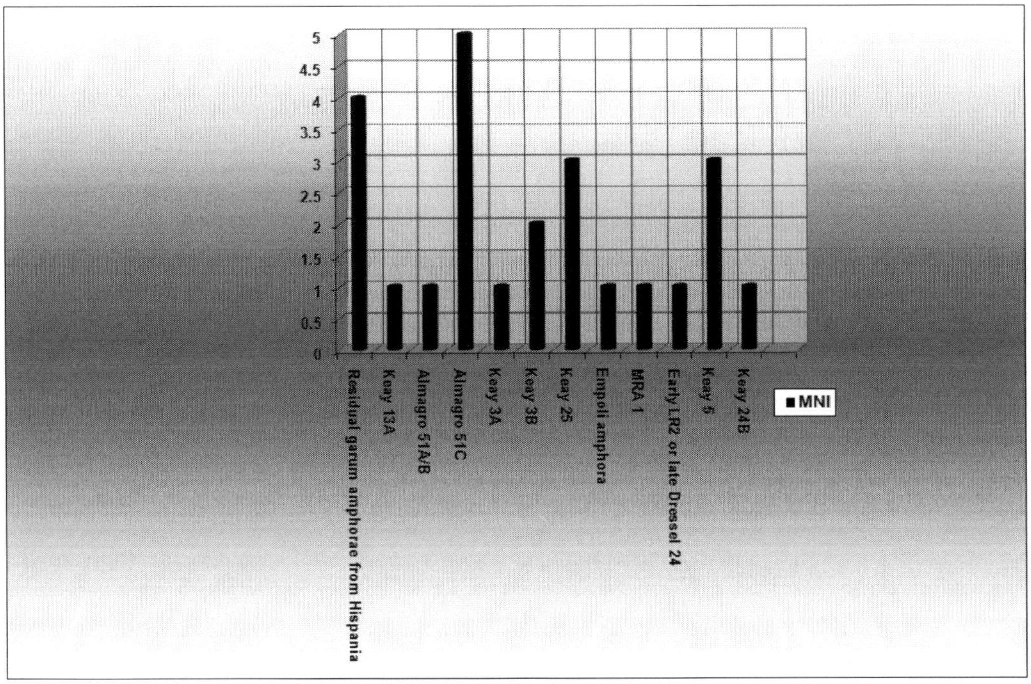

Graph XIV_ Amphorae from USS 5147=5170 and 5141 (Minimum Number of Individuals).

The only open form is a bowl with a markedly everted, thickened and slightly hooked rim, measuring 13 cm in diameter. The body has a convex profile and presents a groove around the middle on the outside, corresponding to a slight ledge on the inside (Pl. VI, no. 5). This type is very similar to *ingobbiata di rosso* forms from Fiesolan contexts of the 4th/early 5th century.[76]

SOAPSTONE

The study of the pottery from context 5147=5170 and context 5141 allowed us to identify a minimum of 1 bowl made of soapstone (Pl. VI, no. 6). This consists of two large contiguous fragments, weighing 55 and 70 grammes respectively, one from the abandonment layer of the metal-working shop and the other from the collapse. This object has a flat rim measuring 21 cm in diameter, with two light grooves on the upper surface. The walls are fairly flaring and 0.7 cm thick. The base is flat and the maximum height of the body is 6.5 cm. The outer wall is decorated with two light grooves immediately beneath the rim. Our object is one of the late Roman wares made from talc schists in the central Alps, as indicated by the properties of the lithotype used.[77] The fabric is grey and fairly fine-grained with the exception of a few yellowish inclusions; the fracture is uneven and feels soapy to the touch. The bowl stands out for its fine workmanship, clearly involving the use of a wheel, as demonstrated by the light but densely packed wheel marks on the inside. The walls are carefully smoothed and the rim appears to have been shaped with considerable skill. It has been suggested that these wares were made with aesthetic as well as functional aims in mind, perhaps in imitation of fineware.[78] The absence of any traces of fumigation on the Roselle specimen suggests that it was used for the consumption and/or presentation of food at table. Similar products are well documented in contexts in Lombardy and the Canton Ticino between the 4th and 5th centuries,[79] perfectly in line with the Rosellan context. There are close parallels with pottery from Santa Giulia in Brescia, where similar wares are documented in Period IIIB (AD 568-680) contexts,[80] and with productions attested between the 4th and 5th centuries in the excavations for the Milan MM3 underground line.[81] The presence of this carefully made form and the general rarity of soapstone vessels in the study area is further evidence of the extent to which Roselle was integrated into interregional trade circuits.[82]

AMPHORAE

Contexts 5147=5170, and to a far more limited extent context 5141, yielded a large quantity of amphora materials. This sample is of enormous help in determining the characteristics and volume of commercial trade reaching the city of Roselle between the 4th and the early years of the 5th century (Graph

[76] Bianchi-Palermo 1990a, p.369, Pl.24, no.23.
[77] For a comparison of the lithotype see Group C, probably from the Valtellina or Val Bregaglia in Alberti 1999, p.262.
[78] Lusuardi Siena-Sannazzaro 1994, p.172.
[79] *Ibidem*, p.172.
[80] For a comparison see Alberti 1999, pp.261-270 and p.625, Pl. CIX, no.2.
[81] Bolla 1991, p.31, Type 4.
[82] A fragment of a soapstone pot was found during the field survey in the upper Osa valley, near two Roman sites which were abandoned in the late 5th/early 6th century AD; other unpublished fragments were found on the hilltop site of Talamonaccio, at the mouth of the Osa river.

XIV). The two layers in question yielded a total of 44 fragments belonging to a minimum number of 26 forms, 24 of which are of known typology. 80% of the identifiable specimens come from context 5147=5170 whilst the remainder were found in context 5141. The coherence and homogeneity of the pottery from these two contexts leads us once again to present this class in a single section.

Among the productions certainly residual from the early and middle Empire are a minimum of at least 4 containers used to transport fish sauces from Baetica, including 2 Dressel 14, a Pelichet 46 and a Dressel 7-13.

The chronology of the remaining minimum number of 20 forms is in part compatible with their presence in phase in a context of the 4th/early 5th century. However, there are strong doubts regarding the Tunisian Africana IIA/Keay V amphorae (Pl. VII, nos 1 and 3); these present close affinities with the variants produced at the d'el-Assa workshop,[83] whose chronology does not seem to go beyond the second half of the 3rd century AD.[84] It is more likely that the specimen shown in Pl. VII, no. 2 was in phase; it can be identified as an Africana I/Keay IIIB. The late variants of this typology were produced up to the second half of the 3rd or 4th century.[85]

Both Africana I and Africana II amphorae began production in the late 2nd century AD and continued to circulate between the 3rd and 4th centuries, whilst conclusive evidence for their continuing production into the early 5th century is lacking.[86] One exception is the data from Aquileia; however, we have no accurate information on the minimum number of specimens attested at this context, making it impossible to evaluate all the amphora materials. At Aquileia, the very large number of rim fragments belonging to Keay III (219 pieces) and Keay V (88 pieces) amphorae, attested prevalently in contexts dating to between the 4th and mid-5th centuries,[87] may suggest that production and export continued into the early years of the 5th century. However, it is also possible that we are dealing with the large-scale reuse of these containers in a period following that of their circulation.

In the Roselle context, the proportionally fairly high number of minimum forms, 3 for each type or 24% of the total minimum number of forms identified, leaves open the possibility that they were in phase. On the other hand, it should be noted that here, as at Aquileia,[88] these amphorae are associated with other types of Tunisian amphorae such as Keay XXV which began to circulate in the early 4th century, gradually becoming extremely widespread until the mid-5th century.

The amphora associations at the Tunisian production site of El Hri near the coast south-west of *Sullecthum* are interesting but do not definitively resolve the problem. The amphora types produced by this workshop during its long period of activity, between the late 2nd and the late 4th/early 5th century, included Keay III, IV, V and XXV.[89] However, as these data come from surface surveys it is impossible to determine whether these types continued to be produced after the introduction of the Keay XXV in the early 4th century and until the 5th century, or if the different typologies belong to two distinct phases in the activity of the same workshop.

In light of all this information we can say that at least 15 amphorae out of a total of 24 were definitely found in phase. The problem of the Keay III and Keay V amphorae remains unresolved whilst awaiting other contemporary contexts in Roselle with associations of transport containers able to clarify this issue. An examination of the goods documented through the amphorae finds provides some helpful evidence on the consumption of foodstuffs at Roselle in the late Roman period.

Two types of amphorae reflect a "peak" in the consumption of Portuguese fish sauces: Keay XIX/Almagro 51 A-B and especially Keay XXIII/Almagro 51C,[90] with 1 and 5 specimens respectively. The Keay XXIII amphora has an everted and thickened rim, shaped on the inside and ranging in diameter from 8 to 10 cm.[91] The neck may be more or less narrow and the wall thickness ranges from 0.8 to 1.2 cm. The handles are always strap-shaped and present a light central groove on the upper surface; they may be set on the rim or at the junction between the rim and the neck (Pl. VIII, nos 3-4). The only spike found is small (4 cm in diameter), hollow and cylindrical (Pl. VIII, no. 6).[92] The Keay XIX is attested by a single conical spike, solid, 8.2 cm long (Pl. VIII, no. 7).

Southern Spain also contributed some oil, although in negligible quantities compared to the more substantial acquisitions from Tunisia. A very thickened and

[83] Bonifay 2004, pp.39-41.
[84] *Ibidem*, pp.107-111.
[85] *Ibidem*, p.107.
[86] For the Keay III amphora see Keay 1984, pp.108-108, for the Keay V, *ibidem* p.115. Reynolds suggests that the production of these two amphora types ceased during the 4th century AD, see Reynolds 1995, pp.47-48. Bonifay tends to rule out a continuity of production of the latest variants of Africana I and Africana II after the 4th century AD: see Bonifay 2004, pp.107-119.
[87] *Aquileia I*, pp.419-423.
[88] *Ibidem*, pp.426-433.
[89] Peacock *et alii* 1989, pp.190-192.
[90] For the general patterns of production of these two amphora types see Alarcão-Mayet 1990 (eds.).
[91] For comparisons see Keay 1984, p.175, Fig.70 no.2 and p.176, Fig.71 no.1.
[92] For a precise comparison with a Keay XXIII spike see *Aquileia I*, p.397, Pl.62, AS 16.

externally pointed rim measuring 14 cm in diameter appears to belong to a Keay XIIIA (Pl. VIII, no. 5).[93]

Wine and/or *salsamenta* from Tunisia seem to be a far more well-documented foodstuff at Roselle in the 4th/early 5th-century context with at least 3 specimens of Keay XXV.[94] This type is represented by an "a corolla" rim with an externally convex profile and an "a becco" lip with a diameter of 12 cm, comparable to variant G (Pl. VII, no. 5).[95] Whilst this minimum individual is made using fabric Anf 25, two other solid conical spikes, slightly thickened in the middle and with a thickened base (Pl. VII, no. 6) are made of fabric Anf 24 and appear comparable with spike variant 5 described by Keay.[96]

The context also yielded a specimen of the fairly rare Keay XXIVB amphora, with a characteristic subvertical rim, barely thickened and presenting grooves on the outer surface (Pl. VII, no. 4). However, conclusive evidence as to the provenance of this amphora is lacking: Simon Keay has proposed a North African origin, but ruled out both Tunisia and Libya as possible production areas.[97] It has recently been suggested, on the basis of a visual comparison, that this type may have been a Tripolitanian amphora introduced between the mid-4th and the mid-5th century, definitively replacing the well-known types of Tripolitanian amphorae documented from the early imperial period.[98] Were this to be confirmed by further research, we could suggest that this "new" type of Tripolitanian amphora was used to transport oil, given the region's main productive specialization.

Although the consumption of wine is documented only by 3 amphora specimens, these nonetheless reveal a fairly complex picture for the wines reaching the Rosellan market, with at least three exporting areas involved.

An "Empoli amphora" comes from the middle Arno valley or the Volterra area.[99] It has a ring-shaped rim with a diameter of 8.5 cm, a fairly narrow cylindrical neck and a thickened strap handle set on the neck (Pl. VIII, no. 1).

A type of amphora from eastern Sicily, on the other hand, has a shaped and barely incurving rim with a diameter of about 9 cm, identifiable as a MRA 1 (Pl. VIII, no. 2). This amphora type is closely linked to wine supply to Rome in the 4th century but continued to circulate in the 5th century.

Finally, the presence of imports from the eastern Mediterranean is attested by a possible early variant of the LR 2, an amphora used to transport surplus wine from the Aegean which is well-documented in western Mediterranean contexts between the 5th and 6th centuries.[100] The specimen from context 5147=5170 has a subvertical rim, tending to become flattened on the upper surface and thickened on the inside (Pl. VII, no. 7). This variant differs slightly from the more common LR 2 which has a slightly more everted and rounded rim;[101] it is documented in mid-6th-century contexts in the north-east sector of the *Domus Tiberiana* in Rome[102] and at the complex of Santa Giulia in Brescia in phases of the 6th/early 7th century.[103] Early attestations of the LR 2 are documented in the excavations undertaken during the construction of the Milan underground,[104] in contexts dated to between the 4th and the 5th century and in southern Italy at Naples and Metaponto where these amphorae are present in phases of the late 4th/early 5th century.[105]

AFRICAN KITCHENWARE

Very few pieces of African kitchenware were found, only 5 fragments belonging to a minimum of 4 forms. The dish/lid of type *Atlante I*, Pl. CIV, no. 2 is almost certainly residual since this form is attested exclusively in contexts of the first half of the 3rd century.[106] The other 3 minimum forms (2 dish/lids of type *Atlante I*, Pl. CIV, no. 6[107] and 1 casserole of type *Atlante I*, Pl. CVI, no. 10[108]) may be in phase, although this is uncertain given the long period of circulation of the two typologies, between the Antonine period and the late 4th/early 5th century.

LOCAL AND REGIONAL KITCHENWARE

Kitchenware is documented in contexts 5147=5170 and 5141 by 153 fragments belonging to a minimum of 64

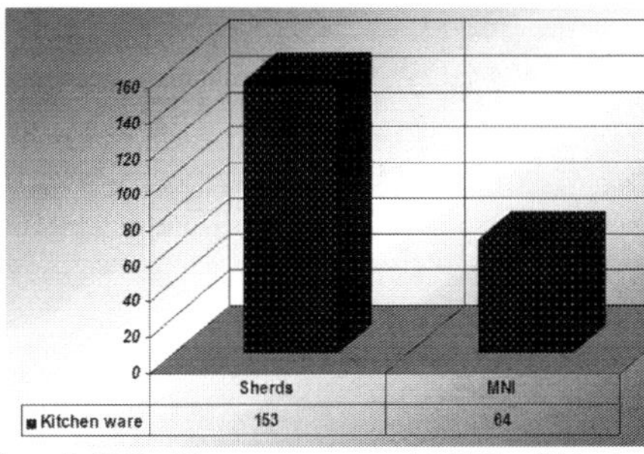

Graph XV_ Fragments and MNI of kitchenware.

[93] Keay 1984, p.144, Fig.55 no.2.
[94] On the foods possibly contained in Keay XXV amphorae see Bonifay 2007, p.24, Fig.8.
[95] Keay 1984, p.202 Fig.80, no.1.
[96] Keay 1984, p.211, Fig.89, no.5.
[97] Keay 1984, p.184.
[98] See Macías-Remolà 2005, p.127.
[99] For the typological comparison see Cambi 1989, p.567, Pl.2, no.3.

[100] Reynolds 1995, pp.75-83.
[101] Keay 1984, pp.352-357.
[102] Munzi *et alii* 2004, p.116, Pl.X, no.89.
[103] Bruno-Bocchio 1999, Pl.XCIX, no.6 and pp.237-238.
[104] MM3, Vol.4, Pl.CXX, no.163.
[105] Arthur 1998, p.168.
[106] *Atlante I*, p.212.
[107] *Ibidem* , p.212.
[108] *Ibidem*, p.217.

forms. The vast majority of pieces (89%) and minimum forms (91%) come from context 5147=5170 (Graph XV). The range of kitchenware forms is extremely varied and comprises generic closed forms, cooking pots, generic open forms, casseroles, bowl/lids, lids and pans (Graph XVI).

These wares, all made on a fast wheel, stand out for their thin walls and the careful shaping of the rims. The outer surfaces show no signs of burnishing, with the exception of 1 bowl specimen, nor traces of decorations. The fabrics indicate that the internal temperature of the kiln was not carefully managed, giving rise to numerous two-coloured pieces, fired in both reducing and oxidizing atmospheres. At least ten different fabrics have been identified, four of which were used to produce both closed and open forms; a further four fabrics were used exclusively to make cooking pots, whilst one fabric is associated only with wide-mouthed pans and one with lids.

Cooking pots, casseroles and lids appear to be replicated in slightly different sizes and with minor variations that nonetheless in most cases make reference to shared formal patterns. Similar forms produced using different fabrics may suggest the existence of several workshops using similar manufacturing techniques. This in turn may be explained by the circulation, probably on a regional scale, of specialized potters who passed their skills on to local artisans. This theory seems more plausible than a pottery trade dominated by a few workshops producing for a large market. Despite their points of contact with a well-defined model the forms suggest no real attempt at standardization. Rather, each form presents different variants, more or less faithful to the prototype; this is not in keeping with a production system based on nucleated workshops.[109]

The repertoire of closed forms is dominated by the cooking pot, present with four main types. The most common has a fairly everted band-shaped rim, shaped internally to host the lid (Type 1, Pl. IX, nos 1,2,3,5). The only relatively intact specimen has a globular body whilst the bases associated with this type are flat. A fairly distinctive peculiarity of the rims belonging to this type is the presence of a light groove on the outer surface, giving them a slightly forked profile; there is also a variant with a smooth rim (Pl. IX, no. 4). These cooking pots vary in size from a minimum of 15 to a maximum of 17 cm. Type 1 is extremely common in numerous late antique contexts in the area between the Alma and Osa valleys, albeit with some variations in the degree to which the rim is everted and its thickness. In Tuscany it is extremely widespread in numerous urban and rural contexts in phases dating to between the 5th and 6th centuries. Among the places with most attestations are Siena, where it is present in the late 5th- to mid-6th-century phases of Santa Maria della Scala,[110] the northern Siena area, where numerous 5th/6th-century settlements have yielded kitchenware assemblages dominated by this type,[111] the urban context of the first half of the 5th century at Pionta ad Arezzo,[112] Fiesole in layers of the 4th and 5th centuries,[113] and finally the 5th-century layers of the villa of Torre Tagliata in the Cosa area.[114] The large-scale regional distribution of this cooking pot, which we have named Type 1, makes it one of the most characteristic indicators of the late antique *facies* of the *Tuscia*. This form, with fairly limited morphological variations, appears to be documented from at least the 5th century up to the mid-6th century, as indicated both by the specimens from context 1260 at Roselle (second half of the 6th century) and those found in Siena at Santa Maria della Scala.[115] A second type of cooking pot which is common at Roselle already in this phase has a markedly everted rim, shaped internally to host the lid and ending in a pointed lip. This form is present in two versions which

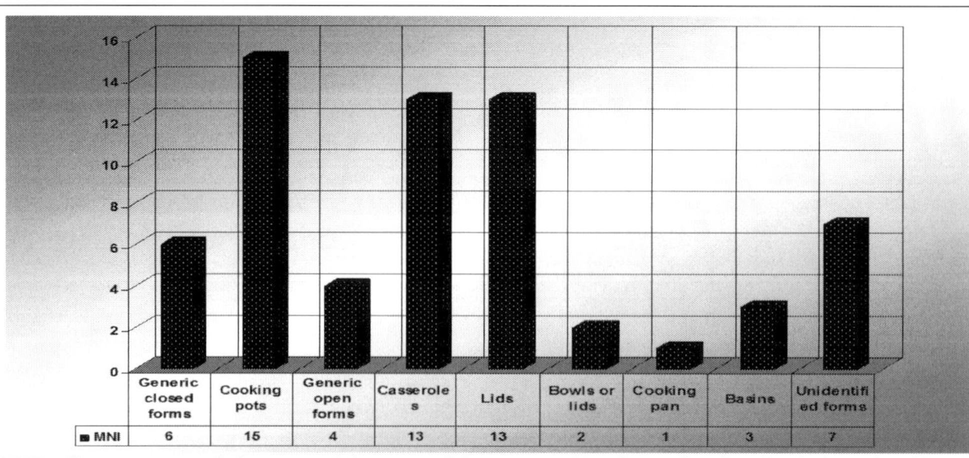

Graph XVI_ Comparison of functional forms and Minimum Number of Individuals (MNI) of kitchenware.

[109] On this issue see Peacock 1982, pp.13-21.

[110] Cantini 2005a, p.140, Pl.27, nos 5.45-49.
[111] Valenti 1996a, Types A1 and A2, p.146.
[112] Saguì-Paroli 1991, p.142, no.13.
[113] Bianchi *et alii* 1990, p.231, nos 27-28.
[114] Ciampoltrini-Rendini 1989, p.527, Fig.8, no.11.
[115] Cantini 2005a, p.140, Pl.27, nos 5.50-51 and p.141, Pl.28 no.5.52.

can be differentiated on the basis of the outer profile of the rim, which may be vertical (Pl. IX, no. 6) or rounded (Pl. IX, no. 7). Both variants are fairly large, between 21 and 23 cm in diameter. In this case, too, the area of distribution covers not only the area around Roselle but also some contexts in the lower Bruna valley, whilst it is absent south of the Ombrone. It is well-documented in other Tuscan sites, including the urban context of Santa Maria della Scala in phases between the late 5th and the early 7th century,[116] some rural houses of the late 4th/5th and 6th centuries in the Chianti Senese,[117] and Fiesole between the 4th and 5th centuries.[118] Less frequent at Roselle are Types III and IV, characterized respectively by an everted, thickened and hooked rim with a diameter of 22 cm (Pl. IX, no. 8) and by a fairly everted and almost plain rim measuring 21 cm in diameter with a light groove on the upper surface, perhaps to better host a lid (Pl. IX, no. 9). The territorial distribution of both these types is fairly limited, and they do not appear to be found in sites south of the Ombrone: some Type III specimens were found in the late antique phase of the village of San Martino *de plano*, in the lower Bruna valley, and a minimum of at least 1 form of Type IV comes from a farmstead in the Alma valley inhabited until the end of the 5th century.

The open forms include some which appear typical of a local production, perhaps between the lower Ombrone valley and the Cosa area. These are the casseroles with a slightly hooked flat rim and a deep carinated body (Pl. X, nos 1-3). They always have a characteristic groove on the rim, probably to host a lid. The walls are extremely thin and well-finished, indicating that they were made by competent potters. Also significant is the degree of standardization evident in the forms from the context on the north slope and those documented in the late Roman layers of the *Domus dei Mosaici*.[119] A possible variant has a slightly more hooked rim, shaped on the upper surface (Pl. X, no. 4). On the outside, near the carination, there is always a light groove. All 8 minimum individuals belonging to this typology present obvious traces of fumigation on the outer surface. The base profile, as indicated by some fragments which are not illustrated, must have been slightly convex, suggesting that these pots were probably set directly onto the embers in the fireplace.

The rim widths vary from a minimum of 22 to a maximum of 33 cm, without any change in shape of the vessels. Whilst at Roselle these casseroles appear to be concentrated mainly in contexts of the 4th/early 5th century, and possibly into the 6th century,[120] further south the sites of Cosa and Settefinestre provide some useful information on their initial period of production. At Cosa, comparable casseroles are already present in phases of the first half of the 1st century AD,[121] and they continue to be common at least until the late 3rd century.[122] However, this type is no longer found in the Forum cistern deposit of the first half of the 6th century,[123] and the little data available on material culture in Cosa between the 4th and 5th centuries does not help to determine if production continued into the late imperial period. Also significant is the attestation of this type at Settefinestre both in imperial phases and during the late antique occupation.[124]

If, as appears likely when we analyse the distribution of this casserole, it was in fact made in the coastal belt between Roselle and Cosa, the fabrics AG 13, 17, 18, 20 and 23 used to make the various specimens found at Roselle can be used as indicators for the workshops manufacturing them. This would mean that the same workshops also produced the whole range of cooking pots (Types I-IV),[125] alongside a broad range of open forms (Table V). Fabric AG 13 is used to make the casserole with an incurving rim, pointed on the upper surface and probably with a globular body (Pl. X, no. 5), documented by a single specimen. The same fabric is also associated with two main types of lids with strongly flaring walls that may either have a plain, flattened rim (Pl. XI, nos 1-2) or a rim slightly

Fabrics	Forms
AG 13	Casseroles, cooking pots, generic open forms, lids, generic closed forms
AG 18	Cooking pots, casseroles
AG 24	Cooking pots
AG 17	Generic closed forms, bowls or lids, cooking pans/tegami, cooking pots, bowls
AG 10	Lids
AG 11	Lids and cooking pots
AG 25	Cooking pans/tegami and lids
AG 8	Cooking pots
AG 19	Cooking pots
AG 20	Cooking pots

US 5147=5170

Tab. V_ Kitchen ware: comparison of fabrics and functional vessels.

[116] Cantini 2005a, p.141, Pl.28, nos 5-57-58.
[117] Valenti 1996a, p.146, Type L1.
[118] Bianchi et *alii* 1990, p.232, no.34.
[119] Michelucci 1985, p.146, Pl.XXII,no.592.
[120] This type of casserole is not documented in context 1262 (first half of the 6th century AD) nor in context 1260 (second half of the 6th/ early 7th century AD).

[121] At least 13 specimens, all similar to the type from Roselle, were yielded by the deposit of Room 22, belonging to the workshops adjacent to the *Atrium Publicum I*. See Brown 1976, Figs 42-43, 22II 1-13.
[122] 14 specimens were yielded by Deposit 7-Late Shops, corresponding to the 2nd to 3rd century AD living layers of one of the workshops near the *Atrium Publicum I*. See Brown 1976, Figs 56-57, LS 17-30.
[123] For the detailed publication of the ceramic assemblage from the Forum cistern see Fontana 2003, pp.307-319, especially pp.313-317.
[124] Papi 1985, p.97, Pl.25, no.8.
[125] Fabric G13 was used to make Types I and II, fabric G17 for a single specimen of Type III, and G18 for Types I and IV. Some specimens of Type I cooking pots were also made with fabrics G8, G19 and G20, whose provenance is uncertain.

thickened on the outside and with an indentation on the inside allowing it to sit better on the cooking pot (Pl. XI, no. 4): both types of lid have button-shaped handles (Pl. XI, nos 6-7). The diameters and morphology of these lids suggest that the type with a flattened rim (23-25 cm) was intended for use with casseroles, whilst the second type with an internal indentation (21 cm) was meant to be used with Type I or more probably Type II cooking pots.

Fabric AG 17, on the other hand, is associated with a flat-bottomed pan with a slightly incurving rim measuring about 15 cm in diameter (Pl. X, no. 6) and with a type of bowl-lid with an internally thickened and externally pointed rim (Pl. X, no. 7).

The remaining open forms of identifiable typology are made using fabrics of unknown provenance. Fabric AG 10 is associated with another lid with a thickened and rounded rim measuring 18 cm in diameter (Pl. XI, no. 3), similar to one documented in fabric AG 13.

Finally, fabric AG 25 is used to make a type of pan with fairly flaring thick walls, a thickened rim rounded on the outside with a diameter ranging from 24 to 34 cm (Pl. XI, nos 8-9), and a form which can be interpreted as a pan-lid with a very thickened rim, shaped externally and flattened on the upper surface, measuring 23 cm in diameter (Pl. XI, no. 5).

CONCLUSIONS: CAN POTTERY BE USED AS A SOCIO-ECONOMIC INDICATOR?

The picture of context 5147=5170 outlined above reveals that this sector of the late Roman city had access to an extremely varied and complex range of pottery. What are the deeper socio-economic implications of this?

First, we should stress the nature of the site where this pottery was found: a modest artisan's workshop established in a space which lost its central importance in the 4th century for a period of about two hundred years. Only in the second half of the 6th century, or perhaps the early 7th century, did this area of the town regain some importance within the topography of Roselle and its status as a city with the construction here of the cathedral church. This project was clearly determined by the potential for reusing some of the surviving bath buildings, including the peristyle. As had happened slightly earlier, or perhaps contemporaneously, in the *Domus dei Mosaici*, this building's loss of its original function did not lead to abandonment, but to a new phase of life without any apparent interruption but with absolute functional discontinuity.

The new occupation did not entail any significant building work, but simply the exploitation of a small room well-suited to a modest manufacturing activity. However, the building's loss of status and of its original function is not reflected in an impoverishment of its pottery assemblages nor in a simplification of food consumption. The stratigraphic data, with the collapse layer (context 5141) sealing the building's abandonment layer, rule out the idea that materials from other areas of the city are present here. The large quantities of scrap metal and ash found in association with the pottery confirm our proposed interpretation.

In light of the material culture yielded by the abandonment layer, a simplistic theory would be that the craftsman working inside this structure had a good quality of life. He was able to choose from a broad range of products: Sicilian, Tuscan and Eastern wines, Portuguese fish sauces, North African *salsamenta* and/or wine and Spanish oil; he could choose to consume his meals from three different types of tableware: the more valuable type imported from the Mediterranean, a good quality service in Italic *sigillata chiara tarda* or everyday *ingobbiata di rosso* ware. What is the real explanation for this broad availability of goods? Certainly craftworking in late antique Roselle may have represented a good source of income, sufficient to justify the potential on the part of the group of people working in this manufacturing sector to access a broad range of imported products.

However, the quality of the goods which this artisan was able to consume should perhaps be ascribed to a factor other than the metalworker's living standards. The most plausible explanation, given the anything but elite nature of the context, is that the pottery and foodstuffs found in context 5147=5170 were in fact readily available in late Roman Roselle. The town market must have been lively, dynamic, and well-integrated into the distribution network for Mediterranean goods. This can only be explained by the existence of a fairly wealthy urban elite which, thanks to its economic power and a well-structured demand for products imported from elsewhere in Italy and from overseas, was able to forge a solid network of trade links, ensuring the influx of numerous goods destined for mass consumption.[126] Most of these must have been consumed by those same local elites whose existence allowed for the creation and consolidation of the trade circuit, whilst another portion may have been purchased by less wealthy sectors of society, at prices which were nonetheless accessible given the high levels of demand. In this case, pottery would not be not simply, or simplistically, an indicator of the socio-economic status of the context in which it was found, but rather a lens through which to read the economic situation in the city as a whole and to evaluate the development and complexity of the market which formed as a response to the demand for foodstuffs and craftworking products by the town's elite classes.

---

[126] On the role played during classical antiquity by local elites in determining a broader distribution of many different goods see also Morley 2007, pp.44-45

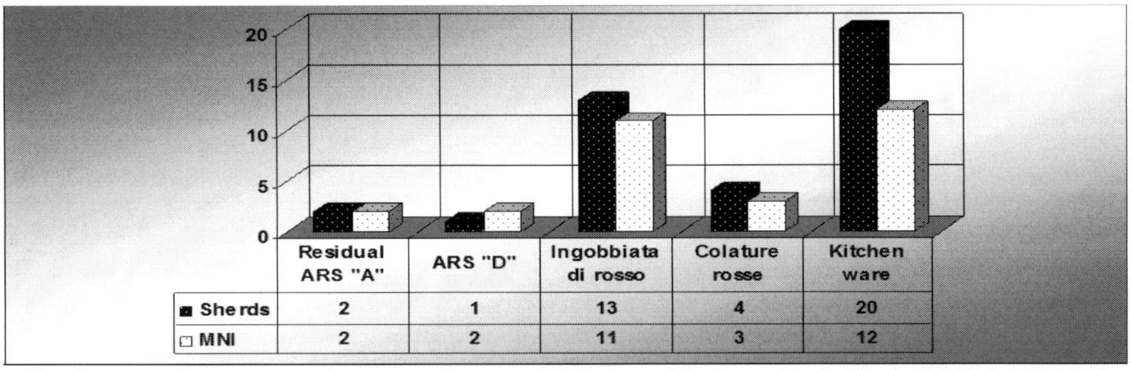

Graph XVII_ Comparison of ceramic classes and Minimum Number of Individuals (MNI) in US 1262.

4.4. The Pottery From Context 1262: Collapse of the Bath Complex (First Half of the Sixth Century)

The abandonment and collapse layer of the bath complex yielded a small quantity of pottery which is nonetheless of help in dating this activity and for an initial evaluation of changes in material culture between the 4th/early 5th century (context 5147=5170) and the first half of the 6th century. In total this context yielded 41 fragments for a total minimum number of 29 forms.

Four pottery classes are documented: African red slip ware with a minimum of 4 forms, *ingobbiata di rosso* with 13, *colature rosse* ware with 3, making its first appearance in this context, and *acroma grezza* with 20 individuals (Graph XVII). The absence of transport containers appears to be due to the limited size of the sample since their circulation is fairly well-documented in the later context 1260.

AFRICAN RED SLIP WARE

Of the minimum number of 3 specimens of African red slip ware only 1 was in phase: a Hayes 99 bowl, with fairly flaring walls and a slightly thickened almond-shaped rim measuring 19 cm in diameter. Our bowl belongs to variant B, dated to between the early decades of the 6th century and 570/580 (Pl. I, no. 6).[127] The other 2 specimens are an unidentifiable production A form which is certainly residual and a production D form which is too fragmentary to be assigned to a specific typology.

INGOBBIATA DI ROSSO AND COLATURE ROSSE WARES

The small quantities of ARS attested correspond to a high percentage of *ingobbiata di rosso* ware, with about 65% of the tableware. This class sees the continuing use of at least three of the fabrics already attested between the 4th and early 5th centuries (AD 7, AD 40 and AD 42), evidence that the kilns manufacturing about a century earlier were still operational or that they had been replaced with others also specializing in red-slipped wares which had access to the same clay quarries. Another two fabrics (AD 41 and Sel 40) are documented here for the first time (Table VI).

As in the pottery assemblages from the late Roman metal-working shop, *ingobbiata di rosso* ware is represented by both open and closed forms, with the repertoire of products presenting a degree of variety. The disappearance of the large flat-based dishes and the basins with thickened rims is compensated for at least in part by the introduction of new types of dishes and a new form: the flanged bowl. The latter, like the type of deep dish with a thickened incurving rim, are obviously modelled on African red slip ware prototypes; however these imitations are not slavish but indicate a complex and original reworking of their models.

A typical instance is the dish mentioned above (Pl. XII, no. 1), reminiscent of Hayes 61B for the incurving rim and external ledge;[128] however, other features such as the rounding of the edge and of the external ledge seem to suggest a knowledge of the Hayes 104A deep dish,[129] manufactured by the Tunisian potters from the early 6th or perhaps even the late 5th century onwards and which inherited the functions previously performed by Hayes 61.

The 2 specimens of flanged bowls are extremely fragmentary and do not allow us to determine which variant of Hayes 91 they were inspired by (Pl. XII, nos 4-5). No. 4, characterized by thin and strongly flaring walls, a barely distinct rim and a flange tending to be hooked set immediately beneath the rim appears similar to the earlier variant Hayes 91A, which ceased production in around 500.[130] By contrast, the dish with a flat base and markedly everted, almost flat rim with a groove on the upper surface, perhaps to host a lid, belongs to a completely independent production tradition not influenced by Mediterranean slip wares (Pl. XII, no. 2). This form is extremely similar to red-

[127] Tortorella 1998, p.43 and p.48, Fig.5, no.42.

[128] A comparison is with form Deneauve 1972, C870; see Bonifay 1998, p.76, Fig.2, no.1.

[129] For the chronology of the Hayes 104A large dishes see Tortorella 1998, p.43.

[130] *Atlante I*, p.106.

slipped wares from contemporary contexts of the late 5th/first half of the 6th century at Santa Maria in Siena[131] and to a type of dish which sometimes presents an impressed decoration of toothed rings found at 5th-century rural sites in the Chianti Senese.[132]

The repertoire of open forms is completed by a large bowl with a flat rim, slightly thickened and hooked at the edge and a fairly deep hemispherical body (Pl. XII, no. 3). The distribution of the orange slip on the outer surface is unusual; it appears to have been applied with a brush, following a slight carination, probably with a specific decorative intent. This large bowl is similar in morphology to kitchenware forms widely attested in Roman contexts of the 6th century on which it may have been modelled,[133] but with a different purpose, for use at table rather than in the kitchen.

A distinctive closed form is a juglet with a barely everted and thickened rim, and a handle of pseudo-rectangular section presenting a groove; the handle is set on the rim, but on a plane immediately below its edge (Pl. XII, no. 6). This type is represented by a minimum of at least 2 forms, assuming that the fragment of a grooved handle with an attachment to the body can be ascribed to this typology (Pl. XII, no. 7). The bases of the closed forms are fairly thick compared to the bodies, with a ratio of 2 to 1, and have a slightly concave profile. The slip is distributed over almost all of the outer surface including the base, but is not always present on the inner surface (Pl. XII, no. 8).

Context 1262 also yielded a minimum number of 3 forms with a partial slip consisting of drips of bright red paint. However, these are represented by wall fragments and 1 base fragment which provide no useful information on the typology to which they belonged. It can be observed that all 3 minimum forms are made from fabrics also attested in wares with a partial or total slip and that these same fabrics were already in use between the 4th and early 5th centuries (Table VII). This suggests that the red drip technique, at least in some cases, was a novelty introduced by the same workshops which traditionally manufactured red-slipped pottery during a late phase of their activity. This new technique gradually spread, being faster to execute and able to create casual decorative effects; however, it never replaced the wares with a more or less systematically applied red slip which continued to dominate. The technique used to apply these two types

MNI	Fabrics
4	AD 7
4	AD 40
1	AD 42
1	AD 41
1	SEL 40

Tab. VI_ Comparison of Minimum Number of Individuals (MNI) and fabrics in ingobbiata di rosso.

MNI	Fabrics
2	AD 7
1	AD 42

Tab. VII_ Comparison of Minimum Number of Individuals (MNI) and fabrics in colature rosse.

of coating is identical: in both cases the pottery form was dipped partially or completely into the slip. In those wares with red drips, a smaller portion of the surface was dipped into the slip; the form was then turned over, allowing it to drip towards the base. This innovation may initially have been accidental, with some vessels being dipped only partly into the recipient containing heavily diluted iron-rich clay. Later on, the pleasing aesthetic effect and the potential for saving time in the execution of the decoration dictated the success of this new type of coating.

KITCHENWARE

The kitchenware is dominated by cooking pots, which account for most of the specimens which can be assigned to a specific typology (Tables VIII-IX). The exceptions are a minimum of 2 casseroles with flat rims presenting a groove and a carinated wall, indicating that the type documented between the 4th and early 5th centuries continued to be manufactured.

Among the most frequently attested cooking pots are some variants of Type II, characterized by a more markedly everted rim, still shaped on the inside to host a lid; the lip is more rounded than in the older specimens. Two different versions can be identified on the basis of the rim diameter, ranging from 18 cm (Pl. XIII, no. 1) to 23 cm (Pl. XIII, no. 2). Another Type II variant has a less inclined rim with a rounded and thickened lip, measuring 18 cm in diameter (Pl. XIII, no. 3).

Functional forms	Fabrics
Cooking pot, casserole	AG 19
Cooking pot, casserole	AG 13
Generic closed form	AG 17
Generic closed forms	AG 20
Cooking pots	AG 23
Cooking pot	AG 14

Tab. VIII_ Comparison of functional forms and fabrics in kitchenware production.

[131] Cantini 2005a, p.156, Pl.38, no.6.1.
[132] Valenti 1996a, p.155, Pl.V, nos 1-3.
[133] I refer to a type of casserole, possibly used for roasting meat, documented in the contexts of the first half of the 6th century AD at the *Basilica Hilariana* on the Caelian Hill (cfr. Pacetti 2004, p.449, Pl.VII, no.47), in those of the late 5th/mid-6th century at the Conservatorio di San Pasquale, near Trastevere (Fogagnolo 2004, p.591, Pl.VII, nos 48-49), in the mithraeum of the Crypta Balbi in the second half of the 6th century (Saguì-Coletti 2004, p.267, Pl.XVI, no.87) and finally in the Casa delle Vestali, in contexts dating to the first half of the 6th century AD (Filippi *et alii* 2004, p.172, Pl.III, no.27).

MNI	Fabrics
3 (of which 1 is a waster)	AG 19
2	AG 13
1	AG 17
3	AG 20
2	AG 23
1	AG 14

Tab. IX_ Comparison of Minimum Number of Individuals (MNI) and fabrics in kitchenware production.

Type V, on the other hand, appears for the first time in this context. It is characterized by a short, everted and externally oblique rim also measuring 18 cm in diameter (Pl. XIII, no. 4). That this type was introduced later is confirmed by the Sienese data from Santa Maria della Scala, where similar wares are found in layers of the second half of the 6th and first half of the 7th century.[134]

Type VI, with an everted and barely thickened rim with a vertical external profile is also attested in context 1262 for the first time (Pl. XIII, no. 5). However, unlike the above typology it is no longer documented in the later context 1260. This type is well attested in sites with late antique phases in the hinterland of Roselle and in the lower Bruna valley.

The cooking pots have thin flat bases, usually about 0.7 cm thick like the walls (Pl. XIII, no. 6).

All the kitchenware was made on a fast wheel and is undecorated. As with the *ingobbiata di rosso* wares we can note the continuing use of some fabrics, including AG 19, AG 13, AG 17 and AG 20 and the introduction of two new fabrics, AG 14 and AG 23. Particularly important is the presence in this context of a fragment of a kiln discard from a closed form with an everted plain rim made using fabric AG 19: this is the same fabric used to make one of the variants of the Type I cooking pot and a casserole of the type with a flat rim and carinated wall. We can therefore suggest that the pottery made using this fabric was manufactured locally, probably in Roselle itself.

4.5. The Pottery From Context 1260: Arrangement and Levelling of the Collapse of the Baths (Second Half of the Sixth/Early Seventh Century)

Context 1260, which yielded a total of 173 fragments belonging to a minimum number of 110 forms, allows us to identify some novelties and a series of constants in pottery consumption at Roselle during the transitional period between the first and second half of the 6th century (Graph XVIII).

RESIDUAL AFRICAN RED SLIP WARE

The first feature of some importance is the complete absence in phase of African red slip ware. This class is documented exclusively by residual forms such as Hayes 58B no. 11 and production D Hayes 59 deep dishes, which ceased production more than a century before the formation of context 1260, and by even earlier forms such as the production C Hayes 50 dish, the production A Hayes 3C flat-based dish and Hayes 9B bowl.

The absence of ARS mirrors the decline in the consumption of imported fineware which, as we have seen, is characteristic of this context during the second half of the 6th century; by the early 7th century links with Mediterranean trade circuits had been completely severed.

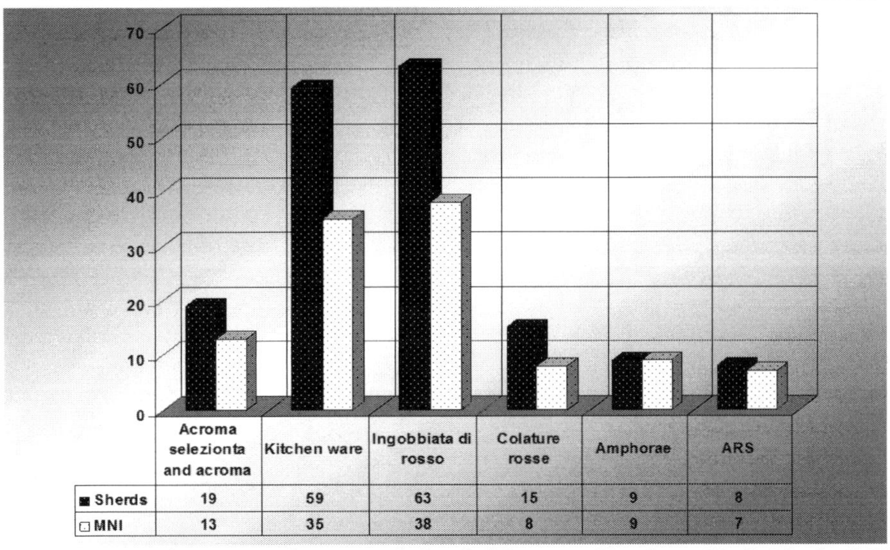

	Acroma selezionta and acroma	Kitchen ware	Ingobbiata di rosso	Colature rosse	Amphorae	ARS
■ Sherds	19	59	63	15	9	8
□ MNI	13	35	38	8	9	7

Graph XVIII_ Comparison of ceramic classes and sherds/Minimum Number of Individuals (MNI) in US 1260.

[134] Cantini 2005a, p.142, Pl.29, no.5.67.

AMPHORAE

Roselle's connection with overseas commercial trade circuits is still documented in this phase thanks to the amphora finds.

Of the minimum of 9 forms documented, at least 3 are in phase, indicating sporadic relations with at least three different areas of supply: the eastern Mediterranean, north-western Sicily or *Bruttium*, and Tunisia. These three areas are represented respectively by an LR1 (Pl. XIV, no. 1), a Keay LII (Pl. XIV, no. 2) and a Keay LXI (Pl. XIV, no. 3). The presence of the Keay LXI is one of the most reliable indicators on the basis of which to date this pottery context to a time no earlier than the second half of the 6th century and possibly between the late 6th and early 7th century. Variants D and B of this amphora, morphologically the most similar to the specimen from context 1260, have recently been ascribed by Bonifay to the late 6th/first half of the 7th century AD.[135] The LR1[136] from context 1260 appears similar to the standard type, widespread from the second half of the 5th century until the early 7th century;[137] however, some features such as the handle with longitudinal ridges and the rim diameter (8.4 cm) are reminiscent of variant 1A, documented from the first quarter to the end of the 5th century.[138] The neck, which is fairly wide, not narrow as in the 5th century specimens for which we have a reliable sample from *Portus Scabris*, allows us to attribute it to the late phase of production.[139] The attestation of Keay LII amphorae at Roselle also appears to be occasional. Along the Tyrrhenian and Ligurian coast north of Rome, the main destination of these containers from the late 4th century onwards, the distribution of this type of amphora covers a variety of settlement contexts: larger towns like Luni,[140] fortified coastal sites such as Cosa,[141] villas which probably acted as support structures for navigation such as Torre Tagliata in the Cosa area,[142] and harbours like *Portus Scabris* near Scarlino and Vada Volterrana.[143] This picture, complemented by the attestations at Roselle, suggests that this container had a fairly varied distribution. However, the related trade flows seem to have been targeted at a series of "privileged" settlements, with smaller rural sites being systematically excluded. Given its relatively short widened neck our Keay LII may date to the latest production phase, between the 6th and the early 7th century,[144] perfectly compatible with the date of the context. The fabric used to make the specimen from Roselle (Anf 30) seems identical to a fabric from *Portus Scabris* associated with an amphora from the Keay LII "family"; both belong to the generic MA1 subgroup defined by Capelli.[145] However, it is impossible to determine if these amphorae came from what is now Calabria or from north-western Sicily. The presence of a Tunisian oil container is unsurprising and simply serves to confirm the vital role played by supplies of Tunisian foodstuffs throughout the long period for which the north slope context provides information. More significant is the presence of the two wine amphorae: one from southern Italy and one from the eastern Mediterranean. We have already noted the probable existence of a local wine production destined for circulation in barrels or in containers which were not perishable but which remain unidentified, given the small quantities of wine amphorae documented after the 2nd/3rd century AD. In light of the anomalous concentration in context 1260 and the overall quality and variety of the pottery yielded by this layer we can therefore suggest that it in some way reflects the food and pottery consumption of a privileged context near the bath area.

The overall picture of the pottery documented in this context seems comparable, for the variety of forms and types of table and kitchenware and for their high quality workmanship, only with that from an abandonment layer of the settlement context of Paduline at Castiglione della Pescaia. By contrast, there are no close affinities with the objects found at the rural sites that survived until the end of the 6th century, where the small number of different forms available seems to indicate a pottery repertoire which was becoming progressively simpler and limited to a few functional types.

INGOBBIATA DI ROSSO AND COLATURE ROSSE WARE

The dominant type of tableware attested in context 1260 still appears to be *ingobbiata di rosso* ware with a minimum of 38 specimens, compared to *colature rosse* ware with 8 specimens (Tables X-XI). There is still a differentiation between the forms produced in these

[135] See Bonifay 2004, p.139, Fig.75, Type Keay 61, no.1 (D) and no.4 (B). See also p.141 for the date.

[136] For a precise comparison see Keay LIII B, Fig.118, no.10; Keay LIII C, Fig.120, no.8.

[137] For the standard form and its chronology see Arthur 1998, pp.164-165.

[138] For the A1 variant see the typology in Pieri 1998, pp.20-21.

[139] The fabric (Anf 15) of the specimen from context 1260 is comparable to fabric Anf 123 used to make a LR1 amphora (variant B of Pieri's typology) from *Portus Scabris*.

[140] *Luni II*, p.198, Pl.129, nos 10-11.

[141] 1 specimen of LII is documented in the ceramic assemblage from the Forum Cistern at Cosa see Fontana 2003, p.312, Fig.141, no.1.

[142] See Ciampoltrini-Rendini 1988, p.531, Fig.11, no.4. In the report the amphora was not identified as a Keay LII, but as an Aegean amphora similar to forms 230, 234, 302, 323 from the Athenian Agora. In my view, both morphology and fabric suggest an identification as a Keay LII.

[143] In the *horrea* of San Gaetano di Vada the wine amphora Keay LII, along with the Empoli type, accounts for about 44% of the materials dating to between the 4th and the 6th century AD. See Del Rio-Vallebona 1996, p.490.

[144] See for comparison the specimen from the *Domus* of Gaudentius in Rome, Pacetti 1998, p.202, Fig.10 no.2.

[145] The generic MA1 subgroup includes various fabrics which can be assigned to the Keay LII type. These differ for the presence of micro-fossils, the ratio of iron oxides to carbonates and finally the presence of limestone inclusions in the matrix. See Capelli 1998, p.336. The Anf 30 fabric from Roselle is iron-rich and does not include micro-fossils in the matrix.

MNI	Fabrics
7	AD 7
1	AD 40
2	AD 42
2	AD 41
9	AD 6
9	AD 44
1	AD 43
1	SEL 40
6	AD 6

Tab. X_ Comparison of fabrics and Minimum Number of Individuals (MNI) in ingobbiata di rosso.

MNI	Fabrics
1	AD 41
4	AD 42
1	AD 44
2	AD 6

Tab. XI_ Comparison of fabrics and Minimum Number of Individuals (MNI) in colature rosse.

two classes: whilst the *ingobbiata di rosso* ware includes both open and closed forms, with the flanged bowls, large bowls and jugs presenting a degree of variety, *colature rosse* ware is represented exclusively by closed forms, too fragmentary to determine their exact typology. An analysis of the fabrics reveals that the workshops producing *ingobbiata di rosso* ware between the 4th/early 5th and the early 6th century continued to remain active. The *colature rosse* ware is made from other fabrics, hitherto used only for *ingobbiata di rosso* ware (AD 6, AD 41, AD 44).

This suggests that new workshops, copying those which manufactured pottery using fabrics AD 7 and AD 42, had also begun to make objects with red drips, albeit in smaller quantities than *ingobbiata di rosso* (Table XII).

Functional forms	Fabrics
Generic closed forms	AD 44
Flanged bowl, generic closed forms, dish	AD 42
Flanged bowl, jugs and generic closed forms	AD 4
Flanged bowl, jug, large bowl/dish and generic closed forms	AD 6
Generic closed forms	AD 7
Generic closed forms	AD 41
Generic closed forms	AD 43
Generic open forms	SEL 40

Tab. XII_ Comparison of functional forms and Fabrics ingobbiata di rosso

The flanged bowls with a red slip are the most frequently documented tableware forms;[146] the main variants can be distinguished by the greater or lesser development of the flange and the depth of the body. The African prototypes used as models are without doubt the late variants of the Hayes 91 flanged bowl, whose widespread distribution and highly functional nature led to their imitation on the part of Italian potters. Hayes 91C, widespread between AD 520 and 570/580, is the model for the type with fairly flaring walls and a short and slightly hooked flange set beneath the rim (Pl. XV, no. 1). The type with a sub-vertical rim and an almost atrophied flange presents fairly obvious analogies with the ARS variant 91D, which began production in around 580 and continued to the 7th century (Pl. XV, no. 2).[147] However, in my opinion a direct derivation from the North African prototype Hayes 91D remains highly dubious given that this form is very rarely found in Tuscany, with the exception of the sites of Cosa and Vada Volterrana.[148] That this variant was a rarity is evident from its absence among the finds from *Portus Scabris*, where the influx of ARS between the late 6th and 7th century is documented. Although we cannot completely rule out that potters working in the *Tuscia* were familiar with this prototype it is more likely that the more common variant 91C underwent a further process of development.

Alongside the flanged bowls we see the continued attestation, with a minimum of at least 1 individual, of the type of large bowl with a slightly incurving and rounded rim, already documented in context 1260. There is also a novelty in the form of the carinated bowl with a sub-vertical rim, pointed on the upper surface and measuring 13 cm in diameter (Pl. XV, no. 3). The profile of the rim and wall and the size of the body are clearly reminiscent of other models in African red slip ware and in particular type *Atlante I*, Pl. LII, no. 6 and Hayes 102, both dating to between the late 5th/early 6th and the mid-6th century.[149]

Among the closed forms is a type of juglet or bottle with a barely everted rim measuring 7.4 cm in diameter, with a short flange of rectangular section set beneath it (Pl. XV, no. 4). This object presents a triple spiral decoration covering the central portion of the neck, the shoulder and the widest part of the body. A number of grooves separate the band of spirals on the shoulder from that on the body. The arrangement of this decoration is very similar to that of some red-

[146] For the distribution of flanged bowls modelled on ARS prototype Hayes 91 see Fontana 1998, pp.83-100.
[147] See Tortorella 1998, p.43.
[148] At Cosa this type is documented by a single specimen, while the generic presence of the type at Vada Volterrana is mentioned with no quantified data. For Cosa see Fentress *et alii*, 1991, p.215; for Vada Volterrana see Pasquinucci *et alii* 1998b, p.638.
[149] For the chronology of these two types see Tortorella 1998, p.43; the *Atlante I*, Pl.LII, no.6 type is well documented at Carthage during the first half of the 6th century; see Fulford-Peacock 1984, p.76, Fig.22, no.78.

slipped pieces from the Crypta Balbi mithraeum in Rome, in phases of the late 6th/early 7th century.[150] The shape of the rim, on the other hand, resembles that of the bottles from the Forum Cistern deposit at Cosa which can be dated to the first half of the 6th century.[151]

As already mentioned, all of the *colature rosse* ware is highly fragmentary but can be ascribed exclusively to closed forms. Alongside various wall fragments we also found two different types of bases: one with a low disk foot measuring 8.5 cm in diameter belonging to a tankard or a bottle with an ovoid body (Pl. XV, no. 5); the other with a flat base measuring 11 cm in diameter and 1 cm thick probably belonging to a jug with a globular body (Pl. XV, no. 6).

The tableware repertoire thus appears to be fairly complete, with various functional forms, both open (large bowls, bowls and flanged bowls) and closed (bottles and jugs). Missing are the large plates used for meat and fish dishes; these were well-documented both in imported and Italic fineware between the 4th and early 5th centuries.

This difference may be due to a change in eating habits between the 5th and the mid-6th century, with semiliquid foods becoming more common and solid foods becoming less so. The production of tableware had to adjust to this cultural change, manufacturing more forms with a deeper body such as flanged bowls and large bowls in place of shallow forms such as plates.

MNI	Fabrics
6	AD 4
2	AD 7
1	AD 3
1	AD 41
1	SEL 4
2	SEL 3

Tab. XIII_ Comparison of Minimum Number of Individuals (MNI) and fabrics in acroma depurata and selezionata.

ACROMA DEPURATA AND ACROMA SELEZIONATA WARE

With respect to the requirements of the table we found relatively few products in *acroma depurata* and *acroma selezionata* ware, represented by a total of 19 fragments belonging to a minimum number of 13 forms (Table XIII). This material is also highly fragmentary, making it impossible to determine typologies; the only certain fact emerging from an analysis of the walls is that these fragments belong exclusively to closed forms. Additionally, the thickness of the fragments suggests that they belonged both to forms destined for use at table like jars and to objects intended for the storage of liquids such as table jars.

KITCHENWARE

Compared to the tableware, the repertoire of kitchenware suggests no particular functional changes with respect to that documented in the first half of the 6th century. Kitchenware, represented by 59 fragments for a total minimum number of 35 individuals, is still characterized by a very varied repertoire of forms reminiscent, albeit with some significant typological differences, of that in use between the 4th and early 5th century.

A new form has been added to the repertoire: the flanged bowl in its kitchenware version. Closed forms continue to be represented exclusively by cooking pots; among these we can note the continuing production of Type II, with an everted and thickened rim, shaped internally to host the lid (Pl. XVI, nos 1-2). In this context we also found a small variant of Type II, whose handle is level with the rim and presents an indented decoration (Pl. XVI, no. 7).

Type V, already present in the context dated to the first half of the 6th century, is also documented with a minimum of 1 form, morphologically identical to the prototype from context 1262 and with the same rim diameter of 18 cm (Pl. XVI, no. 5). This specimen has a hole immediately beneath the shoulder, probably due to repair.

Types VII and VIII are new. The latter has an ovoid body and barely everted rim, pointed on the upper surface and with a vertical external profile (Pl. XVI, no. 6). The narrow mouth, only 12.5 cm in diameter, makes this the smallest type of cooking pot, suggesting that it was intended for individual use rather than for the collective preparation of food. Type VII, which exists in two variants, has a slightly everted rim, shaped on the inside and with a flange of triangular section on the outside; this may be straight (variant I: Pl. XVI, no. 3) or slightly hooked (variant II: Pl. XVI, no. 4). The rim diameters range from 16 to 21 cm. The morphological characteristics of Type VII suggest that it represents a development of Type I, well-

[150] Saguì-Coletti 2004, p.273, Pl.XXI, no.121.
[151] Fontana 2004, p.315, Fig.143, nos FC36-37.

documented at Roselle in the first half of the 5th century. The overall profile seems fairly similar, with the difference that in Type VII the rim tends to be less everted and to develop a flange. The possible chrono-typological evolution from no. I to no. VII may be documented, as well as at Roselle, by the important urban context of Santa Maria della Scala, where cooking pots with an outer flange appear only from the first half of the 7th century, whilst those similar to our Type I are well-attested between the late 5th and mid-6th century.[152] The walls of the cooking pots sometimes present a dense decoration of lines made using a "comb" (Pl. XVI, no. 8) or multiple spiral decorations inside bands bounded by parallel lines (Pl. XVI, no. 9); this decorative motif is reminiscent of that attested during the same period on some bottles or jugs in *ingobbiata di rosso* ware.

Whilst the cooking pots appear to have been intended for cooking semiliquid foods such as *puls*, also the main foods consumed off the tableware, or for boiling dried meats, the series of open forms comprising casseroles, pans and bowl-lids completed the kitchenware repertoire, supplying forms used for frying or stewing.[153]

As already noted, the most original open kitchenware form of the second half of the 6th century is the flanged bowl, attested by a specimen with a plain vertical rim measuring 19 cm in diameter and a flange of rectangular section turned slightly downwards; the outer wall presents a combed decoration (Pl. XVII, no. 1). The use of the flanged bowl for cooking is not well documented, but the presence of obvious traces of fumigation on the outer wall of our specimen is evidence of its exposure to fire. Another function possibly performed by this form in the kitchen, alongside the cooking of semiliquid foods, is as a lid: turned upside down it could be placed on cooking pots or casseroles and then removed using the flange as a handle. A similar kitchenware version comes from a context generically dated to the 6th/7th century in the urban excavations at Grosseto.[154]

Functional forms	Fabrics
Generic closed forms (including a waster), casserole and cooking pot	AG 13
Flanged bowl, cooking pot	AG 14
Generic closed forms, cooking pot, bowl or lid	AG 8
Cooking pot, lid	AG 6
Generic closed forms	AG 19
Generic closed forms, casserole	AG 11
Generic closed forms, cooking pot, casserole	AG 20
Cooking pot, cooking pans/*tegami*	AG 17
Lid, coking pot	AG 18
Cooking pot	AG 24

Tab. XIV_ Comparison of functional forms and fabrics in kitchenware.

Two clearly distinct types of casserole are documented; however, both are related to forms already attested in earlier contexts. The production of the type with a flat rim and forked outer profile already seen between the 4th and early 5th century continues (Pl. XVII, no. 6). The variant from context 1260 has a less marked carination and has lost the characteristic grooves on the rim which made it easier to host the lid.

The other type, presenting an incurving, thickened rim, flat on the upper surface with a diameter of 24 cm (Pl. XVII, no. 7) is vaguely reminiscent of a specimen from context 5147=5170. Similar casseroles, but made by hand, are well-documented in contexts of the mid-6th and 7th century at Carthage, although these were made locally in northern Tunisia.[155] It has been suggested that similar forms found at Cosa were imported from southern Italy or more probably from Sardinia.[156] Comparable products are also frequently attested in Roman contexts, including a type from the late 7th-century waste heap in the Crypta Balbi, characterized by a rim profile fairly similar to that from context 1260 but with small handles on the shoulder; it has been suggested that this may be an import from North Africa.[157] The specimen from Roselle, certainly made on the fast wheel, was likely produced locally or regionally since its fabric (AG 13) does not appear to have been used by workshops outside this region. This observation seems to be confirmed by the presence in context 1260 of a rim from a closed form, probably a cooking pot, made of fabric AG 13 and which appears to be a kiln discard. Evidently the workshop which used this fabric must have been located in the city centre or in its immediate vicinity.

The type of pan with a thickened and rounded rim measuring 29 cm in diameter, with a flat base and gently flaring walls (Pl. XVII, no, 4) is reminiscent of forms in use in the late Roman levels already analysed, though it differs from these for its less everted walls.

152 For the cooking pots comparable to Type I see Cantini 2005a, p.140, Pl.27, nos 5.45-49; for those comparable to Type VII *ibidem*, p.141, Pl.28, nos 5.53-54.

153 On the late Roman transformation of the kitchenware repertoire see also Fontana 2004, pp.316-317.

154 I identified this ceramic type in 2002 when I was responsible for studying the late Roman and early medieval ceramics from the urban excavations at Grosseto.

155 For a comparison see Fulford-Peacock p.162, Fig.58, no.19.3; for a discussion of the possible identification of the workshops see *ibidem* pp.11-12, nos 3-5.

156 Fontana 2004, pp.314-315, Figs 142-143, nos FC 23-24.

157 Ricci 1998, p.353, Fig.1, no.7.

Again there are strong affinities with a piece from the late 7th century deposit in the Crypta Balbi.[158]

The repertoire of open kitchenware forms is completed by two main types of lid: that with a slightly thickened and rounded rim (Pl. XVII, no. 2) and a more complex type with a rim of triangular section presenting a groove to ensure better adherence to the edge of the cooking pot and a slightly carinated body (Pl. XVII, no. 5). The lids generally have button-shaped handles (Pl. XVII, no. 3). The macroscopic analysis of the fabrics allows us to note the continued use of those previously documented in contexts 5147=5170 and 1262, with the exception of fabric AG 6, present for the first time in this context and used to make cooking pots and lids (Table XIV).

4.6. The Pottery from Context 1310: Evidence of Help in Dating the Abandonment of the Small Circular Hut

The only layer of the small circular structure west of the church to have yielded materials of use for dating purposes is the fill of a post hole: context 1310.

An initial fact worth noting is the small overall number of minimum forms documented, only 12, and the large proportion of these which are residual, as much as 72% of the total.

The residual transport containers include a minimum of at least 2 Dressel 1 amphorae, a Baetic Dressel 7-13 amphora, and a Keay XXV from Tunisia. The only amphora in phase is a late version of the LR4 (Pl. XVIII, no. 3). The LR4 from context 1310 has a plain vertical rim with a diameter of 9.5 cm, comparable with the variants in use from the late 5th/early 6th century;[159] it is also characterized by the large quantities of clay added to the rim, a typical feature of late specimens.[160]

All of the African red slip ware is residual and consists of a minimum of 2 production D forms; the only identifiable specimen is a Hayes 59 deep dish, dated to between AD 320 and 400/420.

The only materials of help in dating the structure, alongside the "Gaza amphora", are a dish and a flanged bowl, both in *colature rosse* ware. The dish has an internally thickened rim, flattened on the upper surface and presenting a fairly marked groove; the diameter of the mouth is 27 cm (Pl. XVIII, no. 2). The shape of this object is similar to common productions well-documented by the British excavations at Carthage in contexts of the late 5th and early 6th century,[161] and to kitchenware from the Roman Vigna Barberini context of the mid-/late 6th century.[162]

The bowl with a flange of rectangular section, inclined slightly downwards, and a vertical rim measuring 25 cm in diameter (Pl. XVIII, no. 1) appears to be modelled on the African prototype Hayes 91C and presents affinities with similar forms in *ingobbiata di rosso* ware from context 1260. A close point of comparison for the version in *colature rosse* ware comes from objects documented in contexts of the first half of the 7th century at Santa Maria della Scala in Siena.[163]

4.7. Brief Remarks on the Importance of a Pottery Deposit on the South Hill at Roselle

The fill of a cistern on the south hill at Roselle yielded some vessels in *colature rosse* ware now in the Museo Archeologico in Grosseto. The minimum number of 3 forms dating to between the mid-6th and the first half of the 7th century must have belonged to a much larger deposit of late antique and early medieval materials, suggesting that the cistern was used as a refuse heap.[164]

The 3 pottery specimens are a flanged bowl, a jug and a bottle.The flanged bowl has a large rim diameter, almost 27 cm, a horizontal, slightly pointed flange and a spout. The walls are gently flaring and the body is extremely deep (Pl. XVIII, no. 4). The closest morphological points of comparison are with similar pieces, with no slip, from the late 7th century deposit in the Crypta Balbi; this context also yielded a similar specimen painted with stripes, probably imported from the Tyrrhenian area of central or southern Italy.[165] The type of jug with a barely everted trilobed rim of rectangular section (Pl. XVIII, no. 5) resembles a specimen of the first half of the 7th century from the urban context of Santa Maria della Scala.[166] Finally, we should note a type of bottle with a tall cylindrical neck, 3.5. cm wide, with a handle set at the junction between the rim and the neck (Pl. XVIII, no. 6).

An analysis of the coatings has revealed an interesting way of applying the paint to the flanged bowl. In contrast to the other two pieces, which present obvious traces of dripping, the paint seems to cover only a strip beneath the rim, where two parallel horizontal drips can be seen. It is possible that this difference is due to the use of a brush rather than simply a random effect of dripping the slip onto the piece. A similar technique

---

158 *Ibidem*, p353, Fig.1, no.11.
159 For the LR4 amphora and its variants see Pieri 1998, pp.22-23.
160 Arthur 1998, p.162 and p.163, Fig.4, no.1.
161 Fulford-Peacock, 1984, p.176, Fig.65, no.36.1.
162 For the archaeological context of the Vigna Barberini on the Palatine Hill see Rizzo *et alii* 2004, p.86, Pl.IV, no.30.
163 Cantini 2005a, p190, Pl.51, no.8.32 and no.8.35.
164 These ceramics, held at the Museo Archeologico e di Storia dell'Arte Sacra di Grosseto, were selected for exhibition as part of a large ceramic assemblage dating to the 6th and 7th centuries AD; personal communication by the Museum Director M.G.Celuzza.
165 For comparisons see Ricci 1998, p.361, Fig.5, no.8 (unpainted specimen), p.378, Fig.16, no.2 (specimen in *colature rosse* ware).
166 Cantini 2005a, p.188, Pl.49, no.8.14.

was used to decorate a flanged bowl, without a spout, from the abandonment phase of the second half of the 6th/early 7th century of the Paduline complex at Castiglione della Pescaia. However, the tentative nature of this theory, which is not currently supported by other similar specimens, has led us to include both these pieces in the *colature rosse* ware category. The 3 specimens described above seem to belong to a period between the late 6th and the late 7th century, indicating the importance of the pottery context yielded by the cistern on the south hill, which should be the subject of in-depth research in future studies.

Appendix A_ identified ARS types from the North Hill in Roselle (data used for the Individual Weighted Means analysis)

FORM	TYPE	PRODUCTION	MNI
BOWL	HAYES 7A	A	2
BOWL	HAYES 9A	A	1
BOWL	HAYES 9B	A	2
BOWL	HAYES 14A	A	3
BOWL	HAYES 14B	A	9
BOWL	HAYES 14/17	A	1
DISH	HAYES 26	A	6
DISH	HAYES 27	A	1
DISH	HAYES 27, N.7	A	1
DISH	HAYES 3A	A	1
DISH	HAYES 3B	A	1
DISH	HAYES 3C	A	4
DISH	HAYES 6C	A	1
BOWL	HAYES 8A	A	7
BOWL	HAYES 8B	A	2
DISH	HAYES 32	A/D	1
PLATE	HAYES 48, n.13	C	1
LARGE DISH	HAYES 50	C	23
LARGE BOWL/DISH	HAYES 45A	C	3
LARGE BOWL/DISH	HAYES 58B, n.11	D	2
LARGE BOWL/DISH	HAYES 59	D	11
DISH	HAYES 50B	D	4
NON ID.	ATLANTE I, stamp no 29 + no 112	D	1
BOTTLE	FULFORD CLOSED FORMS 2	D	1
LARGE BOWL/DISH	HAYES 61A	D	2
LARGE BOWL/DISH	HAYES 61B	D	10
LARGE BOWL/DISH	HAYES 63	D	1
LARGE BOWL	HAYES 67	D	1
LARGE BOWL/DISH	HAYES 87A	D	1
FLANGED BOWL	HAYES 91A/B	D	2
FLANGED BOWL	HAYES 91B	D	2
FLANGED BOWL	HAYES 91C	D	1
LARGE BOWL	HAYES 93B	D	1
DISH	HAYES 104A	D	3
DISH	HAYES 104B	D	1
BOWL	HAYES 99A	D	2
BOWL	HAYES 99C	D	1
DISH	ATLANTE I, Tav. XLVI, 1-2	D	1
Stamp Hayes A(ii)		D	2
BOWL	HAYES 99B	D	1

5. Ceramics and Rural Areas: the Socio-Economic Differentiation of Settlement Contexts Between the Fourth and Early Seventh Centuries

The period between the 4th and the early 7th century saw profound transformations in settlement patterns and economic structures. The analytical study of the pottery contexts from both excavations and surface surveys represents the main tool allowing archaeologists to attempt an overall interpretation of economic systems.[1] Although the available sample may be more or less representative depending on whether it is produced by a stratigraphic excavation or by an archaeological survey, ceramic data allow us not only to study different settlement types but above all to attempt broader reconstructions on the regional scale.

Until at least the 7th century, when production and trade systems underwent a marked process of simplification and localization throughout the western Mediterranean,[2] pottery represents an excellent archaeological marker for the economic complexity of a site or an area and for the extent of its integration into medium- and long-range trade circuits.

Using pottery as our guide, this chapter will attempt to analyse the economic systems of the study area in terms of three fundamental aspects:

- the relations between settlements and maritime trade circuits;
- the degree of complexity of the circulation of goods on a regional and interregional scale;
- the possible function of some classes of ceramics as socio-economic markers.

Focusing on these three lines of inquiry, our study was conducted mainly at two different levels of resolution: first, at the regional scale, with the aim of defining the salient aspects of pottery consumption and at identifying socio-economic hierarchies among settlements; second, at the site level, with an analysis of the complexity presented by some elite ceramic contexts from different types of site.

The proximity of this area to long-distance maritime trade circuits allows us not only to develop some reflections on the region's general permeability to overseas maritime trade, but also to determine the receptive capacity of each individual context in the period between the 4th and the early 7th century AD by means of a comparative analysis.[3]

[1] For an extremely broad approach covering the Mediterranean and northern Europe see Wickham 2005.
[2] Ward-Perkins 2005, pp. 104-110.
[3] On the problem of interpreting pottery from surveys see in general Keay 2000, pp. 100-109.

5.1. Imported Mediterranean Fineware and Its Distribution in Rural Areas (Fourth to Early Seventh Centuries AD)

As we have already seen for the town of Roselle, the demand for imported Mediterranean fineware in rural areas was also met exclusively by African products; the only exceptions are the maritime villa at Santa Francesca, near Talamone, and the site of Talamonaccio. On the basis of the surface data, the late antique phase of the villa yielded no specimens of African red slip ware, but only a few forms of *Dérivées-des-Sigillées Paléochrétiennes* (henceforth DSP.), fired under reducing conditions with a dark-grey slip (Munsell Gley 2, 5/1 bluish grey); these can be ascribed to the workshops of southern Gaul.[4] The items found include two base fragments with poorly developed ring-shaped feet, measuring 14.4 and 15 cm respectively, and a stamped decoration on the bottom (Pl. XIX, nos 1-2). The walls are flaring. The morphological structure of the minimum number of 2 individuals suggests that they belong to a single type of indeterminate nature. Both bases present two concentric grooves enclosing the stamped decoration. In one case the decoration consists of palm branches copied from stamps *Atlante I*, Pl. LVII(b), nos 47-49, typical of African red slip ware with decorations belonging to Hayes style A(i)-(ii) from between AD 320 and 420. The motif on the Narbonese slip ware is enriched by a circular element at either end of the plant motif.[5] This decoration is well-documented on forms from the *castrum* of Saint Blaise in Provence dating to between the 6th and early 7th centuries.[6] By contrast, the motif on the second specimen is a more original interpretation of the palm branch, taking the form of an irregular rhombus with horizontal and vertical ridges intersecting to join the opposite corners; two circular elements are present in the smaller outward-facing portion. This type of palm branch also finds analogies on a piece found at Saint Blaise in a context of the first half of the 6th century and on another from the early 7th century.[7]

The fineware finds from the villa on the Gulf of Talamone are similar to those from the fortified settlement on the hill at Talamonaccio.[8] The exclusive presence at these two sites, at least as far as we can tell from the surface survey, of DSP may indicate that these materials were redistributed from the port of Cosa, given the significant presence of this class among the unstratified materials from Brown's excavations on the *Arx*,[9] and a minimum number of at

[4] *Atlante I*, p. 5.
[5] On the decoration see *Atlante I*, Pl. XI, no. 116.
[6] See Rigoir-Rigoir 1994, p. 155, Fig. 109, nos 212-214 and p. 158, Fig. 113, no. 4375.
[7] *Ibidem*, p.158, Fig.113, no.3728.
[8] For Talamonaccio we have only generic information regarding the presence of some fragments, in Fentress 2002, pp. 248-249.
[9] This information was provided by Elizabeth Fentress, whom I thank.

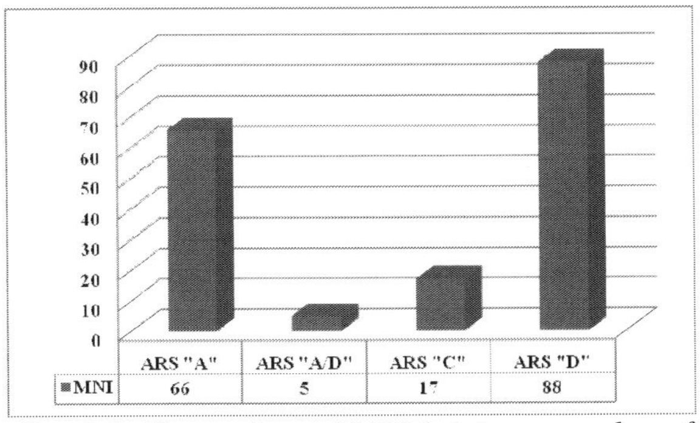

Graph I_ Comparison of MNI (minimum number of individuals) of ARS productions in the territory (the ARS data from the villa site at Aiali is not included).

least 1 individual in the construction phase of the 6th-century *castrum*.[10]

The distribution of DSP seems to be occasional on the Tyrrhenian coast south of Liguria; in Liguria it is fairly common in the late antique contexts of Ventimiglia and Luni. Sporadic finds are documented at Cosa, the villa at Talamone and at Talamonaccio, as well as at Vada Volterrana,[11] Rome, Ostia, Sperlonga, Naples and at Cagliari, Porto Torres and Cornus in Sardinia.[12] The presence of this pottery class at the Ligurian sites and at Vada can be explained by the existence of a *cabotage* route linking southern Gaul, via the Ligurian Sea, with the northern Tyrrhenian. Supply to sites further south, by contrast, may have been guaranteed by a sea route running from Marseilles to Porto Torres and thence to Rome, passing through the Strait of Bonifacio. Two different redistribution circuits may then have led away from Rome: one towards the north and one towards the south.

Despite the exceptions described above, Tunisian products dominate the imported Mediterranean fineware found in rural areas. The survey allowed us to identify a significant number of fragments of African red slip ware belonging to productions A, A/D, C and D; however, only a minimum number of 176 individuals can be ascribed with certainty to a specific type.[13] 37.5% of individual types belong to A production workshops, only 2.84% to A/D production workshops, 9.65% to C production workshops and 50% to production D workshops (Graph I).

The study of African red slip ware, essential for determining the chronology of imperial and late antique settlements, was aimed both at determining the degree to which the study area was integrated into Mediterranean trade networks and at identifying any differences between the capacity of various sites to access these goods. The territorial distribution of this pottery class over the long term presents a series of extremely interesting features: these can in part be ascribed to changes in settlement patterns and the gradual selection of some sites to the detriment of others, but also to different commercial choices made by contemporary settlements.

Fig.1 shows the distribution of ARS between the 2nd and 3rd centuries AD, during a phase which saw a decrease in the total number of rural sites compared to the late Republic and early Empire. A and A/D production forms, and the earliest specimens introduced by the new workshops of central Tunisia specializing in production C can be found throughout the study area in considerable numbers. At least 49 settlements yielded a minimum of one or more individuals. The highest concentrations were found in areas nearest the coast, where the settlement density is in any case higher. Specifically, significant quantities were recorded along the flat strip overlooking the north-west bank of Lake Prile. By contrast, finds were scarce in the areas closest to Vetulonia and in the urban area near Sestinga Nuova, where a surface survey was carried out. Here we found only 2 fragments of a Hayes 8 bowl, whilst the recent excavations in via Garibaldi, inside the modern village, yielded a hitherto indeterminate number of production A forms.[14] Another area yielding significant finds is located along the lower Ombrone river, between Alberese and the harbour at Scoglietto. Throughout this phase, ARS is found without distinction at all the settlement types attested: villas, villages and small and medium-sized farmsteads.

Among the most commonly documented forms are various production A bowls (Hayes 14A, 14B, 8A and 9A) and the production C Hayes 50A deep dish (Pl. XX, no. 1), introduced during the first half of the 3rd century and produced up to the early decades of the following century. Other specimens belonging to 3rd-century productions C1 and C2 are rare: among these we could mention the flat-based dish Hayes 49, no. 1 and the deep dish *Atlante I*, Pl. XXVIII, 7 (Pl. XX, no. 2). In keeping with what we have already seen in the deposit from the north slopes at Roselle, production A/D is not commonly documented in rural areas; the only finds from this production are 3 specimens of the Salomonson A25 and 2 of the Hayes 31, nn.1, 4 bowls, both manufactured during the first half of the 3rd century.

The picture of the distribution of Tunisian fineware changes slightly between the 4th and 5th centuries (Fig.2). The decrease in the number of contexts

[10] Fentress *et alii* 1991, p. 215.
[11] Pasquinucci *et alii* 1998, p. 619.
[12] On the distribution of DSP see Reynolds 1995, pp. 36-37 and Soricelli 1994, p. 141.
[13] This first level of analysis did not include the extraordinarily large number of ARS finds from the villa at Aiali, a wholly atypical context compared to the general trend for rural areas with a total of 214 minimum individuals ascribable to specific typologies. On the late antique pottery from this site see also Vaccaro-Campana-Ghisleni 2009.

[14] The latter piece of information was provided by M.Çygielman (SBAT) whom I thank.

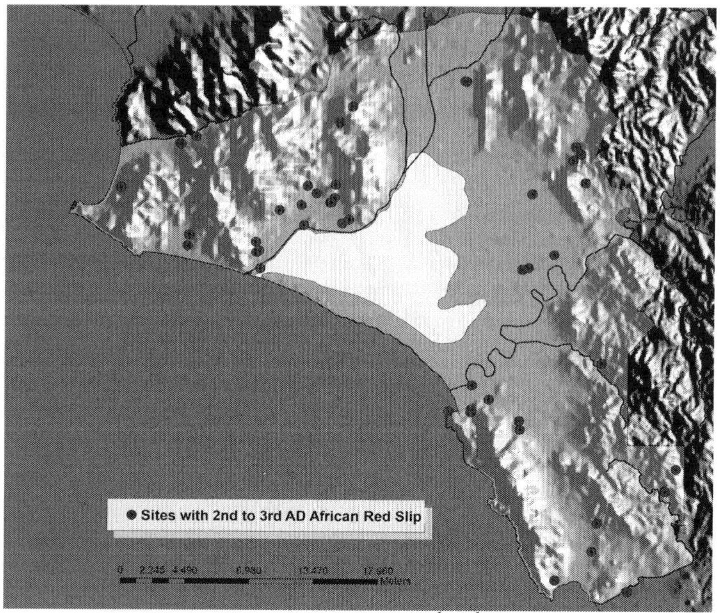

Fig.1_ ARS distribution in the 2nd-3rd centuries AD.

yielding ARS from this period, down from 49 during the preceding phase to 27, a drop of about 45%, does not, however, appear to be due to a decrease in the capacity to purchase Tunisian tableware; rather, it is an effect of the settlement selection process resulting from the middle imperial crisis.

This becomes apparent if we note that, with the exception of two contexts in the lower Ombrone valley,[15] where North African transport containers indicate that the site was frequented during the 4th-5th centuries, all the remaining settlements attested during this period yielded specimens of ARS. Evidence of the ease with which African red slip ware was still obtainable between the 4th and 5th centuries and its broad distribution even in smaller settlement contexts is supplied by the finds from the excavations in the town of Grosseto.[16] This settlement became a true village only in the High Middle Ages; only slight traces of frequentation can be found for the late antique period. The discovery of residual African red slip ware (types Hayes 84, 61, 67, 76 and 91A) in medieval layers demonstrates that ARS also reached small rural settlements such as this. During the course of the 5th century, Grosseto must still have been a seasonal settlement, perhaps connected to the exploitation of the land on the left-hand bank of the Ombrone river for agriculture and/or animal husbandry, and to the extraction of salt. Significant quantities of ARS were also found during the excavations in via Garibaldi, indicating the persistence of relations between the ancient town of Vetulonia and Mediterranean trade circuits in late Antiquity.[17] The most frequently documented forms in rural areas between the 4th and 5th centuries can be ascribed to the production D workshops of northern Tunisia, with 10 different types and at least 14 variants. Among the most common are the deep dishes Hayes 61A and 61B (Pl. XX, nos 6-7), 67 (Pl. XX, no. 4) and 76 (Pl. XX, no. 5). To these we should add, for production C5, the Hayes 84 deep dish (Pl. XX, no. 3), which represents the last experiment by the Byzacene workshops of Sidi Marzouk Tounsi and which was made from the 5th to the early decades of the 6th century.[18] The uniform distribution of 4th- and 5th-century ARS in all types of settlement context allows us to identify these as commodities which during this phase continued to be destined for mass consumption.

However, this picture is destined to change with the transition to the 6th century, when we see a marked decrease in ARS finds, attributable only in part to the further decline in population levels which characterized the turn of the 5th century. The decrease can be ascribed principally to the exclusion from overseas trade flows of a series of more modest rural settlements, principally late frequentations of villas or small farmsteads; as such, these contexts tended to obtain their supply of tableware from local and regional markets. Only 16 settlements yielded types of African red slip ware introduced in the mid-5th century and still produced during the 6th century, or types and variants typical of the mid-6th century (Fig.3). Compared to the previous period, there is a drop of about 41% in ARS finds; compared to the first phase of distribution of African red slip ware the decrease is about 67.4%. In more general terms, however, this data nonetheless show that

[15] The settlements in question are the harbour at Scoglietto and a house, covering a surface area of 150 m2 at the foot of the Monti dell'Uccellina on the Strada degli Olivi.

[16] The excavations were conducted between 1998 and 2005 by the Faculty of Medieval Archaeology of Siena University, directed by Riccardo Francovich and coordinated by Carlo Citter.

[17] By far the most common form is the production D deep dish Hayes 67 (information provided by M. Çygielman).

[18] On the Hayes 84 deep dish and the production site of Sidi Marzouk Tounsi see Mackensen 1998, pp.26-30.

Fig.2_ ARS distribution in the 4th-5th centuries AD.

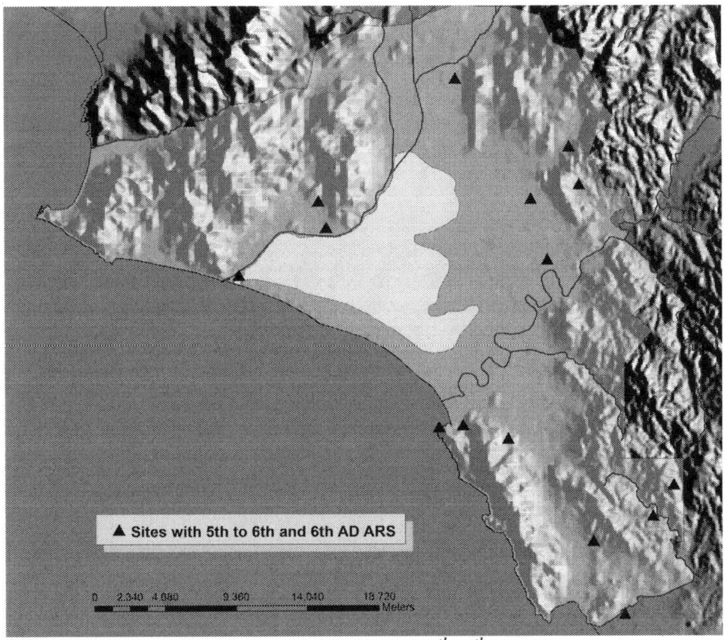

Fig.3_ ARS distribution in the 5th-6th centuries AD.

rural areas remained fairly well integrated into Mediterranean trade networks, especially when compared with the values for the diachronic distribution of ARS in other nearby areas, such as those investigated during the South Etruria surveys. Here, the African slip ware dating to between AD 470 and 550 is a third of that circulating between the early and mid-5th century and a tenth of that dated to the 4th century.[19]

Even during the early 6th century, then, the study area maintained constant relations with Mediterranean trade circuits, sufficient to allow for the redistribution of overseas pottery, albeit more selectively than during previous periods. The overall contraction in the volumes of ARS available seems to be due to two different factors. The first relates to the structure of the western Mediterranean economy which saw a loosening of the close interregional ties of dependence after the fall of Rome; these had remained solid even after the loss of the North African region to the Vandals.[20] The second factor, only partially connected to the first, is the strengthening of local and regional productions, able to meet a demand for pottery which had remained high and which could no longer be fully satisfied by imported pottery, now more difficult to access. The 4th- and 5th-century data from the town of Roselle showed high percentages of Italic tableware (*ingobbiata di rosso* and *sigillata chiara tarda dell'Italia centro-settentrionale*), found in greater quantities than Tunisian wares. The vigorous growth of Italic manufacturing activities is thus a phenomenon which had already begun in the 4th century, at a time when Tunisian fineware was still easily accessible both in the town and in rural areas. Of particular importance

[19] Hayes 1998, p.13.

[20] Panella 1993, pp.641-648.

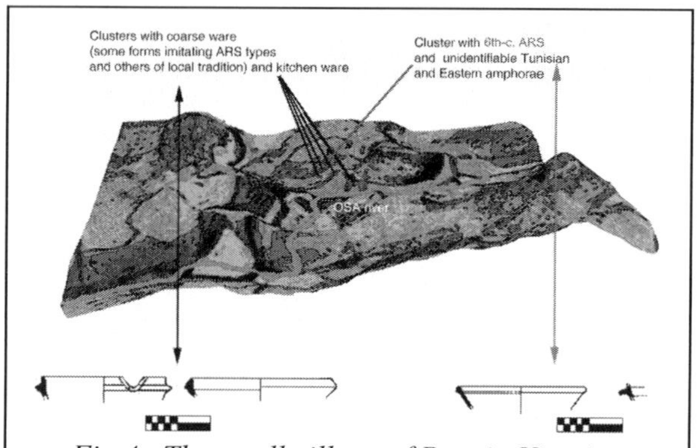

Fig.4_ The small village of Poggio Vicarina (along the upper Osa valley) and the pottery distribution (after Vaccaro 2008).

are the quantitative data: in other words, between the 5th and the early 6th century, what percentage of the tableware consumed in towns and rural settlements in the politically and economically more "marginal" areas of the western Mediterranean consisted of ARS? Was African red slip ware still a product available *en masse* or, as the data from Roselle would seem to suggest, did it already occupy a privileged position among tablewares where it continued to be present, albeit in smaller quantities than regional pottery? This question is currently difficult to answer for our study area and more generally for areas investigated through topographical surveys; this is because the finds yielded by surface contexts do not necessarily form a representative sample of the pottery consumed at a site.

As such, a quantitative approach is viable only for excavated contexts and for those surface sites which have been subjected to intensive and repeated surveys allowing for the collection of a large quantity of ceramics. Generally speaking, we can say that between the 5th and 6th centuries African red slip ware systematically accounts for a smaller percentage of fineware than Italic productions. However, there are some exceptions to this rule which seem essentially to be located near the coast; examples are the late antique occupation of the Scoglietto cave (*infra*), or that of a farmstead established *ex novo* between the 4th and 5th centuries at Vacchereccia, on the northern slopes of the Monti dell'Uccellina. In the latter context, the tableware forms found consist almost exclusively of ARS, with Hayes types 61A, 61B, 67 and 91B. The trend for rural areas nonetheless shows a constant and gradual increase in the supply of tableware from regional markets, starting already in the 4th century; this increase becomes more marked with the turn of the 5th-6th century when trade flows from North Africa begin to decrease.

As Chris Wickham has shown, it is possible that in the long history of the production and trade of ARS, lasting around six centuries, there were times when the marginal costs of exporting Tunisian pottery increased, leading to a drop in demand for this product.[21] The demand for tableware, which remained high, must therefore have been directed towards other supply channels which were already in place, thus leading to a growth in Italic productions. African red slip ware continued to circulate and to remain widespread at coastal sites throughout the 5th century, but in smaller percentages than the tableware made by regional workshops. During the 6th century, the social and political upheaval caused by the Greek-Gothic war further reduced the penetrative capacity of Mediterranean products, to the extent that African red slip ware became a luxury commodity, accessible almost exclusively to elite contexts.

In this context, it is worth mentioning the settlement established during the 6th century on the Poggio Vicarina hill in the upper Osa valley (Fig.4). Here the pottery associations suggest that the uppermost topographical unit was of central importance; it was located at 80 m above sea level, higher up than the four houses found on the south-eastern slopes of the hill, at 70 m above sea level. Possible evidence of this pre-eminence is the exclusive presence of African red slip ware (types Hayes 91C and 80B/99) and imported Tunisian amphorae on the highest point of the hill. These two imported classes are absent from the other four clusters where, by contrast, we find imitations of African prototypes (Hayes 61 and 91) in *acroma selezionata*, alongside local or regional small storage amphorae rather than true amphorae. The African red slip ware and transport containers, found exclusively at the surface site in the best strategic position within this hamlet, might suggest that it played a privileged role, perhaps connected to the presence of a storeroom housing overseas foodstuffs; its owner, or someone closely connected to the owner, probably had access to imported Mediterranean fineware. Within the overall picture for the distribution of 5th- and 6th-century ARS in rural areas we can observe that some forms are preferred to others (Graph II). Particularly common are Hayes 91 flanged bowls, present with variants B (Pl. XXI, no. 1) and C (Pl. XXI, nos 2-3), and Hayes 99 bowls, present with variants A (Pl. XXI, no. 4) and B (Pl. XXI, no. 5). Other forms typical of the 6th century are less well documented; these include the deep dishes Hayes 104A (Pl. XXI, no. 7), Hayes 80B/99 (Pl. XXI, no. 6) and Hayes 93, and the Hayes 12/110 bowl. Another type of bowl, Hayes 94, is present in significant quantities, but only at the Scoglietto cave context (*infra*).

[21] See most recently Wickham 2005, pp.712-713; and Wickham 1989, p.113.

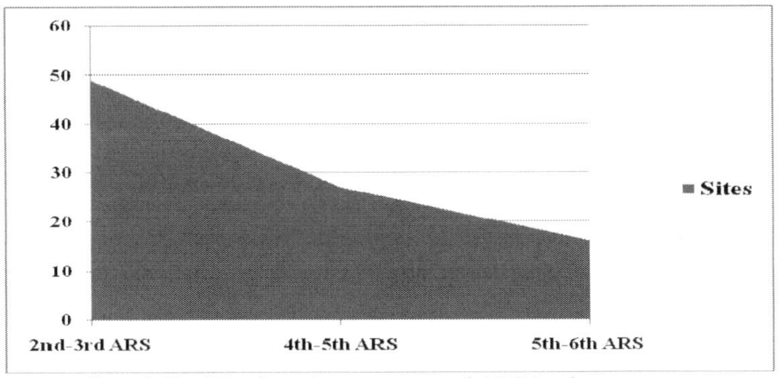

Graph II_ Diachronic presence of ARS in the territory.

5.1.1. The Distribution Trend for African Red Slip Ware Over Time: Rural Areas

The analysis of the distribution of African red slip ware over the long term allows us to identify some interesting analogies and differences with what we have already seen regarding the supply of Tunisian pottery in the town of Roselle. As in the urban context, the countryside also sees a significant increase in attestations of ARS from the early 2nd century AD (Graph III). This is due to three closely interconnected factors: first, the intensification of the trade in foodstuffs paid as taxes in kind to Rome and thus a corresponding increase in the commercial redistribution of the surplus goods reaching the Roman markets. To this we should add the important role of the trade carried out by the North African *navicularii* on their own behalf alongside that for taxation purposes.

The increase in attestations is exponential, reaching an absolute peak in the early 3rd century. Later, in the second half of the 3rd century, we see a marked drop in the circulation of goods coinciding on the one hand with a crisis in rural population patterns and on the other with a decline in production A, not counterbalanced by the wares of the production C workshops established in central Tunisia. From the second half of the 4th century onwards, distribution again picks up significantly thanks to the enormous success of the production D workshops re-established in the northern part of Tunisia. Between the mid-4th and the early decades of the 6th century the trend is generally positive, but with some brief periods of decline resulting from adverse political conditions. These occur in the 430s and at the end of the 5th century and coincide with the Vandal conquest of Carthage which suddenly interrupted the flows of fiscal goods from Tunisia to Rome and with the collapse of the western Empire. A comparison with Roselle shows strong analogies in the supply of African red slip ware between the mid-4th and the early decades of the 6th century. The only notable differences are the more marked increase in attestations during the second half of the 4th century in the town compared to the countryside and a more marked decrease in the supply of pottery to the countryside following the Vandal conquest of Carthage. These two facts are important because they indicate that the urban market was the main target of supply flows. These continued to reach the town even when trade was most difficult to organize, such as when Tunisia fell to the Vandals. During phases of increased production and demand, for example when production D wares became popular during the 4th century, pottery arrived in enormous quantities, in part to meet the needs of urban consumption and in part for redistribution to the countryside.

Subsequently, the most interesting period, when the distribution curve for ARS in rural areas is out of line with that for the town, is between the 530s and 550s. At Roselle there was a slight but significant increase in attestations of African red slip ware starting from the 520s and 530s which remained constant until the middle of the century. The probable reason for this was

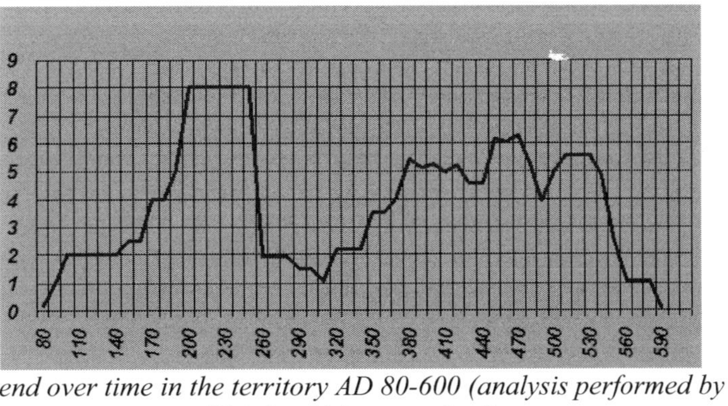

Graph III_ The ARS trend over time in the territory AD 80-600 (analysis performed by using the Individual Weighted Means method).

the strategic and military role played by the site during the Gothic war, giving the state a vested interest in ensuring that supplies remained as constant as possible. The picture for rural areas at this time is very different. From the 530s we see a sudden drop in the Tunisian fineware in circulation which appears to be closely linked to a general contraction in trade due to the widespread devastation caused by the Greek-Gothic war; the war had a dramatic impact on economic and settlement structures in most of the Italian peninsula.[22]

From the mid-6th century onwards both town and countryside once again start to present similar trends. At Roselle there is a slight drop in circulation compared to the preceding decades, whilst in rural areas we see a phase of stagnation lasting around twenty years, preceded by a sharp drop. The progressive crisis in acquisitions of Tunisian fineware beginning in the countryside in the second and third decades of the 6th century and two decades later in the town is a structural phenomenon. This trend began long before the 590s, when the Lombard conquest of the area merely succeeded in interrupting links with the Mediterranean world that had already lost their stability and continuity and become merely episodic.

After the 580s/590s African red slip ware forms no longer reach rural areas, not even those contexts which were in more direct contact with the coast such as the settlement of Paduline at Castiglione della Pescaia where transport containers and overseas coarseware continue to be attested between the mid -6th and early 7th centuries. ARS had become an extremely rare and valuable product and although it continued to circulate along the routes used for *cabotage* as indicated, though weakly, by the data from *Portus Scabris*, it was no longer redistributed to rural sites.

5.1.2. The Villa at Aiali (*Ager Rusellanus*): a Case of Early Contraction in Acquisitions of African Red Slip Ware

The settlement complex of Aiali, about 4 km south-west of the town of Roselle, represents a case study of enormous interest for research into the transformations undergone by the villa between the imperial period and late Antiquity. Among the various research methodologies and techniques adopted, the intensive analysis of this context entailed the systematic collection of ceramic finds in the field using a system of virtual grids uploaded to DGPS handsets in order to record the exact topographical localation of moveable materials. The pottery record resulting from these replicated surveys is significant, amounting to over 1100 fragments of identifiable typology, and a total

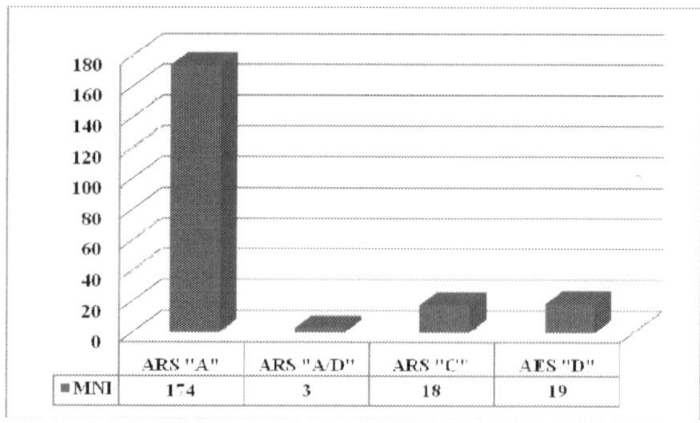

Graph IV_ Comparison of MNI (minimum number of individuals) of ARS productions at the villa site in the locality of Aiali.

minimum number of 1044 individuals.[23] Hitherto, the analytical study has concerned both fineware and coarseware and the medieval materials with the main aim of investigating the site's varying intensity of occupation over the long term.

African red slip ware, documented with productions A, C and D, accounts for about 20.5% of the minimum number of individuals identified (Graph IV and Appendix B.). The extraordinarily large quantities of ARS collected during the surface surveys made it necessary to deal with this context separately since the exceptional nature of the data posed the risk of distorting our interpretations of the overall distribution trend for this pottery class in rural areas. The history of supplies of tableware at this site seems highly unusual, to the extent that it requires a detailed analysis and a reflection on the settlement history of this context during the long period between the 2nd and 6th centuries AD.

The most striking fact when compared with the African red slip ware "curve" for rural areas is the sharp drop in acquisitions starting in the last quarter of the 3rd century, contrasting with the massive presence during the period between the early 2nd and mid-3rd centuries (Graph V). Starting from the 4th century, the number of African red slip ware specimens appears negligible in comparison with the huge quantities attested in the 2nd and mid-3rd century. Were we to read these data without comparing them with attestations of Italic tableware from the period between the 4th and 6th centuries, we would be forced to assume a crisis in the settlement and probably a strong contraction in the surface area inhabited following the middle imperial crisis. The presence of African slip ware A and A/D, respectively with a minimum number of 174 and 3 individuals of identifiable typology, is significant and, as is apparent from an analysis of its distribution within the context, covers practically the whole area where systematic grid-based collection was carried out (Fig.5). By contrast, both productions C and D are documented to a far more limited extent, with a

[22] On the impoverishment of markets and the localization of economic systems in Italy from 530 see Wickham 2003, pp.390-393, with bibliography.

[23] The material was recorded by Mariaelena Ghisleni and the author; of the distribution of the main classes of tableware can be found in Vaccaro-Ghisleni-Campana 2009, pp.303-324.

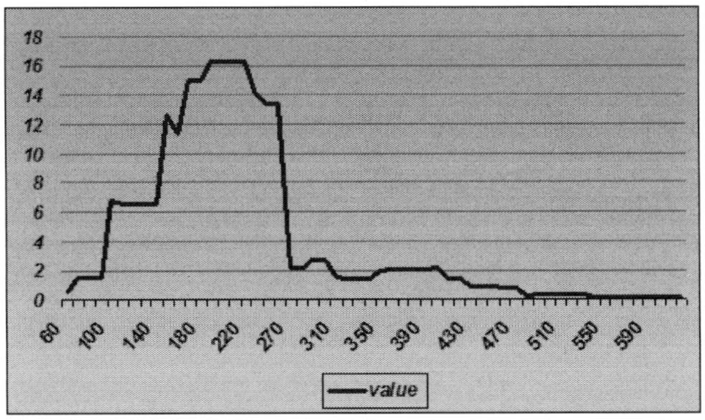

Graph V_ The ARS trend over time at Aiali AD 80-600 (analysis performed by using the Individual Weighted Means method).

minimum number of 18 and 19 individuals respectively. Furthermore, the distribution of C and D forms appears to be circumscribed to some areas of the settlement, contrasting with the systematic presence of production A specimens. However, it should be noted that the distribution of some specimens of African red slip ware dated to the 5th-6th century covers both the main settlement complexes identified at Aiali. Specifically, the grid covering the building with side corridors and square rooms at the corners yielded two flanged bowls belonging respectively to a generic Hayes 91 form and to a Baradez 1961, Plate II, no. 7; the latter is not documented at other sites in the study territory. To these we should add a fragment of a Hayes 99 bowl. The other settlement complex with a central courtyard yielded four late African red slip ware forms, belonging to types Hayes 99, Hayes 91A/B (2 specimens) and a rim probably from a flat-based dish of type *Atlante I*, Pl. XLVI, no. 6, also attested in the deposit on the north hill at Roselle.

Since we are dealing with surface evidence a degree of caution is called for, but we cannot ignore this sudden decrease in the supply of African red slip ware after the mid-3rd century. There appears to have been a decrease in the capacity or the interest on the part of the site's inhabitants in acquiring imported Mediterranean goods starting from the 4th century. At this time these goods, albeit to a smaller extent than in previous centuries, still reached numerous sites in rural areas and in particular the town of Roselle and the town of Vetulonia with some continuity.

If our general argument that the African red slip ware of the late 5th and 6th centuries held symbolic value as a "weak sign" of power and a means of self-representation through eating practices holds true (*infra*), we can suggest that the site of Aiali, whilst still representing a focal point in the settlement network, was no longer the stable residence of an elite, but rather a sort of large village inhabited by peasants dependent on a land owner who was present only occasionally. This theory is based on the analysis of the surface ceramics and in particular the emergence of a "hierarchy" among the different classes of tableware: as such it should be considered a working hypothesis rather than an exhaustive explanation for our observations. At Aiali, the continuity of settlement throughout late Antiquity is clearly indicated by the significant presence and capillary distribution of coarsewares and of regional colour coated ware (*ingobbiata di rosso* and *sigillata chiara tarda dell'Italia centro-settentrionale* wares). From the 4th century onwards, and perhaps as early as the 3rd century, the site sees a massive influx of tableware, likely produced regionally, which seems fully able to counterbalance the marked decrease in Tunisian fineware (Figs.6-7). In this context, a quantitative comparison of African red slip ware and regionally produced tableware in the pottery assemblages of the 4th-early 5th centuries on the north hill at Roselle is instructive. Here, the supply of tableware is clearly dominated by regional productions like *ingobbiata di rosso* and the so-called *sigillata chiara tarda dell'Italia centro-settentrionale*;[24] in comparison, far smaller quantities of ARS are attested.

It is likely that the marked increase in regionally produced red-slipped wares and those with a bright red impermeable slip, more similar to the traditional *sigillata italica*, reflects high levels of demand for fineware and semi-fine tableware. This demand could be met only in part, and mainly in coastal areas and major inland towns, by fineware imported from Tunisia, which between the 5th and 6th centuries had generally become rarer. As we have seen, in our study area African red slip ware continues to be documented in significant quantities up to the early years of the 6th century, albeit in smaller quantities than Italic tablewares. African red slip ware still reaches the site of Aiali in the 6th century, but only occasionally; though the quantitative comparison of surface pottery calls for immense caution, the data from Aiali suggest a massive predominance of Italic tableware, both red-slipped and plain, over Tunisian imports. Worth noting is the presence at Aiali of a minimum number of at least 7 individuals which can be ascribed to the *sigillata chiara tarda dell'Italia centro-settentrionale:* this pottery class is well documented in the urban context of Roselle, less than 4 km east of Aiali, but is much rarer in the countryside. In any case, the most

[24] On its distribution in the towns of *Tuscia* see Michelucci 1985 (Roselle), Bianchi-Palermo 1990a, pp.158-168 (Fiesole), Tortorella 1991, pp. 103-114 (Arezzo).

frequently attested tableware at Aiali is *ingobbiata di rosso*, generally easy to identify given the larger number of different forms produced and the often poor quality of the slip, frequently deteriorated to form an extremely fine film which detaches with ease. This class is present with about 652 fragments and at least 100 specimens of identifiable typology. This clearly demonstrates that the marked decrease in fineware does not in any way constitute a sign of a crisis in the settlement or a contraction in the surface area occupied. Rather, it results from different choices in the acquisition of tableware, now oriented more towards regional wares than towards overseas pottery.

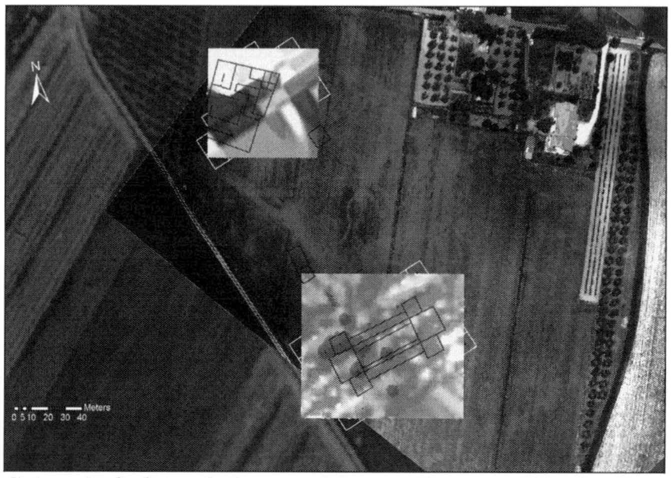

Fig.5_ Density map of ARS A at Aiali through the use of Inverse Distance Weighted interpolation (after Vaccaro-Ghisleni-Campana 2009).

Fig.6_ Density map of the 4th to 6th AD Ingobbiata di Rosso Ware at Aiali through the use of Inverse Distance Weighted interpolation (after Vaccaro-Ghisleni-Campana 2009).

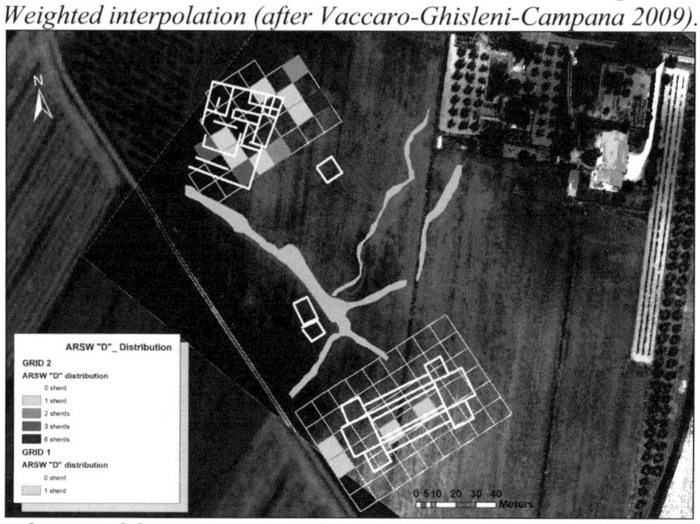

Fig.7_ Infra-site distribution of the minimum number of ARS D individuals at Aiali (4th-6th centuries AD). (After Vaccaro-Ghisleni-Campana 2009).

The workshops which produced *ingobbiata di rosso* wares were capable of making a fairly broad and diverse repertoire of forms, comprising a significant variety of open forms and a large number of closed forms; the latter are rarely attested among the imported fineware in this area.[25]

The repertoire of open tableware forms was in part influenced by some Tunisian archetypes. Generally, though, we can note the significant presence of specimens which belong to an independent tradition that could be termed at the very least sub-regional, if not a genuine "koiné" of Tuscany and part of central Italy. Among the forms modelled on Tunisian archetypes found at Aiali we could mention various deep dishes inspired both by Hayes 61A and the later 61B, some bowls with a short and slightly hooked flange modelled on Hayes 91C and finally a pair of large bowls with an almond-shaped rim resembling the earlier variant of Hayes 99 with a more pronounced rim. In other cases, it is more difficult to identify a specific and direct connection with Tunisian prototypes. This is true of some deep dishes with more or less inclined flat rims which are sometimes reminiscent of Hayes 58 and Hayes 59 and at others more similar to Hayes 67. The same can be said of a various types of bowls and deep dishes with a sub-vertical or slightly incurving rim. Although these present some similarities with Hayes 62 and Hayes 64, they may in fact, given their morphological simplicity, belong to a regional tradition, wholly or partly independent of the influence of Tunisian fineware. However, it should be stressed that in many cases we cannot identify a direct relationship with African red slip ware given the absence of even partially intact specimens allowing us to see the whole body profile. The series of carinated basins, documented with variants that differ in the morphological structure of the rim, usually more or less thickened and either rounded or flattened on the upper surface, is completely independent of the influences of Tunisian tableware. Given its characteristics, this form doubtless served for the consumption of liquid or semi-liquid foods and is the most frequently attested of the red-slipped pottery found at Aiali. On the basis of comparisons with the materials from excavations in the town of Roselle, it can be ascribed to the period between the 4th and the early 5th century AD.[26]

A comparison of the distribution of late antique red-slipped pottery and that of African red slip ware within the two collection grids allows us to make some interesting observations. In grid no. 1 *ingobbiata di rosso* ware was found in at least 27 grid squares out of a total of 54 and is thus more widespread even than African red slip ware A, documented in 22 grid squares. The distribution values for grid no. 2 are very similar to those for grid no. 1: here *ingobbiata di rosso* is attested in 27 out of 32 grid squares whilst African red slip ware A was found in 28 grid squares.

Although in quantitative terms African red slip ware A is more common than late antique red-slipped pottery in both grids, the widespread distribution of Italic tableware in the Aiali context is of enormous help in understanding the size of the site in its late antique phases. On the basis of the surface evidence, we can suggest that the areas occupied between the 4th and 5th and perhaps up to the early 6th century coincided with those occupied in the early and middle imperial period. After this, the evidence for the continuous use of the villa becomes progressively weaker and more episodic until the context is abandoned at a point apparently no later than the late 6th century. Naturally, not even an in-depth analysis of the distribution of surface materials such as that attempted for Aiali can be considered truly exhaustive in terms of a reconstruction of the long term dynamics of the site. If we compare the distribution of pottery and the plans of the buildings reconstructed on the basis of geophysical surveys, we can obtain a hypothetical picture of the areas occupied at any given time. However, only excavation will be able to supply the evidence needed to determine any functional transformations undergone by the site in the long term.

What we can say, with a good degree of certainty, is that the site of Aiali, despite transformations in the composition of the pottery assemblages and in particular the different choices in the source of tableware between the early imperial period and late Antiquity, must have been one of the major population centres in the A*ger Rusellanus* until at least the 5th-early 6th century, and probably also an important centre for the administration of the various forms of exploitation of the area's resources. Without doubt at the centre of a substantial landholding between the early and middle imperial period and likely the residence of a *possessor*, between the 4th and early 6th century the site still hosted a large population which mainly consumed regionally manufactured pottery but which occasionally – and this may represent weak evidence of the episodic presence of the owner – still imported African red slip ware between the 4th and 6th century and Tunisian amphorae of types Keay XXV, LV and LXII.

[25] It is important to note that the late antique bottle of type Fulford closed forms 2 produced in ARS is currently documented only in the urban context on the north slope at Roselle and in the Portus Scabris dump, with a single minimum individual each.

[26] On the presence of this type of basin in the contexts under examination here and on the north slope see above; this form is also well documented in the late antique reoccupation phases of the Domus dei Mosaici, south of the Forum, with the same chronology. Some Roman and late antique contexts in the Domus dei Mosaici are currently being studied as part of two undergraduate theses supervised by the author.

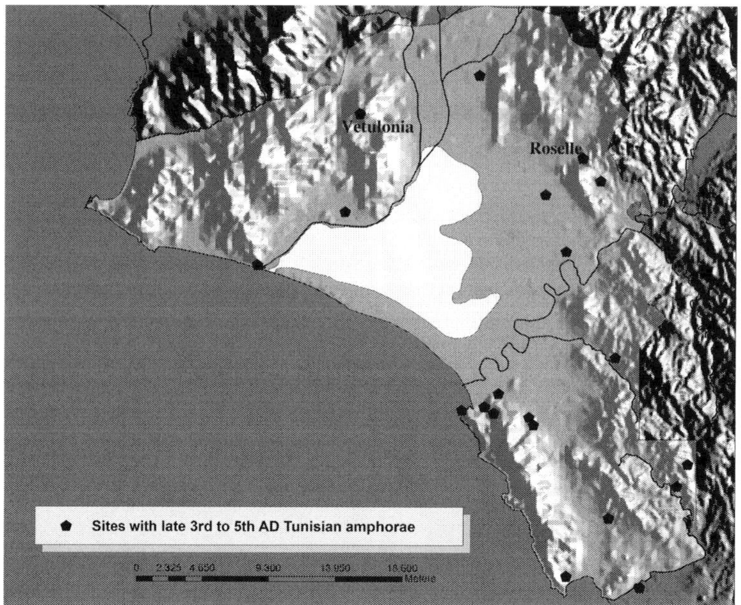

Fig.8_ Sites yielding late 3rd to 5th AD Tunisian amphorae (total number of the sites: 20).

5.2. Transport Containers in Rural Areas Between the Fourth and Sixth Centuries

The distribution trend for imported Mediterranean amphorae in late Antiquity presents numerous similarities with that for overseas fineware. The first significant fact is the virtually exclusive presence of Tunisian amphorae for the transport of fish sauces, wine and oil (Fig.8). Other areas of supply seem to be represented only to a fairly limited extent, even for products like wine, which were not major production specialities of North Africa. This is important because it suggests a specific and deliberate choice of the foodstuffs for import, probably a result of their scarce availability *in loco* and at the same time the potential for acquiring other foodstuffs, such as wine, locally; these were thus not sought from maritime trade networks.

Even compared to the town of Roselle the goods attested are less varied, with few *garum* amphorae from Lusitania; by contrast, these are well-documented in the town between the 4th and early 5th centuries. At Roselle we saw a significant presence of Keay XXIII/ Almagro 51C containers; in the study area these were present only at the site of *San Martino de plano*. Between the 3rd and 5th centuries Keay IIIA and Keay IIIB amphorae are widespread in rural areas (Pl. XXII, nos 1-4). Variant A is present in most contexts with 4th and 5th-century phases. However, the predominance of imported Tunisian foodstuffs (in all likelihood wines and fish sauces) mainly concerns those products transported in Keay XXV medium-sized cylindrical amphorae. At least 70% of the sites for which the pottery indicators suggest an occupation during the 4th-5th centuries have yielded this type of amphora. Keay XXV is documented with variants B, C, G and L (Pl. XXII, nos 6-9) with one or more specimens at all 20 sites where late 3rd-5th-century Tunisian amphorae were found. To these we should add some attestations of Keay VII (Pl. XXII, no. 5), which began production already in the early 3rd century, probably continuing up to the early decades of the 5th century.[27] Rare on the other hand are attestations of fish sauce amphorae from southern Spain, of type Keay XVIA/ Almagro 50 (Pl. XXIV, no. 2), common between the late 2nd/early 3rd and the early 5th century;[28] these are documented exclusively at the harbour town of Serrata Martini at Castiglione della Pescaia and at the Roman and late antique village of *San Martino de Plano* near Montepescali. The presence of other Tunisian containers possibly used for the transport of oil such as Keay XXXIII (Pl. XXIII, no. 5) is more episodic; an amphora of this type is documented only at the village with late antique phases at Quercia Grossa in the upper Osa valley. Keay XLI was found at the village of *San Martino de plano* in the Bruna valley and the site overlooking the last bend in the Osa river, at 10 m above sea level (Pl. XXIV, nos 4-5). Finally, a specimen of Keay XXXVA is documented at a medium-sized farmstead near Alberese,[29] on the *Via Aurelia Vetus* (Pl. XXIII, no. 6). The chronology of this amphora has recently been recalibrated, suggesting that it was manufactured in the 5th century AD.[30] However, its association with materials dated to before the end of the 5th century suggests that it was not imported after this date. Between the 4th and 5th centuries, imports of foodstuffs from other areas of the western Mediterranean were a marginal phenomenon. The presence of a single specimen of the Lusitanian fish-sauce container Keay XIIIC/ Almagro 50 at the harbour

[27] Keay 1984, pp.121-126; on the production sites of El Mokaïda, El Hri1, El Hri2, Salata, El Maklouba and Dahar Slima in the Sahel see Peacock *et alii* 1989, pp.189-198.

[28] Keay 1984, pp.149-155, for a morphological comparison p.153, Fig.59, no.1.

[29] I refer to the Bruna-Osa Survey site no. 65.3; for further information see the Catalogue of Sites.

[30] See Bonifay 2004, p.135.

village of Serrata Martini and another at the late antique settlement near the bend in the Osa river are clear evidence of this (Pl. XXIV, no. 3).

Products from Tunisia continue to be the most popular foodstuffs between the mid-5th and 6th centuries (Fig. 9), with a documented presence at as many as twelve sites. The most common containers are Keay XXVI *spatheia* (Pls XXII, no. 10 and XXIII, nos 1-4),[31] present in numerous contexts including the village of Serrata Martini-Paduline, the villa of San Martino near the Ombrone river, the village with late Roman phases at Podere Serratone and the town of Roselle. The versatility of this vessel, used to transport different types of food, currently makes it impossible to determine which product was purchased by the sites where specimens have been found. We can suggest that some types, also documented in our study area, were used to transport oil or fish-sauce: these include Keay LXII (Pl. XXIII, nos 8-10), LV and XXXVIB (Pl. XXIII, no. 7). The Keay LXII amphora is documented in various rural contexts, including Serrata Martini-Paduline, the village of San Martino *de plano* in the Bruna valley, a late Roman farmstead at Vacchereccia, and the Scoglietto cave in the lower Ombrone valley. In the Osa valley it is present at the site located near

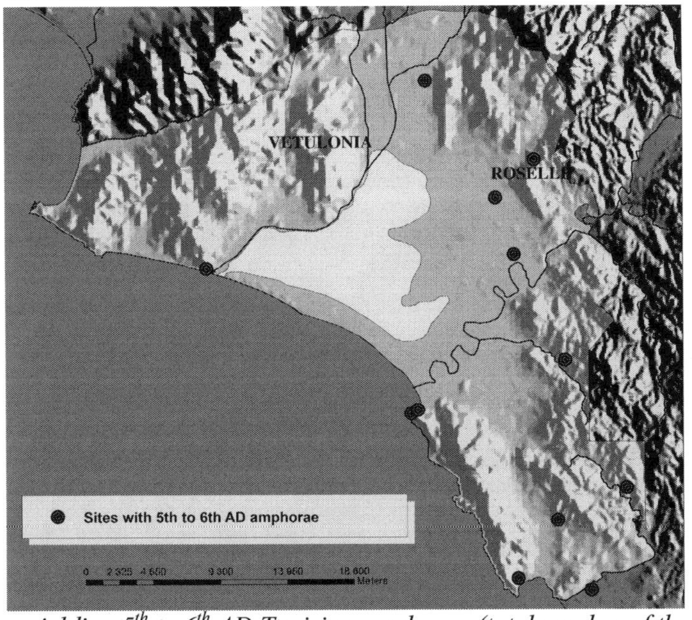

Fig.9_ Sites yielding 5th to 6th AD Tunisian amphorae (total number of the sites: 12).

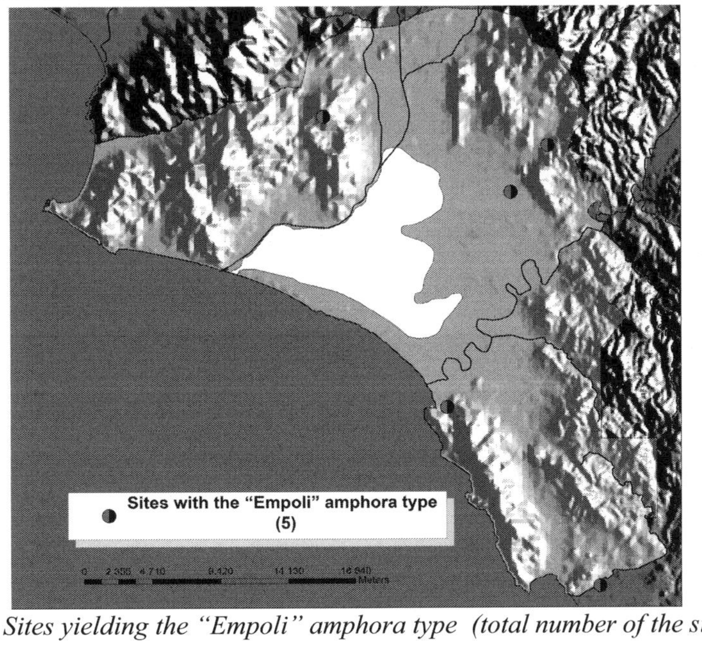

Fig.10_ Sites yielding the "Empoli" amphora type (total number of the sites: 5).

the last bend in the river and, further upstream, at the village of Poggio Vicarina. In the village with late antique phases of San Martino *de plano*, a specimen of Keay LXIIG was found together with a Keay XXXVIB

[31] In rural contexts Keay XXVI is often found in association with 5th and 6th century African red slip ware. It is therefore possible that specimens of this type were purchased alongside the most recent types of ARS. On the date of the Keay XXVI see Keay 1998, p.145.

amphora. By contrast, the Keay LV amphora, also present at Roselle, has been identified in the countryside only at the villa of Aiali, in use up to the 6th century.

The similarities between the town of Roselle and the area between the Alma and Osa valleys thus concern not only the popularity of Tunisian amphorae but also the scarce attestations of Italic and eastern Aegean wines. The Empoli amphora (Pl. XXIV, nos 6-7), used to trade the wine produced mainly in *Tuscia annonaria*, is attested only in a very few rural contexts and in all cases with only a small number of specimens (Fig.10). At Vetulonia, the recent excavations in Via Garibaldi revealed the presence of at least 1 specimen of this container in 4th-century phases.[32]

Generally, however, regionally produced wine is not well-documented in rural areas; this finding is in line with what we have seen at the context on the north slopes at Roselle, where a minimum number of only 2 forms destined for its transport were found. Still more infrequent are attestations of containers from the eastern Aegean. In most cases, these were identified not on the basis of diagnostic fragments allowing for a precise attribution but only on that of a very few poorly preserved fragments of grooved walls, typical of these vessels (Fig.11); given the properties of the fabric they probably belong to LR1 amphorae. Except in a minority of cases this makes it extremely difficult to determine the area of provenance of the products in question.[33] Overall, at least eight sites yielded one or more fragments of amphorae which can be ascribed to the eastern Mediterranean, but if we ignore the town of Roselle where the presence of LR1, LR2 and LR4 has already been noted, only 2 specimens can be assigned to a specific typology. The rim of an LR1 was found at the late antique site on the river Osa, a short distance from the river mouth, in association with other fragments belonging to generic eastern Aegean amphorae (Pl. XXIV, nos 8-9);[34] another comes from the village of *San Martino de plano*. A specimen found at the Scoglietto harbour belongs to type LR2, used to trade Aegean wine (Pl. XXIV, no. 1). This is a shoulder fragment characterized by a semi-purified fabric with rare limestone inclusions and a reddish fracture (Munsell 7.5YR 7/4 pink).

Given the fundamental role played by wine in the ancient diet, the small quantities of Italic and eastern wine imports documented may represent an *argumentum ex silentio* suggesting that wine was produced locally. It is entirely plausible that local wine was destined for a limited circulation, for which wooden barrels may have been used; their use in late Antiquity now seems certain. However, it cannot be ruled out that redistribution on overland routes may have made use of pottery forms such as small flat-bottomed amphorae, more suitable for loading onto carts for transportation. Unfortunately the likelihood of identifying these forms, produced *in loco*, is minimal given the difficulties of identifying containers with this specific function within the varied repertoire of closed storage forms made in *acroma depurata* or *acroma* *selezionata* ware. In this context, it is worth stressing the recent report of 2 small two-handled amphorae from the deposit dating to the first half of the 6th century in the Cosa forum cistern (Pl. XXXI, no. 7).[35] The properties of the fabric of these 2 vessels, similar

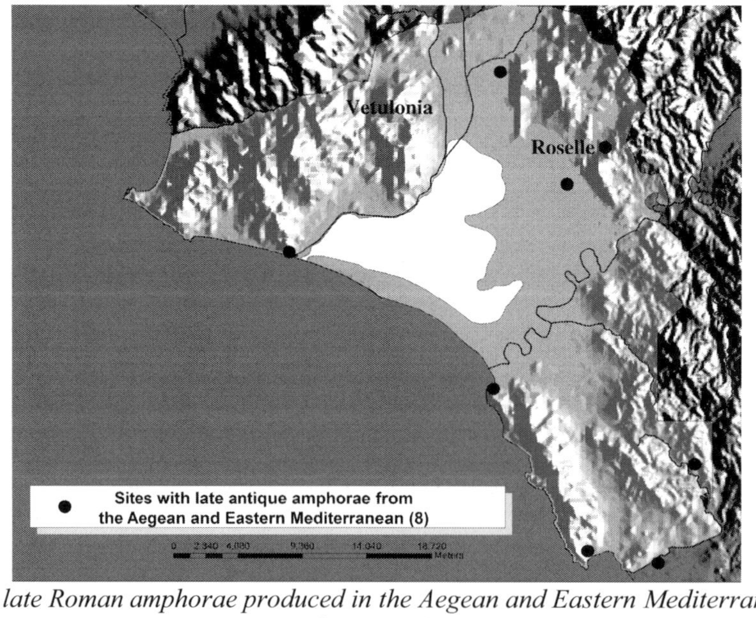

Fig.11_ Sites yielding late Roman amphorae produced in the Aegean and Eastern Mediterranean (total number of the sites: 8).

[32] Information provided by Mario Çygielman.

[33] Not even the examination of the body clays and a comparison with those analysed using an optical microscope from LR1, LR2 and LR5 documented at *Portus Scabris* provided further information. This is probably due to the fact that several production sites located in individual areas of provenance were involved in the production of the different types of eastern amphorae; as a consequence different types of clay were used to make the same types of vessel. On the latter aspect see Saguì *et alii* 2001, pp.287-292.

[34] See Ciampoltrini-Rendini 1990, p.519, Fig.4, nos 6-9.

[35] Fontana 2003, p.311 and p.312, Fig.141, nos 2-3.

to numerous specimens of Cosan coarseware, suggest that they were made locally. Their morphological structure, generically similar to Empoli amphorae, may suggest that they were also used to transport and trade wine. Neither the surface contexts investigated nor excavations have hitherto brought to light this type of form. A closed form, probably a jug or a small amphora, from the late antique frequentation of the Spaccasasso cave has a similar profile but there is no certainty that we are dealing with the same two-handled type or more importantly that it played the same functional purpose. In any case, we can note the significant presence in the two contexts with late antique phases of Poggio Vicarina and Poggio Quercia Grossa, in the upper Osa valley, of numerous thickened strap handles with a longitudinal groove on the lower surface, a marked ridge on the upper surface and a ridge on the side, morphologically very similar to those of the 2 small Cosan amphorae (Pl. XXXI, nos 4-6). Given the highly distinctive shape of the handles and their association with a fairly coarse fabric like that of the coarseware found at the two settlements, we cannot rule out that these do in fact belong to specimens similar to the Cosan vessels, probably used for wine. If this theory is confirmed by future research, it would not only represent valuable evidence of the existence of a late antique productive specialization of this area, but would also encourage a careful "reinterpretation" of the ceramic data collected during earlier studies in order to define the area of distribution of these containers.

5.3. Regional Tableware and Storage Ware: *Ingobbiata di Rosso*, *Acroma Depurata* and *Acroma Selezionata*

The regional production of pottery in late Antiquity presents a complex variety of classes and forms. At the top of the hierarchy in terms of the organization of production and the market was the *sigillata chiara tarda dell'Italia centro-settentrionale*, immediately followed by *ingobbiata di rosso* wares. The manufacture of both these types must have been based on nucleated workshops[36] operating on a regional scale and producing vessels with very similar formal characteristics, though using slightly different, but usually well-purified, clays. It cannot be ruled out that both these classes were made by the same workshops, given the similarities of some forms and, on the basis of preliminary research, of some fabrics. The distinctive feature, allowing for a sometimes problematic identification, is the quality of the slips; in *sigillata chiara tarda dell'Italia centro-settentrionale* ware the slip tends to be more even, shiny and impermeable, sometimes tending towards the sintered even if this effect is only actually achieved rarely;[37] to this we should add the presence in various cases of overpainted decorations. However, it should be stressed that the *sigillata chiara tarda dell'Italia centro-settentrionale* is rarely attested at rural sites in the study area, though it is present in large quantities in the town of Roselle and at Vetulonia.

At a lower level of this "hierarchy" is *acroma depurata* wares (purified and unpainted), which must in many cases have been produced by the same workshops as *ingobbiata di rosso*, as demonstrated by the similarities between the fabrics identified at Roselle and in rural areas. In terms of the morphological repertoire, there are recurrent affinities between these two classes, both as regards products copied from African red slip ware and forms which can be ascribed to an independent tradition. Often the only significant difference is the coating, used by the potters to supply the markets with higher quality products, competitive with African red slip ware. Above all, these products aimed to meet a demand for tableware which remained high even at times when adverse political and economic circumstances combined to cause a decline in the exports of Tunisian fineware and a lower and more selective capacity to penetrate rural markets.

By contrast, *acroma selezionata* wares (semi-purified and unpainted) appear to have been made by individual workshops, which were nonetheless able to create objects of reasonable quality using the fast wheel. The products of the potters who used coarser fabrics seem to have taken two main forms: open forms made in imitation of African prototypes and closed forms such as jugs and small amphorae aimed at meeting food storage and preservation needs. The fact that these open forms are constantly and accurately modelled on African red slip ware forms indicates that the potters had full knowledge of these and were fairly skilled in copying their morphological structure. The fabrics are often comparable with those of the wares of the early medieval period found in other rural contexts, indicating that in all probability *acroma selezionata* wares were manufactured directly *in loco*.

[36] In general on methods of pottery production see Peacock 1982, pp.13-21.
[37] On the differences between sintered and non-sintered red-slipped wares see Cuomo di Caprio 2007, pp.305-373.

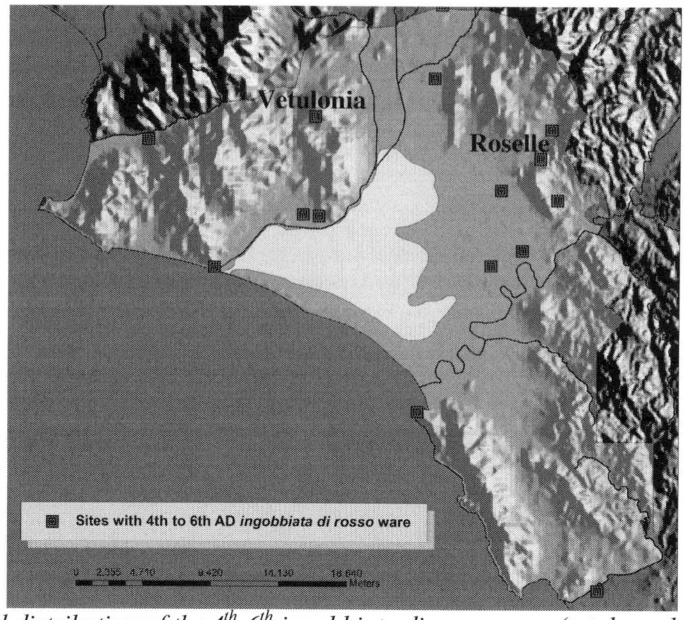

Fig.12_ Territorial distribution of the 4th-6th ingobbiata di rosso ware (total number of the sites: 13).

5.3.1. Territorial Distribution

As already mentioned above, from the 4th century onwards there is an increasing divergence between the pottery assemblages documented in towns and major rural sites on the one hand and at smaller contexts on the other. In the late imperial period, some rural sites present an economy oriented increasingly towards the consumption of their own produce, as indicated by the rare attestations of ARS and imported amphorae of the 4th – 6th centuries. Between the 5th and the late 6th/early 7th centuries some settlements manage to meet not only their own food needs but also those linked to the acquisition of tableware and storage vessels. The pottery made in imitation of African wares, both *ingobbiata di rosso* and uncoated, represents a wholly satisfactory substitute for North African fineware from the 4th-early 5th century onwards (Figs.12-13).

If we analyse the distribution of pottery copied from Mediterranean slip wares we can observe a higher density of attestations of wares with a red slip in the area around Lake Prile, between Roselle and Castiglione della Pescaia, where these are present both in urban areas and in the countryside. Further south, by contrast, only one settlement in the Osa valley has yielded this class. In this case, as for ARS and imported amphorae, the urban market appears to have been more receptive towards the regional trade in these products. The town of Roselle must have acted as a hub for redistribution flows of these wares towards the countryside. Like the red-slipped imitations, those made in *acroma depurata* and *acroma selezionata* are particularly well documented between the Bruna and Ombrone valleys, although they have also been found occasionally further north in the Alma valley and further south in the Osa valley. In the latter, the village of Poggio Vicarina has yielded specimens of flanged bowls and large bowls with incurving rims reminiscent of ARS prototypes Hayes 61B and 91B/C (Figs.14-15).

Overall, the most interesting fact is the gradual increase in the quantities of Italic tableware between the 4th and 6th century in all settlement types. However, there are differences between major sites in the rural settlement network, such as villages, the last surviving villas and some particularly active farmsteads where specimens of 5th/6th-century ARS are found in association with numerous contemporary forms in both *ingobbiata di rosso* and *acroma* wares, and a series of smaller contexts where only regional tableware is present, both slipped and uncoated, made in imitation of some popular forms of African red slip ware. In this context, two particularly important instances are those of a villa frequented up to the 6th century in the Alma valley and a long-lived farmstead, apparently inhabited continuously from the 2nd century BC to the 6th century AD in the lower Bruna valley.[38] In both cases, the presence of African red slip ware is attested at least up to the 4th-5th century with specimens of Hayes 67 deep dishes. The subsequent absence of ARS does not, however, appear to indicate an abandonment of the sites. In fact, both the villa and the farmstead surveys revealed some evidence of continued use in the 6th century, circumscribed to a limited area of the settlement, indicating a possible contraction in the surface area inhabited. In these two cases, the continuity of occupation can be confirmed by both *acroma* and *ingobbiata* wares, with flanged bowls being particularly well-represented.

Imitation products begin to appear from the 4th century onwards. At this time deep dishes with incurving rims modelled on Hayes 61 A and B are widely attested and can be dated to between AD 325 and 420, and between

[38] C.d.P. Survey sites 14.2 and 67.1 respectively.

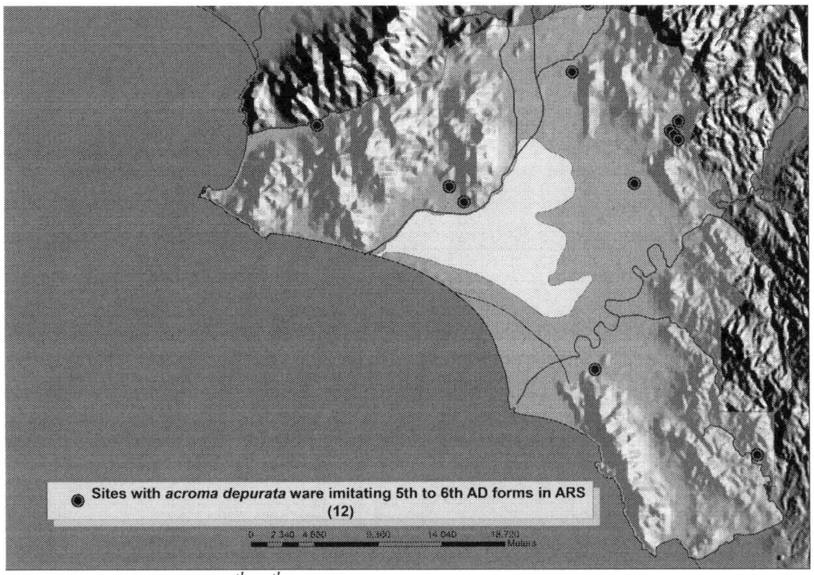

Fig.13_ Territorial distribution of the 5th-6th acroma depurata ware imitating types in ARS (total number of the sites: 12).

380 and the late 5th century respectively.[39] Surface contexts do not provide reliable information on the chronology of the vessels influenced by African fineware; in the case of imitations of Hayes 61 we can note, on a purely indicative basis, their presence in contexts alongside African red slip ware of the 5th and 6th centuries. Far more significant is the attestation of a deep dish in *ingobbiata di rosso* modelled on Hayes 61B in the Roselle context 1262, dating to the first half of the 6th century. The notable practical usefulness of this form, suited to holding semiliquid and solid foods, may have caused its production to be prolonged into the 6th century with the repetition of the same formal schemes as in the preceding century, albeit with some slight variations.[40] Following the formal revamping of African red slip ware between the late 5th and early decades of the 6th century, we see the introduction of new forms inspired by production D models. The Hayes 91C flanged bowl is doubtless an important reference point for regional wares, to the extent that the constant attestation of imitations in 6th-century contexts has made it one of the main "indicators" for this period.

OPEN FORMS MODELLED ON AFRICAN RED SLIP WARE: INGOBBIATA DI ROSSO

The largest number of open forms modelled on African red slip ware prototypes are made in *ingobbiata di rosso* ware. The repertoire of these forms is vast and includes numerous types for use at table: small and medium-sized bowls, deep dishes and flanged bowls. Essentially, thanks to the considerable variety of shapes produced, the *ingobbiata di rosso* workshops were able to supply the markets with a repertoire identical to that of African red slip ware, but significantly enriched with independent forms not belonging to the repertoire of the Tunisian potters.

Hayes 61, especially variant B, is the most frequently imitated prototype (Pl. XXV, nos 6-8). A type of deep dish with a thinned and pointed rim seems, on the other hand, to derive from Hayes 50B (Pl. XXV, nos 1-2). Another specimen of deep dish is reminiscent of Hayes 104, probably variant B, typical of the 6th century (Pl. XXV, no. 10). Some specimens are fairly faithful imitations of the Hayes 80A bowl, dating to the 5th century,[41] attested both with the variant whose rim is not distinct from the wall and with that presenting a slightly thickened rim (Pl. XXV nos 4-5). Finally, we should note specimens of flanged bowls modelled on Hayes 91, documented both in a version with a thickened and receding rim (Pl. XXVI, no. 5) and in another with an almost atrophied flange and vertical rim reminiscent of the late variant D of the late 6th-7th century (Pl. XXVI, no. 6).

ACROMA DEPURATA

Among the *acroma depurata* wares the form most frequently imitated is the Hayes 91 flanged bowl, attested in numerous different versions. Both that with an incurving rim and a straight or slightly hooked flange (Pl. XXVIII, no. 10; Pl. XXIX, nos 1, 4), and that with a pointed or externally oblique flange and a vertical rim (Pl. XXVIII, no. 9; Pl. XXIX, nos 2-3) are well documented. There is also a less common variant with an almost atrophied flange and vertical rim (Pl. XXVIII, nos 7-8). Hayes 61B is also occasionally imitated in *acroma depurata*; these copies are modelled mainly on the version with a pointed and barely incurving rim, and a slight external ledge (Pl. XXVIII,

---

39 On the lowering of the final chronology of some late variants of Hayes 61 to the very late 5th century see Bonifay 1998, pp.71-77.

40 This phenomenon of continuing production is also noted in Fontana 1998, p.84.

41 *Atlante I*, p.104.

no. 3). Another type of deep dish, documented exclusively at the village of San Martino *de plano*, seems to be influenced mainly by the Hayes 104A prototype, characterized by a thickened and rounded, slightly hooked rim; however, the slightly incurving rim suggests a connection with Hayes 61 (Pl. XXVIII, no. 4). The deep dish with a slightly pointed and upturned rim, separated from the wall by a fairly marked groove, appears to be modelled on the Hayes 87B prototype.[42] This type was found only at the village with major early medieval phases at Podere Serratone; here, the most ancient forms also included fragments of flanged bowls made using the same purified fabric (Pl. XXVIII, n.5).[43] Finally, among the imitation wares we should note the presence of a base with a disc foot, with an incised decoration on the inside in the form of a stylized plant motif (Pl. XXVIII, no. 6). It seems plausible that this represents a fairly rough and ready copy of the palm fronds characteristic of the broad repertoire of Hayes style A decorations.[44] The execution of the decoration presents similarities with the motif consisting of three branches inside concentric circles found on the base of a large bowl in *acroma depurata* modelled on Hayes 103B (early 6th-570/580) found in a context at *Albintimilium* datable to between the 5th and 8th centuries.[45] Interestingly this specimen, as is often the case with both flanged bowls and forms related to Hayes 61, indicates a process of

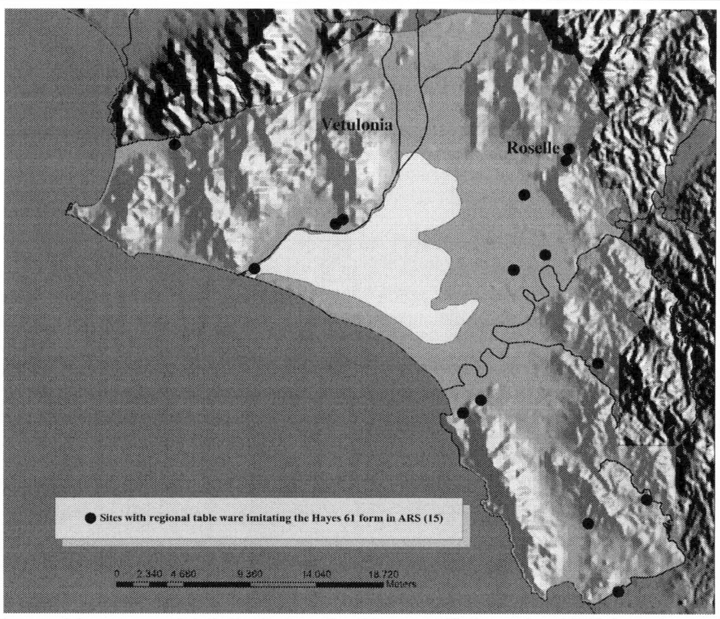

Fig.14_ Sites yielding table ware which imitates the Hayes 61 form in ARS (total number of the sites 15).

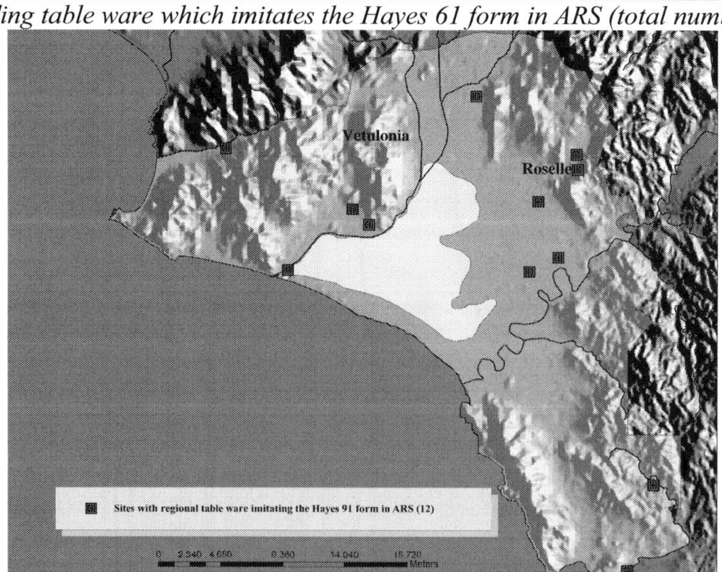

Fig.15_ Sites yielding table ware which imitates the Hayes 91 form in ARS (total number of the sites 12).

[42] Specifically it is highly reminiscent of the variant *Atlante I*, Pl.XXXIX, no.9.

[43] The association of imitations of the Hayes 91C flanged bowl and the Hayes 87B deep dish is important evidence on the basis of which to determine the initial chronology (mid-6th century) of the context abandoned in the late 9th century.

[44] Palm brances are typical of all of Style A stamped decorations for ARS (AD 320-470). See *Atlante* I, pp.123-124 and pp.127-128.

[45] Olcese 1993, p.257, Fig.60, no.219.

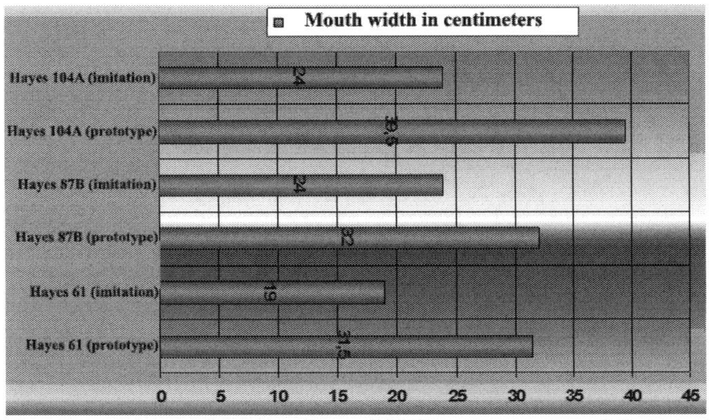

Graph VI_ Mouth width: comparison of a selection of ARS prototypes and their imitations in the regional tableware.

reworking of the formal models used in Tunisia. In part, as in this case, this is due to a failure to adhere faithfully to the original model and in part, as in many other cases, to an attempt to introduce variations on the archetype and thus to "personalize" the imitation.

ACROMA SELEZIONATA

In *acroma selezionata* ware, too, numerous open forms derive from the same prototypes which inspired *ingobbiata di rosso* and *acroma depurata* wares. The Hayes 61B large bowl, in the version with a pointed and barely incurving rim and a slight external ledge, once again represents a highly successful production experiment (Pl. XXX, nos 1-2). Also well documented are the bowls with a vertical or slightly everted rim and a short flange (Pl. XXX, nos 3, 5), including one version with a spout (Pl. XXX, no. 4). The deep dish with a thickened, rounded and hooked rim based on Hayes 104 (Pl. XXX, no. 6) is a faithful copy of its prototype. Other forms made in *acroma selezionata* include a type of bowl with a barely thickened and almond-shaped rim, pointed on the upper surface, reminiscent of Hayes 99 in the versions with a more flaring wall and thinner rim (Pl. XXX, no. 7).

GENERAL REMARKS ON IMITATIONS OF AFRICAN RED SLIP WARE

One important feature, probably related to a specific functional aim, is the systematic reduction of the rim widths of bowls belonging to the three classes described above with respect to their Tunisian prototypes (Graph VI). Taking as an example the deep dish described above and reminiscent of Hayes 104, we can see that, with its rim diameter of 24 cm, this bowl is far smaller than its reference model. Variant A, for example, which appears to be the original most similar to the imitation, has diameters ranging from 29 to 50 cm,[46] indicating that it was used for the collective consumption of meals. The same can be said of the other type of deep dish, made in imitation of the ARS archetype Hayes 87B. The copy has a diameter of less than 24 cm, whilst the originals have apertures ranging from 28 to 36 cm in diameter.[47] This is also true of imitations of Hayes 61, where the *acroma depurata* copies have a diameter of less than 20 cm, those in *acroma selezionata* of less than 22 cm, whilst those made in *ingobbiata di rosso* present diameters ranging from a minimum of 14 cm to a maximum of 24 cm. The prototype, by contrast, has diameters ranging from 22 to 41 cm. It is thus clear that, even when the copy is fairly faithful to the reference model in terms of morphological structure, there is a marked tendency to decrease the rim diameter. This was probably a response to a demand for pottery forms destined for individual rather than collective use.

OPEN FORMS BELONGING TO AN INDEPENDENT TRADITION: INGOBBIATA DI ROSSO

Various open forms in *ingobbiata di rosso*, including large bowls, deep dishes and basins, present no obvious connections with Tunisian models but rather belong to an independent manufacturing tradition. This tradition appears aimed towards marketing products not characteristic of the ARS repertoire and which, at least in the case of basins, respond to a demand for deep pottery vessels used to hold semiliquid foods.

The most frequently attested type of large bowl presents a slightly receding rim which is not distinct from the wall (Pl. XXV, no. 3). This form presents some notable similarities with wares from Fiesolan contexts dated to between the second half of the 4th and the early 5th century.[48] To this we should add another two typologies attested by a single specimen each. In the harbour village of Serrata Martini-Paduline a bowl was found with walls over one cm thick, a pointed rim and a slip covering the inside and present externally only on the rim and on a strip beneath it (Pl. XXV, no. 11). This type is comparable with a specimen from the Chianti Senese area found in association with other forms in *ingobbiata di rosso* of the 6th-early 7th century.[49] The fine carinated bowl with a vertical and slightly thinned rim has a highly original morphological structure. This form was found in a farmstead with phases dating to until the 6th century

46 *Atlante I*, p.94.

47 *Atlante I*, p.91.

48 Bianchi-Palermo 1990, p.371, Pl.26, nos 46, 48.

49 Valenti 1996a, p.151, Pl.I, no.3.

near the west bank of Lake Prile (Pl. XXV, no. 12).[50] This artefact stands out in the general context of *ingobbiata di rosso* ware for the high quality of the slip which adheres closely to the surface of the vessel and which is a brighter red. A close parallel can be found in a similar form, albeit presenting an overpainted decoration, from the well at Savignano sul Panaro in the province of Modena, dated to the first half of the 7th century.[51] Not even the deep dish with a squared and externally thickened rim seems directly related to Tunisian prototypes (Pl. XXV, no. 9). This type is attested in various settlements in the lower Bruna valley and in the Ombrone valley; it is generically similar to pottery from contexts in Fiesole of the second half of the 4th century.[52] Among the *ingobbiata di rosso* forms not deriving from ARS an extremely successful form is the hemispherical basin with a thickened and rounded rim, flattened on the upper surface (Pl. XXVI, nos 1-3). An analysis of the distribution of this type shows a high density of attestations in the hinterland of Roselle, where some specimens were present at the two villas of San Martino and Casette di Motta; a very large minimum number of individuals was found at the villa of Aiali. A single specimen, on the other hand, is documented at the harbour village of Serrata Martini-Paduline (Fig.16). In the urban deposit on the north slopes at Roselle it is attested between the 4th and early 5th centuries (SU 5147=5170). However, its presence in contexts of the second half of the 6th-early 7th century at Santa Maria della Scala in Siena seems significant.[53] This may indicate that its production continued even after the 5th century, though we lack definitive stratigraphic information on the basis of which to state that this was also the case in the Roselle area. Another type of basin with an everted rim, slightly thickened and flattened on the upper surface, is documented exclusively at the villas of Aiali, San Martino and Casette di Mota near Roselle (Pl. XXVI, no. 4). Fairly close points of comparison are found in contexts of the Chianti Senese dated to between the 4th and early 7th centuries.[54]

ACROMA DEPURATA AND ACROMA SELEZIONATA WARES

Only a few forms in *acroma depurata* and *acroma selezionata* are not directly influenced by African red slip ware, suggesting that the morphological repertoires of these productions were less varied than those of *ingobbiata di rosso* ware.

The territorial distribution of these few forms is also extremely sparse; they are attested with only a single specimen only at two settlements. In the villa frequented during the 6th century in the Alma valley we found two types of large bowl, one with a thin rim, indistinct from the wall (Pl. XXVIII, no. 1), and another with a thinned vertical rim with a diameter of 26 cm (Pl. XXVIII, no. 2).[55] Both specimens come from a black layer identified in the highest portion of archaeological stratigraphy brought to light by a trench about 1.60 m deep, used as a ditch for farming purposes. The trench cut through the central part of the villa, allowing us to identify traces of a late antique frequentation of the context, indicated by a layer of dark earth mixed with charcoal covering a stone wall. The two bowls were found in association with a specimen of flanged bowl with an atrophied flange and fragments of closed forms in *ingobbiata di rosso*. Similar specimens have also been found in rural contexts in the Chianti Senese in association with imitations of the Hayes 61 deep dish and the Hayes 91 flanged bowl.[56] The villa of San Martino, on the other hand, yielded a bowl made in *acroma selezionata* with a receding rim, flattened on the upper surface, and a spiral decoration on the outer wall (Pl. XXX, no. 8). This typology presents some similarities with a late antique kitchenware form from the same site and with specimens of early medieval pottery (late 8th-late 9th centuries) from the Casa Andreoni context. There are also close parallels with artefacts from sites dating to the 6th-7th centuries from the Roccastrada area.[57]

CLOSED TABLEWARE AND STORAGE FORMS

In morphological terms, closed tableware forms are completely independent of the influence of African red slip ware. The workshops making ARS, although they did produce closed forms,[58] albeit in extremely modest quantities compared to open forms, almost exclusively exported the latter.

---

[50] C.d.P. Survey site 21.1.
[51] Gelichi-Giordani 1994, p.125, Fig.103, no.1.
[52] Bianchi-Palermo 1990, p.370, Pl.25, no.29.
[53] Cantini 2005a, p.157, Pl.39, nos 6.13-14.
[54] Valenti 1995a, p.162, Pl.LXXXII, no.1 and p.76.
[55] C.d.P. survey site 14.2.
[56] Valenti 1995a, p.162, pl.LXXXII, no.8 and Pl.LXXX, no.15.
[57] Guideri 2000a, p.17, Pl.V, no.1.
[58] See in particular the series of one- and two-handled flasks and bottles attested at Carthage in contexts of the 5th and 6th centuries excavated by the British Mission, in Fulford-Peacock 1984, p.82, Fig.25, nos 1-5 p.86, Fig.26, nos 6-22.

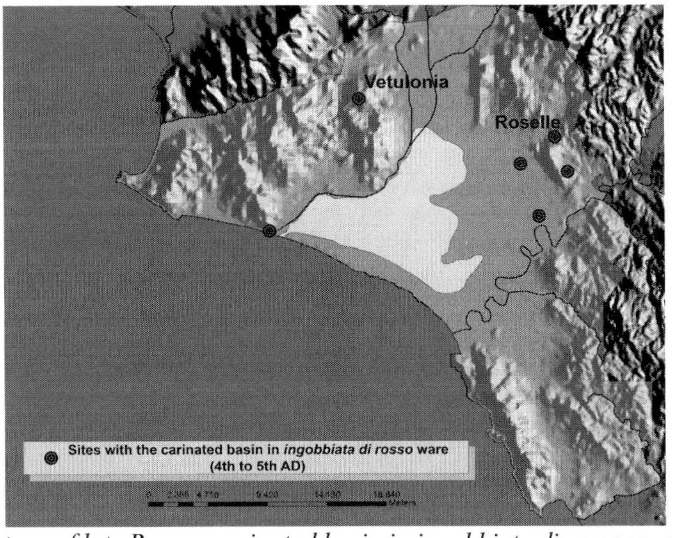

Fig.16_ Sites yielding the type of late Roman carinated basin in ingobbiata di rosso ware(total number of the sites 6).

CLOSED FORMS IN INGOBBIATA DI ROSSO WARE

The wares with a red slip present a greater variety of different forms than *acroma* wares; these consist of one-handled jugs, tankards with three-lobed rims, pitchers and small jars for use at table.

In the harbour village of Serrata Martini, at least two main versions of the one-handled jug are attested. The first has an everted and rounded rim, presenting a groove on the outside (Pl. XXVII no. 1). The other has an almost vertical thickened rim (Pl. XXVII, no. 2). Both have a strap-shaped handle presenting longitudinal grooves on the upper surface. The handle is set immediately beneath the rim. Fairly similar 5th-century materials were found on the Colle del Pionta at Arezzo.[59] Another typology also attested in the Bruna valley, but this time at the village of *San Martino de plano*, presents a short flat rim with a grooved strap-handle, level with the rim (Pl. XXVII, no. 4). Well documented at the village of Serrata Martini is a type of small jar with a markedly everted rim ranging in diameter from 7 to 11 cm, a globular body and disc foot (Pl. XXVII, nos 5-6). This typology is not attested in other settlements in the study area, but presents close similarities with wares from the Emilia area found in a mid-5th-century waste heap in the farmhouse at Casalecchio di Reno.[60] A type of table jar with a hooked rim, presenting a spiral decoration on the inner part of the rim, is documented at the villa of Casette di Mota near Roselle (Pl. XXVII, no. 3). Externally, the slip covers the entire fragment but inside is present only on the band holding the decoration. A generic point of comparison can be found with wares from the Lucanian kiln at Calle di Tricarico, active between the 4th and 6th centuries AD.[61]

Among the slipped tableware in use before the mid-7th century we should also note a flask from the Lombard burial ground discovered some years ago on the hill at Castiglione della Pescaia.[62] This is a peculiar object belonging to a transitional phase during which forms were produced whose morphology was probably based on models from outside the region, but which must have been made at regional workshops given the properties of the fabric and the surface treatment. These regional workshops still had significant technological capabilities and were able to produce wares aimed at a fairly demanding clientele. The object in question is a flask, which finds close parallels among Lombard wares,[63] whilst the coating, in the form of a few red drops, and the technical properties of the well-purified fabric are reminiscent of the regional tradition of the late Roman period. The everted rim is set on a neck with a concave profile, the body is ovoid and sagging whilst the base is slightly concave. There are notable similarities with a bottle of the Lombard period now in the Fiesole Museum, characterized by a decoration consisting of three undulating lines alternating with three straight lines.[64] Unlike the specimen from Fiesole, though, the Castiglione flask has a comb decoration and presents traces of red drips, so minute as to suggest an occasional nature, on the base of the neck and the widest point of the body (Pl. XXVII, nos 7a-b). This object is currently attested only in this context and it is thus impossible to formulate theories as to its distribution; a production specifically for funerary purposes cannot be ruled out.

[59] Paroli-Saguì 1991, p.145, no.58.
[60] Negrelli 2002, p.33, Pl.7, nos 9-10.
[61] Di Giuseppe 1998, p.742, Fig.7, no.4.
[62] Citter 1995a, p.216 and notes.
[63] See in particular specimens nos 1111 and 1113 from Santa Giulia in Brescia, in Vitali 1999, p.218.
[64] Francovich 1984, pp.618-619, Drawing.no.1.

CLOSED FORMS IN ACROMA DEPURATA AND ACROMA SELEZIONATA

Attestations of late antique closed forms in *acroma depurata* are rare. They include a type of jug with a barely everted and rounded rim and a strap handle level with the rim from a farmstead with late antique phases on the western bank of Lake Prile (Pl. XXIX, no. 5).[65] The morphology of the rim and the handle, which presents longitudinal grooves, allows us to associate this jug with contemporary handled wares in *ingobbiata di rosso*. The village of San Martino *de plano* yielded another specimen of jug with a vertical rim, presenting a slightly hooked flange on the outside (Pl. XXIX, no. 6). The structure of the rim is reminiscent of that of a bottle in *ingobbiata di rosso* from context 1260 at Roselle, although it differs from the latter in the greater width of the mouth. The same village yielded wall fragments with impressed motifs inside bands presenting a combed decoration (Pl. XXIX, no. 7) and multiple spiral decorations (Pl. XXIX, no. 8); these belong to late antique closed forms. Sites in the hinterland of Roselle have yielded closed forms in *acroma selezionata* with thickened strap handles level with the rim or set beneath it (Pl. XXXI, nos 1-3). The version with a handle level with the rim finds exact parallels in the coarseware from 6th-7th-century contexts in the area around the villa del Saraceno at Giglio Porto.[66] The 6th-century village of Poggio Vicarina in the upper Osa valley yielded an unusual variant of the jug with a strap handle level with the rim, characterized by two marked fingerprints: one marking the junction with the rim and the other lower down, but also on the handle (Pl. XXXI, no. 2).

5.4. Kitchenware

The analysis of the kitchenware forms distributed among the late antique rural contexts reveals close parallels with the morphological repertoire typical of 4th/early 5th- and 6th-century contexts at Roselle. However, some settlements such as the Scoglietto cave and Paduline-Serrata Martini demonstrate the existence of contacts with the commercial trade in kitchenware from outside the region, and sometimes from elsewhere in the Mediterranean (*infra*). The most frequently documented kitchenware form is the cooking pot, to which we should add casseroles and lids. Interesting data emerge from the study of the distribution of some types of cooking pots from Roselle, present in rural sites with fabrics similar to those of the urban context; most of these wares are made using fabrics G13 and G19, for which we have proposed a possible local origin, perhaps even an urban one, on the basis of some wasters.

Type II from Roselle is the most widespread in the study area, and has been found at various contexts in the Bruna, Ombrone and Osa valleys (Fig.17). The most frequently attested versions have a strongly everted rim, with the typical internal shaping and hooked on the outside (Pl. XXXII, nos 1-3), although variants with a less markedly everted rim do exist (Pl.

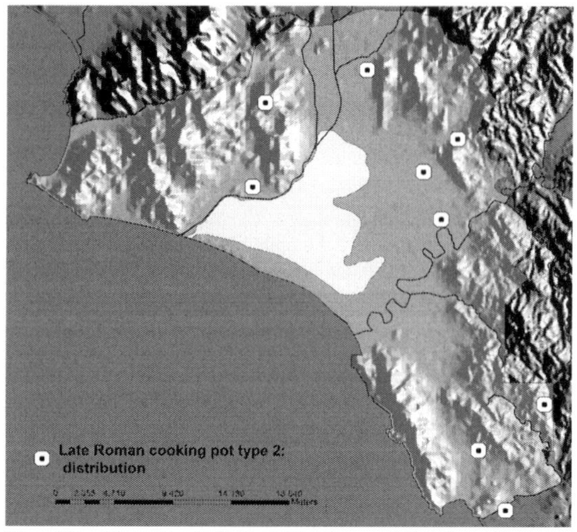

Fig.17_ Territorial distribution of the late Roman cooking pot type 2.

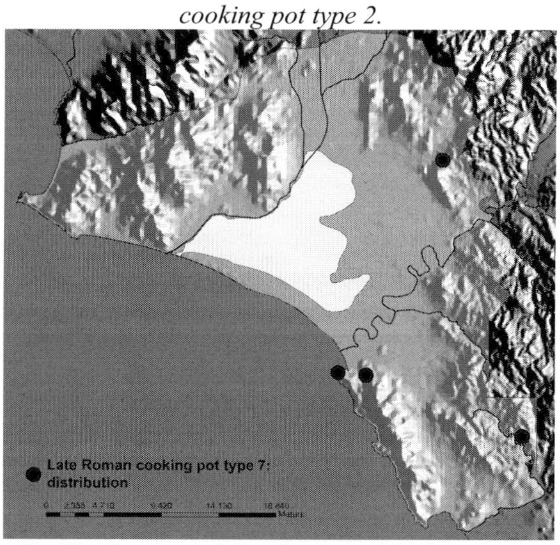

Fig.18_ Territorial distribution of the late Roman cooking pot type 7.

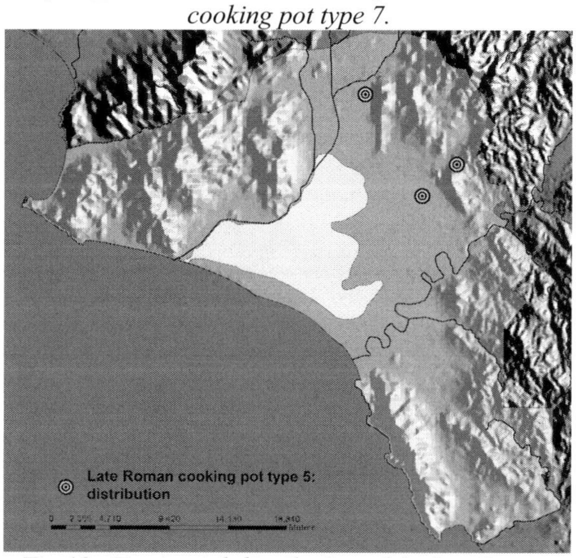

Fig.19_ Territorial distribution of the late Roman cooking pot type 5.

[65] C.d.P. Survey site 21.1.

[66] Rendini 1998, p.641, Fig.2, no.10.

XXXII, no. 4). A farmstead with late antique phases on the western bank of Lake Prile yielded a specimen with a spiral decoration on the widest part of the body (Pl. XXXII, no. 8).[67]

The distribution pattern for cooking pot Type VII is also fairly complex (Fig.18). This type is characterized by a short external, more or less hooked flange, and is well attested both at Roselle and in the late antique phases of occupation of the Spaccasasso and Scoglietto caves (*infra*). A variant with an almost atrophied flange was found in the 6th-century village of Poggio Vicarina, in the upper Osa valley (Pl. XXXII, no. 10).

The distribution of Type V (Fig.19), with a markedly everted rim, pointed on the upper surface (Pl. XXXII, nos 6-7), is limited to Roselle, the villa of Aiali and the village of San Martino *de plano* (Pl. XXXII, no. 5). The latter site also yielded a specimen with a slightly incurving and hooked rim which is generically similar to Type III from context 5147-5170 at Roselle, ascribed to the 4th-early 5th century (Pl. XXXII, no. 9).

Belonging to Type IV from the same deposit in Roselle are the two cooking pots with an everted rim, oblique on the outside, and in one case with a slight indentation to host the lid (Pl. XXXIII, nos 3-4). Both were found at a farmstead in the Alma valley, frequented occasionally between the 5th and 6th centuries.[68]

Other types of cooking pots have hitherto been found only at some rural contexts but not in the town. Particularly interesting is the almost exclusively coastal distribution of the type with an everted rim of rectangular section, with an internal edge, found in large quantities in the Scoglietto cave and at the harbour site of Serrata Martini-Paduline (Pl. XXXIII, no. 1). In inland areas near Roselle, by contrast, only a single specimen was found at the villa of San Martino (Pl. XXXIII, no. 2). This suggests that this type may have been imported by sea, a theory confirmed in part by the optical microscope analysis of the fabrics from the Scoglietto cave (*infra*).

Other types, by contrast, come from the 5th/6th century phases of farmsteads located near the west bank of Lake Prile. A site near Mortelle,[69] frequented during late Antiquity after a period of abandonment between the 3rd and 4th centuries, yielded a type of two-handled cooking pot with a slightly everted plain rim, found in association with flanged bowls. The body is globular and the handles, set beneath the rim and at the widest point of the body, are rectangular in section and present two light grooves, one on the upper and one on the lower surface (Pl. XXXIII, no. 7). This type is identical to vessels dated to between the 5th and 7th century found at *Albintimilium*.[70] Another farmstead frequented uninterruptedly between the 2nd century BC and the 6th century AD, despite the decrease in the area occupied,[71] yielded a cooking pot which represents another *unicum* in the study area. It has a slightly everted plain rim and an external decoration consisting of impressed oblique short lines beneath the rim, whilst the walls are burnished on the outside (Pl. XXXIII, no. 6). This pot, found in association exclusively with *ingobbiata di rosso* ware of the 4th-6th centuries and African red slip ware of the 4th-5th centuries, comes from a concentration belonging to the latest phase of the site, identified within the larger surface scatter. The only close parallels for the decorative motif are with productions from northern Italy, and in particular 4th/8th-century materials from Invillino,[72] and others from the late Roman phase of Santa Giulia in Brescia.[73] There are also strong analogies with late antique and early medieval pottery from the central and eastern Alpine belt.[74]

A last type of cooking pot characterized by a vertical rim, with a "collarino" profile, measuring 21 cm in diameter, is attested by a single specimen from the late antique frequentation level identified in the occasional section running through the villa in the Alma valley (Pl. XXXIII, no. 5).[75] The latter finds close parallels in wares documented in 5th- and 6th-century contexts in the Chianti Senese.[76]

Also well attested in the Bruna valley is a type of cooking pot with a flat and sometimes slightly hooked rim (Pl. XXXIV, nos 1-2). This type is common at the port site of Serrata Martini, but also in contexts with late antique phases located along the western bank of Lake Prile.[77] Close comparisons can be made with productions from *Albintimilium* dated to between the 4th and 7th centuries.[78]

Among the open forms we should note the scarce presence of casseroles, with the sole exception of the Scoglietto site (in general a unique context in the study area for the variety of its pottery assemblages). This may indicate an overall simplification of kitchenware types in the countryside compared to the town. The type with a flat rim with a groove and a carinated wall, well documented at Roselle in the 4th-early 5th century deposit, is present only at the villa of San Martino, just outside Roselle (Pl. XXXIV, no. 3). This site also yielded a different type whose rim is flat on the upper surface and thickened internally (Pl. XXXIV, no. 4), a morphological structure identical to that of a bowl in

[67] C.d.P. Survey site 21.1.
[68] C.d.P. Survey site 12.2.
[69] C.d.P. Survey site 50.1.
[70] Olcese 1993, p.207, Fig.38, no.65.
[71] C.d.P. Survey site 67.1.
[72] Bierbrauer 1990, p.63, Pl.II, no.13 and p.72, Pl.V, nos 1-5.
[73] Massa-Portulano 1999, Pl.LXVI, no.5.
[74] Rodriguez 1992, p.161, Pl.1, no.25 and p.173, Pl.6, no.4.
[75] C.d.P. Survey site 14.2.
[76] Valenti 1995a, p.139, Pl.LIX, no.21 and p.71.
[77] The type with a band-shaped rim is typical of late frequentations of C.d.P. Survey sites 50.1 and 47.1.
[78] Olcese 1993, p.209, Fig.39, no.70.

acroma selezionata attested at the settlement. The village of San Martino *de plano* in the Bruna valley yielded a casserole with a markedly everted and slightly hooked rim, with a slight groove on the upper surface to host a lid (Pl. XXXIV, no. 5), very similar to wares from the deposit dating to the first half of the 6th century in the Cosa forum cistern.[79]

Bowl-lids are rarely attested; one type with an almond-shaped rim is documented at the villa with 6th-century phases of San Martino near Roselle (Pl. XXXV, nos 8-9). Among the lids, we can note the widespread distribution, in both the Bruna and Ombrone valleys, of the type with an everted and forked rim, sometimes with a slight groove allowing it to fit the pot better, as shown by a variant from the site of Serrata Martini at Castiglione della Pescaia (Pl. XXXV, no. 13). The handles are generally button-shaped (Pl. XXXV, nos 10-11). Fairly close points of comparison for the rim structure can be found in lids from 6th/7th-century contexts in the Priamar at Savona.[80] A type with a slightly thickened rim, flattened on the upper surface, is found exclusively at the late antique village of San Martino *de plano*; it is similar to specimens found at Santa Maria della Scala in Siena in contexts of the first half of the 7th century (Pl. XXXV, no. 12).[81] The distribution of another type of lid with a strongly everted rim, rectangular in section, oblique or rounded externally and sometimes presenting an internal thickened edge (Pl. XXXV, nos 1-7) is limited to the upper Osa valley and was thus probably made locally in this area. This type is present at the 6th-century village of Poggio Vicarina with a large minimum number of forms, whilst at least 3 were found at the settlement with late antique phases at Podere Quercia Grossa.

5.5. Infra-Site Analysis (Scoglietto, Spaccasasso and Paduline)

5.5.1. The Late Antique Occupation of the Scoglietto Cave: Analysis of an Elite Pottery Context

Foreword

The natural cavity of Scoglietto, in the north-western part of the Monti dell'Uccellina, has been the object of archaeological research since the 1930s, aimed mainly at studying the context's prehistoric and protohistoric occupation phases.[82] The large size of the cave,[83] about 40 m long, and its large and well-lit entrance area,[84] represented the main reasons for its use even in subsequent periods, including the Roman and late antique eras. An excavation trench dug between 1948 and 1950 led to the identification, above the prehistoric phases of frequentation, of a deposit about 40 cm deep, characterized by "loose brown soil with ash lenses and large fireplaces, Roman-Etruscan and Roman pottery; in the innermost area, where all the layers are thicker, noteworthy burials were found in large amphorae with funerary equipment consisting of glass and bronze artefacts of the Roman period".[85] Little information is available on this discovery, but nonetheless forms an important reference point with which to compare the data collected during the study of the ceramic deposit recovered during the 2005 excavations, aimed at understanding how the cave was used between the Roman period and late Antiquity. In the early months of 2005, a new excavation was carried out at the Scoglietto cave, limited to part of the spoil heap consisting of discarded materials from earlier studies, which had accumulated on the entrance ramp leading to the site (Fig.20).[86]

As concerns the time frame of interest to this study, the recent survey made it possible to recover a large pottery assemblage in its secondary context, belonging to the late antique phase of the use of this natural cavity which was excavated without regard to stratigraphy during earlier surveys. Though they were not found *in situ*, the analysis of the ceramic materials allows us to formulate some valuable hypotheses on the site's function during late Antiquity and on the nature of pottery consumption during this phase of the settlement. The material in question forms a coherent and homogeneous context which can be ascribed to the period between the mid-5th and mid-6th centuries. It is particularly important because it provides a series of new facts on the Mediterranean and extra-regional circulation of fineware and coarseware during late Antiquity. The frequent presence of traces of fumigation on the numerous items of kitchenware represents clear evidence that this pottery assemblage belongs to a settlement phase.

It seems far more likely that the materials analysed here belong to the large number of fireplaces identified during the 1948-1950 excavations, rather than to the phase during which the site was used for funerary purposes. This is confirmed by a further two pieces of evidence: the lack of references to pottery among the goods belonging to the *enchytrismos* burials,[87] and the large quantity of kitchenware belonging to a broad range of functional forms, including pots, cooking pots, casseroles, lids, pans and bowl-lids. The minimum number of amphorae is also fairly small, despite the

---

[79] Fontana 2003, p.314, FC 12-13.

[80] Lavagna 1998, p.587, Fig.2, CSD15164 and PL 31088.

[81] Cantini 2005a, p.135, Pl.22, no.5.14.

[82] For a detailed summary of the various phases of this research, which have in common a desire to understand the nature and chronology of the frequentations of the site between the Neolithic and the Early Bronze Age see Cavanna-Cavanna 2006, pp.84-87.

[83] From a geomorpholofical point of view the cavern differs from the cave for its larger entrance area and shorter length. On this see Sgherri-Costantini 2004, p.38.

[84] Sestini-Cardini 1935

[85] Rittatore 1951, p.27.

[86] Cavanna-Cavanna *op.cit.*, p.86.

[87] Rittatore *op.cit.* refers only to funerary equipment consisting of glass and bronze materials.

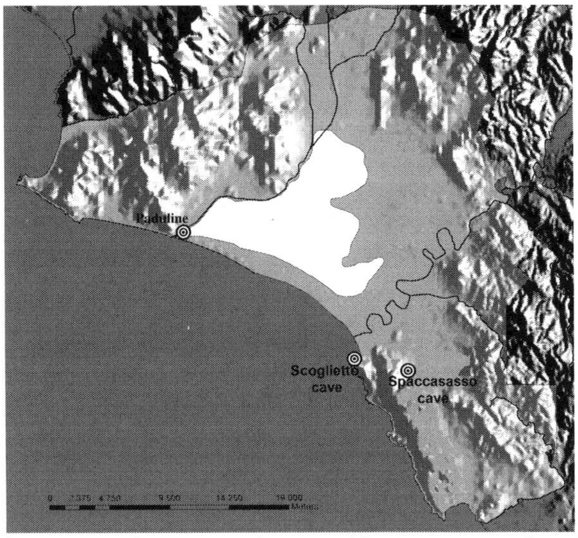

Fig.20_ Location of the three sites whose ceramic assemblages were analysed separately and in detail.

numerous fragments found: only 4, of which only one can be assigned to a specific typology.

Taken together, these facts would seem to indicate that the 2005 excavations mainly allowed us to recover pottery materials belonging to an occupation for the purposes of settlement and probably trade during late Antiquity, rather than to the occupation for funerary purposes which saw the use of amphorae as burial vessels. It is also worth noting that the recent survey brought to light numerous coins, only 4 of which belong to the period from the late Republic to the early Empire.[88] The early imperial frequentation of the cave is also documented by a bowl in *sigillata italica* of type Goudineau 38a/Conspectus 33.1, datable to between 20 AD and the late 1st and probably the early 2nd century.[89] This may mean that the use of the cave as a burial place dates to this period, given the possible use of the four coins as Charon's obols.

We would thus have two different phases of occupation between the Roman period and late Antiquity, with the late antique phase seeing a reuse of the cave for residential and trading purposes. This theory is supported by the assemblage of late antique pottery, with the conspicuous presence of Tunisian fineware, coarseware imported from overseas and from outside the region, and as many as 66 coins dating to between the mid-3rd and 5th centuries.[90] This large quantity of coins appears to belong to the occupation of the cave between the late 5th and mid-6th centuries, given that late Roman bronze coins continued to be used for everyday transactions even in later periods. A further confirmation that activities linked to exchange and trade were carried out here comes from the analysis of other materials found inside the cave: alongside the coins, the Scoglietto excavations also brought to light two bronze coin weights corresponding respectively to the *solidus aureus* and perhaps the *tremissis*.[91] The large quantity of pottery imported from overseas, the attestation of late Roman bronze coins and the two coin weights all combine to suggest not only a context linked to maritime trade flows but probably also to a small market-place. This may have been at the nearby Scoglietto harbour and served to sort and redistribute overseas goods arriving here between the late 5th and mid-6th centuries towards inland areas.

More generally, the late antique reoccupation of the cave finds immediate confirmation not only in the nearby context of Spaccasasso, but above all in a series of caves and grottos in western Liguria and Finale Ligure. These were also characterized by late antique and early medieval reoccupations, prevalently for settlement purposes but also for burials.[92] Of special interest is a comparison with the prehistoric cave of Arene Candide,[93] characterized by two occasional frequentations during the early and middle imperial period and by a significant and stable occupation between the 6th and the first half of the 7th centuries. The latter yielded an extremely varied range of goods, including Tunisian transport containers (Keay LXIIA, D, Q, Keay LVA, Keay LVIB types, Keay XXVI G *spatheia*, and amphorae with a *fondo umbonato ed ombelicato*), an Eastern amphora, specimens of ARS, North African and Middle Eastern coarseware, locally produced coarseware, soapstone, glass items, metals, and a millstone from the volcanic area of Campania/Lazio. At Scoglietto, as at Arene Candide, the late antique reoccupation of the cave, inhabited already in prehistory, does not appear to have been determined by defensive requirements but seems rather to respond to economic and cultural changes which in Liguria led to the reinforcement of silviculture and pastoral activities, sometimes to the detriment of agriculture, and to the shift of some settlements to

[88] See De Benetti 2007.
[89] For a comparison see *Atlante II*, Pl.CXXXI, 11.
[90] De Benetti 2007.
[91] *Ibidem*.
[92] Murialdo *et alii* 1992, p.296 and Pastorino 1997, p.632.
[93] Pastorino 1997, pp.623-634.

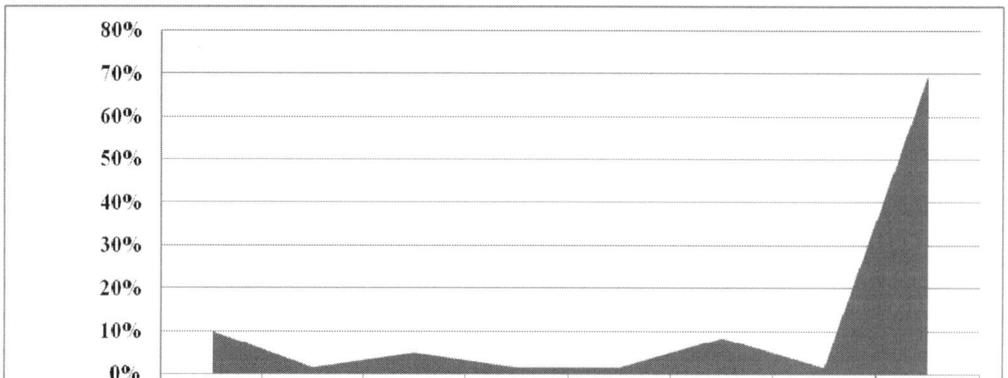

	ARS	Tunisian amphorae	Ingobbiata di rosso ware	Colature rosse ware	Sigillata chiara tarda	Tunisian coarse ware	Mediterranean (?) coarse ware	Regional (Tuscany) and extra-regional (Lazio) coarse ware
■ % of MNI	10%	1,70%	5%	1,70%	1,70%	8,50%	1,70%	69,50%

Graph VII_ Quantified ceramics (relative frequencies of ceramic classes measured by MNI) from the mid 5th-mid 6th AD occupation of the cave site at Scoglietto.

areas in closer contact with newly exploited resources. At Scoglietto, by contrast, the reoccupation appears to be due more to the search for a new site which could be used as a base for fishing and which above all was closely connected to the maritime cabotage trade touching on the Tyrrhenian coast during late Antiquity.

The Mid-Fifth- To Mid-Sixth-Century Pottery Deposit at Scoglietto

The analysis of the pottery materials was conducted by selecting all the diagnostic fragments and examining all the fabrics identified under a sterescopic microscope. This made it possible to determine the minimum number of individuals attested without needing to systematically record every single fragment.[94]

In total we identified a minimum number of at least 61 individuals belonging to specific typologies and ascribable to different pottery classes. Some of these certainly belong to a phase preceding that under investigation here: this is true of the hemispherical bowl in *sigillata italica* with a short external flange and a rouletting decoration on the rim and the outer wall above the flange (Pl. XXXVII, no. 1) of type Goudineau 38a/Conspectus 33.1.[95] A production D ARS form also predates the mid-5th/mid-6th century phase: this is a flat-based dish with a plain vertical rim presenting two grooves beneath the rim, of type Hayes 63, datable to between AD 375 and 400.[96]

The remaining minimum number of 59 forms belong to the phase of late antique occupation of the cave (Graph VII). Among the tableware we should mention the prevalence of North African imports, thanks to the close relations between this site and maritime trade, accounting for 10% of the individuals. These are followed by *ingobbiata di rosso* with 5% of specimens and *colature rosse* pottery with an extremely low 1.7%. The Italic tableware documented includes *sigillata chiara tarda dell'Italia centro-settentrionale*, also with 1.7%. This type of ware, which may have been produced up to but not beyond the mid-5th century, may represent a clue of help in dating the initial phase of the late antique use of the cave. Tunisia also plays a vital role in supplying foodstuffs, as demonstrated by the fact that a minimum number of at least 4 amphorae originating in this area were identified. However, only one has been included in Graph VII since it is the only amphora which can be ascribed to a specific typology. The most surprising fact is the presence of coarseware imported from North Africa, clearly belonging to the phase between the mid-5th and mid-6th century, attested with 8.5%. From this point of view the Scoglietto context, like Serrata Martini, seems to be an exception to the rule. After the 4th or early 5th century, imports of North African coarseware seem to cease both in the town of Roselle and in rural areas.[97] Most of the material identified, accounting for 69.5% of the total, consisted of

[94] Since these are materials from a secondary context, whose context of provenance can only be guessed at on the basis of the materials themselves, this method was considered preferable as it allowed us to optimize the time required for analysis without losing the most important information for the study of pottery consumption and the circulation of goods.

[95] The fabric of our specimen, brick red with an even fracture, seems comparable to body clay no.15 of the sigillata italica attested at Settefinestre, where it is also associated with a Goudineau 38a/Conspectus 33.1 bowl, see Regoli 1985, pp.138-144.

[96] See *Atlante I*, Pl.XXXVI, 5 and pp.85-86.

[97] The context of *Portus Scabris*, where coarsewares imported from the Mediterranean are well documented, cannot be considered alongside other coastal sites as part of an examination of the inland distribution of these wares, given its nature as a harbour dump.

coarseware not imported from elsewhere in the Mediterranean. A comparison with the fabric of a kiln discard from context 1260 in Roselle suggests that at least some of this was produced locally; for the remaining specimens we can currently suggest a regional or possibly extra-regional provenance.

AFRICAN RED SLIP WARE

The African red slip ware belonging to the late antique phase at Scoglietto consists of 5 bowls and 1 deep dish. The latter, of type Fulford 65.2/Hayes 104A2,[98] is characterized by a thickened rim with an external ledge and an internal groove at the junction with the wall; the mouth is 26.5 cm wide (Pl. XXXVI, no. 1). This form, traditionally dated to between AD 470/480 and 570/580, now has a more precise chronological range between the second quarter to the mid-6th century.[99] The specimen produced using the common fabric Sig 2 is overfired, to the extent that both the fabric, which is usually light red in colour and the slip, generally a brilliant orange, have taken on a brown tone. This is currently the only specimen of ARS with obvious firing defects; it nonetheless documents the enormous commercial importance of African red slip ware and the high levels of demand even for imperfect products.

All 3 bowls, despite some slight morphological differences, are of type Mackensen 24.[100] This is a small type of bowl with a flat horizontal (Pl. XXXVI, no. 4) or slightly hooked (Pl. XXXVI, nos 2-3) rim with a diameter ranging from 15 to 17 cm. The outer wall often presents a groove. The chronology of this type has been established by Mackensen as between the early 6th century and AD 580,[101] whilst Tortorella sets its production within a shorter time frame, between the late 5th or early 6th century and the mid-6th century.[102] Scoglietto is the only site in the study area to have yielded bowls of this type; it is important to note that they are not documented among the finds from *Portus Scabris*. The type is also absent from another important coastal site of late antique and early medieval *Tuscia*, Vada Volterrana,[103] indicating that it was not widely distributed. However, it is attested with a minimum of at least 1 individual at the Sienese context of Santa Maria della Scala, where it may still be in context in a layer dating to the second half of the 6th-early 7th century.[104]

The Scoglietto cave represents an anomaly compared to the rest of the study area also for the presence of another small bowl with a subvertical forked rim measuring 7 cm in diameter, belonging to type Hayes 12/102 (Pl. XXXVI, no. 6) and datable to between the second half of the 5th and AD 530/550.[105]

Finally, we note the presence of another bowl with a thickened and slightly hooked rim of triangular section with a diameter of 19 cm which seems to belong to a variant of Hayes 93/Fulford 52.2 (Pl. XXXVI, no. 5).[106] The specimen in question presents a stamped decoration with a probable association of a bird and a cross in Hayes style E (i),[107] dated to between the late 5th and mid-6th century. There are very close parallels with a type of bowl, also decorated with a stamped cross, from the *castrum* of Saint Blaise near the mouth of the Rhone, where it is attested both in phase III (second half of the 5th-early 6th century) and in phase VII (580-600).[108] In the British excavations at Carthage this form is well documented in contexts datable to between 500 and 550, though its *floruit* seems to fall between AD 525 and 530.[109] The bowl found at Scoglietto is made of fabric Sig 103, associated with two Hayes 61B deep dishes and a Hayes 93B bowl from *Portus Scabris*. This fabric is not documented either at Roselle or in the area between the Alma and Osa rivers.

One fact which appears worthy of note in the study of the African red slip ware from Scoglietto, is the constant presence of small forms used for the individual consumption of liquids (?) whilst larger forms destined for solid or semiliquid foods such as deep dishes, large bowls and flat-based dishes are completely absent with the exception of Fulford 65.2/Hayes 104A2.

ARS is the main indicator of help in defining the chronology of the late antique occupation of the site, which we can thus date to between the mid-5th and mid-6th centuries.

ITALIC TABLEWARE

As for African red slip ware, locally or regionally produced tableware is also dominated by small forms, both open and closed.

Ingobbiata di rosso ware, documented with a minimum number of 3 individuals, all produced using fabric AD 4, well attested at Roselle, is represented by two types of bowl and a basin for use at table. Despite their morphological simplicity, the bowls do not present close analogies with the materials from the excavation on the north slope at Roselle, whilst they are similar to productions from other late antique sites in the territory between the Alma valley and the lower Ombrone

98 Fulford-Peacock 1984, p.70, Fig.20, no.65.2.
99 For the date see Bonifay 2004, p.183.
100 This form is identical to Hayes 94. For comparisons see Mackensen 1993, Pl.65, nos 24.1 and 24.2 and pp.606-607.
101 Mackensen 1998, p.33.
102 Tortorella 1998, p.43.
103 Pasquinucci *et alii* 1998, p.618.
104 Cantini 2005a, p.66 and p.70, Pl.2, no.3.16.
105 On the chronology and a comparison see Tortorella 1998, p.43 and p.45, Fig.3, no.27.
106 See Barraud *et alii* 1998, p.146.
107 For a similar decoration see *Atlante I*, Pl.LIX (b), no.38).
108 Cavaillès Llopis-Vallauri 1994, p.100, Fig.55, no.86.
109 Fulford-Peacock 1984, p.68, Fig.52.2, and p.69.

valley. Both bowls have a hemispherical body, whilst they differ in the shape of the rim, which may be plain with a slight internal groove (Pl. XXXVII, no. 2) or slightly receding (Pl. XXXVII, no. 3). The two variants are fairly similar to bowls attested in late antique contexts in the Volterra area.[110] The type of basin found, which has a rounded and slightly incurving rim with a diameter of 17 cm, is the only item of tableware from the whole context to have a deeper body, making it suitable for the consumption of semiliquid and perhaps solid foods (Pl. XXXVII, no.4). This form presents no close analogies with the late antique pottery documented in the Maremman coastal belt; it is similar to a piece of *acroma depurata* ware from a context of the first half of the 7th century at Santa Maria della Scala in Siena.[111]

Sigillata chiara tarda dell'Italia centro-settentrionale is represented by a single specimen of a deep dish with an everted and pointed rim with a diameter of 19 cm (Pl. XXXVII, no. 5), made from fabric AD 45 and belonging to the production already identified at Roselle.

Colature rosse ware is also documented by a single closed form, perhaps a small tankard or a flask, with fairly everted walls and a flat base measuring 7 cm in diameter (Pl. XXXVII, no. 6).

TUNISIAN TRANSPORT CONTAINERS

The only minimum amphora form ascribable to a specific typology is a possible variant of Keay LXII produced in the first half of the 6th century AD.[112] It is characterized by a slightly everted rim, thickened and presenting a narrow external space at the junction with the neck (Pl. XXXVIII, no. 1). The fabric is identical to Anf 114 from *Portus Scabris*, used to produce various types of Tunisian amphorae present at the harbour site, including some specimens of variant A of Keay LXII.

COARSEWARE IMPORTED FROM TUNISIA

The optical microscope analysis of fabrics and the comparison with fabrics certainly belonging to transport containers and coarseware produced in Tunisia allowed us to identify a minimum number of at least 5 individuals identifiable as imports from North Africa. As already mentioned above, this is important because within the study area the circulation of Tunisian coarseware becomes infrequent at the end of the 4th and beginning of the 5th century, when the production of wares with a blackened surface and rim, well attested from the Antonine period onwards, comes to an end. A redistribution of North African coarseware is attested only at the harbour town of Paduline-Serrata Martini and the Scoglietto cave. No specimens are attested in the town of Roselle, an indication of the rarity and the probably occasional nature of the introduction of these wares into the area.

Among the kitchenware forms is a type of casserole and a lid, whilst a one-handled jug, a large jug and a small bowl were destined for use at table or for storage. As concerns the fabrics identified, we can note the presence of a single fabric attested exclusively at this site (Com Imp 4), whilst a further two are also present at *Portus Scabris* (Com Imp 3 and Anf 114). The large jug made of fabric Com Imp 4 is characterized by a fairly everted, thickened and rounded rim with a diameter of 19 and a barely raised disc foot; the fairly flaring walls present external grooves (Pl. XXXVIII, no. 3). The outer surface of the body is brown (Munsell 10YR 4/2), probably the result of a special and deliberate treatment of the clay during firing.[113] This form appears similar to Fulford CW Jars 1.1/1.2, well documented at Carthage in contexts dated to between AD 500 and 540.[114] This specimen does not present any obvious traces of fumigation.

A type of jug which can be partly reconstructed was likely used to hold and preserve liquid foods. It has a markedly everted and rounded rim with a diameter of 9 cm, a narrow neck, unpronounced shoulder, and probably an ovoid body. The strap handle presents two grooves on the upper surface and is set on the widest point of the body. At the base of the neck are two shallow external grooves (Pl. XXXVIII, no. 2). This piece is also made using fabric Com Imp 4, but unlike the pot described above it presents a characteristic two-coloured fracture, which ranges from red (Munsell 2.5YR 5/8) to grey (Munsell 2.5YR 4/1). Externally, the form is covered with a reddish brown (Munsell 5YR 4/4) clay slip which is uniformly distributed on the neck and body but which appears to be absent from part of the rim. The slip adheres closely to the fabric and is difficult to scratch. On the basis of its morphology, the jug can be ascribed to the Carthaginian type Fulford CW closed forms 77, dated to between AD 500 and 525. However, the latter differs in the surface treatment; in the Carthage specimen the surface was lightened by mixing salt water into the clay or by adding coarse salt to the fabric.[115]

The type of casserole with a thickened and everted rim and the lid with extremely flaring walls and a rounded rim can also be assigned a Tunisian provenance on the basis of a fabric generally associated with amphorae (Anf 114). The type of casserole with a mouth measuring 19 cm, despite its fragmentary nature, appears generically similar to the two-handled form Fulford CW Casseroles 18.1, documented in the British excavations at Carthage in contexts dated to between

[110] Lupi 1998, p.626, Fig.1, nos 3-5.
[111] Cantini 2005a.
[112] For the date see Bonifay 2004, p.140.

[113] For the comparison see Keay 1984, p.313, Fig.138, no.3.
[114] Fulford-Peacock 1984, p.16.
[115] *Ibidem*, p.192, Fig.73, no.1.2.

AD 450/475 and 500/520 (Pl. XXXVIII, no. 4).[116] The use of the same fabric – 2.1 – characterizing numerous amphorae and all ARS wares has also been identified in some of the specimens from Carthage.[117]

This fabric (Anf 114) is also used to produce a lid with a rounded rim measuring 17 cm in diameter and walls presenting light grooves on the outside (Pl. XXXVIII, no. 6). This type is identical to Fulford CW lids 4.3, for which a chronology between the 4th century and AD 525/550 has been proposed on the basis of finds at Carthage.[118]

The kitchenware picture is completed by a type of deep dish or dish-lid with a flat and upwardly inclined rim with a diameter of 16 cm, strongly flaring walls and a base with an atrophied ring foot. The outer surface of the body presents light horizontal grooves, whilst the rim is blackened (Pl. XXXVIII, no. 5). The Tunisian provenance of this form is certified by fabric Com Imp 3, attested at *Portus Scabris* in Tunisian casseroles belonging to types Fulford 19 and 20.[119] The treatment of the outer surfaces of the body and rim is fairly unusual; these are brownish (Munsell 5YR 4/2), clearly distinct from the colour of the internal surfaces of the pot which is identical to that of the fabric in the fracture (Munsell 2.5 YR 5/6). This type of casserole is not closely comparable to the forms found during the British excavations at Carthage, although there are some analogies with the two forms Fulford CW dishes or lids 4 and 8, dated to the early and the second half of the 6th century respectively.

It is obvious that the dates of the Tunisian coarseware are fully in line with those of ARS and the only amphora of certain typology found at Scoglietto. This confirms the validity of the chronological range established for the late antique occupation of the cave and the clearly "connected" nature of the context, which had access to the primary, secondary and tertiary products of North Africa (oil or fish sauces in the Keay LXII amphora, ARS and coarseware respectively).

KITCHENWARE OF POSSIBLE MEDITERRANEAN PROVENANCE

This is the definition given to a type of two-handled cooking pot which can be partly reconstructed, and characterized by an everted, thickened and rounded rim with a diameter of 22 cm. The base is flat and the outer walls are ribbed from the shoulder to the base. The thickened strap handles present two light grooves on the upper surface. This item was made on a fast wheel and the base presents marks indicating that it was detached from the wheel using a string (Pl. XXXIX, no. 1).

The pot was fired in a reducing atmosphere and has a brown fabric (Munsell 10YR 5/3), containing quartz and calcite inclusions. Fabric AG 100 has not been found in association with other pottery forms either at Scoglietto or in other sites in the study area, suggesting that it may have been imported from overseas, although its area of provenance is difficult to determine. Overall its morphological characteristics would appear to rule out an import from the Aegean since our specimen does not have the umbonated base typical of many pots from this area.[120] The rim and body profile, but not the base, present some generic affinities with Abruzzese kitchenware dated to between the late 6th and 8th; it has been suggested that these were imported from the eastern Mediterranean or made locally after models from overseas.[121] The pot presents some fairly marked similarities with a specimen from the Roman context of the *Basilica Hilariana* and dated to between the 6th and early 7th century,[122] although no information on the fabric or provenance of the latter are available. The properties of the fabric and the atmosphere in which the Scoglietto specimen were fired tend to rule out an import from Liguria, and specifically one of the late antique and early medieval productions from Ventimiglia, where similar forms with a ribbed globular body are attested.[123] The issue of the provenance of this specimen thus remains open and we can suggest that it was a Mediterranean import of hitherto unidentified provenance.

LOCALLY PRODUCED KITCHENWARE

A minimum number of 4 individuals made using fabric AG 109, identical to AG13 from Roselle, can be ascribed to a production which was almost certainly local and possibly located in the town of Roselle itself. A fragment of a kiln discard made with this fabric found in context 1260 from the excavation on the north slope indicate the presence of a workshop inside the town or in its immediate hinterland. At Scoglietto this production is represented by three different forms which serve the most important cooking purposes: a wide-mouthed pot to boil meat or make soups, a pan and a casserole to stew or roast food. The pots are all of the same type, with a more or less thickened and hooked rim and measuring 18 to 19 cm in diameter (Pl. XL, nos 5-6). This type is also attested in the late antique and early medieval phase of the village of San

[116] For the comparison see *Ibidem*, p.214, Fig.84, no.77; for the surface whitening technique see pp.263-264.
[117] *Ibidem* p.182. Fig.68, no.18.2.
[118] *Ibidem*, pp.14-15.
[119] This type is also made from two types of fabric, one of which (2.1 *fabric*) has already been mentioned for its association with amphorae and ARS found during the British excavations. See Fulford-Peacock 1984, p.196, Fig.75, no.4.3.

[120] For an overview of the distribution of Aegean cooking pots which influenced Otranto wares see Arthur-Patterson 1998, pp.518 and 521.
[121] See Staffa 2004, p.214, Fig.10, no.71b; and Staffa 1998, pp.463-471.
[122] Vatta-Bertoldi 2004, p.468, Pl.VIII, no.65.
[123] There are some similarities with cooking pots made locally using fabric 1 which systematically presents micaceous inclusions or fabric 4, always fired in an oxidizing atmosphere. See Olcese 1993, pp.166-168, p.212, Fig.40, no.78 and p.214, Fig.41, no.92.

Martino *de plano*. Similar forms are also present in the urban deposit of Santa Maria della Scala in Siena in phases of the late 5th- mid-6th century, indicating the success of these pots and the possible existence of workshops capable of producing them for a regional market. The distribution of this type also covers contexts outside the region, with a concentration of attestations in the Sabina, as shown by its presence in the late antique and early medieval phases of Casale San Donato, near Farfa.[124] Clearly, the circulation of this type of pot in both coastal and inland areas seems to be linked to the existence of workshops operating in different areas but using similar formal models, determined by the functional nature of the types produced. The cooking pot made using fabric AG 109 has a fairly everted rim of rectangular section with a diameter of 18 cm; the walls have a slightly convex external profile (Pl. XXXIX, no. 5). The inside presents pronounced grooves made by throwing on the wheel. This type presents similarities with specimens from Cosa found in the late 5th – mid-6th century deposit in the forum cistern,[125] and in a dump of material covering the collapse of the garden of the *domus* of Diana, dated to between the late 5th and early 6th century.[126] However, the Scoglietto specimen differs clearly from the Cosa pieces in the properties of the fabric, which does not present mica inclusions. The same type, produced using different fabrics in two contexts in close proximity to one another represents further proof of the local and regional complexity of production activities.

At Scoglietto, much of the kitchenware found presents fabrics which are more or less rich in mica; the morphological repertoire produced using these fabrics comprises pots and casseroles whose formal characteristics are similar to the pottery from Cosa. The main exception is represented by types made using fabric AG 109, characteristic of the Roselle area.

The last form attested at Scoglietto and ascribable to the AG 109 "workshop" is a pot with gently flaring walls and a plain rim rounded on the upper surface and measuring 24 cm in diameter. Before firing, the external surfaces were decorated with a light combed decoration; a spiral motif was later impressed on them using a pointed tool (Pl. XLI, no. 4). A similar specimen with a wave decoration was found in the mid-5th-century levels of the maritime villa of Torre Tagliata in the A*gro Cosano.*[127] The latter was made using a fabric which, on the basis of the description,[128] is similar to that of our specimen, possible proof of the local circulation of wares which were presumably made at the Roselle workshop.

[124] Patterson-Roberts 1998, p.429, Fig.6, nos 2-4.
[125] Fontana 2003, p.314, Fig.142, FC18.
[126] Gusberti 2003, p.306, Fig.139, no.2.
[127] Ciampoltrini-Rendini 1990, p.527, Fig.8, no.17.
[128] The fabric used to make the specimen from Torre Tagliata is "di colore bruno-nerastro, granuloso e soggetto a sfaldarsi", *ibidem* p.530.

KITCHENWARE OF PROBABLE REGIONAL PROVENANCE

We have included within this category some closed and open forms made from three fabrics which share a texture characterized by a predominance of calcite granules (AG 106, AG 110, AG 111).

One of these, containing an abundance of ground spathic calcite, added to the clay to increase the heat resistance of the vessels (AG 106), presents close analogies with the fabrics attested in contexts of the central centuries of the Middle Ages between the Alma valley and the lower Ombrone valley.[129] Fabric AG 106 is used to make a type of pot with a band-shaped rim documented by 2 specimens with diameters of 17 and 19 cm (Pl. XL, nos 1-2), identical to the 4th-early 5th-century Type I from Roselle. The same fabric is employed for two types of lid characterized respectively by a rounded and thickened rim, pointed on the outer surface (Pl. XLII, no 5) and by a slightly incurved rim (Pl. XLII, no. 6 and Pl. XLIII, no. 1). The diameters, ranging from 17 to 18 cm, and the rim structures appear wholly compatible with the pots made from the same fabric. This suggests that the regional workshops using fabric AG 106 specialized in the production of cooking pots with band-shaped rims and lids.

Fabric AG 110 is used to make a single type of pot with a thickened rim of triangular section measuring 17 cm in diameter. The outer surface presents a few light grooves (Pl. XL, no. 7). The morphology of the rim is comparable to Type VII from Roselle attested in a context of the second half of the 6th-early 7th century.

The last fabric in this category (AG 111) is used to make two large lids with diameters of 26 and 28 cm characterized in one instance by a thickened and rounded rim (Pl. XLIII, no. 5) and in the other by a plain rim (Pl. XLIII, no. 6); these must have belonged to large cooking pots or casseroles.

KITCHENWARE PRODUCED OUTSIDE THE REGION (?) WITH MICACEOUS FABRICS

Belonging to this category are a series of kitchenware items characterized by fabrics all of which contain biotite and muscovite inclusions, albeit in varying proportions. On the basis of the ratio between the various inclusions documented in the fabrics we can

[129] Identical fabrics containing spathic calcite are associated with cooking pots with a dense external ribbing documented in 11th and 12th-century phases at Grosseto and Castel Maus (Alma valley) in a surface context of the central centuries of the Middle Ages. Thin section analysis of a cooking pot from Grosseto allowed us to determine that the medieval wares were fired at 700°. The mineral phases include a predominance of calcite, smaller amounts of quartz, rare muscovite, some oxides and secondary calcite. It was probably made regionally. I would like to thank Consuelo Fortina of the Department of Earth Sciences at Siena University for these data.

subdivide these into two sub-categories. The first, consisting of fabrics AG 105, 107, 108 and 112, presents a predominance of mica inclusions. The second, consisting of fabrics AG 101, 102 and 103, contains similar inclusions, but in far more modest quantities compared to the other mineralogical phases identified.[130] This subdivision is important for archaeological purposes because these two sub-categories also present interesting differences in the functional forms produced compared to the pottery which can be ascribed to local workshops. The morphological properties of the objects made from these two sub-categories of fabrics seem to suggest that they were made by workshops located in the Tyrrhenian coastal belt between the very southern Maremma and Lazio, as we will see below. Of particular significance is a series of similarities in morphology and fabric between the objects found at Scoglietto belonging to this category and the local productions of the area around Rome (*infra*). This is an extremely important piece of evidence since it may document an unexpected interregional circulation of kitchenware along the central Tyrrhenian coast, following a south-north route.

A) VERY MICACEOUS FABRICS

Among the forms belonging to this sub-category is a type of cooking pot characterized by a thickened rim of pseudo-rectangular section, squared (Pl. XXXIX, no. 3) or pointed (Pl. XXXIX, no. 4) on the outer surface. The upper part of the first specimen presents a slightly concave profile to host the lid. The mouths are fairly wide, ranging in diameter from 21 to 24 cm. This type of cooking pot is well documented at the site of Paduline-Serrata Martini, whilst it is absent from contexts further inland, including those hitherto identified in the town of Roselle. Further south, this type is systematically present at Cosa, where it is frequently attested in the forum cistern deposit,[131] in the construction phase of the *castrum* on the Arx[132] and in the debris dump from the *domus* of Diana.[133] The materials from Cosa also present abundant biotite, alongside volcanic and quartz inclusions, possibly suggesting that they were manufactured in northern Lazio or southern Etruria.[134] This type of cooking pot also finds exact parallels in materials from the late antique phases of Mola di Monte Gelato in the Roman Campagna,[135] and in various contexts in the city of Rome itself; these include the *Basilica Hilariana* on the Caelian in phases of the first half of the 6th [136] and of the 6th-early 7th century,[137] and the Conservatory of San Pasquale between the late 5th and second half of the 6th century.[138] It is worth noting the area of distribution of this type of cooking pot. Between the Bruna and Albegna valleys it is found exclusively in settlements which were in direct contact with harbour facilities (Serrata Martini, Scoglietto and Cosa). This may be evidence that this type of cooking pot circulated by sea and was distributed by the production centres, perhaps located in Lazio, along *cabotage* routes; the same routes also used to transport the excess goods imported from the Mediterranean reaching the Roman markets. These goods may have been carried in the boats which transported Mediterranean foodstuffs and fineware from the harbours of Rome to the rural sites of the Tyrrhenian coast north of the city.

A trade mechanism similar to that just described may also explain the presence at Scoglietto of another type of cooking pot with a fairly everted and thickened rim, concave on the upper surface to host the lid (Pl. XLIV, nos 2-3). This type is also characterized by a wide mouth, measuring up to 22 and 23 cm in the 2 specimens documented. The cooking pot is similar to materials from Cosa found in the late antique debris dump in the garden of the *domus* of Diana,[139] whilst comparable forms have not been found in the late antique phases hitherto analysed at Roselle, nor in other sites in the study area. It is, on the other hand, comparable to productions well attested at *Portus* (Rome) in the 7th century and which, according to the analysis of the fabrics, can be ascribed to workshops in the Rome area.[140]

By contrast, the type of cooking pot characterized by a strongly everted plain rim with a diameter of 21 cm (Pl. XLIV, no. 1) finds no morphological parallels in the late antique contexts in this or neighbouring areas.

Another form presenting numerous close analogies with materials from Roman contexts is the small cooking pot destined for individual use and presenting a short flat rim, upwardly rising and with a diameter of 13 cm. This form has an ovoid body, a shoulder decorated with parallel grooves and a small disc foot (Pl. XLIV, no. 4). This type is documented both in a context of the first half of the 6th century in the *Basilica Hilariana* on the Caelian,[141] and in another context of the late 5th-second half of the 6th century at the Conservatory of San Pasquale in Trastevere.[142] To these we should add a one-handled version attested in the late 7th-century deposit in the Crypta Balbi.[143]

Among the open forms belonging to this sub-category is a pan with subvertical walls, a pointed rim with a diameter of 26 cm, a flat base measuring about 25 cm

[130] For a description of the fabics see the Catalogue.
[131] Fontana 2003, p.314, Fig.142, FC20-22.
[132] Fentress *et alii* 1991, p.220, Fig.19, nos 18a-b. Import from an unspecified area has been suggested for the two specimens made from fabric "D", containing quartzite.
[133] Gusberti 2003, p.306, Fig.139, no.1.
[134] Fontana 2003, p.316.
[135] Patterson-Roberts 1998, p.424, Fig.2, no.4.
[136] Pacetti 2004, p.448, Pl.VI, no.44.
[137] Vatta-Bertoldi 2004, p.466, p.465, Pl.V, no.37.
[138] Fogagnolo 2004, p.594, Pl.IX, no.73.
[139] Gusberti 2003, p.306, Fig.139, nos 3-4.
[140] Coletti 1998, p.405, Fig.8, no.5 and p.404.
[141] Pacetti 2004, p.449, Pl.VII, no.53.
[142] Fogagnolo 2004, p.593, Pl.VIII, no.59.
[143] Ricci 1998, p.353, Fig.1, nos 3-4.

and a maximum depth of 8.4 cm (Pl. XLI, no. 5). The pan presents a characteristic dark grey clay slip (Munsell 10R 4/3) and obvious traces of burnishing on the outer surface. The few fumigation marks, alongside the unusual slip, might suggest that it was used not only for cooking but also to prepare or consume food.

The lids found present a thickened rim, flattened on the upper surface (Pl. XLIII, no. 4) or internally oblique (Pl. XLIII, no. 3), and strongly flaring walls with grooves on the outer surface which make their profile fairly complex. The rim diameters range from 21 to 24 cm and are thus perfectly compatible with the broad mouths of the pots belonging to this production. The only documented handle is button-shaped (Pl. XLIII, no. 7).

The unusual morphology of these lids is reminiscent of type Fulford CW, lids 4.3, made in Tunisia,[144] attested at Scoglietto in its original version (Pl. XXXVIII, no. 6). It thus seems fairly plausible that these were imitated from Tunisian coarseware prototypes at the workshops which made their own pieces using the fabrics in this sub-category.

B) FABRICS WITH SMALL QUANTITIES OF MICA INCLUSIONS

Among the forms most characteristic of this sub-category we should note a type of casserole characterized by strongly flaring walls and a thickened incurving rim with a more or less pronounced ledge on the outside. These forms often have wide mouths, between 22 and 28 cm in diameter, although a smaller version measuring 17 cm is also documented (Pl. XLV, nos 1-5). The structure of the rims is strongly reminiscent of forms of African kitchenware such as variant 3 of the dish or lid with a blackened rim of type Fulford CW, dishes or lids 9, dating to between the 3rd-4th and early 5th century, and the lid Fulford CW, lids 6.5, in turn typical of Carthaginian contexts dated to between AD 575/600 and 650.[145] The frequent presence of traces of fumigation on the specimens found at Scoglietto is evidence that they were used for cooking; some flat bases, which are not illustrated and which can be ascribed to the rims in question on the basis of the fabric and the thickness of the walls, seem to suggest that they were used as casseroles to cook stews or other similar dishes. In Tuscany the only close points of comparison are with two forms found in the fill of the Cosa forum cistern dating to the late 5th- mid-6th century.[146]

In Rome numerous specimens comparable to the casseroles made using the fabrics in this subgroup are attested in late antique and early medieval contexts. In the phases of the first half of the 5th century in the *Schola Praeconum* pottery similar to ours is well documented; this was made locally and using micaceous fabrics similar to those of Scoglietto.[147] Other close points of comparison are with wares from the mid-5th century context of the Crypta Balbi *mithraeum*,[148] with pottery from the Vigna Barberini in mid-late 6th century phases[149] and with forms from the late 5th-second half of the 6th century deposit in the Conservatory of San Pasquale.[150] It is highly likely that the objects of this type found at Scoglietto were imports from Rome, as described above for other forms. This theory appears to gain further support from the identification of another type of casserole, attested in two different variants, one with an incurving rim (Pl. XLV, no. 6) and one with an incurving and folded rim (Pl. XLV, no. 7). In the case of this form, the similarities with wares from Roman contexts are even closer. Specifically, for the first variant we can mention some 5th century bowls/lids from the *Schola Praeconum*[151] and others of the first half of the 6th century from the *Basilica Hilariana*;[152] the latter, on the other hand, is identical to a casserole found in the mithraeum of the Crypta Balbi in phases of the mid-5th century.[153]

A third type of medium-small casserole is characterized by a rim flattened on the upper surface and thickened on the inside, measuring 17 cm in diameter. The exterior presents a light groove beneath the rim (Pl. XLI, no. 1). This type presents generic morphological similarities with a piece of kitchenware from a context of the first quarter of the 4th century in drainage ditch VII in the northeast sector of the *Domus Tiberiana*,[154] and with another hemispherical casserole from the Crypta Balbi mithraeum in phases of the late 6th-early 7th century.[155]

A final type of casserole or lid belonging to this sub-category presents fairly flaring walls, and has a slightly receding rim, pointed on the upper surface, measuring 25 cm in diameter; the rim presents a light combed decoration on the outside (Pl. XLI, no. 3). Reliable points of comparison once again come from the 5th century context of the *Schola Praeconum*, where similar forms are made using micaceous fabrics identical to ours.[156]

The broad repertoire of open forms belonging to this sub-category also comprises a series of medium and large-sized lids, for use with the large casseroles and cooking pots made from the same fabric. The lid with

---

144 Fulford-Peacock 1984, p.196, Fig.75, nos 4.2, 4.3.
145 *Ibidem*, p.190, Fig.72, no.3 and p.196, Fig.75, no.6.5.
146 Fontana 2003, p.314, Fig.142, nos FC7-8.
147 I refer in particular to the pottery made using fabrics 7, 8 and 9. See Whitehouse *et alii* 1982, p.70, Fig.6, nos 74-75 e p.58.
148 Saguì-Coletti 2004, p.251, Pl.VI, no.31.
149 Rizzo *et alii* 1998, p.86, Pl.IV, no.26.
150 Fogagnolo 2004, p.595, Pl.X, nos 83-84.
151 Whitehouse *et alii* 1982, p.75, Fig.9.116.
152 Pacetti 2004, p.451, Pl.VIII, no.62.
153 Sagui-Coletti 2004, p.251, Pl.VI, no.32.
154 Munzi *et alii* 2004, p.108, Pl.VI, no.58.
155 Saguì-Coletti 2004, p.274, Pl.XXII, no.127.
156 Whitehouse *et alii* 1982, p.70, Fig.6, nos72-73.

fairly everted walls, a thickened rim pointed on the upper surface and presenting an external ledge (Pl. XLI, no. 2), is similar to a type with an identical profile but presenting light grooves on the outer surface of the rim, attested in the late 5th-second half of the 6th century phase of the Conservatory of San Pasquale in Trastevere.[157]

The very simply shaped medium-sized lid, with a slightly thickened rim measuring 18 cm in diameter (Pl. XLIII, no. 2), must have been used with closed forms with narrow mouths, probably with the cooking pot with a band-shaped rim also belonging to this sub-category (Pl. XL, no. 3).

The various lids with rims flattened on the upper surface and thickened on the inside, with diameters ranging from 22 and 32 cm (Pl. XLII, nos 1-3), must have belonged to the large casseroles with shaped rims or to the larger cooking pots.

Closed forms were also made using the fabrics in this sub-category, albeit less frequently than open forms. These are represented by three different types of cooking pot, each of which is documented by a minimum number of only 1 individual, and by a type of one-handled tankard. Among the forms used to cook *puls* or to boil meats is the wide-mouthed cooking pot with an everted and thickened rim; the same type was also produced by the workshops using very micaceous fabrics. This type of cooking pot has a mouth about 30 cm in diameter, compatible with the larger lids (Pl. XXXIX, no. 2).

The cooking pot with a band-shaped rim, shaped internally to host the lid (Pl. XL, no. 3), is morphologically similar to Type I from Roselle, although the properties of the fabric are different. Similar forms made from micaceous fabrics are common in the context of the first half of the 5th century of the *Schola Praeconum I*,[158] and in the 7th-century context of the *Schola Praeconum II* in Rome.[159] This type is widespread in Roman contexts, mainly in phases of the 6th and 7th centuries.[160]

The type presenting a rim with a short external pointed flange (Pl. XL, no. 4) is morphologically similar to forms documented at Roselle and ascribable to a local or regional workshop.[161] However, it differs from these in the fabric, which is that used in the Rome-Lazio area. There are close parallels from contexts of the first half of the 6th century at Cosa, with materials produced using mica-rich fabrics and therefore belonging to productions of the volcanic areas of the central sector of the Tyrrhenian coast,[162] and from Roman layers of the 6th and 7th centuries.[163]

The repertoire of closed forms ends with a type of small tankard for individual use, employed both for cooking and for use at table, probably for cooking dried meat in wine or water or for warming wine to be consumed directly at table. It presents an everted and thickened rim, rounded on the upper surface and measuring 10 cm in diameter, a strap handle rising above the rim and a disc foot, 8 cm in diameter. The body is ovoid and the maximum height is about 12.5 cm (Pl. XLIV, no. 5).

KITCHENWARE WITH A FOSSIL-RICH FABRIC

We have decided to devote a separate section to this category, although it is represented only by a single fabric and a minimum number of only 1 individual. The highly distinctive fabric (AG 104) presents a high proportion of fossilized *cardium* fragments, including some whole valves measuring 0.4-0.5 cm across, associated with rare fragments of quartz and chalk. This is an absolutely unprecedented fabric in the late antique and early medieval contexts of the study area and thus almost certainly belongs to an imported object, probably from overseas. The form associated with fabric AG 104 is a lid with fairly flaring walls, a thickened and flattened rim with a diameter of 23 cm and presenting an internal indentation making it easier to position on a cooking pot (Pl. XLII, no. 4). The piece is made by hand and presents a characteristic addition of brown clay on the outer surface, smoothed to make the fabric less rough. A very generic point of comparison for the fabric is fabric 1.8 used to produce a type of casserole and a type of lid documented at Carthage in contexts of the late 5th-early 7th centuries, ascribed to a possible import from Italy and more precisely Sicily.[164]

5.5.2. The Cave Shelter of Spaccasasso: the Material Culture of the Late Antique Occupation

A system of three cavities originating with the geological formation of the Calcare Massiccio has been identified on the summit of the Poggio di Spaccasasso near Alberese, at 130 metres above sea level.[165] Work

[157] Fogagnolo 2004, p.595, Pl.X, no.81.
[158] Whitehouse *et alii* 1982, p.74, Fig.8, no.110.
[159] Whitehouse *et alii* 1985, p.183, Fig.7, no.36.
[160] Attested in the north-east sector of the Domus Tiberiana, in phases of the early 7th century, in Ambiente D of the Roman Forum dating to between the late 6th and late 7th century and in the Basilica Hilariana on the Caelian between the 6th and early 7th century. See respectively Munzi *et alii* 2004, p.109, Pl.VII, nos67-68; Paganelli 2004, p.189, Pl.III, no.40; Pacetti 2004, p.467, Pl. VII, nos53, 56.
[161] I refer in particular to cooking pot Type VII from context 1260 in Roselle.
[162] Items made from fabrics A and B identified at Cosa belong to this production. For an exact parallel for the cooking pot with an external flange see the type in Fig.18, no.13a, in Fentress *et alii* 1991, on the two fabrics *A* and *B* see *ibidem*, p.218.
[163] There are analogies with a cooking pot from the Basilica Hilariana on the Caelian in phases of the 6th and early 7th century and with one from a context on the Aventine of the mid-7th century. See Vatta-Bertoldi 2004, p.467, Pl.VII, no.54 and Fontana *et alii* 2004, p.554, Pl.IV, no.38.
[164] Fulford-Peacock 1984, p.13 e p.164, Fig.59, nos30-31.
[165] Sgherri-Costantini 2004, pp.134-136.

to clear the space in front of the "Buca di Spaccasasso no. 2" cave allowed for the identification of materials ascribable to different phases of occupation of this context,[166] including a pottery assemblage belonging to what was probably an inhabitation of the site during the 6th century.

The assemblage of late antique ceramic materials consists of a minimum number of 4 tableware forms and 2 coarseware forms, to which we should add a minimum number of 2 North African amphorae: these present a surface discolouration and cannot be ascribed to a specific typology since they are represented only by wall fragments. The small quantity of pottery belonging to this phase seems to suggest occupation by a single family, probably in connection with the exploitation of woodland resources given the position of the cave.

TABLEWARE

ARS is attested by a specimen of bowl with a short flat rim, measuring about 22 cm in diameter and presenting two grooves on the upper surface. The bowl has a fairly deep hemispherical body and belongs to type Hayes 93B, datable to between the mid-5th century and 530/550 (Pl. XLVI, no. 1).[167] This type is not attested in other rural contexts or in the town of Roselle, whilst it is well documented at the harbour site of *Portus Scabris*.

The tableware certainly imported from elsewhere in the Mediterranean includes various wall fragments and a handle belonging to a single unidentifiable closed form. Both the walls and the handle present a decoration consisting of a zig-zag motif impressed with a spatula and a poorly preserved red-orange slip (Pl. XLVI, nos 4a-b). The semi-fine fabric is olive-yellow in colour and contains quartz, very hard black inclusions, rare calcite and biotite.[168] The zig-zag decorations are typical of a class of pottery produced in the eastern Mediterranean, with the major workshops being located at Gerasa and other hitherto unidentified sites in southern Palestine. These objects were distributed mainly to areas of the eastern Mediterranean, including some contexts in what is now Palestine, Syria, Jordan, Iraq and Iran, and were exported principally between the 6th and the early 7th century.[169] The import of these products is also attested sporadically in the western Mediterranean and an interesting concentration of finds has been identified on the Tyrrhenian coast.[170] This class has been found in late 7th-century deposits in the Crypta Balbi,[171] at *Portus*, Cosa and the maritime villa of Torre Tagliata in the *Ager Cosanus*.[172] The specimens from Torre Tagliata were considered by the authors to be a probable residual presence in a 5th-century context; however, according to Uscatescu they can be dated to the early years of the 6th century, when the production of this class began.[173] The minimum form from Spaccasasso presents close analogies in terms of fabric and decoration with the specimens found at Cosa and Torre Tagliata. However, the impossibility of reconstructing the profile even in part makes it impossible to go beyond a generic morphological comparison with the walls of the indeterminate closed forms from Cosa.[174] A significant characteristic of the distribution of the pottery with zig-zag decorations in the western Mediterranean is its constant association with eastern wine amphorae; the exception to this rule is Castel Trosino.[175] Similarly, at Spaccasasso this pottery class is not associated with eastern transport containers, but only with African red slip ware and Tunisian amphorae. Indeed, the area between the lower Ombrone valley and the Alma valley is characterized by the infrequent attestation of eastern amphorae.

Certainly belonging to italic tableware productions are a carinated bowl in *ingobbiata di rosso* and a closed form in *colature rosse* ware. The bowl has a conical body and a pointed rim with a diameter of 23 cm presenting two grooves on the outside. It is made using an extremely fine, soft, porous suede-coloured fabric (Pl. XLVI, no. 2). The slip, distributed evenly on both the inside and the outside, is dark red in colour. Similar bowls are also attested in late antique contexts in the Volterra area.[176]

The small closed form with a ring foot measuring 7 cm in diameter and an ovoid body, on the other hand, appears to be a small tankard with a *colature rosse* coating (Pl. XLVI, no. 3). This specimen presents analogies, in terms of the fabric as well, with a fairly similar piece from the Scoglietto cave, although the morphology of the base is different.

The tableware forms, few in number but varied in function, can thus be ascribed to at least three different areas of origin: a probable regional provenance, with the *ingobbiata di rosso* ware and the *colature rosse* ware, and two overseas area of provenance (Tunisia and southern Palestine). This may suggest that the context in question was economically somewhat

[166] Preliminary research was conducted by the Società Naturalistica Speleologica Maremmana coordinated by Carlo Cavanna. From 2004 excavations have been underway, organized by the Faculty of Prehistory and Protohistory of Siena University, with the scientific direction of Lucia Sarti.
[167] Tortorella 1998, p.43.
[168] For a detailed description of fabric Com Imp 5 see the Catalogue.
[169] For the definition of this class see the important article by Alexandra Uscatescu, in Uscatescu 1996, pp.625-646.
[170] *Ibidem*, p.641, Fig.8.

[171] Ricci 1998, p.368, Fig.10, no.1.
[172] Ciampoltrini-Rendini 1990, p.528, Fig.9.
[173] Uscatescu 1996, p.637.
[174] The forms attested at Cosa and Torre Tagliata have different fabrics and morphologies than those from other contexts such as the Crypta Balbi, Castel Trosino and Oderzo, and are ascribed to a generic origin in central-southern Palestine. See Uscatescu, pp.635-637. On the closed forms attested at Cosa see *ibidem*, p.638, Fig.5, nos3, 5-7.
[175] *Ibidem*, p.643.
[176] Lupi 1998, p.625.

complex; though modest in size it was nonetheless fairly receptive to maritime and overland trade flows.

COARSEWARE

The only 2 specimens of coarseware are a globular cooking pot and a multi-purpose jar/small amphora (?) which was probably used both at table and for storage. Both are made using fabrics which belong to the strongly micaceous sub-category of kitchenware attested at the Scoglietto cave.

The cooking pot, made from fabric AG 108, presents a slightly everted rim with a diameter of 23 cm, shaped on the inside to host the lid and with a short external flange of triangular section. The body is globular and the flat base measures 13 cm (Pl. XLVII, no. 1). This typology, morphologically similar to cooking pot type VII from Roselle, also finds exact parallels at Scoglietto with a specimen made from a similar but less micaceous fabric (AG 102).

The jar, made using fabric AG 105, is characterized by a barely everted rim, thickened and rounded and measuring 9 cm in diameter; the handle presents a longitudinal ridge on the upper surface and is set immediately beneath the rim (Pl. XLVII, no. 2). This type appears identical to late antique and early medieval productions identified in surface contexts in the Farfa area in the Sabina[177] and to a type of small amphora, perhaps used for wine, recently found in the cistern deposit at Cosa (late 5th-mid-6th century), for which a local or sub-regional production has been proposed.[178] However, the fragmentary nature of the Spaccasasso specimen makes it impossible to determine if this is a one- or two-handled form.

5.5.3. The Materials from the Rubbish Dump at Paduline (Castiglione della Pescaia): a Mid-Sixth to Early Seventh-Century Ceramic Deposit

In the early 1980s the Soprintendenza per i Beni Archeologici della Toscana opened a series of test pits in the imperial settlement and bath complex at Paduline in the Castiglione della Pescaia area, near the mouth of the Bruna river.[179] The archaeological surveys, concentrated inside three contiguous rooms, named A, E and F, completely uncovered room A, at the north-west end of the bath building, bringing to light a *praefurnium* used to heat the surrounding rooms. This structure, built between the late 1st and the first half of the 2nd century AD,[180] was sealed by a layer of earth containing numerous pottery wasters which was interpreted as a rubbish dump. This ceramic deposit is important because of its potential for dating the last phase of frequentation of the Paduline complex and the information it provides on the nature of pottery consumption during the period between the 6th and 7th centuries at a site which, during the imperial and late antique period, certainly played an important role in the system of intermediate harbours in the central and northern Tyrrhenian.

MEDITERRANEAN IMPORTS

A first important feature is the absence of African red slip ware definitely in context. The analysis of the ceramic deposit allowed us to identify only a minimum of 1 form, consisting of an overfired body fragment from a deep dish in ARS production D; the impossibility of identifying this object leaves it open to question whether it is a residual presence or in context.

A problem which is in some respects similar concerns the transport containers, of which a minimum number of 9 individuals were found, in 8 cases ascribable to imports from North Africa and in 1 to eastern Mediterranean productions. In this case, too, most of the fragments belonging to these 9 individuals are wall fragments, with only a few diagnostic pieces. Whilst it was relatively easy to ascertain the North African origin of these vessels given the properties of the fabrics, identical to those of Tunisian forms from *Portus Scabris*, in at least 6 cases no typological attribution was possible. The presence of a possible small *spathion* from Tunisia should also be noted (*infra*).

The 2 certain Tunisian amphorae identified are in phase and residual respectively. The specimen with a vertical rim, slightly thickened at the edge and presenting a slight ledge marking the junction with the neck appears to belong to type Keay XXVA, dating to the 4th century AD (Pl. XLIX, no. 3).[181] The only Tunisian oil or fish sauce transport container found in context is a possible Keay LXII. Of this form we found a cylindrical neck, with handles with an elliptical section presenting two longitudinal grooves on the lower part, set on a broad shoulder, and a hollow spike with a thickened base, characterized by a raised circular element joining the base to the wall (Pl. XLIX, nos 1-2). These characteristic features make it possible to attribute the specimen to a generic Keay LXII type, datable to between the first half of the 6th and the early 7th century AD.[182] The fabric used to make this form is Anf 104, characteristic of numerous Tunisian amphorae from *Portus Scabris* (types Keay XXV, XXVI, XXXIII, LVA).

Another minimum individual to which 8 wall fragments have been ascribed, made using a reddish

[177] Patterson-Roberts 1998, p.430, Fig.7, no.1.
[178] Fontana 2003.
[179] Çygielman 1982, pp.367-368.
[180] See Bonifay 2004, p.122 for the date.

[181] For the general date of the Keay LXII amphora type see Bonifay 2004, p.140.
[182] For the comparison with type Keay LXIIB see Keay 1984, p.320, Fig.144, no.8 and p.341, Fig.159, nos13-15; on the chronology of this type see Keay 1998, p.145.

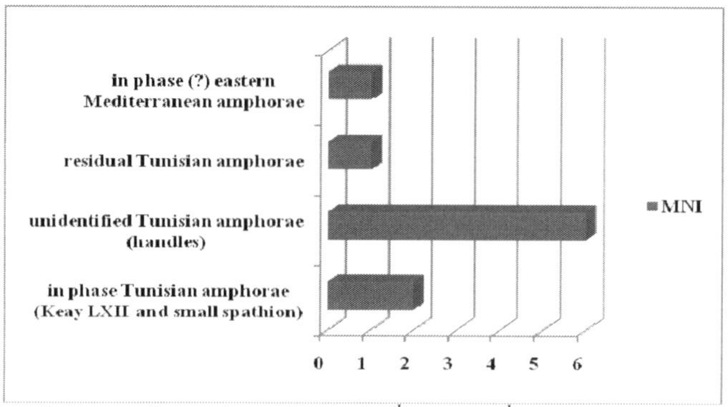

Graph VIII_ Amphora evidence from the mid 6th-early 7th AD ceramic dump at Paduline.

fabric rich in limestone and quartz inclusions, some of which present light rilling, can be ascribed to an import from the eastern Mediterranean which cannot be identified with certainty but which may possibly be a LR 2 amphora (Graph VIII).

STORAGE COARSEWARE OF PROBABLE TUNISIAN ORIGIN

This description has been given to a single closed form identified in the Paduline deposit. It is made from a semipurified fabric with an even fracture, fairly porous and characterized by the presence of white inclusions, quartz and iron oxides. The fabric takes on a two-tone appearance ranging from orange (Munsell 2.5 YR 6/8 light red) to cream (Munsell 10YR 8/4 very pale brown) and appears similar to the carbonatic fabrics associated with some of the North African transport amphorae found at S. Antonino in the phases of the *castrum* dating to the late 6th-7th century.[183] The form is that of a small amphora or bottle with a subvertical rim, shaped externally to form a double ledge, with a diameter of 7 cm, set on a short cone-shaped neck (Pl. XLVIII, no. 3). After firing a zig-zag motif was incised on the shoulder, but this is only partially visible. Though the structure of the rim and the properties of the fabric are identical to those of a variant of the late S. Antonino 18b *spatheion*[184] from the site of the same name in the Finale Ligure, the absence of handles, which on small cylindrical containers are set at the base of the rim and on the shoulder, makes this identification doubtful. However, we should note the existence of some late variants of *spatheia* which had no handles; one specimen was found at S. Antonino,[185] and another in the collapse of church A at the complex of San Giusto di Lucera in Puglia, ascribed to the second half of the 6th-early 7th century.[186] There are also some significant morphological similarities with Tunisian coarseware used for storage purposes, such as type Fulford Closed forms 72.2, attested at Carthage from 535 onwards[187] and made from a fabric similar to that of the Paduline specimen.[188] At S. Antonino some bottles similar to Fulford type 72.2 were also present, though these were made with a ferrous fabric.[189] These data, although they do not definitively clarify the functional attribution of the specimen concerned – small *spatheion* or bottle – do provide further confirmation of the primacy of North African wares in the overseas supply of Paduline, even between the late 6th and early 7th century.

ITALIC TABLEWARE

The repertoire of tableware and storage forms, belonging to pottery classes produced in Italy, coated or otherwise, is fairly varied, with some interesting novelties with respect to the picture for contemporary or slightly earlier contexts in rural areas.

A) ACROMA DEPURATA WARE

Acroma depurata ware is represented by a minimum of at least 5 closed forms. Among these was a jar with a band-shaped rim, shaped inside and fairly everted, measuring 11.6 cm in diameter (Pl. XLVIII, no. 2). The jar has a thickened strap handle (Pl. XLVIII, no. 6). A type of small two-handled small amphora or bottle was also found with a small mouth measuring 4 cm and elbow handles set on the rim (Pl. XLVIII, no. 4). The jug/small amphora with a tall band-shaped rim finds close parallels in Roman contexts, where this type seems to appear as early as the mid-5th century, as indicated by a version with a slightly everted rim from the Crypta Balbi *mithraeum*;[190] the type reaches its maximum diffusion between the 6th and first half of the 7th century.[191] No particularly close comparisons have

[183] Murialdo 2001a, p.261.
[184] *Ibidem*, p.272, Pl.12, no.115.
[185] *Ibidem*, p.276, Pl.14 no.152.
[186] Biffino *et alii* 1998, p.276, no.10.
[187] Fulford-Peacock 1984, p.214, Fig.84, no.72.2.

[188] This type is made from fabric 2.5 of probable Tunisian origin, characteristic of the pottery described as cream sandy ware for the typical carbonatic clays. On the fabric see Fulford-Peacock 1984, p.17.
[189] Murialdo 2001c, p.349, Pl.27, nos36-37.
[190] Saguì-Coletti 2004, p.250, Pl.V, no.25.
[191] A one-handled version comes from the Crypta Balbi *mithraeum* in phases of the late 6th-early 7th century (Saguì-Coletti 2004, p.272, Pl.XX, no.113), specimens similar to ours are also documented in the deposit of the first half of the 6th century in the House of the Vestal Virgins (Filippi *et alii* 2004, p.170, Pl.II, no.13) and in the mid-7th-century context of Via Sant'Alberto Magno-Largo Arrigo VII on the Aventine (Fontana *et alii* 2004, p.552, Pl.III, no.25).

been found for the two-handled narrow-mouthed bottle, although there are some similarities with a specimen from the Lombard necropolis of Castel Trosino; however, the handles are set on the neck and not on the rim.[192] The only base in *acroma depurata* ware has a small disc foot (Pl. XLVIII, no. 8), whilst a further two handles have a different structure to that of the jug with a band-shaped rim: one has a rectangular section and a longitudinal groove on the upper surface (Pl. XLVIII, no. 5), the other has a circular section (Pl. XLVIII, no. 7). *Acroma depurata* ware accounts for the largest number of closed forms for use at table or for storage found at Paduline. This may indicate the beginning of a specialization of the workshops producing this class of pottery; during the central part of the early Middle Ages these mainly manufactured small amphorae, jugs and tankards.

B) INGOBBIATA DI ROSSO WARE

The *ingobbiata di rosso* class also includes some closed forms with handles. One of these, which can be reconstructed in part, is a one-handled bottle or juglet with a pear-shaped body and a disc foot, rounded on the outside. The handle, which has not survived, was set beneath the widest part of the body and the outer surface presents a series of light parallel grooves. The slip, red/orange in colour, is only partially preserved, but it must have covered the whole of the outer surface; the inside of the vessel only presents some drips which do not go beyond the shoulder (Pl. LI, no. 1a-b). Similar forms with a red slip are well documented in some well-deposits of the first half of the 7th century in the Modena area,[193] but also in the urban context of the Crypta Balbi. The latter context has yielded a similar juglet, albeit with a wider body, forming the funeral equipment of a child's tomb in the late 6th-century cemetery in the exedra.[194]

The flanged bowl is also well documented in *ingobbiata di rosso* ware, as we have also seen in late antique rural contexts and the town of Roselle during the 6th century. In the Paduline rubbish dump two versions are attested which differ in morphology and above all in size; this may be due to the fact that they served different purposes at table. The type with a short flange and a vertical rim with a diameter of 17 cm (Pl. LI, no. 3) is very similar to the specimen in Pl. XV, no.2 from context 1260 at Roselle, whose size appears compatible with individual use for the preparation of food. The same cannot be said for the large variant, with a pronounced flange and a barely everted rim measuring 32 cm in diameter (Pl. LI, no. 4). This wide-mouthed version is unique among the types of flanged bowl present in the territory and was likely used for the preparation of dishes for collective consumption, which may have taken place directly from this vessel. In both cases, the fineness of the fabrics and the smoothing of the internal surfaces rule out a use for chopping foods, suggesting that these may instead have been mashed using a pestle.[195]

C) RED PAINTED WARE

At Paduline we note for the first time the appearance of a pottery class characterized by a painted decoration of subhorizontal stripes covering either an external strip immediately beneath the rim or the widest part of the body.

4 specimens belong to this class, representing 2 functional forms: the flanged bowl and the basin. The form deriving from the ARS prototype Hayes 91, as we have seen, represents a typical product of the late antique and early medieval contexts in the study area, and numerous versions are known in *acroma depurata*, *ingobbiata di rosso* and *colature rosse* ware.

The specimen from Paduline, with a thickened and rounded rim measuring 29 cm in diameter and a well-developed horizontal flange (Pl. L, no. 1) may have had the same functions suggested for the large flanged bowl in *ingobbiata di rosso* ware shown in Pl. LI, no. 4, whilst the characteristics of the slip find a close parallel only in the type shown in Pl. XVIII, no. 4, from the fill in the cistern on the south hill at Roselle. There are also some similarities in the distribution of the decoration with a bowl with an almost atrophied flange and a spout found in a late 7th-century context in the Crypta Balbi, an import from the southern or central Tyrrhenian area of Italy.[196]

At least two versions of basin are attested. One has a cylindrical spout and a body which reaches its maximum width immediately beneath the spout (Pl. L, no. 2) or level with it (Pl. L, no. 3). The other version has a slightly everted rim, rounded on the upper surface and pointed on the outside, and a strap handle with a light external groove set on the rim and at the widest point of the body (Pl. L, no. 4). The latter presents impressed dots made before firing on the upper surface of the rim. The painted decoration differs somewhat in these two versions: the basin with the impressed decoration on the rim is also characterized by a fairly narrow painted band beneath the rim, similar to that of the flanged bowl, whilst the two spouted specimens present painted decorations made using a broader brush. In morphological terms, the type with a cylindrical spout generically resembles some 7th- and 8th-century forms from the urban context of Santa Maria della Scala in Siena;[197] however these are decorated with drips and not with stripes. The decorative characteristics of the Paduline basins seem

---

[192] Paroli 1995, pp.317-318.

[193] See well VI at Gorzano, well Rubiera 1, Vr VI at Cognento, in Gelichi-Giordani (eds) 1994, pp.125-132, and especially the specimens in Fig.104, no.2, Fig.112, no.4 and Fig.113, nos3-4.

[194] Ricci-Saguì 2001, p.249, no.I.13.6a.

[195] In general on the uses of flanged bowls see Olcese 1993, p.308.

[196] Ricci 1998, p.378, Fig.16, no.2.

[197] Cantini 2005a, p.191, Pl.53, nos8.41-42.

to suggest that they were made in southern Italy, where painted pottery has a well-established tradition starting from the late antique period and continuing into the early Middle Ages and later centuries without any apparent interruption.[198] Among the most important wares hitherto identified are those of the Calle Tricarico kiln in Basilicata, active between the 4th and 6th centuries,[199] and a number of manufacturing centres in Campania,[200] in particular the early medieval workshop of Capo Miseno, near Naples.[201] The macroscopic and steromicroscopic analysis of the very fine fabrics used to make the red painted wares found at Paduline did not allow for the identification of any mineral phases of help in determining their provenance. However, it remains plausible, in light of the characteristics of the slip, that these were imports from central or southern Italy. If confirmed by future archaeometric research, this may be evidence of the existence of commercial ties with the Byzantine areas in the centre and south of the peninsula during a phase in which the study territory was passing under Lombard control. This theory also appears to be confirmed by the study of the kitchenware, whose forms and fabrics mostly resemble those of Lazio and Campania.

COLATURE ROSSE WARE

This class is documented at Paduline by a minimum number of only 1 individual: an open form, probably a basin or a handled basin. Belonging to this specimen are a base with a small disc foot measuring 13 cm in diameter and strongly flaring walls, decorated on the outside with orange coloured drips (Pl. L, no. 5), and a strap handle with a profile concave on the upper surface (Pl. L, no. 6).

KITCHENWARE

In total, kitchenware is represented by a minimum number of at least 10 forms; on the basis of their fabrics these can be ascribed to two different areas of provenance: one local or sub-regional and one identifiable with the central and southern Tyrrhenian.

Belonging to the sub-regional group are 2 cooking pots and a generic closed form made using a fabric similar to AG 109 from Scoglietto. The first type of cooking pot presents a strongly everted rim, rounded on the upper surface and shaped inside, with a diameter of 22 cm (Pl. LII, no. 2); it is identical to Type V from Roselle attested in contexts of the first half of the 6th century (context 1262) and of the second half of the 6th-early 7th century (context 1260).

A second type, not attested in other contexts in the territory, is characterized by a slightly everted and almost vertical rim, thickened and rounded on the upper surface and shaped on the inside (Pl. LII, no. 1). The body is globular. This typology presents close morphological analogies with productions documented at Lucca in the early medieval context of Galli-Tassi.[202]

The group of possible imports from the central-southern Tyrrhenian area consists of pottery whose fabrics are rich in mica and fragments of probably volcanic rock, similar to those of the "micaceous" group from Scoglietto. The body structures also present some similarities with the pottery from Scoglietto, and above all with local pottery from Lazio. Among the most well-documented forms is the type of cooking pot with a rim of rectangular section, barely concave on the upper surface (Pl. LII, no. 3). The small tankard presenting obvious traces of fumigation was destined for use both for cooking and at table. It has a rounded and thickened rim with a diameter of 9 cm and a strap handle set immediately beneath the rim. The body is ovoid and the base has a ring foot with a central *omphalos* (Pl. XLVIII, no. 1). The specimen appears comparable with productions for domestic and kitchen use attested in the *vicus* with late antique and early medieval phases at Madonna del Passo in the Sabina.[203] A casserole and a pan attested at Paduline with a single specimen each belong to productions well documented in Rome. The casserole has a flat rim, oblique on the outside, with a diameter of 24 cm and a globular body (Pl. LII, no. 4). This form is comparable to forms from contexts of the second half of the 6th century in the Crypta Balbi *mithraeum*[204] and with wares of the first half of the 6th and late 6th-early 7th centuries from the *Basilica Hilariana* on the Caelian.[205] An identical specimen, made in Lazio, is attested at *Portus* in the 7th century.[206] The hemispherical pan with a thickened and rounded rim, presenting obvious wheel marks on the inside, also finds numerous points of comparison in Roman contexts of the 6th and 7th centuries (Pl. LII, no. 5). This type is fairly common in the Crypta Balbi in phases of the second half of the 6th and late 6th-early 7th centuries,[207] in the *mithraeum* and adjacent areas, and in the late 7th-century deposit in the exedra.[208]

Final Remarks on the Paduline Context

Calibration of the chronologies of the pottery found in the rubbish dump makes it possible to ascribe the formation of the deposit to the period between the mid-6th and the early decades of the 7th century. During this phase, some significant transformations took place in

[198] On this aspect see Romei 2004, pp.286-287.
[199] Di Giuseppe 1998, pp.735-752.
[200] Arthur-Patterson 1994, pp.412-423.
[201] De Rossi 2004, pp.253-264.

[202] Ciampoltrini 2004, p.155, Fig.6, no.5.
[203] Patterson-Roberts 1998, p.431, Fig.8, no.4.
[204] Saguì-Coletti 2004, p.266, Pl.XV, no.83.
[205] Pacetti 2004, p.448, Pl.VI, nos43-44 and p.456, Pl.XI, no.83.
[206] Ciarrocchi *et alii* 1998, p.405, Fig.8, no.6.
[207] Saguì-Coletti 2004, p.266, Pl.XV, no.81, and p.275, Pl.XXIII, no.137 (the latter has a slighter broader rim than ours).
[208] Ricci 1998, p.353, Fig.1, no.9.

both settlement and economic patterns in this area. The material culture from Paduline still presents a fairly varied range of goods; however, the absence of Tunisian fineware is highly significant. The gradual decrease of ARS in the second half of the 6th century, before supply was definitively interrupted in the 580s and 590s, has been clearly documented by the distributional analysis of this class in urban and rural areas, through the analysis of individual weighted means. In this respect, context 1260 in Roselle presents some close analogies with Paduline. A further point of contact between these two deposits is the continuing attestation of transport containers: Tunisian and eastern Mediterranean at Paduline, Tunisian, eastern Mediterranean and Italic in context 1260 excavated on the north slopes at Roselle. However, there are some fairly substantial differences in the assemblages of Italic tableware and kitchenware and in the presence of coarseware used for storage imported from the Mediterranean. At Roselle, the assemblages of tableware and kitchenware of the second half of the 6th century are dominated by local and regional productions, whilst forms ascribable to imports from outside the region and from overseas are absent. At Paduline, by contrast, the attestation of *dipinta di rosso* ware is in all likelihood related to imports from central and southern Italy; the same may also be true of some forms in *acroma depurata*, such as the small two-handled amphora and the jug with a band-shaped rim. Given their form and fabrics, some pieces of kitchenware may also be ascribed to productions active in the Rome area. Also worth noting is the presence of a small *spathion*, possibly imported from Tunisia, which may have arrived alongside the transport containers from the same region of origin, including a specimen of Keay LXII. It is thus obvious that some of the evidence agrees in suggesting that the Paduline context was more closely integrated into Tyrrhenian maritime trade than Roselle.

This connection may in part be explained by the fact that the Paduline-Serrata Martini site acted as an intermediate harbour, and also had a closer relationship with Rome at the turn of the 6th century. Furthermore, the mention of a *curtis Piscariae*, which can be identified with Castiglione della Pescaia, among the Papal landholdings in Rosellan territory in the early decades of the 8th century[209] is indisputable evidence that the Catholic Church purchased lands in the Maremma at some point before this; these properties included the complex of Serrata Martini-Paduline. It is fairly likely that the Papacy no longer had free use of these landholdings and their rents after the Roselle area fell into the hands of the Lombards, when the new property interests of Lucca and Chiusi combined to create a complex mosaic of ownership. However, it does seem plausible, in accordance with the theory advanced by Kurze, that the Papacy regained control of its properties in the territories of Lucca, Pisa, Volterra and Roselle during the reign of Aripert II, when the church of Rome was once again able to exploit its properties in the Cottian Alps. This is the first contact between Rome and the Lombards attested in the *Liber Pontificalis* after a century of silence.[210] Between 720 and 730, the combination of Liutprando's expansionist policies and the iconoclastic crisis between the Eastern Empire and the Papacy created conditions favourable to the Church of Rome's adoption of a leadership role in the political events of the peninsula, to the detriment of the Exarchate and thus of Byzantine interference.[211] One important point remains to be clarified: by what process did the Papacy acquire the properties in question?

For the *curtis Piscariae* we can advance an hypothesis based on archaeological evidence. A series of clues seem to agree in suggesting that the settlement complex of Paduline-Serrata Martini originally formed part of the large imperial landholdings along the Tyrrhenian coast. On the one hand the monumental nature of the context and the high formal quality of its decorative programme, known from the detailed reports of the late 19th-century excavations and the few remains brought to light by excavations in the 1970s and 80s, do not in themselves form sufficient evidence to resolve this issue. However, other hitherto neglected clues may help to support this theory. A first direct link with Rome is indicated by the presence of stamped bricks in the walls of the *praefurnium* from the *Domitianae Minores* and *Tonneianae Viccinae* workshops in the city, datable to between the late 1st century AD and the first half of the 2nd century.[212] Secondly, we should mention the ceremonial marble bust of the Emperor Hadrian (AD 76-138) found during the 19th-century excavations at Serrata Martini. The baths excavated by Ademollo must have been private and not public given that the bust of Hadrian did not have the canonical properties of an image destined for the public veneration of the emperor but rather those typical of a private cult.[213] This type of self-promotion was perfectly in keeping with a villa belonging to the imperial landholdings. Indeed, it is precisely in this period that we see a significant increase in the number of private properties owned by the emperor; in many cases these include the maritime

[209] The reference to the *curtis Piscariae* can be found in the collection of Church rents compiled by Cardinal Deusdedit in around the late 11th century. For the document see Von Glanvell Von Glanvell 1905, Lib.III, cap.191, pp.353-355.

[210] Kurze opts for a date in the early decades of the 7th century of the various Pauscia rented out and belonging to section 191 of Book III of Deusdedit's compilation. Through a detailed analysis which also makes use of numismatic history, the German scholar identifies the Popes John and Gregory mentioned in the document as John VII and Gregory III. King Aripert II's return of a series of lands in the territories of Lucca, Pisa, Volterra and Roselle is thus dated Papacy, must have continued under Gregory III (734-736), at a time when the taxes from Tuscia must have become more important given the impossibility of the Pope of using the lands in Calabria and Sicily, confiscated by the Emperor Leo III the Isaurian in around 733 after the iconoclast crisis. For this theory see Kurze 2002b, pp.397-414.

[211] Marazzi 1998, p.110.

[212] Cygielman 1982, p.368.

[213] Curri, unpublished work, p.72.

villas placed at strategic points along the coastal belt, sometimes near the Via Aurelia, at others near other roads able to ensure rapid and safe connections with major transport networks.[214] A further clue which I believe may confirm the hypothesis that part or all of the complex of Paduline-Serrata Martini formed part of the emperor's landholdings, at least between the 1st and 3rd centuries AD, is epigraphical in nature. The 19th-century excavations at Serrata Martini also brought to light a marble funerary inscription. This was dated on palaeographic grounds to between the late 2nd and early 3rd century AD[215] and consists of a funerary dedication by an *Agapomenus*, who describes himself as *augusti nostri verna*, to his deceased wife *Aurelia Felicitas*. The man's social status as an imperial servant represents further support for the theory that Paduline-Serrata Martini was an imperial property.

At this point it remains to be clarified when the imperial lands at Castiglione della Pescaia came to form part of the *patrimonium sancti Petri*. Although no direct information is available, we can deduce the political circumstances most favourable to this property transfer on logical grounds. The most favourable conditions were without doubt during the Constantinian period and in particular after the Edict of Milan in 313. At this time, Constantine undertook a series of actions in support of the Church, including large donations which significantly enlarged its properties. However, it cannot be ruled out that the donation may have been later in date, although the *terminus ante quem* remains that of the Greek-Gothic war.[216] In light of this reconstruction hypothesis, we may be able to better contextualize the pottery context of the late 6th-early 7th centuries from Paduline and the relations which these materials appear to suggest with the Rome-Lazio area. It is worth noting that from the Papacy of Gregory the Great onwards, the Church of Rome took over the role of the state in the control and organization of the taxation system. Though the public distribution of foodstuffs was abolished definitively in the first quarter of the 7th century, a direct link with the Papacy might nonetheless have ensured privileged access to otherwise inaccessible goods imported from outside the region and from the Mediterranean.

In conclusion, it seems likely that the complexity of the pottery assemblage found in the Paduline rubbish dump may be due at least in part to the fact that the site fell into the sphere of the Papacy's property interests and that the Church may have played an important role in organizing the commercial redistribution of goods for mass consumption towards its outlying landholdings.[217]

[214] Celuzza 2002b, p.204.
[215] Unpublished inscription in the Museo Archeologico e di Arte Sacra di Grosseto. A preliminary descriptive note for the display of this artefact in the museum has been compiled by Stefano Conti.
[216] This position is also expressed in Citter 2005 (ed.), p.77.
[217] On the role of the Church in managing the *annona* see Marazzi 1993, pp.269-270.

5.6. Reflections on the Circulation of Mediterranean Goods Between the Late Fifth and Mid-Sixth Century and on The Potential Use of Pottery as a Socio-Economic and Cultural Marker

Between the late 5th and mid-6th century we see a gradual decrease in the number of rural settlements in with access to North African fineware, which nonetheless continued to circulate in significant quantities.[218] This decline is mirrored by an exponential increase in regional tableware which, especially at medium-small-sized contexts, represented the most accessible source of supply and in the majority of cases the only type documented. African red slip ware datable to between the mid-5th and 6th centuries is attested in about 46% of the sites still inhabited, whereas during the period between the 4th-mid-5th century as many as 27 out of 32 sites (about 84%) yielded specimens. Even more interesting is the move towards local autonomy in food supply: only 12 sites, as compared to 20 between the 4th and mid-5th century, now avail themselves of imported goods, mainly from Tunisia and occasionally from the eastern Mediterranean.

As is known, the pottery yielded by surveys poses significant problems of quantification: in many of the long-lasting sites analysed here the total minimum number of forms belonging to the period between the 5th and 6th centuries is only 10 or just over. The impossibility of assessing the degree to which surface pottery assemblages, as opposed to buried deposits, are actually representative raises methodological issues which must be taken into consideration when comparing different contexts. Nonetheless, this does not mean that it is impossible to identify broad trends when, in cases such as this, the territorial sample analysed is fairly large. The data appears to indicate that between the mid-5th and mid-6th centuries Tunisian fineware and imported transport containers were distributed almost exclusively in larger contexts, such as long-lived villas, villages and cave settlements. Defunctionalized villas, farmsteads and late reoccupations of previously abandoned sites, by contrast, only very rarely yield these types of materials. If we compare the position in the territory of the settlement contexts with African red slip ware of the second half of the 5th-6th centuries and contemporary transport containers, with the sites that prevalently depended on local and sub-regional trade circuits, it is impossible to identify differences depending on the greater or lesser proximity to the coast, to harbour structures or road networks. Essentially, the feature which makes a difference does not seem to be the distance from maritime or overland infrastructure and thus a more rapid access to goods imported from overseas. As such, it seems likely that the interpretative key may lie in the differing economic resources

[218] Between the late 5th and the first two/three decades of the 6th century the sample area shows a slight recovery in the total quantities of ARS circulating.

available and essential to ensure a minimum supply of those Mediterranean products which during the 6th century continued to be sold along the coast of *Tuscia*.[219]

ARS and commercial amphorae may have been goods of low-medium prestige during the early decades of the 6th century, still being fairly readily available and widespread, especially in coastal areas. However, it is fairly certain that compared to the period before the Vandal conquest of North Africa, when the fiscal system linked to the supply of taxes in kind had created a system of linked industries which also encouraged free trade, the marginal costs of moving these goods must have increased. Goods destined for mass consumption thus became rarer and more prized.[220]

One working hypothesis might thus be to see these indicators as "weak signs"[221] of the existence of a social hierarchy in the southern Tuscan countryside, where an albeit lower level of demand from the elites still allowed for the influx of Mediterranean goods.[222] From a cultural point of view, the potential for consuming meals on Tunisian fineware and availing oneself of imported foodstuffs may have been a way of making direct reference to the cultural values of a Roman and Mediterranean tradition. It is an objective fact that, between the late 5th and 6th centuries, the diocesan territories of Roselle and Sovana were fairly marginal in socio-economic terms. In this context, the supply of imported fineware and foodstuffs still reaching major settlements, albeit in smaller quantities, may not have been simply a sign of the continuity of the distribution network for these products. Above all it may represent an indication of the presence of weak elites still active in the study area, which expressed their socio-cultural status in part through the consumption of overseas goods.

Appendix A. African Red Slip ware from the countryside (data used for the Individual Weighted Means analysis).

FORM	TYPE	PRODUCTION	MNI
BOWL	HAYES 9A	A	7
BOWL	HAYES 9B	A	4
BOWL	HAYES 14A	A	18
BOWL	HAYES 14B	A	7
BOWL	HAYES 10A, n.3	A	1
BOWL	HAYES 16, n.16	A	1
BOWL	HAYES 17B	A	2
DISH	HAYES 6A	A	1
BOWL	HAYES 6C	A	1
BOWL	HAYES 8A	A	21
BOWL	HAYES 8B	A	2
DISH	HAYES 33	A	1
BOWL	HAYES 31, nn.1, 4	A/D	2
BOWL	SALOMONSON A25	A/D	3
DISH	HAYES 50A	C	9
DISH	HAYES 49	C	2
BOWL	ATLANTE I, TAV. XXVIII, 7	C	1
BOWL	HAYES 57	C	1

[219] Indicative of the intensity of flows of overseas goods along the Tuscan coast are the data from the excavation of the *horrea* of Vada Volterrana: see Pasquinucci *et alii* 1998 and Pasquinucci et alii 1999; similar results are emerging from the study of late antique materials from the harbour dump of *Portus Scabris* at Portiglioni (Chapter 6).
[220] On this see Zanini 1996 and Wickham 2005, pp.708-713.
[221] Recently Zanini has proposed a threeway subdivision of indicators of power into markers of "explicit self-representation" (monumental iconography, donations) and "implicit self-representation" (private houses and personal clothing), to which we should add "weak signs", for difficult to read and interpret, of which pottery is the main component. See Zanini 2007, especially pp.29-42. This analysis has been applied to Byzantine areas in Italy during the 6th-8th centuries but provides interestinfig food for thought for the phase immediately preceding the Greek-Gothic war as well.
[222] On the role of demand expressed by the elites in activating long-range commercial trade see Wickham 2005, pp.707-708 and pp.718-720; and Valenti 2007, p.211, especially note 26.

BOWL	HAYES 75	C	1
BOWL	HAYES 84	C	3
LARGE BOWL	HAYES 58B	D	1
LARGE BOWL/DISH	HAYES 59	D	2
DISH	HAYES 60	D	2
LARGE BOWL/DISH	HAYES 61A	D	5
LARGE BOWL/DISH	HAYES 61B	D	16
DISH	HAYES 63	D	2
LARGE BOWL	GENERIC HAYES 67	D	5
LARGE BOWL	HAYES 67 (ATLANTE I, Tav.XXXVIII, 2)	D	1
LARGE BOWL	HAYES 67, nos.5-6, 17	D	10
LARGE BOWL	HAYES 76	D	5
BOWL	HAYES 80	D	2
BOWL	HAYES 80B/99	D	1
BOWL	HAYES 87	D	1
FLANGED BOWL	HAYES 91A	D	3
FLANGED BOWL	HAYES 91B	D	6
FLANGED BOWL	HAYES 91C	D	3
LARGE BOWL	HAYES 93	D	1
BOWL	HAYES 94	D	3
LARGE DISH	HAYES 56 (?)	D	1
BOWL	HAYES 99A	D	7
BOWL	HAYES 99B	D	4
LARGE DISH	HAYES 104A	D	3
LARGE DISH	HAYES 104B	D	1
SMALL BOWL	HAYES 12/110	D	1
GENERIC OPEN VESSEL	STAMP ATLANTE I, TAV. LVI (a), n.23	D	1
GENERIC OPEN VESSEL	STAMP ATLANTE I, TAV. LVI (a), n.23	D	1
GENERIC OPEN VESSEL	STAMP ATLANTE I, TAV. LVIII(b), nn.35-37	D	1
GENERIC OPEN VESSEL	STAMP ATLANTE I, TAV. LVI (a), n.42	D	1
GENERIC OPEN VESSEL	STAMP ATLANTE I, TAV. LVII (b), n. 50	D	1

Appendix B. African Red Slip ware from the villa site at Aiali

FORM	TYPE	PRODUCTION	MNI
BOWL	HAYES 2	A	3
BOWL	HAYES 9A	A	17
BOWL	HAYES 9B	A	4
LARGE BOWL	HAYES 10	A	1
BOWL	HAYES 14A	A	29
BOWL	HAYES 14B	A	7
BOWL	HAYES 14C	A	13
BOWL	Generic Hayes 14	A	22
BOWL	HAYES 14/17	A	1
DISH	HAYES 26	A	7
DISH	HAYES 27	A	6
BOWL	HAYES 16	A	6
BOWL	HAYES 17A	A	3
DISH	HAYES 3B	A	2
DISH	HAYES 3C	A	10
BOWL	Generic Hayes 6	A	2
BOWL	HAYES 6A	A	2
BOWL	HAYES 6B	A	4
BOWL	HAYES 7A	A	2
BOWL	HAYES 7B	A	2
BOWL	HAYES 8A	A	21
BOWL	HAYES 8B	A	9
DISH	HAYES 34	A	1
DISH	HAYES 32	A/D	1
DISH	HAYES 31, nn.1, 4	A/D	2
DISH	HAYES 50A	C	15
LARGE BOWL/DISH	HAYES 45	C	3
LARGE BOWL/DISH	HAYES 58B, n.11	D	1
LARGE BOWL/DISH	HAYES 59	D	2
LARGE BOWL/DISH	HAYES 61	D	1
LARGE BOWL	HAYES 65	D	1
LARGE BOWL	HAYES 67	D	4
BOWL	BARADEZ 1961, Tav. II, n.7/ATLANITE I, Tav. L, 6-7	D	1
FLANGED BOWL	HAYES 91A/B	D	4
LARGE DISH	ATLANTE I, Tav.XLVI, n.7	D	1
BOWL	Generic HAYES 99A	D	1
GENERIC OPEN VESSEL	STAMP ATLANTE I, TAV. LVI (a), n. 21.	D	2
GENERIC OPEN VESSEL	STAMPS ATLANTE I, TAV.LVI (a),n.33 AND TAV LVII(b), n.54	D	1

6. *Portus Scabris*-Portiglioni: Analysis of Maritime Trade and the Redistribution of Goods to Rural Areas Between Late Antiquity and the Middle Ages

According to a consolidated scholarly tradition,[1] the site of *Portus Scabris*, described in the *Itinerarium Maritimum* as being located between the *Alma positio* to the south and the *Falesiae portus* to the north, can be identified with the place known as Portiglione or Portiglioni, west of the Puntone di Scarlino (Fig.1).

The presence of a substantial archaeological deposit, recently identified a few metres from the coast, is clear evidence that the harbour was exploited more or less intensively from the late 3rd century BC until the modern period.

Work to construct the new Puntone di Scarlino marina began in 2000; from the summer of 2000 until the end of 2001 the heritage authorities monitored the construction work and undertook preventive research on the seabed affected by the dredging operations needed to reach the depth required by the new marina facilities.[2]

6.1. The Construction of the Puntone di Scarlino Marina and Research to Understand and Safeguard Its Archaeological Heritage

During the design phase,[3] the harbour basin was subdivided into a virtual grid with grid squares measuring 100x100 m, each of which was identified by a letter of the alphabet. Grid squares A to I, M to P and S to U were dredged to lower the level of the seabed (Fig.2). Archaeological deposits were found in only some of these.

Piles (iron tubes with electrical resistance) were driven into the seabed around the internal perimeter of the harbour basin; the quay was subsequently built on top of these. The sinking of the piles entailed digging to a depth of between 12 and 30 m, followed by the removal of the material inside using an impact drill. Here, archaeological research entailed monitoring the removal of earth from the interior of each tube to a depth of 1.5 m and the study of the debris from the tubes. At the same time, a preliminary underwater survey of the areas at greatest risk was undertaken by the local heritage authority's Underwater Unit.

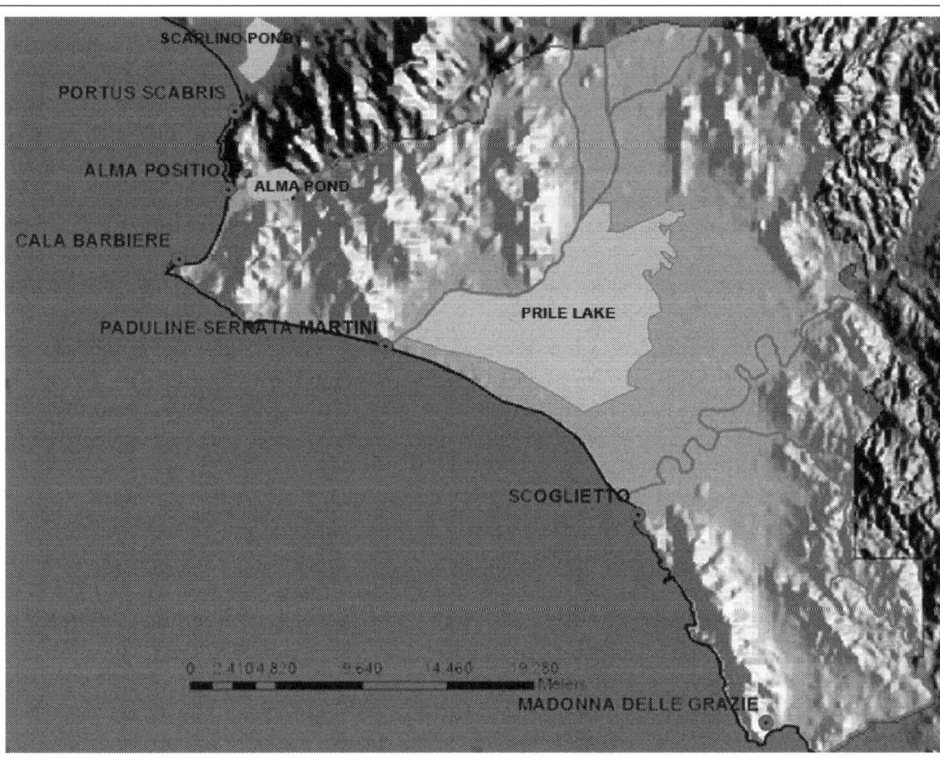

Fig.1_ Portus Scabris and the system of Roman sea-ports and landing places between the Osa and Pecora valleys.

[1] For the identification of the site see Cristofani 1983, p.34; Gambogi 2003, p.27; Pasquinucci 2004, p.79; Camilli-Gambogi 2004.

[2] The archaeological rescue operations at *Portus Scabris* were carried out by the Soprintendenza per i Beni Archeologici della Toscana and directed by Biancamaria Aranguren and Pamela Gambogi. For a preliminary report on the archaeological research see Gambogi 2003, pp.25-29.

[3] I would like to thank Samata Castelli for allowing me to use the final report produced by the Cooperativa Archeologia di Firenze, essential for the exact location of the finds and a better understanding of the archaeological context.

This phase of the project was of enormous importance for the evaluation of the overall archaeological potential of the harbour basin.

At a later stage, the seabed was dredged to remove an average 50 cm of material. Along the docks this depth reached up to 3.5/4 m, essential in order to construct the embankments. Archaeological research included the systematic study of the deposit removed, which was heaped into 9 strips. In two cases, the strips located east of no. VII, the materials were removed as these strips served exclusively to store the sand removed by dredging. In the other seven cases (strips I to VII), it was necessary to record the exact position and provenance of the sand in order to ensure the more accurate positioning of the archaeological materials recovered.

Following these emergency archaeological operations, dredging was forbidden exclusively in two zones in front of the landward dock. These were: a strip of seabed between piles 17 and 27, stretching for 60 m inside the harbour basin; and another between piles 27 and 30, stretching to a distance of 40 m from the landward dock.

Digging operations to sink the piles and lower the seabed revealed the enormous importance of the archaeological deposit in some grid squares. *Grid square A* was particularly rich in finds, with a major concentration in the area in front of piles 27-29, as was the intersection of *grid squares G-B-F* and the vicinity of piles 26 and 27. The further lowering of the seabed to a depth of 3.5 m for the construction of the landward dock led to the recovery, in the vicinity of piles 25/27, of numerous transport containers, identified as Empoli amphorae.

Inside *grid square B* the highest density of finds was yielded by the area between *strips III* and *IV*, although significant finds were also made in the area between *strips V* and *VI* and in the area affected by digging operations for the landward dock embankment. In *grid square C*, too, the contexts of greatest interest were uncovered when the seabed was lowered to construct the embankment. Along this strip the most significant archaeological deposit was found at a depth of 3.5/4 m.

Grid square E brought to light some interesting pottery contexts dating to between the late Republican period and the modern period in the vicinity of piles 12-15 and 18-19, and between *strips I* and *II*. Other finds dating to between the Roman period and the Middle Ages were recovered west of the *Sales strip* between *strip I* and the landward and breakwater docks.

Also of special importance were the archaeological finds from *grid square F*, systematically uncovered in the areas between *strips I* and *II* and *II-III*, to the extent that work was stopped up to a distance of 60 m from the landward dock. The highest concentration of archaeological finds came from the area between piles 24 and 26 and an area 20 m north-east of the dock.

Grid square G also contained a significant concentration of archaeological deposits between *strips II-III* and *III-IV*.

In *grid square M*, by contrast, the finds came principally from the strip in front of the landward dock,

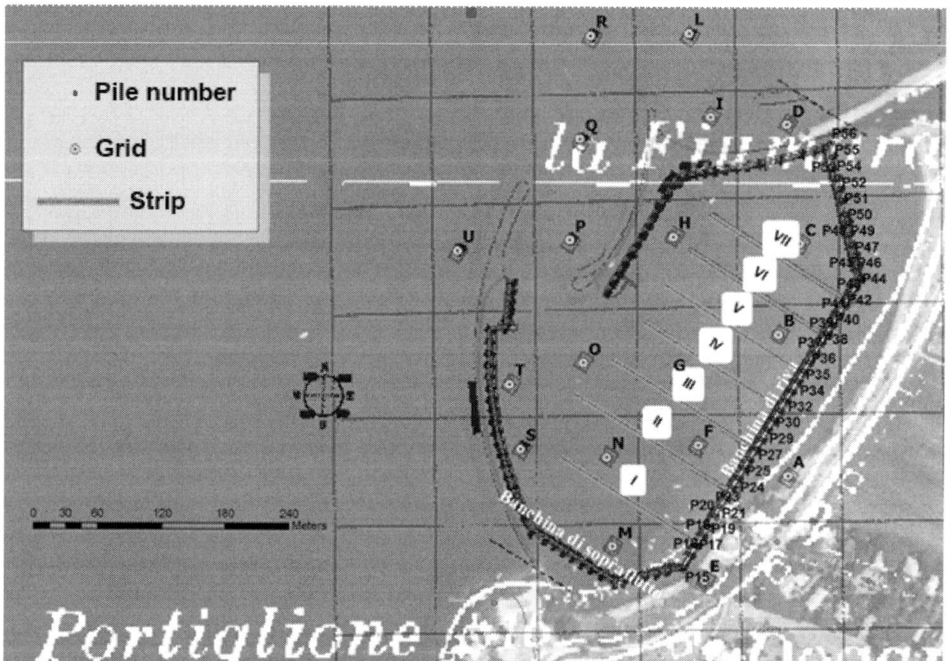

Fig.2_ Plan of the Puntone marina: grids, strips and piles.

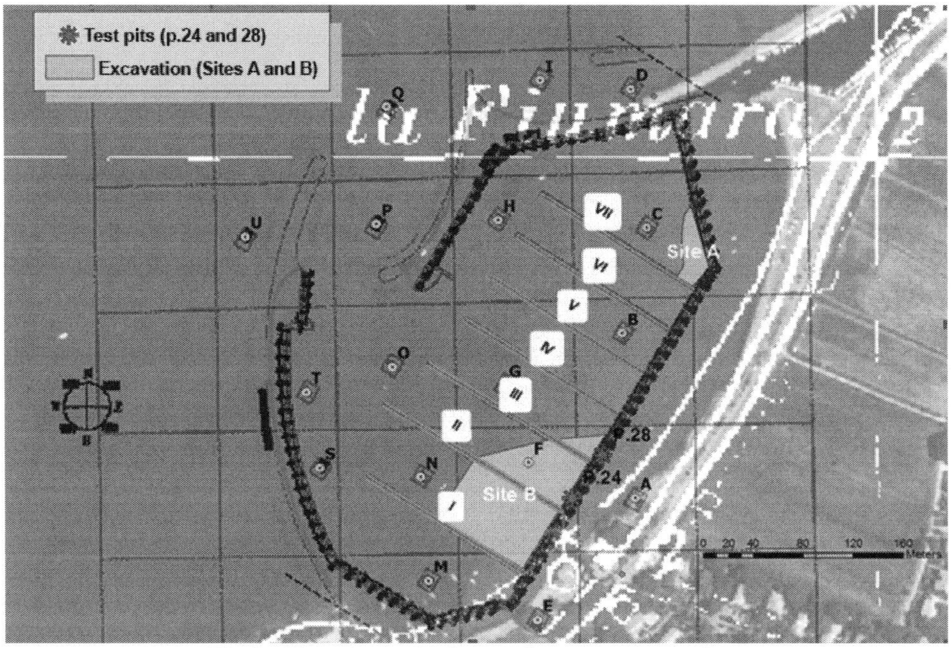

Fig.3_ Test pits and other underwater excavations.

and covered a broad time span between the late Republic and the modern period. Numerous pottery fragments, dating mainly to between the late Republic and the early Empire, were uncovered by dredging for *strip I* inside *grid square N. Grid squares S* and *T* yielded materials covering the long period between the late Republic and the modern period, with a higher concentration in the latter than in the former.

Investigations in *grid squares D, H-I, O-Q*, and *U*, on the other hand, brought to light few or no archaeological materials of significance.

Following this preliminary research and the underwater surveys, some exploratory excavations were carried out in the contexts which seemed most promising. Excavations thus concentrated on four different areas in front of the landward dock, mainly between *strips I* and *III*. In the south-east portion of the harbour basin lie "site B" and test-pits P-28 and P-24, in the vicinity of the *piles* of the same name, whilst "site A" lies further north.[4] Whereas the excavation of "site A" failed to contribute significantly to our understanding of ancient port activities in the Portiglioni bay,[5] the data collected from the other contexts studied are of considerable interest (Fig.3).

Overall, the stratigraphic excavations allow us to date the harbour's initial period of use to the end of the 3rd century BC and to identify a significant intensification in port activities during the late Republican period. The larger size of the late Republican archaeological deposit compared to that of the early imperial period suggests a slight decrease in the quantities of goods passing through between the 1st and 2nd centuries AD, although the port continued to be used.

The information collected on the volume of trade passing through *Portus Scabris* during the late imperial period is less accurate. The presence of Keay XXVI *spatheia* and Tunisian Africana II amphorae in the contaminated layers of test pits P-24 and P-28 tell us that the port was used continuously at least until the 4th-5th century. However, they do not allow us to determine if trade was episodic or systematic during this period.

Of particular importance for determining the material structure of the harbour is the fact that no concrete structures were found, neither during digging with grab dredgers nor during the underwater stratigraphic excavations. However, it is worth noting that the early imperial phase of test-pit P-24 and the late Republican phase of "site B" yielded wooden poles which were probably used to moor ships.[6] This might be evidence that the bay of *Portus Scabris*, naturally well-protected from winds from the third and fourth quadrants, was an anchor point equipped only with infrastructure in perishable materials, sufficient to dock ships sailing coast to coast. In this context, it is important to distinguish between true ports, equipped with concrete structures such as piers, wharves and breakwaters, and simple harbours which only had modest facilities generally made of perishable materials.[7] The site of *Portus Scabris* seems to fall clearly into the latter category, although it differs from other harbours on Italy's Tyrrhenian coast[8] for the unusual vigour of the

4 See Bargagliotti-Cibecchini 2003, pp.43-59.
5 *Ibidem*, p.45.

6 *Ibidem*, pp.50-53.
7 Camilli-Gambogi 2004, with bibliography.
8 For an analytical description of the Roman and late antique sea-ports and harbours along the Tuscan coast see Camilli-Gambogi 2004 and Pasquinucci 2004.

trade taking place here and for its long period of use. Also of importance is the positioning of the harbour, which seems to have remained unaltered over the long term (Figs 4-5).

Fig.4_ Portiglioni before the construction of the marina (Orthophoto year 1996).

Fig.5_ Portiglioni during the construction of the marina (Orthophoto year 2002).

On the basis of the excavation data and the distribution of the materials recovered during the construction of the marina, we can see a significant concentration of finds in the area between *strips I* and *III*, in *grid squares A* and *G-F*; the most intensive and continuous port activities seem to have taken place here. The location of the port took advantage of the natural shelter provided by the outline of the coast. It is highly likely that the port of *Portus Scabris* was also the only access route to the inland saltwater lagoon, known up to the 19th century as the Stagno di Scarlino (Scarlino lake) and which has now shrunk to a small marsh covering an area of about 3 km^2. Environmental conditions on this stretch of coast appear suitable for the installation of docks for two reasons. First, because the geomorphology of the coastline ensured that the bay was naturally sheltered from winds and currents. Second, the presence of the mouth of the river Pecora leading from the Stagno di Scarlino about a km to the north represented a further attraction as it allowed boats to penetrate further inland. Environments characterized by inland lagoons, separated from the sea by the rapid flow of sediments along the shore and not subsequently silted up by debris from rivers historically represent the contexts most frequently used for port activities along the Tuscan coast.[9]

6.2. The Study of Late Antique and Early Medieval Pottery: New Data on Commercial Trade Between the Fourth and Eighth Centuries

The study which follows covers all the late antique and early medieval pottery contexts extrapolated from the large quantities of material collected during archaeological research accompanying digging work for the construction of the marina. The lack of a systematic inventory of the materials made it necessary to undertake exhaustive research in the storage facilities where these materials had been placed after work was completed. Since the aim of this study is to determine the extent to which this port site formed an integral part of maritime trade routes, and its capacity to redistribute Mediterranean products to markets inland, all the pottery classes potentially able to answer our starting questions were sampled.

Our analysis thus concentrates on transport containers, on fineware and on the coarseware which, on the basis of forms and fabrics, could be immediately attributed to overseas productions. The time span covered by the study runs from the 4th to the 8th century, the period to which the majority of the materials described belong. To this main group we should also add some coarseware from the Pisa area and two amphorae belonging to the period between the $10^{th}/11^{th}$ and the 13th century; these represent the first archaeological indicators that the port was in use after over two centuries of silence from the material sources. Naturally, as will become apparent, not all the material examined was destined for trade; some of it probably formed part of the onboard equipment used by the crews who visited the harbour. The harbour of *Portus Scabris* is thus enlightening and rich in new and unexpected insights into the trade in foodstuffs and other goods which, to a greater or lesser extent, touched on the coasts of the study area between late Antiquity and the Middle Ages. One methodological problem encountered was linked to the informative potential of the pottery contexts given the way in which these were recovered. The materials analysed here do not come from the limited underwater stratigraphic excavations but were brought to the surface by digging work using grab dredgers in various parts of the harbour basin. As such, although the original underwater location of the materials is known, we have no information on the stratigraphic contexts from which they come. On the one hand this means that these materials do allow for a detailed study of their means and periods of circulation, since we are dealing with classes that are well known thanks to a consolidated scholarly tradition. On the other hand,

9 On the relations between the geomorphology of the Tuscan shore and their potential to provide safe harbours see Pasquinucci-Pranzini-Silenzi 2004, pp.92-98.

however, they do not provide us with new chronological or typological data, or information on the associations between different productions. As a consequence, for example, we are unable to determine if the containers used to transport oil and Tunisian fish sauces circulated alongside eastern Mediterranean wine vessels or if these belonged to different cargoes and different ships. It is equally difficult to study the associations between different types of African red slip ware since we have clear evidence that types whose chronologies do not overlap were discovered in the same area. This material must therefore be analysed in the same way as a multi-period surface context, which may provide valuable information on the chronology of its use and on its economic systems but which is of little use for an accurate analysis of the chronology of individual types; it therefore does not allow us to refine the chronological framework available for the typologies analysed or to determine with greater accuracy the time at which they reached the context.

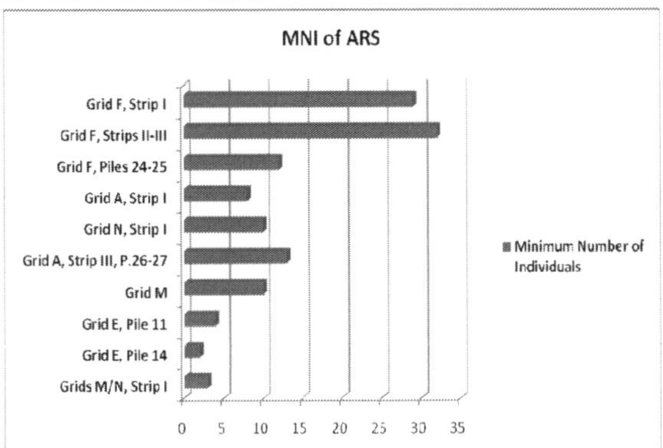

Graph I_ Distribution of ARS in the underwater deposits.

6.2.1. *African Red Slip Ware Between the Fourth and Seventh Centuries AD*

As we have seen clearly for the town of Roselle and its territory, for the port of *Portus Scabris* dealing with the distribution of late antique red slip wares also means dealing exclusively with ARS.

The analysis of this class concentrates on types which can be ascribed to the period between the 4th and 7th centuries. As a consequence, we systematically studied all of production D and those production C forms which, though they came into use earlier, continued to be produced for part of the time period under consideration here. In total, we identified a minimum of at least 128 individuals which can be ascribed to the period in question. Of these, as many as 120 specimens belonged to production D whereas only 8 can be ascribed to the later forms made by the central Tunisian workshops specializing in production C. The study of African red slip ware involved two different levels of analysis. The first aim was to identify accurately the contexts of provenance of each individual specimen. Secondly, we attempted to interpret diachronic trends in the distribution of ARS during the period between the early 5th and 7th centuries, with the aim of identifying any affinities and divergences with our findings for the study area as a whole.

The study of the distribution of this class within the harbour basin was aimed principally at understanding any alterations in the location of the port during the late antique period (Graph I and Fig.6). This approach allowed me to rule out any change in the location of the port between the 4th and 7th centuries since, at least as far as ARS is concerned, later forms were found in the same areas as earlier ones, indicating that the same waters were frequented continuously.

Essentially, the data on the distribution of African red slip ware confirms that emerging from underwater stratigraphic excavations and indicating a higher density of port activities in the area immediately north of the Portiglioni promontory. This allows us to estimate that the portion of the bay which was exploited intensively for port activities covered approximately 22,000 m^2.

Some significant data comes from the diachronic analysis of African red slip wares from the early 5th century. The large quantities of material which can be dated to after this period makes it possible to undertake a fruitful analysis of the volume of trade passing through the port during the late antique period and to suggest some thought-provoking comparisons with the similar quantitative analyses undertaken in inland contexts.

Ports like *Portus Scabris* are ideal contexts for the application of quantitative evaluation methods to determine the volume of goods imported from elsewhere in the Mediterranean circulating along Tyrrhenian coastal routes. As we will see, the port is not just a place where these products were commercially redistributed to surrounding areas but may also have been used simply as a temporary mooring place for boats in difficulty, whose cargoes were destined for other ports. Under such circumstances, the removal from the hull of materials

Fig.6_ Map of ARS distribution.

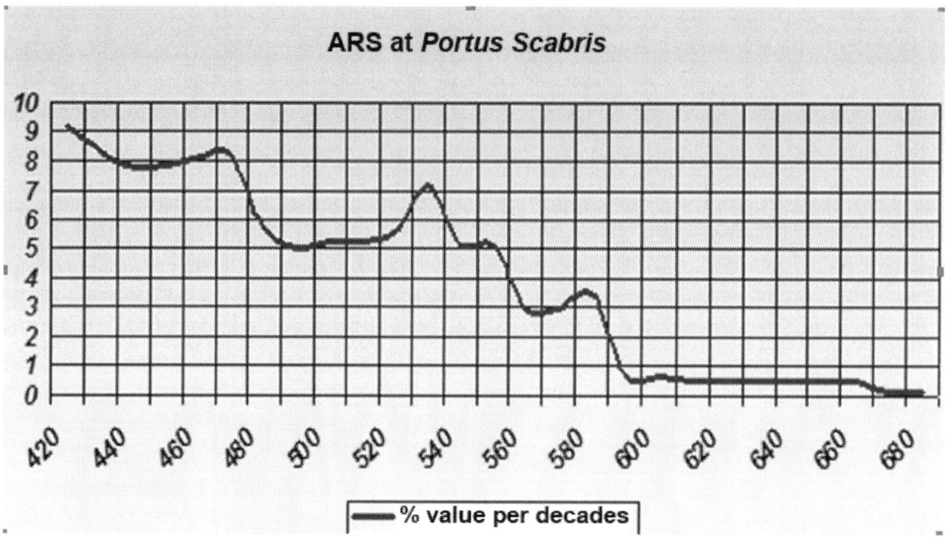

Graph II_ Individual Weighted Means Analysis of the ARS at Portus Scabris during the period AD 400-680.

broken during the voyage led to the presence in the underwater deposit of pots and transport containers which were not destined for this site or for inland contexts. By its very nature, then, the port provides far more in-depth and detailed information on the maritime trade routes plied by small and medium-sized craft than can be obtained from inland contexts, where the presence of imported materials is determined by the process of commercial redistribution aimed directly at that specific context.

If we observe the curve in Graph II we can see firstly that the quantities of finds from the 420s represent the peak in ARS during the study period. This is due to an increase in purchases of Tunisian fine tableware which is clearly confirmed by the town of Roselle and its hinterland and which was in all probability triggered by the commercial success of production D wares.

McCormick has recently claimed that the decrease in the volumes of African red slip wares culminating in the years of the Vandal conquest of Carthage actually began a few years prior to this event.[10] Both the data from *Portus Scabris* and those from the study area indicate a positive trend in the early years of the 5th century. This confirms the theory that the Vandal conquest of North Africa and the interruption of the fiscal axis between Rome and Carthage were the structural causes of the decrease, following a trend which, after the 4th century peak, had remained entirely positive. We can see that the flows of ARS from Tunisia began to be affected by the adverse political circumstances triggered by the early Vandal conquests, following the landing in Mauretania Tingitana in 429 of the troops led by Genseric. After this phase of contraction in the volumes of ARS reaching *Portus Scabris* we see a phase of stagnation and a brief period of slight recovery between the 460s and early 470s. The fall of the Western Empire and the interruption of the economic and commercial integration of the western Mediterranean led from this point onwards to an abrupt and dramatic drop in purchases of African red slip wares. This decline appears to be marked and long-term, as also indicated by the overall picture for rural areas and the finds from Roselle. Certainly, after this phase, although later points when circulation recovered are documented, the distribution of ARS and the extent of its penetration into rural areas no longer equalled or even came close to the peaks reached between the 2nd and first half of the 3rd century and later in the 4th. This is evidence of a contraction in maritime trade which is also clearly reflected by the decrease in shipwrecks between AD 300 and 700 in the western Mediterranean basin.[11] After the decline in African red slip ware during the last quarter of the 5th century, there appears to be a significant recovery in trade flows in the 530s and 540s, followed by another sudden decline from the mid-550s onwards. During the same period we see a decrease in the quantities of ARS attested in the area between the Alma valley and the Osa valley; by contrast there is a slight increase in the urban context of Roselle which matches that at *Portus Scabris*. The increase in ARS in the Portiglioni harbour, as at Roselle, seems to be directly related to the events of the Greek-Gothic war.

[10] McCormick 2001, p.100.

[11] See Parker 1992 and McCormick 2001, p.66.

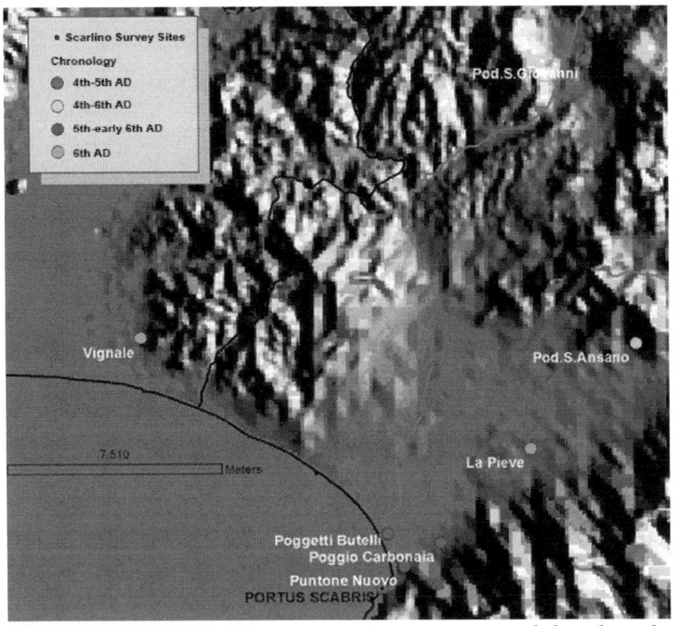

Fig.7_ Late antique sites found during the Scarlino Survey and dated on the basis of ARS.

During military operations, the coastal areas of the *Tuscia* were of enormous strategic importance to the Byzantines. They used the ports which had fallen under their control to send the necessary supplies to the troops deployed in central Italy. The Tuscan ports also played a fundamental role in providing foodstuffs to Rome, as demonstrated by an episode of 544 related by Procopius.

We know that, after Totila's conquest of Tivoli, following an act of treason on the part of the city, food supplies from Tuscany were no longer able to reach the river routes of the Aniene or the Teverone and thence travel to Rome, which was under siege.[12] The Tuscan ports must also have acted as intermediate harbours for the movement of people and goods en route to the coasts of Liguria, where the port of Genoa was one of the most important Byzantine strongholds on the Tyrrhenian sea. The contingent of 1000 soldiers, comprising both Isaurans and Thracians, sent by Belisarius for military operations in the Po valley disembarked here in 538. After landing at Genoa, the troops, which had set sail from Rome, moved towards the town of Pavia which was still held by the Goths.[13]

Whilst on the one hand the Greek-Gothic war had disastrous effects on the economic and settlement systems of the Italian peninsula, the events of the war also required a reinforcement of maritime circulation for the movement of troops and victuals for the army. Belisarius' reconquest of Carthage in 533 provided an opportunity to re-establish the circulation of fiscal goods sent to Rome from North Africa. This opportunity must have been exploited rapidly and fairly systematically in order to respond to the immediate needs of the military tax destined for the Byzantine army engaged in Italy. The increase in finds of ARS at *Portus Scabris*, coinciding with a positive trend in the presence of Tunisian transport containers, seems to be due to an increase in the circulation of foodstuffs crossing the Tyrrhenian sea and destined to feed the troops sent from Byzantium.

The trade reaching the harbour at Portiglioni was not primarily commercial in nature, as clearly indicated by the significant decrease in the volumes of ARS and transport containers reaching nearby areas during the Gothic war. Instead, trade was triggered by the new organization of the fiscal system decided by the Byzantine state.

Essentially, there does not seem to have been a large-scale redistribution of Tunisian wares either towards the nearby areas to the south, between the Alma and Ombrone valleys, or towards the few settlement contexts which continued to flourish in the Pecora valley and around the gulf of Follonica. Here, the surface surveys undertaken roughly twenty-five years ago revealed,[14] alongside the fragility of settlement structures during late Antiquity, the presence of only three contexts of villa or *mansio* type still able to purchase African red slip ware in the 5th-6th centuries. This tells us that the Tunisian wares reaching Portiglioni in large quantities did not penetrate inland to any significant extent (Fig.7).

---

[12] Procopius, *De Bello Gothico, Lib.III, X.* In this passage, as noted by Elio Bartolini, Procopius does not provide the reader with precise topographical information. In fact, he confuses the Tiber - *Τίβουριν* in the original text –, named as the river along which foodstuffs from Tuscany reached Rome, with either the Aniene or Teverone. Procopius, *De Bello Gothico, Lib.III, X.*

[13] Procopius, *De Bello Gothico, Lib.II, XII.*

[14] On the Scarlino survey see Francovich 1985 (ed.), particularly sites nos 21, 26, 47, 118, 153 232, 235.

After the mid-6th century, *Portus Scabris* also saw a fairly marked decline in volumes of ARS; however, this decrease did not reach the dramatic levels seen in the area between the Alma and Osa valleys and the town of Roselle itself. This would seem to suggest that the harbour retained a role of some importance in the context of maritime trade in the central and northern Tyrrhenian at the end of the 6th century.

Compared to the other contexts studied, we can observe a slight reversal of this trend between the 580s and 590s, with some forms not documented elsewhere, such as the Hayes 105 deep bowl, reaching the port site in limited quantities. This is a short-lived recovery which cannot be plausibly explained by a purely occasional use of the harbour since some amphora indicators also provide evidence of the continuous exploitation of the site between the late 6th and 7th centuries and perhaps, on an occasional basis, up to the early years of the 8th century.

The general decrease in maritime trade after the early 5th century is well documented by the distributive analysis of shipwrecks between the 4th and 7th centuries. From the 6th century onwards shipwrecks are almost systematically located in that part of the Mediterranean basin falling into Byzantium's sphere of political influence, with a particularly high density in the area between the North African coast to the south, the Italian peninsula to the north and the Maltese islands to the east.[15] The large numbers of ships in circulation thus appears to be closely linked to the resumption of navigation within the Byzantine political and economic system. When the Maremma came under Lombard control in the early 590s, it was excluded from this integrated commercial and fiscal trade system; however, the system continued to prevail in areas under the influence of Constantinople. In any case, the favourable geographical location of *Portus Scabris*, halfway between the Byzantine territories of central and southern Italy and the Ligurian coastal belt, still controlled by the Byzantines until Rotari's military campaigns of 643, ensured its continuous use during the 7th century as well.

This fate is in many ways similar to that of the harbour of Giglio Porto, an important reference point for trade routes in the north and central Tyrrhenian. The pottery contexts of the 6th-7th centuries document the harbour's vitality at the time of the Lombard conquest of the Maremma coast and its importance for links between Rome and Byzantine Liguria.[16]

Forms and Types of African Red Slip Ware From Portus Scabris (4th-7th Centuries): Preliminary Remarks

The typological analysis of the African red slip ware found at the Portiglioni context allowed us to identify a minimum number of 128 individuals. Of these, 118 belong to 22 different known types, which can in turn be subdivided into 30 variants dating to between the 4th and 7th centuries. For a further minimum number of 10 individuals, no typological identification proved possible, although the presence of a stamped decoration on the base allowed us to assign these to the time-frame of interest to this study.

The time-frame covered by this study led us to systematically record all pottery types belonging to production D and some pieces belonging to the later phases of production C (C^3, C^4, C^5).

The visual study of body clays allowed us to identify two fabrics attributable to production C and as many as seven belonging to production D; these can be differentiated mainly on the basis of the quantity of quartz inclusions, hardness and the properties of the fracture.[17] As Graph III and Table I show clearly, the dominant fabric in production D is Sig 2, for which we

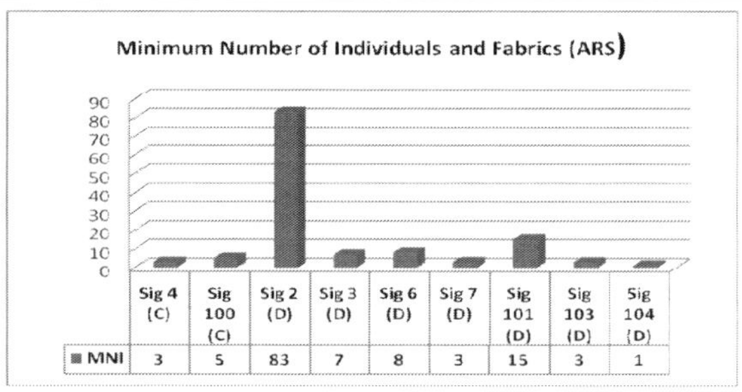

Graph III_ relations between MNI of ARS (productions C and D) and fabrics.

Fabrics	Identified forms
Sig 2	Hayes 58B, 59, 61A-B, 63, 67, 76, 91A-B-C, 93A-B, 99A-B, 103B, 104A-B, *Mackensen 33.2/34*, *Mackensen 17*, *Mackensen 16*, Hayes 80A, *Mackensen 22*
Sig 6	87B/109, 91C, 99B, 104 A, 105
Sig 3	Hayes 61B, 67
Sig 7	Hayes 61B, 79, 91B
Sig 101	Hayes 59, 87A, 91B-C, 93B, 103B, *Fulford ARSW closed forms 2.8*
Sig 103	Hayes 61B, 93B
Sig 104	Hayes 109

Tab. I_ Relations between identified ARS forms and fabrics.

[15] Zanini 1996, p.682.

[16] Ciampoltrini-Rendini 2004, pp.88-90.

[17] See the Catalogue of Fabrics.

have proposed an identification with the "fabric" most commonly used by the kilns of El Mahrine. This fabric is associated with a significant proportion of the catalogue of typical forms produced by these workshops, covering the entire period from the early decades of the 4th century to the 7th century. The other body clays, by contrast, are restricted to shorter periods (Sig 3, Sig 6, Sig 7, Sig 101, Sig 103, Sig 104). Particularly interesting is the association between the only specimen of a Hayes 109 dish and a type of fabric (Sig 104) which is a *unicum* at *Portus Scabris* and which is absent both from the African red slip ware found at Roselle and from that of rural areas, where form Hayes 109 is not documented. This dish, produced between the late 6th and the 7th century, did not belong to the rich catalogue of forms produced by the El Mahrine workshops,[18] whose products reached Portiglioni between the 4th and the 7th centuries. Given the characteristic polished striped decoration, also found on specimens of Hayes 87 and on some intermediate Hayes 87/109 variants, it has been suggested that this form was made at the *Pheradi Maius* production site.[19]

Production C

A minimum number of 4 individuals belong to productions C^3 and C^4; these can be ascribed to two types of bowl and one type of deep dish which were common between the 4th and 5th century.[20] The Hayes 71B bowl, two specimens of which were found, is characterized by its flat rim, ending in a thickened lip, rounded on the upper surface, with a diameter of about 22 cm; the body is cone-shaped (Pl. LIII, no. 1).[21] The Hayes 73A bowl, by contrast, has a flat rim presenting a series of light grooves and a slightly hooked lip. In this case the body has a barely convex, rather than rectilinear, profile. The specimen found has an isolated motif on the rim, characteristic of applied relief decorations; the subject cannot be clearly identified due to the fragmentary nature of the piece (Pl. LIII, no. 3).[22] The applied relief technique, a speciality of the production C workshops in central Tunisia, was one of the reasons that forms from Byzacena were so popular when they were introduced onto the Mediterranean markets, and helped to ensure their considerable success. The production of forms with this type of decoration seems to have come to an end with the Vandal conquest of Carthage and the subsequent reorganization of manufacturing activities.[23] The Hayes 75 dish is also characterized by a flat rising rim, but presents a typical outer groove on the outside and a slightly thickened lip which is clearly distinguished from the rim by a ledge on the outside (Pl. LIII, no. 2).[24] Whereas the first two forms are absent from the study area, a specimen of the third form is also documented at the harbour village of Serrata Martini-Paduline.

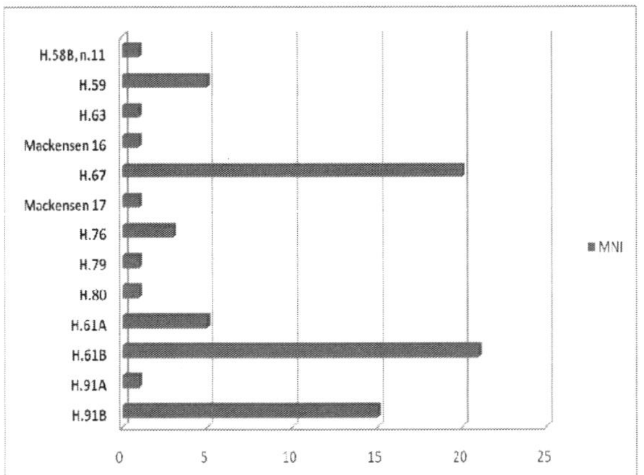

Graph IV_ ARS forms and variants circulating in the 4th-5th centuries AD.

The most recent production C form documented at *Portus Scabris*, with at least 4 specimens, is the Hayes 84 deep dish. This is the last form tested by the Byzacene workshops located near Sidi Marzouk Tounsi, active until the first quarter of the 6th century.[25] During their final phase of activity, these workshops introduced two types of deep dish and one type of dish (Hayes 82A-B, 84 and 85B), often with stamped decorations on the base, all belonging to production C^5. However, it is worth recalling that Hayes 84, with variants similar to two documented at *Portus Scabris*, was also manufactured at the smaller workshop of Nabeul-Sidi Zahruni, specializing in the production of amphorae and characterized by the use of a fabric which was coarser than that generally used for ARS.[26]

Hayes 84 was a very successful form which is systematically attested at major contexts in the western Mediterranean, albeit often in modest quantities compared to contemporary production D forms.[27] Of the 4 specimens documented at *Portus Scabris*, 2 can be ascribed to the classic, more common version of Hayes 84, with a rim of triangular section presenting two grooves on the outside and a rouletting decoration on the wall (Pl. LIII, no. 4). A further 2 specimens, though belonging to the same type, present some variations in the morphological structure of the rim and in the positioning of the external rouletting. In these two cases, the rim is thinner and more pointed and lacks the two grooves, whilst the decorative motif seems to be absent from that part of the body beneath the rim. In the only specimen with a surviving base, it has a ring-shaped foot of triangular section (Pl. LIII, nos 5-6). These two possible "variants" are comparable

[18] Mackensen 1998, pp.30-39.
[19] Murialdo 2001b, p.334.
[20] See the Appendix at the end of this chapter.
[21] *Atlante I*, Fig. XXX, no.19.
[22] *Atlante I*, Fig. XXXI, no.1.
[23] Reynolds 1995, p.13.
[24] *Atlante I*, Fig. XXIX, no.7.
[25] On the workshop at Sidi Marzouk Tounsi see Mackensen 1998, pp.26-30.
[26] Bonifay 2004, p.57.
[27] On the Mediterranean distribution of ARS types dating to between the 5th and early 6th century AD see Reynolds 1995, pp.19-25.

in every respect with the two specimens of Fulford ARS, open forms 27.1-2 documented in the British excavations at Carthage in phases of the early 6th century and attributable to imports from Byzacena, which are in fact fairly rare in northern Tunisia.[28] The classic version of Hayes 84 is present in the study area, both in the Bruna valley and the lower Ombrone valley.

D Production:

Forms and Types in Use Between the Fourth and Fifth Centuries

Below we will discuss a series of 11 forms with their variants which came into production before the Vandal conquest of Tunisia but which in at least eight cases continued to be manufactured afterwards, during the early and middle Vandal era (AD 430-475). Only four types ceased production before the capture of Carthage (Hayes 58B, no. 11, 59, 61A, Mackensen 17), whilst a further three were manufactured even after the chronological watershed of the last quarter of the 5th century (Hayes 61B, 80A, 91A, 91B). Within this group, represented at *Portus Scabris* by a total minimum number of 76 individuals, we can identify some interesting differences in the frequency of attestation of individual types, in turn determined by their differing degrees of commercial success (Graph IV).

The significant presence of the Hayes 61B bowl (27.6% of the total specimens dating to this period), of the Hayes 67 deep bowl (26.3%) and the Hayes 91B flanged bowl (19.7%) provides clear confirmation of the considerable Mediterranean distribution of these three functional forms,[29] due to their potential for creating an almost complete service. Less well-represented are the other two functional forms, the dish and the bowl, in the shape respectively of Hayes 58B, no. 11 and Hayes 63, and the Mackensen 16 and Mackensen 17 types.

a) Forms Produced From the Fourth Century Onwards Which Ceased Production Before the Vandal Era

Among the most ancient production D forms, we should note the Hayes 58B dish, no. 11, characterized by a short flat rim with a groove, measuring 25 cm in diameter (Pl. LIV, no. 1). This form, identical to Mackensen no. 1,[30] is well documented at Ostia in contexts of the late 4th-early 5th century, although a more restricted chronology of the third quarter of the 4th century has been proposed for variant no. 11.[31] The second form which does not appear to survive beyond the early 5th century is the Hayes 59/Mackensen 2 deep dish,[32] which has a flat upturned rim, sometimes with grooves, and a shallow body often decorated with ridges on the outside. At *Portus Scabris* this type is documented by 5 highly fragmentary specimens whilst an almost intact specimen was found in a primary context at Roselle in Context 5147=5170, dated to the 4th to early 5th century.

It seems clear that the Hayes 61A dish, with an incurving rim of triangular section (Pl. LV, no. 1), was not produced after the first two decades of the 5th century,[33] and was then replaced by the new and more common variant Hayes 61B. Of the 5 specimens attested at Portiglioni, most have rims with a diameter ranging from 32 to 35 cm, although a smaller version with a 23 cm rim is also attested.

Finally, the Mackensen 17 bowl is characterized by a flat rim, rising upwards and ending in a hooked lip. Both the upper surface of the lip and the junction between the rim and the wall present a groove; the wall has a rectilinear profile (Pl. LIV, no. 5). This type, well documented at El Mahrine,[34] has an identical morphological structure to the Hayes 52B bowl, belonging to productions C^1, C^2 and C^3 and dating to between the first half of the 4th and the early 5th century.[35]

b) Forms Produced Up to the Early and Middle Vandal Era (AD 430-470)

Four forms belong to a small group introduced before the Vandal conquest of Tunisia and still produced between the second and third quarters of the 5th century. These are a type of dish (Hayes 63), two deep dishes (Hayes 67, 76) and a bowl (Mackensen 16). All these forms belong to the production repertoire of El Mahrine, to which we have tentatively ascribed body clay Sig. 2. However, the presence at *Portus Scabris* of 3 of the total of 21 specimens of the Hayes 67 bowl produced using the Sig 3 fabric suggests that this form was also made at other Tunisian workshops.[36]

The minimum number of individuals which can be ascribed to the other four forms are all made from fabric Sig 2. Hayes 67 is the most well-represented in this group. This deep bowl is attested at Portiglioni in at least two main variants, which can be differentiated on the basis of their rims. The rim may be rounded and thickened as in the specimen shown in Pl. LVI, no. 2 (Mackensen 9.4 variant), or thickened, slightly hooked and bearing a groove on the upper part as in those shown in Pl. LVI nos 1, 3 (Mackensen 9.1 variant). The rim is always joined to the wall by a flat member,

[28] Fulford-Peacock 1984, p.56, Fig.14, nos 27.1-2.
[29] Reynolds 1995.
[30] Mackensen 1993, p.398.
[31] *Atlante I*, p.82.
[32] Mackensen 1993, p.399-401, and *Atlante I*, pp.82-83.
[33] *Atlante I*, p.84.
[34] Mackensen 1993, pp.601-602.
[35] *Atlante I*, p.71, on Hayes 52B.
[36] Bonifay 2004, p.171.

slightly rising. The shallow body has a height of 5 to 6 cm, whilst the base has an almost atrophied ring-shaped foot. The versions documented differ significantly in size, but the rims always have a diameter ranging between a minimum of 25 cm and a maximum of 36 cm. The stamped decoration of Hayes A(ii) type, on the sole specimen where it is present, consists of a motif with concentric circles at the centre of the base, surrounded by alternating palm branches and concentric circles.[37]

The other type of deep dish, Hayes 76/Mackensen 10, has a slightly rising flat rim ending in a thickened lip of oval section, sometimes decorated with impressed dentils. This type is documented by 3 highly fragmentary specimens; only in one case was it possible to estimate the diameter of the rim as measuring 34 cm.

The only specimen of the Hayes 63/Mackensen 6 dish has a plain vertical rim with a diameter of 26 cm, with three grooves on the outside. The body is about 4.5 cm deep (Pl. LIV, no. 2).

Whereas the three forms described above are well documented not only at *Portus Scabris* but also in the area between the Alma and Osa valleys, the Mackensen 16 bowl is currently attested only at Portiglioni, indicating that it had a fairly limited circulation compared to other types.

This form, with a slightly rising flat rim, bearing grooves and ending in a thickened lip (Pl. LIV, no. 3) is identical to the Hayes 73 bowl, made in African red slip ware C^4. On the basis of a number of contexts including Sperlonga, Carandini and Tortorella have claimed that this type is far more common in production C than in production D.[38] However, its frequency at El Mahrine, where at least four variants were made,[39] and the fair number of attestations of production D types at Carthage, greater in number than the versions in African red slip ware C, would appear to suggest that the northern Tunisian production of this type may have been more significant than hitherto thought.[40]

c) Forms Which Continued Production into the Late Vandal Era (AD 475-535)

This subgroup includes four types and their variants which came into production before the 430s and which remained widespread until the end of the century or during the first half of the 6th century. These types belong to four different functional forms: the bowl, the large bowl, the deep dish and the flanged bowl.

Of some interest is the presence of a specimen which can be identified as the rare Hayes 79 deep dish, made using fabric Sig 3 by a workshop whose repertoire of wares also included two other forms belonging to this subgroup: the Hayes 61B bowl and the Hayes 91B flanged bowl. Hayes 79 presents a slightly carinated body and an everted and thickened rim with a fairly deep groove on the upper surface giving it a forked profile (Pl. LIV, no. 4). A fairly generic date of the 5th century has been proposed for this form,[41] although some contexts in the British excavations at Carthage allow its chronology to be defined more accurately. Hayes 79 is in fact identical to Fulford ARSW, 35,[42] introduced between 425 and 450 and widespread particularly in the late 5th century up to the year 500, after which it is present in secondary contexts in phases dated to between AD 525 and 530. The uncertainties regarding the initial chronology of this type leave open the question of whether it was introduced before the Vandal conquest or after manufacturing activities were reorganized starting in the 430s.

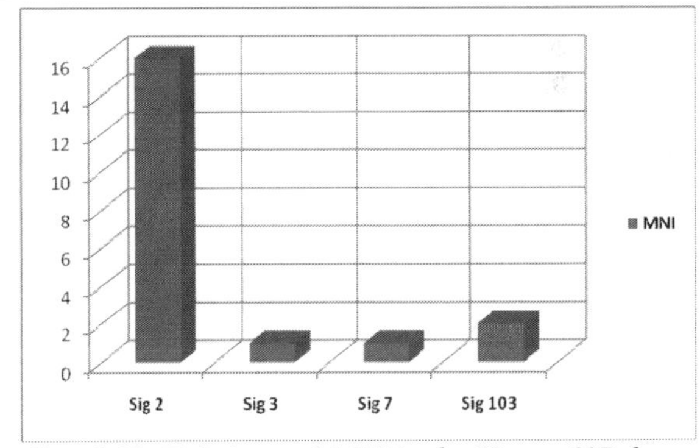

Graph V_ Fabrics and MNI in the Hayes 61B form.

Much debated, on the other hand, is the final chronology of the Hayes 61B dish, the most frequently documented at *Portus Scabris* with at least 21 specimens (Graph V). Traditionally, the production of Hayes 61B is dated to between 380 and 450,[43] but thanks to data from a series of surveys in southern France and at Carthage we can now lower the final chronology of some "sub-variants" by half a century.[44] Of particular importance are the occasional

[37] On the palm branch and concentric circle motifs see respectively *Atlante I*, Fig.LVII (b), no.54 and ibidem, Fig. LVI (a), no.18. Hayes style A(ii) was documented between AD 350 and AD 420.
[38] *Atlante I*, pp.72-73.
[39] Mackensen 1993, p.601.
[40] Reynolds 1995, p.9.

[41] *Atlante I*, p.90.
[42] Fulford-Peacock 1984, p.61 and p.58, Fig.15, nos 35.1-7.
[43] *Atlante I*, p.84.
[44] On the evidence from Marseille see Bonifay 1998, pp.71-77; on that from the castrum of Saint-Blaise see Cavaillès Llopis-Vallauri 1994, p.90.

associations of some variants of Hayes 61B with African red slip ware C^5 and D^2 of the late 5th-early 6th century and with Tunisian and eastern amphorae.[45] At Carthage, Fulford noted the appearance of this form from the late 4th-early 5th century onwards, whilst stressing that it is attested most frequently between AD 475 and 500.[46]

At least five variants are documented at Portiglioni; these are characterized by differences in the structure of the rim and in the profile of the wall. The size of the mouth, ranging from 26 to 38 cm, makes it possible to identify two main versions: a smaller version with rims measuring between 26 and 29 cm and a larger version with rims measuring between 31 to 38 cm.

Identical to the Bonifay 1 variant is the version presenting a rim of triangular section, rounded or slightly pointed on the upper surface, with an internal groove where it joins the wall and a fairly marked, but not hooked, external step.[47] The mouth may range from 32 to 36 cm in diameter (Pl. LV, no. 4).

Clearly identifiable with Bonifay no. 2 is the variant with a slightly thickened vertical rim separated from the wall on the outside by a slight ledge.[48] This version has a mouth measuring about 36 cm (Pl. LV, no. 2). The flat base presents three series of grooves; the inner two enclose the stamped decoration consisting of a combination of the geometrical grille figure of type *Atlante* I, Pl. LVI (b) no. 49 and the concentric circle motif *Atlante* I, Pl. LVI (a), no. 10.[49] Ascribable to variant 3 is the type which also has a vertical rim, but more thickened and rounded, with a diameter of 35 cm.[50] In this case, the wall has a fairly concave profile and the external step appears less marked (Pl. LVII, no. 5). Variant no. 4,[51] by contrast, has a rim of triangular section, even more thickened and slightly incurving. The outer step is extremely pronounced and slightly hooked. In one case, the diameter reaches 38 cm, whilst the body is always fairly shallow, no more than 4.5 cm deep (Pl. LV, no. 3 and Pl. LVII, no. 4).

Finally, we note the existence of a late version, also well attested at Marseilles, and documented at Portiglioni with a minimum number of at least 3 individuals.[52] This variant has a thickened and rounded rim, with a less pronounced external ledge reminiscent of some specimens of the Hayes 104A and 104B deep dish.[53] The most obvious distinguishing feature is the profile of the wall, which is slightly concave and presents a slight flange. The rims range in width from 29 to 31 cm (Pl. LVII, nos 1-3).

Interesting food for thought is provided by the analysis of the fabrics associated with the various Hayes 61B variants. First, about 76% of the minimum number of individuals, including specimens of all five variants, were made using fabric Sig 2. This is fairly surprising, considering that the repertoire of the El Mahrine kilns, to which this body clay has hypothetically been attributed, did not include the various versions of Hayes 61B but only 61A and a variant described as "transitional".[54] An identification of the site of provenance of the late Hayes 61B variants with the production context of Sidi Khalifa, about 70 km south east of El Mahrine, has been proposed.[55] On the basis of the distribution data currently in our possession, the late versions of Hayes 61B are well documented in the western Mediterranean, with finds at Ravenna and in the Port Miou and Cap Dramont E shipwrecks,[56] in the Monreale area of Sicily,[57] the city of Brescia, the Mantovan countryside,[58] *Portus Scabris*, the Provencal coast at the sites of Marseilles and Saint Blaise,[59] and the Alicante area and the Balearic islands.[60]

The association between fabric Sig 2 and forms that did not belong to the rich morphological repertoire of El Mahrine does not seem to be due to a failure on Mackensen's part to identify late variants of Hayes 61B. Rather, it suggests that clay deposits with similar properties may have been used by the manufacturing sites of the Medjerda area and by those located further south-east, on the gulf of Hammamet; this may be why it is difficult to differentiate between the two fabrics without recourse to mineralogical and petrographical analyses.

By contrast, the last two forms belonging to this group, the Hayes 80A/Mackensen 12 bowl and the Hayes 91 flanged bowl with variants A and B, are well documented in the production repertoire of El Mahrine.

The Mackensen 12 bowl, made using body clay Sig 2, is characterized by its everted plain rim measuring 23 cm in diameter, with three grooves on the outside, and its fairly deep conical body (Pl. LIV, no. 6). This form is rarely documented in the study area, with only two specimens of the variant with a smooth outer wall found at the village of Serrata Martini at Castiglione della Pescaia.

[45] Bonifay 1998, p.76.
[46] For the data from Carthage see Fulford-Peacock 1984, p.49.
[47] Bonifay 2004, p.74, Fig.1, no.3.
[48] *Ibidem*, p.74, Fig.1, no.4.
[49] These motifs are typical of styles Hayes A(ii) and A(iii), documented between AD 350 and AD 470.
[50] Bonifay 1998, p.74, Fig.1, no.5.
[51] *Ibidem*, p.76, Fig.2, nos 1-4.
[52] *Ibidem*, p.76, Fig.2, no.5.
[53] *Atlante I*, Fig. XLII, nos 2, 5.
[54] On form Hayes 61 from the workshop at El Mahrine see Mackensen 1993, Figs 53-54, nos 4.1-4 and related text.
[55] See Mackensen 1993 and Bonifay 2004, pp.55-56.
[56] Bonifay 1998.
[57] Reynolds 1995, p.24.
[58] Massa 1999, p.109.
[59] Bonifay 1998, pp.71-77.
[60] Reynolds 1995, pp.19-21.

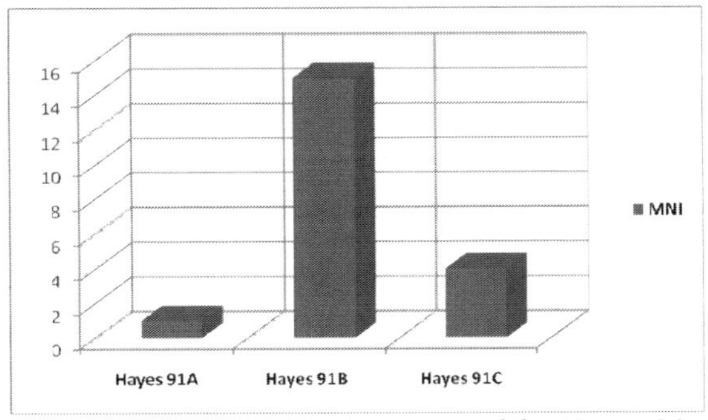

Graph VI_ MNI of each variant of the Hayes 91 flanged bowl.

The flanged bowl was an enormously successful form in the production history of African red slip ware D; with its four different variants it covers the entire history of this manufacturing activity, from the 4th to the late 7th century. The three variants A, B and C (Graph VI) are well documented at *Portus Scabris*, whereas D is absent; this variant was introduced in around 580 and is typical of the 7th century.[61] The earliest variant, Hayes 91A, possibly produced from the early decades of the 4th century until around 500 is attested by a single specimen.[62] It is characterized by a fairly thick flange, not angled, set immediately beneath the rim. The walls are flaring. Well-documented, on the other hand, is variant 91B, which is the third most common form of African red slip ware of the 4th to 7th centuries found at Portiglioni. This form was introduced shortly before the Vandal conquest and continued production until the mid-6th century, overlapping in part both with the earlier variant A and the later variant C. In the harbour at least four different versions are present, and the specimens found vary significantly in size, with rims ranging in diameter from 17 to 27 cm. This difference may be due to different types of use, *pro capite* for the smaller items and collective for the larger specimens. A large version (25-27 cm in diameter) is characterized by a long flange set immediately beneath a barely rounded rim (Pl. LVIII, nos 1-2). The specimen similar to the Mackensen 52.3 variant is smaller,[63] with a strongly everted rim and hooked flange. The body is less than 8 cm deep and the base has an almost atrophied ring-shaped foot (Pl. LVIII, no. 3). Inside we can see a meticulously applied rouletting decoration covering about half the wall. Finally, an even smaller version is attested which, with its shorter flange, seems to pave the way for the later variants C and D. This specimen is characterized by the even squatter body and the presence of a very carefully made roulette decoration covering almost all of the inner surface (Pl. LVIII, no. 4). The morphological structure finds a parallel in a flanged bowl attested in an early 6th-century context at the *castrum* of Saint Blaise.[64]

d) Fourth-Fifth Century Stamped Decorations

Alongside the specimens analysed above are a minimum number of 9 unidentifiable individuals represented by base fragments. These are equally interesting from a typological and chronological point of view, since they present stamped decorations typical of Hayes style A.[65]

The most common decorative motifs are concentric circles and concentric circles with dot fringes, attested in 3 and 2 cases respectively (Graph VII). The former, belonging to Hayes style A(ii), can be dated roughly to between AD 350 and 420 (Pl. LIX, no. 5),[66] whilst the latter are typical of both Hayes style A(ii) and A(iii), and thus cover a broader time span, between AD 350 and 470 (Pl. LIX, nos 1-2).[67] A further three motifs are attested on 1 minimum individual each: clover-leaves, circles with dot fringes and volutes. The most ancient of the three is the clover-leaf motif,[68] typical of Hayes style A(ii) (Pl. LIX, no. 4), whilst the circle with dot fringes seems typical of styles A(ii) and A(iii) (Pl. LIX, no. 6).[69] Finally, the volute motif[70] is generally associated with an unidentifiable cross and above all with a palm-branch motif which is recurrent in styles A(iii), C/D and E(i).[71] This decoration is dated to between the mid-5th and early 6th century (Pl. LIX, no. 3). Given its small size, it is impossible to ascertain which decoration the fragment from Portiglioni bearing this stamped decoration is associated with.

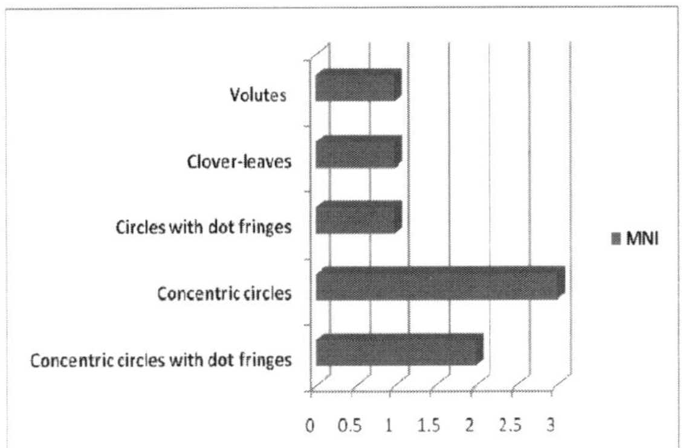

Graph VII_ MNI presenting different types of stamped decoration.

[61] On the final period of production of form Hayes 91 see Tortorella 1998, p.43.
[62] *Atlante I*, p.106.
[63] Mackensen 1993, Fig.75, no.52.3.

[64] Cavaillès Llopis-Vallauri 1994, p.97, Fig.52, no.63.
[65] On Hayes style A and its different phases see *Atlante I*, pp.122-124.
[66] *Ibidem*, Fig. LVI (a), nos 11-12.
[67] *Ibidem*, Fig. LVI (a), no.32
[68] *Ibidem*, Fig. LVIII(a), no.35
[69] *Ibidem*, Fig. LVI(a), no.4.
[70] *Ibidem*, Fig. LVII(a), no.15.
[71] *Ibidem*, Fig. LVIII(a), no.23.

Productions Introduced Between the Middle and Late Vandal Period (Mid-Fifth to Early Decades of the Sixth Century)

Belonging to this group are all the forms in African red slip ware belonging to production D, introduced during the Vandal rule of North Africa and present with a total minimum number of 30 individuals. Some of these forms were developed during the reorganization of the workshops taking place in the mid-5th century and continued to be widespread in later years; others represent the final experiments carried out by the Tunisian potters coming into production immediately before the Byzantine conquest of Carthage.

a) Forms Produced From the Second Half of the Fifth Century

A further minimum number of 8 individuals documented at Portiglioni can be ascribed to five types introduced in the second half of the 5th century which ceased production after AD 530/550;[72] an exception is Fulford, ARS, C.F. 2.8, which continued to be made even in the 7th century. These comprise three different types of deep dish (with four variants), one type of bowl and one type of flask (Graph VIII).

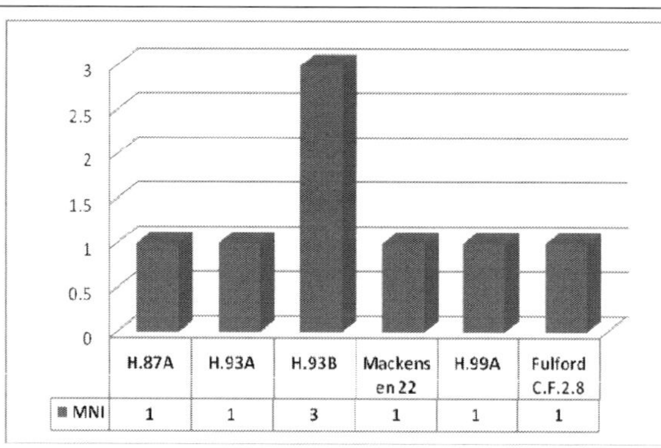

Graph VIII_ MNI of types produced from the second half of the 5th AD onwards.

The Hayes 87 deep dish is not a form known from the production of El Mahrine and should probably be ascribed to the repertoire of the Sidi Kahlifa workshops.[73] The specimen found at *Portus Scabris* belonging to variant A (Sig 101) is in fact made using a fabric different from Sig 2. Hayes 87A has a thickened rim of triangular section; the join with the wall is marked internally by a groove and on the outside by a step with a rounded profile (Pl. LX, no. 6).

The Hayes 93 deep dish is present with a minimum number of four individuals and both variants A and B. Belonging to variant A is the specimen with a flat, slightly down-turned rim with a diameter of 25 cm and conical body (Pl. LX, no. 1).[74] This type, produced using fabric Sig 2, is identical to Mackensen form 21.1 from El Mahrine.[75] More frequently attested, however, is variant Hayes 93B; the harbour of Portiglioni yielded at least three specimens belonging to versions which differ slightly in the structure of their rims. In two cases the rim is short and flat (Pl. LX, no. 4) or barely down-turned (Pl. LX, no. 3). The walls are curved and the ring-shaped foot, in the only specimen on which it survives, is high and flaring. Although these forms are well documented in the El Mahrine repertoire,[76] their association with fabrics – Sig 103 and Sig 101 – also typical of other forms such as Hayes 61B and Hayes 87A, not attested at the production context of the Mejerda valley, suggests that they were also produced at other manufacturing sites. The last specimen has a more thickened rim with a light groove on the upper surface (Pl. LX, no. 2). This specimen, made using body clay Sig 2, is comparable with variant Mackensen 20.3.[77] Overall, the rims of the Hayes 93B deep dishes have a diameter of between 25 and 27 cm.

The Hayes 99A bowl, much rarer at Portiglioni than variant 99B, is documented by a single highly fragmentary specimen, with a thickened almond-shaped rim, similar to type *Atlante I*, Pl. L, no. 12.

Finally, we note the presence of one specimen of a one-handled flask, with a fairly everted, thickened and slightly hooked rim, measuring 7 cm in diameter. The handle is set on the neck, which has a slightly convex profile, immediately beneath the rim. The handle is strap-shaped with five fairly pronounced longitudinal grooves on the upper surface. The slip, light orange in colour and not particularly thick, is found on the outer surface, whilst on the inside it is visible only on the rim (Pl. LX, no. 7). This form is identical to Fulford ARS, Closed Forms, 2.8, well-documented at Carthage between 425/450 and 500/550, in contexts excavated by the British mission.[78] The fact that it is common in phases of the late 6th – 7th century at the *castrum* of Sant'Antonino in Liguria suggests that its production continued up to the 7th century.[79] This form, associated with fabric Sig 101 at Portiglioni, may also have been produced at El Mahrine, although the finds from this manufacturing site did not include specimens ascribable with certainty to this form. The presence among the materials analysed by Mackensen of fragments of handles and a neck which are fully compatible with those of Fulford Closed Forms 2 leaves the issue open.[80]

[72] For the dates see Tortorella 1998, p.43.
[73] Mackensen 1998, p.30; Bonifay 2004, pp.55-56; Wickham 2005, pp.720-721.

[74] *Atlante I*, Fig. XLVII, no.4
[75] Mackensen 1993, Fig.65, no.21.1.
[76] Some close similarities have been observed with form Mackensen 20.1, see Mackensen 1993, Fig.64, no.20.1.
[77] *Ibidem*, Fig.84, no.20.3.
[78] Fulford-Peacock 1984, p.84 and p.82, Fig.25, no.2.8.
[79] Excavations at the *castrum* of Sant'Antonino yielded several variants: Closed Forms 2.3, 2.6, 2.7 and 2.8, see Murialdo 2001b, p.337.
[80] Mackensen 1993, Fig. 79, no.62 (4-7).

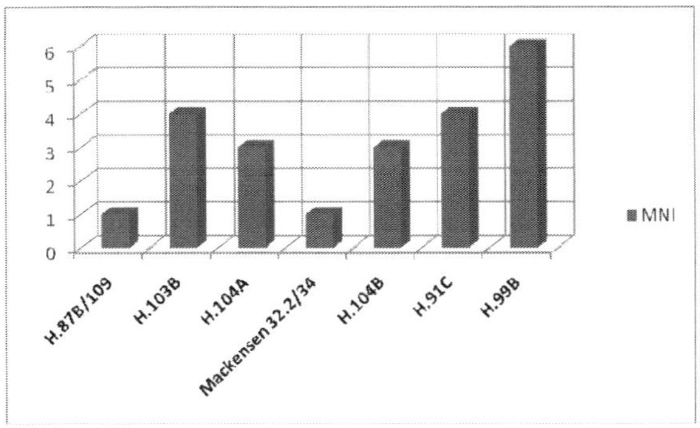

Graph IX_ ARS forms produced from the late 5th/early 6th onwards.

b) Forms Produced from the Late Fifth and Early Sixth Century Onwards (Late Vandal Era)

This subgroup is composed of a minimum number of 22 individuals which can be ascribed to forms and variants that came into production between the last two decades of the 5th century and the first two decades of the following century, and which continued to be made during the Byzantine period up to AD 570/580. These include four new types of deep dish, with five variants, a variant of the flanged bowl and one of a bowl (Graph IX). One of the most frequently documented forms is the Hayes 99B bowl, whose production chronology, from the early decades of the 6th century to AD 570/580,[81] overlaps for about thirty years with the earlier variant A. The most common version found at Portiglioni, with at least three specimens, presents the characteristic almond-shaped rim and strongly flaring walls. The rims have diameters of between 18 and 19 cm (Pl. LXI, nos 2-4). Alongside this more "classic" version is a variant with a rim presenting a barely visible depression at the junction with the wall and characterized by a greater width, up to 20/21 cm (Pl. LXI, nos 5-6). This form is clearly comparable to Fulford ARS, Open Forms 60, attested at Carthage between AD 475/500 and 500/525.[82] It has also been found at several sites in Provence, including Marseilles and especially the *castrum* of Saint Blaise,[83] where specimens similar to those of *Portus Scabris* are attested from the early 6th century; however, larger quantities are found between the last quarter of the 6th and the early 7th century.

The last documented variant is characterized by its decidedly thickened almond-shaped rim, with an internal groove, and by its very flaring walls (Pl. LXI, no. 1). An identical specimen is attested at Carthage in the excavations of *Insula E 218*,[84] and some similar forms are found in the pottery repertoire of El Mahrine.[85]

Another form which is well-attested at *Portus Scabris* is the Hayes 91C flanged bowl, present with 4 specimens. Compared to the earlier variants A and B, variant C presents a progressive lowering of the point of attachment of the flange, which also becomes shorter. The rims, measuring 18-20 cm in diameter, are subvertical or slightly everted; only in one case does the rim present an internal groove. The rouletting decoration, on the only specimen where it is visible, seems less densely packed and less carefully made (Pl. LVIII, nos 5-7).

Equally well-attested is the Hayes 103B deep dish, of which a minimum number of 4 individuals were identified. Two versions of this bowl were found at Portiglioni, which can be differentiated on the basis of the morphology of the rim: this may fairly everted, thickened and rounded (Pl. LXII, no. 1) or a more markedly triangular and hooked section (Pl. LXII, no. 2). The first version is identical to a form attested at Delos,[86] whilst the latter is very similar to Mackensen 26.2 from El Mahrine.[87] The width of the rims ranges from 27 to 31 cm.

A base, whose identification is doubtful (Mackensen 18[88]?), is characterized by a low ring-shaped foot with a diameter of 12 cm; the fairly flaring wall presents a slight carination. The base presents two concentric grooves, of which the innermost encloses the stamped decoration (Pl. LXII, no. 3). This decoration is an isolated cross motif, typical of Hayes style E(i) in use between AD 480 and 540.[89]

Within this subgroup, the most frequently documented form is the Hayes 104 deep dish, present with variants A, B and a transitional variant between Mackensen 32 and Mackensen 34. Version 104A is documented by a minimum of 2 individuals of certain attribution and another which appears to be a transitional version between 104A and 104B. Variant A is characterized by a thickened and rounded rim of pseudo-triangular section and a diameter of 36 cm. The walls are strongly flaring (Pl. LXIII, no. 1).[90] Another, smaller, version is characterized by even more flaring walls and a less thickened rim (Pl. LXIII, no. 2). The latter is clearly comparable with specimens from the English excavations at Carthage dating to between around AD

[81] On the dates of this form and others in this sub-group see Tortorella 1998, p.43.
[82] Fulford-Peacock, p.68, Fig.19, nos 60.1-2.
[83] Cavaillès Llopis-Vallauri 1994, p.101, Fig.56, nos 95-96.
[84] Mackensen 1993, Fig.83, n.10.

[85] Close similarities have been observed with the form Mackensen 28.2: Mackensen 1993, Fig.67, no.28.2.
[86] *Atlante I*, Fig. XLV, no.7.
[87] Mackensen 1993, Fig.66, no.26.2.
[88] Mackensen 1993, Fig.63, nn.5-15.
[89] On the stamped decoration see *Atlante I*, Fig. LIX(b), no.42; on the shape of the base see *Atlante I*, Fig. XLV, no.7.
[90] *Atlante I*, Fig. XLII, no.2.

500 and 600.[91] Both the specimens described were made using fabric Sig 2 (Table II).

Form	Fabric
Hayes 104A	Sig 2 (two specimens) Sig 6 (one specimen)
Mackensen 32/34 (Hayes 104A, late variant)	Sig 2 (one specimen)
Hayes 104B	Sig 2 (three specimens)

Tab. II_ Relations between fabrics and MNI referable to the Hayes 104A-B types.

Also probably belonging to Hayes 104A is a base made using body fabric Sig 6, characterized by a flaring ring-shaped foot, with a diameter of about 22 cm, crossed inside by two closely-placed grooves enclosing the stamped decoration of type Hayes E (i). The stamped motif consists of a central cross surrounded by a series of hearts (Pl. LXIII, no. 3).[92]

A further specimen was found at Portiglioni whose morphological structure presents some similarities to types Mackensen 32 and Mackensen 34,[93] which I have therefore decided to describe as a "transitional" form. It is characterized by a markedly thickened rim, rounded and hooked, and by a wall with a slightly concave profile. The rim is 34 cm wide (Pl. LXIII, no. 6). Mackensen claims that form 34 is a late variant of Hayes 104A, still produced during the 7th century as shown by its presence in contexts dated to after AD 650 in the excavations at Carthage conducted by the University of Michigan.[94]

The Hayes 104B variant presents a more everted wall, whilst the rim tends to take on a more rounded profile. Sometimes the wall presents three grooves on the inner surface (Pl. LXIII, nos 4-5). Of the minimum number of 3 individuals found at *Portus Scabris*, only in two cases were we able to ascertain the diameter, between 30 and 36 cm. All the specimens of Hayes 104B are made using fabric Sig 2 and present close analogies with form Mackensen 37 from El Mahrine.[95]

The last form is a type of deep dish with a rim diameter of 30 cm; the rim is barely thickened on the outside with an indentation at the point at which it joins the very flaring wall (Pl. LXII, no. 4). This type, documented at Portiglioni by 1 specimen made using fabric Sig 6, can be associated with Hayes 87C/109,[96] introduced at the end of the 5th/ early 6th century and still widespread during this century. Since both the Hayes 87 deep dish and the Hayes 109 dish are among the specialities of the factories near Sidi Khalifa, we can assume that the transitional variant Hayes 87C/109 was also made by these workshops.

Productions Introduced In the Middle Byzantine Period (Late Sixth-Seventh Century)

Only 3 of the total minimum number of individuals in African red slip ware attested at Portiglioni belong to productions introduced during the last twenty years of the 6th century and which remained widespread during the 7th century. These are 2 specimens of the large dish Hayes 105, produced using fabric Sig 6, and 1 specimen of the smaller Hayes 109 dish made using body clay Sig 104.

Both these types are well represented in those early medieval contexts in the Tyrrhenian area which maintained political and economic ties to the Byzantine world during the 7th century. The presence of these two types in a secondary context in 8th-century layers at the Carminielli ai Mannesi in Naples is significant.[97] In Rome, in the late 7th-century deposit in the Crypta Balbi, the Hayes 109 dish and the Hayes 105 dish are respectively the most frequent and the third most frequent forms among the large quantities of African red slip ware.[98] Large quantities are also documented in the *castrum* of Sant'Antonino in the Finale Ligure, where these two forms are present with minimum numbers of 8 (H105) and 12 (H109) individuals.[99] Again in Liguria, some specimens were found in the urban contexts of Luni and Albenga.[100] In Tuscany, with the exception of those found at Portiglioni, some specimens of Hayes 105 are found in the late 6th –7th-century phase of the villa at Giglio Porto.[101] It is clear that, during the 7th century, flows of African red slip ware systematically penetrated areas under Lombard control, indicating the fundamental role of the Byzantine state in supplying those settlement contexts which were of structural importance for the control over the Italic territories remaining in their possession after the late 6th century.

The 2 specimens of the Hayes 105 dish found at Portiglioni belong to two slightly different versions. One version has a thickened rim, flattened on the inside and with a slight indentation at the point where it joins the wall (Pl. LXIV, no. 1).[102] The other also has a thickened rim, flattened on the inside, but slightly more hooked on the outside (Pl. LXIV, no. 2).[103] In both

[91] Fulford-Peacock 1984, p.70, Fig.20, nos 65.3 and 65.5.
[92] On the two stamped decorations see respectively *Atlante I*, Fig. LIX (b), no.58 and *Atlante I*, Fig. LVII(a), no.23.
[93] Mackensen 1993, Fig.68, no.32 and Fig.70, no.34.
[94] Mackensen 1998, p.37, and bibliography in footnote no.57.
[95] Mackensen 1993, Fig.70, no.37.
[96] On this form see Reynolds 1995, Fig.33, nos 40-44.
[97] Soricelli 1994, p.133.
[98] Saguì 1998, p.310, Fig.5.
[99] Murialdo 2001b, p.324, Fig.29.1.
[100] Gandolfi 1998, pp.260-271.
[101] Rendini 1998, p.639.
[102] *Atlante I*, Fig. XLIII, no.5.
[103] *Ibidem*, Fig. XLIV, no.2.

cases, the walls are strongly flaring and the rims reach a diameter of between 34 and 36 cm.

The only specimen of Hayes 109 is characterized by very flaring thin walls and by a rounded and almost plain rim, marked on the inside by a light groove at the point where it joins the wall (Pl. LXIV, no. 3). The diameter of the rim is 22 cm. Inside is a polished striped decoration, poorly preserved due to the long time spent in seawater; this also explains the poor preservation of the brick red slip, which originally covered the inner surface of the fragment and is present externally only in a strip beneath the rim. Our specimen appears to belong to variant 109A described by Bonifay and finds a parallel in a version documented at Ostia.[104]

6.2.2. Lamps in African Red Slip Ware

Lamps in African red slip ware are documented at *Portus Scabris* by a minimum number of only 3 individuals belonging to type Hayes 1/ *Atlante* VIII. The large-scale production and export of this form dates to between the mid 4th and the late 5th/early 6th century AD.[105]

Pl. LXV, no. 1. Lamp characterized by an elongated body and a cylindrical spout that is not clearly distinct from the body. The thick handle is set vertically and presents a longitudinal groove. The shoulder is decorated with moulded plant motifs, probably a schematic palm leaf. The base is circular and slightly concave with a not particularly evident ring-shape. The discus is decorated with volute motifs. The lamp has two off-centre asymmetrical filling holes. *Date*: mid-4th -late 5th century AD. *Parallels*: at Ostia with products dating to between the late 5th and mid-6th century. *Bibliography*: *Atlante I*, Pl. XCVI, no. 1. Form VIII A1a. On Ostia see Barbera *et alii* 2001, p. 186, 1.4.25

Pl. LXV, no. 2. Upper part of a lamp with an elongated body and a cylindrical spout only a tiny part of which survives, but which does not seem to be clearly distinct from the body. There are two symmetrical filling holes on the discus. The shoulder is decorated with a double band of ovoli motifs in relief. The mould is extremely worn. *Date*: 5th century. *Bibliography*: *Atlante I*, Pl. XCVII, no. 6, Form VIII, C2c.

Pl. LXV, no. 3. Lamp with a rounded body and cylindrical spout which is somewhat distinct from the body. The discus presents a decoration of a monogrammed cross with *RHO* reading right to left. The decoration on the shoulder is impossible to interpret given the very worn mould. There is a filling hole high up on the right. Thick handle with a central groove. The decoration is identical to that on a Hayes IIB/ *Atlante* X lamp from a late 7th -century context in the Crypta Balbi in Rome. *Date*: 5th - early 6th century. *Bibliography*: *Atlante I*, Pl. CLVII, no. 6, Form VIII, C1a; on the decoration see also Saguì *et alii* 2001, p. 278, no. II.3.72.

6.2.3. Mediterranean Coarseware

The harbour yielded a minimum number of at least 8 coarseware forms which can be ascribed to Tunisian productions, and one of uncertain provenance dating to the 5th century onwards. The limited number of specimens identified does not allow us to determine whether these were wares destined for commercial circulation or whether these finds are simply indicative of the fact that coarseware was used on board the ships docking at *Portus Scabris* (Table III).

One feature which may lead us to prefer the latter theory is the evident imbalance between the significant quantities of African kitchenware dating to the 2nd – late 4th /early 5th century and the scarce finds of North African or other Mediterranean coarseware dating to subsequent periods. Although the series of productions with a blackened surface, blackened rim and a striped polished decoration has not been analysed,[106] since it largely fell outside the chronological scope of this study, we easily and immediately noted the large quantities of these found whilst working in the storerooms to research and record the materials belonging to the chronological context under examination.

It was possible to ascribe the minimum number of 8 individuals extrapolated from the imported coarseware since they belong to typologies dated with certainty to the 5th century onwards to Tunisian factories on the basis of a morphological examination. The analysis of the fabrics and their affinities with the body clays of amphorae certainly made in Tunisia allowed us to determine their area of provenance.[107]

Tunisian Kitchenware

Kitchenware is represented exclusively by a single form, the casserole, of which at least two types are attested. The most documented type, with at least 3 specimens, is the Fulford 19 casserole,[108] known at Carthage before the Vandal conquest, from the late 4th century onwards, but attested mainly between AD 475

[104] Bonifay 1998, p.79, Fig.3, no.5; Bonifay 2004, p.186, Fig.99, nos 14 and 16.
[105] On the chronology and variants of the lamp Atlante VIII see *Atlante I*, pp.192-194; and Mackensen 1993, pp.111-122.
[106] On the typologies and chronologies of Tunisian kitchen ware related to ARS see *Atlante I*, pp.208-211.
[107] I refer to the following fabrics: Com imp 4 (Munsell 2.5YR 4/6 red), Com imp 1 (Munsell 2.5YR 5/6 red), Com imp 2 (5YR 5/4 reddish brown) similar to Anf 119, and Com imp 3 (Munsell 2.5YR 5/8 red) similar to Anf 103; see the Fabrics Catalogue for further details.
[108] Fulford-Peacock 1984, p.184, Fig.69, nos 19.1-2; Bonifay 2004, pp.239-242.

and 500. This product was commonly traded in the western Mediterranean, and fairly large quantities have been found in the Iberian peninsula dating to the 5th century,[109] at Marseilles in contexts of the first half of the 5th century and at Toulon.[110] In Italy, by contrast, this type is absent both from Sardinia and from the northern and central Tyrrhenian coast at the 5th century contexts of Cosa and Ventimiglia, whilst it is probable that at least one specimen is attested in deposit I of the *Schola Praeconum* in Rome, dating to between 430 and 440.[111] It is more difficult to determine the provenance of some specimens which morphologically belong to this type, found in the Neapolitan context of the Carminiello ai Mannesi, in phases dating to between the mid-5th and the first third of the 6th century.[112]

Type	MNI	Fabric	Find Area
Fulford 19 Casserole	3	Com imp 1 (2), Com imp 3 (1)	Grid F, Strips I-II
Fulford 20.1/20.3 Casserole	1	Com imp 3	Grid F, Strip II
Casserole of uncertain origin (Eastern Mediterranean?)	1	Com imp 5	Grid A
Flanged bowl, Fulford mortaria 2	2	Com imp 3, Com imp 4	Grids A/F, Piles 23-27
Fulford, Closed Forms 16.3 *similis*	1	Com imp 1	Grid A, Strip I
Tunsian basin with inverted rim	1	Com imp 2	Grid A, Strip I, Piles 24-26

Tab.III_ Tunisian and Eastern Mediterranean (?) coarseware at Portus Scabris (5th-7th AD).

Given the macroscopic properties of the fabric, these forms have hypothetically been ascribed to local productions.[113]

Of the minimum number of 3 individuals from Portiglioni, only in one case was it possible to reconstruct an almost complete form. It is characterized by a slightly everted rim, thickened and barely rounded on the upper surface. Inside, the rim is shaped to hold the lid. The two handles, with a strap-shaped section, are set directly onto the edge, rising slightly above it. The globular body presents grooves on the outside and a blackening of the surface which was deliberately obtained during the firing phase (Pl. LXVI, no. 2). The other 2 specimens, whose handles have not survived, have a slightly more everted and rounded rim with a more marked inner edge, whilst the body profile and the treatment of the surfaces are identical (Pl. LXVI, no. 1). The width of the mouths is between roughly 13 and 15 cm.

The second type of casserole attested is identical to form Fulford 20 from Carthage, produced during the Vandal period and the early Byzantine period, between AD 450/475 and 535/550.[114] This form was sometimes sold commercially, though to a far lesser extent than Fulford 19, in some contexts of the western Mediterranean basin: the town of *Pollentia* in the Balearic Isles and the town of Valencia have yielded some specimens.[115] The morphological structure of this type is characterized by a fairly everted and flattened rim, shaped internally to host the lid and with a pronounced projection where it joins the wall. The body tends to have a cylindrical profile (Pl. LXVI, no. 3).

Coarseware Produced in Tunisia: Tableware and Storage Ware

Tunisian coarseware, excluding kitchenware, is represented by three different functional forms: the small-medium flanged bowl used to prepare food and serve it at table; the jug/small amphora for the storage of liquid or solid foodstuffs and the basin used to serve liquid or semiliquid foods.

The small amphora or jug made using fabric Com Imp 1, has a slightly everted rim, slightly thickened and rounded, with a diameter of 13 cm, set on a fairly tall conical neck. The thickened strap handle is level with the rim and set on the shoulder at the lower end (Pl. LXVII, no. 1). This form presents some generic similarities with the type Fulford, Coarse Ware, closed

[109] Some specimens were found in excavated contexts at Vila/Roma in *Tarraco* dating to between AD 400 and AD 450/470; one specimen comes from the Vinalopó valley and four from Cartagena, see Reynolds 1995, pp.87-89.
[110] *Ibidem* , p.90.
[111] *Ibidem*, p.91-92.
[112] Carsana 1994, p.237, Fig.112, nos 33.1-4.

[113] These specimens are made of fabric 1, which is described as: "dura, ben depurata, di colore arancio o nocciola (2.5YR 5/8), superfici ruvide, generalmente annerite. Frattura irregolare. Inclusi: vulcanici (pirossene), calcarei, bianchi, micacei piccoli e medi, di media frequenza." *Ibidem*, p.222.
[114] Fulford-Peacock 1984, p.184, Fig.69, nos 20.1 and 20.3.
[115] Reynolds 1995, p.97.

forms, 16, dated at Carthage to between AD 550 and 575/600.[116]

Among the open forms it is worth noting the flanged bowl Fulford, mortaria and flanged bowls 2, present with 2 specimens. This form has a hooked flange set immediately beneath a fairly everted plain rim. The mouths measure between 17 and 19 cm (Pl. LXVII, nos 3-4). This form, belonging to the coarseware similar to African red slip ware, appears in Carthage in the early 6th century, but is still attested in large quantities at the end of this century and the early decades of the following century.[117] Its presence at Sant'Antonino di Perti between the late 6th and 7th centuries seems fully compatible with the final chronology proposed for the specimens from Carthage.[118] This type was commercialized fairly heavily; it has been found both in other African sites such as Benghazi and Bir el Knissia, and in western Mediterranean contexts in Spain, Provence, Liguria, Sardinia and the central Tyrrhenian coast.[119] A specimen attested at Cosa in phases of the late 5th - first half of the 6th century, initially ascribed to this typology, has recently been associated with a possible Spanish production.[120]

A basin with an incurving rim of triangular section, measuring 22 cm in diameter and a fairly deep hemispherical body probably comes from Tunisia, although it presents no clear points of comparison with the coarseware attested at Carthage (Pl. LXVII, no. 2). However, the fabric used to make it (Com Imp 2) is comparable with body clay Anf 119 used to make two Keay LXII amphorae also attested at Portiglioni. On the basis of this piece of evidence our attribution appears convincing. On the other hand, the morphology of this vessel, which presents close analogies with Hayes 61 deep dishes, suggests that forms with an incurving rim may have formed part of the coarseware repertoire correlated with ARS.

Cooking Pot of Possible Eastern Origin

A single minimum individual documents a cooking pot with an everted rim, flat on the upper surface and barely shaped on the inside. The body profile is globular and bag-shaped. The surfaces are blackened on the outside but present no grooves. The handle, of pseudo-rectangular section, is set horizontally on the shoulder (Pl. LXVI, no. 4). The morphological structure of the rim and the bag-shaped body are reminiscent of a type of two-handled cooking pot produced in the Eastern Aegean and frequently imported to contexts in the western Mediterranean between the 5th and the 6th century.[121] However, our specimen has a completely different handle. Similar forms are attested at Kellia in Egypt in phases of the 6th century.[122] The properties of the fabric used to produce the Portiglioni vessel nonetheless resemble those of the kitchenware of eastern origin attested in Naples in the Carminiello ai Mannesi context, from the late 5th to the first third of the 6th century.[123] The body clay Com Imp 5 presents numerous inclusions of quartz, including polycrystalline quartz, biotite and volcanic rock, whilst its colour is reddish brown (5YR 5/4). We can also suggest a parallel between this fabric and Anf 130 fabric, used to make an amphora of possible Aegean provenance, also documented at Portiglioni (*infra*, amphora similar to P72 type from the Yassi Ada shipwreck).

6.2.4. Commercial Amphorae at Portiglioni Between the Mid-Fourth and the Late Seventh/Eighth Centuries

During the emergency excavations which took place alongside dredging in the harbour basin, a large number of transport amphorae were collected. These cover the entire period between the Hellenistic/late-Republican period and the late antique to early medieval periods.

According to a preliminary estimate made by the archaeologists in charge of recording the materials produced by digging operations, the total minimum number of individuals amounts to 1250. This calculation was made using the criterion of minimum and maximum forms, evaluating the total number of diagnostic fragments (rims, necks, handles and spikes) not belonging to the same vessel.[124] On the basis of a preliminary study, 52% (650) of the vessels recovered belong to typologies certainly dating to the late Republican period, whilst the information which can be extrapolated from initial counting operations on the minimum number of individuals belonging to the time period of greatest interest to this study is less accurate. We know that a minimum number of 290 individuals can be generically attributed to the imperial period without any further specification of phase. This means that a large number of specimens (310) escaped preliminary identification.

[116] Fulford-Peacock 1984, p.206, Fig.80, no.16.
[117] *Ibidem*, p.200 and p.198, Fig.76, no.2.
[118] Murialdo 2001b, p.344.
[119] On the distribution of this type see *ibidem*, p.244, and also Reynolds 1995, p.97.
[120] Fontana 2003, p.315, Fig.143, no.FC34.
[121] Carsana 1994, p.250 and p.251, Fig.120, no.106.

[122] Egloff 1977, p.101 and Fig.48.5.
[123] *Ibidem*, fabrics 6 and 7 on p.222.
[124] The method used for quantifying the minimum number of individuals belonging to each amphora type is explained in detail in the report produced by the Cooperativa Archeologia di Firenze, and supplied to me by Samanta Castelli.

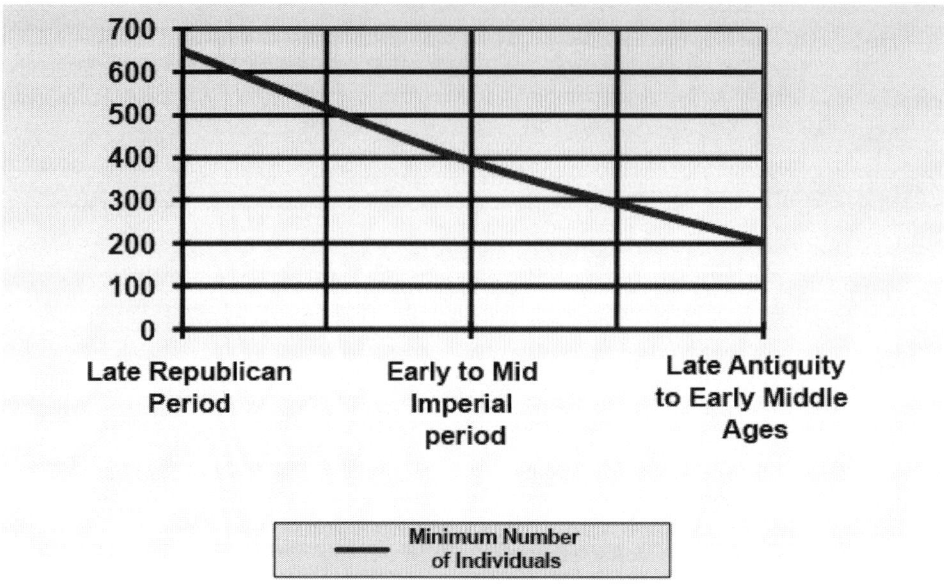

Graph X_ Hypothetical trend over time in amphora circulation from the Late Republican period to late Antiquity and the early Middle Ages at Portus Scabris.

However, the fact which most needs to be stressed is the impossibility, at the current state of knowledge, of accurately assessing oscillations in the flow of foodstuffs reaching *Portus Scabris* between the 3rd century BC and the 7th -early 8th century AD: this is the period in which almost all the identifiable forms are concentrated. My research made it possible to determine that a total number of 207 transport containers date to the 4th – 7th/early 8th century AD.[125] Considering that a minimum number of 650 forms date to the late Republican period and at least 207 to the period between late Antiquity and the early middle ages, it remains to be seen how many of the other amphorae are to be ascribed to the early and middle imperial period, in order to draw a graph of amphora circulation through the site of Portiglioni. If, purely hypothetically, we imagined that all the remaining specimens could be assigned to this period, we could obtain a preliminary picture of the trends over time in the offloading (and loading?) activities at the harbour of *Scabris* (Graph X). Naturally, in the absence of a systematic catalogue of the materials predating those analysed here, these are necessarily rough calculations, which may nonetheless be extremely helpful for a preliminary evaluation of trends in the circulation of amphorae at this site. The diachronic reconstruction of trade flows proposed has also found preliminary confirmation in the stratigraphic excavations, which suggested that late Republican contexts were larger and more complex than those of the early Empire and that late antique finds were significantly fewer in number.[126] The trend identifiable at Portiglioni is in line with the general trend for trade and production in the western Mediterranean, which registers a significant drop from the 4th-5th century, reaching a low point in the 7th century.[127] The diachronic analysis of

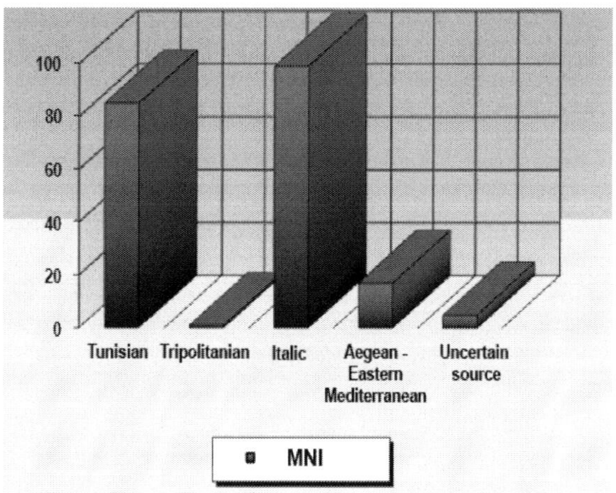

Graph XI_ 4th to late7th/early 8th AD amphorae at Portus Scabris and their origins.

the shipwrecks attested along the coasts in the vicinity of *Portus Scabris* similarly reveals a peak in trading activities between the late Republic and early Empire, and a consistently high level of trade up to the middle imperial period followed by a marked decline in late Antiquity.

The Circulation of Amphorae at Portiglioni Between the Fourth and the Late Seventh/Eighth Centuries: An Overview

The conditions under which finds were made at Portiglioni, with no stratigraphic information, make it impossible to subdivide amphora flows through this context into phases on the basis of relative chronologies and associations between the various transport containers attested. The study of the large quantity of wares belonging to late Antiquity and the less significant finds from the early Middle Ages was thus based solely on the "absolute" chronologies available for each individual type of vessel. However,

125 My study was based on the RB (Rims & Bases) criterion.
126 Bargagliotti-Cibecchini 1993, pp.43-59.
127 Volpe 1998, p.363.

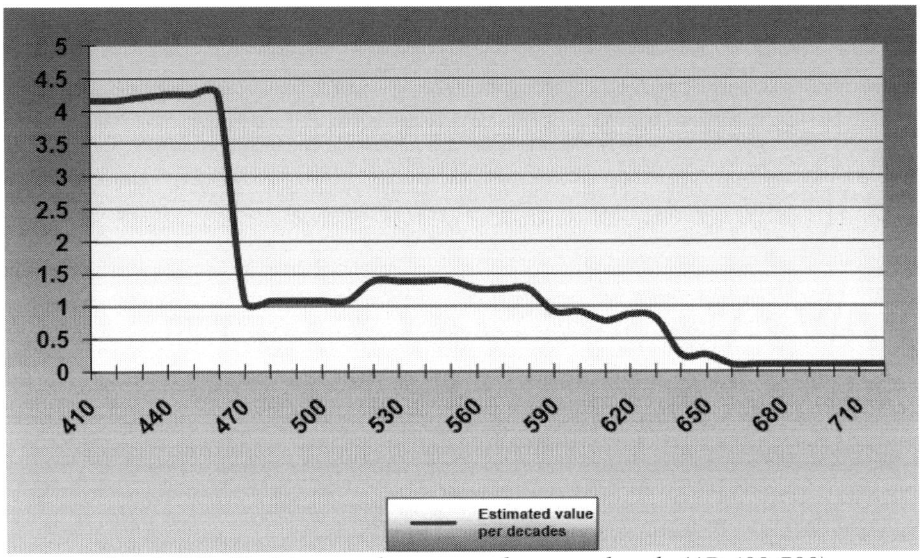

Graph XII_ Tunisian amphorae: numbers per decade (AD 400-700).

the existence of some extremely well-defined chrono-typological sequences allowed me to subdivide the goods arriving into broad time periods and to establish long-term trends for some wares (Graph XI).

The chronological range covered by this study led me to select systematically all those transport containers which, on the basis of their morphological properties, could be ascribed to types in use between the 4th and late 7th /early 8th century. As such, I analysed not only all those materials clearly falling into this chronological range but also those wares which, despite having been introduced during an earlier phase, continued to be common during part of the period in question. An observation of all the 207 amphorae analysed provided some interesting data on their areas of provenance. The first significant fact is the apparent absence of the Portuguese vessels destined for the fish sauce trade,[128] which, by contrast, are well-documented at Roselle between the 4th and early 5th centuries. Still more surprising, given our findings at Roselle and in the study area as a whole, is the predominance of wares from Italy, accounting for 47.8% of the total of those reaching Portiglioni in the period under investigation.

However, these data should be weighted correctly, considering the probable presence of a beached shipwreck carrying Empoli amphorae which has created an imbalance in the proportions of wares from different areas of provenance. It is also important to note that, of the 99 amphorae of Italian production, as many as 94 can be ascribed specifically to the Empoli amphora which appears to be well-represented not only at the point where the possible shipwreck lies but also in other parts of the bay, as we will see below. This container, for which a lowering of the final chronology to the first half of the 6th century has recently been proposed,[129] was nonetheless most common between the 4th and late 5th century AD,[130] and its presence cannot provide any information of significance to the reconstruction of the later trade history of Portiglioni, between the mid 6th and 7th century. Also very high, as expected, are the quantities of Tunisian wares, accounting for about 41% of the specimens found. Oil amphorae and fish sauce amphorae from Tunisia are well-documented by types covering the entire chronological range between the 4th and 7th centuries; given the large quantities involved and the fairly narrow chronologies, these make it possible to track trends over time. The supply of oil from Tripolitania, on the other hand, is attested only by a single amphora specimen.

Fairly common are containers used to trade wines from the eastern Mediterranean, representing 8.2% of the total.

Finally, we should mention 5 amphorae of uncertain provenance which, on the basis of their morphological characteristics, can be ascribed to productions dating to between late Antiquity and the early Middle Ages. At least 3 of these present convincing parallels with amphora types in use between the 7th and 8th centuries.

---

128 During the rescue archaeological research at least 4 specimens of the Portuguese amphora Alamgro 51C were collected from the grid square A and the crossing among grid squares A, B, G, F. Unfortunately it was not possible to find these specimens on the occasion of my laboratory research.

129 In the excavation at via de' Castellani, in Florence, some specimens of Empoli amphora have been yielded by contexts dating to the first half of the 6th century AD: see Francovich-Cantini 2006, p.133 and Cantini 2007, pp.235-236 and 252-257.

130 Concerning the first proper identification and suggested date of this amphora type see Cambi 1989. A preliminary interregional trade pattern for this type between the 4th and late 5th/early 6th centuries AD can be found in Pasquinucci et alii 1999, p.60.

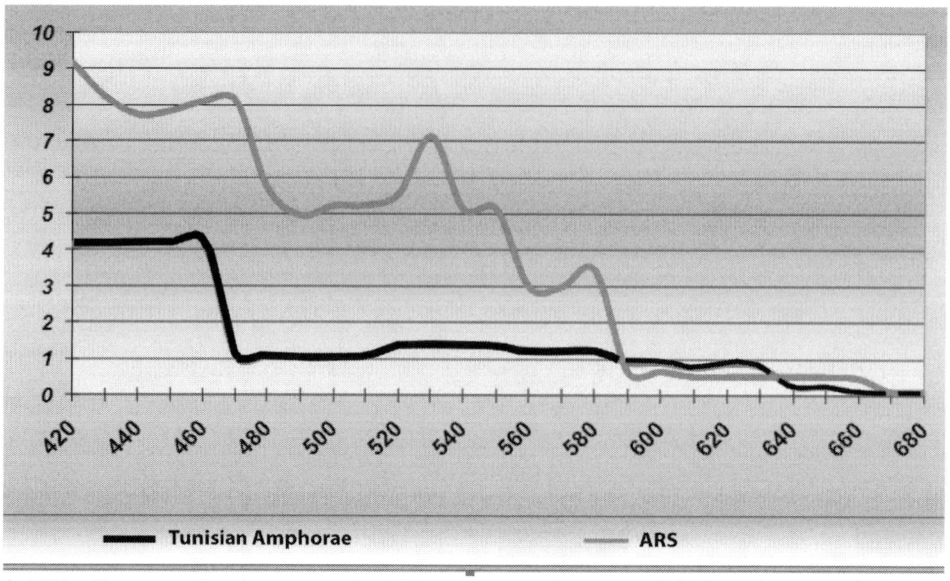

Graph XIII_ Comparative data: trends in Tunisian amphorae and ARS in the period AD 400-700.

Tunisian Productions

a) Diachronic Analysis of North African Amphorae

As already mentioned, the amphorae of North African provenance, covering the whole time period under examination with a fairly large minimum number of individuals, are the only ones which allow me to attempt an interpretation of trade trends over the long term (Graph XII). The diachronic analysis of Tunisian imports made it possible to appreciate some important features of the transformation of trade flows affecting Portiglioni between the early 5th and late 7th centuries. The subsequent comparison between imports of foodstuffs and imports of fine tableware from Tunisia was of great help in the reconstruction of economic patterns (Graph XIII). The curve for North African transport containers presents very high values at the beginning of the 5th century which do not seem to be affected in any way by the interruption of the fiscal axis between Rome and Carthage. By contrast, African red slip ware presents a slight decrease in circulation coinciding precisely with this event. In this case, we can assume that fineware allows for a more accurate assessment of oscillations in trade activities over short periods of time, since their chronologies are more detailed chronologies than those of amphorae. In fact, the peak in Tunisian transport containers in the first half of the 5th century is determined by the conspicuous presence of cylindrical vessels of type Keay XXV (as much as 64.7% of all Tunisian amphorae), whose production covers a broad time period, between the early 4th and mid-5th centuries. By contrast, during the same period African red slip wares, even in the absence of stratigraphic data, allow for more accurate and specific chronological subdivisions.

Starting from the 470s, the curve for Tunisian amphorae mirrors that for ARS: we see a significant drop in imports which coincides, with extraordinary precision, with the fall of the Western Empire. Subsequently, there is a long phase of stagnation lasting about half a century. From the 520s and 530s the curve shows an extremely interesting reversal of this trend which lasts, despite a slight downturn at the beginning of the second half of the 6th century, up to the 580s. The agreement of the trends for these two classes of imported materials from Tunisia supports the theory outlined above concerning the important role played by the harbour in the context of Byzantine military policy in Italy. In the 590s, coinciding with the Lombard conquest of this area, we see a new decline in the goods reaching *Portus Scabris*. However, this did not result in the almost total interruption of contacts with the Mediterranean world, as seen at Roselle and the study area; rather, the decrease in the flow of goods seems to reflect a general downturn in maritime activities in the western Mediterranean (Graph XIV).[131]

The Lombardization of this area put an end to the redistribution of foodstuffs and fineware towards inland areas, whilst the port site continued to serve its purpose at least until the 630s/640s, for as long as it met Constantinople's need to guarantee control over the intermediate harbours necessary for maritime connections between Rome and Byzantine Liguria.

[131] For an overview of the development of sea trade in light of the evidence from ancient shipwrecks see Zanini 1996.

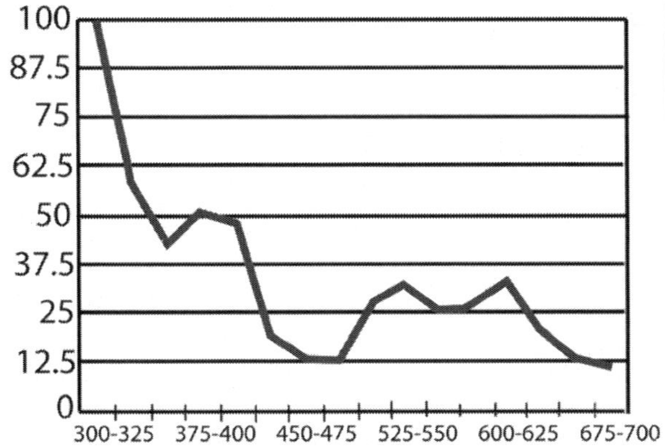

Graph XIV_ Trends in Mediterranean shipwrecks AD 300-700 (from Zanini 1996, p.684).

The curve for Tunisian amphorae at Portiglioni even shows a slight recovery of flows in the first quarter of the 7th century, coinciding with a slight increase in the number of shipwrecks attested in the areas crossed by Byzantine trade.[132] This does not appear to be a simple coincidence, but rather represents further evidence that the site of *Scabris* still played a role of some importance in the context of coastal navigation using small and medium-sized vessels.

b) Tunisian Amphorae between the Fourth and Seventh Centuries AD: Aspects of Production and Details on their Spatial Distribution at *Portus Scabris*

Before proceeding with a detailed description of the individual types of North African amphorae analysed and their variants, it is worth considering again some features of production structures and their spatial distribution within the context.

b.1. Hypothesis on the Organization of Production Based on the Microscopic Analysis of Fabrics

The systematic interpretation of fabrics using a stereoscopic microscope made it possible to acquire some interesting information on the organization of activities linked to the production of Tunisian amphorae. The first fact worthy of note is the large number of fabrics identified (19) which can be distinguished either on the basis of the properties of the fracture, the hardness of the fabric and the firing atmosphere, or sometimes on the mineralogical phases attested. This would seem to confirm the existence of numerous workshops involved in the production of amphorae[133] and linked, at least in part, to the exploitation of different clay quarries. Whilst a large group of body clays is documented on a merely occasional basis, being associated with between 1 and 5 minimum individuals,[134] at least 4 pottery fabrics are characteristic of a larger number of specimens and different typologies (Table IV, Graph XV).

Fabrics	Types
Anf 114	Keay XXV, Keay XXXV, Keay LXII, Keay XXVIIB, Keay VII
Anf 100	Keay XXV
Anf 101	Keay XXV
Anf 104	Keay XXVI, Keay LV *similis* (?), Keay XXV
Anf 105	Keay XXVIIB
Anf 25	Keay XXV
Anf 107	Keay XXV
Anf 108	Keay XXV
Anf 110	Keay LXII, Keay XXV
Anf 103	Keay XXVI
Anf 111	Keay XXVI
Anf 16	Keay VII, Keay XXV
Anf 113	Keay XXV, Keay XXVI
Anf 119	Keay LXII
Anf 24	Keay XXV

Tab.IV_ Fabrics and typologies of Tunisian amphorae at Portus Scabris.

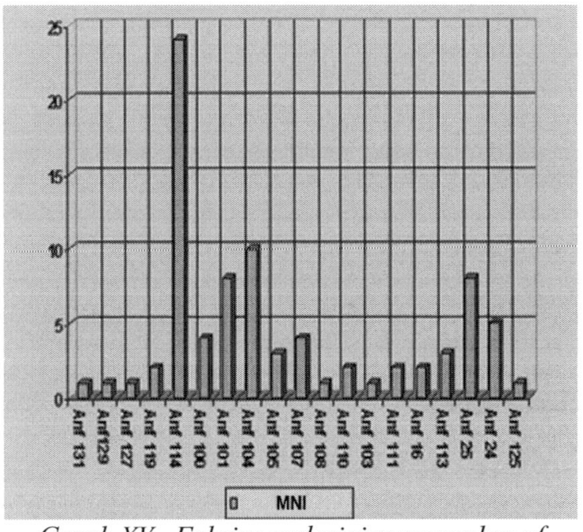

Graph XV_ Fabrics and minimum number of individuals of the Tunisian amphorae documented at Portus Scabris.

b.2. Distribution of Tunisian Amphorae in the Portiglioni Bay

The distribution of Tunisian amphorae seems to mirror that of African red slip ware, being concentrated particularly inside grid squares A and F near the landward dock. Fairly interesting is the spatial distribution of cylindrical Keay XXV vessels, the most frequently attested type of Tunisian amphora of those

[132] *Ibidem*, pp.683-685.

[133] Field surveys in the Sahel identified several production centres, in two different areas: the first along the coast and the second inland, see Peacock *et alii* 1989, pp.179-222. An exhaustive and up-to-date survey of the Tunisian workshops involved in the production of amphorae is in Bonifay 2004, pp.9-44.

[134] These fabrics are: Anf 131, Anf 129, Anf 127, Anf 119, Anf 100, Anf 105, Anf 107, Anf 108, Anf 110, Anf 103, Anf 111, Anf 16, Anf 113, Anf 125, Anf 24.

dating from the 4th century onwards (Graph XVI). Of the 55 specimens of Keay XXV identified, over 58% come from the area between *piles* 23 and 27 (Fig.8). It is fairly obvious that the location of the minimum number of individuals belonging to this type of amphora supports the theory, advanced on the basis of the areas where ARS was found, that most cargo offloading and hull cleaning activities took place in the central part of the bay. However, it cannot be ruled out that some higher concentrations in this segment of the harbour basin, such as that of Keay XXV, may in fact be evidence of the deliberate beaching of vessels,[135] undertaken in times of significant difficulty in order to save the crews and at least part of the cargo. The recovery of at least some of the goods transported would have been facilitated by the shallow waters and the vicinity of the coast.

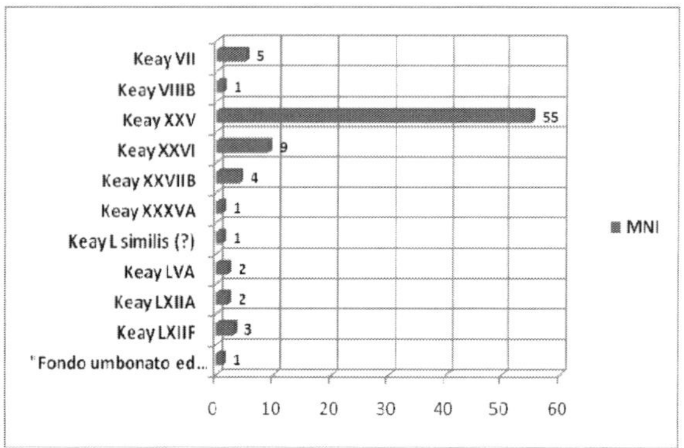

Graph XVI_ Minimum number of individuals of Tunisian amphorae typologies.

C) Types and Variants of Tunisian Amphorae between the Fourth and Late Sixth/Early Seventh Centuries

c.1. Forms Coming Into Use Before the Vandal Conquest of Carthage

Belonging to this category are a significant percentage (about 88%) of the minimum individuals belonging to types of Tunisian amphorae introduced before the Vandal conquest of Carthage but which in large part continued production during the Vandal era and in some cases into the Byzantine period.

KEAY VII

This type of amphora, attested at *Portus Scabris* with a minimum number of at least 5 individuals, dates to between the first half of the 3rd century and the 4th century.[136] It was generally used to transport fish sauces.[137] Among the production sites for this typology we could mention El Hri 1, El Hri 2 and Salakta, in the Ksour-el-Saf area south of the Gulf of Hammamet and the sites of Sahar Slima and the Punic Necropolis further north near the town of Leptis Minor.[138] The morphological structure of this type of amphora is characterized by a band-shaped rim with a convex internal profile and an outer groove marking the point of junction with the neck (Pl. LXVIII, nos 1-3). Sometimes we observe a slight development of the lip (Pl. LXVIII, no. 4). The rim diameter ranges from a minimum of 10 to a maximum of 12 cm. The "ear-shaped" handles are set on the neck immediately beneath the rim or at the junction between these two elements. The bottom of the handles is set on the end of the neck. The handles may have an elliptical or thickened strap section. Three out of five specimens present a lightening of the surface colour.

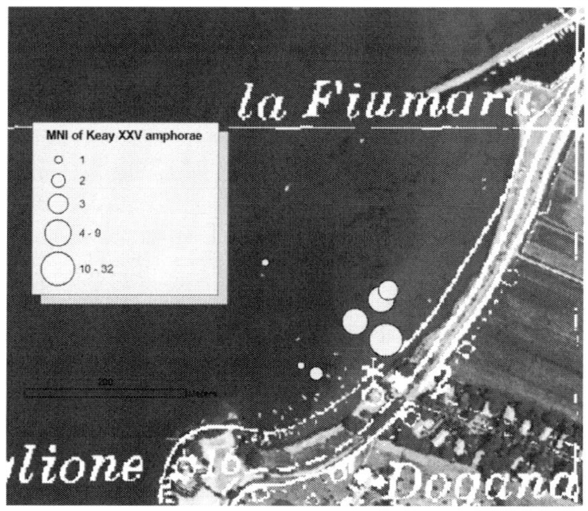

Fig.8_ Distribution of Keay XXV amphorae at Portus Scabris.

KEAY XXV

This is the most frequently attested Tunisian transport vessel at Portiglioni and is one of the most common amphorae both at Roselle and in the study area, indicating the significant commercial success of the foodstuffs transported in these vessels (Fig.8). In this case, as for Keay VII, the available evidence does not allow us to specify the nature of the contents with certainty; they probably consisted both of fish-based products and of wine.[139] The main production centres for Keay XXV currently known are those identified over twenty years ago in the Sahel region and more specifically: the contexts of El Hri 1 and Salakta Catacombes near the coast, and possibly Henchir ech Chekaf further inland.[140] To these we should add the production site of Oued El-Akarit in southern Byzacena, identified more recently, and that of *Thaenae*/Thyna a few tens of km further north along the coast. Another production site for Keay XXV amphorae has recently been identified at Sidi Zahruni, along the coast north of the Gulf of Hammamet in

[135] On the practice of deliberate beaching see Beltrame 1998, pp.144-146.
[136] Bonifay 2004, pp.115-117.
[137] *Ibidem* p.474, Tab.4
[138] Peacock *et alii* 1989.
[139] See Bonifay-Garnier 2007, p.24, Fig.8.
[140] Peacock *et alii* 1989.

Zeugitana.[141] At least six variants are documented at *Portus Scabris* alongside a form generically ascribable to the Keay XXV family.

VARIANT B

At Portiglioni this variant is the most common version of Keay XXV. It is characterized by a slightly everted and thickened rim, sometimes ending in a barely pointed lip, set on a tall cylindrical neck. The mouth has a diameter of between 11 and 13 cm. The handles, with a thickened strap section, are set on the highest and lowest parts of the neck, immediately above the shoulder (Pl. LXIX, no.1 and Pl. LXX, no. 3). One specimen presents a *post cocturam* graffito in the shape of an 'X' (Pl. LXIX, no. 2).

VARIANT D

A version characterized by an everted "a corolla" rim ending in a slightly thickened and rounded lip. The internal profile of the rim is convex. The mouth may be between 12 and 13 cm wide (Pl. LXIX, no. 3).

VARIANT G

This variant has a more everted rim, which presents an "a corolla" structure similar to that of the preceding variant. The lip is fairly well-developed and has an "a becco" profile (Pl. LXXI, no. 3 and Pl. LXIX, no. 4). Sometimes there is a slight groove on the inner surface of the rim. The mouth is 13 cm wide in most specimens, although in one case it reaches 15 cm. The neck and handles are identical to the variants described above.

VARIANT H

This variant presents a strongly everted rim with an "a corolla" profile and a thickened hooked lip, clearly distinct from the neck (Pl. LXXI, no. 1). The rims attested have a diameter ranging from 13 to 15 cm.

VARIANT M

This version is attested by a single specimen with a very thickened rim, tending to become oblique on the inside, ending in a barely pronounced, rounded lip. The rim is set on a high conical neck. The "ear-shaped" handles are thickened and set beneath the rim and at the junction between the neck and the shoulder. The mouth is 14.5 cm wide (Pl. LXX, no. 2).

VARIANT W

This version is also attested by a single specimen with a thickened and rounded rim with a hooked profile (Pl. LXXI, no. 2). On the basis of the fragment found we cannot rule out a possible identification with type Keay XXXVA, whose rim has a similar morphological structure.

KEAY XXV SIMILIS

We have used this name to describe a type of cylindrical amphora generically reminiscent of both Keay VI and Keay XXV, in particular of some versions of variant B. Particularly similar to Keay VI are the shape of the short conical neck and the "ear-shaped" handles set immediately beneath the rim and on the shoulder;[142] by contrast, the flat, barely everted and internally convex rim and the narrower body are reminiscent of Keay XXVB. The specimen found presents a stamp on the neck consisting of two concentric circles, with impressed dots between the first and second circles and a broader impression inside the innermost circle (Pl. LXX, no. 1). A possible morphological point of comparison for this amphora is a Keay XXV from *Thaenae* in south-eastern Byzacena.[143] This type is produced using fabric Anf 101, also used for another 7 specimens of Keay XXV.

KEAY XXVI SPATHEION

This is a cylindrical transport vessel, more tapered in shape than Keay XXV. The production of this type, which began in the 5th century, and is thus partly contemporary with Keay XXV, continued until the late 6th century,[144] long past the final chronology of wider cylindrical containers, dated to the mid-5th century. Between the end of the 6th and the 7th century Keay XXVI *spatheia* were replaced by far smaller *spatheia*, which generally account for a significant percentage of vessels in the North African amphorae assemblages in contexts dating to the early Middle Ages.[145] There are still numerous uncertainties regarding the contents of Keay XXVI *spatheia* and their later developments. The smaller capacity of Keay XXVI and the truly minimal capacity of the little *spatheia* would tend to rule out their use for the transport of oil, since it would have been uneconomical to trade small quantities of a product destined for such widespread commercialization. It therefore seems more probable, given also the information provided by the written sources,[146] that other foodstuffs such as wine, fish sauce, olives, honey, lentils or valuable products such as unguents were transported in these. At Portiglioni, *spatheia* are documented only by the larger versions dating to the 5th-6th centuries, which also appear

[141] Bonifay 2004, pp.31-39.

[142] On Keay VI see Keay 1984, p.117, Fig.44, no.6.

[143] Bonifay 2004, p.118, Fig.63, no.13.

[144] Bonifay 2004, pp.125-127, especially *spatheion 1* and *spatheion 2* types.

[145] To mention but a few examples, the urban context of the Crypta Balbi in Roma and the two *castra* at Sant'Antonino in Finale Ligure and Saint Blaise in Provence, where these types are documented in the 7th century AD. On these sites see Saguì 1998, p.312, Fig.6, Murialdo 2001a, pp.273-278 and Villedieu 1994, pp.133-135.

[146] See Keay 1984, p.215, quoting Manacorda 1977.

sporadically at Roselle, Serrata Martini and in a few contexts of the lower Ombrone valley. Of the 9 specimens attested, at least 6 can be identified with one of the variants described by Keay.[147] Variant XXVIF has a strongly everted rim, thickened and hooked, with a diameter of about 10-11 cm (Pl. LXXII, nos 1, 5). Keay XXVIG has a less everted rim which does not always end in a hooked lip (Pl. LXXII, nos 2, 6) Finally, variant Keay XXVIi presents a rim with a slightly squarer shape, with one or two light grooves on the outside and always ending in a fairly hooked lip (Pl. LXXII, nos 3-4). The necks are almost cylindrical and very tall, and the small handles are set beneath the rim and on the lower part of the neck. The very tapering bodies, burnished on the outside, end in a long, solid and tapering spike (Pl. LXXIII, nos 1-3).

KEAY XXVII

Attested by a minimum of 4 individuals, all ascribable to variant B, this type of Tunisian amphora presents strong analogies in terms of size and shape with Keay XXV amphorae.[148] On the basis of finds in Catalonia, its chronology has been set between the 4th and mid-5th century;[149] however, the significant finds at Carthage, in phases dating to between 450 and 525,[150] which Keay ascribes to a distribution limited exclusively to local markets, may also be evidence that these amphorae were traded regionally even after AD 450. The specimens from Portiglioni present necks of average height and barely thickened rims with an almost plain lip. The handles, similar in shape to those of Keay XXV, are set on the rim and at the junction between the neck and the shoulder. The latter may be unpronounced or pronounced (Pl. LXXIV, nos 1-2). The diameter of the rims ranges from 11 to 13 cm.

KEAY XXXVA

This type of large amphora was produced and traded in the 5th century AD.[151] The only specimen found at *Portus Scabris* has a very thickened rim, rounded on top and hooked, with a diameter of 12 cm. The conical neck presents four fine grooves on the outer surface beneath the rim. The "ear-shaped" handles have a thickened strap section and are set on the upper part of the neck and on the shoulder. A lightening of the outer surface, with a yellow-cream colour, can be observed (Pl. LXXV, no.1).

c.2. Forms Coming Into Use During the Vandal Period

This subcategory consists of a minimum number of 10 transport vessels introduced during the Vandal era and produced continuously during the Byzantine period, sometimes up until the very beginning of the 7th century. 9 of the specimens found belong to large types of amphora (Keay LXII, Keay VIII, and Keay LV), whilst 1 is a medium-sized amphora (Keay L *similis*).

KEAY LV

A large amphora present with 2 specimens at *Portus Scabris*. This type is also attested in the urban context of Roselle and at the villa with late antique phases of Aiali, in the countryside near Roselle. The minimum number of 2 individuals from Portiglioni have a vertical rim with an internal swelling, rounded on the upper surface; the lip is plain or unpronounced. The sub-cylindrical neck presents a series of light but closely packed horizontal incised comb decorations on the outside, at the point where the neck joins the rim. The "ear-shaped" handles are set on the neck and shoulder. The rims have a diameter between 12 and 13 cm. In one case, the outer surface was lightened in colour (Pl. LXXVI, nos 1-2). This amphora dates to between the end of the 5th and the mid-6th century AD, although its production may have continued slightly after this.[152]

KEAY L SIMILIS (?)

This is a medium-sized amphora which, given its morphology, probably descends from Keay L; on the basis of the evidence from Catalonia it has been dated to between the 4th and mid-5th centuries.[153] Thanks to a series of finds of similar forms, in contexts of the late 6th and 7th centuries,[154] a possible evolution of Keay L into a smaller variant has been proposed, produced in Tunisia between the middle and late Byzantine period. The only specimen found at Portiglioni has a rather everted plain rim, flattened on the upper surface. The handles, pseudorectangular in section, present a light longitudinal groove on their upper surface and are set on the shoulder and at the junction between the rim and the neck. The diameter of the rim is 8 cm (Pl. LXXVI, no. 3). The identification is uncertain.

KEAY VIII

A large cylindrical amphora dated to between the late 5th and the 7th century, with two documented variants (A and B).[155] At Portiglioni a single specimen was

[147] Keay 1984, pp.212-219.
[148] Keay, in light of some similarities in height, width and rim diameters, pointed out the similar size of types Keay XXV and XXVII. See Keay 1984, p.224.
[149] *Ibidem* p.224.
[150] Fulford-Peacock 1984, p.133, n n.53-55.
[151] Bonifay 2004, p.135.
[152] On the date see Bonifay 2004, p.137.
[153] On Keay L type see Keay 1984, p.265, Fig.115, no.1.
[154] It is worth noting the evidence from Sant'Antonino in Liguria, Santa Giulia in Brescia, Marseilles, Carthage and Sidi Jidi in Tunisia, see Murialdo 2001a, p.271.
[155] Keay 1998, p.147.

found which seems to belong to variant B given its morphological properties. It has a flat vertical rim, about 12 cm wide, ending in a thickened and pointed lip and with a fairly marked ledge separating it from the cylindrical neck (Pl. LXXVI, no. 4). This amphora has hitherto never been found with an internal pitch coating and, according to Bonifay's recent remarks, appears to have been used to export oil.[156] The proposed date of variant Keay VIIIB is between the second half of the 5th to the first third of the 6th AD.[157]

KEAY LXII

This large container, certainly produced in the subcoastal workshops of Byzacena,[158] was a typology of considerable success within the amphora production of the Vandal and Byzantine eras. Given the morphological structure of the rims, Keay has proposed a subdivision of this type into 21 variants, covering a broad time-range between the mid-5th and the 7th centuries.[159] There is ample evidence for the considerable commercial success of this type, even in the area under examination here, given its systematic presence in sites with 6th and early 7th century phases in the lower Bruna valley, the lower stretches of the Ombrone river, the Osa valley and the town of Roselle. A subdivision of Keay LXII's long production history into two main phases has recently been proposed: an initial phase during the Vandal era, continuing into the Byzantine period, and a second phase restricted to the Byzantine period.[160] This distinction is reflected in a diversification of the variants attested. Specifically, we can say that variants F, G, O and M were introduced at a later date, from the late 6th century onwards.[161] Given the absence of variant A from the late 6th/7th century stratigraphy at Sant'Antonino di Perti, where numerous other versions of Keay LXII are attested, we can suggest that the production of this variant ceased by the end of the 6th century.[162] A minimum number of at least 5 individuals are documented at Portiglioni belonging to variant A (1 specimen), to variant Q=Albegna 11-12 and Keay LXIIR[163] (3 specimens) and to a generic Keay LXII attested by a spike fragment.

VARIANT A

This version has a barely everted band-shaped rim, rounded on the upper surface and slightly thickened, with a light groove on the outside marking the point where it joins the neck. The outer surface of the rim is slightly concave and the neck appears to be conical. The rim is 13 cm wide (Pl. LXXVII, no. 1).

VARIANT KEAY LXIIQ=ALBEGNA 11-12 AND KEAY LXIIR

This variant presents a band-shaped rim which may be either vertical or slightly flaring. The rim ends in a barely thickened and slightly hooked lip. The inner surface of the edge presents a fairly marked indentation, whilst the outer profile is convex. There is a ledge at the point of junction between rim and neck. The handles are set on the neck immediately beneath the rim (Pl. LXXVII, nos 2-3).

GENERIC KEAY LXII

This name has been given to a spike probably belonging to a Keay LXII given its shape. The fragment is 4.4 cm high and 2.6 cm wide at the base, and presents a band in relief with a convex profile and a "button-shaped" end (Pl. LXXVII, no. 4) The shape suggests an association with variant F:[164] one of the 15 possible versions of the spikes belonging to this type identified by Keay.

c.3. Forms Coming Into Production in the Byzantine Period

Some scholars have recently suggested that some variants of Keay LXII and other large cylindrical vessels, mainly Keay LXI, should be ascribed to the phase of reorganization of production activities during the Byzantine period which led to the introduction of new typological models.[165] It seems entirely plausible that the reconquest of Tunisia would have led to the re-establishment of the fiscal links between Carthage on the one hand and Rome and Constantinople on the other.[166] Specifically, the resumption of food supply to Rome once again created that system of linked industries, which also encouraged the commercial circulation of goods, characteristic of trade in the Mediterranean before 439. A subsequent alteration in the amphora production of the Byzantine period can be dated to the late 6th and early 7th centuries, when a new typology characterized by its smaller size, globular body and "fondo convesso ombelicato" was introduced.[167] This formal innovation seems to have been influenced to some extent by the influx of contemporary productions used in the eastern Mediterranean, where amphorae with a globular body appear in some instances to represent a development of older forms.[168] The gradual establishment of this new type was doubtless closely linked to the reorganization of trade: smaller forms without a spike appear unsuitable for the large-scale maritime trade in the

156 Bonifay-Garnier 2007, p.19.
157 Bonifay 2004, p.132.
158 Peacock *et alii* 1989.
159 Keay 1984, pp.309-350 and Keay 1998, pp.144-153.
160 Murialdo 2001a, pp.264-267.
161 Keay 1998, p.147.
162 Murialdo 2001a, p.266.
163 On this definition see Bonifay 2004, p.137.

164 Keay 1984, p.343, Fig.161, no.1.
165 Keay 1998, pp.148-149.
166 *Ibidem*, p.151; Wickham 2005, pp.723-728.
167 See Keay 1998, pp.148-149; Murialdo 2001a, pp.289-291.
168 See, for example, the morphological links between amphora type 2 from the Yassi Ada shipwreck dated to the early decades of the 7th AD near Bodrum in Turkey and the LRA2. On the early 7th AD amphorae from Yassi Ada see Bass 1982, pp.155-165.

foodstuffs transported in these containers. Certainly the absence of the spike indicates a change in the way the containers were stored. It is possible that demand decreased from a quantitative point of view but remained widespread and linked mainly to major centres of consumption, both on the coast and inland, thus leading to an increasing preference for smaller containers which could be transported by different means, both by sea (ships of medium tonnage), by river (barges) and by land (carts).

The recent definition of this new type of amphorae does not allow us to shed full light on its areas of production, although the significant evidence gathered in the Ligurian context of Sant'Antonino[169] and in the Crypta Balbi in Rome[170] suggest that Tunisia was an important region of provenance at least until the late 7th century.

GLOBULAR AMPHORA "A FONDO CONVESSO OMBELICATO"

A single specimen of this type is attested, consisting of a base "a fondo convesso ombelicato" with a diameter of about 13 cm, with fairly flaring walls (Pl. LXXVII, no. 5). This form is made using a fairly purified red fabric (10R 5/8 red), characterized by an inclusions to matrix ratio between 5% and 10%.[171] A few quartz granules with an average diameter of 0.2 mm were identified. The piece appears to have been well-fired in an oxidizing atmosphere and presents no obvious firing defects.[172] This body clay, which appears to be identical to that used in Tunisian wares given its properties, presents similarities with fabric A1a from S.Antonino, whose Tunisian origin has been confirmed by thin-section analysis.[173]

Amphora of Tripolitanian Origin

Only a single minimum individual of the Tripolitanian III amphora is attested at Portus Scabris. It is a rim sherd characterized by a slightly everted rim, with a double ledge profile, ending in a pointed hanging lip. The rim, with a diameter of about 15 cm is set on a short conical neck (Pl. LXXV, no. 2). The specimen found is identical to one attested at Carthage in a context dated to between AD 450 and 500;[174] however, it has been suggested that this was a residual find.[175] Both Tripolitanian I and III amphorae were manufactured at the same workshops, located in the hinterland of the coastal cities of Leptis Magna and Oea, modern Tripoli, and in the vicinity of major agricultural production areas.[176] However, we cannot rule out that amphorae morphologically similar to Tripolitanian III/Keay XI were also produced by at least one of the workshops located in the Tunisian Sahel region: the site of Salakta has yielded one specimen made using the same fabric employed for the transport containers manufactured *in loco*.[177] The Mediterranean distribution of these amphorae, generally fairly limited, suggests that they were destined essentially for the provision of foodstuffs to Rome and only to a minimal extent for trade on the free market.[178] Whereas Tripolitanian I appears to circulate mainly between the Augustan period to the mid-2nd century AD,[179] Tripolitanian III circulated especially during the second half of the 2nd and the 3rd centuries AD; later, in the 4th century, it was replaced by some

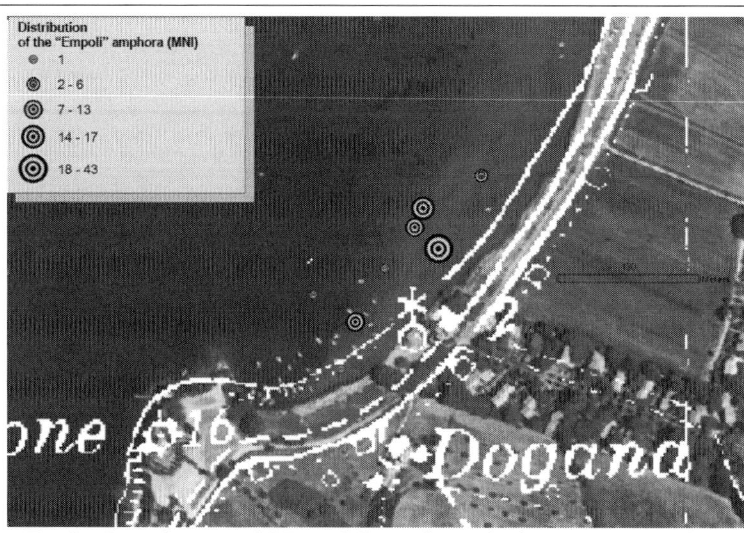

Fig.9_ Distribution of "Empoli" amphora finds at Portus Scabris.

[169] Murialdo 2001a, pp.291-293.
[170] Saguì 1998, pp.315-317.
[171] See Fabric Anf 109 in the Catalogue.
[172] Several specimens from Crypta Balbi deposit present some firing defects: Saguì 1998, p.315.

[173] On this fabric from the Sant'Antonino ceramic assemblages see Murialdo 2001a, p.260.
[174] Fulford-Peacock 1984, p.132, Fig.41, no.85.
[175] Anselmino *et alii* 1986, p.177.
[176] *Ibidem*, p.130; for the economy of Tripolitania see in particular Mattingly 1995, pp.138-159.
[177] Peacock *et alii* 1989, p.193 and Fig.16, no.9.
[178] Manacorda 1977.
[179] Bonifay 2004, p.105.

late variants circulating well into the 4th AD.[180] I cannot rule out that the only specimen from *Portus Scabris* can be assigned to a 4th AD variant.

Italic Transport Vessels (Fourth to Sixth/Early Seventh Centuries)

The Italic transport containers found at Portiglioni are represented mainly by the Empoli amphora,[181] accounting for about 95% of the specimens belonging to this category. The remaining 5% consists of 1 MRA1 type, of probable Sicilian origin, 3 specimens of Keay LII and a late variant of this type. All these amphora types were used to transport wine.

Empoli Amphora

Some written sources indicate the importance of the wine production of *Tuscia* between the 4th and 6th centuries, not only for regional consumption but also for export. In around the mid-4th century, an anonymous geographer, speaking of Tuscany, described this as an agriculturally rich region, particularly renowned for its wine production.[182] For the early 6th century phase a passage from Cassiodorus, part of which discusses *Tuscia*, is of particular importance, although it is impossible to determine whether his discussion refers to a specific area or to the region as a whole. During the reign of Theodoric, various regions of Italy had attained a production capacity such that they were able to set aside their surplus for export; these regions, as well as Campania and Lucania, also included *Tuscia*. From these areas, *victualia* or various foodstuffs, could be exported to the *Galliae*.[183] It is entirely plausible that these foodstuffs included wine from the region. Later on, during the Greek-Gothic war, the agricultural production of Tuscany must still have been registering a partially positive trend, since boats laden with foodstuffs bound for Rome, under siege by the Gothic forces, sailed from its shores. In the late antique sources, *Tuscia* is never mentioned as being among the regions of note for the large-scale production of grain. In any case, the geomorphology of this area did not allow for the

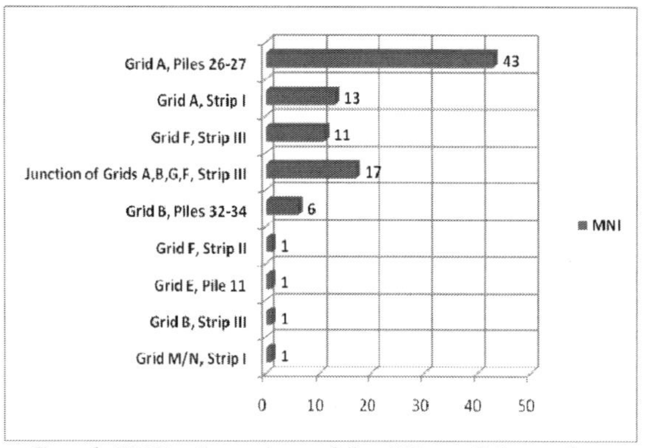

Graph XVII_ Location of the "Empoli" amphora finds in the Portiglioni Bay.

development of cereal farming on a sufficiently large scale to ensure the necessary surplus for export, as was the case in other regions such as Puglia, Calabria, Sicily and also Sardinia.[184] Viticulture, far more suited to the natural environment, must therefore have been one of the main, if not the principal, agricultural resource. Archaeology provides valuable information on the capillary regional distribution,[185] and a medium-distance circulation outside the region, of the Tuscan wine produced in the middle Valdarno area[186] and in the Agro Volterrano.[187] Particularly interesting are recent finds in some Roman contexts, where the wine transported in Empoli amphorae represented a commodity that was sometimes consumed in large quantities.[188] Specimens of this type of amphora have also been identified at Porto Torres in Sardinia[189] and at Luni and Ventimiglia in Liguria.[190]

The substantial minimum number of individuals documented at Portiglioni nonetheless represents an anomaly in the distribution patterns for this typology in the contexts studied here. The number of specimens attested at this site is completely out of line with the limited diffusion of this type in the areas covered by the survey and in the town of Roselle.

[180] *Ibidem*, pp.105-107.

[181] A specific and analytical study of the Empoli amphorae from *Portus Scabris* was undertaken by Sergio Bargagliotti and Franca Cibecchini and its publication is forthcoming. My study of the Empoli amphorae is mainly aimed at proposing a complete overview of amphora finds at *Portus Scabris* in late Antiquity, rather than at providing a specific discussion of the type and its morphological variants both the object of an in-depth investigation in Bargagliotti and Cibecchini's work.

[182] See De Robertis 1972, p.55.

[183] "*...in Gallicana igitur regione victualium cognovimus caritatem, ad quam negotitatio sempre prompta festinat, ut empta angustiare pretio largius distrahantur. sic eventi ut et venditoribus satisfiat et illis provisio nostra subvenit. Atque ideo devotio tua presenti auctoritate cognoscat omnes navicularios Campanile, Lucaniae sive Tusciae fideiussoribus idonei se debere commettere, ut cum victualibus speciebus tantum proficiscantur ad Gallias, abituri licentiam distrahendi sic ut inter emptorem venditoremque convenerit.*" Cassiodorus, *Variae, IIII, V, 1-2.*

[184] For the main Italic regions specializing in grain production see De Robertis 1972, p.88 and pp.105-115.

[185] The regional circulation of Empoli amphorae is aimed at coastal areas (rural sites in the Albegna valley, Cosa, Vada Volterrana and some rural settlements in Versilia) as well as inland towns (Fiesole, Florence, Lucca, Pistoia and Siena). See Francovich-Cantini 2006; Cantini 2007; Del Rio-Vallebona 1996; Villa 1994, pp.359-361; Faggella 1990, pp.249-250 and pp.255-257; Cambi 1989.

[186] Cambi 1989.

[187] Del Rio-Vallebona 1996, p.490.

[188] In the *mithraeum* of the Crypta Balbi in Rome, in contexts dating to the mid-5th century AD, this amphora is second only to Keay LII among the amphorae imported from Italic areas. See Saguì-Coletti 2004, p.244, Graph no.3. The Empoli amphora is less well documented between AD425 and AD475 in the *Domus Tiberiana*: Munzi *et alii* 2004, p.111, Tab.2. Finally, it is rare in the *Magna Mater* context, where it reaches only 1% of the total documented amphorae of the period between AD420 and AD 440: see Reynolds 1995, Appendix D.21.

[189] For *Turris Libisonis* see Villedieu 1986, pp.157 and 159.

[190] For these two sites see Villa 1994, pp.360-361.

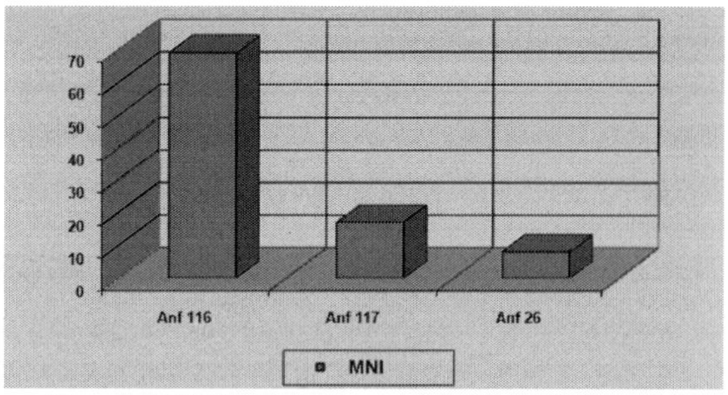

Graph XVIII_ Fabrics and MNI of "Empoli" amphorae.

One possible explanation for this anomaly may be found by analysing the characteristics of the finds from Portiglioni (Fig.9 and Graph XVII).

The minimum individuals ascribable to this amphora type were recovered, in around roughly 48% of cases (43 specimens), in the vicinity of *piles* 26-27, and thus in an extremely circumscribed area.

The minimum vessels from this site were in all probability broken during digging operations, as suggested by the presence of fresh fractures and the identification of rims, bases and bodies belonging to the same vessels. Yet more interesting is the discovery of cork stoppers in many of the individuals found. A further two significant concentrations were found in close proximity to that described above. 11 and 17 specimens come from the excavation of *strip III* in *grid-square* F and from the intersection of *grid-squares* A, B, G, F: two sites, one less than 30 and one about 40 m from the point of maximum concentration. The nature of the finds at the first site and the presence of numerous other specimens in its immediate vicinity seem to me to represent valid evidence of the presence of a probable beached shipwreck. Indeed, the heavy concentration of materials and especially the significant presence of cork stoppers is inconsistent with loading and unloading activities or with the disposal of materials damaged during the voyage. The point at which the ship sank should probably be placed near *piles* 26 and 27, whilst the presence of similar amphorae at the two nearby sites may be due to the movement of the material from the wreck site caused by waves breaking on the shore.

FABRICS AND TYPOLOGY

An examination of the fabrics of the Empoli amphorae made it possible to identify at least three fabrics (Anf 26, Anf 116 and Anf 117), with fairly similar properties (Graph XVIII). In all three cases the fabric is fairly purified and non-porous, hard-fired and with a clean or even fracture. In two cases (Anf 26 and Anf 117) microfossils are present in the clay; in one of these, Anf 26, there are also a few quartz inclusions, whilst the other two share the presence of rare limestone.[191] The amphorae were evenly fired in an oxidizing atmosphere, although in some cases firing defects have been observed, indicated by the presence of a grey core in the fracture or by a bichrome colouring. This property has been identified especially in specimens produced using fabric Anf 26, which varies in colour from light red (2.5 YR 6/8) to light grey (2.5YR 6/1 reddish gray). The other two fabrics, by contrast, as well as presenting some slightly different mineralogical phases, have a light red and generally even colouring, though one over-fired specimen has been identified for each of the two. Claudio Capelli's minero-petrographic analysis of some sample specimens will determine more accurately whether they were manufactured in the middle Valdarno or in the workshops identified in the Livorno area.[192]

Portus Scabris	**Cambi 1989, p.567, Pl.2**
Variant 1	Pl.2, no.5 similis
Variant 2	Pl.2, no.1
Variant 3	Not identified
Variant 4	Not identified
Variant 5	Pl.2, no.6 similis

Tab.V_ The "Empoli" amphora typology: the evidence from Portus Scabris compared with that in Cambi 1989.

As concerns the typology of the Empoli amphora, the specimens found at *Portus Scabris* indicate a significant variation in the morphology of rims, necks and shoulders.[193] The existence of various versions which nonetheless belong to a single form and the large number of specimens made it advisable to attempt a typological definition taking into consideration the theories already formulated in the past (Table V).[194]

Our analysis initially concentrated on the variants attested at the site identified near *piles* 26-27, which, according to our theory, come from a single cargo. It is important to note the association of morphologically diverse versions within a context that probably formed in a unitary and coherent way. The first variant identified is characterized by a rounded rim, slightly thickened on the outside, narrow neck and pronounced

[191] For the detailed microscopic analysis see the Catalogue.
[192] I was informed by Sergio Bargagliotti and Franca Cibecchini that the thin section analysis of some specimens of Empoli amphorae from Portus Scabris was planned in 2006. For a minero-petrographic description of the two main groups of fabrics, from the Arno valley and the Livornò area see Roman Amphorae: a Digital Resource (University of Southampton) http://ads.ahds.ac.uk/catalogue/archive/amphora_ahrb_2005/petrology.cfm?id=129, and also Pasquinucci *et alii* 1999, p.59 for the discovery of a kiln site in the Livorno area.
[193] The determination of the minimum number of individuals belonging to this amphora type was mainly based on the study of each single rim fragment and subsequently on that of the bases.
[194] Cambi 1989, p.564, Figs 1-6 and p.567.

wide shoulder. The rim, only 7 cm in diameter, is the smallest attested (Pl. LXXVIII, no. 1). The second variant has a ring-shaped rim, thickened on the outside and presenting a light groove on the inside; the neck generally tends to be wider whilst the shoulder may be either unpronounced or pronounced (Pl. LXXVIII, nos 2-3, Pl. LXXIX, no. 1). Variant 2 also includes a version with a rim similar to the most-widespread version but with a slightly "a becco" profile (Pl. LXXIX, no. 2). Variant 3, on the other hand, has a more flaring rim, with a clearly "a becco" section, whilst the neck is similar to the preceding variant (Pl. LXXIX, no. 3). Variant 4 shares many features with no. 1 and no. 2, but differs from the former for its more thickened rim and from the latter for the absence of the inner groove. Its narrow neck is reminiscent of that of variant 1 (Pl. LXXIX, no. 5). Variant 5 has a fairly everted rim, more squashed than the other variants; only in one case is there a fairly marked groove on the upper surface (Pl. LXXX, nos 1-3).

On average the mouths are about 9 cm wide, with a minimum of 7 cm and a maximum of 10 cm. The handles are on the whole more standardized: in variants 1, 2 and 5 they are strap-shaped with a pseudo-rectangular section and two longitudinal grooves on the upper surface. In variants 3 and 4, on the other hand, they tend to take on a thickened strap shape and lose the double groove. In all the documented variants the handles are set on the neck, immediately beneath the rim, and on the shoulder.

The specimens from the other sectors of the Portiglioni deposit allow us to note a larger number of amphorae belonging to variant 2 (Pl. LXXXI nos 1-3, Pl. LXXXII, nos 1-2, Pl. LXXXIII, nos 1-2) and 5 (Pl. LXXXIII, no. 3, Pl. LXXXV, nos 1-3, Pl. LXXXIV, no. 1) whilst variants 3 and 4 are much rarer, the latter being attested by a version that stands out, in particular, for its large size and pronounced shoulder (Pl. LXXXIV, no. 2).

MR1 Amphora

Among the Italic amphora 1 minimum individual belonging to type MR1 is also documented. This is a wine amphora produced in eastern Sicily and exported mainly between the 3rd and 4th centuries AD.[195] It is probable that this type was still widespread in the early 5th century, if the specimen documented at Roselle in US 5141 is in phase. The only specimen found at Portiglioni has a rim shaped on the inside with a diameter of 5 cm set on a narrow cylindrical neck, with clear wheel marks inside. The handles have a circular section and are set on the neck immediately beneath the rim (Pl. LXXXVI, no. 1). The fabric used to produce this amphora seems to be the same as that of the MR1 found at Roselle (Anf 18).

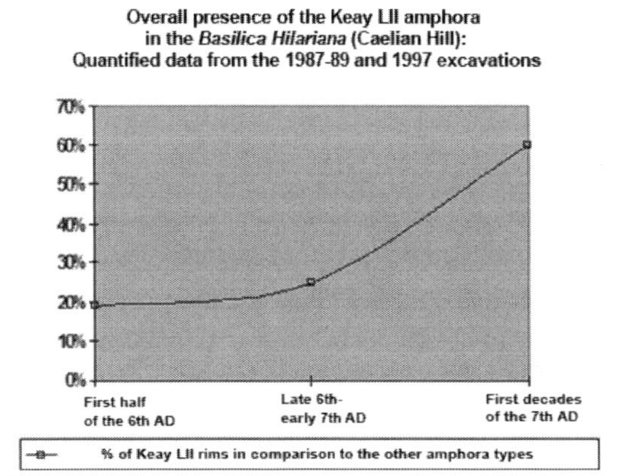

Graph XIX_ Keay LII in the Basilica Hilariana in Rome (based on Pacetti 2004).

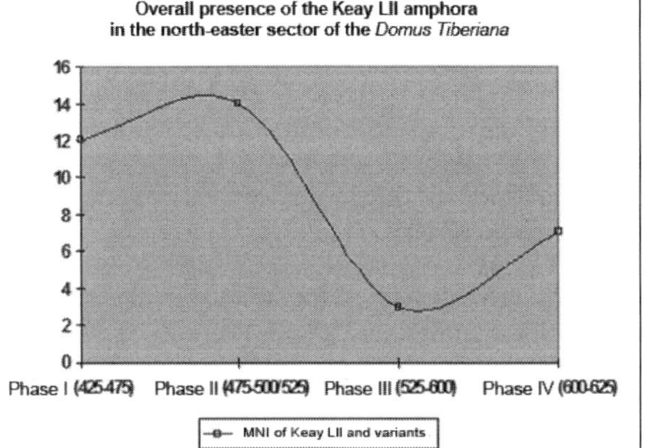

Graph XX_ Keay LII in the north-eastern sector of the Domus Tiberiana in Rome (based on Munzi et alii 2004).

Keay LII and Late Variant

In the Portiglioni context at least 3 specimens of Keay LII were found, alongside 1 specimen which can be ascribed to a late variant belonging to the so-called "Keay LII family".[196] This container for the transport of wine produced in southern Calabria and north-eastern Sicily came into production from the first half of the 4th century but became truly widespread only from the mid-5th century.[197] The type continues to be well-documented during the 6th century, reaching the late 7th with a series of variants.[198] Some Roman contexts provide fairly clear evidence of the importance of Sicilian and Calabrian wine between the mid-5th and 7th centuries, despite differences in the quantities found, probably due to differences in wine

[195] For this type see Chapter 4.

[196] Saguì 1998, p.323, Fig.11.

[197] Reynolds 1995, p.68, mentioning Arthur 1989, p.135 and p.137. The case of Naples is very significant as Keay LII is not documented in contexts dating to the end of the 4th century AD, but starts to be attested at the beginning of the 5th and then reaches a considerable peak in the mid-5th century AD. In Rome, in the context of the Temple of Cybele on the Palatine, Keay LII is well documented as early as the mid-4th century AD: see Pacetti 1998, p.191, Tab.1.

[198] Saguì *et alii* 2001, p.292.

consumption within the deposits (Graphs XIX and XX).[199]

Both in *Bruttium* and in Sicily, wine production must have represented an important agricultural specialization. In Calabria viticulture was already well-developed from the 4th century, to the extent that the region produced the surplus needed for export, and further increased during the 6th century.[200] It is fairly probable, as noted by C. Panella,[201] that the development of viticulture and the commercialization of the wine produced around the Straits of Messina and in the surrounding area was strongly influenced by the imposition of a wine tax paid to Rome by *Bruttium*, Sicily and other regions of central and southern Italy.

The morphological similarities between Keay LII and MR1 and the partial overlapping of their areas of provenance may suggest that these two forms developed one from the other. Their chronology also seems to confirm this theory: Keay LII begins to be widely attested in western Mediterranean contexts from the 5th century, when the production of MR1 ceases. Reynolds has suggested that Keay LII had a more circumscribed sphere of distribution than MR1, directed mainly at Rome and secondarily at Marseilles, and which on a smaller scale also touched on other cities such as Naples and Tarragona.[202] However, the circulation of Keay LII also reached both the western and eastern coasts of the Adriatic, with finds in contexts at Classe and Aquileia in the west and Zara and Spalato in the east;[203] to these we should add the recent finds at Butrint in Albania.[204] In Tuscany, too, finds of Keay LII appear to be fairly significant, especially in the urban and rural sites of the coastal belt and the Tuscan archipelago. In addition to the contexts examined here, Keay LII is documented in the town of Cosa,[205] in phases of the first half of the 6th century, in the villa of Torre Tagliata in phases of the mid-5th century or possibly slightly later,[206] on the island of Gorgona,[207] and in the *horrea* of S. Gaetano,[208] at Vada Volterrana, between the 4th and 6th/7th century. Finds in inland areas seem to be more limited, with a single minimum individual from the urban stratigraphy of

MNI	Location	Fabric
1	Grid F, Strip I	Anf 120
1	Grid A, Strip III, Piles 26-27	Anf 128
1	Grid F, Strip II	Anf 128
1 (late variant)	Grid F, Strip I	Anf 132

Tab.VI_ Keay LII amphorae and late variant: MNI/Location/Fabrics.

Siena[209] and a few specimens in the archaeological deposit of Via de' Castellani in Florence.[210]

MORPHOLOGICAL PROPERTIES OF THE PORTIGLIONI SPECIMENS

The scarce standardization of productions belonging to the Keay LII family has already been stressed by others,[211] as has the probable connection between this morphological differentiation and the existence of a number of production centres dependent on various rural wine-producing sites.

At sites such as Portiglioni, where we have no stratigraphical information on the contexts of provenance of the individual specimens, it becomes essential to attempt an association between the variants identified and one of the phases characterizing the development and morphological transformation of Keay LII amphorae between the 4th and 7th centuries. It now appears evident that the earliest specimens of the 4th and 5th centuries present a taller neck, often tubular in shape, which in most 6th century variants becomes shorter, conical and more flaring (Table VI).[212]

One of the versions attested at *Portus Scabris* is characterized by its long tubular neck; the pseudo-triangular rim, 8 cm wide, is set on the neck. The handles are set on the neck and on the unpronounced shoulder and have a circular section, with two lateral grooves (Pl. LXXXVII, no. 1). This specimen presents close similarities with one attested in the north-east sector of the *Domus Tiberiana* in Rome, in a phase dated to between AD 425 and 475.[213] A second version presents a rim with a triangular profile, 7 cm in diameter, and a cylindrical neck which is shorter than that of the variant described above. The handles, which have a circular section with a central band in relief, are set beneath the rim and elbow-shaped (Pl. LXXXVI no. 2). Particularly interesting is the presence of residues, visible under a microscope, of an internal dark-green pitch coating which represents further evidence that the amphora may have contained wine.

---

[199] On the *Basilica Hilariana* on the Caelian Hill see Pacetti 2004, pp.435-457; on the north-eastern sector of the *Domus Tiberiana* see Munzi et alii 2004, pp.91-128.
[200] On the written sources mentioning wine production in *Bruttium* see De Robertis 1972, p.107.
[201] Panella 1993, pp.647-648.
[202] Reynolds 1995, pp.69-70.
[203] Pacetti 1998, p.192.
[204] Reynolds 2004a, p.229.
[205] Fontana 2003, p.311 and p.312, Fig.141, no.1.
[206] Ciampoltrini-Rendini 1989, p.531, Fig.11, no.4.
[207] Firmati-Gambogi 1998, p.636.
[208] Del Rio-Vallebona 1996, p.490.

[209] A residual specimen was found in a mid-7th to 8th century context from the urban context of Santa Maria della Scala in Siena: Cantini 2005, p.201.
[210] Cantini 2007.
[211] Pacetti 1998.
[212] Ibidem, pp.193-197.
[213] Munzi *et alii* 2004, p.112, Fig.VIII, no.72.

This specimen also has features in common with forms from the *Domus Tiberiana*, in this case both from phases dated to between AD 420 and 475 and from a later phase dating to AD 475/500.[214] A third variant has a rim measuring 8 cm in diameter, of pseudotriangular section, ending in a slightly hooked lip. The neck is broader and shorter than in the other specimens found. The thickened strap handles present two light longitudinal grooves and are set immediately beneath the rim (Pl. LXXXVI, no. 3). In this case too, there is an internal pitch coating. Once again, comparable specimens have been found in the *Domus Tiberiana* deposit, in a phase dated to between roughly 600 and 625.[215] The potential for establishing a precise point of comparison between our specimens and those documented in Roman contexts of the 5th to early 7th centuries, where stratigraphic reference points have made it possible to develop a chrono-typology for Keay LII, allowed us to provide a more accurate chronological context for the versions documented at our site.

Finally, we note a minimum individual characterized by an "a becco" rim with a diameter of 7 cm, set on a short conical neck. The handles are of circular section and are set immediately beneath the rim (Pl. LXXXVII, no. 2). The fabric used to make this specimen (Anf 132) is fairly similar to body clay Anf 128, used to make two Keay LII.[216] Its morphology presents close analogies with a late variant belonging to the Keay LII family and found in the late 7th century deposit in the Crypta Balbi.[217] A generic comparison can also be made with a still later production from Calabria or Calabria/Sicily, again attested in the Crypta Balbi, but this time in the 8th-century context.[218] The Portiglioni specimen, regardless of whether it belongs to a late 7th-century or an early 8th-century transport container nonetheless represents important evidence of the circulation of southern Italian foodstuffs north of Rome during the early Middle Ages. The Rome market doubtless represented the main outlet for the flows of foodstuffs from southern Italy, at least while the Church estates in *Bruttium* and Sicily continued to play a fundamental role in the provisioning of Rome and its Church.[219] Obviously this specimen represents a first piece of evidence, albeit episodic, of the possible existence of trade flows leading in other directions than their main target.

Transport Containers from the Eastern-Aegean Area (Fourth-Seventh Centuries)

At least 18 amphorae were found at Portiglioni which come from the eastern Mediterranean basin. Of these the most frequent were LR 1 amphorae, with over 66% of the total, followed by two variants belonging to the heterogeneous Agorà M 273 group, whilst the Agorà P16074, LR 2, LR 5 and Samos Cistern types are present with a single specimen each (Graph XXI and Table VII).

Generally speaking, the distribution in the western Mediterranean of amphorae from the *pars orientalis* becomes truly significant only from the late 4th/5th century onwards. From that time until the end of the 6th century, and in a more selective way during the 7th century, there was a systematic flow of eastern wines to a large number of western sites.[220] The increased circulation of wines from the Levant is certainly a consequence of the growth and strengthening of agricultural production, triggered by the foundation of Constantinople which, alongside Rome, becomes the

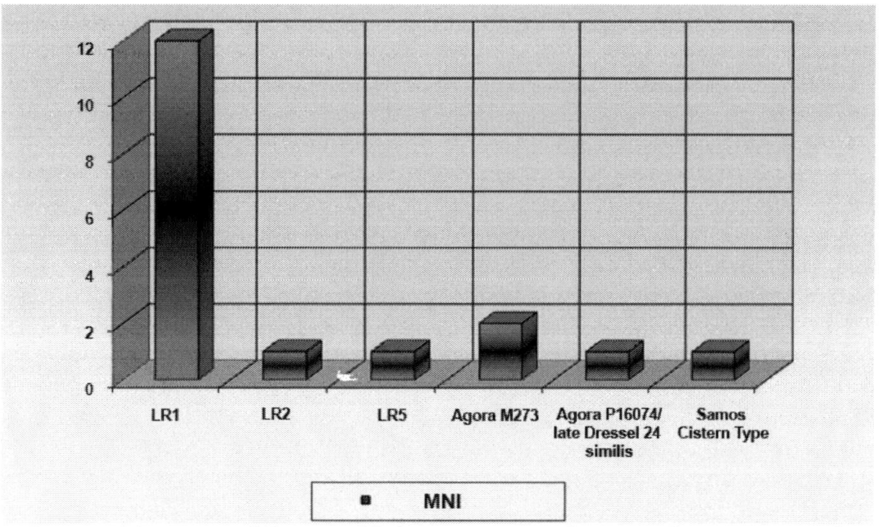

Graph XXI_ Typologies of Aegean and Eastern Mediterranean amphorae and minimum numbers of individuals.

214 *Ibidem*, p.112, Fig.VIII, n.73, and pp.110, 114.
215 *Ibidem*, p.116, Fig.X, nos 91,93.
216 See the Catalogue for details.
217 Saguì 1998, p.32, Fig.11, no.6.
218 Romei 2004, p.280, Fig.1, no.3.
219 In 730s the papal estates in Sicily were confiscated by the Byzantine emperor Leo III, as a consequence of the iconoclast crisis: see Marazzi 1991.
220 Reynolds 1995, p.71; Panella 1993, pp.654-673.

Mediterranean's main centre of consumption.[221] The trade route linking the *pars orientalis* centred around Constantinople on the one hand and Rome on the other, followed a route which had already existed for some time: that which, from the early imperial period up until the foundation of Byzantium had allowed grain supplies from Alexandria to reach Rome. The commodities crossing the Mediterranean basin from east to west, during late Antiquity and the early Middle Ages, independently of their exact point of departure, moved mainly along coastal routes. The first intermediate stops were Cyprus and Crete for trade flows from the southern part of the Levant, or the port of Malvasia (*Monemvasìa*) for those from the Aegean. Subsequently, after crossing the Ionian Sea, the cargoes were directed towards the Straits of Messina and thence through the southern Tyrrhenian to Rome.[222] This was obviously a highly complex axis with an equally complex series of branch routes, for which the widespread dissemination of eastern amphorae in the Adriatic provides ample evidence.[223] As for goods arriving from other regions, Rome must have acted as a redistribution point, making use of a navigation system based on small ships to ensure supply to contexts in the northern Tyrrhenian and in Liguria.

Amphorae from the Aegean Sea and the Black Sea

Agorà P16074/late Dressel 24 *similis*

This name has been given to a single specimen, of problematic identification, similar to an amphora identified by Robinson in contexts of the Athenian agora.[224] This form is characterized by a funnel-shaped and slightly everted rim with a diameter of 13 cm, set on a fairly tall cylindrical neck. The strap handles are set on the neck, immediately beneath the rim and on the shoulder. The amphora has a fairly pronounced external ribbing (Pl. LXXXVIII, no. 2). The specimen is made from a fairly purified fabric, light reddish/brown in colour (5YR, 6/3) which contains rare small volcanic rock inclusions (Anf 115). The volcanic fragments appear macroscopically similar to those identified in the body clay of an Aegean LR2 amphora from Portiglioni. Robinson has noted a close morphological similarity between type P16074 and type Agorà M235, attested at Athens in the 4th century and in turn resembling form Agorà M272/LR2 for the morphological structure of the body. It therefore seems possible that type P16074 may belong to the same production tradition as LR2, to the extent that the two forms share some morphological characteristics, and, if the similarity between the inclusions in the two body clays is confirmed, the same area of origin. Since it has proved impossible to identify other contexts in the western Mediterranean where similar specimens have been found, we can currently suggest an occasional distribution of this type, dated to the 4th century on the basis of the chronological information provided by the Athenian excavations. Evidence on the contents is currently lacking; however, considering the affinities between this amphora and Dressel 24 (*infra*) olive oil be the main foodstuff transported. It is worth noting that Opait has recently identified a possible line of evolution which starts with Dressel 24, produced in the Aegean area, and leads to LR2.[225] The specimen found at *Portus Scabris* presents some close affinities with the late variant of a Dressel 24 *similis* found in the north of Dobrudja on the western coasts of the Black Sea, probably dating to the late 3rd century AD.[226]

Location	***Type (and MNI)***
Grid F, Strips II-III	LR1 (1)
Junction of Grids A, B, G, F, Strip III	LR1 (1), Agora P16074 (1), Agora M273 (1), Samos Cistern Type (1)
Grid F, Piles 24-25	LR 1 (1)
Grid F, Pile I	LR1 (1), LR2 (1), LR5 (1), Agora M273 (1)
Grid A, Strip III, Piles 26-27	LR1 (7)
Grid F, Strips I-II	LR1 (1)

Tab.VII_ Location of the finds of Aegean and Eastern Mediterranean amphorae.

LR2

This type of Aegean amphora is well documented in western Mediterranean contexts, principally between the late 4th and 6th centuries.[227] The distribution of LR2 is in fact dated to between the last quarter of the 4th century and the end of the 6th century although two later specimens, belonging to a variant which has lost the traditional splayed and rounded rim, are attested at Emporio and at S. Antonino di Perti in the early decades of the 7th century.[228] The area of provenance can be identified with a good degree of certainty as the Aegean region, as demonstrated by the discovery of kilns at Chios and Porto Cheli and at Kounoupi in the Argolis.[229] LR2 amphorae were probably used mainly to transport wine.

221 Panella 1983.

222 For the sea-route connecting Constantinople and Rome and the written sources mentioning the possible stops along it see McCormick 2001, pp.502-508.

223 For the distribution of late antique Eastern Mediterranean amphorae along the Adriatic coasts see Villa 1994, p.400 and more recently Gelichi-Negrelli 2007 (eds.).

224 Robinson 1958, Plate 40, no.P16074.

225 Opaiţ 2007, pp.627-643.

226 *Ibidem*, p.632.

227 Reynolds 1995, pp.72-75.

228 Arthur 1998, p.169.

229 *Ibidem*, p.168.

A single specimen was found at Portiglioni characterized by the typical slightly everted rim, thickened on the inside and rounded on the upper surface, and a conical neck with ribbing on the lower part. The thickened strap handles are set on the neck, immediately beneath the rim, which measures 11 cm in diameter (Pl. LXXXVIII, no. 1). The fabric used to make LR2 is light red in colour (2.5 YR, 6/6) with very rare quartz inclusions and minute fragments of volcanic rock (Anf 122).

Agorà M273

Ascribable to this type are 2 amphorae which present affinities with a type of transport container with a wide body, identified by Robinson in the excavations of the Athenian agora in late 4th-century contexts.[230] Amphorae similar to the M273 are common between the 3rd and 6th centuries in the Aegean and the Black Sea, and many of these were probably manufactured in mainland Greece and the Greek islands, whilst others may have been made on the island of Samos.[231] Although one of the two versions presents some differences with respect to the typical morphology of M273, it was decided to attribute it to this form on the basis of a comparison with amphorae of this type from other excavation contexts.[232] It is important to note that we do not as yet have a detailed typological definition of this form to facilitate its identification. The version of Agora M273 found at *Portus Scabris* is characterized by a short vertical neck, on which a rounded rim with a diameter of 10 cm is set. The handles have a rectangular section and are about 2 cm thick and 3 cm wide. They are attached at the junction between neck and rim and on the shoulder. Starting from the shoulder there is a light and fairly sparse rilling (Pl. LXXXIX, no. 1). This specimen is made using fabric Anf 112, dark yellow in colour (5 YR 7/4 reddish yellow), fairly purified, with inclusions of limestone, quartz and especially fragments of volcanic rock (Table VIII). The second version documented, on the other hand, presents a thickened and rounded rim with a diameter of 8 cm, with a barely visible outer spigolo set on a short vertical neck. The strap handles are set immediately beneath the rim and on the shoulder. In this case, too, rilling is present from the shoulder down (Pl. LXXXIX, no. 2). The fabric contains the same mineralogical phases as the preceding specimen, from which it differs mainly in its light brown colour (7.5 YR 6/4).

Type	Fabric
Agora M273	Anf 112
Agora M273 similis	Anf 121

Tab.VIII_ Fabrics of the Agora M273 type.

Samos Cistern Type

The definition of this type is due to Arthur, the first to identify the Samian provenance of an amphora attested at Naples in the 7th-century context of S.Maria La Nova, morphologically similar to a type found, with various specimens, in the fill of a cistern on the island of Samos.[233] This form circulated between the mid-6th and 7th centuries, and its presence in western Mediterranean contexts has been ascribed to a deliberate attempt by the Byzantine state to supply the areas of greatest strategic importance to its own political and military interests.[234] In Italy, the amphora is attested mainly in large towns such as Luni and Naples on the Tyrrhenian coast, Ravenna, Oderzo and Udine in the northern Adriatic, and at secondary settlements such as Kaukana in Sicily and Marano Lagunare in the province of Udine.[235] Recently, large numbers of this type have also been identified in the Roman stratigraphy of the Crypta Balbi: one specimen was used for an *enchytismos* burial in the 6th-century necropolis[236] and various minimum individuals are attested in the late 7th-century deposit.[237] The Samos amphora is also documented in the north-east sector of the *Domus Tiberiana*, in phases dated to between 525 and 600 and between 600 and 625,[238] in the layers of Ambiente D of the Roman Forum between the late 6th and late 7th centuries,[239] in the *Basilica Hilariana* between the late 6th and early 7th centuries,[240] and finally in an Aventine context dating to the mid-7th century.[241] The large number of Roman finds seems to represent clear confirmation of the privileged destination of the wine contained in this type of amphora.

The Portiglioni specimen is characterized by a vertical neck and slightly thickened and rounded rim with a diameter of about 10 cm, with an internal groove. On the outside it presents distinctive rilling from the neck down; this becomes more dense on the shoulder. The strap handle presents a groove on the upper surface. It is set on the neck, immediately beneath the rim and on the shoulder. The interior presents extremely marked wheel lines (Pl. LXXXIX, no. 3). The yellowish red fabric (5YR 4/6) mainly presents inclusions of muscovite and lime, and more rarely of quartz and biotite (Anf 119 bis).

[230] Robinson 1956, p.109, Plate no.29, M273.
[231] Arthur 1998, p.167.
[232] See *Scavi ad Aquileia I*, pp.458-459 and in particular the vessel illustrated in Fig.72, AIA 18.
[233] Arthur 1985, pp.247-259.
[234] Arthur 1989, p.83 and Arthur 1990, coll. 288-290.
[235] Arthur 1990, coll.291-292.
[236] Ricci-Saguì 2001, p.249.
[237] Saguì 1998, p.312, Fig.6.
[238] Munzi *et alii* 2004, p.115, Tab.4 and p.117, Tab.5.
[239] Paganelli 2004, p.191, Graph 4.
[240] Pacetti 2004, p.441, Tab.5.
[241] Fontana *et alii* 2004, p.556, Tab.1.

Amphorae from the Anatolian and Syro-Palestinian Region

LR5

This amphora was manufactured in ancient Palestine, although the production centres hitherto identified tend to suggest an area more circumscribed than the entire region, between Tel Rasile, near Tel Aviv, and Horvat 'Uza in the western part of the Akko valley. Although LR5 were used in Palestine to store various types of foodstuffs, such as oil, figs, fish preserves, grain, beans, nuts, barley and olives, the evidence available on the export of LR5, like LR4, tends to associated these containers with the transport and trade in Palestinian wine.[242] LR5 amphorae were produced from the 2nd to the 7th century, with some evidence of continuity into the Ummayad period.[243] The large-scale export of Palestinian wine seems to have begun towards the end of the 4th century, with an acceleration in the early 5th century. However, it has been observed that the large scale maritime trade in LR4 must have preceded that in LR5 amphorae.[244] In Italy, "bag-shaped" amphorae of types LR5/6 – it is not always possible to make a clear distinction between these two types (LR5 and LR6), which are morphologically similar and produced in the same region – begin to appear in the early 5th century and in some rare cases their export continues until the 7th century.[245]

A single specimen is documented at Portiglioni with a slightly "bag-shaped" body profile, a rounded shoulder and "ear-shaped" handles set on the shoulder; the outer surface presents a closely packed and fairly pronounced ribbing, with only a narrow strip being left plain (Pl. XC, no. 1). The fabric is yellowish red in colour (5YR 5/6) and fairly purified; it presents some inclusions of quartz, limestone and rare limestone. On the outer surface the colour is greenish grey (Gley 1 5/1). The morphological structure of the body and the handles makes it possible to ascribe this specimen to variant 1 of the typology proposed by Pieri on the basis of finds in the south of Gallia, where it is attested mainly in the first half of the 6th century AD.[246]

LR1

With a minimum number of 12 individuals, LR1 is the most frequently attested late antique eastern amphora at *Portus Scabris*. This form was manufactured at various sites located mainly between Cilicia and northern Syria, on the islands of Cyprus and Rhodes and at Datça in the Knidos peninsula.[247] The product most frequently transported in these amphorae was certainly wine, although it is highly likely that they were also used for the trade in olive oil and other non-liquid foodstuffs.[248] It seems probable that a large range of products could have been transported in these amphorae, especially as concerns the wares manufactured in northern Syria. In this region, olive farming was particularly well-established and flourished in the areas controlled by Antioch, Apamea and Chalcis between the 5th and the early 7th century. Without doubt the production of oil represented the main trade specialization and thus the main source of income. Benefiting from this generalized wealth was a substantial class of small and medium-sized landowners who lived in villages, characterized by their high-quality housing, and who were directly involved in olive farming.[249] The presence near Seleucia Pieria at the mouth of the Orontes of the largest LR1 production area hitherto identified, with kiln wasters covering an area of over ten hectares, suggests that these amphorae were used to export the oil produced further inland. This site represents the direct outlet for the foodstuffs arriving from the territory of Antioch.[250] In Italy, between the 5th and the early 7th century, LR1 represent the most frequently attested amphorae overall, and are widespread in both urban and rural contexts.[251] Along the Tuscan coast south of the study area, these amphorae are attested at Cosa in the first half of the 6th century,[252] and in the late antique phases of the villa at Torre Tagliata.[253] In the Tuscan archipelago the form is documented in the 5th-7th-century contexts of the maritime villa at Limiti on the island of Gorgona[254] and in the villa at Giglio Porto.[255] Further north, LR1 is the most frequently documented type of eastern transport container in the second phase (mid-4th – 6th/7th centuries) of the *horrea* of San Gaetano, with 8.9% of the total amphora assemblage.[256]

Moving on to the typological characteristics of LR1, we find, alongside a degree of morphological standardization, the existence of variants characterized by a fairly well-defined chronological differences. This is particularly important, since even in the absence of a

[242] See in particular Kingsley 2001, pp.50-51. The author lists several convincing pieces of evidence for the use of LR4 and LR5 amphorae for holding and trading wine. First of all the presence in both types of circular blowholes identified on the lower part of the shoulder. These were aimed at preventing the pressure produced by carbon dioxide during the fermentation process from breaking the amphora itself. Secondly, the presence of large and highly complex wine presses nearby the Third Mile Property, near Askalon, in association with LR4 amphorae. Finally the presence of pitch inside many specimens of LR4 and LR5 amphorae suggests a use for the wine trade.
[243] Pieri 2005.
[244] Kingsley 2001, p.53.
[245] Pacetti 1995, pp.286-287.
[246] Pieri 1997, pp.23-25.

[247] Pacetti 1995, p.273.
[248] Arthur 1998, p.164.
[249] Wickham 2005, pp.443-454 with previous bibliography.
[250] Pacetti 1994, p.273.
[251] Pacetti 1994, pp.274-276; Reynolds 1995, pp.73-77.
[252] Fontana 2003, p.313.
[253] Ciampoltrini-Rendini 1988, p.533.
[254] Gambogi-Firmati 1998, p.636.
[255] Rendini 1998, p.642.
[256] Del Rio-Vallebona 1996, pp.491-492.

stratigraphic context of provenance it allows for a fairly accurate positioning of specimens within a specific time frame. Paul Arthur[257] and Dominique Pieri[258] have proposed an extremely convincing chrono-typology for this form, based on constant stratigraphic references. Specifically, they suggest the existence of an earlier variant typical of the 5th century, comparable with form 169 from the Egyptian site of Kellia identified by Egloff.[259] This form is the same as Pieri's variant LR1A, characterized by a narrow neck, vertical, slightly thickened rim with a diameter ranging from 4.5 to 7.5 cm, and wide and pronounced shoulder. This form is thought to have been widespread particularly between the late 4th and 5th centuries. From the second half of the 5th century onwards, there was a gradual move towards another variant (LR1B) which tends to take on a barrel-shaped body profile, whilst the neck and rim tend to become longer with the latter having a diameter between 10 and 12 cm. This version, known as Kellia 164, is thought to have remained in use in the 6th and 7th centuries as well. The final variant, LR1C, represents a further evolution of the preceding variant, characterized mainly by a smaller capacity, now ranging from 3.5 to 9 litres, much lower than Kellia 169 and Kellia 164 which could hold from 15 to 19 litres. LR1C is typical of 7th- and perhaps also of 8th-century contexts.

On the basis of this typology, we were able to subdivide the minimum number of 12 individuals found at Portiglioni into two groups, belonging to variants A and B respectively, each present with 6 specimens (Graph XXII).

LR1 A amphorae are characterized by their generally tall narrow necks, with a slightly thickened sub-vertical rim, rounded on the upper surface, whose diameter does not exceed 8 cm. The handles have a pseudo-circular section and present one or two longitudinal ridges. They are set immediately beneath the lip (Pl. XCI, nos 1-4).

LR1B, by contrast, have wider necks, rims which are sometimes barely thickened and rounded, often with a pointed rim projection. The width of the mouth ranges from 8 to 10 cm. In those specimens where it has survived, the shoulder seems to be more pronounced. The handle almost forms a right angle whilst in LR1A the handles are less angled (Pl. XCII, nos 1-3 and Pl. XCIII, nos 1-3).

This morphological diversification does not always correspond to differences in the fabrics (Table IX). The LR1 from *Portus Scabris* are made using three different fabrics, of which the most frequently attested is Anf 118, present in 75% of specimens. This fabric is

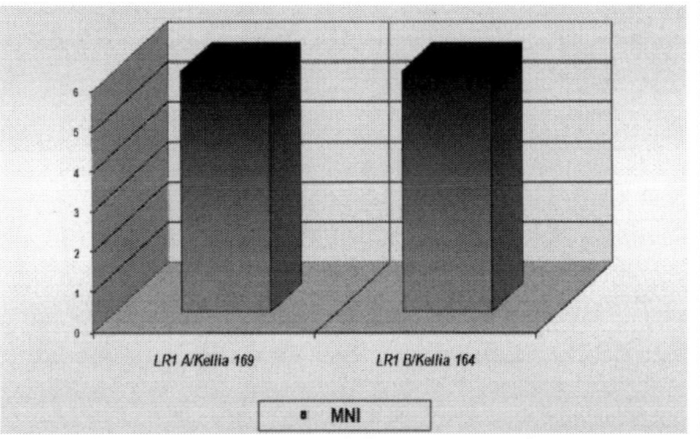

Graph XXII_ Variants of the LRA1 and minimum numbers of individuals.

Variant	Fabrics (and minimum number of individuals)
Kellia 164	Anf 118 (5), Anf 126=106 (1)
Kellia 169	Anf 126=106 (1), Anf 118 (4), Anf 123 (1)

Tab.IX_ LR1 variants and fabrics.

documented both in forms belonging to the earlier variant and in that typical of the 6th century. The same is true of Anf 106=126, documented both in a specimen of Kellia 169 and in one of Kellia 164. By contrast, Anf 123 was found only in a variant of the late 4th –5th century.

The two fabrics Anf 118 and Anf 123 have in common the presence of inclusions of limestone, rare muscovite and biotite, but are distinguished by the presence in one (Anf 118) of numerous quartz clasts and in the other (Anf 123) of fragments of volcanic rock. They also differ in colour: greenish grey for the former (Gley1 4/1 dark greenish gray) and light brown for the latter (10YR 6/3 pale brown). The third body clay, on the other hand, differs clearly from the other two for the mineralogical phases attested. Granules of rock fragments have been identified, associated with quartz-feldspar and pyrites. In this case, the colour of the fracture is grey (10YR 6/1) whilst the outer surface takes on a yellow hue (10YR 7/6). The diversity of fabrics attested at Portiglioni once again raises the issue of the probable existence of a large number of sites engaged in the manufacture of this type of amphora. It seems probable that the workshops were numerous and that they were located in the vicinity of the many agricultural areas able to produce a surplus sufficient for trade.[260]

[257] Arthur 1998, pp.164-165.
[258] Pieri 1999, pp.20-21.
[259] On the forms Kellia 169 and Kellia 164 see Egloff 1977, pp.109-114, nos 164 and 169.

[260] Panella 1993, p.663.

Late Transport Containers of Uncertain Provenance (Seventh/early Eighth to Tenth Centuries)

Overview

We have included in this category a minimum of 4 individuals of uncertain provenance (Table X). Despite this, the morphological structure of these specimens made it possible, by comparison, to ascribe at least three of them to a late period between the 7th and the early decades of the 8th century. These are extremely interesting forms because, along with some African, Italian and Eastern amphorae which survive into the 7th century, they allow us to shed some light on the structure of the trade networks touching on the site of Portiglioni during the early centuries of the High Middle Ages. Later on, between the early decades of the 8th and the mid-10th centuries, the site yielded only a single amphora which makes it possible to posit a minimal (perhaps occasional) use of the site as an intermediate harbour. This does not in itself mean that the site was completely excluded from maritime trade; other trade flows connected with the transport of perishable goods may have continued to make use of the harbour at Portiglioni without leaving any material traces. The *Portus Scabris* data, however, seems to be at least partly in line with the reconstruction of maritime trade in the western Mediterranean based on documentary sources. Some years ago, Tangheroni dated the most significant contraction in Mediterranean commercial exchange to the late 7th and early 8th centuries,[261] coinciding with the gradual development of a new continental economic axis between the Loire and the Rhine. The gradual re-establishment of overland trade between the 8th and 9th centuries, to the detriment of maritime trade, is well-documented by the relations between Rome and France and can be supported by an analysis of the distribution of the Papal correspondence sent to continental Europe.[262] McCormick has noted that in the late 6th and 7th century Papal missives travelled mainly during the periods most suitable for navigation, between spring and summer, and significantly less during the *mare clausum* period between November and March. From the 8th century onwards, however, the letters are evenly distributed throughout the year, probably indicating that alternative communication routes, other than sea routes, were used.[263] Naturally, this does not mean that maritime trade ceased altogether, but it did certainly decrease significantly. Unmistakeable evidence that overseas trade continued in those parts of Italy falling into the Byzantine political and economic sphere of influence can be found in the transport amphorae which came into use between the late 7th and early 8th century; these have been found both in major centres of consumption[264] and in sites still actively involved in regional and interregional trade such as Otranto[265] and Comacchio.[266] The data from *Portus Scabris* seem to suggest that some episodic long-distance trade continued in the northern Tyrrhenian even after the Lombard conquest of the Byzantine strongholds in Liguria. The routes followed by the few goods which have left traces in the archaeological record and which reached Portiglioni between the mid-7th and 8th centuries must have coincided, at least in the central-southern sector, with the route continuing to the north-west to reach the French coast. The trade in globular amphorae reaching the rural site of San Peyre (40 km north of Nimes) from one of the Byzantine contexts of the western or eastern Mediterranean must have run north-south, through the Tyrrhenian and the Ligurian Sea, passing through the harbour of Marseilles and then the Gulf of Lyons, before travelling up the Rhone.[267] At present, the most commonly used globular transport containers of Italian origin seem to be those made at the production sites of Ischia, Cuma and Miseno,[268] and at Otranto.[269] This fact allows us to shed new light on the patterns of foodstuff circulation between the mid-7th and the 8th century.[270] Finds of these amphorae, mainly restricted to Byzantine territories in Italy, are evidence of a medium and long-range commercial circulation mainly in the central and southern

Location	*Type*
Grid F, Strip I	Generic globular amphora and globular amphora similar to the “Miseno” type
Grid E, Pile 11	Small amphora similar to Yassi Ada P72
Grid F, Piles 24-25	Amphora similar to the type Saraçhane 52

Tab.X_ Late amphorae of uncertain provenance and their location.

[261] Tangheroni 1996, pp.73-88.
[262] McCormick 2001, pp.79-82.

[263] *Ibidem*, in particular p.80, Graph 3.1.
[264] The 8th century AD dump at the Crypta Balbi in Rome is important because it yielded a few amphorae possibly imported from North Africa, but especially a considerable number of globular amphorae from southern Italy: see Romei 2001, pp.503-506.
[265] Arthur 2004, pp.313-317; Leo Imperiale 2004, pp.327-333; Arthur 1999, pp.9-18.
[266] Gelichi *et alii* 2006, pp.119-122.
[267] Citter *et alii* 1996, pp.122-123 and pp.129-131.
[268] On the production of the Miseno amphora see De Rossi 2004, pp.253-264; in general on the production of early medieval amphorae in Campania see Arthur 1993 and De Rossi 2006.
[269] Leo Imperiale 2004, pp.327-333; Arthur-Patterson 1998, pp.511-530.
[270] It is also worth mentioning a production of early medieval amphorae along the central-southern Tyrrhenian coast of Calabria. Amphorae from this area are documented in the 8th-century AD dump in the Crypta Balbi (Romei 2003, p.506; Di Gangi-Lebole 1998, pp.761-768). In addition a production of globular amphorae has recently been identified in the Northern Adriatic, possibly near Comacchio (Gelichi *et alii* 2006a, pp.119-122; Gelichi 2008).

Tyrrhenian where Rome, on the basis of available data, still represents the main destination.[271]

In an overall context characterized by a contraction and simplification of trade, the distribution pattern of globular amphorae seems to rule out a large-scale redistribution of goods among broad swathes of the population. These finds appear to suggest elite exchange mechanisms rather than genuine trade; it is thus probable that these wares circulated as luxury products, not available on the local markets, and whose contents were destined for a consumption which we could qualify as elite. Speaking of the northern Tyrrhenian, McCormick has noted that in around 700 "the old shipping circuits had shrunk to a shadow of their former selves". This statement is supported by the tiny number of ships which, according to the documentary sources, crossed the northern part of the Tyrrhenian sea during the 8th century.[272] The scarce finds of high medieval globular amphorae north of Rome and the equally few mentions of maritime activities along the Tuscan coast in the written sources make it extremely difficult to attempt a socio-economic contextualization of the few, but significant, late finds at Portiglioni. We can certainly rule out the idea that these products were destined for redistribution among contexts of the Maremman coastal area, since none of the early medieval contexts studied stratigraphically yielded specimens of this type.[273] However, relations between settlements in our study area and overseas trade circuits seem to have been interrupted as early as the late 6th century and certainly no later than the early 7th century. The most plausible theory is currently that the finds at *Scabris* represent evidence of a sea route, little used in the 8th century, linking Italy with southern France.[274] The site of Portiglioni may have continued to play, in part, the role of intermediate harbour on this route. It is also worth noting that genuine "trading" activities were carried out along the Tuscan coasts by the Byzantine merchants who bought slaves from the Lombards for later resale to the Arabs. This must have been a well-established trade considering that between 775 and 776 we see a fairly intense correspondence between Pope Adrian I and Charlemagne aimed at putting a stop to this situation.[275] It is likely that foodstuffs also circulated within the context of this trade, although we have no documentary evidence of this.

Typologies

Late Globular Amphora

The only Portiglioni specimen ascribable with certainty to this form has a slightly everted and barely thickened rim with a diameter of 6 cm. The rim is set on a fairly narrow conical neck, with clear wheel marks inside. The handles are set immediately beneath the rim and on the shoulder and have a pseudo-triangular section. The shoulder is fairly wide (Pl. XCIV, no. 4). The fabric used to make this amphora (Anf 124) is associated exclusively with this form. This fabric is semi-purified and non-porous, with inclusions of both hyaline and opaque quartz. Its colour is red (10R 5/8). The specimen presents numerous analogies with similar artefacts from early medieval contexts. The closest morphological affinities are with one of the types of amphora produced at the kilns of Fondo Mitello at Otranto between the late 7th and 8th centuries,[276] with a flaring lipped globular amphora from the site of San Peyre in Languedoc[277] and with another documented at Saraçhane in Istanbul in deposit 35, dated to between the late 8th and early 9th century.[278]

Small Amphora Comparable with Form P72 from Yassi Ada

We found a single specimen of a small amphora, presenting a slightly thickened rim, flattened on the upper surface, with a diameter of 8 cm, set on a vertical neck with a few light external grooves. The strap handles are set beneath the rim and on the unpronounced shoulder. These present two finger grooves on the upper surface (Pl. XCIV, no. 3). We can suggest a comparison with a storage amphora belonging to the cargo found on board the Yassi Ada wreck,[279] dating to the early decades of the 7th century. This amphora is very similar to the Portiglioni form in terms of dimensions and the diameter of the rim is identical. The colour of the fabric of the Yassi Ada specimen is orange-ochre and contains generic grey and brick red granules. The body clay of the Portiglioni specimen (Anf 130), on the other hand, is light red in colour (2.5 YR 6/6) and presents limestone, quartz and rare muscovite inclusions.

---

[271] In addition to the finds from the Crypta Balbi dump, it is worth bearing in mind the globular amphorae dating to the late 7th-8th century AD, from the sea-port of Portus, see Ciarrocchi *et alii* 1993, pp.237-243.
[272] McCormick 2001, pp.515-516.
[273] I refer mainly to the urban site of Rusellae, the rural villages of Poggio Cavolo and Scarlino and finally the early medieval proto-urban site of Grosseto (for the latter see Valdambrini 2006, pp.474-479).
[274] The sea-route was certainly used in AD 753, when two Byzantine officials went to Rome and afterwards to Marseille; the same route was used in AD 773, when Pope Adrian I sent his ambassadors to Charlemagne: see McCormick 2001, p.518, p.872, n.162 and p.876, n.183.
[275] For the written source see McCormick 2001, p.877, n.186 and p.519.

[276] Arthur-Patterson 1998, p.519, Fig.4, no.2.
[277] Citter *et alii* 1996, p.130, Fig.6, no.4.
[278] Hayes 1992, p.177, Fig.57, n.34.
[279] For the comparison see Bass-Van Doornick 1982, p.182, P72 and p.183.

Amphora Comparable with Saraçhane Type 52

A single minimum individual was found of an amphora with a rim about 10 cm in diameter, rounded on the upper surface, set on a pseudo-cylindrical neck. The thickened strap handles are set on the neck, immediately beneath the rim, and on the shoulder. There are a few light grooves on the outer surface of the neck (Pl. XCIV, no. 2). The specimen is made from a fabric (Anf 133) which is red in colour (2.5 YR 5/6) and which presents inclusions consisting of fragments of volcanic rock, quartzes, feldspars, biotite and pyroxenes. The properties of the body clay suggest a generic volcanic area of provenance which cannot be identified more specifically in the absence of mineral and petrographical analyses: both the Aegean region and central-southern Italy are valid possibilities. Our specimen is morphologically similar to type 52 attested at Sarachane (Istanbul) in an early 10th-century deposit.[280]

Miseno-Type Amphora (?)

This is a type of amphora characterized by a slightly everted rim of triangular section, with a diameter of about 9 cm. Despite the fragmentary nature of this piece, the neck appears to be conical. The massive circular handles are set between the neck and the rim, but are not level with the latter. They form a wide elbow profile and seem to be oversized with respect to the neck (Pl. XCIV, no. 1). The most significant analogies are with early medieval transport amphorae. Specifically, we can see some similarities with the morphological structure of the rim and handle of type Dragonara 2, made at the workshop at Miseno (Naples) and dated to the 8th century.[281] The *Scabris* specimen presents close points of comparison with 2 specimens from the Bay of Naples, found respectively in the excavations in the courtyard of the Archivio Storico del Banco di Napoli and at the monastery of SS. Nicandro e Marciano, in phases of the late 7th or 8th century.[282]

This form is documented with certainty both in Campania[283] and in contexts dating to the 8th century in western Sicily,[284] in the 8th-century deposit of the Crypta Balbi in Rome,[285] at Ostia between the late 7th and 8th centuries,[286] at *Portus* and, finally, at Cagliari, again in 8th-century phases.[287] These finds indicate a fairly intensive circulation mainly in the central and southern Tyrrhenian where the Catholic Church had substantial land holdings. It is interesting to note that the Miseno amphora is mainly found at sites linked to monasteries, indicating an elite trade circuit for wine from the Bay of Naples, the virtually exclusive province of important Church institutions.[288] The find at *Portus Scabris*, the only one hitherto known north of Rome, may represent evidence of a wider circulation, though this was probably occasional in nature.

6.3. Diagonistic Pottery of the Mid-Tenth to Twelfth Centuries

6.3.1. Foreword

As already mentioned, the study of the Portiglioni pottery deposit revealed the complete absence of archaeological data documenting a use of the harbour between the mid-8th and 9th centuries. Whilst the lack of material (and documentary) evidence does not in itself constitute definitive proof of the total interruption of maritime activities at the port, since operations to load and offload perishable goods may have continued without leaving any archaeological traces, it is nonetheless significant. The importance of this silence of material sources during the later High Middle Ages is amplified by the fact that archaeological data reappears at least from the mid-10th-11th century, preceded by the import from an unknown source of the amphora comparable to type Saraçhane 52, dating to the early 10th century. The resumption of the circulation of goods through the harbour during the central centuries of the Middle Ages nonetheless seems to have been fairly slow and is not comparable, in terms of quantities, to the large quantities of products reaching Portiglioni during late Antiquity. Naturally, this comparison cannot be made on the basis of foodstuffs circulating in amphorae. The containers used for maritime transport continued to be manufactured, on a smaller scale, only in some parts of southern Italy,[289] characterized by economic and production structures which were more similar to those of the Byzantine world, where commercial amphorae remained in use at least until the 14th century.[290] In central and northern Italy, by contrast, we have no evidence for the local production of transport containers after late Antiquity. On the Mediterranean scale, we should also take into consideration the marked decline in the practice of storing foodstuffs in

[280] See Hayes 1992, p.73 and p.72, Fig.25, no.9.
[281] On this type see De Rossi 2004, p.257, Fig.2, "a" type and related text.
[282] For the precise parallel see Arthur 1993, p.234, Fig.2, nos 7-8.
[283] *Ibidem*, pp.231-244.
[284] Ardizzone 2000, pp.402-407.
[285] Saguì *et alii* 2001, p.505-506 (specimens IV.5.13-17).
[286] Ciarrocchi *et alii* 1993, p.240, Fig.4, no.4.
[287] De Rossi 2006, p.543, Fig.2.

[288] The Miseno amphora is documented in the 8th-century AD dump at the Crypta Balbi, related to the monastery of San Lorenzo *in Pallaciniis* in Rome, in the convent of the Saints Nicandro and Marciano in Naples, in a rubbish dump in Cagliari, which was produced by the monastery in the Bonaria area, in an area near the *xenodochium* of Pomacchio, perhaps the cathedral of the sea port of Portus, and finally along the coasts of the Egadi islands and Sicily. This distribution reflects the well developed maritime links between Rome and the papal estates in Sicily and southern Italy along which the grain supply moved towards Rome. See in general De Rossi 2006, pp.547-548.
[289] See Arthur 1999, pp.9-18. The author particularly refers to the 10th to 13th c. amphora production at Otranto and also to some specimens very similar to those produced in Otranto, but found at coastal sites in Calabria and underwater sites along the Ionic and Calabrian coasts.
[290] Villa 1994, pp.414-416 and p.419.

amphorae, a generalized phenomenon especially in comparison with the intensive circulation of amphorae during the late antique period.

There is thus a structural obstacle which prevents us from drawing a comparison between the overall picture of the central centuries of the Middle Ages and that of the preceding period. The Portiglioni context yielded only a single specimen of a maritime transport container dating to between the mid-10th and the 11th century. The diagnostic pottery most significant in terms of quantity thus consists of a small group of coarse tableware and storage containers which, given their morphological characteristics and fabrics, were certainly made by the workshops active in Pisan territory.[291] This tableware is documented systematically in rural and urban contexts between the Alma valley to the north and the lower Ombrone vallley to the south,[292] as early as the late 10th century[293] but with greater frequency between the 11th and 12th centuries, reaching a true quantitative peak during the following century. The vigour of medium-distance trade between the Maremman coast and Pisa forms part of that more general process which between the 11th and 12th century sees the gradual establishment of this city, alongside Genoa, as the main player in maritime activities in the Tyrrhenian. During this phase, these two cities were the focal points of an intense Mediterranean-wide trade, and stand out for their increasing ability to compete with the Arabs for maritime supremacy as far away as the coasts of Spain, the Balearic Isles and North Africa.[294] The expansion of Pisa into the Maremman as early as the mid-11th century is well documented in its 12th-century phases.[295] Confirming the city's political and territorial power in the Maremma, the Emperor Henry VI, with a deed of 1 March 1191, renewed the privilege conceded to the Pisans by his father in 1162, in which Castiglione della Pescaia and the Abbey of San Pancrazio al Fango represented the southern boundaries of the Pisan *contado*.[296] Portiglioni must therefore have played an important role as a commercial harbour in sea links between the city and its outlying land holdings. Some documents of the 14th century attest the movement of foodstuffs such as salt and cereals from Portiglioni towards Pisa.[297]

Location	Form (MNI)
Grid E, "Sales" Strip	Pisan jug (1)
Grid F, Strip II	Pisan jug (1)
Grid A, Strip III, Piles 23-26	Pisan jug (1)
Grid E, Pile 11	Pisan jug (1)
Grid E, Pile 14	Pisan jug (2), Otranto type 1 amphora (1)
Grid F/E, Piles 17-20	Pisan jug (2)

Tab. XI_ 10th to 13th ceramics and their location in the Portiglioni Bay.

6.3.2. Distribution of Materials from the Central Centuries of the Middle Ages

Laboratory research allowed us to identify a minimum number of at least 8 individuals consisting of medium-sized and small jugs which can be ascribed to workshops in the Pisa area. This is a fairly small number which might nonetheless increase significantly after further targeted searches among the materials recovered from the harbour basin. The selection of objects for analysis exclusively concerned fragments of rims with the junction where the handle was attached, potentially allowing for a more accurate typological identification of the piece. Despite the small quantities of materials which can be ascribed with certainty to the central centuries of the Middle Ages, it is interesting to note their distribution within the harbour of Portiglioni (Table XI). If we compare Fig.10 with the distribution maps for late antique materials above, we can see that there is a higher concentration of tableware from this phase in an area a few tens of metres further south of that most intensely exploited between the 5th and 7th centuries. There thus seems to have been a slight shift in the loading and offloading activities towards an area of the Portiglioni harbour which had hitherto been used for port activities only to a limited extent. The small amount of data at our disposal does not allow us to formulate hypotheses regarding the real reasons for this possible move; the only certain fact is that the area chosen during this phase seems to be located in a position more sheltered from south-west winds by the Portiglioni promontory.

An interesting theory, which is not currently supported by definitive evidence, suggests a relationship between the concentration of port activities in the vicinity of the Portiglioni hill and the presence here of the *curtis* of *Portilione*, attested for the first time in 1055.[298] The desire to manage port operations more directly, and perhaps to facilitate the storage of the supplies arriving

[291] Berti-Menchelli 1998.
[292] *Acroma depurata* ware imported from Pisa is well documented at rural sites investigated in the Alma valley (Castel Maus, Punta Fortezza and Poggio Castellaccio), in the lower Bruna valley (Castellaccio del Prile, Castiglione della Pescaia, Abbazia di San Pancrazio al Fango), in the lower Ombrone valley (Poggio Cavolo) and the urban site of Rusellae. Recently a broad range of *acroma depurata* vessels were found in the urban excavations at Grosseto in contexts dating from the 11th to the 13th centuries onwards (for Grosseto see Valdambrini 2006, pp.474-479.
[293] At Poggio Cavolo, a mid- to late 10th-century AD context yielded a flat base of a jug that, according to its fabric, was imported from Pisa see Vaccaro-Salvadori 2006, p.481.
[294] Tangheroni 1996, pp.137-147.
[295] For a detailed reconstruction of the complex expansion process of the Pisan countryside into the Maremma see Ceccarelli Lemut 1985, pp.58-62.
[296] *Ibidem*, p.60.
[297] *Ibidem*, p.71, note 54.
[298] The document is dated 14 June 1055: see Manaresi 1960, vol.3, pp.222-224.

here, may have led to the harbour being moved to an area closer to the village on the hill.

6.3.3. Typologies

Medium-Sized and Small Pisan Jugs

At least 4 specimens of jug are documented, characterized by a vertical or slightly incurving and rounded rim. The edges have a diameter of 10 cm. The strap handle is from 5 to 6 cm wide and 0.5/0.6 cm thick. It is set immediately beneath the rim and almost forms an elbow profile. In two cases, the handles present single stamps in the form of a toothed ring, in one case stamped with 16 dots in the other with 21. In the first specimen the ring is surrounded by a circle of tooth (Pl. XCV, nos 1-2, 6, 8). At Grosseto this type is attested from the 12th century, with continuous finds in 13th-century stratigraphies as well.[299]

2 specimens document a type of jug with a slightly more raised rim, flat on the upper surface, whose diameter ranges from 11 to 12 cm. The handle is still strap-shaped and set beneath the rim, but it forms a narrower loop, bending rapidly downwards. These handles are also 0.5 cm thick, whilst their width ranges from 4 to 5 cm (Pl. XCV, nos 3, 5). This form finds parallels in Pisa in the Piazza dei Cavalieri context, in phases of the second half of the 11th - first half of the 12th century.[300]

A final type of small jug or tankard, attested by a minimum of 2 individuals, is characterized by a rim which is rounded or almost flat on the upper surface, with a diameter of about 9 cm. The attachment point of the handle, immediately beneath the rim, is marked by a finger print. In this case, too, the handle is strap-shaped, but it is less wide and thick than those of the specimens described above, measuring 4 and 0.4 cm respectively (Pl. XCV, nos 4, 7). This type is well attested at Pisa in phases from between the first half of the 11th and the first half of the 12th century.[301]

The analysis of the fabrics allowed me to identify three very purified and fairly porous fabrics, characterized by the presence of extremely rare quartz inclusions and a colour ranging from brick red (10R 5/6) to light reddish brown (2.5 YR 6/4) to yellowish red (5YR 5/6).

Transport Amphora

A type of amphora is attested by a part of its body. It is ovoid in shape, with a maximum width of 30 cm. On the outer surface the wall presents fairly marked ribbing covering the entire preserved surface, tending to become less dense on the lower part. A spiral decoration, impressed before firing, adorns the central portion. This motif was made after the external finishing (Pl. XCVI, no. 1). The specimen was made using a fairly purified and porous body clay, brownish yellow in colour (10 YR 6/6). The Portiglioni fragment finds a plausible point of comparison, in terms of morphological structure and the size of the body, and for the characteristics of the decoration and external finishing of the wall, with the Otranto 1 type amphora.[302] The specimens from Otranto present a fabric of similar colour. Scholars have proposed that this type of amphora was made in the area between Bari and Brindisi, given the similarities of the body clay with that of the Apuleian productions of the Roman period.

The chronology of type 1, on the basis of the Otranto stratigraphy, runs from the 10th to the first half of the 11th century. The distribution of this form and of type 2, in use between the late 11th and 12th centuries and continuing into the following century, seems to cover

Fig.10_ 10th to 13th AD ceramics in the Portiglioni Bay: distribution.

[299] Valdambrini 2006, p.477-478, no.26, and also Berti-Menchelli 1998 for the typology.
[300] Menchelli-Renzi Rizzo 2000, p.147, Fig.1, MGC9.
[301] *Ibidem*, p.137, Fig.III, nos 7.4, 8.5.
[302] For the Otranto 1 type see Arthur 1992, pp.206, 208 and Fig.7.3, n.824.

southern Puglia to Barletta and the Dalmatian coast, including Albania where a specimen of type 1 was found at Durazzo, whilst significant finds are documented in the urban context of Butrint between the 11th and 13th centuries.[303] Possible finds are also attested at Athens, Çanakkale on the strait of the Dardanelles, Venice, Genoa, Marseilles and southern Corsica.

Appendix A. Late 4th to 7th AD analysed ARS from the underwater finds at *Portus Scabris*
(data used for Individual Weighted Means analysis)

FORM	TYPE	MNI
SMALL BOWL	HAYES 73 A	1
DISH	HAYES 75	1
SMALL BOWL	HAYES 71B	2
LARGE BOWL/DISH	HAYES 84	4
DISH	HAYES 58B, NO 11	1
LARGE BOWL/DISH	HAYES 63	1
LARGE BOWL	HAYES 67	20
BOWL	MACKENSEN 16	1
BOWL	MACKENSEN 17	1
LARGE BOWL/DISH	HAYES 76	3
LARGE BOWL/DISH	HAYES 79	1
LARGE BOWL/DISH	HAYES 61A	5
LARGE BOWL/DISH	HAYES 61B	21
SHALLOW BOWL	MACKENSEN 12/HAYES 80A	1
LARGE BOWL/DISH	HAYES 87A	1
LARGE BOWL/DISH	HAYES 87C/109	1
LARGE BOWL	HAYES 93A	1
LARGE BOWL	HAYES 93B	3
LARGE BOWL	MACKENSEN 22	1
LARGE BOWL/DISH	HAYES 103B	4
DISH	HAYES 105	2
DISH	HAYES 104A	3
DISH	MACKENSEN 33.2/34	1
DISH	HAYES 104B	3
FLANGED BOWL	HAYES 91A	1
FLANGED BOWL	HAYES 91B	15
FLANGED BOWL	HAYES 91C	4
BOWL	HAYES 99A	1
BOWL	HAYES 99B	6
SHALLOW DISH	HAYES 109	1
STAMPED BASE (NOT RELATED TO OTHER DIAGNOSTICS)	Stamp Atlante I, Tav. LVIII (a), n.35	1
STAMPED BASE (NOT RELATED TO OTHER DIAGNOSTICS)	Stamp Atlante I, Tav. LVI (a), n.4	1
STAMPED BASE (NOT RELATED TO OTHER DIAGNOSTICS)	Stamp Atlante I, Tav. LVI (a), n.11	1
STAMPED BASE (NOT RELATED TO OTHER DIAGNOSTICS)	Stamp Atlante I, Tav. LVI (a), n.12	1
STAMPED BASE (NOT RELATED TO OTHER DIAGNOSTICS)	Stamp Atlante I, Tav. LVI (a), n.32	3
STAMPED BASE (NOT RELATED TO OTHER DIAGNOSTICS)	Stamps Atlante I, Tav. LVI (a), n.40; Tav. LVI (b), n.51	1
STAMPED BASE (NOT RELATED TO OTHER DIAGNOSTICS)	Stamp Atlante I, Tav. LVII (a), n.15	1
BOTTLE	FULFORD CLOSED-FORMS 2.8	1

[303] See Reynolds 2004b, pp.270-271.

7. Shipwrecks and the Circulation of Overseas Goods in the Mid and Late Imperial Period: the Cala del Barbiere Harbour at Punta Ala in Its Territorial Context

7.1. Foreword

The analysis of the shipwrecks discovered along the coastal belt in our study area is an important tool for a fuller understanding of commercial dynamics in this region over the long term. The starting point for any in-depth research of this type is the book by A.J. Parker, which provides an extremely detailed catalogue of ancient shipwrecks, both in the Mediterranean basin and in the seas off other Roman provinces.[1] Although it remains a valuable source of information, this work has been criticized for the method used to date the shipwrecks, calculated as the mean of the most ancient and most recent finds transported on board.[2] As has been pointed out, this criterion is of little use for those contexts which present a narrower chronological range and for small samples, such as those which characterize many late antique shipwrecks.[3] However, in more general long-term studies these limitations tend to become less important and the subdivision of the wrecks into distinct phases is both feasible and informative. This approach allows us to analyse general trends in the numbers of vessels in circulation on the basis of the number of shipwrecks documented for each phase.

To investigate trends in commercial trade along the coastal belt between the Osa and Alma valleys we selected all the wrecks in that area of the Tyrrhenian Sea between the Monte Argentario promontory to the south and the promontory of Populonia to the north, including all reports for the waters around the islands of the Tuscan archipelago (Fig.1). Parker records a total of 72 shipwrecks in this area of water,[4] whose dates range from the Etruscan-Archaic period to the late Middle Ages. A long-term analysis shows a clear peak in the number of vessels circulating between the late Republic and early Empire, with 50% of all reports (Graph I). To these we should add at least some of the six shipwrecks generically assigned to the Roman period, but for which no more precise date is available.

During the middle Empire the number of contexts suggests that intense trading activities continued, with seven shipwrecks belonging to this period and three dated more generically to the early or middle Empire.

The subsequent period sees a sudden drop in the number of vessels in circulation, with only one shipwreck ascribed with certainty to the late Empire. The shipwreck off the small island of Le Scole, south-

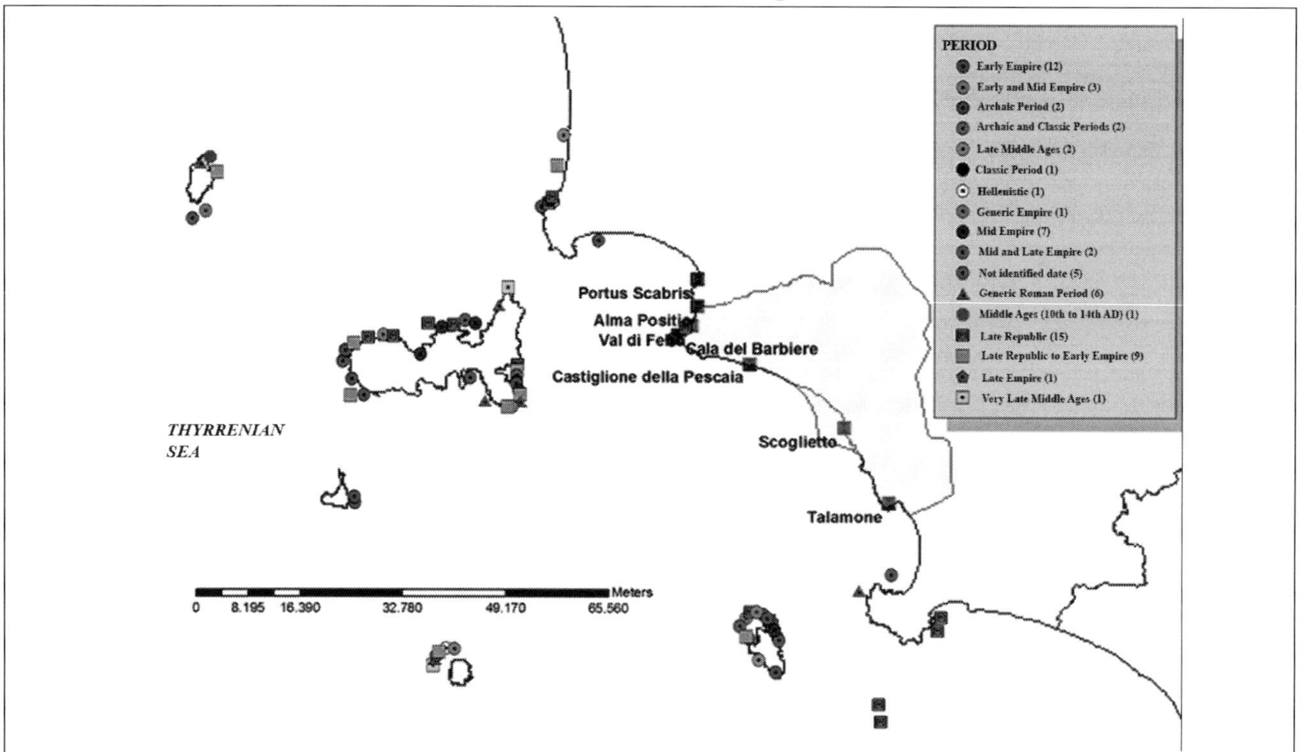

Fig.1_ Location of the ancient shipwrecks published in Parker 1992 and concerning the investigated sea stretch. The main shores and sea-ports are indicated.

[1] Parker 1992.
[2] Volpe 1998, pp.566-567.
[3] Parker's catalogue includes a total record of 1259 shipwrecks; only 16% of which can be ascribed to the period between the 3rd and the 7th centuries AD. See Parker 1992 and Volpe 1998.
[4] See Parker 1992, Fig.7, North-West Italy.

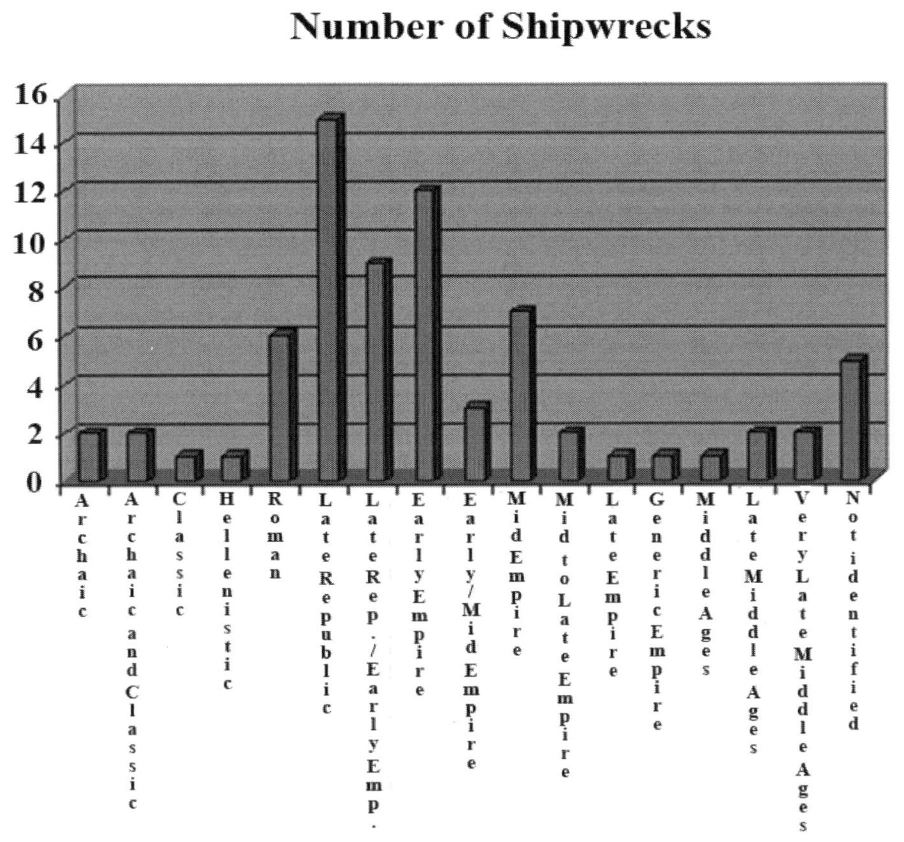

Graph I_ Diachronic distribution of the seventy-two shipwrecks.

east of the Isola del Giglio,[5] at a depth of about 50 m, was carrying a cargo of Keay XXVG/Africana IIIC Tunisian amphorae. Since the report does not mention any associated fineware, the only chronological information available is that provided by the amphorae themselves, datable to between the late 4th and mid-5th centuries.[6] It is more difficult to assess the reliability of Parker's report of a hoard of silver and copper coins, perhaps minted under Valens, contained in a sort of wooden box.[7] Were this report to be confirmed, it would provide a *terminus post quem* for the shipwreck of 364-378 AD.

7.2. The Cala del Barbiere Harbour (Punta Ala) and the So-Called "Site D"

Alongside the Le Scole A shipwreck, we can report another possible shipwreck with a cargo consisting mainly of Tunisian amphorae, recently identified in the Cala del Barbiere near the Punta Ala promontory, at a depth of 4/4.5 m. The existence of this shipwreck is suggested by some of the materials excavated at Site D (Fig.2).[8] This context is of enormous interest for a study of the processes by which Tunisian foodstuffs and production C African red slip ware were redistributed from major ports to smaller towns on the Tyrrhenian coast. Unfortunately, only part of the context has been excavated and, although portions of the ship's wooden planking have been recovered, no accurate information is available on the structure of the hull and the size of the cargo; given the shipwreck's proximity to the coast and the fact that it lies in shallow waters it has probably been looted by clandestine divers.

As we will see below, the materials recovered during the excavation of Site D allowed us to identify three main phases: an initial phase between the 2nd and 3rd centuries; a later phase, to which the majority of materials belong and which may consist of part of the cargo of a shipwreck dating to the first half of the 4th century; and, finally, a more recent phase datable to the 5th century and represented by a few pottery finds.

Below we will discuss the pottery materials in accordance with these three phases:

- Phase 1: 2nd-3rd centuries AD;
- Phase 2: first half of the 4th century AD;
- Phase 3: 5th century AD.

---

5 See Celuzza-Rendini 1992, pp.106-108.
6 For the date of the Keay XXVG see Bonifay 2004, p.122.
7 Parker 1992, p.391.
8 The underwater archaeological research at Cala del Barbiere was carried out in 2003 by the Nucleo Subacqueo of the Soprintendenza per i Beni Archeologici della Toscana and directed by Pamela Gambogi. I would like to thank the scientific director for allowing me to process the ceramic finds from Site D.

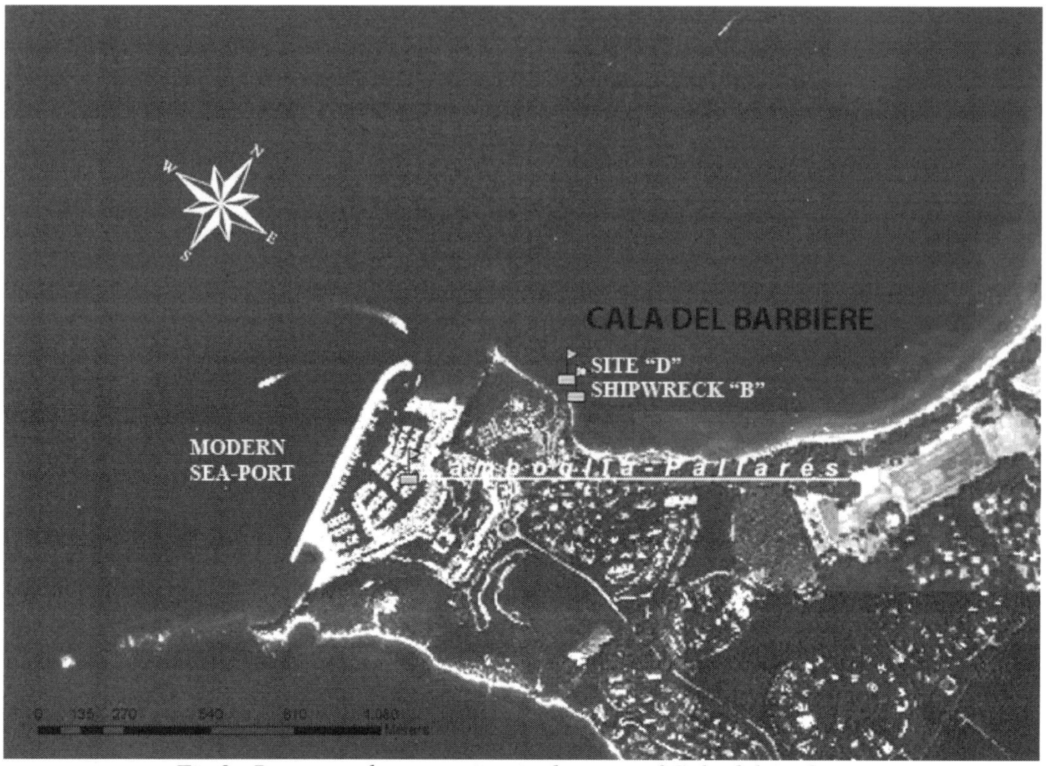

Fig.2_ Roman underwater sites in the area of Cala del Barbiere.

The underwater archaeological excavation only covered part of Site D and as such the materials brought to light represent only a sample of the whole context. The pottery finds sampled have nonetheless provided some valuable information on the chronological phases of the site, suggesting the possible presence of part of a shipwreck belonging to Phase 2.

We will concentrate here on the hitherto unpublished materials from Site D which, as already mentioned, help to shed new light on the long continuity of use of the Cala del Barbiere harbour; we have also considered it necessary to attempt an exhaustive contextualization of this site within the Punta Ala area as a whole.

Given its good location, well-protected from winds from the third and fourth quadrants (*Libeccio*, *Mezzogiorno* and *Scirocco*) the Cala del Barbiere must have been a well-known natural harbour for those sailing along the coasts of the central and northern Tyrrhenian, where vessels could anchor to carry out repairs or take shelter during storms. The outline of the coast ensured protection for the ships which cast anchor here. Cala del Barbiere was thus a harbour in the strict sense of the word: a point on the coast which allowed ships to reach shore but which may have had simple wooden wharves rather than more complex infrastructure in *opus coementicium*.[9] Furthermore, the harbour does not seem to have belonged to a large settlement, but was instead connected to a series of small and medium-sized production contexts located immediately to the north (*infra*).

The practicality of this harbour is the main reason for its long period of use. The earliest evidence for the passage of ships through the waters just off Punta Ala date to between the late 6th and the mid-5th century BC, as indicated by the so-called wreck "A",[10] not to be confused with the other wreck "A", recently published and dated to the mid-3rd century AD (*infra*). Wreck "B",[11] on the other hand, seems to date to the 2nd century AD; this was a medium-large annonary vessel of which two substantial portions of the hull have been brought to light. The ship's extremely varied cargo consisted of Baetic Dressel 20 oil amphorae, Dressel 2/4 wine amphorae from Tarragona, Gallic Gauloise 4 and 5 wine amphorae, Italic Forlimpopoli B wine amphorae and Spello amphorae. These transport containers were found in association with late Italic sigillata ware, both undecorated and decorated, production A African red slip ware, thin-walled ware and African kitchenware. However it is unclear which, if any, of these pottery classes were destined for trade and which simply for use on board ship.

The shipwreck identified during the construction of the Punta Ala marina and now buried under its infrastructure is later in date.[12] The context south of

[9] For a typological differentiation between Roman sea-ports see Camilli-Gambogi 2004, with bibliography.

[10] On this shipwreck see Çygielman 1998, pp.91-92.

[11] On the so-called wreck "B" see Gambogi 2004, p.78; Bargagliotti-Cibecchini-Gambogi 2004, pp.93-103; Bargagliotti-Cibecchini-Gambogi 2002, pp.243-246.

[12] See Lamboglia-Pallarés 1983, pp.172-176; Parker 1992, p.345 and also Dell'Amico-Pallarés 2006.

Punta Hidalgo, a few hundred metres from Cala del Barbiere, consists of a beached shipwreck, 25 m in length and lying at a depth of only 2 metres. This vessel was carrying an extremely varied cargo of Lusitanian, Baetic and Tunisian amphorae (*infra*). Also belonging to the cargo were two *sacculi* of coins, one of which, hidden between the inner and outer planking of the hull, contained coins from the mid-3rd century AD. Phases 2 and 3 of Site D, discussed below, date to the 4th and 5th centuries respectively and demonstrate the harbour's long continuity of use, even into the late imperial period. The uninterrupted use of the Cala del Barbiere harbour up to the 6th century, by contrast, is demonstrated by the sporadic presence in various areas of the bay of amphorae belonging to this chronological horizon.[13] Some of the materials recovered during the 2003 research campaign are particularly noteworthy: the spike of a Tunisian Keay LXII amphora (Pl. CII, no. 2),[14] and the body with the shoulder and part of the handle of an Aegean LR2 amphora made from fabric Anf 122, also documented at *Portus Scabris* in association with the same type of amphora (Pl. CII, no. 1).

7.2.1. The Amphorae From Site D

The amphorae recovered during the excavation of Site D represent the main instrument for subdividing the context into different phases and for the possible identification of part of the cargo of a shipwreck from the first half of the 4th century, in Phase 2 (Table I). A total minimum number of 16 amphorae were recovered, most of which are variants on the medium-sized cylindrical container Keay XXV/Africana III (Figure 3).

Phase 2 Amphorae

Bonifay has grouped the numerous variants of the Keay XXV/Africana III amphora into three main subtypes spanning the whole period between the late 3rd and the mid-5th century.[15] At least 10 specimens belong to this type, to which we should add a transitional form between Africana IID and Keay XXV.

These 11 amphorae seem to form part of a fairly homogeneous cargo of Tunisian transport containers and, as we will see below, can be assigned with a good degree of certainty to Phase 2. The transitional Africana IID/Keay XXV type is characterized by a near vertical, slightly thickened and rounded rim. The handles have a pseudo-elliptical section and are larger than those of Keay XXV amphorae (Pl. XCVII, no. 1). This variant can be dated to between the mid-3rd and

Fig.3_ Specimens of Tunisian amphorae, Dressel 20 and Empoli type from Site D at Cala del Barbiere.

the first third of the 4th century and beyond (?).[16] The five amphorae belonging to the variant Keay XXVB/Africana IIIA have a thickened and gently everted rim ending in a rounded or slightly pointed edge. The neck is always fairly tall and presents a cone-shaped profile, whilst the shoulder is unpronounced. The handles are generally thickened and strap-shaped; these are attached about halfway up the neck and slightly above the junction between the neck and the shoulder. The width of the mouths ranges from 11 to 12.8 cm (Pl. XCVII, nos 2-3, 6-8). Two specimens of Keay XXVC/Africana IIIA were identified; these differ from the above variant for their thinner rim, which has a slightly more everted profile and ends in a more pointed edge. The mouth measures about 12 cm in diameter (Pl. XCVII, nos 4-5). Both variants Keay XXVB and Keay XXVC, grouped together in Bonifay's Africana IIIA, are dated to the 4th century on the basis of finds in Tunisian contexts.[17] A single specimen belongs to the variant Keay XXVP/Africana IIIB. This type has a wider cone-shaped neck than the forms described above, with a thickened rim ending in a hooked lip; the mouth measures 9.5 cm in diameter (Pl. XCVII, no. 9). This variant is also dated to the 4th century.[18] Two spikes can be generically ascribed to Keay XXV amphorae;[19] based on the microscopic analysis of the fabrics (Table I) these do not belong to any of the specimens described above but to another two minimum forms (Pl. XCVII, nos 11-12). At least four specimens of Keay XXV are characterized by the presence of a whitish skin resulting from the use of salty water.

Interestingly, several medium-sized cylindrical containers of the type described above still contain the preserved remains of the cork plug used to seal the contents and prevent them spilling out during transport.[20] Since the remains of the contents have not

[13] See Bargagliotti-Cibecchini-Gambogi 2004, pp.93-94, for a preliminary overview of the harbour's long period of use.
[14] For a comparison see Keay 1984, p.342, Fig.160, nos 7-8.
[15] Bonifay 2004, pp.118-122.

[16] *Ibidem*, p.117.
[17] *Ibidem*, p.122.
[18] *Ibidem*, p.122.
[19] See Keay 1984, p.210, Fig.88, no.3 and p.211, Fig.89, no.5.
[20] The use of cork plugs appears to be characteristic mainly of Africana II and Keay XXV amphorae, see Bonifay-Garnier 2007, pp.16-17.

been subjected to archaeometric research we cannot at present suggest any theories as to the contents of these amphorae, which on the basis of the available sample seem to have formed the vast majority of the cargo belonging to the hypothetical shipwreck. However, it is worth noting that in 8 out of 10 cases the Keay XXV/Africana III amphorae, like the only transitional Africana IID/Keay XXV specimen, present significant traces of black pitch on the inside, at times forming a genuine coating of varying thickness, clearly visible in the fracture. In at least 6 cases the pitch has spilled out and can be seen clearly on the rims and necks.

An important recent essay by Bonifay and Garnier has attempted to reexamine all the Tunisian amphorae of the Roman and late antique periods and their possible contents, considering the relations between the amphora type, the presence or otherwise of an internal pitch coating and the foodstuff transported, using new types of archaeometric analysis.[21] The authors noted that Keay XXV amphorae are the most commonly documented type in contexts along the French coast and that a large number of specimens present an internal pitch coating. Starting from the theory, apparently confirmed by the ancient sources but not always by archaeometric analysis,[22] according to which pitch was incompatible with food oils, its presence represents a valid basis on which to distinguish between the contents of amphorae: pitch-coated amphorae for fish sauces and wine, amphorae without a pitch coating for food oils. The gas chromatograph analysis of some fragments of Keay XXV amphorae from shipwrecks found along the French coast appeared to confirm the absence of any traces of oil, suggesting that these containers were used to transport other food products (*salsamenta* or wine).[23] Whilst awaiting the results of archaeometric analysis we can thus suggest, on the basis of this evidence, that the Keay XXV amphorae found at Site D were used to transport fish sauces or more probably Tunisian wine.[24]

The specimens described above are associated with different fabrics (Anf 100 with 4 specimens, Anf 101 and Anf 102 with 1 specimen each, Anf 114 with 3 specimens, Anf 131 with 2 specimens). A preliminary study suggests that these fabrics may have been used by two different workshops located in close proximity to one another north of the Gulf of Hammamet: Nabeul-Sidi Aoun (fabric Anf 114) and Sidi Zahruni (fabrics Anf 100, 101, 102 and 131). These two sites specialized in the production of Africana I, IIA, IIC, Keay XXV, XXXVA and Dressel 30 amphorae (Nabeul-Sidi Aoun), and of Keay XXV, XXXVA, LV, LVI, LVII and LXIIA amphorae (Sidi Zahruni) respectively.[25] The fabric used at Sidi Aoun, very similar to our Anf 114, is "jaune orangé, assez granuleuse, avec une surface blanche assez homogène" and according to petrographic analyses appears fairly similar to that used at Sidi Zahruni.[26] The analysis of a sample of the fabric of a Keay XXXVA from Sidi Zahruni shows that it is: "characterized by the presence of an abundant lower granulometric fraction (<0.1 mm), consisting mainly of angular quartz (the higher granulometric fraction, by contrast, is fairly scarce and well-sorted) and by an iron-rich matrix which is not entirely homogeneous. Limestone and fossils are present in small quantities alongside rare fine micas"[27] The description of the body clay used at Sidi Zahruni appears comparable to our Anf 100, 101, 102 and 131.[28] The Tunisian amphorae from Phase 2 of Site D

Amphora Type	Fabric	Pitch	MNI	Phase
Keay 35A	Anf 1008	No	1	3
Keay 25P/Africana IIIB	Anf 114	Yes	1	2
Keay 25B/Africana IIIA	Anf 100	Yes	3	2
Keay 25C/Africana IIIA	Anf 100	No	1	2
Keay 25C/Africana IIIA	Anf 114	Yes	1	2
Keay 25B/Africana IIIA	Anf 114	Yes	1	2
Keay 25B/Africana IIIA	Anf 101	Yes	1	2
Transitional Africana IID/Keay 25	Anf 102	Yes	1	2
Generic Keay 25	Anf 131	Yes	2	2
Almagro 51C	non id.	Yes	1	2 (?)
Empoli Type	Anf 117	No	1	2 (?)
Dressel 20	Anf 1009	No	1	1

Tab. I_ Amphora types from Site D.

[21] *Ibidem*, pp.8-31.
[22] The residue analysis applied to a Keay LXIIA amphora from the shipwreck of La Palud I revealed the presence of vegetable oil although the amphora was pitched, *Ibidem*, pp.28-29.
[23] *Ibidem*, p.27.
[24] I am grateful to Michel Bonifay for reading this.
[25] Bonifay 2004, p.37.
[26] On this fabric see *Ibidem*, p.37.
[27] See Bonifay *et alii* 2005, p.181.
[28] The fabric associated with the ceramic production of Sidi Zahruni is described as follows: "la pâte de ces amphores est orange à rouge brique, avec quelques inclusions blanches ou jaunes, parfois des stries de la même couleur et de rares inclusions anguleuses rouge-violet (...). On a déjà mentionné la présence, apparue en lame mince, d'inclusions ferriques et surtout de minéraux de grès quartzeux qui semblent caractéristiques dé l'argile de cet atelier (...). La surface

thus appear to form part of the cargo of a vessel which sank in the first half of the 4th century and which was carrying Tunisian amphorae used to trade fish sauces or more probably wine and, as we will see below, Hayes 50 flat-based dishes in African red slip ware C.

Given their overlapping chronology, we have decided to include in this section a further two amphorae, from two different areas of provenance and which, in our opinion, may have either belonged to the cargo or been intended for use by the ship's crew. A hollow cylindrical spike can be ascribed to an Almagro 51C amphora from Lusitania (Pl. CI, no. 4).[29] The specimen with traces of pitch visible on the inside must have been used for trading Portuguese fish sauces. Of particular interest is the presence of an Empoli amphora among the transport containers recovered during the excavation. This container has the typical ring-shaped rim with a rounded profile, narrow neck and thickened strap handles presenting two longitudinal grooves on the upper surface; these are set on the shoulder and on the neck, immediately beneath the rim (Pl. CI, no. 3).

Assuming that this specimen did indeed form part of the cargo we need to explain its presence onboard a vessel which almost exclusively carried Tunisian products. We can imagine two equally plausible scenarios. Before it sank, the vessel was sailing northwards along the coast to redistribute surplus North African foodstuffs from a large port to the smaller contexts along the Tyrrhenian coast. We have already noted the fundamental role played by Rome in organizing this redistribution process on several occasions; we can thus suggest that smaller craft left the ports of Rome laden with foodstuffs and then sailed along the coast towards secondary destinations. As McCormick has rightly noted, there must have been a fairly marked difference between the major routes used to transport goods used as taxes in kind, most of which lay some distance from the coast in deep waters, and secondary shipping routes through coastal waters.[30] This difference must have corresponded to a difference in the vessels in circulation, with larger and more robust ships being used for the former type of trade and smaller and therefore more manoeuvrable vessels for the latter.[31] In any case, the central and northern Tyrrhenian coastline, given its ancient morphology with coastal lagoons and plentiful river mouths large and small, offered numerous places in which to moor small and medium-sized vessels.[32]

extérieure présente un éclaircissement blanc jaunâtre, parfois nuancé d'orange ou de brun-violet en correspondance avec certains coups d'estèque verticaux; l'intérieur est orange, souvent zébré de bandes plus ou moins blanches parallèles au tournage" ; Bonifay 2004, p.39.

[29] Keay 1984, p.176, Fig.71, no.7.

[30] McCormick 2001, p.93.

[31] *Ibidem*, pp.95-96.

[32] Torelli 1984, p.18.

If our vessel was sailing northwards, the most likely theory is that its point of departure was one of Rome's two ports and that the Empoli amphora was brought on board during operations to load the cargo. However, if this explanation is correct, the amphora cannot have been intended for trade; it was probably one of the containers holding wine destined for consumption by the crew. This is in no way surprising, given the importance of the flows of wine from the Arno valley towards Rome, clearly documented by the finds from some Roman contexts of the 4th and 5th centuries.[33] It would be absurd and uneconomical to assume that wine was transported southwards from central-northern Tuscany for trade and then redistributed back northwards. Such a process would have entailed taking the wine to the Roman markets and then returning some of it back to the north, destined for the coastal sites near its area of production.

The second, equally plausible, scenario sees *Portus Scabris* as one of the possible sites to which secondary trade flows from Rome may have been directed, given the importance of this harbour in the Roman and late antique period. Smaller boats could then have left *Portus Scabris*, directed both south and north to supply nearby sites. Were this the case, the Empoli amphora may have been put on board at *Portus Scabris*. The wine inside it may have been destined for consumption by the sailors transporting Tunisian foodstuffs or for supply to one of these smaller sites. These two hypotheses also help to explain the presence of the Portuguese Almagro 51C container for fish sauces.

Phase 3 Amphora

Site D also yielded a fairly atypical amphora specimen, perhaps a Keay XXXVA. This specimen, which has no pitch coating, has a thickened and rounded rim ending in a pointed lip; the neck is cone-shaped and the thickened strap handles present a groove on the underside and are attached to the neck, immediately beneath the rim, and to the junction between shoulder and neck. The specimen presents a whitish external slip (Pl. XCVII, no. 10). Keay XXXVA amphorae are dated to the 5th century on the basis of Tunisian finds.[34] As such, the specimen from Site D is not in phase with the presumed shipwreck but must indicate later activity at the site.

[33] Empoli amphorae are continuously documented in the ceramic assemblages of the *Magna Mater* temple, albeit in small quantities, from the mid 4th to the early 5th century AD. Even more interesting is the data from the mid 5th-century context of the Crypta Balbi *mithraeum*, where Empoli amphorae are very well documented, being second only to Keay LII amphorae in the repertoire of late Roman amphorae produced in Italy; they are the third most important imported amphora in terms of absolute percentage values. For this data see Reynolds 1995, pp.333-336, Appendix D.21 and Saguì-Coletti 2004, p.244, Graph III.

[34] Bonifay 2004, pp.134-135.

Phase 1 Amphora

An amphora with a massive, internally concave rim of pseudo-triangular section, a short cylindrical neck and thick handles of circular section set beneath the rim can be identified as a Dressel 20 used to carry Baetic oil. The mouth is 12.8 cm wide (Pl. CI, no. 5). The amphora is made from a greyish fabric containing an abundance of limestone and quartz fragments (Anf 1009); this specimen may have been overfired. This type of amphora was produced at least from the Tiberian period onwards and became widespread under Claudius; its production continued up to the late 3rd century and perhaps even into the 4th.[35] Given the morphological structure of the rim and handles, our specimen is generically comparable with a Dressel 20 from the nearby shipwreck "A" at Punta Ala, dated to the mid-3rd century.[36]

7.2.2. Production C African Red Slip Ware

Fineware is represented by a minimum number of only 11 forms, all Hayes 50 deep dishes in African red slip ware C. All the specimens have a shiny red-orange slip, very similar to the well-purified fabric (tiny inclusions of quartz and limestone measuring about 0.06-0.1 mm); the fracture is very clean and some fragments make a metallic sound, an indication of the high temperatures reached during firing. Overall the material appears to be well preserved despite its contact with the geological and biochemical elements of the seabed and its long period of immersion in sea water.

The Hayes 50 flat-based dish is represented by two versions of different sizes: one with rim widths falling into the range 20-24 cm and a larger version with rims measuring between 28 and 34 cm in diameter. The walls appear strongly flaring and fairly thin, no thicker than 3 mm. The specimens from Site D at Cala del Barbiere seem to belong to Hayes' variants A/B and B given their morphology and the size of the base. In two cases the small bases present an almost atrophied ring-foot similar to that of variant A/B dated to between 300 and 360 AD (Pl. XCVIII, nos 9-10).[37] The bases with no foot are marked by a ledge and present a slightly arched profile identical to that of the later variant Hayes 50B, ascribed to the second half of the 4th-early 5th century and perhaps slightly later (Pl. XCVIII, nos 4, 6-7).[38]

It is more difficult to determine which variant a specimen belongs to on the basis of the morphological structure of the rims; these are generally plain and end in a slightly pointed lip (Pl. XCVIII, nos 1-3, 5, 8), as in variant A/B and the more ancient variant A. In one case the rim is rounded (Pl. XCVIII, no. 6); in another it is oblique on the outer surface and resembles that more typical of the late variant B (Pl. XCVIII, no. 7).

The African red slip ware C appears to suggest that the wreck dates to the 4th century. Finally, it is difficult to say if the fineware recovered during excavations was part of the cargo, like the amphorae, or if it was used by the crew. The exclusive presence of minimum forms of Hayes 50 flat-based dishes, the most widespread African red slip ware C form in the Mediterranean, might suggest that it was intended for trade.

7.2.3. Tunisian Kitchenware

The excavation yielded a total minimum number of 11 forms of Tunisian coarseware. These can be subdivided into:

- a bottle for use at table/storage;
- three casseroles;
- seven dish-lids for kitchen use.

At least three fabrics have been identified;[39] two of these – the samples "Tunisian coarseware 1" and "Tunisian coarseware 3" – are associated with a minimum of only three forms: a lid and a dish-lid for the former and the only bottle for the latter. All the other minimum forms, both casseroles and dish-lids, are made using the more common fabric "Tunisian coarseware 2", constantly associated with the African kitchenware found at surface sites in the territory between the Alma and Osa valleys.

The only specimen of a bottle has two handles and an everted and rounded rim, with a thickened external ledge marking the junction with the neck (Pl. CI, no. 1). The rim diameter measures 10 cm. The strap handles are small (about 2 cm wide) and present two light longitudinal grooves. The neck is cylindrical, with a slightly convex profile at the point where the handles are attached. A whitish slip is distributed over both the external and internal surfaces. This type of bottle presents some generic similarities with Fulford, CW, closed forms 24.1,[40] attested in the British excavations at Carthage and datable to a later phase than our specimen, between 450/475 and 500/525. Given their morphological affinities, the bottle from Site D at Cala del Barbiere may be an earlier variant of the type documented at Carthage. Its chronology suggests that it belongs to Phase 3 of Site D.

Moving on to the kitchenware, we can identify two types of casserole, attested with a minimum number of one individual each; the fragmentary nature of the third specimen, by contrast, makes it impossible to ascribe it to a specific typology.

[35] Peacock-Williams 1986, p.136.
[36] Dell'Amico-Pallarés 2006, p.66, Fig.22.
[37] Hayes 1972, p.68, Fig.12, no.65.
[38] *Ibidem*, p.68, Fig.12, no.56.
[39] For the fabrics see the Catalogue.
[40] Fulford-Peacock 1984, p.206, Fig.80, no.24.1.

The first type has an everted thickened rim with a narrow gap between the rim and the wall; the body is shallow and the base is grooved (Pl. XCIX, no. 6). This form is similar, but not identical, to type *Ostia III, 324*,[41] documented at Ostia in contexts datable to the Flavian period in the mid-2nd century AD,[42] and in the Tarragona area both in contexts of the Domitian period and in others contemporary with those at Ostia.[43] Its chronology allows us to ascribe this specimen to Phase 1 of Site D.

The second type has an internally thickened rim, gently flaring walls and an outer flange marking the junction between the walls and the grooved base (Pl. XCIX, no. 7). This type can be identified as a Hayes 23B, documented at Ostia from the first half of the 2nd century to the late 4th/early 5th century.[44] Given this specimen's thin walls and the shallow profile of the base it seems to belong to a 3rd-century AD production, and therefore to Phase 1.

The last casserole specimen can be ascribed with certainty to Phase 2. This specimen is characterized by its large size and by its grooved and footless base. This form resembles a fairly late large variant of Hayes 197 (Pl. XCIX, no. 8). Despite its complex typological evolution, this type of casserole is attested throughout the long period between the late 2nd and the first half of the 5th century.[45] The Site D specimen appears similar to a variant datable to between the late 3rd and the early 4th century.[46]

Some of the African coarseware dish-lids, like the casseroles, present traces of smoke, indicating that they were used by the crew. Among these the most common type is Hayes 196, with a minimum of at least 5 individuals characterized by thickened almond-shaped rims whose widths range from 23 to 28 cm. The base is preserved only in one case; it has a very low ring foot. This form is well documented at Ostia from the Antonine period onwards, but becomes more common from the Severan period until the late 4th-early 5th century.[47] In the Tarragona area, this type and other similar forms are well attested from the Claudian period up to the end of the 5th century.[48]

The wall profiles allow us to subdivide this group into two variants which can be ascribed to two different phases. The specimens with markedly flaring walls, a shallow body and less thickened rims belong to Phase 1 of Site D (Pl. C, nos 2-3). These find exact parallels in materials from Nabeul of the mid-3rd century AD.[49]

By contrast, the three specimens with much deeper bodies and a thickened rim can be ascribed to Phase 2 (Pl. C, nos 4-6).

A specimen of lid with an externally thickened rim ending in a barely pointed edge measuring 19 cm in diameter (Pl. C, no. 1) is similar to a variant of Hayes 185, termed *culinarie type 9C* by Bonifay.[50] This variant is well documented at the Tunisian contexts of Nabeul/*Neapolis* and Hammamet/*Pupput* between the late 2nd and the mid-3rd century.[51] Its chronology allows us to ascribe the specimen to Phase 1 of Site D.

Finally, a specimen of lid with strongly flaring walls presenting light horizontal grooves, and an everted, thickened and rounded rim (Pl. C, no. 7) is comparable with type Fulford CW, lids 4.3; in the British excavations at Carthage this type was found in contexts datable to between the 4th century and 525/550 AD.[52] Comparisons with materials from Tunisia were of no assistance in clarifying whether our specimen belongs to Phase 2 or 3 of Site D.

7.2.4. Tableware of Uncertain Provenance

The excavation yielded a minimum number of one closed form, perhaps a juglet or small tankard in *ingobbiata di rosso* ware. Only the slightly concave base and part of the wall are preserved; the wall presents light external grooves (Pl. CI, no. 2). The fabric (AD 1006) is purified and presents a substantial quantity of inclusions (<5%). These are mainly quartz and iron oxides, with a smaller amount of limestone. Similar forms are documented among the materials belonging to the crew of shipwreck "A" at Punta Ala (*infra*) dated to the mid-3rd century AD.[53] It is currently impossible to determine with certainty where this piece came from; however, we can note its similarity with forms in *ingobbiata di rosso* ware from the late Roman sites in the study area, probably made by regional workshops.

7.2.5. Kitchenware of Tyrrhenian Provenance

This group consists of a minimum number of 6 lids made using fabrics different to those used by Tunisian workshops and which must therefore have come from one or more production areas outside North Africa.

All the specimens analysed appear to present more or less obvious differences in their fabrics, although

[41] Atlante I, Pl.CVII, no.6.
[42] *Ibidem*, p.218.
[43] Aguarod Otal 1991, p.279.
[44] Atlante I, Pl.CVI, no.10.
[45] Bonifay 2004, p.225.
[46] *Ibidem*, p.224, Fig.120, no.5.
[47] Atlante I, p.212.
[48] Aguarod Otal 1991, p.250.
[49] Bonifay 2004, p.226, Fig.121, nos 5 and 7.
[50] *Ibidem*, p.222, Fig.118, no.7.
[51] *Ibidem*, p.221.
[52] Fulford-Peacock 1984, p.196, Fig.75, no.4.3 and p.197.
[53] For comparisons see Dell'Amico-Pallarés 2006, p.113, Fig.69, nos 3-4.

examination under an optical microscope and the comparison with fabrics from other sites (especially those of the late antique phase of the Scoglietto cave and context 5147 in the excavation on the north slopes at Roselle) make it possible to subdivide these into different categories and formulate an hypothesis on their provenance.

Fabrics AG 1003 and AG 1009 are both characterized by the prevalence of calcite, alongside iron oxides and quartzes; both fabrics also contain micaceous inclusions (biotite in AG 1009 and muscovite in AG 1003). The only difference between the two is the presence in AG 1009 of feldspars, absent from AG 1003. Given the affinities of these fabrics with some documented at Roselle in contexts of the 4th-early 5th century and the close similarities with those attested in some 10th-century kitchenware forms from the hilltop village of Poggio Cavolo, it is likely that these fabrics were used by workshops located between southern Tuscany and Lazio.

These two fabrics are used to make three specimens of dish-lids. The two made from fabric AG 1003 are characterized by rims of pseudo-triangular section, with a rounded edge and internal ledge (Pl. C, no. 8), and by their plain rim, cone-shaped body and ring foot (Pl. XCIX, no. 5). The dish-lid associated with fabric AG 1009, by contrast, has a slightly thickened rim and extremely flaring walls with a convex profile (Pl. XCIX, no. 2). The first specimen is very similar to a type attested in the mid-5th-/mid-6th-century phase of the Scoglietto cave, whilst both the second and third are generically reminiscent of specimens attested at Roselle in context 5147 (4th-early 5th century).

We can also ascribe the lid made using the spathic calcite-enriched fabric AG 106 to a local or sub-regional production; this fabric is documented in kitchenware forms from the Scoglietto cave and cooking pots from medieval contexts in the territory between the Alma and Osa valleys. This type of lid has a barely thickened rim and a button-shaped handle (Pl. XCIX, no. 1). It is difficult to ascertain the exact chronology of these types of lid; given their simplicity they may have been produced over a long period. At *Albintimilium*, for example, similar forms appear from as early as the 2nd century BC or from the Augustan period onwards.[54] Comparisons with materials from that part of southern Tuscany studied here, however, allow us to suggest that they belong to Phase 2 or 3 of Site D.

Finally, the two lids made from fabrics AG 1010 and AG 1011 respectively may come from the volcanic areas of Lazio or Campania. Their fabrics present extremely hard, shiny black inclusions of volcanic origin (augite in both fabrics?). One lid has an everted and thickened rim (Pl. XCIX, no. 3) and the other an almost plain edge and low ring foot (Pl. XCIX, no. 4). The lid shown in Pl. XCIX no. 3 is comparable with form *no. 5 Celsa 19.15* attested in the Tarragona area from the late 1st century BC to the early 2nd century AD.[55] According to Aguarod Otal, in her typology of the pottery with an internal red slip produced in Campania, this lid was used together with dish no. 5.[56] The properties of the fabric of our specimen (AG 1010) do not seem to differ significantly from fabric no. 2 identified by Aguarod in both pottery with an internal red slip and unslipped wares produced in the Vesuvian area.[57] We can therefore suggest that lids similar to those of the early imperial period continued to be produced into the late Roman period, as perhaps demonstrated by the specimen from Site D at Punta Ala. To recapitulate, then, the six lids described above can be ascribed in four cases to workshops operating between southern Tuscany and Lazio and in two cases to workshops in Campania/Lazio.

7.2.6. Concluding Remarks on Site D

In light of the evidence presented above, we can suggest that Phase 2 of Site D, ascribed to the first half of the 4th century, may represent part of the severely looted cargo of a shipwreck. This theory appears to be supported by the recovery of wooden planking in the same area as the underwater deposit. The long period of continuous use of the Cala del Barbiere harbour explains why the materials from Site D are of different dates. However, only the materials from Phase 2 are sufficiently homogeneous to allow these to be ascribed to a vessel transporting a cargo of Tunisian amphorae, probably manufactured in the Nabeul area and used to trade North African wine or fish sauces. It is possible that the Lusitanian Almagro 51C amphora and an "Empoli amphora" also belonged to the cargo, although the fact that these types are attested with a single minimum form each makes it impossible to rule out that they were in fact used by the crew. The African red slip ware C, well attested with a minimum number of 11 forms, all Hayes 50 flat-based dishes, variants A/B and B, may also have belonged to the cargo. Overall, then, we have a cargo represented by a sample of a minimum of 11 Tunisian amphora forms and 11 African red slip ware C dishes. To these materials we can add, on a purely hypothetical basis, the Almagro 51C and Empoli amphorae.

The African kitchenware and the various dish-lids in kitchenware ascribed to a production in the "Tyrrhenian area", chronologically compatible with Phase 2, must have been part of the equipment used by the crew, as demonstrated by the evident traces of smoke. The same can be said for the juglet in purified ware with a red slip, which must also have belonged to the sailors.

[54] Olcese 1993, p.336, Pl.12, p.337, Pl.13, p.338, Pl.14.

[55] Aguarod Otal 1991, pp.117-118.

[56] *Ibidem*, pp.117-118.

[57] *Ibidem*, pp.40-41.

The characteristics of this partially reconstructed cargo allow us to draw some comparisons with two well-known 4th-century shipwrecks: that at Femmina Morta, west of Punta Secca in Sicily, and that of Pampelonne, near Saint Tropez. The former, dated to the early 4th century, mainly carried Africana IIB-D amphorae and a further six types of Tunisian cylindrical containers. Also belonging to this cargo were some specimens of Lusitanian Almagro 51C amphorae and Baetic Dressel 23 amphorae. Some African red slip ware D of the early 4th century has been ascribed to the cargo.[58] The Pampelonne wreck, dated to the first half of the 4th century, was carrying a partially similar cargo, mostly Tunisian cylindrical amphorae with an internal pitch coating and Almagro 51C amphorae. In this case, the size of the deposit suggests that the vessel was a small one, although definite data on its structure is lacking.[59]

There are some obvious parallels between the possible shipwreck in Phase 2 of Site D and the two described above. In particular, all three sites present an association of Tunisian amphorae and Lusitanian Almagro 51C amphorae. Additionally, both in the Femmina Morta site and the Site D wreck, the Tunisian amphorae were associated with African red slip ware as a secondary cargo, also destined for trade. This is important because, contrary to what we might think, it is not a particularly common occurrence.

There are also some interesting parallels with materials from another, slightly more ancient, shipwreck also found near Punta Ala a few tens of metres from Site D.[60] The so-called shipwreck "A", ascribed to the mid-3rd century on the basis of numismatic evidence, was transporting an extremely heterogeneous cargo. This consisted of Africana II amphorae (especially variants C and D), Lusitanian Almagro 51 A-B, Almagro 51C and Beltran 72 amphorae and a variant of a Lusitanian amphora whose rim is similar to a Keay XXIVA, and finally Baetic Dressel 20 and Dressel 23 amphorae. The supposed attestation of variants of Keay XXV, on the other hand, appears doubtful on the basis of the materials illustrated.[61]

All the Lusitanian amphorae are characterized by their internal pitch coating, a characteristic which they share with numerous specimens of Tunisian cylindrical containers. Given what we have already said, these amphorae must have been used to transport fish sauces from Lusitania and *salsamenta* and wine from Tunisia. The Baetic amphorae, on the other hand, present no trace of an internal pitch coating, in keeping with their use to transport oil. The cargo included some *dolia*, also with an internal pitch coating.

The 37 fragments of African red slip ware C belonging to various specimens of Hayes 50 flat-based dishes (variants A and A/B) have been ascribed to wares used by the crew;[62] however, as for the shipwreck at Site D, it cannot be ruled out that these also formed part of the cargo.

Finally, the African kitchenware, some wares with a purified fabric, both with an external red and orange slip and uncoated, destined for use at table and for storage, and a series of kitchenware forms of uncertain provenance must have formed part of the equipment used by the crew. The same can perhaps be said for some containers probably manufactured in Tunisia, characterized by an umbonated base and an internal pitch coating.[63]

The parallels between shipwreck "A" and the hypothetical shipwreck at Site D are clear, although the latter is at least half a century later in date. Though in the case of shipwreck "A" the quantitative ratios of the different types of amphorae lean decidedly in favour of Lusitanian rather than Tunisian materials, it is important to note that here, as at Site D, food supplies from both these provinces coexist. Furthermore, the association of African red slip ware C and Tunisian amphorae, perhaps made by the workshops in the Nabeul area on the basis of the fabrics and slips, albeit with slightly different typologies, represents another interesting analogy between the two wrecks.

The complex variety of primary goods characterizing shipwreck "A" has led us to formulate at least two hypotheses regarding the redistribution port where these Lusitianian, Baetic and Tunisian goods could have been loaded onto the annonary vessel which later ran aground at Punta Ala. A first possibility is that the port in question was either Cádiz or Cartagena; from here the vessel may have sailed via the Balearic Islands and Sardinia towards the Tyrrhenian coast. According to the second and equally plausible hypothesis, the vessel originally set sail from northern Tunisia, reached one of the aforementioned ports and unloaded part of its cargo. The cargo still on board was then supplemented with Baetic and Lusitanian foodstuffs which had previously reached the port of redistribution. The vessel then sailed on, following the same route as in theory one.[64]

[58] Parker 1992, p.177, no.398.
[59] *Ibidem*, p.301, no.783.
[60] For shipwreck "A" at Punta Ala see Dell'Amico-Pallarés 2007.
[61] See *ibidem*, pp.77-80 for the supposed Keay XXV amphorae.
[62] *Ibidem*, pp.101-103.
[63] *Ibidem*, pp.103-119 and pp.80-82.
[64] *Ibidem*, pp.161-163.

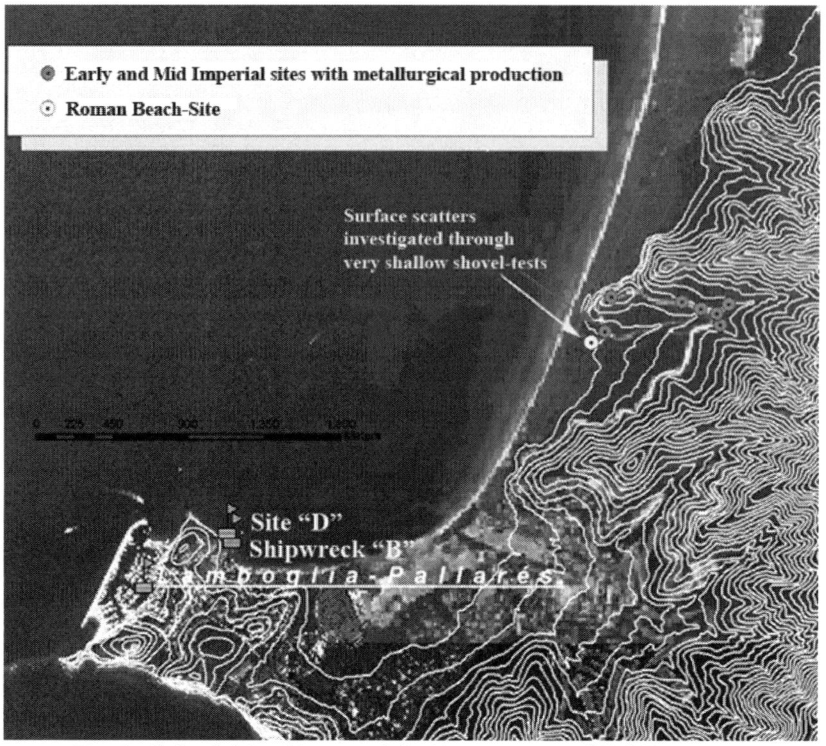

Fig.4_ Cala del Barbiere and the Roman sites of Val Piastrone.

In the case of the Site D shipwreck, on the other hand, we do not have sufficient information to determine if this was a vessel carrying taxes in kind or if it was a smaller boat destined for the redistribution of foodstuffs and Tunisian fineware along a coastal route. As noted above, the presence of the "Empoli amphora" might lead us to prefer the latter theory, but in the absence of more thorough excavations and in light of the significant looting undergone by the underwater deposit this issue seems destined to remain unresolved.

7.3. Cala del Barbiere and Its Relations With the Roman Production Context at Val Piastrone

During the early and middle Empire, the Cala del Barbiere harbour was probably linked to a settlement and production complex consisting of various small sites forming part of a larger cluster with buildings and warehouses for the storage of imported foodstuffs. Surface surveys and two very shallow shovel tests conducted in the Val Piastrone, immediately north of Cala del Barbiere, have shown the existence of a substantial Roman settlement along the small watercourse which gives its name to the area. The sites are found mainly along a belt at the foot of the hills between 10 and 50 m above sea level. In six out of eight cases these sites consist of small scatters of surface materials, measuring 5x5 m on average, with associations of pottery, bricks, slag from the smelting of iron and haematite from Elba. The only finds that can be dated with certainty are fragments of Arretine sigillata, *terra sigillata tardo-italica* and African red slip ware A, which make it possible to date these contexts to between the 1st and 3rd centuries AD. Two larger clusters, 7-8 m above sea level, consisted in one case of a significant concentration of bricks and in another of large quantities of wall fragments from Gallic amphorae associated with Arretine sigillata ware and African red slip ware. Two shovel tests were carried out inside these clusters, in an area measuring 50x50 cm and reaching a depth of 5cm, aimed at assessing the depth of the contexts and at documenting any later surface materials in the top layer of sand. Both sites, less than 200 m from the current coastline, are located along a minor road running through dense Mediterranean scrub. As the two shovel tests and an occasional section showed, the archaeological sediment was identified virtually at the surface, at a depth of only 5 cm beneath the current land level. In the case of the northernmost TU, a layer of roof tiles was uncovered very partially; this probably belongs to the collapse of the roof of a building (Figure 4).

The morphology and fabric of the roof tiles were similar to those found at the other surface clusters, suggesting, in the absence of pottery evidence, that they were contemporary with the other TUs. Of greater interest was the layer uncovered by the shovel test at the other surface cluster. This brought to light a layer of dark earth containing numerous fragments of amphorae and bricks, and a fragment of an African red slip ware A Hayes 9A bowl, datable to between 100 and 160 AD. Among the transport containers, we identified a so-called small Italic Spello amphora, datable to between the 1st and 3rd century, and a Gallic Gauloise 4 amphora, widespread between the mid-1st and the 3rd centuries AD;[65] both were used to trade the wines produced in their respective areas of provenance

[65] Peacock-Williams 1986, pp.142-143.

(Figure 5). These amphora finds are perfectly in line with those from shipwreck "B" at Cala del Barbiere, evidence of the close relations between this site and maritime trade circuits. Only further archaeological excavations can provide definitive proof, but it is likely that the layer uncovered by the shovel test belonged to a warehouse for the storage of foodstuffs. The complex settlement at Val Piastrone seems to have had a specific productive purpose linked to the smelting of haematite from Elba. This activity also seems to have taken place at another two contexts located a few km to the north along the Alma river: the villa frequented in late Antiquity at Pian d'Alma and the late 5th-6th-century settlement at Val Molina. The favourable location of the Punta Ala bay, "open" to the mining district of Elba, allowed for direct connections with the island, ensuring rapid commercial links and the transfer of its resources from the Etruscan period until the end of the Middle Ages.[66]

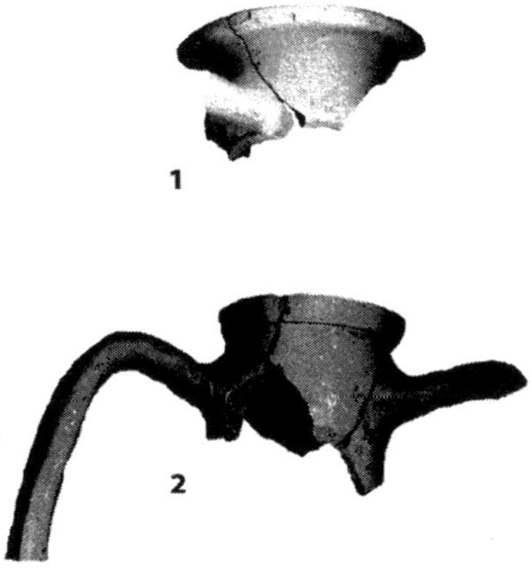

Fig.5_ Gauloise 4 amphora (1) and "Spello" amphora (2) types from the Roman beach-site of Val Piastrone.

Another harbour reached by these coastal routes was located at the mouth of the Alma river in the Torre Civette area; this must have been the location of a *positio* mentioned in the *Itinerarium Maritimum*.[67] This harbour provided access for vessels to the brackish Lake Alma, mentioned for the first time in a sales contract of 1074 but certainly also extant in the Roman period,[68] and thence the inland sites along the river. The settlements in the Val Piastrone do not show any signs of a continuity of life after the 3rd century AD and they are probably among that large number of settlements which were abandoned as a result of the middle imperial crisis.

Although this period saw the demise of one of the major settlements to which the Punta Ala-Cala del Barbiere harbour made reference, it continued to be used constantly for at least another three centuries, until trade with small and medium-sized vessels became well integrated into a larger-scale maritime trade network.

[66] For the long continuity of metal production in this area see Cucini Tizzoni-Tizzoni 1992.

[67] For the location of the *positio* near the Alma river mouth see Camilli-Gambogi 2004.

[68] For the document see C.A.S.P., 2, no.17, pp.28-30.

8. The Countryside in the Early Middle Ages

8.1. The Centralization of Settlement Between the Eighth and Early Tenth Centuries: Villages on Hilltops and in the Plains

Foreword

A few preliminary remarks are in order before we attempt to provide a general outline of population patterns during the High Middle Ages (8th-9th centuries) in the coastal and sub-coastal belt between the Alma valley to the north and the Osa valley to the south. The data presented here come mainly from intensive surface surveys undertaken both in zones with good visibility inside the various sample areas and in wooded areas where anomalies on aerial photographs or archive sources suggested the likely presence of medieval fortified villages. Only in three cases did our research agenda aim to take the study further to the analytical level, with stratigraphic excavations at the hilltop village of Poggio Cavolo, the early medieval farmstead of Casa Andreoni and the multi-period site of San Martino in Piano. Our objectives in these three cases were to investigate: the formation processes of the village of Poggio Cavolo; the topographical layout of a settlement feature belonging to a non-centralized settlement at Casa Andreoni; and the dynamics of the late antique and medieval occupation at San Martino in Piano. Given the quantitative imbalance between survey data and excavation data it is difficult to draw meaningful comparisons between these different structures, especially for the early medieval phase. This is due essentially to a problem of "visibility" affecting this period and closely linked to the nature of 8th and 9th century settlements. The extensive stratigraphic excavations conducted over the past thirty years on a representative sample of twelve Tuscan fortified sites have demonstrated the existence of structured villages on hilltops preceding the fortification process.[1] This makes it impossible, or at least extremely difficult, to find surface evidence of help in identifying features predating the construction of the castles, whose stone structures necessarily "conceal" any earlier phases. Surface surveys provide only a small amount of information of help in identifying early medieval hilltop villages and this is an objective limitation which must be borne in mind since these long lasting contexts probably played a key role in 8th- to 10th-century settlement patterns.[2] The limitation is a significant one considering the overall picture emerging from the surface surveys undertaken in the past; between the provinces of Grosseto and Siena these covered an area of about 1979 km^2, equivalent to about 8.6% of Tuscan territory, but failed to discover more than a handful of features dating to the High Middle Ages. The features discovered, moreover, were found exclusively in failed contexts prematurely abandoned before the 11th century and located in non-urbanized areas.[3] Nonetheless, this finding, superficially fairly discouraging as to the informative potential of surveys, was confirmed only partially by the results of our own surface surveys in the study area. There are a series of "lucky" exceptions: hilltop villages which, despite their monumentalization during the late Middle Ages, have yielded slight traces of earlier settlements dating to between the late 9th and the 10th century in the form of pottery indicators documented in exposed sections. Naturally these data are occasional and partial, and provide neither information on the spatial and topographical layout of the hilltop settlement preceding the construction of the castle nor a date for its foundation. The presence of a few pieces of late 9th-/10th-century pottery clearly indicates that the site was in use during this phase, but not that this was when the settlement began to develop. In other cases, surveys of low-lying and hilly areas with good archaeological visibility allowed us to identify some early medieval contexts by systematically analysing the entire sample of surface pottery. Despite their short life-span these contexts provide a glimpse of the complexity and variety of settlements in this area during the 8th-9th centuries. The picture emerging from the study area examined here appears to suggest that equating the early medieval settlement network with part of that system of hilltop sites which were later fortified fails to represent adequately the complexity and fluidity of population dynamics during the High Middle Ages; the settlement network comprised a series of more or less centralized settlements in the plains which have hitherto been underestimated or even ignored.

A case apart are those late 9th- and 10th-century sites which were established after an apparent gap or with only slight traces of continuity at population centres that had remained in use up to the 6th or early 7th century. In these cases surface surveys, supported by the distributional analysis of pottery, allowed us to acquire some data on the processes of topographical transformation undergone by settlements between the transitional period and the Middle Ages.

[1] The excavations organized by the Department of Medieval Archaeology of the University of Siena took place at the villages of Montarrenti, Poggibonsi and Miranduolo in the province of Siena; Scarlino, Rocchette Pannocchieschi, Grosseto, Cugnano, Montemassi and more recently Poggio Cavolo in the province of Grosseto; and finally Suvereto, Campiglia Marittima and Donoratico in the province of Livorno. On these sites see Francovich-Hodges 2003, Cantini 2003 (Montarrenti); Valenti 2004, Salvadori-Valenti 2003, Valenti 1996 (Poggibonsi); Nardini-Valenti 2005, Valenti 2004, Valenti 2008 (ed.) (Miranduolo); Francovich-Hodges 2003, Marasco 2002-2003 (Scarlino); Valenti 2004; Boldrini-Grassi 2003 (Rocchette Pannocchieschi); Citter 2007c, Citter 2005 (ed.), Francovich *et alii* 2000 (Grosseto); Grassi 2006, Belli-Francovich-Grassi-Quirós Castillo 2005 (Cugnano); Grassi 2006 (Montemassi); Salvadori-Vaccaro-Ghisleni-Chirico 2006 (Poggio Cavolo); Valenti 2004, Ceglie *et alii* 2006, Cuteri 1990 (Suvereto); Bianchi 2004a (Campiglia Marittima); Francovich-Bianchi 2006, Bianchi 2004b (Donoratico).

[2] See especially Francovich-Valenti 2005; Francovich 2004; Valenti 2004; Francovich-Hodges 2003.

[3] See Valenti 2004, p.72 and p.80.

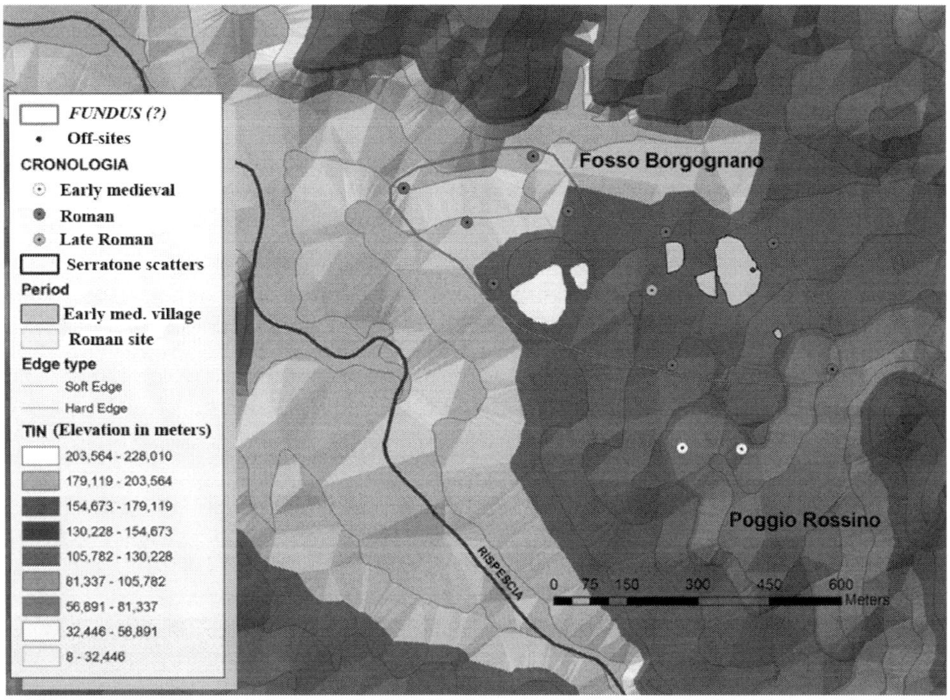

Fig.1_ The early medieval village at Podere Serratone and its historical and geographical context.

The period between the 8th and the 10th centuries thus appears to be far more complex than previously thought, with forms of settlement hitherto unknown to archaeological research in the Tuscan countryside. These settlement types tend to share a common feature: given the political and economic situation, still in its formative phase, the tendency to concentrate human energies seems to have been an essential strategy if people were to support and feed themselves (Synoptic Table I,). Dispersed settlements, on the other hand, appear to have contributed little to population patterns, being documented with three isolated houses and a probable medium-large farmstead within an intensively surveyed sample territory of 68 km^2.

8.2. Settlement Contexts Abandoned Before the Tenth Century: Types and Interpretations

8.2.1. The Village of Podere Serratone

The survey supplied some important data on the formation of sizeable aggregated or nucleated population centres established in the vicinity of areas with good agricultural soils. Two of these, which probably had fairly large populations, continued to exploit areas which had previously hosted Roman and late antique structures between the 8th and 9th centuries, albeit without any direct topographical continuity.

At Podere Serratone, near the Rispescia river, we identified a village consisting of three features which, on the basis of the pottery evidence, appear to be contemporary. These occupy an area of about a hectare in total within a small valley, bounded to the north and west by the Fosso di Borgognano,[4] to the east by the slopes of Poggio Rossino and to the south by the Rispescia river. The settlement appears to have formed prevalently between the 8th and 9th centuries, although some pottery indicators suggest that the context may initially have been frequented between the late 6th/7th centuries. We cannot rule out a connection between the foundation of the early medieval village and a phenomenon of population shift on the part of the group previously established at the late Roman settlement, about 200 m to the south. The latter was abandoned no later than the 5th century and presents a surface scatter covering almost a hectare, an area more or less identical to that of the later village. Equally, the topographical proximity of these two contexts and the matching dates for the abandonment of the former and the development of the latter also offer convincing support for the theory that the settlement shifted within the same area of farmland. If we analyse the spatial distribution of the off sites yielding Roman and late antique materials, systematically georeferenced in the field,[5] we can identify an area of farmland belonging to the Roman and late antique settlement of about 26 hectares; within this lies the zone later occupied by the early medieval village of Podere Serratone (Fig.1). This reconstruction hypothesis finds further

[4]This toponym is documented in the *Catasto Leopoldino* of 1823 (Grosseto - Section K of Poggio Cavallo, Grancia, and Volta di Sacco, Sheet V), from which we can see that in the 19th century the stream followed the same course as today.

[5] The accurate georeferencing of off-site ceramics using a handheld GPS and further processing of their fabrics using an optical microscope was a successful approach to studying the exploitation of the territory around village sites. A similar approach was adopted to attempt a reconstruction of the extent of the landholdings in the *Ager Brundisium* in Apulia owned by Visellius, a wealthy late Republican aristocrat who also owned some kilns: see Cambi 2000, pp.177-179.

confirmation in the praedial toponym Borgognano, which probably derives from the Roman name *Verconius* or *Verconnius*.[6] The early medieval village may thus have been established within the settlement/economic space of a pre-existing Roman settlement, perhaps a *vicus*.[7] In this context, it is interesting to note the attestation, inside the main surface feature of the $8^{th}/9^{th}$-century village, of *acroma depurata* ware belonging to the transitional phase between late Antiquity and the High Middle Ages. These pottery fragments consist of a minimum of 3 bowls with incurving rims modelled on the ARS prototype Hayes 61, a flanged bowl made in imitation of Hayes 91C and a bowl with a rim pointed on the upper surface and a groove beneath the rim, possibly modelled on the ARS prototype Hayes 87B. To these we should add 8 amphora fragments with a white outer slip, probably imported from North Africa and belonging to a minimum of at least one form.[8] Some off sites consisting of 8th- and 9th-century pottery seem to suggest that the area of farmland expanded southwards during the High Middle Ages, eventually reaching the western slopes of Poggio Rossino. Between the late 6th and the 7th century the population of this new settlement must have been fairly small; there are relatively few pottery forms ascribable with certainty to this phase compared to the copious pottery finds dated to between the 8th and 9th centuries.

The surface survey suggests that the village of Podere Serratone consisted of a central unit, a small and probably residential structure to the south on the lower slopes of Poggio Rossino, and a larger unit, perhaps composed of several buildings, to the west. Altogether the Topographical Units belonging to the early medieval village cover a surface area of just over a hectare, although it should be noted that natural and anthropic factors may have increased the size of the surface scatter with respect to that of the buried deposit. Aerial surveys in the Grosseto area revealed a soil mark in correspondence with the main surface feature of the Serratone village, confirming at least in part that the buried archaeological deposit and the surface evidence coincide (Fig.2).[9]

The surface surveys at Podere Serratone failed to identify any definite traces of defensive structures, suggesting that this was an open settlement. The geomorphology of the area occupied by the early

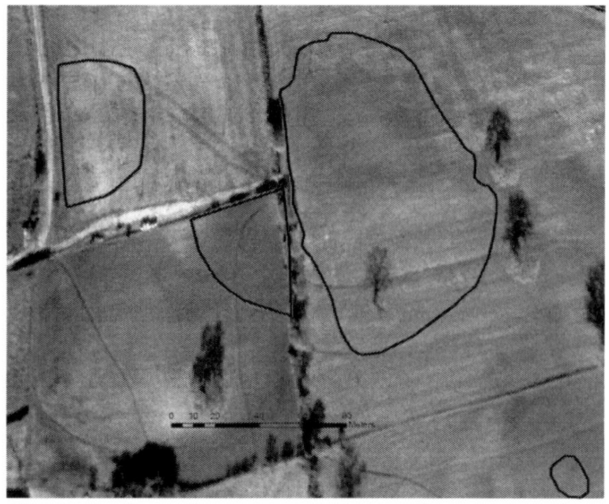

Fig.2_ Soil mark corresponding to the main surface scatter at Podere Serratone.

medieval village, in the middle of a narrow valley, did not even provide natural protection.

The buildings in the village of Podere Serratone must have been earth houses or wooden huts given the extremely low density of reused stones and bricks from the Roman settlement found inside the features: the density of small and medium-sized limestone blocks is about one per m^2, whilst bricks are virtually absent. The odd dark colouring of the soil in the main Topographical Unit may be interpreted as resulting from the decay of structures made of perishable materials cut through by ploughs. A comparison with other surface contexts of the transitional period and the early part of the High Middle Ages between the lower Bruna valley and the Osa valley allows us to identify Podere Serratone as the site with the lowest density of reused bricks and stone blocks (Graph I). A peculiarity of this village was without doubt the presence here of craftworkers, as demonstrated by the existence of a pottery kiln specializing in the production of morphologically highly standardized coarseware. This manufacturing activity is documented by the presence of fired clay, overfired pottery sherds and some wasters found exclusively in a circumscribed area on the east side of the main surface scatter. Magnetometric data also appear to confirm the results of the survey: a strong anomaly was found at this point which can be

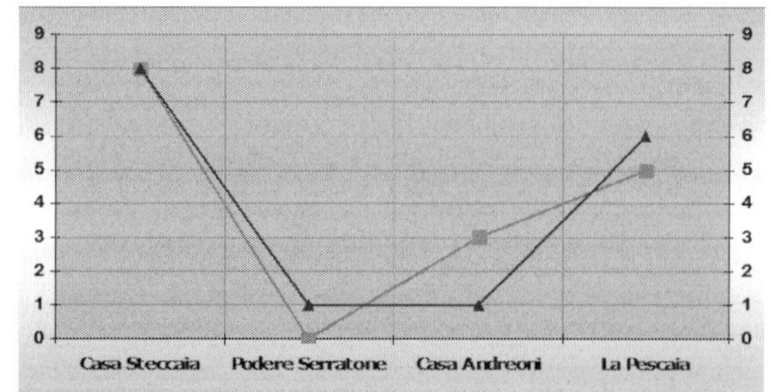

Graph I_ Quantification of the building materials (per m2) from four early medieval sites.

---

[6] For the Roman origin of this toponym see Pieri 1969, p.139.

[7] On the role of late Roman *vici*, located at the centre of large private estates and inhabited by small to medium land owners and *coloni* see Arthur 2004b, p.105.

[8] The prototypes Hayes 91C and Hayes 87B are dated to AD 500-570/580 and from the second half of the 5th century to AD 530/550 respectively. For the dates of 6th-century AD African Red Slip ware circulating in Italy see Tortorella 1998, pp.41-69.

[9] The aerial survey was directed by Stefano Campana as part of a larger project aimed at surveying and monitoring archaeological sites in the provinces of Siena, Grosseto and Florence. For the Serratone case-study see also Campana 2005, p.463, Fig.1.

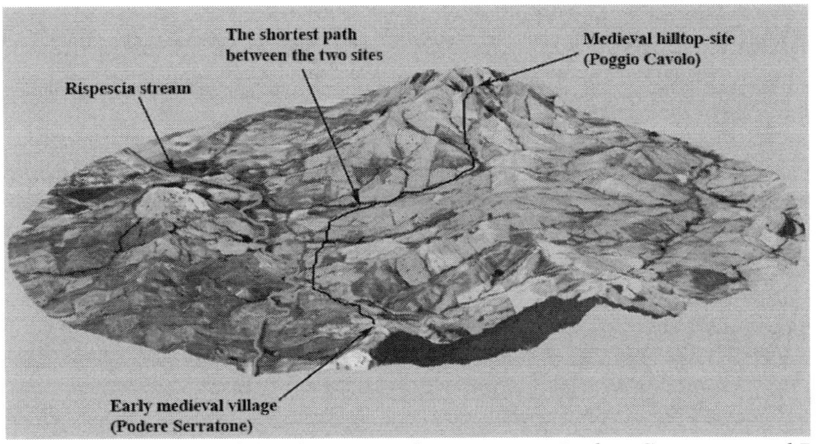

Fig.3_ GIS-based reconstruction of the shortest path connecting Podere Serratone and Poggio Cavolo.

interpreted as residual thermal activities.

After developing significantly in the 8th and 9th centuries, the pottery indicators suggest that the Podere Serratone context underwent an abandonment process which was completed by the early 10th century. In an attempt to understand why this village failed to develop we investigated the topographical relations between this settlement and the castles documented from the 10th century onwards on the basis of archaeological data and documentary sources. This told us that the nearest hilltop village was that of Monte Calvi-Poggio Cavolo.[10] This site consists of a wall circuit enclosing the flat hilltop, with a surface area of 0.46 hectares, and of an outer structure, perhaps a second wall circuit or a broad terrace, which in turn surrounded the whole village, covering a total of 1.24 hectares. The settlement was in an excellent strategic position overlooking the Grosseto plain and the lower Ombrone river down to its mouth. Excavations between 2005 and 2007 covered too limited an area of the site to reach any definitive conclusions on its initial chronology and topographical layout. However, the discovery of a church rebuilt in the second half of the 10th century is of enormous importance for the argument proposed here; the north and south sides of the church rested against the wall circuit enclosing the hilltop. The stratigraphic relations currently do not allow us to determine exactly when the defensive structure and the church were built, but they certainly formed part of a significant construction project dating to no later than the early 10th century and probably slightly earlier (9th century?). Obviously the construction of a massive structure like the wall circuit, which has a perimeter of about 280 m and an average thickness of 1.7 m, must have required a significant investment on the part of the *dominus*, indicating that it belonged to a site of some importance both as a population centre and perhaps for strategic purposes.[11]

The shortest route between the villages of Podere Serratone and Poggio Cavolo was determined on a GIS base using a three-dimensional model of the area, with the greatest importance being given to height above sea level and the slope.[12] The final outcome was a shortest route of 4.6 km, corresponding to the distance a person could travel on a daily basis to reach farmed areas from a central site (Fig.3).

Ethnographical studies have shown that farming communities tend to exploit lands located within a radius of 5 km or one hour's walk from the village.[13] The practical applicability of this analysis was tested experimentally by walking the shortest possible route between the site of Poggio Cavolo and that of Podere Serratone calculated using GIS, with the aim of determining the time needed. It took just over an hour to cover this distance, making it likely that there was a spatial relationship between the hilltop site and the area occupied by the early medieval settlement of Podere Serratone.[14]

The final objective of studying the relations between these two sites was to understand whether or not the village population may have shifted from Podere Serratone to Poggio Cavolo. The period between the late 9th and early 10th century was a time when the significant development of the landowning nobility and the establishment of local aristocracies led to a more marked concentration of the rural population.

The phenomenon of settlement shift is still little studied in Italy whilst it is a fairly characteristic feature of the early medieval villages of northern and western Europe, where it may take two distinct forms:[15]

[10] See also Farinelli-Vaccaro-Salvadori 2008.

[11] At the early medieval hilltop village of Donoratico in the Cornia valley (province of Livorno), a single-apsed church and wall circuit with a perimeter of about 353 m enclosing 8374 m^2 of site surface were both built in the 9th century AD, see Francovich-Bianchi 2006, pp.110-111.

[12] See Macchi Janica 2001, pp.61-82.

[13] Renfrew-Bahn p.224.

[14] The shortest route between the two sites was checked in the field by covering the distance on foot; a vector feature representing the path itself was downloaded onto a handheld GPS for ease of navigation.

[15] For these aspects see Hamerow 2002, pp.104-106.

- the gradual shift of a site within its territorial boundaries;
- the complete refoundation of a site in an area that may be a considerable distance from its original location.

Ethnographical studies have shown that settlement shift within an area of farmland may be due to reasons of health and hygiene (e.g. the need to move houses periodically to avoid epidemics), and above all to economic reasons, making it possible to farm areas previously occupied by the settlement and rendered particularly fertile by the accumulation of organic matter.

The 10th century seems to have seen a reversal of this trend in central and western Europe with settlements gradually stabilizing. This was probably due to the introduction of new systems for the exploitation and centralized management of land which required an intensification of labour and entailed the production of larger food surpluses.

In Tuscany the 10th- and 11th-century *incastellamento* materially and juridically consolidated a tendency to choose hilltops as the preferred place for settlement which had begun in the early Middle Ages;[16] however, this did not prevent the simultaneous development, between the 7th and 10th centuries, of some settlements of various sizes still located in the plains, served by major roads and in the vicinity of lands which were fertile and easy to farm.

In the late 9th century the coastal belt between the lower Ombrone valley and the Osa valley seems to have seen a gradual selection of settlements, with the widespread abandonment of the few settlements still located in the plains. Their populations thus moved to nearby hilltop sites, where concentrated and organized forms of settlement must have developed during the High Middle Ages.[17] In light of the data currently in our possession, for example, Poggio Cavolo must have become a fully structured settlement from as early as the late 9th/early 10th century. This period saw the completion of the process of consolidation of village elites, a development clearly expressed by the emergence of a spatial hierarchy.[18] At Poggio Cavolo the building of a massive wall circuit and a church with an apsidal chamber demonstrates the existence of a local elite able to organize and fund this type of expensive construction work.

Compared to Podere Serratone, this village was certainly a better expression of the principle of a more rational and wide-reaching exploitation and control of the land between the lower Ombrone river to the north and the Rispescia river to the south; this also encouraged the organization of diversified agriculture around the centralized site.[19]

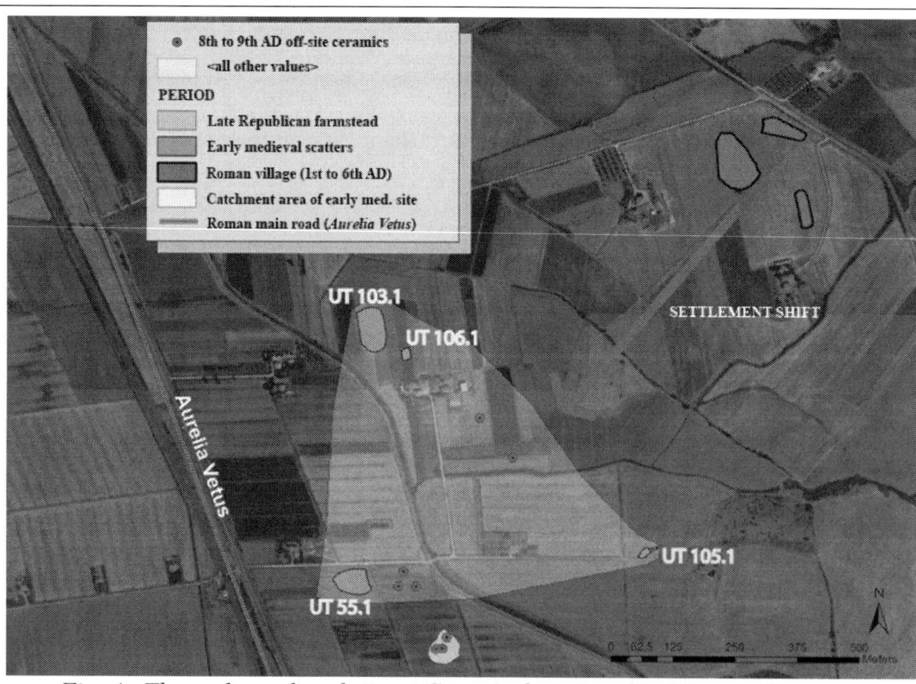

Fig. 4_ The early medieval site at Casa Andreoni and its historical context.

[16] Francovich 1998, pp.17-18.

[17] For the reconstruction of early medieval settlement patterns in Tuscany based on the central role played by hilltop villages which later became *castelli* see Valenti 2004 and Francovich-Hodges 2003.

[18] Valenti 2007.

[19] On the development of a variety of farming activities around castles see in general Francovich 2004, pp.XIV-XVI.

Topographic Unit (UT)	Surface size in m2
55.1	3100 m2
105.1	381 m2
103.1	4000 m2
106.1	388 m2

Tab. I_ Surface size of the early medieval surface scatters composing the semi-nucleated site at Casa Andreoni.

As concerns the management of the agricultural resources within their productive space, one of the major novelties resulting from the establishment of population centres on hilltops was the development of intensive diversified agriculture in nearby areas; the extensive cultivation of cereal crops probably continued in lowland areas, which had been used for this purpose for some time. It is thus possible that, after the abandonment of the village of Podere Serratone, its lands were incorporated into the catchment area of Poggio Cavolo and used for extensive cultivation and/or pasture.

8.2.2. The Casa Andreoni Site: a Non-Centralized Eighth/Ninth-Century Settlement On the Via Aurelia

Overview of the Context

The settlement discovered near Casa Andreoni lies on that stretch of the *Via Aurelia Vetus*[20] immediately north of the Gulf of Talamone. In this case, too, the foundation and development of the settlement can probably be ascribed to a phenomenon of settlement shift on the part of the population of the village of Podere Laschi, in a protected position on a small hill about 800 m to the east (Fig.4). As at Serratone, some pottery indicators found at Podere Andreoni suggest that the site was first used in the late Roman period,[21] although it developed most markedly between the 8th and 9th centuries; after this the settlement was abandoned.

In terms of topographical layout, the settlement consists of three/four surface features identifiable as houses (Table I), on average 380 m apart and arranged within an area of about 26 hectares which may have represented the catchment area of this system of small farms. The presence of some off sites with pottery materials contemporary with those from the main site (8th-9th centuries) suggests that these areas were used for agricultural purposes. However, in at least one case it cannot be ruled out that the superimposition of a minimum of three early medieval pottery forms on a feature forming part of a large farm abandoned by the end of the 1st century AD indicates that the ruins of the Roman building were reused for residential purposes.

Excavations and the Interpretation of the Site

The peculiarity of this context, whose topographical and spatial characteristics currently appear to be unique, led us to open some test pits into the main surface feature.[22]

The geoarchaeological study of the site to be excavated allowed us to place the area of land on which it stands at 6 metres above sea level, between the terraces linking the system of scattered hills to the east and the plain to the west.[23] Thanks to this observation we can deduce that the area in which the village of Casa Andreoni stood was not subject to problems of water-logging in ancient times and that the minimal impact of accumulation and erosion processes characterizing this type of landscape led to a fairly slight change in the land level between the High Middle Ages and the present. Additionally, the presence of significant numbers of proto-historical settlements on the terraces allows us to state with a good degree of certainty that the whole belt remained passable at least between the Final Bronze Age and the High Middle Ages. Any swamping phenomena of the type affecting the area around Lake Prile to the north must have taken place after the late Middle Ages when the human impact on the countryside decreased, resulting in a failure to

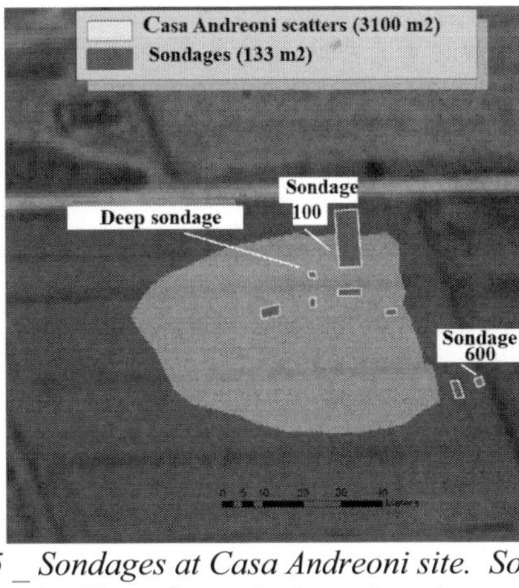

Fig.5 _ Sondages at Casa Andreoni site. Sondages 100 and 600 are better indicated as they produced the most interesting results.

[20] For the Roman road network along the Tuscan coast see Citter 2007b.

[21] It is worth noting the presence of two specimens of bowl with an inverted rim, in imitation of African Red Slip type Hayes 61.

[22] The excavation at Casa Andreoni was co-directed by Dr P.Gambogi (Soprintendenza per i Beni Archeologici della Toscana) and the author. This took the form of a rescue excavation in July 2005, and involved students from various Italian universities.

[23] I am grateful to Antonia Arnoldus Huyzendveld for her assessment of the geoarchaeological context. For a geological map of the area see Van Berghem *et alii* 1991, p.70.

maintain canals and banks.[24]

Our excavation involved mechanically digging a series of eight test pits into the main feature of the early medieval settlement. The aim was to evaluate the degree of conservation and informative potential of the deposit by obtaining a sample which was as representative as possible of the whole structure. A total area of 133 m^2 was investigated, about 4.3% of the Topographical Unit intercepted by the survey, which covers an area of 3100 m^2. In six out of eight cases the excavation reached an average depth of 50/60 cm beneath the current land surface without intercepting archaeological layers, merely indicating the significant depth of soil disturbed by ploughing.

Fig.6_ Section from the deep sondage (1,2 meters in depth). Here, the ploughed soil is immediately on top of the natural layer.

Fig.7_ View of some post-holes cut through SU 103.

The soil covered an inorganic yellow-brown layer, with a clayey-sandy matrix, 20 cm deep; this in turn covered the pedogenetic substratum consisting of clays and Holocene clayey limestone deposits (Figs.5-6).[25] For an understanding of the settlement structure, the most interesting finds come from test pit 100 and to a lesser extent test pit 600. The former, measuring about 15 x 6 m, runs north-south along the north-east corner of the surface feature. Here, beneath the layer of ploughsoil, 35-45 cm deep, were the clearly visible traces of an anthropic layer which had been severely disturbed by mechanical ploughing (context 101). This layer covered about ¾ of the test pit, with the exception of the south segment where we found a completely inert sandy-clayey layer (context 102) under the ploughsoil, at a depth of 45 cm. In the rest of the test pit, underneath context 101 which was on average 10-12 cm deep, was a layer with a dark brown clayey-sandy matrix containing various pottery fragments and reused bricks on the interface (Fig.7). Context 103, pseudo-horizontal and sloping slightly from south to north with a maximum height difference of 10 cm, can be interpreted as a probable levelling into which at least 42 post holes had been cut. Thanks to the thermoluminescence dosimetry of four pottery samples from this layer we can propose a calibrated date of 830±50 AD. Unfortunately, deep ploughing had completely removed the living and abandonment layers belonging to the settlement features identified by the excavations; as a result the test pits only intercepted the negative imprint of the structures represented by the alignment of post holes. It seems entirely likely that here, as in test pit 600, agricultural activities at least in part "spared" the buried deposit because the surviving stratigraphy lay on the edges of the field; the space needed to turn the mechanical ploughs thus prevented the ploughshare from reaching a depth of over 40 cm.

---

[24] These considerations are fundamental for an accurate evaluation of the data collected during excavations. The Casa Andreoni area, like most of the coastal countryside of the southern Maremma, was affected by massive land reclamation works and introduction of mechanized farming in the 1950s, promoted by the Ente Maremma. As a result of this vast reclamation project, ploughing reached a depth of 50-60 cm for the first time; archaeological sites in ploughed areas which were not sealed by post-depositional accumulation processes were severely damaged. Some useful information on farming in the coastal areas of southern Tuscany, and especially around the present day towns of Grosseto, Magliano in Toscana and Orbetello, come from a careful reading of the publications by Francesco Vivarelli Colonna, who owned a huge estate and recorded details of agricultural work on his properties (including the depth of ploughing). Describing the systematic use of deep mechanical ploughs which he promoted on his estates, Francesco Vivarelli Colonna says: "*Quando nel 1905, entrato nella maggiore età, iniziai la bonifica di questa vasta zona di terreno, l'agricoltura predominante era quella comune alla regione, e cioè l'estensiva. I concimi chimici erano sconosciuti ... Mancava qualsiasi razionale rotazione e solo dopo aver lasciato un numero rilevante di anni il terreno a pascolo, questo veniva maggesato per seminarvi grano e poi, sulla stoppia, avena, per ritornare dopo, per molti e molti anni di seguito, ancora a pascolo. Aratri e coltrine di legno lavoravano il suolo alla profondità di cinque cm. Circa*" (Vivarelli Colonna 1926); details of the use of deep ploughs can also be found in Vivarelli Colonna 1937: "*Le maggesi venivano fatte con delle piccole coltrine di legno con puntale di ferro, che intaccavano il terreno a qualche centimetro di profondità, cinque, sei centimetri al massimo*". In the 1937 note we also read: "*Mi preoccupai di approfondire al massimo possibile la coltratura e per ottenere questo dotai ogni fattore di potente aratro dissodatore e di un ripuntatore, e così potei raggiungere una profondità di cm. 40 circa*". Apparently the introduction of very deep ploughing in the Casa Andreoni area, part of the huge Vivarelli Colonna estate, predated the Ente Maremma reclamation project of the 1950s. I am indebted to Giampaolo Bonora for drawing my attention to these texts.

[25] For the natural layer and its description see Van Berghem *et alii* 1991, p.70.

The absence of fireplaces and anthropic layers related to the post holes forced us to refine our interpretative criteria considerably to obtain an explanation which was as accurate as possible of the function of and relations between each individual post hole in order to identify potential structures.[26] We therefore proceeded to interpret the post holes using GIS, cross-referencing the data on the depth and diameter of each individual hole. We were thus able to divide 32 of the 42 holes into three functional categories (Fig.8):

- holes for posts serving as reinforcements or decorations with a diameter of 16-18 cm and a depth of 28-35 cm;
- holes for reinforcement or small load-bearing posts with a diameter of 17-26 cm and a depth of 36-42 cm;
- holes for load-bearing or other posts, with a diameter of 27-60 cm and a depth of 43-51 cm.

The phasing of these features on the basis of their function suggests the existence of at least two structures, one of which may have been an oval residential hut, oriented east-west and with an opening to the south on the long side (S1). If we observe that portion of the floor plan uncovered by excavations, we can identify two lines of post holes inside the structure which probably served to support it internally and to separate interior spaces with different functions. If the door was halfway along the south side of the building, as the structural data in our possession appear to suggest, the hut's total size was probably about 20 m^2.[27] The hut appears to have had internal furnishings, as demonstrated by 5 post holes arranged in a cross shape near the door. A fence, whose presence is indicated by five narrow, deep post holes, closed the *sedimen* on the south side (S2).

A further 10 post holes, concentrated in the southern portion of the test pit, are extremely shallow, on average no more than 10 cm deep despite a diameter ranging from 25 to 40 cm, compatible with load-bearing or reinforcement posts.[28] These holes seem to be related to a small pseudo-trapezoid structure with the long side measuring about 3.8 m, the short side 2.5 m and the width 2.3 m; this structure can be interpreted as a functional annexe or as an enclosure (S3). The fact that the post holes belonging to this structure are shallower than the other 32 may suggest that it was later in date, since it was certainly built at a higher level than the others. However, on the basis of the evidence collected it is impossible to assign a precise date to the outbuilding.

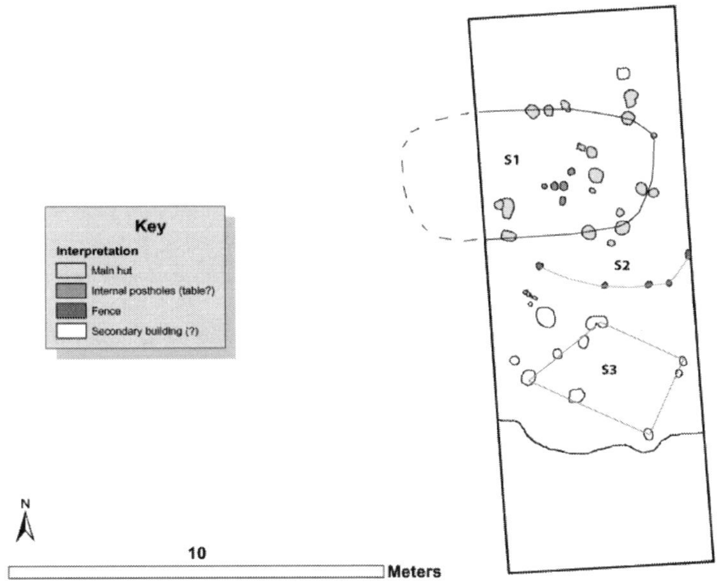

Fig.8_ GIS-based interpretation of the excavated data from sondage 100; the three possible structures are S1, S2 and S3.

[26] For the analysis of early medieval post holes based on their depth and width see Fronza-Valenti 2000, pp.21-27 and Francovich-Valenti 2000, pp.14-20.

[27] A two-square module has been suggested for a series of Early to Mid Saxon huts in England. According to this reconstruction model, domestic huts tended to be twice as long as they were wide, ideally forming two adjacent squares of almost identical size. This calculation has been attempted for the hut at Podere Andreoni. For this reconstruction method and the Saxon village at Mucking (Essex) see Hamerow 1993, pp.9-10, with bibliography.

[28] In the interests of clarity, the depth of each post hole belonging to the third structure (S3) identified at Casa Andreoni is as follows: 5 cm (contexts 162, 107, 146); 6 cm (contexts 148, 156); 8 cm (context 154); 10 cm (context 106); 13 cm (context 160); 15 cm (contexts 122, 127).

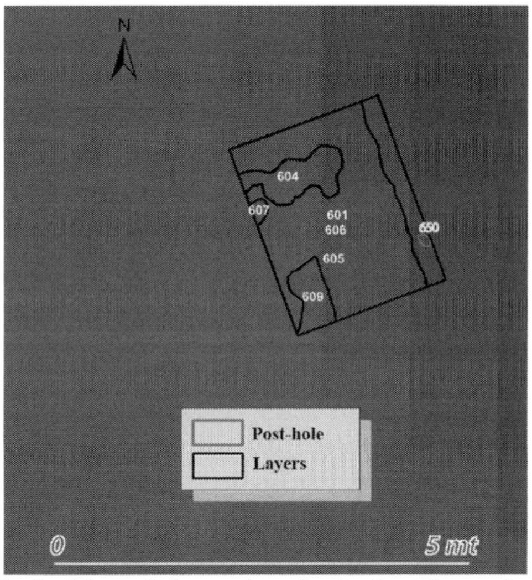

Fig.9_ Map of the archaeological evidence from sondage 600.

Fig.10_ Possible wall in beaten earth from sondage 600.

We also documented repair work on at least three holes belonging to the oval hut, with new circular cuts superimposed on the earlier holes. This may suggest that the structure remained in use, with some minor maintenance work, for two or three generations, within the chronological range between the late 8th and late 9th century.

The data from test pit 600, measuring 1.8 x 2.3 m, are less clear (Figs.9-10). This test pit was located 10 m to the east of the surface feature, near a small country lane, not significantly affected by agricultural activities over the past 40 years.[29] The objective was to check if the settlement also developed towards the areas surrounding the Topographical Unit documented by the survey. In this case, too, the layer of ploughsoil reached an average depth of 40/45 cm beneath the land surface (context 601). The ploughed layer covered a situation which remains difficult to interpret given the small size of the test pit. The first archaeological layer intercepted, context 605, had a clayey matrix and was interpreted as a levelling, with an average depth of 8-10 cm. This context yielded some pottery indicators ascribable to the 8th-9th centuries. An oval post hole with a maximum width of 14 cm and a depth of 10 had been cut into context 605, near the east side of the test pit. The fill of the post hole yielded no material of help in dating it; because it is so shallow it seems certain that, like levelling layer 605, the post hole was disturbed to some extent by ploughing. Beneath this was a layer of very compact brown clayey soil running east-west, which can probably be interpreted as the decay of an earth wall, preserved to a height of 10-15 cm and with a maximum width of 38 cm. This structure must have been related to a beaten earth floor, whose existence is indicated by two patches (contexts 607=609) preserved near the south-west corner of the test pit and near the earth wall. The floor lies about 10 cm below context 604. These contexts overlie a levelling layer: context 606, 15 cm thick and horizontal, covering the whole test pit. Context 606 yielded various reused Roman bricks, a small early medieval Type 2 amphora and an early medieval Type 6 cooking pot.[30] Finally, context 606 covered a very compact yellowish-brown inert layer of natural origin (context 615).

The evidence uncovered in test pit 600 currently remains impossible to interpret.

It is unclear if the two different phases, evidenced in one case by the post hole and the levelling layer (context 605) and in the other by the earthen structure and beaten earth floor, belong to residential buildings or subsidiary structures. However, it is important to note that, according to the pottery evidence, the features in test pits 100 and 600 appear to be contemporary. The two contexts lie about 50 m from one another and suggest the existence of a fairly complex settlement structure of single farmstead type.[31] Recent anthropological studies have shown that all agricultural activities were based around single farmsteads. These generally consist of a residential building, buildings for animals, a warehouse for forage

Fig.11_ Topographic Unit 105.1. View of the surface scatter and soil mark.

[29] Information provided by the landowner.

[30] See Chapter 9.

[31] On early medieval single farmsteads in northern Europe see Hamerow 2002, pp.79-86.

Fig.12_ Hypothetic 3D reconstruction of the hut at Casa Andreoni, based upon the excavation data (elaborated by Matteo Sordini – LAP&T).

and cereals, production areas, courtyards, enclosures and open spaces, all bounded by fences and access roads.[32]

Podere Andreoni appears to be an anomaly within the context of population patterns in early medieval Tuscany but within the study area it finds a possible parallel with the Casa Steccaia context in the upper Osa valley (see below). The surface survey indicated no obvious differences between the various Topographical Units belonging to the early medieval dispersed settlement. Despite the significant damage to the buried deposit caused by ploughing, the stratigraphic excavation brought to light a fairly complex and varied settlement structure which appears to have survived for a few generations. If we cross-reference the surface area of the 4 features composing the settlement with the excavation data it seems probable, given its size, that TU 103.1 was a single farmstead. About 40 m to the south-east lies a far less extensive feature, characterized by a high concentration of table/storage ware and kitchenware which suggests a residential structure, perhaps a hut similar to that in test pit 100. The other residential unit is TU 105.1, intercepted by the survey inside a recently planted vineyard (Fig.11). Interestingly, the scatter of pottery materials, which coincides perfectly with a dark patch of soil resulting from the mixing of anthropic layers, is oriented east-west, the opposite direction to the vineyard, which runs north-south. It therefore seems likely that the TU in question, measuring about 26 x 12 m, was a large residential building or several buildings next to one another, whose orientation is identical to that of the hut in test pit 100 (Fig.12).

To recap, the Casa Andreoni complex represents a unique type of settlement, similar in terms of topographical characteristics to the semi-nucleated settlements documented mainly in central and northern Europe during the High Middle Ages.[33] We could describe this context as a nucleated site consisting of at least four distinct units, although it cannot be ruled out that other structures, not visible during the surface survey, may have existed in between those already intercepted. The farmsteads and houses are arranged within what was probably a common space used for subsistence farming. The close relations between the settlement and the road network, like the significant presence of small amphorae used to store/transport foodstuffs, also suggests that local trade networks reached this site.

Although the Casa Andreoni settlement has an extremely unusual topographical layout, it is clear that here, too, there was a tendency to develop a distinctive social and settlement identity. This is conveyed by the potential for exploiting the same farmland albeit probably in a more extensive and less incisive way given the available manpower: on the basis of the data collected no more than 20 people.[34]

8.2.3. The Eighth/Ninth-Century Casa Steccaia Settlement (Upper Osa Valley)

The early medieval settlement of Casa Steccaia lies on a plateau just over 100 m above sea level, about 2 km south-west of Poggio Castellaccio, home to the *castellare de Scopertorio* documented in the *Tavola delle Possessioni* of AD 1320 covering the district of Montiano castle.[35]

The three main surface features are grouped into two clusters 100 m apart (Fig.13). The first and more complex cluster consists of two features with an association of small and medium-sized fragments of limestone and sandstone, pottery finds, bricks made from rose-coloured and yellow fabrics, probably

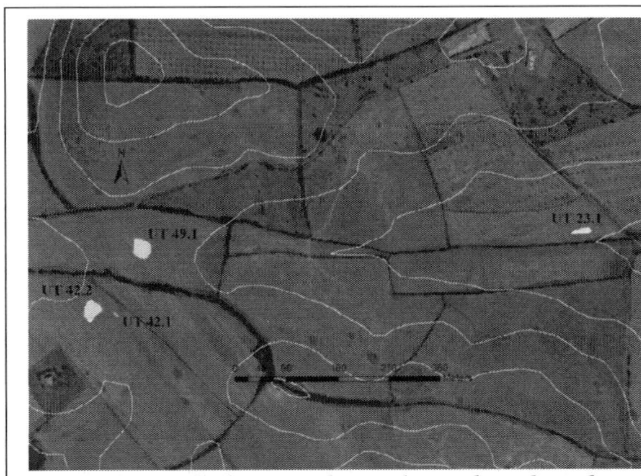

Fig. 13_ In light gray the early medieval surface scatters composing the semi-dispersed site at Casa Steccaia.

[32] See in general Roberts 1996, pp.15-16.
[33] See the examples of poly-focal settlements at Flögeln-Eekhöltjen (Lower Saxony) and Speyer-Vogelgesang (North Rhine-Westphalia) in Hamerow 2002, pp.75-78.
[34] Each unit may have hosted a group of 4-5 people, considering the possible size of the hut excavated.
[35] For the identification of the site of *Scopertorio* see Farinelli 2007, data sheet no.9501.

Fig.14_ Surface materials collection on TU 42.2. The high density of ceramics, tiles and stones can be noted.

reused, and some fragments of *incannicciata*[36] suggesting a construction technique which at least in part made use of perishable materials. The largest Topographical Unit (TU 42.2) is polygonal in shape (c. 34 x 27 m) and covers an area of about 900 m^2. About 20 m to the east is a second feature (TU 42.1) with a far better defined outline, oriented NW-SE, measuring 6 x 12 m and elliptical in shape. This feature presents the same stone, pottery and brick materials on the surface. If, as seems likely on the basis of the surface evidence, TU 42.1 belongs to a single residential building or annexe, TU 42.2, also characterized by a high density of finds per square metre – 8 brick fragments, 10 pottery fragments – seems to correspond to a larger building which was probably the core of this cluster (Fig.14). In light of these observations, the complex can be interpreted as a small farmstead with at least one residential building and one or more annexes. Despite the considerable amount of pottery present, few diagnostic materials were found; however, we can date the complex to the 8th/9th centuries.

The second cluster, contemporary with that described above, consists of a single feature of pseudo-circular shape covering an area of 1000 m^2 (TU 49.1). In this case the characteristics of the surface scatter, with a low density of fragments per square metre (2-3), suggests that the original deposit covered a far smaller area, probably in the central part of the feature; the feature is circular in shape and has a diameter of about 10 m, with a find density of 5-6 per square metre. A third settlement unit, on the basis of the pottery evidence contemporary with the above features, lies about 700 m to the east on a flat area slightly lower down at 80 m above sea level. TU 23.1 was intercepted where there is a dark-coloured patch of land, probably due to the presence of layers rich in organic materials disturbed by ploughing. Here, as for TU 49.1, the characteristics and morphology of the scatter allow us to interpret the context as a residential unit whose original size has been altered by farming activities. The east-west orientation of the surface feature, perfectly in line with the direction of ploughing, and the higher density of finds in the central area of the TU, measuring about 12 x 14 m,[37] is fully compatible with the theory of one large building or several modest buildings made of perishable materials.

In the case of TU 42.1 and TU 42.2 we are almost certainly dealing with a mixed construction technique using small blocks of stone, both limestone and sandstone, to build the bases of walls whilst their elevations were probably made of perishable materials as suggested by the presence of fragments of beaten clay. A building material peculiar to these two TUs is the abundant brick, certainly reused given the similarities in terms of morphology and fabric with the roof tiles from nearby Roman and late antique features identified at the foot of Poggio Castellaccio and on the south-eastern slopes of Poggio Vicarina. In these two TUs bricks are present with on average 8 fragments per square metre whilst in TUs 23.1 and 49.1 they are attested with an average of three and five fragments per square metre respectively. Generally speaking, the quantities of roof tiles found in all four features are extremely high, at least in the first two cases the highest of all the early medieval surface contexts identified between the lower Bruna valley and the Osa valley (Graph I). The small size of the fragments, generally no more than 10 cm in length, does not in itself provide any evidence on their functional purpose. They may have been recovered almost intact from the nearby Roman and late antique deposits for reuse to roof buildings; their extremely poor state of conservation may be due simply to crushing by ploughing in the modern period. An informative point of comparison is the Casa Andreoni context, also dated to between the 8th and 9th centuries, where excavations indicated the presence of various brick fragments in the levelling layer (context 103) and their reuse, in at least four cases, as simple fills inside post holes. The relative ease with which this material could be recovered locally may have led the inhabitants of the Casa Steccaia settlement clusters to collect brick fragments and use them as a construction material for the stone and brick wall bases of houses built using a mixed technique. Three of the four TUs are found in areas where no earlier settlement features existed;[38] only TU 23.1 is located in a zone already densely populated in the Etruscan and late Republican period. The space occupied by these clusters was probably mainly unfarmed; the absence of other medieval population centres in the immediate vicinity suggests that these lands had not been farmed previously. These sites may therefore have been intended to cultivate new low-lying areas which were easier to exploit, located in the vicinity of a modest road network (the country lane crossing the Casa Steccaia area) which would have facilitated the local transportation of foodstuffs. The significant presence among the domestic pottery in use at the houses of small amphorae used to store agricultural products and perhaps for their transport may confirm this theory.

[36] Some fragments of beaten clay with straw footprints revealing the presence of straw/clay walls were collected during the intensive field survey.

[37] The surface scatter, as a whole, covers an area of about 400 m^2.

[38] TUs 42.1, 42.2 and 49.1.

It is unlikely to be a coincidence that the various early medieval clusters at Casa Steccaia are lined up along a secondary road running through the area and descending to the Osa river in the form of a path. The small population units at Steccaia may well have fallen into the context of that slow and difficult process of turning the outfield back into the infield. This process was fairly generalized in Mediterranean and continental Europe and appears to have had some significant precedents in the southern regions of Europe in as early as the 9th century.[39]

The material culture of the settlement complex allows us to state with a good degree of certainty that it was abandoned before the 10th century, with the exception of TU 49.1 which yielded a minimum of at least two pottery forms ascribable to the central centuries of the Middle Ages. This very limited data may, however, indicate either a more ephemeral and seasonal reoccupation of the context after a period of abandonment or a decrease in the number of people living at the site between the 10th and 12th centuries, reflected in a decrease in the amount of pottery in use during this period.

What is certain, on the other hand, is that the significant development of the nearby village of Poggio Castellaccio between the late 9th and the 12th century led to the abandonment of the settlement clusters in its hinterland and the concentration of the population on the hill. However, the surface survey is unable to tell us if the village of Poggio Castellaccio was established at the same period as the Casa Steccaia clusters or if it began to attract the population of surrounding areas only at a later date, when the village was incorporated into the system of *curtes*.

8.2.4. Eighth/Ninth-Century Dispersed Settlements in Their Territorial Context

We have already noted the small number of scattered and isolated forms of settlement in the population dynamics of the High Middle Ages. Only two evidently isolated features were intercepted: one at Alberese, at the foot of the Monti dell'Uccellina, and another slightly further south, at the 163rd kilometre of the Via Aurelia. These two contexts share a close relationship with the major road network of Roman times, represented in this area by the *Aurelia Vetus* (Fig.15). The Alberese settlement, in an area which was intensely inhabited between the late Republic and late Antiquity, appears on the surface as a medium-large isolated site, covering just under half a hectare but with an extremely low density of finds (c. 1 per m^2); we failed to identify any concentrations belonging to different residential units (Fig.16).

Despite the settlement's large total surface area we can suggest that its population was small given the small amount of pottery found during replicated collections. Although visibility conditions are optimal and ploughing reaches to an average depth of about 50 cm, we documented the presence of only 39 pottery fragments belonging to a minimum number of 11

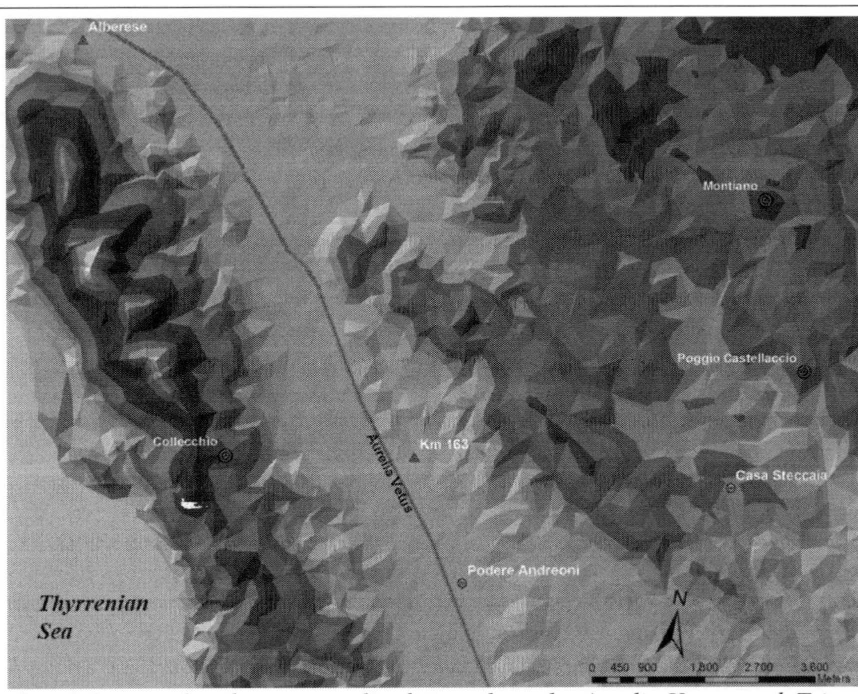

Fig.15_ Early medieval dispersed and non-centralized sites along the Aurelia Vetus road. Triangles correspond to the single farmstead and isolated house; light colour circles are non-centralized sites; dark colour circles are castles.

[39] In general on this phenomenon see Fossier 2004 with bibliography, pp.1157-1171.

Fig.16_ The early medieval scatter and off-site ceramics at Alberese along the Aurelia Vetus; a linear anomaly, corresponding to the Roman road, can be seen in the 1944 Royal Air Force picture georeferenced on GIS.

forms. In light of comparisons with the material culture of other contemporary sites intercepted under similar land use and visibility conditions, such as Casa Andreoni, this allows us to say that this was very likely a single settlement unit of farmstead type. Given the very low find density, the large size of the surface scatter may be the consequence of deep and frequent ploughing rather than an indication of the actual extent of the site.

In connection with this settlement are three off sites which yielded a total of 6 pottery fragments similar to those of the main feature, at a distance of between 300 and 370 m from it, and probably indicating the use of the land around the site for farming.

An evaluation of the characteristics of this 8th/9th-century structure suggests that it may be a "single farmstead",[40] a settlement type which is well documented in central and northern Europe. A single farmstead consisted of one or more residential huts and some smaller structures arranged inside a courtyard, which was usually fenced; some of the smaller structures could also be located outside the enclosure. Generally speaking, for the isolated farmsteads of continental and northern Europe it is impossible to rule out a connection with nearby villages not intercepted by surveys or excavations. An example is Mørup in the Jutland peninsula, which confirms a significant trend towards the aggregation of settlements.[41] The Alberese context cannot at present be connected to contemporary village-type features, although the 9th- and 10th-century documentary sources indicate the existence of large settlements not yet identified by surface surveys; given their names these must have been located on the lower Ombrone river. One of these was the *locus* of Caliano, first mentioned in 803 and which by this period must already have been an important population centre given the interest of the Aldobrandeschi in ensuring control over it. Their interest can probably be explained by the site's good position on the Ombrone river, making it a potential

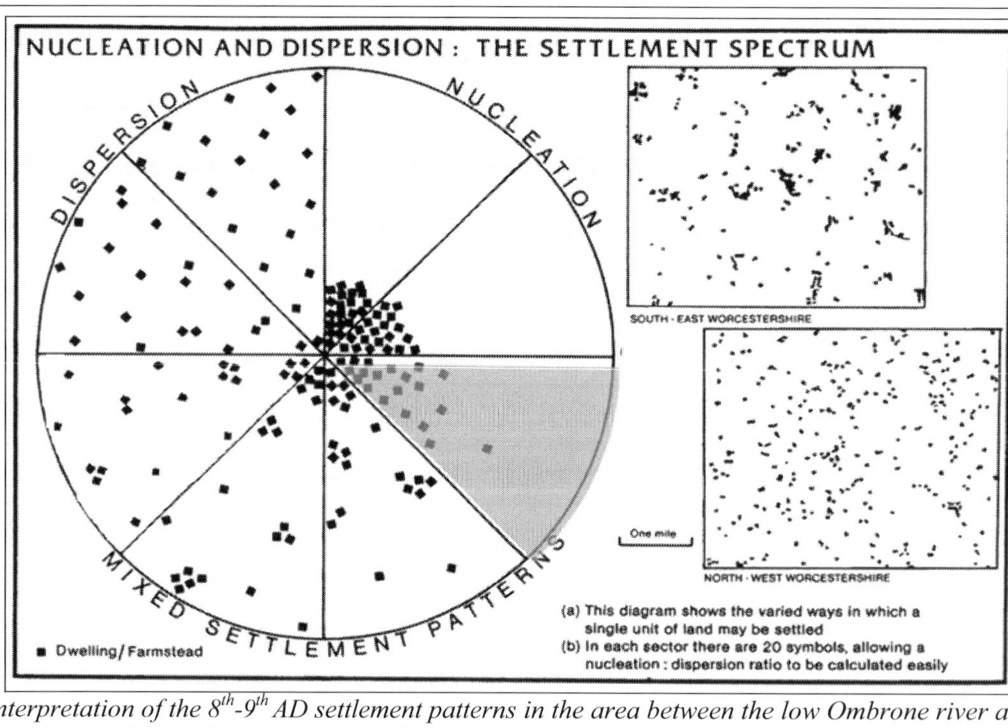

Fig.17_ Interpretation of the 8th-9th AD settlement patterns in the area between the low Ombrone river and the Gulf of Talamone (gray colour). The reconstruction hypothesis is based upon the settlement models proposed in Roberts 1996, p.20, Fig.2.1.

[40] Two well-known cases of single farmsteads excavated in northern Europe, Mørup (Denmark) and Dalen (Netherlands), have a surface area of up to about 2600 m² and 3600 m² respectively. These sites are generally composed of one or two longhouses and a few out-buildings; some are sunken-featured buildings. The single farmstead at Dalen is highly emblematic as it represents the only case of a completely isolated unit. See Hamerow 2002, pp.80-85.

[41] Hamerow 2002, pp.79-80.

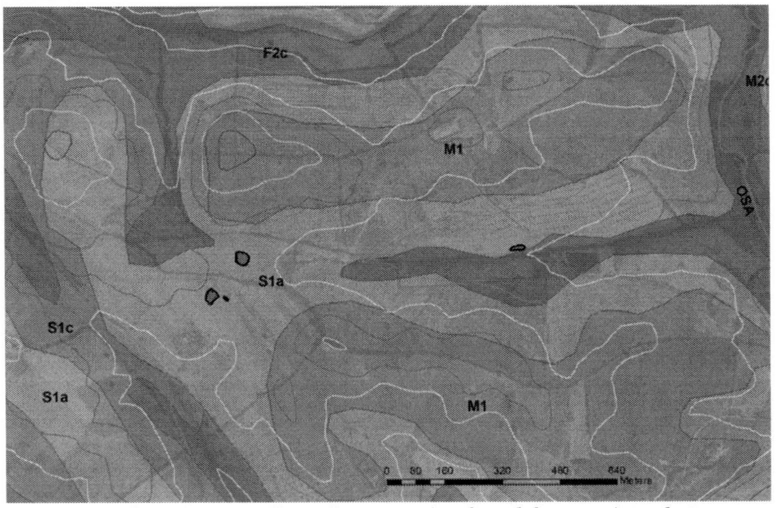

Fig.18_ The 8th-9th AD Topographic Units at Casa Steccaia (outlined features) in their geopedological context. The surface scatters are located on the most favourable soil (S1a) of the area. The geopedological map (after Van Berghem et alii 1991) has been georeferenced on the GIS base.

base from which to manage and organize trade along the river.[42] We know that the settlement played a strategic role from a document of 973, in which Caliano is described as the only one of the forty-four *curtes* owned by Lamberto, a member of the Aldobrandeschi family, to have a tower.[43] This document also mentions a *curtis Astiano*, again owned by the Aldobrandeschi, which must have been located in the Alberese area; the place name suggests that this town inherited not only the name but in part also the population and the task of controlling the ancient road network previously performed by the *mansio* of *Hasta*, identified in the field near Alberese.

The other apparently isolated settlement unit must have had an even smaller population. This settlement is located further south and is also in direct contact with the major road network. About 500 m east of the SS 1 Aurelia, which in this area follows the same route as the ancient *Aurelia Vetus*, a surface feature oriented east-west and measuring about 18 x 5 m was identified at the 163rd km. The feature lies on the edge of a recently planted vineyard and is characterized by small quantities of pottery dating to the 8th and 9th centuries, a few brick fragments and small stones, all associated with a soil mark anomaly which is clearly visible in the field. In total a minimum of only 5 pottery forms were documented: these are a *testo*, a cooking pot, a small amphora and two small jugs. Considering the type of soil use, the buried deposit has probably been severely disturbed by trenching, making the material culture present in the surface layer a highly representative sample, not only of the range but also of the quantities of pottery in use at the site. If we cross-reference the size of the TU with the pottery data,[44] we can propose that this was a single house made of perishable materials, probably belonging to an individual family unit. The context's apparent isolation is counterbalanced by its proximity to the road network and its possible relations with the contemporary settlement of Casa Andreoni, only 1.6 km to the south.

It therefore seems likely that the considerable complexity of the 8th/9th-century settlement network in the area between the lower Ombrone river and the Gulf of Talamone may somehow be due to the presence of a still functioning road network, based on the Roman *Aurelia Vetus* which may have acted as a genuine *trait d'union* in a settlement network dominated by aggregated sites. However, this did not preclude the occasional presence of scattered settlements, given the area's excellent farming potential (*infra*).

If we wished to sum up this situation, we could suggest that this area follows a "complex" population model, similar to one of the possible forms of land occupation proposed by B. K. Roberts, in which village-type clusters coexist with single farmsteads or isolated rural houses (Fig.17).[45]

8.3. Relations Between Eighth- and Ninth-Century Settlements in the Plains and the Farming Potential of Soils

The fairly widespread presence between the lower Ombrone valley and the Osa valley of settlements in the plains, distant from the main medieval population centres on the hilltops, suggests the need to contextualize these in a geopedological reference framework in order to attempt a definition of their

[42] See *C.L.A.*, Lucca I, no.27, pp.94-95; M.D.L. - T.V/2, no.CCCXIII, p.186.

[43] The AD 973 document mentions: *Caliano cum castello et eclesia seu turre ibidem consistente super ripa fluviis Umbron.* See C.D.A. II, n.203, pp.9-13.

[44] TU 110.1 found during the Bruna-Osa *Survey*. See the Catalogue for details.

[45] Roberts 1996, p.19 and p.20, Fig.2.1.

salient economic characteristics.[46] To this end we made a comparative analysis of the geological and pedological features of the areas where these settlements were founded *ex novo* during the High Middle Ages; this analysis took account especially of access to water resources and the agricultural potential of the soils, defined on the basis of the slope,[47] stoniness, drainage and the potential for using ancient farming tools.[48] This is an experimental approach which requires further refinement with the extensive excavation of the sites examined and the immediately adjacent areas, with the systematic application, for example, of palynological analyses. Nonetheless it has provided data of some interest allowing us to identify the features shared by the places chosen for this type of settlement.

8.3.1. The Casa Steccaia Context

The geopedological analysis of the Casa Steccaia area revealed that this was one of the contexts with best accessibility (in other words the potential for accessing a site to establish a stable settlement for agricultural exploitation) in the entire upper Osa valley (Fig.18).

The TUs lie on a slightly undulating plateau with a gradient of 6-8% where the rapid drainage prevents problems related to watter-logging. The extremely slow surface runoff of this soil, typical of the broad plateaux of the Macigno (S1a), allows water to seep into the soil whilst the risk of erosion is virtually nil.[49] The soil is moderately deep and somewhat stony; neither its internal drainage nor its density are such as to impede trafficability, in other words the passage of rudimentary farming tools like hoes. This is a useful clue to determining the area's agricultural potential, though farming would have required considerable effort: the soil conditions are such that crops could have been grown on the modest plateau although the relatively shallow soil and its stoniness may have represented an objective limitation to its workability in the High Middle Ages. Overall, given the area's pedological characteristics we can imagine a context which during the early medieval period may have been mainly outfield, associated with *colturae* of some size, and an economy directed towards silviculture and pastoral activities alongside small-scale farming. A feature weighing decidedly in favour of the accessibility of this area is the presence of numerous springs, including one located in one of the 8th/9th-century TUs.[50] Naturally this is purely coincidental; of greater significance is the establishment of the settlement in an area which, in as well as presenting favourable pedological conditions, was also rich in water, making this one of the economically most promising areas in the upper Osa valley.

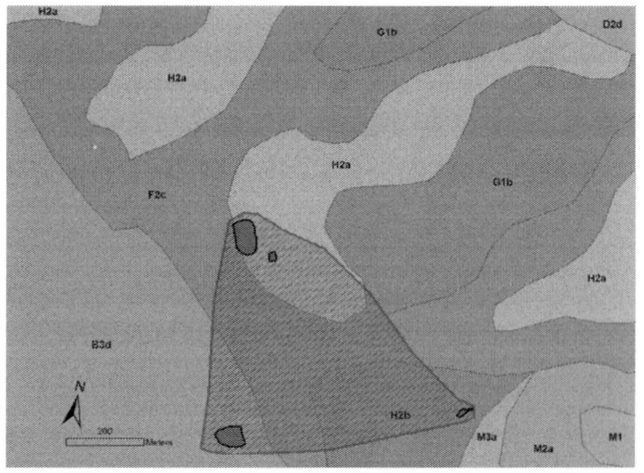

Fig.19_ The non-centralized site at Casa Andreoni in its geopedological context. Soils within the hypothesised catchment area of the site are H2a, H2b e B3d.

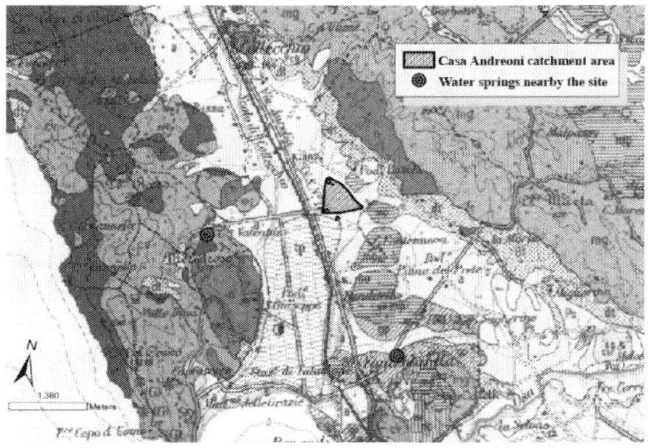

Fig.20_ Visualisation of the early medieval site at Casa Andreoni on the 1:100000 geological map: the water springs are indicated with circles.

8.3.2. The Casa Andreoni Settlement

The settlement units forming the scattered settlement of Casa Andreoni lie in a flat area with a very shallow gradient of 1.5-3%. Although this area is generally flat, the land probably belonging to the settlement does slope, preventing problems related to the flooding of cultivated areas.

The soils on which the four settlement units hitherto identified stood present three distinct types of pedogenetic subsoils; however, in terms of agricultural potential they can be treated together. The soils range in depth from moderately deep to deep, their internal drainage from medium to fast and stoniness is nil or so low as to present no noticeable impediment to the use of rudimentary farming tools (Fig.19). Overall, the soils in the catchment area of the Casa Andreoni settlement are potentially suitable for all types of crops,

46 I am indebted to Antonia Arnoldus Huyzendveld for reading and commenting on this section.
47 In order to evaluate the slope at each site and its surroundings, a 1-metre resolution Digital Terrain Model was created on the GIS base.
48 For the role played by these characteristics in determining the potential of soils for cultivation see Van Berghem *et alii* 1991, pp.119-125.
49 For a detailed description of this soil type see Van Berghem *et alii* 1991, pp.37-38; p.83.
50 For the distribution of springs see Sheet 135 (Orbetello) of the *Carta Geologica d'Italia* 1:100000.

Fig.21_ Thiessen Polygons analysis applied to the catchment area of the early medieval site at Casa Andreoni.

even assuming a very low level of technology and a modest workforce such as that available at this site.

The site's productive and economic potential was also increased by its proximity to the *Aurelia Vetus*, this stretch of which at least doubtless continued to be used during the High Middle Ages since it was the only way through the valley running between the Monti dell'Uccellina to the west and the hilly belt between Poggio Aquilone and Monte Cornuto to the east. Rapid access to the road network may have encouraged the local circulation of foodstuffs produced at the site.

The only potential limitation was represented by access to water resources, given the absence of natural springs in the immediate vicinity. The nearest springs are about 1.7 km to the west near La Valentina or about 3 km to the south on the southern slopes of Poggio Civitella near Fonteblanda (Fig.20).[51]

The Casa Andreoni contest is also of special interest for the results of the Thiessen polygon analysis applied to the site's catchment area. The objective of this approach was to determine the area of farmland available to each of the settlement units making up this non-centralized settlement. On the basis of this reconstruction hypothesis, we calculated that three of the four settlement units had a large area of land, between about 6 and 10 hectares;[52] only the feature in TU 103.1 had a smaller area, no more than 1.6 hectares (Fig.21). This apparent discrepancy can be explained by the proximity of settlement contexts TU 103.1 and TU 106.1 which may have formed a single farmstead unit. Were this the case, we would have a more equitable subdivision of farmland with three large plots measuring 6.3, 9.1 and 11.4 hectares respectively. The affinity between these values and the typical *manso* measurement may be no coincidence: according to Leicht,[53] supported by Montanari,[54] this must have been around 12 *iugeri* or 9.4 hectares, assuming an area of about 7900 m^2 for the Carolingian *iugero*.

8.3.3. The Village of Podere Serratone

Most of the village stands on one of the soils typical of Pleistocene alluvial deposits.[55] It has an optimal gradient of 6.5-8% and good drainage. These characteristics prevent problems of both flooding and erosion. Its coarse sandy-loam texture, its depth and the absence of sand and gravel on the surface would certainly have made it easier to farm using rudimentary tools during the High Middle Ages. Additionally, the high proportion of organic material in the upper part of the soil profile increases its agricultural potential (Fig.22).

Only TU 10.1, a house slightly off-centre with respect to the village, is located in a slightly less advantageous position, despite the good drainage. Here the gradient is steeper – about 13.5% - and the soil is less fertile,[56] moderately deep, stony and gravely. These data suggest that the area immediately surrounding the house had a modest farming potential, although its proximity to the village area, where conditions were far better, means that this unit may have had access to more promising areas for its own *colturae*, in other words to the fields belonging to the village community. It is likely, given the pedological data, that the outfield began in the vicinity of TU 10.1 and that the construction of the house itself involved clearing an area which contains no traces of settlement features predating the early Middle Ages. This may mean that between the 8th and the 9th century the area exploited for agriculture or more probably

Fig.22_ The early medieval village (outlined features corresponding to surface scatters) and early medieval off-site ceramics (light colour circles) at Podere Serratone in their geopedological context.

[51] See Sheet 135 (Orbetello) of the *Carta Geologica d'Italia* 1:100000.
[52] TU 55.1 theoretically managed an area of 9 hectares, TU 106.1 about 9.9 hectares and TU 105.1 about 6.3 hectares.
[53] Leicht 1964, pp.61-62
[54] Montanari 1979, pp.197-199
[55] For the soil named F1b in the Podere Serratone area see Sevink *et alii* 1986, pp.58-59.
[56] For the soil named S3b see *ibidem*, p.100.

silviculture/pastoralism expanded modestly compared to the area farmed in Roman times and linked to the settlement some 300 m to the south-west. Confirmation of this theory comes from the two off sites identified south-east of the village on the western slopes of Poggio Rossino. These consist of a few but informative sporadic materials: fragments of handles and bases in a purified and selected fabric similar in terms of typology and fabric to the domestic pottery documented at the site. These traces, related to the exploitation of the village hinterland, are found in areas where the slope is more marked than in the village, between 12 and 15%. The stoniness, medium texture and steeper gradient of most of these soils must have represented a minor limitation to the use of these spaces for farming;[57] more probably they were exploited as an *incultum*.

8.3.4. The Farmstead at Alberese

The isolated farmstead near Alberese stood in an area with a gradient of 2-6% which prevented any problems due to swamping. This location falls perfectly into line with the trend characteristic of Roman and late antique population patterns in this area near the lower Ombrone river; settlements developed on land with a slope of over 2%, systematically avoiding the wide plain which fans out near Alberese, between the northern hills of the Monti dell'Uccellina to the west and Monte Querciola to the east. The plain has a gradient of less than 1% and is therefore subject to frequent floods. The site stands in an area of deep well-drained soil, with a silt-loam texture, generally suitable for farming (Fig.23).[58] Interestingly, the three off sites with pottery materials contemporary to those of the feature and probably related to the frequentation of the area north-west of the site for farming purposes are found on the same type of soil.

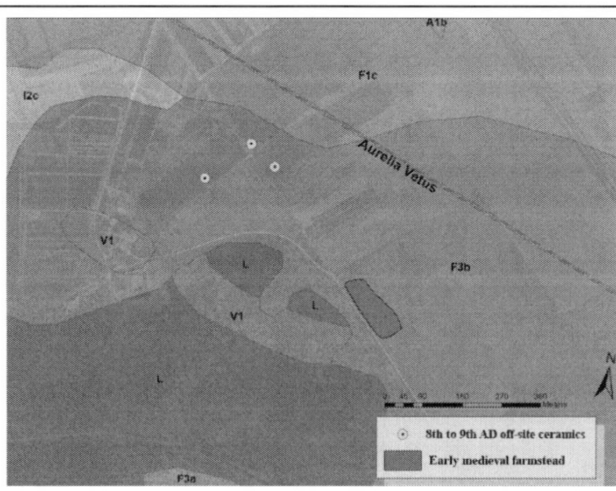

Fig.23_ The early medieval farmstead at Alberese in the geopedological context.

8.3.5. Final Remarks on the Relations Between Soil Types and Eighth/Ninth-Century Settlements in the Plains

The study described above allowed us to identify some interesting features shared by settlement choices in $8^{th}/9^{th}$-century contexts in low-lying coastal areas and on inland plateaux. Although the land was occupied in various different ways, with centralized villages, dispersed settlements and isolated farmsteads, there is a marked tendency to settle in the most promising areas of the territory. Compared to the Roman period, for example, when the population was more evenly distributed and the areas chosen were not always those with the greatest agricultural potential, between the 8th and 9th centuries settlement choices seem to obey an extremely rigid rationale, optimizing the relationship between available manpower and soil fertility. A good example is the 1st-5th-century settlement a short distance from the Podere Serratone context, which stands on a decidedly more stony and less fertile soil than that characterizing the central area of the nearby $8^{th}/9^{th}$-century village.[59] Probably the lesser potential for altering the landscape by exploiting its resources, due to both technological limitations and the smaller available workforce compared to the Roman period, triggered a tendency during the High Middle Ages to select the areas used for farming with enormous common sense and care.

Fig.24 _ The late 9th to 12th centuries AD sites on the plain between Roselle and Grosseto. The Roman to medieval road network is that proposed in Citter 2005 (ed.), p.73, Tav.13.

[57] For the soil named P4 see *ibidem*, p.89.
[58] For the soil named F3b see *ibidem*, p.65.

[59] P4 soil type, *ibidem*, p.89.

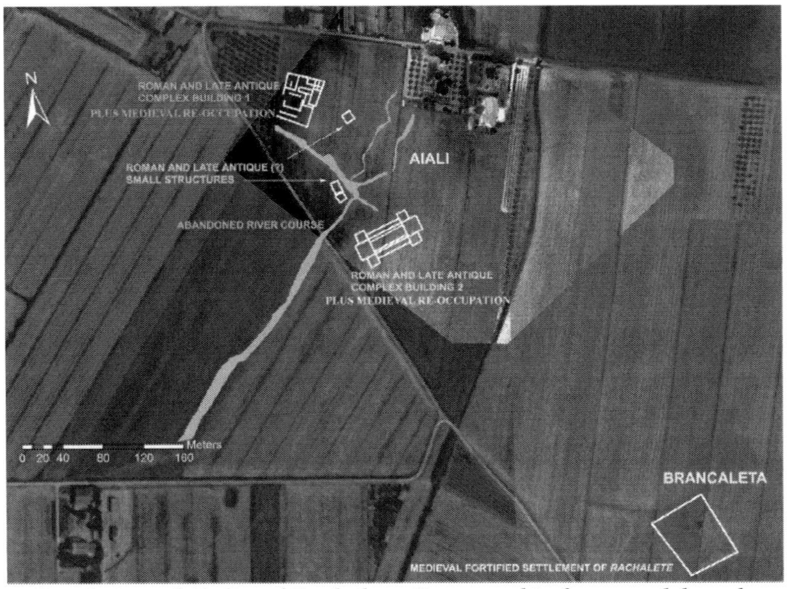

Fig.25_ The two medieval sites of Aiali and Rachalete. Topographic framework based upon field survey and geophysical data (after Vaccaro- Ghisleni-Campana 2009).

8.4. Centralized Population Centres in the Plains Between the Late Ninth and Twelfth Centuries and Their Relationship with Late Antique Settlements

At the end of the High Middle Ages, but perhaps even earlier, population centres gradually developed in the vicinity of the Roman road network running around Lake Prile and its inland tributaries. Most of these centres were fairly large and were established on top of contexts which had been abandoned or shrunk considerably after the mid-6th/early 7th century. The feature common to this series of new settlements between the lower Ombrone valley and the Bruna valley is their close relationship with the ancient road network.[60] Particularly interesting are the population dynamics in the small area north of the town of Grosseto, between Casoni del Terzo and Aiali, and, slightly further north, in the middle Bruna valley (Fig.24).

8.4.1. The Countryside Between Grosseto and Roselle: Reoccupation of Sites at the End of the High Middle Ages or Uninterrupted Life?

Toponymic data allow us to place the Papal *curtis* of *Flacianum, cum caio suo qui dicitur tertio* in the Casoni del Terzo area. The *curtis* is mentioned in the collection of censuses compiled by Cardinal Deusdedit in around the 1080s, but the section in question relates more specifically to property issues during the early years of the 8th century.[61] This document lists a series of properties arranged in an arc around Lake Prile, starting at Castiglione della Pescaia; immediately after *Flacianum* it mentions a *villa magna et fossa, que vocatur Flexu*. The archaeological evidence collected during recent and past surface surveys has made it possible to identify a dynamic settlement network in this area which appears to be based on large population centres dating to the period between the late 9th and the 12th centuries.[62] Unfortunately, the archaeological record for the flat strip between Aiali and Casoni del Terzo does not allow us to match the settlement features discovered in the field with those mentioned in the documents. More importantly, though, there is a close correspondence between the material and written sources, both of which indicate that this area was densely populated.

In the Casoni del Terzo area, at a site located 10 m above sea level already used during the Roman period, new analyses of the small amounts of pottery collected during surveys at the end of the last century made it possible to record a frequentation dating to between the late 9th and the 11th centuries. In this case, the failure to georeference the medieval pottery means that it is impossible to determine the spatial extent of this phase and therefore whether it belongs to a small permanent or seasonal settlement. Certainly we cannot identify the *curtis* of *Flacianum*, which must have been in the Casoni del Terzo area, with this feature; at the same time we cannot rule out that it was a settlement unit in some way related to the *curtis*.

There appear to have been two settlement contexts with sizeable populations in the area immediately north of Grosseto: that established on top of the large Roman and late antique villa of Aiali and probably also in its

[60] For the Roman road network in the study area see Citter 2007b.

[61] For the document see Von Glanvell 1905, Vol.III, ch.191; for its interpretation and precise chronological and political framework see Kurze 2002b, pp.397-414.

[62] A sample area between Grosseto and Roselle was investigated by Carlo Citter in the second half of 1980s. I am grateful to him for having allowed me to further process the surface ceramics with the aim of identifying new late Roman and early medieval phases, previously missed due to a poor understanding of 5th- to 9th-century AD coarsewares.

Fig.26_ Distribution of the medieval ceramics at Aiali after the gridded collection. (After Vaccaro-Ghisleni-Campana 2009).

vicinity, and a motte-and-bailey castle at Brancaleta, identifiable with the *castellare* of Rachalete first mentioned in a boundary document of 1262.[63] The two sites lie just under 700 m apart along the Roman *Aemilia Scauri* road.[64]

On the surface the Aiali context takes the form of a large scatter of pottery, bricks and construction materials covering an area of about 4 hectares with no apparent gaps. Here the systematic collection of finds, supported by a system of virtual grids,[65] allowed us to position the material collected accurately in space (Fig.25).[66]

The subsequent analysis of the pottery deposit allowed us to extrapolate from this extraordinary record, dating mainly to the imperial and late antique period, a minimum of at least 30 forms ascribable to specific typologies and certainly dating to the period between the late 9th and the 11th century (Fig.26). In light of the data currently in our possession, the pottery evidence records a gap of about three centuries following the abandonment of the villa between the late 6th and the early 7th century. A new settlement was then established above the Roman structures, perhaps reusing them at least in part. The most significant information comes from the distribution of the materials, superimposed both on the main building and the surrounding secondary structures. This may mean that the medieval phase of Aiali in some way mirrored the topographical layout of the Roman and late antique complex; however, on the basis of the ceramic evidence, the population density appears to be much lower than in earlier periods. This apparent coincidence may, here as elsewhere, be due to the opportunity for intercepting structures which were still potentially usable and above all construction materials which could be employed in new buildings. The close relationship with the road network also represented a significant attraction, especially given the potential for carrying out economic activities aimed not merely at self-sufficiency but at a small-scale local trade in products. At Aiali the surface archaeology yielded no traces of continued settlement between late Antiquity and the medieval period, as we were unable to identify diagnostic materials from the period between the 7th and the late 9th century. However, the presence of a fairly large settlement in the vicinity of the site may be indicated by a documentary source of the early 8th century which mentions a *villa magna* belonging to the Pope. If, as seems clear, the *curtis* of *Flacianum* was in the Casoni del Terzo area, the *villa magna* mentioned immediately afterwards was probably at Aiali, whose large Roman and late antique complex is one of the most important monuments in the Roselle area. Possible confirmation that the early medieval *villa* was indeed near Aiali may come from a comparison of the documentary and archaeological data. Aerial surveys of the site allowed us to identify clear traces of an ancient riverbed running alongside the Roman and late antique settlement structures and clearly visible in the AIMA flight of 1996. Where the villa stands, this ancient riverbed bends abruptly, almost at right angles; the two adjacent rectangular buildings are also near this point. The Papal source speaks of a *villa magna et fossa que vocatur Flexu*, in other words a settlement and a ditch named *Flexu*, probably for its winding course. This appears to be something more than a mere coincidence, potentially indicating that the early 8th-century settlement was in the vicinity of or at the site of Aiali. However, this theory must necessarily remain

[63] This site was first identified in autumn 2006 during field surveys carried out in the area between Roselle and Grosseto by the Laboratory of Landscape Archaeology and Remote Sensing (University of Siena); for preliminary information see also Campana 2006a, pp.131-132. On the written sources mentioning this site see Farinelli 2007, data sheet no.12920, and also Farinelli 2000, p.160, Tab.1.II.c.
[64] For a hypothetical reconstruction of the Roman road crossing this area see Citter 2005 (ed.), p.73, Pl.13.
[65] For the collection method see Vaccaro-Ghisleni-Campana 2009.
[66] Gridded collection covered two main areas with a total surface area of about 8000 m^2, equivalent to 20% of the surface scatter as a whole.

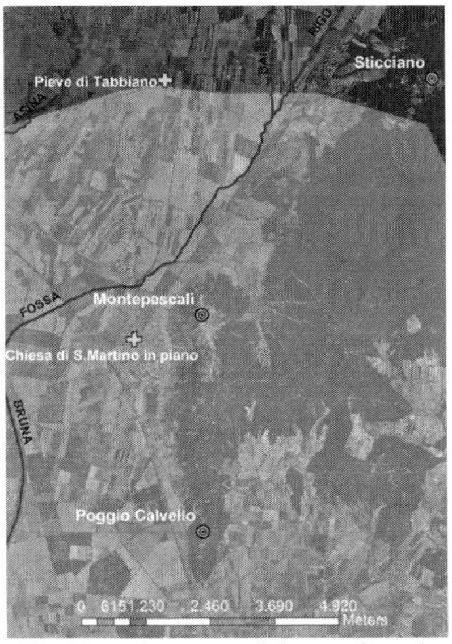

Fig.27_ Visualisation of the medieval rural churches with small associated sites (crosses) and nearby castles (circles) in the investigated area (transparent feature) along the mid Bruna valley.

tentative whilst awaiting extensive excavation of the context.

The settlement of *Rachalete* is located only about 390 m south-east of the Aiali complex, in an area named Brancaleta on the cadastral 1:5000 maps; the name clearly derives from that of the *castellare* attested in 1262 (*supra*). In the boundary document of that year it is clearly stated that the site, demoted to the status of *castellare*, indicating that it had been or was in the process of being precociously abandoned,[67] was to all effects and purposes the property of the Bishop of Grosseto. As Farinelli has observed, the context had probably already lost control over a castle district before 1179 since it is not mentioned in the deed of that year concerning the transfer of properties between the Bishop of Grosseto and Ildebrandino VII Aldobrandeschi. Attempting to define the territory of *Montecurliano*, the document mentions the lands belonging to the nearby castles of Istia and Roselle, but not those of *Rachalete*.[68] In any case, the preliminary chronology supplied by the pottery materials, which are still being studied, seems to suggest that this was a "failed site" inhabited between the late 9th/early 10th and the 11th/12th centuries.

The site, which presents an obvious microrelief identifiable as a motte, is also characterized by what is probably a defensive structure, rectangular in shape and clearly visible on satellite images and the vertical aerial photograph taken in 2001.[69] This trace surrounds a fairly large surface area of almost 2700 m^2, comparable in size to the summit of numerous castles in the area, including Poggio Cavolo (c. 4600 m^2), Calvello (3800 m^2), Castel Maus (c. 2400 m^2), Castellaccio del Prile (c. 3400 m^2) and Montepescali (4775 m^2), to mention but a few examples. The site thus appears to be a fortified village with a sizeable population established in an area which had a well-structured settlement pattern between the 9th and 11th centuries, with this settlement and that of Aiali as its main hubs.

8.4.2. San Martino In Piano: Surface Data and Rescue Excavations

Other contemporary features intercepted during recent surveys conducted in the low-lying areas of the middle Bruna valley can be ascribed to religious buildings associated with small population centres (Fig.27).

The Survey

The village of San Martino in Piano, at the foot of the medieval castle of Montepescali, saw an expansion of the area occupied for settlement between the 5th and the early 7th century, and then, after an apparent gap of almost two centuries, a new occupation from the 9th/early 10th century. The AD 1320 *Tavola delle Possessioni* of Montepescali notes the existence of a place named *San Martino de plano* located in precisely this area.[70] Since this is a multi-period context we proceeded to record the features, distinguishing them on the basis of their chronological horizon as determined by diagnostic pottery.

After systematically analysing the finds this procedure allowed us to obtain a preliminary reconstruction of the site's topographical layout in its various phases. During the period between the 9th/early 10th century and the 12th century, the features covered an area of about 3400 m^2, indicating a contraction compared to the late antique phase, which occupied over half a hectare (Fig.28). Taken together, a series of archaeological data appear to suggest the presence here of a religious building from at least the central centuries of the Middle Ages or more probably the High Middle Ages. Specifically, the survey intercepted associations of surface materials consisting of squared stone blocks, human bones and pottery dating to the 9th-12th centuries. Further confirmation of this hypothesis comes from a piece of 10th-century marble sculpture with rosette motifs, walled into the facade of the farmstead only 100 m away (Figs.29-30).[71] During this phase the church, which clearly had a funerary purpose, was associated with a modest settlement of no more than two or three houses.

[67] For the meaning of the term *castellare* in 12th- to 14th-century Tuscan written sources see Farinelli 2000, p.184.
[68] Farinelli 2007, data sheet no.12920.
[69] See also Campana 2006a, p.132, Figs 1-2.

[70] See *ASS, Estimo del Contado di Siena, Montepescali, n.5; Tavola preparatoria n.236.*
[71] The marble sculpture was analysed by Riccardo Belcari, who suggested this date on a comparative basis.

Fig.28_ Visualisation of the late 9th to 12th centuries AD surface scatters at San Martino in piano. The modern farmhouse to the north is the one with the reused marble sculpture walled into the facade.

Fig.29_ The modern farmhouse and reused sculpture into the wall.

Fig.30_ Detail of the 10th century AD marble sculpture with rosette motif, originally belonged to the church of San Martino in piano (?).

It should be noted that there is no correspondence between the chronology supplied by the documentary source and that provided by archaeological data, which indicates that the context was abandoned no later than the 12th century. We have no definitive evidence that settlement continued until the 14th century, when the site is attested in the written documentation. The only indications that the context may have been frequented in the 14th century are two sporadic fragments of *maiolica arcaica*.

For the time being, the lack of references to this church in more ancient sources and in the *Rationes Decimarum* leaves open the question as to whether and when this building acted as a parish church and meeting place for the inhabitants of the nearby hilltop villages, also located near the Roman road network running around Lake Prile and lacking church buildings until at least the 13th century.[72] Among these is the castle of Montepescali, whose church is attested only from the last quarter of the 13th century, and Poggio Calvello, 4 km further south.[73]

The Rescue Excavations

The 2008 rescue excavations already mentioned concentrated on four main areas, three of which yielded features ascribable to the Middle Ages (Fig.31). The data emerging from the excavation of Area 2000 (c. 44 m^2) are currently less detailed as concerns the medieval occupation of the site; the main features here belong to the 6th-5th centuries BC in the form of a rural building, and subsequently to between the 1st century BC and the 1st century AD, during which period a basin was in use, probably for making oil or wine.[74] However, the identification of some burials in earth graves, certainly post-dating the classical period and belonging to at least two distinct, though chronologically proximate, cemetery phases appears to be ascribable to the medieval occupation of San Martino in Piano, probably in connection with the presence of a parish church.

The data emerging from the excavation of Areas 4000 and 5000 are far more detailed. These on the one hand provide more information on the site's function between the 9th and 11th centuries and on the other a clearer picture of the chronological phasing of the medieval period; as such they deserve to be discussed in greater detail.[75]

AREA 4000

Area 4000 corresponds to a scatter of pottery materials from the central centuries of the Middle Ages identified during the archaeological survey conducted in various stages between 2004 and 2007.

Initially, an area of 5 x 3 m was excavated. Underneath the ploughsoil we identified context 4002, covering the entire area and characterized by a clayey matrix with abundant pottery dating to between the 10th and the 11th centuries. Specifically, we noted a predominance of forms in *acroma depurata* ware such as tankards and jugs. Underneath context 4002 was context 4003, a layer of river pebbles and sub-rounded stones of medium to large size, "bound" by clay and small pottery fragments. Only at some points did this layer

[72] In 1276-1277 the *Rationes Decimarum* for the Grosseto area, Montepescali included the parish churches of San Niccolò and Santo Stefano. See Guidi 1932 (edited by), p.144.

[73] The first church documented at Montepescali is that of Santo Stefano. It was mentioned in the AD 1188 privilege issued by Clement III (*infra*). This church is characterized by the presence of some early medieval architectural features reused in the building, see Citter 1996a.

[74] For the site see also Çygielman-Vaccaro-Agricoli-Ghisleni 2009.

[75] Data from the excavations of Area 4000 and 5000 are also published in Çygielman-Vaccaro-Agricoli-Ghisleni 2009.

present gaps which we interpreted as places from which stones had been removed. Only small portions of layers 4004-4005-4006 and 4008 are preserved; these are covered by context 4002 and cover context 4003. Contexts 4004, 4005 and 4008 are identical, virtually horizontal layers with a very compact clayey matrix and charcoal fragments on the surface; context 4006 consists of small stones with soil and tiny fragments of bricks and pottery as a binder. Context 4003 can be interpreted as a preparatory layer, a loose stone foundation for the construction of a floor made partly of beaten earth (contexts 4004-5-8) and partly of tiny stones and pottery fragments bound by clay (context 4006) to form an extremely compact and virtually horizontal layer (Fig.32). The theories that this may have been an open space or the internal floor of a structure were evaluated by enlarging the excavated area. The theory that area 4000 intercepted part of a *platea* and thus the arrangement of an open space belonging to a $10^{th}/11^{th}$-century and probably early medieval settlement may be confirmed by the aforementioned *Tavola delle Possessioni* of Montepescali of 1320 which mentions the toponym *San Martino de plano*. This document makes no reference to a church located in this area whilst the *Rationes Decimarum* list two churches at Montepescali, San Niccolò and Santo Stefano, but none dedicated to San Martino. However, thanks to deep ploughing in the area the replicated surface surveys brought to light large numbers of human bones, some of which were still anatomically connected; these were found in association with large squared stone blocks and pottery from the central centuries of the Middle Ages. Additionally, part of a cemetery intercepted in Area 2000 represents a valid confirmation of the surface survey data.

These data led us to postulate the presence of a religious building with a funerary function although it does not appear to be mentioned in the archive documents known at present. At the current state of research we can say that Area 4000 did not intercept the interior of the church and therefore its floor, but rather an area outside the church used by the religious building; on the basis of the survey data this was located north-east of Area 4000. Confirmation that Area 4000 was the result of arranging an open area comes from the abandonment layers, rich in pottery and therefore unlikely to belong to the interior of a religious building. The excavation of the loose stone foundation allowed us to recover numerous pottery fragments dated to the late 10th-11th centuries, the period at which the building appears to have been abandoned in light of the pottery fragments from context 4002; some residual materials from the 9th-10th centuries were also found. Underneath context 4003 we identified context 4009, interpreted as the preparatory layer for the loose stone foundation with a clayey matrix containing small stones and pottery fragments dating to the 9th-early 10th centuries alongside some residual materials. The properties of this layer and the fact that it lies immediately beneath the loose stone foundation (context 4003) suggest that this may have been a drainage layer, serving for the setting of 4003. Furthermore, the presence of pottery dating to the 9th-early 10th century makes it likely that this arrangement exploited an earlier situation and that context 4009 represented an arrangement of the pre-existing layer (context 4010). Context 4010, covering almost all of the test pit, has a clayey matrix with small stones and abundant pottery inclusions dated to the 9th-early 10th centuries on the basis of their forms. The layer also yielded some residual pottery, mainly of the 4th-6th centuries, and a coin which is probably late antique. This is the abandonment layer of an earlier

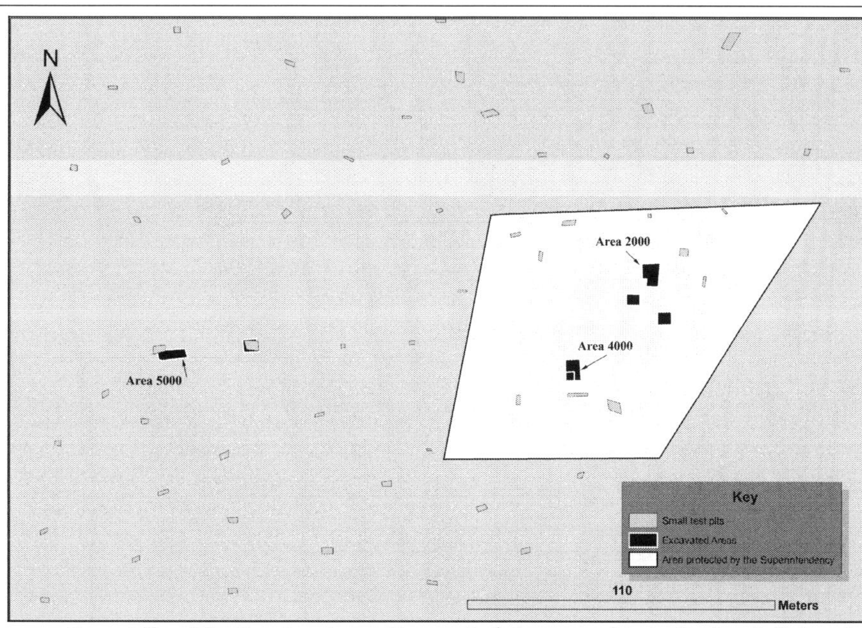

Fig.31_ Rescue excavation at San Martino in piano. Excavated Areas and test pits for defining the actual size of the site through the ages.

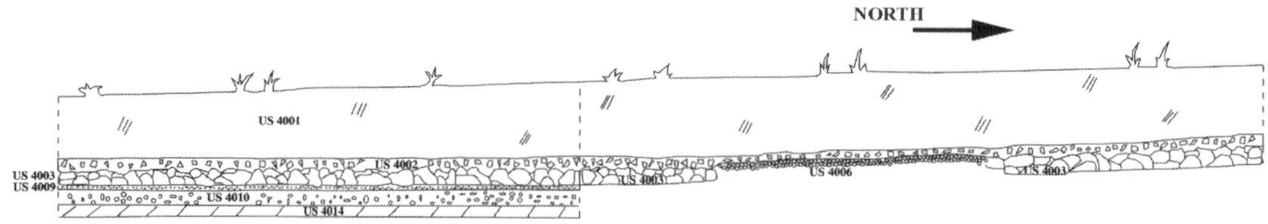

Fig.32_ Section of the medieval platea and early medieval levelling layers from Area 4000 (length 7,7 meters). (After Çygielman-Vaccaro-Agricoli-Ghisleni 2009).

arrangement of the area; two small patches of the beaten earth floor may have survived (contexts 4011 and 4016). These two layers and the others visible beneath the 9th/early 10th-century abandonment layers have yet to be excavated. Of these context 4013, a stone setting with mortar inclusions in a clayey matrix, appears very similar to context 4003, suggesting that it may be the loose stone foundation from an earlier phase. It is obvious that the *platea* was relaid at least twice in three centuries; of these arrangements we fully excavated the stratigraphic sequence of the most recent 10th /11th-century floor and identified the earlier 9th/early 10th-century phase. The stratigraphic sequence revealed that the construction technique remained unaltered over the centuries, with stones and pottery fragments being used to arrange and drain a clayey soil subject to flooding even in recent times.

AREA 5000

Area 5000 lies about 105 metres to the west of the main archaeological features belonging to the multi-period site of San Martino in Piano, whose surface area, thanks to a combination of data from excavations and mechanically dug test pits, can be estimated as 8500 m^2. Our research strategy moved along two distinct but parallel lines – stratigraphic excavation in areas chosen on the basis of the information provided by the archaeological survey and geophysical surveys, and small test pits aimed at understanding the true extent of the buried deposit. This allowed us to collect valuable information not only on the characteristics of the settlement and the settlement sequence over the long term, but also on its actual size and possible relations with the infrastructure found in the immediate vicinity, as in the case of Area 5000.

In this area the archaeological surface survey identified no noteworthy features, with the exception of small numbers of stones not associated with pottery materials. One of the test pits dug around the site, however, indicated the presence at precisely this point of a layer with a clayey-sandy matrix underneath the ploughsoil. This layer contained numerous charcoal fragments and a few worn ceramic fragments and covered the remains of a roadbed consisting of limestone blocks and some fragments of sandstone and gravel well cemented together. We therefore decided to excavate an area of about 11 x 3.5 metres stratigraphically (Fig.33).

The archaeological deposit is much deeper here than in the main part of the site, up to a metre. The excavation allowed us to determine the exact extent of the layer with a brownish-grey clayey-sandy matrix (context 5002), deposited throughout the excavated area and sealing the roadbed. This layer, 15-20 cm deep, yielded a few pottery and brick fragments which do not allow us to date it accurately. A very small amount of pottery was found: a mere 36 fragments, all poorly preserved. These clearly belong to two main chronological horizons. First, the period between the 9th and the 11th century AD; it is impossible to make a more accurate distinction given the absence of types of identifiable typology, though the pottery finds are comparable in terms of fabrics and handle shapes to the abundant finds from Area 4000. Second, late Antiquity, represented by a minimum of two African red slip ware forms: the rim of a production C Hayes 50B flat-based dish and the rim of a production D Hayes 67 dish; to these we should add wall fragments from Lusitanian and Tunisian amphorae.

This very limited evidence may suggest that the road was abandoned between the late and middle part of the High Middle Ages. However, the probably alluvial nature of the clayey-sandy layer sealing it, resulting from the chance deposition of materials from nearby stratigraphies, means that we do not have a completely reliable *terminus ante quem* for the construction of the roadbed.

Fig.33_ Area 5000 and the ancient road.

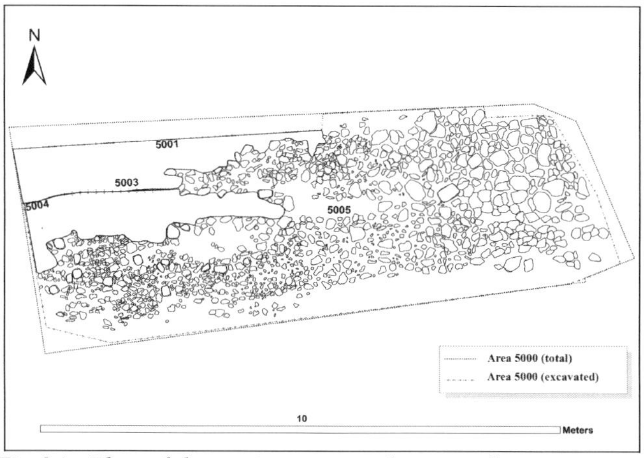

Fig.34_ Plan of the ancient strata glareata after excavation.

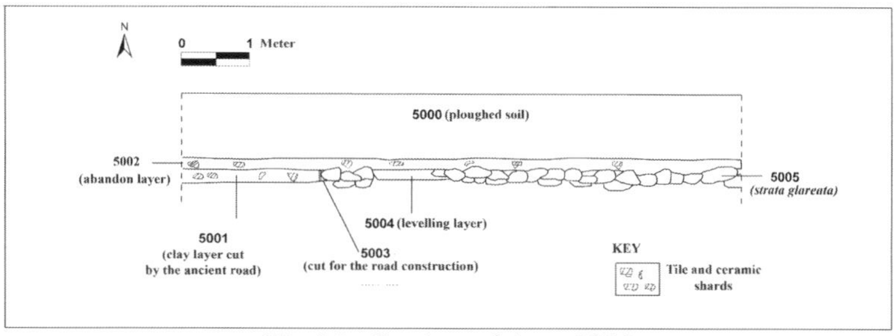

Fig.35_ Section of Area 5000.
(After Çygielman-Vaccaro-Agricoli-Ghisleni 2009).

Context 5002 lay immediately above the road, which ran east-west and was just over 3 m wide in the excavated area; however, its actual width may have been greater since it continues into the north sections. The road was made of river stones of varying size, generally rounded in the form of cobblestones, some fragments of red granite and a few Roman roof tiles, pieces of which are sometimes used to fill the gaps between the larger stones. These materials appear to have been put in place with some care to make the surface as flat as possible; however, the road is still fairly uneven. In the central portion of the roadbed we observed a strip with a lower density of materials forming a dip between 15 and 20 cm deep beneath the sides of the road; this was probably intended to drain water from its surface. In the western portion of the excavation area we found clear evidence of an extremely even cut (context 5003), at least 2 m long, into context 5001, the layer with a yellowish-brown clayey-sandy matrix on which the road was laid. The cleaning of this layer, which was uncovered but not excavated, yielded only a tiny number of pottery fragments in very poor condition which provided no information of help in establishing a *terminus post quem* for the construction of the road surface. The roadbed rested on an arrangement obtained with a fill of clayey brown soil (context 5004), also uncovered but not excavated. In the excavated area, we observed that the road was virtually horizontal, with slight changes in level clearly due to the few gaps in the road. The generally good state of conservation of the stretch brought to light is due essentially to the considerable depth of the foundations, which in turn ensured the good conservation of the abandonment layer context 5002 sealing the road surface throughout the area excavated. The few gaps must be due to heavy use of the road during antiquity (Figs.34-35).

The archaeological evidence tells us that the road uncovered just to the west of San Martino in Piano was certainly a "*via glareata*". This construction technique was highly suited to an area like this, where the nearby rivers, and especially the Bruna, provided an abundance of river stones. No evidence of help in pinpointing the chronology of the road emerged from the stratigraphy and it is likewise impossible to formulate hypotheses on the basis of the technology: "*vie glareate*", given their relative simplicity of construction, were common throughout the Roman period; their reuse or maintenance are also documented in late Antiquity and the High Middle Ages.[76] The construction technique of the road intercepted in Area 5000 presents some interesting analogies with another road in the eastern suburbs of Lucca, and more specifically the archaeological area of San Ponziano. Here a Roman *via glareata* remained in use until late Antiquity and the High Middle Ages, after which the installation of a burial ground led to a gradual reduction in its width. The *via glareata* lost its function after the construction of the church of San Bartolomeo which came to occupy the road surface during the Lombard period; a passable road must then have been

[76] For comparisons from the eastern *Cispadana* area (part of the Po valley) see Ortalli 1999, pp.155-160.

moved just to the south of the Roman road.[77] Our *via glareata* seems to have been a sort of east-west link road, probably leading from the major road network (in the shape of the *Aurelia Vetus* and the *Aemilia Scauri*) crossing the plain north of Lake Prile. According to a recent analytical reconstruction of the Roman road network, much of which remained in use up to the early Middle Ages, both these roads ran around the lake on the inland side, probably joining to form a single road before crossing an ancient riverbed of the Bruna and then continuing to Badia Vecchia-*Salebrone/Saleborna*.[78] Given its orientation, the road recently intercepted at San Martino in Piano would appear to be one of the secondary routes essential for the local circulation of people and goods; it branched off the main Roman road, perhaps at Badia Vecchia, running east to reach the Montepescali area and possibly continuing north-east towards La Pescaia, where both Roman and early medieval settlements are documented together with Lombard burials. A road first documented in 1298 with the name *via dei Muriccenghi*, but probably of pre-Roman origin, ran around the La Pescaia area, home to both an early medieval settlement and burials ascribable to the second half of the 7th century, and thence to inland areas of the *Ager Rusellanus*.[79]

8.4.3. Podere Selvaccia-Tabbiano

A context similar to that of San Martino in Piano, but for which far less archaeological data is available, lies 5 km to the north near Selvaccia, south-west of Monte Lattaia (Fig.36). This area was once home to the *silvam Tabbianensem*, attested in a document of 1272[80] which says that it was crossed by a public road, probably a *diverticulum* of the main Roman road running towards the interior. The privilege of 12 April 1188 issued by Pope Clement III to Gualfredo, Bishop of Grosseto, mentions eighteen parish churches belonging to the diocese located between the Alma and Ombrone valleys.[81] The list is generally in topographical order and mentions the *plebem de Tabiano cum capella sua* between that of Sticciano and that of Fornoli. The parish church, first attested on 23 July 1071, must therefore have been in the area between Fornoli and Sticciano, where the *silvam* mentioned in 1272 and which takes its name from the religious building was also located (*supra*). As we can see on the IGM 1:25000 maps, there are still numerous places with names like Selvaccia and Selvello in the area where the Asina flows into the Bruna river and it therefore seems likely that the *silvam Tabbianensem* was in this very area. A careful examination of a field at Podere Selvaccia led to the identification of a large surface feature covering about half a hectare along the road leading from the SS1 to the foot of Montemassi.[82] Unfortunately visibility was not optimal due to the growing crops and did not allow us to undertake an in depth infra-site survey as was done in other cases. The diagnostic materials collected appear to suggest that the context was frequented for a long time between the imperial period and the 6th/early 7th century.[83] Preliminary analyses of the small amount of pottery collected indicate the presence of some forms belonging to the chronological horizon between the 10th and the 12th century AD (Fig.37). Also extremely important is the presence at the nearby farm of "Le Selvacce" of numerous perfectly squared cornerstones reused in a building which is now in ruins. These data allow us to suggest that the country church of San Giovanni Battista di Tabbiano was located in precisely this area, perhaps where the surface feature described above is found, reoccupying an area with a sizeable Roman and late antique village abandoned between the late 6th and the early 7th century AD.

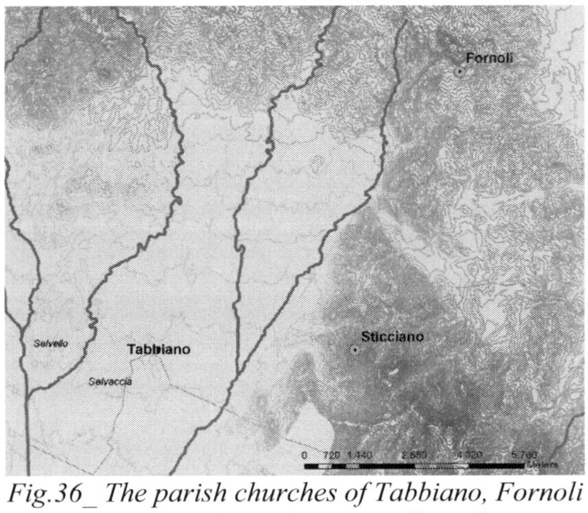

Fig.36_ The parish churches of Tabbiano, Fornoli and Sticciano in the mid Bruna valley. They were all mentioned in the AD 1188 privilege.

The religious building, which may have attracted a small settlement to form around it as at San Martino in Piano, stood near a road network crossing the plain north of Lake Prile from east to west, ensuring communications between the coast and inland areas. The 1071 document which first mentions the country church of Tabbiano also refers to a road of *lupo inpiso* which, on the basis of Prisco's reconstruction, ran along a route of probable Etrusco-Roman origin between the inland Siena area and the Maremman coast.[84] The country church is no longer attested in the *Rationes Decimarum* of 1276-1277,[85] nor in those of 1302-1303,[86] indicating that the site had been abandoned or at least lost its baptismal function, perhaps taken over by other religious buildings in the

[77] Ciampoltrini 2006 (ed.), pp. 13-34.
[78] Citter 2007b.
[79] See Vaccaro 2005, pp.21-26.
[80] For the location of the *silvam* and the document see Prisco 1994, p.279, particularly footnote no.703.
[81] Pflugk-Harttung, III, no.414, pp.359-361.
[82] Garzella 2001, p.10, footnote 17.
[83] The late antique occupation of the site is documented by the presence of coarseware made in imitation of ARS prototypes Hayes 91 and 104, and by one specimen of Hayes 99B in ARS.
[84] For the document see Prisco 1994, pp.276-277.
[85] Guidi 1932 (ed.), pp.143-144.
[86] Giusti-Guidi 1942 (ed.), pp.185-189.

area. This seems to be in line with the chronology of the medieval materials from the surface feature at Podere Selvaccia, which yielded no pottery indicators of the 13th and 14th centuries.

Fig.37_ Detail of the surface scatter corresponding to the long-lasting site of Tabbiano.

8.4.4. Conclusions: The (Re)Occupation of Lowland Sites Between the Carolingian and Ottonian Periods

To sum up, the features examined above seem indicative of an important aspect of settlement patterns between the Carolingian period and the central centuries of the Middle Ages. Obviously it is important to distinguish between the contexts of San Martino in Piano, Aiali and Brancaleta, which must have had fairly large populations, and that of Tabbiano where the church is associated with a small site. However, the constant relations between the medieval phase, the late antique settlement and the road network emerging from some contexts should not be underestimated in the population structure of the High Middle Ages and the central centuries of this era.

In future, our research agenda will clearly need to include the systematic excavation of some of these contexts with a view to understanding first of all if the absence of features from the later part of the High Middle Ages is due to an actual gap in the occupation of sites or simply to a greater difficulty in extrapolating 8th-century pottery indicators when these represent a minority with respect to the larger quantities of pottery from the 5th-early 7th centuries and from the period between the 9th and the 10th centuries.

In light of our current good knowledge of early medieval coarsewares from the Grosseto area, it seems more likely that there was in fact a gap between the late antique phase and the later part of the High Middle Ages. However, we cannot rule out that surveys alone failed to intercept evidence from a period during which the settlement, assuming it was still in use, covered a smaller surface area or had a smaller population. The case of San Martino in Piano, where the excavation of Area 4000 brought to light a stratigraphic sequence running from the late 10th/11th century to at least the 9th century and perhaps even earlier, calls for a degree of caution in stating that there was a discontinuity of occupation in the light of field survey data alone.

Were a gap in settlement to be confirmed, we would need to reflect on the deeper reasons for the reoccupation, for very different purposes, of central places such as Aiali and San Martino in Piano, which played a fundamental role in the hierarchy of late antique-early medieval population centres and which had been abandoned over two centuries earlier. We could imagine a series of interrelated causes, including their location along an important local road and the presence of some at least partially visible structures which could be used as quarries for building materials; at this time stoneworking technologies were coming back into large-scale use, at least for religious buildings and sometimes wall circuits.[87]

At San Martino in Piano and Tabbiano the proximity of local roads and hilltop villages where churches are not attested until a later date might suggest a process of selection perhaps taking place as early as the Carolingian period and resulting from an intent to construct religious buildings to meet the spiritual needs of the populations of nearby villages.

The reasons for the selection of other sites immediately north of Grosseto like Aiali and Casoni del Terzo are more complex. Here we are probably dealing with the attempt to reorganize land ownership promoted by the papal authorities at a time, between the 8th and 9th centuries, when documentary sources indicate the existence of large peripheral landholdings in the Maremma area forming part of the *patrimonium sancti Petri*; these were probably acquired during late Antiquity through the practice of imperial donations.

8.5. The Birth of Central Places on Hilltops: the Contribution of Archaeological Surface Surveys

The extensive stratigraphic excavations conducted at a representative sample of 10 fortified sites (*supra*) have revealed the existence of villages established on hilltops during the long period between the 8th and the 9th centuries, with some appearing as early as the 7th century.[88] The settlements founded *ex novo* during the High Middle Ages are generally large, occupied by several tens of inhabitants. These came to be a focal

---

87 Strong evidence for the re-introduction of stone buildings between the 9th and early 10th century AD in the study area is supplied by the wall circuit and first church at Poggio Cavolo, which can be dated to an earlier phase than the mid-10th AD; also important is the early medieval church of San Pietro in Grosseto, which was built in the late 8th-early 9th and then enlarged in the late 9th-early 10th century AD; for San Pietro in Grosseto see Citter 2005 (ed.). It is also worth bearing in mind the early medieval hilltop village of Scarlino, located a few km to the north in the Pecora valley; here, between the 8th and 9th centuries AD, a wall circuit in mixed materials (stone and perishable materials) was built alongside a single-apsed church in local stone (on this site see Valenti 2004, p.59).

88 In particular the hilltop villages of Montarrenti, Poggibonsi and Scarlino, discussed in Valenti 2004, pp.47-56.

point for the rural population network and underwent a continuous transition from the 8th-9th century settlement, to the fortified settlement of the 10th-11th centuries to the 13th-14th century village; the villages underwent significant urban development and some have survived until the present in their late medieval form. In Tuscany the contribution of long lasting hilltop villages to shaping the settlement patterns of the High Middle Ages must be taken into consideration when attempting to define the population structure of an area between the 8th and the 10th centuries. Important in this context are some recent statistical data on Tuscany, starting from the total number of excavated castles with High Medieval phases. About 62% of the castles excavated stratigraphically yielded traces of medieval settlements "underneath" the castle structures.[89] If we extend this percentage to the total number of fortified sites in Tuscany, 1554, as many as 960 of these may be long lasting sites stably occupied from the High Middle Ages. In my opinion this working hypothesis, though based on solid excavation evidence, requires further confirmation; projecting a datum which is currently limited to only part of Tuscany (especially the central and southern segment) onto other areas may lead to the unthinking attribution of what may in fact be a micro-regional model to much larger areas. We might thus underestimate the diversity of different areas and their possible variants, such as those which emerged clearly for the period between the 8th and 10th centuries from the sample discussed here.

Stratigraphic archaeology is in the process of developing a rural settlement model for central and southern Tuscany with long lasting hilltop villages as its central places,[90] and it is thus worth reflecting on the capacity of surface surveys to find the features needed to identify this phenomenon within the study area as well. The limited capacity of archaeological surveys to identify indicators of genuine help in finding early medieval settlement structures is well known.[91]

This may be due in part to the nature of 7th-9th-century settlements. On the basis of the data from the excavation of castles, hilltops were chosen as the preferred places for the establishment of permanent settlements. In these areas, problems of visibility due to the presence of later stone structures which obliterated earlier deposits and tree cover usually represent insurmountable obstacles to surveying. In the study area, systematic surface surveys and test pits have in fact documented numerous settlement features other than hilltop sites which are of undoubted importance for the reconstruction of settlement patterns in the 8th-9th centuries.

As concerns the study of hilltop landscapes, the survey ran into objective difficulties in identifying phases preceding the construction of the castles. Despite this, the application of a multi-stage approach to 6 hilltop sites,[92] fortified between the 10th and 11th centuries and abandoned precociously by the late Middle Ages, allowed us to document probable frequentations from

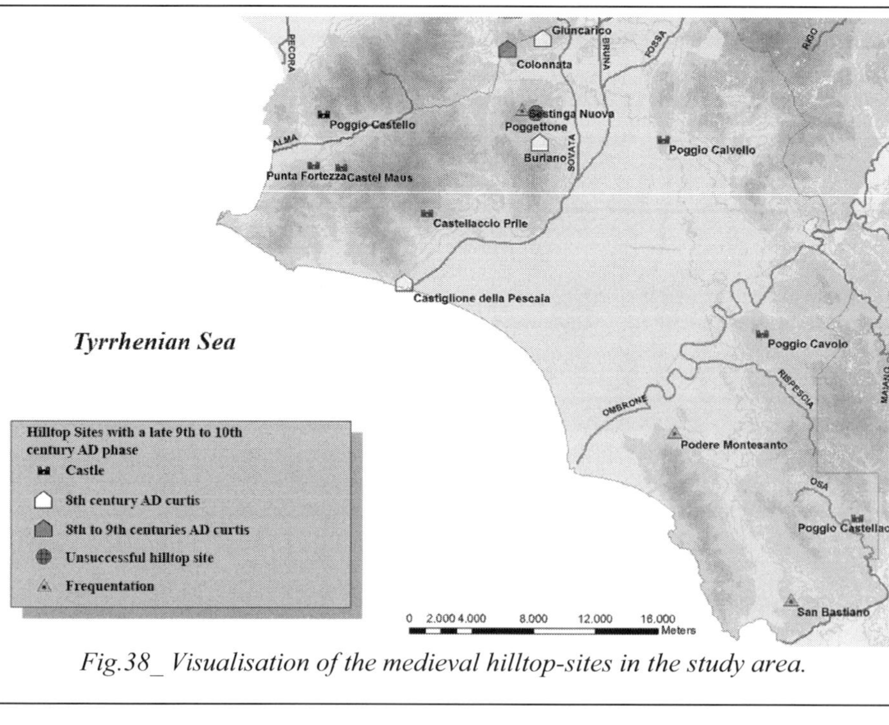

Fig.38_ Visualisation of the medieval hilltop-sites in the study area.

[89] For this calculation see Valenti 2004, p.127.

[90] For the so-called Tuscan model see Francovich-Valenti 2005.

[91] See Valenti 2004, pp.11-15.

[92] The infra-site survey of six medieval hilltop sites (Castel Maus, Punta Fortezza, Poggio Castello, Castellaccio del Prile, Calvello and Poggio Castellaccio-Scopertorio) was integrated with data from aerial photography and the analysis of written sources, as well as from the clearing of opportunistic sections.

the late 9th/early 10th century onwards; this is at least one phase, probably the final one, in the long process leading to the establishment of fully structured villages on hilltops (Fig.38).

The study of three castles in the Alma valley provided important information for a preliminary evaluation of pre-existing early medieval settlements. In the north-western sector of the village of Castel Maus we identified an occasional section; cleaning this section allowed us to document a layer with materials dating to between the late 9th/early 10th and the 11th century. Although this provided no information on the actual size of the settlement during this period it did nonetheless indicate that the context was occupied at least from the late part of the High Middle Ages.

More interesting are the data acquired on the two hilltop villages of Poggio Castello and Punta Fortezza, both crossed by firebreaks which, especially in the former case, damaged part of the deposit but also brought to light sections and materials belonging to the earliest phases of frequentation. At both contexts, kitchenware and table/storage wares were documented, dating from the late 9th century onwards. The precocious abandonment of the two sites, no later than the 12th century, and the consequent lack of monumental stone structures (with the exception of the wall circuits and a probable tower at Punta Fortezza) helped us to study the entire surface area, allowing us to find some early medieval pottery indicators in other zones as well. The data in our possession suggest that the area occupied during the later part of the High Middle Ages and that in use between the 11th and 12th centuries was identical, just over 5000 m^2 at Punta Fortezza and 6000 m^2 at Poggio Castello.

At Castellaccio del Prile, a monumental fortified village abandoned between the 13th and 14th centuries, the presence of yet another firebreak, in this case crossing part of the settlement from north to south, brought to light sections with significantly disturbed stratigraphies and pottery materials, including kitchen and *semidepurata* wares dating to between the late 9th and the 10th century. Here, as at Castel Maus, the information supplied by the survey simply provides clues as to the period during which the hilltop was stably occupied.

Further south, in the middle Bruna valley, replicated collections at the village of Poggio Calvello, 9 km north of Grosseto, brought to light kitchenware and table/storage wares dating to between the late 9th and the 10th century in various parts of the area enclosed by the wall circuit, measuring about 9000 m^2. This suggests that the area occupied at the end of the High Middle Ages was the same as that of the 11th-12th century castle.[93]

Obviously, the information acquired at these contexts consists of ephemeral traces, often found entirely by chance. This makes it extremely difficult to formulate hypotheses as to the actual size of the early medieval village; nor can this type of evidence be considered sufficient for an evaluation of how and when the hilltop village was established.

This is nonetheless precious information which highlights a fundamental aspect of the rural population structure during the High Middle Ages. The settlement dynamics of the hilltop village of Poggettone, on the slopes of the hill on which Vetulonia lies, are clearer. In this case the reading of aerial photographs led to the discovery of a settlement occupying a plateau measuring just over 1300 m^2 and enclosed by an elliptical wall-circuit, a stretch of which is barely preserved on the east side. The wall circuit is fairly roughly made using simply broken local sandstone blocks arranged in subhorizontal courses and connected with an earthy mortar.

The site is easy to read on the surface and yielded pottery indicators covering the period between the 9th and the 11th centuries, allowing us to ascribe it to that category of small "failed" sites which, after a fairly limited period of use, were neither fortified nor evolved into open villages.

The abandonment of the Poggettone site was probably due to the shift of the population towards the town of Vetulonia which regained vigour in the mid-12th century thanks to the initiative of the Abbey of San Bartolomeo di Sestinga.[94] The fortification of Vetulonia probably also led to the abandonment of another population centre, this time inside the city's Etrusco-Roman wall circuit; that of *Castelvecchio*,[95] for which we lack clear archaeological indicators of stable frequentation during the central part of the High Middle Ages (Fig.39). This series of abandonments clearly forms part of that process of marked settlement

[93] The site was mentioned as a *castellare* (in the process of abandonment or already abandoned) as early as AD 1262, while it was first attested in a document of AD 1121 mentioning an individual by the name of *Gerardinus de Calvello*. See Farinelli 2000, p.158, Tab.1.II.c.

[94] The castle of *Colonna* (Vetulonia) is first mentioned in AD 1233, although its foundation by the monks from the monastery of Sestinga can be dated to the 2nd half of the 12th century AD. After AD 1181, the monks moved the seat of the abbey from its original location (still known as Badia Vecchia) to one of the hilltops in the hilly area of Vetulonia, within the wall circuit protecting the Etrusco-Roman town. For the document mentioning Colonna see Ceccarelli Lemut 1985, p.40; for the foundation of the castle of Colonna in the 12th century AD see Cardarelli 1932, pp.234-235, and also Farinelli 2007, data sheet no.14162.

[95] Cardarelli 1932, pp.152-155 and pp.160-161 identifies this site with the *castellum di Vitulonnio* mentioned in the AD 1181 exchange of land between Ranieri, abbot of Sestinga, and Giovanni, abbot of San Pancrazio al Fango.

Fig.39_ Archaeological context of the hilltop-site at Poggettone in the hilly area of Vetulonia. The background orthophotograph was draped on the DTM.

concentration typical of the second *incastellamento* in the 12th-13th century.[96] Contemporary with the Poggettone site is a feature identified near Sestinga Nuova, 60 m from the abbey. This is a concentration of medieval pottery materials and stones covering about 1000 m^2, intercepted within a large scatter of brick fragments belonging mainly to the period between the 3rd century BC and the 2nd century AD. The medieval phase, probably a settlement, covers a fairly long time span with the highest concentration of recognizable pottery fragments dating to the late Middle Ages. However, some minimum individuals indicate that the area was in use from the late 9th/10th century, well before the seat of the abbey was moved from Badia Vecchia. Despite the scarcity of data currently available on the early medieval phase of Vetulonia, this new information tells us that, although there was an indisputable contraction in the area inhabited compared to the Etrusco-Roman city, some areas continued to have a fairly substantial population. These were probably on the three hills of Castelvecchio, Vetulonia and Convento inside the wall circuit which, according to the written documents of the 12th century, hosted sizeable settlements. To these we should add the Poggettone context which reveals a tendency towards the stable occupation of hilltops in the hinterland of the ancient city in the form of centralized settlements.

At Poggio Castellaccio, in the upper Osa valley, the formation process of the hilltop village emerged clearly from surface surveys (Fig.40). Between the late 6th and the early 7th century the village on the slopes of Poggio Vicarina, 70 m above sea level, was abandoned, whilst the farmsteads on the Casa Steccaia plateau were deserted at the end of the 9th century. Later, between the late 9th and 11th centuries, a far more complex and well-structured population centre was established on Poggio Castellaccio (160 m above sea level), 1 km from Poggio Vicarina and 2 km from Casa Steccaia. On the hilltop we identified a ring-shaped stone wall circuit enclosing an area of about 7800 m^2. On the small hill beneath this (130 m above sea level) at least four contemporary features were found which can be identified as houses. These stand on the flat surface of terraces, perhaps created specifically to allow the slopes of the hill to be used for settlement. A further two features, west of Poggio Castellaccio, lie at 110 and 90 m above sea level respectively and yielded pottery materials belonging to the same chronological horizon. In this case, the formation of the village did not just involve occupying the hilltop plateau, where a stone wall circuit was constructed, but also entailed a fairly complex and varied distribution of the houses, which were also built on the southern and western slopes (Fig.41). On the basis of the data collected, it seems probable that the population residing in the modest settlements of the area began to concentrate on the hilltop already by the middle part of the High Middle Ages. A topographically well-structured village is documented on Poggio Castellaccio from the late High Middle Ages and certainly had a sizeable population. However, during the 9th century the hilltop

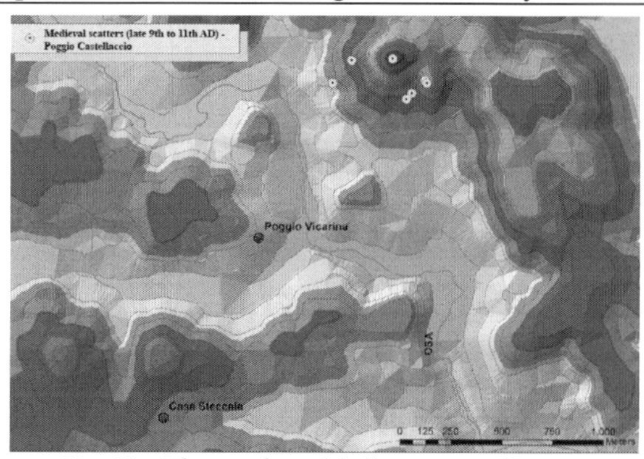

Fig.40_ The medieval hilltop site of Poggio Castellaccio and early medieval surface sites along the upper Osa valley.

[96] In general on the so-called *secondo incastellamento* see Farinelli-Giorgi 2000, pp.239-284.

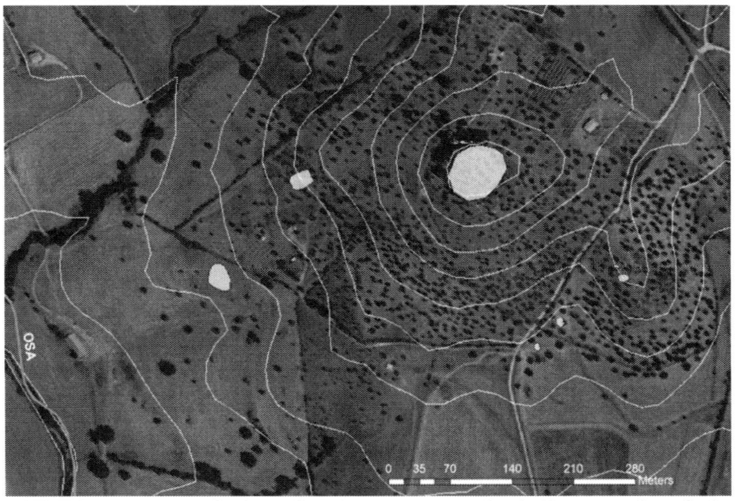

Fig.41_ The medieval surface scatter (light colour) composing the hill-top and mid-slope village of Poggio Castellaccio.

village seems to have coexisted with the nucleated site exploiting the favourable economic and settlement conditions offered by the Casa Steccaia plateau. The pedological properties of the area in which this dispersed settlement developed are among the most promising for agriculture in the whole upper Osa valley (*supra*).

It is worth reflecting on the late attestation of the fortified village in the written sources: Farinelli identifies it with the *castellare de Scopertorio* mentioned in the *Tavola delle Possessioni* of Montiano of 1320,[97] and it is possible that the context is the anonymous farmstead on the Osa mentioned in the mid-11th century.[98]

As well as the development of new early medieval sites on low-lying strips of land, a series of documentary data help to confirm the model which from the 8th century sees the birth of settlements in the form of hilltop villages. Examples are the papal *curtes* of *Piscaria* (Castiglione della Pescaia), *Burrianum* (Buriano),[99] and the Lucchese Colonnata, attested as a *curtis* in 831,[100] but already mentioned in a leasehold contract of 762.[101] Both Buriano and Castiglione della Pescaia were fortified from at least the 11th/12th century,[102] and are still inhabited today, demonstrating that these were successful and long-lived settlements within the population dynamics of the lower Bruna valley. At Castiglione della Pescaia, furthermore, the occupation of the hilltop where the *curtis* and later the fortifications were found is demonstrated by the discovery of a burial ground with at least 10 graves on the side of the hilltop facing the sea. Given the typology of the grave goods it can be ascribed to the mid-7th century.

Contemporarily with the establishment of a stable settlement on the hilltop, material traces of inhabitation at the Paduline-Serrata Martini complex near the Prile estuary are interrupted. The lowland settlement may have been frequented after this to carry out production activities linked to the salt-water lagoon, such as the extraction of salt and fishing.

The identification of the *curtis* of Colonnata near Giuncarico, where the toponym l'Incoronata still exists today, is facilitated by a document of 790 concerning the sale by a certain Tasso di Lunata to Giovanni, Bishop of Lucca, of a piece of land described as *gahagio Subperitulo* located *in loco Columnata*.[103] The document states that the land is bounded on one side by a public road and on the other by the Bruna river, an area which may in part be that at the foot of the hill of Giuncarico.[104] Cardarelli, citing an 18th-century description by Pecci, suggested that the *curtis* of Colonnata was located on the site of l'Incoronata.[105] A careful survey of the hill overlooking the area of this name on the IGM 1:25000 map led to the identification of a large scatter covering about 1700 m^2 and consisting of small and medium-sized pieces of broken local stone from the collapse of one or more structures. These were associated with some pottery fragments of the late 9th-10th century. The archaeological surface feature allows us to state that the site was frequented during the High Middle Ages but only stratigraphic excavations will be able to clarify if this was in fact the

97 Farinelli 2007, data sheet no.9501.
98 Fentress-Wickham 2002b, pp.67-68.
99 The list of papal estates required to pay rent was drawn up in the 1080s by cardinal Deusdedit, see Von Glanvell 1905, Vol.III, Ch.191; for the presence of early 8th century AD papal estates in southern Tuscany, including the aforementioned *curtes*, see Kurze 2002, pp.397-414.
100 M.D.L. - TV/2, DXIV, p.308.
101 For the AD 762 document see *C.L.A.*, Lucca, IV, n.974, pp.86-87.
102 A *castellum* at Buriano was first mentioned in AD 1049 and at *Castellione de Piscaria* in AD 1163. See Farinelli 2007, data sheets no.14158 and no.14233 respectively.

103 M.D.L.-TIV/1, CVIII.
104 Prisco 1994, p.401.
105 Cardarelli, quoting Pecci's description, writes: *sulla cima di mezzo, che è la più alta e la più appariscente dopo la quota 112...evidenti ruderi di un minuscolo castello, o forse semplicemente di una grossa torre medievale.* See Cardarelli 1932, pp.164-166.

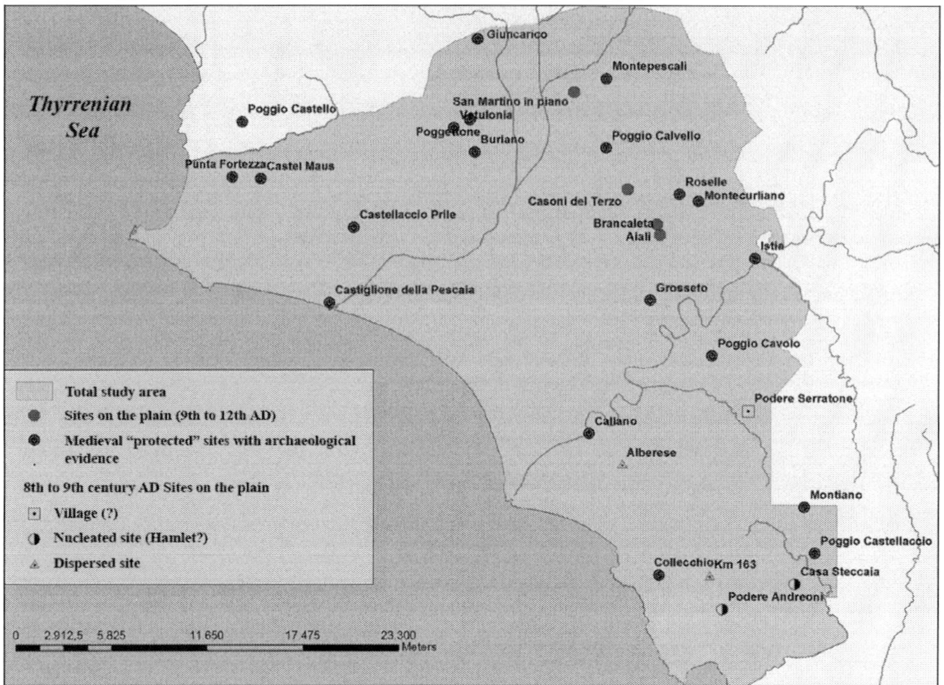

Synoptic Table I_ The main archaeological sites (8th to 11th AD centuries) in the study-area.

curtis of Colonnata. The name of this area may provide a further piece of circumstantial evidence: the hill on which the settlement was found is still called San Martino today, perhaps suggesting a connection with the cathedral church of Lucca.

In at least two cases the surface survey of hilltops not occupied by castles revealed the presence of traces of modest settlements also dated to the late part of the High Middle Ages. These are small settlements established on low hills, between 30 and 50 m above sea level, which nonetheless offer a protected position within their geomorphological context. Near Podere Montesanto, at Alberese, about 200 m west of the 8th/9th-century farmstead (*supra*), a feature was identified covering an area of about 260 m^2 and identifiable as a single building. This may in some way have inherited the functions of the single farmstead, moving to the vicinity of wooded areas in order to exploit them more effectively.

Further south, on the southern slopes of Poggio di San Bastiano, we identified a second surface feature covering an area of almost 100 m^2; given the low density of pottery per m^2 this does not appear to represent a settlement of more than one or at most two buildings. We cannot rule out that this site was a religious building since a document of 1097 concerning the donation of properties located west of the nearby Poggio Civitella notes that these pieces of land stretched *ad sancto Sebastiano*.[106]

These two apparently isolated features are also located along the road network running between the Monti dell'Uccellina to the west and the hills between Poggio Civitella and Monte Querciola to the east, in accordance with a settlement model which, as we have seen, became characteristic of this area already in the 8th and 9th centuries.

8.6. The Grosseto Model: Full Development of the Village From the Carolingian Period

The data emerging from excavations in the city of Grosseto[107] indicate with a degree of clarity the point at which the village began to stabilize and take on a definite form.[108] The earliest traces of a settlement which was no longer seasonal, as it had been from about 400 and probably up to the late 6th century, seem to appear from the early 7th century, after the Lombards took definitive control of this area in the early 590s, under the reign of Agilulf. On the basis of the published data, however, the settlement appears to have remained scattered and fluid at least until the late 8th century, as indicated mainly by the scarce attestation of stratigraphies belonging to this phase.

An exception is the hut of uncertain function dating to between the late 7th and the 8th century identified during the excavation of San Pietro. Far more data is available on the long period between the late 9th and the 11th centuries, the time at which the village began to grow significantly. A crucial turning point in the social, topographical and economic structure of the village appears to have occurred between the late 8th

[106] For the document see Farinelli 2007, data sheet no.19063.

[107] The 1997-2005 excavations in the town of Grosseto were organized by the Chair of Medieval Archaeology of the University of Siena and directed by Riccardo Francovich and Carlo Citter.

[108] See Citter 2007c, but also Citter 2005 (ed.) and Francovich *et alii* 2000.

and the early 9th century. During this phase at least two churches are present at the site, one known from archaeological evidence and the other from documentary sources; this is indicative of a large population and the existence of a well-defined social structure. Beneath the 12th-century church of San Pietro an older religious building has been excavated, with a single nave and semi-circular apse, measuring 12 x 5 m and dating to the second half of the 8th-early 9th centuries; the building was later extended backwards by a further 2.10 m during the 9th century.[109]

Another church is mentioned in 803, in this case dedicated to San Giorgio and located in *loco Grossito*,[110] part of the private property of Iacopo, Bishop of Lucca. The appearance of complex architecture in the village can be explained by an initiative undertaken not by the local community, but by political powers, perhaps the Papacy in the case of the more ancient church of San Pietro as suggested by Citter,[111] and the Diocese of Lucca in that of San Giorgio. This intervention can be explained by their interest in controlling Grosseto, which was undoubtedly experiencing a phase of growth and able to ensure the large-scale and organized exploitation of local salt deposits. Between the 10th and 11th centuries the site expanded constantly and as a result took on a proto-urban form, to the extent that it was given the title *civitas* to the detriment of the nearby Roselle.[112]

8.7. Concluding Remarks on Settlement Patterns in the Eighth and Ninth Centuries

The encouraging results of our study, which succeeded in identifying various early medieval settlements in the plains, thought on the grounds of region-wide studies to contain few or no settlements from this period,[113] suggest that we should reconsider the importance of other forms of settlement, more or less complementary to hilltop sites. In this area, too, these "new" settlement types, extremely important for a complete reconstruction of the complex settlement network of the High Middle Ages, coexist with the establishment of centralized sites on hilltops. This process was already in progress from at least the 9th/early 10th century, as demonstrated by the limited data from the survey of some precociously abandoned castles and in part by the excavation of Poggio Cavolo.The poor visibility of the period between the 8th and 9th centuries, with the exception of some failed contexts, makes it essential to extensively excavate successful sites, fortified from the 10th and 11th centuries: this is a fundamental tool for the study of early medieval population dynamics as concerns its social, topographical and economic aspects.A significant, but not definitive, confirmation of the tendency to establish early medieval settlements on hilltops comes, in this area as well, from the excavations conducted between 2005 and 2007 at the site of Poggio Cavolo. Here the construction of the wall circuit enclosing the hilltop plateau and the single-naved church with a polygonal apse date to a time prior to the mid-10th century, perhaps between the late 9th and early 10th century (if not earlier).[114] The existence of definitive proof of the occupation of hilltops between the late 9th and early 10th century, immediately preceding fortification, whilst often minimal given the limitations of surface surveys, confirms a trend in settlement which for Tuscany has been reconstructed on the basis of a significant archaeological record. However, it should be stressed that in this area the population patterns of the 8th-early 10th centuries are extremely complex, diverse and rich in variants, to a much greater extent than hitherto thought. Certainly the long-term success of hilltop villages suggests that even before the fortification process these played a primary role as the genuine hubs of the early medieval settlement network. The tendency towards nucleation is a feature shared by hilltop villages and some of the 8th/9th-century settlements discovered in the plains; this is true both of markedly centralized sites such as Podere Serratone and those with a less centralized distribution of individual houses, as at the Casa Steccaia and Casa Andreoni contexts. Anthropological research has shown that the distance between the individual farmsteads forming a settlement may be up to 150 or even 300 m without any loss of socio-economic cohesion.[115] The real difference lies in the intensity and means with which an area's various resources were exploited. We have seen clearly that the 8th/9th-century contexts in coastal lowland areas or on inland plateaux reveal a constant tendency to occupy potentially better areas, considering factors such as the availability of water resources, the presence of farmable agricultural lands and wooded areas, and the relationship with the road network. Compared to hilltop villages, the topographical layout of these settlements tends to be shaped as a direct function of the availability of resources within the context. Hilltop villages, by contrast, must have exploited the resources of the surrounding countryside according a system which we can visualize as a series of concentric circles, each of which corresponds to one or more production activities depending on its potential.[116] In these cases there was probably a tendency towards diversified farming, a good compromise between the availability of fertile

---

[109] Citter 2005 (ed.).

[110] MDL TV/2, no.CCCXIII.

[111] Citter 2005 (ed.), pp.81-82.

[112] The papal bull of 9 April 1138, with which Pope Innocent III authorized Roland, Bishop of Roselle, to move the bishop's seat from the ancient town (Roselle) to the medieval *civitas* of Grosseto is published in Ughelli 1717-1722, X, coll.268-269

[113] The minimal (or nonexistent) presence of early medieval settlements in the plains was first suggested in Francovich-Hodges 2003 and later restated in Valenti 2004.

[114] See Farinelli-Vaccaro-Salvadori 2008.

[115] See Roberts 1996, p.24 and p.35.

[116] For the schematic diagram of a typical rural site see *ibidem*, p.30, Fig.2.5.

soils, optimization of the workforce and achievement of production levels capable of ensuring self-sufficiency. At the scale of the study area, the hilltop village of Poggio Cavolo could more easily exploit the hill slopes by planting vegetables and intensive crops such as vines and olives, reserving part of the *saltus* for hunting, pasture for animals and the collection of wild fruits and berries. At the same time, the nearby village of Podere Serratone was located in an environmental and pedological context probably more suited to extensive crops such as cereals. It is likely that the range of economic options available to hilltop settlements was one of the reasons for their success. We should ask ourselves why a context such as Podere Serratone, which between the 8th and 9th century probably had a population density not dissimilar to that of early medieval hilltop villages, was destined for precocious abandonment by the end of the 9th century. Certainly the *incastellamento* played an important part in determining a marked selection of settlements in favour of those which ensured better management of an area's resources. Again, however, this does not mean that after the late 9th/early 10th century centralized sites on hilltops represent the only settlement option available. This is clearly demonstrated by contexts dated to after this period, but which may also be more ancient, such as the 9th-century phases of San Martino in Piano, in the vicinity of the road network running eastwards around Lake Prile. In the cases of Brancaleta and Aiali the size and population density of these settlements must have been in line with those of hilltop sites. At Brancaleta we saw that the site's topographical features are reminiscent, for the presence of defensive structures, of the hilltop village model, where the construction of wall circuits predated the fortification process. One new element which emerges forcefully from the study area is the presence of more or less sizeable settlements, in the form of villages as at Aiali or religious buildings associated with a small settlement, as at San Martino in Piano and Tabbiano, built on top of late antique villas and *vici* connected to the road network.

The feature common to the various settlement types in use between the 8th and the early 10th centuries is the tendency towards nucleation; however, this also leaves room for other, less centralized, forms of occupation and exploitation of the land, as at the sites of Casa Andreoni and Casa Steccaia.

The most successful pattern is the aggregated site, with the individual settlements representing optimal production units where the close relationship between socio-economic identity and productive space provides the necessary means for achieving subsistence. In physical terms, this relationship is not always expressed in the centralized village set at the centre of its own catchment area; sometimes, as at Casa Steccaia and Casa Andreoni, we find a settlement model consisting of distinct units. In these cases, too, the potential for exploiting shared spaces and resources may have provided the necessary opportunities for social interaction and the creation of a group identity. In any case, the distances between individual residential units are never so great as to impede either visual and/or vocal communication, and therefore the potential for mutual assistance in the event of need.

One last consideration concerns the contribution of very scattered settlements; whilst these had little impact on the settlement network, some such settlements did nonetheless exist during the long period between the 8th and the 10th/11th centuries. Belonging to this category are the single farmstead near Alberese of the 8th-9th century, the house identified at the 163rd km of the SS1 Aurelia, that of the late 9th-11th century near Casoni del Terzo and, finally, that at Podere Montesanto, also dating to the late 9th/early 10th and 11th centuries.

It should be stressed that these apparently isolated units are systematically located in the vicinity of centralized settlements. The 8th/9th-century farmstead and the small house at Podere Montesanto, both near Alberese and only 200 m apart, are near large population centres attested in written documents. The Alberese area, specifically, must have hosted the *curtis Astiano* documented in 973 (*supra*) whilst about 3 km to the north-east, near the Tenuta La Trappola estate, lies the site of Caliano, already documented as a *locus* in 803 and as a castle with a tower in the 973 document.

The site of Casoni del Terzo in turn lies in the area of the papal *curtis* of *Flacianum* and about 2 km north-west of the complexes of Aiali and Brancaleta, along the Roman road also in use during the Middle Ages.

The isolated house at the 163rd km of the SS1 is just over 1 km from the settlement of Casa Andreoni, to which it was linked directly by the *Aurelia Vetus*.

The constant relationship between the few scattered sites and contemporary aggregated settlements, facilitated in all the cases analysed by the presence of roads, allows us to contextualize this settlement pattern within a hierarchy of the population pattern which sees the former in close and probably subordinate relation to the latter.

The isolated settlement was probably a sort of productive offshoot of the nucleated site within a network of socio-economic relations that allowed it to survive even when the harvests of the individual unit failed. In the context of this relationship it is fairly likely that the families living at isolated sites were periodically replaced. The leasehold contracts of the 8th-9th centuries clearly demonstrate that the direct succession from father to son in the management as tenants of a *manso* was an exception to the rule; generally peasant settlements are discontinuous, with the arrival of a new tenant farmer with their *familia* and/or *consortes* after the death of the previous tenant.[117]

[117] This concluding remark is based on the analysis of the aforementioned written sources.

9. Production and Exchange Structures Between the Eighth and Ninth Centuries in Light of the Pottery Evidence

9.1. Preliminary Remarks

We have already dealt in depth with the severance of links between the study area and Mediterranean commercial exchange circuits between the late 6th and early 7th century following a process of marked decline in the flows of Tunisian foodstuffs and fineware already fairly evident from the late 5th century. Within this general context, though, there are also cases in which relations with the Mediterranean world clearly persist; we ascribed this to political and military circumstances at Roselle and Portiglioni, and to privileged relations with areas under Byzantine control at Castiglione della Pescaia. Of particular importance are the data provided by the study of late antique and early medieval amphorae from *Portus Scabris*. These confirmed that North African, eastern Mediterranean and southern Italian foodstuffs continued to arrive throughout the 7th century and the early decades of the 8th century, albeit in far smaller quantities. However, at least in light of the data currently in our possession, these products were not redistributed to inland contexts. Surface surveys and excavations have provided a series of important data on the High Middle Ages, although these are probably not exhaustive given the complexity of an area as large as that studied here. The data acquired allow us to propose not only a preliminary reconstruction of settlement dynamics but also a fairly accurate analysis of production and trade structures based on the pottery indicators. As Chris Wickham has shown,[1] pottery indicators are in many ways the only analytical tool which enables us to compare archaeological contexts of differing socio-economic status and geographical location. Non-perishable and intended for mass consumption, pottery allows us to study production structures in depth simply by analysing these artefacts, and to determine its distribution with a good degree of accuracy by using a classic supply and demand model.[2] However, if we wish to exploit its undeniable potential for reconstructing exchange and production structures pottery data must be evaluated with extreme caution. By its very nature pottery is a product manufactured for mass consumption and as such it is aimed at all levels of the social hierarchy. In a generally simplified context like that of ceramic production in the High Middle Ages this often leads to a fairly marked standardization of pottery consumption; it is therefore difficult to distinguish clearly between contexts which might nonetheless have differed considerably in economic status. Between the late 5th and the early 7th century the distribution of foodstuffs contained in amphorae and of Mediterranean fineware continued to be organized on a fairly large scale. These products may therefore represent useful markers for testing the socio-economic vigour of the settlement contexts in a given area (on a more analytical and detailed level) or for suggesting analogies and differences between different regions (in a more general perspective). The capacity of local markets to access these products must be considered on a case by case basis, in the context of the geographical location (coastal/inland) of the site or area and its distance from road networks or river routes: the presence of imported products does not necessarily mean a high level of socio-economic well-being.[3] In my view, a particularly fruitful approach, applied experimentally in this study, is to compare contemporary settlement contexts within a given area in order to identify genuine differences in status and reduce to a minimum the danger of seeing other factors, such as geographical location, as having the greatest influence on the formation process of pottery contexts. For the High Middle Ages this type of research is particularly problematic: the collapse of regular interregional trade flows led to the disappearance throughout the Italian peninsula (with the exception of some areas where trade was unusually vigorous[4] and some centres of consumption),[5] of those markers which allow us to distinguish between settlement contexts that depended exclusively on sub-regional or more frequently local markets and those that remained open to imported goods.

Broadly speaking, the production and distribution of early medieval pottery in Tuscany appears to have seen a marked regionalization of manufacturing and exchange structures and a significant decrease in the range of classes and forms produced; this makes it extremely difficult to use pottery data as a marker for the economic vigour of a site or an area. However, despite its simplification, the pottery record does present some interesting features of help in studying production and exchange structures. One peculiarity which is beginning to emerge clearly is the constant presence at 8th- to 10th-century sites on the Maremman coast and areas immediately inland[6] of small amphorae with a flat or convex base; these appear not only to have been used to store the foodstuffs required by individual settlements but may also indicate a circulation of goods on at least a sub-regional scale.[7] However, our ability to trace trade circuits on anything more than a purely local scale is significantly hindered by the lack of a standard criterion for describing pottery fabrics. When dealing with similar

[1] Wickham 2005, pp.700-706.

[2] Generally on the system of exchange see Manca 1993, pp.23-24. For a recent analysis of the patterns of ceramic production, trade and consumption in early medieval Italy see Gelichi 2007.

[3] See also Molinari 2003.

[4] I refer mainly to some market towns, such as Comacchio (Gelichi *et alii* 2006a, Gelichi *et alii* 2006b, Gelichi 2008), Venezia (Gelichi 2008, Toniolo 2007), Otranto (Leo Imperiale 2004; Arthur 1992), and those in the Bay of Naples (De Rossi 2004).

[5] During the 8th century AD, Rome continued to be supplied with considerable quantities of foodstuffs contained in amphorae from southern Italy and Sicily, see Romei 2004, pp.278-284.

[6] For a very recent sub-regional overview see Vaccaro 2009, with bibliography.

[7] On this hypothesis see also Vaccaro 2005d, p.474.

morphologies, only the analysis of the fabric can determine whether the object was made at a local workshop or imported. The second, equally thorny, problem concerns the identification of the foodstuff or foodstuffs contained within these amphorae (depending on whether there is a direct relationship between the pottery form and a specific foodstuff or whether the amphorae were used to hold several foodstuffs depending on the production specializations of individual sites).[8] Although this issue has never been the object of specific research, we can nonetheless attempt a preliminary analysis of distribution for the contexts in our study area dating to between the 8th and the 9th century thanks to the fairly substantial numbers of small early medieval amphorae found. Possible confirmation that the small amphorae in use during this period had a "commercial" function may come from the frequency with which the word *amphora* is used as a synonym for the measurement unit equivalent to about 26 litres and used to stipulate wine supplies in early medieval leasehold contacts. Although it seems certain, on the basis of the materials in our possession, that the amphorae attested in 8th/9th-century settlement contexts had a much smaller capacity, not even half of the measurement unit for liquids, this practice still seems significant at a period long after that which saw the great success of these commercial transport containers. A fairly similar process seems to occur in the eastern Mediterranean during the Byzantine period, when the transport amphora was known as a *μεγαρικόν* or *μαγαρικόν* by metonymy: this was the name of a type of amphora produced at Megara. Still more significant is the fact that the word *magariki* or *megariko* was used not only for the commercial container but also for a measurement unit typical of the Byzantine world.[9] At a regional scale it seems probable that, if the early medieval small amphora was indeed used to trade foodstuffs, it must have been intended for liquid or semi-liquid substances rather than solid foods such as grain, traditionally transported in sacks.

9.2. The Eighth-Ninth Centuries

9.2.1. The Contexts Analysed

For the period between the 8th and 9th centuries our study of pottery production and consumption covered five main contexts, identified during surface surveys. Of these, the two settlements of Podere Serratone, on the Rispescia river, and Casa Andreoni, near the Gulf of Talamone, yielded pottery assemblages of considerable interest and great help in reconstructing early medieval pottery production in the study area. A further two sites, one at Alberese on the lower Ombrone river and another at Casa Steccaia in the upper Osa valley, yielded smaller quantities of pottery which nonetheless allowed us to test the local distribution of forms and types and acquire further data on the proportions of different pottery classes present. Finally, we considered the pottery from the settlement of San Martino in Piano, in the middle Bruna valley, which was the object of repeated infra-site surveys between 2004 and 2007 and of a rescue excavation in 2008. Stratigraphic excavation brought to light layers dated to between the 9th and 11th centuries and an interesting sample of materials from the 9th/early 10th centuries AD (Fig.1).

In three out of five cases our study concerned surface features whilst at the sites of Podere Andreoni and San Martino in Piano we were able to compare analyses of the material yielded by replicated collections with the later excavation data.

The significant potential of the surface pottery assemblages from Podere Serratone, Casa Andreoni, Casa Steccaia and Alberese was immediately apparent thanks to the narrow chronological range of these contexts. A systematic study of all the finds collected on various occasions and the comparison of the principal types found allowed us to date these to a period which sees the maximum peak in attestations between the 8th and the 9th century.

In all the cases investigated, with the exception of one Topographical Unit at the Casa Steccaia settlement which yielded a minimum of 2 forms from the central centuries of the Middle Ages, we noted the absence of pottery indicators belonging to horizons after the 9th century. The Podere Serratone and Casa Andreoni contexts, on the other hand, yielded a few minimum individuals dating to between the 6th and 7th centuries. An extremely important fact, possibly suggesting that the two contexts were first frequented in the late 6th century, is the total absence of African red slip ware which, as we have seen, becomes extremely rare in the territory after mid-century. At the village of Podere Serratone a minimum of 1 amphora was found, characterized by a whitish skin and a fabric which is certainly Tunisian; its typology remains uncertain given the absence of diagnostic fragments.

San Martino in Piano is different, since it was inhabited, albeit intermittently, between the Etruscan-Archaic period and the 11th/12th century AD.[10]

9.2.2. Research Methodologies Applied to the Eighth- and Ninth-Century Surface Pottery Contexts

The systematic study of pottery finds from surface collections must necessarily take into consideration some general characteristics of these contexts; the more

[8] On the importance of residue analysis applied to medieval ceramics see Pecci 2010.

[9] Bakirtzis 1989, p.73.

[10] On this site see also Çygielman-Vaccaro-Agricoli-Ghisleni 2010.

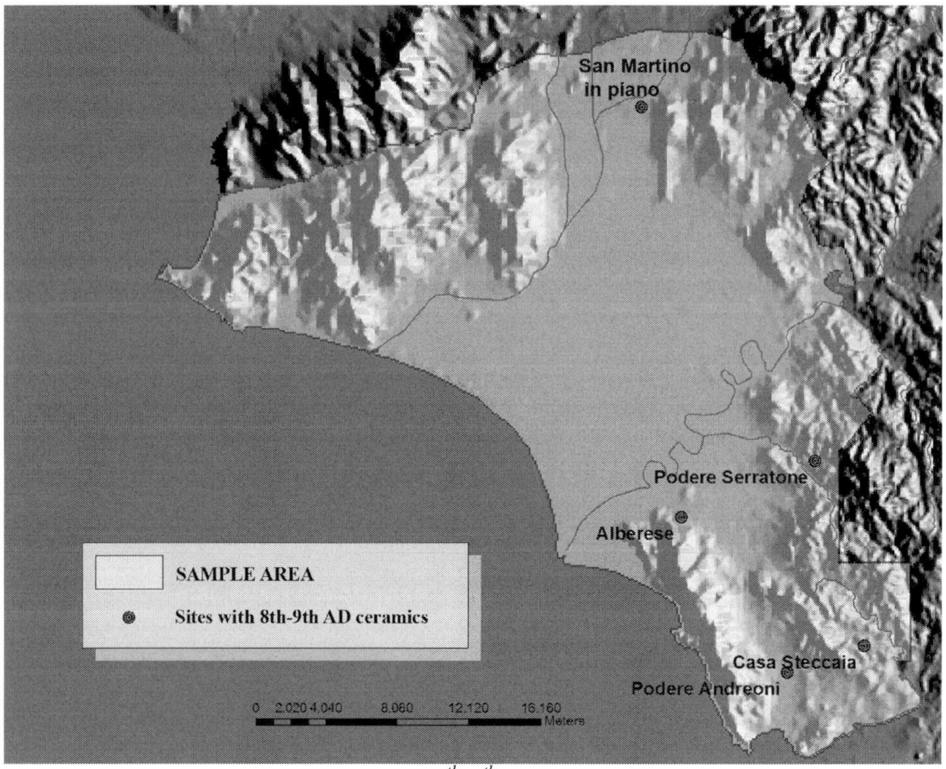

Fig.1_ Distribution of the main 8th-9th centuries AD sites on the plains.

analytical and detailed the study aims to be, the greater their importance:[11]

- in the absence of stratigraphic reference points, when materials belonging to different chronological horizons are found together surface pottery can be subdivided into phases only on the basis of typological criteria;
- pottery samples exposed to ploughing are the outcome of continuous processes of transformation and alteration linked to climatic and mechanical factors whose impact on the state of conservation of different classes[12] and different portions of an individual vessel may differ;[13]
- it is usually impossible to postulate a direct correspondence between the traces of the settlement visible on the surface and the true extent of the buried deposit; this premise also reflects on the pottery sample brought to the surface by ploughing. There are no *a priori* criteria which allow us to determine the degree of reliability of the quantitative relationships between the classes and types attested at a site through surveys and the pottery materials originally belonging to the context. As such, the results of the analysis of pottery finds, however carefully conducted, must be treated with appropriate caution;
- in some cases a combination of replicated surface surveys and the systematic collection of materials present in the field allows us to obtain a fairly representative sample of the pottery actually consumed at a given context.[14]

The most commonly used quantification methods,[15] such as counting and weighing the total fragments, subdivided into classes and forms, or the more analytical evaluation of the minimum number of identifiable individuals, present some objective limitations when applied to surface contexts.

Counting fragments and weighing depend heavily on the properties of individual classes. For example, fineware dishes, which are usually fine walled, generally produce a larger number of fragments than thicker-walled amphorae; additionally, the dish will weigh far less than the amphora. The application to surface contexts of a combination of both these

[11] On these aspects see especially Millett 2000.

[12] Colour-coated wares, such as *ingobbiata di rosso* or *colature rosse* wares, tend to lose their slip very quickly, especially when poor slips are associated with porous fabrics fired at low temperatures which did not lead to a process of sinterization.

[13] Diagnostic fragments (rims, bases and handles) in general and rims in particular are more difficult to find in a good state of preservation than walls. This is due not only to the larger surface area of the body of vessels, but also to the generally more complex shape of rims which are consequently more liable to fragment into pieces which are no longer recognizable.

[14] This is true especially of those sites which were settled for a short period.

[15] On the various methods for quantifying surface ceramics see Millett 1991; Millett 2000; Mattingly 2000; Fentress 2000; Patterson 2000, Campana-Francovich-Vaccaro 2005 and Cirelli 2006. In general on ceramic quantification in archaeology see Orton *et alii* 1993. I am particularly grateful to Martin Millett for his suggestions towards developing this method of analysis.

classification methods, whose significant limitations in the study of excavated materials have been noted,[16] is even less fruitful since disturbance by farm vehicles leads to further fragmentation of the material compared to the time at which it came to form part of the archaeological deposit.

The concept of minimum forms, on the other hand, is difficult to apply to non-stratified deposits containing highly fragmentary materials; this is because it is difficult to ascribe non-diagnostic fragments to a single individual even after a careful examination of fabrics and manufacturing techniques.

At the two contexts of Podere Serratone and Casa Andreoni, the large quantities of pottery present on the surface led us to adopt a complex research strategy from the outset, allowing us to exploit to the full the informative potential of the material culture documented. As such, during the survey we opted for a systematic collection of all the pottery fragments on the surface, analysing their distribution within individual features. Since these contexts are not subdivided into various phases, but, as was apparent even from a rapid preliminary examination, belong to a chronological horizon between the late 6th/7th century and the 9th century, we decided to proceed with an analytical study. We therefore applied both the criteria generally used for surface materials such as the weight and number of fragments for each class and form, and the determination of the minimum number of individuals for each individual form and, where possible, for individual types based on the observation of diagnostic finds (rims, bases and handles). The likely presence of a pottery kiln at the Podere Serratone site, signalled both by the identification on the surface of overfired ceramics associated with overfired clay pieces (part of the kiln?) in one specific part of the feature and by a residual heat anomaly in the same area identified by magnetometry, allowed us to suggest that most if not all of the early medieval coarseware found was produced by this local workshop (see *infra*). This facilitated the overall study of the materials, allowing us to proceed with a detailed analysis of the proportions of different classes, forms and fabrics found. Our probable identification of a production structure also allowed us to identify local distribution circuits for the materials from Podere Serratone after a systematic microscope analysis of the fabrics of forms from other 8th- and 9th-century contexts.

The high degree of morphological standardization of the pottery present at these contexts was fundamental for the accurate determination of the minimum number of forms found at each individual site. At the two contexts yielding a large number of finds (Podere Andreoni and Podere Serratone), we first calculated the total minimum number of forms and then concentrated our analysis on pottery which could be ascribed to a specific typology.

Having selected the sample of typifiable individuals, we proceeded to search for the most reliable points of comparison, attempting to establish links with pottery contexts from early medieval sites in Tuscany[17] and Lazio,[18] with a preference for those dated on a stratigraphic basis.

Unfortunately, no direct points of comparison were found in the Grosseto area, although we were able to acquire some indirect information from the lack of attestations of the pottery typical of Podere Serratone and Casa Andreoni in the 6th/early 7th-century layers on the north slopes at Roselle and in the urban deposits of Grosseto dating to the period between the late 9th/early 10th and 12th centuries.[19]

In order to determine the true chronological duration of the two sites and the period of maximum settlement growth on the basis of the number of pottery specimens attested, we decided to use the method of individual weighted means. This method is generally applied to fineware for which an extremely accurate chronology is available or to other classes, like transport containers, for which detailed studies of their periods of attestation are available.[20]

In our case, however, the pottery repertoires turned out to consist exclusively of coarsewares;[21] it is far more difficult to narrow down the chronological range of attestation for individual types belonging to this class beyond a century and a half, even in excavated contexts. We attempted to resolve this problem satisfactorily by selecting all the individuals belonging to identifiable typologies and for which several morphological points of comparison were available.

[16] See Molinari 2003.

[17] I refer in particular to the excavated sites of Montarrenti (SI), (Cantini 2003), Santa Maria della Scala in Siena (Cantini 2005a) and San Pietro in Grosseto (Valdambrini 2005), but also to surface sites which have yielded interesting late antique and early medieval ceramic assemblages such as those in the Roccastrada area (GR) (Guideri 2000a, pp.11-37) and the early medieval surface site at Podere Aione (Follonica-GR), (Cucini 1989, pp.499-512).

[18] There are some notable affinities with early medieval ceramic assemblages from *Latium* and especially with the late 8th to 9th century AD wares made at Mola di Monte Gelato, see Patterson 1997, pp.366-383.

[19] I would like to thank Carlo Citter for allowing me to analyse the medieval ceramics from the 1998-2003 excavations in the town of Grosseto for comparative purposes. The 8th/9th-century typologies in *acroma depurata* and *acroma selezionata* documented at the surface sites discussed in this chapter are completely absent from the stratigraphic contexts at San Pietro in Grosseto, dating to the second half of the 8th/early 9th century AD. Here, in contrast to our sites, kitchenware is in the overwhelming majority compared to table/storage wares (see Valdambrini 2005, pp.36-47).

[20] For this statistical method and its applications see Terrenato-Ricci 1998, pp.89-104.

[21] The only exception is a minimum vessel in early medieval red-painted ware from the site of Casa Andreoni.

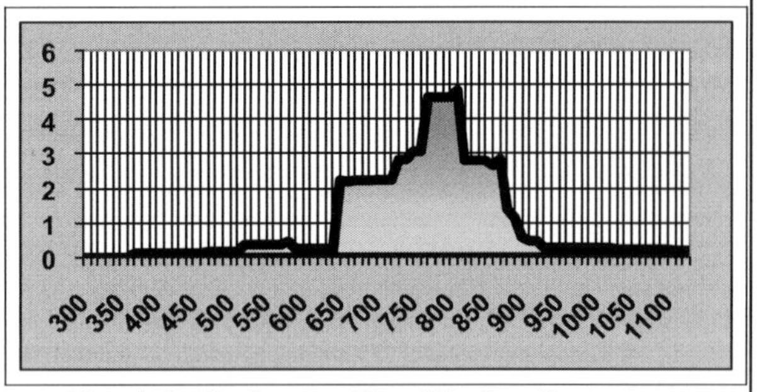

Graph I_ Dating profile of Podere Serratone. Individual Weighted Means analysis applied to surface ceramics.

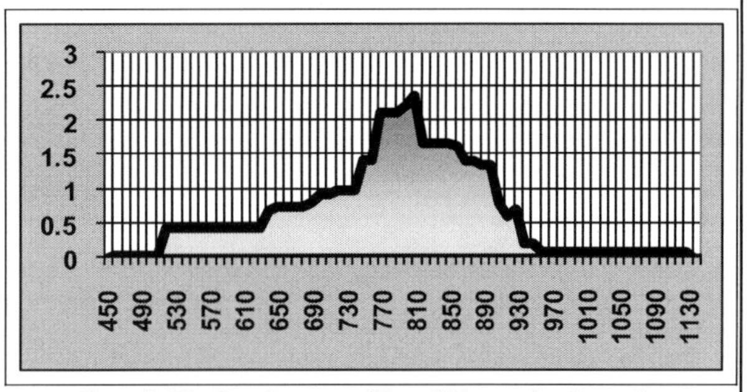

Graph II_ Dating profile of Casa Andreoni. Individual Weighted Means analysis applied to surface ceramics.

Cearmic sample	Date (years B.P.)	Absolute date
D2028-inv.699; Pl. CVII, no. 1	1155±65	AD 850±65
D2029-inv.700; Pl. CVII, no. 2	1210±70	AD 795±70
D2030-inv.701; Pl. CVII, no. 4	1190±60	AD 815±60
D2031-inv.703; Pl. CVIII, no.4	1150±50	AD 855±55
	Average date	AD 830±50

Tab. I_ Absolute dates of four sampled ceramics from context 103. Results of the thermoluminescence dosimetry analysis.

After determining the initial and final chronologies for each of these comparative materials, the next step was to calculate the mean. This allowed us to identify the probable chronological limits of attestation for each pottery type attested at Podere Serratone and Casa Andreoni (for specific data see Appendices I and II).

We then proceeded to assign the value calculated to each group of finds of identical chronology, using the fraction of the number of specimens belonging to a given type and its chronological range of attestation. The result represents the value of that pottery type for each year of its period of attestation. In order to make data management more efficient we decided to multiply this value by ten to obtain a decimal fraction.

After applying this method to all identifiable types we added up the values for each decade to obtain a graph describing and presenting the chronological distribution of the artefacts present at the contexts (Graphs I and II). As we can see, the curves for the two settlements are virtually identical, given their fairly homogeneous material culture. There is an initial slight increase in attestations in around the mid-7th century, with the trend remaining positive until the last quarter of the 9th century. If we examine the two curves more closely we can see a maximum peak at both sites between the last quarter of the 8th century and the 870/880s. It is therefore reasonable to assume that, aside from the few pottery indicators suggesting an initial frequentation of the two contexts during the 7th century, the sites were most intensively settled between the late 8th and late 9th centuries, as indicated by the larger number of pottery fragments found. This theory is fully confirmed by the results of thermoluminescence dosimetry applied to a minimum of four pottery forms from context 103 excavated at Casa Andreoni, interpreted as a levelling on which the hut and its annexes were built. We employed this type of absolute analysis in order to test the validity of the method used to study the early medieval pottery from the contexts examined here and to acquire accurate chronological information on their life phases.[22] The results of the thermoluminescence analysis confirmed the validity of the method used to analyse the early medieval pottery deposits.

All four absolute dates for the minimum individuals found in phase in context 103 fall within the 8th and 9th centuries, with a mean calibrated date of AD 830±50 (Table I); this is in line with the chronology proposed for the period of maximum attestation of pottery materials yielded by the two contexts of Casa Andreoni and Podere Serratone.

[22] The thermoluminescence dosimetry analysis of the early medieval ceramics from Casa Andreoni was carried out in 2006 by Marco Martini and Emanuela Sibilia (University of Milan-Bicocca, Department of Materials Science).

9.2.3. The Analysis of "Podere Serratone-Type" Pottery

The Study of Production Properties

At the Podere Serratone context we identified features probably belonging to a pottery workshop and documented the attestation of pottery of similar morphology in other sites within the study area, leading us to study the distribution of this pottery in depth. We therefore analysed the fabrics present at the production site and compared them with those associated with similar materials from other contexts. After analysing the fabrics from Podere Serratone under an optical microscope and identifying the principal mineral phases we sampled the clays along the course of the Rispescia river near the site in order to determine if there was a correspondence between the geological material used to make the fabrics and those available *in loco* (Fig.2).

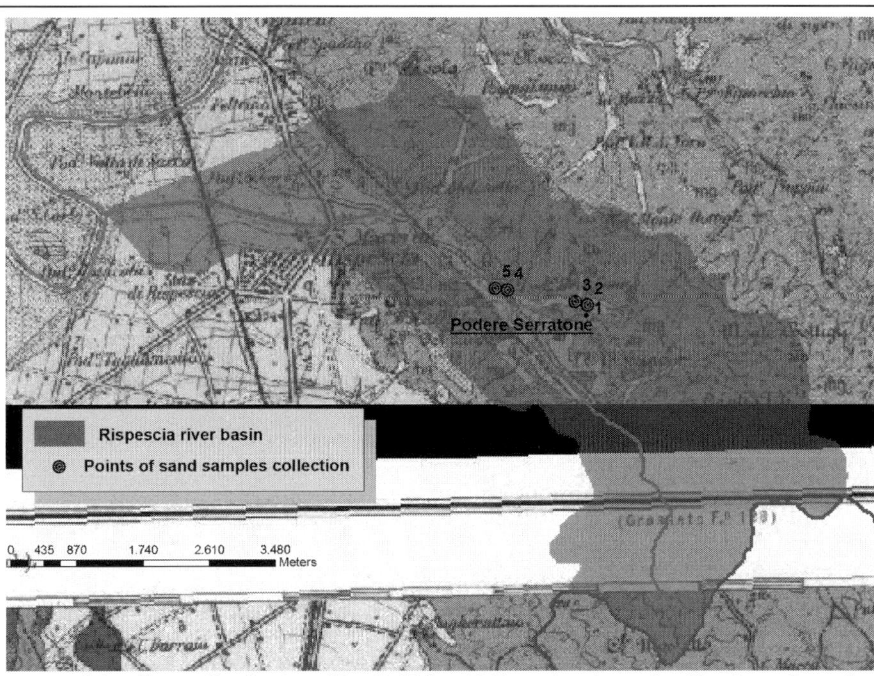

Fig.2_ Visualisation of the Carta Geologica (Fogli 128 e 135) and points of collection along the Rispescia river.

Between Podere Serratone and its source on the Mosfatto hill north-west of Montiano, the catchment basin of the Rispescia river crosses various geological formations, with a clear predominance of quartz-rich feldspar sandstones.[23] In the vicinity of Serratone, a fairly large lens of marly limestone cuts through these sandstones, whilst a few tens of metres to the south, near Poggio Rossino, we find the high terrace conglomerates of inland areas and, along the river, the loose reddish-brown conglomerates commonly found along water courses. Our study of the geological materials available for pottery production concentrated on the properties of the sandstone and its typical facies in this area.

The predominant lithotype in the Rispescia basin is sandstone, whilst sand-schists are present, in limited areas, only at the foot of Poggio del Lupo, about half a kilometre south-west of Podere Serratone. This is extremely important because the mineralogical composition of these two lithotypes presents some fairly significant differences, linked particularly to the much larger quantity of phyllosilicates, such as biotite and muscovite, present in sand-schists (Graph III).[24] The microscopic analysis of the materials sampled along the river indicated a scarcity of phyllosilicates, documented only in one sample, and an abundance of quartzes, alongside a smaller quantity of feldspars (orthclase) and calcite. When we compared these data with those from the optical microscope analysis of the coarse, selected and purified fabrics, the most widely attested at Podere Serratone, we found a strong similarity in the mineral phases. Quartzes are particularly frequent, followed by feldspars, calcite and generic sandstone fragments, documented both in coarse and purified/selected fabrics; micaceous inclusions, which never appear in the more purified fabrics and which are present in lower proportions in kitchenware compared to other mineralogical phases, are rarer.[25] These data and in particular the parallels

[23] For the geological formations of the Rispescia river basin see Foglio no.128 (Grosseto) and Foglio no.135 (Orbetello) of the Carta Geologica d'Italia and the relevant notes in Motta 1969 and Signorini 1967 respectively. I would like to thank Antonia Arnoldus Huyzendveld for discussing this section with me.

[24] The comparison was made possible by the surveys presented in Motta 1969, pp.32-33, citing Cipriani 1961. These data cover the Rapolano area in the province of Siena (Foglio no 121 (Montepulciano), adjacent to Foglio no. 128 (Grosseto)).

[25] The main ceramic fabrics identified in the pottery production of Podere Serratone were given the following codes: AD 30, AD 31 (*acroma depurata*); Sel 30, Sel 32 (*acroma selezionata*); G 31, G32,

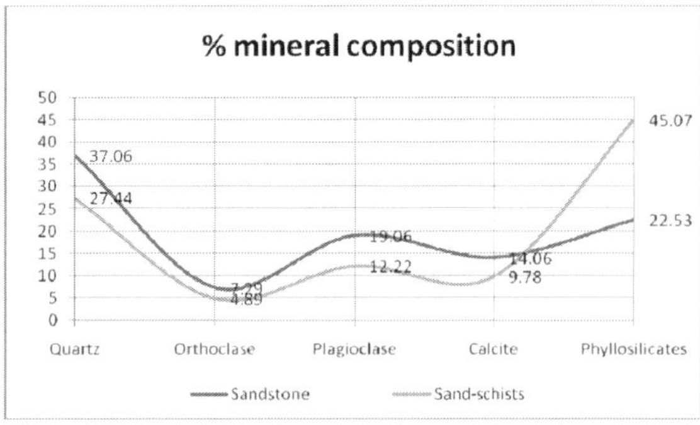

Graph III_ Mineral composition of sandstone and sand-schist.

between the minerals attested in the clays and sands of the Rispescia river and those identified in the fabrics from Podere Serratone appear to indicate that the raw materials used to make pottery were available locally, transported and deposited by the river. Further confirmation of this comes from the profile of the granules, always rounded to sub-rounded, and highly spherical. This is compatible with a direct use of the geological material collected along the Rispescia river, rounded by river transport with no need for a subsequent grinding process.

The Organization of Production

Repeated surveys at the Podere Serratone site led to the identification, under different land use conditions, of some kiln wasters, overfired fragments and overfired clay pieces in a fairly circumscribed area of about 5x5 m inside the main surface feature. The first features belonging to a probable pottery kiln found at least partial confirmation from geophysical surveys. In a fairly small area roughly in the centre of the Topographical Unit and exactly where the production indicators were found, we noted a strong anomaly due to the presence of residual heat activity, fully compatible with a kiln (Fig.3). Even without excavating the area these clues allowed us to state that there was almost certainly a pottery workshop in the centre of the settlement. It is important to note the exclusive presence, among the minimum of 6 overfired individuals and 3 kiln wasters, of small amphorae and jugs made from fine and selected fabrics, and the lack

Fig.3_ Correspondence between the geophysical anomaly and both over-fired clay and over-fired ceramic fragments on the surface.

of conclusive evidence allowing us to ascribe the kitchenware documented at the site to a local workshop. However, the fact that the same mineral phases were identified in the *acroma depurata/selezionata* wares and the kitchenwares, with the only real differences being the proportion of inclusions to matrix and the more constant presence of phyllosilicates in the kitchenware, may represent a valid argument in support of the theory that the kitchenware was also produced here. Were this craftworking activity to have met the needs not only of this settlement but also of various nearby contexts, it would make better economic sense to produce as broad a range of coarseware as possible to reduce the risk of local competition.

G33, G34 (kitchenware); for further details see the Catalogue of Fabrics.

Furthermore, another medieval production structure, the small kiln discovered in the Lucca area near the hill of Pieve Santo Stefano, represents a fairly convincing point of comparison: this workshop produced both cooking pots and one-handled storage jugs for a fairly restricted rural area between the 11th and early 12th centuries.[26]

The production unit at Podere Serratone seems to correspond to the individual workshop type, in accordance with the model developed by Peacock.[27] Essentially, an individual workshop provides a significant income for the person working there but does not represent the only source of income. Since in this type of organization craftworking did not continue full time all year round, the income generated could be supplemented in less intensive periods of production with agricultural labour. This level of organization, simple but professional, entailed a degree of technological sophistication, with the systematic use of the fast wheel as revealed by the whole pottery sample from Podere Serratone. The wares manufactured here must have been destined for a relatively circumscribed circulation, exploiting the commercial opportunities provided by a local demand for pottery. Their area of distribution currently appears to be comprised between the catchment basins of the Ombrone and Osa rivers.

Going on to examine the pottery assemblages in greater detail, we noted the presence of 983 fragments weighing over 10 kg in total resulting from two surface collections.[28] There are a total minimum number of 149 recognizable forms: 34.5% belong to the class of kitchen ware whilst the remainder consists of *acroma depurata* with 37.5% and *acroma selezionata* with 28% of the total (Graph IV). A quantitative analysis of the proportion of fragments presenting a grey core in the fracture suggests that the potters' capacity to control the kiln temperature throughout the firing process was limited (Graph V). In simple production structures such as that operating at Podere Serratone the different colouring probably results from the differing position of the pieces inside the kiln.[29] The beige pieces must have been fired at a constant temperature whilst those with a brighter red-orange colour were probably placed near the hole in the roof allowing combustion gases to escape. Finally, the large number of products with a grey core indicate uneven ventilation inside the kiln, with an alternation between oxidizing and reducing atmospheres resulting in the different colouring of the surface and internal parts. The presence of more or less marked kiln defects seems to be a common feature among wares destined for rural markets; this is evident if we compare the

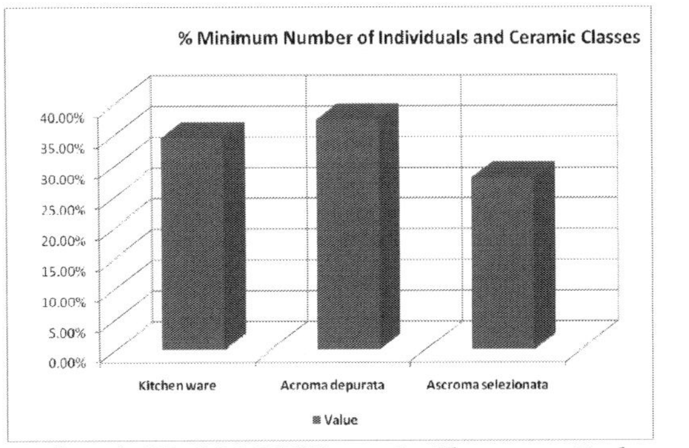

Graph IV_ % MNI/Ceramic Classes at Podere Serratone.

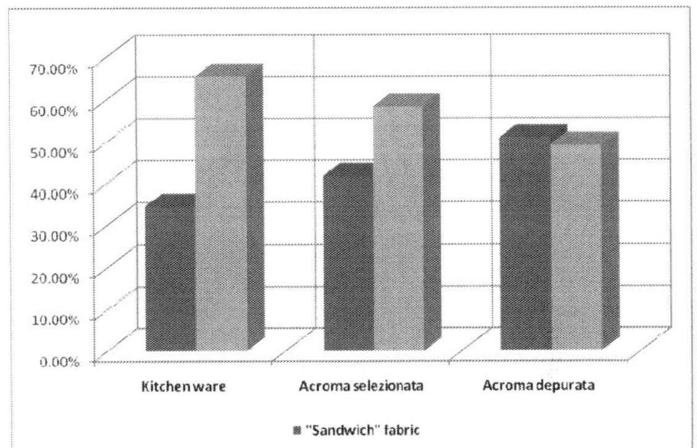

Graph V_ % of "sandwich" fabric per each ceramic class at Podere Serratone.

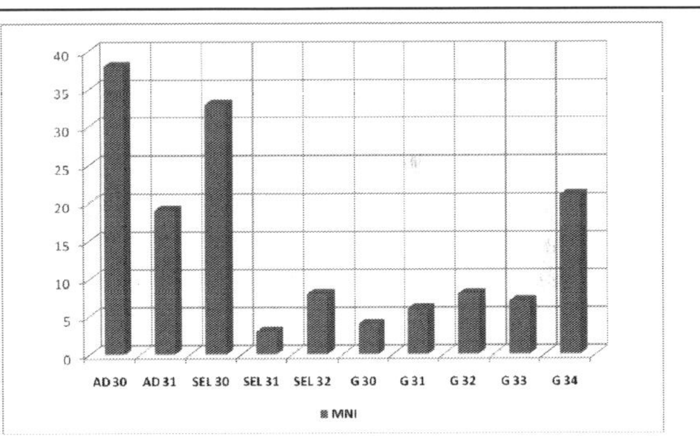

Graph VI_ Fabrics and minimum number of individuals (MNI) at Podere Serratone.

acroma depurata and *acroma selezionata* wares in use between the 7th and the 9th century at Montarrenti, near Siena, with the products consumed at the same time inside the town of Siena at Santa Maria della Scala.[30] During this period the *acroma depurata* and *acroma selezionata* pottery reaching the country village presents a grey core in the fracture more often than that destined for the urban Sienese market. This probably indicates not only a socio-economic difference between these two contexts but also a possible structural difference in the commercial objectives of the production centres in this area.[31] At the Serratone site, we documented at least 5 different body clays used to make the *acroma depurata* and *acroma selezionata* wares and at least as many destined for the production of kitchenware (Graph VI). This apparently large

[26] Ciampoltrini 2004, pp.159-161.
[27] See in general Peacock 1982, pp.13-43 and more recently Gelichi 2007, pp.58-60.
[28] To the ceramic record we should add a total minimum number of 17 bricks (25 fragments weighing 3.350 Kg) and 50 overfired clay pieces, weighing about 570 grams.
[29] On this aspect see Nicholson-Patterson 1989.

[30] Cantini 2005a, pp.245-248.
[31] *Ibidem*, p.246.

number of fabrics is in fact induced by the analytical study of the fabrics; these were assigned to different samples even when they contained identical mineral phases but presented a different degree of hardness or slightly different properties of the fracture. The minerals documented and the morphology of the granules suggest no real differences in the areas from which the geological material was sourced but rather different proportions of temper. For the purified and selected fabrics there did not appear to be any direct relationship between any given form and a specific fabric: all the fabrics attested seem to have been used interchangeably to manufacture the two main forms, the jug and the small amphora (Graph VII). Coarsewares appear to be more complex and varied, with a closer link between forms and fabrics. The common fabric G34 is used to make cooking pots and a type of jug; G31 is used for small open forms like bowl/lids and G30 for *testi*. The other two fabrics, G32 and G33, are used to make closed forms such as cooking pots and small amphorae, and in an entirely occasional fashion for a generic open form (G32) and a *testo* (G33).

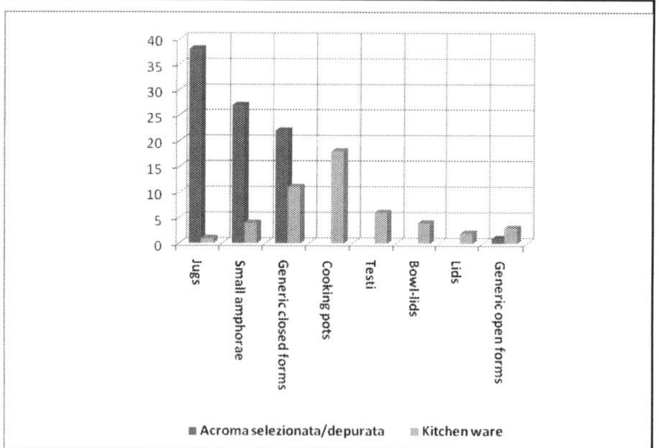

Graph VII_ Functional vessels and MNI at Podere Serratone.

The Pottery from Podere Serratone in its Tuscan and Italian Context

Before describing the pottery forms and typologies documented at the Podere Serratone context in detail, we should stress the complex relations between classes. Altogether, there is a larger quantity of *acroma depurata* and *selezionata* wares than kitchenware, with 65.5% of total specimens. This is important, as we will see below, because it appears to be a typical feature of 8th- and 9th-century contexts in this area. The disproportionate quantity of table/storage ware compared to kitchenware is a constant in the rural villages of early medieval Tuscany,[32] with the exception of the site of Poggibonsi[33] and perhaps Grosseto.[34]

This imbalance should be ascribed to the existence of both urban and rural consumers with cultural ties to the late antique pottery tradition. Demand for pottery remained high during the transition to the early Middle Ages, fuelling a production which still manufactured a complex and diverse range of forms and classes with different functions. In contrast to much of northern Italy, where simplification and the localization of production structures were far more marked, leading to the gradual decline of *acroma depurata* ware in favour of kitchenware,[35] in Tuscany we see a cultural and food consumption model more similar to the contexts of central and southern Italy where pottery production continued to maintain high quality standards.[36] Nonetheless, the obvious differences between the pottery repertoires of northern Italy on the one hand and those from the central and southern regions of the peninsula on the other do not seem to be a direct consequence of a lesser degree of economic well-being and a more limited propensity towards trade on the part of the northern elites compared to those of the centre-south.[37] Other indicators, such as the foundation or refurbishment of religious buildings or the construction of private funerary areas are indicative of the large capital investments made by the Lombard aristocracies of northern Italy and thus their economic capacity.[38] This is not to deny that there was a wealth gap between the ruling classes of the north and the south of Italy; rather, it is simplistic and over-schematic to make this assertion on the basis of the pottery evidence alone. Research currently underway in the northern Adriatic area is in any case beginning to reveal the existence of an intense trade in foodstuffs transported in commercial amphorae reaching major urban contexts north of the Po river between the 8th and 9th centuries.[39] A further aspect worth mentioning, in this case directly connected to our study area, is that there does not appear to be a direct relationship between pottery production, which remains diverse and professional though very localized, and the demand for high quality pottery on the part of local elites. At least on the basis of current evidence, within our study area the early medieval city of Roselle does not seem to have acted as a catalyst for a local production of pottery to be sold on a dynamic and active urban market. We do not have sufficient evidence for the existence of a town aristocracy whose demand for pottery may have laid the structural foundations for a production activity

[32] In the villages of Campiglia Marittima, Rocchette Pannocchieschi, Donoratico, Montemassi and Scarlino, kitchenware did not predominate over *acroma depurata* and *acroma selezionata* wares (see Grassi 2006, p.461). In the hilltop village of Montarrenti, between the second half of the 8th and the 9th century AD, the overall quantities of kitchenware are equivalent to those of *acroma depurata* and *acroma selezionata* wares (see Cantini 2003, p.160).

[33] From this point of view the early medieval village of Poggibonsi represents a marked anomaly, with kitchenware being in the overwhelming majority over other pottery classes, accounting for 83% of the total (*acroma depurata* and *acroma selezionata* wares account for 14% and 2% respectively, and Forum Ware for 3%) see Valenti 1996, p.111.

[34] See Valdambrini 2005.

[35] Wickham 2005, pp.731-734.

[36] Saguì-Ricci-Romei 1997.

[37] Wickham 2005, pp.739-741.

[38] Gelichi 2006b.

[39] Gelichi *et alii* 2006a; Gelichi *et alii* 2006b, Gelichi 2008.

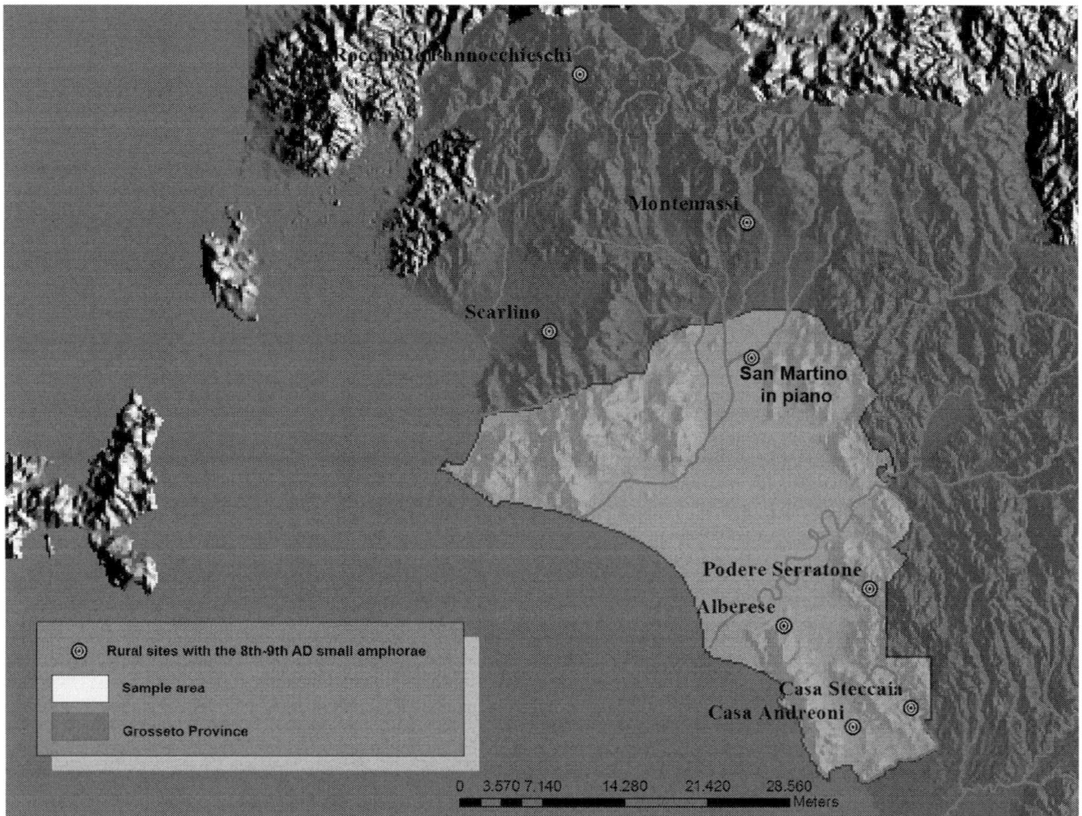

Fig.4_ Rural sites with the 8th to 9th AD small amphorae in the sample area and surrounding territory.

which continued to be complex. Certainly the area between the Alma valley and the Osa river stands out for the presence of various major powers acting through their peripheral landholdings, such as the Diocese of Lucca, the city of Chiusi and the Roman Catholic Church. However, it is impossible to establish a link between this and the production of good quality pottery after late Antiquity. It is more plausible that the affinities between the pottery context of Podere Serratone and the material culture of central and southern Italy can be explained on a purely cultural basis. The pottery deposits of the 8th and 9th centuries intercepted in this area, like most of the urban and rural contexts of the early medieval *Tuscia*,[40] suggest that links to the late antique manufacturing tradition were never irreversibly severed, despite an often systematic selection of the pottery classes and forms produced. Certainly the transition affected craftworking activities to the same extent as population patterns, but the characteristically local nature of early medieval pottery production structures does not prevent us from identifying more or less close links with the past. Specifically, Lombard Tuscany appears to be out of line with the trend for much of northern Italy, preserving solid links with late antique production structures; this does not appear to be due to economic factors but rather to profound socio-cultural factors.

Going on to examine the salient features of pottery production during the 8th and 9th centuries within the study area in further detail, some important characteristics allow us to identify affinities and differences with respect to other deposits inside and outside the region.

A comparison with the morphological and functional repertoire from elite urban contexts like the Crypta Balbi in Rome[41] or, on a smaller scale, Santa Maria della Scala in Siena,[42] indicates a strong selection process affecting the number of forms attested; in rural contexts like Podere Serratone these are reduced to a few, often multi-purpose, types. Indicative in this sense is the jug which, in a fairly simplified morphological repertoire such as that in use between the 8th and 9th centuries, served a variety of different purposes. These included not only the pouring out of liquid foods at table and their storage in storerooms, the traditional functions of this form, but also at least a partial use in

[40] On Lucca see Ciampoltrini 2004; on Montarrenti, Cantini 2003; on Siena, Cantini 2005a; for a preliminary overview of early medieval ceramics from the hilltop villages of Donoratico, Campiglia Marittima, Rocchette Pannocchieschi, Montemassi and Scarlino see Grassi 2006.

[41] It has been noted that the closed *acroma depurata* forms from the 8th-century AD context of the Crypta Balbi in Rome present a considerable degree of typological variety. Closed forms account for 97.6% of *the acroma depurata* ware as a whole, while open forms are documented with a very low 2.4%. See Romei 2004, pp.291-294.

[42] In the 8th- and 9th-century ceramic assemblages at Santa Maria della Scala, the *acroma depurata* repertoire includes not only several types of closed forms but also both wide- and narrow-mouthed open vessels, such as flanged bowls, bowls and basins. As a consequence, the repertoire of ceramic forms for use at table and for storage is more diverse than in the rural contexts of southern Tuscany. On the urban site of Santa Maria della Scala see Cantini 2005a, p.94 and pp.100-101.

the kitchen. The presence of slight traces of smoke on some bases and walls of jugs made from purified and selected fabrics at Podere Serratone suggests that these forms were also used in the kitchen, probably for cooking liquids and perhaps for the preparation of *puls*.

An interesting characteristic of the 8th and 9th century repertoires is the constant attestation of small amphorae, documented with at least two main types. Outside the study area, the presence of two-handled containers, probably used for transport as well as for the storage of surplus agricultural produce, is documented at the hilltop villages of Rocchette Pannocchieschi, Montemassi and Scarlino (Fig.4).[43] By contrast, vessels of this type have not been found in the early medieval urban deposits of Lucca and Siena, for which reliable pottery sequences are available. On the basis of published data, recent excavations and surface surveys, the map of distribution shows that small amphorae are concentrated in the coastal and subcoastal belt between the Milia valley to the north and the Osa valley to the south during the 8th and 9th centuries.

In morphological terms, these two-handed forms are very similar to the small amphorae attested in Rome in the 8th- to 10th-century layers of the Crypta Balbi,[44] and in other early medieval contexts in the city.[45] The formal differences between the specimens from the Grosseto area and those from Rome lie essentially in the base profile (flat in the former whilst in the wares from Lazio the base remains umbonated from the High Middle Ages until the 14th century)[46] and in the absence of incised comb decorations on the specimens from the study area. There are also close analogies with the wares made at the small production structure on Monte Gelato between the late 8th and early 9th century.[47] This kiln specialized in the manufacture of small one-handled amphorae and jugs made of a purified fabric, typologically similar to those of the contemporary deposits of the Crypta Balbi and the Roman Campagna; this suggests that the pottery made here was probably also sold on the city market (Graph VIII). A perhaps insufficiently studied but nonetheless telling clue as to the functional purpose of the little amphorae manufactured at Monte Gelato comes from the identification of this site as one of the production companies belonging to the *domusculta* of *Capracorum*, founded by Pope Adrian I between 774 and 776.[48] This papal project, aimed at reorganizing and increasing agricultural production in the Roman Campagna, was a practical response to the economic weakening of the Church of Rome caused by Leo II the Isaurian's confiscation of its lands in Calabria and Sicily in the 730s.[49] Essentially, Adrian I intended the *domuscultae* to guarantee that the Roman Church received the agricultural supplies sufficient not only to meet its own needs but also to continue public distributions of food and thus ensure popular consensus for the papacy's political control over the city of Rome. As we have already stressed, the Roman context presenting the closest parallels with the pottery produced at Mola di Monte Gelato is the Crypta Balbi and this is probably no accident. By the 7th century, the exedra of the Crypta was already being used as a refuse heap and it served this purpose for a long period. Given the privileged nature of the finds from this deposit, dating to between the late 7th and the 10th century, it has been suggested that this was the rubbish heap of the nearby monastery of San Lorenzo *in Pallacinis*.[50] The pottery documented in the exedra thus reflects the consumption of a wealthy city monastery and this is of particular interest for the argument proposed here. The fact that the Crypta Balbi deposits have yielded small 8th- and 9th- century amphorae morphologically similar to those manufactured at Monte Gelato suggests that the occupants of the monastery were in all probability among those who consumed the pottery produced at the Faliscan workshop. Evidently some of the pottery reaching the city must have been destined for use at table and for storage, but the amphorae probably also served to transport foodstuffs such as wine or oil. The confiscation of lands in southern Italy and Sicily must have led to a marked contraction in wine supply from these areas, forcing people to fall back on locally produced wine. This long digression supplies some interesting clues on which to reflect and demonstrates the informative potential of studies of the distribution of small coarseware amphorae for the analysis of local and sub-regional trade.

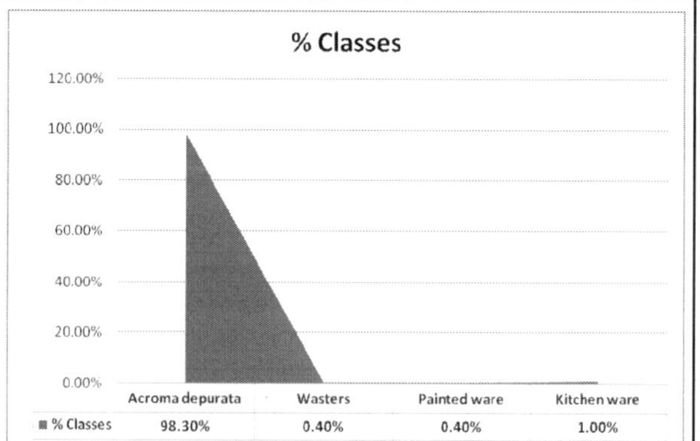

Graph VIII_ Ceramic classes (%) at Mola di Monte Gelato (data after Patterson 1997 Tab.64).

[43] See especially Vaccaro 2009 for an overview of the distribution of early medieval small amphorae in southern Tuscany. For the presence of this amphora type at the sites of Rocchette Pannocchieschi, Montemassi and Scarlino see also Grassi 2006, p.464.

[44] Romei 2004, pp.291-308.

[45] See in particular the late 8th-/9th-century AD ceramic assemblages from Santo Stefano Rotondo on the Caelian Hill in Martin 2004, pp.506-516 and the 8th-century AD deposits at San Clemente, in Mandarini-Paganelli 1998, p.29, Fig.5, no.13

[46] Saguì *et alii* 2001b, p.520.

[47] On the early medieval ceramic kiln at Mola di Monte Gelato and its products see Patterson 1997, pp.366-374.

[48] See Potter-King 1997, pp.78-79.

[49] Marazzi 1993, pp. 267-286.

[50] See Arena *et alii* 2001, pp.266-267 and p.498.

The morphological structure of the small "amphorae" attested in the Maremma area, with a flat base and fairly wide body, may have made them suitable for a variety of means of transport: barges along the coast or on rivers, and carts and mules for overland transport. Particularly interesting are the possible functional similarities between these forms and the various small amphorae produced between the 9th and the 13th/14th centuries in the Aegean region and the areas facing onto the Black Sea; their peculiarity was that they could be carried by one man on his back.[51] In central-southern Italy and especially the Rome and Salerno areas, there is a measurement unit for liquid capacity, frequently documented from the 10th century until the dawn of the modern age, not fully standardized and known as the *lagena*.[52] It is possible that this measurement unit corresponded to a pottery container for the transport and particularly the storage of liquids, especially wine and oil, in line with the theory formulated by Bakirtzis, who identified functional similarities between the Byzantine *magarikè* and a series of small amphorae documented between the 9th and 10th centuries in Rome and the Roman Campagna, although the Roman specimens have a smaller capacity.[53] This suggests that between the 8th and 9th century other pottery forms inherited the functions typical of commercial amphorae, albeit on a smaller scale both as concerns their range of distribution and the amount of produce stored. This reconstruction hypothesis would thus be evidence for the existence of trade circuits which remained vigorous and well-structured during the early Middle Ages, albeit restricted to commercial interaction between neighbouring rural sites (as in the area between the lower Ombrone and Osa valleys) or between cities and their production space (as appears to be the case between Rome and the Roman Campagna). Within our study area it appears clear that the pottery produced at the village of Podere Serratone was distributed locally. Jugs and small amphorae, whose morphology and fabrics are similar to those produced at the site, have been identified at the 8th/9th-century settlement near Alberese and at the two dispersed settlements of Casa Andreoni and Casa Steccaia. There is currently no definitive evidence that these small amphorae also had a commercial function but it is entirely plausible that they were used for a local trade in agricultural surplus, probably wine or oil, produced at Podere Serratone (see *infra*).

[51] Bakirtzis 1989, especially p.73.
[52] Sereni 1995, p.272.
[53] See *ibidem*, pp.274-275, and also Bakirtzis 1989.

Forms and Types Attested at the Podere Serratone Site

ACROMA DEPURATA AND ACROMA SELEZIONATA WARES

Since the same objects were made using both purified fabrics (AD 30-31) and selected fabrics (Sel 30-32) we decided to treat these two classes together. Of the total of 81 typifiable forms identified at the site, 36 are Type 1 jugs. This form is characterized by a sub-vertical rim, often shaped internally, and a handle which is sometimes level with the edge but more commonly set immediately beneath it (Pl. CIII, nos 8-12). The width of the handles ranges from 4 to 4.5 cm, and they are usually no more than 1 cm thick. Their morphology is fairly variable, with slightly or very thickened strap handles presenting light longitudinal grooves (Pl. CIV, nos 3-5), incurved handles (Pl. CIV, nos 1-2), and, more rarely, simple but never markedly thin strap handles (Pl. CIV, no. 6). The mouths are fairly narrow, between 8 and 10 cm in diameter. This type of jug finds close parallels with specimens dated to the 6th/7th centuries from surface features in the Roccastrada area,[54] with mid-7th to 8th-century forms from Santa Maria della Scala in Siena[55] and with jugs of the same period attested at Montarrenti.[56] We should also note the close affinities with some specimens made between the late 8th and early 9th century at the Mola di Monte Gelato kiln.[57]

The Type 2 jug is less common, with a minimum of only 2 individuals. This form has a band-shaped rim which may be either fairly everted (Pl. CIII, no. 13) or slightly flaring (Pl. CIII, no. 14). In the only specimen where it can be reconstructed the mouth diameter is 10 cm. This typology is extremely similar to the jugs with band-shaped rims attested in the late antique contexts of the area, although the narrow mouth appears to be a distinctive feature of the early medieval forms. However, given the presence of a minimum of 5 forms[58] belonging to the initial frequentation of the site between the 6th and 7th century, it cannot be ruled out that the 2 juglets with band-shaped rims belong to the first phase of occupation of the context. The available points of comparison also point to a late antique and early medieval chronology,[59] whilst only some of the

[54] Guideri 2000a, p.14, Pl.II, nos 1-4. In light of the chrono-typological data now available for southern Tuscan coarsewares we can suggest that the surface pottery from the Roccastrada area dates to the 7th -9th centuries AD rather than to the 6th -7th centuries.
[55] Cantini 2005a, p.95, Pl.7, no.4.11
[56] Cantini 2003, p.125, Pl.25, no.II.6.1
[57] Patterson 1997, p.377, nos 41 and 51.
[58] I refer to three specimens of bowl with an inverted rim, modelled on ARS form Hayes 61B, a flanged bowl modelled on Hayes 91C (ARS) and finally a deep dish modelled on the prototype Hayes 87B (ARS). All 5 vessels are made in *acroma depurata* ware.
[59] Similar small jugs are well documented in the Crypta Balbi *mithraeum* between the late 6th and early 7th century AD (Saguì-Coletti 2004, p.272, Pl.XX, no.113); in the first half of the 6th century AD deposit of the Casa delle Vestali (Roman Forum) (Filippi et alii 2004, p.170, Pl.II, nos 12-13); and finally in a context dated to the

specimens attested at surface contexts of the 7th and 8th centuries in the Roccastrada area belong to the central period of the High Middle Ages.[60]

A juglet with a strongly everted rim ending in a rounded lip is documented by a single specimen. As in the above typologies the mouth measures 10 cm in diameter (Pl. CIII, no. 7). This type has no distinctive morphological characteristics and finds some generic parallels at Santa Maria della Scala with one-handed jugs of the first half of the 7th[61] and the 9th century.[62]

A series of small bases in all likelihood belong to Type 1 and 2 jugs. All of these are flat with highly standardized diameters, between 10 and 11 cm. The walls, between ½ and 1 cm thick, are slightly flaring, indicating that the bodies probably had an ovoid profile.

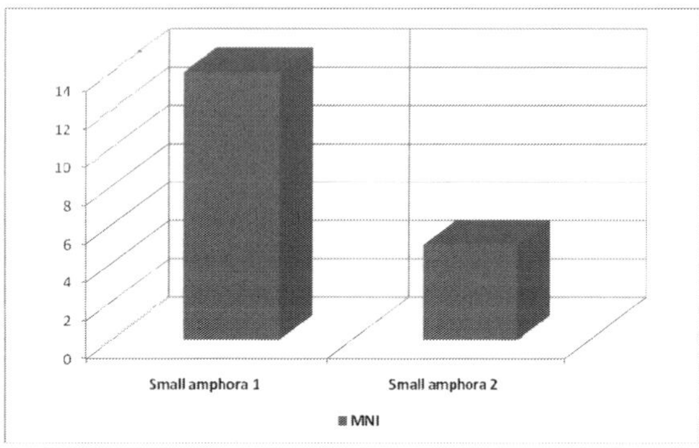

Graph IX_ Minimum number of individuals per each type of small amphora.

The other very successful form within the Podere Serratone production repertoire is the small amphora, already discussed at length for its possible commercial implications. A morphological analysis allowed us to identify two possible typologies which, on the basis of the fragments, differ essentially for the neck profile (Graph IX).[63] The Type 1 small amphora has a short everted rim, rounded on the upper surface and set on a cylindrical neck (Pl. CIII, nos 1-4). Type 2, by contrast, has a conical neck, whilst the rim profile cannot be determined; on the basis of the junction it would appear to be vertical or slightly incurving (Pl. CIII, nos 5-6). There are no differences between the handles of these two typologies, which are between 5 and 6 cm wide and 1 to 1.5 cm thick. Their morphological structure is identical to that of Type 1 jugs, with more or less thickened strap shapes, sometimes presenting light longitudinal grooves, and more rarely quite thin strap handles. The small amphorae always have flat bases and gently flaring walls, 1 or 1.5 cm thick. Their average diameter is 15 cm (Pl. CIV, nos 12-13) though there is a large version, attested by a single specimen, with a diameter of 26 cm (Pl. CIV, no. 14). With their respective versions and variants the jug and the small amphora seem to account for virtually the whole Podere Serratone production repertoire in *acroma depurata* and *acroma selezionata* ware. However, we should note the presence of an unidentifiable minimum individual, made from fabric Sel 30; given the inclination of the walls this must have been an open form. There is no evidence for pieces used for the direct consumption of foods; this must be due not only to changes in eating habits compared to those still documented in the early 7th century but also to the replacement of pottery tableware with items made of other materials such as wood, at least as concerns the objects destined to hold food at the point of consumption.[64]

One feature common to all the *acroma depurata* and *acroma selezionata* wares from Podere Serratone is the absence of decorations, surface whitening and burnishing; these features seem to be typical of some of the table and storage wares widespread in the area from the 10th or perhaps the late 9th century.

KITCHEN WARE

The kitchenware repertoire presents that balance between open and closed forms which is lacking in table and storage wares. Although simplified, the morphological range of wares made using a coarse fabric consists of at least 6 functional forms (Graph X). Not all of these, however, were intended for cooking food, as we know from the attestation of at least 4 specimens of small amphorae, including a specimen which is certainly a Type 2 amphora, well-documented

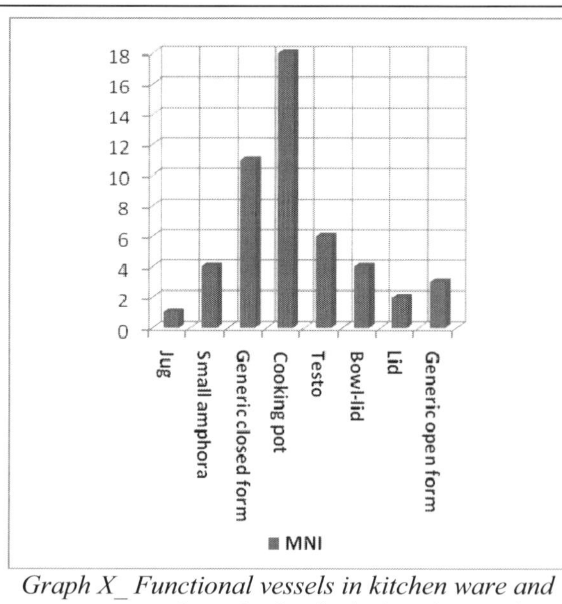

Graph X_ Functional vessels in kitchen ware and minimum number of individuals (MNI) at Podere Serratone.

first half of the 7th century AD on the Aventine (Fontana *et alii* 2004, p.552, Pl.III, no.25).

[60] Guideri 2000a, p.17, Pl.5, no.14.

[61] Cantini 2005a, p.95, Pl.7, no.4.10.

[62] *Ibidem*, p.95, Pl.7 no.4.14.

[63] For comparisons see above and Appendix I.

[64] Arthur-Patterson 1994, p.429.

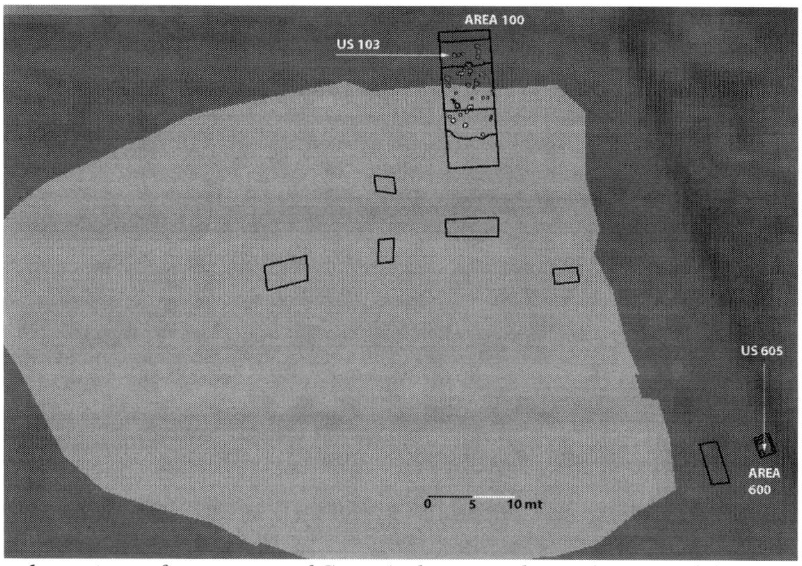

Fig.5_ Excavation at the main surface scatter of Casa Andreoni and visualisation of the two contexts (SU 103 and 605) which yielded well-dated ceramics.

in the version made with a purified/selected fabric (Pl. CV, no. 2). Although highly fragmentary, none of the pieces belonging to small amphorae present any traces of smoke to indicate that they were placed over a fire. The same is true of a minimum form made of a coarse fabric which, interestingly, replicates the formal model of the Type 1 jug for use at table and for storage. The coarseware version loses the slight concave profile inside the rim, which is more everted. The mouth width also changes significantly, reaching 16 cm as compared to the 8-10 cm of the specimens in *depurata* and *selezionata* ware (Pl. CV, no. 1).

However, the predominant form is the cooking pot, documented with a minimum of at least 18 individuals. This is probably an underestimate, since the wall thickness suggests that many of the other 11 unidentifiable closed forms may have been cooking pots. This functional form is attested in the Serratone repertoire with at least three versions which differ for the degree to which the rim is everted and its profile.

The Type 1 cooking pot has a gently flaring plain edge with a slight internal ledge where it joins the wall (Pl. CV, nos 3-4). This typology is also attested in a version whose rim is slightly concave on the inside (Pl. CV, no. 5). The mouth widths range from 13 to 17 cm. The closest points of comparison are specimens attested at Santa Maria della Scala in layers of the second half of the 6th/early 7th century[65] and of the 9th century,[66] and at Montarrenti in phases of the second half of the 8th and 9th century.[67] A second well-documented type resembles the above, from which it differs principally for the more flaring rim and the absence of the slight internal ledge (Pl. CV, nos 6-9). Its mouth measures between 15 and 16 cm. Once again, there are close morphological parallels with wares of the second half of the 8th and the 9th century at Montarrenti.[68] Finally, cooking pot Type 3 is present at Serratone with a single minimum individual. It has a slightly everted rim ending in a pointed lip with a marked internal thickening at the junction between the rim and the wall (Pl. CV, no. 10). This is a small version, measuring only 12 cm. Similar forms come from the late 5th- to mid-6th-century layers at Santa Maria della Scala in Siena[69] and from those of the second half of the 8th/early 9th century at San Pietro in Grosseto.[70]

Among the open forms of recognizable typology the dominant form is the *testo*, documented with a minimum of at least 6 specimens. There are two main versions: one with a rounded plain rim set on a gently flaring wall (Pl. CV, no. 15) and another with a thinned rim, flat on the upper surface (Pl. CV, no. 14). The bases are always flat and plain. Also well-represented are bowl-lids, attested by a single version with a semispherical body and receding rim, flat on the upper surface. The diameter of this form always ranges from 16 to 17 cm, fully compatible with Type 1 cooking pots, with which it may have been used as a lid (Pl. CV, nos 11-12). The type of bowl just described seems to be a possible important chronological marker for the early medieval phases of some Tuscan contexts. It is well attested both in the study area and in layers of the second half of the 8th and 9th centuries at Montarrenti, where the upper surface of the rim and the outer surface of the body present a spiral decoration applied to the raw clay.[71]

[65] Cantini 2005a, p.146, Pl.33, no.5.101.
[66] *Ibidem*, p.146, Pl.33, no.5.103.
[67] Cantini 2003, p.91, Pl.9, no.I.7.10.
[68] *Ibidem*, p.91, Pl.9, no.I.7.10.
[69] Cantini 2005a, p.143, Pl.30, no.5.77.
[70] Valdambrini 2005, p.46, Pl.6, no.5.
[71] Cantini 2003, p.83, Pl.4, no.II.3.1.

9.2.4. The Pottery Contexts of the Casa Andreoni Settlement: Affinities With and Differences From Podere Serratone

Characteristics of the Deposits

The pottery contexts at Casa Andreoni were studied on two different levels: first the systematic analysis of all surface materials, as at Podere Serratone, and second, after the excavation of the main surface feature, the identification of the diagnostic pieces most helpful in determining the deposit's chronology and the range of functional forms present (Fig.5).

Some preliminary remarks on the conditions of the surface and excavated deposits at the time of their discovery are in order. First, the topographical layout of the nucleated site of Casa Andreoni differs markedly from that of Podere Serratone. In the latter, the aggregated nature of the surface features and the homogeneity of the pottery materials allowed us to undertake a unitary analysis; this was impossible at Casa Andreoni from the outset. This site has a nucleated layout with individual farmsteads distributed over an area of about 26 hectares, forcing us first to study each individual feature carefully. Later, after confirming the homogeneous nature of the four pottery assemblages, we were able to proceed with an overall analysis of the entire deposit, allowing us to suggest a preliminary chronological calibration for the site (Graph II). The site's main Topographical Unit was then excavated stratigraphically with the aim of understanding the deposit's state of conservation and acquiring data on the settlement structure. One important feature emerging from the excavations is the marked quantitative imbalance between the numerous pottery finds discovered during the survey and the small quantities documented in the test pits. This anomaly is clearly linked to the complete removal, due to agricultural activities, of the life and abandonment layers of the hut and the other structures intercepted by excavations. As noted above, four pottery samples were subjected to thermoluminescence analysis, with a view to dating some recurrent typologies accurately; the remaining materials in phase were examined for the informative potential of the relationship between forms, functions and fabrics. Particularly significant was the absolute chrono-typological agreement between the large amounts of surface materials and the few pottery finds still *in situ*, essentially from the levelling layers contexts 103 and 605. In light of these findings, we believe that pottery consumption at the Casa Andreoni settlement can be reconstructed mainly by examining the rich surface contexts and subsequently comparing these with the few pottery indicators recovered during excavations. The total pottery record recovered during the replicated surveys of the four Topographical Units amounts to 387 fragments, weighing 5 kg. The total minimum number of forms is 128. The proportions of different pottery classes correspond to those previously found at Podere

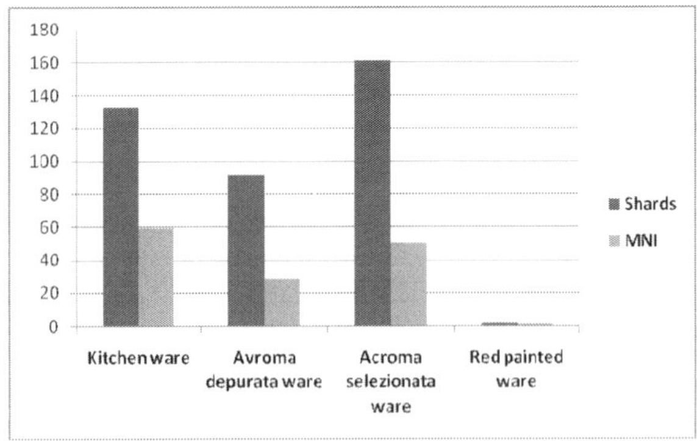

Graph XI_ Relations between fragments and Minimum number of individuals (MNI) per each ceramic class at Casa Andreoni.

Serratone. At the Casa Andreoni settlement, too, table/storage wares predominate over coarsewares, with 56.5% and 42.8% respectively (Graph XI).

Another similarity between the two contexts is the fairly large number of fragments made of purified and selected fabrics presenting a grey core in the fracture (Graph XII). Although the proportion of fragments with a grey core is essentially similar, at Casa Andreoni we see a slight overall decrease if we add up the partial percentages for *acroma depurata* and *acroma selezionata*: 36.4% compared to 46.3% at Serratone using the same calculation (Table III). If this fairly significant difference is not due to pure chance it might indicate a feature of some interest. 88% of the *acroma depurata* and *acroma selezionata* pottery from Casa Andreoni is made of the same fabrics also documented at Podere Serratone (Graph XIII).[72] Since the forms are also essentially identical to those attested at the village with the production structure, as we will see below, it seems fairly certain that the table and storage ware found at Casa Andreoni came directly from the settlement on the Rispescia river. The smaller number of fragments with the grey core found at the consumption site as compared to the production site might thus suggest a tendency to trade principally in uniformly fired pottery rather than that with defects. Naturally this does not imply a systematic selection of products for sale but at the least a possible distinction between first and second class pottery.

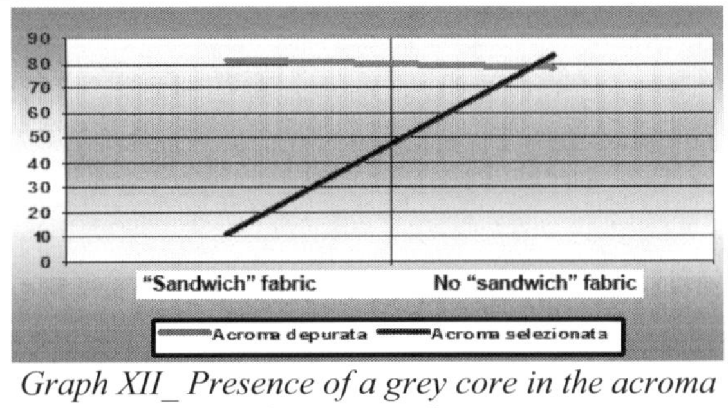

Graph XII_ Presence of a grey core in the acroma depurata and acroma selezionata wares.

[72] I refer to ceramic fabrics AD 30 and AD 31 (*acroma depurata*) and Sel 30, Sel 31, Sel 32 (*acroma selezionata*).

	Acroma depurata with grey core%	Acroma selezionata with grey core %
Casa Andreoni	11,7%	51%
Podere Serratone	50,9%	41,7%

Table III_ Comparison of grey core percentage in the acroma depurata and acroma selezionata wares at Casa Andreoni and Podere Serratone.

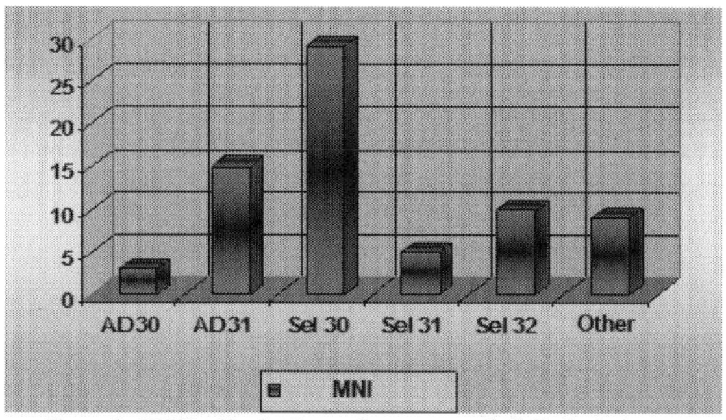

Graph XIII_ Relations between MNI (minimum number of individuals) and fabrics at Casa Andreoni.

A novelty with respect to the Podere Serratone deposit is the appearance of pottery with red painted decorations, attested by two fragments belonging to a single individual. Interestingly, this specimen, a closed handled form, almost certainly a jug, is made from fabric AD 32, not documented among the body clays used to manufacture the Podere Serratone pottery. This fabric is very fine, yellowish in colour (10YR 7/6 yellow) and sometimes presents a grey core in the fracture (10YR 4/1 dark gray);[73] it is attested at Casa Andreoni with 7 fragments and a minimum of 4 forms. Only the minimum individual shown in Pl. CVI, no. 4 presents obvious traces of a red painted decoration; the other 3 specimens, represented by 3 bases and 2 wall fragments, have no such decorations. This is likely due to the fragmentary nature of the pieces; as such these 3 closed forms can probably also be ascribed to the red painted wares. However, this problem is destined to remain unresolved. It is in any case worth noting that this fabric is completely different from those associated with the few pottery specimens of red painted ware from the late 9th- to 11th-century context of Aiali. There are also marked differences from the fabrics of red painted wares of the 10th-12th centuries ascribable to Pisan workshops, which differ clearly from that of Casa Andreoni in colour and the mineral phases documented.[74] This may suggest that the pottery with red painted decoration found at Casa Andreoni came from outside the region, perhaps from workshops in central or southern Italy where the manufacturing tradition of this class appears to be well established throughout the Middle Ages.[75]

As concerns the kitchenware, we can see close affinities at Casa Andreoni with that found at Podere Serratone; it is fairly probable that at least some of the pottery reaching the settlement overlooking the Gulf of Talamone came from this kiln. A morphological analysis and the study of the fabrics seem to indicate that the local circulation of the wares produced at Podere Serratone concerned not only table and storage ware but also some kitchenware. Other kitchenware typologies with no parallels among the pottery manufactured at Serratone are also documented at Casa Andreoni, indicating that there were other local or sub-regional production centres specializing in coarsewares. These workshops must have operated at the artisanal or semi-professional level with a systematic use of the wheel, as revealed by an analysis of the artefacts.

Forms and Typologies of Table/Storage Ware and Kitchenware

The pottery repertoire from Casa Andreoni repeats the simplified scheme already seen at Podere Serratone, albeit with some different functional features (Graph XIV). Among the *acroma depurata* and *acroma selezionata* wares the predominant forms remain the jug and the small amphora, whilst the wide-mouthed jug makes an appearance. We should also note the presence of at least 1 open form, documented by a fragment of a flat rim, possibly belonging to a bowl, with a spiral decoration impressed into the raw clay. Closed forms also predominate among the kitchenware, with the largest number of identifiable specimens being cooking pots. Kitchenware jugs are barely attested, with only 1 minimum individual of Serratone Type 2 with a band-shaped rim. Also uncommon are open kitchenware forms, represented exclusively by 1 specimen of *testo*, 2 Type 1 bowl-lids and 1 pan. In contrast to Podere Serratone, a fairly large number of the fragments belonging to closed kitchen ware forms present an outer surface finishing characterized by a combed decoration which may be densely or loosely packed and is in general fairly light. These suggest a greater decorative intent than the production attested at Serratone (Graph XV).

[73] For a detailed description see the Catalogue of Fabrics.

[74] The medieval red painted ware produced in the Pisa area is characterized mainly by the presence of the following inclusions: quartz (including polycrystalline quartz), plagioclase, orthoclase, muscovite and sandstone; by contrast ceramic fabric AD 32 only contains iron oxides and neo-formation calcite on the edges of some pores. For the red painted ware from Pisa see Abela 1993b, pp.413-418, particularly ceramic fabrics 1, 3-4; Abela 2000b, pp.119-120 and also Pallecchi 2000, p.229, Gruppo IA.

[75] See in general Romei 2004, p.287.

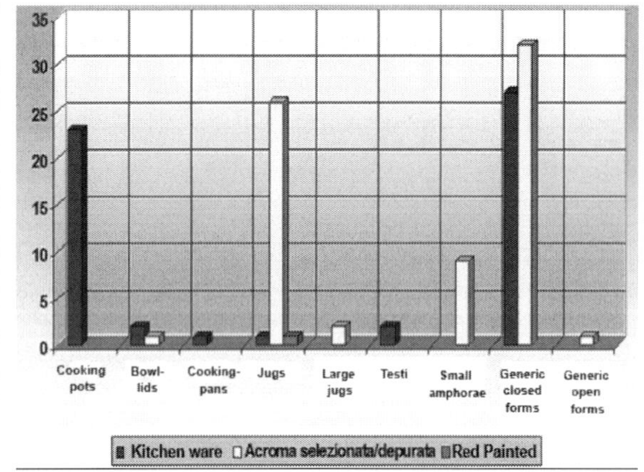

Graph XIV_ Relations between functional vessels and MNI at Casa Andreoni.

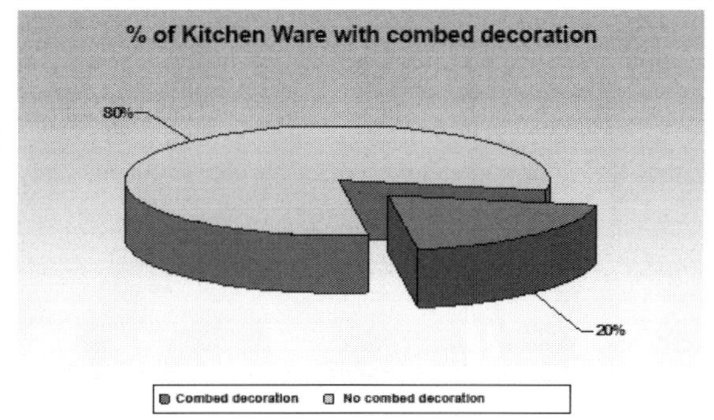

Graph XV_ % of kitchen ware fragments characterised by combed decoration.

Acroma Depurata and Acroma Selezionata: Types

As for the kitchenware, the typological analysis of the table and storage ware entailed comparing the materials found during surface surveys with those from excavations (Table IV). At Casa Andreoni, too, the closed forms ascribable to a specific typology include large numbers of Type 1 jugs, characterized by a thickened strap handle set on the edge. The mouth widths range from 8 to 9 cm, whilst the handles are between 4 and 5 cm wide and 1 cm thick (Pl. CVI, nos 1-2). Also well documented is the Type 2 juglet with a band-shaped rim, 1 specimen of which was found in context 103 in association with materials dating to the late 8th to late 9th centuries (Pl. CVI, no. 3). Various strap handles, some with a central thickening and some thinner, clearly belong to these types of jugs (Pl. CVII, nos 2-4, 6-8 and Pl. CVIII, no. 7). The frequency with which individual fragments of handles with these characteristics were found during surveys and excavations led us to date 2 specimens using thermoluminescence: one fairly broad thin strap handle which may also belong to a small amphora (Pl. CVII, no. 2) and a simple strap handle which can be ascribed to a jug (Pl. CVII, no. 4). The first sample was dated to AD 795±70 and the second to AD 815±60.

Type 1 and especially Type 2 small amphorae are also well documented; the latter has a conical neck and a handle which may be either thin and strap-shaped or

Types	MNI from field survey	MNI from excavation
Jug, Type 1	12	2 (SU 101)
Jug, Type 4	4	1 (SU 103)
Small amphora, Type 1	3	
Small amphora, Type 2	6	1 (SU 103)
Large jug, Type 1	2	1 (SU 103)
Basin, Type 1		1 (SU 605)

Table IV_ Main types in acroma depurata and selezionata from the field survey and excavation.

slightly thickened with longitudinal grooves (Pl. CVI, nos 5-6). A specimen belonging to this typology, found in the levelling layer context 103, was subjected to thermoluminescence dosimetry and dated to AD 850±65 (Pl. CVII, no. 1). Also present at Casa Andreoni is the type of wide-mouthed jar with an everted rim and wide mouth measuring between 19 and 20 cm. The morphological structure of the rim allows us to distinguish between two possible variants, one with a virtually plain lip and one with a thickened lip (Pl. CVI, nos 7-8). Another specimen is documented in context 103, allowing us to date this form to between the 8th and 9th centuries (Pl. CVII, no. 5). Wide-mouthed jars similar to our specimen were found at Santa Maria della Scala in contexts of the 7th-8th century[76] and at Montarrenti in 10th- to 11th-century phases.[77]

As at Podere Serratone, the bases of closed forms are flat with gently or fairly flaring walls 1 cm thick. Large forms such as small amphorae or wide-mouthed jars have a diameter of 19-20 cm (Pl. CVII, nos 9-10) whilst jugs have a diameter of 12-13 cm (Pl. CVIII, no. 1). A form not found at Serratone is the basin with an inturning rim flattened on the upper surface, attested by a single specimen from context 605 where it is associated with materials from the 8th-9th centuries, including a Type 2 small amphora. The mouth of this typology measures about 15 cm in diameter (Pl. CVIII, no. 8). Small basins of identical morphology to that

[76] Cantini 2005a, p.98, Pl.10, no.4.32.
[77] Cantini 2003, p.126, Pl.26, II.7.3.

Fig.6_ Ceramic classes documented in the four surface scatters composing the early medieval site of Casa Andreoni.

from Casa Andreoni are attested at Santa Maria della Scala in contexts of the first half of the 7th century.[78]

Kitchen ware: Types

Compared to Podere Serratone, the cooking pots belonging to the kitchenware repertoires at Casa Andreoni present a greater morphological variety with at least five different typologies as opposed to three at Serratone (Table V). As already mentioned, some forms were probably purchased from among the products made at the kiln on the Rispescia river; the remainder can be ascribed to other workshops not yet identified in the field but which must have been nearby given the similarities in the geological materials used.

Belonging to the Serratone repertoire are the specimens of Type 1 cooking pot (Pl. CVIII, no. 5 and Pl. CIX, no. 7) and Type 2 cooking pot, whose fabrics have been shown to be identical to those from the production site. Alongside these types are another three which have in common a very everted edge. Type 4 has an everted and thickened rim and exists in two versions of different size: one with a narrow mouth measuring about 12 cm (Pl. CIX, no. 2) and one with a rim measuring between 18 and 19 cm in diameter (Pl. CIX, nos 1, 3 and CVIII, no. 9). This typology finds close parallels with cooking pots found at Montarrenti and dating to the long period between the 8th and 11th centuries,[79] and at Santa Maria della Scala in Siena dating to between the second half of the 7th and the 8th century.[80] More rare is Type 5, represented by a single specimen with a short and very everted rim measuring 15 cm in diameter (Pl. CIX, no. 6). Similar cooking pots again come from layers of the second half of the 7th and 8th century at Santa Maria della Scala.[81] Type 6

Types	**Minimum number of individuals from field survey**	**Minimum number of individuals from excavation**
Cooking pot, Type 1	3	1
Cooking pot, Type 2	4	
Cooking pot, Type 4	4	1
Cooking pot, Type 5	1	
Cooking pot, Type 6	3	2
Jug, Type 2	1	
Handled coking-pan	1	1
Bowl-lid, Type 1	2	2

Table V_ Main types in kitchen ware from field survey and excavation.

is well documented; it has a fairly everted rim, rounded lip and barely visible internal ledge (Pl. CIX, nos 4-5 and Pl. CVIII no. 2). This typology also exists in a second version which differs for the slightly concave profile of the upper surface of the rim (Pl. CVIII, no. 3). The mouths have a diameter of between 13 and 16 cm. The presence of at least 2 specimens in context 103 helps to date this type to between the late 8th and late 9th century. However, it should be noted that this was an extremely successful version which continues to be attested systematically in 10th-century contexts, as revealed by the numerous minimum individuals found at the village of Poggio Cavolo in layers dated to the second half of this century.

As at Serratone, Type 1 bowl-lids with an inturning rim and flat upper edge continue to be well documented among the open forms. At Casa Andreoni, however, 2 of the 4 specimens of this type have a light combed decoration on the outer surface of the body and the upper surface of the edge (Pl. CVIII, no. 4 and Pl. CIX, no. 9). The fabric (G 33) and formal properties of the 2 undecorated specimens allow us to ascribe them to the workshop at Podere Serratone (Pl. CVIII, no. 6). The rim diameter, 17-18 cm, is also compatible with the products of this kiln. By contrast, the specimens with a combed decoration have much wider mouths, between 22 and 24 cm, compatible with a use as casseroles.

[78] Cantini 2005a, p.100, Pl.12, no.4.5.2.
[79] Cantini 2003, p.93, Pl.10, no.I.7.24.
[80] Cantini 2005a, p.143, Pl.30, no.5.75.
[81] *Ibidem*, p.146, Pl.33, no.5.106.

Despite the similarities between their fabrics and those used at the kiln on the Rispescia river they were probably made at another production site given the differences in morphology and decorations. A combed bowl-lid from context 103 was subjected to thermoluminescence analysis and dated to AD 855±55 (Pl. CVIII, no. 4). Finally, we should note a type of pan with a rim flat on the upper surface with a diameter of 24 cm, and a small horizontal handle set immediately beneath the rim (Pl. CIX, no. 8).

9.2.5. *The Eighth- and Ninth-Century Pottery Contexts at Alberese and Casa Steccaia*

The surface contexts intercepted at Alberese and Casa Steccaia are two interesting case studies for the analysis of pottery consumption during the 8th and 9th centuries at settlements with a smaller population than the two villages discussed above. These sites are an apparently isolated farmstead at the foot of the Monti dell'Uccellina, a short distance from the Ombrone river, and a small nucleated site identified in the upper Osa valley consisting of three houses and a probable functional annexe. The small population of these settlements obviously explains the limited quantity of pottery found during surface surveys. However, it is precisely the different size of these two settlements compared to Casa Andreoni and Podere Serratone that allows us to develop some interesting reflections after a careful comparison of their pottery assemblages. The Casa Steccaia context, located in a sub-coastal area at a minimum distance of about 12 km from the village of Podere Serratone, has also provided some important data for the study of the local distribution of the pottery produced here.

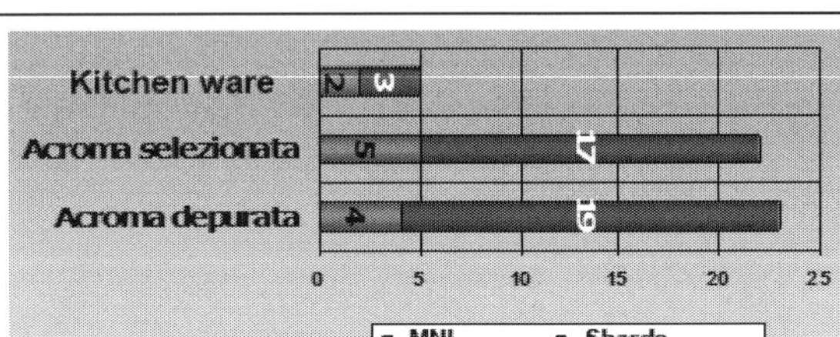

Graph XVI_ Relations between shards and MNI per each ceramic class at Alberese.

The Farmstead at Alberese: the Pottery Context

Only a fairly small amount of material was collected during the two surface surveys carried out at the site, a total of only 39 fragments and a minimum of 11 forms.

Despite this, the proportions of these belonging to different pottery classes and the various functional forms attested provide some interesting information. First, we again noted the predominance of *acroma depurata* and *acroma selezionata* wares over coarsewares, even more marked here with 81% of minimum forms and as much as 92% of the total fragments (Graph XVI). Almost half of the table and

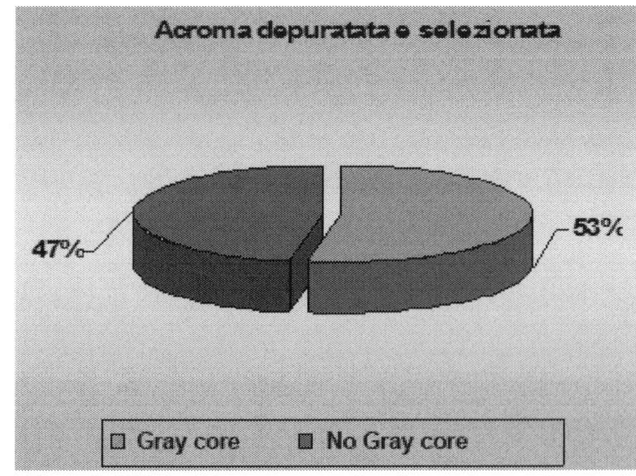

Graph XVII_ % gray core in the acroma depurata and selezionata wares at Alberese.

Fabric	Shards	MNI
Sel 30	18	5
AD 30	18	4
G31	2	1
G32	1	1

Table VI_ Fabrics/MNI at Alberese.

storage wares present a grey core in the fracture, in line with the trend observed at Podere Serratone (Graph XVII). On the basis of the reconstruction proposed after the analysis of the surface materials, the domestic repertoire in use at a small-medium context such as this may have consisted of 7 jugs, 2 small amphorae and 2 cooking pots. Interestingly, here, as at Serratone, the walls of some jugs made of purified/selected fabrics present traces of fumigation, proof that this form was often used for cooking. The morphological analysis and above all that of the fabrics suggests that the entire repertoire in use at this site was almost certainly purchased from the production context of Podere Serratone, only 8 km away (Table VI).

The Settlement of Casa Steccaia: the Pottery Context

The Casa Steccaia settlement has a dispersed topographical layout with three housing modules. These are arranged in two main clusters about 700 m apart on the upper Osa river (Fig.7). We have already discussed the possibility that the function of these sites was to cultivate new lowlying areas of land, easier to exploit and located in the vicinity of a modest road which would have facilitated the transportation of foodstuffs. The analysis of the pottery documented at the various surface features allowed us to determine that these were contemporary and possibly date to the $8^{th}/9^{th}$ centuries on the basis of ceramics of known date. Given the pronounced morphological homogeneity and identical fabrics found at the various features we decided to examine the pottery record from the Casa Steccaia as a group, noting any micro-differences between the various settlement modules on a case by case basis. As shown in Graph XVIII, only a few materials were documented at the three houses intercepted by the survey; however, these provide a glimpse into the nature of pottery consumption. A first

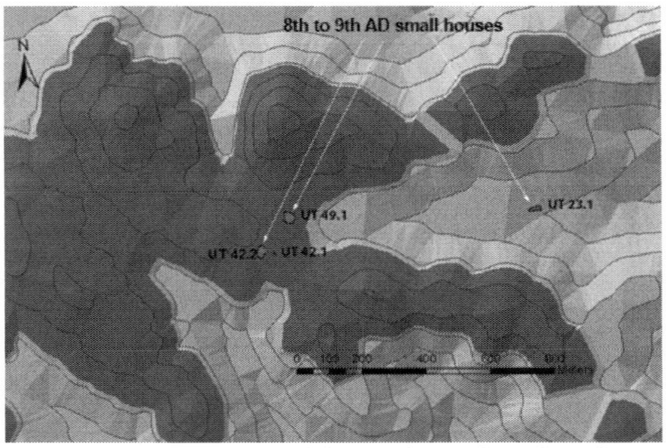

Fig. 7_ Visualisation of the early medieval surface scatters at Casa Steccaia (upper Osa valley).

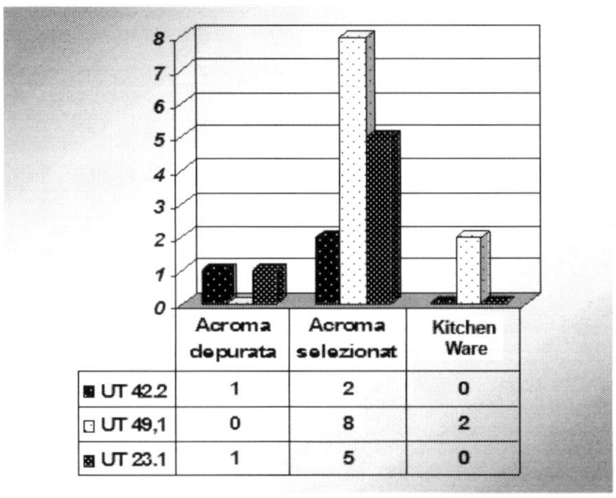

	Acroma depurata	Acroma selezionat	Kitchen Ware
UT 42.2	1	2	0
UT 49,1	0	8	2
UT 23.1	1	5	0

Graph XVIII_ Relations between shards and ceramic classes at Casa Steccaia.

important observation concerns the scarcity of kitchenware, represented exclusively by 2 minimum forms of cooking pots. Table and storage ware thus predominates, with a total of 17 minimum individuals. Among these we should again note the large numbers of jugs and small amphorae, to which we can add the wide-mouthed jug and small bowl with a minimum of 1 individual each (Graph XIX).

Large numbers of fragments again present a grey core in the fracture, in this case around 35% of the total fragments made from purified/selected fabrics. The morphological characteristics of the materials analysed here are similar to those from Podere Serratone and Casa Andreoni with the exception of a minimum of 2 forms, obviously not considered in the overall total of materials from the 8th/9th century found at house 49.1. These are: a jug or tankard whose walls are decorated with a spiral motif which finds close parallels, in terms of fabric and decoration, at Poggio Cavolo in contexts of the 11th/12th century; a cooking pot with a slightly everted thickened and pointed rim and an edge flat on the upper surface with a diameter of 12 cm (Fig.8).[82] These 2 minimum individuals testify to a frequentation of the settlement, at least on an occasional basis, into

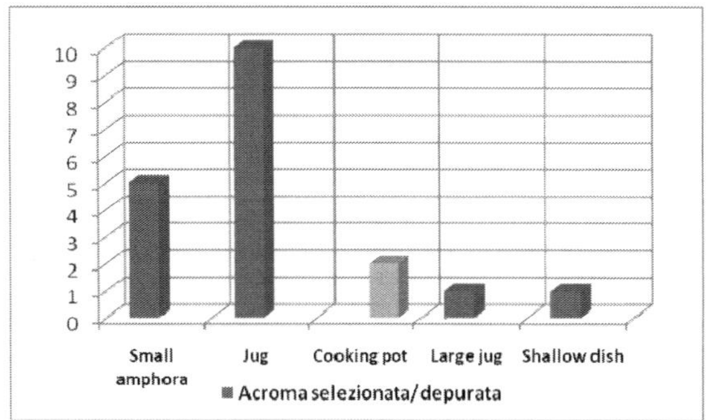

Graph XIX_ Relations between functional forms and ceramic classes: comparative analysis of the surface assemblages at Casa Steccaia.

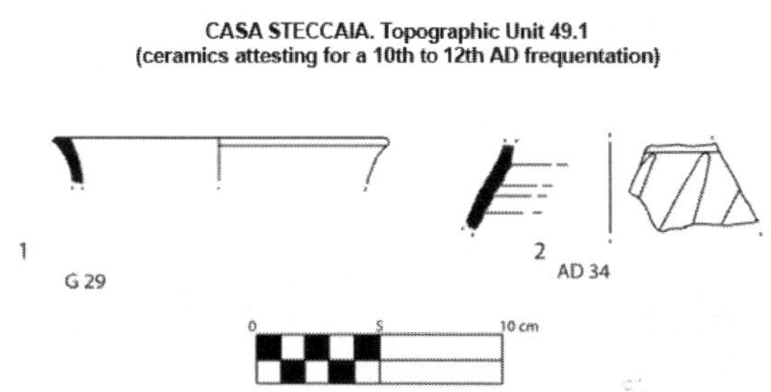

Fig.8_ 10th to 12th centuries AD coarse ware from TU 49.1 at Casa Steccaia.

the central centuries of the Middle Ages. The rest of the material, by contrast, can be dated with a good degree of certainty to between the 8th and 9th centuries. Among the most frequently attested forms are Type 1 jugs (Pl. CX, no. 9), to which we should add a number of handles probably belonging to this form or to small amphorae, made from the fabrics used at Podere Serratone (Pl. CX, nos 1-3, 5, 7-8). Also well documented are Type 1 (Pl. CX, no. 4) and Type 2 amphorae (Pl. CX, nos 6, 12); however, whereas the Type 2 specimens are made of fabrics Sel 30 and Sel 32 from Serratone, the minimum individual belonging to Type 1 is made from a different fabric – similar to AD 33 – which is well documented at Poggio Cavolo in association with materials from the Pisa area and which may be evidence of early contacts. The same fabric is also used to make a specimen of wide-mouthed jug with a short, barely everted and rounded rim; it is impossible to determine the mouth width (Pl. CX, no. 11). This specimen is reminiscent of a type attested at Santa Maria della Scala in a context of the first half of the 7th century.[83] Among the open forms we should note a type of shallow bowl made from a purified fabric and characterized by an externally oblique and receding rim with a diameter of 17 cm and a flat, plain base (Pl. CX, no. 10). Its morphological characteristics make it particularly well-suited to holding sauces or flat breads. As already noted, the scarce kitchenware is represented only by 2 specimens of cooking pots; their typology was impossible to determine given the fragmentary nature of the pieces.

[82] At Montarrenti, this type is dated to between the 10th and 11th centuries AD; see Cantini 2003, p.101, Pl.15, no.I.7.60.

[83] Cantini 2005a, p.97, Pl.9, no.4.29.

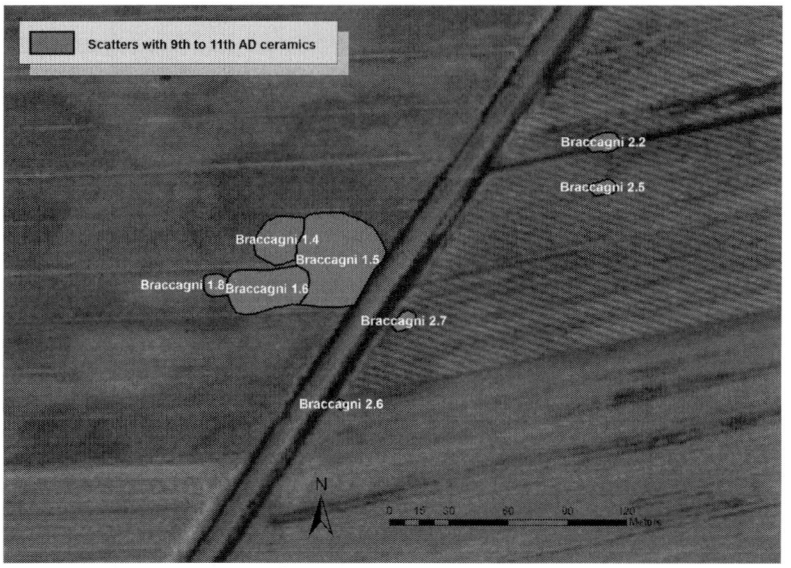

Fig.9_ Surface scatters with medieval occupation at San Martino de plano.

9.2.6. The Site of San Martino De Plano During the High Middle Ages: the Pottery Indicators

San Martino in Piano allows us to undertake a valuable comparison between the picture of pottery consumption between late Antiquity and the Middle Ages emerging from surface pottery and that emerging from the recalibration of these data after rescue excavations. Given the importance of this comparison it is worth outlining the interpretative picture for early medieval pottery before and after excavations. The settlement of San Martino *de plano*, at the foot of Montepescali castle, presents numerous similarities with the settlement at Aiali. Both contexts were larger during the Roman and late antique phases than during the Middle Ages, with a possible interruption in settlement between the late 6th/early 7th and 9th century. However, it should be noted that in the case of San Martino *de plano* the surface survey brought to light a few pottery indicators possibly suggesting that the site continued to be frequented during the early Middle Ages, though in an ephemeral and occasional way. The analysis of the ceramic materials allowed us to identify a minimum of at least 45 forms definitely belonging to a chronological horizon between the later part of the early Middle Ages and the central centuries of this period; its surface distribution, in association with stone blocks and bricks, allows us to estimate that a total area of about 3470 m^2 was occupied at this time (Fig.9).

The Possible Frequentation of the Site Between the Eighth and Ninth Centuries: the Limited Surface Pottery Evidence

A comparative study suggests that, of the minimum of 45 forms dating to the medieval period, at least 3 individuals appear to be ascribable to phases of the 8th and 9th centuries. These include a specimen of wide-mouthed jug with an everted, thickened and rounded rim, presenting a wavy decoration on both the inner and outer surface of the edge (Pl. CXI, no. 8). This typology, not documented in contexts of the late 9th-11th century in the study area, finds close parallels with a specimen attested in layers of the second half of the 7th/8th century at Santa Maria della Scala in Siena.[84] A small strap handle, made from one of the fabrics in use at Podere Serratone (AD 30), can be ascribed to the period between the mid-8th and the mid-9th century. The morphology of this handle resembles that of some variants of the Type 1 jug, frequently attested especially at Serratone and Casa Andreoni (Pl. CXI, no. 11). The cooking pot with a short, everted and barely thickened rim measuring 15 cm in diameter and made from fabric G34 used at the Serratone workshop is identical to Type 5 from Casa Andreoni (Pl. CXII, no. 8).

Naturally a mere 3 minimum forms are insufficient evidence to state with certainty that the context of San Martino *de plano* continued to be occupied even during the early Middle Ages. Here, as in many other cases, identifying traces from the 8th and 9th centuries is extremely difficult on the basis of surface surveys alone. Subsequent excavations, albeit limited in duration, demonstrated that the site was occupied at least during the 9th century whilst for the 8th century the evidence is still inconclusive. Despite this we should stress that excavations in Area 4000 stopped short at the 9th-century layers; these cover layers which have not yet been excavated but which, given the characteristics of the few pottery materials visible at the interface but not collected, might suggest a longer continuity of use of at least part of the site during the High Middle Ages.

[84] *Ibidem*, p.98, Pl.10, no.4.34.

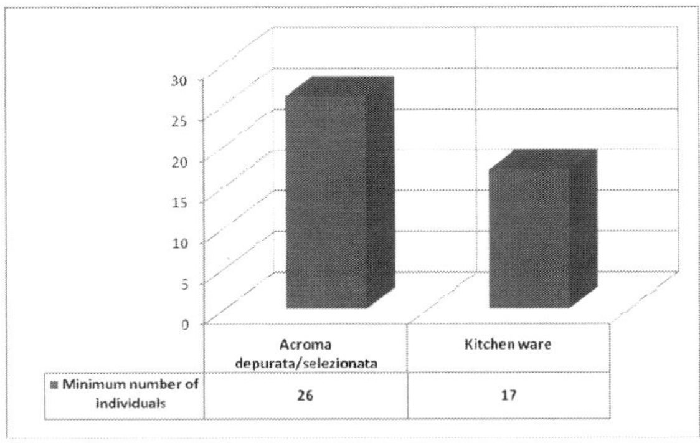

Graph XX_ MNI and medieval ceramic classes at San Martino de plano.

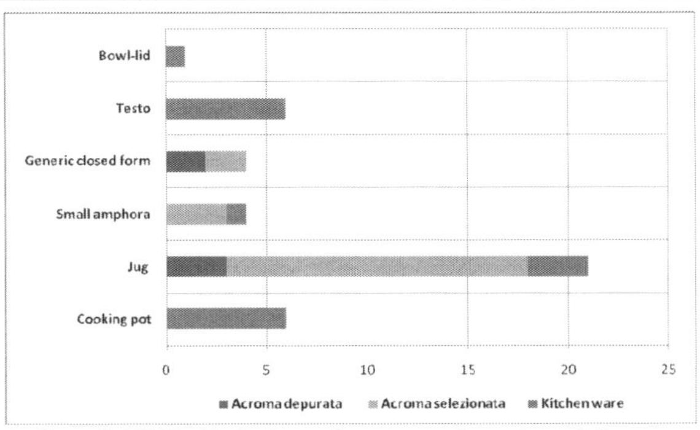

Graph XXI_ Relations between functional forms and ceramic classes in the late 9th to 11th ceramic assemblages at San Martino de plano.

The Late Ninth- to Eleventh-Century Phases: the Pottery Indicators

A far larger number of surface pottery finds belonged to the chronological horizon between the late 9th/early 10th and the 11th century, with at least 42 minimum forms. Although the sample analysed here may not actually be representative of pottery consumption at the site during this phase, we can nonetheless extrapolate some interesting features of help in developing an initial reconstruction hypothesis for the contents of the repertoires and acquiring new data on the local circulation of pottery. It is worth noting that 90% of the pottery was made using fabrics already documented at the hilltop site of Poggio Cavolo. Another two fabrics – Sel 45 and AD 41 – used to make generic closed forms for table/storage use and absent at Poggio Cavolo are well attested among the *acroma depurata* and *acroma selezionata* wares dating to between the late 9th and the 11th century from the Poggettone site in the hilly Vetulonia area. Only fabric AD 45, used to make a single closed specimen, appears to represent a novelty with respect to the other contexts studied. Assuming that this is not a distortion induced by the sample itself, the material examined presents a degree of imbalance between table/storage wares, with about 62% of specimens, and kitchenware, with 38% of the total individuals (Graph XX). The presence of the grey core in the fracture is also limited, being documented in 24% of all fragments of *depurata* and *selezionata* ware. The technological standards indicated by the materials seem to be in line with other contexts, with only wheel-made pottery being found. Also important is the clear separation between the pottery repertoires for table/storage use and those reserved for cooking. This appears to be a characteristic feature of the period between the late 9th and the 11th century, to the extent that it represents a distinctive factor with respect to the $8^{th}/9^{th}$ centuries, when forms in *acroma depurata* or *acroma selezionata* were also used to cook or heat liquid foods (Graph XXI).

ACROMA DEPURATA AND ACROMA SELEZIONATA WARES

The repertoire of table/storage ware consists exclusively of closed forms like jugs and small amphorae, which served all the functions of storing foodstuffs and probably consuming liquid substances. The jug is the single most common form, with at least 15 specimens in *acroma selezionata* and 3 in *acroma depurata* ware. The most common typology has an everted plain rim, rounded edge and thin strap handle level with the rim, 5 cm wide and 1 cm thick (Pl. CXI, nos 1-3). These jugs are similar to the specimens which appear at Poggio Cavolo between the late 10th and the early 11th century. Also attested are another two versions which have an everted rim with a pointed edge (Pl. CXI, no. 5) and a thickened strap handle set on a rim slightly concave on the inside (Pl. CXI, nos 4, 6). The latter version presents close parallels with the jugs typical of the "Galli Tassi Phase III" pottery repertoire from Lucca, in use between the late 8th/early 9th and the early years of the 11th century.[85] Overall the width of the mouths ranges from 9 to 11 cm, whilst the handles are on average 5 cm wide and between 0.8 and 1.3 cm thick (Pl. CXI, nos 9-10, 12). The bases are always flat and may be burnished on the outside (Pl. CXI, no. 14) or unfinished (Pl. CXI, no. 13).

The presence of small amphorae is signalled almost exclusively by large fragments of strap handles, on average 6-6.5 cm wide with thickened edges and longitudinal grooves, similar to those of the forms identified in the contexts discussed above. The plain rounded rim of a single specimen is preserved, measuring 12 cm and set on a cylindrical neck. It presents three light horizontal grooves on the outside, whilst the inside was burnished using a stick (Pl. CXI, no. 7). In morphological terms this specimen is very similar to a two-handled form from Mola di Monte Gelato, belonging to productions in use between the late 9th/early 10th and the early 12th century.[86]

KITCHEN WARE

Alongside vessels specifically intended for cooking foods (cooking pots, *testi* and bowl-lids), we also found vessels for the storage of foodstuffs (small amphorae)

[85] Ciampoltrini 2004, p.156 and p.154, Fig.5, no.8.
[86] Patterson 1997, p.381, Fig.247, no.101.

and vessels for heating/pouring out liquid foods (jugs); these combine to form a fairly varied repertoire of kitchenware.

The morphological structure of the *acroma grezza* jugs, with an everted rim and strap handle set level with the rim, is identical to that of specimens made of purified and selected fabrics; the width of the mouths is also identical, between 9 and 12 cm (Pl. CXII, nos 1-3). The only specimen of small amphora or large jug is represented by a fragment of a thickened strap handle, 6 cm wide and 1.3 cm thick.

The range of cooking pots, consisting of forms with a mouth width between 13 and 16 cm, comprises at least five main versions. The first has a markedly everted rim and rounded lip and is comparable to artefacts of the late 9th/early 10th century from Grosseto (Pl. CXII, no. 4).[87] The two types with a fairly flaring rim of pseudo-rectangular section, with a rounded or externally oblique lip, are similar to wares from contexts of the second half of the 10th century at Poggio Cavolo (Pl. CXII, nos 5-6). Also resembling forms in use at the village of Poggio Cavolo, this time between the late 10th and early 11th century, are the two versions with a strongly flaring rim and pointed lip (Pl. CXII, no. 7)[88] and a barely everted and rounded rim (Pl. CXII, no. 9).

At least two types of *testi* are present: that with a plain rounded rim, common between the 10th and the 11th century at Poggio Cavolo (Pl. CXII, no. 12) and the other with a slightly thinned rim set on a strongly flaring wall (Pl. CXII, nos 10-11, 13), already documented at Poggettone. The mouth widths range from 20 to 25 cm; the bases are generally plain and flat, although a version which is shaped on the inside is also documented.

The bowl-lid appears in a version with fairly flaring walls and a rim flattened on the upper surface measuring 19 cm in diameter and presenting three light grooves on the outside (Pl. CXII, no. 14). This form is made from a fabric (G57) generally associated with cooking pots and is comparable to specimens of the second half of the 10th century from Poggio Cavolo[89].

Ninth Century Pottery Contexts and Residual Late Antique Finds From Area 4000

Area 4000 yielded the vast majority of the pottery recovered during the 2008 rescue excavations at San Martino in Piano. The clear stratigraphic sequences allowed us to identify at least two phases of the construction and use of an open space interpreted as a *platea*; its abandonment layers, contexts 4010 and 4002 (see above), yielded pottery dated to between the 9th and early 10th century[90] and to between the late 10th and 11th century respectively on the basis of comparisons with materials from Tuscan excavations and some contexts outside the region. Thanks to the good quality of the stratigraphy and the typological changes characterizing the transition between the pottery assemblages of context 4010 and context 4002 we were able to propose a fairly accurate sequence for the pottery vessels in use at the site between the 9th and 11th centuries.

In this study we have decided to focus on the main 9th- and early 10th-century context 4010, subsequently extending our analysis to the smaller quantity of materials from context 4009. This was probably a levelling for the construction of the second *platea* which reused materials from context 4010 that can also be dated to between the 9th and 10th centuries.

As we will see below, one very interesting feature apparently characteristic of the early medieval contexts of San Martino in Piano is the large quantity of residual materials dating mainly to the 5th and 6th centuries. The rescue excavation concentrated mainly on the areas which, according to surface surveys, held features of the Roman and medieval periods, and only partially covered those belonging to the late antique reoccupation; nonetheless, judging from the size of the surface scatters, the latter must have covered a large area.

Alongside Area 6000, a few metres to the east of Area 5000, where late Roman levels were uncovered but not excavated, and Area 3000, where the two 5th/6th-century burials were studied, significant confirmation of the large-scale occupation of the site between the 4th and 6th centuries comes from residual materials in the early medieval layers. Whilst awaiting more extensive excavations, these residual materials provide a partial confirmation of the site's vigour during late Antiquity and its integration into the overseas trade system, already demonstrated by the archaeological survey.

Going on to deal in depth with the materials from context 4010, we see a marked preponderance of wares made from purified and selected fabrics. These two classes are documented respectively with 481 fragments weighing 6440 grammes and equivalent to a minimum number of 43 forms and with 46 fragments weighing 1219 grammes corresponding to a minimum number of 10 individuals. By contrast, kitchenware is attested with a total of 26 fragments weighing 510

[87] Valdambrini 2006, p.46, Pl.6, no.2.
[88] Materials processed by the author and precisely dated through the association with Sparse Glaze Ware B imported from *Latium*.
[89] See Vaccaro-Salvadori 2006 for comparisons.

[90] We have suggested a date between the 9th and early 10th century AD for context 4010 in light of generic comparisons with pottery from the sites of Podere Serratone and Casa Andreoni (8th to 9th century AD) and from unpublished contexts at the hilltop site of Poggio Cavolo which can be dated to before the mid-10th century on the basis of the stratigraphic sequence.

grammes and equivalent to a minimum of only 6 forms (Graph XXII).[91]

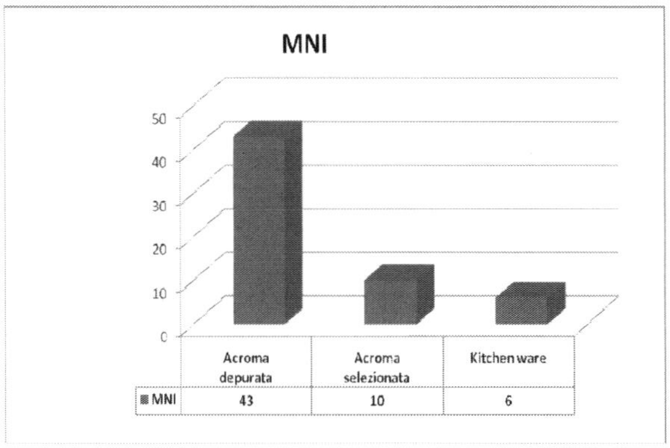

Graph XXII_ Minimum number of individuals (MNI) and ceramic classes documented in the 9th century AD context 4010 at San Martino de plano.

To these we should add the residual materials: a minimum of 1 form of African red slip ware, a Tunisian amphora, a few fragments of unidentifiable amphorae and some walls belonging to *ingobbiata di rosso* vessels.

The other context discussed here – context 4009 – yielded a far smaller quantity of materials but is equally interesting since it marks the transition from the 9th/early 10th-century phase to that of the late 10th/11th century. The characteristics of the pottery assemblages are identical to those from context 4010 with some interesting residual finds from the 5th and 6th centuries.

In this context, too, *acroma depurata* is the most commonly attested class with 35 fragments weighing 1040 grammes in total and equivalent to a minimum of 9 forms; this is followed by *acroma selezionata* ware with 8 fragments weighing 220 grammes and corresponding to a minimum of 4 individuals. Finally, kitchenware is once again present in smaller quantities, with 4 fragments weighing 150 grammes and corresponding to a minimum of only 3 forms. The predominance of *acroma depurata* and *acroma selezionata* wares, destined mainly for use at table, for storage and transport, over kitchenware was already clear in the 8th- and 9th-century contexts at Podere Serratone, Casa Andreoni, Casa Steccaia and Alberese but at San Martino the primacy of the former two classes over the latter becomes overwhelming. This trend seems to continue into the late 10th and 11th centuries, although the contexts of this period have not yet been systematically studied. The reasons for the absolute dominance of purified and selected pottery, which appears to be in some ways exceptional among the 8th- to 10th-century contexts excavated in Tuscany, should perhaps be sought in different food consumption practices at this settlement due to specific productive specializations and perhaps the wider availability of these pottery classes on the local market.

The latter factor should be evaluated in particular in light of the close analogies between the most common type of jug found at San Martino in Piano, made from both selected and purified fabrics, and a similar form for table and storage use widely attested in the neighbouring Roccastrada area; however in the latter these materials have been dated to a much earlier 6th/7th-century phase.[92] Although the chronology of the one-handled jugs with a band-shaped rim recovered during the survey in the Roccastrada area, along the upper and middle Bruna valley, should be post-dated by at least two centuries, their frequent attestation in this area suggests the presence here of hitherto unidentified production structures. The large-scale availability of these materials *in loco* may thus have contributed at least in part to the imbalance between the pottery classes in favour of *acroma depurata* and *acroma selezionata* wares.

As at other early medieval contexts, we observed a significant simplification of the pottery repertoires at San Martino in Piano, translating into the presence of only a few functional forms: the jug, the basin and the small amphora for use at table and for storage and perhaps also the transport of foodstuffs, and the cooking pot for cooking. By contrast, we found no obvious evidence that table/storage ware forms such as jugs served a variety of purposes; at other contexts like Podere Serratone these sometimes appear to have been used for cooking or heating liquid or semi-liquid foods.

As concerns the technology used to manufacture *acroma depurata* and *acroma selezionata* wares, we identified 6 slightly different fabrics (3 purified and 3 selected); however, since identical typologies are made using different fabrics, these may have been used by one or more small workshops operating at a local or sub-regional scale which obtained their clay from the same quarries. The vessels were all made on the fast wheel and fired in an oxidizing atmosphere. Among the *acroma depurata* wares firing defects resulting from the failure to maintain a constant temperature inside the furnace and leading to the presence of a grey core are extremely rare, with only a minimum of 2 forms of the 43 found in context 4010. This "sandwich" fabric is attested far more widely among *acroma selezionata* wares, with as many as 9 out of 10 minimum individuals presenting this defect. The proportions are similar in context 4009, where only 2 of the 9 forms in *acroma depurata* have a grey core compared to 3 out of 4 forms in *acroma selezionata*. The pottery materials

[91] The calculation of the MNI (minimum number of individuals) is based on the analysis of all diagnostic fragments (rims, bases, handles); however, we also counted and weighed all the wall fragments for a more comprehensive data record.

[92] Guideri 2000, p.14, Pl.II. As already noted, some of what were thought to be 6th- and 7th-century ceramic assemblages from the Roccastrada area are probably later in date (7th-9th century) in light of the new data from stratified contexts in southern Tuscany, such as Casa Andreoni and San Martino in Piano.

are generally of high quality and present no surface finishings: the surface whitening and burnishing which seem to be typical of the 10th-century materials from the hilltop sites of Poggio Cavolo and Capalbiaccio are completely absent.[93]

Going into further detail on the forms documented among the *acroma depurata* and *acroma selezionata* wares we should note the predominance of the jug, with a minimum of 19 forms in context 4010 and 2 in context 4009, and at least five different typologies. The first type, by far the most common with a minimum of at least 14 individuals, is characterized by a band-shaped rim, slightly concave on the inside, and a strap handle which is generally but not invariably thickened, set about 2 mm beneath the rim. All the specimens documented have flat bases (Pl. CXIII, nos 1-3). This type finds close parallels at the aforementioned surface contexts in the Roccastrada area, especially the sites of Podere Serratone and Casa Andreoni between the Ombrone and Osa valleys. These points of comparison provide valuable evidence on the basis of which to establish the chronology of San Martino Type 1: identical artefacts from the settlement of Casa Andreoni have been dated to between the late 8th and late 9th century using thermoluminescence dosimetry.

Type 1 is the most successful typology, and is made from both purified and selected fabrics; the other types are made exclusively from purified fabrics and are documented with only a single minimum individual each.

Type 2 has an everted and barely thickened rim, and a strap handle set level with the edge and presenting three grooves (Pl. CXIII, no. 4); it generically resembles specimens from contexts of the mid-7th to 9th centuries at Montarrenti.[94]

Type 3 has a slightly thickened, rounded and gently everted rim and a strap handle set level with the edge, measuring about 4 cm in width (Pl. CXIII, no. 5). It is comparable to 9th-century materials from Santa Maria della Scala in Siena.[95]

Type 4 has a gently everted rim and a strap handle with light longitudinal grooves set on the edge. This type is similar to Type 2, although the handle inclines downwards more markedly (Pl. CXIII, no. 6).

Finally, Type 5 has a narrower mouth than the typologies described above; the fairly narrow handle is again set on the rim but is more incurved than in the other specimens (Pl. CXIII, no. 7). It presents some similarities with a jug attested in 10th-century phases at the village of Campiglia Marittima (Livorno).[96]

A particularly successful form at San Martino, as at other 8th/9th century sites in southern Tuscany, is the small two-handled amphora, documented with a minimum of at least 8 forms in context 4010 and 2 in context 4009; most of these are made from purified and selected fabrics, although a coarseware specimen was also found. Of particular importance is San Martino's inclusion in the network of medieval hilltop and lowlying sites to have yielded specimens of two-handled amphorae dating to between the 8th and the 11th.[97] We believe that these forms were not used exclusively to store foodstuffs for the subsistence of individual sites. Given their medium-small size, flat or slightly convex base, globular body and two broad handles, they may also have served to transport goods (probably wine and oil) on a local and perhaps sub-regional scale. The attestation of these forms at San Martino thus implies that the site formed part of a trade circuit for foodstuffs carried in small amphorae and covering a fairly large area of southern Tuscany between the Val di Cornia to the north and the Valle del Melone to the south, between the High Middle Ages and the central centuries of the Middle Ages. Three fairly distinctive types of small amphora are documented at San Martino. The first type, shown in Pl. CXIV, nos 2, 4, has a fairly thickened strap handle set between the shoulder and the short neck; the rim, preserved in only one specimen, is band-shaped and reminiscent of the rims of Type 1 jugs, but more everted. This type is fairly similar, especially for the characteristics of the shoulder, neck and handles, to the late 8th- to late 9th-century specimens from the sites of Podere Serratone and Casa Andreoni. The type shown in Pl. CXIV, no. 1 appears to be a variant; it is larger, with massive and markedly incurved handles. Finally, we found a specimen which has a narrow neck (6 cm in diameter) and handles of circular section presenting a longitudinal groove; this specimen currently presents no analogies with known materials from other early medieval contexts in southern Tuscany (Pl. CXIV, no. 3).

The repertoire of table and storage ware is completed by a single *acroma depurata* basin characterized by an incurving rim flattened on the upper surface and a mouth measuring about 25 cm (Pl. CXIII, no. 8). It is similar to a smaller version from the 8th/9th-century contexts at Casa Andreoni.

The kitchenware attested in contexts 4010 and 4009 consists exclusively of closed forms made on the fast wheel: these include 2 Type 1 jugs, similar to the specimens in *acroma depurata* and *acroma selezionata* ware, a small amphora and 6 cooking pots of which

93 Vaccaro 2009.
94 Cantini 2003, p.125, Pl.25, no.II.6.2.
95 Cantini 2005a, p.95, Pl.7, no.4.14.
96 Grassi 2006, p.464, Fig.4, no.18.
97 See Vaccaro 2009 for an up-to-date picture of the distribution of small amphorae in southern Tuscany.

only 4, with rim widths ranging from 14 to 15 cm, can be assigned to a specific typology.

The specimens in Pl. CXIV, nos 6-7 seem to belong to the same typology, characterized by an everted and rounded rim, in one case with a light groove on the outside. This type is well documented in the 8th/9th-century phases at Casa Andreoni and at San Pietro in Grosseto in contexts of the second half of the 8th/early 9th century.[98] The cooking pot with a flat upwardly inclined rim, thickened internally at the junction with the neck (Pl. CXIV, no. 8) is generically similar to a type attested at the village of Campiglia Marittima in phases of the 9th/10th century.[99] Finally, the cooking pot with an everted rim, slightly thickened on the outside and almost flat on the upper surface (Pl. CXIV, no. 5), finds a close point of comparison in the late 9th/early 10th-century levels at San Pietro in Grosseto.[100]

As already noted, both contexts 4010 and 4009 yielded interesting residual materials from the 5th and 6th centuries which help to determine the chronology of the late antique occupation of San Martino. Production D African red slip ware, abundant among the surface finds, is documented by a single minimum form of Hayes 61B/Bonifay Sigillée type 38 B2 (Pl. CXIV, no. 12) dated to the first half of the 5th century, and by a Hayes 99 A bowl with an almond-shaped rim dating to the late 5th/mid-6th century (Pl. CXIV, no. 13). A specimen of Tunisian amphora, with a slight surface whitening, thickened and gentle everted rim and a slightly hooked edge can be identified as a Keay 62A (Pl. CXIV, no. 9), a type recently dated to the first half of the 6th century.[101] The 2 minimum specimens of LR1 amphorae come from the eastern Mediterranean and more specifically from Cilicia given the properties of the fabric; these are represented by two handles which, given the differences in the typical ridges, cannot belong to a single specimen (Pl. CXIV, nos 10-11). The morphological structure of the handles suggests that these are variants dating to the 6th rather than the 5th century.[102]

9.3. Final Remarks on Pottery Consumption and the Local Distribution of Pottery Between the Eighth and Ninth Centuries

As we have already noted on several occasions, the pottery repertoires in use between the 8th and 9th centuries underwent a marked selection process in favour of a few forms able to meet all the needs of cooking and food preparation and the storage of foodstuffs. By contrast we have no definitive evidence for the use of open forms like flat-based dishes and large deep dishes for the consumption of food at table. Also limited is the use of basins with incurving rims; these may have been used to hold and prepare food rather than for its consumption. It should be noted that in the rural contexts of this area, from as early as the 6th century, we see a gradual decline in the use of pottery vessels for fish or meat courses, indicating that a transformation in eating habits was already underway. The most obvious difference with respect to late antique domestic repertoires is thus the disappearance of deep-bodied forms such as large bowls, deep dishes and flanged bowls for use at table and intended for holding and serving liquid and semi-liquid foods. A partial explanation for this may be the use of other materials, such as wood, to manufacture tableware. However, we should note the lack of evidence for this, even where post-depositional conditions are such as to ensure the conservation of perishable materials.[103] It therefore seems more helpful to reflect on the true extent of changes in the foods consumed and above all in eating habits. Small cooking pots, generally measuring no more than 15-16 cm in diameter, are constantly attested at the contexts studied in this chapter. It is possible that the kitchenware specimens, with narrower mouths, were used to boil small pieces of dried meat or to heat flat breads in water or spiced wine to soften them.[104] On the basis of this hypothesis, it is likely that these small cooking pots for individual use were also used directly to consume the foods cooked in them. This may also help to explain the absence of open forms used to serve foods at table.

Alongside the simplification of pottery repertoires we also see a marked standardization of the pottery used, which provides no useful clues on the basis of which to differentiate between the socio-economic status of consumers. Coarseware, widespread in the area between the 8th and 9th centuries, remains of fairly high quality but does not allow us to grasp any fundamental differences in access to locally available wares on the part of the sites analysed. The absence of fineware and of imported products more generally does not allow us to rank contexts hierarchically on the basis of their economic means and capacity to access valuable pottery or imported foodstuffs. The attestation at Casa Andreoni of a single specimen of jug decorated with red stripes, possibly imported from outside the region, only indicates the existence of episodic contacts with other areas. It is therefore of greater interest to attempt to define the trade network at a micro-local and sub-regional level. The coarseware produced at Podere Serratone seems to have been an important source of supply for the settlements identified between the lower Ombrone river and the Osa valley.

98 On Grosseto see Valdambrini 2005, p.46, Pl.6, no.7.

99 Grassi 2003 p.281, Pl.II, no.I.2.1b.

100 Valdambrini 2005, p.46, Pl.6, no.6.

101 Bonifay 2004, p.138, Fig.74, no.5.

102 For the differences between the 5th- and 6th-century variants of the LRA1 documented at Butrint (Albania) see Reynolds 2004a, pp.230-231 and Reynolds 2004c.

103 In Tuscany an interesting instance is the hilltop village of Miranduolo where the excavation of a 10th-century AD storeroom yielded a few fragments of wooden bowls; however, the very small quantities found are insufficient evidence to postulate an exclusive use of these vessels for food consumption. On the finds from Miranduolo see Valenti 2008 (ed.).

104 On the different use of wide-mouthed cooking pots and *pro capite* cooking pots see Giovannini 1998, pp.15-22.

The 9th- and early 10th-century pottery assemblages from San Martino in Piano in the middle Bruna valley, whilst sharing some features with the pottery productions documented at Podere Serratone, clearly indicate the existence of other production centres active on the local scale.

Another open question is whether the widespread attestation of small two-handled amphorae simply reflects the circulation of empty pottery vessels or if their local distribution also indicates a trade in surplus foodstuffs. The attestation of these small 8th/9th-century amphorae, morphologically well-suited to the local transport of liquid foodstuffs such as oil and wine, is important for a study of the area's economy. In this context, the results of the recent application of gas chromatography coupled with mass spectrometry[105] to a Type 2 amphora sample from the Podere Serratone site take on a special importance. Alongside the characteristic markers for the internal coating of *Pinaceae* resin, the archaeometric study identified large quantities of olive oil markers and to a lesser extent wine markers.[106] This tells us that the vessel was used for at least two purposes (holding oil and wine): to store two of the most important liquid foods in use during the Middle Ages. Naturally the archaeometric data are unable to show whether or not the small amphora also had a commercial function; they can only tell us what types of substances it contained. Clearly, our future research agenda should pursue this line of inquiry further, analysing the relationship between early medieval amphorae and the foodstuffs stored inside them on a case by case basis. The informative potential of these pottery vessels is of great importance for the study of the structure and organization of early medieval trade. By combining studies of their morphology and fabric with the spatial distribution of specimens and the analysis of their contents we may be able to gain a clearer picture of the complexity of the circulation of commodities on a micro-regional scale.

---

[105] The archaeometric analysis was carried out by Alessandra Pecci at the Archaeometric Laboratory (University of Siena) in collaboration with the *Centro per le Analisi e Determinazioni Strutturali* (CIADS).

[106] Wine markers are: tartaric acid, cinnamic acid, vanillic acid, hydroxybenzoic acid, succinic acid and anisaldehyde. See also Pecci 2009.

Appendix A. Ceramics from Podere Serratone: types and compared chronologies

Type	Minimum Number of Individuals	Comparisons	Initial date (AD)	Final date (AD)
Small amphora, type2	5	Mola di Monte Gelato (p.381, n.103)	875	1125
		Cencelle (p.181, Fig.3, b)	800	899
		Crypta Balbi, p.296, n.50	700	799
Average date			792	941
Small amphora, type 1	14	Mola di Monte Gelato (p.377, nn.30,31,32)	775	899 d.C
		San Clemente, Rome (p.30, n.7 e p.28, n.9)	775	825
Average date			775	862
Jug, Type 1	36	Mola di Monte Gelato (p.377, nn.41, 51)	775	899
		Santa Maria della Scala (p.95, Tav.7, n.4.11)	650	799
		San Genesio	700	999
		Roccastrada territory (p.14, Tav.II, nn.1-4)	500	699
		Montarrenti (p.125 Tav.25, n.II.6.1)	650	799
Average date			655	839
Jug, Type 2	2	Casa delle Vestali, Rome (p.170, Tav.II, nn.12-13)	500	550
		Mithraeum in the Crypta Balbi, Rome (p.272, Tav. XX, n.113)	575	625
		Aventino, Rome (p.552, Tav.III, n.25)	600	650
		Roccastrada territory (p.17, Tav.5, n.14)	600	799
Average date			550	644
Testo with rounded rim	3	Montarrenti (p.54, Tav.5, n.1.5.7)	900	1099
		Santa Maria della Scala (p.148, Tav.35, n.5.128)	600	650
Average date			750	875
Testo with flattened rim	1	Santa Maria della Scala (p.148, Tav.35, n.5.126)	900	1199
Average date			900	1199
Flanged bowl in acroma depurata imitating the type Hayes 91C in ARS	1	Chronology of the Tunisian prototype and its imitations in the investigated area	520	625
Average date			520	625
Bowl imitating the type Hayes 87B in ARS	1	Chronology of the Tunisian prototype	450	530/ 550
Average date			450	540
Bowl with inverted rim, possibly imitating the type Hayes 61in ARS	3	Santa Maria della Scala (p.94, Tav.6, n.4.3)	550	625
		Chronology of the vessel documented in the territory of Roselle	375	550
Average date			463	587
Bowl-lid with flattened rim	2	Montarrenti (p.83, Tav.4, n.1.3.1)	750	899
		Poggibonsi (p.131, Tav.VII, n.9)	875	925
Average date			813	912

Cooking pot, Type 1	10	Montarrenti (p.91, Tav.9, n.I.7.10)	750	899
		Mola di Monte Gelato (p.379, n. 111)	875	1125
		Santa Maria della Scala (p.146, Tav.33, n.5.101)	550	625
Average date			725	883

Cooking pot, Type 2	2	Montarrenti (p.91, Tav.9, n.I.7.9)	750	899
Average date			750	899

Cooking pot, Type 3	1	Grosseto-San Pietro (p.46, Tav.6, n.5)	750	825
		Santa Maria della Scala (p.143, Tav.30, n.5.77)	475	550
Average date			613	688

Total 81 Minimum Number of Individuals (MNI) which can be assigned to a typology

Appendix B. Surface ceramics from Casa Andreoni: types and compared chronologies

Type	**Minimum Number of Individuals**	**Comparisons**	**Initial date (AD)**	**Final date (AD)**
Jug, Type 2	4	Casa delle Vestali, Rome (p.170, Tav.II, nn.12-13)	500	550
		Mithraeum of the Crypta Balbi, Rome (p.272, Tav. XX, n.113)	575	625
		Aventino, Rome (p.552, Tav.III, n.25)	600	650
		Territory of Roccastrada (p.17, Tav.V, n.14)	600	799
Average date			569	656

Cooking pot, Type 5	1	Santa Maria della Scala (p.146, Tav.33, n.5.106)	650	799
Average date			650	799

Cooking pot, Type 5	4	Montarrenti (p.93, Tav.10, n.I.7.24)	750	1099
		Santa Maria della Scala (p.143, Tav.30, n.5.75)	650	799
Average date			700	949

Cooking pot, Type 2	4	Montarrenti (p.91, Tav.9, n.I.7.9)	750	899
Average date			750	899

Cooking pot, Type 1	3	Montarrenti (p.91, Tav.9, n.I.7.10)	750	899
		Mola di Monte Gelato (p.379, n. 111)	875	1125
		Santa Maria della Scala (p.146, Tav.33, n.5.101)	550	625
Average date			725	883

Cooking pot, Type 6	3	Montarrenti (p.97, Tav.12, n.I.7.42)	750	899
		Grosseto (p.46, Tav.6, nn.1 e 4)	750	825
Average date			750	862

Handle of a closed form in Red Painted Ware	1	Santa Maria della Scala (p.193, Tav.54, n.9.4)	800	899
Average date			800	899

Small amphora, Type 1	3	Mola di Monte Gelato (p.377, nn.30,31,32)	775	899
		San Clemente, Rome (p.30, n.7 e p.28, n.9)	775	825
Average date			775	862

Small amphora, Type 2	6	Mola di Monte Gelato (p.381, n.103)	875	1125
		Cencelle (p.181, Fig.3, b)	800	899
		Crypta Balbi, p.296, n.50	700	799
Average date			792	941

Jug, Type 1	12	Mola di Monte Gelato (p.377, nn.41, 51)	775	899
		Santa Maria della Scala (p.95, Tav.7, n.4.11)	650	799
		San Genesio	700	999
		Territory of Roccastrada (p.14, Tav.II, nn.1-4)	500	699
		Montarrenti (p.125 Tav.25, n.II.6.1)	650	799
Average date			655	839

Bowl-lid with flattened rim	2	Montarrenti (p.83, Tav.4, n.1.3.1)	750	899
		Poggibonsi (p.131, Tav.VII, n.9)	875	925
Average date			813	912

Large jug with everted rim	2	Pisa, Piazza Dante (p.514, n.14)	Late 10th	Mid 12th
		Montarrenti (p.126, Tav.26, II.7.3)	10th	11th
Average date			938	1125

Handled coking pan with flattened rim	1	Poggibonsi (p.133, Tav.IX, nn.1-2)	875	925
Average date			875	925

Bowl with inverted rim, possibly imitating the type Hayes 61 in ARS	1	Santa Maria della Scala (p.94, Tav.6, n.4.3)	550	625
		Chronology of the vessel documented in the territory of Roselle	375	550
Average date			463	587

Total 47 Minimum Number of Individuals (MNI) which can be assigned to a typology

Bibliographical comparisons:

Aventino, Rome = Fontana *et alii* 2004
Casa delle Vestali, Rome = Filippi *et alii* 2004
Cencelle (Latium) = Prandi-Silvestrini 2004
Crypta Balbi (Rome) = Romei 2004
Grosseto, San Pietro (southern Tuscany) = Valdambrini 2005
Mithraeum of the Crypta Balbi, Rome = Saguì-Coletti 2004
Mola di Monte Gelato (Latium) = Patterson 1997
Montarrenti (central Tuscany) = Cantini 2003
Pisa, Piazza Dante (northern Tuscany) = Menchelli 1993
Poggibonsi (central Tuscany) = Valenti 1996
San Clemente, Rome = Mandarini-Paganelli 1998
San Genesio (northern Tuscany) = as per information by F.Cantini
Santa Maria della Scala (central Tuscany) = Cantini 2005a
Roccastrada territory (southern Tuscany) = Guideri 2000a

10. Conclusions: Connecting a Micro-Region to the Wider Western Mediterranean context (AD 300-900)

The analysis of economic and settlement patterns in the study area as a whole provides us with a series of data which need to be understood in a broader context. This context comprises not only the Italian peninsula but also, where appropriate, the western Mediterranean basin as a whole, in order to develop a preliminary historical and geographical interpretative model. Since our study area is located on the coast, we need to investigate relations between local economic systems and the trade in people and goods along Tyrrhenian routes between the 4th and 10th centuries AD and how these changed over time.

Between the 4th and mid-6th century, the study area, like much of the Italian peninsula,[1] saw a gradual decrease in the number of sites attested: the number of villas drops suddenly already after the 3rd century as does that of small scattered dwellings; by contrast, villages and medium-sized settlement clusters which can be interpreted as farmsteads seem more resistant to this process of decline. Property ownership systems seem to indicate a prevalence of large estates managed by the few surviving villas, including those of Talamone and Paduline-Serrata Martini belonging to the imperial landholdings. This landscape of large estates, however, coexisted with medium-sized properties, which from the late Republican period had sprung up between the lands belonging to the villas, thus creating the highly variegated picture typical of this area and, further north, of the *Ager Volterranus*.[2]

In the sub-coastal belt, by contrast, where villas were few and far between even during the period of significant demographic growth between the 2nd century BC and the 1st century AD, villages appear to be the dominant form of settlement. From the time of their foundation, often in the late Republican era, these do not appear to have been subordinate to villas in the population hierarchy. Whilst it is currently impossible to determine their social make-up,[3] and thus to understand if their inhabitants were free or dependent peasants, or more plausibly both, the distance which generally separates these clusters from the villas makes it unlikely that they were inhabited by dependent share-croppers who worked on the large estates.

Between the 4th and 5th centuries the towns of Roselle and Vetulonia continued to develop along different lines, already apparent by the early imperial period: whilst the former maintained its role as an administrative centre with a complex urban topography,[4] Vetulonia appears to have lost its function as a central place and as a magnet for the population of its hinterland between the late 1st century BC and the 1st century AD. During this period, the area around the city saw a marked population decline, counterbalanced by a significant and sudden increase in the number of sites around the western banks of nearby Lake Prile. Although epigraphical evidence tells us that the *municipium* survived up to the early 3rd century AD, the town must have lost its urban nature some centuries previously, with a strong contraction in the area occupied within the wall circuit.[5] The features recently brought to light by excavations in Via Garibaldi[6] clearly show that the main indications of a continuity of settlement lie inside today's village, in an area which cannot have covered more than about 2 hectares in total.

By contrast, mid-4th century Roselle saw the construction of a bath complex within the town but some distance from the Forum,[7] near the Etruscan wall circuit and in the vicinity of one of the city gates along the south-east Roman road, a clear sign of its "openness" towards the surrounding area. The centre of the urban area shows clear signs that at least two important and recently excavated contexts were converted to perform a new function.[8] Between the 4th and the early 5th century the *Domus dei Mosaici*[9] in the southern area of the Forum and the Hadrianic bath complex on the slopes of the north hill see the establishment of workshops involved in the recycling and transformation of scrap metal. This is evidence of the transformation of residential and service areas into manufacturing areas, probably responding to the consumption needs of a community which remained lively. A process of marked transformation of the urban landscape was certainly underway in as early as this period, but the town still maintained a satisfactory level of economic and productive vitality. The ceramic finds from late Roman contexts, found in the workshop established in the Hadrianic baths, indicate not only a supply of Tunisian fineware but above all the considerable variety of Mediterranean foodstuffs reaching the town, including Lusitanian and North

[1] Exceptions, to mention only the most significant examples, are Apulia, which underwent a true phase of economic and demographic growth between the 4th and early 6th century (Volpe 2006); it is also worth noting the exceptional vigour of the villages in the Segesta area of Sicily, again between the 6th and early 7th century (Cambi 2006).

[2] On the territory of Volterra in late Antiquity see Motta 1997 and Terrenato 1998. On this comparison see also Vaccaro 2008.

[3] On the possible social components of late antique *vici* see most recently Vera 2006.

[4] For an overview see Rizzitelli 1999 and Nicosia-Poggesi 1998 (eds).

[5] See Vaccaro 2008 with bibliography.

[6] Çygielman 2006a

[7] De Marinis 1998b.

[8] A full understanding of the dynamics of the transformation of Roselle's urban fabric over the *longue durée* is hindered by the small amounts of published data available and above all by the small number of contexts excavated stratigraphically and with due attention to the late antique and early medieval phases.

[9] Michelucci 1985 .

African fish sauces, possibly Tunisian oil, and eastern wines alongside the wines of *Tuscia* and of Sicily.[10]

The surrounding area, between the 4th and the 5th century, also saw the import of large quantities of overseas goods; these are mainly African red slip ware, attested in up to 25 of the 32 rural settlements still inhabited, but also Tunisian oil and fish sauces, whose containers are documented at 17 sites. Full integration into Mediterranean trade systems was ensured by an efficient system of harbours, represented along this stretch of coast, from south to north, by: the harbour of Talamone, the river port of Scoglietto at the mouth of the Ombrone river, the harbour of Paduline-Serrata Martini in the Prile estuary, the harbour of Cala del Barbiere near Punta Ala and the Alma harbour. Slightly further north, in the Portiglioni bay, lay the important site of *Portus Scabris*, which alone has yielded significant archaeological evidence that it was still integrated into the Tyrrhenian trade routes that remained in use between the 7th and the early decades of the 8th century. Between the 4th and the early decades of the 5th century, coastal ports represented the access points to inland areas for secondary trade routes branching off the main Rome-Carthage axis; the latter was a mostly fiscal trade route dependent on the Roman *annona* at least until the Vandal conquest of Tunisia. The solidity of this south-north fiscal channel, linked to Rome's supply of grain and oil, created favourable conditions for the trade in other products, both from North Africa itself, such as fish sauce, wine and finewares, and from other areas, such as the eastern Mediterranean which specialized mainly in the export of wine. Products such as wine, fish sauces and Tunisian and eastern Mediterranean slip wares, though they circulated together with fiscal commodities, were traded commercially.[11] The *navicularii* engaged in the distribution of goods for the *annona* enjoyed a series of tax incentives which allowed them, after fulfilling their obligations to the state, to sell surplus foodstuffs, ceramics and other products like textiles directly at relatively low prices, thanks to the low transport costs.[12] Essentially, the existence of the fiscal supply route also multiplied the opportunities for free trade, at least along the Carthage-Rome axis and the secondary routes branching off it.

Commercial trade with the regions of Carthage and *Hadrumentum*, however, must have played an important role after the establishment of the oil *annona* between the 2nd and 3rd century AD;[13] it would otherwise be difficult to explain the large quantities of foodstuffs and craftworking products imported from this area, even after it came under Vandal control following the conquest of Carthage in 439. Probably the fiscal links between Rome and the regions of modern Tunisia allowed for the consolidation of a rapport of which trade formed an important and long-lasting component. After the capture of Carthage, goods continued to circulate with a degree of ease even without the support of the fiscal trade axis.

The data emerging from our study area show a decrease in the quantities of ARS and Tunisian transport containers between the 420s and 430s, but this is immediately followed by a slight recovery. Probably the decrease in the overall volume of goods in circulation, coinciding precisely with the years of the conquest between 429 and 439, was a side-effect of the war; however, as the data for the following decades show, this does not appear to have damaged the organization of commercial relations with the rest of the Mediterranean. Between the 4th and 6th centuries, ARS and Tunisian foodstuffs are clearly predominant among the imported products reaching the markets in the area between the Alma and Osa valleys. This is probably due to the characteristics of the economy of this area.

The process for redistributing goods from the Roman ports of Ostia and Portus was essentially linked to the demand expressed by local elites, whose purchasing power played an essential role in triggering large-scale commercial circulation.[14] The establishment of these relations created a system of linked industries which encouraged a broader territorial distribution of imported goods, which could thus be accessed by groups of lesser socio-economic status. Oil, fish sauces and Tunisian wine were clearly products in high demand between the 4th and 5th centuries among all sectors of society. By contrast, eastern Aegean amphorae of the 5th and 6th centuries, linked essentially to the trade in wines from this area, are attested only at a few privileged contexts, including the town of Roselle, the seaside villas of Paduline-Serrata Martini and Talamone, the large villa of Aiali, the port of Scoglietto and only in two instances at smaller sites in the Osa valley. This distribution, with rare exceptions, seems to be a direct response to the demand of local elites able to stimulate trade mechanisms. The scarcity of wine containers in the study area, including regional ones like the Empoli amphora, is probably proof that sufficient wine was produced locally to meet demand. Only the wealthiest individuals were able to access eastern wines which, according to late antique documentary sources, must have been highly prized.[15] Further confirmation of this may come from the finds at *Portus Scabris*, where eastern wine amphorae are attested in fairly large numbers; this is true particularly

[10] See Chapter 4.

[11] On the differences between the products destined mainly for the *annona* and those intended for commercial trade see McCormick 2001, p.99.

[12] Wickham 2005, pp.710-711.

[13] On the oil *annona* and the African supplies connected to it see Panella 1993, pp. 625-627.

[14] On the important role played by aristocratic powers in activating and consolidating long-range trade systems see Wickham 2005, pp.706-707 and p.719.

[15] On the late antique sources attesting the quality of the eastern wines transported in LR1, LR4 and LR 5/6 amphorae see in particular Pacetti 1994.

of the LR1, both in the earlier late 4th-5th century version (LR1A-Kellia 169) and in the later version dating to the second half of the 5th-6th/7th century (LR1B-Kellia 164). These products are attested in the underwater deposit formed by the dumping of products damaged during the voyage, but were not redistributed to coastal areas except in the few instances mentioned above. An identical trend can be seen for the data on Empoli wine amphorae, the most frequently attested type at the harbour site, and for Keay LII, both of which are documented only rarely in the contexts immediately inland.

Overall, the picture for overseas imports of foodstuffs at major sites in the Tyrrhenian is characterized, between the 4th and 6th centuries, by large quantities of African products, accompanied by significant amounts of eastern Mediterranean and southern Italian products.[16] At Marseilles, by contrast, the picture for overseas foodstuffs shows a predominance of African products during the 4th century, complemented from an early stage by eastern wines, which reach 40% of the goods stored in amphorae by the mid-5th century. These then decrease after the late 6th century when North African imports once again increased vigorously.[17] From the mid-6th century, after the Byzantine reconquest of Carthage, a privileged relationship appears to have been established between Tunisia and the markets of Merovingian Gaul, leading to an increase in the numbers of North African amphorae. Further information of importance for our study comes from the analysis of the transport containers found in the 6th-century shipwreck of La Palud, near the island of Port-Cros, about thirty km south-east of Toulon.[18] About 90% of the ship's cargo consisted of Tunisian amphorae without an internal pitch coating (perhaps used to trade oil). Smaller numbers of containers for the transport of eastern wines were also attested (LR1, LR2, LR4 and LR5 amphorae). A careful analysis of this cargo made it possible to estimate the total quantity of foodstuffs stored, between 12,000 and 18,000 litres. What is interesting is that, according to the excavators' interpretation, these goods were not destined for the Provençal markets directly connected to the port of Marseilles. Rather, it has been suggested that the amphorae were unloaded for temporary storage, after which they were loaded onto other vessels bound for other destinations. It is probable that during this period local Provençal oil sufficed to meet the city's needs. This hypothesis is supported by the constant presence of a pitch coating inside the Tunisian amphorae found at late antique contexts in Marseilles, believed by some scholars to be more compatible with the transportation of fish sauces than of oil.[19] The same line of reasoning suggests that high levels of demand for eastern wines were due to the inability of domestic production to meet the demands of the Marseillaise market.

This fact may help to support, though for different commodities, our hypothesis on the Maremma area where, unlike Provence, it is likely that sufficient wine was produced locally to meet demand, thus explaining the reduced need to purchase overseas products and more prized regional wines; although these cargoes reached harbour sites in this area, as we know from *Portus Scabris*, the goods were only redistributed to the surrounding area in very limited quantities.

As we have seen, overall imports, mainly from Tunisia, remained at a high level, though lower than previously, even during the decades following the interruption of the fiscal axis between Carthage and Rome. There is a phase of significant discontinuity in the flows of amphorae and ARS reaching both the town of Roselle and *Portus Scabris* in the final quarter of the 5th century. The overlap with the Ostrogoth conquest of Italy, which dealt a severe blow to the overall integration of the western Mediterranean, seems unlikely to be a coincidence. Immediately afterwards, however, the total attestations of African amphorae and ARS in both rural areas, the urban context of Roselle and at the port site of *Scabris,* begin to recover. The years of the Greek-Gothic war led to another crisis in imports, at least at rural settlements. By contrast, at Roselle and Portiglioni, these same years appear to see a slight increase in Tunisian foodstuffs and African red slip ware, probably due to the importance of these two contexts for Byzantine military strategy. Between 533 and 534 the conquest of North Africa by Belisarius' troops provided an opportunity for the reestablishment of fiscal links between the producing area of Tunisia and the large centres of consumption of Constantinople and Rome. The need to ensure the victualling of the Byzantine army engaged in Italy led, in the short term, to the reestablishment of the military *annona*. During this phase Roselle, like the city of Cosa further to the south, probably became a *castrum*, whilst *Portus Scabris* was a site of primary strategic importance for control over the Tyrrhenian coastal belt. It therefore seems likely that the slight recovery in Tunisian imports was determined by the policies of the Byzantine state and the events of the Gothic war, rather than by initiatives of a purely commercial nature. Immediately after the Greek-Gothic war the quantities of foodstuffs and Tunisian fineware attested at Roselle fall back into line with those of the surrounding area, indicating a gradual decline in imports leading to the definitive interruption of organized links with the Mediterranean world; this, on the basis of the trend for African red slip ware, can be dated to the 580s/590s. The Lombard conquest, then simply exacerbated an economic and commercial situation which had already been seriously compromised by the Greek-Gothic war, severing the weak commercial links between the town and overseas trade routes. It is no accident that the urban context excavated on the north hill at Roselle

[16] For a comprehensive study see Reynolds 1995, pp.38-85.
[17] On trends in amphora imports at Marseilles between the 4th and 7th centuries see Bonifay-Carre-Rigoir (eds) 1998, pp. 379-420.
[18] Long-Volpe 1998, pp.317-342 for a provisional publication of the wreck.
[19] *Ibidem*, pp.340-341.

yielded only a single specimen of ARS which came into production after the mid-6th century.[20] Even the rural settlement network appears to have emerged from the Greek-Gothic war profoundly damaged and compromised, as indicated by the existence of only 12 sites, as opposed to 33 during the period between the 5th and the early decades of the 6th century.

Somewhat different is the case of *Portus Scabris*, which continues to yield mainly Tunisian imported materials from up to the 7th century. The site obviously maintained an important strategic role for the Byzantines, even after the Lombard conquest of the Maremma, as an intermediate harbour able to guarantee the supply of foodstuffs to the Ligurian territories still under Byzantine control. This harbour, then, seems to have maintained a minimum of functionality and continuity of use thanks to the military *annona* destined for the Ligurian strongholds, such as S. Antonino di Perti.[21] The relations between the harbour and areas further inland, however, seem to have been definitively severed by the arrival of the Lombards from Lucca,[22] as demonstrated by the complete absence of imported 7th-century materials in the surrounding area. The settlement of Paduline, near the Lake Prile estuary, also shows a slight continuity of overseas supply between the mid-6th and the early decades of the 7th century, linked to the presence of a harbour and the privileged relations between this site, which probably already at this time belonged to the *patrimonium Sancti Petri*, and Rome.[23]

After losing control over the strongholds on the Ligurian coast following Rotari's incursions of the early 640s, the Byzantine state no longer had any reason to keep the subcoastal route through the central and northern Tyrrhenian operational. After this, attestations of imported goods along this route become progressively rarer until they become virtually invisible, at least on an archaeological level. By contrast, the southern segment of the Tyrrhenian axis remained fully functional until the 8th century, as is evident from the late 7th-[24] and 8th-century[25] deposits of the Crypta Balbi in Rome. However, the composition of supplies changed significantly even in privileged contexts, such as this Roman one, with the transition from the 7th to the 8th century. The Arab conquest of Carthage in 698 led to the interruption of supplies of Tunisian food and fineware to Rome and other large centres of consumption in the Mediterranean, like Marseilles.[26] These products, which had dominated the markets of the western Mediterranean during the second half of the 7th century and had continued to reach Constantinople throughout the century,[27] begin to disappear from the deposits of the period immediately after at the same sites.[28] Among the goods which continued to be exported by Tunisia during the 7th century are grain, as we know from the Saint Gervais 2 shipwreck at Fos-sur-Mer, about 40 km west of Marseilles. This vessel, which sank in the first quarter of the 7th century or slight afterwards, was carrying a cargo of cereals weighing about 21 tonnes, about half the ship's total capacity. That the ship came from Tunisia is evident from the fineware (types Hayes 108 and 109) used by the crew and from the amphorae which, though only present in tiny quantities, indicate a prevalence of North African products (types Keay VIIIA, Keay LXIA and two small late *spatheia*) over eastern amphorae (one specimen of LR5/6).[29]

The Islamic conquest interrupted this link, partly fiscal and partly commercial, which in the 7th century continued to connect Tunisia with the major towns of the Mediterranean. The Arab advance had a huge impact not only on the way trade was structured; in Tunisia it also appears to have had a significant affect on the settlement network and production activities. As Wickham has rightly observed,[30] North Africa was the region best integrated into the system of Mediterranean trade and as a consequence was heavily affected by the collapse of this system. Tunisia's status as an exporting region was not counterbalanced by lively commercial circulation at a regional level; instead, production structures and domestic trade were highly localized. As a consequence, when Tunisia lost its central role in the Mediterranean, we see a gradual disappearance of those archaeological indicators characteristic of the preceding centuries (ARS and amphorae), whose large-scale production was triggered by close integration into the Roman commercial and fiscal system. In this context, it is worth noting the picture emerging from recent surface surveys conducted along the Tunisian coast, from the border with Libya to that with Algeria. On the one hand these have shown the widespread presence of late antique settlements up to the end of the 7th century, whilst on the other they have indicated, over the long term, a strong localization of the domestic trade in fineware and foodstuffs which thus appears to be a structural feature typical of this region.[31] A similar picture emerges from the pottery

[20] The dish is *Atlante* I, Pl.XLVI, nos.1-2, dated to between 580 and the 7th century.

[21] On the site of S.Antonino see Mannoni-Murialdo (eds) 2001.

[22] On the Lombard conquest of the Maremma see Kurze 2002a.

[23] See Chapter 5 for a specific discussion of the site and its relations with the Rome area.

[24] Sagui 1998.

[25] Romei 2004.

[26] Bonifay-Carre-Rigoir (eds) 1998, p.390, Tab.XXIV (context from the excavation of *La Bourse*).

[27] At Saraçhane (Istanbul), deposit 30, dated to between 655 and 670, has yielded late forms of ARS (Hayes 109) and Tunisian amphorae of type Keay LXI; see Hayes 1992, pp.100-105 and p. 167, Fig.47, nos 199-200 for the amphorae identified.

[28] At Saraçhane see for example deposit 32 of the 8th century, in Hayes 1992, p.107.

[29] On the wreck see Jézégou 1998, pp.343-351.

[30] On these aspects see Wickham 2005, pp.720-728.

[31] Studies conducted between 1987 and 1997 led to the identification of as many as 210 sites, of which a large percentage belong to the late antique period (4th-7th c. AD), with a significant number of both contexts founded *ex novo* during the Vandal or Byzantine period and of sites frequented without interruption up to the 6th-7th centuries. An overview of the circulation of amphorae and ARS allows us to

finds from the late antique phases excavated in the south Basilica of Sidi Jdidi, about 14 km from the Gulf of Hammamet.[32] In this case, the ceramic evidence provides a picture of a town which, between the 5th and 7th century, was turned in on itself and its hinterland. This site, equidistant between the ARS workshops of Oudna and Sidi Khalifa, was supplied almost exclusively by the latter. Even the amphorae indicate a tendency towards genuine isolation, suggested by the prevalent attestation of traditional Punic transport containers, produced uninterruptedly between the 2nd and the 7th century AD in the Gulf of Hammamet area. Only at the end of the Byzantine era did the commodities present at Sidi Jdidi change slightly, with a greater openness towards regional markets. Hammamet amphorae, for example, are gradually replaced by the more common large cylindrical containers Keay LXI and by other local products like the Sidi Jdidi 2 amphora; by contrast, the influx of eastern wine amphorae remains at the same modest level as in preceding phases.

The Arab conquest of Tunisia, then, seems to have hastened a process of trade localization already characteristic of this region over the *longue durée*. Moreover, during the 7th century the total volume of craftworking and foodstuff production seems to have fallen significantly, as revealed by the low degree of morphological variety presented by the African red slip ware and transport containers attested in Rome in the late 7th century, belonging to a few types still in use.[33] In any case, some important *ateliers*, such as that of El Mahrine,[34] had ceased production well before the fall of Carthage. The interruption of the vital bond between the Tunisian production system and the system of maritime trade put an end to the economic vigour which, though already in decline, had allowed for the continuation of productive specializations aimed at meeting demand from the main markets in the Mediterranean basin. From the late 7th century African red slip ware disappears, and the transport containers typical of the 6th and 7th centuries cease production. In Rome, the 8th-century context of the *Crypta Balbi* yielded only two types of North African amphorae, one globular and the other with a small ovoid body; albeit with some doubts these can be considered to be in phase.[35] Excluded from the few Mediterranean routes which remained operational, Tunisia was unable, given the weakness of its domestic trade,[36] to draw new productive vigour from the circulation of products on a regional scale. This strong decline is reflected both in the settlement network, which presents a strong contraction compared to the late Byzantine period,[37] and in the production of ceramics. When African red slip ware ceased production it was not replaced by other classes of fineware destined to meet the requirements of demanding aristocratic classes. Rather, there was a more marked localization of coarsewares, indicators of an economic structure which was without doubt simplified and which makes it very difficult to identify ceramic markers for the 8th century. The attestation of a possible local production of glazed ware, documented by a very few specimens from late 7th-century phases found during the American excavations at Carthage remains fairly isolated and somewhat dubious.[38] The morphological characteristics of the few minimum individuals (hemispherical bowls with a sub-vertical pointed edge, bowls with a thickened rim and some jugs) and their internal slips, ranging from greenish-brown to purplish-black in colour, seem comparable to those of Byzantine wares of the 7th-8th century, known as Glazed White Ware I

identify at least 5 sub-regions which seem, in terms of trade, to be organized fairly independently of one another:
- the sites in the Gulf of Gabes turn mainly to the markets of southern Tunisia from the 4th century onwards, as indicated by the prevalence of southern Tunisian slip wares, though products from central and northern Tunisia are also found;
- the Sahel area is highly active in late Antiquity thanks to the presence of the cities of *Thaenae*, *Sullecthum*, *Leptiminus* and *Hadrumentum*. This area produced Africana I and II amphorae and the medium-sized cylindrical containers of type Keay XXV. Even after the mid-5th century, this area remained highly productive, as indicated by the presence of workshops linked to the production of Keay LXI and LXII. More limited, by contrast, was the circulation of Keay XXXIV, mainly found in the El-Jem *Acholla* area;
- the Gulf of Hammamet produced amphorae of Punic type for the long period between the 2nd to the 6th century AD, whilst ARS is supplied mainly by the workshops of Sidi Kahalifa;
- in the Cap Bon area, 6 km from the city of *Neapolis*, was a workshop which made Keay XXV, XXXVB and LVA. ARS acquisitions can be ascribed mainly to the wares from the urban area of Oudna;
- along the northern coast the most well-attested wares are ARS produced in the nearby Mejerda valley, at the El Mahrine workshop; the most common amphorae, by contrast, are those from Cap Bon.
For this data see Bonifay *et alii* 2005, especially pp.171-173, and also Bonifay 2004.

32 On the context of the S basilica of Sidi Jdidi between the 5th and 7th centuries see Ben Abed-Ben Khader *et alii* 2004, especially pp.315-316 for an overview of pottery circulation.

33 See Saguì 1998, for an overview of ARS and Tunisian amphorae attested in Rome in the late 7th century; see also Mannoni-Murialdo 2001 (eds.) for the finds from Sant'Antonino between the late 6th and the 7th century.

34 According to Mackensen the El Mahrine workshops ceased production immediately after the mid-7th century (Mackensen 1998, p.33).

35 Romei 2004, pp.279-280. The doubts are linked to the possibility that these two specimens may be residual (*ibidem*, p.279). In fact, the entirely different typology compared to the Tunisian amphorae of the late 7th century deposit may suggest that they are in phase in the 8th-century context.

36 Wickham 2005, pp.720-721.

37 It is extremely important to note that surface surveys along the Tunisian coast led to the identification of only 11 out of the total of 210 sites with indications of an Arab occupation: 6 of these may perhaps indicate a continuity of settlement with respect to the late Byzantine period (sites no.77-78, 105, 137, 160-161). See Bonifay *et alii* 2005, pp.198-201, Tab.1. Traces of discontinuity between the Vandal-Byzantine phase of the 6th century and the Arab phase of the 10th-13th centuries have been identified at the site of *Uchi Maius*, about 100 km south-west of Tunis (see Gelichi-Milanese 1999, pp.271-284).

38 The local origin of this production, probably made in imitation of Byzantine glazed wares, was suggested by Hayes on the basis of the similarities between these fabrics and those of ARS. On the pottery from the excavations at Carthage conducted by the University of Michigan see Hayes 1978, pp.93-95.

and Early Plain Glazed Ware with a red fabric.[39] It is therefore possible that these were imported items rather than locally-produced pottery, considering also their absence from other contexts.

In our study area, with the few exceptions already mentioned, the influx of Mediterranean goods seems to have been interrupted in the second half of the 6th century as a result of the weakening of socio-economic structures due mainly to the Greek-Gothic war and only slightly exacerbated by the Lombard conquest. During the period between the 4th and the late 6th/early 7th century, the circulation of regionally produced tableware, both with and without a red slip, reached significant proportions; suffice it to note the extent to which Italic tableware dominated over African red slip ware in the urban context on the north hill at Roselle by as early as the 4th century. During the 6th century, items made by regional workshops gradually replaced ARS in most medium-sized and small rural contexts indicating that these were increasingly falling back on domestic markets, able to supply good quality products at lower prices. Even before the Greek-Gothic war, African red slip ware seems to have become a more valuable and less accessible commodity, whose redistribution from coastal ports was mainly directed at major settlement contexts such as villas and villages, and even here in smaller quantities than regional products. After about the year 600, tableware modelled on Tunisian formal prototypes also vanished; this makes it very difficult to identify new 7th-century settlements or later frequentations of sites already inhabited in the late 6th century through surface surveys. This appears to be due mainly to two orders of factors: on the one hand new population trends which, on the basis of the data currently available, seem to be oriented towards the selection of new areas, sometimes close to late antique sites but not coinciding with them; on the other the localization of early medieval pottery production structures led to a marked reduction in morphological repertoires, making it difficult to distinguish 7th-century guide fossils from those of the following two centuries. Nonetheless, ceramic products remained of good quality, with the systematic use of the fast wheel for both wares made using purified and selected fabrics and for kitchenware. By contrast, for almost three centuries, up to roughly the mid-10th century, we find virtually no certain evidence, in the whole area between the Osa and Alma valleys, of tableware imported from outside the region; this becomes common again only with the introduction of Sparse Glazed Ware from Rome, accompanied by unslipped wares. This was probably a consequence of the decreasing economic power of the local elites, which in the absence of the state as a driving force capable of organizing fiscal trade flows, were no longer able to activate long-range commercial circulation mechanisms. A probable secondary cause were the cultural changes which affected the area's governing groups after the Lombard conquest. Imported fineware no longer appears to have aroused the interest of the elites which, in the second half of the 7th century, tended to express their social standing through grave goods, characterized by local peculiarities to the extent that they marked their belonging to a ruling group.[40] Nonetheless the impact of cultural factors must have been limited in comparison to economic factors, given that in the nearby city of Siena, for example, also in the Lombard period, the range of tableware forms yielded by the deposit of Santa Maria della Scala is characterized by a significant degree of variety and by the presence of slip wares (prevalently *colature rosse* ware) as late as the 7th and 8th centuries.[41]

The close relationship between the wealth of the elites and the complexity and variety of regional pottery trades has been studied in depth in northern France.[42] Here the formation process of the aristocracies and their consolidation were extremely rapid, to the extent that in the 8th century, when the Mediterranean world saw the greatest localization of trade, northern France shows clear signs that its elites were accumulating wealth linked to land ownership. The long continuity of production of Mayen pottery and its broad distribution between the late 4th and the 11th century cannot be explained without a constant demand expressed by rural communities and above all by the aristocracy. From the 8th century, two new and very successful pottery classes appeared – Badorf and Tating wares –; rather than replacing Mayen pottery, these coexisted with it. In 8th-century France, the organization of domestic trade was extremely complex as we know both from the pottery evidence and from the distribution of foodstuffs and other commodities: grain travelled down towards the coast along the Rhine, wine reached the areas near the mouth of this river by routes some of which were overland, woollen clothing, a specialization of the area near the Rhine delta, were sent back north. Alongside local circulation, then, regional and sub-regional trade also flourished. The driving force behind this complex trade system was the nobility, whose power was based from the 7th century onwards on large landholdings, which had no equivalents in the western Mediterranean.[43]

In other instances in northern Europe, trade based on *emporia* determined the success of the ceramic classes which were widespread at the regional scale. A typical instance is that of Ipswich pottery, a specialized production of considerable importance which seems to have begun in the early 7th century and which continued during the subsequent two centuries, with an increasing capacity for penetration. Its large area of regional distribution is not merely an indicator of high production levels but above all reflects the role played

[39] On these classes see the overview in Vroom 2005, pp.62-65.

[40] See Chapter 3.

[41] On Santa Maria della Scala see Cantini 2005.

[42] Wickham 2005, pp.794-805.

[43] *Ibidem.*

by the Ipswich *emporium* in organizing trade in south-eastern England.[44] It is no coincidence that Ipswich pottery saw an increase in the scale of production and distribution when the site was transformed from a "type A" *emporium* to a "type B" *emporium* in the late 8th century.[45] This phase saw a transition from an occasional market place, reserved for the trade in prestige goods destined exclusively for elite customers, to a large central place where regional products were traded; the central authorities invested heavily in the town with a view to controlling and simultaneously encouraging production activities and trade through a specifically created customs system.[46] The complex network of trade based around Ipswich ensured that its pottery enjoyed a wide distribution, not restricted to East Anglia but also reaching Yorkshire, Lincolnshire, Cambridgeshire and Essex.[47]

In the Maremma, the circulation of pottery seems to be heavily localized throughout the early Middle Ages: it must have been based on the activity of small individual workshops, whose products were destined for markets with a limited range of distribution, probably no more than a few tens of kilometres. The trade in pottery thus principally made use of overland routes, although we cannot rule out the use of barges for distribution to sites along the coast. The maritime trade which still sporadically touched on the central and northern segment of the Tyrrhenian does not appear to have led to any form of redistibution to the study area at least until the 10th century. The presence of the harbour of *Portus Scabris*, still partially used for long-range trade between the 7th and the early decades of the 8th century, did not represent a preferential access point for Mediterranean goods towards inland areas, as had been the case up to the 6th century. The underwater surveys carried out in Portiglioni Bay yielded a minimum of at least 3 transport containers dated with certainty to this phase. We know from their area of origin that the late 7th- or 8th-century amphora modelled on the Keay LII and the Misenum amphora, imported from Calabria and Campania respectively, contained wine. By contrast we were able to determine the presence of wine in the globular specimen only after a gas chromatograph analysis coupled with mass spectrometry. Two different fragments of the same amphora were examined:[48] one had a blackish incrustation on the internal wall of the neck; the other is a wall fragment. For the former, the analyses indicated that the substance was *pinaceae* resin, perhaps transformed into pitch directly by the distillation of the wood. The location of the resin, found only inside the neck, and the characteristic drips suggest that it was used to seal the amphora using a cork. Inside the wall, by contrast, we found clear traces of a coating (*pinaceae* resin) alongside wine markers (tartaric, hydroxybenzoic, fumaric and succinic acid). The circulation of wine and other foodstuffs along the axis between southern Italy and Rome between the late 7th and early decades of the 8th century essentially responded to the demand expressed by the clergy rather than genuine commercial transactions involving broader sectors of society.[49] It is therefore difficult to explain why trade flows continued north of the city of Rome, especially during a phase characterized by strong regionalism due to the separation between Lombard and Byzantine areas. Certainly, from the year 700 onwards, the stabilization of the Lombard control of Italy created a more relaxed social and political climate which might have encouraged increased movement of both people and goods by land and sea.[50] However, it is equally true that the period between the late 7th and the early 8th century saw the most significant contraction in Mediterranean commercial trade,[51] including that based around the Tyrrhenian Sea.[52] As such, the scarce early medieval amphora finds from *Scabris* may indicate the persistence of residual forms of long-distance trade with Provence and Languedoc, attested by the presence of globular amphorae in contexts of the late 7th-early 8th century at Marseilles[53] and in the early medieval phases at San Peyre.[54]

Between the 8th and 9th centuries, the Tyrrhenian route continued to be partially used for communications between the Papal see and the Frankish court, although overland communications were preferred: this is clearly indicated by the continuity, throughout the year, of Papal embassies sent between 700 and 900, and not only during the seasons most favourable to sailing, as was the case between the late 6th and the late 7th century.[55]Telling is the information on the embassy sent by Hadrian I to Charlemagne in 773, in which the biographer stressed, as if this was an unusual situation, that recourse was made to the maritime route.[56] The

[44] Hodges 1982, pp.146-147.
[45] Hodges 2000, p.97.
[46] *Ibidem*, pp.76-92.
[47] On the distribution of Ipswich pottery see Wickham 2005, pp.810-811.
[48] The analyses were carried out by Alessandra Pecci in collaboration with the Centro per le Analisi e Determinazioni Strutturali of the University of Siena.

[49] On these aspects see De Rossi 2006; Romei 2004 and Arthur 1993.
[50] McCormick 2001, p.82.
[51] Tangheroni 1996, pp.73-88.
[52] McCormick 2001, pp.515-516.
[53] Phase E of the excavations at La Bourse in Marseilles, dated to between the second half of the 7th and early 8th century (?) provides an overview of the commodities reaching this large port at the beginning of the early Middle Ages. The picture for amphorae is still dominated by large North African containers of types Keay LXI and Keay VIIIA, which share their country of origin with the medium-sized containers of type Keay L and the small *spatheia*. The novelty is represented by the appearance of globular amphorae of uncertain origin (southern Italy, North Africa or the eastern Mediterranean). ARS is well documented by the Hayes 109B dish and by lamps of type *Atlante* X. In two contexts, the commodities just mentioned are associated with coins of Heraclius and Childeric II. In the latter instance, the coin is a silver *denarius* from the mint of Bayeux dating to between 670-680 which provides a valuable *terminus post quem*, see Bonifay-Carre-Rigoir 1998 (eds.), p.358.
[54] Paroli *et alii* 1996.
[55] On this aspect see McCormick 2001, pp.79-82.
[56] *Ibidem*, p.876, n.182.

Tyrrhenian route was also used occasionally for communications between Charlemagne and the Abbasid Caliph Harun al'Rashid, although the most frequently used route was that between Venice, Jerusalem and Baghdad.[57] In 801, an embassy sent by Harun al'Rashid, led by the governor of Egypt, disembarked at Pisa and reached Charlemagne on the road between Vercelli and Ivrea to inform him of the death of two of his emissaries sent to Baghdad in 797 and to tell him that the third was still in Africa with the white elephant Abu l'Abbas and the other gifts presented to him by the Caliph.[58] At this point Charlemagne instructed Ercanbald to travel to Liguria and arrange for a fleet able to sail to Africa and bring both the elephant and the other gifts to Europe.[59] This episode tells us of the presence along the northern Tyrrhenian coast of a network of functioning ports, based around Pisa and probably Genoa, and above all the availability of ships of sufficient tonnage to carry such a large "gift". The success of the expedition is proof of the effectiveness of this network of connections. Long-range navigation cannot, however, have been a common practice in the early decades of the 9th century considering that the expedition by sea against the Saracens, organized in 828 by Bonifacio II of Lucca and other counts of the *Tuscia*, after reaching Corsica and finding no enemies, was forced to make use of local navigators who knew the route to Africa in order to reach the Gulf of Tunis.[60] It seems clear that, at least until the early decades of the 9th century, the northern sector of the Tyrrhenian route must have been used primarily for operations of political type (the exchange of gifts) or of military nature (Saracen raids and the counter-offensives of the counts of *Tuscia*), rather than for genuine trade. Archaeology and documentary sources provide little information on the existence of organized commerce. However, it is worth noting the trade in Christian slaves bought by Byzantine merchants along the Tuscan coasts and then sold to the Arabs. This must have been a fairly consolidated practice given that between 775 and 776 Pope Adrian I and Charlemagne communicated frequently to find an appropriate solution to the problem.[61]

A very different picture is emerging for the Adriatic route, whose importance in medium and long-range maritime trade has a direct impact on the features of trade and commerce, thanks to the central role played above all by the *emporia* of Comacchio and Torcello between the 7th and 8th centuries and by Venice from the turn of the 8th century onwards.[62] The amphora finds from Torcello and Comacchio allow us to see the complexity of the flows of regional and extra-regional commodities reaching these two sites in the early centuries of the High Middle Ages. Thanks to the results of recent archaeological studies,[63] we know that Comacchio was a genuine crossroads for maritime trade between the Po valley on the one hand and the Adriatic region and the eastern Aegean on the other. In this context, it is particularly interesting to note the widespread presence in 8th- and early 9th-century contexts, of globular amphorae probably made in different areas, which include southern Italy, the Aegean and the Black Sea,[64] and belonging to two main typologies clearly modelled on types from the Byzantine area.[65] A no less important role in large-scale maritime trade was played by Torcello,[66] where the Polish excavations have revealed the frequent presence of early medieval transport containers. In the excavated contexts in the cathedral and "piazza" areas, in phases of the late 7th-8th [67] and 9th-10th century,[68] transport containers were found similar to type 1 from the Yassi Ada wreck, which are not definitely in phase,[69] amphorae with an *ombelicato* base[70] and globular containers similar in terms of morphological characteristics and surface treatment to the specimens from Comacchio.[71] A recent overview of the circulation of early medieval globular amphora in the Venetian Lagoon has demonstrated the frequent presence of these vessels,[72] indicative of a broad range

[57] The use of the Adriatic route is indicated by the embassies of 797 and perhaps by that of 802, and certainly those of 806 and 807. On the reference sources see Mc Cormick 2001, pp.887-894.

[58] The episode of Charlemagne's elephant is indicative of trade in the Mediterranean. Although this is an exchange of gifts between the two most powerful individuals in the entire Mediterranean basin, it is symbolically highly charged as it indicates the quest for contacts and a new input to the resumption of connections in the Mediterranean. On these aspects see Hodges 2000, pp.35-40 and Hodges 1989, pp.155-168.

[59] McCormick 2001, pp.890-891.

[60] For the edition of the *expeditione contra Sarracenos facienda*, see Boretius-Krause 1897 (eds), no.203, c.9, p.67.

[61] McCormick 2001, p.519 and p.877, n.186.

[62] See Negrelli 2007 and Gelichi 2008.

[63] Gelichi *et alii* 2006a, Gelichi *et alii* 2006b, Gelichi 2008.

[64] Gelichi 2008, p.92.

[65] Gelichi *et alii* 2006a, pp.120-122.

[66] Particularly significant for their long-range trade implications is the attestation of a *denarius* of Charlemagne and an Arab *dirham* in layer IV of the excavation of the "piazza". On the two coins see Leciejewicz *et alii* 1977, p.57 and most recently Gelichi 2006a.

[67] I refer in particular to layers VII and VIII of the excavations of the cathedral (dated to between the second half of the 7th and first half of the 8th century) and to layer V from the excavation of the "piazza" (7th/8th-early 9th century). See Leciejewicz *et alii* 1977, pp.27 and 57-73 .

[68] Layer VI of the cathedral excavations (dated to the 8th-10th c.) and context IV of the 9th-10th century from the excavations of the "piazza"; on these see Leciejewicz *et alii* 1977, pp.23-27 and 42-57

[69] The contexts published by the Polish excavators present large quantities of residual materials. Indicative for example is layer IV in the "piazza" where in a 9th-10th century phase the excavators documented the Tunisian amphorae Keay XXV, Keay LXI and Keay LV, and Keay LII imported from Calabria (see respectively Leciejewicz *et alii* 1977, p.51, Fig.46, nos 3, 15-16 and 5). Amphorae similar to type Yassi Ada 1, of the 7th century, are present especially in layer VI, for drawings of the finds see Leciejewicz *et alii* 1977, p.26, Fig.23, nos 1, 4).

[70] See the specimen in Leciejewicz *et alii* 1977, p.71, Fig.75, no.7, attested in a 7th/8th-early 9th century layer.

[71] Fragments of globular bodies with sets of horizontal lines come from layer IV of the "piazza" excavations whilst layer V yielded an amphora specimen comparable to the type published in Gelichi *et alii* 2006a, p.120, Fig.5, no.4. On these materials see Leciejewicz *et alii* 1977, p.52, Fig.47, no.9 and p.71, Fig.75, no.17.

[72] Toniolo 2007, p.101.

of economic connections largely unexpected until a few years ago. They appear to be widespread throughout northern and north-western Italy, not just in coastal settlements (Comacchio, Venice, Rimini, Cervia and Grado) but also inland towns (Verona, Brescia, Milan and possibly Pavia) ,[73] suggesting a sophisticated redistribution network mainly based on the river route provided by the Po.

At the end of the 8th century, the true trade hub of the Mediterranean was Venice, which took over the role played by Marseilles up until the late 7th century.[74] Its crucial function is clearly illustrated by Charlemagne's repeated attempts to conquer the Lagoon between the 780s and 810. After the treaty of Aix-la-Chapelle of 812, marking the peace between the Franks and the eastern Empire and thus creating favourable conditions for the resumption of trade between these two areas,[75] the coins issued by Venice and the other cities of northern Italy were commonly used for economic transactions north of the Alps. From the 820s, there was a recession in the trade which had been organized around the *emporia* of the North Sea and Venetian coins became even more common.[76] Byzantium's new commercial interests in the Adriatic area and the favourable relations with the Carolingians led to the beginning of a new phase of intense maritime trade which, via the Adriatic and its ports,[77] linked the Frankish world to the East and especially Constantinople.

The central and northern Tyrrhenian did not benefit from the new and vigorous commercial contacts between the Byzantine and Frankish worlds; it was only when Pisa's maritime economy began to grow substantially in the mid-10th century that large-scale trade became re-established along this route.[78] Despite the localization of production structures and its effective isolation from long-range trade routes, the settlement network in the Maremma, after a lack of data for the mid-7th century, shows signs of renewed vitality between the 8th and 9th centuries. Population patterns are characterized by the development of more or less nucleated sites in the plains and a few scattered sites located in areas with the highest agricultural potential. The development of centralized hilltop sites represents a phenomenon which is difficult to identify through surface surveys, however detailed. However, by combining the data from the excavation of the hilltop village of Poggio Cavolo and those from some "lucky" surveys at castles abandoned precociously by the 12th or 13th century, we were able to demonstrate that this phenomenon also occurred in this area during the early Middle Ages, as emerges clearly from the excavations at numerous fortified sites of central and southern Tuscany. Between the Lombard period and the early decades of the Carolingian period, the study area was at the heart of the political and economic interests of the cities of Lucca and Chiusi, on the one hand, as a consequence of the Lombard conquest in the 590s,[79] and of the Church of Rome on the other as a result of the late antique donation of imperial properties to the Papacy. This complex web of powers interested in exploiting the area's numerous agricultural and woodland resources, and above all its salt pans, must have led to a fairly substantial presence of local elites linked to urban aristocratic groups, both laymen and churchmen. However, for much of the 8th century archaeology provides no obvious traces of hegemonic powers organized at the local level. By contrast, the documentary sources from Lucca and Chiusi indicate that fairly heavy pressure was exerted on the dependent farmers of the Maremman estates in the dioceses of Roselle and Sovana from the mid-8th century. The control over the production activities taking place in these estates must have been fairly close, as we know from the extent of the taxes in kind and the services in manual labour (*angaria*) paid. The silence of the archaeological sources, then, does not seem to correspond, at least during the late Lombard period, to a weakness on the part of the aristocracy, which must have managed its outlying properties through *actores* able to organize the collection of taxes.[80]

With the Carolingian period, however, the written and archaeological sources agree in suggesting an increase in the economic means and investment capacity of the local aristocracies. The transformations triggered by the Frankish conquest had an impact on both social and economic structures. The elites consolidated their position in the hierarchy of public power, thus becoming yet more powerful and able to exert absolute control over the peasant masses. The excavation of monasteries and Tuscan villages indicates that rural aristocratic residences first appeared during this very phase.[81] In the Maremma, the construction of churches appears to be a recurrent feature, through which we can read the extent of aristocratic investments. In Grosseto, one religious building was constructed between the late

[73] For a recent review of the distribution of early medieval globular amphorae in the north-western Adriatic and northern Italy see Gelichi 2008, p.91.
[74] Gelichi 2006a, pp.171-176.
[75] Brogiolo 2001, p.21.
[76] Hodges 2000, p.62. On the commercial role of Venice see also Hodges 2008.
[77] See for example the case of Pescara, which appears to have undergone a phase of "comprehensive reorganization and a probable relaunch of the settlement" during the Carolingian period (Staffa 2005, p.145). The harbour on the Golena was still in use in the 9th century when the city, undergoing a phase of growth, began to take on a new form, due to the absorption into the early medieval urban fabric of the ancient structures; layers of black soil were deposited on these with construction materials being mainly perishable or mixed (Staffa 2006, p.409 and Staffa 2005, p.156).
[78] On Pisa and its key role in Tyrrhenian trade see Tangheroni 1996, pp.137-147.

[79] For the Lombard conquest of this area in Tuscany see See Kurze 2002a, p. 138 and pp.142-149.
[80] See the documents discussed in Chapter 3, notes 48-49.
[81] On these aspects see Hodges 2008; Valenti 2008; Francovich-Valenti 2005; Wickham 1997; Hodges 1994.

8th and the early 9th century[82] whilst a second, dedicated to San Giorgio, is documented in 803. The construction of the wall circuit surrounding the village of Poggio Cavolo and the single-naved single-apsed church resting against it can be dated to the late 9th-early 10th century or perhaps even earlier. At the bishops's seat of Roselle, between the late 8th and early 9th century[83] an ambitious sculptural redecoration project was undertaken in the city cathedral, built between the late 6th and early 7th century. These episodes, despite the considerable differences between their contexts (two villages, of which one, Grosseto, was soon to take on a proto-urban nature, and an ancient city) ushered in a new era of stone constructions, made possible by the economic means of the local elites. This accumulation of wealth can be explained, alongside the major role played by members of the elites in the Carolingian political system, by a more organized and solid relationship with the peasant classes, translating into a greater capacity to exact taxes and to manage and exploit the available workforce. The transformations of the Carolingian period thus seem to have had a radical effect on the ways in which landholdings were managed, becoming more careful and systematic. A clear indication of this can be found in the new policies pursued by the bishop of Lucca Peredero in the inland area of the diocese of Sovana (to the south of the investigated area) after his trip to France.[84] Probably influenced by the methods of land and workforce management characteristic of the Carolingian world, the new regulations as expressed by the contracts issued after his return from France indicate a greater care in specifying the true extent of the work to be carried out by tenant farmers in the lands directly managed by the various *curtes.*[85]

Indirect proof of the intensification of farming activities during the Carolingian period can be found in the frequency with which early medieval storage/transport amphorae made of uncoated pottery, both purified and selected, are found in contexts of the 8th-9th centuries in this area. These amphorae are well documented in early medieval settlements between the Osa and Bruna valleys, but they are also a constant presence in other villages (Scarlino, Rocchette Pannocchieschi, Montemassi) of the coastal and sub-coastal belt north of the study area, and at least from the 10th century at Capalbiacco, a few tens of kilometres further south in the Cosa area.[86] The surface contexts in the study area which have yielded these materials mainly date to between the 8th and 9th centuries, but it is impossible to narrow their chronology further. However, a significant piece of evidence comes from the excavation of one of the farmsteads making up the dispersed settlement of Casa Andreoni, near the Gulf of Talamone. The luminescence dosimetry analysis of a specimen of small amphora, identical to those common throughout this area, supplied an absolute date of AD 850±65, potential proof that this form was introduced no earlier than the late 8th century, perhaps compatible with a new intensification of farming and the availability of larger surpluses for trade. This working hypothesis requires further refinement in the near future with a systematic comparison of the chronologies of the contexts in which these forms are found. An issue which remains open is the identification of the places where these products were traded, for which no clues are forthcoming either from the archaeological or the written documentation. During the late antique period a key role may have been played by the city of Roselle and the coastal harbours; the former may have hosted periodic markets for the redistribution of regional products and the latter for Mediterranean goods in the latter. The problem arises for the phase between the 8th and 10th centuries, when we know very little about the city of Roselle; the features brought to light by archaeological investigations at Grosseto have provided no evidence of help to this discussion. It is in any case worth remembering that two land rental contracts, of 770 and 777 respectively, specify that the obligations of the tenants, resident in *mansi* in the hinterland of the diocese of Sovana, included taking the animals to be paid to the Bishop of Lucca as rent to Roselle. Clearly there must have been a facility, run by the Bishop of Lucca through an *actor*, used for the temporary accumulation of the produce destined for the Luccan diocese.[87] The only early medieval pottery kiln hitherto identified in this area is in the village of Podere Serratone; it manufactured coarseware for use at table and for storage, and perhaps also kitchenware. This must have been one of the workshops which produced the small amphorae discussed above, used both for storage and probably also for the trade in foodstuffs such as oil and wine.

With the transition to the 10th century, the re-establishment of long-distance trade in the Tyrrhenian thanks to the initiatives of Pisa and Genoa created favourable conditions for the reactivation of the extra-regional pottery trade at the site of *Portus Scabris* and some hilltop villages in the coastal belt and immediately inland. The harbour of Portiglioni may

[82] Citter 2006a, p.153.

[83] The church furnishings have recently been analysed by Riccardo Belcari, whom I thank for the information on their chronology.

[84] On this see Andreolli-Montanari 1983, pp.57-63.

[85] It is interesting to note that in a lease contract drawn up in AD 777, the tenants who rented an estate in *Tuciano* (in the diocese of Sovana to the south of the study area), are expected to contribute specified unpaid labour (*corvée*), corresponding to five working days, in the Bishop's *curtis* located *in Lusciano*. Previously, as mentioned in two contracts dating to AD 762 and 770, the tenant farmers are merely expected to carry out unpaid labour according to the needs of the directional site (*curtis*), with no further specifications. The three documents are mentioned in Chapter 3 note 48.

[86] On the materials from Rocchette Pannocchieschi and Montemassi see Grassi 2006; on those from Scarlino see Marasco 2002-2003; on Capalbiaccio see Vaccaro 2009 and *ibidem* for a sub-regional overview.

[87] See Chapter 3, note 48 for a discussion about the two documents.

also have remained in use between the late 8th and the 9th century, although we have no definitive archaeological evidence that it was frequented during this phase. It is likely that this harbour, which lay in an area where the diocese of Lucca had large landholdings, remained operational to link Lucca with its outlying properties in the Maremma and to transfer the foodstuffs produced by the estates in *Maritima*. The harbour at *Scabris* may still have been important for the exchange of goods within the vast properties of the diocese of Lucca between the 8th and 9th centuries, like the unidentified *portum illum* to which two sailors from the Val di Cecina travelled, as was customary, to transport grain and salt to Lucca, as we know from a document of 768.[88] New but scarce archaeological markers appear from the 10th century indicating that the harbour formed part of an extra-regional trade network. At present these markers consist of a minimum of only two amphorae, one of type Otranto 1 from the Salento, and one similar to type Saraçhane 52,[89] both common from the 10th century onwards. Whereas the former's area of provenance is known thanks to the identification of a workshop,[90] the latter's area of origin is more difficult to determine, although its presence at Istanbul and its absence from other published contexts may suggest an eastern Aegean origin. The albeit extremely limited attestation of containers used for overseas transport at this very late phase requires further study, especially in light of the low frequency with which commercial amphorae of the central phase of the Middle Ages are documented in the central and northern Tyrrhenian.[91] The strong contraction in the number of amphorae ascribable to this phase is unsurprising considering the scarce use of pottery containers for maritime trade, compared to the situation at least up to the 7th century. Only a few towns, traditionally more closely linked to the Byzantine world like those in the Adriatic, maintained a well-structured amphora production until the central Middle Ages.[92] By contrast, in the Aegean area the practice of transporting goods in amphorae remained unchanged until the 14th century, probably thanks to the existence of a solid state organization able to ensure a high level of demand for foodstuffs, destined largely to meet the consumption needs of Byzantium but also thanks to a complex regional trade network.[93] The long production tradition of maritime transport containers is clearly indicated by the variety and complexity of amphorae types still in use between the 9th and 13th centuries, which on the basis of the materials held in Turkish museums[94] alone can be ascribed to at least 4 types, and by the large number of wrecks attested between the 11th and 13th centuries in the Sea of Marmara.[95]

Heavily marginalized from the late 6th century in terms of archaeologically visible economic links, the study area in the Tuscan Maremma had to wait for the emergence of Pisa as a maritime power, from the 10th century onwards, before it once again became part, albeit initially to a very limited extent, of a maritime trade network capable of "broadening" the localized system of exchanges characteristic of the 8th and 9th centuries.

To sum up, the pottery evidence has provided a lens through which to read economic and production patterns in this area between the 4th and 9th centuries, and the various phases of integration into Mediterranean trade networks. After a phase of intensive and complex medium and long-range trade characteristic of the 4th-6th centuries, and despite its vicinity to the coast and the presence of port structures which were still partially in use such as that of *Portus Scabris*, the study area seems to have been excluded from long-range commercial contacts from the 7th century to the early 10th century. Between the 7th and 9th centuries, the pottery indicates a marked localization and simplification of production structures which, however, continue to maintain good quality standards. The range of distribution of the wares manufactured by local workshops seems to fall to a few tens of kilometres as indicated by the pottery from Podere Serratone. Only from the Ottonian period onwards did this area once again develop a complex inter-regional and regional trade network, in part promoted by the economic policies of Pisa, which in

88 For the document see *C.L.A.*, Lucca V, no.1005, pp.76-77; for a discussion of relations between Lucca and the Maremma area see also Chapter 3.

89 For a discussion of the two typologies see Chapter 6.

90 Arthur 1992.

91 An exception seems to be Pisa, one of the main players in the relaunch of large-scale maritime trade. Here the so-called *a cannelures* amphorae made in western Sicily or North Africa between the 10th and 12th centuries are well attested. For attestations in Pisa see Menchelli 1993, p.520 no.1 and p.522, nos 2-5 and Menchelli-Renzi Rizzo 2000, pp.160-162.

92 See especially the case of Otranto where amphorae production is well attested between the early and late Middle Ages. See especially Arthur 2004a; Arthur 1998; Arthur 1992; Leo Imperiale 2004.

93 On the complexity of trade and exchange during the early Middle Ages in the Aegean area see Wickham 2005, pp.780-794.

94 The examination of the amphorae in Turkish museums led Günsenin to identify 4 different typologies:
- type 1, dated to between the 9th and 11th century, is attested in Turkey, as well as in the Sea of Marmara, Bulgaria, Romania and the former Soviet Union;
- type 2 is dated to between the 10th and 11th century and is well documented between the Aegean and the Black Sea;
- type 3, of the 12th-13th century, is attested in the Black Sea, Bulgaria, Romania, the former Soviet Union, Cyprus, Israel and Greece;
- type 4, also of the 12th-13th century is present in the Black Sea, Bulgaria and the former Soviet Union. See Günsenin 1989, pp. 267-276.

95 Günsenin's excavations conducted in recent years along the shores of the Black Sea led to the identification of 11 shipwrecks, 4 of which can be dated to the 6th/7th century, 6 to the 11th and one to the 13th. The latter (Çamalti Burnu I) contained an extremely varied cargo of amphorae, with types ranging from 47 to 80 cm in height and with capacities between 17 and 115 litres, probably linked to the existence of multiples (and submultiples?) of a standard measurement. See Günsenin 2001, pp.252-256.

the second half of the 12th century extended the southern borders of its *contado* up to the Bruna river.[96]

[96] On the enlargement of Pisan territories in the Maremma see Ceccarelli Lemut 1985.

Appendix 1. Catalogue of Sites: the Main Archaeological Features Identified During the Survey (Fourth-Eleventh Century)

1.1. T.U.s from the Castiglione della Pescaia Survey (C.d.P. Survey)

SITE.T.U. C.d.P. 12.2
Municipality: Castiglione della Pescaia
Location: Pian d'Alma
Description of T.U.: Area of ceramic fragments with abundant pottery and brick. Black Glaze ware is scarce, but both *sigillata italica* and production A African red slip ware are well attested; production D ARS is represented by a single specimen. The soil in the area of the concentration is a dark colour and the soil mark is visible immediately upon entering the field. The analysis of the finds allowed us to identify some pottery typologies ascribable to the 6th c. AD.
Interpretation: Farmstead
Finds of help in dating:
Black Glaze ware : A few fragments of unidentifiable typology
Sigillata italica: Various fragments including a dish with two grooves of type Conspectus 3.2. with a thickened rim and ovoid section; there is a groove on the inside underneath the rim
Sigillata tardo-italica: One fragment of unidentifiable typology
African kitchenware: Dish-lid with a blackened rim of type *Atlante* I, Pl.CIV, 7
African red slip ware A: Various fragments, including a Hayes 14A bowl
African red slip ware C: Hayes 50 dish
African red slip ware D: A single fragment belonging to a Hayes 61B deep dish
6th-c. AD pottery: Kitchenware and an *acroma depurata* flanged bowl
Concentration of finds per m^2: 12
Period: Roman and late antique
Phase: The phase of most intensive settlement can be dated to between the 1st c. BC and the 3rd c. AD; after this the site appears to be frequented between the 4th and 5th c. AD; in the 6th c. AD the site may have been occupied seasonally

SITE.T.U. C.d.P. 14.1
Municipality: Castiglione della Pescaia
Location: Pian d'Alma
Description of T.U.: Area of ceramics measuring about 130 x 180 m, characterized by an abundance of bricks, coarseware and tableware, amphorae and fragments of lime mortar mixed with crushed brick. In the northern part we found a large quantity of slag from the smelting of iron; however it is impossible to determine the exact extent of this area
Interpretation: Roman villa
Finds of help in dating:
Black Glaze ware : Very few fragments of unidentifiable typology
Sigillata italica: This appears to be the most widely attested ceramic class. Recognizable forms include a hemispherical bowl with a flange and vertical rim of type Conspectus 34.1 and a bowl with a thinned rim of type Pucci XIII. During the survey carried out by C. Cucini, Goudineau 1 and 4 dishes and Goudineau 24, 33 and 38 bowls were found
Terra sigillata tardo-italica: Various fragments of unidentifiable typology. During the survey carried out by C. Cucini, Dragendorff-Watzinger 663 dishes and Dragendorff 28 bowls with a rouletting decoration were found
African red slip ware A: Numerous fragments including a Hayes 14B, no.8 bowl
African red slip ware C: The only identifiable form is the Hayes 50A deep dish with a plain rim
African red slip ware D: Various fragments including a Hayes 67 dish
African kitchenware: Casseroles with a more or less thickened rim of type *Atlante* I, Pl.CVII, 7
Amphorae: Numerous unidentifiable fragments
Concentration of finds per m^2: 15
Period: Roman
Phase: Late Republic-late Empire (1st c. BC-mid-5th/early 6th c. AD)

SITE.T.U. C.d.P. 14.2
Municipality: Castiglione della Pescaia
Location: Pian d'Alma
Description of T.U.: In the spring of 2002 a trench about 1.6 m deep, running N-S, was dug for an irrigation channel in the field where T.U. 14.1 was found. Thanks to the occasional section thus created, we were able to observe and to a limited extent document the properties of the archaeological deposit. The T.U. consists of a layer of black earth, identified in the highest part of the stratigraphic sequence. This layer was particularly rich in charcoal and contained numerous fragments of *ingobbiata di rosso* ware dated to the 6th c. AD. Further indications of both relative and absolute chronology come from the discovery of a fragment of an ARS Hayes 67 deep dish in the layer beneath
Interpretation: Probable late frequentation of the Roman villa T.U. 14.1
Period: Late Antiquity
Phase: 5th/6th c. AD

SITE.T.U. C.d.P. 14.3
Municipality: Castiglione della Pescaia
Location: Pian d'Alma
Description of T.U.: The interpretation of the stratigraphic sequence allowed us to identify, in section, a stone wall made from the river stones present *in loco*, bound with a limestone-rich mortar. We also observed a layer composed of numerous brick fragments, located above the wall and probably resulting from the collapse of the roof
Interpretation: Walls belonging to the Roman villa T.U. 14.1
Period: Roman

SITE.T.U. C.d.P. 18.1
Municipality: Castiglione della Pescaia
Location: Castel Maus
Description of site: Hill known as Castel Maus, at 310 m above sea level in the Alma valley
Historical data: The vast area known as *Alma* in the Middle Ages was home to three castles, also named Alma in the modern period; this makes it difficult to determine which of the two is meant when dealing with mentions of individual sites indicated only by the toponym Alma. In 1293 Ranieri dei Pannocchieschi d'Elci acquired lands and rights over the castle of Alma; in the early 14th c. the Counts Pannocchieschi d'Elci, together with the "sons of Ciantino" are recorded as being the owners of a castle which may be Castel Maus. Were this identification to be correct, this is also the site mentioned in a deed of 1479, with which Achille son of the deceased Antonio d'Elci ceded to Andrea Piccolomini the "castrum, roccam seu arcem, quemadmodum ad praesens reperitur castri, cassari seu rocce de Alma veteri superiori de montanea dicta Alma de poggio, et omnes et singulas eius possessiones [...] cum dominatione, signoria, iurisdictione meri et mixti imperii"
Description of T.U.: The castle has two wall circuits: one surrounding the castle proper and enclosing an area of about 0.23 ha, and another surrounding the village and enclosing an area of a hectare. The outer circuit is made of fairly large blocks, although these are not of identical size, and appears to date to the Romanesque monumentalization of the settlement; however, some parts of the wall circuit appear to be less carefully built, perhaps reflecting different construction phases. On the slopes of the hill inside the outer wall circuit are the remains of partially collapsed structures belonging to houses or service buildings. A structure which is well-preserved in elevation on the northern side underneath the castle area must have had a residential function. This structure has a hollow wall; the wall faces are made of courses of local sandstone blocks, rectangular and elongated, which are not perfectly horizontal. Immediately outside the inner wall circuit surrounding the castle is the single-naved church with a semi-circular apse. The Romanesque structure was certainly built by craftsmen from outside the area, since the formal quality of both the inner and outer wall faces, with the careful "*a nastrino*" finishing of the ashlars used in the interior walls of the apse, does not seem to be in keeping with local technical skills. The central nucleus of the castle is preceded by an area hosting functional annexes and service buildings, such as the cistern, located in the south-western part of the settlement. It is rectangular in shape and is covered with a barrel-vault; it is built of squared blocks, laid in horizontal courses with broad joins and bound in copious yellow

mortar. Originally the cistern must have had an internal cladding of lime mortar with crushed brick, in part still visible. The castle has a flat area in the central part whilst some walls survive on the S, E and W sides
Interpretation: Castle
Period: Middle Ages
Phase: Central and late Middle Ages (11th/12th-14th/15th c. AD)
Bibliography: Farinelli 2007, Entry no.14240; Prisco 1998, pp.181-190; Cucini 1989a, pp.8-12 and 24-27; Cardarelli 1932, p.179

SITE.T.U. C.d.P. 18.2
Description of T.U.: In the western area of the village, near the wall circuit, we identified an exposed section with numerous pottery fragments. Kitchenware is absolutely predominant, with only a small amount of *acroma depurata* ware. Most identifiable forms were cooking pots of types dating to the late 9th/10th c.
Interpretation: Evidence for an early medieval phase
Period: Middle Ages
Phase: late 9th-10th c. AD

SITE.T.U. C.d.P. 18.3
Description of T.U.: A few metres from the outer wall circuit is an area measuring about 40 x 14 m, characterized by a large quantity of slag, haematite, fragments of vitrified refractory clay and sherds dating to the central centuries of the Middle Ages
Interpretation: Iron-working area belonging to the castle
Period: Middle Ages
Phase: Central-late Middle Ages

SITO.UT C.d.P. 19.1
Municipality: Castiglione della Pescaia
Location: Castellaccio del Prile
Description of site: Hill known as Castellaccio del Prile on the IGM maps, at 287 m above sea level
Historical data: No documentation
Description of T.U.: The site known as Castellaccio del Prile lies on a hill which reaches a height of 287 m above sealevel, overlooking the plain of Castiglione. The placename is certainly modern and derives from the presence of a ruined castle in a strategic position overlooking the plain of the ancient Lake Prile. The best way of accessing the site is via a firebreak which runs from the Palazzo Prile estate to the castle. The firebreak appears to have disturbed a series of structures located in the south-western area of the village. Only some stretches of the second wall circuit can be identified. In the N-W part of the village the wall circuit appears to be about 1.6 m thick; it is made of irregularly shaped stones bound with an earthy mortar, currently in a poor state of preservation. The sandstone used in the castle buildings must have been obtained locally, as demonstrated by the presence along the access road to the castle of outcrops presenting large cuts where stone was removed. In the northern and western sectors, the village seems to develop in a series of concentric circles around the top of the hill, arranged according to the contours. The layout of the village presents clear evidence that building activities were planned, with the preparation of flat areas for building by constructing terracing walls, and the use of standardized modules for the sizing of the most common dwellings. Unfortunately the dense vegetation made it impossible to record the structures; this might have provided a clearer picture of the layout of the castle. In the western sector of the village is a well-preserved wall of a dwelling; the wall face, made of fairly well-squared and evened stones, though of different sizes, bound with a good quality lime mortar, appears identical to other stretches identified in the area left of the access road. Here, as at Castel Maus, the church, located on the northern side "linked" the castle area to the village. The church is currently well below the current land level; however, we can see its single nave plan with a semicircular apse. The wall structures do not appear to be more carefully built than the more clearly visible village walls, except in the apse whose stones are roughly squared and evened, again the result of local technical know-how. The inner wall circuit is made of stones of different sizes but all fairly large; these were certainly hewn with greater care than the blocks used to build the outer wall circuit. Of particular interest is a sloping defensive structure protecting the western side of the summit area. This structure is about 15 m high and exploits the slope of the hilltop. This type of defensive structure does not appear to find parallels in the Maremman area. A few metres above it is the cistern, entirely covered in hydraulic mortar and with a barrel vault
Surface area: The inner wall circuit encloses a surface area of about 0.33 ha; the outer wall circuit an area of 2 ha
Interpretation: Castle
Period: Middle Ages
Phase: Central-late Middle Ages

SITE.T.U. C.d.P. 19.2
Description of T.U.: In the northern sector of the castle the shape and size of the residential structures are easier to read; these appear to have been fairly small (30-40 m^2). In this area we observed a strong concentration of pottery fragments and grindstones
Interpretation: Part of the village
Finds of help in dating: Kitchenware dating to between the 12th and 13th c. AD
Concentration of finds per m^2: 6
Period: Middle Ages
Phase: Central-late Middle Ages

SITE.T.U. C.d.P. 19.3
Description of T.U.: On the north-eastern side of the castle area we identified an occasional section, probably the work of wild animals. Cleaning this section allowed us to identify a strong concentration of fragments of *acroma* wares whose edges were not at all worn, though they were extremely small.
Finds of help in dating: *Acroma depurata* ware of the 12th-13th c. AD
Period: Middle Ages
Phase: Central-late Middle Ages (12th-13th c. AD)

SITE.T.U. C.d.P.19.4
Description of T.U.: The creation of the firebreak cut fairly deeply into part of the west sector of the castle, as a result of which mobile finds from the disturbed layers are fairly frequent in this area. Among these sporadic materials we identified some fragments of cooking pots similar to wares of the late 9th and early 10th c.
Interpretation: Evidence of an early medieval phase
Finds of help in dating: Kitchenware of the late 9th-10th c. AD
Concentration of finds per m^2: 3
Period: Middle Ages
Phase: late 9th-10th c. AD

SITE.T.U. C.d.P.19.5
Description of T.U.: In the south-western sector of the village were some houses still partially preserved in elevation. In this area we identified a vast concentration of pottery and fragments of grindstones
Interpretation: Portion of the village
Finds of help in dating: *Acroma depurata* ware and kitchenware of the 12th-13th c. AD
Concentration of finds per m^2: 6
Period: Middle Ages
Phase: Central-late Middle Ages (12th-13th c. AD)

SITE.T.U. C.d.P.19.6
Description of T.U.: Following the firebreak leading to Castellaccio del Prile, about 20 m before reaching the remains of the village wall circuit we identified a strong concentration of slag from the production of iron, fragments of refractory clay, haematite from Elba and a few ceramic fragments, measuring at least 15 x 35 m. This production area seems to have been established in an abandoned quarry, as indicated by the obvious cuts in the sandstone outcrops; the discovery of some post holes cut straight into the rock suggests the existence of one or more wooden structures, inside which the iron must have been produced
Interpretation: Iron-working area
Finds of help in dating: *Acroma depurata* ware of the 12th-13th c. AD
Concentration of finds per m^2: 10
Period: Middle Ages
Phase: Central-late Middle Ages (12th-13th c. AD)

SITE.T.U. C.d.P.20.1
Municipality: Castiglione della Pescaia
Location: Podere Le Querce

Description of site: Near the crossroads leading to Punta Ala, in the field surrounding the Podere Le Querce, on the S side of the field
Description of T.U.: We observed a vast scatter of slag from the production of iron measuring at least 100 x 50 m. The surface in the area of the T.U. is also much darker in colour. Few materials were collected and these consist of some fragments of *acroma selezionata* ware with a sandwich fabric
Interpretation: Iron-working area
Concentration of finds per m^2: Slag 5; pottery not calculable
Period: Middle Ages
Phase: Early-central Middle Ages (?)

SITE.T.U. C.d.P.21.1
Municipality: Castiglione della Pescaia
Location: Badiola farmstead
Description of site: Ploughed field about 630 m S-W of the Badiola farm. The field can be reached either via the road to Podere S. Enrico or via the road leading directly to the Badiola farm. This field is separated from another adjacent to the farm by a ditch whilst to the S it borders the SP Castiglionese road
Description of T.U.: The field survey allowed us to identify an obvious soil mark in the northern part of the field, consisting of an evident microrelief where the ground is darker in colour than in the rest of the area. This is an area of ceramic fragments extremely rich in finds and measuring about 50 x 60 m. The finds discovered include two fragments of open forms made of *bucchero*, Black Glaze ware , *sigillata italica*, *sigillata tardo-italica*, production A, C and D African red slip ware, African kitchenware, amphorae, coarseware and *ingobbiata di rosso* ware. Among the construction materials were numerous fragments of roof tiles of semi-circular section and imbrices with raised edges; various fragments of lime mortar mixed with crushed brick are also present. We also found some iron slag
Interpretation: Medium-large farmstead
Concentration of finds per m^2: 12
Finds of help in dating:
Bucchero: Two fragments of unidentifiable typology
Black Glaze ware : Numerous fragments of open forms, including a fragment of a bowl with a slightly incurving rim, Serie Morel 2766 dating to between the 3rd and 2nd c. BC
Terra sigillata italica: Numerous small fragments, both plain and decorated, including a hemispherical bowl with a flange and vertical rim of type Conspectus 34, decorated "a la barbotine" with a decorative motif of dolphins
Decorated sigillata tardo-italica: A few fragments including a wall belonging to a carinated bowl of type Dragendorff 29, characterized by a decoration of erotes
African red slip ware A: Numerous fragments including a Hayes 14 A bowl with a slightly thickened rim, a Hayes 14 B no. 8 bowl with an internally oblique rim, and a Hayes 8A bowl with a rim characterized by a central lobe presenting a rouletting decoration and a slightly everted lower flange
African red slip ware C: Hayes 50 dish
African red slip ware D: This production is even more widely attested than the above; the recognizable forms include various specimens of Hayes 59 large deep dishes with flat rims presenting two grooves on the upper surface and one Hayes 67 deep dish with a rim inclined towards the outside and a convex internal profile, with a bright orange slip of excellent workmanship; finally, we found a fragment of a Hayes 104A deep dish
African kitchenware: Dish lids of type *Atlante* I, Pl. CIV, 9-10; "A a strisce" casseroles of type *Atlante* I, Pl.CVI, 10-11
Amphorae: Dressel 2-4 amphorae; African Keay IIIA and IIIB and Keay XXV containers
Ingobbiata di rosso ware: A fragment modelled on a Hayes 61 deep dish, various specimens of open forms including a carinated bowl of the 6th/early 7th c. AD
Acroma depurata: A fragment of a flanged bowl of the 6th c. AD
Period: Multi-period
Phase: From the Etrusco-Roman phase to late Antiquity without gaps (3rd/2nd c. BC-6th c. AD); possible pre-existing Etruscan settlement, indicated by two fragments of bucchero

SITE.T.U. C.d.P. 47.1
Municipality: Castiglione della Pescaia
Location: Le Mortelle
Description of site: Recently planted vineyard, about 300 m N-E of the Le Mortelle farm
Description of T.U.: The survey allowed us to identify a large scatter of ceramics and construction materials, brought to light by recent earthmoving work for the planting of the vineyard. The building materials include sandstone blocks, fragments of lime mortar with crushed bricks, square bricks, imbrices with raised edges, semi-circular roof tiles, small bricks for *opus spicatum* floors, fragments of mortar. There is an abundance of tableware but in a highly fragmentary state, making it difficult to determine typologies with accuracy. Also present are Black Glaze ware , *sigillata italica*, African red slip ware A and a fragment of African red slip ware D, two fragments of *ingobbiata di rosso* ware. Coarseware is represented mainly by African kitchenware and by some kitchenware pieces resembling materials of the 5th/6th c. AD. Some amphorae were found including at least two Dressel 2/4. Various fragments of iron slag were found
Surface area of T.U.: 8455 m^2
Interpretation: Roman villa
Concentration of finds per m^2: 12
Period: Roman
Phase: Late Republic-middle Empire (2nd c. BC-2nd/3rd c. AD)
Observations: The presence of a few materials dating to between the 5th and mid-6th c. AD indicates reoccupation during this phase

SITE.T.U. C.d.P. 50.1
Municipality: Castiglione della Pescaia
Location: Le Mortelle
Description of site: Field about 70 m E of the Fosso Cortigliano and about 500 m E of the Le Mortelle farm
Description of T.U.: Fairly large area of ceramic fragments measuring about 50 x 80 m, characterized by an abundance of roof tiles. Pottery finds are also numerous and are represented by a fragment with a bucchero-like fabric, Black Glaze ware , *sigillata italica*, African red slip ware A and African kitchenware. We also found a group of three pottery forms (two flanged bowls and a cooking pot) of the 5th/6th c. AD
Interpretation: Large farmstead
Concentration of finds per m^2: 10
Degree of reliability: 4
X-Y coordinates: 1660245; 4740915
Period: Roman
Phase: Late Republic-middle Empire (2nd c. BC-3rd c. AD); a fragment with a bucchero-like fabric may indicate a pre-existing Etruscan settlement
Observations: The 6th c. AD material indicates a late antique reoccupation of the site

SITE.T.U. C.d.P. 53.2
Municipality: Castiglione della Pescaia
Location: Il Convento (Badia Nuova di Sestinga)
Description of site: Field about 50 m S of the Abbey of San Bartolomeo di Sestinga. The land is mostly used for pasture, but at the time of our survey had been ploughed, making the area easy to read
Description of T.U.: Within the large T.U. 53.1 (dating to the Hellenistic/late Republican and early imperial period) we observed a concentration of medieval pottery measuring about 20 x 40 m. Although the finds belonging to these two periods were juxtaposed, we were able to distinguish fairly clearly between the concentration of medieval materials and that of classical materials. Among the finds present in T.U. 53.2 were archaic majolica finds of Sienese workmanship. Also present were fragments of jugs with strap handles set immediately beneath the rim, made by Pisan workshops. A fairly small group of cooking pots and jugs is not contemporary with the late medieval materials, but dates to between the 9th and 11th c. AD
Interpretation: Early medieval frequentation and late medieval occupation
Concentration of finds per m^2: 12
Period: Middle Ages
Phase: Early-late Middle Ages

SITE.T.U. C.d.P. 57.1/58.1
Municipality: Castiglione della Pescaia
Location: Serrata Martini

Notes: Initially we identified two distinct T.Us, due less to the diversity of the contexts as to field divisions and the different crops present. In this definitive treatment, however, we have opted to treat the settlement found at Serrata Martini as a single T.U. This is due in part to the failure to identify any boundaries within the site and/or specific functional distinctions between the two areas of ceramic fragments identified in the field. The numerous surveys undertaken here, always under optimal visibility conditions, allowed us to acquire a large quantity of data on the material culture present at the Serrata Martini site

Description of site: Fields at Serrata Martini, where we noted various pieces of land with different crops, all belonging to a single property bounded to the W by the Canale Essiccatore drainage canal, to the N by a line of trees and to the E by an embankment

Description of T.U.: A vast scatter of ceramic fragments characterized by some areas with a higher concentration whose boundaries are not clearly defined. Among the materials present we observed a few fragments of Black Glaze ware , abundant *sigillata italica* and *sigillata tardo-italica*, production A, C and D African red slip ware and a few fragments of *ingobbiata di rosso* ware. Coarseware is represented mainly by African kitchenware. There were also extremely large quantities of amphorae, with a preponderance of African vessels. Among the construction materials we observed sandstone blocks, large pieces of lime mortar mixed with brick fragments, large pieces of mortar, bricks and a fragment of a marble slab

Surface area of T.U.: c. 4.5 ha

Interpretation: Harbour settlement related to the imperial-owned villa at Paduline

Finds of help in dating: Our analysis concentrated mainly on materials dating to the 3rd c. AD onwards, though a preliminary examination covered all the finds

Black Glaze ware : Very few fragments of unidentifiable typology

Sigillata italica: Numerous plain and decorated fragments

Decorated sigillata italica: Bowls of type *Conspectus* 34, decorated "à la barbotine"; the most common motifs are the rosette with short petals and the dolphin

Plain sigillata italica: *Consepctus* 34 bowls and *Conspectus* 3.2 and 4.3 dishes

Terra sigillata tardo-italica with moulded decorations: Numerous fragments belonging to the Dragendorff 29 bowl, characterized by a sequence of festoons on the upper part and a simple sequence with erotes on the bottom part

African red slip ware A: Hayes 8 A, 9 A and 14 A bowls, a Hayes 31 dish, deep dishes with a flat rim presenting a light groove towards the inside of type *Atlante* I, Pl.XXIV

African red slip ware C: Various specimens of Hayes 50A dishes, at least two specimens of Hayes 84 deep dishes

African red slip ware D:

1) Hayes 67 nos 5-6, 17 deep dishes;
2) Hayes 61B deep dishes;
3) Hayes 80 bowl;
4) *Atlante* I, Pl.XLVI, 7 dish;
5) Hayes 99B bowl;
6) Hayes 104B deep dish;
7) Hayes 91C flanged bowl

Late antique glazed ware: One wall fragment

Ingobbiata di rosso ware: Numerous fragments of closed and open forms modelled on Hayes types 61, 80 and 91

African kitchenware: Casseroles with raised rims of type *Atlante* I, Pl.CVI, 10-11, or those with a more or less thickened rim of type *Atlante* I, Pl.CVII, 7; dish lids of type *Atlante* I, Pl.CIV, 7; dishes with an abnormally large rim of type *Atlante* I, Pl.CIV, 10 and other similar forms characterized by their hooked rim resembling type *Atlante* I, Pl.CV no.3

Kitchen ware: Some fragments of cooking pots and casseroles comparable to late antique and early medieval materials

Amphorae: Among the best attested containers from the middle imperial period onwards are the Keay IIIA and IIIB amphorae, numerous specimens of which were found; also present were various specimens of Keay XXV, Keay XXVI *spatheia* and Keay LXII late cylindrical amphorae

Concentration of finds per m^2: 25

Period: Multi-period

Phase: Late Republic-late Antiquity (2nd/1st c. BC– 6th/early 7th c. AD)

SITE.T.U. C.d.P. 62.1

Municipality: Castiglione della Pescaia

Location: Poggio Petriccio

Description of site: Hill located N of Castiglione della Pescaia, with a maximum height of 330 m above sealevel. The summit is crossed by three firebreaks

Description of T.U.: The detailed survey aimed at checking an anomaly on an aerial photograph consisting of a semi-elliptical mark with others in a concentric pattern around it, allowed us to find an archaeological deposit in part disturbed by the firebreaks crossing it. We observed a fairly thin stratigraphy on top of the sandstone which partly outcrops on the summit of the hill. Kitchenware and *acroma depurata* wares are present. Some fragments of *acroma depurata* ware present a grey core in the section. The only structure surveyed is the remains of a wall, razed to ground level

Surface area of T.U.: Not determinable with accuracy due to the presence of Mediterranean scrub

Interpretation: Centralized hilltop site

Finds of help in dating: No fragments of identifiable typology were found; the *acroma depurata* ware suggests a date of the 10th-12th c. AD

Period: Middle Ages

Phase: Central centuries

SITE.T.U. C.d.P. 67.1

Municipality: Castiglione della Pescaia

Location: Badiola farm

Description of site: Field located S of the Badiola farm, bounded to the E by the unpaved road leading to the farmhouse. The field was recently ploughed in order to plant a vineyard

Description of T.U.: Area of ceramic fragments measuring about 60 x 30 m, characterized by a very high concentration of materials. In the area of the scatter the soil is greyish. We observed numerous fragments of brick and local stones of medium size probably used to construct the walls of the building. Fragments of lime mortar with crushed brick are also present. Since this deposit has recently been disturbed we were able to carry out a collection aimed at determining the presence of partitions inside the building. We observed that in the southern portion of the building there was an abundance of *dolia* and kitchenware alongside brick fragments. In the northern part, by contrast, we observed the highest concentration of tableware, including various fragments of Black Glaze ware , *sigillata italica* and especially production A, C and D African red slip ware. In a fairly circumscribed area of about 10 x 10 m we collected various fragments of *ingobbiata di rosso* ware and late antique kitchenware. In the central part of the site we collected fragments of *bucchero grigio* belonging to a carinated bowl which we managed to reconstruct in part

Interpretation: Farmstead

Finds of help in dating:

Bucchero grigio: Various fragments of a carinated bowl dating to the 6th c. AD

Black Glaze ware : Fragments of open forms of unidentifiable typology

Sigillata italica:

1) Two specimens of *Conspectus* 3.2 dishes
2) Large hemispherical bowl with a flange of type *Conspectus* 34.1

African red slip ware A:

1) Hayes 14A bowl
2) A fragment of a deep dish with a flat rim and a light groove towards the inside which seems very similar to Salomonson A25 (Cfr. *Atlante* I, Pl.XXIV, 13)
3) Hayes 8A carinated bowl
4) Hayes 9A bowl

African red slip ware C: Various fragments of Hayes 50 A dishes and a Hayes 73A bowl

African red slip ware D:

1) Deep dish of type *Atlante* I, Pl.XXXVIII, 2
2) Specimens of Hayes 67 deep dishes

Ingobbiata di rosso: Open and closed forms dating to the 5th-6th c. AD

African kitchenware: Casseroles of type *Atlante* I, Pl.CVII no.6

Concentration of finds per m^2: 20

Period: Multi-period

Phase: Late Republic-late Antiquity (2nd c. BC-6th/early 7th c. AD)

Observations: The presence of *bucchero grigio* allows us to state that the site was frequented during the Etruscan/archaic period

SITE.T.U. C.d.P. 68.1
Municipality: Castiglione della Pescaia
Location: Punta Fortezza
Description of site: Hill with a maximum height of 200 m above sealevel, located S-E of Pian d'Alma, accessible via a firebreak which in part crosses the summit of the hill. The top of the low hill is covered with Mediterranean scrub
Description of T.U.: On the top of the hill we identified the remains of a sizeable settlement, elliptical in shape. In some places there are still remains of a fairly coarsely built wall circuit surrounding the settlement, made of roughly hewn sandstone blocks of medium to large size, bound with earthy mortar. There are no obvious traces of houses inside the walls, only heaps of stones which come in part from the collapse of the wall circuit. We cannot rule out that the houses were built with a mixed technique or were made entirely of perishable materials. What is certain, however, is that the layout of the settlement was not altered in accordance with Romanesque models. In the upper part of the settlement we observed the remains, at considerable depth beneath the land surface, of a structure which probably had a circular floor plan, perhaps a tower. The wall face is made of local stones of variable size laid in sub-horizontal courses and bound with mortar poor in lime. Various pieces of iron slag were found in the area covered by the settlement
Surface area of T.U.: 0.5 ha
Interpretation: Castle
Period: Middle Ages
Phase: Central centuries

SITE.T.U. C.d.P. 68.2
Description of T.U.: Area of ceramic fragments on the northern edge of the settlement. The materials were brought to light in that part of the site crossed by the firebreak. The pottery finds collected include *acroma depurata* and kitchenwares, fragments of *vetrina sparsa* ware and imported amphorae
Kitchen ware: Open and closed forms dating to between the late 9th and 10th c. AD;
Acroma depurata: Fragments of jugs dating to between the 9th and 11th c. AD
Sparse glaze ware: Fragments of jugs of the 11th-12th c. AD
Amphorae: Fragments of *a cannelures* amphorae imported from North Africa or Norman Sicily
Period: Middle Ages
Phase: Early-central Middle Ages (9th-12th c. AD)

SITE.T.U. C.d.P. 69.1
Municipality: Castiglione della Pescaia
Location: Poggettone
Description of site: Low hill W of the monastery, only 700 m as the crow flies from Sestinga Nuova. The site has been flattened in the summit area and the slopes are covered by an olive grove
Description of T.U.: The survey undertaken with the aim of checking a soil mark on a vertical aerial photograph led to the discovery of an extremely interesting settlement. In the field we observed a large dark grey mark, rich in charcoal, which corresponds almost exactly to the summit area; fragments of kitchenware, *semidepurata* and *depurata* wares of the 9th-11th c. were present. In some places a wall circuit was still visible, though collapsed and almost completely buried; it was made of stones of varying sizes, built using a dry stone technique or bound with an earthy mortar of which no trace survives. A modest *shovel test*, measuring about 40 x 40 cm and no more than 15 cm deep, allowed us to identify a dark layer rich in charcoal with some small but not at all worn ceramic fragments. The absence of stones belonging to the houses suggests that these were built entirely using perishable materials
Surface area of T.U.: 1200 m^2
Interpretation: Centralized hilltop site
Concentration of finds per m^2: 5
Period: Middle Ages
Phase: Early-central Middle Ages

SITE.T.U. C.d.P. 80.1
Municipality: Scarlino
Location: Val Molina
Description of site: Section along the unpaved road at La Zinghera, W of the Alma river, and the field below it
Description of T.U.: The cleaning of the section running along the road aimed to check the data reported in Cucini 1989a on the presence of disturbed stratigraphies and the remains of burials. This investigation allowed us to identify an anthropic layer black in colour, rich in fragments of kitchen and *semidepurata* wares, whilst no trace of burials was found; however, the fairly reliable information collected locally suggests that these did exist. A fairly large quantity of materials was found, including some in the strip of field next to the road, about 100 m long, roughly the same length as the stratigraphies visible in section. Among the materials it is worth noting a rim certainly from an ARS Hayes 99B deep dish; coarseware is abundant but highly fragmentary: however we did identify a specimen of flanged bowl in *acroma depurata* and a cooking pot with a band-shaped rim, frequent indicators in the 6th-c. layers at Roselle.
Interpretation: Village (?)
Period: Late Antiquity
Phase: 6th c. AD
Observations: The hypothesis advanced in Cucini 1989a, which identifies the disturbed stratigraphies as the cemetery of a church of Santo Stefano, attested in 1160 and destroyed when the road was built, does not rule out the presence of a pre-existing late antique village

SITE.T.U. C.d.P. 82.1
Municipality: Scarlino
Location: Poggio Castello
Description of site: Poggio Castello is a hill 140 m above sealevel in the Scarlino part of the Alma valley. The hill can be reached via a firebreak which leads off the internal Pian d'Alma road. The summit of this low hill has been profoundly disturbed by the firebreak which turns at a 90° angle on the hilltop, turning S towards the valley
Description of T.U.: The deposit has been severely compromised by the firebreak cutting through it, which has led to the almost complete removal of the archaeological sediment and exposing the bare rock. On the southern and western slopes are some heaps of small to medium-sized roughly hewn stones and some stretches of walls which have completely collapsed and are visible at ground level. There is no trace of mortar. This settlement, like that of Punta Fortezza, was not rebuilt in the Romanesque period. Numerous pieces of slag from the smelting of iron were found. Among the pottery founds collected, alongside 9th/10th c. kitchenwares, were fragments of jugs with strap handles, made of both *acroma selezionata* and *acroma depurata*, comparable to typologies of the late 9th/10th c.
Surface area of T.U.: 6000 m^2
Interpretation: Castle
Degree of reliability: 5
Period: Middle Ages
Phase: Early-central Middle Ages

1.2. T.U.s from the Forma Italiae-Vetulonia Project (Curri 1978)

Site number/T.U.: Curri 75
Municipality: Castiglione della Pescaia
Location: Fosso Cortigliano
Description of site: Field about 380 m S-E of the Podere S.Enrico, bounded to the E by the Fosso Cortigliano and to the N by the unpaved road leading from the Badiola farm to Casa Fornace
Description of T.U.: The analysis of the data supplied by Curri allows us to identify this as one of the most interesting sites in the Castiglione area, especially for the late antique and early medieval period given the presence of burials superimposed on the residential area of the Roman villa. Unfortunately poor visibility and above all the levelling of the field a few years ago meant that only a few fragments of bricks and pottery were found; these provided no further information to supplement that provided by Curri.
Curri 1978, pp.135-143 informs us of the discovery of a Roman villa measuring about 100 x 150 m; on the basis of the pottery finds, its construction can be dated to the 2nd c. BC, whilst it appears to have been abandoned no later than the 5th c. AD. Inside the scatter, farm work brought to light numerous mosaic tesserae. An excavation

campaign in 1974 brought to light some burials on top of the villa. The upper part of tomb no. 1 consisted of a rectangular stone platform, which gave it the appearance of a brick caisson, oriented S-E, measuring 2.9 x 1.4 m and 0.85 m deep. Tomb no. 1 was built using the wooden coffin as a framework; the boards of which it was made gave it a polygonal section. The imprint of the coffin was preserved in the layer of mortar applied around it to hold the stones of the side walls in place. The space needed to host the coffin was created by damaging the villa structures. The roof was made by pouring mortar on top of the wooden caisson to form a low vault; two rows of five trapezoid-shaped roof tiles with raised edges were placed on top of this. These were reinforced at the sides with stones placed so as to fill the gap. Inside the tomb the well-preserved skeleton of a male adult aged about 40-45 old was found in a supine position, together with some fragments from the skull of a child; there were no grave goods. Ten m S-W of tomb no. 1 is a rectangular platform of sandstone slabs, perhaps the remains of a wall foundation; at the edge of this, in a transverse position, was tomb no. 2: a simple grave, shallow and 2 m long, bounded by a row of stone slabs stuck into the ground. The grave was covered by a layer of small unevenly shaped stones, placed above a row of 4 irregular slabs of larger size. On the outside the tomb must have been sealed with large limestone slabs, only one of which remained *in situ*. In the grave, facing S-W, was the skeleton of a man aged 40-45, in a supine position and with the hands placed over the pubis; there were no grave goods. According to local sources at least another two tombs similar to no. 2 were destroyed during farm work

Interpretation: Roman villa (on top of which a late antique burial ground was established)

Finds of help in dating: Black Glaze ware , sigillata italica, African red slip ware

Period: Roman

Phase: Late Republic-late Empire ($3^{rd}/2^{nd}$ c. BC-$4^{th}/5^{th}$ c. AD)

Observations: The initial date of the burial ground cannot be ascertained but on the basis of the tomb typology it appears to belong to the late antique and early medieval period

Bibliography: Curri 1978, Site no.75

Site number/T.U.: Curri 88

Municipality: Castiglione della Pescaia

Location: Poggio Franco

Description of site: Field about 200 m S-E of the Poggio Franco estate, S of the unpaved road leading to the estate. When first surveyed the field had lain fallow for at least a year and was difficult to survey given the fairly dense vegetation. The second survey was carried out in September 2001, shortly after radical farmwork had taken place in order to plant a vineyard here

Description of T.U.: Here Curri identified one of the largest villas in the Castiglione area, with a wealth of materials, some of which were valuable. During an initial survey, when the field had lain fallow for a long time (2001), we only found some sporadic fragments of large bricks, visible where the land surface was exposed. Among the ceramic finds only one fragment of *sigillata italica* was collected. In the ditch next to the road a large column drum was noted, which must have belonged to the villa. The second survey, after the addition of large quantities of earth to plant a vineyard, was not much more fruitful. As soon as ploughing intercepted large structures, it was decided to add large amounts of earth; this was then levelled and the vineyard planted on top of it. The second survey yielded only sporadic fragments of *sigillata italica* and ARS. Given the site's current illegibility, its correct definition of necessity relies on the data reported in Curri 1978, which allow us to reconstruct the dimensions of the Roman villa (c. 50 x 100 m) and to define its material culture at least in part

Construction materials:

1) Trachyte column drum (height 40 cm, diameter 41 cm. Hole running through the middle)

2) Numerous fragments of tiles, pieces of lime mortar, fragments of plaster painted a purple colour and small bricks from *opus spicatum* floors

3) Fragments of terracotta facing slabs with a geometrical decoration stamped on one of the faces

Copper-alloy finds:

1) Ring with grooves of elliptical section, diameter 5.8 cm

2) Lock mechanism

3) Nail with a rounded head, lacking the point

Lead finds:

1) Cap shaped like a *cardium* valve. Max diam. 3.7 cm

2) Fragment consisting of two irregular oval plates, joined by a piece of smaller section. Dimensions 6.5 x 5 cm, height 2.7 cm

Glass finds:

1) Straight horizontal strap handle in pale green glass, ending in a disk. Length 11.5 cm, width 1.6 cm

2) 4 fragments of blueish-green and whitish glass, including a ring foot and two other fragments of ring feet

3) 8 fragments of flat slabs of whitish and pale green glass for windows, obtained by melting in a mould. Two fragments still have a straight margin with rounded edges. A third has two straight margins at right angles

Coin finds:

1) *As* of Augustus. Corroded surfaces. Obv/ Head of the emperor Rev/ illegible

2) *As* of Vespasian. Very corroded surfaces Obv/ head of the emperor Rev/ illegible

3) Silver *denarius* of Vespasian of AD 79

4) Coin of Constantine or Crispus. Providentia Augustea type. AD 324/330

5) Reduced maiorina of Constantius II. Minted in AD 531 for Siscia or Sirmio

Functional objects in terracotta:

1) Loom weight made of a reddish-brown fabric with sandy inclusions, of flattened biconical shape with a rounded end. Diam. 4.7 cm, height 2.9 cm

Pottery finds:

1) Fragment of bucchero-like fabric; black surface, grey in section. Decoration of impressed rings with a straight groove

2) 12 fragments of Black Glaze ware

3) 166 fragments of *sigillata italica* belonging to small cups, paterae and large bowls. The clay is always very fine, of reddish-light brown colour, and the slip is of good quality

4) 55 fragments of ARS

5) 25 fragments of red or yellowish-brown coarseware

Surface area of T.U.: 5000 m^2

Interpretation: Roman villa

Period: Roman

Phase: Late Republic-late Empire (2nd c. BC-5th c. AD)

Bibliography: Curri 1978, Site no.88

Site number/T.U.: Curri 97

Location: Castellaccio del Prile

Municipality: Castiglione della Pescaia

Description of site: At the foot of a hill at 287 m above sealevel, overlooked by the medieval ruins of Castellaccio di Prile and to the E of the farmstead of the same name, near the recently built dam of a small artificial lake

Description of T.U.: The archaeological area was partly destroyed by earthmoving work for the construction of the dam. Abundant pieces of roof tiles and ceramic fragments are scattered on the surface, in an E-W direction, for a stretch of about 200 m, with two or three areas of higher concentration towards the eastern end above a slight ridge where the remains of an *opus spicatum* and lime mortar and crushed brick floor, lumps of lime mortar and fragments of plaster can be seen on the surface. N of the villa, near a brick cabin, is a mass of trachyte cut into a circular shape

Interpretation of T.U.: Roman villa

Period: Roman

Phase: Late Republic-late Empire (without apparent gaps)

Initial chronology: 2nd c. BC

Final chronology: 5th c. AD

Motivation for dating: Finds

Materials found:

Building materials: Numerous small flooring bricks made of yellowish clay, fragments of lime mortar and crushed brick floors, fragments of tile made of a rose-coloured fabric with mortises at the sides, bricks, roof tiles

Coin finds: *As* of Nero, poorly preserved. Diam. 25 mm; weight 6.7 g. Obv/ NERO CAESAR AUG GERM IMP. Head of the emperor wearing a crown right Rev/ Flying Victory on the left, preceded by a globe. At the sides of the script: S C.; diam. 25.5 mm; weight 6.751 g. *Sestertius* of Otacilia (AD 244-249). Corroded surfaces. Obv/ MARCIA OTACIL SEVERA AUG. Head of the empress right Rev/

PUDICITIA AG Representation of enthroned Pudicitia left. Under the throne, the initials S C., diam. 31 mm; weight 15.459 g.
Copper-alloy finds: Small rod of square section; both ends are pointed. Length cm 52.8 cm; thickness 0.35 cm
Lead finds: A fr. of foil. Length 4.9 cm
Metalworking activities:
Slag: 5 small pieces of lead slag
Glass finds: A fr. of turquoise glass, 9 frs of small vessels made of greenish-blue glass, 5 frs of flat slabs of whitish, whitish-purple and greenish-blue glass, made by pouring into a mould, two of which still have a straight, rounded edge. Thickness ranges from 0.4 to 0.6 cm. A fragment of a strap-handle with a double groove on the back. Length 11 cm
Terracotta tools: Biconical loom weight with a rounded end. Grey clay with a brownish-red surface with sandy inclusions. Hole off-centre. Poorly made. Diam. 4.5 cm; height 3.1 cm
Architectural decorations: Fr. of a flat slab with one face decorated by bundles of grooves intersecting at right angles. Compact rose-coloured clay with silica inclusions
Pottery:
Black Glaze ware : 3 frs of Black Glaze ware paterae, five made of a light brown-yellowish clay with an opaque black slip and one made of reddish clay with a shiny blackish-blue slip
Sigillata italica: 222 fragments belonging to small cups and large paterae with different grades of more or less shiny and diluted slip
African red slip ware: 112 fragments of African red slip ware
Hayes types: 10A, no.3; 182, no.2; 197, no.24; 49, no.1; 67/28; 185, no.3; 23, no.24; 16, no.16; 57, no.1; 8A, no.1; 8A, no.30; 9A, no.2
Coarseware: Numerous fragments of Roman coarseware, including various types of handles: shaped and grooved strap handles, single and double handles of circular section and twisted handles
Bibliography: Curri 1978, Site no.97

1.3. T.U.s from the *Ager Rusellanus* Project (Citter 1988-1989)

SITE/T.U. GR 1
Municipality: Grosseto
Location: Strada del Serpaio
Description of site: At the southern end of a flat field, at 78 m above sealevel
Description of T.U.: Area of ceramic fragments measuring about 400 m^2. Numerous bricks are present. Among the tableware it is worth noting 7 fragments of Black Glaze ware , 9 of *sigillata italica* including one of type Goudineau 1968, no.17/18 and 2 fragments of *sigillata tardoitalica*. Also present is coarseware for use at table and in the kitchen. African red slip ware is attested by 5 fragments of unidentifiable typology, whilst African kitchenware is present with 3 fragments. Among the identifiable amphorae are 4 fragments of Dressel 1 and 2 of Dressel 2/4. A fragment of window glass is also documented
Interpretation: Farmstead
Period: Roman
Phase: Late Republic-early/middle Empire
New data: A review of the pottery materials allowed us to identify a minimum number of at least 4 forms (an *acroma depurata* flanged bowl modelled on ARS type Hayes 91 and three cooking pots of the 5th/6th c. AD) which represent evidence of frequentation in the 5th/6th c. AD, after the site's abandonment
Second Phase: Late antique frequentation

SITE/T.U. GR 8
Municipality: Grosseto
Location: Poggio Mosconcino-Podere La Vigna
Description of site: Flat field used for pasture; 38 m above sealevel
Description of T.U.: Area of ceramic fragments measuring about 40 x 20 m. 46 fragments of coarseware jugs were collected, with different types of handles, together with 22 fragments of kitchenware, a fragment of a *dolium* and an Africana II amphora
Interpretation: Farmstead
Period: Roman
Phase: Generic imperial period
New data: A review of the pottery materials allowed us to identify various specimens of jugs made from both purified and selected fabrics with strap handles with thickened edges level with the rim, in addition to several fragments of flat bases (similar wares are found at Poggio Cavolo between the 10th and the 11th c.). Among the kitchenware we identified cooking pots with a strongly everted rim of the 9th/10th c.
Second Phase: Occupation of the end of the early-central Middle Ages reusing the Roman site

SITE/T.U. GR 13.2
Municipality: Grosseto
Location: Casette di Mota
Description of site: The digging of a ditch during work to pave the road leading from the Rosellano estate to the school at Casette di Mota, facing the estate of the same name, brought to light a section of about 40 m in length, where a layer of lime mortar and crushed brick is visible. In the ditch were numerous ceramic fragments and bricks.
Description of T.U.: The settlement must have covered an area of about half a hectare and was divided into several clusters. Mosaics made of black and white tesserae were present at the site, as shown by a fragment now in the nearby school, found in the villa area
Materials found:
Coarseware: 57 fragments of kitchenware
Black Glaze ware : 45 fragments
Sigillata italica: 159 fragments, including types Goudineau 1968, nos 3, 5, 7, 13, 15 , 21, 24, 38 and 41
Sigillata tardoitalica: 17 fragments
Thin-walled pottery: 4 unidentified fragments
African red slip ware A: 12 fragments, including types Hayes 6A, 8A, 17A
African red slip ware C: 2 fragments belonging to type Hayes 50
African red slip ware D: 12 fragments, including types Hayes 56, 58B, 60, 61, 63, 99
African kitchenware: 4 fragments
Ingobbiata di rosso ware: A review of the materials allowed us to identify forms modelled on the Tunisian prototype Hayes 61, as well as typologies belonging to a tradition independent of the influence of ARS
Sigillata chiara tarda dell'Italia centro-settentrionale: A base fragment with an overpainted decoration, comparable to materials from Roselle in context 5147=5170 of the early decades of the 5th c. AD
Amphorae: 1 fragment of Dressel 7/13 and 1 of Dressel 2/4
Lamps: 5 unidentified fragments
Metal finds: One disc shaped copper alloy buckle
Period: Roman
Phase: Late Republic-late Antiquity (without apparent gaps)
Initial chronology: 2nd c. BC
Final chronology: 6th c. AD
Interpretation: Villa

SITE/T.U. GR 24
Municipality: Grosseto
Location: Montebrandoli
Description of site: On the slopes of the low Montebrandoli hill, at 65 m above sealevel
Description of T.U.: Area of ceramic fragments measuring about 40 x 70 m; in fact it is probable that the original site covered a smaller area and that the size of the scatter has been increased by erosion and run-off. This is a residential unit of small farmstead type with an adjacent brick production structure. Two fragments of Black Glaze ware , a Dressel 7/11 and a Dressel 2/4 were collected. Also present were 34 fragments of kitchenware
Interpretation: Residence with a brick kiln
Period: Roman
Phase: Late Republic-early Empire
New data: A review of the ceramic materials allowed us to identify a minimum number of at least two forms (an *acroma depurata* flanged bowl modelled on ARS type Hayes 91 and a cooking pot of the 5th/6th c. AD) indicating frequentation during the 5th/6th c. AD, after the site's abandonment
Second Phase: Late antique frequentation

SITE/T.U. GR 42
Municipality: Grosseto
Location: Poggio Mosconcino-Podere La Vigna

Description of site: Field used for pasture, with a slight slope. At 42m above sealevel, near a dirt track
Description of T.U.: Area of ceramic fragments measuring about 5 x 5 m; presence of bricks and scarce pottery, including 3 fragments of tableware and a base in Black Glaze ware
Interpretation: Frequentation
Period: Etrusco-Roman
Phase: Hellenistic-late Republic
New data: A review of the pottery materials allowed us to identify a minimum number of two forms (an *acroma depurata* flanged bowl modelled on ARS type Hayes 91 and a jug with a thickened strap handle level with the edge, dating to the 6th/7th c. AD) indicating a frequentation in the 6th c. AD, after the site's abandonment
Second Phase: Late antique and early medieval frequentation
Observations: It cannot be ruled out that the isolated fragment of Black Glaze ware belongs to an early frequentation of the site and that the feature documented belongs to a seasonal late antique structure

SITE/T.U. GR 54.1
Municipality: Grosseto
Location: Sterpeto
Description of site: Flat field part of which hosts a vineyard and part of which is fallow
Description of T.U.: In an area of about 2 hectares, at on average 12 m above sealevel, features clearly belonging to a large Roman villa were found. Particularly noteworthy are the remains of pottery pipes perhaps belonging to a bath complex, fragments of black and white mosaics, large and small mosaic tesserae, fragments of whitish floor plaster and one fragment of Pompeiian red plaster from a wall decoration. Also recovered were 17 fragments of Roman brick bearing the stamp *cla(udi) cob(athii) sab(athii) vol(usiani)*. The site must have had facilities for the production of bricks and for the smelting of iron, as demonstrated by the abundant wasters and slag. To the E, covering an area of several hectares, were some scatters of pottery materials and bricks which may relate to the villa's subsidiary structures or the residences of dependent share-croppers
Materials found:
Coarseware: 63 fragments of kitchenware; 21 fragments of open forms and 89 of closed forms of table/storage ware
Black Glaze ware : 2 unidentified fragments and one specimen of type Morel 155
Sigillata italica: 2 individuals of type Goudineau 1968, 38b; one individual of type 38a; 5 of type 43; one type 39c and 17 unidentified fragments
Sigillata tardoitalica: 17 fragments
Thin-walled pottery: unidentified fragments
African red slip ware A: Hayes types 8, 9b, 14 and 14/17
African red slip ware C: Hayes types 49 and 50
African red slip ware D: 43 fragments, including Hayes types 67, 76, 99 and 104
African kitchenware: 11 fragments
Ingobbiata di rosso ware: A review of the materials allowed us to identify forms modelled on the Tunisian prototypes Hayes 61 and 91, alongside typologies independent of the influence of ARS
Amphorae: 5 fragments of Graeco-Italic; 2 of generic Hispanic; 2 of Dressel 1; 6 of Dressel 2/4; 1 of Pelichet 47; 3 of unidentified African; 1 of unidentified Tripolitanian; 1 of *spatheion* and 90 unidentified
Lamps: unidentified fragments
Metal finds: 3 fragments of copper foil; the handle of a small container and a copper buckle
Glass finds: a fragment of window glass; 6 fragments of a chalice
Period: Roman
Phase: Late Republic-late Antiquity (without apparent gaps)
Initial chronology: 2nd c. BC
Final chronology: 6th-early 7th c. AD
Interpretation: Villa

SITE/T.U. GR 113
Municipality: Grosseto
Location: Casoni del Terzo
Description of site: Flat fallow field
Description of T.U.: Area of ceramic fragments measuring 30 x 10 m which yielded bricks and coarseware for both table/storage and kitchen use
Interpretation: Farmstead
Period: Roman
Phase: Generic Empire
New data: A review of the pottery materials allowed us to identify various fragments of strap handles with thickened edges, 5-6 cm wide, belonging to jugs made from similar fabrics to those from Poggio Cavolo, in use between the 10th and 11th c., and a specimen of small medieval amphora with a rounded and thickened rim, a *testo* with a thinned edge and a cooking pot with a strongly everted rim and a pronounced groove, dating to between the 9th and the 10th c.
Second Phase: Reoccupation of the site between the end of the early and the central Middle Ages

SITE/T.U. MP15
Municipality: Grosseto
Location: Zona Tre Fonti
Description of T.U.: Circular tumulus clearly distinct from the rest of the field but impossible to investigate directly given the dense vegetation covering it. Information gathered in the local area refers to the presence of human bones. A few fragments of coarseware were present
Interpretation: Tomb (?)
Period: Not identified
New data: A review of the pottery materials allowed us to identify a minimum of at least two forms (an *acroma depurata* flanged bowl modelled on ARS type Hayes 91 and a juglet with a band-shaped rim dating to the 6th/7th c. AD) indicating a frequentation during the 6th c. AD after the site's abandonment
Second Phase: Late antique frequentation

SITE/T.U. MP17
Municipality: Grosseto
Location: Podere Colombaio
Description of site: On the right-hand side of the dirt track leading to the top of a ploughed field, sloping slightly and at 32 m above sealevel
Description of T.U.: Very dense concentration of ceramic fragments covering an area of 30 x 20 m. Present are coarseware for table/storage and kitchen use. Among the tableware attested are 5 fragments of unidentified Black Glaze ware , and 2 of ARS. A Dressel 1 amphora and 10 unidentified amphora fragments were present
Interpretation: Farmstead
Period: Roman
Phase: Late Republic-early/middle Empire
New data: A review of the ceramic materials allowed us to identify a minimum of at least 3 forms (an *acroma depurata* bowl modelled on ARS type Hayes 99 and two jugs with thickened strap handles, one level with the edge and the other set immediately beneath it), indicating a frequentation during the 6th c. AD after the site's abandonment
Second Phase: Late antique frequentation

1.4 T.U.s from the new Surveys between the Bruna and Osa valleys (code S.2003-2005)

SITE/T.U. ***S.2003-2005*** **no.8.1**
Municipality: Grosseto
Location: Podere Serratone
Description of site: Low hill used for pasture, about 250 m N of the Rispescia stream, between Podere Serratone and Podere Poggio della Pescina
Description of T.U.: Scatter of ceramic fragments measuring about 100 x 110 m, with a particularly high concentration on the top of the hill. The concentration of materials ranges from 10 fragments per m^2 on the flat hilltop to 1-2 fragments per m^2 in the western part of the scatter. The finds include tableware (*sigillata tardoitalica* and ARS), African kitchenware, local/regional kitchenware, *acroma depurata* and fragments of Tunisian amphorae. Also present are various fragments of bricks. The orthophotographic map to a scale of 1:10000 allowed us to identify, in the central area of the hill, an evident soil mark corresponding to the highest concentration of materials; the mark is rectangular and measures 100 x 35 m
Concentration of finds per m^2: 10
Interpretation: Village (?)

Period: Roman
Phase: Early-late Empire
Initial chronology: 1st-2nd c. BC
Final chronology: 5th c. AD

SITE/T.U. ***S.2003-2005*** **no.10.1**
Municipality: Grosseto
Location: Podere Serratone
Description of site: Field on the western slopes of Poggio Rossino, about 500 m from the top of the low hill
Description of T.U.: Area of ceramic fragments measuring about 18 x 15 m. We observed specimens of jugs made from purified and selected fabrics of "Serratone type"; bricks were completely absent. According to information supplied by the owner of the estate, an intact amphora was found in the vineyard about 250 m to the S during the 1930s
Concentration of finds per m^2: 3-4
Interpretation: Individual residential structure of hut type
Period: Middle Ages
Phase: Early Middle Ages
Initial chronology: 7th c. AD
Final chronology: 9th c. AD

SITE/T.U. ***S.2003-2005*** **no.11.1**
Municipality: Grosseto
Location: Podere Serratone
Description of site: Field in a lowlying area, 70 m above sealevel. The area is bounded to the N and W by the Fosso Borgognano, and to the E by the slopes of Poggio Rossino
Description of T.U.: Large scatter of ceramic fragments measuring about 84 x 145 m. No traces of either structures or construction materials such as stone or bricks were noted. The site does not even have natural protection, whilst the water supply appears to be guaranteed by the nearby streams. The structures must have been made of perishable materials. Among the large numbers of pottery fragments we observed cooking pots, a few *testi* and lids, but above all a large quantity of *acroma depurata* and *selezionata* ware with a high proportion of sandwich fabrics. *Acroma depurata* is in the clear majority over kitchenware. Particularly well-represented were jugs with strap handles set either on the rim or beneath it and medieval small amphorae. The finds included a few indicators of the late 6th-7th c.
Concentration of finds per m^2: 15
Interpretation: Central part of the early medieval village of Podere Serratone
Period: Middle Ages
Phase: Early Middle Ages
Initial chronology: Late $6^{th}/7^{th}$ c. AD
Final chronology: 9th c. AD

SITE/T.U. ***S.2003-2005*** **no.11.2**
Municipality: Grosseto
Location: Podere Serratone
Description of T.U.: In the central and eastern part of the scatter we identified a small area whose boundaries were difficult to determine (less than 6 x 6 m), characterized by numerous fragments of fired clay, pottery fragments made from purified and selected fabrics, including strap handles and the walls of small amphorae, some of which were overfired
Concentration of finds per m^2: 8-10
Interpretation: Pottery kiln
Period: Middle Ages
Phase: Early Middle Ages
Initial chronology: Late $6^{th}/7^{th}$ c. AD
Final chronology: 9th c. AD

SITE/T.U. ***S.2003-2005*** **no.12.1**
Municipality: Grosseto
Location: Podere Serratone
Description of site: Field about 60 m S of T.U. 11.1
Description of T.U.: Scatter identified about 40 m from T.U. 13.1 and 62 m from T.U. 11.1. The absence of pottery materials between T.U. 12.1 and the other two T.U.s indicates that this is a distinct site. The ceramic scatter is fairly large (35 x 63 m) and the concentration of finds is lower than in the central part of the village, whilst the typology of the materials is identical. We can suggest a second settlement area belonging to the village, probably a large farmstead, or another cluster of houses. There are no differences between the pottery assemblages to suggest a difference in status between the inhabitants of the two sites
Concentration of finds per m^2: 5-6
Interpretation: Large farmstead
Period: Middle Ages
Phase: Early Middle Ages
Initial chronology: Late $6^{th}/7^{th}$ c. AD
Final chronology: 9th c. AD

SITE/T.U. ***S.2003-2005*** **no.13.1**
Municipality: Grosseto
Location: Podere Serratone
Description of site: Field adjacent to the S side of that of T.U. 11.1, from which it is separated by a net fence
Description of T.U.: Area of ceramic fragments measuring about 50 x 40 m. The material present is identical to that from T.U. 11.1. Probably there is no gap between T.U. 11.1 and 13.1: the two T.U.s are separated only by the net fence and by a narrow ditch
Concentration of finds per m^2: 4-5
Interpretation: Part of the early medieval village of Podere Serratone
Period: Middle Ages
Phase: Early Middle Ages
Initial chronology: Late $6^{th}/7^{th}$ c. AD
Final chronology: 9th c. AD

SITE/T.U. ***S.2003-2005*** **no.23.1**
Municipality: Magliano in Toscana
Location: Casa Steccaia
Description of site: Narrow strip of lowlying land at 80 m above sealevel, about 600 m W of the Osa river and 300 m S of Casa Steccaia
Description of T.U.: In the field near the stream we noted an elongated concentration of ceramics, measuring about 12 x 30 m; the highest density of finds was in an area measuring 12 x 14 m. We collected numerous pottery fragments, almost exclusively *acroma selezionata* and *depurata* ware, and with an abundance of sandwich fabrics. Numerous handles and bases belonging to jugs and medieval small amphorae were found. The handles are strap-shaped. No building stones were found whilst the rare bricks seem to have been taken from nearby Roman sites and reused
Concentration of finds per m^2: 5-6
Interpretation: House made of perishable materials
Period: Middle Ages
Phase: Early Middle Ages
Initial chronology: 8th c. AD
Final chronology: 9th c. AD

SITE/T.U. ***S.2003-2005*** **no.30.1**
Municipality: Magliano in Toscana
Location: Poggio Castellaccio
Description of site: Slightly sloping field on the southern slopes of Poggio Castellaccio, about 400 m W of the Osa
Description of T.U.: Area of ceramic fragments oriented N-S and measuring about 50 x 25 m. We found large numbers of bricks, including roof tiles, local stones and a large quantity of pottery, including *sigillata italica*, production A, C and D ARS, transport amphorae (including Tunisian) and coarseware for table/storage and kitchen use
Concentration of finds per m^2: 10
Interpretation: Farmstead
Period: Roman
Phase: Multi-phase
Initial chronology: late 1st c. BC/1st c. AD
Final chronology: 5th/early 6th c. AD

SITE/T.U. ***S.2003-2005*** **no.30.2**
Municipality: Magliano in Toscana
Location: Poggio Castellaccio
Description of T.U.: Area of ceramic fragments oriented NW-SE and measuring about 60 x 26 m. The T.U. is very close to 30.1, about 20 m away, but there is a clear gap between the two (these may have been two adjacent farmsteads forming a single complex settlement unit). Present were numerous fragments of roof tiles, local stone and

large quantities of pottery, including all the classes found in T.U. 30.1. A series of sporadic materials found about 140 m to the E included a fragment of soapstone
Concentration of finds per m^2: 8-10
Interpretation: Farmstead
Period: Roman
Phase: Multi-phase
Initial chronology: Late 1st c. BC/1st c. AD
Final chronology: 5th/early 6th c. AD

SITE/T.U. *S.2003-2005* no.31.1
Municipality: Magliano in Toscana
Location: Poggio Castellaccio
Description of site: Summit of Poggio Castellaccio, at 160 m above sealevel, about 500 m E of the Osa. Immediately W of the hilltop a house with outbuildings has recently been constructed; judging from the sections still exposed building work appears to have intercepted archaeological layers
Description of T.U.: The summit of Poggio Castellaccio is surrounded by a circular wall circuit (diameter about 60 m), enclosing an area of 0.7 hectares. The mark is clearly visible on vertical and oblique aerial photographs, whilst in the field the remains of the walls are difficult to interpret due to the dense vegetation covering them. The type of stone used is local sandstone. The ceramic materials found are in *acroma* ware for storage/table and kitchen use, dating to the 10th-12th c. AD The site can be identified as the *castellare de Scopertorio* mentioned in the *Tavola delle Possessioni di Montiano* of 1320; it is also possible that this context is the anonymous farmstead on the Osa mentioned in the mid-11th c.
Concentration of finds per m^2: 10
Interpretation: Phase one castle
Period: Middle Ages
Phase: Central centuries
Initial chronology: 10th c. AD
Final chronology: 12th c. AD
Bibliography: Farinelli 2007; Fentress-Wickham 2002b, pp.67-68

SITO/UT *S.2003-2005* n.32.1
Municipality: Magliano in Toscana
Location: Poggio Castellaccio
Description of site: Field about 100 m NW of that of T.U. 30.1 and 30.2. At 100 m above sealevel
Description of T.U.: Small area of ceramic fragments, measuring about 9 x 7 m. Bricks and building stones are absent whilst coarseware is attested with typologies of cooking pots and jugs suggesting a date of the late 9th-11th c.
Concentration of finds per m^2: 6
Interpretation: House (in perishable materials?)
Period: Middle Ages
Phase: Early-central Middle Ages
Initial chronology: Late 9th c. AD
Final chronology: 11th c. AD

SITE/T.U. *S.2003-2005* no.33.1
Municipality: Magliano in Toscana
Location: Poggio Castellaccio
Description of site: Olive grove on the western slopes of a hill at a maximum of 133 m above sealevel, SE of Poggio Castellaccio
Description of T.U.: Area of ceramic fragments measuring about 11 x 7 m. Bricks and building stones are absent whilst coarseware is attested with typologies of cooking pots and jugs suggesting a late 9th-11th c. date
Concentration of finds per m^2: 3-4
Interpretation: House (in perishable materials?)
Period: Middle Ages
Phase: Early-central Middle Ages
Initial chronology: Late 9th c. AD
Final chronology: 11th c. AD

SITE/T.U. *S.2003-2005* no.33.2
Municipality: Magliano in Toscana
Location: Poggio Castellaccio
Description of T.U.: Area of ceramic fragments measuring about 7 x 3.5 m on the summit of the low hill. Bricks and building stones are absent whilst coarseware is attested with typologies of cooking pots and jugs suggesting a date of the late 9th-11th c.; specimens of *testi* and lids were also found
Concentration of finds per m^2: 5
Interpretation: House (in perishable materials?)
Period: Middle Ages
Phase: Early-central Middle Ages
Initial chronology: Late 9th c. AD
Final chronology: 11th c. AD

SITE/T.U. *S.2003-2005* no.33.3
Municipality: Magliano in Toscana
Location: Poggio Castellaccio
Description of T.U.: Area of ceramic fragments measuring about 12 x 8.5 m on the summit of the low hill, 7.5 m S of T.U. 33.2. Bricks and building stones are absent whilst coarseware is attested with typologies of cooking pots and jugs suggesting a date of the late 9th-11th c.; specimens of *testi* and lids were also found
Concentration of finds per m^2: 6-8
Interpretation: House (in perishable materials?)
Period: Middle Ages
Phase: Early-central Middle Ages
Initial chronology: Late 9th c. AD
Final chronology: 11th c. AD

SITE/T.U. *S.2003-2005* no.34.1
Municipality: Magliano in Toscana
Location: Poggio Castellaccio
Description of site: Olive grove on the western slopes of Poggio Castellaccio, about 150 m from the top of the hill
Description of T.U.: Area of ceramic fragments measuring about 25 x 17 m, at 110 m above sealevel. Both bricks and building stones are completely absent. Coarseware for table/storage and kitchen use is attested; we also collected a handle made of sparse glaze B ware from Lazio. The material is highly fragmentary, some cooking pots can be dated to between the late 9th and the 10th c.
Concentration of finds per m^2: 8
Interpretation: House (in perishable materials?)
Period: Middle Ages
Phase: Early-central Middle Ages
Initial chronology: Late 9th c. AD
Final chronology: 11th c. AD

SITE/T.U. *S.2003-2005* no.35.3
Municipality: Magliano in Toscana
Location: Poggio Castellaccio
Description of site: Pasture located between the Osa river and Poggio Castellaccio, at 80 m above sealevel
Description of T.U.: Area of ceramic fragments measuring about 30 x 20 m; construction materials are completely absent. The pottery is highly fragmentary, but nonetheless offers a homogeneous set of coarseware, mainly with purified and selected fabrics. Fragments of jugs with strap handles, similar to 10th-c. types from the village of Poggio Cavolo were found. A cooking pot of the late 9th/10th c. is attested
Concentration of finds per m^2: 4
Interpretation: Farmstead
Period: Middle Ages
Phase: Early-central Middle Ages
Initial chronology: Late 9th c. AD
Final chronology: 11th c. AD

SITE/T.U. *S.2003-2005* no.39.1
Municipality: Magliano in Toscana
Location: Poggio Vicarina
Description of site: Field on a terrace overlooking the Osa river, only 130 m away
Description of T.U.: The T.U., elongated and measuring 17 x 9 m, is located in the southern part of the field, at 70 m above sealevel. We observed numerous brick fragments, mainly imbrices with raised edges made from a rose-coloured fabric; building stones were absent. The ceramic materials found belong to a late antique horizon: particularly worth noting are a large bowl with an incurving rim reminiscent of a Hayes 61 B, made from a selected fabric, a jug with a thickened strap handle level with the edge, made from a purified fabric, lids and cooking pots and fragments of *dolia*.
Concentration of finds per m^2: 3-4

Interpretation: House (in perishable materials?)
Period: Late Antiquity
Initial chronology: 6th c. AD
Final chronology: Late 6th/early 7th c. AD

SITE/T.U. ***S.2003-2005*** **no.39.2**
Municipality: Magliano in Toscana
Location: Poggio Vicarina
Description of T.U.: The T.U., measuring 28 x 12 m, lies about 100 m E of the above T.U., at the same height above sealevel. Fragments of bricks and coarseware were present, among which we identified a jug with a thickened strap handle level with the edge, made of a purified fabric with a grey core, other handles of pseudotriangular section and numerous walls made from both selected and purified fabrics
Concentration of finds per m²: 2
Interpretation: House (in perishable materials?)
Period: Late Antiquity
Initial chronology: 6th c. AD
Final chronology: Late 6th/early 7th c. AD

SITE/T.U. ***S.2003-2005*** **no.39.3**
Municipality: Magliano in Toscana
Location: Poggio Vicarina
Description of T.U.: The T.U., measuring about 38 x 20 m, lies about 40 m from both T.U.39.2 and T.U. 39.1: it is halfway between the two at 80 m above sealevel. The T.U. takes the form of a fairly diffuse scatter of elongated shape. We noted fragments of bricks and a large amount of pottery including: a fragment of a thickened strap handle level with the edge, various wall fragments of closed forms made from selected and purified fabrics, a specimen of flanged bowl with a spout
Concentration of finds per m²: 5-6
Interpretation: House (in perishable materials?)
Period: Late Antiquity
Initial chronology: 6th c. AD
Final chronology: Late 6th/early 7th c. AD

SITE/T.U. ***S.2003-2005*** **no.39.4**
Municipality: Magliano in Toscana
Location: Poggio Vicarina
Description of T.U.: The T.U., measuring about 25 x 50 m, lies at the western edge of the field, in an uncultivated sloping area with rock outcrops. The nearest T.U. is 34.1, 30 m to the SE. We noted brick fragments and walls made of coarseware. The only diagnostic find was a specimen of flanged bowl made from a purified fabric
Concentration of finds per m²: 4-5
Interpretation: House/dwellings (in perishable materials?)
Period: Late Antiquity
Initial chronology: 6th c. AD
Final chronology: Late 6th/early 7th c. AD

SITE/T.U. ***S.2003-2005*** **no.40.1**
Municipality: Magliano in Toscana
Location: Poggio Vicarina
Description of site: Pasture lying at 80-90 m above sealevel, at least 250 m from the Osa river
Description of T.U.: The T.U. lies on a flat part of the field and is pseudocircular in shape with a diameter of 20 m. We found brick fragments, slag from the production of iron, coarseware, African red slip ware D (1 specimen of Hayes 91C flanged bowl and 1 of a Hayes 80B/99 deep dish), and fragments of Tunisian amphorae
Concentration of finds per m²: 4
Interpretation: House (in perishable materials?)
Period: Late Antiquity
Initial chronology: 6th c. AD
Final chronology: Late 6th/early 7th c. AD

SITE/T.U. ***S.2003-2005*** **no.40.2**
Municipality: Magliano in Toscana
Location: Poggio Vicarina
Description of T.U.: The T.U., about 50 m NW of the above, occupies an area of about 24 m². It yielded brick fragments, kitchenware, walls of Tunisian amphorae and the wall of an eastern grooved amphora
Concentration of finds per m²: 2
Interpretation: Functional annexe/storeroom
Period: Late Antiquity

SITE/T.U. ***S.2003-2005*** **no.42.1**
Municipality: Magliano in Toscana
Location: Poggio Verriolo-Casa Steccaia
Description of site: Plateau about 600 m from Casa Steccaia, at 90 m above sealevel
Description of T.U.: Oval area of ceramic fragments (about 70 m²) characterized by the presence of a few bricks and pottery made mainly from purified and selected fabrics, including strap handles from jugs similar to those of Podere Serratone. The soil in the area of the scatter is darker in colour, due to the disturbance of anthropic layers
Concentration of finds per m²: 2-3
Interpretation: House/annexe
Period: Middle Ages
Phase: Early Middle Ages
Initial chronology: 8th c. AD
Final chronology: 9th c. AD

SITE/T.U. ***S.2003-2005*** **no.42.2**
Municipality: Magliano in Toscana
Location: Poggio Verriolo-Casa Steccaia
Description of T.U.: Rectangular area of ceramic fragments (30 x 28 m) about 15 m from T.U. 42.1 and characterized by the presence of bricks and limestone, simply broken into blocks of different sizes, and coarseware for use mainly at table and for storage. We found fragments of strap handles from jugs and small amphorae of "Serratone type", walls of kitchen ware with combed decorations on the outside
Concentration of finds per m²: 6-7
Interpretation: Farmstead (constructed using a mixed technique?)
Period: Middle Ages
Phase: Early Middle Ages
Initial chronology: 8th c. AD
Final chronology: 9th c. AD

SITE/T.U. ***S.2003-2005*** **no.46.1**
Municipality: Magliano in Toscana
Location: Poggio Quercia Grossa
Description of site: The eastern slopes of Poggio Quercia Grossa, part of a field between the contour line at 140 and that at 150 m above sealevel, about 1.8 km SE of Montiano
Description of T.U.: Rectangular area of ceramic fragments measuring about 12 x 16 m. Numerous brick fragments and building stones are attested. Various classes of fineware are documented (Black Glaze ware , *sigillata italica*, production A and C ARS), alongside coarseware and fragments of amphorae
Concentration of finds per m²: 5-10
Interpretation: House belonging to the village of Poggio Quercia Grossa
Period: Roman
Phase: Multi-phase
Initial chronology: 2nd-1st c. BC
Final chronology: 3rd-4th c. AD

SITE/T.U. ***S.2003-2005*** **no.46.2**
Municipality: Magliano in Toscana
Location: Poggio Quercia Grossa
Description of T.U.: The T.U. takes the form of a broad scatter of ceramic materials covering an area of over half a hectare. The edges of the feature are irregular, probably due to the heavy water erosion affecting the soil resulting in the material being swept downhill. We did not notice any obvious gaps inside the T.U. which, given its size, appears to belong to several houses. We found large quantities of pottery (production A, C and D African red slip ware, *sigillata italica*, Black Glaze ware , coarseware and amphorae), together with large numbers of brick fragments. The pottery is fairly worn
Concentration of finds per m²: 15
Interpretation: Houses belonging to the village of Poggio Quercia Grossa
Period: Roman and late antique
Phase: Multi-phase
Initial chronology: 2nd-1st c. BC
Final chronology: 6th c. AD

SITE/T.U. *S.2003-2005* no.46.3
Municipality: Magliano in Toscana
Location: Poggio Quercia Grossa
Description of T.U.: The T.U., measuring about 2100 m^2, lies about 50 m S of the above. In some areas we noted that the grass was unusually high, perhaps due to the presence of buried structures. Large quantities of ceramic materials and bricks are attested. We also found fragments of amphorae, Black Glaze ware , *sigillata italica* and ARS (A, C and D), alongside a fair amount of coarseware. We noted no gaps within the scatter
Concentration of finds per m^2: 10
Interpretation: House(s) belonging to the village of Poggio Quercia Grossa
Period: Roman
Phase: Multi-phase
Initial chronology: 2nd-1st c. BC
Final chronology: 4th-5th c. AD

SITE/T.U. *S.2003-2005* no.47.1
Municipality: Magliano in Toscana
Location: Poggio Quercia Grossa
Description of site: Uncultivated lowlying field adjacent to that of T.U.s 46.1-3, at 150 m above sealevel
Description of T.U.: Area of ceramic fragments occupying an area of about 800 m^2. The scatter is characterized by an abundance of bricks, imbrices and curved roof tiles, fragments of coarseware for table/storage and kitchen use, African amphorae and a fragment of *sigillata italica*. We observed numerous fragments of stone within the scatter. Large blocks are heaped up near the hedgerow
Concentration of finds per m^2: 10
Interpretation: House(s) belonging to the village of Poggio Quercia Grossa
Period: Roman
Phase: Empire
Initial chronology: Late 1st c. BC-1st c. AD
Final chronology: 4th/5th c. AD

SITE/T.U. *S.2003-2005* no.49.1
Municipality: Magliano in Toscana
Location: Poggio Verriolo-Casa Steccaia
Description of site: Field immediately N of that hosting T.U.s 42.1 and 42.2, on the same *plateau*
Description of T.U.: Area of ceramic fragments of pseudoquadrangular shape measuring 400 m^2; however, the highest concentration of finds was in an area measuring 12 x 14 m, which may reflect roughly the true extent of the buried deposit. Among the construction materials, bricks and small stones were attested. Present were coarsewares with purified and selected fabrics which could be assigned to the Podere Serratone workshop on the basis of their typology. Also documented are a minimum of two forms (a jug and a cooking pot) which seem to attest a continuity or reoccupation of the site during the central centuries of the Middle Ages
Concentration of finds per m^2: 5
Interpretation: Farmstead (built using a mixed technique?)
Period: Middle Ages
Phase: Early Middle Ages- central centuries
Initial chronology: 7th-8th c. AD
Final chronology: 11th-12th c. AD

SITE/T.U. *S.2003-2005* no.55.1
Municipality: Orbetello
Location: Casa Andreoni
Description of site: Field at 6 m above sealevel, E of the SS1 Aurelia road, at km 161
Description of T.U.: Area of ceramic fragments of pseudotriangular shape, measuring about 3000 m^2. The soil inside the T.U. is significantly blackened. We documented the presence of numerous fragments of roof tiles, probably reused from nearby Roman sites. Large quantities of coarseware for table/storage use and early medieval kitchenware (including forms similar to those of Podere Serratone are attested). Also present are two fragments decorated with reddish-brown stripes (a handle and a base) probably belonging to a single jug
Concentration of finds per m^2: 15
Interpretation: Farmstead belonging to the early medieval semi-nucleated settlement of Casa Andreoni
Period: Middle Ages
Phase: Early Middle Ages
Initial chronology: 7th c. AD
Final chronology: 9th c. AD

SITE/T.U. *S.2003-2005* no.58.1
Municipality: Magliano in Toscana
Location: SP 3104 road
Description of site: Along the northern edge of a recently planted vineyard, at 20 m above sealevel
Description of T.U.: Small concentration of ceramic fragments, measuring about 18 x 5 m. A few brick fragments and small stones are attested within an anomaly of soil mark type, clearly visible in the field. The site yielded a minimum of only 5 pottery forms: a *testo*, a cooking pot, a medieval small amphora and two early medieval juglets
Concentration of finds per m^2: 1
Interpretation: Isolated house
Period: Middle Ages
Phase: Early Middle Ages
Initial chronology: 7th c. AD
Final chronology: 9th c. AD

SITE/T.U. *S.2003-2005* no.63.1
Municipality: Orbetello
Location: Poggio San Bastiano
Description of site: South-eastern slopes of Poggio San Bastiano, about 240 m from the summit
Description of T.U.: At 40 m above sealevel we intercepted a circular area of ceramic fragments occupying an area of about 116 m^2. A few fragments of brick, perhaps reused, were present alongside a small amount of coarseware, belonging to a late 9th-11th-c. horizon. It is probable that there was also a church in this area since a document of 1097, regarding the donation of properties located to the E of the nearby Poggio Civitella, notes that these pieces of land stretched *ad sancto Sebastiano*
Concentration of finds per m^2: 3-4
Interpretation: House (?)
Period: Middle Ages
Phase: Early-central Middle Ages
Initial chronology: Late 9th c. AD
Final chronology: 11th c. AD
Bibliography: Farinelli 2007, Entry no.19063

SITE/T.U. *S.2003-2005* no.65.3
Municipality: Grosseto
Location: Casa Burraia
Description of site: Field in a lowlying area (6-8 m above sealevel), at the foot of the hill overlooking the village of Alberese, on the SP 362 road
Description of T.U.: Large rectangular scatter occupying an area of about 2500 m^2. It is characterized by the presence of bricks (roof tiles), limestone blocks, medium-small stones and numerous fragments of lime mortar mixed with crushed brick. The soil is a darker colour than in the surrounding area. The pottery materials include numerous fragments of *sigillata italica* some of which is decorated, a fragment of *sigillata tardo italica*, thin-walled pottery, African red slip ware A, C and D, African kitchenware, amphorae and coarseware. We also found two fragments of glass
Concentration of finds per m^2: 5-7
Interpretation: Farmstead
Period: Roman
Phase: Multi-phase
Initial chronology: Late 1st c. BC-1st c. AD
Final chronology: 5th c. AD

SITE/T.U. *S.2003-2005* no.74.1
Municipality: Grosseto
Location: Vacchereccia
Description of site: Field at 4 m above sealevel, W of the hill at Vacchereccia and S of the Strada del Mare road leading to Marina di Alberese
Description of T.U.: Scatter of ceramic materials and bricks covering an area of about 2800 m^2. Along the eastern edge of the

scatter the concentration of finds is higher. The predominant pottery class is African red slip ware D (Hayes types 61, 76 and 91), but imitations of Hayes 61 in *ingobbiata di rosso* and *acroma depurata* wares are also attested. There are still numerous transport containers from Tunisia and an Empoli amphora. The bricks include roof tiles and bricks made from red and rose-coloured fabrics
Concentration of finds per m^2: 15
Interpretation: Farmstead
Period: Roman and late antique
Phase: Multi-phase
Initial chronology: 4th c. AD
Final chronology: 5th-early 6th c. AD

SITE/T.U. *S.2003-2005* no.75.2
Municipality: Grosseto
Location: Vacchereccia
Description of site: Olive grove S of the field hosting T.U. 74.1, at 10 m above sealevel
Description of T.U.: Scatter of ceramic materials oriented N-S, measuring about 30 x 20 m and about 130 m from T.U. 74.1. No construction materials are attested, only coarseware and numerous fragments of Tunisian amphorae
Concentration of finds per m^2: 2-3
Interpretation: Functional annexe/storeroom
Period: Roman
Phase: Multi-phase
Initial chronology: Late 2nd/3rd c. AD
Final chronology: 5th c. AD

SITE/T.U. *S.2003-2005* no.96.1
Municipality: Grosseto
Location: Scoglietto
Description of site: Poggio di Scoglietto, overlooking the Ombrone river. Between the contour lines at 10 and 20 m above sealevel
Description of T.U.: Within an area covered mainly in Mediterranean scrub we identified a broad scatter of bricks and pieces of local limestone covering an area of over 1800 m^2. Among the building materials it is worth noting two fragments of marble architectural decorations. The survey of the site was hindered by the dense vegetation; however, we intercepted pottery finds of help in dating it covering the entire imperial period. These include Italic transport amphorae as well as amphorae from Tunisia and the eastern Mediterranean; by contrast, fineware was scarce, being represented by a few fragments of *sigillata italica* and ARS (A, C and D). The site also yielded an inscription, the first line of which contains a dedication to *Dianae Umbronensi*. On the north-western edge we intercepted a stretch of wall belonging to the Roman site
Concentration of finds per m^2: 4-5
Interpretation: Sanctuary/harbour settlement on the Ombrone
Period: Roman and late antique
Phase: Multi-phase
Initial chronology: Late 1st c. BC-1st c. AD
Final chronology: 5th-early 6th c. AD (?)

SITE/T.U. *S.2003-2005* no.98.1
Municipality: Magliano in Toscana
Location: Podere Laschi
Description of site: Northern slopes of the hill at Podere Laschi, immediately W of the SP 3104 road, at 40 m above sealevel
Description of T.U.: Area of ceramic fragments measuring about 80 x 25 m. We identified roof tiles made of rose-coloured and orange fabrics. The pottery finds include coarseware, African red slip ware A and D, a fragment of *sigillata italica* ware and North African amphorae
Concentration of finds per m^2: 6-7
Interpretation: Part of the imperial and late antique village of Podere Laschi
Period: Roman and late antique
Phase: Multi-phase
Initial chronology: Late 1st c. BC-1st c. AD
Final chronology: 6th c. AD

SITE/T.U. *S.2003-2005* no.98.1
Municipality: Magliano in Toscana
Location: Podere Laschi
Description of T.U.: Broad scatter of ceramic fragments and bricks oriented N-S and covering an area of about 7000 m^2. We identified large amounts of African red slip ware A, C and D, a fragment of *sigillata italica*, coarseware and African kitchenware; the construction materials include numerous bricks, especially those used for *opus spicatum*. The site had a brick production structure, as demonstrated by the presence at this T.U. of roof tile wasters
Concentration of finds per m^2: 6-7
Interpretation: Part of the imperial and late antique village of Podere Laschi
Period: Roman and late antique
Phase: Multi-phase
Initial chronology: Late 1st c. BC-1st c. AD
Final chronology: 6th c. AD

SITE/T.U. *S.2003-2005* no.99.1
Municipality: Magliano in Toscana
Location: Podere Laschi
Description of site: Recently planted vineyard on the eastern slopes of the hill at Podere Laschi, at 40 m above sealevel
Description of T.U.: Area of ceramic fragments oriented N-S, measuring about 70 x 26 m. The scatter contains numerous bricks and pottery; the classes attested include African red slip ware, represented by productions A and D; also present is coarseware for table/storage and kitchen use and African kitchenware; the rare amphora fragments are mainly Tunisian
Concentration of finds per m^2: 3-4
Interpretation: Part of the imperial and late antique village of Podere Laschi
Period: Roman and late antique
Phase: Multi-phase
Initial chronology: 2nd c. AD
Final chronology: 6th c. AD

SITE/T.U. *S.2003-2005* no.103.1
Municipality: Orbetello
Location: Fosso della Cacciarella
Description of site: Lowlying field at 6 m above sealevel, about 260 m N of the Fosso della Cacciarella and 380 E of the SS1 Aurelia road
Description of T.U.: Low density scatter of ceramic fragments covering an area of about 4000 m^2; its low visibility, due to the presence of alfalfa, made it impossible to determine the true extent of the concentration. Roof tiles are present which were probably reused, alongside pottery forms in *acroma depurata* and *selezionata* ware similar to those from Podere Serratone and a few fragments of kitchenware
Concentration of finds per m^2: 2-3
Interpretation: Farmstead belonging to the early medieval semi-nucleated settlement of Casa Andreoni
Period: Middle Ages
Phase: Early Middle Ages
Initial chronology: 7th c. AD
Final chronology: 9th c. AD

SITE/T.U. *S.2003-2005* no.105.1
Municipality: Orbetello
Location: Fosso della Cacciarella
Description of site: Vineyard about 180 m S of the Fosso della Cacciarella, 800 m from km 161 of the SS1 Aurelia road
Description of T.U.: Elongated concentration (about 14 x 70 m) of reused bricks, *acroma depurata* and *selezionata* wares with a grey core in the fracture and kitchenware. We identified typologies similar to those from Podere Serratone. The soil in the area of the concentration of materials clearly changes colour from brown to reddish
Concentration of finds per m^2: 5
Interpretation: Farmstead belonging to the early medieval semi-nucleated settlement of Casa Andreoni
Period: Middle Ages
Phase: Early Middle Ages
Initial chronology: 7th c. AD
Final chronology: 9th c. AD

SITE/T.U. *S.2003-2005* no.106.1
Municipality: Orbetello
Location: Fosso della Cacciarella

Description of site: Field about 40 m W of that hosting T.U. 103.1, at 6-7 m above sealevel
Description of T.U.: Area of ceramic fragments oriented N-S, measuring about 23 x 17 m. Reused bricks and early medieval coarseware for table/storage and kitchen use (typologies similar to those from Podere Serratone) are attested
Concentration of finds per m^2: 3-4
Interpretation: Farmstead belonging to the early medieval semi-nucleated settlement of Casa Andreoni
Period: Middle Ages
Phase: Early Middle Ages
Initial chronology: 7th c. AD
Final chronology: 9th c. AD

SITE/T.U. *S.2003-2005* no.110.1
Municipality: Grosseto
Location: Alberese
Description of site: Lowlying field about 490 m S-E of Podere Montesanto and 540 m W of the SP 362 road; 20 m above sealevel
Description of T.U.: Area of ceramic fragments measuring about 8000 m^2. The highest concentration of finds covering an area of half a hectare seems to be more representative of the actual dimensions of the site. Attested are bricks, probably reused, and small amounts of early medieval coarseware for table/storage and kitchen use
Concentration of finds per m^2: 1-2
Interpretation: Large isolated farmstead
Period: Middle Ages
Phase: Early Middle Ages
Initial chronology: 8th c. AD
Final chronology: 9th c. AD

SITE/T.U. *S.2003-2005* no.111.1
Municipality: Grosseto
Location: Podere Montesanto
Description of site: Lowlying field about 420 m N of Podere Montesanto and 220 m S of the Strada del Mare road; 6 m above sealevel
Description of T.U.: Broad scatter of ceramic fragments and building stones covering an area of 130 x 60 m. This was almost certainly the residential area of the large villa of Podere Montesanto, part of which was intercepted by earthmoving in 1993. Unfortunately the owners of the land prevented a more accurate *infra-site* survey. Despite this, during the 2004 survey we were able to document the presence of pottery indicators covering the entire imperial period, probably up to the early decades of the 6th c. AD. The most representative materials include *sigillata italica*, African red slip ware (A, C, D), Tunisian and Iberian amphorae, forms in *acroma* ware modelled on the Tunisian prototype Hayes 61B, and two specimens of cooking pots comparable with Rosellan typologies of the 5th-6th c. AD. The total surface area of the villa is about 1.6 hectares
Concentration of finds per m^2: 15-20
Interpretation: Villa
Period: Roman and late antique
Phase: Multi-phase
Initial chronology: Late 1st c. BC-1st c. AD
Final chronology: 5th-early 6th c. AD
Bibliography: Poggesi 2004, pp.116-119

SITE/T.U. *S.2003-2005* no.Braccagni 1.1
Municipality: Grosseto
Location: Casa Mancini-*San Martino de plano*
Description of site: Lowlying field at 18 m above sealevel, about 370 m W of Km 196 of the SS1 Aurelia road, opposite the Casa Mancini estate
Description of T.U.: Area of ceramic fragments covering an area of about 66 m^2. We noted numerous bricks, a few pottery fragments, including *sigillata italica* and production A ARS and coarseware
Concentration of finds per m^2: 2
Interpretation: House
Period: Roman
Phase: Early-middle Empire
Initial chronology: Late 1st c. BC-1st c. AD
Final chronology: 2nd-3rd c. AD

SITE/T.U. *S.2003-2005* no.Braccagni 1.2
Municipality: Grosseto
Location: Casa Mancini-*San Martino de plano*
Description of T.U.: Area of ceramic fragments covering an area of 166 m^2. Pottery is represented by *sigillata italica*, production A and C ARS, and coarseware
Concentration of finds per m2: 2
Interpretation: House
Period: Roman
Phase: Empire
Initial chronology: Late 1st c. BC-1st c. AD
Final chronology: 3rd-4th c. AD

SITE/T.U. *S.2003-2005* no.Braccagni 1.3
Municipality: Grosseto
Location: Casa Mancini-*San Martino de plano*
Description of T.U.: Area of ceramic fragments covering 199 m^2. Pottery is represented by production A and C ARS, and coarseware, including a specimen of flanged bowl in *acroma depurata* ware modelled on type Hayes 91 in African red slip ware and a 5th/6th-c. cooking pot
Concentration of finds per m^2: 2-3
Interpretation: House
Period: Roman and late antique
Phase: Multi-phase
Initial chronology: 2nd-3rd c. AD
Final chronology: 6th c. AD

SITE/T.U. *S.2003-2005* no.Braccagni 1.4
Municipality: Grosseto
Location: Casa Mancini-*San Martino de plano*
Description of T.U.: Area of ceramic fragments of pseudocircular shape covering an area of 487 m^2. Numerous bricks, particularly roof tiles with raised edges. The pottery attested includes: fragments of production D ARS, Tunisian amphorae, coarseware of the 5th-6th/early 7th c. and pottery dating to between the late 9th and 11th c. AD
Concentration of finds per m^2: 4-5
Interpretation: House(s)
Period: Multi-period
Phase: Multi-phase
Late antique phase
Initial chronology: 4th-5th c. AD
Final chronology: 6th-early 7th c. AD
Phase: Early-central Middle Ages
Initial chronology: Late 9th-early 10th c. AD
Final chronology: 11th c. AD

SITE/T.U. *S.2003-2005* no.Braccagni 1.5
Municipality: Grosseto
Location: Casa Mancini-*San Martino de plano*
Description of T.U.: Area of ceramic fragments of pseudocircular shape covering an area of about 1700 m^2. Numerous bricks, especially tegulae with raised edges and roof tiles of semicircular section and stone blocks. Numerous human bones were found. The pottery attested includes: fragments of production D ARS, Tunisian amphorae, coarseware of the 5th-6th/early 7th c. and pottery dating to between the late 9th and 11th c. AD
Concentration of finds per m^2: 4-5
Interpretation 1: House(s) during the late antique period
Interpretation 2: Area of the church and cemetery of *San Martino de plano*
Period: Multi-period
Phase: Multi-phase
Late antique phase
Initial chronology: 4th-5th c. AD
Final chronology: 6th-early 7th c. AD
Early/central medieval phase
Initial chronology: Late 9th-early 10th c. AD
Final chronology: 11th c. AD

SITE/T.U. *S.2003-2005* no.Braccagni 1.6
Municipality: Grosseto
Location: Casa Mancini-*San Martino de plano*
Description of T.U.: Area of ceramic fragments of pseudorectangular shape covering an area of over 800 m^2. Numerous bricks, especially tegulae with raised edges and roof tiles of

semicircular section and stone blocks. Human bones were found. The pottery attested includes: fragments of production D ARS, Tunisian amphorae, coarseware of the 5th-6th/early 7th c. and pottery dating to between the late 9th and 11th c. AD
Concentration of finds per m^2: 5
Interpretation 1: House(s) during the late antique period
Interpretation 2: Area of the church and cemetery of *San Martino de plano*
Period: Multi-period
Phase: Multi-phase
Late antique phase
Initial chronology: 4th-5th c. AD
Final chronology: 6th-early 7th c. AD
Early/central medieval phase
Initial chronology: Late 9th-early 10th c. AD
Final chronology: 11th c. AD

SITE/T.U. *S.2003-2005* no.Braccagni 1.7
Municipality: Grosseto
Location: Casa Mancini-*San Martino de plano*
Description of T.U.: Area of ceramic fragments of circular shape covering an area of about 180 m^2. Numerous bricks and pottery of various classes (*sigillata italica*, Black Glaze ware , amphorae and coarseware) are attested
Concentration of finds per m^2: 5
Interpretation: House
Period: Roman
Phase: Multi-phase
Initial chronology: 2nd c. BC
Final chronology: 1st c. AD

SITE/T.U. *S.2003-2005* no.Braccagni 1.8
Municipality: Grosseto
Location: Casa Mancini-*San Martino de plano*
Description of T.U.: Area of ceramic fragments of circular shape covering an area of about 124 m^2. Numerous bricks, especially tegulae with raised edges and roof tiles of semicircular section. The pottery attested includes: coarseware of the 5th-6th/early 7th c. and pottery dating to between the late 9th and the 11th c. AD
Concentration of finds per m^2: 4
Interpretation: House
Period: Multi-period
Phase: Multi-phase
Late antique phase
Initial chronology: 5th c. AD
Final chronology: 6th-early 7th c. AD
Early/central medieval phase
Initial chronology: Late 9th-early 10th c. AD
Final chronology: 11th c. AD

SITE/T.U. *S.2003-2005* no.Braccagni 1.9
Municipality: Grosseto
Location: Casa Mancini-*San Martino de plano*
Description of T.U.: Area of ceramic fragments of rectangular shape covering an area of about 1700 m^2. Numerous fragments of bricks. Pottery is represented by rare *sigillata italica* and above all by production C and D ARS, coarseware of the 5th-6th/early 7th c. and a few amphora fragments
Concentration of finds per m^2: 5-7
Interpretation: House(s)
Period: Roman and late antique
Phase: Multi-period
Initial chronology: Late 1st c. BC-1st c. AD
Final chronology: 6th/early 7th c. AD

SITE/T.U. *S.2003-2005* no.Braccagni 2.1
Municipality: Grosseto
Location: Casa Mancini-*San Martino de plano*
Description of site: Field adjacent to the above, from which it is separated by the railway line
Description of T.U.: Circular area of ceramic fragments measuring about 48 m^2. Bricks, including tegulae and rounded roof tiles are frequent. Pottery is represented by rare *sigillata italica*, African red slip ware A and coarseware of the imperial period
Concentration of finds per m^2: 2
Interpretation: Small house
Period: Roman
Phase: Early-middle Empire
Initial chronology: Late 1st c. BC-1st c. AD
Final chronology: 2nd-3rd c. AD

SITE/T.U. *S.2003-2005* no.Braccagni 2.2
Municipality: Grosseto
Location: Casa Mancini-*San Martino de plano*
Description of T.U.: Oval area of ceramic fragments covering an area of about 134 m^2. Various fragments of bricks, in particular tegulae with raised edges and roof tiles of semicircular section. The pottery attested includes: production D ARS, coarseware of the 5th-6th/early 7th c. and the late 9th-11th c. AD
Concentration of finds per m^2: 2
Interpretation: House
Period: Multi-period
Phase: Multi-phase
Late antique phase
Initial chronology: 4th-5th c. AD
Final chronology: 6th-early 7th c. AD
Early/central medieval phase
Initial chronology: Late 9th-early 10th c. AD
Final chronology: 11th c. AD

SITE/T.U. *S.2003-2005* no.Braccagni 2.3
Municipality: Grosseto
Location: Casa Mancini-*San Martino de plano*
Description of T.U.: Area of ceramic fragments covering an area di 34 m^2. Various fragments of bricks, especially tegulae with raised edges and roof tiles of semicircular section. The pottery attested includes: production D ARS, Tunisian amphorae and cooking pots of the 5th-6th/early 7th c. AD
Concentration of finds per m^2: 2
Interpretation: House
Period: Late antique
Initial chronology: 4th-5th c. AD
Final chronology: 6th-early 7th c. AD

SITE/T.U. *S.2003-2005* no.Braccagni 2.4
Municipality: Grosseto
Location: Casa Mancini-*San Martino de plano*
Description of T.U.: Oval area of ceramic fragments covering an area of about 86 m^2. Pottery is attested dating to between the late 9th and the 11th c. AD
Concentration of finds per m^2: 1-2
Interpretation: House
Period: Middle Ages
Phase: Early-central Middle Ages
Initial chronology: Late 9th-10th c. AD
Final chronology: 11th c. AD

SITE/T.U. *S.2003-2005* no.Braccagni 2.5
Municipality: Grosseto
Location: Casa Mancini-*San Martino de plano*
Description of T.U.: Rectangular area of ceramic fragments covering about 86 m^2. Numerous bricks, especially tegulae with raised edges and roof tiles of semicircular section. The pottery attested includes: coarseware of the 5th-6th/early 7th c. and pottery dating to between the late 9th and 11th c. AD
Concentration of finds per m^2: 1-2
Interpretation: House
Period: Multi-period
Phase: Multi-phase
Late antique phase
Initial chronology: 5th c. AD
Final chronology: 6th-early 7th c. AD
Early/central medieval phase
Initial chronology: Late 9th-early 10th c. AD
Final chronology: 11th c. AD

SITE/T.U. *S.2003-2005* no.Braccagni 2.6
Municipality: Grosseto
Location: Casa Mancini-*San Martino de plano*
Description of T.U.: Area of ceramic fragments of rectangular shape, covering an area of about 25 m^2. Pottery dating to between the late 9th and the 11th c. AD is attested

Concentration of finds per m^2: 1-2
Interpretation: House
Period: Middle Ages
Phase: Early-central Middle Ages
Initial chronology: Late 9th-10th c. AD
Final chronology: 11th c. AD

SITE/T.U. ***S.2003-2005*** **no.Braccagni 2.7**
Municipality: Grosseto
Location: Casa Mancini-*San Martino de plano*
Description of T.U.: Area of ceramic fragments covering an area of about 84 m^2. Pottery dating to between the late 9th and the 11th c. AD is attested
Concentration of finds per m^2: 2
Interpretation: House
Period: Middle Ages
Phase: Early-central Middle Ages
Initial chronology: Late 9th-10th c. AD
Final chronology: 11th c. AD

SITE/T.U. ***S.2003-2005*** **no.Braccagni 2.8**
Municipality: Grosseto
Location: Casa Mancini-*San Martino de plano*
Description of T.U.: Area of ceramic fragments of circular shape covering an area of about 100 m^2. Numerous bricks, especially tegulae with raised edges and roof tiles of semicircular section. The pottery attested includes: production D ARS and coarseware of the 5th-6th/early 7th c. AD
Concentration of finds per m^2: 2-3
Interpretation: House
Period: Late antique
Initial chronology: 4th-5th C. AD
Final chronology: 6th-early 7th c. AD

SITE/T.U. ***S.2003-2005*** **no.Braccagni 2.9**
Municipality: Grosseto
Location: Casa Mancini-*San Martino de plano*
Description of T.U.: Area of ceramic fragments covering about 77 m^2. We noted bricks, a few ceramic fragments, including *sigillata italica* and production A ARS and coarseware
Concentration of finds per m^2: 1-2
Interpretation: House
Period: Roman
Phase: Early-middle Empire
Initial chronology: Late 1st c. BC-1st c, AD
Final chronology: 2nd-3rd c. AD

SITE/T.U. ***S.2003-2005*** **no.La Pescaia 1.1**
Municipality: Roccastrada
Location: La Pescaia
Description of site: Lowlying field at 40 m above sealevel located just under 400 m W of La Pescaia, next to km 5 of the SS 73 Senese-Aretina road
Description of T.U.: Area of ceramic fragments of pseudocircular section covering 318 m^2. This is an association of bricks, medium-sized stones and fragments of *acroma depurata* and *acroma selezionata* wares. The pottery of help in dating the scatter consists of jugs with thickened strap handles both level with the edge and set immediately beneath it
Concentration of finds per m^2: 2-3
Interpretation: House
Period: Late Antiquity-early Middle Ages
Chronology: Late 6th-7th c. AD

SITE/T.U. ***S.2003-2005 no.La Pescaia 1.2***
Municipality: Roccastrada
Location: La Pescaia
Description of T.U.: Rectangular area of ceramic fragments covering 360 m^2. This is an association of bricks, medium-sized stones and fragments of *acroma depurata* and *acroma selezionata* wares. As above the pottery of help in dating the scatter consists of jugs with thickened strap handles both level with the edge and set immediately beneath it
Concentration of finds per m^2: 4
Interpretation: House
Period: Late Antiquity-early Middle Ages
Chronology: Late 6th-7th c. AD

SITE/T.U. ***S.2003-2005 n.La Pescaia 1.3***
Municipality: Roccastrada
Location: La Pescaia
Description of T.U.: Oval area of ceramic fragments covering just over 80 m^2. This is an association of bricks, medium-sized stones and fragments of *acroma depurata, acroma selezionata* and kitchenware. The pottery of help in dating the scatter consists of jugs with thickened strap handles both level with the edge and set immediately beneath it
Concentration of finds per m^2: 2-3
Interpretation: House
Period: Late Antiquity-early Middle Ages
Chronology: Late 6th-7th c. AD

SITE/T.U. ***S.2003-2005 no.La Pescaia 1.4***
Municipality: Roccastrada
Location: La Pescaia
Description of T.U.: Area of ceramic fragments of pseudocircular shape covering 244 m^2. This is an association of bricks, medium and small-sized stones, and fragments of *acroma depurata, acroma selezionata* and kitchenware. The pottery of help in dating the scatter consists of jugs with thickened strap handles both level with the edge and set immediately beneath it
Concentration of finds per m^2: 2
Interpretation: House
Period: Late Antiquity-early Middle Ages
Chronology: Late 6th-7th c. AD

SITE/T.U. ***S.2003-2005 no.La Pescaia 1.6***
Municipality: Roccastrada
Location: La Pescaia
Description of T.U.: Area of ceramic fragments of elliptical shape, covering 95 m^2. This is an association of a few bricks, medium and small-sized stones and fragments of *acroma depurata, acroma selezionata* and kitchenware. The pottery of help in dating the scatter consists of jugs with thickened strap handles both level with the edge and set immediately beneath it
Concentration of finds per m^2: 2
Interpretation: House
Period: Late Antiquity-early Middle Ages
Chronology: Late 6th-7th c. AD

SITE/T.U. ***S.2003-2005*** **no.Selvacce 1.1**
Municipality: Roccastrada
Location: Le Selvacce-Podere Scopatone
Description of site: Lowlying field located along the SP 321 road, near the crossroads with the road leading to Podere Scopatone. At 40 m above sealevel
Description of T.U.: Large concentration of ceramic materials covering an area of over 6000 m^2. Among the construction materials, alongside the large numbers of bricks, we observed some trachyte blocks. The presence of grass prevented a detailed *infra-site* survey. However, the preliminary survey allowed us to determine the size and chronology of the site. The pottery of use for dating purposes consists of production C and D ARS, *ingobbiata di rosso* ware of the 4th-6th c. and coarseware imitating ARS prototypes, including a specimen modelled on Hayes 104 and another similar to type Hayes 91. Also attested was pottery dating to between the late 9th and the 11th c. It was impossible to determine any transformations in the settlement shape over the long term, but it seems that the phase between the middle Empire and late Antiquity covered the entire area of the site. Also located in this area is the *silvam Tabbianensem* mentioned in a document of 1272, where it is said that the wood was crossed by a *strada pubblica*, probably a *diverticulum* leading off the major Roman road network towards the interior. In the privilege of 12 April 1188 issued by Pope Clement III to the Bishop of Grosseto Gualfredo, 18 country churches belonging to the diocese are mentioned; these are located between the Alma and Ombrone valleys. The list is generally organized topographically and mentions the *plebem de Tabiano cum capella sua*, between that of Sticciano and that of Fornoli. The country church, first attested on 23 July 1071, must therefore have been in the area between Fornoli and Sticciano, probably also the site of the *silvam* mentioned in 1272, which takes its name from the religious building. It is probable that

the church at *Tabiano* was at this very site. Numerous stone blocks, including some cornerstones, were reused in a building in the courtyard of the Azienda "Le Selvacce"
Concentration of finds per m^2: 1-2
Interpretation1: Imperial and late antique village
Interpretation 2: Country church of the central centuries of the Middle Ages
Period: Multi-period
Phase: Multi-phase
Late antique phase
Initial chronology: 3rd-4th c. AD
Final chronology: 6th c. AD
Early/central medieval phase
Initial chronology: Late 9th-early 10th c. AD
Final chronology: 11th c. AD
Bibliography: Garzella 2001, p.10, note 17; Prisco 1994, p.279

Appendix 2. Catalogue of Fabrics: Macroscopic and Optical Microscope Analyses

2.1. Macroscopic Descriptions of the Late Antique Fabrics of Pottery Materials from Roselle

2.1.1. Late Antique *ingobbiata di rosso*, *colature rosse*, *acroma depurata* and *acroma selezionata* wares (Roselle)[1]

Sample: AD3
Clay properties: Purified orange clay
Hardness: Very hard
Fracture: Uneven
Porosity: Porous
Voids: Present
Description of voids: Minute
Inclusions: White
Quantity of inclusions: Small
Manufacturing technique: Fast wheel
Firing atmosphere: Oxidizing
Colour: Light orange/grey

Sample: AD4
Clay properties: Purified beige-cream coloured clay, powdery to the touch and porous
Hardness: Soft
Fracture: Even
Porosity: Porous
Voids: Present
Description of voids: Minute
Inclusions: White, quartz
Quantity of inclusions: Small
Manufacturing technique: Fast wheel
Firing atmosphere: Oxidizing
Colour: Cream

Sample: AD5
Clay properties: Purified clay without inclusions
Hardness: Fairly hard
Fracture: Clean
Porosity: Porous
Voids: Present
Description of voids: Very small and round
Inclusions: White
Quantity of inclusions: Small
Manufacturing technique: Fast wheel
Firing atmosphere: Oxidizing/Reducing
Colour: Red/orange

Sample: AD6
Clay properties: Well-purified clay with rare voids and white inclusions
Hardness: Fairly hard
Fracture: Even
Porosity: Compact
Voids: Present
Description of voids: Few and laminar
Inclusions: White
Quantity of inclusions: Small
Manufacturing technique: Fast wheel
Firing atmosphere: Oxidizing
Colour: Light orange

Sample: AD7
Clay properties: Fairly purified clay with various voids and a few white inclusions
Hardness: Hard
Fracture: Clean
Porosity: Compact
Voids: Present
Description of voids: Rare, elongated and of various sizes
Inclusions: White, quartz
Quantity of inclusions: Small
Manufacturing technique: Fast wheel
Firing atmosphere: Oxidizing/reducing
Colour: Orange-rose-grey

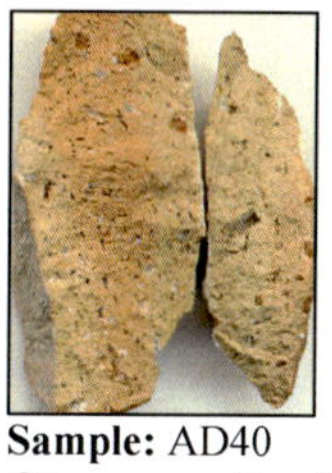

Sample: AD40
Clay properties: Fairly purified light brown clay
Hardness: Fairly hard
Fracture: Uneven
Porosity: Porous
Voids: Present
Description of voids: Tiny and round, very rare
Inclusions: Black, white, red, quartz
Quantity of inclusions: Small
Manufacturing technique: Fast wheel
Firing atmosphere: Oxidizing
Colour: Light brown

[1] Some sample codes are identical to those attributed to early medieval pottery but the fabrics are different. AD = purified fabrics; Sel = selected/semipurified fabrics; G = very coarse fabrics (mainly kitchen ware).

Sample: AD41
Clay properties: Very purified clay with a few white inclusions
Hardness: Fairly hard
Fracture: Clean
Porosity: Compact
Voids: Present
Description of voids: Rare, some round, some larger and laminar
Inclusions: White, quartz. The white inclusions are larger than the quartz grains
Quantity of inclusions: Small
Manufacturing technique: Fast wheel
Firing atmosphere: Oxidizing/Reducing
Colour: Rose/orange/grey

Sample: AD42
Clay properties: Very purified clay, with rare small white inclusions
Hardness: Soft
Fracture: Clean
Porosity: Porous
Voids: Present
Description of voids: Rare and round
Inclusions: White
Quantity of inclusions: Small
Manufacturing technique: Fast wheel
Firing atmosphere: Oxidizing
Colour: Pinky-orange/grey

Sample: AD43
Clay properties: Purified fabric with fairly numerous white inclusions
Hardness: Hard
Fracture: Even
Porosity: Porous
Voids: Present
Description of voids: Very small and laminar
Inclusions: White, quartz
Quantity of inclusions: Medium
Manufacturing technique: Fast wheel
Firing atmosphere: Oxidizing
Colour: Orange

Sample: AD44
Clay properties: Purified clay with some white and quartz inclusions
Hardness: Fairly hard
Fracture: Clean
Porosity: Compact
Voids: Present
Description of voids: Small and shapeless
Inclusions: White, quartz
Quantity of inclusions: Small
Manufacturing technique: Fast wheel
Firing atmosphere: Oxidizing/reducing
Colour: Orange/grey

Sample: Sel3
Clay properties: Semi-purified rose-coloured clay, with rare mainly white inclusions
Hardness: Hard
Fracture: Clean
Porosity: Compact
Voids: Absent
Inclusions: White, quartz
Quantity of inclusions: Medium
Manufacturing technique: Fast wheel
Firing atmosphere: Oxidizing/reducing
Colour: Rose-coloured

Sample: Sel4
Clay properties: Semi-purified beige-cream coloured clay
Hardness: Fairly hard
Fracture: Clean
Porosity: Porous
Voids: Absent
Inclusions: Black, red, quartz
Quantity of inclusions: Small
Manufacturing technique: Fast wheel
Firing atmosphere: Oxidizing
Colour: Beige/cream

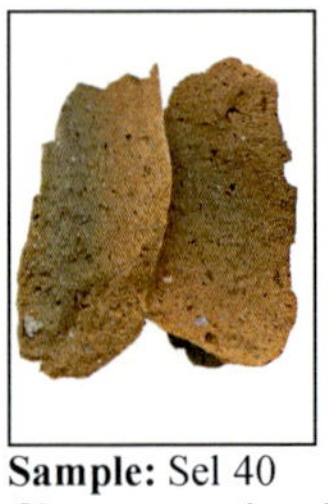

Sample: Sel 40
Clay properties: Selected fabric with fairly numerous inclusions
Hardness: Fairly hard
Fracture: Jagged
Porosity: Porous
Voids: Absent
Inclusions: White, quartz, red
Quantity of inclusions: Medium
Manufacturing technique: Fast wheel
Firing atmosphere: Oxidizing/reducing

Colour: Orange/grey

2.1.2. *Sigillata chiara tarda dell'Italia centro-settentrionale* (Roselle)

Sample: AD 45
Clay properties: Purified clay with very rare white inclusions
Hardness: Fairly hard
Fracture: Even
Porosity: Porous
Voids: Present
Description of voids: Tiny and rounded
Inclusions: White
Quantity of inclusions: Small
Manufacturing technique: Fast wheel
Firing atmosphere: Oxidizing
Colour: Dark orange

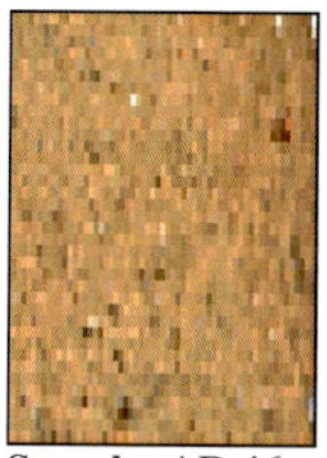

Sample: AD 46
Clay properties: Purified and very porous buff-beige clay
Hardness: Fairly hard
Fracture: Even
Porosity: Porous
Voids: Absent
Inclusions: Absent
Manufacturing technique: Fast wheel
Firing atmosphere: Oxidizing
Colour: From buff to beige

2.1.3. Late antique kitchen ware (Roselle)

Sample: G6
Clay properties: Fairly coarse clay with white inclusions
Hardness: Fairly hard
Fracture: Uneven
Porosity: Porous
Voids: Present
Description of voids: Tiny and round
Inclusions: White, grey and quartz
Quantity of inclusions: Medium
Manufacturing technique: Fast wheel
Firing atmosphere: Oxidizing
Colour: Rose-orange

Sample: G8
Clay properties: Coarse clay with numerous inclusions, some of which are large
Hardness: Soft
Fracture: Uneven
Porosity: Porous
Voids: Present
Description of voids: Small and round
Inclusions: White, quartz
Quantity of inclusions: Medium
Manufacturing technique: Fast wheel
Firing atmosphere: Oxidizing
Colour: Dark brown

Sample: G10
Clay properties: Coarse clay with shiny white inclusions
Hardness: Soft
Fracture: Uneven
Porosity: Porous
Voids: Present
Description of voids: Laminar
Inclusions: White, quartz
Quantity of inclusions: Medium
Manufacturing technique: Slow wheel
Firing atmosphere: Oxidizing
Colour: Orange

Sample: G11
Clay properties: Coarse clay with fairly numerous inclusions and a few voids
Hardness: Fairly hard
Fracture: Uneven
Porosity: Porous
Voids: Present
Description of voids: A few round voids, rare elongated voids
Inclusions: White, quartz, grey
Quantity of inclusions: Large
Manufacturing technique: Fast wheel
Firing atmosphere: Oxidizing/reducing
Colour: Orange/grey/brown

Sample: G13
Clay properties: Coarse clay with numerous inclusions
Hardness: Soft
Fracture: Uneven
Porosity: Porous
Voids: Present
Description of voids: Rare and small
Inclusions: White, grey, quartz
Quantity of inclusions: Large
Manufacturing technique: Fast wheel
Firing atmosphere: Oxidizing/reducing
Colour: Grey/orange

Sample: G14
Clay properties: Coarse clay with some large inclusions
Hardness: Fairly hard
Fracture: Jagged
Porosity: Porous
Voids: Present
Description of voids: Some large round voids, other very small shapeless voids
Inclusions: Grey, white
Quantity of inclusions: Medium
Manufacturing technique: Fast wheel
Firing atmosphere: Oxidizing/reducing
Colour: Chestnut brown/grey

Sample: G17
Clay properties: Coarse clay with numerous inclusions
Hardness: Fairly hard
Fracture: Jagged
Porosity: Porous
Voids: Absent
Description of voids: Round and laminar
Inclusions: White, quartz and black
Quantity of inclusions: Large
Manufacturing technique: Fast wheel
Firing atmosphere: Oxidizing
Colour: Dark orange

Sample: G18
Clay properties: Coarse clay with white and quartz inclusions
Hardness: Fairly hard
Fracture: Even
Porosity: Porous
Voids: Present
Description of voids: Rare, small and round
Inclusions: White, quartz
Quantity of inclusions: Medium
Manufacturing technique: Fast wheel
Firing atmosphere: Oxidizing
Colour: Orange

Sample: G19
Clay properties: Coarse clay
Hardness: Fairly hard
Fracture: Even
Porosity: Porous
Voids: Present
Description of voids: Rare and laminar
Inclusions: White, quartz
Quantity of inclusions: Small
Observations:
Manufacturing technique: Fast wheel
Firing atmosphere: Reducing
Colour: Brown/grey

Sample: G20
Clay properties: Coarse clay
Hardness: Soft
Fracture: Flaky
Porosity: Porous
Voids: Present
Description of voids: Rare, small round voids and larger laminar voids
Inclusions: White, black, quartz
Quantity of inclusions: Medium
Manufacturing technique: Fast wheel
Firing atmosphere: Oxidizing
Colour: Orange

Sample: G23
Clay properties: Coarse clay
Hardness: Fairly hard
Fracture: Even
Porosity: Porous
Voids: Present
Description of voids: Rare and round, very small
Inclusions: White, quartz, brown
Quantity of inclusions: Medium
Manufacturing technique: Fast wheel
Firing atmosphere: Oxidizing
Colour: Dark orange

Sample: G24
Clay properties: Coarse clay
Hardness: Fairly hard
Fracture: Even
Porosity: Porous
Voids: Present
Description of voids: Round
Inclusions: White, quartz
Quantity of inclusions: Large
Manufacturing technique: Fast wheel
Firing atmosphere: Reducing
Colour: Grey/chestnut

Sample: G25
Clay properties: Coarse clay
Hardness: Fairly hard
Fracture: Even
Porosity: Porous
Voids: Present
Description of voids: Rare and round
Inclusions: White, quartz. The quartz grains are much smaller than the white inclusions
Quantity of inclusions: Large
Manufacturing technique: Fast wheel
Firing atmosphere: Reducing
Colour: Grey/green

2.2. Macroscopic descriptions of ARS fabrics from Roselle, *Portus Scabris* and the territory

Fabric code Sig 2
Clay properties Fairly purified clay with some white inclusions
Hardness Fairly hard
Fracture Even
Porosity Porous
Voids Absent
Description of voids
Inclusions White, quartz, red
Quantity of inclusions Medium
Observations
Manufacturing technique Fast wheel
Firing atmosphere Oxidizing
Colour Rose-orange
Observations Production D ARSW

Fabric code Sig3
Clay properties Purified clay, with some white inclusions
Hardness Soft
Fracture Even
Porosity Porous
Voids Absent
Description of voids
Inclusions White
Quantity of inclusions Medium
Observations Most very small, some larger
Manufacturing technique Fast wheel
Firing atmosphere Oxidizing
Colour Rose-orange
Observations Production D ARSW

Fabric code Sig4
Clay properties Very purified clay, virtually free of inclusions
Hardness Fairly hard
Fracture Clean
Porosity Compact
Voids Absent
Description of voids
Inclusions White
Quantity of inclusions Small
Observations
Manufacturing technique Fast wheel
Firing atmosphere Oxidizing
Colour Brick red
Observations Production C ARSW

Fabric code Sig5
Clay properties Purified clay with white and quartz inclusions
Hardness Fairly hard
Fracture Even
Porosity Porous
Voids Present
Description of voids Very rare and very small, mainly laminar
Inclusions White, quartz
Quantity of inclusions Small
Observations Larger quantities of quartz
Manufacturing technique Fast wheel
Firing atmosphere Oxidizing
Colour Orange
Observations Production A ARSW

Fabric code Sig6
Clay properties Purified clay with some white and quartz inclusions
Hardness Soft
Fracture Uneven
Porosity Porous
Voids Present
Description of voids Rare, small and round
Inclusions White, quartz
Quantity of inclusions Small
Observations
Manufacturing technique Fast wheel
Firing atmosphere Oxidizing
Colour Orange
Observations Production D ARSW

Fabric code Sig7
Clay properties Purified fabric with some small white inclusions and quartz grains
Hardness Fairly hard
Fracture Uneven
Porosity Porous
Voids Absent
Description of voids
Inclusions White, quartz, brown
Quantity of inclusions Medium
Observations
Manufacturing technique Fast wheel
Firing atmosphere Oxidizing
Colour Dark orange
Observations Production D ARSW

Fabric code Sig 100
Clay properties Very purified clay with very rare tiny quartz inclusions
Hardness Fairly hard
Fracture Even
Porosity Porous
Voids Absent
Description of voids
Inclusions Quartz
Quantity of inclusions
Observations Very few
Manufacturing technique Fast wheel
Firing atmosphere Oxidizing
Colour Pink
Observations Associated with Production C ARSW (Hayes 84 deep dishes), this fabric may in fact be Sig 4. The differences may be due to discoloration and the decay of the clay due to the long permanence in seawater as this fabric is present only at *Portus Scabris*

Fabric code Sig 101
Clay properties Purified clay with very rare and very small white inclusions and rare quartz
Hardness Soft
Fracture Even
Porosity Porous
Voids Absent
Description of voids
Inclusions White, quartz
Quantity of inclusions Small
Observations
Manufacturing technique Fast wheel
Firing atmosphere Oxidizing
Colour Orange
Observations Production D

Fabric code Sig 102
Clay properties Selected clay with dense white and quartz inclusions
Hardness Fairly hard
Fracture Uneven
Porosity Porous
Voids Absent
Description of voids
Inclusions White, quartz
Quantity of inclusions Medium
Observations
Manufacturing technique Fast wheel
Firing atmosphere Oxidizing
Colour Dark orange
Observations ARSW similar to Sig 7

Fabric code Sig 103
Clay properties Semi-purified clay with very tiny quartz inclusions
Hardness Fairly hard
Fracture Even
Porosity Porous
Voids Absent

Description of voids
Inclusions Quartz
Quantity of inclusions Medium
Observations Dense and very tiny
Manufacturing technique Fast wheel
Firing atmosphere Oxidizing
Colour Red/Orange
Observations Production D

Fabric code Sig 104
Clay properties Selected clay with very numerous and very tiny quartz inclusions
Hardness Soft
Fracture Even
Porosity Porous
Voids Absent
Description of voids
Inclusions Quartz
Quantity of inclusions Large
Observations Tiny and shiny
Manufacturing technique Fast wheel
Firing atmosphere Oxidizing
Colour Dark orange
Observations ARSW D, form Hayes 109

2.3. Optical microscope analysis of the fabrics of the late antique pottery from the Scoglietto and Spaccasasso caves

2.3.1. Imported coarseware

Sample: Similar to Com imp 1 (*infra*)
Texture: Hiatal and homogeneous, inclusions in the order of 10%; well-sorted
Description of inclusions: Inclusions measuring between 0.3 and 1 mm with a modal value of 0.3 mm; quartz grains and rarer calcite, including secondary calcite; sub-rounded and highly spherical inclusions
Description of matrix: Porosity in the order of 5-7%, mainly rounded pores measuring 0.2-0.4 mm
Colour: 2.5 YR 5/4 reddish brown

Sample: Similar to Anf 114 (*infra*)
Texture: Serial and homogeneous, inclusions in the order of 5-10%, well-sorted
Description of inclusions: Inclusions measuring between 0.2 to 1 mm, with all size classes present; predominantly quartz grains (both transparent and opaque), rare secondary calcite. Sub-rounded and highly spherical inclusions
Description of matrix: Porosity 5%, elongated and orientated pores measuring 0.2 mm in length
Colour: Two-coloured

Sample: AG 100
Texture: Hiatal and homogeneous. Inclusions in the order of 10%. Well-sorted
Description of inclusions: Inclusions measuring between 0.2 and 0.5 mm, rounded and highly spherical. Prevalence of calcite, with rare quartz
Description of matrix: Porosity in the order of about 5%. Rounded pores with a diameter of 0.2-0.3 mm
Colour: 5YR 4/4 reddish brown

2.3.2. Regional and extra-regional kitchen ware

Sample: AG 101
Texture: Hiatal and homogeneous, inclusions in the order of 20-25%; well-sorted
Description of inclusions: Inclusions measuring between 0.2 and 1.5 mm; predominantly calcite, rare quartz grains, a fragment of rock with calcite and muscovite, fragments of light-grey rock; sub-rounded inclusions with low sphericity
Description of matrix: Porosity in the order of 10%, small rounded pores measuring 0.1-0.2 mm
Colour: 5YR 5/3 reddish brown

Sample: AG 102
Texture: Hiatal and homogeneous; inclusions in the order of 15%; well-sorted
Description of inclusions: Inclusions measuring between 0.2 and 1.2 mm; predominantly calcite, rare quartz grains, a fragment of rock with calcite and biotite, rare biotite; very rounded inclusions with low sphericity
Description of matrix: Porosity in the order of 5-10%, rounded pores measuring 0.2 mm
Colour: 2.5YR 5/6 red
Observations: this sample appears very similar to the previous one, with the difference that this fabric contains a larger number of inclusions

Sample: AG 103
Texture: Hiatal and homogeneous, inclusions in the order of 15-20%; well-sorted
Description of inclusions: Inclusions measuring between 0.2 and 1/1.5 mm; predominantly quartz grains, including transparent quartz, rare biotite and muscovite, rare fragments of dark grey stone, some polycrystalline mineral aggregates, few iron oxides; sub-rounded inclusions with low sphericity
Description of matrix: Porosity in the order of 5-10%, pores mainly very minute, measuring under 1 millimetre, and rounded; also present are elongated and orientated pores measuring 0.2 mm in length
Colour: 2.5YR 4/6 red

Sample: AG 104
Texture: Hiatal and homogeneous, inclusions in the order of 20-25%, well-sorted
Description of inclusions: Inclusions measuring between 0.2 mm and 1 cm. Numerous microfossils, rare quartz grains, fragments of yellowish rock and perhaps chalk; inclusions sub-rounded with low sphericity
Description of matrix: Porosity in the order of 5%, rounded and measuring 0.1/0.2 mm in width
Colour: From 2.5YR 4/1 dark reddish brown to 2.5YR 4/6 red

Sample: AG 105
Texture: Hiatal and homogeneous, inclusions around 20%, very well-sorted
Description of inclusions: Inclusions measuring between 0.2 and 2 mm, prevalently inclusions of 1 mm. Large quantities of biotite, quartz grains and feldspar, smaller amounts of muscovite. Present are rock fragments with associations of feldspar and biotite and of quartz and biotite. Sub-rounded inclusions with low sphericity
Description of matrix: Porosity between 5 and 10%, pores prevalently rounded and measuring between 0.2 and 0.5 mm
Colour: 7.5YR 5/8 strong brown

Sample: AG 106
Texture: Hiatal and homogeneous, inclusions between 25 and 30%, very well-sorted
Description of inclusions: Inclusions measuring between 0.2 and 1 mm, the smallest inclusions are particularly well represented; large quantities of crushed spathic calcite. The inclusions are angular with low sphericity
Description of matrix: Porosity lower than 5%, rounded pores 0.2 mm wide
Colour: 10YR 3/1 very dark gray

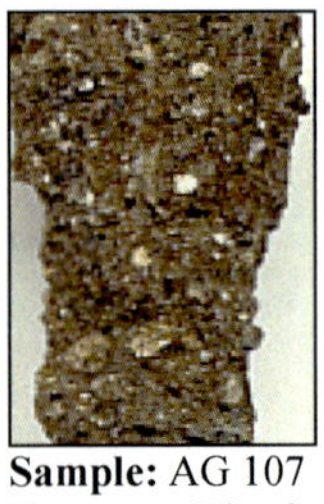

Sample: AG 107
Texture: Hiatal and homogeneous, inclusions about 15%, well-sorted
Description of inclusions: Inclusions measuring between 0.2 and 2 mm, mainly attested are those measuring between 0.2 and 0.5 mm, numerous quartz grains and muscovite inclusions; the inclusions are sub-rounded with low sphericity
Description of matrix: Porosity of 10%, rounded pores prevalently measuring 0.2/0.3 mm
Colour: 2.5YR 3/2 very dark grayish brown

Sample: AG 108
Texture: Hiatal and homogeneous, inclusions about 15%, well-sorted
Description of inclusions: Inclusions measuring between 0.2 mm and 2 mm, modal value 0.2/0.5 mm; predominantly biotite, smaller amounts of muscovite, presence of calcite and quartz, fragments of rock with an association of mica and calcite, rare fragments of grey rock and iron oxides; sub-rounded inclusions with low sphericity
Description of matrix: Porosity in the order of 10%, rounded pores measuring 0.2 mm
Colour: 2.5Y 2.5/1 black

Sample: AG 109 (similar to G13 from Roselle)
Texture: Hiatal and homogeneous, inclusions in the order of 10-15%, very well-sorted
Description of inclusions: Inclusions measuring between 0.3 and 1.5 mm; modal value 0.4/0.5 mm; presence of quartz and calcite, rare fragments of grey rock and iron oxides; sub-rounded inclusions with low sphericity
Description of matrix: Porosity in the order of 5-10%; pores either rounded (0.1 mm) or elongated and orientated (0.3/0.5 mm)
Colour: Gley 1 2.5/1 greenish black

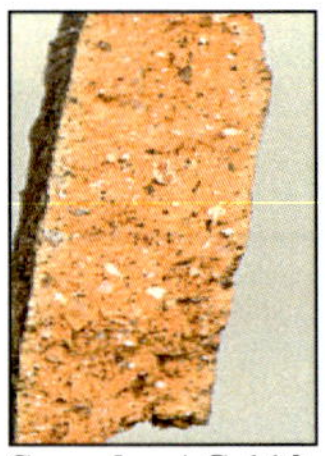

Sample: AG 110
Texture: Hiatal and homogeneous, inclusions in the order of 20-25%; well-sorted
Description of inclusions: Inclusions measuring between 0.2 and 2 mm; numerous calcite crystals, some quartz grains (opaque), very frequent secondary calcite, iron oxides; sub-rounded highly spherical inclusions
Description of matrix: Porosity in the order of 10%; pores both elongated and oriented measuring 0.2-0.4 mm, and rounded measuring 0.1 mm and less
Colour: 5YR 5/8 yellowish red

Sample: AG 111
Texture: Hiatal and homogeneous, inclusions in the order of 10-15%; well-sorted

Description of inclusions: Inclusions measuring between 0.5 and 2 mm, prevalence of those measuring 1 mm; numerous limestone inclusions, rare fragments of grey rock and iron oxides; sub-rounded inclusions with low sphericity
Description of matrix: Porosity in the order of 5-10%, rounded pores with a mean diameter of 0.2 mm
Colour: 5YR 4/4 reddish brown

Sample: AG 112
Texture: Hiatal and homogeneous; inclusions in the order of 20%; well-sorted
Description of inclusions: Inclusions measuring between 0.3/0.4 and 2 mm; prevalence of calcite, widespread biotite and rare quartz grains, some fragments of whitish rock; sub-rounded and highly spherical inclusions
Description of matrix: Porosity in the order of 15%; pores mainly elongated and orientated, measuring 0.2/0.3 mm
Colour: 7.5YR 5/8 strong brown

2.4. Fabrics of the transport amphorae from *Portus Scabris* and other sites: optical microscope analysis

Sample: Anf 100
Texture: Serial and homogeneous, inclusions to matrix ratio of 5%. Well-sorted
Description of inclusions: Very rare inclusions measuring between 0.2 and 0.5 mm. Rounded and highly spherical inclusions. Quartz grains, including aeolian quartz
Description of matrix: Porosity in the order of 5-10%. Rounded pores measuring between 0.1 and 0.2 mm
Colour: Fracture: Gley 1 5/ gray; **Surface:** 10YR 5/4 yellowish brown

Sample: Anf 101
Texture: Serial and homogeneous. Inclusions in the order of 5-10%. Well-sorted
Description of inclusions: Inclusions measuring between 0.2 and 0.8 mm, prevalence of those measuring 0.2-0.5 mm; sub-rounded and highly spherical inclusions. Aeolian quartz, calcite crystals, secondary calcite
Description of matrix: Porosity in the order of 5-10%. Pores prevalently rounded measuring 0.1-0.3 mm
Colour: Fracture: 2.5YR 6/6 light red; **Surface:** 2.5YR 4/1 dark reddish gray

Sample: Anf 102
Texture: Hiatal and homogeneous. Inclusions to matrix ratio of 10%. Moderately well-sorted
Description of inclusions: Inclusions measuring between 0.2 and 1.2 mm (on average 0.2-0.3 mm). Sub-rounded and highly spherical inclusions. Prevalently quartz grains, with secondary calcite in some pores and secondary chalk linked to the permanence in seawater
Description of matrix: Porosity in the order of 25-30%. Pores mainly round, measuring 0.2/0.4 mm on average
Colour: Fracture: 5YR 5/6 yellowish red; **Surface:** Gley 1 5/1 greenish gray

Sample: Anf 103
Texture: Serial and homogeneous. Inclusions to matrix ratio of under 5%. Fairly fine
Description of inclusions: Inclusions measuring between 0.2 and 0.3 mm. Sub-rounded and highly spherical inclusions. Quartz grains, secondary calcite in some pores and probably chalk, rare iron oxides
Description of matrix: Porosity between 15 and 20%. Pores mainly rounded and measuring 0.1-0.2 mm. Some pores are elongated and orientated and measure between 0.4 and 0.5 mm
Colour: 2.5YR 5/6 red

Sample: Anf 104
Texture: Hiatal and homogeneous. Inclusions to matrix ratio of 15-20%. Well-sorted
Description of inclusions: Inclusions measuring between 0.2 and 1 mm, sub-rounded and highly spherical. Quartz grains, some of which are of aeolian type, some secondary calcite
Description of matrix: Porosity between 10 and 15%. Rounded pores, measuring mainly 0.1-0.2 mm
Colour: 10R 4/8 red

Sample: Anf 105
Texture: Hiatal and homogeneous. Inclusions in the order of 5-10%. Well-sorted
Description of inclusions: Inclusions measuring between 0.2 and 0.4 mm, sub-rounded and highly spherical. Quartz and secondary calcite
Description of matrix: Porosity in the order of 5-10%. The pores are prevalently elongated and orientated, and measure between 0.4 and 0.5 mm

Colour: 10R 6/8 light red

Sample: Anf 106
Texture: Hiatal and homogeneous
Description of inclusions: Moderately sorted. Grain size between 0.2 and 1 mm. Some granules consist of rock fragments with an association of quartz-feldspars and pyrites. Firing led to the creation of some voids with a dark coating ascribable to the reaction space. Permanence in seawater led to some cavities filling with chalk and pyrites. Some idreddi di ferro
Description of matrix: Round pores measuring 0.1-0.2 mm, porosity of 5/10%
Colour: Core: 10YR, 6/1 gray; **Outer surface:** 10YR, 7/6 yellow

Sample: Anf 107
Texture: Hiatal and homogeneous, inclusions in the order of 15%, well-sorted
Description of inclusions: Inclusions measuring 0.2-0.4 mm; some clasts of opaque quartz; sub-rounded and highly spherical inclusions
Description of matrix: Porosity in the order of 5%, rounded pores measuring 1 mm in diameter
Colour: 5YR 6/3 light reddish brown

Sample: Anf 108
Texture: Hiatal and homogeneous, inclusions in the order of 5-10%. Well-sorted
Description of inclusions: Inclusions measuring 0.5 mm, rounded and highly spherical. Prevalence of quartz, rare limestone inclusions. Also well-represented is secondary calcite
Description of matrix: Porosity < 5%. Elongated and orientated pores, measuring 0.2/0.4 mm
Colour: Fracture: Gley 2 5/1 bluish gray; **Surface:** 7.5YR 7/6 yellowish red

Sample: Anf 109
Texture: Serial and homogeneous
Description of inclusions: Well-sorted, inclusions to matrix ratio 5-10%; quartz inclusions measuring 0.1 mm; presence of iron oxides measuring between 0.5 and 4 mm. Sub-rounded and highly spherical inclusions.
Description of matrix: Elongated and orientated pores measuring 2 mm; porosity in the order of 10-15%.
Colour: 10R, 5/8 red

Sample: Anf 110
Texture: Hiatal and homogeneous, inclusions in the order of 15/20%, very well-sorted
Description of inclusions: Inclusions measuring between 0.2 and 1 mm, modal value 0.2/0.5 mm; highly spherical sub-rounded inclusions; quartz, including aeolian quartz, secondary limestone in some pores
Description of matrix: Porosity in the order of 5-10%, elongated and orientated pores measuring 0.4/0.5 mm on average
Colour: Fracture: 10R 4/3 weak red; **Surface:** 2.5 YR 5/4 reddish brown

Sample: Anf 111
Texture: Hiatal and heterogeneous, inclusions in the order of 10%, well-sorted
Description of inclusions: Inclusions measuring between 0.2 and 1 mm, on average 0.5 mm, highly spherical and sub-rounded; almost exclusively quartz grains, fragments of unidentifiable rock; secondary chalk (due to permanence in water) in some pores, round iron oxides.
Description of matrix: Porosity 10/15%, elongated and orientated pores measuring on average 0.5 mm
Colour: 5YR 5/4 reddish brown

Sample: Anf 112
Texture: Hiatal, fairly homogeneous.
Description of inclusions: Matrix to inclusions ratio of 40-50%. Moderately sorted, inclusions measuring between 0.2 and 1 mm, mean 0.5 mm. Mineral phases: calcite, prevalence of volcanic inclusions and quartz. Sub-angular and highly spherical inclusions.
Description of matrix: Porosity between 5 and 10%; round pores measuring 0.1 mm.
Colour: 5YR, 7/4 reddish yellow

Sample: Anf 113
Texture: Serial and homogeneous. Inclusions virtually absent. Fine fabric

Description of inclusions: Only very rare quartz grains measuring 0.2 mm, probably already present in the clay. Fairly frequent secondary calcite
Description of matrix: Porosity in the order of about 10%. Round pores measuring 0.1 mm in diameter
Colour: 2.5YR 5/8 red

Sample: Anf 114
Texture: Serial and homogeneous.
Description of inclusions: Inclusions <5%, well-sorted, angular and highly spherical. The matrix contains quartz grains measuring 0.1 mm.
Porosity: Very rare rounded pores measuring 0.1 mm; elongated and rounded pores measuring 2-3 mm.
Colour: 2.5YR, 5/8 red

Sample: Anf 115
Texture: Serial and homogeneous
Description of inclusions: Moderately well-sorted; the inclusions present in the original clay measure between 0.1 and 0.5 mm. Sub-rounded and highly spherical inclusions. Some volcanic inclusions in the original clay; secondary post-depositional chalk crystals.
Description of matrix: Porosity between 5 and 10%, rounded pores measuring about 0.1 mm in diameter.
Colour: fracture: 5YR, 6/3 light reddish brown

Sample: Anf 116
Texture: Serial and homogeneous; inclusions < 5%, well-sorted
Description of inclusions: Inclusions measuring between 0.1 and 0.5 mm; fragments of sandstone and secondary calcite in some pores, rare limestone; sub-rounded and highly spherical inclusions
Description of matrix: Porosity in the order of 5%; elongated and orientated pores measuring 0.5 mm (modal value)
Colour: 2.5 YR 6/8 light red

Sample: Anf 117
Texture: Serial and homogeneous; inclusions < 5%, well-sorted
Description of inclusions: Inclusions measuring between 0.3 and 0.5 mm. Rare limestone inclusions, secondary calcite and iron oxides; numerous microfossils, possibly echinoderms (?); sub-angular and highly spherical inclusions

Description of matrix: Porosity in the order of 5-10%, prevalently elongated and orientated pores measuring 0.2-0.3 to 0.5 mm in length
Colour: 2.5 YR 6/6 light red

Sample: Anf 118
Texture: Hiatal and homogeneous.
Description of inclusions: Inclusions/matrix ratio 30%; well-sorted, inclusions measuring between 0.2 and 0.5 mm. Quartz grains and muscovite, biotite and limestone inclusions. Clear predominance of quartz.
Description of matrix: Rounded pores measuring 0.1-0.2 mm; porosity in the order of 5-7%.
Colour: 7.5YR 5/1 gray

Sample: Anf 119
Texture: Hiatal and heterogeneous.
Description of inclusions: Inclusions 7-15%, moderately well-sorted, inclusions measuring between 0.2 and 1 mm, mean size 0.2-0.5 mm. Inclusions: quartz (aeolian, transparent and opaque) secondary calcite.
Description of matrix: Rounded pores measuring between 0.1 and 0.2 mm and rare elongated and orientated pores measuring 0.3-0.4 mm; porosity 5-10%.
Colour: 2.5 YR, 5/8 red
Observations: Tunisian fabric

Sample: Anf 119bis
Texture: Hiatal and homogeneous; inclusions in the order of 10-15%, well-sorted
Description of inclusions: Inclusions measuring between 0.1 and 0.5 mm, prevalence of those measuring 0.1-0.2 mm; numerous muscovite inclusions and limestone inclusions, rarer quartz and very rare biotite. Secondary calcite, some iron oxides and rare fragments of unidentified rock; sub-rounded inclusions with low sphericity
Description of matrix: Porosity in the order of 5-10%, prevalently rounded pores measuring 0.1-0.2 mm
Colour: 5YR 4/6 yellowish red
Observations: Samos Cistern Type

Sample: Anf 120

Texture: Hiatal and heterogeneous. Inclusions to matrix ratio of 5-10%. Moderately well-sorted
Description of inclusions: Inclusions measuring between 0.1 and 1 mm, with a prevalence of those measuring 0.1 mm. Minute limestone inclusions (prevalent), perhaps belonging to the clay matrix; quartz is also present. The granules are sub-rounded and highly spherical. Some iron oxides.
Description of matrix: Porosity in the order of 20-25%. Small and rounded pores, measuring 0.1 mm in diameter
Colour: 10YR 6/4 light reddish brown

Sample: Anf 121
Texture: Hiatal and homogeneous; inclusions in the range 5-10%, well-sorted
Description of inclusions: Inclusions measuring between 0.3 and 0.5 mm, modal value 0.3 mm; prevalence of quartz and limestone inclusions; some fragments of volcanic rock and iron oxides are present; inclusions rounded and highly spherical
Description of matrix: Porosity in the order of 10/15%, pores prevalently rounded measuring between 0.1 and 0.3 mm.
Colour: 7.5 YR 6/4 light brown

Sample: Anf 122
Texture: Hiatal and homogeneous.
Description of inclusions: Inclusions to matrix ratio 20-30%, moderately sorted, granules measuring between 0.2 and 3 mm, presence of volcanic inclusions in the clay and rare quartz. The granules are sub-rounded and highly spherical.
Description of matrix: The pores are both round and elongated and orientated according to the direction of the wheel. Abundance of pores in the order of 7-10%.
Colour: 2.5 YR, 6/6 light red

Sample: Anf 123
Texture: Hiatal and homogeneous. Inclusions to matrix ratio of 15%. Well-sorted
Description of inclusions: Inclusions measuring between 0.3 and 1.5 mm, modal value 0.2-0.3 mm. Numerous inclusions of probable volcanic origin, but quartz and calcite crystals are also attested. Rarer biotite and muscovite. Secondary calcite and some iron oxides. Sub-rounded and highly spherical inclusions
Description of matrix: Porosity in the order of 5-10%. Pores elongated and orientated, 0.2 mm long
Colour: 10YR 6/3 pale brown

Sample: Anf 124
Texture: Hiatal, heterogeneous.
Description of inclusions: Matrix/inclusions ratio 20%, well-sorted, inclusions measuring between 0.5 and 1 mm. Lighter and darker quartz grains
Description of matrix: Elongated pores following the direction of the wheel; porosity in the order of 5-10%.
Colour: 10R, 5/8 Red

Sample: Anf 125
Texture: Hiatal and homogeneous. Inclusions in the order of 5-10%. Well-sorted
Description of inclusions: Inclusions measuring between 0.1 and 1 mm, modal value 0.3-0.4 mm. Prevalence of quartz, including aeolian quartz, limestone inclusions and fragments of sandstone. Some secondary calcite. Inclusions rounded and highly spherical
Description of matrix: Porosity in the order of 10-15%, pores prevalently elongated and orientated, measuring 0.1-0.2 mm
Colour: Fracture: 5YR 7/4 pink; **Surface:** 10YR 7/3 very pale brown

Sample: Anf 126, very similar to Anf 106 (both associated with LR1)
Texture: Serial and homogeneous, inclusions in the order of 15-20%. Well-sorted
Description of inclusions: Inclusions measuring between 0.2 and 1 mm (prevalence of those measuring 0.2-0.4 mm), rounded and highly spherical. Rare quartz and calcite. Firing led to the creation of voids with a dark coating ascribable to the reaction space. The permanence in water led some cavities to fill with chalk and pyrites. Some idreddi di ferro
Description of matrix: Porosity in the order of 5-10%. The pores are both elongated and orientated, and round. The former measure 0.3-0.5 mm; the latter 0.1 mm
Colour: 10YR 6/4 light yellowish brown

Sample: Anf 127
Texture: Hiatal and homogeneous, inclusions in the order of 10%, well-sorted
Description of inclusions: Inclusions measuring between 0.3 and 0.5 mm, prevalence of quartz grains, both opaque and transparent,

including aeolian quartz, rare feldspars, very rare secondary calcite. Sub-rounded and highly spherical inclusions
Description of matrix: Porosity in the order of 10-15%, pores mainly rounded with a diameter of 0.1-0.2 mm
Colour: 2.5 YR 5/4 reddish brown

Sample: Anf 128
Texture: Hiatal and heterogeneous
Description of inclusions: Inclusions/matrix ratio 10%; moderately well-sorted, inclusions measuring between 0.2 and 2 mm, on average 0.5 mm, sub-rounded and highly spherical. Presence of numerous microfossils. The inclusions include: quartz, feldspars, rare biotite and rare limestone inclusions, iron oxides.
Porosity: Pores elongated and orientated, some round, measuring on average 0.3 mm
Colour: 5YR, 6/1 gray

Sample: Anf 129
Texture: Hiatal and heterogeneous
Description of inclusions: Inclusions/matrix ratio 5-10%; moderately well-sorted. Inclusions measuring between 0.1 and 1 mm, mean 0.2-0.5 mm; rounded and highly spherical; quartz (aeolian and opaque) and limestone inclusions
Porosity: Rounded pores measuring 0.1-0.3 mm; porosity in the order of 5-7%
Colour: Fracture 5YR, 7/6 reddish yellow

Sample: Anf 130
Texture: Hiatal and homogeneous.
Description of inclusions: Inclusions/matrix ratio: 5-10%, well-sorted, measuring between 0.1 and 0.3 mm; sub-angular and highly spherical. Abundant limestone inclusions, quartz and rare muscovite
Porosity: Round pores measuring on average 0.2 mm and elongated pores measuring on average 2 mm, porosity about 10%
Colour: 2.5YR, 6/6 light red

Sample: Anf 131
Texture: Hiatal and homogeneous, inclusions in the order of 20-25%; very well-sorted

Description of inclusions: Inclusions measuring 0.2-0.4 mm; prevalence of quartz, including aeolian quartz and to a lesser extent limestone; inclusions rounded and highly spherical
Description of matrix: Porosity under 5%; pores mainly rounded measuring 0.1-0.3 mm
Colour: Fracture: 2.5YR 5/8 red; **Surface:** 2.5YR 4/1 dark greenish gray

Sample: Anf 132
Texture: Serial and homogeneous, inclusions < 5%. Almost fine fabric
Description of inclusions: Only very rare quartz measuring between 0.5 and 1 mm. Sub-rounded and highly spherical inclusions.
Description of matrix: Porosity under 5%. Elongated pores measuring between 0.2 and 1 mm
Colour: 7.5YR 5/4 brown

Sample: Anf 133
Texture: Hiatal and homogeneous
Description of inclusions: Inclusions to matrix ratio 10-15%, moderately well-sorted, 0.2 to 2 mm, mean 0.5-1 mm, sub-rounded and highly spherical. In order of frequency: fragments of volcanic rocks, quartz, feldspars, biotite and pyroxenes.
Description of matrix: Porosity in the order of 5%, elongated and orientated pores measuring 0.2 mm in length.
Colour: 2.5YR, 5/6 red

Sample: Anf 134
Texture: Serial and homogeneous (purified fabric)
Description of inclusions: Absent
Description of matrix: Porosity in the order of 10-15%; pores both rounded, and elongated and orientated measuring between 0.1 and 0.5 mm
Colour: 10YR 6/6 brownish yellow

Sample: Anf 135
Texture: Serial and homogeneous; inclusions in the order of < 5%; well-sorted
Description of inclusions: Inclusions measuring between 0.1 and 0.2 mm, only quartz; secondary calcite inside many pores, presence of microfossils (?)

Description of matrix: Porosity in the order of 5%, prevalently rounded pores measuring between 0.1 and 0.4 mm
Colour: 5YR 5/6 yellowish red

Sample: Anf 136 (*A cannelures* amphora)
Texture: Hiatal and homogeneous, inclusions in the order of 20-25%; very well-sorted
Description of inclusions: Inclusions measuring between 0.2 and 0.5 mm, modal value 0.2/0.3 mm; feldspars, minute and very rare quartz grains (0.1 mm) probably already present in the clay, secondary calcite inside some pores
Description of matrix: Porosity in the order of 5-10%, the pores are both rounded, and elongated and orientated (though the latter are rarer), measuring between 0.1 and 0.5 mm, modal value 0.1-0.2 mm
Colour: Fracture: 2.5 YR 5/8 red; **Surface:** 10 YR 6/3 pale brown

Sample: Anf 137
Texture: Serial and homogeneous (fine fabric)
Description of inclusions: Very rare calcite and quartz grains measuring 0.1-0.2 mm; iron oxides. Sub-rounded and highly spherical inclusions
Description of matrix: Porosity in the order of 15%. Mainly elongated and orientated pores measuring between 0.1 and 1 mm
Colour: Fracture: 2.5 YR 5/8 red; **Internal and external surface**: 7.5YR 7/1 light gray

2.5. Fabrics of *acroma depurata* ware from *Portus Scabris*: optical microscope analysis

Sample: AD 100
Texture: Serial and homogeneous, inclusions in the order of 5-10%, very well-sorted
Description of inclusions: Inclusions measuring between 0.2 and 0.5 mm; quartz, rare iron oxides; inclusions rounded and highly spherical
Description of matrix: Porosity in the order of 10%; prevalently elongated and orientated pores measuring between 0.2 and 0.4 mm
Colour: 2.5YR 6/4 light reddish brown

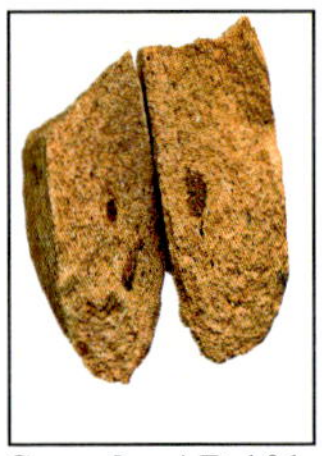

Sample: AD 101
Texture: Very purified fabric, very rare inclusions (less than 5%)
Description of inclusions: Only very rare quartz measuring 0.1-0.2 mm and rare iron oxides; inclusions rounded and highly spherical
Description of matrix: Porosity in the order of 10%; rounded pores measuring 0.1-0.2 mm
Colour: 10R 5/6 red

Sample: AD 102
Texture: Very purified fabric similar to the above but more porous
Description of inclusions: See AD 101
Description of matrix: Porosity in the order of 15-20%, pores both rounded, and elongated and orientated, measuring between 0.1 and 0.5 mm
Colour: 5YR 5/6 yellowish red

2.6. Fabrics of imported coarseware from *Portus Scabris*: optical microscope analysis

Sample: Com imp 1
Texture: Hiatal and homogeneous; inclusions in the order of 10%; very well-sorted
Description of inclusions: Inclusions measuring between 0.2 and 1 mm, modal value 0.2/0.3 mm; quartz, including aeolian quartz, some calcite crystals; sub-rounded and highly spherical inclusions
Description of matrix: Porosity in the order of 5-10%, pores prevalently elongated and orientated measuring 0.2-0.4 mm
Colour: 2.5 YR 5/4 reddish brown

Sample: Com imp 2 = Anf 119
Texture:
Description of inclusions:
Description of matrix:
Colour:

Sample: Com imp 3
Texture: Hiatal and homogeneous; inclusions in the order of 5-10%; well-sorted
Description of inclusions: Inclusions measuring between 0.1 and 0.3/0.4 mm; mainly quartz, some calcite crystals; inclusions rounded and highly spherical

Description of matrix: Porosity in the order of 5-10%, prevalently elongated and orientated pores measuring between 0.2 and 0.4 mm
Colour: 2.5YR 5/8 red

Sample: Com imp5
Texture: Hiatal and homogeneous; inclusions in the order of 15-20%; well-sorted
Description of inclusions: Inclusions measuring between 0.2 and 0.5 mm; quartz, including polycrystalline quartz, and biotite. We also observed fragments of volcanic rock; inclusions rounded with low sphericity
Description of matrix: Porosity in the order of 5-10%; mainly rounded pores measuring 0.1-0.2 mm in diameter
Colour: 5YR 5/4 reddish brown

2.7. Fabrics of the plain and painted wares of the early and central Middle Ages from excavated and surface sites: Optical microscope analysis

2.7.1. Purified fabrics (*Acroma depurata* and red painted wares)

Sample: AD1 PCV
Texture: Serial and homogeneous, absence of inclusions, very fine fabric
Description of inclusions:
Description of matrix: Porosity in the order of 10%. Pores elongated and rounded measuring between ≤ 0.1 mm and 0.5/0.6 mm, prevalence of those measuring 0.2/0.3 mm.
Colour: 2.5 YR light red 6/6

Sample: AD30
Texture: Serial and homogeneous, sorted, fine, inclusions under 5%
Description of inclusions: Rock, oxides, secondary calcite
Description of matrix: Pores elongated and orientated, non-homogeneous, measuring 0.25 ≤ P ≤ 0.5 mm. Secondary calcite around some pores; porosity 20%
Colour: Surface 2.5 YR 5/8 RED, black core Gley 1 5/1 greenish gray

Sample: AD31 Serratone
Texture: Serial and homogeneous, inclusions < 5%, fine fabric
Description of inclusions: Inclusions measuring between 0.1/0.2 and 0.5 mm, mean 0.2 mm, rounded and highly spherical. The only inclusions present consist of secondary calcite inside some pores
Description of matrix: Porosity in the order of 15/20%, pores both rounded and elongated and orientated: the former measure between < 0.1 mm and 0.2 mm in diameter with a mean of 0.1 mm, the latter measure on average 0.2 mm in diameter
Colour: 2,5 YR 6/6 light red

Sample: AD 32 (both *acroma depurata* and red painted wares from Casa Andreoni)
Texture: Serial and homogeneous, very fine fabric
Description of inclusions: The only inclusions present are iron oxides and secondary calcite around the edge of some pores
Description of matrix: Porosity in the order of 15%; pores both rounded, and elongated and orientated; the former measure 0.1 mm in diameter, whilst the latter measure between 0.2 and 0.4 mm
Colour: tending towards yellow (10YR 7/6 yellow), sometimes with a black core (10YR 4/1 dark gray)

Sample: AD33 (*Acroma depurata* and sparse glaze ware from the Pisa area)
Texture: Serial, homogeneous distribution of inclusions, very well-sorted, inclusions <5%, measuring between 0.2 and 0.4 mm
Description of inclusions: Sub-rounded and highly spherical inclusions. Mineralogical nature of inclusions: calcite (the only appreciable mineral phase) granules measuring between 0.2 and 0.5 mm, some iron oxides. The granules seem to belong to the clay, with no significant addition of temper
Description of matrix: Porosity 5/10%, pores both round and elongated in the direction of the wheel measuring between 0.1 and 0.5 mm
Colour: 7.5 YR 5/6 strong brown

Sample: AD34
Texture: Serial, heterogeneous. Inclusions to matrix ratio 5%
Description of inclusions: Inclusions measuring between 0.1 and 0.3 mm. The inclusions are biotite and calcite, with rarer quartz. The inclusions are sub-rounded with low sphericity
Description of matrix: Porosity in the order of 5-10% with a mean pore size of 0.1/0.2 mm; some elongated and orientated pores measuring 0.5 mm
Colour: 5YR 5/3 reddish brown

Sample: AD35
Texture: Hiatal, heterogeneous granulometric distribution, inclusions to matrix ratio 5-10%, inclusions modestly sorted
Description of inclusions: Inclusions measuring between 0.2 and 2 mm, mean size 0.5mm. Angular inclusions with low sphericity. Mineral phases identified: scarce muscovite, 0.2mm; moderate

presence of quartz grains measuring 1 to 2 mm; dominant calcite measuring between 0.2 and 1 mm; rounded iron oxides 0.5 mm
Description of matrix: Porosity 20-25%. Pores prevalently rounded or elongated and orientated in the direction of the wheel. Pores measuring between 0.1 and 0.5 mm. The smallest pores are generally elongated
Colour: 5YR 5/8 yellowish red

Sample: AD36
Texture: Serial and homogeneous. Inclusions to matrix ratio < 5%. Well-sorted
Description of inclusions: Inclusions measuring on average 0.2/0.3 mm, one quartz grain measuring 1 mm, 1 biotite measuring 0.5/0.6mm. Inclusions rounded and highly spherical. Prevalence of quartz, some calcite, rare biotite
Description of matrix: Porosity 5-10%. Prevalence of rounded pores measuring 0.1/0.2 mm, some elongated and orientated pores measuring 0.3/0.5 mm
Colour: 10YR 6/8 brownish yellow

Sample: AD37 (*Acroma depurata* and red painted pottery)
Texture: Hiatal, heterogeneous granulometric distribution, inclusions 5-10%, well-sorted
Description of inclusions: Inclusions measuring between 0.2 and 0.7 mm, mean size 0.4-0.6 mm. Granules angular and highly spherical. Inclusions: quartz 0.4-0.5 mm, calcite 0.4-0.6 mm, muscovite 0.6-0.7 mm, iron oxides 0.3-0.5 mm, secondary calcite around some pores, feldspars 0.3-0.4 mm. Predominant calcite
Description of matrix: Mean pore size of 0.2 to 0.5 mm, prevalently 0.2-0.3 mm
Description of matrix: Pores both rounded and elongated in the direction of the wheel. Porosity 10-15%
Colour: Surface: 5YR 6/8 yellowish red; Fracture: Gley 2 5/1 bluish gray

Sample: AD38
Texture: Serial and homogeneous, inclusions/matrix 10%, very well-sorted
Description of inclusions: Inclusions measuring between 0.1 and 0.5 mm, mean size 0.1-0.2 mm. Inclusions sub-rounded and highly spherical. Only calcite is present, some iron oxides measuring 0.5 mm
Description of matrix: Porosity in the order of 15-20%. Generally rounded pores measuring between < 0.1 mm and 0.1/0.2 mm in diameter, some elongated and orientated pores measuring 0.2/0.3 mm
Colour: 7.5YR 7/6 yellowish red

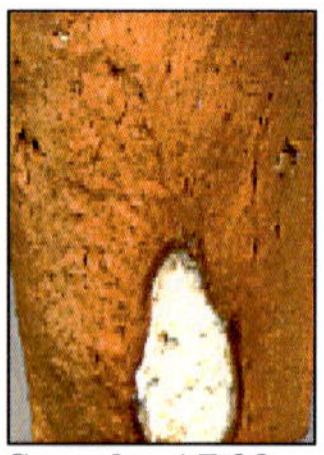

Sample: AD39
Texture: Serial and homogeneous, Inclusions to matrix ratio < 5%, well-sorted.
Description of inclusions: The inclusions present are calcite granules measuring on average 0.2 mm, only one measures 7 mm in diameter and may be an accidental presence. The inclusions are rounded and highly spherical
Description of matrix: Porosity in the order of 5-10%, generally elongated and orientated pores measuring 0.2/0.3 mm. Some rounded pores < 0.1 mm
Colour: 7.5YR 6/8 reddish yellow

Sample: AD40 (sparse glaze ware from Lazio)
Texture: Serial and homogeneous. Inclusions in the order of 5-10% with respect to the matrix. Very well-sorted
Description of inclusions: Between 0.1/0.2 mm and 0,5 mm, with a mean size of 0.2 mm. A fragment of rock with an association of quartz and feldspar has a section of 1 mm. Prevalence of quartz grains, followed by feldspars, biotite and rare calcite, including secondary calcite. Rare iron oxides. Inclusions sub-angular and highly spherical
Description of matrix: Porosity in the order of 10%, pores both round and elongated, measuring between 0.1 and 0.3 mm
Colour: 7.5YR 6/8 reddish yellow

Sample: AD41
Texture: Serial, fine-grained
Description of inclusions: Very well-sorted. The sample contained only one calcite crystal measuring 0.2 mm, sub-rounded and with low sphericity. Some iron oxides
Description of matrix: Porosity in the order of 10%. Pores prevalently rounded measuring between 0.1 and 0.3 mm, elongated and orientated pores measuring 0.2-0.3 mm
Colour: 2.5Y 7/2 light gray

2.7.2. Selected fabrics (*Acroma selezionata* ware)

Sample: SEL1 PCV
Texture: Hiatal and homogeneous. Inclusions to matrix ratio 15-20%. Very well-sorted

Description of inclusions: Inclusions measuring between 0.5 and 2 mm, prevalently between 0.5 and 1 mm, sub-rounded and highly spherical. Quartz, including polycrystalline quartz, and rare iron oxides are attested
Description of matrix: Porosity in the order of 15/20%, essentially rounded pores measuring on average 0.2-0.5 mm
Colour: Black core: GLEY 2 6/1 bluish gray; **Surface:** 2.5 YR 5/8 red

Sample: SEL2 PCV (= SEL 4 PCV?)
Texture: Hiatal and homogeneous, inclusions to matrix ratio 10%, very well-sorted
Description of inclusions: Inclusions measuring between 0.2 and 0.5 mm, prevalently 0.5 mm, sub-rounded with low sphericity. Presence mainly of feldspars, with some quartz
Description of matrix: Porosity in the order of 25/30%. Pores prevalently rounded and small, measuring between <0.1 mm and 2 mm. Some elongated and rounded pores measuring 0.5 mm
Colour: 2.5 YR light red 6/8

Sample: SEL 4 PCV
Texture: Hiatal and homogeneous. Inclusions to matrix ratio 10%. Very well-sorted
Description of inclusions: Inclusions measuring between 0.2 and 1.5 mm, prevalently between 0.5 and 1 mm, sub-rounded and highly spherical. Mainly quartz, with some feldspars
Description of matrix: Porosity in the order of 20/25%, pores measuring between 0.2 and 2 mm, mainly elongated and orientated. The smallest pores are rounded. Mean size of 0.5 mm
Colour: 7.5 YR light brown 6/4

Sample: SEL 8 PCV
Texture: Hiatal and homogeneous. Inclusions to matrix ratio 15-20%. Well-sorted
Description of inclusions: Inclusions measuring between 0.5 and 1 mm, prevalence of those measuring 0.5 mm. Inclusions sub-rounded and highly spherical. Quartz and idreddi di ferro
Description of matrix: Porosity in the order of 25-30%, pores prevalently rounded and measuring 0.2-0.3 mm
Colour: 5Y 7/3 pale yellow

Sample: SEL 30
Texture: Hiatal and homogeneous, well-sorted fabric
Description of inclusions: Inclusions measuring between 0.2 and 0.5 mm, prevalently 0.5 mm. Rare quartz measuring 1 mm. Inclusions sub-angular and highly spherical. Prevalence of quartz with some calcite crystals
Description of matrix: Porosity in the order of 10-15%. Pores both rounded and elongated and orientated, measuring between 0.2 and 0.5 mm, prevalence of those measuring 0.2 mm
Colour: Grey core: Gley 2 5/1 Bluish gray; **Fracture and Surface:** 2.5 YR, 6/6 light red

Sample: Sel 31
Texture: Hiatal and homogeneous, well-sorted fabric
Description of inclusions: Inclusions in the order of 10%; granules measuring between 0.2 and 0.3 mm, rounded and highly spherical. Calcite crystals and rare quartz. Presence of secondary calcite and some iron oxides
Description of matrix: Porosity in the order of 15-20%; elongated and orientated pores measuring between 0.2 and 1 mm
Colour: 2.5YR 4/6 red

Sample: SEL 32
Texture: Hiatal and homogeneous. Inclusions/matrix ratio 10-20%. Well-sorted
Description of inclusions: Inclusions measuring between 0.2 and 1 mm, mean 0.2 to 0.5 mm, sub-rounded and highly spherical. Mainly quartz, both small (0.2 mm) and larger (1 mm) grains, calcite, small fragments of sandstone, rare iron oxides
Description of matrix: Porosity in the order of 15-20%. Pores prevalently elongated and orientated measuring between 0.2 and 1 mm in length, prevalence of those measuring 0.2 mm
Colour: from 2.5 YR 6/3 light reddish brown to 2.5 YR 5/8 red

Sample: SEL 43
Texture: Hiatal and homogeneous. Inclusions in the order of 10-15 %. Well-sorted
Description of inclusions: Inclusions measuring between 0.2 and 1 mm, mean size between 0.5 and 0.6 mm, sub-rounded and highly spherical. Larger quantities of quartz and feldspars, with some biotite and muscovite and secondary calcite. Rare iron oxides
Description of matrix: Porosity in the order of 10/15%. Pores both rounded and elongated and orientated measuring between 0.1 and 0.3 mm
Colour: 5YR 6/6 yellowish red

Sample: SEL 44
Texture: Hiatal and homogeneous. Inclusions/matrix ratio 15-20%. Well-sorted
Description of inclusions: Inclusions measuring between 0.5 and < 1 mm, mean size 0.5 mm, angular and highly spherical. Predominance of quartz, with some calcite crystals, chalk, feldspars and some iron oxides, muscovite (very rare)
Description of matrix: Porosity in the order of 10/15%. Pores elongated measuring between 0.5 and 1 mm, prevalence of those measuring 1 mm
Colour: 10 YR 6/4 light yellowish brown

Sample: SEL 45
Texture: Hiatal and homogeneous. Inclusions to matrix ratio 15-20%. Very well-sorted
Description of inclusions: Inclusions measuring between 0.2 and 1.5 mm, modal value 0.5 mm. Abundance of calcite crystals, both quartz and feldspars are very well attested, mineral associations of quartz and feldspar and of feldspar and biotite were found, some iron oxides
Description of matrix: Porosity in the order of 20%. Pores both round (0.1-0.2 mm) and elongated (0.3-0.5 mm) and orientated
Colour: Black core: Gley 2 6/1 bluish gray; **Surface:** 5YR 6/6 reddish yellow

Sample: Sel 46
Texture: Hiatal and homogeneous, well-sorted
Description of inclusions: Inclusions in the order of 10%; prevalence of quartz with rarer calcite crystals; a fragment of volcanic rock is present. Inclusions measuring between 0.2 and 2 mm (prevalently between 0.2 and 0.5 mm), sub-rounded and highly spherical
Description of matrix: Porosity in the order of 10-15%; pores both elongated and oriented, and rounded, measuring between 0.1 and 0.4 mm
Colour: Beige (2.5Y 7/3 pale yellow) with black core (2.5Y 6/1 gray)

2.7.3. Kitchenware

Sample: G1PCV = G29
Texture:
Description of inclusions:
Description of matrix:
Colour:

Sample: G5PCV = G51
Texture:
Description of inclusions:
Description of matrix:
Colour:

Sample: G7PCV
Texture: Hiatal and homogeneous; well-sorted
Description of inclusions: Inclusions in the order of 15%; prevalently quartz, calcite and numerous iron oxides; inclusions sub-rounded with low sphericity, measuring between 0.2 and 1 mm, prevalently between 0.2 and 1 mm
Description of matrix: Porosity in the order of 5-10%, rounded pores measuring 0.1 mm in diameter
Colour: 10YR 6/3 pale brown

Sample: G8PCV = G29
Texture:
Description of inclusions:
Description of matrix:
Colour:

Sample: G26
Texture: Hiatal and homogeneous. Inclusions to matrix ratio of 30/35%. Moderately well-sorted
Description of inclusions: Inclusions measuring between 0.2 and 1.5 mm, mean size 0.5-1 mm, sub-rounded with low sphericity. Abundant quartz and feldspars (including some polycrystalline); to a lesser extent calcite crystals and clasts of biotite, numerous iron oxides
Description of matrix: Porosity in the order of 10-15%, prevalently rounded pores measuring 0.5 mm
Colour: 5YR, 5/6 yellowish red

Sample: G27
Texture: Hiatal and homogeneous. Inclusions/matrix ratio of 15-20%. Well-sorted
Description of inclusions: Inclusions measuring between 0.2 and 1 mm, mean size 0.5 mm, angular and highly spherical. The inclusions are quartz of different colours, with numerous fragments of sandstone and iron oxides
Description of matrix: Porosity in the order of 10%. Pores elongated and orientated measuring about 0.3-0.5 mm
Colour: 2,5 YR light red 6/8

Sample: G28
Texture: Hiatal and heterogeneous. Inclusions to matrix ratio 15%. Moderately well-sorted
Description of inclusions: Inclusions measuring between 0.5 and 1 mm, mean size 0.5 mm, sub-rounded and highly spherical. Prevalence of quartz, with some biotite, an aggregate of several minerals with an association of quartz and biotite
Description of matrix: Pores prevalently round measuring 0.2/0.3 mm. Some elongated and orientated pores measuring between 0.5 and 1 mm. Porosity 15/20%
Colour: 5YK, yellowish-red 5/6

Sample: G29
Texture: Hiatal and homogeneous; well-sorted
Description of inclusions: Inclusions in the order of 15%; calcite, quartz and biotite; inclusions measuring between 0.2 and 1 mm, rounded with low sphericity
Description of matrix: Porosity in the order of 5-10%; rounded pores measuring 0.1 mm in diameter
Colour: Often two-coloured, from red to reddish-grey (2.5YR 5/8 red – 2.5YR 3/1 dark reddish gray)

Sample: G30
Texture: Hiatal and homogeneous, very well-sorted fabric
Description of inclusions: Inclusions in the order of 25-30%; inclusions measuring between 0.2 and 1.5 mm (prevalence of granules measuring about 1 mm), sub-rounded and highly spherical. Prevalence of feldspars and opaque quartz, some fragments of rock with an association of feldspar and muscovite, of feldspar and biotite and of quartz and biotite. Apparently absent are single phyllosilicates
Description of matrix: Porosity in the order of 10-15%, rounded pores measuring 0.1-0.2 mm
Colour: 5YR 4/6 yellowish red

Sample: G31
Texture: Hiatal and homogeneous. Inclusions/matrix ratio of 25-30%. Well-sorted
Description of inclusions: Inclusions measuring between 0.2 and 1 mm, prevalence of those measuring 0.5 mm. Sub-rounded and highly spherical. Prevalence of quartz and feldspars, a calcite crystal, fragments of rocks with quartz and biotite, biotite
Description of matrix: Porosity in the order of 5/10%. Rounded pores measuring 0.1-0.2 mm
Colour: from 5YR, 5/3 reddish brown to 2.5Y 6/2 light brownish gray

Sample: G32=G36
Texture: Hiatal and homogeneous, well-sorted fabric
Description of inclusions: Inclusions in the order of 20-25%; inclusions measuring between 0.2 and 1 mm (prevalence of granules measuring 0.5-1 mm); the mineral phases documented are quartz, both opaque and transparent, rare feldspars, calcite and very rare biotite. Also present is secondary calcite. The granules are sub-rounded and highly spherical
Description of matrix: Porosity in the order of 10-15%, prevalently elongated and orientated pores measuring between 0.2 and 0.4 mm
Colour: Surface: 5YR 5/6 yellowish red; fracture sometimes: 5YR 4/1 dark gray

Sample: G33
Texture: Hiatal and homogeneous. Inclusions to matrix ratio 20-25%. Very well-sorted
Description of inclusions: Inclusions measuring between 0.2 and 1 mm, mean size between 0.5 and 1 mm, sub-rounded and highly spherical. Prevalence of quartz and feldspars, rarer calcite crystals, some iron oxides, a fragment of rock with an association of feldspars and biotite
Description of matrix: Porosity in the order of 10/15%. Pores elongated and orientated, prevalently measuring between 0.2 and 0.5 mm
Colour: 2,5YR/6/8 light red, the grey core is GLEY2, 6/1 greenish gray
Similar to G26

Sample: G34
Texture: Hiatal, inhomogeneous granulometry, inclusions/matrix ratio 25-30%
Description of inclusions: Quartz grains measuring 0.5-1 mm. Feldspars 0.2-1 mm. Presence of an iron oxide. Moderately well-sorted. Inclusions from sub-angular to sub-rounded
Description of matrix: Porosity 10/15%. Pores measuring between 0.5 and 1 mm, elongated and orientated
Colour: Black core: Gley 2 5/1 bluish gray; Surface 2.5YR 6/8light red

Sample: G51
Texture: Hiatal and homogeneous. Inclusions to matrix ratio 25-30%. Well-sorted
Description of inclusions: Inclusions measuring between 0.2/0.3 and 1 mm, mean size 0.3-0.5 mm, sub-angular and highly spherical. Prevalence of quartz, some feldspars, rare calcite crystals
Description of matrix: Porosity in the order of 10/15%. Pores prevalently elongated and orientated, measuring between 0.5 and 1 mm, prevalence of those measuring 0.5 mm
Colour: Black core: GLEY 2 dark greenish gray 4/1; Surface: 5YR reddish brown 5/4

Sample: G52
Texture: Hiatal, homogeneous granulometric distribution. Inclusions to matrix ratio 20%. Well-sorted
Description of inclusions: Inclusions measuring between 0.2 and 0.5 mm, rarer inclusions measuring 1 mm. Sub-rounded and highly spherical. Dominance of quartz, including some polycrystalline quartz, feldspars, to a lesser extent calcite, very rare biotite and muscovite. A probable inclusion of organic nature
Description of matrix: Porosity 10/15%. Pores prevalently elongated and orientated measuring on average 0.2/0.4mm
Colour: Black core: 5YR 5/1 gray; Surface: 5YR 5/8 yellowish red

Sample: G53
Texture: Hiatal and homogeneous. Inclusions in the order of 20-30%. Well-sorted
Description of inclusions: Inclusions measuring between 0.5 and 1 mm on average, sub-rounded with low sphericity. Only quartz and some secondary calcite
Description of matrix: Porosity of 5/10%. Rounded pores mainly measuring 0.2/0.4 mm
Colour: 7.5YR 5/1 gray

Sample: G54
Texture: Hiatal and homogeneous. Inclusions to matrix ratio 30-40%. Well-sorted fabric
Description of inclusions: Inclusions measuring between 0.3 and 1 mm, mean size 0.5 mm, sub-rounded with low sphericity. Absolute predominance of calcite crystals and quartz, very rare biotite, a few fragments of aggregates of several minerals with an association of quartz and biotite. Rarer pyroxenes, rare iron oxides
Description of matrix: Porosity in the order of 5/10%. Prevalently rounded pores measuring 0.1/0.2 mm
Colour: Black core: Gley1 6/1 gray; Surface: 2.5YR 5/6 red

Sample: G55
Texture: Hiatal and homogeneous
Description of inclusions: Inclusions to matrix ratio 15%, Well-sorted, measuring between 0.2 and 1 mm, mean size 0.5 mm. Angular and highly spherical. Quartz, muscovite and rare calcite
Description of matrix: Pores both elongated and orientated and rounded, measuring between 0.2 and 2 mm
Colour: 2.5Y, 2.5/1 black

Sample: G56 (very similar to G34)
Texture: Hiatal and homogeneous
Description of inclusions: Inclusions to matrix ratio 20-30%, moderately well-sorted, measuring between 0.2 and 1 mm, mean size 0.5 mm. Sub-rounded and highly spherical. Inclusions: mainly quartz and calcite, rare iron oxides
Description of matrix: Pores both rounded and elongated and orientated, measuring between 0.1 and 0.5 mm; porosity in the order of 5-10%
Colour: Surface: 2.5YR, 5/8 red; black core: 2.5YR, 5/1 reddish gray

Sample: G57 (in one instance associated with a form decorated with red stripes)
Texture: Hiatal and heterogeneous. Inclusions to matrix ratio of 25/30%. Well-sorted

Description of inclusions: Inclusions measuring between 0.2 and 1.5 mm, mean size 0.3/0.5 mm, rounded and highly spherical. Calcite, feldspars, quartz, biotite and muscovite. Larger quantities of quartz, feldspars and calcite
Description of matrix: Porosity in the order of 5/10%, prevalently rounded pores measuring 0.1/0.3 mm
Colour: 2.5YR 4/3 reddish brown

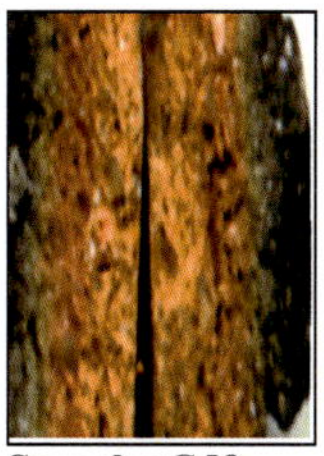

Sample: G58
Texture: Hiatal and homogeneous; well-sorted
Description of inclusions: Inclusions in the order of 10-15%; opaque quartz measuring between 0.2 and 2 mm, sub-rounded with low sphericity
Description of matrix: Porosity in the order of 5-10%, pores elongated and orientated measuring between 0.2 and 0.4 mm
Colour: Two-coloured, from orange-red (5YR 5/6 yellowish red) to dark grey (4/1 dark gray)

Sample: G59 = AG 106 Scoglietto
Texture:
Description of inclusions:
Description of matrix:
Colour: Dark grey (10YR 3/1 very dark gray)

BIBLIOGRAPHY

UNPUBLISHED PRIMARY SOURCES

ASS[1] – *Biblioteca MNS B.62, "Spogli dei contratti dell'Ospedale della Scala", Tomo III, c.244, n.1238, 1335 giugno 4.*

ASS – Capitoli 3, c.223v., 1307 Aprile 25.

ASS – Capitoli 122, secoli XIV-XV, Inventario delle cose del Comune di Siena chessono en certe terre del territorio e giurisdizione nostro. Talamone, cc.3-15.

ASS – Estimo del Contado di Siena, Montepescali n.5; Tavola preparatoria, n.236.

ASS – Ufficiali sui casseri e fortezze 12.

ASS – Vino e terratici 10, 1430 settembre 28.

PUBLISHED PRIMARY SOURCES

Acta Pontificum Romanorum Inedita - Pflugk Harttung J.v. 1958 (ed.), *Acta Pontificum Romanorum Inedita*, Vol.III, Tübingen.

AIMAe – Muratori L.A. 1740 (ed.), *Antiquitates Italicae Medii Aevi*, Milan.

Bartolini 1994 – Bartolini E. (ed.), *Procopio di Cesarea, La Guerra Gotica*, Milan.

C.A.S.P. – Sirolla M.L. 1990 (ed.), *Carte dell'Archivio di Stato di Pisa*, II, 1070-1100, Pisa.

C.D.A. – Kurze W. 1974 (ed.), *Codex Diplomaticus Amiatinus*, Tübingen.

C.D.L. – Schiapparelli L. 1929-1933 (ed.), *Codice Diplomatico Longobardo*, I-II, Rome.

Ch.L.A. – Bruckner A., Marichal R. 1954-1998 (eds.), *Chartae Latinae antiquiores*, 49 voll., Basel, Dietikon-Zurich.

Comparetti 1895 – Comparetti D., *La guerra gotica di Procopio di Cesarea*, Rome.

Giorgetti 1874 – Giorgetti A., *Il cartulario del monastero di San Quirico di Populonia*, in "Archivio Storico Italiano", s.3, XX, pp.209-224.

I Diplomi di Guido e di Lamberto – Schiaparelli L. 1906 (ed.), *I Diplomi di Guido e di Lamberto*, Rome.

Italia Sacra – Ughelli F. 1717-1722 (ed.), *Italia sacra sive de episcopis Italiane*, 2a ed., voll.10, Venice.

Leges Ahistulfi – Beyerle F. 1962 (ed.), *Leges Langobardorum 643-866,* Witzenhausen, pp.194-204.

Le Liber Census de l'eglise romaine - Fabre P., Duchesne L. 1889-1905 (eds.), *Le Liber Census de leglise romaine*, 1, Paris-Rome.

Manaresi 1955 – Manaresi C. (ed.), *I placiti del "Regnum Italiae"*, I, Rome.

M.D.L. – Barsocchini D., Bertini 1837-1841 (eds.), *Memorie e documenti per servire all'istoria del ducato di Lucca*, IV-V, Lucca.

M.G.H. – Mommsen T. 1981 (ed.), *Auctores Antiquissimi 12. Cassiodori Senatoris Variae*, XII, XIV, Munich.

M.G.H. – Boretius A., Krause V. 1897 (eds.), *Capitularia Regum Francorum, I, Capitulare de villis,* Hannover.

M.G.H. – Boretius A., Hrause V. 1897 (eds.), *Capitularia regum Francorum,* II, *Hlotarii capitulare de expeditione contra Sarracenos facienda, M.G.H.*, Hannover.

M.G.H. – Bluhme F. 1868 (ed.), *Legum tom.*4, *Edictus Langobardorum*, Hannover.

M.G.H. – Bethman L., Waitz G. 1878 (eds.), *Scriptores Rerum Langobardicarum et Italicarum sec.VI/IX, Pauli Diaconi, Historia Langobardorum*, Hannover.

Regesto del Capitolo di Lucca – Guidi P., Parenti O. 1910 (eds.), *Regesto del Capitolo di Lucca*, Vol.I, Rome.

Rutilio Namaziano – Fo A. 1992 (ed.), *De reditu suo*, Turin.

Tito Livio – Berzero G. 1943 (ed.), *Ab Urbe condita*, lib.X, , Turin.

Von Glanvell 1905 – Von Glanvell W. (ed.), *Die Kanonensammlung des Kardinals Deusdedit*, Padeborn.

[1] *ASS* = Archivio di Stato di Siena.

SECONDARY SOURCES

Abela 2000a – Abela E., *Ceramica a vetrina pesante (VP)*, in Abela E., Berti G., Bruni S. (eds.), *Ricerche archeologiche medievali a Pisa. I. Piazza dei Cavalieri, la campagna di scavo 1993*, Florence, pp.121-122.

Abela 2000b – Abela E., *Ceramica dipinta a bande rosse (DR)*, in Abela E., Berti G., Bruni S. (eds.), *Ricerche archeologiche medievali a Pisa. I. Piazza dei Cavalieri, la campagna di scavo 1993*, Florence, pp.119-120.

Abela 1993a – Abela E., *Ceramica a vetrina pesante (Forum Ware) (VP) Ceramica a vetrina pesante a macchia (Sparse Glazed) (VPS)*, in Bruni S. (ed.), *Piazza Dante: uno spaccato di storia pisana*, Pontedera, pp.419-424.

Abela 1993b – Abela E., *Ceramica dipinta in rosso (DR)*, in Bruni S. (ed.), *Piazza Dante: uno spaccato di storia pisana*, Pontedera, pp.413-418

Abela *et alii* 2000 – Abela E., Berti G., Bruni S. (eds.), *Ricerche archeologiche medievali a Pisa. I. Piazza dei Cavalieri, la campagna di scavo 1993*, Florence.

Ademollo 1880 – Ademollo A., *Scavi della Serrata Martini presso Castiglione della Pescaia*, in "Ombrone", nn. 27 ss., Grosseto.

Alarcão-Mayet 1990 – Alarcão A., Mayet, F. (eds.), *As ânforas Lusitanas: Tipologia, produção, comércio,* Actas das jornadas de estudo realizadas em Conimbriga em 13 et 14 de Outobro 1988, Coimbra-Paris.

Alberti 1999, *I recipienti in pietra ollare* in Brogiolo G.P. (ed.), *S.Giulia di Brescia gli scavi dal 1980 al 1992,* Florence, pp.261-270.

Alcock-Cherry 2004 (eds.) – Alcock S.E., Cherry J.F. (eds.), *Side-by-Side Survey. Comparative Studies in the Mediterranean World,* Oxford.

Alessi *et alii* 1993 – Alessi D., Bonet P., Spinesi P., *Vasellame da fuoco privo di rivestimento: forme chiuse,* in Bruni S. (ed.), *Piazza Dante: uno spaccato di storia pisana*, Pontedera, pp.427-444.

Ammermann 1985 – Ammermann A.J., *Plow-Zone Experiments in Calabria, Italy*, in "Journal of Field Archaeology", 12, pp.33-40.

Andreolli 1985 – Andreolli B., *La forza del diritto: lo ius libellarium e le sue variazioni durante il Medioevo*, in Andreolli B., Fumagalli V., Montanari M. (eds.), *Le campagne italiane prima e dopo il mille. Una società in trasformazione*, Bologna, pp.275-309.

Andreolli 1983 – Andreolli B., *Uomini nel Medioevo. Studi sulla società lucchese dei secoli VIII-XI*, Bologna.

Angelucci 1977 – Angelucci P., *Ricerche sul sale maremmano nel Medioevo*, in "Ricerche Soriche", anno VII, n.I, gennaio-giugno 1977, Florence, pp. 119-136.

Anselmino *et alii* 1986 – Anselmino L., Coletti C.M., Ferrantini M.L., Panella C., *Ostia. Terme del Nuotatore*, in Giardina A. (ed.), *Società romana e impero tardoantico, Vol.III. Le merci e gli insediamenti*, Bari, pp.45-81.

Aprosio 2005 – Aprosio M., *Paesaggi tardoantichi di Brindisi*, in Volpe G., Turchiano M. (eds.), *Paesaggi e insediamenti rurali in Italia meridionale fra tardoantico e altomedioevo*, Bari, pp.443-454.

Arnoldus Huyzendveld 2007 – Arnoldus Huyzendveld A., *Le trasformazioni dell'ambiente naturale della pianura grossetana. Dati geologici e paloe-ambientali*, in Citter C., Arnoldus Huyzendveld (eds.), *Archeologia urbana a Grosseto. Origine e sviluppo di una città medievale nella "Toscana delle città deboli". Le ricerche 1997 – 2005. I: la città di Grosseto nel contesto geografico della bassa valle dell'Ombrone*, Florence, pp.41-61.

Arnoldus Huyzendveld 2005 – Arnoldus Huyzendveld A., *Il paleoambiente storico di Grosseto*, in Citter C. (ed.), *Lo scavo della chiesa di S.Pietro a Grosseto. Nuovi dati sull'origine e lo sviluppo di una città medievale*, Florence, pp.62-7.

Arthur 2004a – Arthur P., *Ceramica in Terra d'Otranto tra VIII e XI secolo*, in Patitucci Uggeri S. (ed.), *La ceramica altomedievale in Italia*, Florence, pp.313-326.

Arthur 2004b – Arthur P., *From Vicus to Village: Italian Landscapes, AD 400-1000*, in Christie N. (ed.), *Landscapes of Change. Rural Evolutions in Late Antiquity and the Early Middle Ages*, Aldershot.

Arthur 1999 – Arthur P., *Riflessioni intorno ad alcune produzioni di anfore tra la Calabria e la Puglia in età medievale*, in *Atti del XXX Convegno internazionale della ceramica 1997*, Albisola, pp.9-18.

Arthur 1998 – Arthur P., *Eastern Mediterranean amphorae between 500 and 700: a view from Italy*, in Saguì L. (ed.), *Ceramica in Italia: VI-VII secolo*, Florence, pp.157-183.

Arthur 1993 – Arthur P., *Early medieval amphorae, the Duchy of Naples and the food supply of Rome*, "Papers of the British School at Rome", LXI, pp.231-244.

Arthur 1992 – Arthur P., *Amphorae for Bulk Transport*, in D'Andria F.-Whitehouse D. (eds.), *Excavations at Otranto. Volume II: The Finds*, Lecce, pp.199-217.

Arthur 1990 – Arthur P., *Anfore dell'alto adriatico ed il problema del "Samos Cystern Type"*, in "Aquileia Nostra", LXI, coll. 281-295.

Arthur 1989a – Arthur P., *Aspects of Byzantine economy: an evaluation of amphora evidence from Italy*, in Deroch V., Spieser J.M. (eds.), *Recherches sur la céramique byzantine*, Paris, pp.79-91.

Arthur 1989b – Arthur P., *Some observations on the economy of Bruttium under the later Roman empire*, "Journal of Roman Archaeology", 2, pp.133-142.

Arthur 1986a – Arthur P., *Archeologia urbana a Napoli: riflessioni sugli ultimi tre anni*, in "Archeologia Medievale", XIII, pp.515-526.

Arthur 1986b – Arthur P., *Appunti sulla circolazione della ceramica medievale a Napoli*, in AAVV., *La ceramica medievale nel Mediterraneo occidentale*, Florence, pp.545-553.

Arthur 1985 – Arthur P., *Naples: Notes on the Economy of a Dark Age City*, in Malone C., Stoddart S. (eds.), *Papers in Italian Archaeology. IV., Classical and Medieval Archaeology*, Oxford, pp.247-259.

Arthur 1984 – Arthur P., *Rapporto preliminare sullo scavo a Santa Patrizia, Napoli*, in "Archeologia Medievale", XI, pp.315-320.

Arthur-Patterson 1998 – Arthur P., Patterson H., *Local pottery in southern Puglia in the sixth and seventh centuries*, in Saguì L. (ed.), *Ceramica in Italia: VI-VII secolo*, Florence, pp.511-530.

Arthur-Patterson 1994 – Arthur P., Patterson H., *Ceramics and Early Medieval Central and Southern Italy: "a Potted History"*, in Francovich R., Noyé G. (eds.), *La storia dell'Alto Medioevo italiano alla luce dell'archeologia*, Atti del Convegno, Certosa di Pontignano (Siena) 1992, Florence, pp.409-441.

Arthur *et alii* 1992 – Arthur P. *et alii*, *Fornaci altomedievali ad Otranto. Nota preliminare*, in "Archeologia Medievale", XIX, pp.91-122.

Atlante I – *Atlante delle forme ceramiche I. Ceramica fine romana nel bacino mediterraneo (medio e tardo impero)*, (1980), Supplement to *Enciclopedia dell'arte antica*, Rome.

Atlante II – *Atlante delle forme ceramiche I. Ceramica fine romana nel bacino mediterraneo (tardo ellensimo e primo impero)*, (1985), Supplement to *Enciclopedia dell'arte antica*, Rome.

Atlante Sedi Umane 1970 – *Atlante aerofotografico delle Sedi Umane in Italia*, Parte II, Istituto Geografico Militare, Florence.

Augenti 2006 – Augenti A., *Ravenna e Classe: archeologia di due città tra la tarda Antichità e l'alto Medioevo*, in Augenti A. (ed.), *Le città italiane tra la Tarda Antichità e l'Alto Medioevo*, Florence, pp.185-218.

Augenti 2000 – Augenti A., *Dai castra tardoantichi ai castelli del secolo X: il caso della Toscana*, in Francovich R., Ginatempo M., *Castelli. Storia e archeologia del potere nella Toscana medievale*, Vol.I, Florence, pp.25-66.

Azzara-Gasparri 1992 – Azzara C., Gasparri S. (eds.), *Le leggi dei Longobardi. Storia, memoria e diritto di un popolo germanico*, Milan.

Bakirtzis 1989 – Bakirtzis Ch., *Byzantine Amphorae*, in Deroch V., Spieser J.M. (eds.), *Recherches sur la céramique byzantine*, Paris, pp.73-77.

Barbera *et alii* 2001 – Barbera M., Pacetti F., Vatta G., Martin A., *Lucerne*, in Arena M.S., Delogu P., Paroli L., Ricci M., Saguì L., Vendittelli L. (eds.), *Roma dall'antichità al medioevo. Archeologia e storia*, Milan, pp.184-192.

Bargagliotti-Cibecchini 2003 – Bargagliotti S., Cibecchini F., *Il porto romano in località Puntone di Scarlino (Gr): indagini archeologiche subacquee e porti moderni*, in Benini A., Giacobelli M. (eds.), *Atti del II Convegno Nazionale di Archeologia Subacquea*, Castiglioncello, 7-9 settembre 2001, Bari, pp.43-59.

Bargagliotti-Cibecchini-Gambogi 2004 – Bargagliotti S., Cibecchini F., Gambogi P., *The Punta Ala "B wreck": a mixed cargo of the Hadrianic Period*, in Pasquinucci M., Weski T. (eds.), *Close Encounters: Sea and Riverborne Trade, Ports and Hinterlands, Ship Construction abd Navigation in Antiquity, the Middle Ages and in Modern Time*, BAR International Series, 1283, Oxford, pp.93-103.

Bargagliotti-Cibecchini-Gambogi 2002 – Bargagliotti S., Cibecchini F., Gambogi P., *Punta Ala. Relitto "B". La campagna di scavo 1998: relazione preliminare*, in " Archeologia subacquea. Studi, ricerche e documenti", III, pp.243-246.

Barker 1995 (ed.) – Barker G. (ed.), *A Mediterranean Valley. Landscape Archaeology and Annales History in the Biferno Valley*, London.

Barker 1991 – Barker G., *Approaches to archaeological survey*, in Barker G., Lloyd J. (eds.), *Roman Landscapes. Archaeological Survey in the Mediterranean Region*, Archaeological Monographs of the British School at Rome, 2, London, pp.1-9.

Barker 1986 – Barker G., *L'archeologia del paesaggio italiano: nuovi orientamenti e recenti esperienze*, "Archeologia Medievale", XIII, pp.7-30.

Barraud *et alii* 1998 – Barraud D *et alii*, *L'industrie céramique de l'Antiquité tardive*, in Ben Hassen H., Maurin L. (eds.), *La rédecouverte d'une ville antique de Tunisie*, Bordeaux-Paris-Tunis, pp.139-167.

Bartoloni-Ricci 1995 – Bartoloni V., Ricci M., *Produzioni ceramiche da un contesto dei secoli XI-XII a Tarquinia,* in De Minicis E. (ed.), *Le ceramiche di Roma e del Lazio in età medievale e moderna, II*, Rome, pp.100-106.

Bass-Van Doornick 1982 – Bass G.F., Van Doornick F.H. Jr., *Yassi Ada: a Seventh-Century Byzantine Shipwreck I*, College Station Texas.

Belli *et alii* 2005 – Belli M., Francovich R., Grassi F., Quirós Castello A. (eds.), *Archeologia di un castello minerario: il sito di Cugnano (Monterotondo M.mo, Gr)*, Florence.

Bellini 1962 – Bellini L., *Le saline dell'antico delta padano*, Ferrara.

Bellotti *et alii* 2004 – Bellotti P., Caputo C., Davoli L., Evangelista S., Garzanti E., Pugliese F., Valeri P., *Morpho-sedimentary characteristics and Holocene evolution of the emergent part of the Ombrone River delta (southern Tuscany)*, in "Geomorphology", 61, pp.71-90.

Bellotti *et alii* 1999 – Bellotti P. *et alii*, *Lineamenti morfologici e sedimentologici della piana deltizia del Fiume Ombrone (Toscana meridionale)*, in "Boll.Soc.Geol.It.", 118, pp.141-147.

Beltrame 1998 – Beltrame C., *Processi formativi del relitto in ambiente marino mediterraneo*, in Volpe G. (ed.), *Archeologia Subacquea*, VIII ciclo di lezioni sulla ricerca applicata in archeologia, Certosa di Pontignano (Siena) 9-15 dicembre 1996, Florence, pp.141-166.

Ben Abed-Ben Khader *et alii* 2004 – Ben Abed-Ben Khader A., Fixot M., Bonifay M., Roucole S., *Sidi Jdidi I. La basilique Sud*, Rome.

Bernardi-Cappelli-Cuteri 1992 – Bernardi M., Cappelli L., Cuteri F., *Ceramiche a vetrina pesante e a vetrina sparsa in Toscana. Il caso degli insediamnti di Scarlino (GR) e Rocca San Silvestro (LI)*, in Paroli L. (ed.), *La ceramica invetriata tardoantica e altomedievale in Italia*, Florence, pp.295-302.

Berti 1993 – Berti G., *Pisa: dalle importazioni islamiche alle produzioni locali di ceramiche con rivestimenti vetrificati (seconda metà X-prima metà XVII secolo)*, in Bruni S. (ed.), *Pisa. Piazza Dante. Uno spaccato della storia pisana. La campagna di scavo 1991*, Pontedera, pp.119-146.

Berti-Menchelli 1998 – Berti G., Menchelli S., *Pisa, ceramiche da cucina, da dispensa, da trasporto dei secoli X-XV*, in "Archeologia Medievale", XXV, pp.307-333.

Berti-Cappelli-Ciampoltrini 1992 – Berti G., Cappelli L., Ciampoltrini G., *Ceramiche a vetrina pesante e a vetrina sparsa a Lucca e in alcuni insediamenti del territorio*, in Paroli L. (ed.), *La ceramica invetriata tardoantica e altomedievale in Italia*, Florence, pp.279-294.

Bianchi 2004a – Bianchi G. (ed.), *Campiglia: un castello e il suo territorio. II. Indagine archeologica*, Florence.

Bianchi 2004b – Bianchi G. (ed.), *Castello di Donoratico. I risultati delle prime campagne di scavo (2000-2002)*, Florence.

Bianchi 2003 – Bianchi G., *Archeologia dell'architettura nei castelli della Toscana sud-occidentale (val di Cornia-bassa val di Cecina)*, in Fiorillo R., Peduto P. (eds.), *III Congresso Nazionale di Archeologia Medievale*, Florence, pp.567-575.

Bianchi 1997 – Bianchi G., *Rocca San Silvestro e Campiglia M.ma: storia parallela di due insediamenti toscani attraverso la lettura delle strutture murarie*, in Gelichi S. (ed.), *I Congresso Nazionale di Archeologia Medievale*, Florence, pp.437-444.

Bianchi *et alii* 1990 – Bianchi S., Viti L., Gargiani B., *Ceramica acroma grezza*, in De Marinis G. (ed.), *Archeologia urbana a Fiesole. Lo scavo di via Marini-via Portigiani*, Florence, pp.223-241.

Bianchi-Palermo 1990a – Bianchi S., Palermo L., *Terra sigillata chiara italica*, in De Marinis G. (ed.), *Archeologia urbana a Fiesole. Lo scavo di via Marini-via Portigiani*, Florence, pp.158-168.

Bianchi-Palermo 1990b – Bianchi S., Palermo L., *Ceramica a vernice rossa tarda*, in De Marinis G. (ed.), *Archeologia urbana a Fiesole. Lo scavo di via Marini-via Portigiani*, Florence, pp.169-188.

Bierbrauer 1990 – Bierbrauer V., *La ceramica grezza di Invillino-Ibligo, Friuli e i suoi paralleli nell'arco alpino centrale e orientale (secc. IV-VII d.C.)*, in "Archeologia Medievale", XVII, pp.57-83.

Biffino *et alii* 1998 – Biffino A., De Felice G., Custode S.F., Lapadula E., Pietropaolo L., *I materiali ceramici e metallici*, in Volpe G. (ed.), *San Giusto: la villa, le ecclesiae*, Bari, pp.263-276.

Bintliff 2000 – Bintliff J., *The concepts of 'site'and 'off-site'archaeology in surface artefact survey*, in Pasquinucci M., Trement F. (eds.), *Non-Destructive Techniques Applied to Landscape Archaeology*, Oxford, pp.200-215.

Bintliff-Snodgrass 1988 – Bintliff J., Snodgrass M.A., *Off-site Distributions: A Regional and Interregional Perspective*, in "Current Antropology", 29, 3, pp.506-513.

Bizzarri 1920 – Bizzarri D., *Il monopolio del sale a Grosseto*, in "Bollettino senese di storia patria", XXVII, pp.1-32.

Boldrini-Grassi 2003 – Boldrini E., Grassi F., *Alle radici dei castelli: indizi di economia curtense nei reperti ceramici della Toscana meridionale*, in Fiorillo R., Peduto P. (eds.), *III Congresso Nazionale di Archeologia Medievale*, Florence, pp.66-70.

Bolla 1991 – Bolla M., *Recipienti in pietra ollare*, in Caporusso D. (ed.), *Scavi MM3, Ricerche di archeologia urbana a Milano durante la costruzione della linea 3 della Metropolitana 1982-1990,* Voll.3.1, 3.2, 4, Rome, pp.11-37.

Bonacasa Carra-Ardizzone 2001 – Bonacasa Carra R.M., Ardizzone F., *Due fornaci medievali ad Agrigento e la produzione di anfore tra X e XI secolo*, in Patitucci Uggeri S. (eds.), *Scavi medievali in Italia 1996-1999*, Rome, pp.425-440.

Bonifay-Garnier 2007 – Bonifay M.-Garnier N., *Que transportaient donc les amphores africaines?*, in Papi E. (ed.), Supplying Rome and the Empire, Journal of Roman Archaeology-Supplemetary Series, n.69, pp.8-31.

Bonifay 2004 – Bonifay M., *Etudes sur la céramique romaine tardive d'Afrique*, BAR International Series, 1301, Oxford.

Bonifay 1998 – Bonifay M., *Sur quelques problèmes de datation des sigillées africaines à Mareseille*, in Saguì L. (ed.), *Ceramica in Italia: VI-VII secolo*, Florence, pp.71-81.

Bonifay *et alii* 2005 – Bonifay M., Capelli C., Martin T., Picon M., Vallauri L., *Le littoral de la Tunisine, étude géoarcheologique et historique (1987-1997). La céramique*, in AAVV, *L'Afrique du Nord de la protohistoire à la conquête arabe*, Paris, pp.125-202.

Bonifay-Carre-Rigoir 1998 – Bonifay M., Carre M.B., Rigoir Y., (eds.), *Fouilles à Marseille. Les mobiliers (Ier-VIIe s.ap.J.-C.)*, Paris.

Borghi 1978 – Borghi L., *Osservazioni geofisiche*, Curri C. B., *Forma Italiae: Regio VII,volumen IV: Vetulonia*, Florence, pp.41-51.

Brecciaroli Taborelli 1978 – Brecciaroli Taborelli L., *Contributo alla classificazione di una terra sigillata chiara italica*, in "Rivista di studi marchigiani", 1, pp.1-38.

Brogiolo 2005 – Brogiolo G.P., *Risultati e prospettive della ricerca archeologica sulle campagne altomedievali italiane*, in Brogiolo G.P., Chavarria A., Valenti M. (eds.), *Dopo la fine delle ville: le campagne dal VI al IX secolo*, XI Seminario sul Tardoantico e l'Altomedioevo, Mantova, pp.7-16.

Brogiolo 2001 – Brogiolo G.P., *L'Adriatico altomedievale in una nuova prospettiva storiografica*, in Bertelli C., Brogiolo G.P., Jurković M., Milošević A., Stella C. (eds.), *Bizantini, Croati, Carolingi. Alba e tramonto di regni e imperi*, Milan, pp.21-25.

Brogiolo 1999 – Brogiolo G.P., *Modelli archeologici per l'età di transizione (secoli V-VIII) in Italia settentrionale*, in Rotili M. (ed.), *Memorie del passato, urgenza del futuro. Il mondo romano fra V e VII secolo*, Atti delle VI giornate di studio sull'età romanobarbarica, Benevento, 18-20 giugno 1998, Naples, pp.197-210.

Brogiolo-Chavarría Arnau (eds.) 2007 – Brogiolo G.P., Chavarría Arnau A. (eds.), *Archeologia e società tra tardo antico e alto medioevo*, Mantova.

Brogiolo-Chavarría 2005 – Brogiolo G.P., Chavarría Arnau A., *Aristocrazie e campagne nell'Occidente da Costantino a Carlo Magno*, Florence.

Bravetti-Pranzini 1993 – Bravetti L., Pranzini G., *Geomorphological Evolution and Sedimentology of the Ombrone River Delta Italy*, in "Journal of Coastal Research", 9, 2, pp.481-489.

Bravetti-Pranzini 1987 – Bravetti L., Pranzini G., 1987 - *L'evoluzione quaternaria della pianura di Grosseto (Toscana): prima interpretazione dei dati del sottosuolo*, in "Geogr. Fis. Dinam.Quat.", 10 (1987), pp.85-92.

Bruni 1993 – Bruni S. (ed.), *Piazza Dante: uno spaccato di storia pisana*, Pontedera.

Bruno-Bocchio 1999 – Bruno B, Bocchio S., *Le anfore da trasporto*, in Brogiolo G.P.(ed.) 1999, *S.Giulia di Brescia gli scavi dal 1980 al 1992*, Florence, pp.231-260.

Cambi 2005 – Cambi F., *Segesta. I villaggi di età imperiale*, in Volpe G., Turchiano M. (eds.), *Paesaggi e insediamenti rurali in Italia meridionale fra tardoantico e altomedioevo*, Bari, pp.623-640.

Cambi 2003 – Cambi F., *Archeologia dei Paesaggi Antichi: Fonti e Diagnostica*, Rome.

Cambi 2000a – Cambi F., *Pottery and territory: a tormented relationship*, in Francovich R., Patterson H., Barker G. (eds.), *Extracting Meanings from Ploughsoil Assemblages*, Oxford, pp.174-184.

Cambi 2000b – Cambi F., *Quando i campi hanno pochi significati da estrarre: visibilità archeologica, storia istituzionale, multi-stage work*, in Francovich R., Patterson H., Barker G. (eds.), *Extracting Meanings from Ploughsoil Assemblages,* Oxford, pp.72-76.

Cambi 1996 – Cambi F., *Carta Archeologica della Provincia di Siena. Il Monte Amiata (Abbadia San Salvatore)*, Vol.II, Siena.

Cambi 1989 – Cambi F., *L'anfora di Empoli*, in AAVV, *Amphores romaines et historie économique: dix ans de recherches*, Atti del Colloquio Internazionale (Siena 22-24 maggio 1986), Rome, pp.564-567.
Cambi 1986 – Cambi F., *L'archeologia di uno spazio geografico. Il progetto topografico ager Cosanus-Valle dell'Albegna*, in , "Archeologia Medievale", XIII, pp.527-544.
Cambi 1985 – Cambi F., *Catalogo degli impasti-Anfore*, in Ricci A. (ed.), *Settefinestre. Una villa schiavistica nell'Etruria romana. La villa e i suoi reperti*, Vol III, Modena, pp.323-330.
Cambi-Fentress 1989 – Cambi F., Fentress E., *Villas to castles: 1st Millennium A.D. Demography in the Albegna Valley*, in Randsborg K. (ed.), *The Birth of Europe. Archaelogogy and Social Development in The First Millennium A.D.*, Rome, pp.74-86.
Cambi-Terrenato 1994 – Cambi F., Terrenato N., *Introduzione all'archeologia dei paesaggi*, Rome.
Cambi-Volpe 1985 – Cambi F.-Volpe G., *Contenitori da cantina e da trasporto*, in Ricci A. (ed.), *Settefinestre. Una villa schiavistica nell'Etruria romana. La villa e i suoi reperti*, Vol III, Modena, pp.72-92.
Cameron 1996 – Cameron A., *Un impero due destini. Roma e Costantinopoli fra il 395 e il 600 d.C.*, (Italian translation by Ghibellini C. and Siccardi E.), Genova.
Camilli-Gambogi 2004 – Camilli A., Gambogi P., *Porti e approdi della costa toscana*, in Arce X., Camilli A., Hodges R., Urteaga M. (eds.), *Mar Exterior. El occidente atlàntico in età romana/Il mare esterno/L'Occidente atlantico in età romana*, atti del convegno (Pisa novembre 2003), Irun 2004.
Cammarosano 2001 – Cammarosano P., *Storie dell'Italia medievale. Dal VI all'XI secolo*, Bari.
Campana 2006a – Campana S., *Remote sensing at work*, in Campana S., Piro S., Felici C., Ghisleni M., *From space to place: the Aiali project (Tuscany-Italy)*, in Campana S., Forte C. (eds.), *From space to place*, 2nd International Conference on Remote Sensing in Archaeology, CNR, Rome, 4-7 dicembre 2006, Oxford, pp.131-132.
Campana 2006b – Campana S., *DGPS e Mobile GPS per l'Archoelogia dei Paesaggi*, in Campana S., Francovich R. (eds.), *Laser Scanner e GPS. Paesaggi archeologici e tecnologie digitali 1*, Florence, pp.201-225.
Campana 2005 – Campana S., *2. Strategia e metodi del Progetto Carta Archeologica della Provincia di Grosseto*, in Campana S., Francovich R., Vaccaro E. (with a contribution by Frezza B. and Ghisleni M.), *Il popolamento tardoromano e altomedievale nella bassa valle dell'Ombrone. Progetto Carta Archeologica della Provincia di Grosseto*, in "Archeologia Medievale", XXXII, pp.461-463.
Campana 2002 – Campana S., *Carta archeologica della provincia di Siena. Murlo*, Vol.V, Siena.
Campana-Piro 2009 – Campana S., Piro S., *Putting everything together: GIS-based data integration and interpretation*, in Campana S., Piro S. (eds.), *Seeing the Unseen Archaeology. Geophysical and Landscape Archaeology*, London, pp.325-330.
Campana-Francovich-Felici 2005 – Campana S., Francovich R., Felici C., *Large scale magnetic survey and archaeological mapping. The Grosseto and Siena Projects*, in Piro S. (ed.), *6th International Conference on Archaeological Prospection, Roma, 14-17 settembre 2005*, Rome, pp.25-30.
Cantini 2007 – Cantini F. 2007, *Etá classica-altomedioevo*, in Cantini F., Francovich R., Cianferoni C., Scampoli E. (eds.), *Firenze prima degli Uffizi. Lo scavo di via de' Castellani: contributi per un'archeologia urbana fra tardo antico ed età moderna*, Florence, pp.183-286.
Cantini 2005a – Cantini F. 2005, *Archeologia urbana a Siena: l'area dell'ospedale di Santa Maria della Scala prima dell'ospedale, altomedioevo*, Florence.
Cantini 2005b – Cantini F., *Ceramiche dai siti medievali rurali della Toscana (VIII-X secolo): una prima sintesi*, in Gelichi S. (ed.), *Campagne medievali. Strutture materiali, economia e società nell'insediamento rurale dell'Italia settentrionale (VIII-X secolo)*, Mantova, pp.259-276.
Cantini 2003 – Cantini F., *Il Castello di Montarrenti*, Florence.
Capelli 1998 – Capelli C., *Il contributo delle analisi minero-petrografiche allo studio delle anfore Keay LII*, in Saguì L. (ed.), *Ceramica in Italia: VI-VII secolo*, Florence, pp.335-342.
Cappelli 1934 – Cappelli A., *Roccastrada: scoperte di tombe di epoca barbarica*, "Notizie degli Scavi di Antichità", pp.64-66.
Carandini 1993 – Carandini A., *L'ultima civiltà sepolta o del massimo oggetto desueto, secondo un archeologo*, in *Storia di Roma, 3. L'età tardoantica, II, I luoghi, le culture*, Turin, pp.11-38.
Carandini 1989 – Carandini A., *La villa romana e la piantagione schiavistica*, in *Storia di Roma, 4. Caratteri e morfologie*, Turin, pp.101-200.
Carsana 1994 – Carsana V., *Ceramica da cucina tardo antica e alto medievale*, in Arthur P. (ed.), *Il Complesso Archeologico di Carminiello ai Mannesi, Napoli (Scavi 1983-1984)*, Galatina, pp.220-258.
Castagnetti 1976 – Castagnetti A., *La pieve rurale nell'Italia padana. Territorio, organizzazione patrimoniale e vicende della pieve veronese di San Pietro di "Tillida" dall'alto medioevo al secolo XIII*, Rome.
Cavaillès Llopis-Vallauri 1994 – Cavaillès Llopis M.T., Vallauri L., *Les sigillées claires africaines*, in Démians d'Archimbaud G. (ed.), *L'oppidum de Saint Blaise du Ve au VIIe siecle*, Paris, pp.86-114.
Cavanna-Cavanna 2006 – Cavanna C., Cavanna F., *La Grotta dello Scoglietto. Un Nosocomio della Preistoria*, in "Equipèco", III, n.7, pp.84-87.
Ceccarelli Lemut 2004 – Ceccarelli Lemut M.L., *I porti minori della Toscana nel Medioevo*, in Bandini F., Darchi M. (eds.), *La repubblica di Noli e l'importanza dei porti minori del Mediterraneo nel Medioevo*, Giornata di studio (Noli, 29 maggio 2004), Florence, pp. 49-67.
Ceccarelli Lemut 2001 – Ceccarelli Lemut M.L., *Le strutture civili del territorio di Roselle-Grosseto nei secoli XI e XII: contea e signorie territoriali*, in Ascheri M. (ed.), *Siena e Maremma nel Medioevo*, Siena, pp.83-113.
Ceccarelli Lemut 1993 – Ceccarelli Lemut M.L., *I conti Gherardeschi e le origini del monastero di S.Maria di Serena*, in Violante C. (ed.), *Nobiltà e chiese nel medioevo e altri saggi. Scritti in onore di G. Tellenbach*, Rome, pp.47-75.
Ceccarelli Lemut 1985 – Ceccarelli Lemut M.L., *Scarlino: le vicende medievali fino al 1399*, in Francovich R. (ed.), *Scarlino I, Storia e territorio*, Florence, pp.19-74.
Ceglie *et alii* 2006 – Ceglie S., Paris M.F., Venturini F., *Le storie della Rocca di Suvereto tra alto e bsso medioevo attraverso le nuove indagini archeologiche*, in Marcucci C., Megale C. (eds.), *Il Medioevo nella provincia di Livorno. I risultati delle recenti indagini*, Ospedaletto, pp.117-130.
Celuzza 2002a – Celuzza M.G., *Dalla riconversione delle ville alla crisi (50-200 d.C.)*, in Carandini A., Cambi F. (eds.), *Paesaggi d'Etruria. Valle dell'Albegna, Valle d'Oro, Valle del Chiarone, Valle del Tafone*, Rome, pp.196-206.
Celuzza 2002b – Celuzza M.G., *I porti (III-VI secolo d.C.)*, in Carandini A., Cambi F. (eds.), *Paesaggi d'Etruria. Valle dell'Albegna, Valle d'Oro, Valle del Chiarone, Valle del Tafone*, Rome, p.245.
Celuzza 2002c – Celuzza M.G. *La romanizzazione: etruschi e romani fra 311 e 123 a.C.*, in Carandini A., Cambi F. (eds.), *Paesaggi d'Etruria. Valle dell'Albegna, Valle d'Oro, Valle del Chiarone, Valle del Tafone*, Rome, pp.103-113.
Celuzza 1998a – Celuzza M.G., *Roselle: la tarda antichità e il Medioevo*, in Nicosia F., Poggesi G. (eds.), *Roselle. Guida al parco archeologico*, Siena, pp.43-48.
Celuzza 1998b – Celuzza M.G., *L'area alle pendici della collina nord*, in Nicosia F., Poggesi G. (eds.), *Roselle. Guida al parco archeologico*, Siena, pp.147-156.

Celuzza 1994a – Celuzza M.G.-Fentress E., *La Toscana centro-meridionale: i casi di Cosa-Ansedonia e Roselle*, in Francovich R., Noyé G. (ed.), *La storia dell'altomedioevo italiano (VI-X secolo) alla luce dell'archeologia*, Florence, pp.601-613.

Celuzza 1994b – Celuzza 1994, *Etruria romana*, in AAVV., «EAA», Secondo supplemento 1971-1994, II, Rome, pp.549-554.

Celuzza-Rendini 1992 – Celuzza M.G., Rendini P. (eds.), *Relitti di storia. Archeologia subacquea in Maremma*, Siena.

Chavarría Arnau 2007 – Chavarrí Arnau A., *El final de las villae en Hispania (siglos IV-VII D.C.)*, Turnhout.

Ciampoltrini 2004 – Ciampoltrini G., *Produzioni ceramiche lucchesi fra VIII e XI secolo. Evidenze dalle stratigrafie dell'area Galli Tassi*, in Patitucci Uggeri S. (ed.), *La ceramica altomedievale in Italia*, Florence, pp.149-162.

Ciampoltrini 2001 – Ciampoltrini G., *Vetroniano e Vico Leoniano. Insediamenti "protetti" e vici nel Valdarno fra VIII e IX secolo*, "Archeologia Medievale", XXVIII, pp.457-464.

Ciampoltrini 1998 – Ciampoltrini G., *L'orciolo e l'olla. Considerazioni sulle produzioni ceramiche in Toscana fra VI e VII secolo*, in Saguì L. (ed.), *Ceramica in Italia VI-VII secolo*, Florence, pp.289-304.

Ciampoltrini 1994 – Ciampoltrini G., *Città frammentate e città fortezza. Storie urbane della Toscana centro-settentrionale fra Teodosio e Carlo Magno*, in Francovich R., Noyé G., 1994 (eds.), *La storia dell'Alto Medioevo italiano (VI-X secolo) alla luce dell'archeologia*, Florence, pp.615-633.

Ciampoltrini 2006 (ed.) – Ciampoltrini G. (ed.), *In Silice. Lo scavo della chiesa di San Ponziano in Lucca*, Lucca.

Ciampoltrini *et alii* 1991 – Campoltrini G. *et alii*, *Materiali tardoantichi ed altomedievali dalla Valle del Serchio*, "Archeologia Medievale", XVIII, pp.699-715.

Ciampoltrini-Notini 1993 – Ciampoltrini G., Notini P., *Massaciuccoli (Com.Massarosa, Lucca): ricerche sull'insediamento post-classico nella villa romana*, "Archeologia Medievale", XX, pp.393-407.

Ciampoltrini-Notini 1990 – Ciampoltrini G., Notini P., *Lucca tardoantica e altomedievale: nuovi contributi archeologici*, in "Archeologia Medievale", XVII, pp.561-592.

Ciampoltrini-Rendini 2004 – Ciampoltrini G., Rendini P., *Ports and Trade in the ager Cosanus and on Giglio Island from the Mid to Late Imperial Age*, in Pasquinucci M., Weski T. (eds.), *Close Encounters: Sea and Riverborne Trade, Ports and Hinterlands, Ship Construction abd Navigation in Antiquity, the Middle Ages and in Modern Time*, BAR International Series, 1283, Oxford, pp.85-91.

Ciampoltrini-Rendini 1990 – Ciampoltrini G., Rendini P., *L'insediamento tardoantico nella villa marittima di Torre tagliata (Orbetello, Gr), scavi 1988-1989*, "Archeologia Medievale", XVII, pp.625-632.

Ciampoltrini-Rendini 1989 – Ciampoltrini G., Rendini P., *Un insediamento tardoantico nella Valle d'Osa (Orbetello, GR), Indagini di superficie*, in "Archeologic Medievale", XV, pp.513-522.

Ciampoltrini-Rendini 1988 – Ciampoltrini G., Rendini P., *L'agro cosano fra tarda antichità e alto medioevo: segnalazioni e contributi*, "Archeologia Medievale", XVI, pp.519-534.

Ciarrocchi *et alii* 1993 – Ciarrocchi B., Martin A., Paroli L., Patterson H., *Produzione e circolazione di ceramiche tardaontiche ed altomedievali ad Ostia e Porto*, in Paroli L., Delogu P. (eds.), *La storia economica di Roma nell'alto Medioevo alla luce dei recenti scavi archeologici*, Florence, pp.203-246.

Cirelli 2006 – Cirelli E., *Classificazione e quantificazione del materiale ceramico nelle ricerche di superficie*, in Mancassola N., Saggioro F. (eds.), *Medioevo, Paesaggi e Metodi*, Mantova, pp.169-178.

Cirelli 2003 – Cirelli E., *The Medieval Coarsewares*, in Fentress E. (ed.), *Cosa V. An intermittent town. Excavations 1991-1997*, Ann Arbor, Michigan, pp.330-349.

Citter 2007a – Citter C., *La tarda antichità e il medioevo*, in Citter C., Arnoldus Huyzendveld (eds.), *Archeologia urbana a Grosseto. Origine e sviluppo di una città medievale nella "Toscana delle città deboli". Le ricerche 1997 – 2005. I: la città di Grosseto nel contesto geografico della bassa valle dell'Ombrone*, Florence, pp.134-152.

Citter 2007b – Citter C., *La città di Grosseto nel quadro della viabilità romana e medievale della bassa valle dell'Ombrone*, in Citter C., Arnoldus Huyzendveld (eds.), *Archeologia urbana a Grosseto. Origine e sviluppo di una città medievale nella "Toscana delle città deboli". Le ricerche 1997 – 2005. I: la città di Grosseto nel contesto geografico della bassa valle dell'Ombrone*, Florence, pp.156-198.

Citter 2007c – Citter C. (ed.), *Archeologia urbana a Grosseto. Origine e sviluppo di una città medievale nella "Toscana delle città deboli". Le ricerche 1997-2005. II: edizione degli scavi urbani 1998-2005*, Florence.

Citter 2006a – Citter C., *Grosseto fra VIII e IX secolo d.C. La nascita e lo sviluppo di un "central place" nel quadro della formazione della città medievale toscana*, in Francovich R., Valenti M. (eds.), *IV Congresso Nazionale di Archeologia Medievale*, Florence, pp.153-156.

Citter 2006b – Citter C., *Gerarchie sociali ed edifici di culto: il territorio rosellano fra longobardi e carolingi*, in Francovich R., Valenti M. (eds.), *IV Congresso Nazionale di Archeologia Medievale*, Florence, pp.360-363.

Citter 2005 (ed.) – Citter C. (ed.), *Lo scavo della chiesa di S.Pietro a Grosseto. Nuovi dati sull'origine e lo sviluppo di una città medievale*, Florence.

Citter 2002a – Citter C. (ed.), *Castel di Pietra (Gavorrano-Gr): relazione preliminare della campagna 2001 e revisione dei dati delle precedenti*, in "Archeologia Medievale", XXIX, pp.115-167.

Citter 2002b – Citter C. (ed.), *Guida agli edifici sacri. Abbazie, monasteri, pievi e chiese medievali della provincia di Grosseto*, Siena.

Citter 2001 – Citter C. (ed.), *La Roccaccia di Selvena (Castell'Azzara-GR): relazione della campagna 2000 e revisione dei dati delle precedenti*, in "Archeologia Medievale", XXVIII, pp.191-224.

Citter 2000 – Citter C., *Recensione a "Archeologia urbana in Toscana: la città altomedievale, Documenti di Archeologia, 17*", "Archeologia Medievale", XXVII, pp.444-445.

Citter 1997 – Citter C., *I doni funebri nella Toscana longobarda ed il loro inquadramento nelle vicende storico- archeologiche del popolamento*, in Paroli L. (ed.), pp.185-211.

Citter 1996a – Citter C. (ed.), *Guida agli edifici sacri. Abbazie, monasteri, pievi e chiese medievali della provincia di Grosseto*, Siena.

Citter 1996b – Citter C. (ed.), *Grosseto, Roselle e il Prile. Note per la storia di una città e del territorio circostante*, Mantova.

Citter 1996c – Citter C., *Rete portuale e commerci nella Toscana tardoantica e altomedievale*, in Paroli L. et alii, *Commerci nel bacino del mediterraneo occidentale fra VIII e IX secolo*, in Brogiolo G. P. (ed.), *Early Medieval towns in West Mediterranean (IV-IX)* , Atti del convegno, Ravello (SA), 1994, Mantova, pp.133-137.

Citter 1995a – Citter C., *Il rapporto fra Bizantini, Germani e Romani nella Maremma toscana attraverso lo studiuo della dinamica del popolamento - il caso rosellano*, in Boldrini E., Francovich R. (eds.), *Acculturazione e mutamenti. Prospettive nell'archeologia medievale del Mediterraneo*, Florence, pp. 201-222.

Citter 1995b – Citter C., *La frontiera meridionale*, in Kurze W., Citter C., *L'occupazione della Maremma toscana da parte dei Longobardi*, in Brogiolo G.P. (ed.), *Città, castelli, campagne nei territori di frontiera*, atti del 5° seminario di Monte Barro, Monte Barro 1994, pp.170-186.

Citter 1995c – Citter C., *Siti, approdi, viabilità da Alberese a Castiglione della Pescaia dalla preistoria all' eta' moderna*, in Bueti, S. (ed.), *Il forte di San Rocco. Una struttura militare nel litorale maremmano del sec. XVIII*, Grosseto, pp. 127-143.

Citter 1988/1989 – Citter C., *La topografia archeologica del territorio di Roselle-Grosseto*, Unpublished Degree Thesis, University of Siena.

Citter-Arnoldus Huyzendveld 2007 (eds.) – Citter C., Arnoldus Huyzendveld (eds.), *Archeologia urbana a Grosseto. Origine e sviluppo di una città medievale nella "Toscana delle città deboli". Le ricerche 1997-2005. I: la città di Grosseto nel contesto geografico della bassa valle dell'Ombrone*, Florence.

Citter-Vaccaro 2003 – *Le costanti dell'urbanesimo altomedievale in Toscana (secoli IV-VIII)*, in Fiorillo R., Peduto P. (eds.), *Congresso Nazionale di Archeologia Medievale III*, Florence, pp.309-313.

Citter *et alii* 1996 – Citter C., Paroli L., Pellecuer C., Péne J.M., *Commerci nel Mediterraneo Occidentale nell'Alto Medioevo*, in Brogiolo G.P. (ed.), *Early medieval towns in the western Mediterranean*, Mantova, pp.121-142.

Coletti 1998 – Coletti C.M. 1998, *Ceramiche comuni dai contesti di Porto (VI e VII secolo)*, in Ciarrocchi B. *et alii*, *Ceramica comune tardoantica da Ostia e Porto (V-VII secolo)*, in Saguì L. (ed.), *Ceramica in Italia VI-VII secolo*, Florence, pp.401-417.

Collavini 1998 – Collavini S., *«Honorabilis domus et spetiosissimus comitatus». Gli Aldobrandeschi da «conti» a «principi territoriali» (secoli IX-XII)*, Pisa.

Collura-Innocenti-Innocenti 2002 – Collura E., Innocenti M., Innocenti S., *Comune di Castiglione della Pescaia: briciole di storia*, Grosseto.

Conspectus – Ettlinger E. *et alii* (1990) *Conspectus Formarum Terrae Sigillatae Italico Modo Confectae*, Bonn.

Corretti 2000 – Corretti A. 2000, *L'attività metallurgica*, in Abela A., Berti G., Bruni S. (eds.), *Ricerche archeologiche medievali a Pisa. I. Piazza dei Cavalieri, la campagna di scavo 1993*, Florence, pp.83-100.

Corsi 2002 – Corsi L., *La villa di Talamone*, in Carandini A., Cambi F. (eds.), *Paesaggi d'Etruria. Valle dell'Albegna, Valle d'Oro, Valle del Chiarone, Valle del Tafone*, Rome, pp.154-157.

Cristofani 1983 – Cristofani M., *Gli Etruschi del mare*, Milan.

Cucini Tizzoni-Tizzoni 1992 – Cucini Tizzoni C., Tizzoni M, *Le antiche scorie del golfo di Follonica (Toscana). Una proposta di tipologia*, Milan.

Cucini 1989a – Cucini C., *La valle dell'Alma nel medioevo*, Follonica.

Cucini 1989b - Cucini C., *L'insediamento altomedievale del Podere Aione (Follonica-GR)*, in "Archeologia Medievale", XVI, pp.499-512.

Cucini 1985 – Cucini C., *Topografia del territorio delle valli del Pecora e dell'Alma*, in Francovich R. (ed.), *Scarlino I. Storia e territorio*, Florence, pp.147-320.

Cuntz 1929 – Cuntz O., *Itineraria romana*, I, Leipzig.

Cuomo di Caprio 2007 – Cuomo di Caprio N., *Ceramica in archeologia 2. Antiche tecniche di lavorazione e moderni metodi di indagine*, Rome.

Curri 1978 – Curri C. B., *Forma Italiae: Regio VII,volumen IV: Vetulonia*, Florence.

Cuteri 1992 – Cuteri F., *Suvereto (LI)*, in Paroli L. (ed.), *La ceramica invetriata tardoantica e altomedievale in Italia*, Florence, p.303.

Çygielman 2006a – Çygielman M., *Castiglione della Pescaia (GR). Vetulonia: via Garibaldi*, in "Notiziario della Soprintendenza per i Beni Archeologici della Toscana", I/2005, pp.307-308.

Çygielman 2006b – Çygielman M., *Castiglione della Pescaia (GR). Villa romana delle Paduline*, in "Notiziario della Soprintendenza per i Beni Archeologici della Toscana", I/2005, pp.309-312.

Çygielman 2004 (ed.) – Çygielman M. (ed.), *La villa romana di Nomadelfia. Aspetti dell'insediamento rurale nel territorio rusellano*, Grosseto.

Çygielman 1998 – Çygielman M., *Castiglione della Pescaia – Punta Ala*, in Poggesi G., Rendini P. (eds.), *Memorie sommerse, archeologia subacquea in Toscana*, Pitigliano, pp.91-92.

Çygielman 1988 – Çygielman M, *Profilo Storico Archeologico*, in Torelli M. (ed.), *Progetto pilota per la ristrutturazione della rete regionale dei parchi archeologici. Parco Archeologico di Vetulonia.*

Çygielman 1982 – Çygielman M., *Castiglione della Pescaia, loc.Paduline*, in "Studi e materiali", V, Rome, pp.367-368.

Çygielman-Vaccaro-Agricoli-Ghisleni 2009 – Çygielman M., Vaccaro E., Agricoli G., Ghisleni M., *Grosseto. Braccagni, vocabolo San Martino*, in "Notiziario della Soprintendenza per i Beni Archeologici della Toscana", IV/2008, pp.259-277.

Dallai-Farinelli 1998 – Dallai L., Farinelli R., *Castel di Pietra e l'alta valle del Bruna. Indagini storiche e topografiche per la redazione di una carta archeologica*, in "Archeologia Medievale", XXV, pp.49-74.

De Benetti 2007 – De Benetti M., *I reperti numismatici dalla grotta dello Scoglietto (Alberese-Grosseto)*, in Cavanna C. (ed.), *La preistoria nelle grotte del Parco Naturale della Maremma*, Atti del Museo di Storia Naturale della Maremma, suppl.n°22, Grosseto, pp.99-116.

De Dominicis 1993 – De Dominicis V., *La vegetazione*, in Giusti F. (ed.), *La storia naturale della Toscana meridionale*, Siena, pp.247-341.

Del Rio-Vallebona 1996 – Del Rio A., Vallebona M., *Le Anfore (IV-VI/VII sec.) rinvenute negli horrea di S.Gaetano di Vada (Rosignano M.Mo, LI): ricerche archeometriche, morfologiche, quantitative*, in "Archeologia e Calcolatori", 7, pp.487-496.

Dell'Amico-Pallarés 2006 – Dell'Amico P., Pallarés F., *Il relitto «A» di Punta Ala. Castiglione della Pescaia, Grosseto*, Rome.

De Luca 1991 – De Luca D., *La lettura stratigrafica*, in Boldrini E., Parenti R. (eds.), *Santa Maria della Scala. Archeologia ed edilizia sulla piazza dello Spedale*, Florence, pp.179-191.

De Marinis 1998a – De Marinis G., *La strada romana di sud-est*, in Nicosia F., Poggesi G. (eds.), *Roselle. Guida al parco archeologico*, Siena, pp.157-161.

De Marinis 1998b – De Marinis G., *Il « piazzale Roma » e la terma di Betitio Perpetuo Arzygio*, in Nicosia F., Poggesi G. (eds.), *Roselle. Guida al parco archeologico*, Siena, pp.162-164.

De Robertis 1972 – De Robertis F., *La produzione agricola in Italia dalla crisi del III secolo all'età dei Carolingi*, Rome.

De Rossi 2005 – De Rossi G., *Indicatori archeologici della produzione e diffusione del vino della Baia di Napoli in età altomedievale*, in Volpe G., Turchiano M. (eds.), *Paesaggi e insediamenti rurali in Italia meridionale fra tardoantico e altomedioevo*, Bari, pp.541-550.

De Rossi 2004 – De Rossi G., *La fornace di Misenum (Napoli) ed i suoi prodottio ceramici : carattere e diffusione*, in Patitucci Uggeri S. (eds.), *La ceramica altomedievale in Italia*, Florence, pp.253-264.

De Vingo-Fossati 2001 – De Vingo P., Fossati A., *Gli elementi accessori dell'abito e dell'acconciatura femminile*, in Mannoni T., Murialdo G. (eds.), *S.Antonino. Un insediamento fortificato nella Liguria bizantina*, Bordighera, pp.487-529.

Devèze 1961 – Devèze M., *La vie de la forêt française au XVIe siècle*, Paris.

Di Gangi-Lebole 1998 – Di Gangi G., C.M. Lebole, *Anfore Keay LII ed altri materiali ceramici da contesti di scavo della Calabria centro-meridionale (V-VIII secolo)*, in Saguì L. (ed.), *Ceramica in Italia: VI-VII secolo*, Florence, pp.761-768,

Di Giuseppe 1998 – Di Giuseppe H. (with a contribution by Capelli C.), *La fornace di Calle di Tricarico: produzione e diffusione*, in Saguì L. (ed.), *Ceramica in Italia: VI-VII secolo*, Florence, pp.735-752.

Duby 1970 – Duby G., *L'economia rurale nell'Europa medievale*, Vol.I, Bari.

Du Cange 1954 – Du Cange D.F., *Glossarium Mediae et Infimae Latinitatis*, Graz.

Egloff 1977 – Egloff M., *Kellia, la poterie copte. Quatre siècles d'artisanat et d'échanges en Basse-Egipte*, I, Genève.

Faggella 1990 – Faggella F., *Contenitori da trasporto*, in De Marinis G. (ed.), *Archeologia urbana a Fiesole. Lo scavo di via Marini-via Portigiani*, Florence, pp.249-274.

Falce 1930 – Falce A., *La formazione storica della marca di Tuscia (secoli IX-X)*, Florence.

Farinelli 2007 – Farinelli R., *I castelli nella Toscana delle "città deboli". Dinamiche insediative e potere rurale nella Toscana meridionale (secoli VII-XIV)*, Florence.

Farinelli 2000 – Farinelli R., *I castelli nei territori diocesani di Populonia-Massa e Roselle-Grosseto (secc. X-XIV)*, in Francovich R., Ginatempo M. (eds.), *Castelli. Storia e archeologia del potere nella Toscana medievale*, vol.I, Florence, pp.141-185.

Dallai-Farinelli 1998 – Dallai L., Farinelli R., *Castel di Pietra e l'alta valle del Bruna. Indagini storiche e topografiche per la redazione di una carta archeologica*, in "Archeologia Medievale" XXV, pp.49-74.

Farinelli 1996a – Farinelli R., *Grosseto: origini e sviluppo di un castrum aldobrandesco*, in Citter C. (ed.), *Grosseto, Roselle e il Prile. Note per la storia di una città e del territorio circostante*, Mantova, pp.65-66.

Farinelli 1996b – Farinelli R., *Il castello di Montemassi nel quadro dei rapporti tra Aldobrandeschi e "conti di Siena" (secc.X-XII)*, in "Bollettino della Società storica maremmana", 68-69, pp.65-83.

Farinelli-Vaccaro-Salvadori 2008 – Farinelli R., Vaccaro E., Salvadori H., *"Le chiese" nel villaggio: la formazione dell'abitato medievale di Poggio Cavolo (Gr)*, in Campana S., Felici C., Francovich R., Gabrielli F. (eds.), *Chiese e insediamenti nei secoli di formazione dei paesaggi medievali. Il rapporto fra le chiese e gli insediamenti tra V e X secolo*, Florence, pp. 169-197.

Farinelli-Giorgi 2000 – Farinelli R., Giogi A., *Fenomeni di accentramento insediativo nella Toscana meridionale tra XII e XIII secolo: il "secondo incastellamento" in area senese*, in Francovich R., Ginatempo M. (eds.), *Castelli. Storia e archeologia del potere nella Toscana medievale*, vol.I, Florence, pp.29-284.

Fasoli 1960 – Fasoli G., *Adalberto di Toscana*, in AAVV, *Dizionario biografico degli italiani*, Vol.I, Rome, p. 216.

Felici 2004 – Felici C., *Carta Archeologica della Provincia di Siena. Pienza*, Vol.VI, Siena.

Fentress 2003 (ed.) – Fentress E. (ed.), *Cosa V. An Intermittent Town, Excavations 1991-1997*, Supplements to the Memoirs of the American Academy in Rome, Supplementary Volume II, Ann Arbor-Michigan.

Fentress 2002 – Fentress E., *Zona D. Talamone*, in Carandini A., Cambi F. (eds.) 2002, *Paesaggi d'Etruria. Valle dell'Albegna, Valle d'Oro, Valle del Chiarone, Valle del Tafone*, Rome, pp.248-249.

Fentress 2000 – Fentress E., *What are we counting for?*, in Francovich R., Patterson H., Barker G. (eds.), *Extracting Meanings from Ploughsoil Assemblages*, Oxford, pp.44-52.

Fentress-Wickham 2002a – Fentress E., Wickham C. , *La Bassa Valle dell'Albegna*, in Carandini A., Cambi F. (eds.), *Paesaggi d'Etruria. Valle dell'Albegna, Valle d'Oro, Valle del Chiarore, Valle del Tafone*, Rome, pp.259-261.

Fentress-Wickham 2002b – Fentress E., Wickham C., *La Valle dell'Albegna fra i secoli VII e XIV*, in Ascheri M. (ed.), *Siena e Maremma nel Medioevo*, Siena, pp.59-82.

Fentress *et alii* 2004 – Fentress L., Fontana S., Hitchner R.B., Perkins P., *Accounting for ARS: fineware and sites in Sicily and Africa*, in Alcock S.E., Cherry J.F. (eds.), *Side-by-Side Survey. Comparative Studies in the Mediterranean World*, Oxford, pp.147-162.

Fentress *et alii* 1991 – Fentress E., Clay T., Hobart M, Webb M., *Late Roman and medieval Cosa I: the arx and the structure near the Eastern Height* , "Papers of the British School at Rome", LIX, pp.197-230.

Fentress-Perkins 1988 – Fentress E., Perkins P., *Counting African Red Slip Ware*, in *L'Africa romana*, Atti del V Convegno di studio (Sassari 1987), Sassari 1988, pp.205-214.

Filippi *et alii* 2004 – Filippi D., Ricci G., Di Giuseppe H., Capelli C., Delussu F., La casa delle Vestali: un immondezzaio di VI secolo d.C., in Paroli L., Venditeli L. (eds.), *Roma dall'antichità al medioevo II. Contesti tardoantichi e altomedievali*, Milan, pp.164-179.

Fiumi 1953 – Fiumi E., *Economia e vita privata dei fiorentini nelle rilevazioni statistiche di Giovanni Villani*, in "Archivio Storico Italiano", CXI, pp.207-241.

Fogagnolo 2004 – Fogagnolo S., *Trastevere. Conservatorio di San Pasquale: dal quartiere romano all'occupazione medievale*, in Paroli L., Venditeli L. (eds.), *Roma dall'antichità al medioevo II. Contesti tardoantichi e altomedievali*, Milan, pp.579-597.

Fontana 2005 – Fontana S., *Le ceramiche da mensa italiche medio-imperiali e tardo-antiche: imitazioni di prodotti importati e tradizione manifatturiera locale*, in Gandolfi D. (ed.), *La ceramica e i materiali di Età Romana. Classi, produzioni, commerci e consumi*, Istituto Internazionale di Studi Liguri, Bordighera, pp.259-278.

Fontana 2003 – Fontana S., *Il deposito della Forum Cistern e la cultura materiale di Cosa agli inizi del VI secolo d.C.*, in Fentress E. (ed.), *Cosa V. An Intermittent Town, Excavations 1991-1997*, Supplements to the Memoirs of the American Academy in Rome, Supplementary Volume II, Ann Arbor-Michigan, pp.307-319.

Fontana 1998 – Fontana S., *Le "imitazioni" della sigillata africana e le ceramiche da mensa italiche tardo-antiche*, in Saguì L. (ed.), *Ceramica in Italia: VI-VII secolo*, Florence, pp.83-100.

Fontana *et alii* 2004 – Fontana S., Munzi M., Beolchini V., de Luca I., Del Vecchio F., *Un contesto di VII secolo dell'Aventino*, in Paroli L., Venditelli L. (eds.), *Roma dall'antichità al medioevo II. Contesti tardoantichi e altomedievali*, Milan, pp.544-568.

Forni 1993 – Forni G., *Dall'agricoltura dei Goti a quella italiana al tempo dei Goti*, in AAVV, *Teoderico il Grande e i Goti d'Italia*, Atti del XIII Congresso Internazionale di studi sull'Alto Medioevo, Milan 2-6 novembre 1992, Tomo II, Spoleto, pp.679-719.

Fortina-Memmi Turbanti 2003 – Fortina C., Memmi Turbanti I., *Caratterizzazione mineralogico-petrografica di alcuni impasti ceramici provenienti dalla Rocca di Campiglia*, in Bianchi G. (ed.), *Campiglia: un castello e il suo territorio. II. Indagine archeologica,* Florence, pp.337-340.

Francovich 2004 – Francovich R., *Villaggi dell'altomedioevo: invisibilità sociale e labilità archeologica*, in Valenti M., *L'insediamento altomedievale nelle campagne toscane. Paesaggi, popolamento e villaggi tra VI e X secolo*, Florence, pp.IX-XXII.

Francovich 1984 – Francovich R., *Rivisitando il Museo Archeologico di Fiesole: in margine ad alcune ceramiche di epoca longobarda*, in AA.VV., *Studi di Antichità in onore di Guglielmo Maetzke*, Milan, pp.617-628.

Francovich-Bianchi 2006 – Francovich R., Bianchi G., *Capanne e muri in pietra. Donoratico nell'altomedioevo*, in Marcucci C., Megale C. (eds.), *Il Medioevo nella provincia di Livorno. I risultati delle recenti indagini*, Ospedaletto, pp.105-116.

Francovich-Cantini 2006 – Francovich R., Cantini F., *Nuovi dati sulla cultura materiale della città di Firenze tra età imperiale ed altomedioevo: i contesti dello scavo di via de' Castellani*, in Francovich R., Valenti M. (eds.), *IV Congresso Nazionale di Archeologia Medievale*, Florence, pp.132-135.

Francovich-Campana-Felici 2005 – Francovich R., Campana S., Felici C., *Dal satellite allo scavo. Reti insediative, questioni di metodo e record archeologico*, in *Innovazioni tecnologiche per i beni culturali in Italia*, Atti del convegno nazionale, 16-17-18 febbraio 2005, Caserta, Reggia Vanvitelliana, (Poster).

Francovich-Valenti 2005 – Francovich R., Valenti M., *Forme del popolamento altomedievale nella campagna Toscana (VII-X secolo)*, in Gelichi S. (ed.), *Campagne medievali. Strutture materiali, economia e società nell'insediamento rurale dell'Italia settentrionale (VIII-X secolo)*, Atti del Convegno Nonantola (MO), San Giovanni in Persicelo (BO) 14-15 marzo 2003, Mantova, pp.245-258.

Francovich-Hodges 2003 – Francovich R., Hodges R., *Villa to Village*, London.

Francovich-Valenti 2001 – Francovich R., Valenti M., *Cartografia archeologica, indagini sul campo e informatizzazione. Il contributo senese alla conoscenza ed alla gestione della risorsa culturale del territorio*, in Francovich R., Pellicanò A., Pasquinucci M. (eds.), *La carta archeologica. Fra ricerca e pianificazione territoriale*, Atti del seminario di studi organizzato dalla Regione Toscana Dipartimento delle Politiche Formative e dei beni Culturali, Firenze 6-7 maggio 1999, Florence, pp.83-116.

Francovich-Ginatempo 2000 – Francovich R., Ginatempo M., *Introduzione*, in Francovich R., Ginatempo M. (eds.), *Castelli. Storia e archeologia del potere nella Toscana medievale*, vol.I, Florence, pp.7-24.

Francovich-Valenti 2000 – Francovich R., Valenti M. 2000, *La piattaforma GIS dello scavo ed il suo utilizzo: l'esperienza di Poggibonsi*, in Brogiolo G.P. (ed.), *II Congresso Nazionale di Archeologia Medievale*, Florence, pp.14-20.

Francovich *et alii* 2000 – Francovich R., Citter C., Damiani S., Farinelli R., Terrosi G., Serafini L., *Archeologia urbana a Grosseto. Rapporto preliminare degli scavi 1998-1999,* in Brogiolo G.P. (ed.), *II Congresso Nazionale di Archeologia Medievale*, Florence, pp.87-94.

Francovich-Gelichi 1989 – Francovich R., Gelichi S., *Archeologia e storia di un monumento mediceo. Gli scavi nel "cassero" senese della Fortezza di Grosseto*, Bari.

Fronza-Valenti 2000 – Fronza V., Valenti M., *L'utilizzo della griglia di riferimento per lo scavo di contesti stratigrafici altomedievali: elaborazione di una soluzione informatica,* in Brogiolo G.P. (ed.), *II Congresso Nazionale di Archeologia Medievale*, Florence, pp.21-27.

Fulford-Peacock 1984 – Fulford M.G., Peacock D.P.S. 1984, *Excavations at Carthage: The British Mission. The Avenue du President Habib Bourguiba, Salammbo. The Pottery and other ceramic objects from the site*, Sheffield.

Fumagalli 1974 – Fumagalli V., *La tipologia dei contratti d'affitto con coltivatori al confine fra Langobardia e Romania (secoli IX-X)*, in "Studi Romagnoli", XXV, pp.205-214.

Fumagalli 1970 – Fumagalli V., *Coloni e signori nell'Italia Superiore dall'VIII al X secolo*, in AAVV., *A Giuseppe Ermini*, Studi Medievali, 3ª serie, X, 1969, Spoleto 1970, I, pp.423-446.

Gabrielli 2001 – Gabrielli R., *Introduzione all'uso dei GPS in archeologia*, in Campana S., Forte M. (eds.), *Remote Sensing in Archaeology*, XI ciclo di lezioni sulla ricerca applicata in archeologia. Cerosa di Pontignano (Siena), 6-11 dicembre 1999, Florence, pp.329-354.

Galetti 1997 – Galetti P., *Abitare nel Medioevo. Forme e vicende dell'insediamento rurale nell'Italia altomedievale*, Florence.

Gambogi 2004 – Gambogi P., *Soprintendenza Archeologica della Toscana: ricerca e tutela del patrimonio sommerso*, in Giacobelli M. (ed.), *Lezioni Fabio Faccenna*, Conferenze di archeologia subacquea, (III-V ciclo), Bari, pp.77-85.

Gambogi 2003 – Gambogi P., *Porti antichi e porti moderni: tutela dei beni archeologici e sviluppo del territorio*, in Campolongo M. (ed.), *Scarlino. Arte, Storia e Territorio*, Follonica, pp.25-29.

Gambogi-Firmati 1998 – Gambogi P., Firmati M., *Frequentazione taqrdoantica e altomedievale nell'isola di Gorgona*, in Saguì L. (ed.), *Ceramica in Italia VI-VII secolo*, Florence, pp.635-638.

Gandolfi 2005 – Gandolfi D. (ed.), *La ceramica e i materiali di Età Romana. Classi, produzioni, commerci e consumi*, Istituto Internazionale di Studi Liguri, Bordighera.

Gandolfi 1998 – Gandolfi D., *Ceramiche fini di importazione di VI-VII in Liguria. L'esempio di Ventimiglia, Albenga e Luni*, in Saguì L. (ed.), *Ceramica in Italia: VI-VII secolo*, Florence, pp.253-274.

Garzella 2001 – Garzella G., *Le strutture ecclesiastiche della diocesi di Roselle-Grosseto: chiesa vescovile, sistema pievano, monasteri*, in Ascheri M. (ed.), *Siena e Maremma nel Medioevo*, Siena, pp.7-26.

Gasparri 2008 – Gasparri S. (ed.), *774. Ipotesi su una transizione*, Turnhout.

Gasparri 1990 – Gasparri S., *Il Regno Longobardo in Italia*, in Cammarosano P., Gasparri S. (eds.), *Langobardia*, Udine, pp.237-306.

Gelichi 2008 – Gelichi S., *The eels of Venice. The long eight century of the emporia of the northern region along the Adriatic coast*, in Gasparri S. (ed.), *774. Ipotesi su una transizione*, Turnhout, pp.81-117.

Gelichi 2007 – Gelichi S., *Gestione e significato sociale della produzione, della circolazione e dei consumi della ceramica nell'Italia dell'alto medioevo*, in Brogiolo G.P., Chavarría Arnau A. (eds.), *Archeologia e società tra tardo antico e alto medioevo*, Mantova, pp.47-69.

Gelichi 2006a – Gelichi S., *Venezia tra archeologia e storia: la costruzione di un'identità urbana*, in Augenti A. (ed.), *Le città italiane tra la Tarda Antichità e l'Alto Medioevo*, Florence, pp.151-184.

Gelichi 2006b – Gelichi S., Una discussione con Chris Wickham, "Storica", 34, XII, pp.134-147.

Gelichi-Negrelli (eds.) – Gelichi S., Negrelli C. (eds.), *La circolazione delle ceramiche nell'Adriatico tra tarda antichità e alto medioevo. III Incontro di studio CER.AM.IS*, Mantova.

Gelichi *et alii* 2006a – Gelichi S., Negrelli C., Calano D., Grandi E., *Comacchio tra IV e X secolo: territorio, abitato e infrastrutture* in Francovich R., Valenti M. (eds.), *IV Congresso Nazionale di Archeologia Medievale*, Florence, pp.114-123.

Gelichi *et alii* 2006b – Gelichi S., Calaon D., Grandi E., Negrelli C., *"...Castrum ingne combussit...": Comacchio tra tarda antichità ed alto medioevo*, in "Archeologia Medievale", XXXIII, pp.19-48.

Gelichi-Milanese 1999 – Gelichi S., Milanese M., *Dall'Antichità al Medioevo nell'Africa Proconsolare. Spunti di ricerca dallo scavo di Uchi Maius (Tunisia)*, in Rotili M. (ed.), *Memorie del passato, urgenza del futuro. Il mondo romano fra V e VII secolo*, Atti delle VI giornate di studio sull'età romanobarbarica, Benevento, 18-20 giugno 1998, Naples, pp.271-284.

Gelichi-Giordani 1994 – Gelichi S., Giordani N. (eds.), *Il tesoro nel pozzo. Pozzi deposito e tesaurizzazioni nell'antica Emilia*, Modena.

Giannichedda 2004 – Giannichedda E., *Un atelier medievale nell'Appennino Parmense*, in Giannichedda E. (ed.), *Metodi e pratica della cultura materiale. Produzione e consumo dei manufatti*, Bordighera, pp.95-106.

Giannichedda *et alii* 1995 – Giannichedda E., Ghiretti A., Biagini M., *La lavorazione della steatite: dalle ricognizioni allo scavo di un atelier medievale a Pareto di Bardi (PR)*, in "Archeologia Medievale", XXII, pp.147-190.

Ginatempo 1987 – Ginatempo M., *Per la storia degli ecosistemi e dell'alimentazione medievali: recenti studi di archeozoologia in Italia*, in Francovich R. (ed.), *Archeologia e storia del medioevo italiano*, Rome, pp.173-197.

Giovannini 1998 – Giovannini F., *Funzioni delle forme ceramiche e modelli alimentari medievali,* in De Minicis E. (ed.), *Le ceramiche di Roma e del Lazio in età medievale e moderna, III,* Rome, pp.15-22.

Giusti-Guidi 1942 – Giusti M., Guidi P. (eds.), *Rationes Decimarum Italiane nei secoli XIII e XIV. Tuscia II: le decime degli anni 1295-1304*, Vatican City.

Goffredo-Volpe 2005 – Goffredo R., Volpe G., *Il "Progetto Valle dell'Ofanto": primi dati sulla Tarda Antichità e l'Altomedioevo*, in Volpe G., Turchiano M. (eds.), *Paesaggi e insediamenti rurali in Italia meridionale fra tardoantico e altomedioevo*, Bari, pp.223-240.

Grassi 2006 – Grassi F., *La ceramica tra VIII e X secolo nella Toscana meridionale: le tipologie, le funzioni, l'alimentazione*, in Francovich R., Valenti M. (eds.), *IV*

Congresso Nazionale di Archeologia Medievale, Florence, pp.461-467.
Grassi 2003 – Grassi F., *Ceramica da cucina,* in, Bianchi G. (ed.), *Campiglia: un castello e il suo territorio. II. Indagine archeologica,* Florence, pp.276-284.
Grassi-Liguori 2004 – Grassi F., Liguori S., *Per un preliminare catalogo dei reperti ceramici: i contesti di ante X-XI secolo,* in Bianchi G. (ed.), *Castello di Donoratico. I risultati delle prime campagne di scavo (2000-2002),* Florence, pp.115-138.
Guideri 2000a – Guideri S., *Il popolamento medievale attraverso un'indagine di superficie*, in Guideri S., Parenti R. (eds.), *Archeologia a Montemassi. Un castello fra storia e storia dell'arte,* Florence, pp.11-37.
Guideri 2000b – Guideri S., *Trasformazioni dell'insediamento nel territorio di Roccastrada. Cenni di archeologia dei paesaggi*, in AAVV., *S.Salvatore di Giugnano. Un monastero tra storia e architettura nel territorio di Roccastrada*, Roccastrada, pp.7-33.
Guidi 1932 – Guidi P. (ed.), *Rationes Decimarum Italiane nei secoli XIII e XIV. Tuscia I: la decima degli anni 1274-1280*, Vatican City.
Günsenin 2001 – Günsenin N., *Çamalti Burnu I Wreck*, in "Istanbul University's Contributions to Archaeology in Turkey (1932-2000)", pp.252-256.
Günsenin 1989 – Günsenin N., *Recherches sur les amphores byzxantines dans les musées turcs*, in Deroch V., Spieser J.M. (eds.), *Recherches sur la céramique byzantine*, Paris, pp.267-276.
Gusberti 2003 – Gusberti E., *La tarda età imperiale (Fase VII)*, in Fentress E. (ed.), *Cosa V. An Intermittent Town, Excavations 1991-1997*, Supplements to the Memoirs of the American Academy in Rome, Supplementary Volume II, Ann Arbor-Michigan, pp.305-307.
Hamerow 2002 – Hamerow H., *Early Medieval Settlements.The Archaeology of Rural Communities in Northwest Europe 400-900*, Oxford.
Hamerow 1993 – Hamerow H., *Excavations at Mucking. The Anglo-Saxon settlement*, Vol.2, London.
Harris 1971 – Harris W.V., *Rome in Etruria and Umbria*, Oxford.
Hayes 2000 – Hayes J.W., *The current state of Roman ceramic studies in Mediterranean survey, or handling pottery from surveys*, in Francovich R., Patterson H., Barker G. (eds.), *Extracting Meanings from Ploughsoil Assemblages,* Oxford, pp.105-109.
Hayes 1998 – Hayes J.W., *Introduction. The study of Roman pottery in the Mediterranean: 23 years after Late Roman Pottery*, in Saguì L. (ed.), *Ceramica in Italia: VI-VII secolo*, Florence, pp.9-21.
Hayes 1992 – Hayes J.W., *Excavations at Saraçhane in Istanbul. II. The Pottery*, Princeton.
Hayes 1978 – Hayes J.W., *Pottery Report – 1976*, in Humprey J.H. (ed.), *Excavations at Chartage 1976, conducted by the University of Michigan*, Ann Arbor, pp.23-98.
Hayes 1972 – Hayes J.W., *Late Roman Pottery*, London.
Hobart 1992 – Hobart M.M., *Ceramica invetriata da Cosa (Ansedonia – Orbetello)*, Paroli L. (ed.), *La ceramica invetriata tardoantica e altomedievale in Italia*, Florence, pp.304-309.
Hodges 2008 – Hodges R., *AD 774 and after: the archaeology of Charlemagne's age in Italy,* in Gasparri S. (ed.), *774. Ipotesi su una transizione*, Turnhout, pp.161-171.
Hodges 2000 – Hodges R., *Towns and Trade in the Age of Charlemagne*, London.
Hodges 1994 – Hodges R., *In the Shadow of Pirenne: San Vincenzo al Volturno and the revival of Mediterranean commerce*, in Francovich R., Noyé G. (eds.), *La storia dell'Alto Medioevo italiano alla luce dell'archeologia*, Atti del Convegno, Certosa di Pontignano (Siena) 1992, Florence, pp.109-127.
Hodges 1989 – Hodges R., *Charlemagne's Elephant and the Beginning of Commodisation in Europe*, in "Acta Archaeologica", Vol.59-1988, pp.155-168.
Hodges 1982 – Hodges R., *Dark Age Economics: The Origins of Towns and Trade, AD 600-1000*, London.
Hodges 1978 – Hodges R., *Ports of Trade in Early Medieval Europe*, in "Norwegian Archaeological Review", Vol.11, n.2, pp.97-101.
Hodges 1977 – Hodges R., *Some Early Medieval French Wares in the British Isles: An Archaeological Assestment of the Early French Wine Trade with Britain*, in Peacock D.P.S. (ed.), *Pottery and Early Commerce Characterization and Trade in Roman and Later Ceramics*, Londra-New York-San Francisco, pp.239-255.
Hodges-Bowden-Lako (eds.) – Hodges R., Bowden W., Lako K. (eds.), *Byzantine Butrint. Excavations and Surveys 1994-99*, Oxford.
Hodges-Bowden 1998 (eds.) – Hodges R., Bowden W. (eds.), *The sixth century. Production, Distribution and Demand*, Leiden.
Horden-Purcell 2000 – Horden P., Purcell N., *The Corrupting Sea: A Study of Mediterranean History,* London.
Innocenti 1998 – Innocenti M., *Alberese: mille anni di storia*, Grosseto.
Keay 2000 – Keay S., *Ceramic cronology and Roman rural settlement in the lower Guadalquivir Valley during the Augustan period*, in Francovich R., Patterson H., Barker G. (eds.), *Extracting Meanings from Ploughsoil Assemblages*, Oxford, pp.162-173.
Keay 1991 – Keay S., *The Ager Tarraconensis in the late Empire: a model for the economic relationshipof town and country in eastern Spain?*, in Barker G., Lloyd J. (eds.), *Roman Landscapes. Archaeological Survey in the Mediterranean Region*, Archaeological Monographs of the British School at Rome, 2, London, pp.79-87.
Keay 1984 – Keay S., *Late Roman Amphorae in the Western Mediterranean. A typology and economic study: the Catalan evidence,* BAR International Series, 196, Oxford.
Kingsley 2001 – Kingsley S.A., *The Economic Impact of the Palestinian Wine Trade in Late Antiquity*, in Kingsley S.A., Decker M. (eds.), *Economy and Exchange in the East Mediterranean during Late Antiquity*, Proceedings of a Conference at Somerville College, Oxford 29th May, 1999, Oxford, pp.44-68.
Kurze 2002a – Kurze W., *L'occupazione della Maremma toscana da parte dei Longobardi*, in Kurze W., *Studi toscani. Storia e Archeologia*, Castelfiorentino, pp.133-158.
Kurze 2002b – Kurze W., *Notizie dei Papi Giovanni VII, Gregorio III e Benedetto III nella raccolta dei canoni del Cardinal Deusdedit*, in Kurze W., *Studi toscani. Storia e Archeologia*, Castelfiorentino, pp.397-414.
Kurze 2002c – Kurze W., *Il monastero di San Salvatore al Monte Amiata e la sua proprietà terriera*, in Kurze W., *Studi toscani. Storia e Archeologia*, Castelfiorentino, pp.361-396.
Jézégou 1998 – Jézégou M.P., *Le mobilier de l'épave Saint-Gervais 2 (VIIe s.) à Fos-sur-Mer (B.-du-Rh.)*, in Bonifay M., Carre M.B., Rigoir Y., (eds.), *Fouilles à Marseille. Les mobiliers (Ier-VIIe s.ap.J.-C.)*, Paris, pp.343-351.
Lamboglia-Pallarés 1983 – Lamboglia N., Pallarés F., *Due campagne di scavo sul relitto di Punta Ala, in Forma Maris Antiqui*, 11-12, pp.172-176.
Leciejwicz *et alii* 1977 – Leciejwicz L., Tabaczyńska E., Tabaczyński S., *Torcello. Scavi 1961-62*, Rome.
Leicht 1969 – Leicht P.S., *Studi sulla proprietà fondiaria del Medio Evo*, Milan.
Leo Imperiale 2004 – Leo Imperiale M., *Otranto, cantiere Mitello: un centro produttivo nel Mediterraneo bizantino*, in Patitucci Uggeri S. (ed.), *La ceramica altomedievale in Italia*, Florence, pp.327-342.
Lewit 2005 – Lewit T., *Bones in the Bathhouse: re-evaluting the notion of "squatter occupation"in 5th-7th century villas*, in Brogiolo G.P., Chavarria A., Valenti M. (eds.), *Dopo la fine delle ville: le campagne dal VI al IX secolo*, XI Seminario sul Tardoantico e l'Altomedioevo, Mantova, pp.251-262.
Long-Volpe 1998 – Long L., Volpe G., *Le chargement de l'épave 1 de la Palud (VIe s.) à Port-Cros (Var.). Note préliminaire*, in Bonifay M., Carre M.B., Rigoir Y., (eds.), *Fouilles à Marseille. Les mobiliers (Ier-VIIe s.ap.J.-C.)*, Paris, pp.317-342.

Lupi 1998 – Lupi S., *La ceramica a vernice rossa nel Volterrano*, in Saguì L. (ed.), *Ceramica in Italia VI-VII secolo*, Florence, pp.625-628.

Lusuardi Siena-Sannazzaro 1994 – Lusuardi Siena S, Sannazzaro M., *La pietra ollare*, in Lusuardi Siena S. (ed.), *Ad mensam. Manufatti d'uso da contesti archeologici fra tarda antichità e medioevo*, Udine, pp.157-188.

Luzzati 1979 – Luzzati M., *Vescovato di Lucca*, in Castagnetti A., Luzzati M., Pasquali G., Vasina A. (eds.), *Inventari altomedievali di terre, coloni e redditi*, Rome.

Macchi Janica 2001 – Macchi Janica G., *Sulla misurazione delle forme d'occupazione sociale nello spazio medievale*, in "Archeologia Medievale", XXVIII, pp.61-82.

Macías-Remolà 2005 – Macías J.M.-Remolà J.A., *La cultura material de Tarraco-Tarracona (Hispania Tarraconensis-Regnum Visigothorum): cerámica común y áanforas*, in Gurt i Esparraguera J.Mª., Buxeda i Garrigós J., Cau Ontiveros M.A. (eds.), *LRCW1. Late Roman Coarse Wares, Cooking waress and Amphorae in the Mediterranean. Archaeology and Archaeometry*, BAR International Series, 1340, Oxford, pp.125-135.

Mackensen 1998 – Mackensen M., *Centres of African red slip ware prodution in Tunisia from the late 5th to the 7th century*, in Saguì L. (ed.), *Ceramica in Italia: VI-VII secolo*, Florence, pp.23-39.

Mackensen 1993 – Mackensen M., *Die spätantiken Sigillata-und Lampentöpfereien von El Mahrine (Nordtunesien). Studien zur nordafrikanischen Feinkeramik des 4. bis 7. Jahrunderts*, Voll.I-II, Munich.

Maetzke 1959 – Maetzke G., *Necropoli barbariche nel territorio grossetano*, in "Notizie Scavi", 1959, pp.66-88.

Manacorda 1977 – Manacorda D., *Testimonianze sulla produzione e il consumo dell'olio tripolitano nel III secolo* , in "DArch" 9-10, 1-2, pp.542-555.

Manca 1995 – Manca C., *Introduzione alla storia dei sistemi economici in Europa dal feudalesimo al capitalismo. Il sistema economico feudale,* Padova.

Manca 1993 – Manca C., *Introduzione alla storia dei sistemi economici in Europa dal feudalesimo al capitalismo. Gli strumenti dell'analisi,* Padova.

Mandarini-Paganelli 1998 – Mandarini L.V., Paganelli M., *Note preliminari sulla ceramica comune del saggio E* della basilica di San Clemente, Roma,* in De Minicis E. (ed.), *Le ceramiche di Roma e del Lazio in età medievale e moderna*, Rome, pp.23-33.

Mangani 1998 – Mangani E., *Le botteghe lungo il decumano massimo*, in Nicosia F., Poggesi G. (eds.), *Roselle. Guida al parco archeologico*, Siena, pp.143-146.

Mannoni 1997 – Mannoni T., Il *problema complesso delle murature storiche in pietra 1. Cultura materiale e cronotipologia*, in "Archeologia dell'Architettura", II, pp.15-24.

Marasco 2002/2003 – Marasco L., *Il castello di Scarlino tra VII e XIII secolo. Elaborazione e analisi dello scavo archeologico*, Unpublished Degree Thesis, University of Siena.

Marazzi 1998 – Marazzi F., *L'Italia del VI e VII secolo*, in AAVV, *Storia medievale*, Rome, pp.106-111.

Marazzi 1993 – Marazzi F., *Roma, il Lazio, il Mediterraneo: relazioni fra economia e politica dal VII al IX secolo*, in Paroli L.-Delogu P. (eds.), *La storia economica di Roma nell'alto Medioevo alla luce dei recenti scavi archeologici*, Florence, pp. 267-286.

Marazzi 1991 – Marazzi F., *Il conflitto tra Leone III Isaurico e il papato tra il 725 e il 733, e il "definitivo" inizio del medioevo a Roma: un'ipotesi in discussione*, in "Papers of the British School at Rome", 59, pp.231-257.

Martini 2004 – Martin A., *Santo Stefano Rotondo: stratigrafia e materiali*, in Paroli L., Venditeli L. (eds.), *Roma dall'antichità al medioevo II. Contesti tardoantichi e altomedievali*, Milan, pp.506-516.

Martin 1998 – Martin A., *La sigillata focese (Phocaean Red-Slip/Late Roman C Ware)*, in Saguì L. (ed.), *Ceramica in Italia: VI-VII secolo*, Florence, pp.109-122.

Marrucchi 1998 – Marrucchi G., *Chiese medievali della Maremma grossetana. Architettura e decorazione religiosa tra la Val di Farma e i Monti dell'Uccellina*, Empoli.

Massa-Portulano 1999 – Massa S., Portulano B., *La ceramica comune*, in Brogiolo G.P. (ed.), *S.Giulia di Brescia gli scavi dal 1980 al 1992*, Florence, pp.143-174.

Mattingly 2000 – Mattingly D., *Methods of collection, recording and quantification*, in Francovich R., Patterson H., Barker G. (ed.), *Extracting Meanings from Ploughsoil Assemblages*, Oxford, pp.5-15.

Mattingly 1995 – Mattingly D., *Tripolitania*, London.

McCormick 2001 – McCormick M., *Origins of the Eurpean Economy. Communications and Commerce AD 300-900*, Cambridge.

Menchelli-Renzi Rizzo 2000 – Menchelli S., Renzi Rizzo C., *Ceramica priva di rivestimento: forme chiuse*, in Abela A., Berti G., Bruni S. (eds.), *Ricerche archeologiche medievali a Pisa. I. Piazza dei Cavalieri, la campagna di scavo 1993*, Florence, pp. 123-162.

Menchelli 1993 – Menchelli S., *Vasellame privo di rivestimento per usi vari. Forme chiuse (MAC)*, Bruni S. (ed.), *Pisa. Piazza Dante. Uno spaccato della storia pisana, la campagna di scavo 1991*, Pontedera, pp.473-524.

Michelucci 1985 – Michelucci M., *La domus dei mosaici*, Montepulciano.

Michelucci 1998 - Michelucci M., *L'area a sud del foro: le botteghe, il tempietto e la domus dei mosaici*, in Nicosia F., Poggesi G. (eds.), *Roselle. Guida al parco archeologico*, Siena, pp.122-137.

Millett 2000 – Millett M., *Dating, quantifing and utilizing pottery assemblages from surface survey*, in Francovich R., Patterson H., Barker G. (eds.), *Extracting Meanings from Ploughsoil Assemblages*, Oxford.

Millett 1991 – Millett M., *Pottery: population or supply patterns? The Ager Tarraconensis approach*, in Barker G., Lloyd J. (eds.), *Roman Landscapes. Archaeological Survey in the Mediterranean Region*, Archaeological Monographs of the British School at Rome, 2, London, pp.18-26.

Molinari 2003 – Molinari A., *La ceramica medievale in Italia ed il suo possibile utilizzo per lo studio della storia economica*, in "Archeologia Medievale", XXX, pp.519-528.

Montanari 2003 – Montanari M., *Alimentazione*, in Le Goff J., Schmitt J.C. (eds.), *Dizionario dell'Occidente medievale*, Turin, pp.17-28.

Montanari 1999 – Montanari M., *Strutture di produzione e sistemi alimentari nell'alto Medioevo*, in Flandrin J.L., Montanari M. (eds.), *Storia dell'alimentazione*, Bari, pp.217-225.

Montanari 1979 – Montanari M., *L'alimentazione contadina nell'alto Medioevo*, Naples.

Mor 1986 – Mor C.G., *Sui poteri civili dei vescovi dal IV al secolo VIII*, in Mor C.G., Schmidinger H. (eds.), *I poteri temporali dei vescovi in Italia e in Germania nel medioevo*, Annali dell'Istituto storico italo-germanico, Quaderni, 3, pp.7-33.

Mordini 1995 – Mordini M., *Statuto del comune di Grosseto del 1421*, Grosseto.

Morel 1981 – Morel J.P., *Céramique campanienne. Les formes*, Rome.

Morley 2007 – Morley N., *Trade in Classical Antiquity*, Cambridge.

Motta 1997 – Motta L., *I paesaggi di Volterra nel Tardoantico*, in "Archeologia Medievale", XXIV, pp.245-267.

Motta *et alii* 1993 – Motta L., Camin L.,Terrenato N., *Un sito rurale nel territorio di Volterra*, "Bollettino di Archeologia", 23-24, pp.109-116.

Motta 1969 – Motta S., *Note illustrative della Carta Geologica d'Italia. Foglio 128. Grosseto*, Ercolano.

Munzi 2004 – Munzi M., *Goti e Bizantini a Vada Volterrana alla luce della documentazione numismatica*, in "ΑΓΩΓΗ", I, Atti della Scuola di Specializzazione in Archeologia, Università di Pisa, pp.289-295.

Munzi et *alii* 2004 – Munzi M., Fontana S., de Luca I., Del Vecchio F., *Domus Tiberiana: contesti tardoantichi dal settore nord-orientale*, in Paroli L., Venditeli L. (eds.), *Roma dall'antichità al medioevo II. Contesti tardoantichi e altomedievali*, Milan, pp.91-128.

Murialdo 2001a – Murialdo G., *Le anfore da trasporto*, in Mannoni T.-Murialdo G. (eds.), *S.Antonino. Un insediamento fortificato nella Liguria bizantina*, Bordighera, pp.255-296.

Murialdo 2001b – Murialdo G., *La suppellettile da mensa e da cucina in età tardoantica a S.Antonino*, in Mannoni T.-Murialdo G. (eds.), *S.Antonino. Un insediamento fortificato nella Liguria bizantina*, Bordighera, pp.311-316.

Murialdo 2001c – Murialdo G., La ceramica comune, in Mannoni T.-Murialdo G. (eds.), *S.Antonino. Un insediamento fortificato nella Liguria bizantina*, Bordighera, pp.339-362.

Murialdo 2001d – Murialdo G., *La ceramica grezza da cucina*, in Mannoni T.-Murialdo G. (eds.), *S.Antonino. Un insediamento fortificato nella Liguria bizantina*, Bordighera, pp.369-380.

Murialdo 2000 – Murialdo G., *La ceramica come indicatore socio-economico. L'esempio di un sito fortificato nella Liguria occidentale: il castrum di Sant'Antonino (fine VI-VII secolo)*, in Atti del XXXII e del XXXIII Convegno Internazionale della Ceramica di Albisola, pp.313-324.

Murialdo *et alii* 1998 – Murialdo G., Olcese G., Palazzi P., Parodi L., *La ceramica comune in Liguria nel VI e VII secolo*, in Saguì L. (ed.), *Ceramica in Italia VI-VII secolo*, Florence, pp.227-252.

Murialdo *et alii* 1992 – Murialdo G., Castiglioni E., Capelli G., Falcetti C., Ferretti F., Fossati A., Giovinazzo R., Mannoni T., Palazzi P., Panizza M., Parodi L., Ricci R., Vicino G., *Il "castrum" tardo-antico di S.Antonino di Perti, Finale Ligure (Savona) : terze notizie preliminari sulle campagne di scavo 1982-1991*, in "Archeologia Medievale", XIX, pp.279-377.

Nardini 2001 – Nardini A., *Carta Archeologica della Provincia di Siena. Chiusdino*, Vol.IV, Siena.

Nardini-Valenti 2004 – Nardini A., Valenti M. (eds.), *Il castello di Miranduolo. Guida breve allo scavo archeologico (anni 2001-2004)*, Florence.

Negrelli 2007 – Negrelli C., *Vasellame e contenitori da trasporto tra tarda antichità ed alto medioevo: l'Emilia Romagna e l'area Medio-Adriatica*, in Gelichi S., Negrelli C. (eds.), *La circolazione delle ceramiche nell'Adriatico tra tarda antichità e alto medioevo. III Incontro di studio CER.AM.IS*, Mantova, pp.297-330.

Negrelli 2006 – Negrelli C., *Rimini tra V ed VIII secolo: topografia e cultura materiale*, in Augenti A. (ed.), *Le città italiane tra la Tarda Antichità e l'Alto Medioevo*, Florence, pp.219-272.

Negrelli 2002 – Negrelli C., *Ceramiche tardoantiche da alcuni contesti stratigrafici dell'Emilia occidentale*, in Negrelli C., Curina R. (eds.), *1° Incontro di studio sulle ceramiche tardoantiche e alto medievali*, Mantova, pp.25-53.

Nicholson-Patterson 1989 – Nicholson P.T., Patterson H., *Ceramic technology in Upper Egypt: a study of pottery firing*, in "World Archaeology", 21, 1, pp.71-86.

Nicosia-Poggesi 1998 – Nicosia F., Poggesi G. (eds.), *Roselle. Guida al parco archeologico*, Siena.

Olcese 1996 – Olcese G., *Problemi metodologici e indirizzi di ricerca nello studio deklle ceramiche archeologiche in Italia settentrionale: alcune considerazioni*, in Brogiolo G.P., Gelichi S. (eds.), *Le ceramiche altomedievali (fine VI-X secolo) in Italia settentrionale: produzione e commerci*, VI seminario sul tardoantico e l'altomedioevo in Italia settentrionale, Mantova, pp.217-220.

Olcese 1993 – Olcese G. 1993, *Le ceramiche comuni di Albintimilum. Indagine archeologica e archeometrica sui materiali dell'area del Cardine*, Florence.

Ortalli 1996 – Ortalli J., *La fine delle ville romane: esperienze locali e problemi generali*, in Brogiolo G.P. (ed.), *La fine delle ville romane: trasformazioni nelle campagne tra tarda antichità e altomedioevo*, Mantova, pp.9-20.

Orton 2000 – Orton C., *Sampling in Archaeology*, Cambridge.

Orton *et alii* 1993 – Orton C., Tyers P., Vince A., *Pottery in Archaeology*, Cambridge.

Pacetti 2004 – Pacetti F., *Celio. Basilica Hilariana: scavi 1987-1989*, in Paroli L., Venditeli L. (eds.), *Roma dall'antichità al medioevo II. Contesti tardoantichi e altomedievali*, Milan, pp.418-434.

Pacetti 1998 – Pacetti F., *La questione delle Keay LII nell'ambito della produzione anforica in Italia*, in Saguì L. (ed.), *Ceramica in Italia: VI-VII secolo*, Florence, pp.185-208.

Pacetti 1994 – Pacetti F., *Appunti su alcuni tipi di anfore orientali della prima età bizantina. Centri di produzione, contenuti, cronologia e distribuzione*, in AAVV, *Agricoltura e commerci nell'Italia antica*, Atlante Tematico di Topografia Antica, I Supplemento, Rome, pp.273-294.

Paganelli 2004 – Paganelli M., *Area a N-O del Foro Romano: l'ambiente D nell'alto medioevo*, in Paroli L., Venditeli L. (eds.), *Roma dall'antichità al medioevo II. Contesti tardoantichi e altomedievali*, Milan, pp.180-203.

Pallecchi 2000 – Pallecchi P., *Indagini mineralogico-petrogrfiche sulle ceramiche provenienti dallo scavo di Piazza dei Cavalieri-Pisa*, in Abela E., Berti G., Bruni S. (eds.), *Ricerche archeologiche medievali a Pisa. I. Piazza dei Cavalieri, la campagna di scavo 1993*, Florence, pp.229-231.

Panella 1993 – Panella C., *Merci e scambi nel Mediterraneo tardoantico*, in Carandini A., Cracco Ruggini L., Giardina A. (eds.), *Storia di Roma 3. L'età tardoantica. II. I luoghi e le culture*, Turin, pp.613-697.

Panella 1983 – Panella C., *Le anfore di Cartagine: nuovi elementi per la ricostruzione dei flussi commerciali del Mediterraneo in età romana*, in "Opus", II, pp.53-73.

Paolucci 1992 – Paolucci G., *Ceramica invetriata da Chiusi a Cianciano Terme*, in Paroli L. (ed.), *La ceramica invetriata tardoantica e altomedievale in Italia*, Florence, pp.314-318.

Papi 2000 – Papi 2000, *L'Etruria dei Romani*, Rome.

Papi 1985 – Papi E., *Ceramica comune*, in n Ricci A. (ed.), *Settefinestre. Una villa schiavistica nell'Etruria romana. La villa e i suoi reperti*, Vol III, Modena, pp.93-105.

Pardi 1993 – Pardi F., *Trasgressioni e regressioni. I lineamenti evolutivi della costa toscana*, in Greppi C. (ed.), *Quadri ambientali della Toscana. III. Paesaggi della costa*, Venice, pp.13-48.

Parker 1992 – Parker A.J., *Ancient Shipwrecks of the Mediterranean & the Roman Provinces*, BAR International Series, 580, Oxford.

Paroli 1995 – Paroli L. (ed.), *La necropoli altomedievale di Castel Trosino: Bizantini e Longobardi nelle Marche*, Cinisello Balsamo.

Paroli 1992a – Paroli L. (ed.), *La ceramica invetriata tardoantica e altomedievale in Italia*, Florence.

Paroli 1992b – Paroli L. *Ceramica invetriata a macchia dagli scavi di Pionta – Arezzo*, in Paroli L. (ed.), *La ceramica invetriata tardoantica e altomedievale in Italia*, Florence, pp.310-313.

Paroli 1990 – Paroli L., *Ceramica a vetrina pesante altomedievale (Forum Ware) e medievale (Sparse Glazed)*, in Saguì L., Paroli L. (eds.), *Archeologia urbana a Roma: il progetto Crypta Balbi 5.L'esedra della Crypta Balbi nel Medioevo (XI-XV secolo)*, Florence, pp.328-353.

Paroli 1985 – Paroli L., *Ceramica a vetrina pesante (Forum Ware). Ceramica a vetrina pesante a macchia (Sparse glazed)*, in Manacorda D. (ed.), *Archeologia urbana a Roma: il progetto Crypta Balbi 3.Il giardino del Conservatorio di S.Caterina della Rosa*, Florence, pp.206-224.

Pasquinucci 2004 – Pasquinucci M., *Paleogeografia costiera, porti e approdi in Toscana*, in De Maria L., Turchetti R. (eds.), *Evolución paleoambiental de los puertos y fondeaderos antiguos en el mediterráneo occidental*, Soveria Mannelli, pp.61-86.

Pasquinucci *et alii* 2004 – Pasquinucci M., Pranzini E., Silenzi S., *Variazioni del livello marittimo ed evoluzione della costa in epoca storica: opportunità di porti e approdi*, in De Maria L., Turchetti R. (eds.), *Evolución paleoambiental de los puertos y fondeaderos antiguos en el mediterráneo occidental*, Soveria Mannelli, pp.87-102.

Pasquinucci *et alii* 1999 – Pasquinucci M., Del Rio A, Menchelli S., *Contenitori da trasporto e da magazzino nella fascia costiera alto-tirrenica dal tardoantico al medioevo*, in Atti del XXX Convegno Internazionale della ceramica (Albisola, 1997), Florence, pp.59-65.

Pasquinucci et alii 1998b – Pasquinucci M., Alessi D., Bianchini S., Cherubini L., Del Rio A., Menchelli S., Spinesi P., Vallebona M, *La ceramica di VI-VII secolo da Vada Volterrana (horrea in loc.S.Gaetano di Vada)*, in Saguì L. (ed.), *Ceramica in Italia VI-VII secolo*, Florence, pp.617-623.

Pastorino 1997 – Pastorino A.M., *Roman and late roman layers in the cave of Arene Candide*, in Maggi R. (ed.), *Arene Candide: a functional and environmental assessment of the Holocene sequence. (Excavations Bernabò Brea-Cardini 1940-50)*, Rome, pp.623-634.

Patitucci 2001 – Patitucci S., *Evidenze archeologiche della provincia Maritima bizantina in Toscana*, in Rotili M. (ed.), *Società multiculturali nei secoli V-IX. Scontri, convivenza, integrazione nel Mediterraneo occidentale*, Atti delle VI giornate di studio sull'età romanobarbarica, Benevento, 18-20 giugno 1998, Naples, pp.191-222.

Patterson 1997 – Patterson H., *The early medieval and medieval pottery*, in Potter T.W., King A.C. (eds.), *Excavations at the Mola di Monte Gelato*, London, pp.366-383.

Patterson *et alii* 2004 – Patterson H, Di Giuseppe H., Witcher R., *Three South Etrurian "crises": first results of the Tiber Valley Project*, in "Papers of the British School at Rome", LXXII, pp.1-36.

Peacock 1982 – Peacock D.P.S., *Pottery in the Roman world: an ethnoarchaeological approach*, London.

Peacock *et alii* 1989 – Peacock D.P.S., Bejaoui F., Belazreg N., *Roman amphora production in the Sahel region of Tunisia*, in AAVV, *Amphores romaines et historie économique: dix ans de recherches*, Atti del Colloquio Internazionale (Siena 22-24 maggio 1986), Rome, pp.180-222.

Pecci 2009 – Pecci A., *Analisi funzionale della ceramica e alimentazione medievale*, in "Archeologia Medievale", 36, pp.21-42.

Peduto 1986 – Peduto P., *Modalità e tipologia del quotidiano dallo studio della ceramica campana nell'alto Medioevo*, in AAVV., *La ceramica medievale nel Mediterraneo occidentale*, Florence, pp.555-572.

Pieri 2005 – Pieri D., *Le commerce du vin oriental à l'époque Byzantine*, Bibliothèque d'Archéologie et d'Histoire. Institut Français du Proche Orient, vol.172, Beirut.

Pieri 1999 – Pieri D., *Les importations d'amphores orientales tardives en Gaule méridionale (IVe-VIIe siècles). Typologie, chronologie et contenu*, in *Atti del XXX Convegno internazionale della ceramica 1997*, Albisola, pp.19-29.

Pieri 1969 – Pieri S., *Toponomastica della Toscana meridionale (valli della Fiora, dell'Ombrone, della Cécina e fiumi minori) e dell'Arcipelago toscano*, Siena.

Piponnier 1999 – Piponnier F., *Dal fuoco alla tavola: archeologia dell'attrezzatura alimentare alla fine del Medioevo*, in Flandrin J.L., Montanari M. (eds.), *Storia dell'alimentazione*, Bari, pp.408-416.

Possenti 1994 – Possenti E., *Gli orecchini a cestello altomedievali in Italia*, Florence.

Potter-King (eds.) 1997 – Potter T.W., King A.C. (eds.), *Excavations at the Mola di Monte Gelato*, London.

Prandi-Silvestrini – Prandi S., Silvestrini G., *Un contesto di ceramica altomedievale da Cencelle*, in Patitucci Uggeri S. (ed.), *La ceramica altomedievale in Italia*, Florence, pp.177-188.

Prisco 1998 – Prisco G., *Castelli e potere nella Maremma grossetana nell'alto medioevo*, Grosseto.

Prisco 1994 – Prisco G., *Grosseto da corte a città, Vol.II, L'acquisizione aldobrandesca del locus Grossito, Tomo 2. Topografia storica*, Grosseto.

Prisco 1989 – Prisco G., *Grosseto da corte a città*, Vol.I, *Roselle e Grosseto nel 1138*, Grosseto.

Regoli 2002a – Regoli E., *Il paesaggio delle ville (II secolo a.C.-metà I a.C.)*, in Carandini A., Cambi F. (eds.), *Paesaggi d'Etruria. Valle dell'Albegna, Valle d'Oro, Valle del Chiarone, Valle del Tafone*, Rome, pp.145-154.

Regoli 2002b – Regoli E., *Dalla villa schiavistica al latifondo (III-IV secolo)*, in Carandini A., Cambi F. (eds.) 2002, *Paesaggi d'Etruria. Valle dell'Albegna, Valle d'Oro, Valle del Chiarone, Valle del Tafone*, Rome, pp.218-227.

Regoli 1992 – Regoli E., *Il progetto di ricognizione topografica della Valle del Cecina*, in Bernardi M. (ed.), *Archeologia del Paesaggio*, atti del IV ciclo di lezioni sulla ricerca applicata in archeologia, Certosa di Pontignano (Siena) 14-26 gennaio, Florence, pp.545-560.

Regoli 1985 – Regoli E., *Sigillata italica* in Ricci A. (ed.), *Settefinestre. Una villa schiavistica nell'Etruria romana. La villa e i suoi reperti*, Vol III, Modena, pp.138-144.

Rendini 1998 – Rendini P., *Ceramiche del VI e VII secolo nell'area della villa di Giglio Porto (isola del Giglio-Gr)*, in Saguì L. (ed.), *Ceramica in Italia VI-VII secolo*, Florence, pp.639-644.

Renfrew-Bahn 1995 – Renfrew C., Bahn P., *Archeologia. Teorie, metodi, pratica*, Bologna.

Reynolds 2005 – Reynolds P., *Levantine amphorae from Cilicia to Gaza: a Typology and Analysis of Regional Production Trends from the 1st to 7th Centuries*, in Gurt i Esparraguera J. M^{a}., Buxeda i Garrigós J., Cau Ontiveros M. A. (eds.), *LRCW I. Late Roman Coarse Wares, Cooking Wares and Amphorae in the Mediterranean: Archaeology and Archaeometry*, BAR International Series, 1340, Oxford, pp.563-612.

Reynolds 2004a – Reynolds P., The Roman pottery from the Triconch Palace, in Hodges R., Bowden W., Lako K. (eds.), *Byzantine Butrint. Excavations and Surveys 1994-99*, Oxford, pp.224-269.

Reynolds 2004b – Reynolds P., *The medieval amphorae*, in Hodges R., Bowden W., Lako K. (eds.), *Byzantine Butrint. Excavations and Surveys 1994-99*, Oxford, pp.270-277.

Reynolds 2004c – Reynolds P., *Appendix 1. Catalogue of Roman ceramics and selected medieval pottery from Butrint 1994-99*, in Hodges R., Bowden W., Lako K. (eds.), *Byzantine Butrint. Excavations and Surveys 1994-99*, Oxford, pp.270-277.

Reynolds 1995 – Reynolds P., *Trade in the Western Mediterranean, AD 400-700: the ceramic evidence*, BAR International Series, 604, Oxford

Ricci 1983 – Ricci A., *La documentazione scritta nella ricerca archeologica sul territorio: un nuovo sistema di schedatura*, in "Archeologia Medievale", X, pp.495-506.

Ricci 2001 – Ricci M., *Abbigliamento e ornamento*, in Arena M.S., Delogu P., Paroli L., Ricci M., Saguì L., Vendittelli L. (eds.), *Roma dall'antichità al medioevo. Archeologia e storia*, Milan, pp.174-177.

Ricci 1998 – Ricci M., *La ceramica comune dal contesto di VII secolo della Crypta Balbi*, in Saguì L. (ed.), *Ceramica in Italia VI-VII secolo*, Florence, pp.351-382.

Ricci 1990 – Ricci M., *Ceramica acroma depurata 2.Brocche, catini, orcioli ed altre forme minori*, in Saguì L., Paroli L. (eds.), *Archeologia urbana a Roma: il progetto Crypta Balbi 5.L'esedra della Crypta Balbi nel Medioevo (XI-XV secolo)*, Florence, pp.288-307.

Ricci-Saguì 2001 – Ricci M., Saguì L., *Crypta Balbi* in Arena M.S., Delogu P., Paroli L., Ricci M., Saguì L., Vendittelli L. (eds.), *Roma dall'antichità al medioevo. Archeologia e storia*, Milan, pp.245-249.

Ricci-Luccerini 2001 – Ricci M., Lucherini F., *Oggetti di abbigliamento e ornamento*, in Arena M.S., Delogu P., Paroli L., Ricci M., Saguì L., Vendittelli L. (eds.), *Roma dall'antichità al medioevo. Archeologia e storia*, Milan, pp.351-352.

Rigoir-Rigoir 1994 – Rigoir Y., Rigoir J., *Les dérivées des sigillées paléochrétiennes*, in Démians d'Archimbaud G. (ed.), *L'oppidum de Saint Blaise du Ve au VIIe siecle*, Paris, pp.136-160.

Rittatore 1951 – Rittatore F., *Scoperte di età eneolitica e del Bronzo nella Maremma Tosco-Laziale*, in "Rivista di Scienze Preistoriche", VI, 1951, pp.3-33.

Rizzitelli 1999 – Rizzitelli C., *Roselle*, in Gelichi S. (ed.), *Archeologia urbana in Toscana. La città altomedievale*, Mantova, pp.105-116.
Rizzo *et alii* 2004 – Rizzo G., Capone M., Costantini C., Gafà R., Pentiricci M., Munzi M., *Vigna Barberini, settore D, Periodo IV: 540/550-580/590 d.C.*, in Paroli L., Venditelli L. (eds.), *Roma dall'antichità al medioevo II. Contesti tardoantichi e altomedievali*, Milan, pp.72-90.
Roberts 1996 – Roberts B.K., *Landscapes of Settlement. Prehistory to the present*, New York.
Robinson 1959 – Robinson H.S., *The Athenian Agorà. Pottery of the Roman Period*, Princeton.
Rodriguez 1992 – Rodriguez H., *Bemerkungen zur relativchronologischen Gliederung der südostalpinen spätrömisch-spätantiken Gebrauchskeramik*, in Brogiolo G.P., Castelletti L. (eds.), *Il territorio tra tardoantico e altomedioevo. Metodi di indagine e risultati*, 3° seminario sul tardoantico e l'altomedioevo nell'area alpina e padana, Florence, pp.159-178.
Romano-Volpe 2005 – Romano A.V., Volpe G., *Paesaggi e insediamenti rurali nel comprensorio del Celone fra Tardoantico e Altomedioevo*, in Volpe G., Turchiano M. (eds.), *Paesaggi e insediamenti rurali in Italia meridionale fra tardoantico e altomedioevo*, Bari, pp.241-264.
Rombai 1986 – Rombai L., *Le ultime "Zone Umide" della Maremma e la "Casa Ximenes". Geografia storica e beni culturali e ambientali*, in Guerrini G. (ed.), *Ecologia Maremma*, Atti dell'incontro di Castiglione della Pescaia 12-13 aprile 1986, Grosseto, pp.13-20.
Romei 2004 – Romei D., *Produzione e circolazione dei manufatti ceramici a Roma nell'altomedioevo*, in Paroli L., Venditeli L. (eds.), *Roma dall'antichità al medioevo II. Contesti tardoantichi e altomedievali*, Milan, pp.278-311.
Romei 2001 – Romei D., *Anfore*, in Saguì L., Ricci M., Romei D., *La cultura materiale a Roma tra VIII e X secolo: i depositi nell'esedra della Crypta Balbi*, in Arena M.S., Delogu P., Paroli L., Ricci M., Saguì L., Vendittelli L. (eds.), *Roma dall'antichità al medioevo. Archeologia e storia*, Milan, pp.498-528.
Romei 1990 – Romei D., *Ceramica acroma depurata 1. Anfore, coperchi, piedistalli*, in Saguì L.-Paroli L. (eds.), *5.L'Esedra della Cripta Balbi nel Medioevo (XI-XV secolo)*, Florence, pp.264-287.
Rossetti 1981 – Rossetti G., *Gli Aldobrandeschi*, in AA.VV., *I ceti dirigenti in Toscana nell'età precomunale*, Atti del I convegno del «Comitato di studi sulla storia dei ceti dirigenti in Toscana», Firenze, 2 dicembre 1978, Pisa, pp.151-63.
Rossetti 1973 – Rossetti G., *Società e istituzioni nei secoli IX e X: Pisa, Volterra, Populonia*, in AA.VV., *Lucca e la Tuscia nell'alto medioevo*, Atti del V Congresso internazionale di Studi sull'alto Medioevo (Lucca, ottobre 1971), Spoleto, Centro Italiano di Studi sull'Alto Medioevo, Spoleto, pp.209-338.
Saguì 1998 – Saguì L., *Il deposito della Crypta Balbi: una testimonianza imprevedibile sulla Roma del VII secolo*, in Saguì L. (ed.), *Ceramica in Italia VI-VII secolo*, Florence, pp.305-330.
Saguì-Coletti 2004 – Saguì L., Coletti C.M., *Contesti tardoantichi dall'area a S-E della cripta Balbi*, in Paroli L., Venditeli L. (eds.), *Roma dall'antichità al medioevo II. Contesti tardoantichi e altomedievali*, Milan, pp.242-277.
Saguì et alii 2001a – Saguì L., Ricci M., Romei D., Rovelli A., De Grossi Mazzorin J., Minniti C., *La circolazione delle merci: il deposito della fine del VII secolo nell'esedra della Cripta Balbi*, in Arena M.S., Delogu P., Paroli L., Ricci M., Saguì L., Vendittelli L. (eds.), *Roma dall'antichità al medioevo. Archeologia e storia*, Milan, pp.266-330.
Saguì *et alii* 2001b – Saguì L., Ricci M., Romei D., *La cultura materiale a Roma tra VIII e X secolo: i depositi nell'esedra della Crypta Balbi*, in Arena M.S., Delogu P., Paroli L., Ricci M., Saguì L., Vendittelli L. (eds.), *Roma dall'antichità al medioevo. Archeologia e storia*, Milan, pp.498-528.
Saguì-Ricci-Romei 1997 – Saguì L., Ricci M., Romei D., *Nuovi dati ceramologici per la storia economica di Roma tra VII e VIII*, in, La céramique médiévale en Méditerranée, Actes du VIéme Colloqui (13-18 Novembre 1995) Aix en Provence, pp.35-48.
Saguì-Paroli 1991 – Saguì L., Paroli L., *La ceramica acroma tardoantica e medievale*, in Melucco Vaccaro A. (ed.), *Arezzo. Il colle del Pionta. Il contributo archeologico alla storia del primo gruppo cattedrale*, Arezzo, pp.127-148.
Salvadori-Valenti 2003 – Salvadori F., Valenti M., *Il periodo altomedievale di Poggio Imperiale (Poggibonsi – SI): dal villaggio all'azienda curtense*, Fiorillo R., Peduto P. (eds.), *III Congresso Nazionale di Archeologia Medievale*, Florence, pp.325-330.
Salvini *et alii* 2004 - Salvini L., Valdambrini C., Pecci A., Citter C., Giorgi G., *Medieval vessels from Grosseto and Castel di Pietra: organic residues and functions*, Poster presented at the *International Symposium on Mass Spectometry 2004*, Bari.
Scavi ad Aquileia I –Verzár Bass M. (ed.) 1991, *Scavi ad Aquileia I. L'area a Est del Foro. Rapporto degli scavi 1988*, Rome.
Scavi MM3 – Caporusso D. (ed.) 1991, *Scavi MM3, Ricerche di archeologia urbana a Milano durante la costruzione della linea 3 della Metropolitana 1982-1990, Voll.3.1, 3.2, 4*, Rome.
Schwarzmaier 1973 – Schwarzmaier H., *Società e istituzioni nel X secolo: Lucca*, in *Atti del 5° Congresso Internazionale di Studi sull'Alto Medioevo*, Lucca, 3-7 ottobre 1971, Spoleto, pp.143-162.
Sereni 1995 – Sereni A., *Contenitori, suppellettile domestica, spazi funzionali: spunti di riflessione attraverso la documentazione scritta altomedievale*, in De Minicis E. (ed.), *Le ceramiche di Roma e del Lazio in età medievale e moderna, II*, Rome, pp.270-279.
Sevink *et alii* 1986 – Sevink J., Beemster J., Van Stiphout T., *Soil survey and land evaluation of the Grosseto area*, Part I, Amsterdam.
Sestini-Cardini 1935 – Sestini A., Cardini L., *Relazione di alcuni sopraluoghi eseguiti nei monti dell'Uccellina*, Istituto Italiano di Paleontologia Umana, Florence.
Sfameni 2005 – Sfameni C., *Le villae-praetoria: i casi di San Giovanni di Ruoti e di Quote San Francesco*, in Volpe G., Turchiano M. (eds.), *Paesaggi e insediamenti rurali in Italia meridionale fra tardoantico e altomedioevo*, Bari, pp.609-622.
Sgherri-Costantini 2004 – Sgherri D., Costantini A., *Piedi a terra. Guida geologica ai sentieri del Parco Regionale della Maremma*, Grosseto.
Signorini 1967 – Signorini R., *Note illustrative della Carta Geologica d'Italia. Foglio 135. Orbetello*, Ercolano.
Sordini 2000 – Sordini B., *Il porto della "gente vana". Lo scalo di Talamone tra il secolo XIII e il secolo XV*, Siena.
Soricelli 1994 – Soricelli G., *Terra Sigillata della prima, media e tarda età imperiale*, in Arthur P. (ed.), *Il Complesso Archeologico di Carminiello ai Mannesi, Napoli (Scavi 1983-1984)*, Galatina, pp.109-168.
Staffa 2006 – Staffa A., *I centri urbani dell'Abruzzo adriatico fra tarda antichità ed altomedioevo*, in Augenti A. (ed.), *Le città italiane tra la Tarda Antichità e l'Alto Medioevo*, Florence, pp.345-476.
Staffa 2005 – Staffa A., *Insediamento e circolazione nelle regioni adriatiche dell'Italia centrale fra VI e IX secolo*, in Brogiolo G.P, De Logu P. (eds.), *L'Adriatico dalla Tarda Antichità all'Età Carolingia*, Florence, pp.109-182.
Staffa 2004 – Staffa A., *Le produzioni ceramiche in Abruzzo nell'altomedioevo*, in Patitucci Uggeri S. (ed.), *La ceramica altomedievale in Italia*, Florence, pp.205-234.
Staffa 1996 – Staffa A. 1996, *Le produzioni ceramiche in Abruzzo fra V e XII secolo*, in Brogiolo G.P., Gelichi S. (eds.), *Le ceramiche altomedievali (fine VI-X secolo) in Italia settentrionale: produzione e commerci*, VI seminario sul tardoantico e l'altomedioevo in Italia settentrionale, Mantova, pp.171-215.

Staffa 1998 – Staffa A. 1998, *Le produzioni ceramiche in Abruzzo tra fine V e VII secolo*, in Saguì L. (ed.), *Ceramica in Italia VI-VII secolo*, Florence, pp.437-480.

Stea-Tenerini 1996 – Stea I., Tenerini B., *L'ambiente naturale della pianura grossetana e la sua evoluzione dalla preistoria alla cartografia rinascimentale*, in Citter C. (ed.), *Grosseto, Roselle e il Prile. Note per la storia di una città e del territorio circostante*, Mantova, pp.13-24.

Stoddart-Whitehead 1991 – Stoddart S., Whitehead N., *Cleaning the Iguvine Stables: Site and off-site Analysis from a central Mediterranean Perspective*, Schofield J. (ed.), *Interpreting Artefacts Scatters. Contribution to Plowzone Archaeology*, Oxford, pp.141-148.

Tangheroni 2003 – Tangheroni M. (ed.), *Pisa e il Mediterraneo. Uomini, merci, idee dagli Etruschi ai Medici*, Milan.

Tangheroni 1996 – Tangheroni M., *Commercio e navigazione nel Medioevo*, Rome-Bari.

Taylor 2000 – Taylor J., *Cultural depositional processes and post-depositional problems*, in Francovich R., Patterson H., Barker G. (eds.), *Extracting Meanings from Ploughsoil Assemblages,* Oxford, pp.16-28.

Terrenato 2000 – Terrenato N., *The visibility of sites and the interpretation of field survey results: towards an analysis of incomplete distribution*, in Francovich R., Patterson H., Barker G. (eds.), *Extracting Meanings from Ploughsoil Assemblages*, Oxford, pp.60-71.

Terrenato 1998 – Terrenato N., *Tam firmum municipium: The Romanization of Volaterrae and Its Cultural Implications*, in "Journal of Roman Studies", 88, pp.94-114.

Terrenato-Ricci 1998 – Terrenato N., Ricci G., *I residui nella stratificazione urbana. Metodi di quantificazione e implicazione per l'interpretazione delle sequenze: un caso di studio dalle pendici settentrionali del Palatino*, in Guidobaldi F., Pavolini C., Pergola Ph. (eds.), *I materiali residui nello scavo archeologico*, Rome, pp.89-104.

Terrenato-Ammermann 1996 – Terrenato N., Ammerman A.J., *Visibility and Site Recovery in the Cecina Valley Survey, Italy*, in "Journal of Field Archaeology", 23, pp.91-109.

Toniolo 2007 – Toniolo A., Anfore dall'area lagunare, in Gelichi-Negrelli (eds.), *La circolazione delle ceramiche nell'Adriatico tra tarda antichità e alto medioevo. III Incontro di studio CER.AM.IS*, Mantova pp.91-106.

Torelli 1984 – Torelli M., *Storia degli Etruschi*, Bari.

Tortorella 1998 – Tortorella S. 1998, *La sigillata africana in Italia nel VI e nel VII secolo d.C.: problemi di cronologia e distribuzione*, in Saguì L. (ed.), *Ceramica in Italia VI-VII secolo*, Florence, pp.41-69.

Tortorella 1991 – Tortorella S., *La ceramica fine da mensa di età romana*, in Melucco Vaccaro A. (ed.), *Arezzo. Il colle del Pionta. Il contributo archeologico alla storia del primo gruppo cattedrale*, Arezzo, pp.103-114.

Toubert 1995 – Toubert P., *Dalla terra ai castelli. Paesaggio, agricoltura e poteri nell'Italia medievale*, Turin.

Uscatescu 1996 – Uscatescu A., *Un tipo di decorazione orientale nelle ceramiche del periodo tardoantico rinvenute in Italia*, in "Archeologia Medievale", XXIII, pp.625-646.

Vaccaro 2009 – Vaccaro E., *Cultura materiale e circolazione di merci: riflessioni su un contesto ceramico di X secolo d.C. da Capalbiaccio-Tricosto*, in Hobart M., Cerri L., Mariotti E., Corti I., Acconcia V., Vaccaro E., Valdambrini C., Salvadori H., *Capalbiaccio (GR) nel tempo: dalla preistoria all'età moderna. Le indagini archeologiche dagli anni '70 al nuovo progetto di ricerca*, in "Archeologia Medievale", XXXVI, pp.93-104.

Vaccaro 2008 – Vaccaro E., *An overview of rural settlement in four river basins in the province of Grosseto on the coast of Tuscany (200 B.C.-A.D.600)*, in "Journal of Roman Archaeology", n.21, 2008, pp.225-247.

Vaccaro 2007 – Vaccaro E., *L'occupazione tardoantica delle grotte di Scoglietto e Spaccasasso nei Monti dell'Uccellina (GR)*, in Cavanna C. (ed.), *La preistoria nelle grotte del Parco Naturale della Maremma*, Atti del Museo di Storia Naturale della Maremma, suppl.n°22, Grosseto, pp. 227-242.

Vaccaro 2005a – Vaccaro E., I*l popolamento rurale tra fine V ed inizi X nella Maremma grossetana: indagini di superficie tra la valle dell'Alma e la valle dell'Osa*, in Brogiolo G.P., Chavarría Arnau A., Valenti M. (eds.), *Dopo la fine delle ville. Evoluzione delle campagne tra VI e IX secolo*, Mantova, pp.179-192.

Vaccaro 2005b – Vaccaro E., *Il sepolcreto di età longobarda presso la Pescaia nel quadro delle evidenze insediative e funerarie tardoantiche e altomedievali della valle del Bruna*, in Farinelli R., Marrucchi G. (eds.), *Roccastrada e il suo territorio. Insediamenti, Arte, Storia, Economia*, Empoli, pp.21-26.

Vaccaro 2005c – Vaccaro E., *Castiglione della Pescaia Survey*, in Francovich R., Valenti M. (eds.), *Relazione del Progetto Archeologia dei Paesaggi Medievali (Anno 2000 - 2004)*, Siena, pp.270-273.

Vaccaro 2005d – Vaccaro E., *.3 Dinamiche insediative; .4 I manufatti ceramici di Podere Serratone: metodi di analisi dei materiali da superficie per lo studio della cultura materiale di un abitato di pianura*, in Campana S., Francovich R., Vaccaro E. (with a contribution by Frezza B. and Ghisleni M.), *Il popolamento tardoromano e altomedievale nella bassa valle dell'Ombrone. Progetto Carta Archeologica della Provincia di Grosseto*, in "Archeologia Medievale", XXXII, pp.461-480.

Vaccaro 2001/2002 – Vaccaro E., *La Formazione dei Paesaggi Medievali nell'Area del Prile: il Caso di Castiglione della Pescaia*, Unpublished Degree Thesis, University of Siena.

Vaccaro-Ghisleni-Campana 2009 – Vaccaro E., Ghisleni M., Campana S., *The site of Aiali from late republican period to middle ages in the light of surface pottery analysis*, in Campana S., Piro S. (eds.), *Seeing the Unseen Archaeology. Geophysical and Landscape Archaeology*, London, pp.303-324.

Vaccaro-Salvadori 2006 – Vaccaro E., Salvadori H., *Prime analisi sui reperti ceramici e numismatici di X secolo dal villaggio medievale di Poggio Cavolo (GR)*, in Francovich R., Valenti M. (eds.), *IV Congresso Nazionale di Archeologia Medievale*, Florence, pp.480-484.

Valdambrini 2006 – Valdambrini C., *Ceramiche depurate e semidepurate prive di rivestimento dagli scavi urbani di Grosseto: considerazioni preliminari*, in Francovich R., Valenti M. (eds.), *IV Congresso Nazionale di Archeologia Medievale*, Florence, pp.474-479.

Valdambrini 2005 – Valdambrini C., *Il materiale ceramico proveniente dallo scavo della chiesa di S.Pietro a Grosseto. Osservazioni preliminari*, in Citter C. (ed.), *Lo scavo della chiesa di S.Pietro a Grosseto. Nuovi dati sull'origine e lo sviluppo di una città medievale*, Florence, pp.33-47.

Valdambrini 2003/2004 – Valdambrini C., *La ceramica ad impasto depurato e selezionato privo di rivestimento da tre contesti della Toscana Meridionale: Grosseto, Castel di Pietra (Gavorrano-Gr), Selvena (Castell'Azzara-Gr). Studio archeologico e applicazioni archeometriche*, Unpublished degree thesis, University of Siena.

Valenti 2008 – Valenti M., *La Toscana prima e dopo il 774. I segni delle aristocrazie in ambito urbano e rurale*, in Gasparri S. (ed.), *774. Ipotesi su una transizione*, Turnhout, pp.221-261.

Valenti 2007 – Valenti M., *Aristocrazie ed élites, deboli e forti, nella Toscana tra VI e X secolo* in Brogiolo G.P., Chavarría Arnau A. (eds.), *Archeologia e società tra tardo antico e alto medioevo*, Mantova, pp.205-240.

Valenti 2005 – Valenti M., *La formazione dell'insediamento altomedievale in Toscana. Dallo spessore dei numeri alla costruzione di modelli*, in Brogiolo G.P., Chavarria A., Valenti M. (eds.), *Dopo la fine delle ville: le campagne dal VI al IX secolo*, XI Seminario sul Tardoantico e l'Altomedioevo, Mantova, pp.193-220.

Valenti 2004 – Valenti M., *L'insediamento altomedievale nelle campagne toscane. Paesaggi, popolamento e villaggi tra VI e X secolo*, Florence.

Valenti 1996a – Valenti M., *La ceramica comune nel territorio settentrionale senese tra V-inizi X secolo*, in Brogiolo G.P.-Gelichi S. (eds.), *Le ceramiche altomedievali (fine VI-X secolo) in Italia settentrionale: produzione e commerci*, VI seminario sul tardoantico e l'altomedioevo in Italia settentrionale, Mantova, pp.143-169.

Valenti 1996b – Valenti M., *Poggio Imperiale a Poggibonsi (Siena). Dal villaggio di capanne al castello di pietra. I. Diagnostica archeologica e campagne di scavo 1991-1994*, Florence.

Valenti 1995a – Valenti M., *Carta archeologica della provincia di Siena. Il Chianti senese (Castellina in Chianti, Castelnuovo Berardenga, Gaiole in Chianti, Radda in Chianti*), Vol.I, Siena.

Valenti 1995b - Valenti M., *Il patrimonio archeologico sommerso del territoro senese. Esperienze e sperimentazioni dei primi anni '90 nell'attività di ricerca del Dipartimento di archeologia e storia delle arti dell'Università di Siena*, in Francovich R., Boldrini E. (eds.), *Acculturazione e mutamenti. Prospettive nell'archeologia medievale del Mediterraneo*, Florence, pp.63-106.

Valenti 2008 (ed.) – Valenti M. (ed.), *Miranduolo in Alta Val di Merse (Chiusdino - SI). Archeologia su un sito di potere del Medioevo toscano*, Florence.

Valenti 1999 (ed.) – Valenti M. (ed.), *Carta archeologica della provincia di Siena. La Val d'Elsa (Colle di Val d'Elsa e Poggibonsi)*, Vol.III, Siena.

Van Berghem et *alii* 1991 – Van Berghem J.W., Meijvogel T., Windmeijer P.N., *La valle dell'Albegna*, Venice.

Vatta-Bertoldi 2004 – Vatta G., Bertoldi T., *Celio. Basilica Hilariana: scavi 1997*, in Paroli L., Vendittelli L. (eds.), *Roma dall'antichità al medioevo II. Contesti tardoantichi e altomedievali*, Milan, pp.458-479.

Vera 2005 – Vera D., *I paesaggi rurali del Meridione tardoantico: bilancio consuntivo e preventivo*, Volpe G., Turchiano M. (eds.), *Paesaggi e insediamenti rurali in Italia meridionale fra tardoantico e altomedioevo*, Bari, pp.23-38.

Vera 1999 – Vera D., *I silenzi di Palladio e l'Italia: osservazioni sull'ultimo agronomo romano*, in "Antiquité Tardive", 7, pp.283-297.

Vera 1998 – Vera D., *Le forme del lavoro rurale: aspetti della trasformazione dell'Europa romana fra Tarda Antichità e Alto Medioevo*, in *Morfologie sociali e culturali in Europa fra Tarda Antichità e Alto Medioevo*, XLV Settimane di Studio del Centro Italiano di Studi sull'Alto Medioevo, Spoleto, pp.293-338.

Vera 1993 – Vera D., *Proprietà terriera e società rurale nell'Italia gotica*, in AAVV, *Teoderico il Grande e i Goti d'Italia*, Atti del XIII Congresso Internazionale di studi sull'Alto Medioevo, Milano 2-6 novembre 1992, Tomo II, Spoleto, pp.133-166.

Vera 1992 – Vera D., *Massa fundorum. Forme della grande proprietà e poteri della città in Italia fra Costantino e Gregorio Magno*, in "MEFRA", 111, pp.991-1025.

Vera 1983 – Vera D., *Strutture agrarie e strutture patrimoniali nella tarda antichità: l'aristocrazia romana fra agricoltura e commercio*, in "Opus", II, 2.

Villa 1994 – Villa L., *Le anfore tra tardoantico e medioevo*, in Lusuardi Siena S. (ed.), *Ad Mensam. Manufatti d'uso da contesti archeologici fra Tarda Antichità e Medioevo*, Udine, pp.335-431.

Villedieu 1994 – Villedieu F., *Les amphores : observations préliminaires*, in Démians d'Archimbaud G. (ed.), *L'oppidum de Saint Blaise du Ve au VIIe siecle*, Paris, pp.133-135.

Villedieu 1986 – Villedieu F., *Turris Libisonis – Porto Torres (Sardegna). Il contesto delle mura* in Giardina A (ed.), *Società romana e impero tardoantico. III. Le merci e gli insediamenti*, Rome-Bari, pp.145-162.

Vita Finzi 1969 – Vita Finzi C., *The Mediterranean Valleys*, Cambridge.

Vitali 1999 – Vitali M., *La ceramica longobarda*, in Brogiolo G.P. (ed.), *S.Giulia di Brescia gli scavi dal 1980 al 1992*, Florence, pp.175-220.

Vivarelli Colonna 1937 – Vivarelli Colonna F., *Venticinque anni di lavoro nelle mie terre di Maremma. 1910-1935*, Estratto dagli Atti della Reale Accademia dei Georgofili, Memoria letta nell'adunanza del 13.6.1937, Florence.

Vivarelli Colonna 1926 – Vivarelli Colonna F., *Bonifica, colonizzazione e trasformazione culturale compiuta dal 1906 al 1926 nelle fattorie di Magliano, Montiano, San Giusto, Collecchio e Barca in provincia di Grosseto*, Relazione alla Regia Accademia dei Georgofili per il concorso da essa bandito con circolare del 10/11/1925, Florence.

Volpe 2007 – Volpe G., *Il ruolo dei vescovi nei processi di trasformazione del paesaggio urbano e rurale*, in Brogiolo G. P., Chavarría Arnau A. (eds.), *Archeologia e società tra Tardo Antico e Alto Medioevo*, Mantova, pp. 85-106.

Volpe 2005 – Volpe G., *Paesaggi e insediamenti rurali dell'Apulia tardoantica e altomedievale*, in Volpe G., Turchiano M. (eds.), *Paesaggi e insediamenti rurali in Italia meridionale fra tardoantico e altomedioevo*, Bari, pp.299-314.

Volpe 1998a – Volpe G., *Archeologia subacquea e commerci in età tardoantica*, in Volpe G. (ed.), *Archeologia Subacquea*, VIII ciclo di lezioni sulla ricerca applicata in archeologia, Certosa di Pontignano (Siena) 9-15 dicembre 1996, Florence, pp.561-626.

Volpe 1998b – Volpe G. (ed.), *San Giusto: la villa, le ecclesiae*, Bari.

Volpe et alii 2005 – Volpe G., De Felice G., Turchiano M., *Faragola (Ascoli Satriano). Una residenza aristocratica tardoantica e un "villaggio" altomedievalenella valle del Carapelle: primi dati*, in Volpe G., Turchiano M. (eds.), *Paesaggi e insediamenti rurali in Italia meridionale fra tardoantico e altomedioevo*, Bari, pp.265-297.

Von Hessen 1975 – von Hessen O., *Secondo contributo alla archeologia longobarda in Toscana*, Accademia Toscana di Scienze e Lettere "La Colombaria", Studi, XLI, Florence.

Von Hessen 1971 – von Hessen O., *Primo contributo alla archeologia longobarda in Toscana*, Accademia Toscana di Scienze e Lettere "La Colombaria", Studi, XVIII, Florence.

Von Vacano 1985 – von Vacano O.W., *Gli Etruschi a Talamone, la baia di Talamone dalla preistoria ai giorni nostri*, Bologna.

Vroom 2005 – Vroom J., *Byzantine to modern pottery in the Aegean. An introduction and field guide*, Utrecht.

Ward Perkins 2005 – Ward Perhins B., *The fall of Rome and the end of civilzation*, Oxford.

Wickham 2005 – Wickham C., *Framing the early Middle Ages: Europe and the Mediterranean 400-800*, Oxford.

Wickham 2003 – Wickham C., *Studying long-term change in the West*, in Lavan L., Bowden W. (eds.), *Theory and Practice in Late Antique Archaeology*, Leiden, pp.385-403.

Wickham 2000 – Wickham C., *Overview: production, distribution and demand, II*, in Hansen I.L., Wickham C. (eds.), *The Long Eight Century*, Leiden, pp.345-378.

Wickham 1998a – Wickham C., *A che serve l'incastellamento?*, in Barcelo M., Toubert P. (eds.), *L'incastellamento: acts de rencontres de Gerone (26-27 nov.1992) et de Rome (5-7 mai 1994)*, Rome, pp.31-41.

Wickham 1998b – Wickham C., *Overview: production, distribution and demand*, in Hodges R., Bowden W. (eds.), *The sixth century. Production, Distribution and Demand*, Leiden, pp.279-292.

Wickham 1997 – Wickham C., *The feudal revolution: comment IV*, in "Past and present", 155, pp.196-207.

Wickham 1988a – Wickham C., *Le strutture dell'economia e del potere*, in Delogu P. (ed.), *Periodi e contenuti del Medio Evo*, Seminari dell'Istituto di Storia Medievale, Università degli Studi di Roma La Sapienza, Rome, pp.75-86.

Wickham 1988b – Wickham C., *L'incastellamento e i suoi destini undici anni dopo il Latium di P.Toubert*, in Noyé G. (ed.), *Castrum 2. Structures de l'habitat et occupation du sol dans les pays mediterranées: les methodes et l'apportt de l'archéologie extensive*, Rome-Madrid, pp.411-420.

Wilson 2009 – Wilson A., *Approaches to Quantifying Roman Trade*, in Bowman A., Wilson A. (eds.), *Quantifying the Roman Economy. Methods and Probelms*, Oxford, pp.213-258.

Whitehouse 1982 – Whitehouse D., *Medieval pottery from South Etruria,* in, Andrews D., Osborne J., Whitehouse D., *Medieval Lazio. Studies in architecture, painting and ceramics*, BAR International Series, 125, Oxford, pp.320-321.

Whitehouse 1980 – Whitehouse D., *The medieval pottery from S.Cornelia,* in "Papers of the British School at Rome", 48, pp.125-156.

Whitehouse *et alii* 1982 – Whitehouse D., Barker G., Reece R., Reese D., *The Schola Praeconum, I. The Coins, Pottery, Lamps and Fauna*, in "Papers of the British School at Rome", 50, pp.53-101.

Wolfram 1985 – Wolfram H., *Storia dei Goti*, Rome.

Zanini 2007 – Zanini E., *Archeologia dello status sociale nell'Italia bizantina: tracce, segni e modelli interpretativi*, in Brogiolo G.P., Chavarría Arnau A. (eds.), *Archeologia e società tra tardo antico e alto medioevo*, Mantova, pp.23-46.

Zanini 2003 – Zanini E., *La ceramica bizantina in Italia tra VI e VIII secolo. Un sistema informativo territoriale per lo studio della distribuzione e del consumo*, in VIIe Congrès International sur la Céramique Médiévale en Méditerranée, (Thessaloniki 1999), pp.381-394.

Zanini 1996 – Zanini E., *Ricontando la terra sigillata africana*, in "Arcehologia Medievale", XXIII, pp.677-688.

ARS D from the North Hill at Roselle: main types

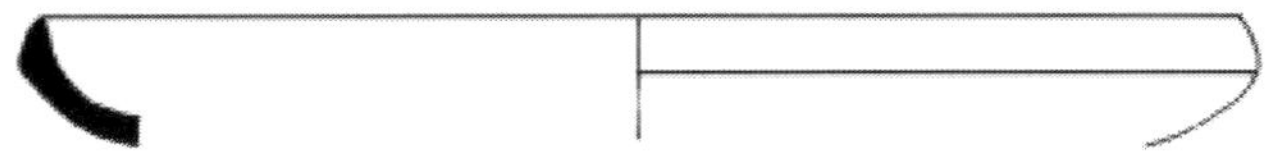

1 Hayes 61A

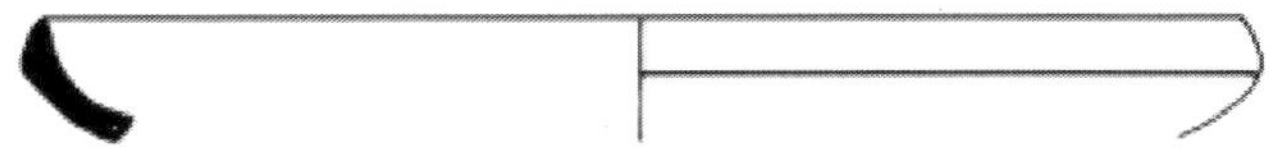

2 Hayes 61A

3 Hayes 61B

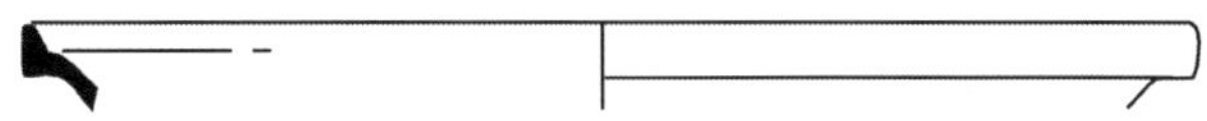

4 Hayes 61B

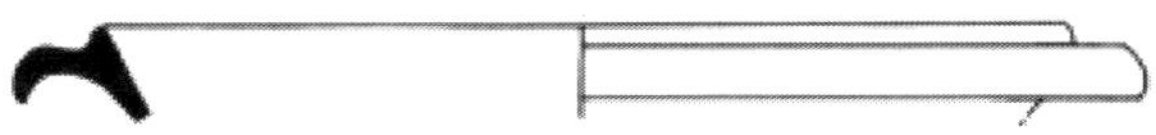

5 Hayes 91B

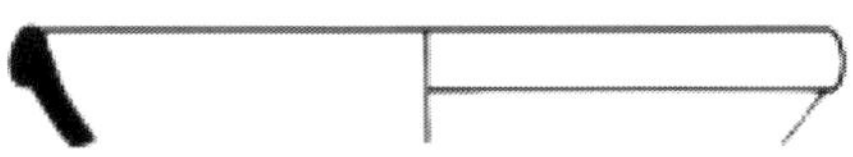

6 Hayes 99B

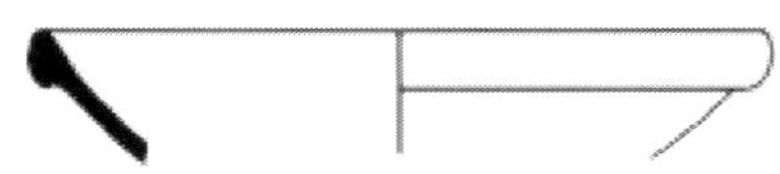

7 Hayes 99B/C

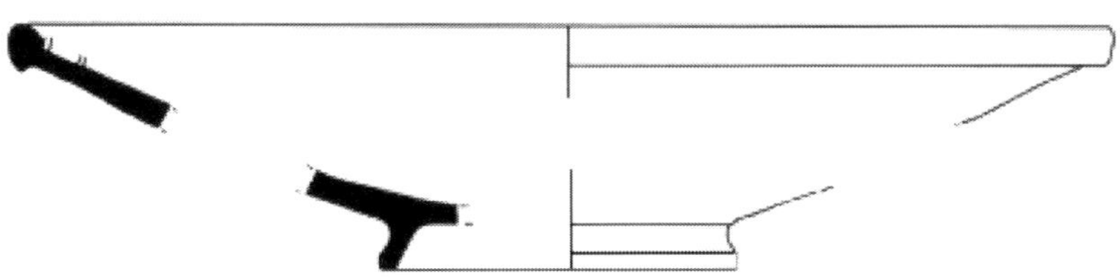

8a Hayes 104A

8b Hayes 104B (decoration)

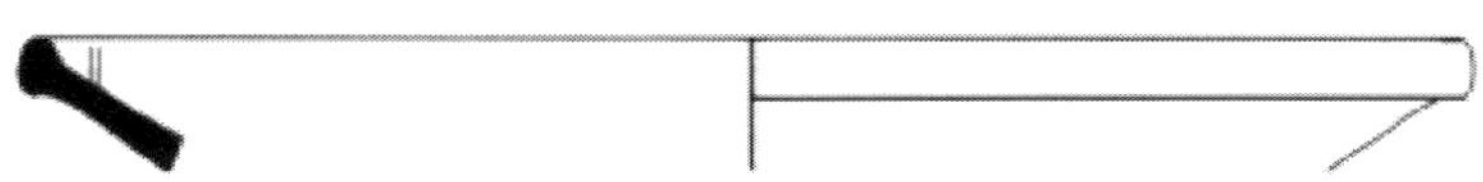

9 Hayes 104B

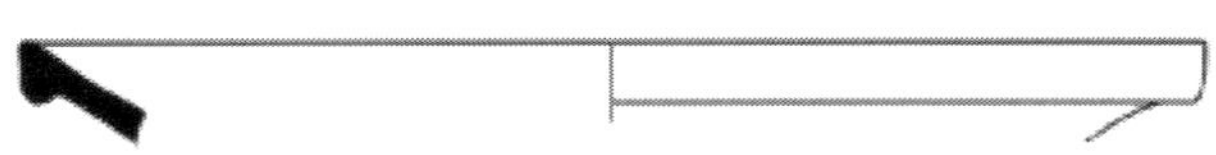

10 Atlante I, Pl. XLVI, 1-2

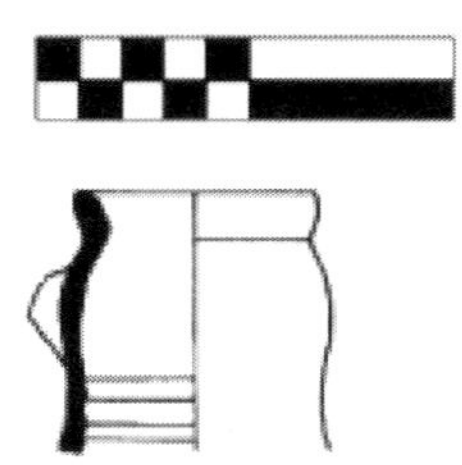

11 Fulford, Closed Forms 2

PLATE I

ARS and *Sigillata chiara tarda dell'Italia centro-settentrionale* from contexts 5147=5170 and 5141 (Roselle, North Hill)

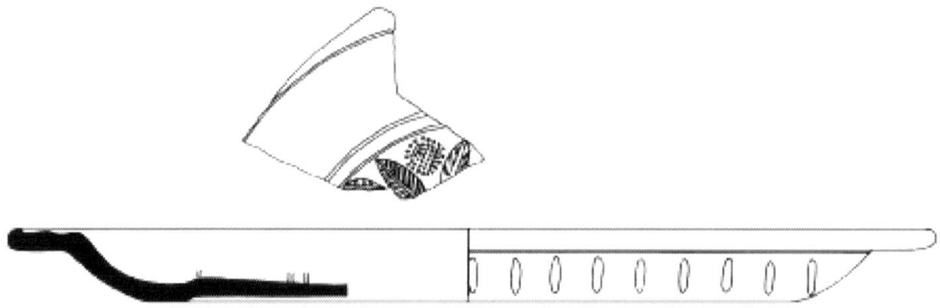

1 Hayes 59

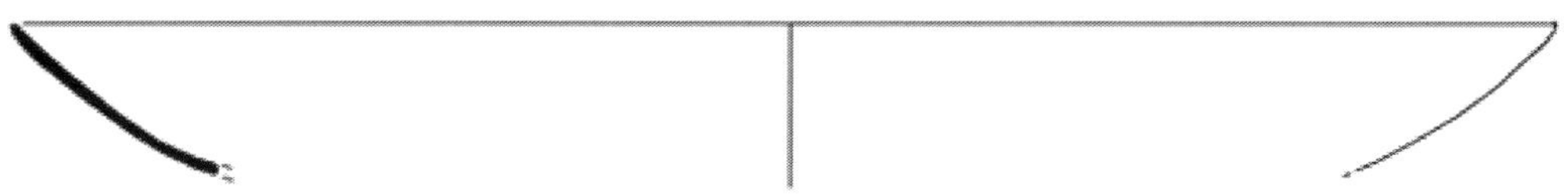

2 Hayes 50B (granular fabric)

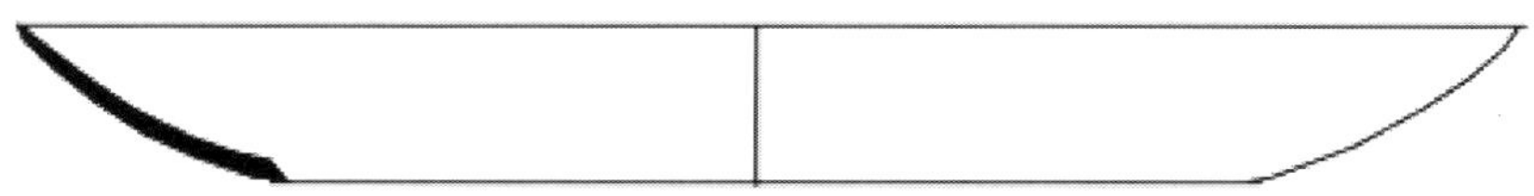

3 Hayes 50B (granular fabric)

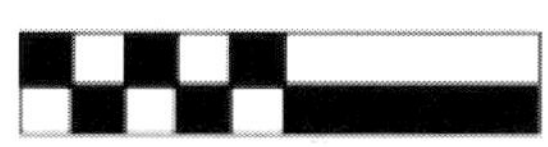

4-5 Overpainted decoration of *sigillata chiara italica tarda*

4

5

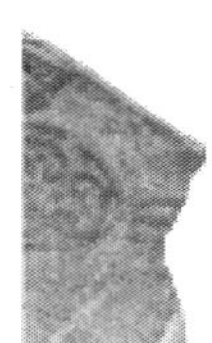

6 ARS C
with applied decoration

PLATE II

Sample types of *Sigillata chiara tarda dell'Italia centro-settentrionale* from the *Domus dei Mosaici* in Roselle

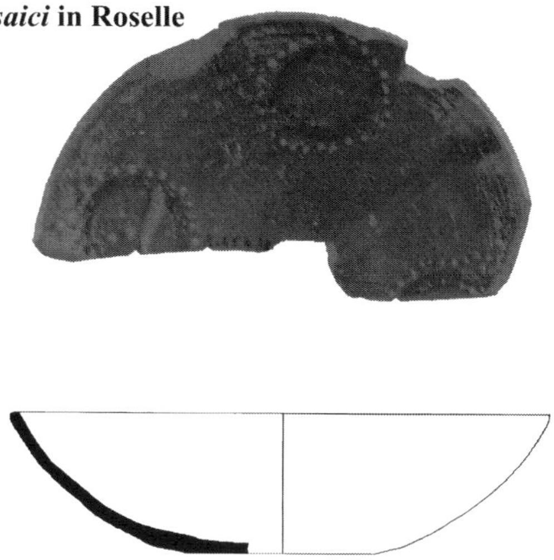

1 Dish imitating a small version of the ARS prototype Hayes 50

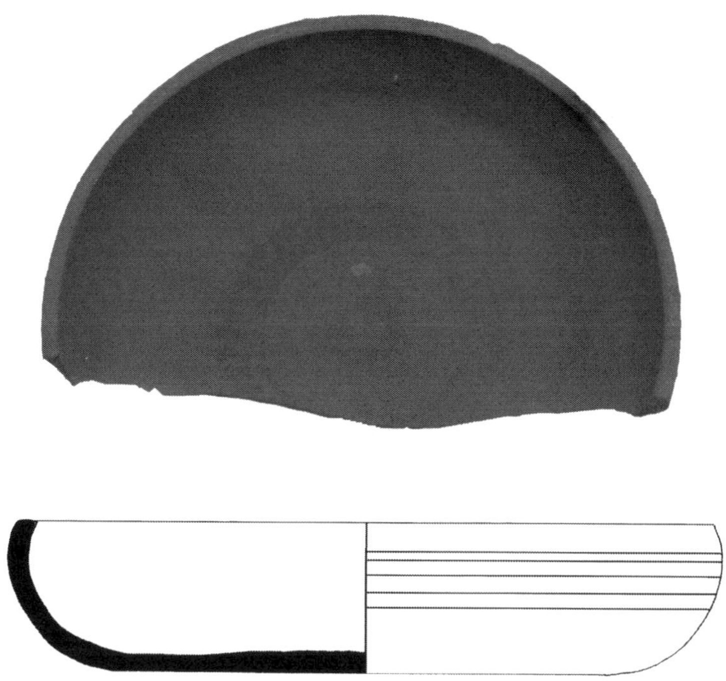

2 Large dish imitating the ARS prototype Hayes 63

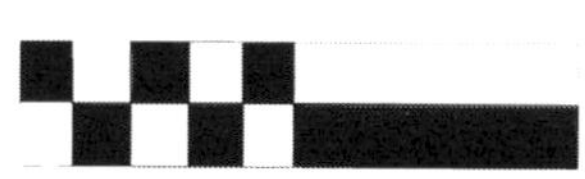

PLATE III

***Sigillata chiara tarda dell'Italia centro-settentrionale* from contexts 5147=5170 and 5141**
(Roselle, North Hill)

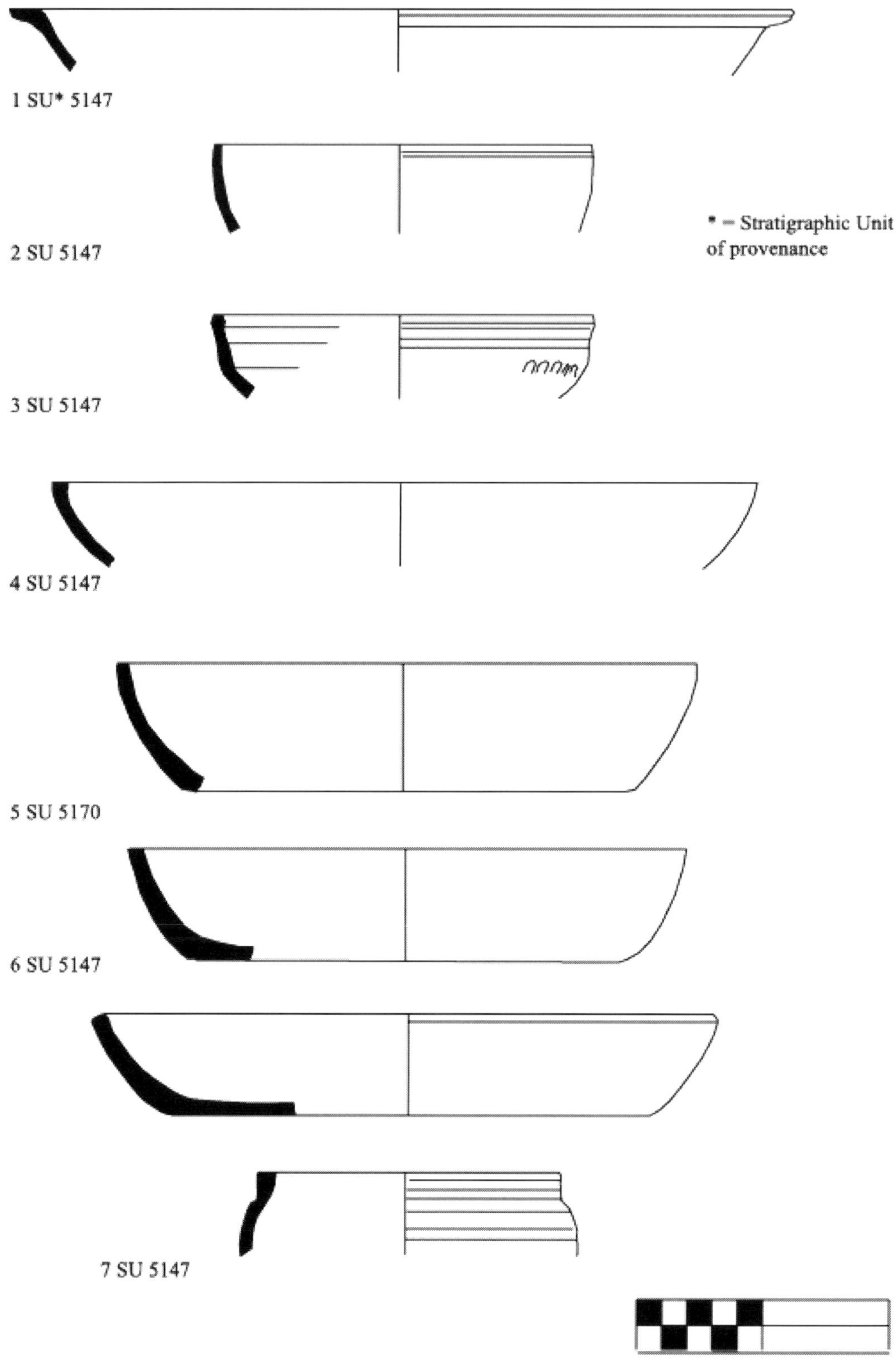

PLATE IV

Ingobbiata di rosso **ware from contexts 5147=5170 and 5141 (Roselle, North Hill)**

* = Stratigraphic Unit of provenance

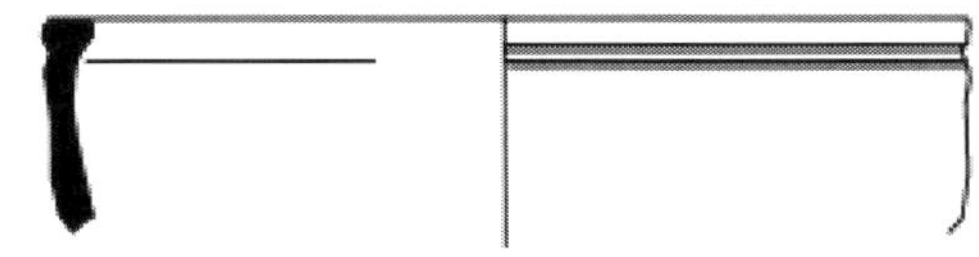

1 SU 5170*

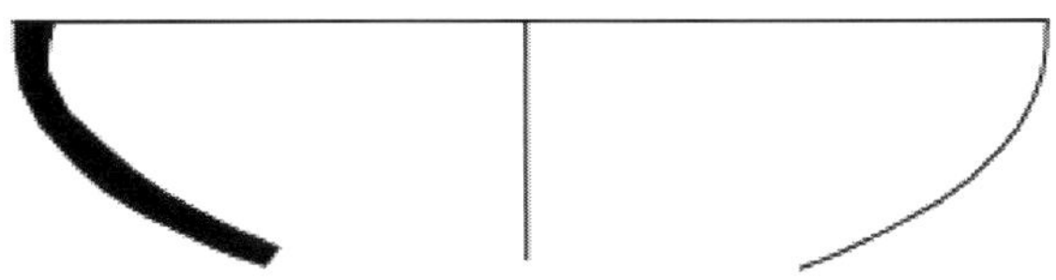

2 SU 5141

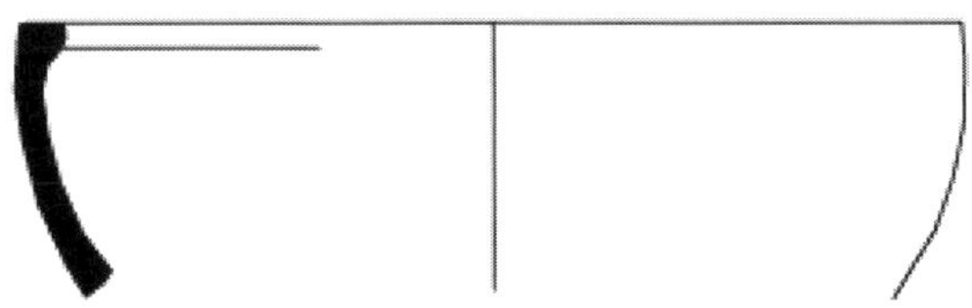

3 SU 5170

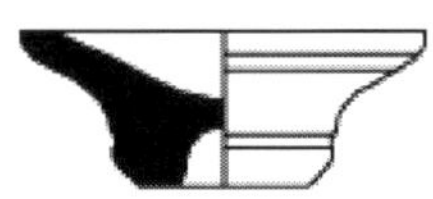

4 SU 5147

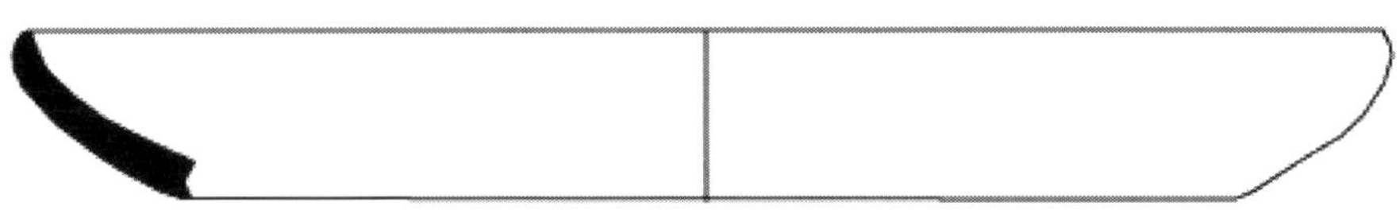

5 SU 5170

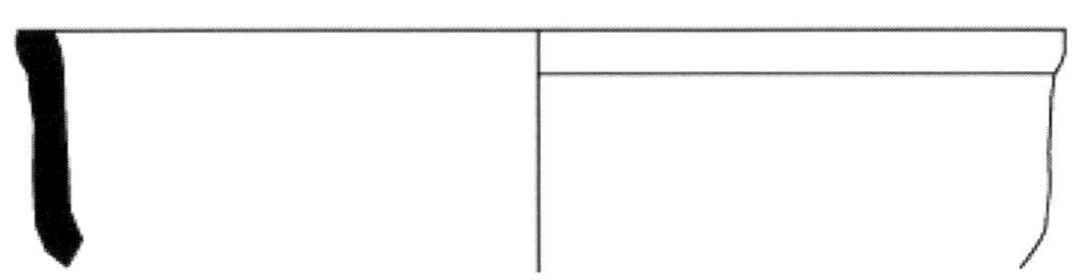

6 SU 5147

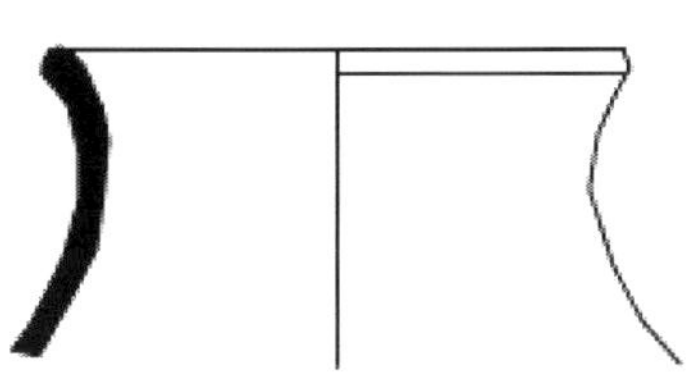

7 SU 5147

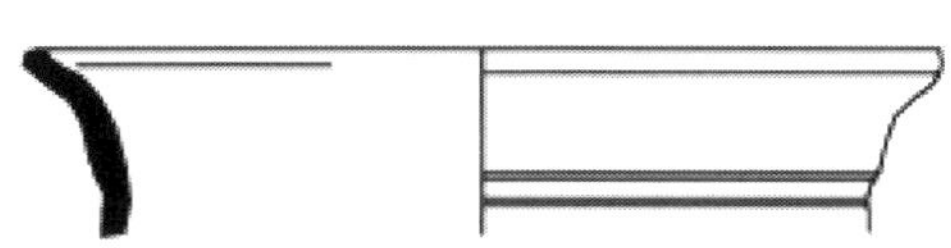

8 SU 5147

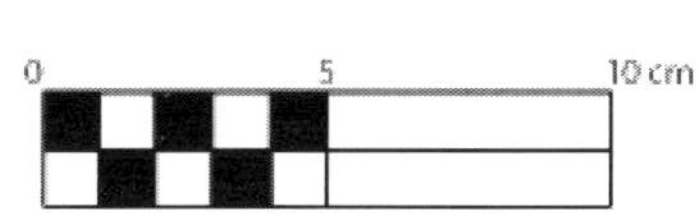

PLATE V

***Acroma depurata* ware and Soapstone from contexts 5147=5170 and 5141 (Roselle, North Hill)**

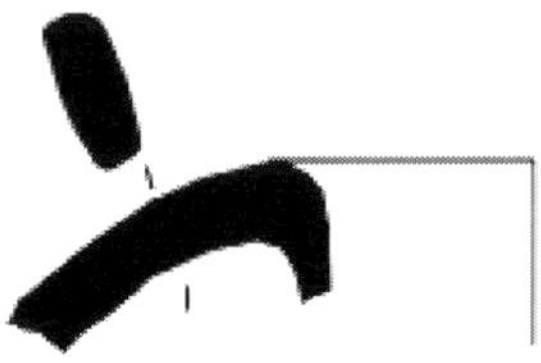

1 *Acroma Depurata* SU 5147*

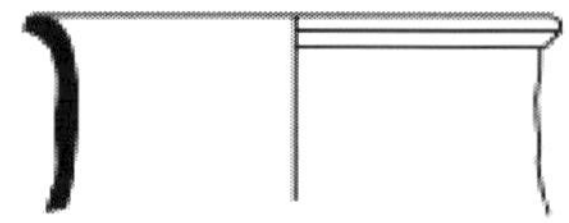

2 *Acroma Depurata* SU 5147

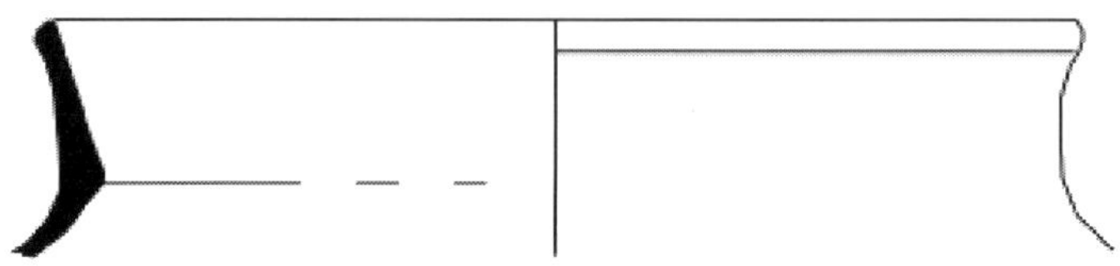

3 *Acroma Depurata* SU 5147

* = Stratigraphic Unit of provenance

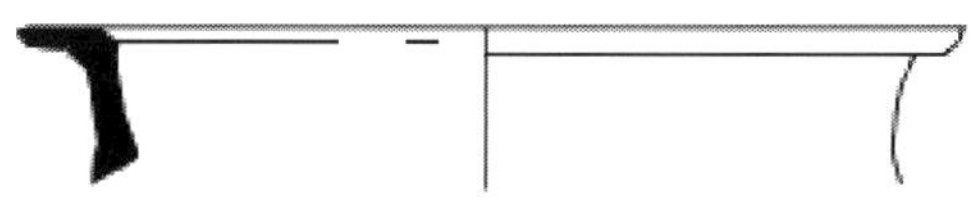

4 *Acroma Depurata* SU 5147

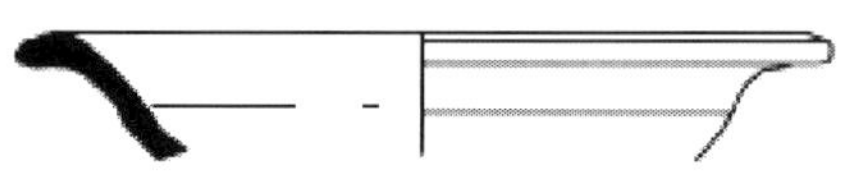

5 *Acroma Depurata* SU 5147*

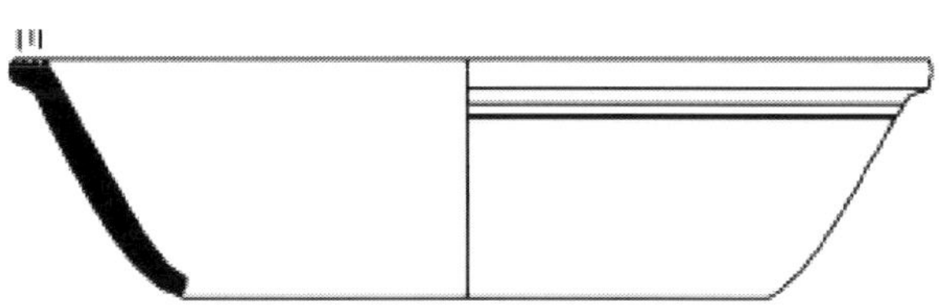

6 Soapstone SU 5147 + SU 5141

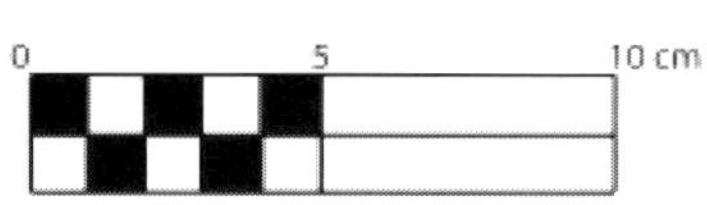

PLATE VI

Amphorae from contexts 5147=5170 and 5141 (North Hill, Roselle)

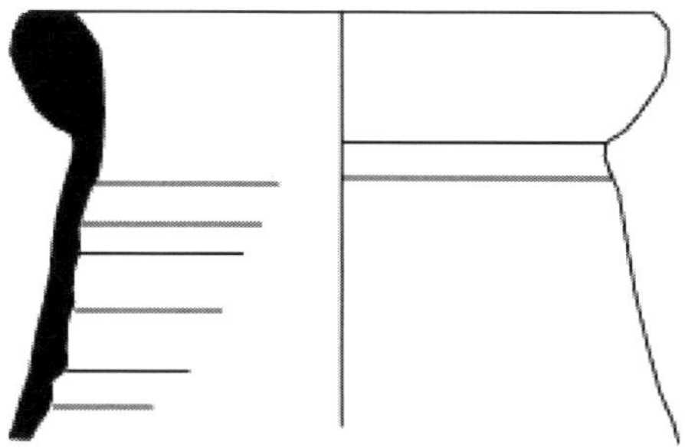

1 Keay V

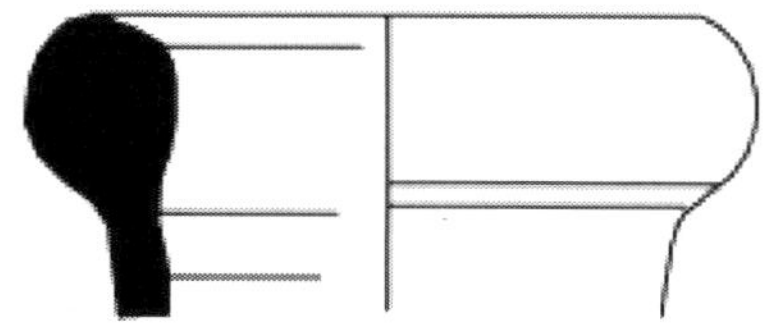

2 Keay IIIB

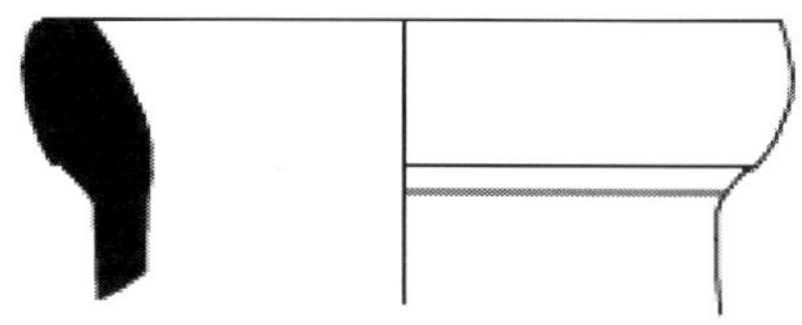

3 Keay V

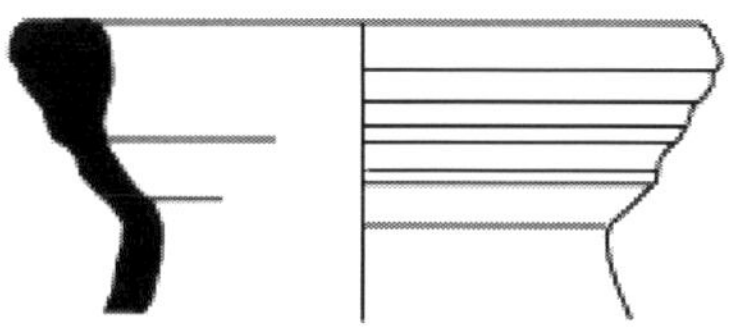

4 Keay XXIVB

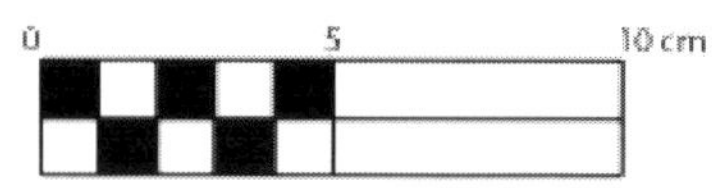

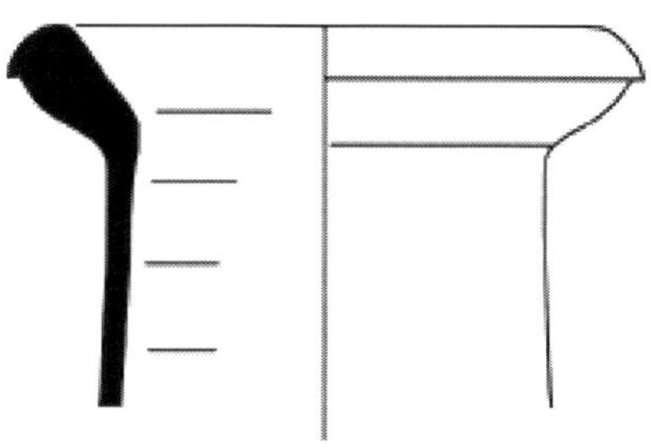

5 Keay XXVG

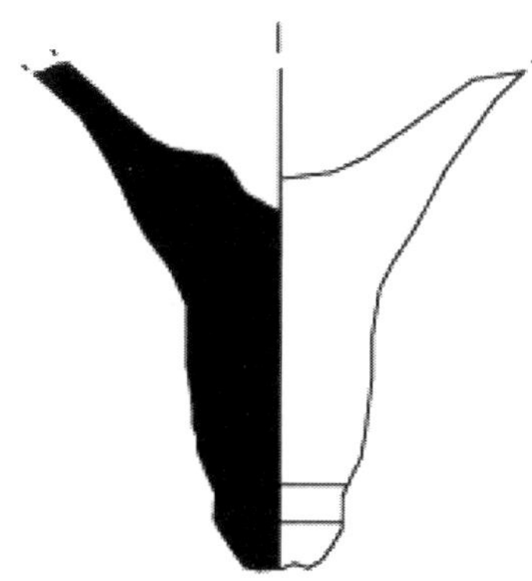

6 Possible Keay XXV spike

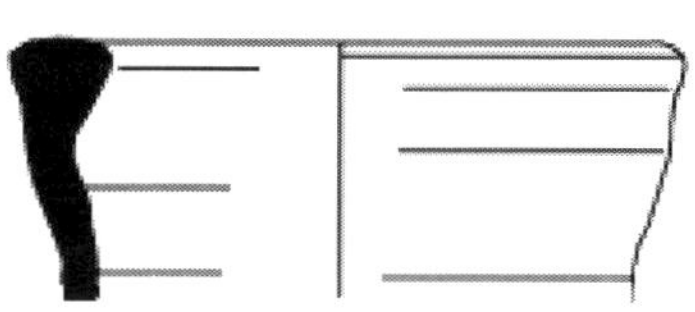

7 Early LR2

PLATE VII

Amphorae from contexts 5147=5170 and 5141 (Roselle, North Hill)

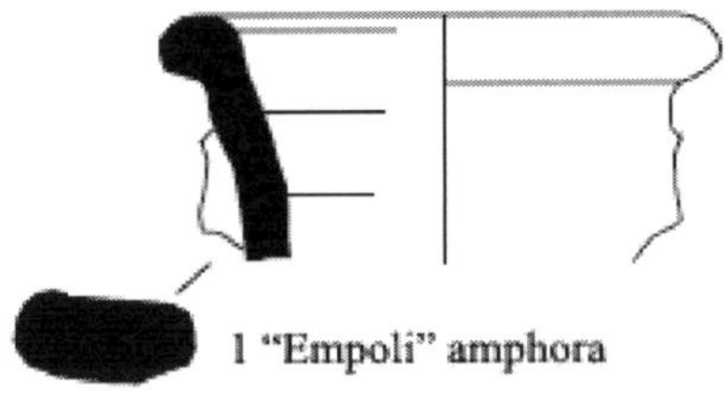

1 "Empoli" amphora

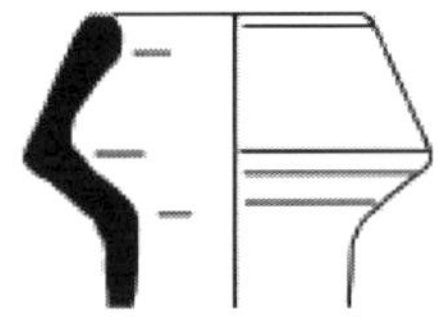

2 MR1 amphora

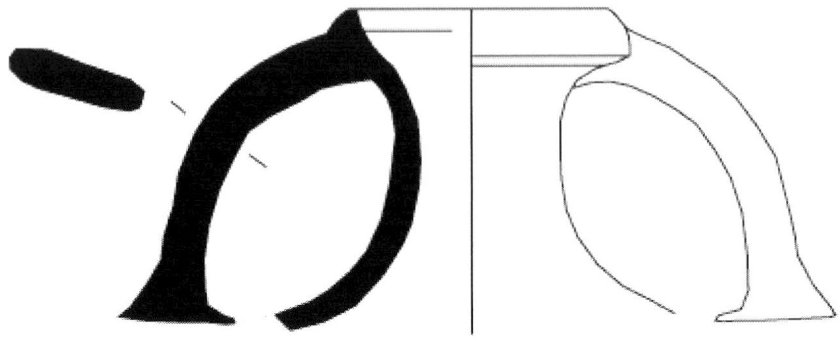

3 Keay XXIII/Almagro 51C

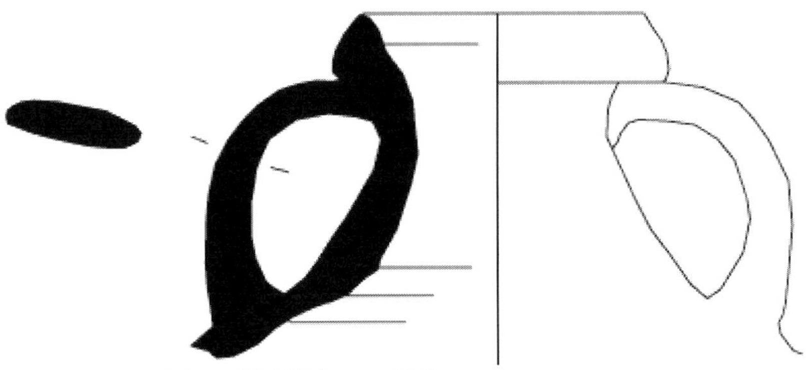

4 Keay XXIII/Almagro 51C

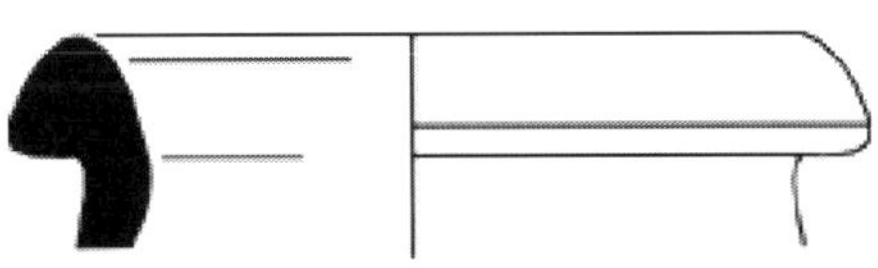

5 Keay XIIIA/Dressel 23

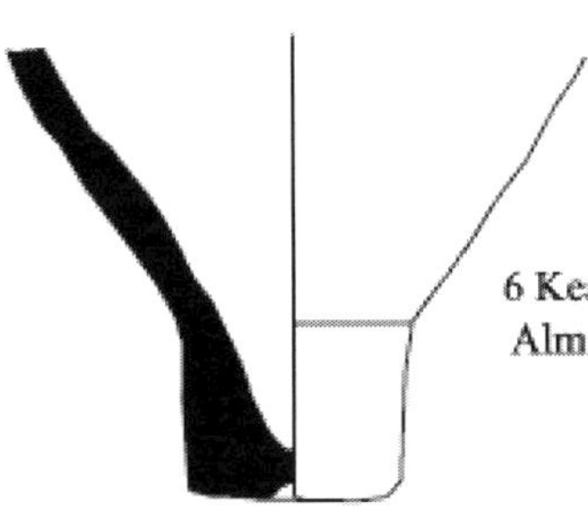

6 Keay XXIII/ Almagro 51C

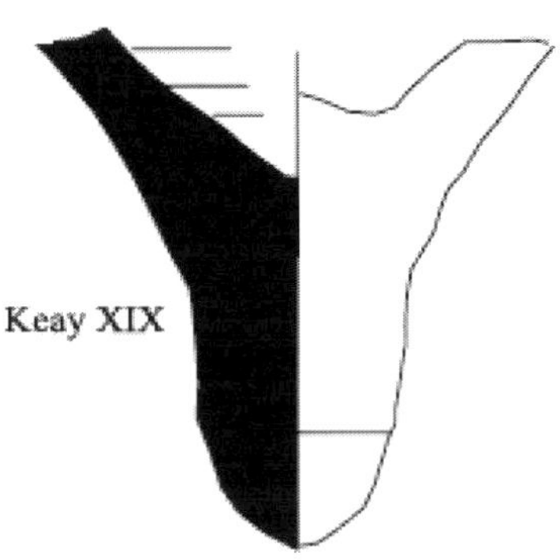

7 Keay XIX

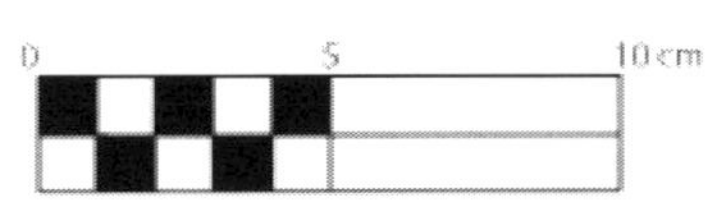

PLATE VIII

Cooking pots in kitchen ware from contexts 5147=5170 and 5141 (Roselle, North Hill): types

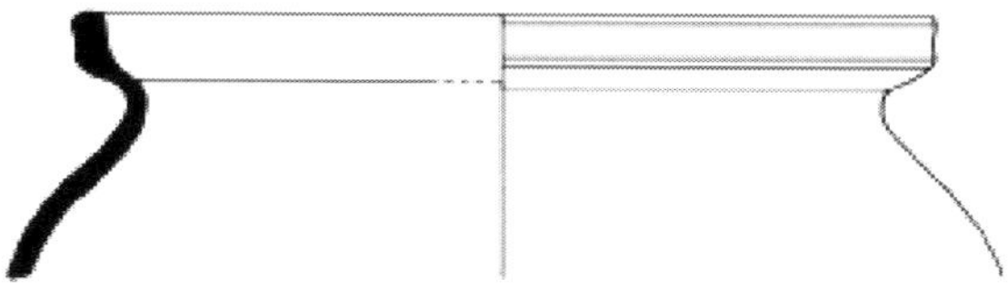

1 Type 1, SU 5147*

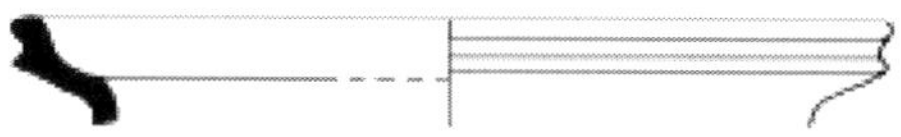

2 Type 1, SU 5147

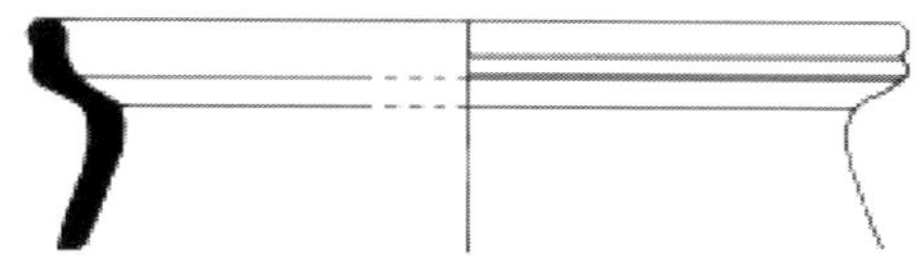

3 Type 1, SU 5147

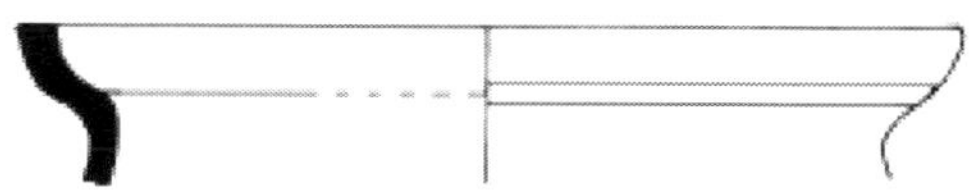

4 Type 1 (variant), SU 5147

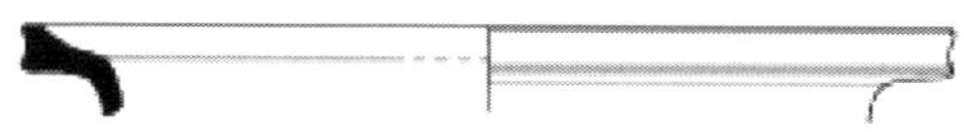

5 Type 1, SU 5147

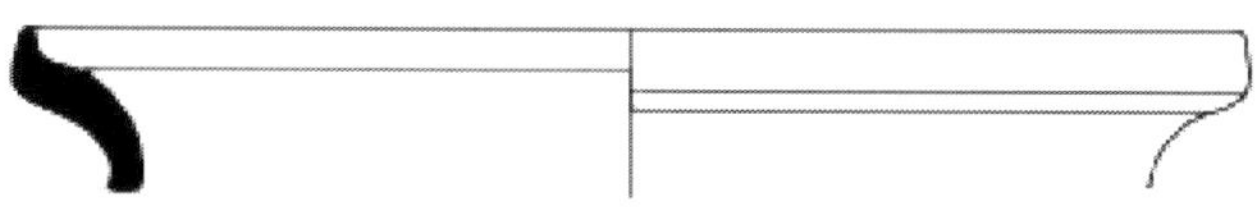

6 Type 2, SU 5147

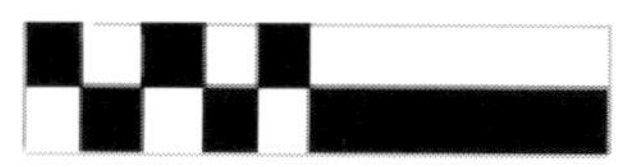

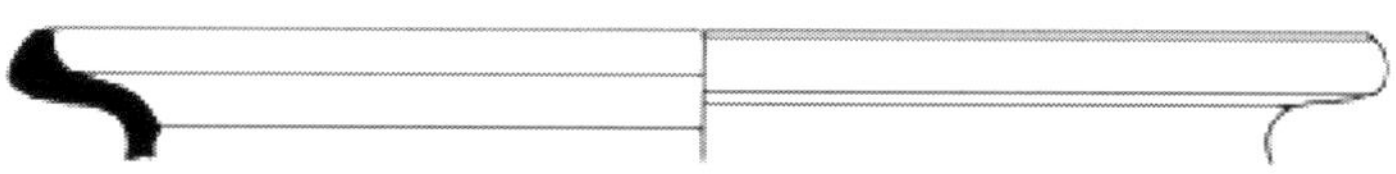

7 Type 2, SU 5147

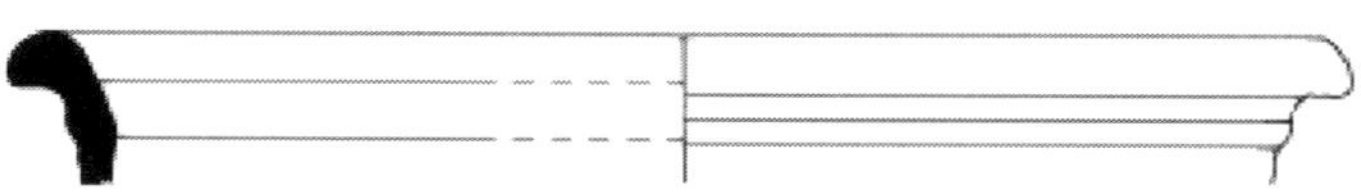

8 Type 3, SU 5147

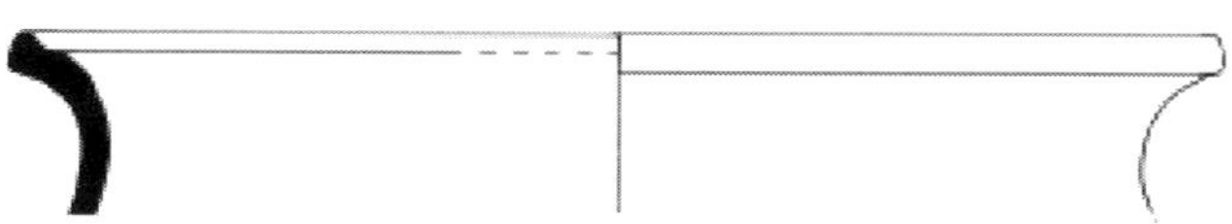

9 Type 4, SU 5147 and SU 5141

* = Stratigraphic Unit of provenance

PLATE IX

Casseroles, cooking-pans and bowl-lids in kitchen ware from context 5147=5170 (Roselle, North Hill)

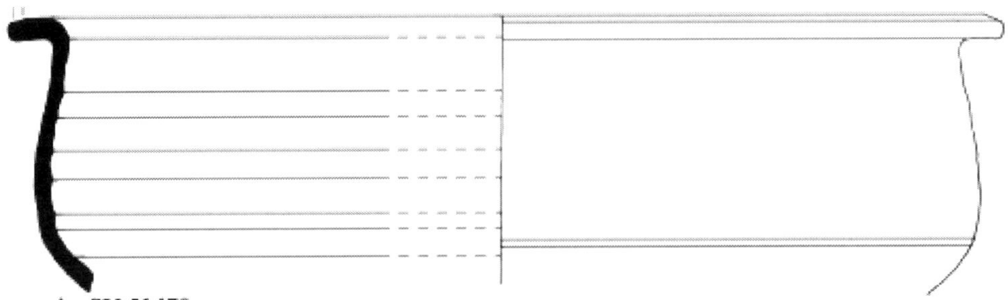

1 Casserole, SU 5147*

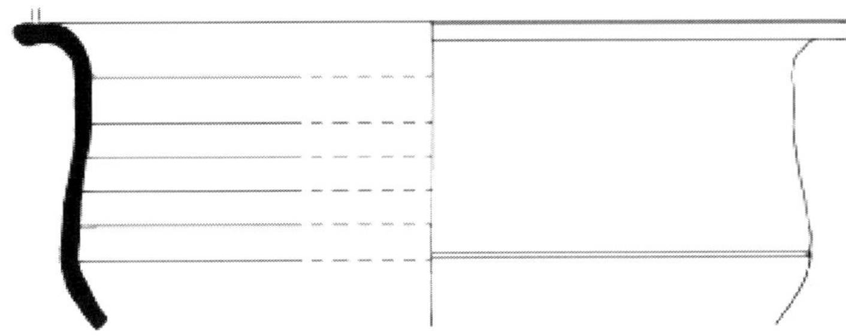

2 Casserole, SU 5147

*SU = Stratigraphic Unit of provenance

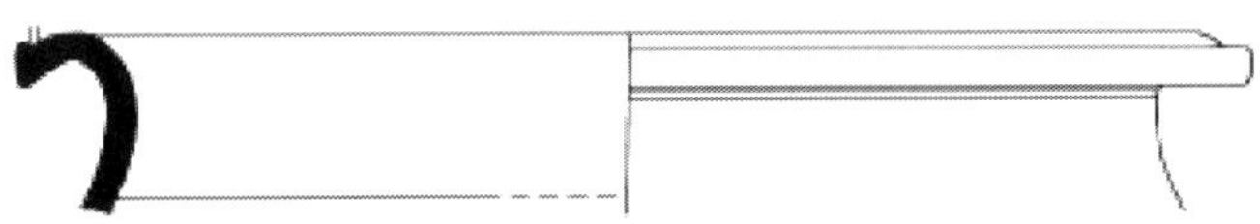

3 Casserole, SU 5147

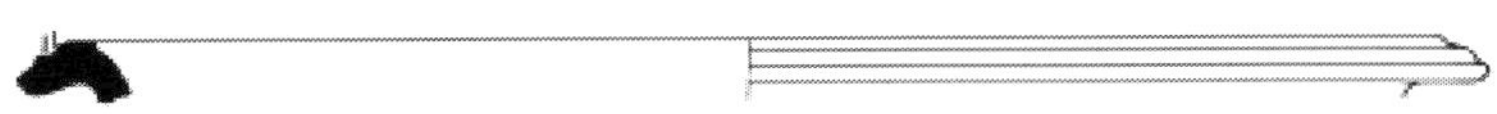

4 Casserole, SU 5147

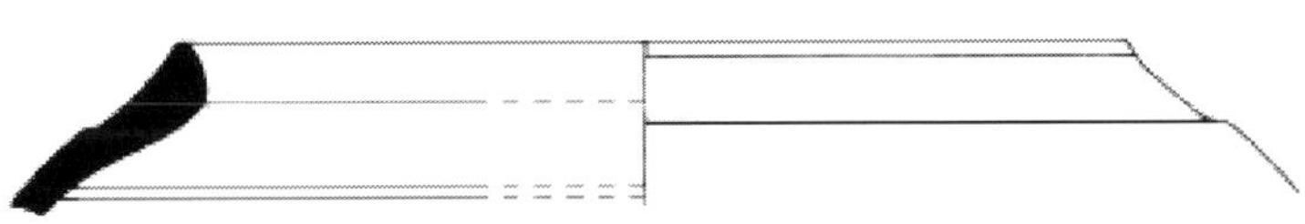

5 Casserole, SU 5147

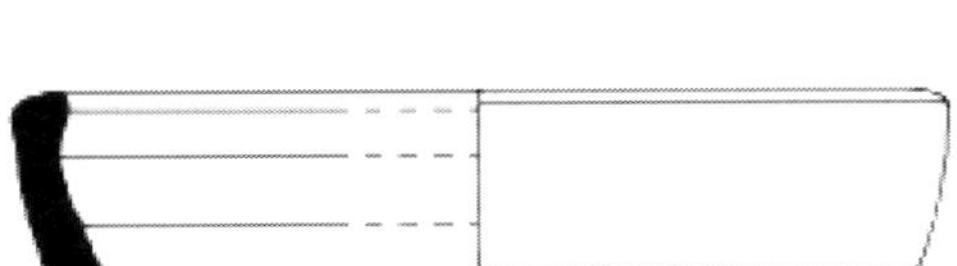

6 Cooking pan, SU 5147

7 Bowl-lid, SU 5147

PLATE X

Cooking-pans and lids in kitchen ware from context 5147=5170 (Roselle, North Hill)

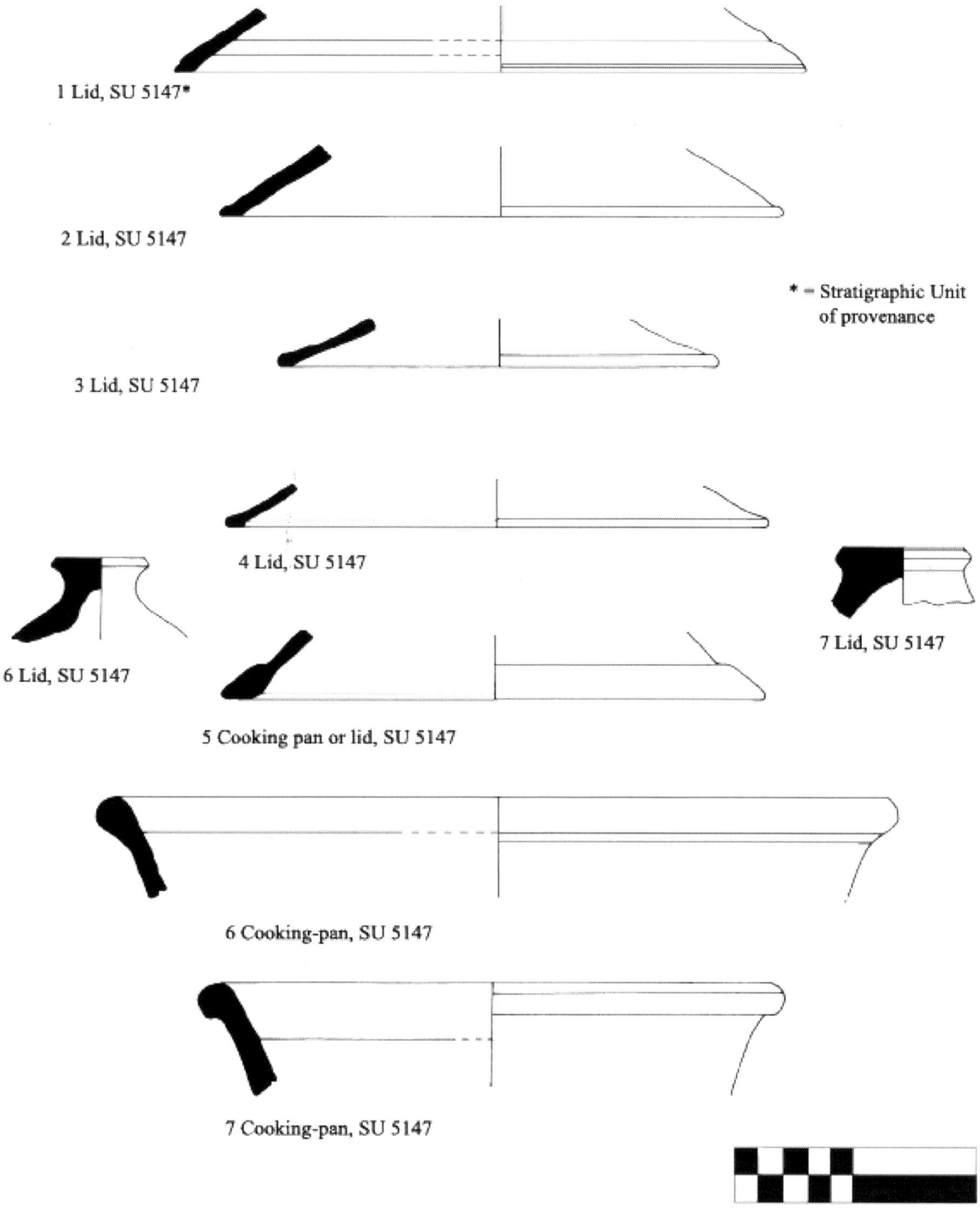

PLATE XI

Ingobbiata di Rosso and _Colature Rosse_ wares from context SU 1262 (AD 500-550)
(Roselle, North Hill)

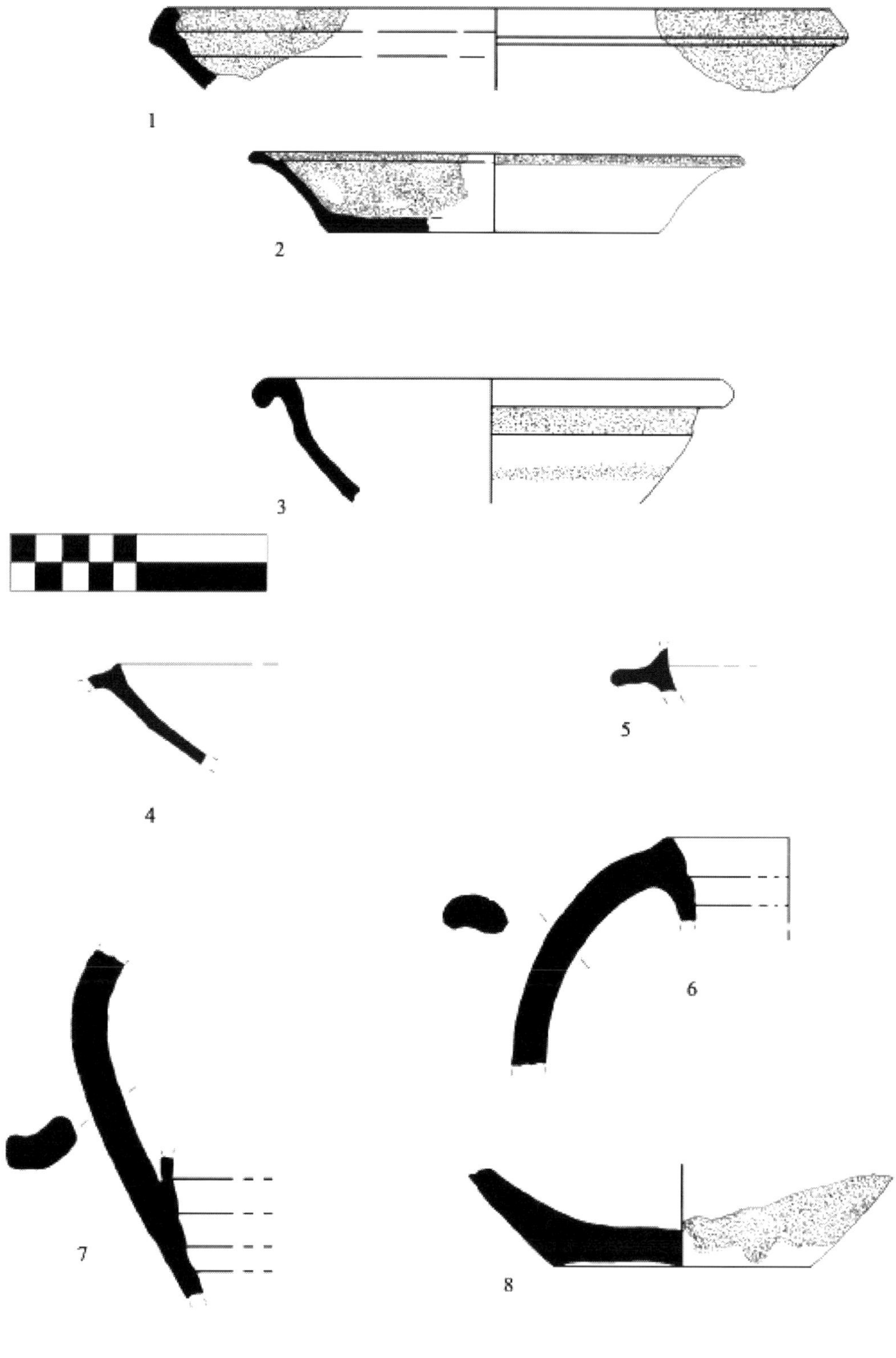

PLATE XII

Cooking pots in kitchen ware from context SU 1262 (AD 500-550)
(Roselle, North Hill)

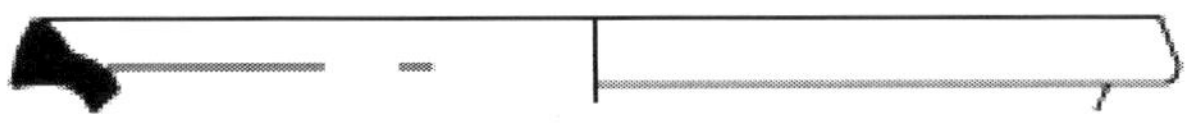

1 Cooking pot, Type 2

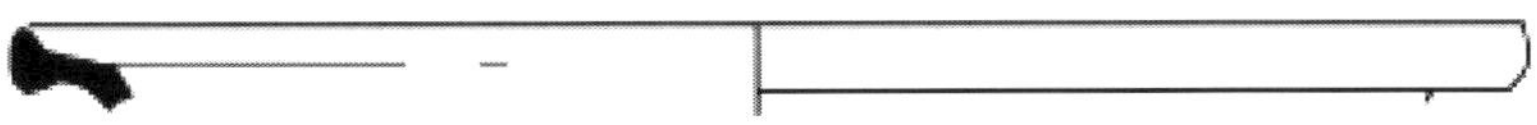

2 Cooking pot, Type 2

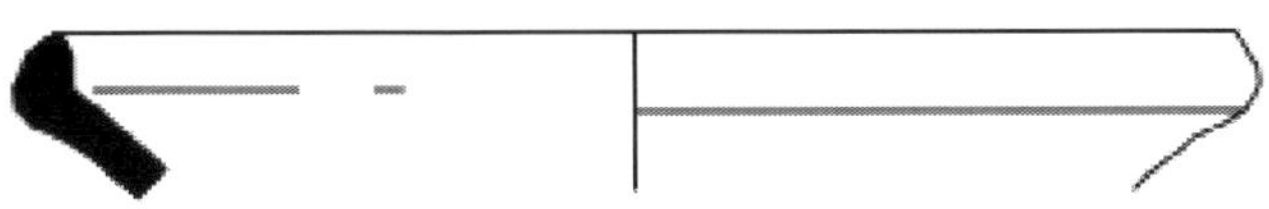

3 Cooking pot, Type 2

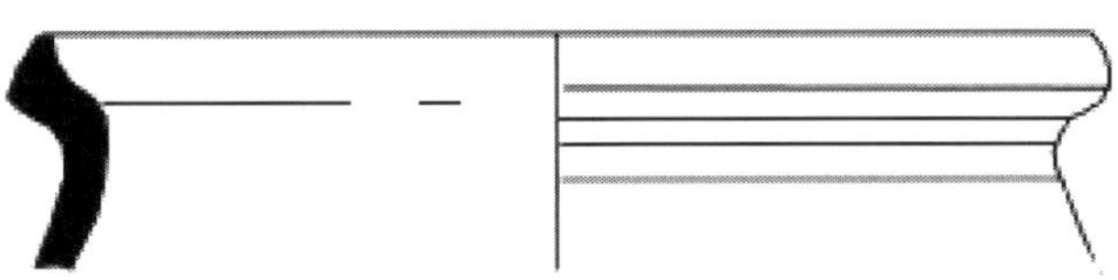

4 Cooking pot, Type 5

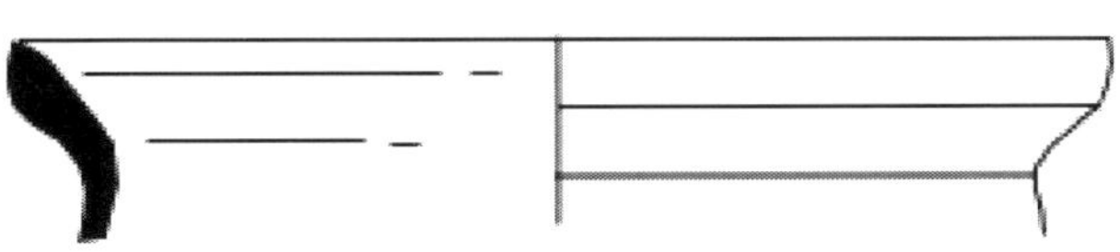

5 Cooking pot, Type 6

6 Cooking pot, flat base

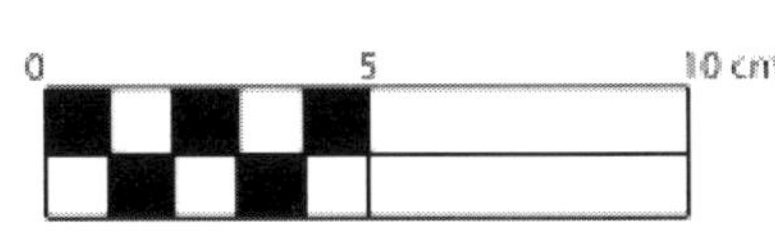

PLATE XIII

Amphorae from context SU 1260: AD 550-600 (Roselle, North Hill)

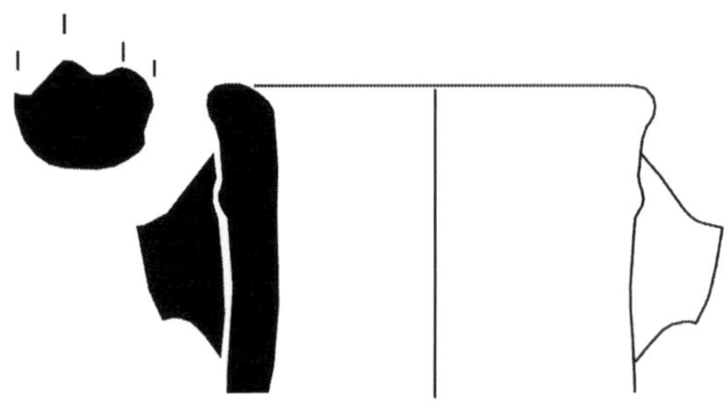

1 LR1 amphora

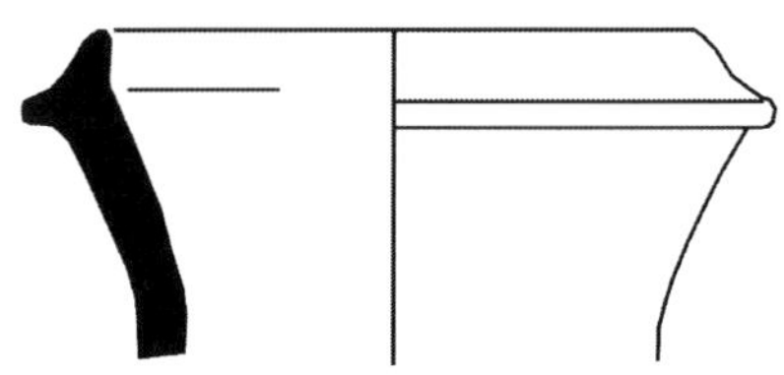

2 Keay LII

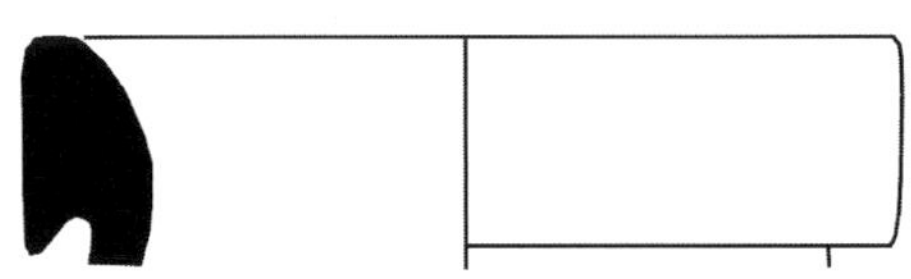

3 Keay LXI

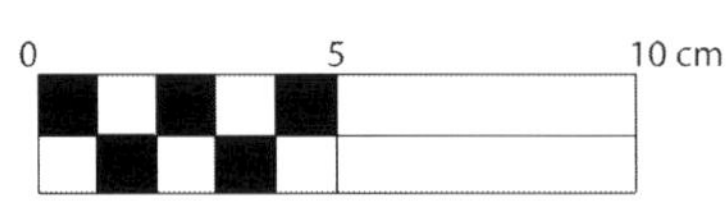

PLATE XIV

Ingobbiata di Rosso and *Colature Rosse* wares from context SU 1260 (AD 550-600)
(Roselle, North Hill)

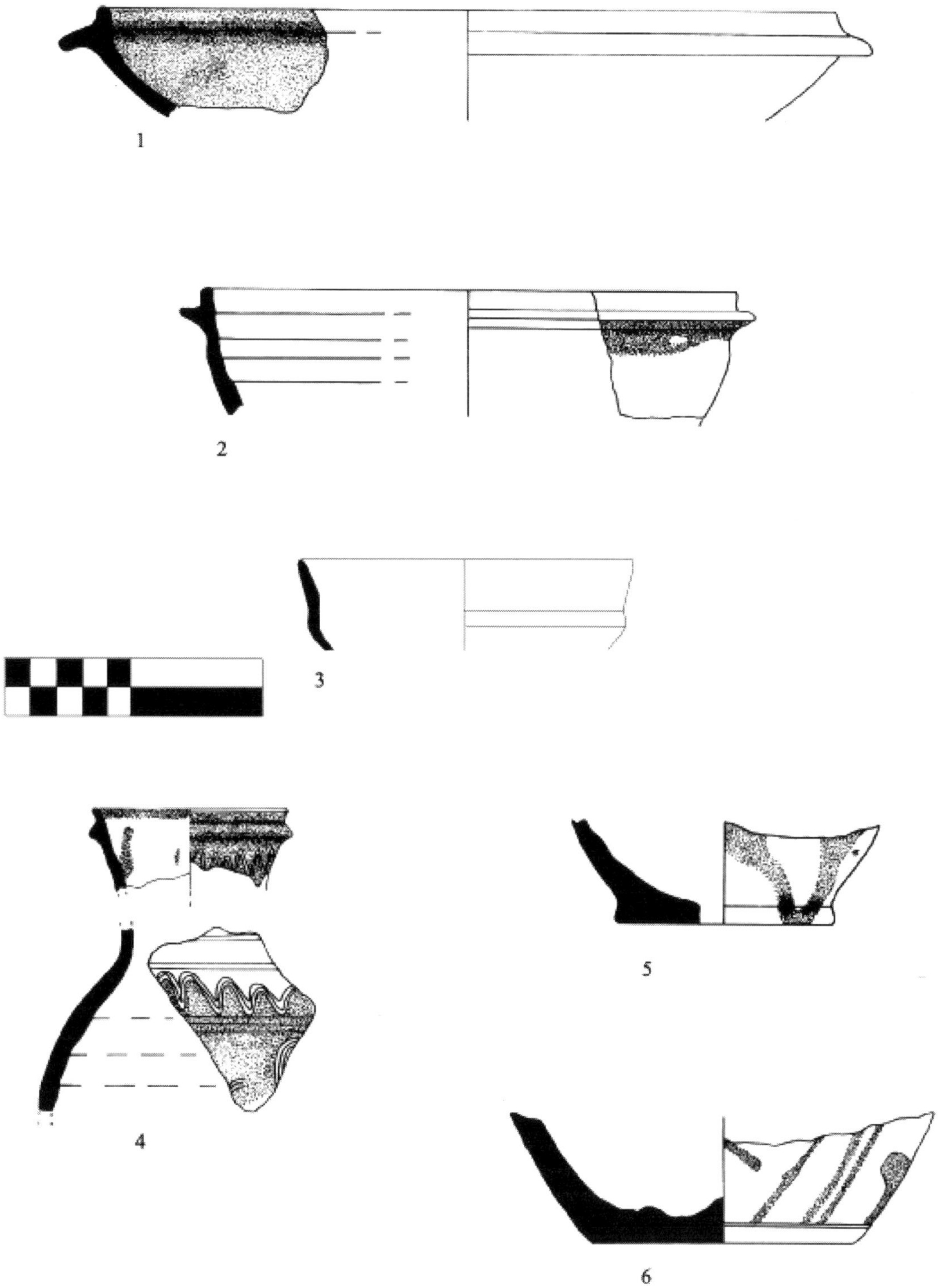

PLATE XV

Cooking pots in kitchen ware from context SU 1260 (AD 550-600)
(Roselle, North Hill)

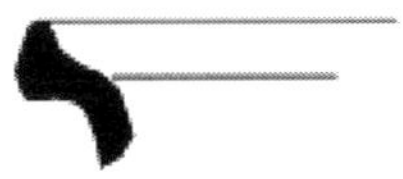

1 Cooking pot, Type 2

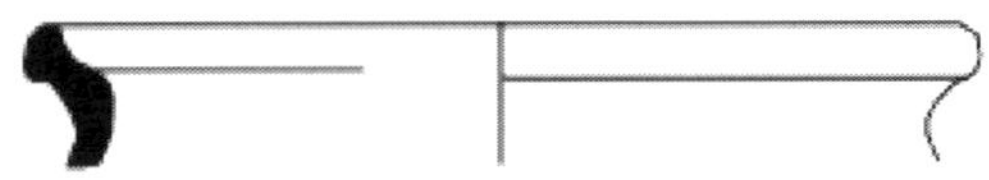

2 Cooking pot, Type 2

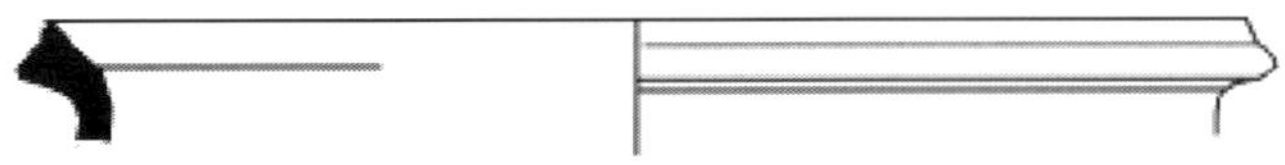

3 Cooking pot, Type 7 (variant 1)

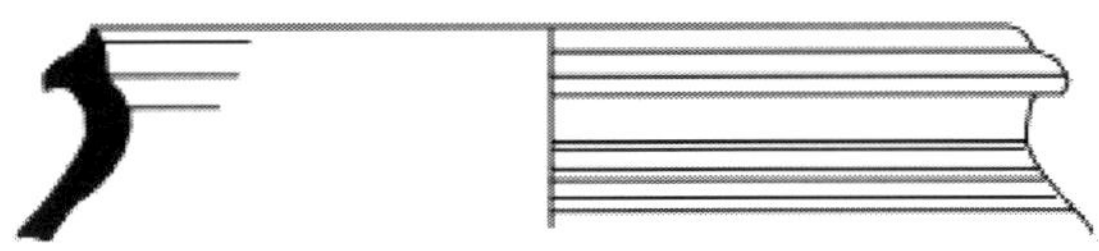

4 Cooking pot, Type 7 (variant 2)

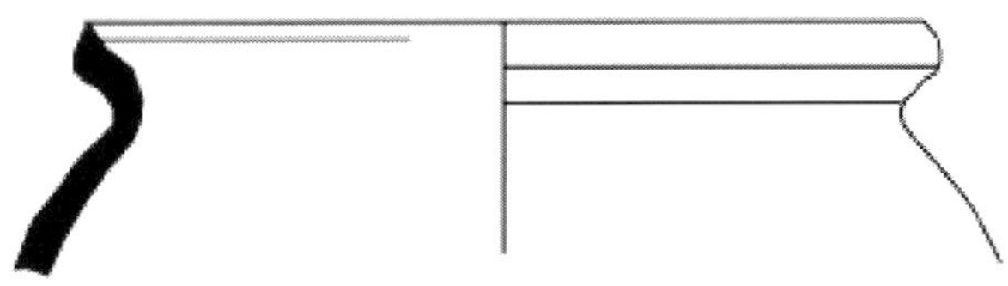

5 Cooking pot, Type 5

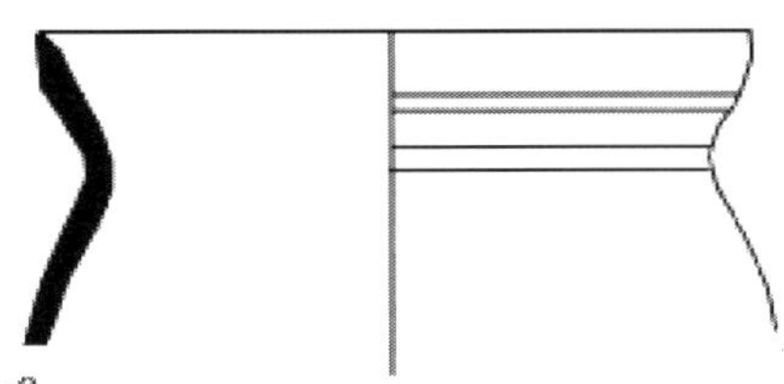

6 Cooking pot, Type 8

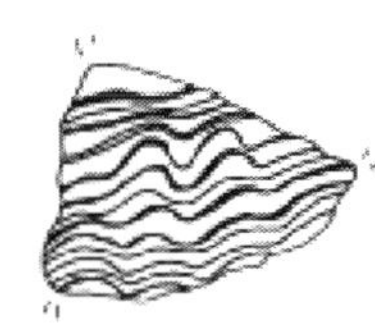

9 wall with weavy lines

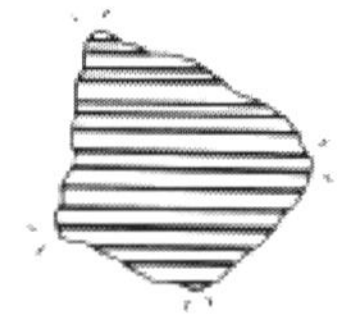

8 wall with combed decoration

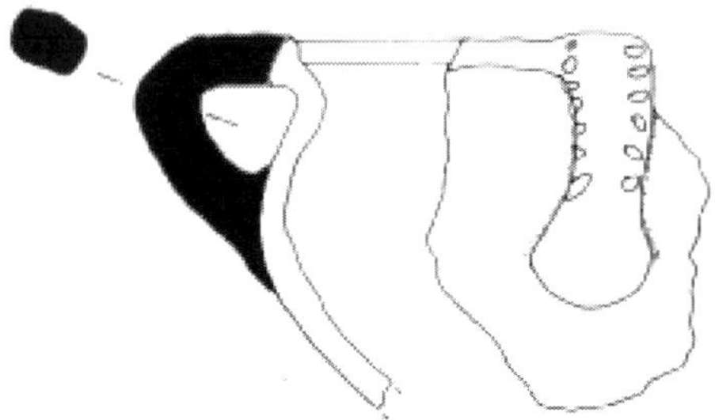

7 Cooking pot, Type 2 (variant)

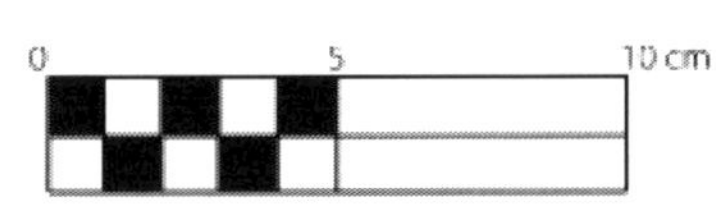

PLATE XVI

Open forms in kitchen ware from context SU 1260 (AD 550-600)
(Roselle, North Hill)

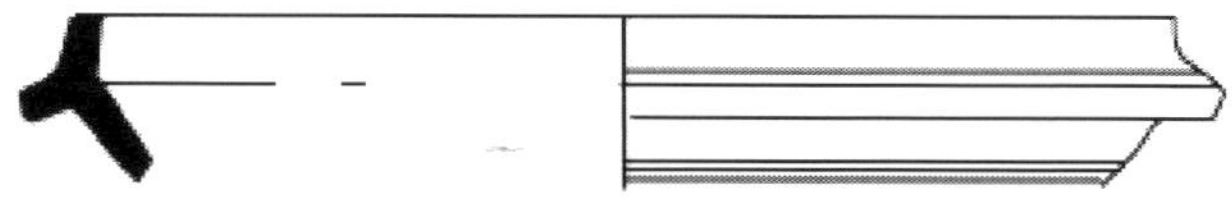

1 Flanged-bowl

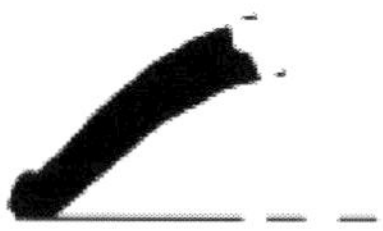

2 Lid

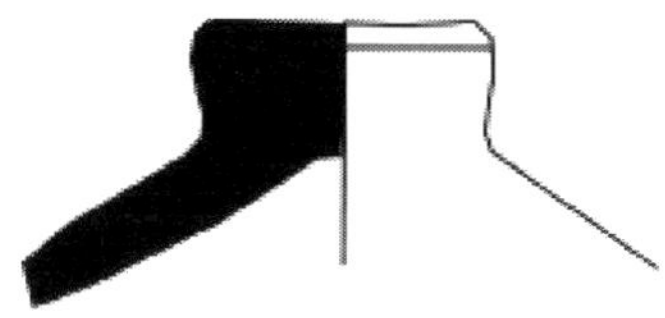

3 Lid

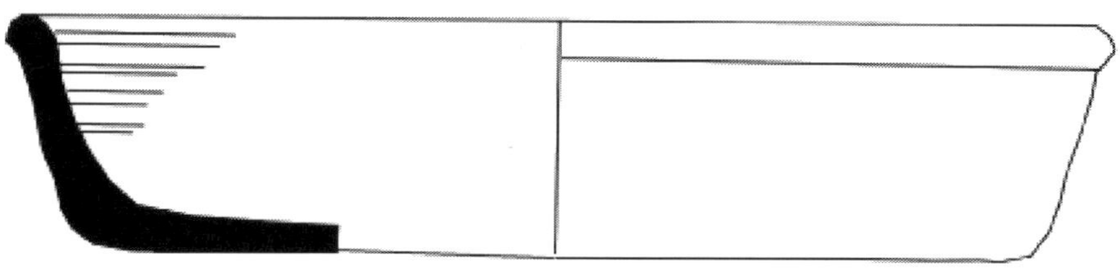

4 Cooking-pan

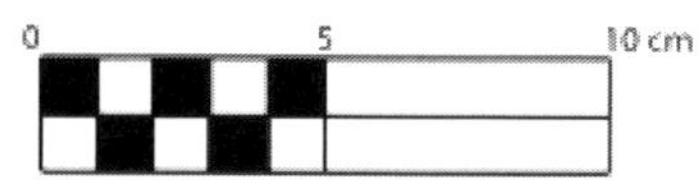

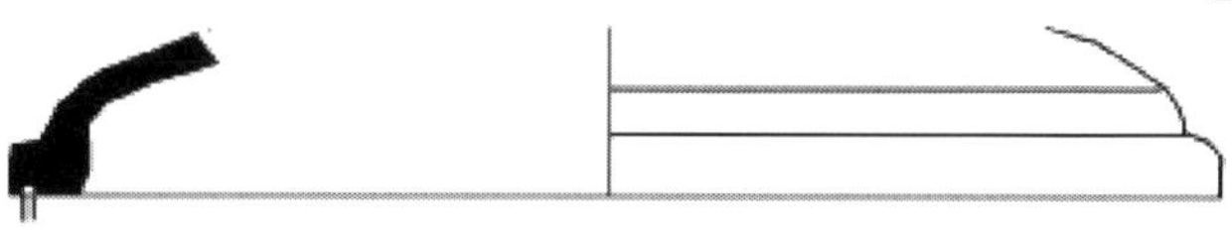

5 Bowl-lid

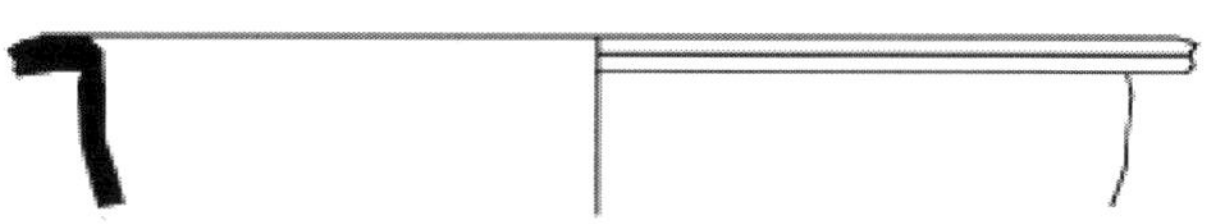

6 Casserole

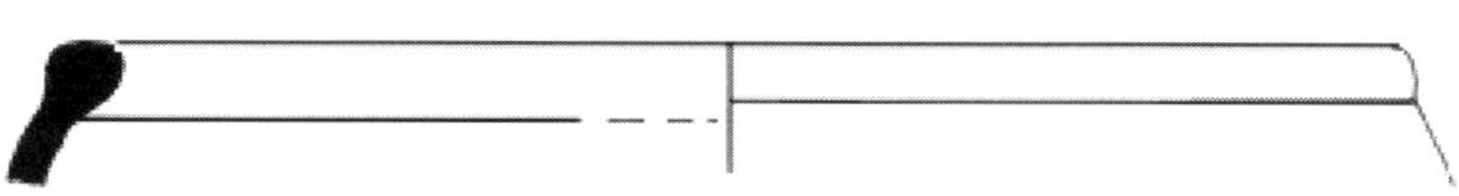

7 Casserole

PLATE XVII

Miscellaneous forms in *Colature Rosse* ware and one amphora from other contexts in Roselle: ca. AD 550-600

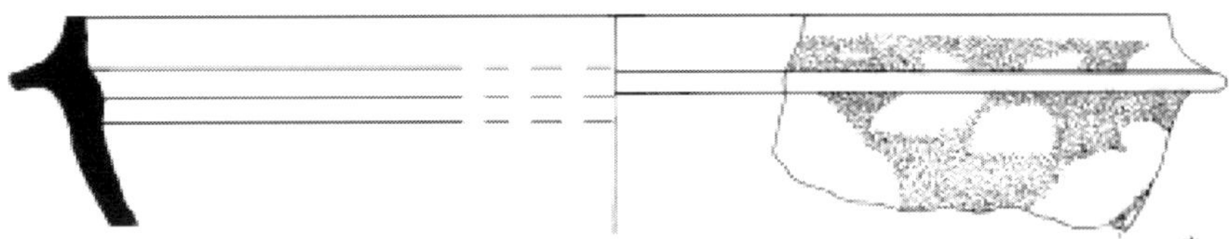

1 Flanged-bowl in *Colature Rosse* ware from SU 1310* (North Hill)

* = Stratigraphic Unit of provenance

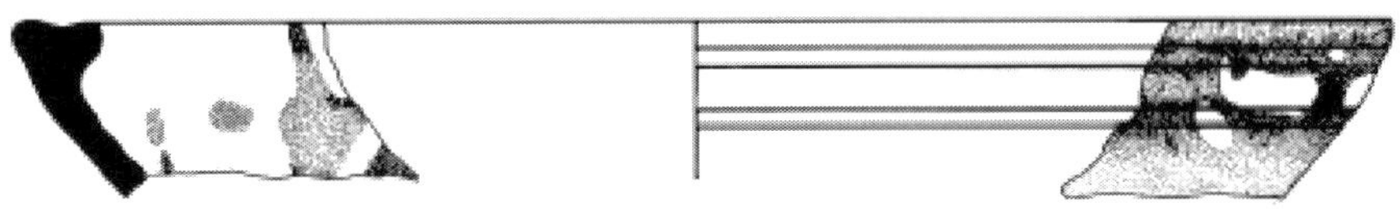

2 Bowl in *Colature Rosse* ware from SU 1310 (North Hill)

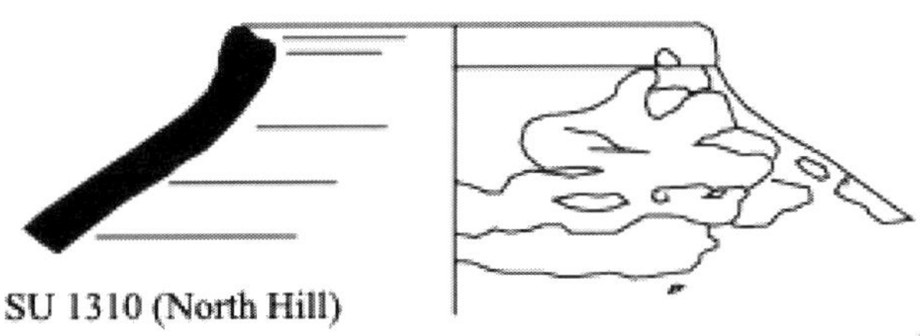

3 LR4 amphora from SU 1310 (North Hill)

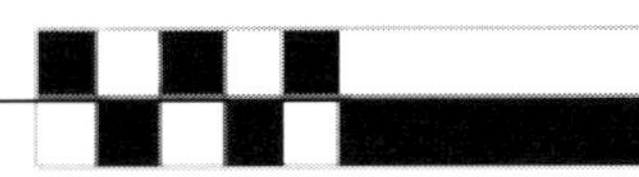

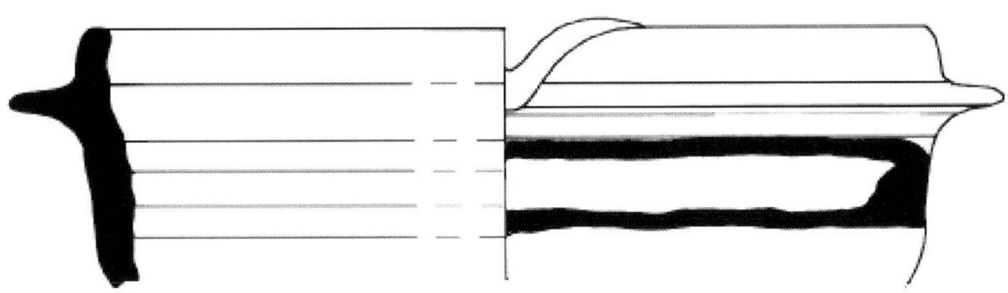

4 Flanged-bowl in *Colature Rosse* ware from the Cistern on the South Hill (late antique dump)

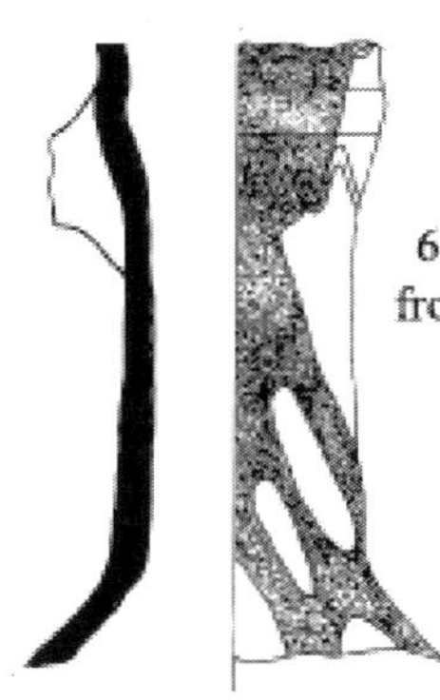

6 Bottle in *Colature Rosse* ware from the Cistern on the South Hill (late antique dump)

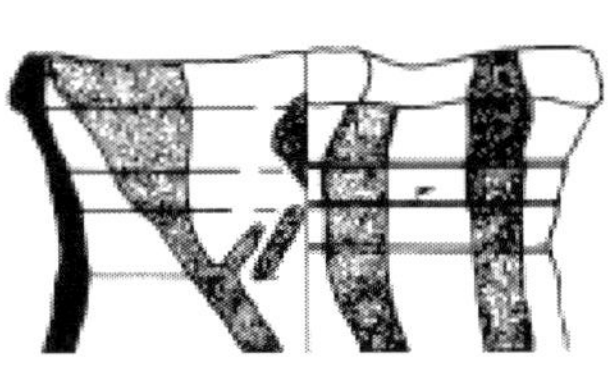

5 Jug in *Colature Rosse* ware from the Cistern on the South Hill (late antique dump)

PLATE XVIII

Dérivées des sigillées paléochrétiennes (DSP)
from the villa site of Santa Francesca
(Talamone)

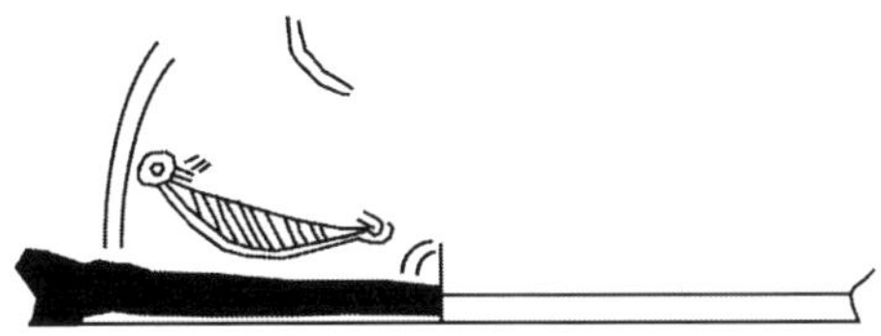

1

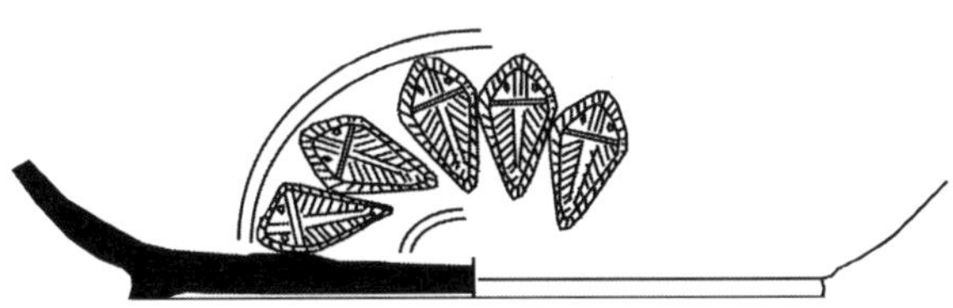

2

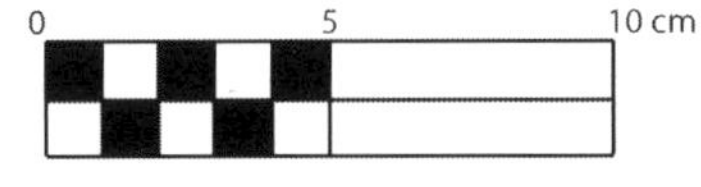

PLATE XIX

ARS types
(3rd to 5th/early 6th AD)
from the territory

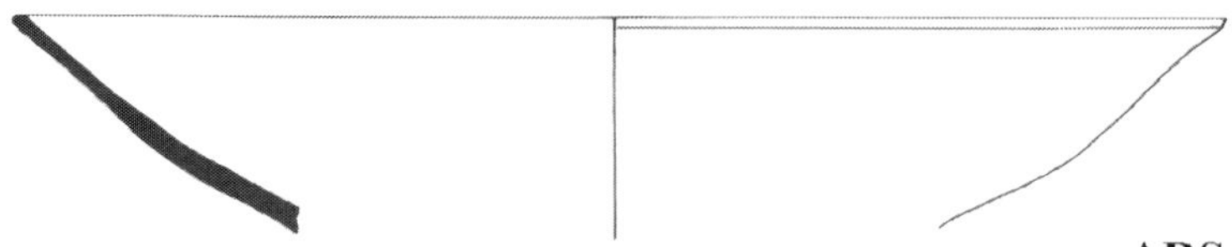

1 Hayes 50A

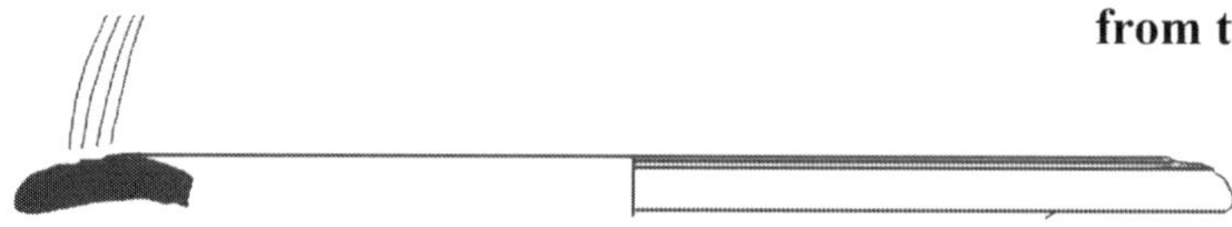

2 Atlante I, Pl.XXVIII, 7

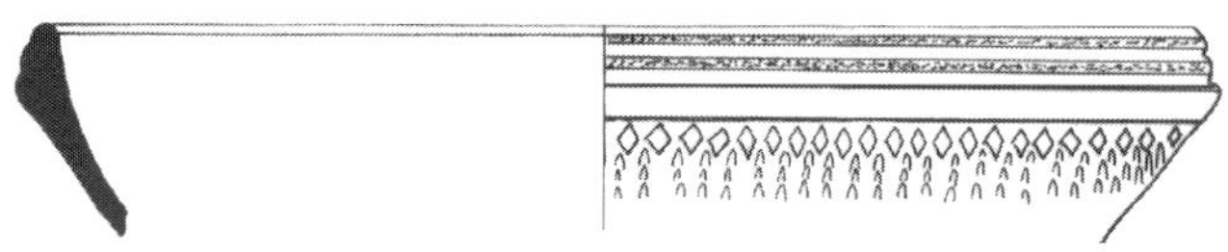

3 Hayes 84

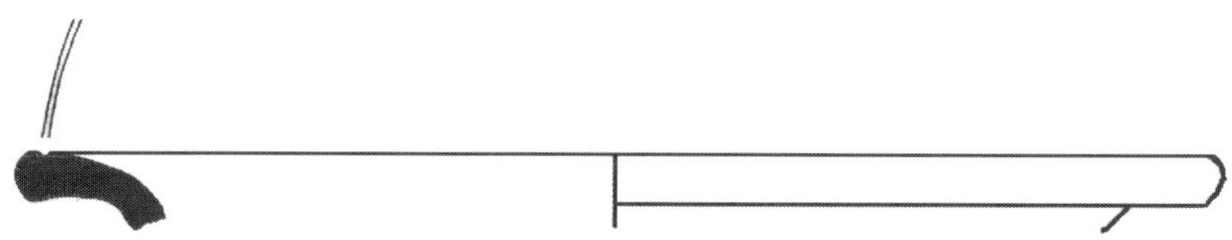

4 Hayes 67

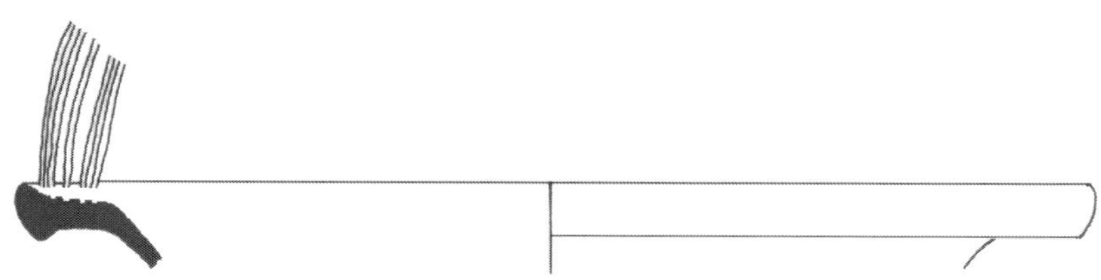

5 Hayes 76

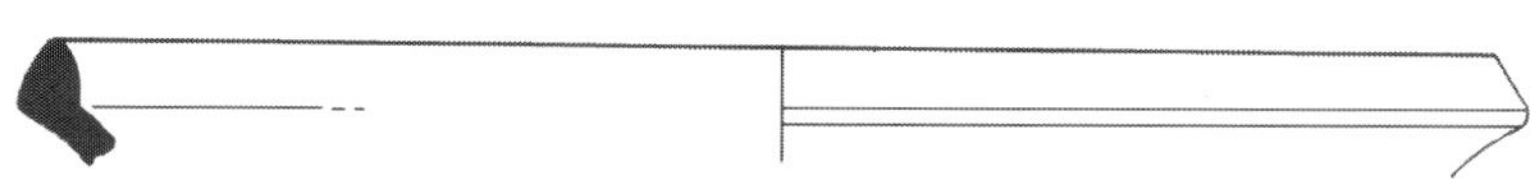

6 Hayes 61B

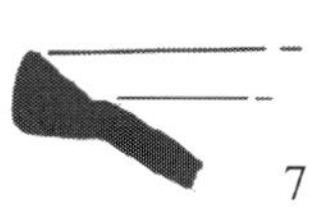

7 Hayes 61B

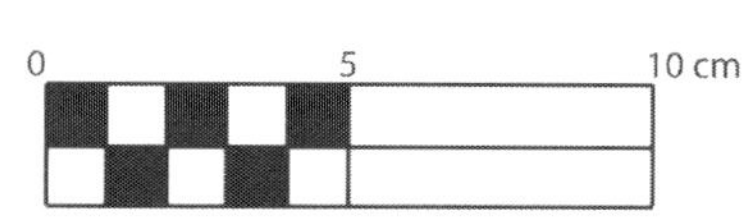

PLATE XX

ARS types (5th to 6th AD) from the territiry

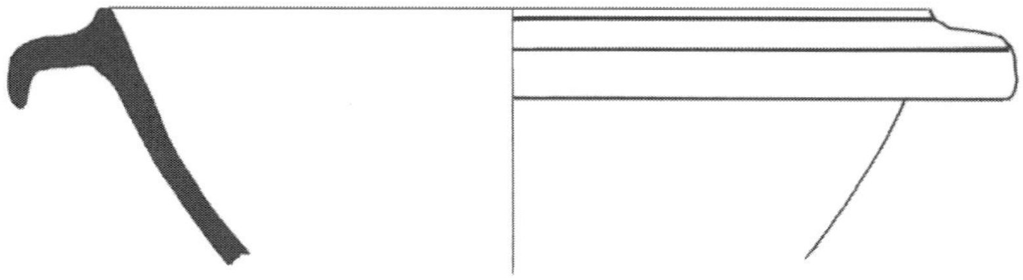

1 Hayes 91B

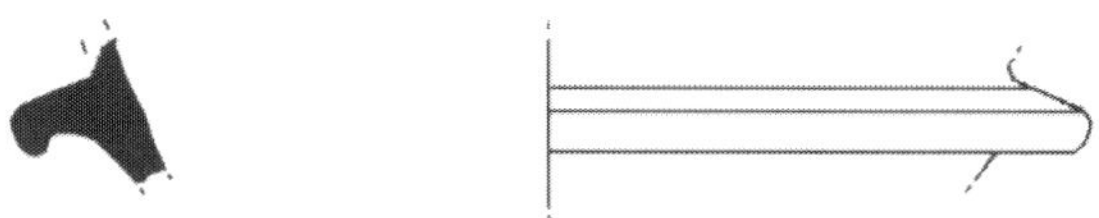

2 Hayes 91C

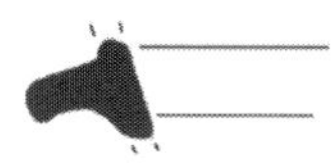

3 Hayes 91C

4 Hayes 99A

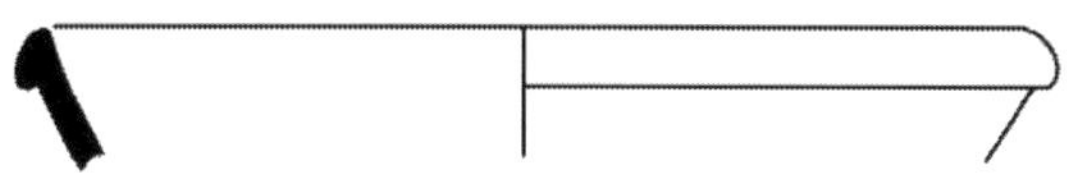

5 Hayes 99B

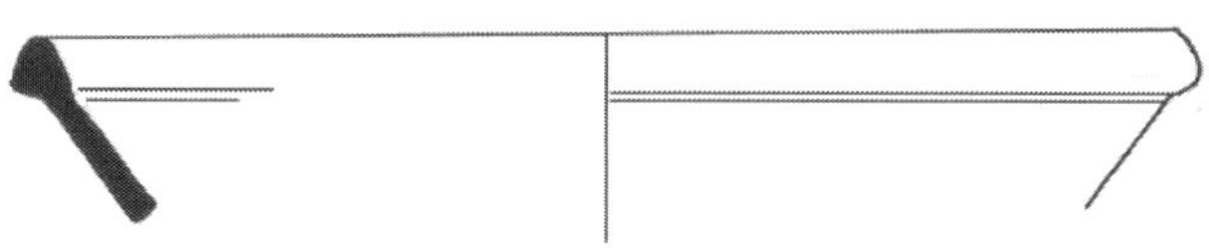

6 Hayes 80B/99

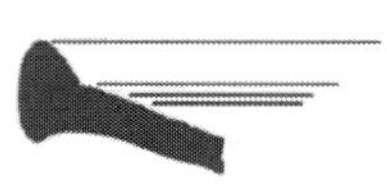

7 Hayes 104A

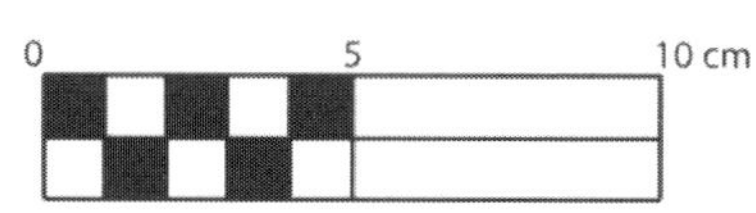

PLATE XXI

Mid to Late Roman Tunisian amphorae from the territory

(*) Re-drawn after
Ciampoltrini-Rendini 1990

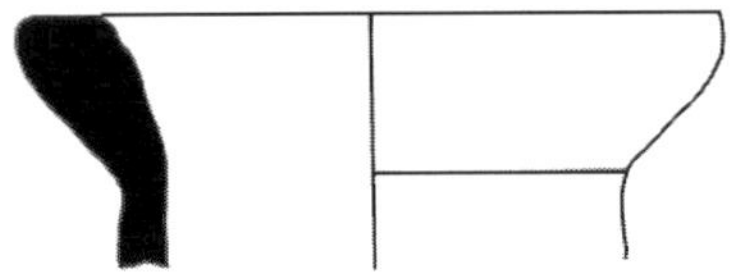

1 Keay IIIA

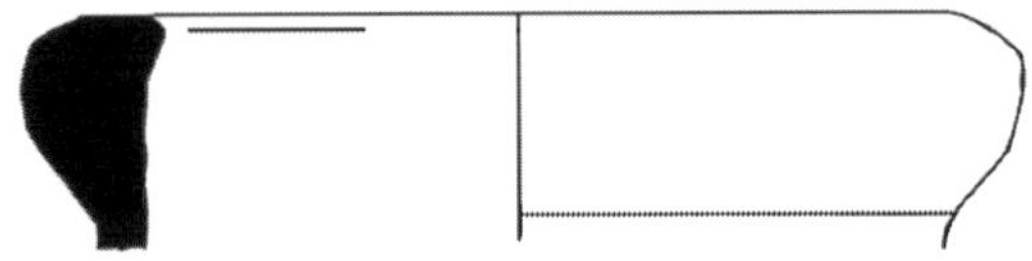

2 Keay IIIB

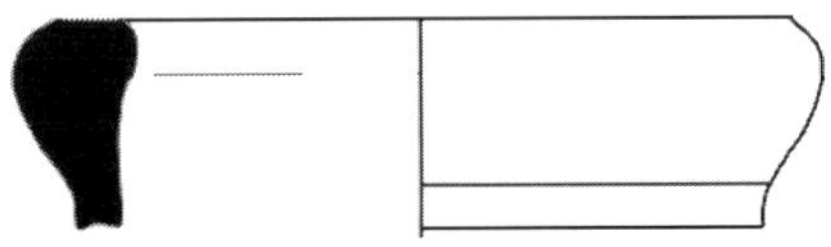

3 Keay IIIB

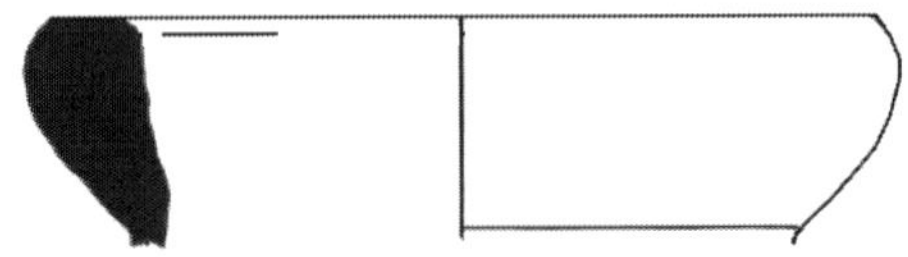

4 Keay IIIB

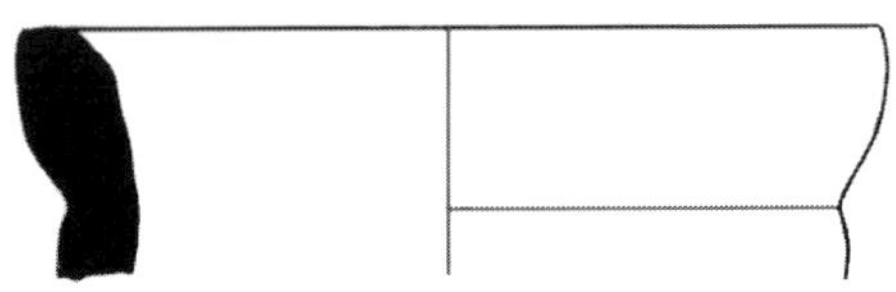

5 Keay VII

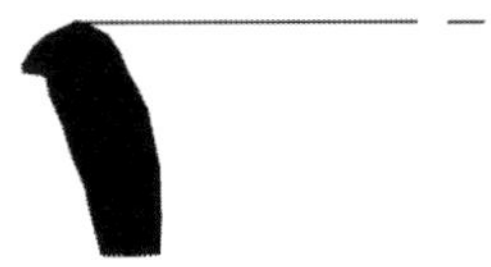

6 Keay XXVB (*)

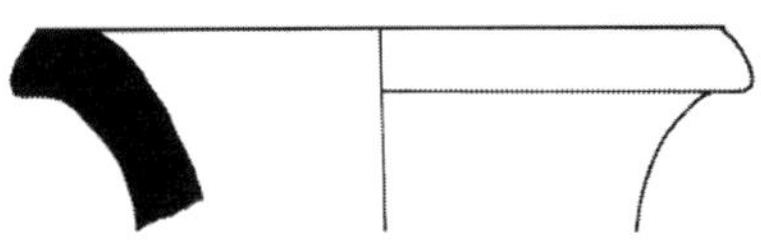

7 Keay XXVG

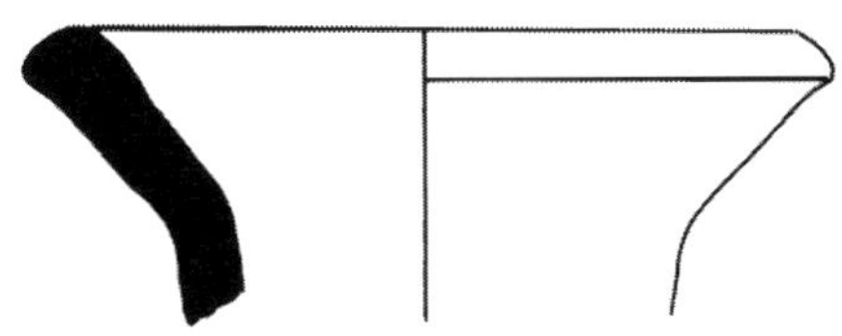

8 Keay XXVL

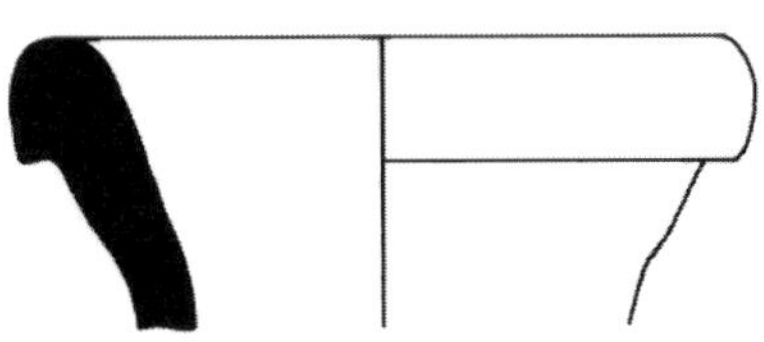

9 Keay XXVC

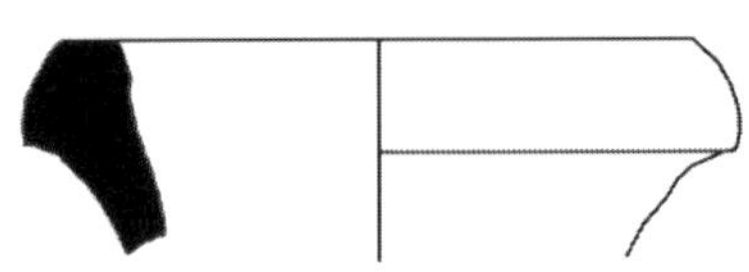

10 Keay XXVI

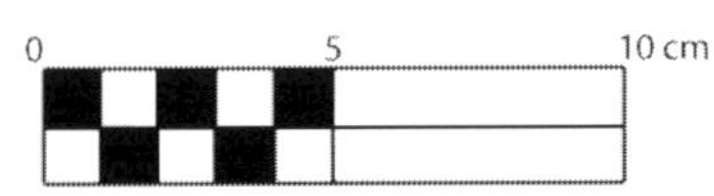

PLATE XXII

Late Roman Tunisian amphorae from the territory

(*) Re-drawn after
Ciampoltrini-Rendini 1990

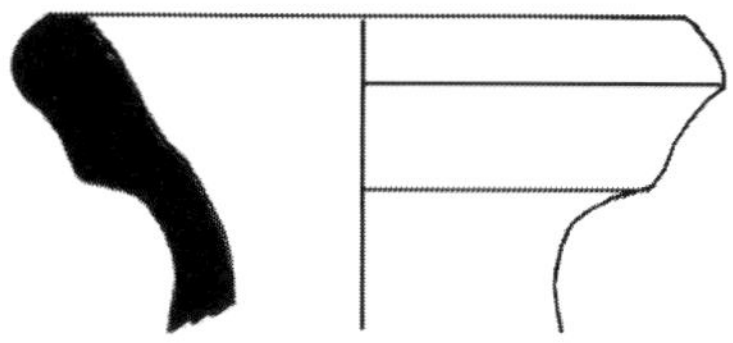

1 Keay XXVI

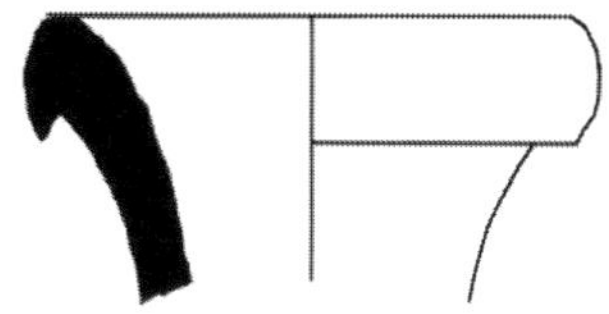

2 Keay XXVI

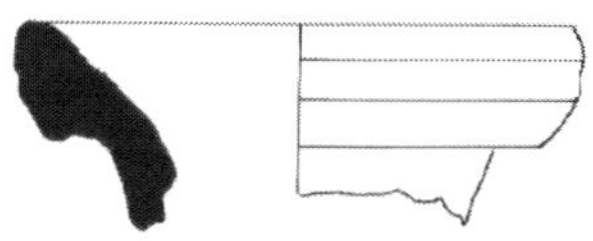

3 Keay XXVI

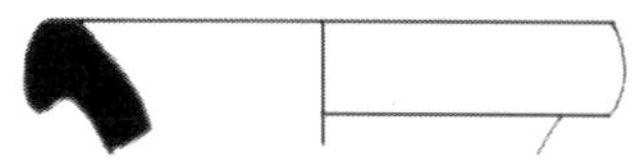

4 Keay XXVI

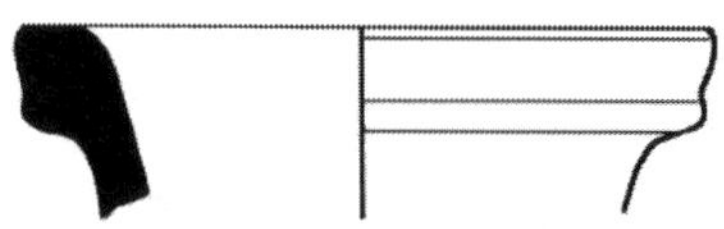

5 Keay XXXIII

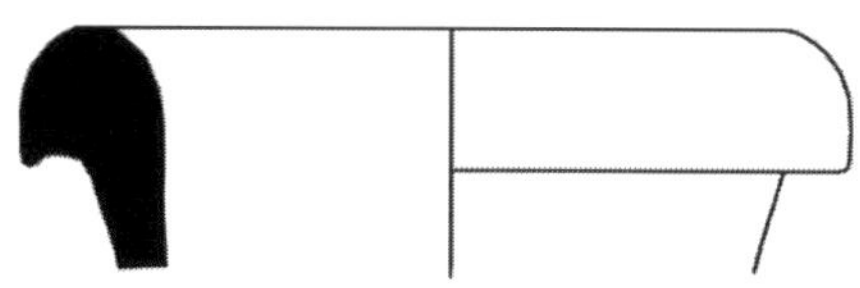

6 Keay XXXVA

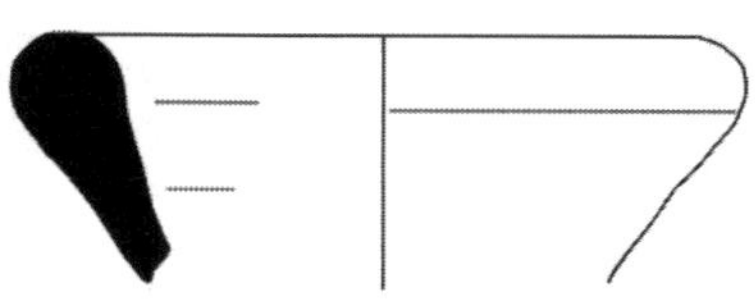

7 Keay XXXVIB

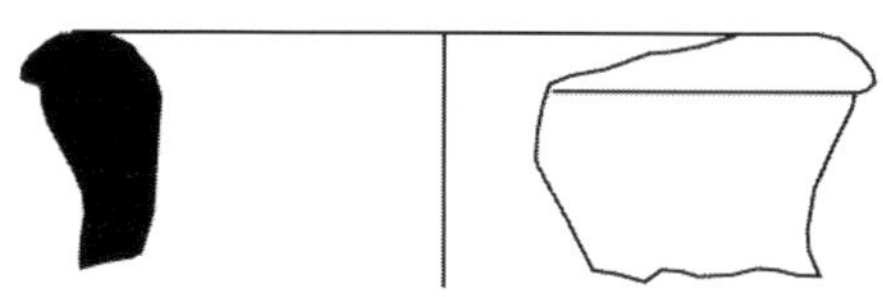

8 Keay LXIIA similis (*)

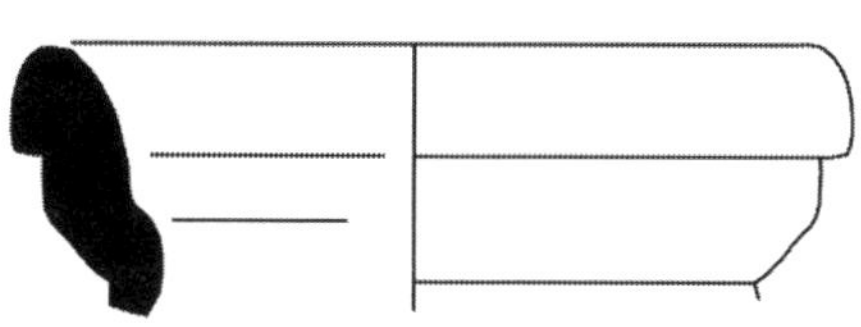

9 Keay LXIIQ

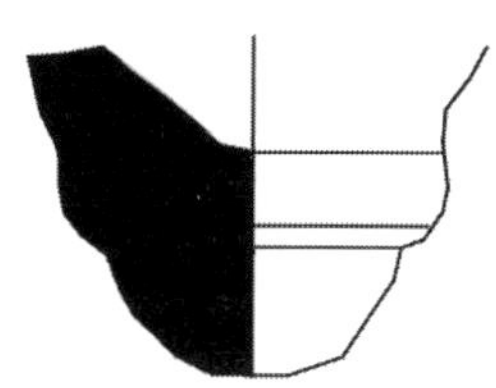

10 Keay LXII

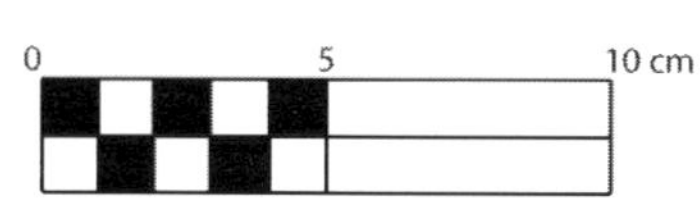

PLATE XXIII

Late Roman amphorae from the territory (Mediterranean and regional sources)

(*) Re-drawn
after Ciampoltrini-Rendini 1990

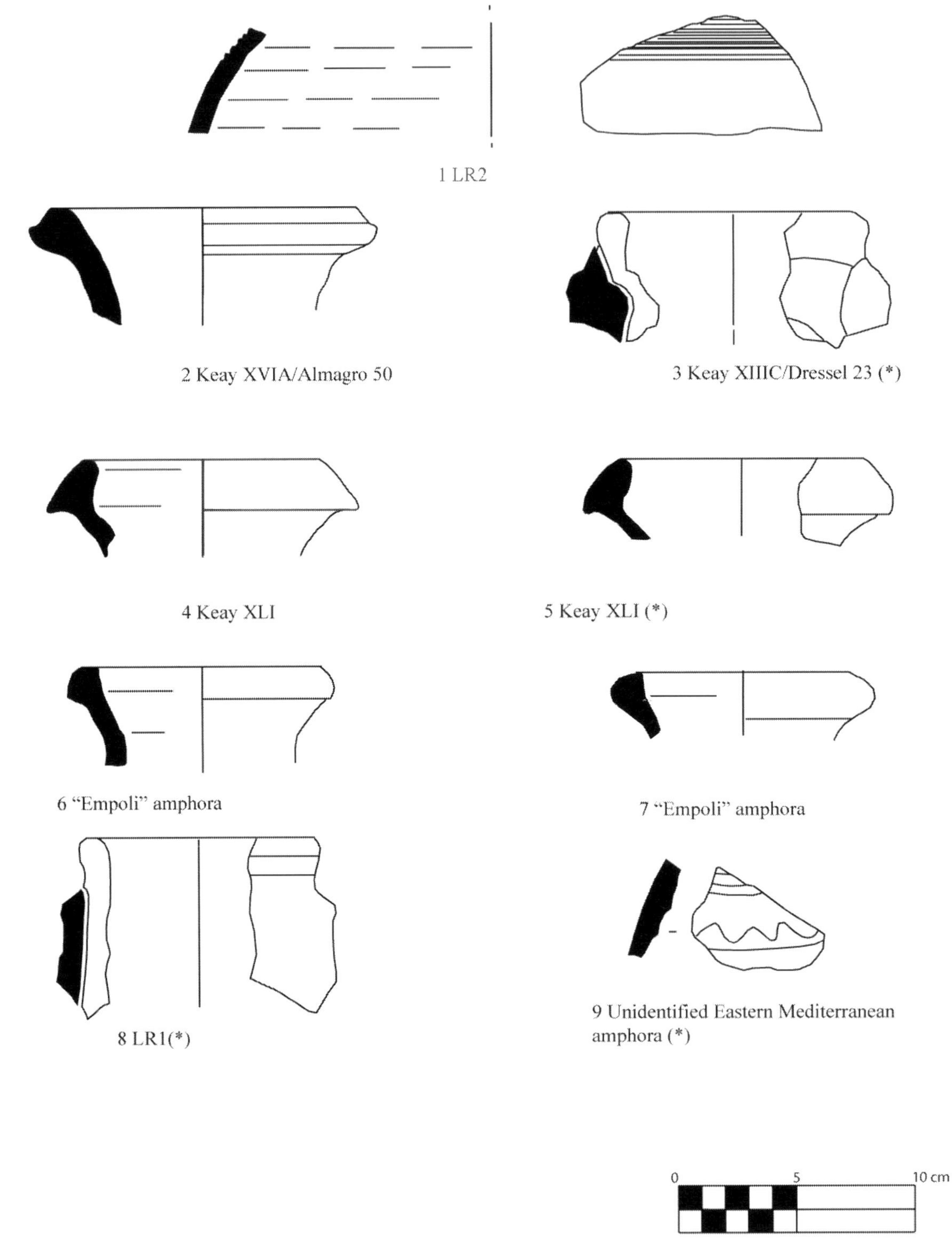

PLATE XXIV

Ingobbiata di rosso ware in the countryside: typologies

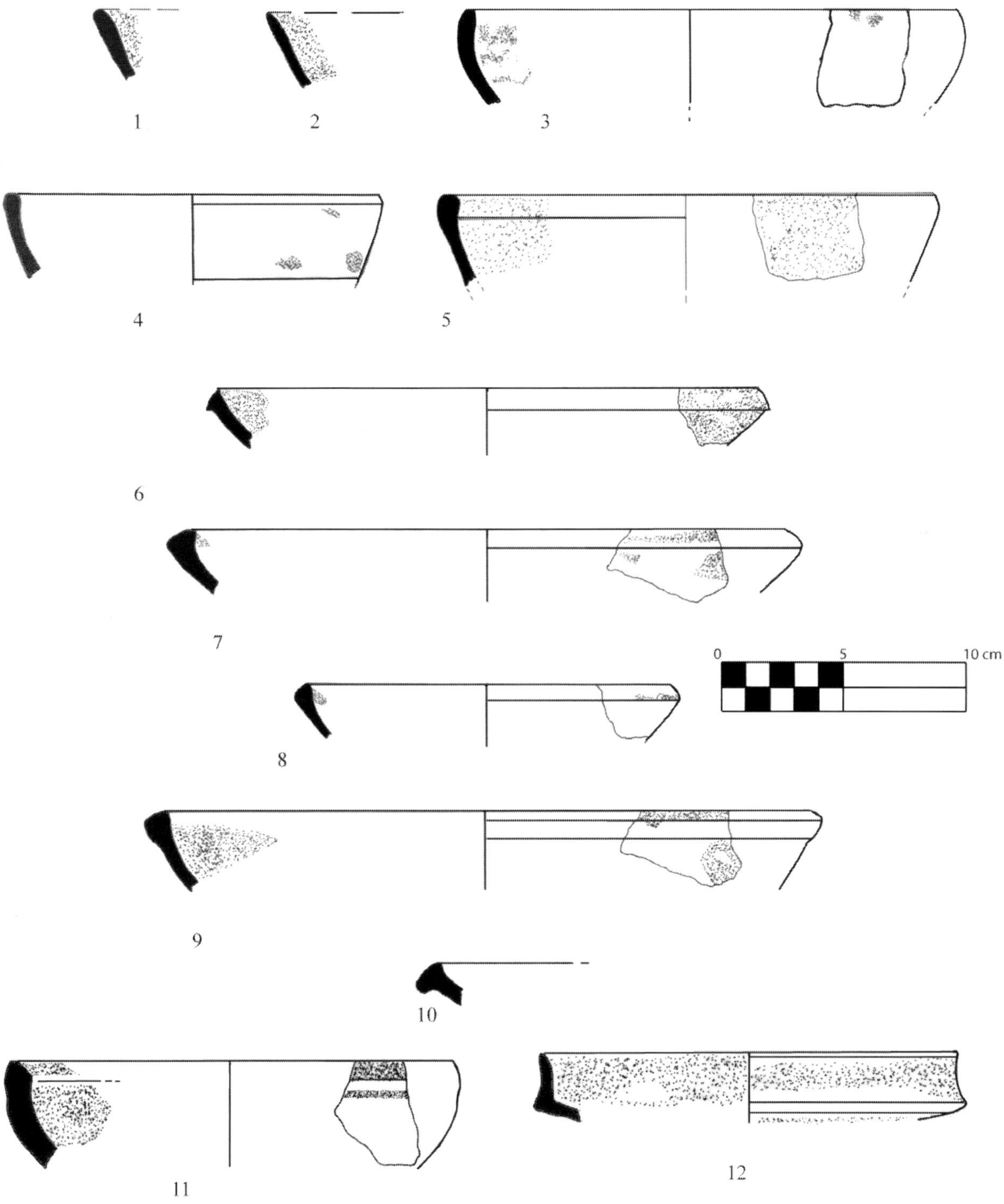

PLATE XXV

Ingobbiata di rosso **ware in the countryside: tipologies**

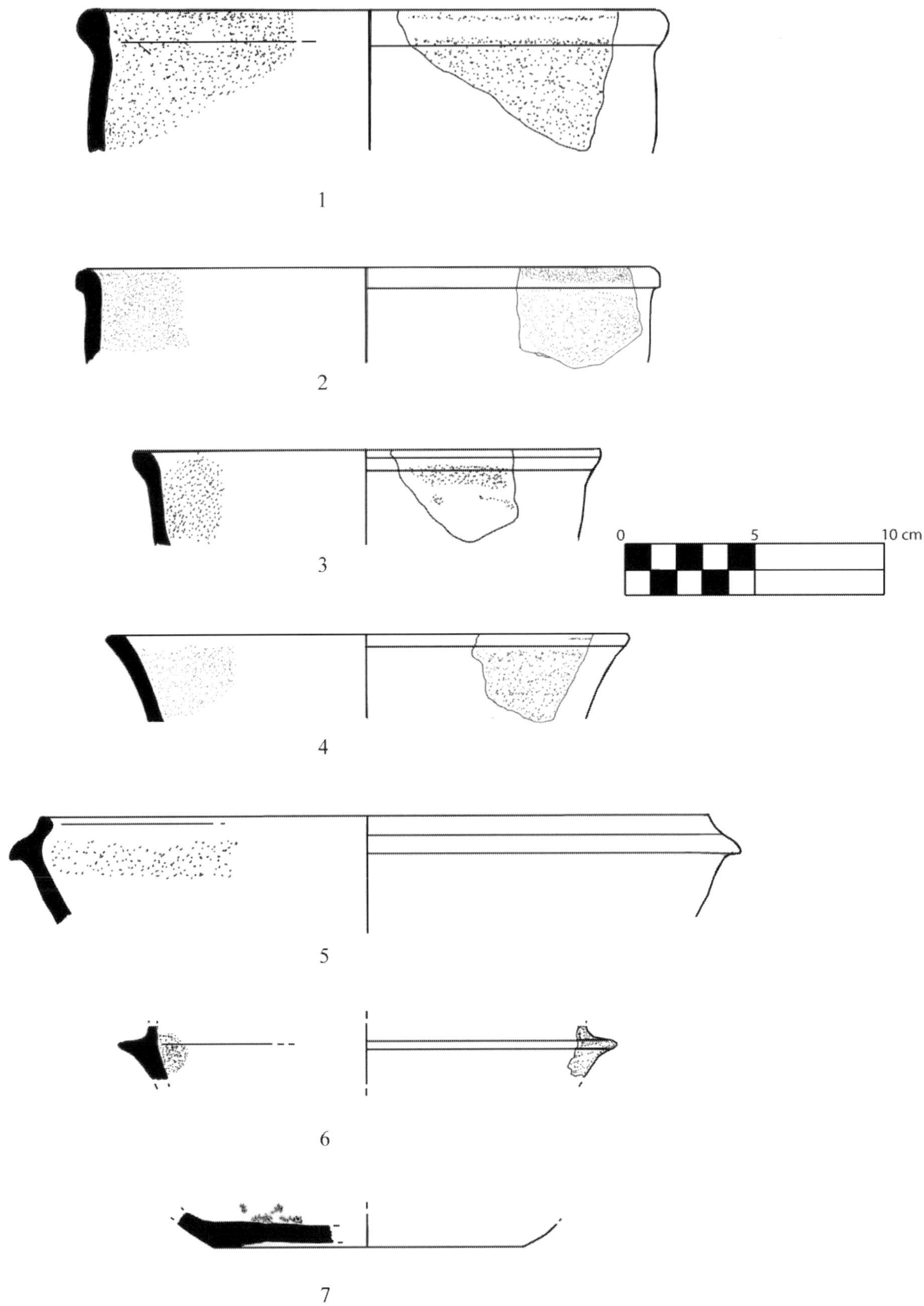

PLATE XXVI

***Ingobbiata di rosso* ware from the countryside: typologies**

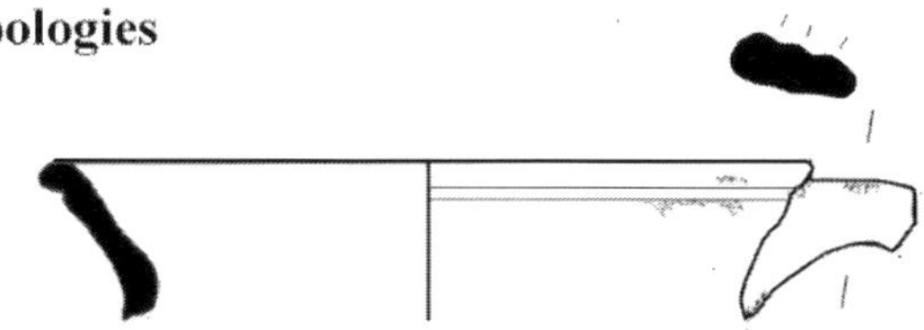
1

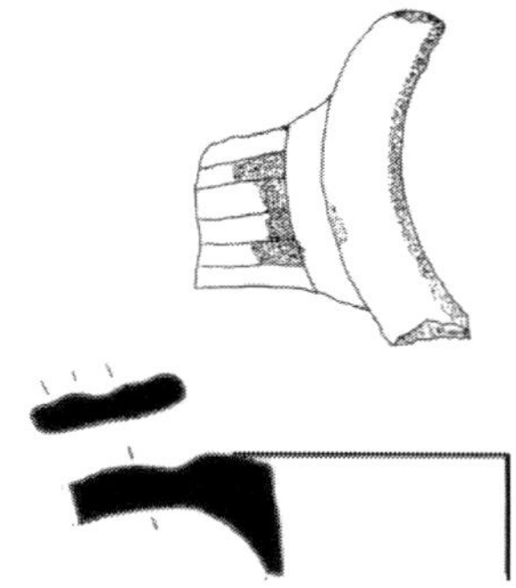
2

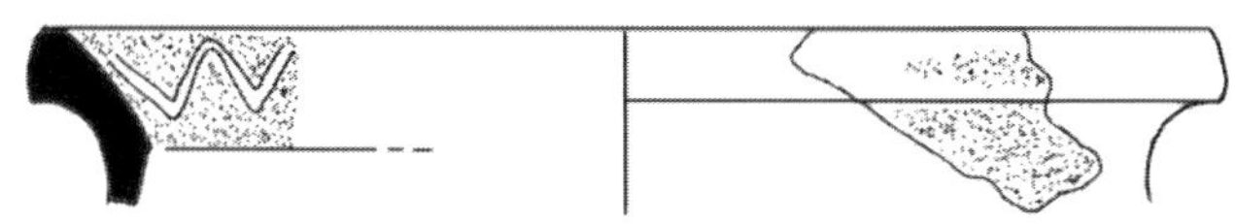
3

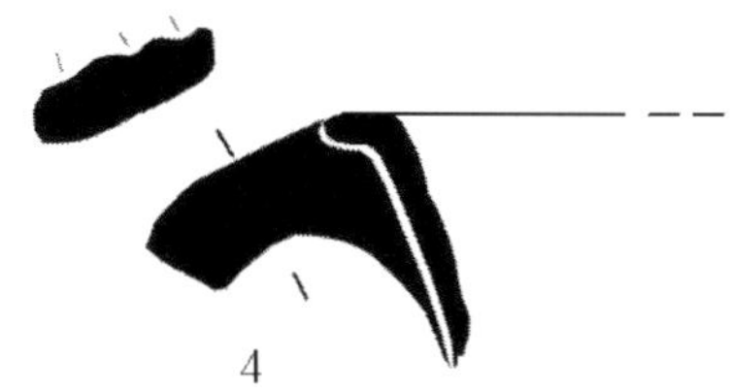
4

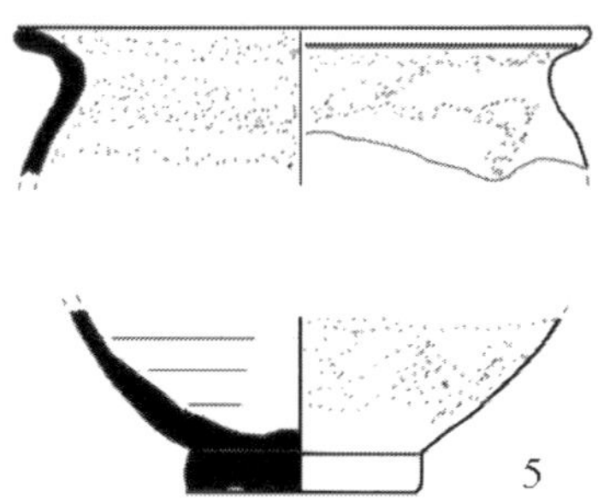
5

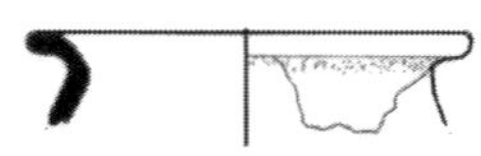
6

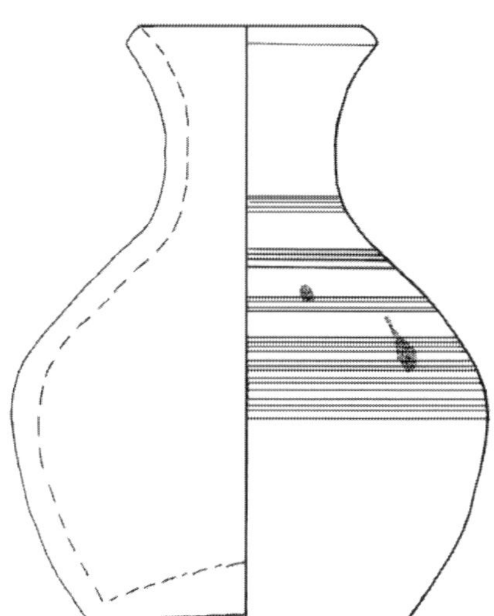
7a

7b

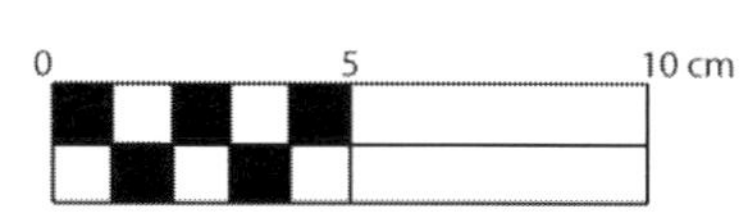

PLATE XXVII

Late Roman *Acroma Depurata* ware in the countryside: typologies

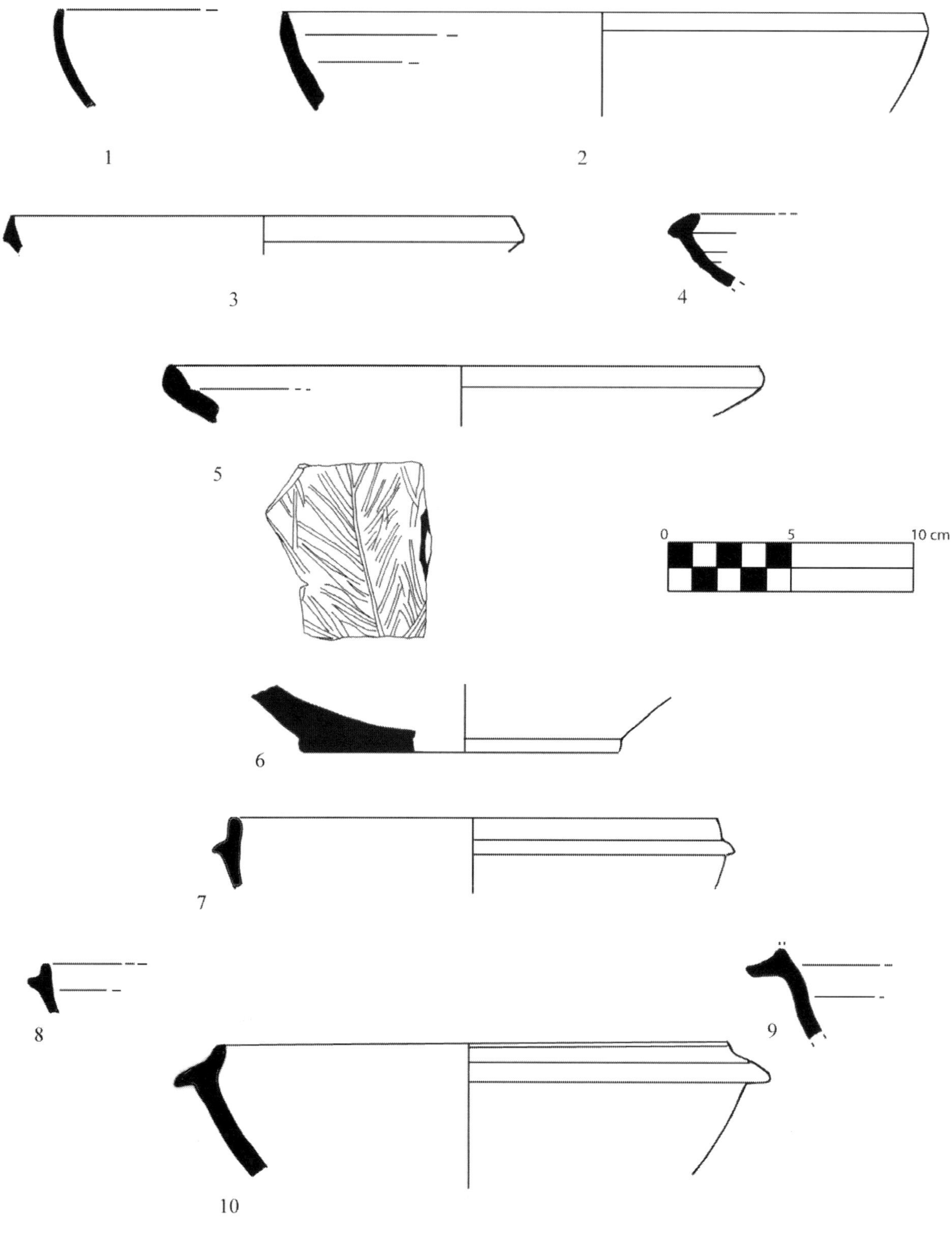

PLATE XXVIII

Late Roman *Acroma Depurata* ware in the countryside: typologies

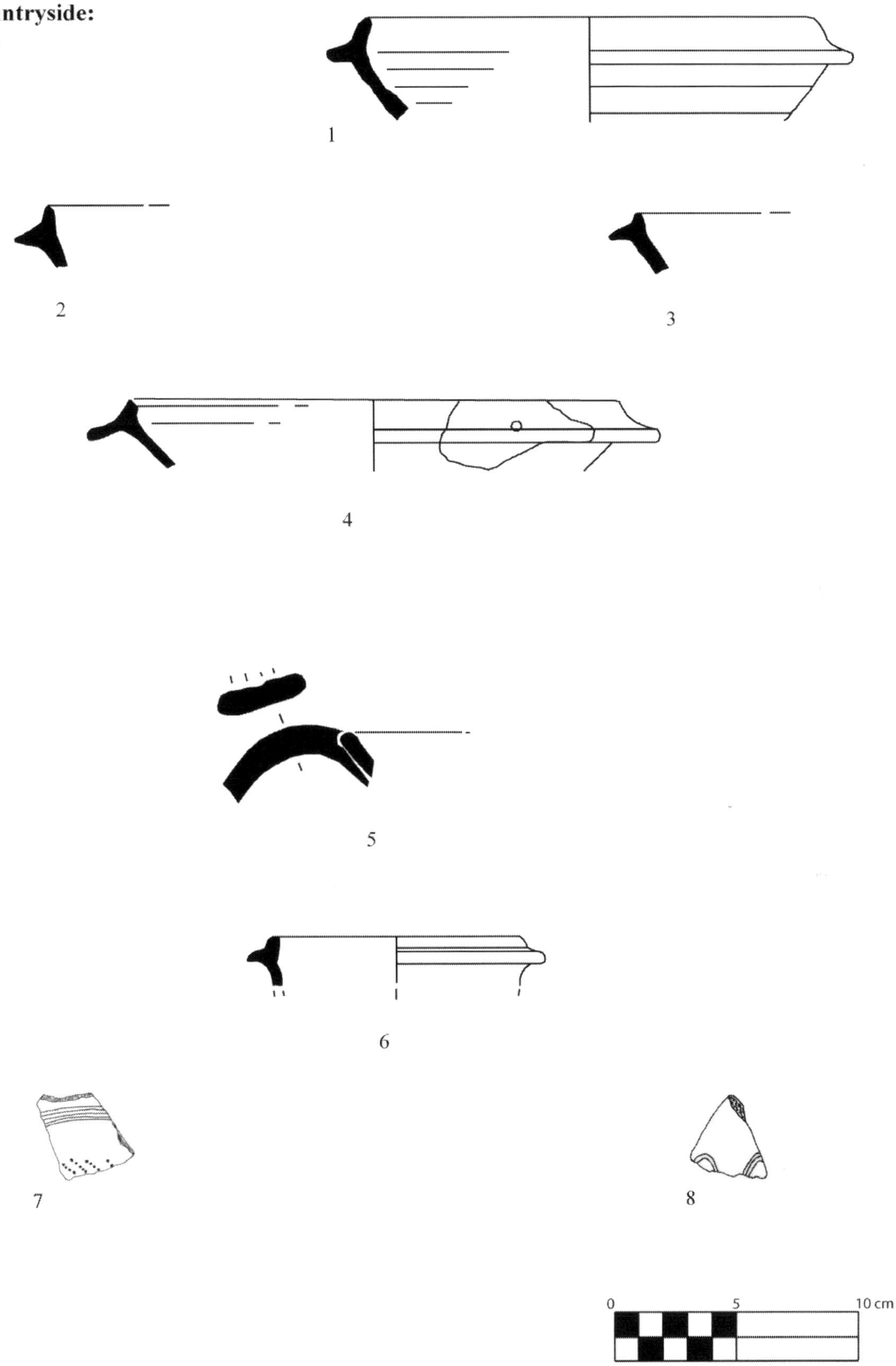

PLATE XXIX

Late Roman *Acroma Selezionata* ware in the countryside: typologies

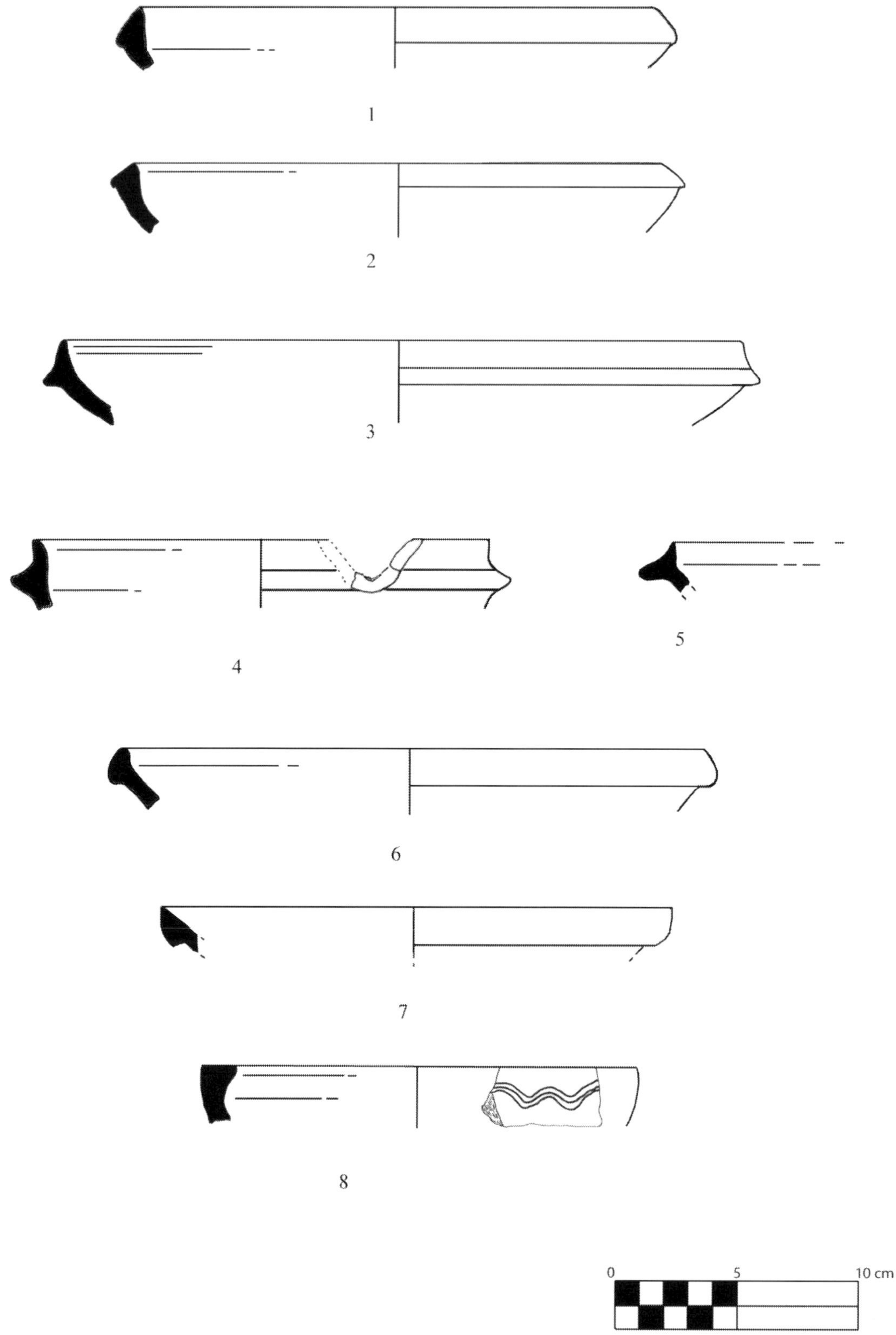

PLATE XXX

Late Roman *Acroma Selezionata* ware in the countryside: typologies

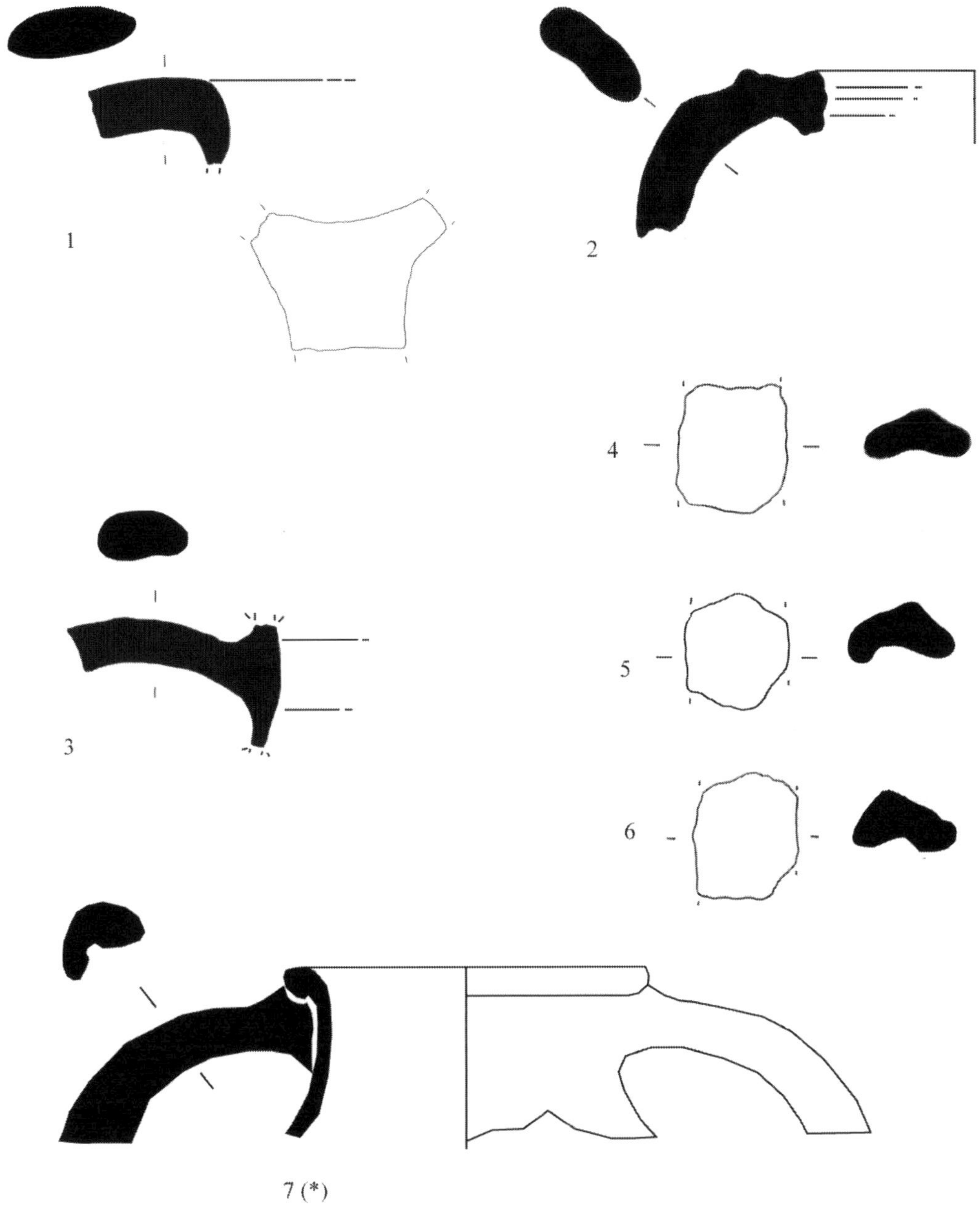

(*) after Fontana 2003 , p.312, Fig.141, n.2

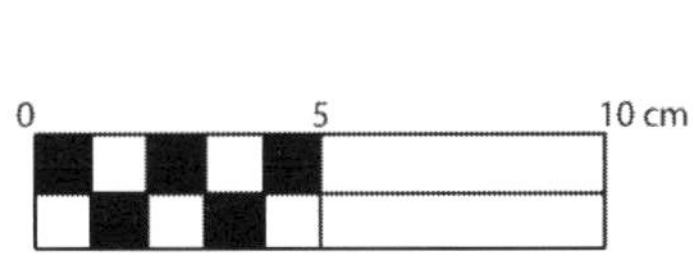

PLATE XXXI

Late Roman Cooking Pots in Kitchen Ware from the Countryside

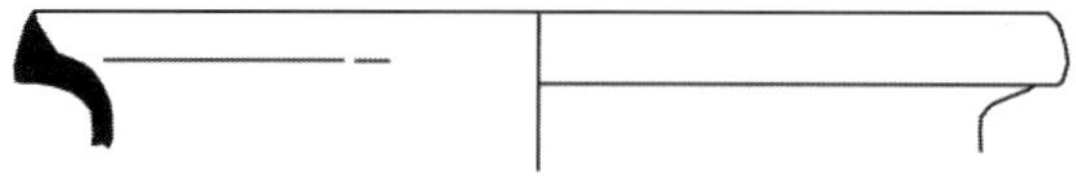

1

LR Cooking pot, "Roselle Type 2"

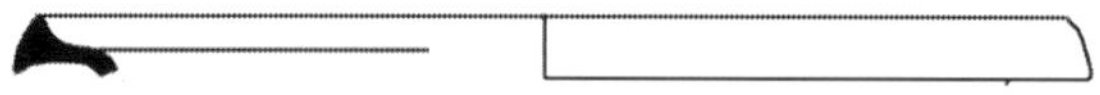

2

LR Cooking pot, "Roselle Type 2"

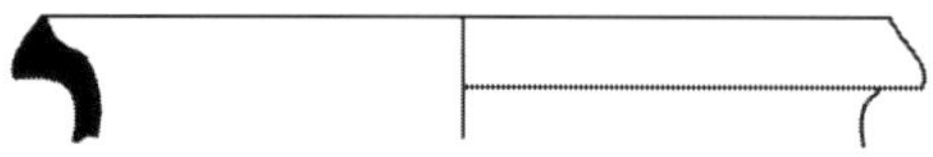

3

LR Cooking pot, "Roselle Type 2"

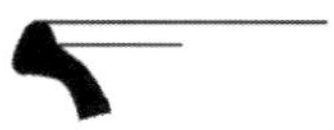

LR Cooking pot, "Roselle type 2" 4

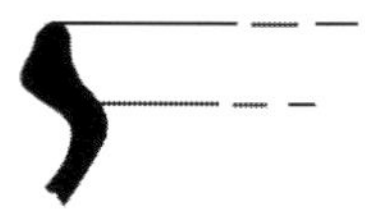

5

LR Cooking pot, "Roselle Type 5"

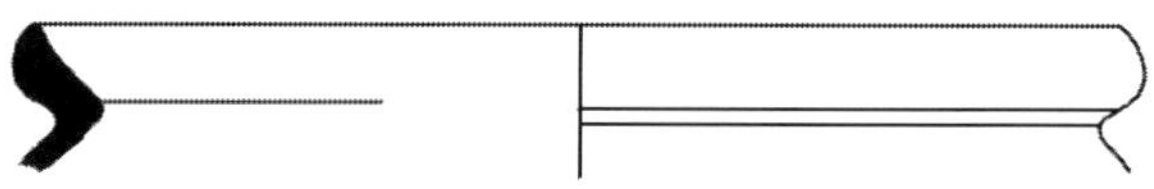

6

LR Cooking pot, "Roselle Type 5" *similis*

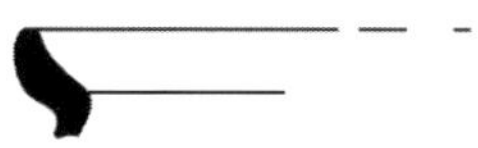

7 LR Cooking pot, "Roselle Type 5" *similis*

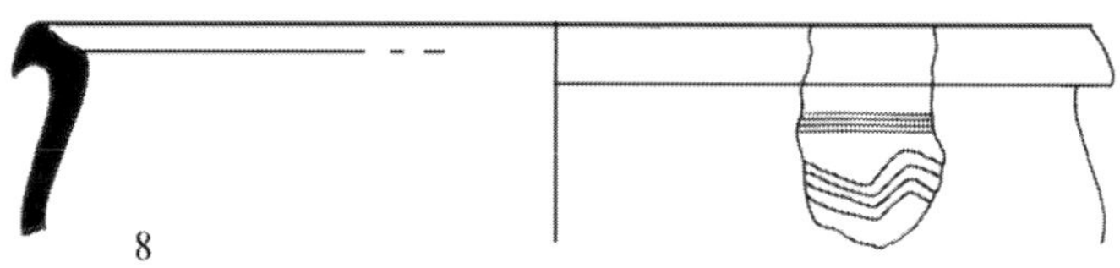

8

LR Cooking pot, "Roselle Type 2" *similis*

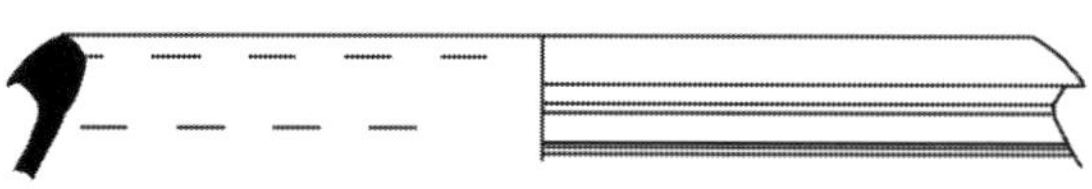

9

LR Cooking pot, "Roselle Type 3" *similis*

10

LR Cooking pot, "Roselle Type 7" *similis*

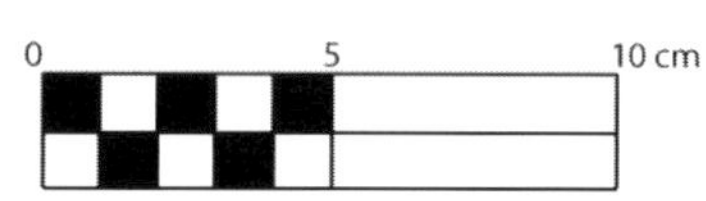

PLATE XXXII

Late Roman Cooking Pots in Kitchen Ware from the Countryside

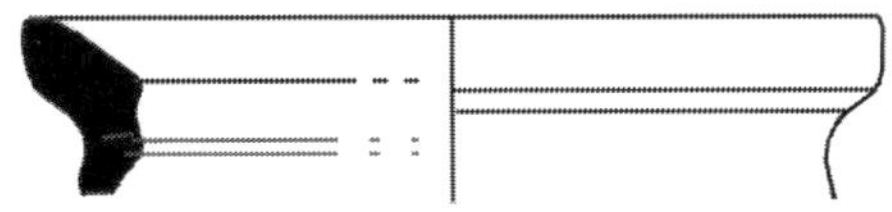

1

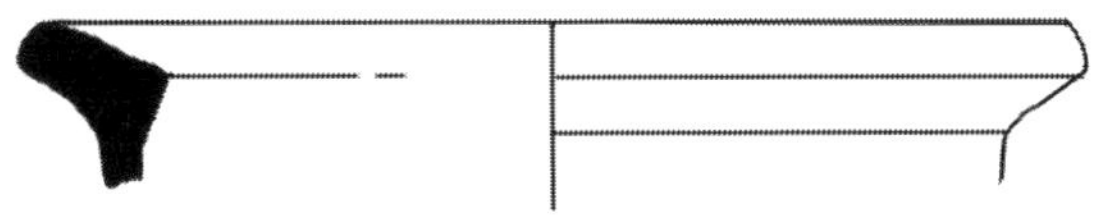

2

3

"Roselle Type 4" *similis*

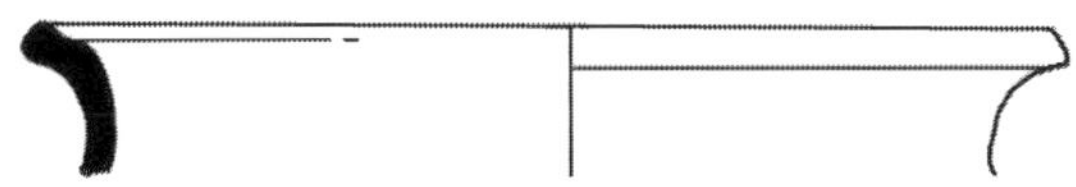

4

"Roselle Type 4"

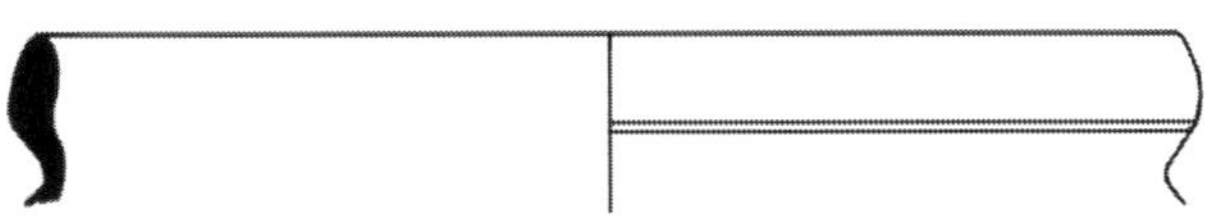

5

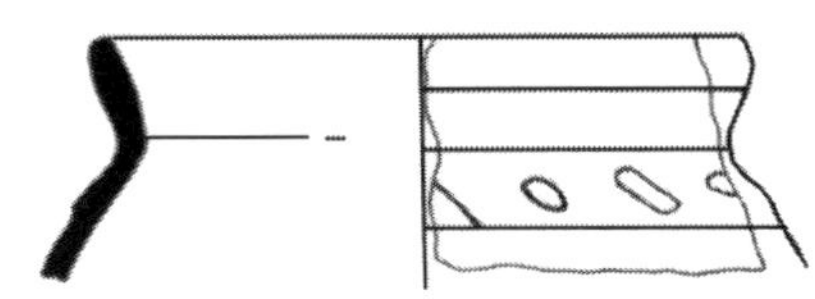

6

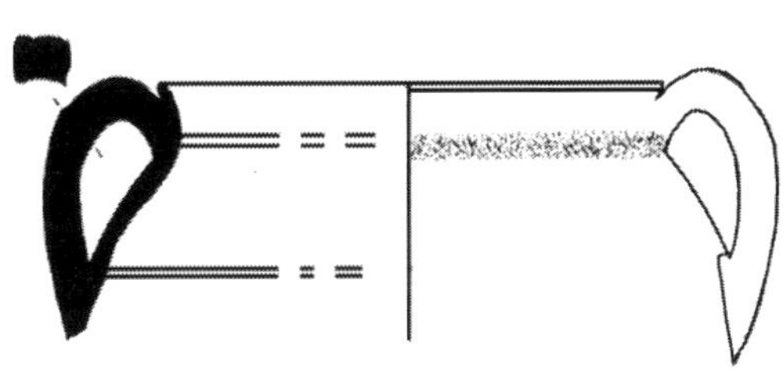

7

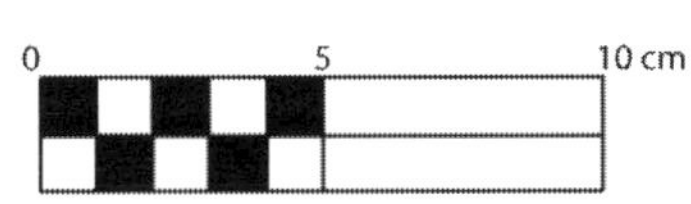

PLATE XXXIII

Late Roman Cooking Pots and Casseroles in the Countryside

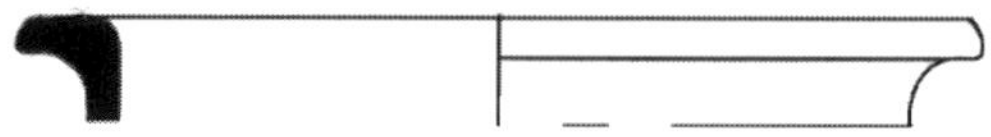

1 Cooking Pot

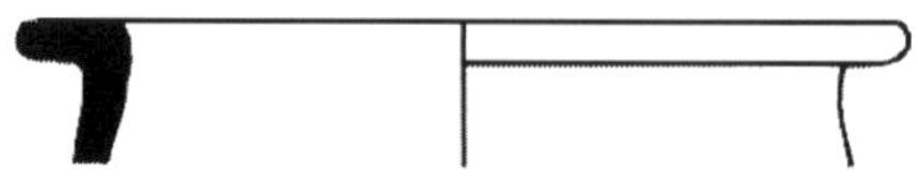

2 Cooking Pot

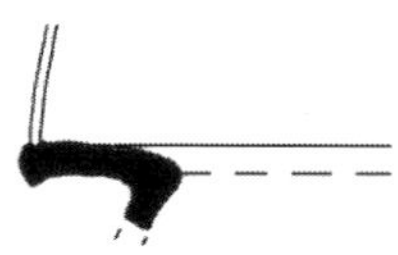

3 Casserole (?)

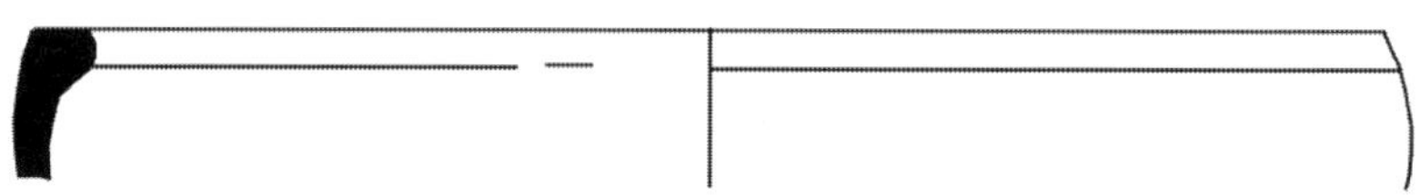

4 Casserole

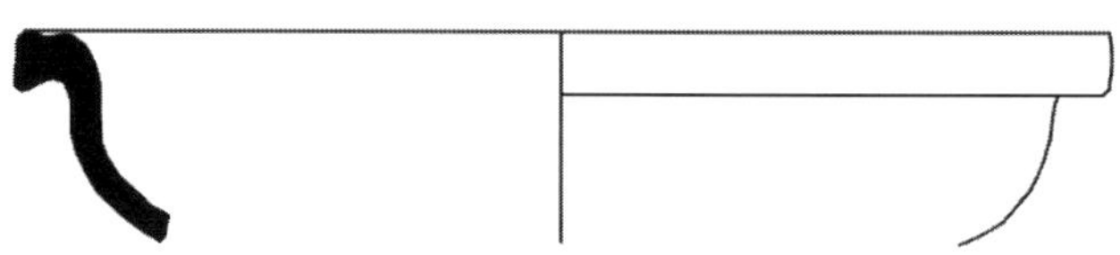

5 Casserole

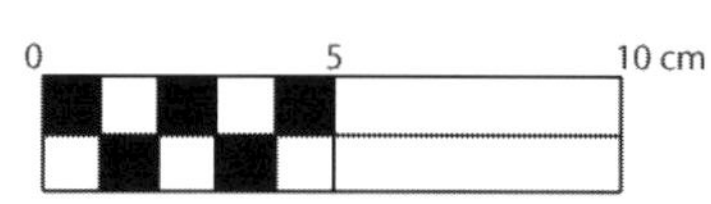

PLATE XXXIV

Late Roman Lids and Bowl-Lids from the Countryside

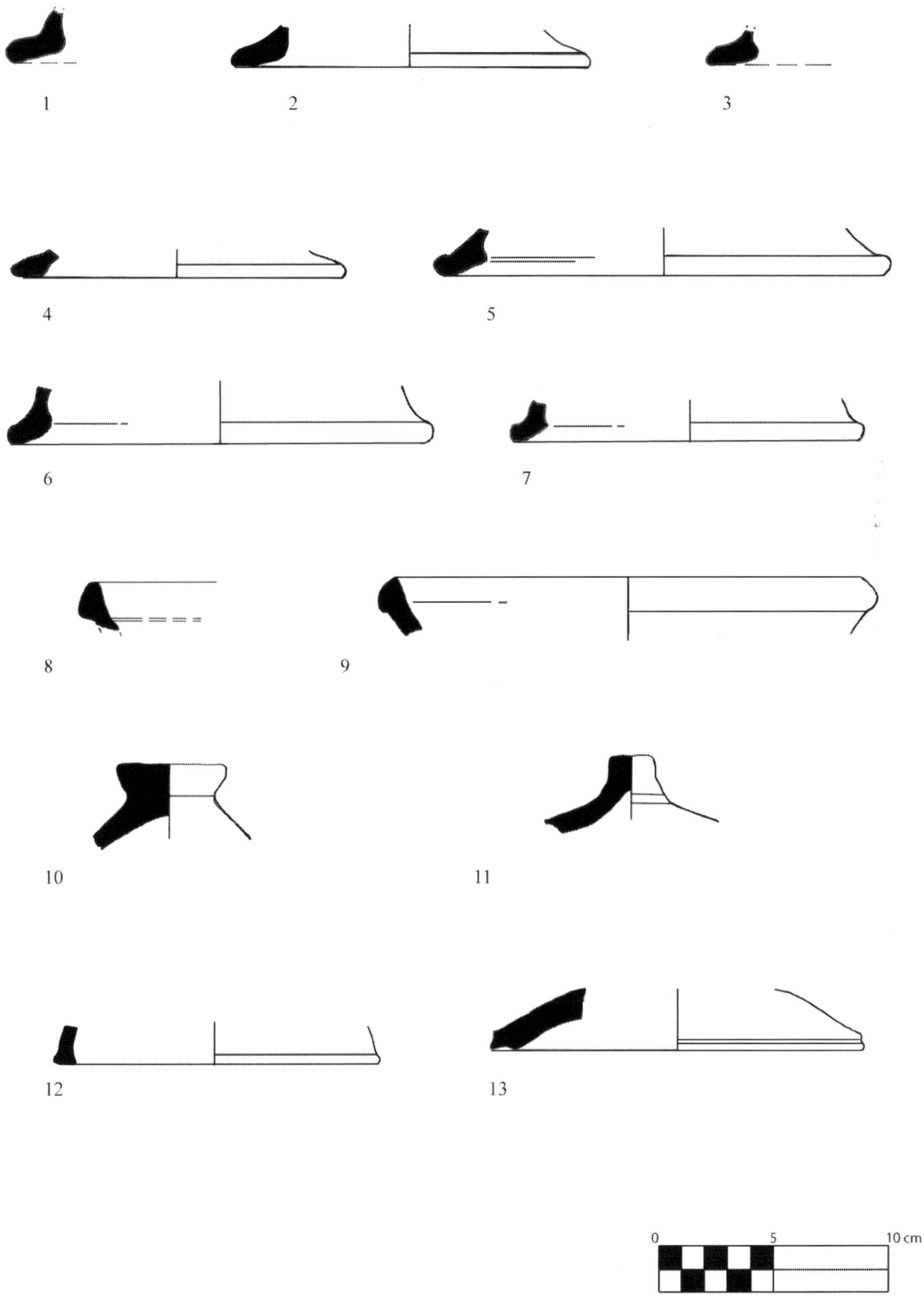

PLATE XXXV

ARS from the cave at Scoglietto (AD 450-550)

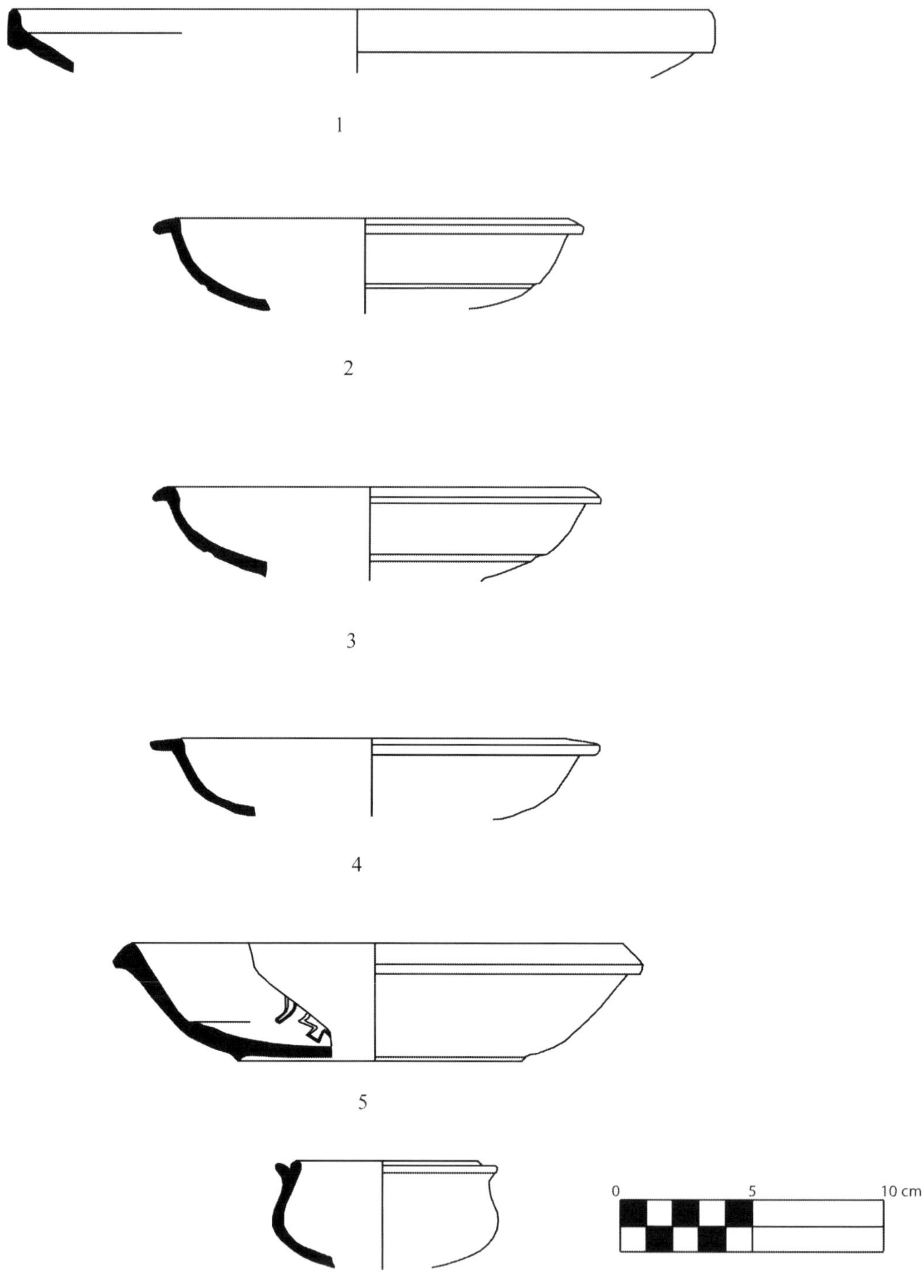

PLATE XXXVI

Italic finewares
(Early Roman and late antique occupation of the cave at Scoglietto)

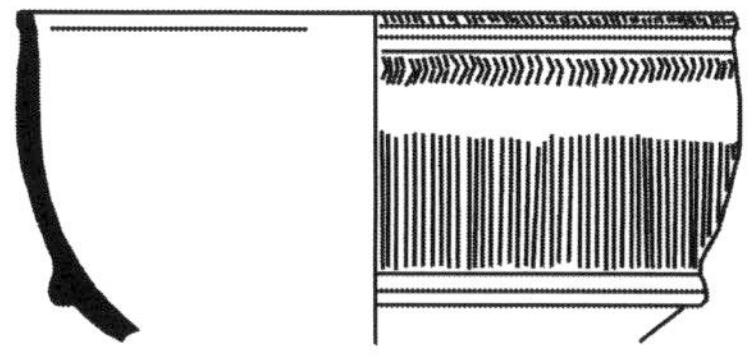

1 Arretine sigillata (Early Roman occupation)

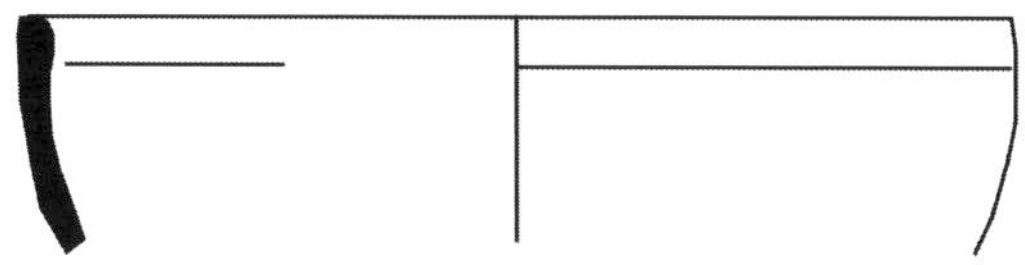

2 *Ingobbiata di rosso* ware (late antique occupation AD 450-550)

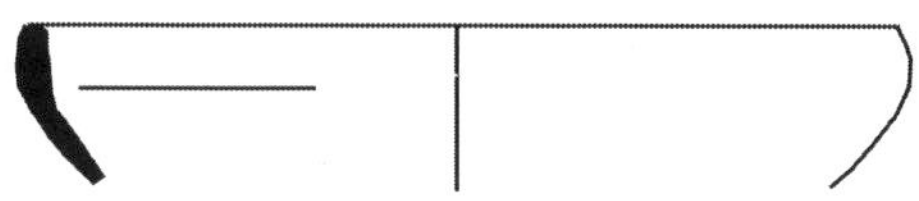

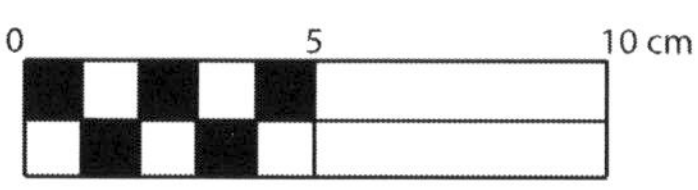

3 *Ingobbiata di rosso* ware (late antique occupation)

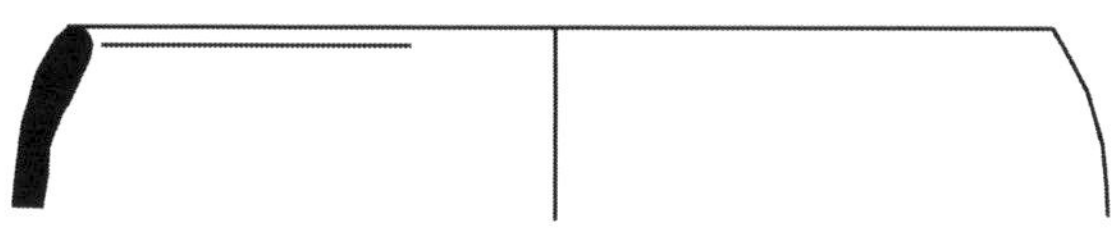

4 *Ingobbiata di rosso* ware (late antique occupation)

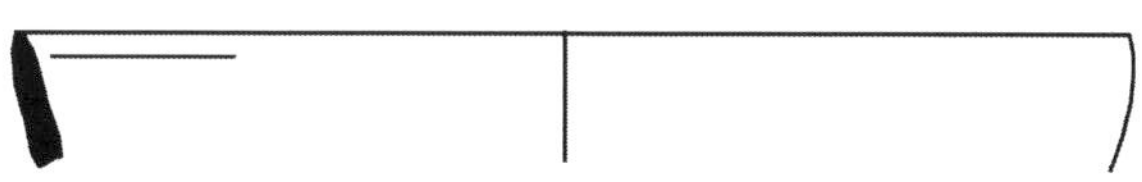

5 *Sigillata chiara tarda dell'Italia centro-settentrionale*
(late antique occupation)

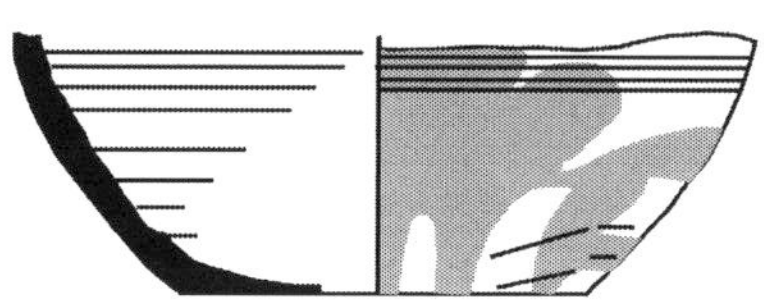

6 *Colature rosse* ware (late antique occupation)

PLATE XXXVII

Mediterranean ceramics (Scoglietto cave)

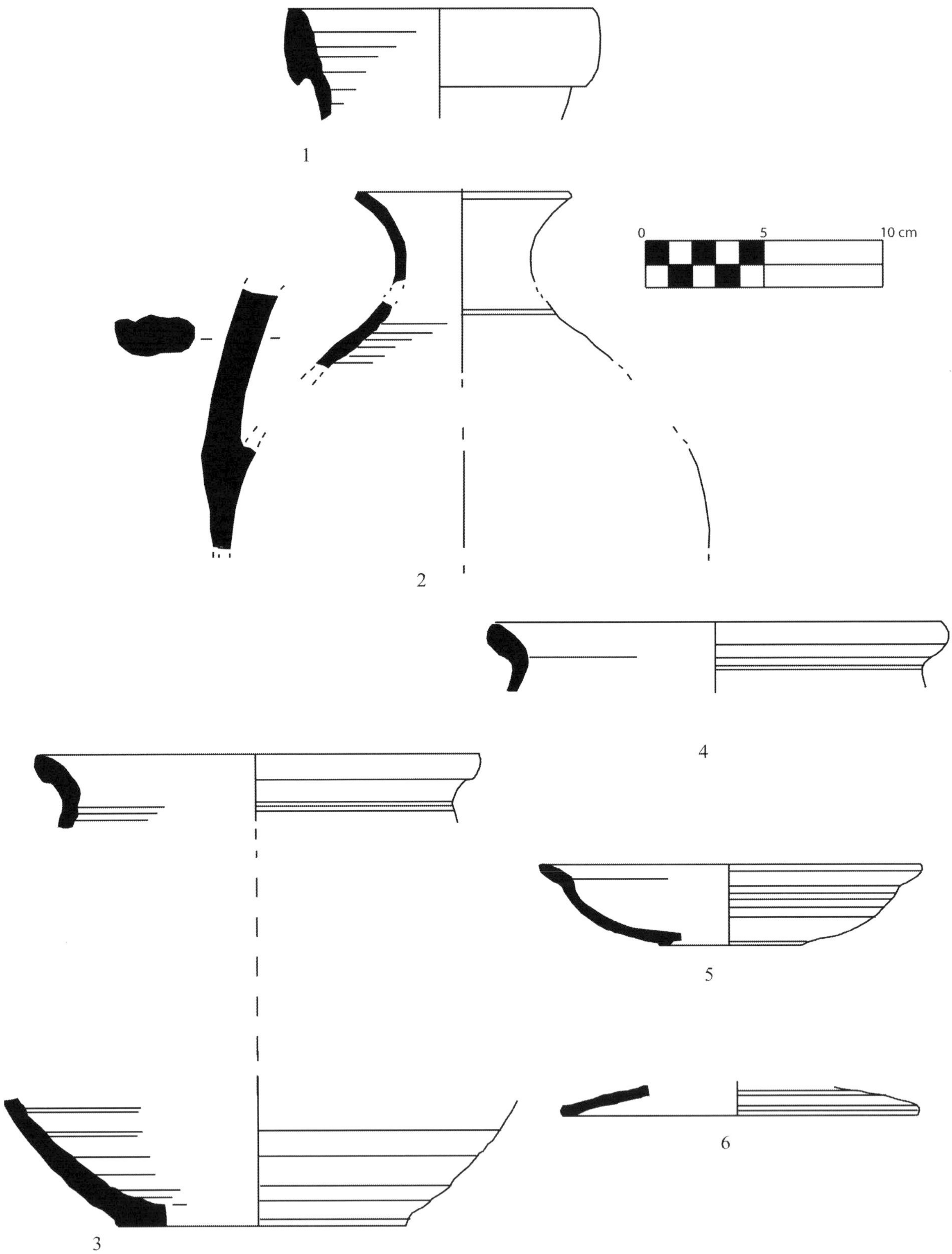

PLATE XXXVIII

Deep cooking pots in kitchen ware and corresponding fabrics from the cave at Scoglietto (AD 450-550)

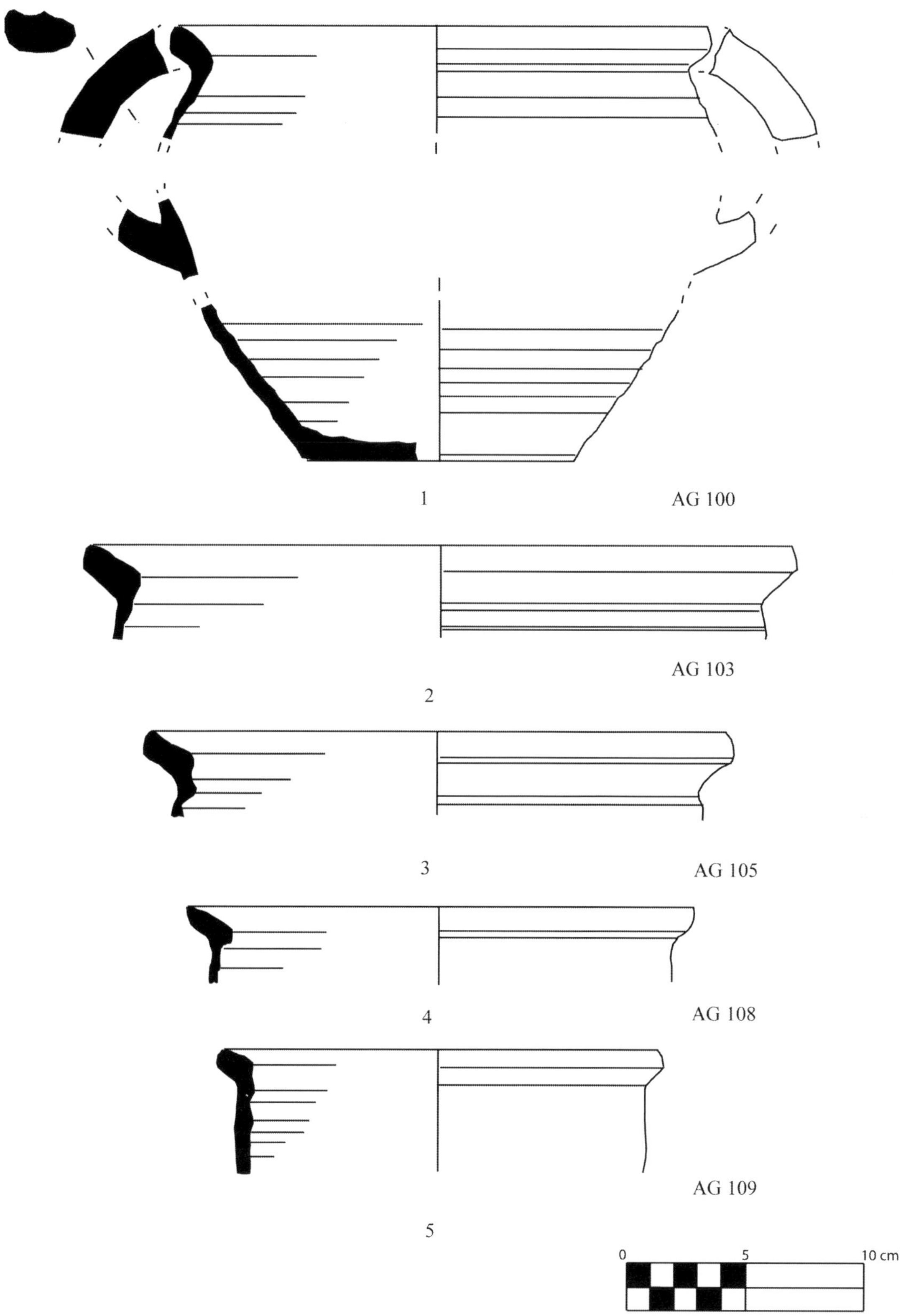

PLATE XXXIX

Cooking pots in kitchen ware and corresponding fabrics from the cave at Scoglietto (AD 450-550)

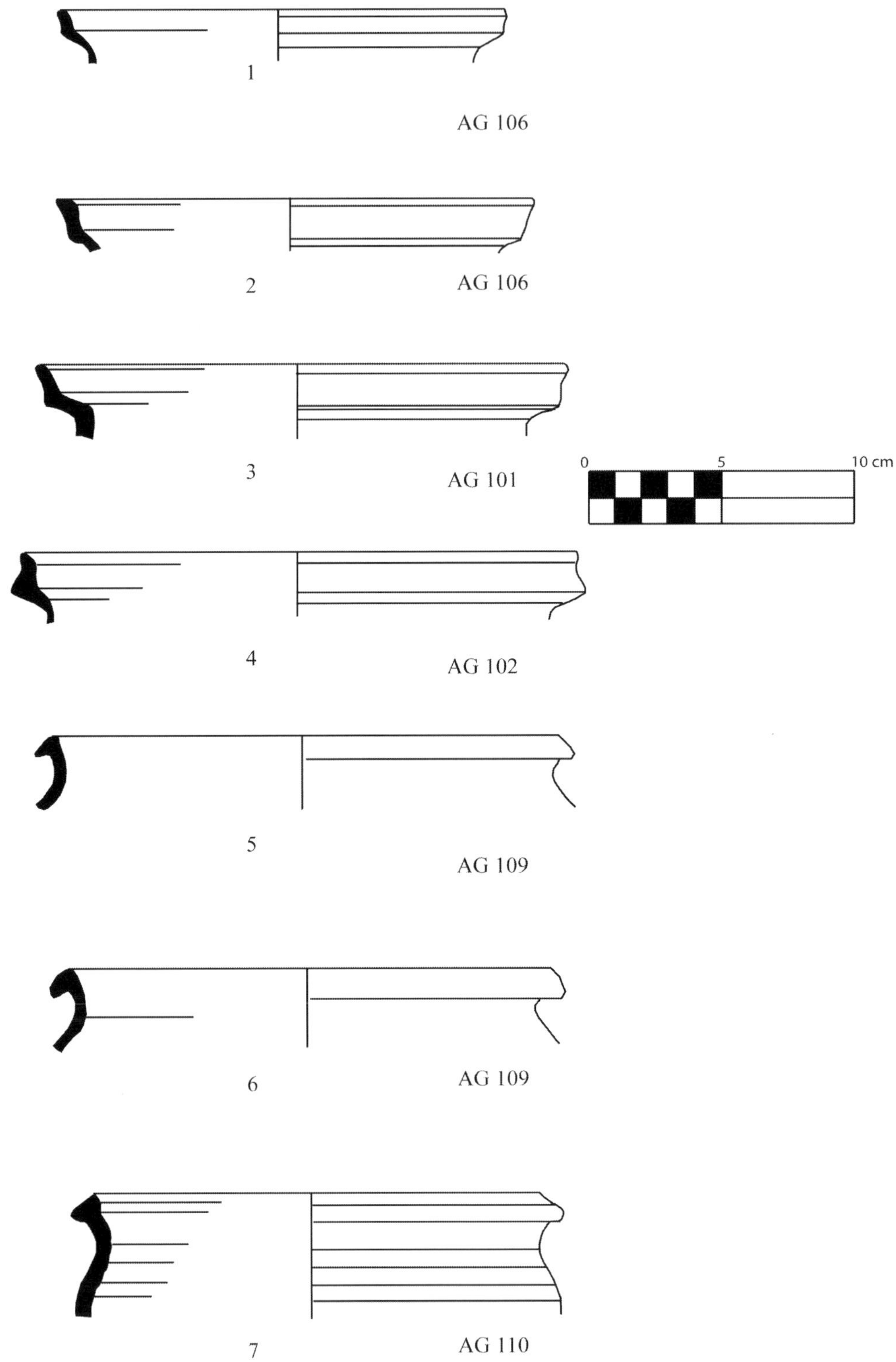

PLATE XL

Cooking-pans and bowl-lids in kitchen ware and corresponding fabrics from the cave at Scoglietto (AD 450-550)

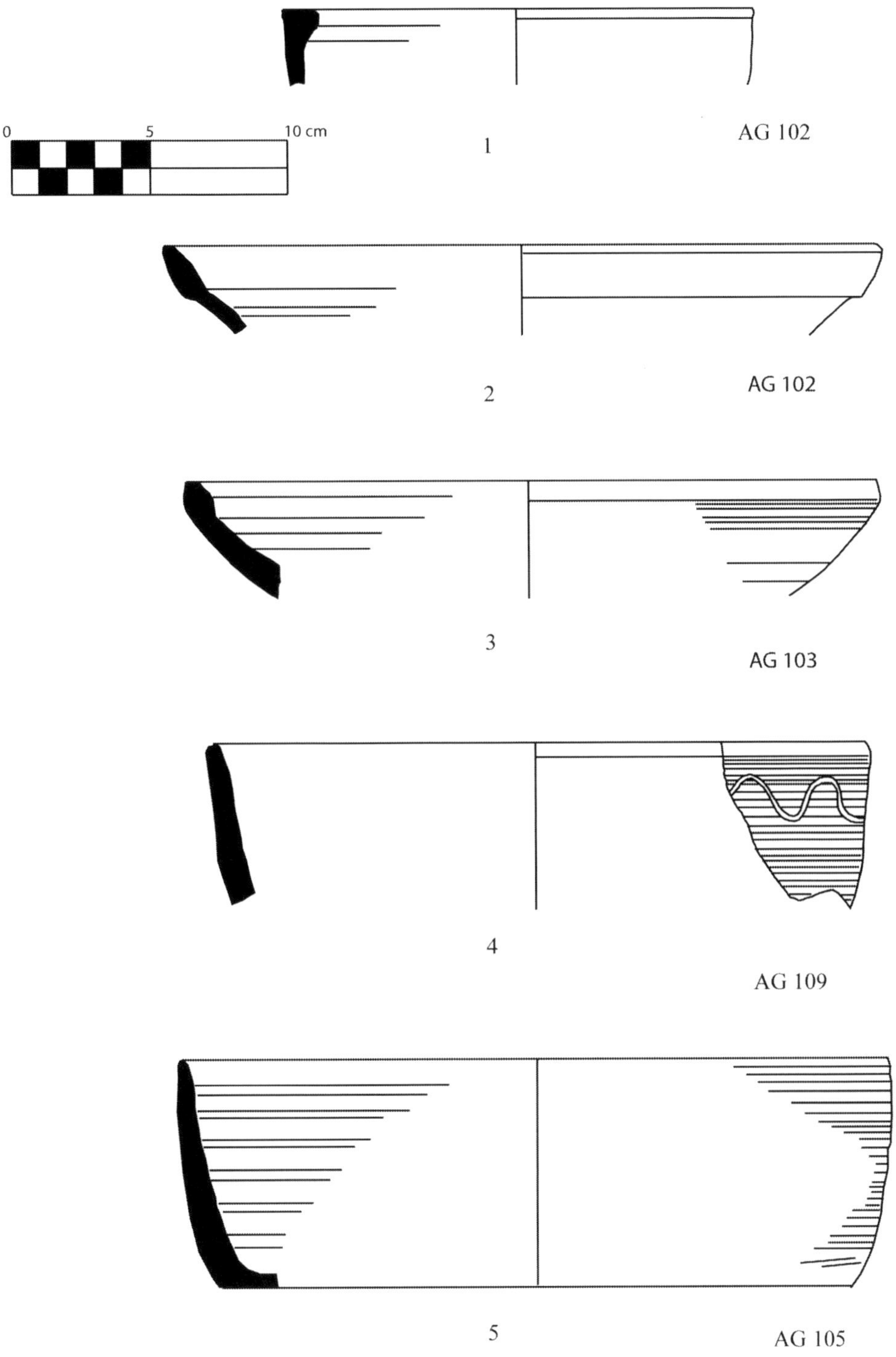

PLATE XLI

Lids in kitchen ware and corresponding fabrics (Scoglietto cave)

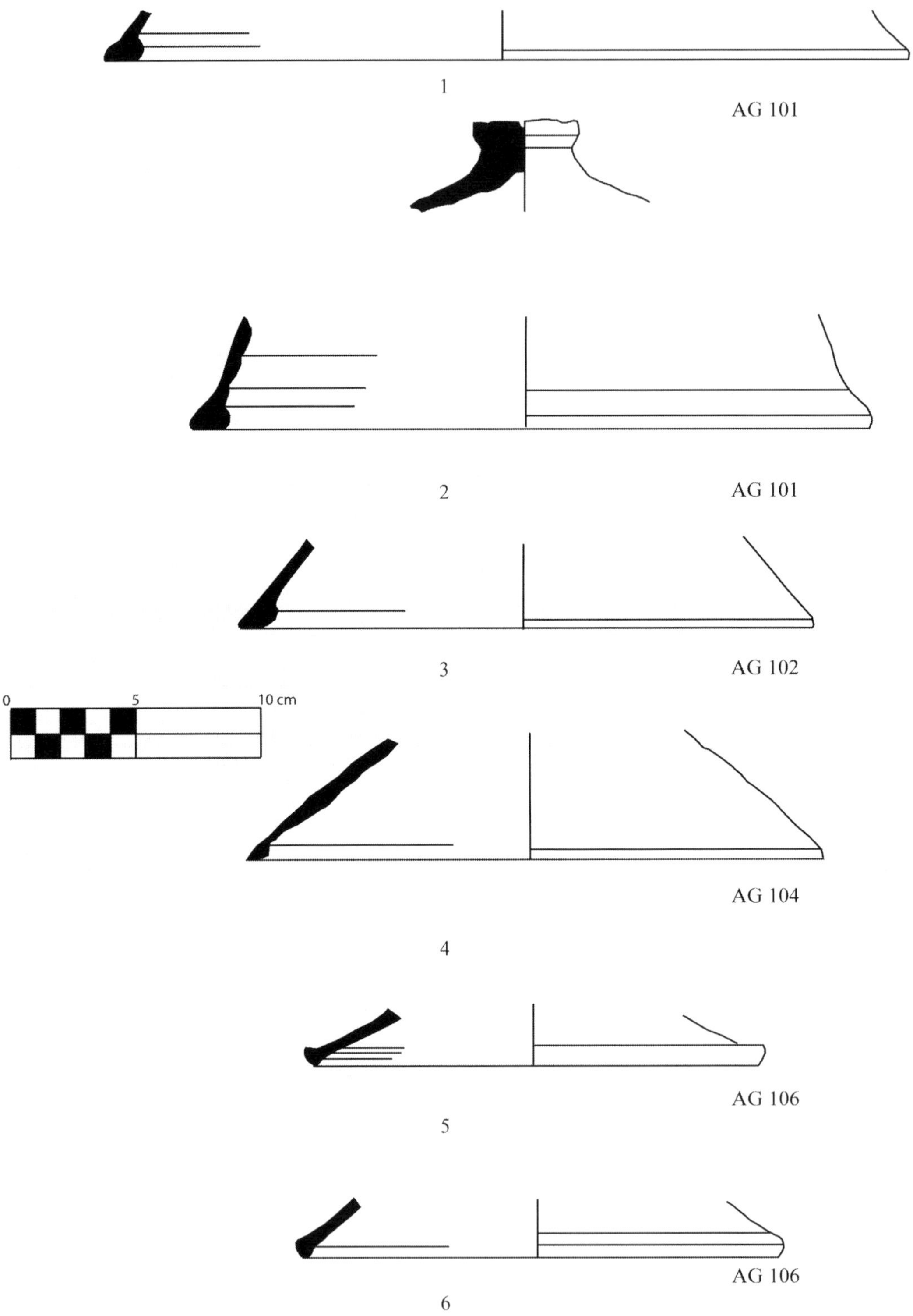

PLATE XLII

Lids in kitchen ware and corresponding fabrics (Scoglietto cave)

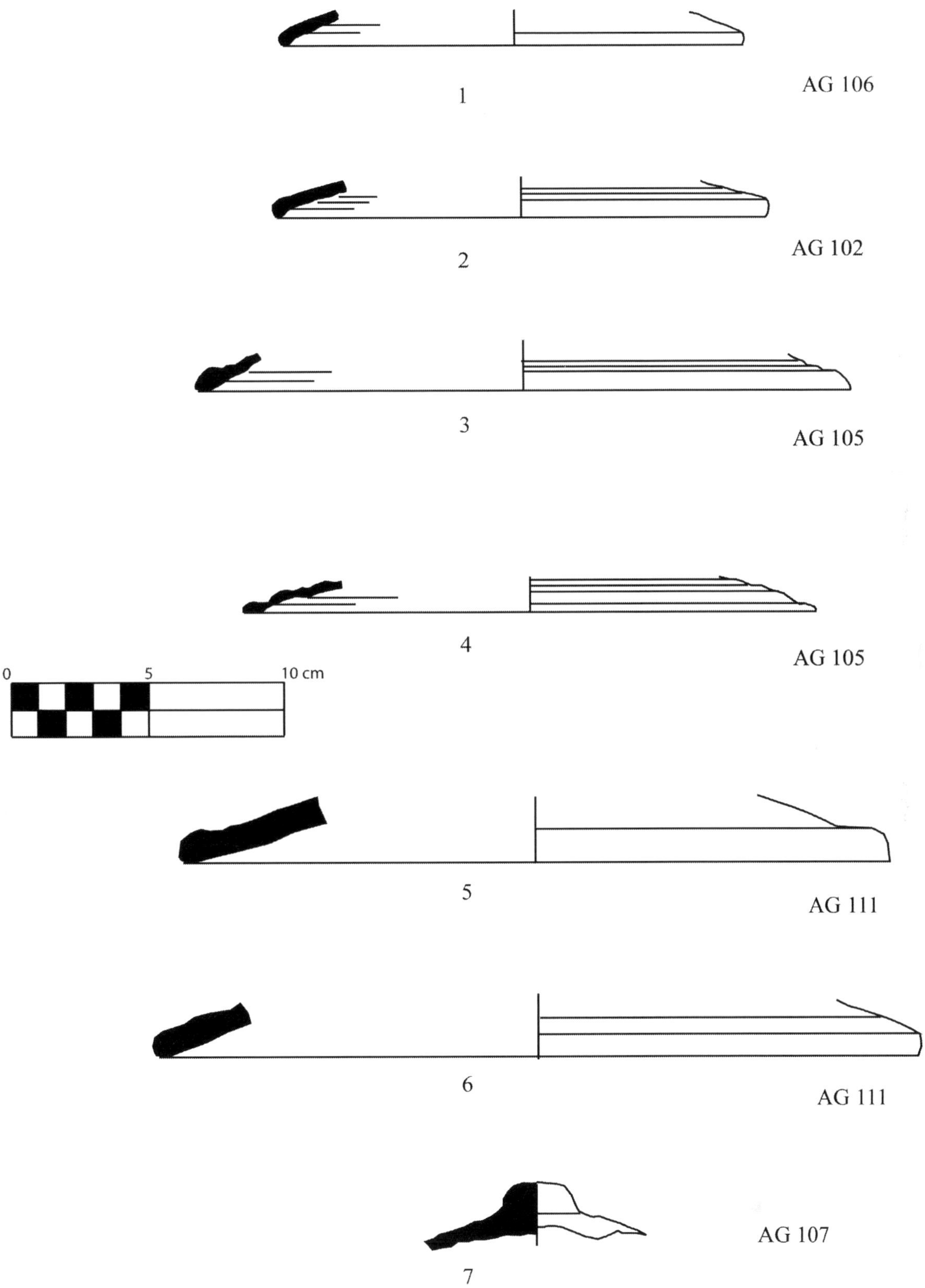

PLATE XLIII

Cooking pots in kitchen ware and corresponding fabrics from the cave at Scoglietto (AD 450-550)

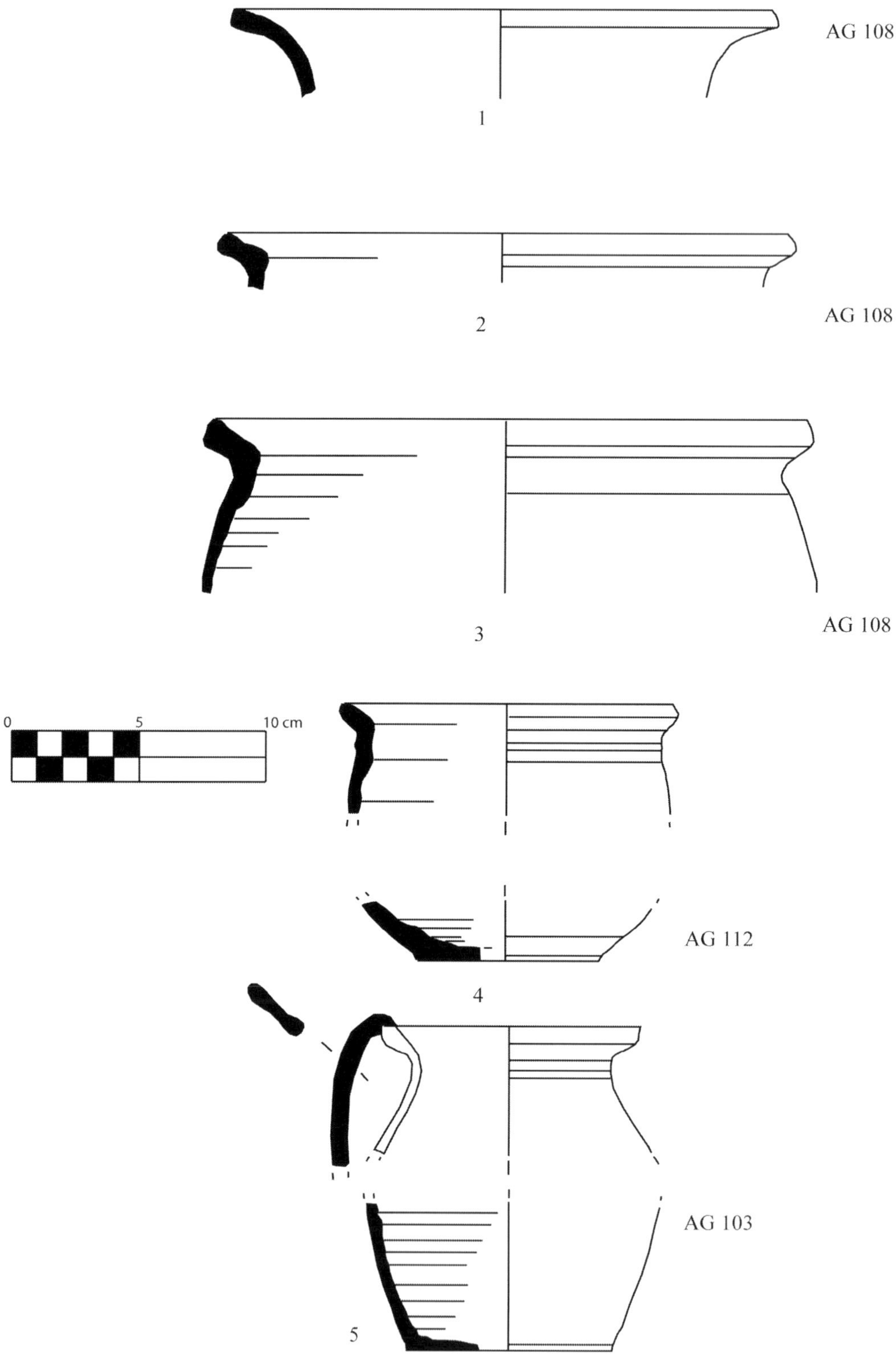

PLATE XLIV

Casseroles in kitchen ware and corresponding fabrics (Scoglietto cave)

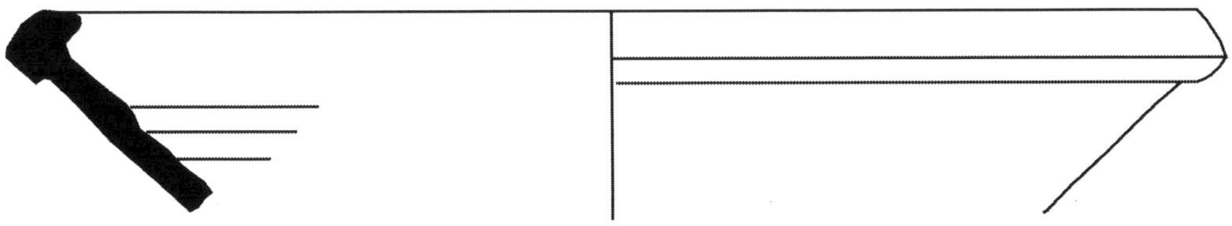

1

AG 101

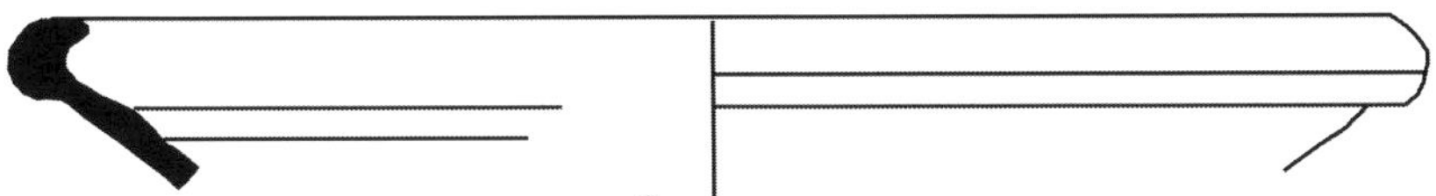

2

AG 101

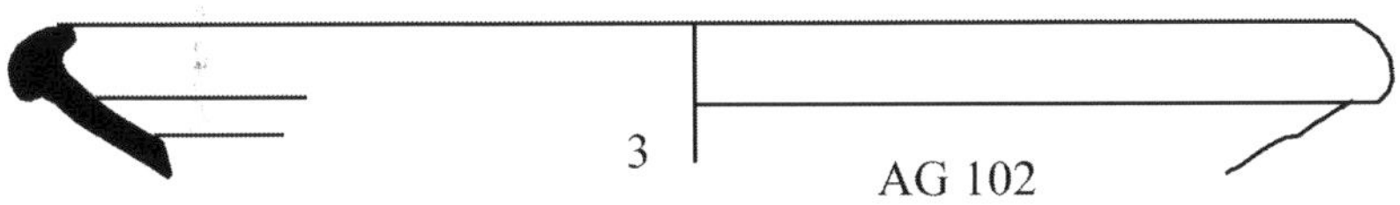

3

AG 102

AG 102

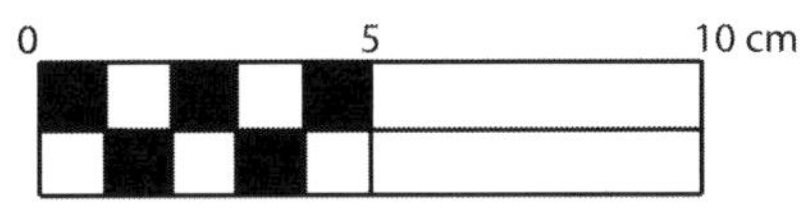

4

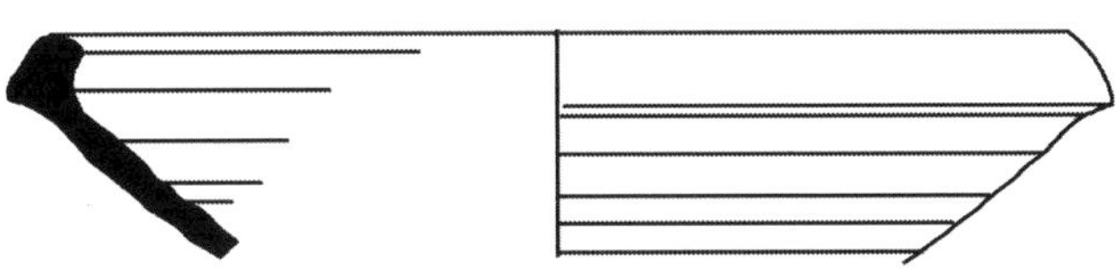

5

AG 103

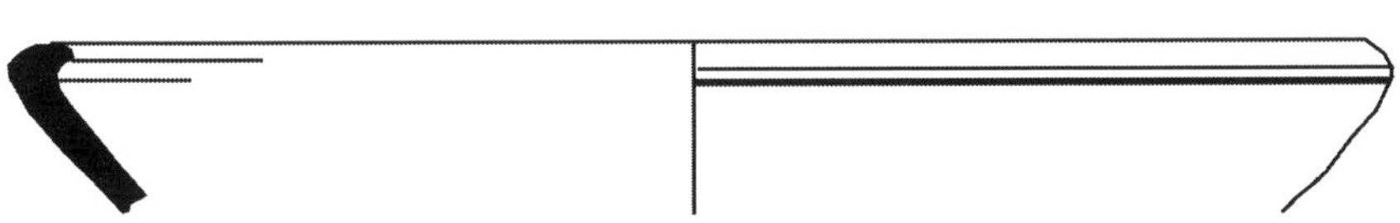

6

AG 102

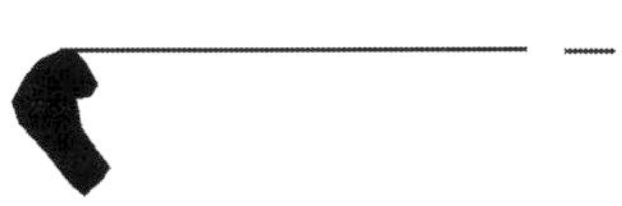

7

AG 101

PLATE XLV

Fine wares from the late antique occupation of the cave at Spaccasasso

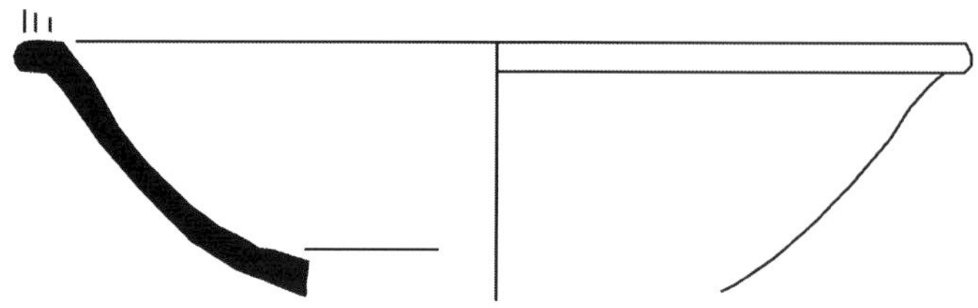

1 Hayes 93B (ARS)

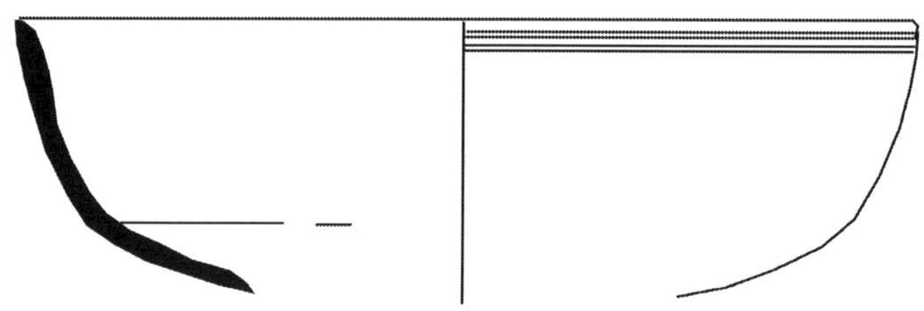

2 *Ingobbiata di rosso* ware

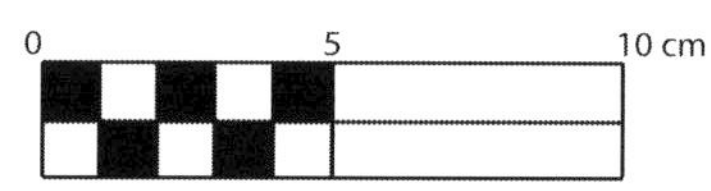

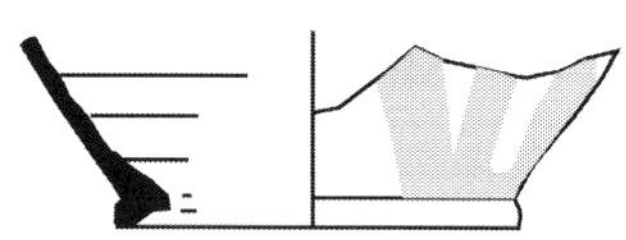

3 *Colature di rosso* ware

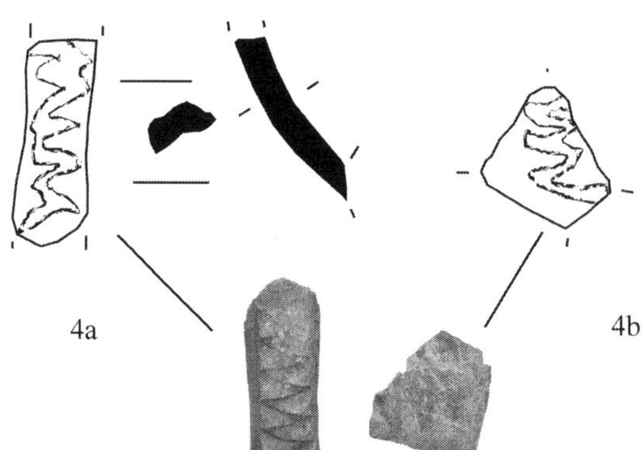

4a

4b Zig-zag ware (Palestine?)

PLATE XLVI

Coarsewares from the late antique occupation of the cave at Spaccasasso

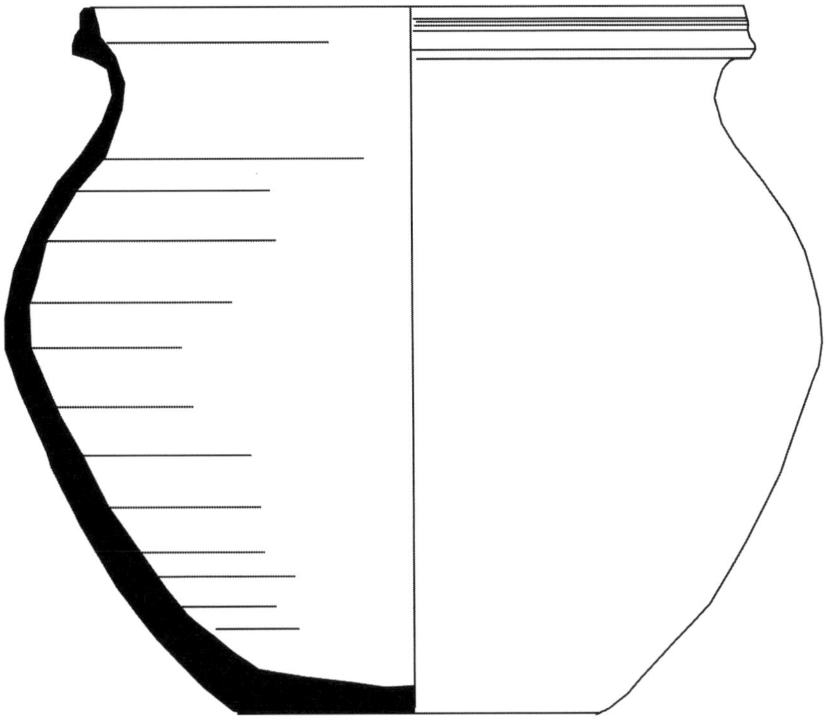

1 Cooking pot AG 108

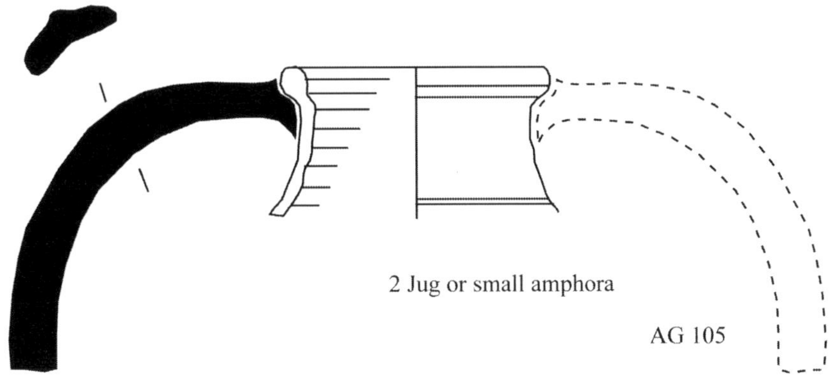

2 Jug or small amphora

AG 105

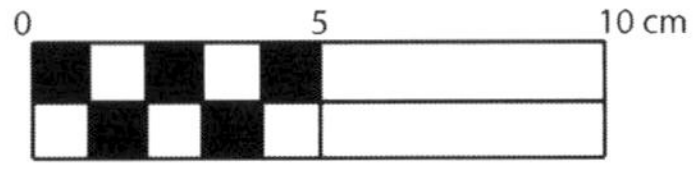

PLATE XLVII

Mediterranean and regional coarse wares from the mid 6th to early 7th AD ceramic assemblage at Paduline

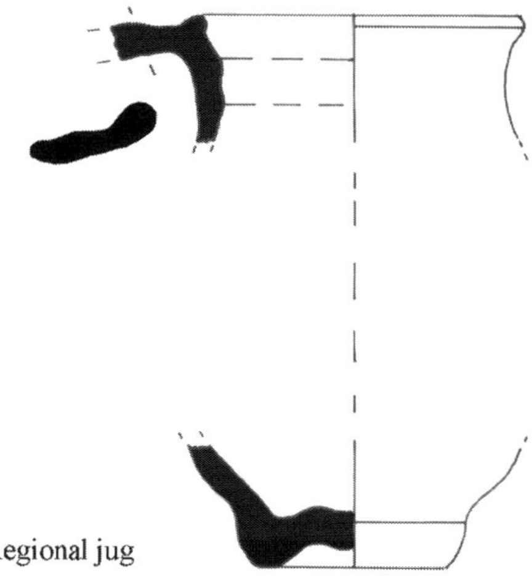

1 Regional jug

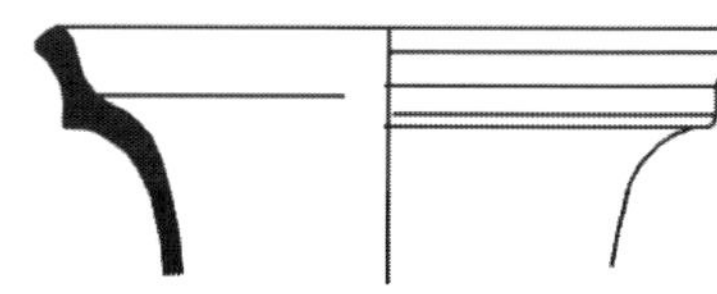

2 Regional jug

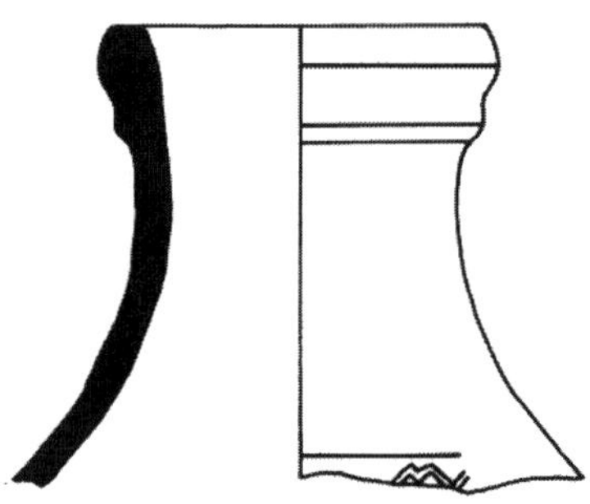

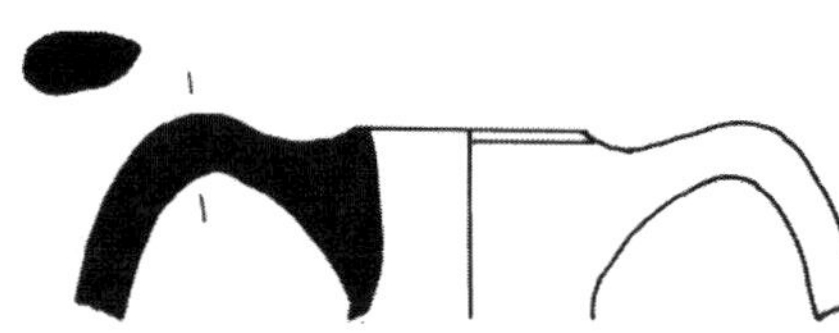

4 Regional bottle

3 Tunisian bottle or small spathion (carbonatic fabric)

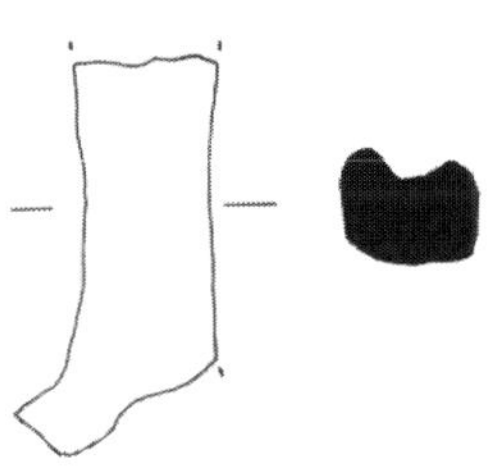

5

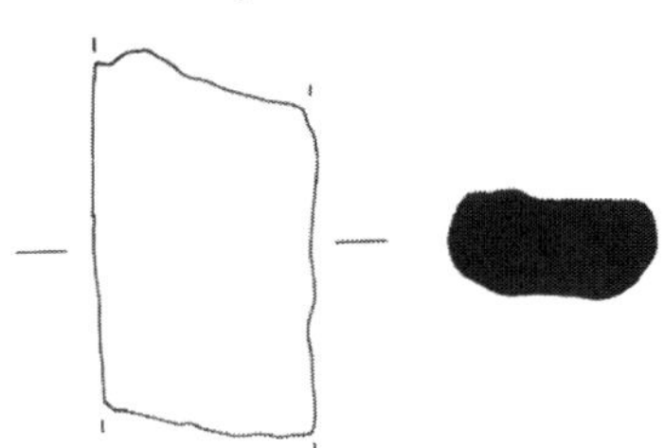

6

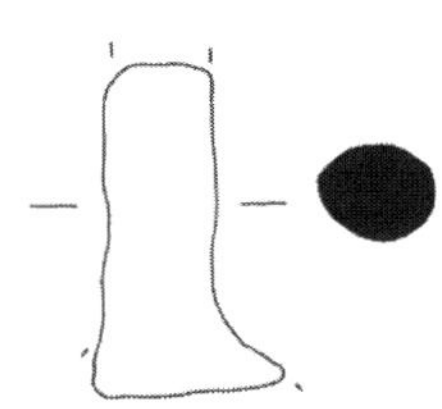

7

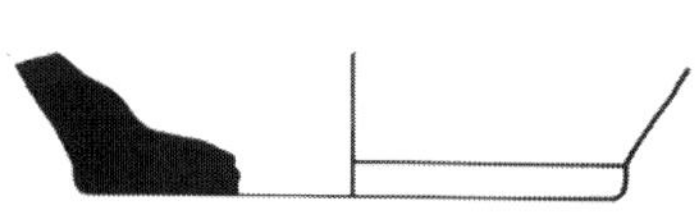

8

PLATE XLVIII

Tunisian amphorae (in phase and residual) from the mid 6th to early 7th AD context at Paduline

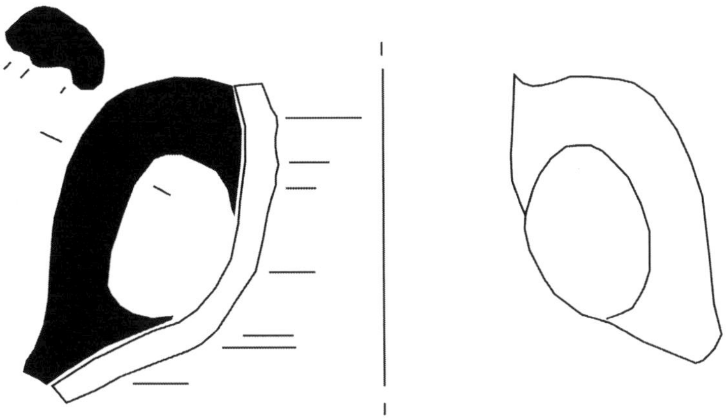

1 Possible Keay LXII neck (in phase)

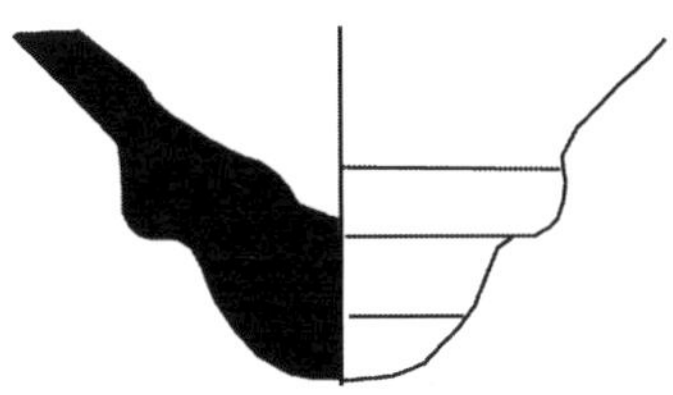

2 Keay LXII spike (in phase)

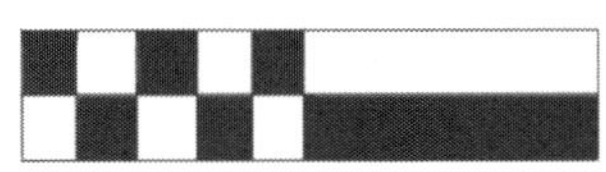

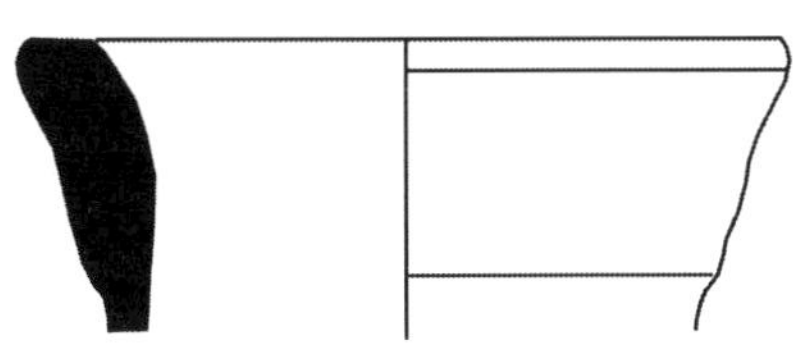

3 Keay XXV B (residual)

PLATE XLIX

Red painted and *colature rosse* wares from the mid 6th to early 7th century AD ceramic dump of Paduline

PLATE L

Ingobbiata di rosso **ware from the mid 6th to early 7th AD ceramic assemblage at Paduline**

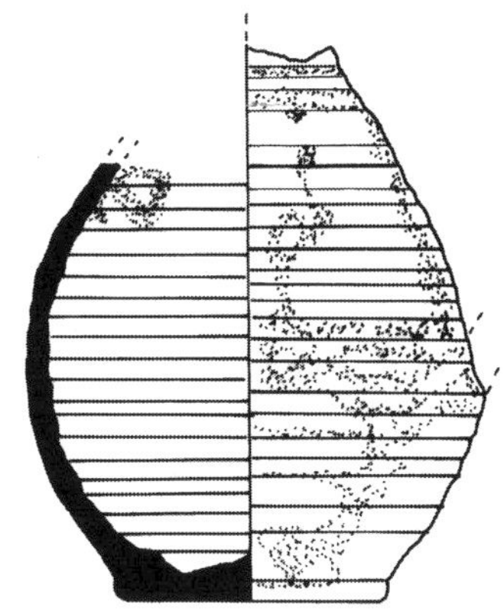

1a

1b

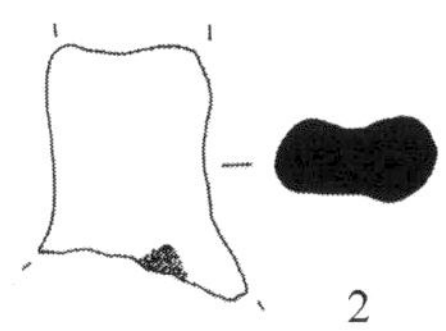

2

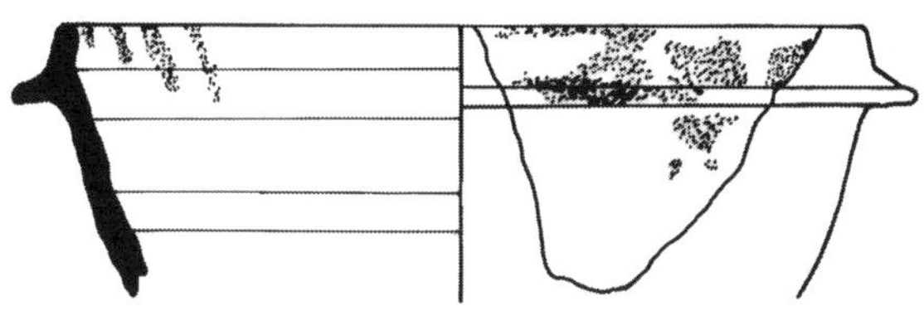

3

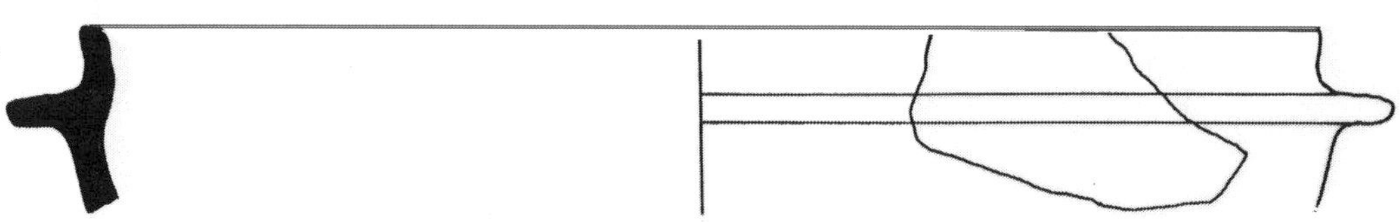

4

PLATE LI

Kitchen ware from the mid 6th-early 7th ceramic assemblage at Paduline

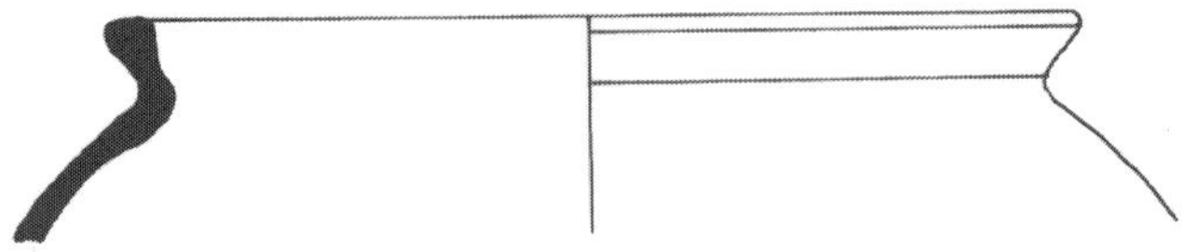

1 Cooking pot

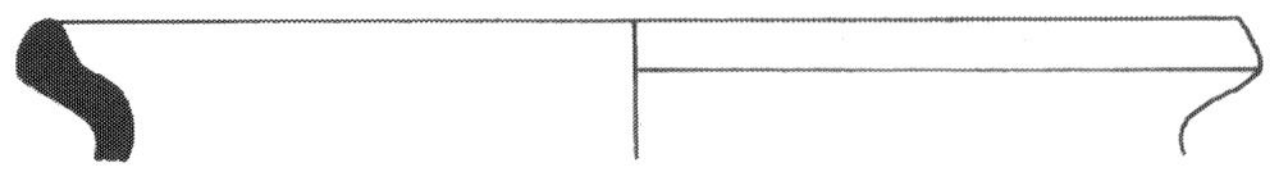

2 Cooking pot

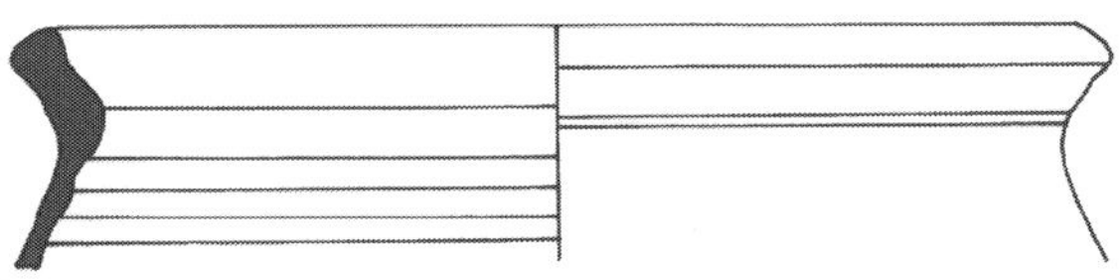

3 Cooking pot

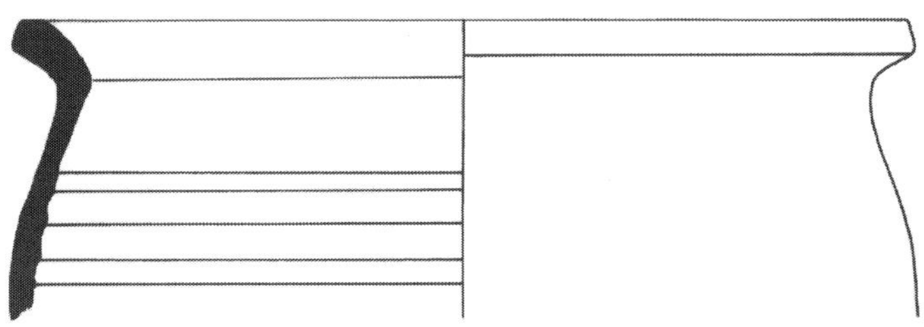

4 Deep cooking pot

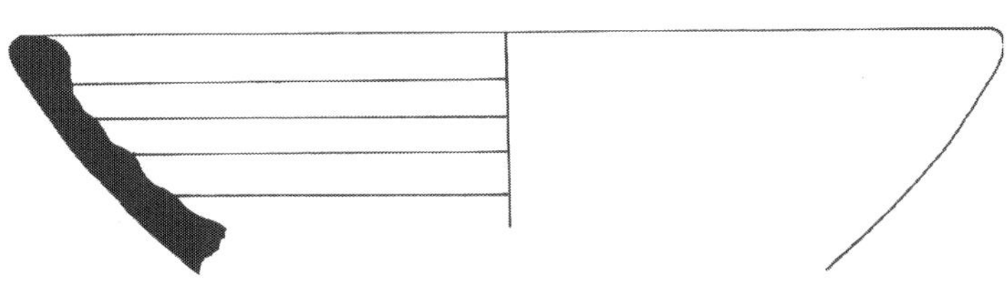

5 Cooking-pan (*tegame*)

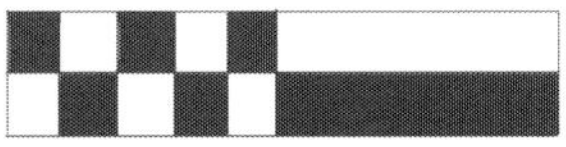

PLATE LII

ARS C from Portus Scabris:
main types (late 4th to early 6th AD)

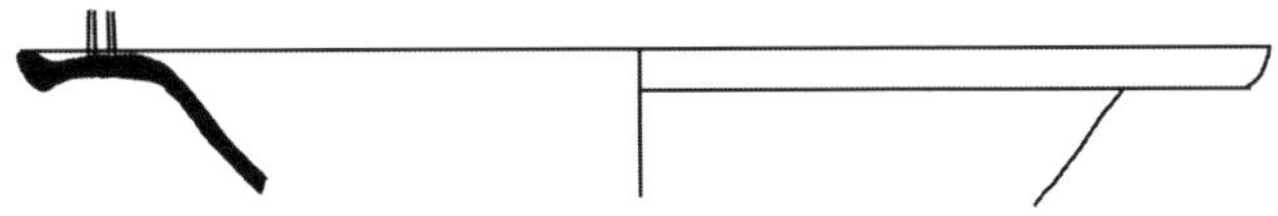

1 HAYES 71B

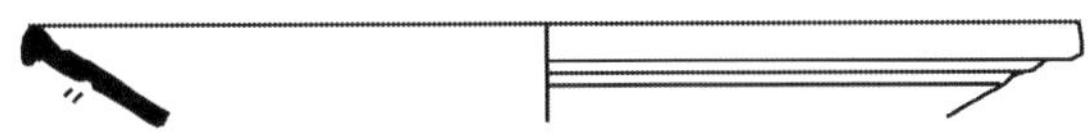

2 HAYES 75

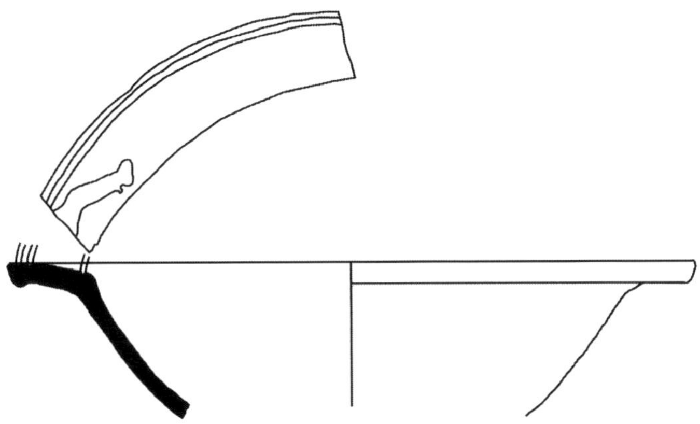

3 HAYES 73A

4 HAYES 84

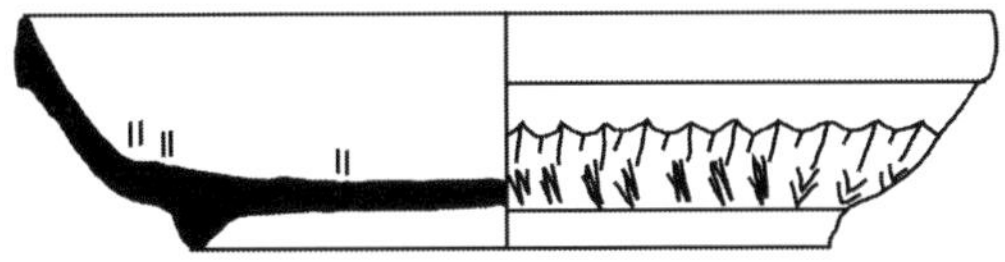

5 FULFORD ARS 27.2 - HAYES 84 *similis*

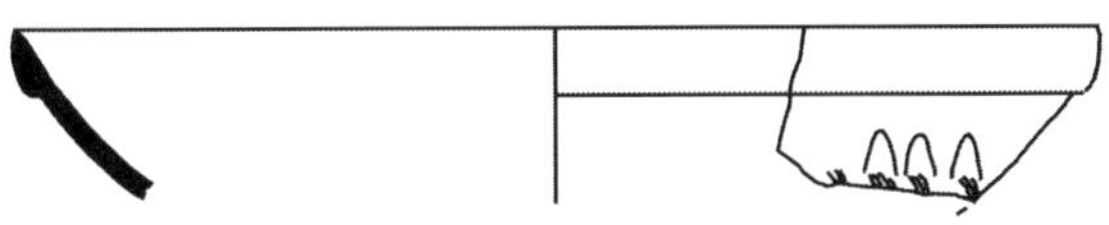

6 FULFORD ARS 27.2 - HAYES 84 *similis*

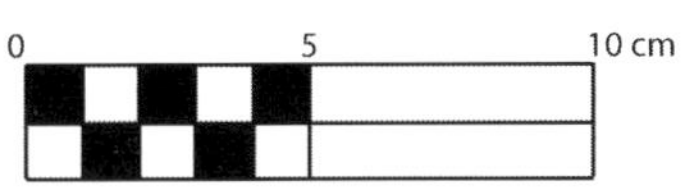

PLATE LIII

**ARS D from Portus Scabris:
4th and 5th centuries types**

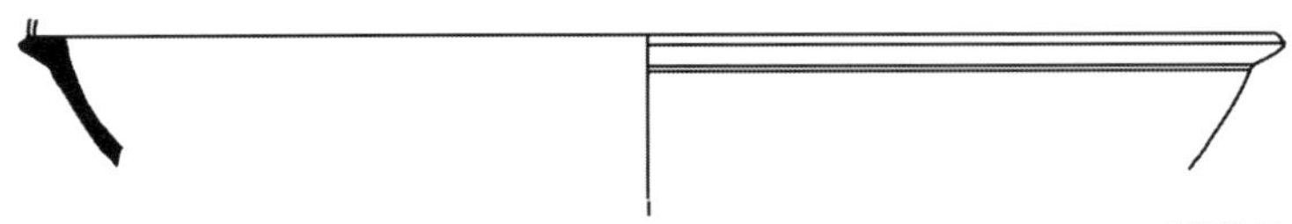

1 Hayes 58B, n.11

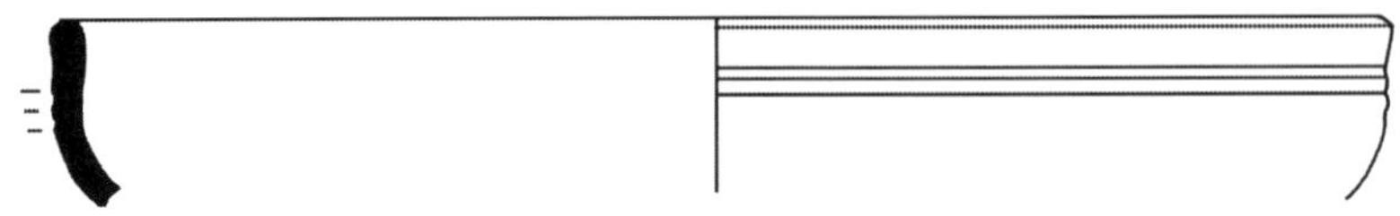

2 Hayes 63

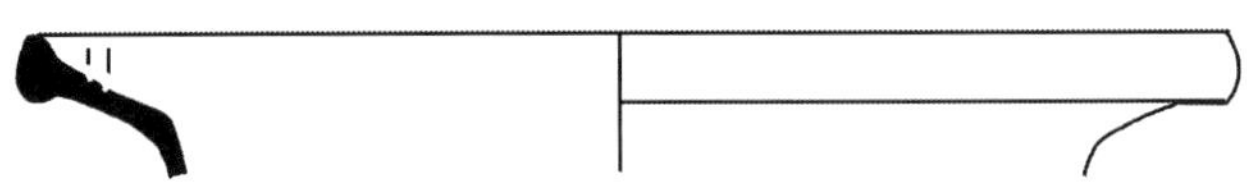

3 Mackensen 16

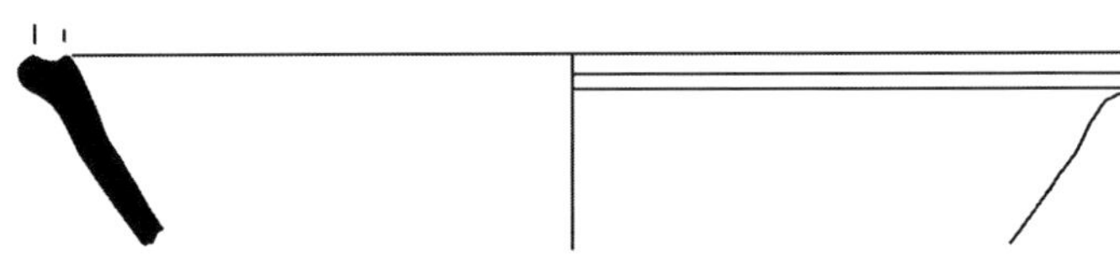

4 Hayes 79

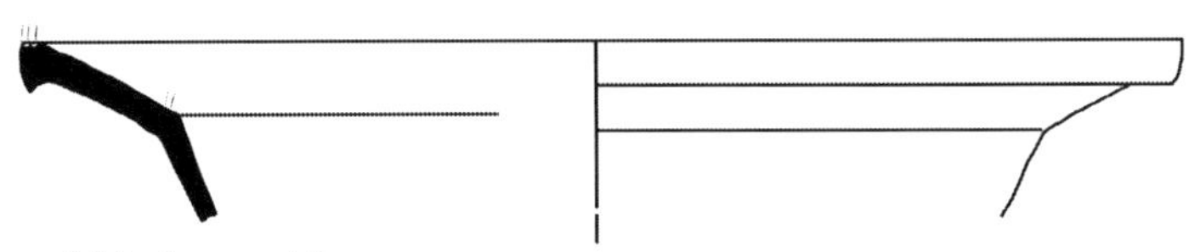

5 Mackensen 17

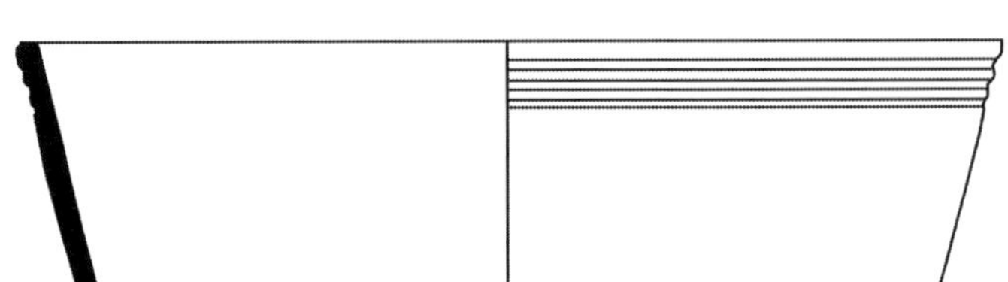

6 Hayes 80A

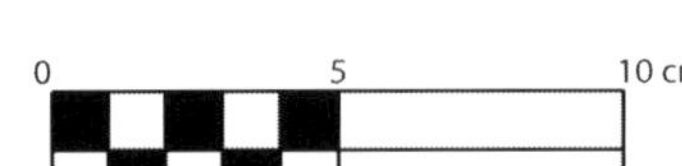

PLATE LIV

ARS D from Portus Scabris: variants A and B of the Hayes 61 large bowl

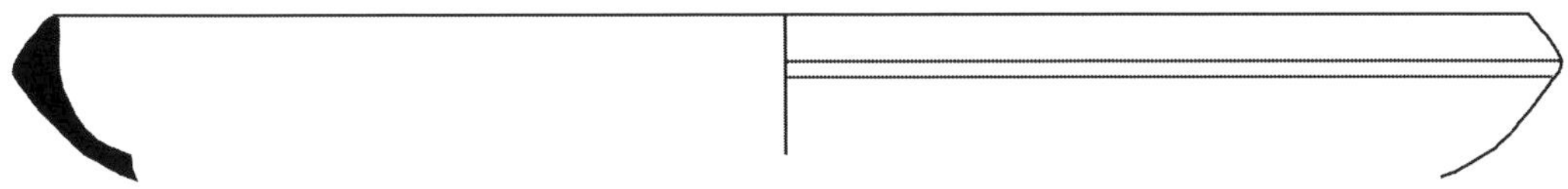

1

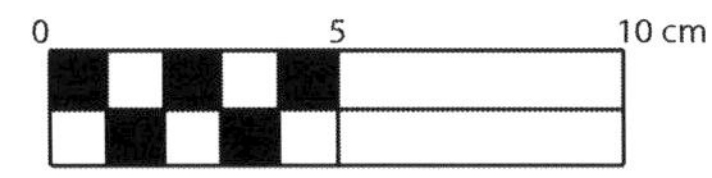

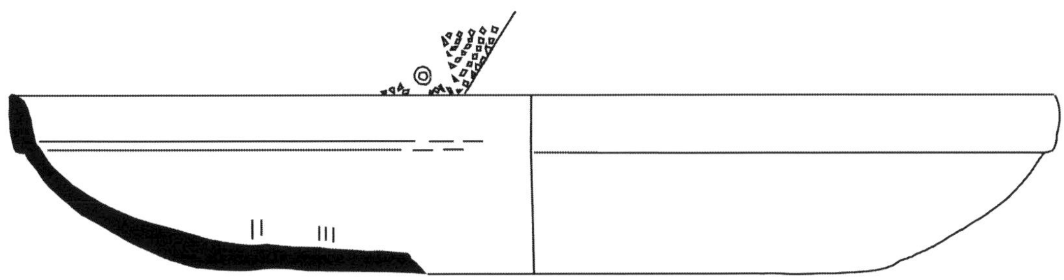

2

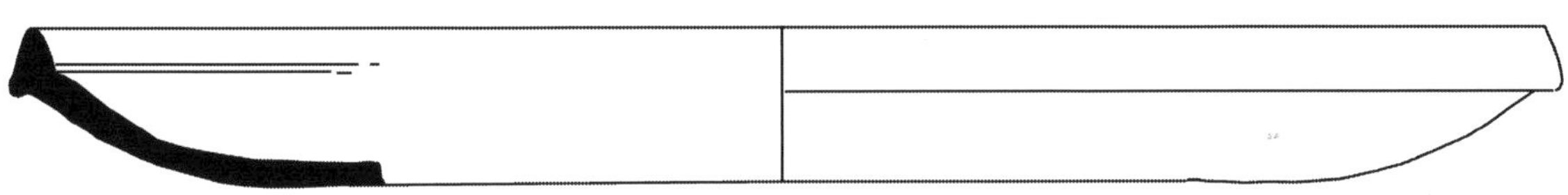

3

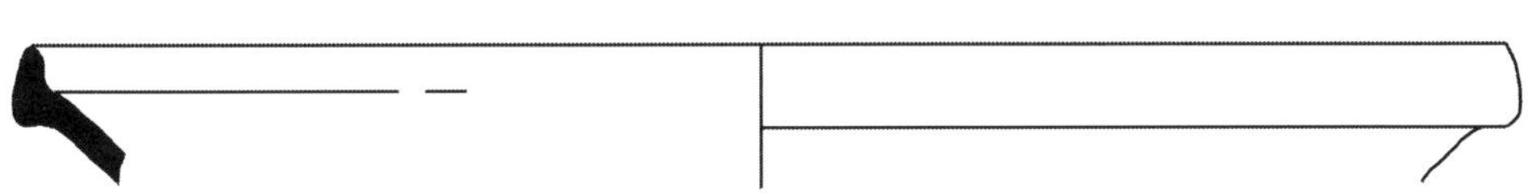

4

PLATE LV

ARS D from Portus Scabris: Hayes 67

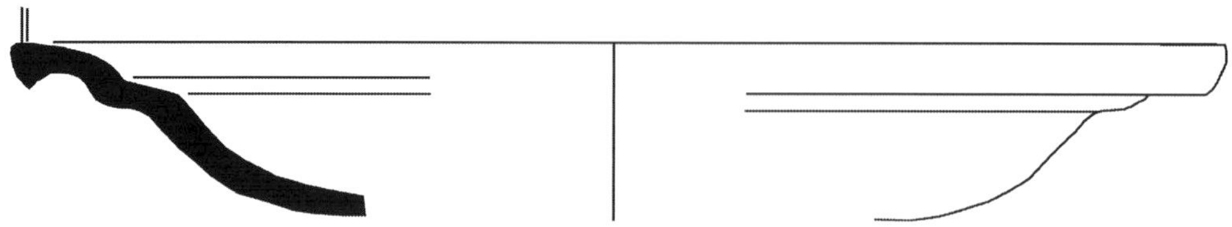

1 Hayes 67

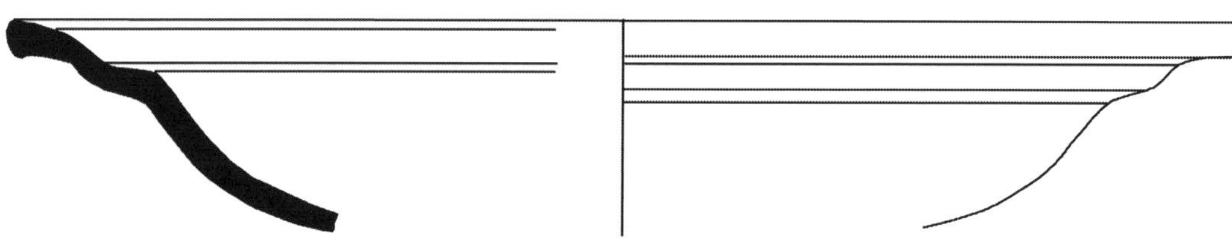

2 Hayes 67

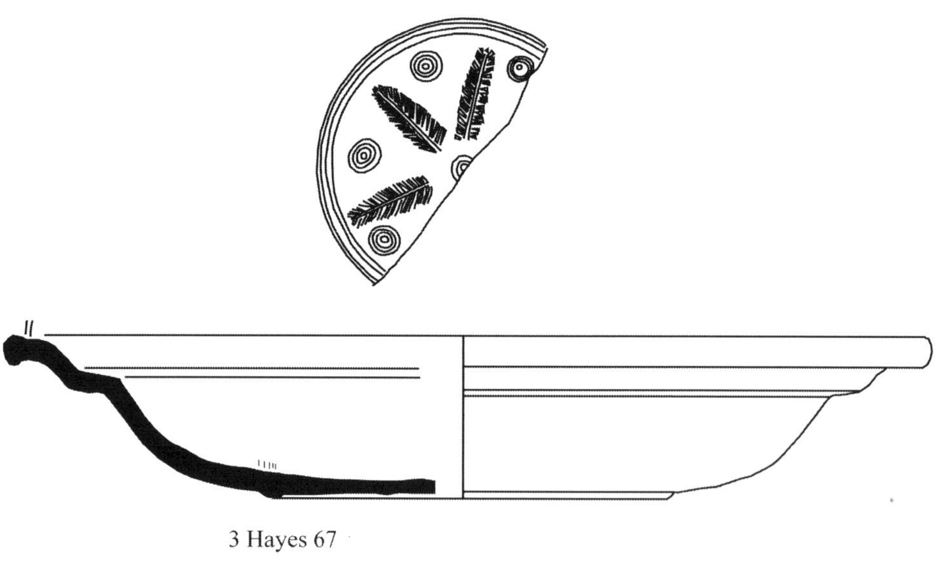

3 Hayes 67

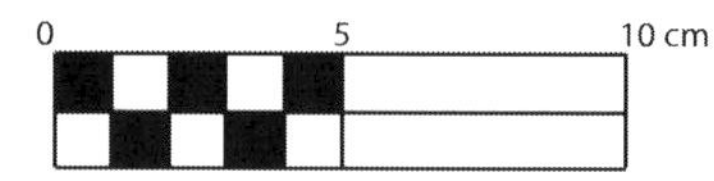

PLATE LVI

Late variants of the Hayes 61B bowl

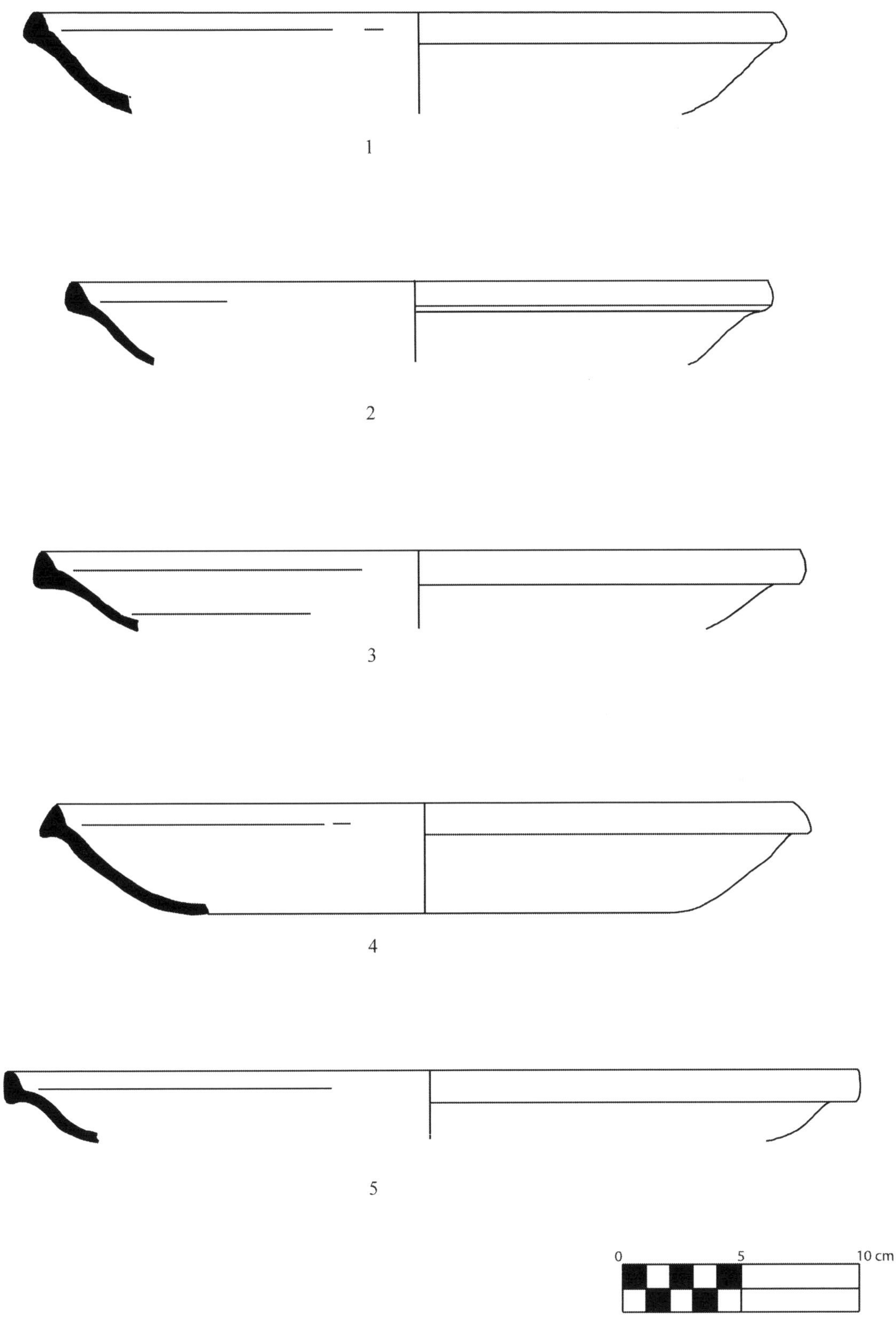

PLATE LVII

ARS D from Portus Scabris: Hayes 91 and variants

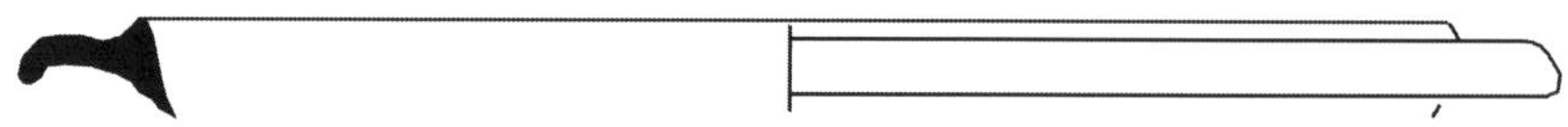

1 Hayes 91B

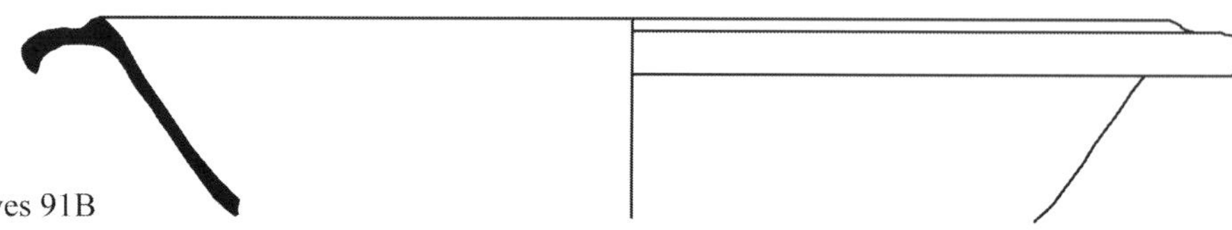

2 Hayes 91B

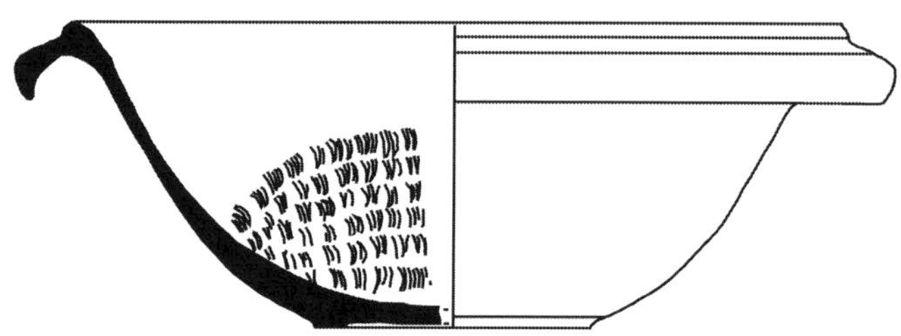

3 Hayes 91B

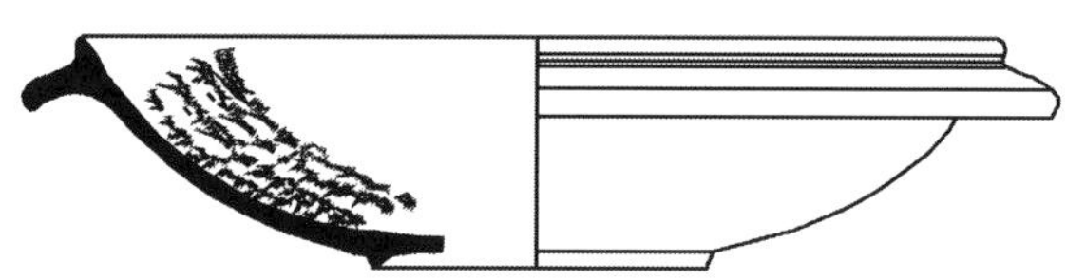

4 Hayes 91B

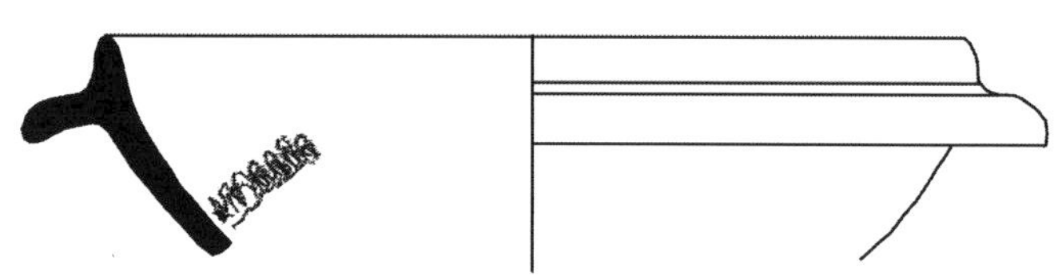

5 Hayes 91C

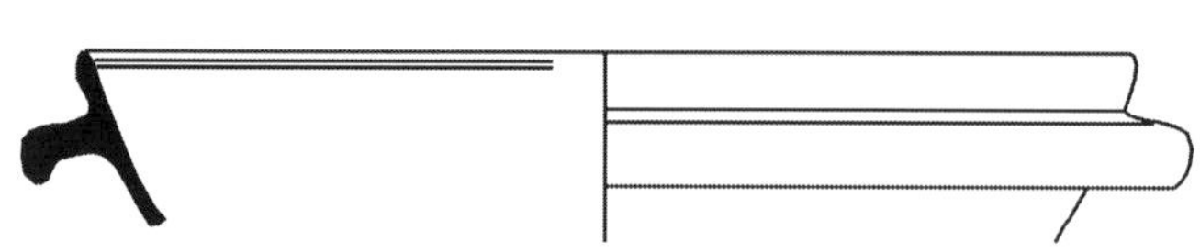

6 Hayes 91C

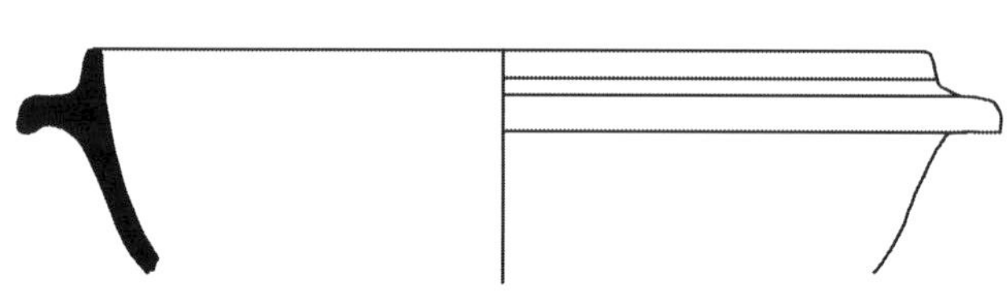

7 Hayes 91C

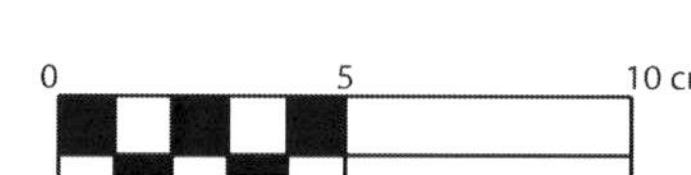

PLATE LVIII

ARS from Portus Scabris:
selection of stamps

1

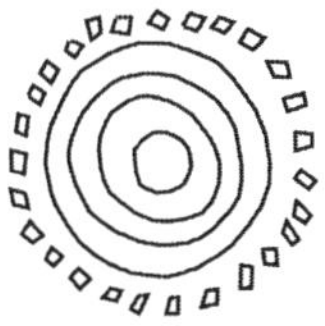

2

3

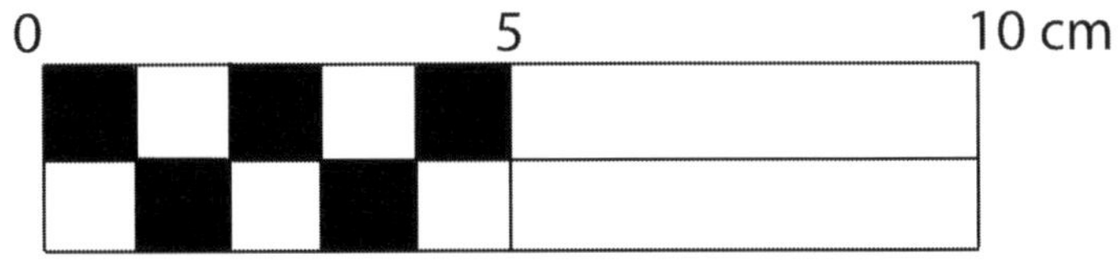

4

5

6

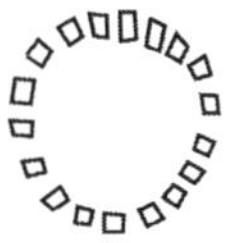

PLATE LIX

ARS D from Portus Scabris: selection of types produced from the second half of the 5th AD onwards

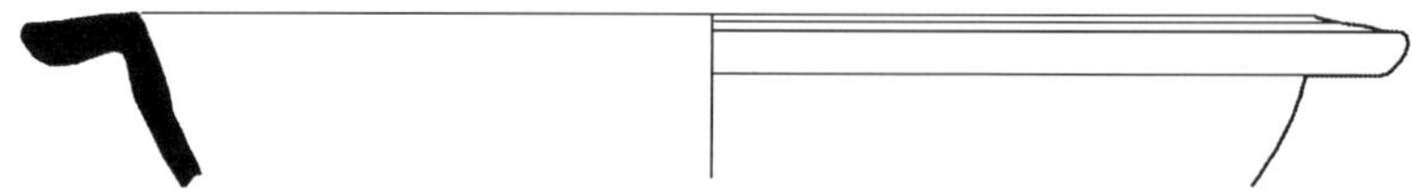

1 Hayes 93A

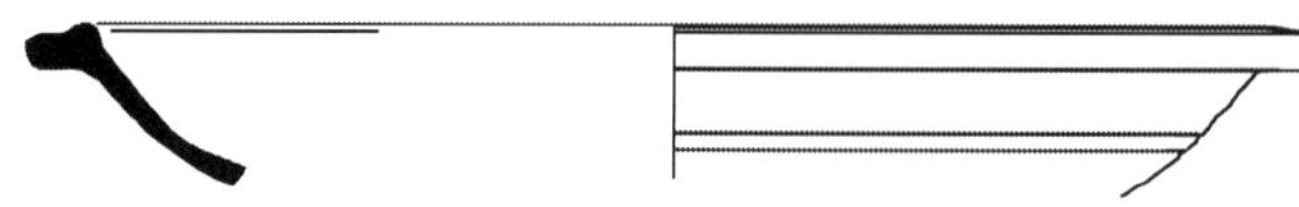

2 Hayes 93B *similis*

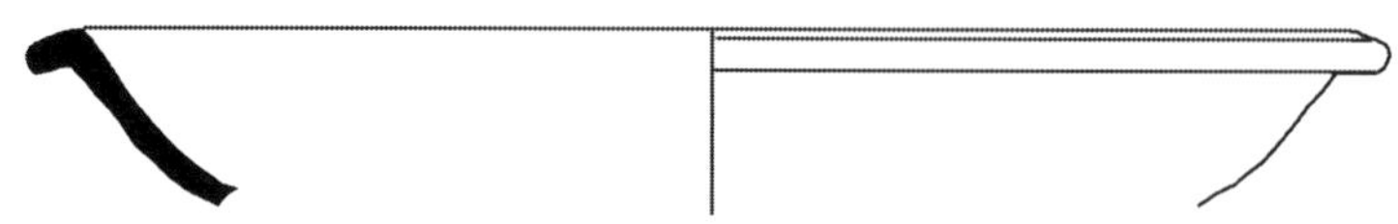

3 Hayes 93B

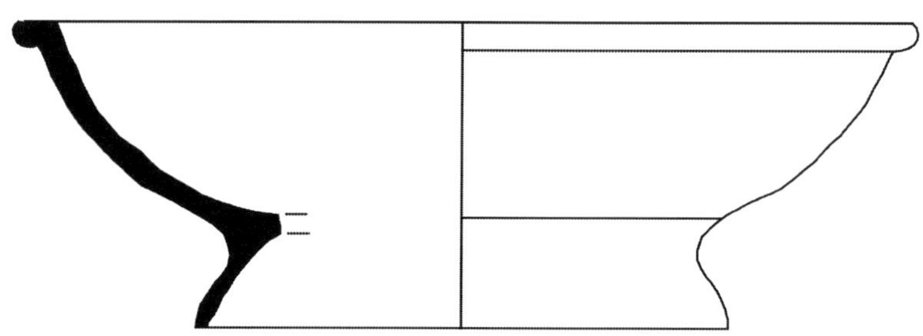

4 Hayes 93B

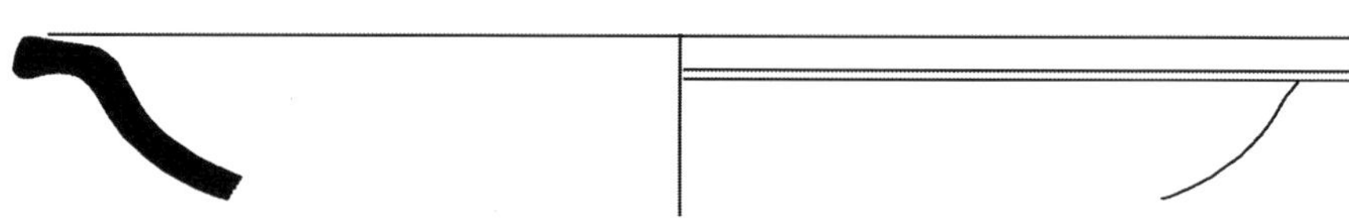

5 Mackensen 22

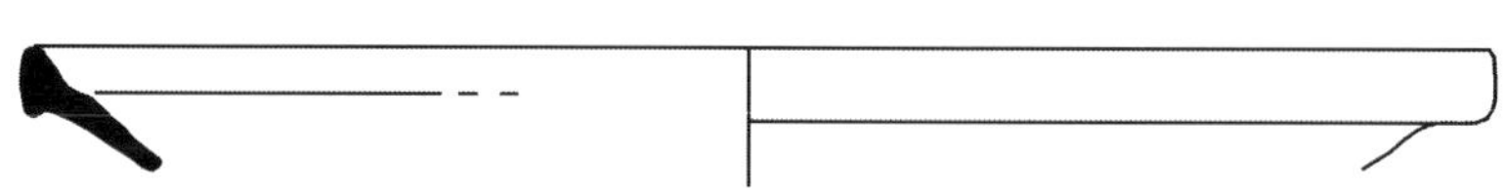

6 Hayes 87A (*similis*)

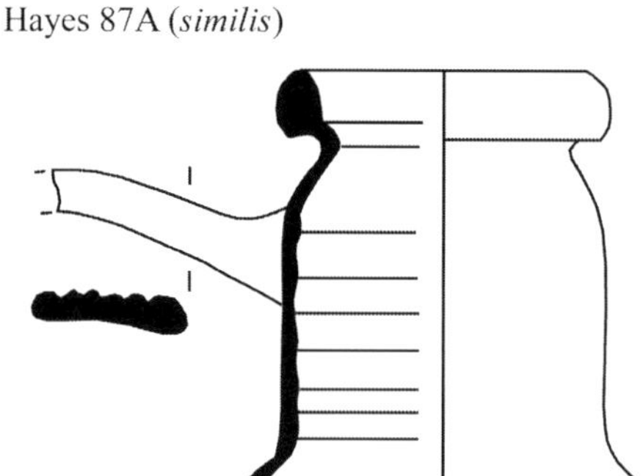

7 Fulford, ARSW, C.F.2.8

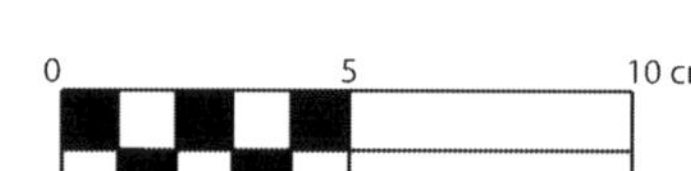

PLATE LX

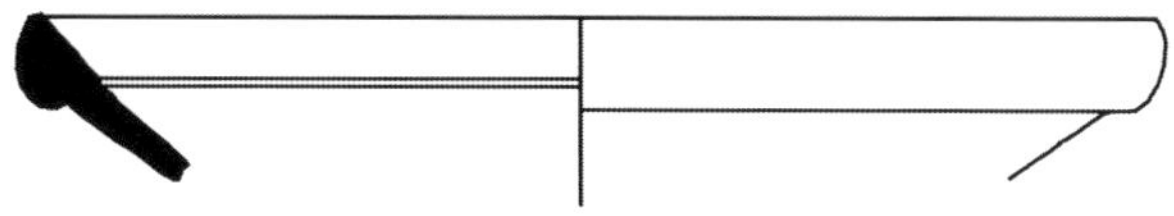

1 Hayes 99 variant/ Mackensen 28.2

ARS D from Portus Scabris: Hayes 99 and variants

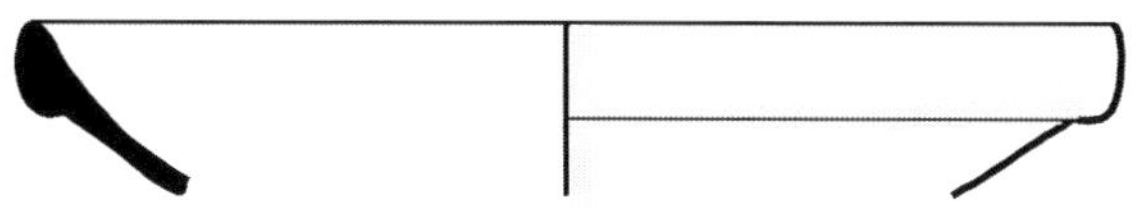

2 Hayes 99B/Mackensen 29.2

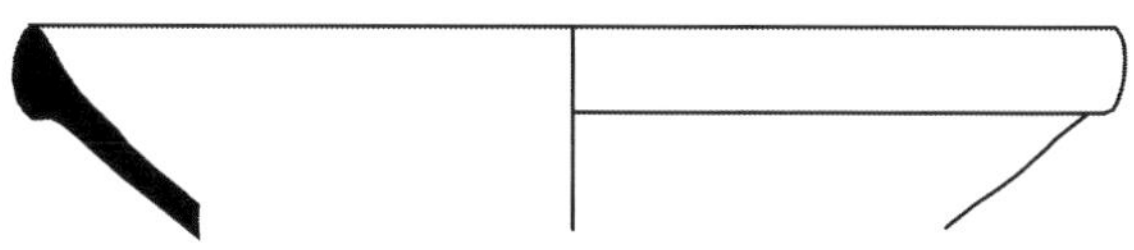

3 Hayes 99B/Mackensen 29.2

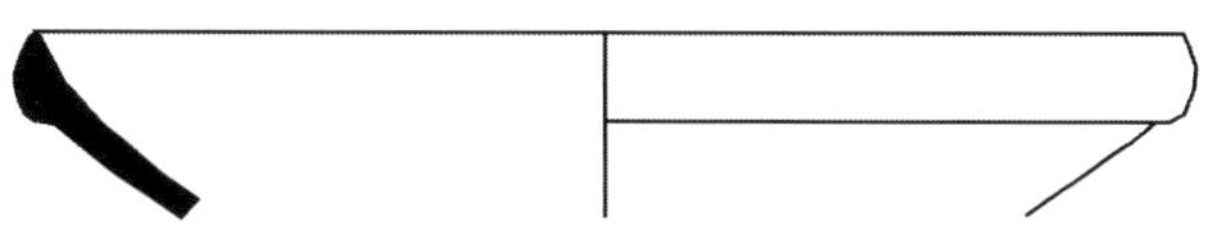

4 Hayes 99B/Mackensen 29.2

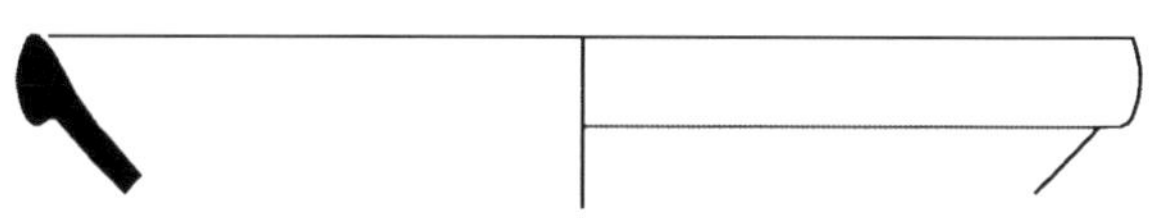

5 Hayes 99B variant

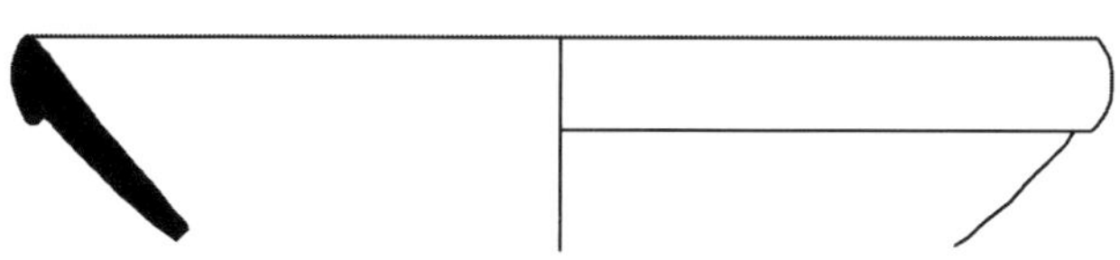

6 Hayes 99B variant

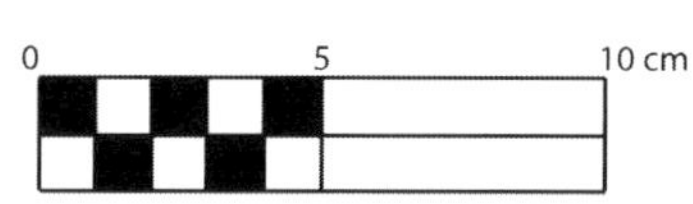

PLATE LXI

ARS D from Portus Scabris:
Hayes 103, Mackensen 18 (?) and Hayes 87C/109

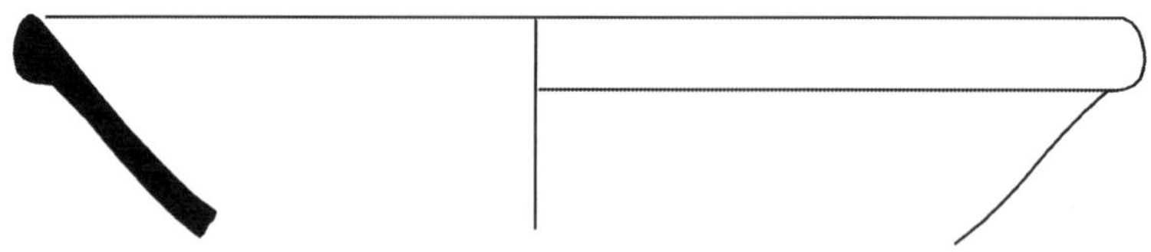

1 Hayes 103B/Mackensen 26

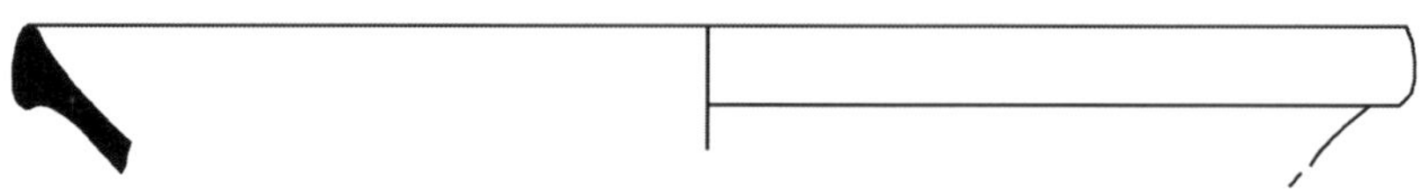

2 Hayes 103B

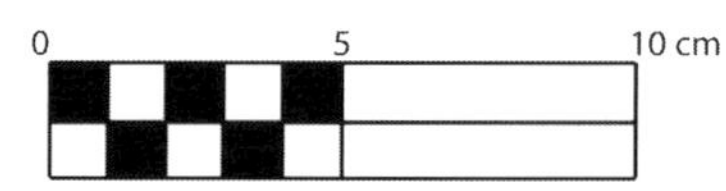

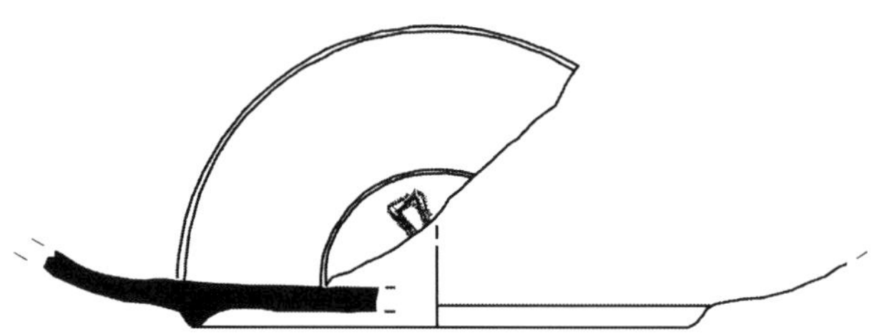

3 Mackensen 18 (?)

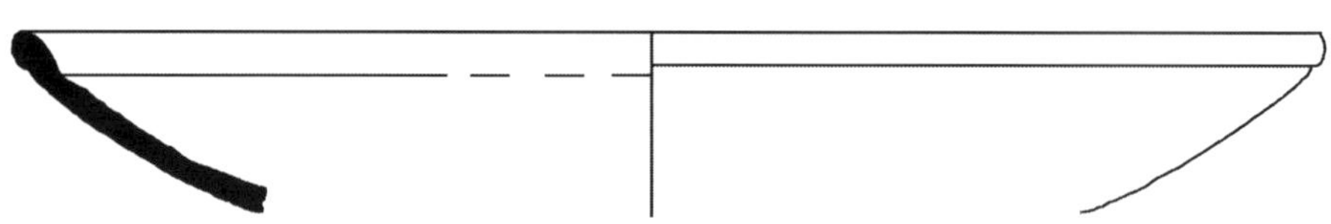

4 Hayes 87C/109

PLATE LXII

ARS D from Portus Scabris:
Hayes 104 and variants

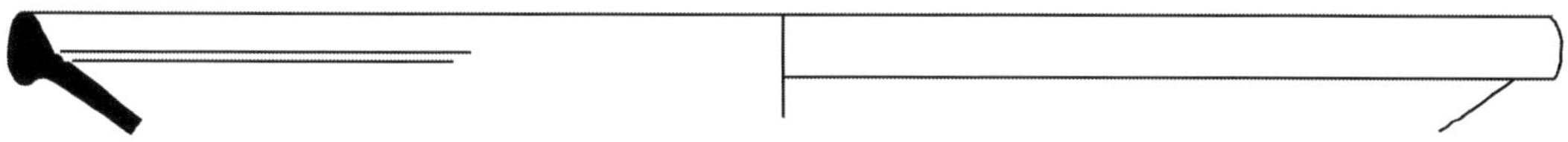

1 Hayes 104A

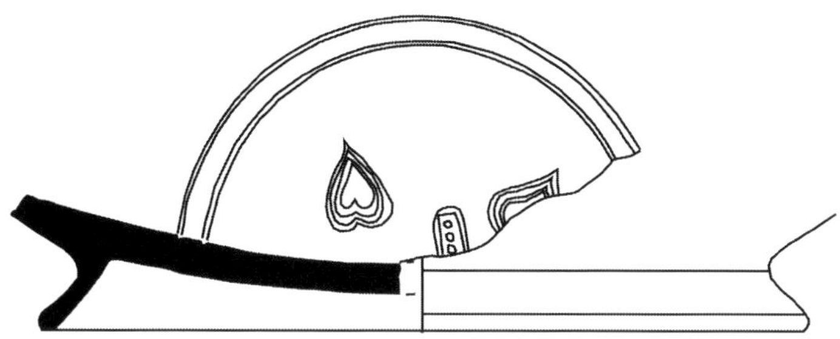

2 Hayes 104A

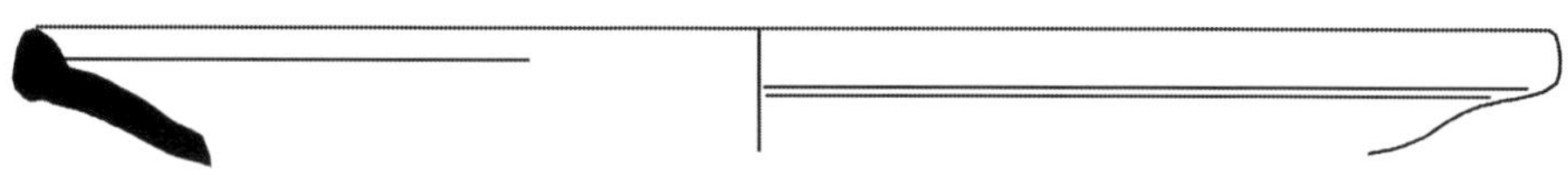

3 Fulford ARSW, Open Forms 65.5/Hayes 104A/B *similis* (?)

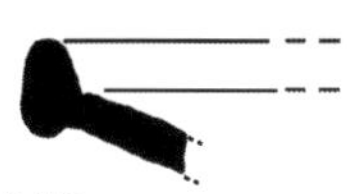

4 Hayes 104B

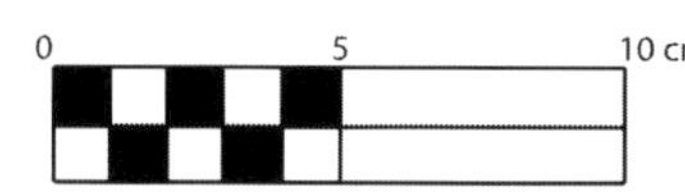

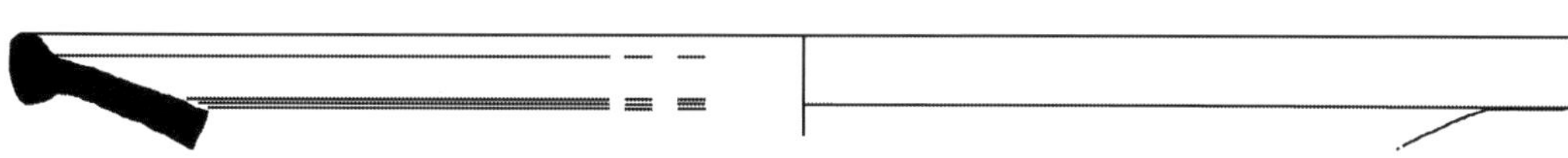

5 Hayes 104B

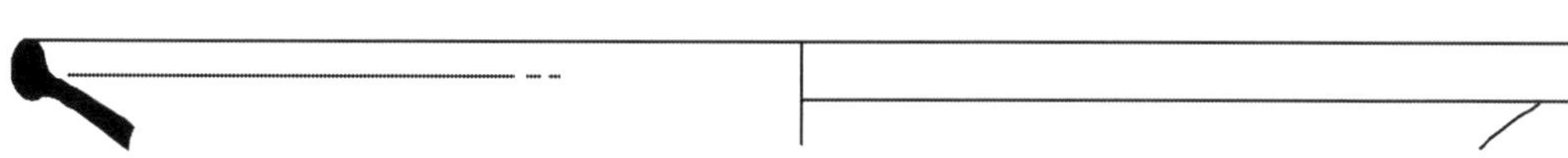

6 Mackensen 32/34-Hayes 104 (late variant)

PLATE LXIII

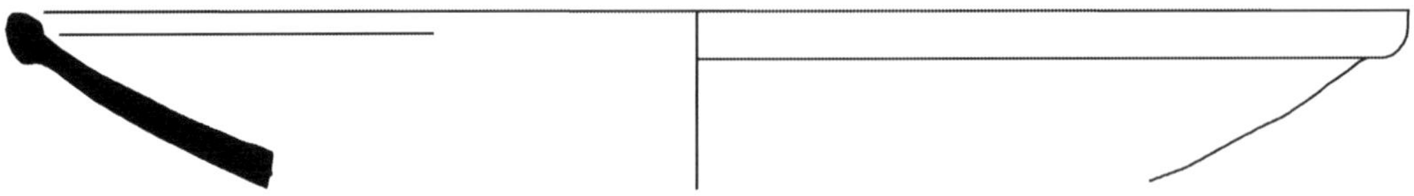

1 Hayes 105, n.17

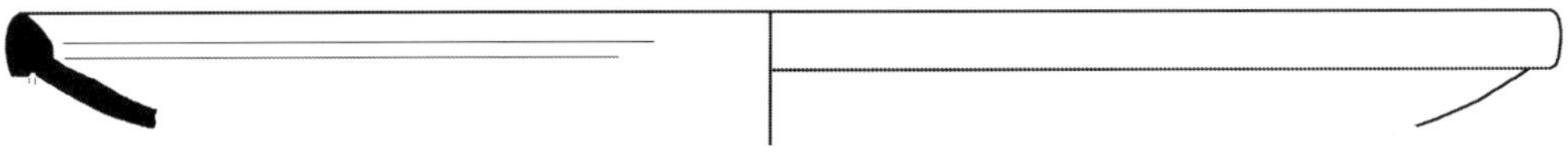

2 Hayes 105, n.7 or n.13

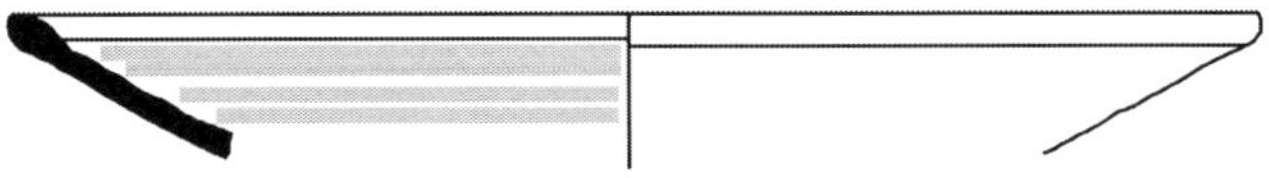

3 Hayes 109

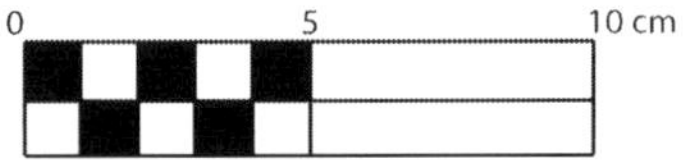

PLATE LXIV

ARS Lamps from Portus Scabris

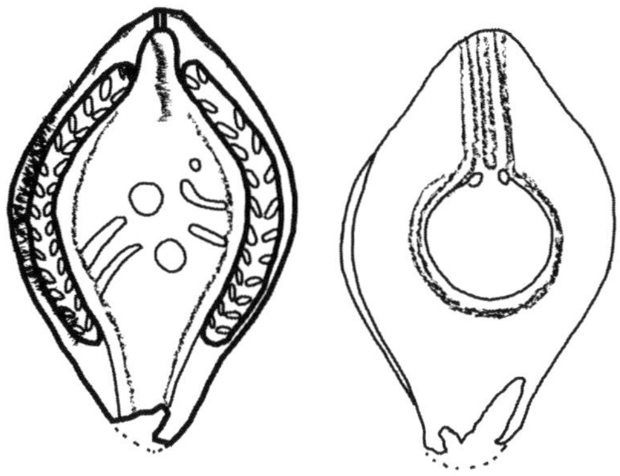

1 Atlante VIII A1 Form

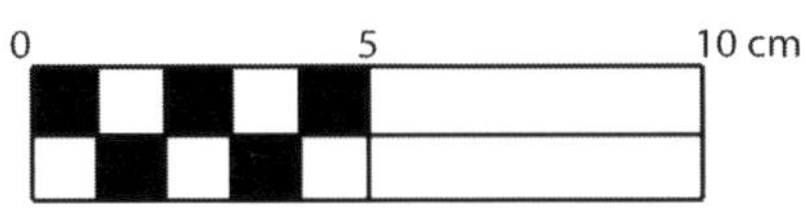

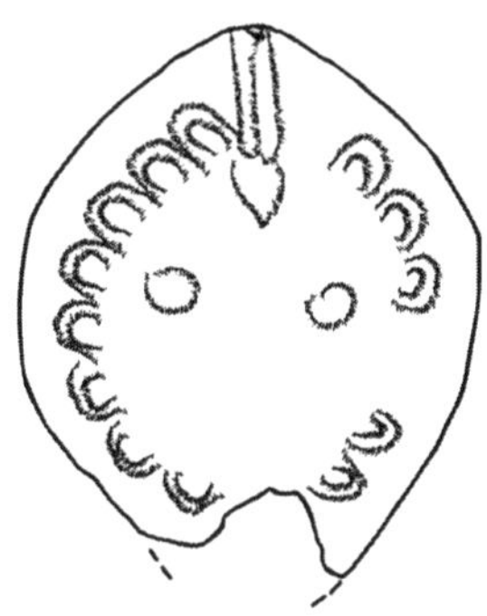

2 Atlante VIII C2 Form

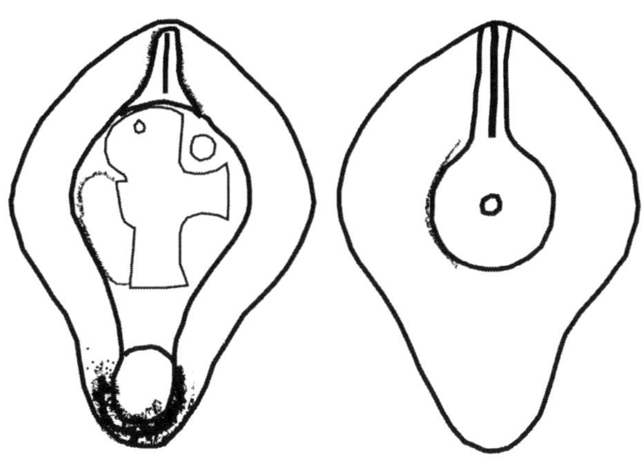

3 Atlante VIII C1 Form

PLATE LXV

Tunisian and Eastern Mediterranean (?)
kitchen ware from Portus Scabris

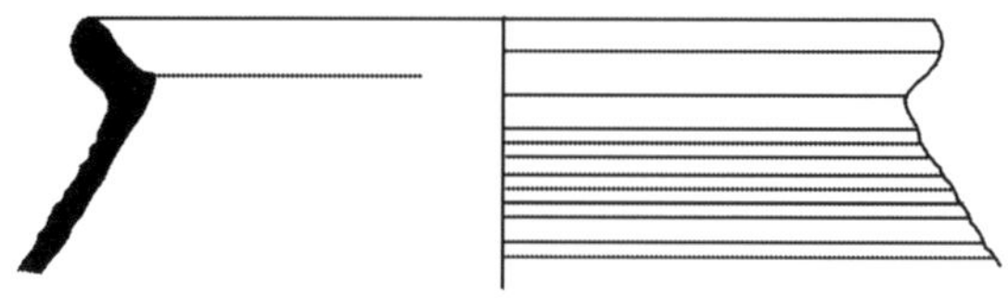

1 Fulford
Casserole 19

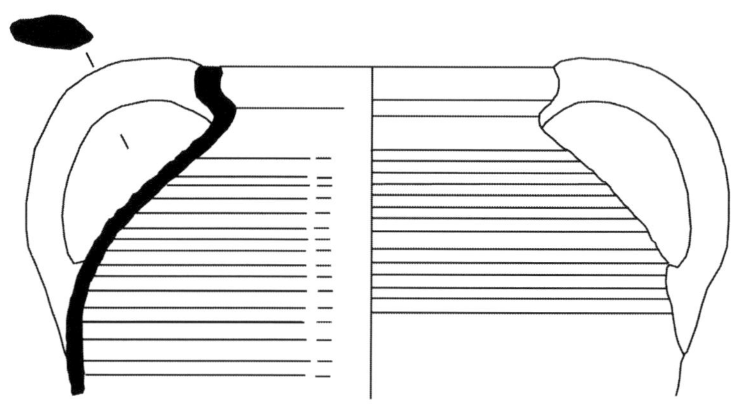

2 Fulford
Casserole 19

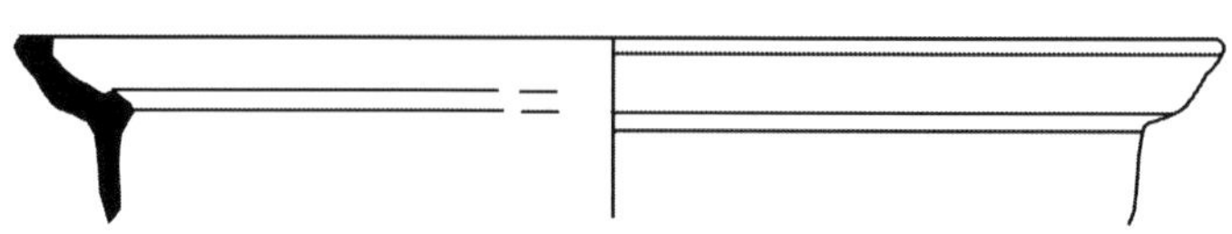

3 Fulford
Casserole 20.1/20.3

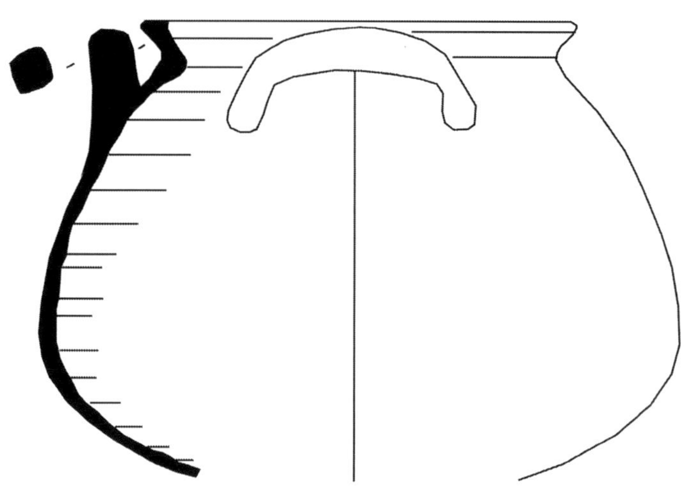

4 Casserole from
an unknown source
(possibly Eastern
Mediterranean)

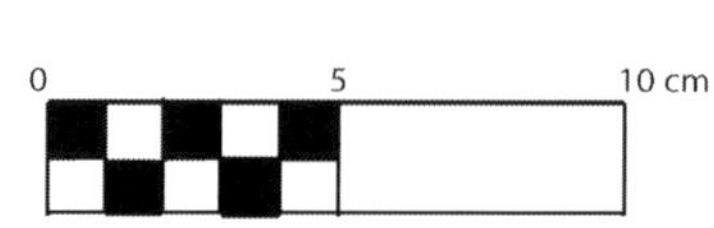

PLATE LXVI

Tunisian coarse ware from Portus Scabris

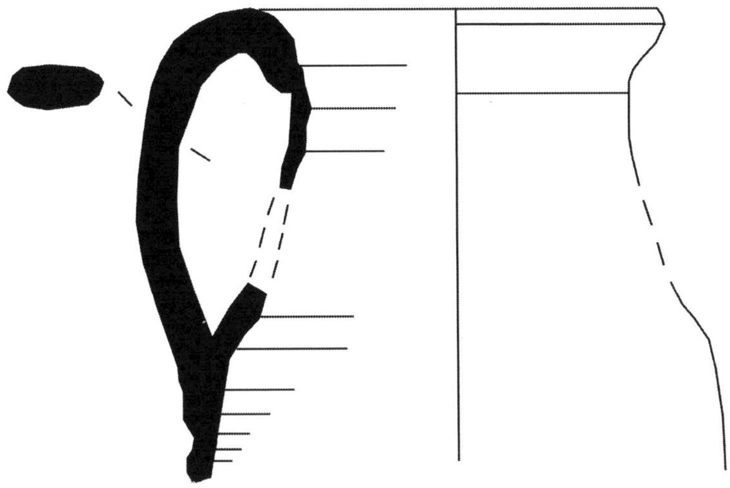

1 Fulford, Closed Forms 16.3 (*similis*)

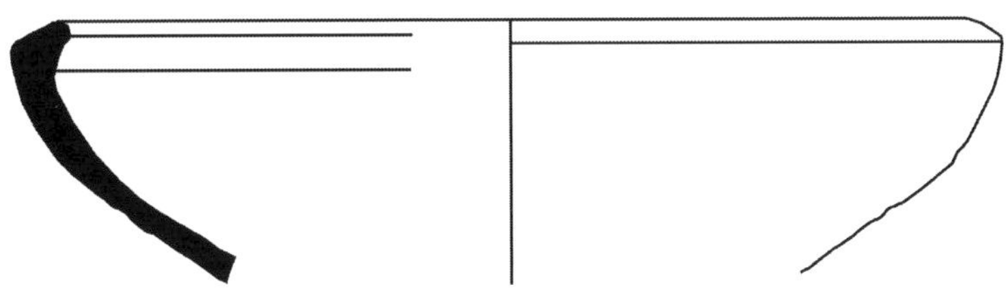

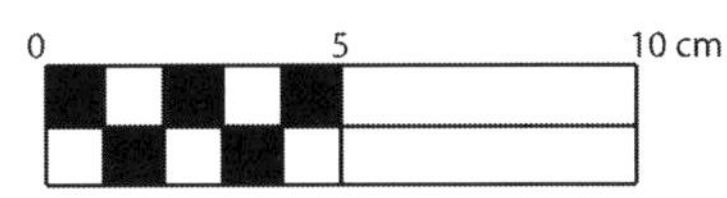

2 Tunisian (?) basin

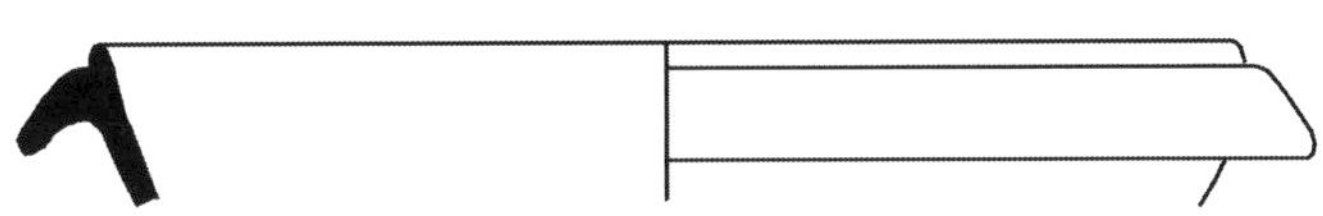

3 Fulford, mortaria 2

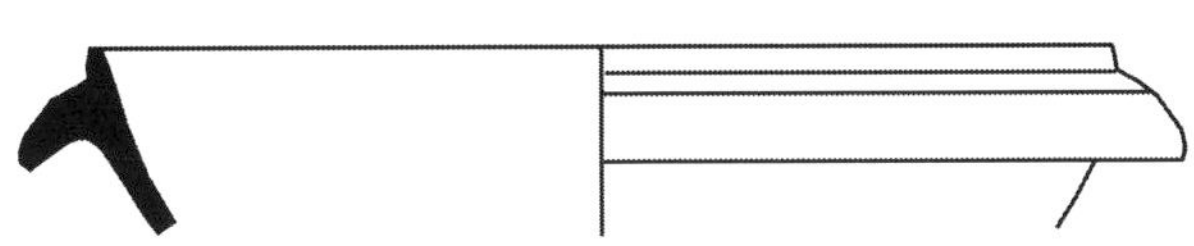

4 Fulford, mortaria 2

PLATE LXVII

Tunisian amphorae from Portus Scabris: Keay VII

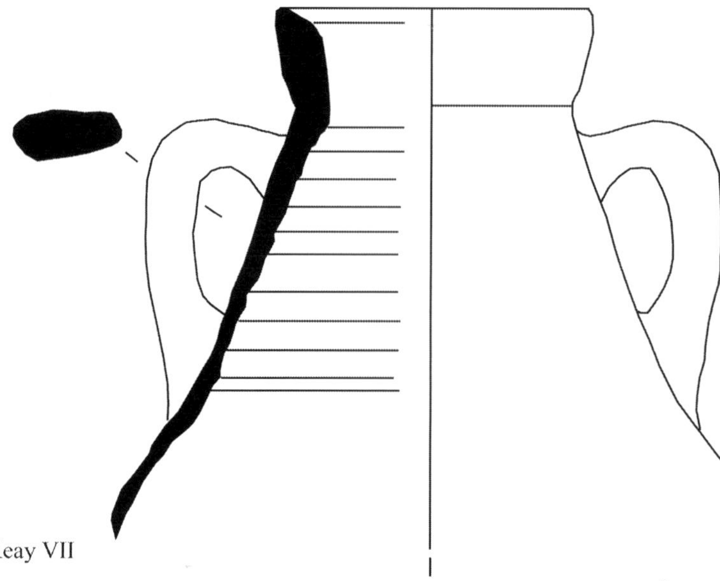

1 Keay VII

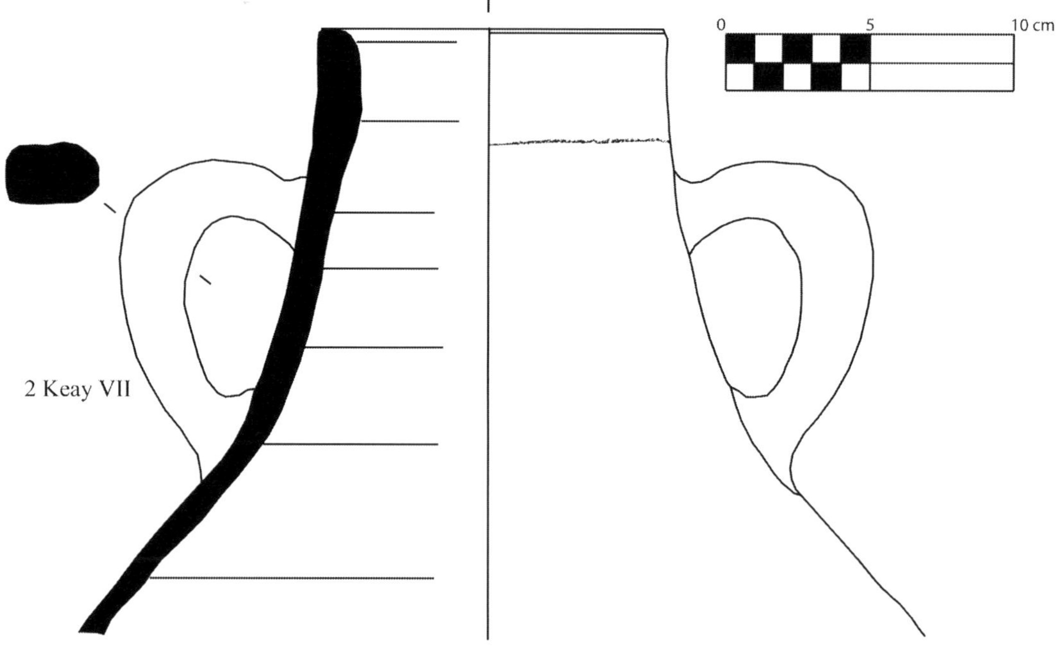

2 Keay VII

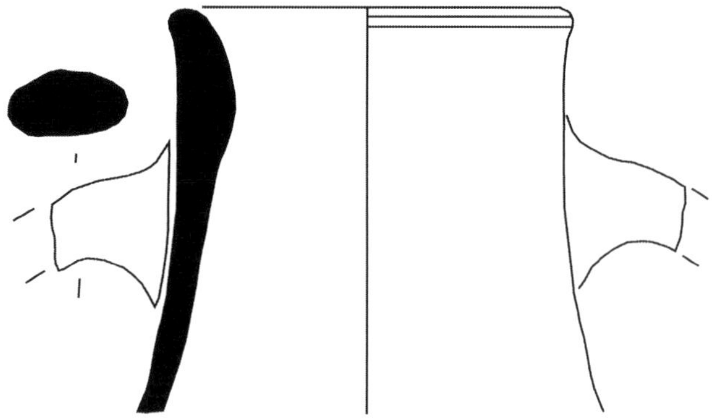

3 Keay VII

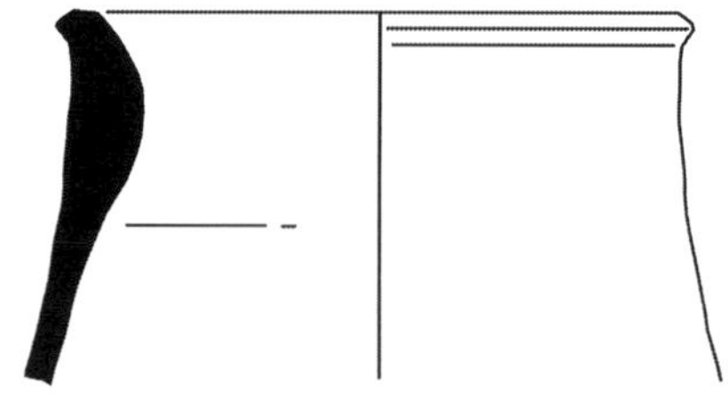

4 Keay VII *similis*

PLATE LXVIII

Tunisian amphorae from Portus Scabris: Keay XXV

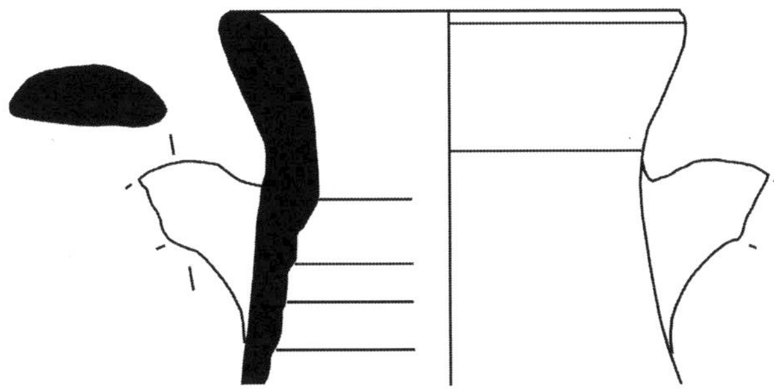

1 Keay XXVB

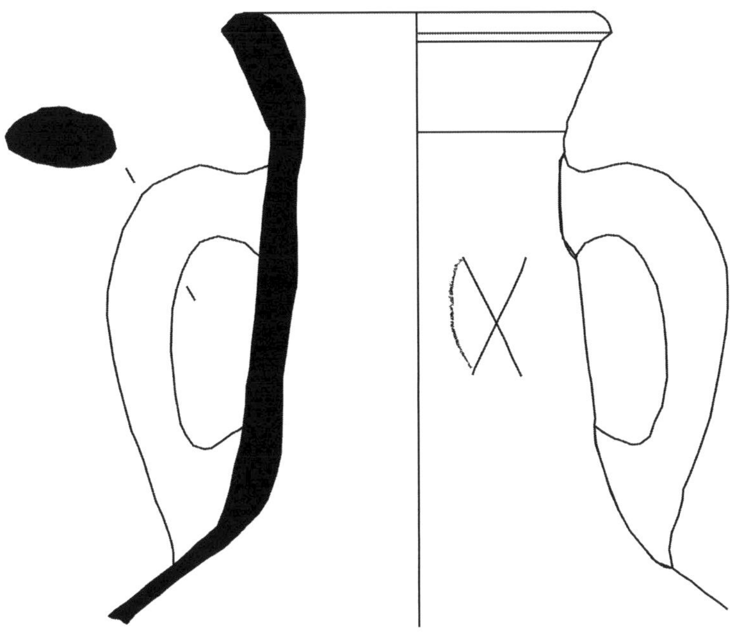

2 Keay XXVB

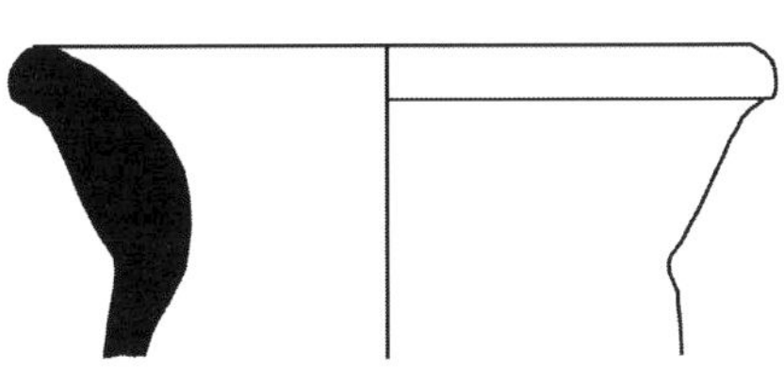

3 Keay XXVD

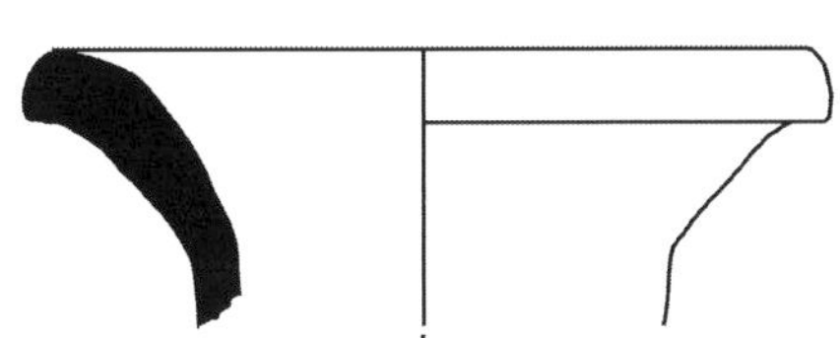

4 Keay XXVG

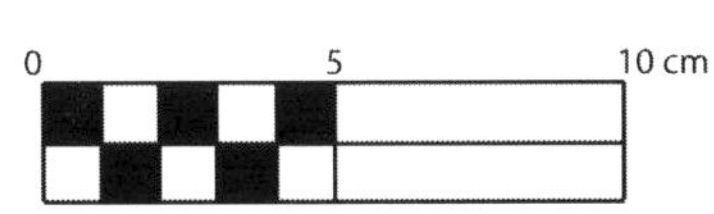

PLATE LXIX

Tunisian amphorae from Portus Scabris: Keay XXV

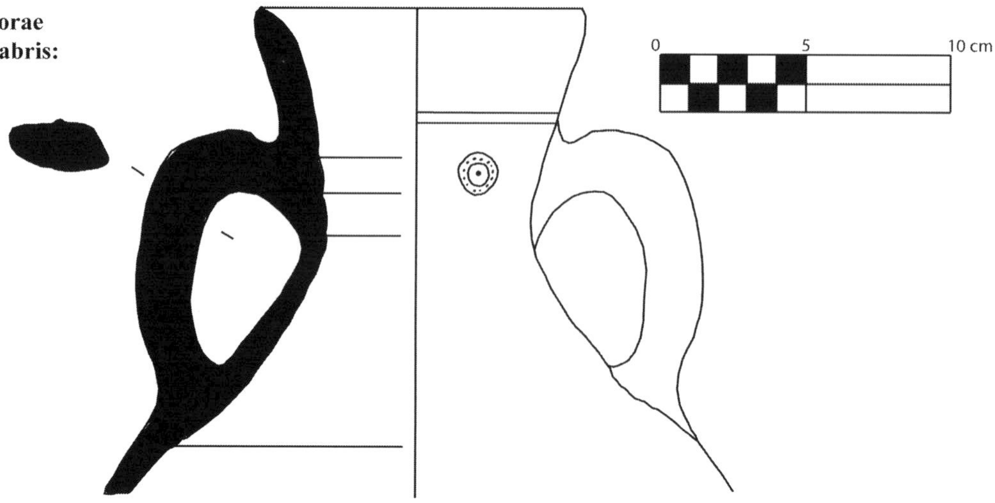

1 Keay XXV *similis*

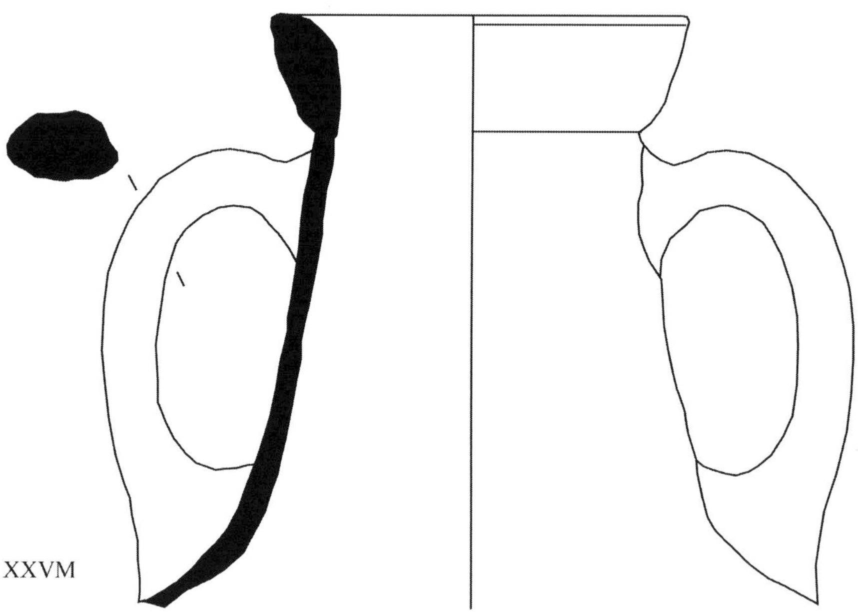

2 Keay XXVM

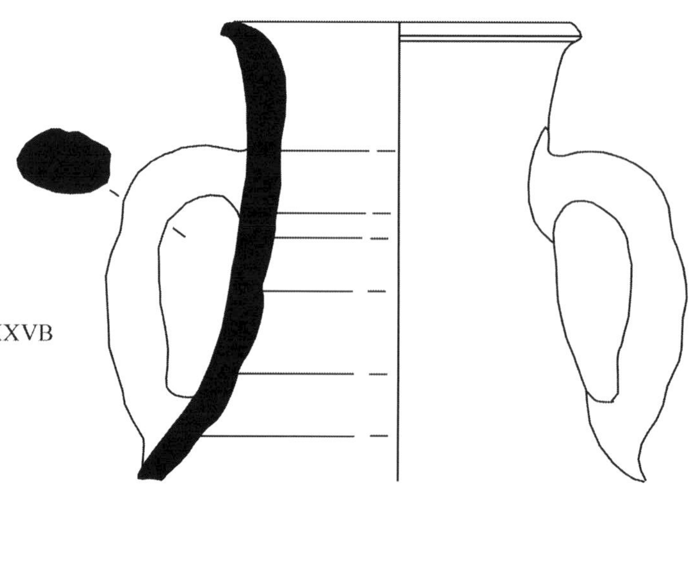

3 Keay XXVB

PLATE LXX

Tunisian amphorae from Portus Scabris: Keay XXV

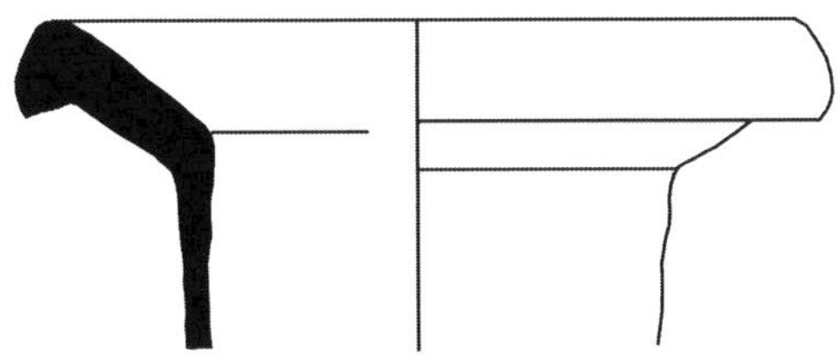

1 Keay XXVH

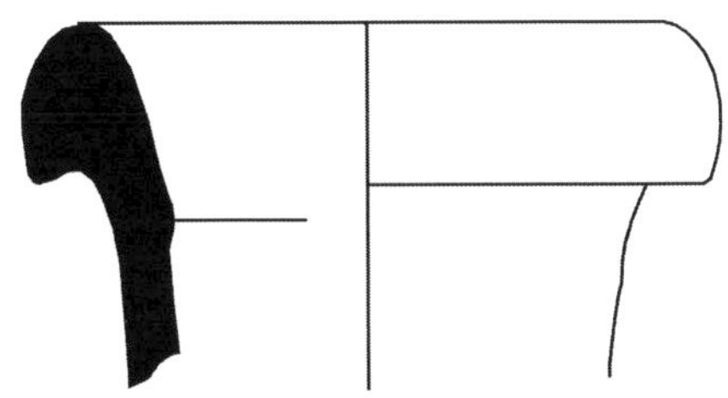

2 Keay XXVW (or Keay XXXVA)

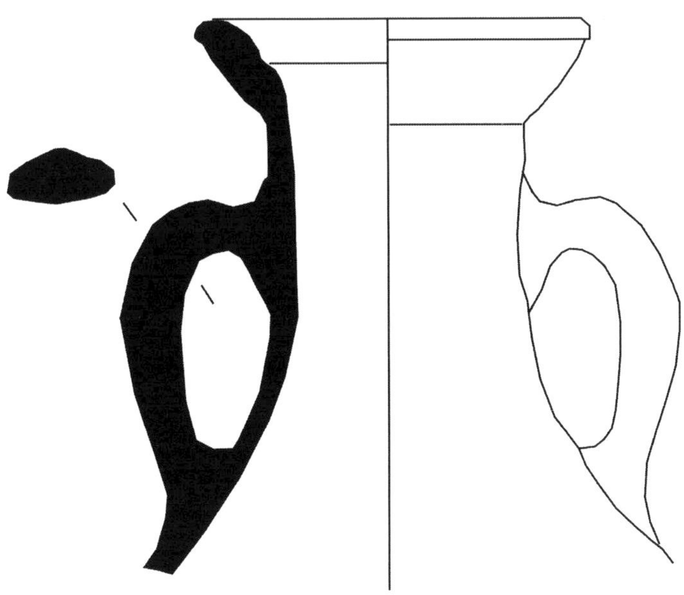

3 Keay XXVG

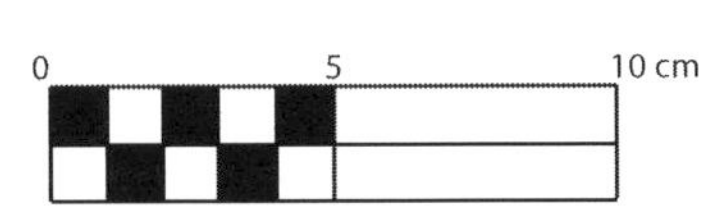

PLATE LXXI

Tunisian amphorae from Portus Scabris:
Keay XXVI

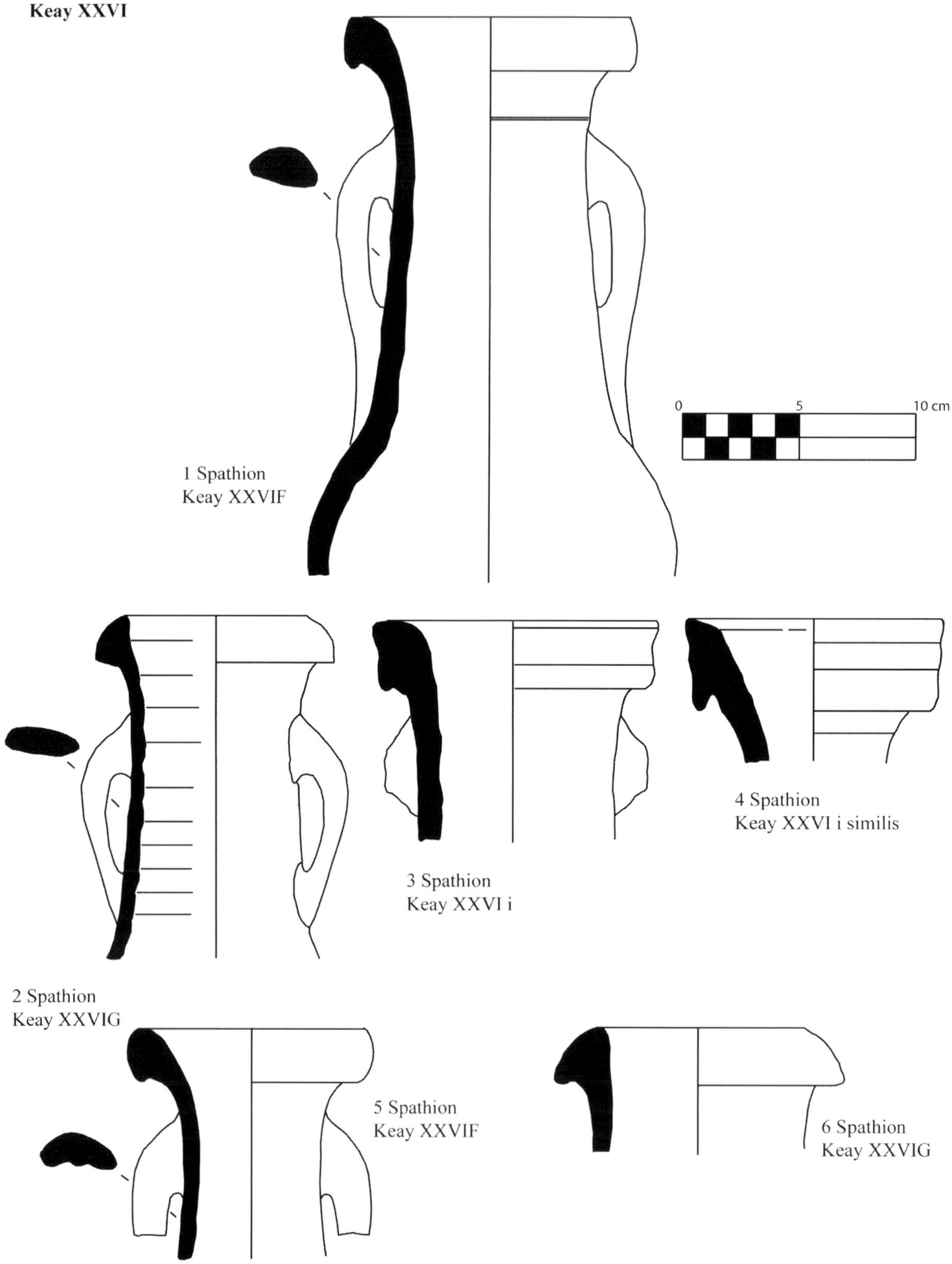

PLATE LXXII

Tunisian amphorae from Portus Scabris:
Keay XXVI

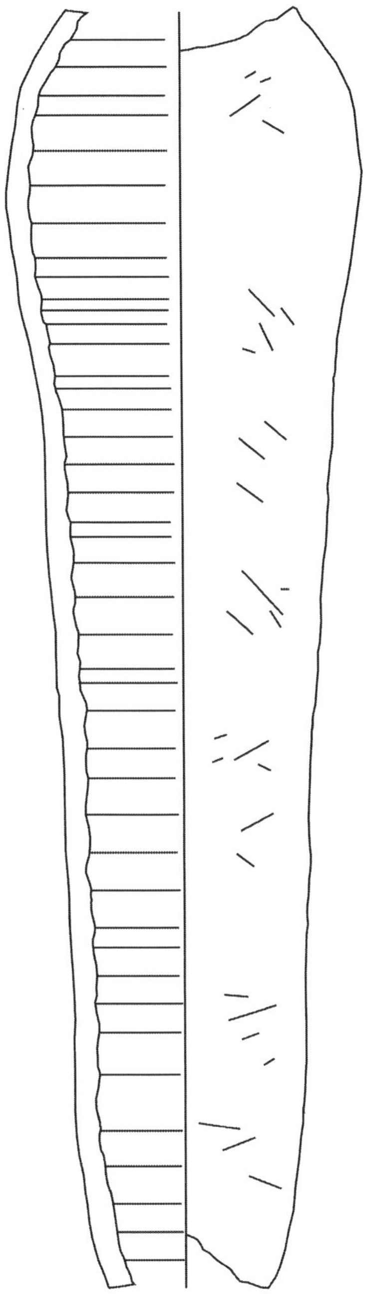

1 Spathion Keay XXVI

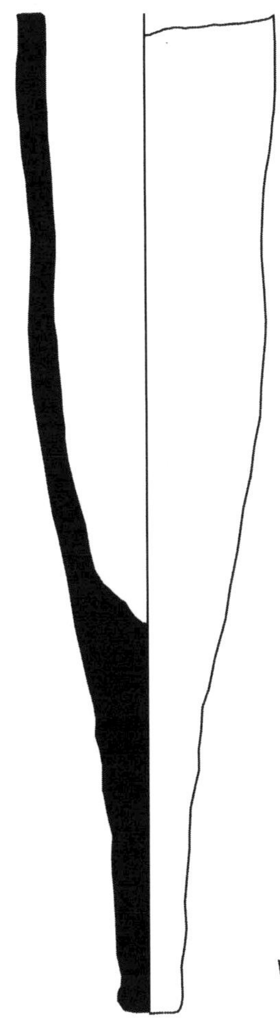

2 Spathion Keay XXVI

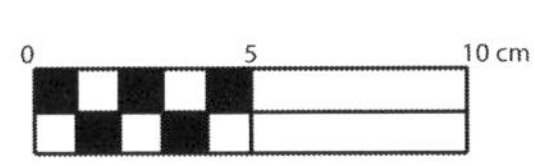

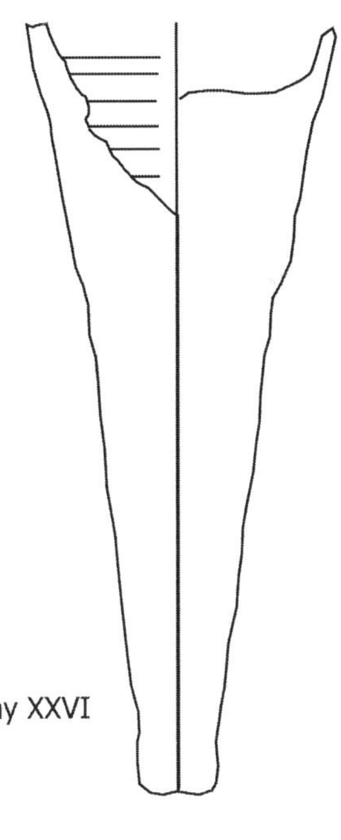

3 Spathion Keay XXVI

PLATE LXXIII

Tunisian amphorae from Portus Scabris: Keay XXVII

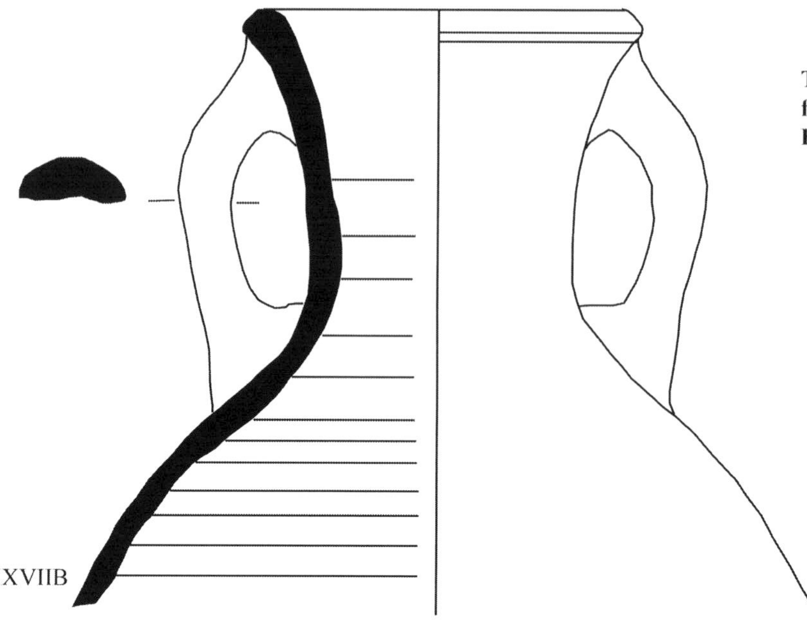

1 Keay XXVIIB

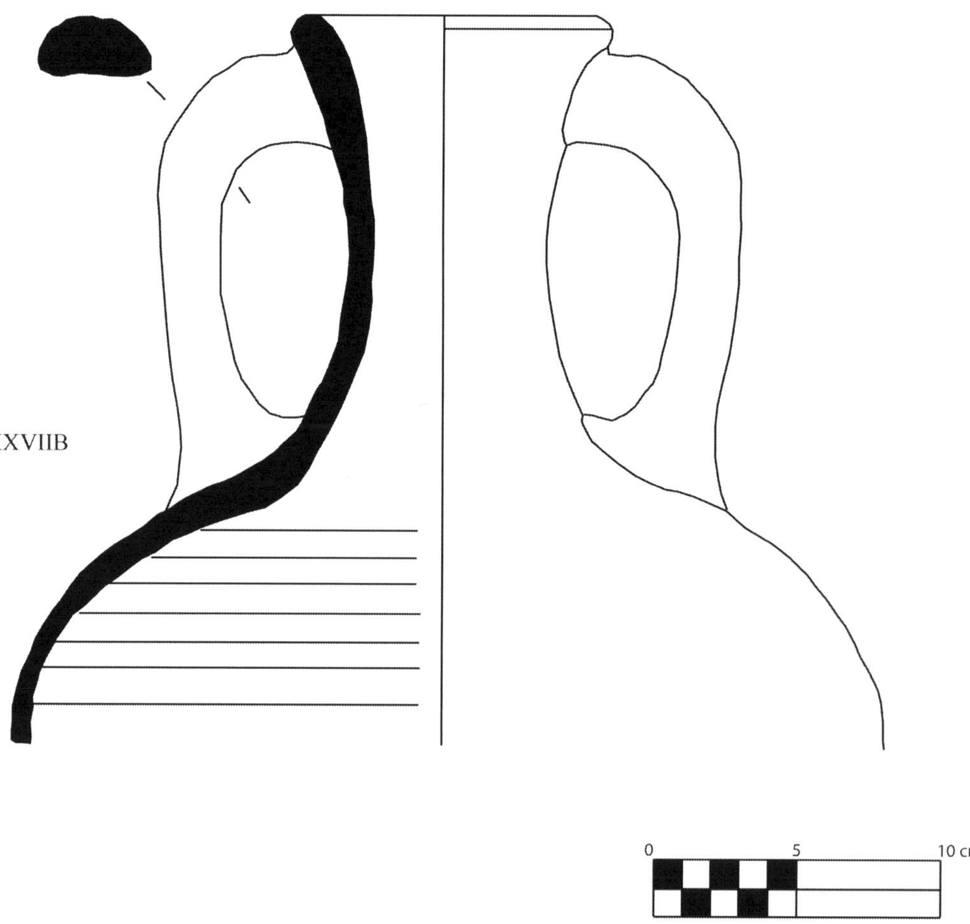

2 Keay XXVIIB

PLATE LXXIV

Tunisian and Tripolitanian amphorae from Portus Scabris: Keay XXXVA and late (?) Tripolitanian III

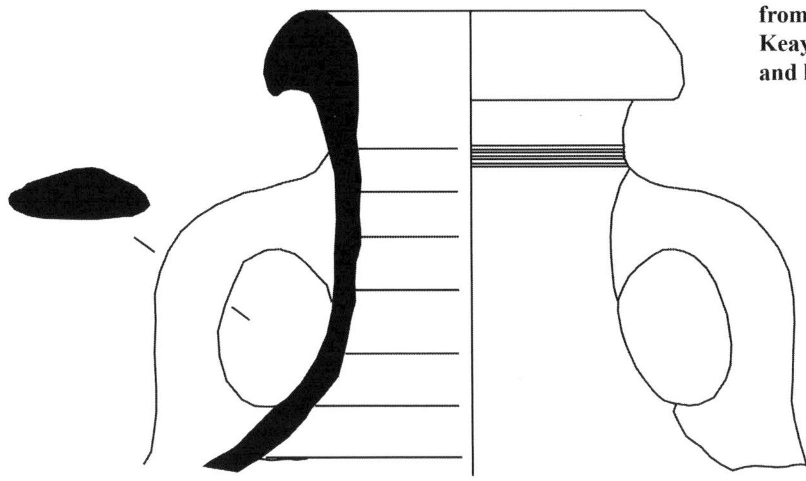

1 Keay XXXVA

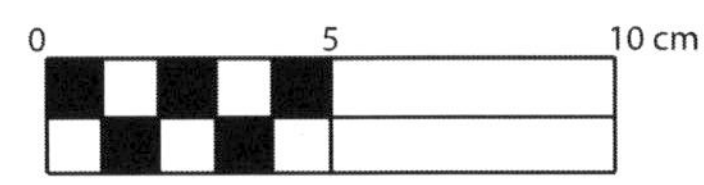

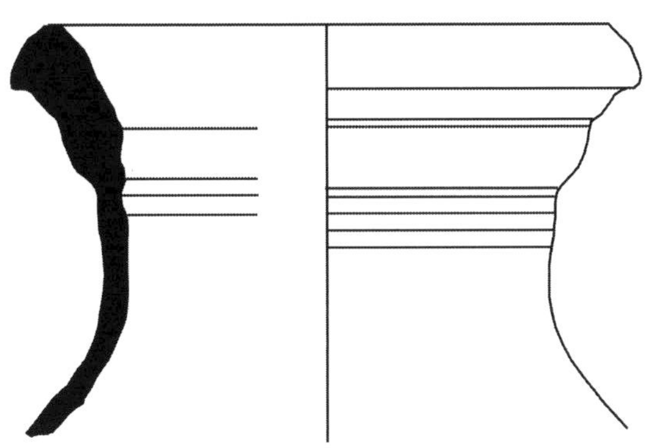

2 Peacock 1984, Fig.41, n.85/Tripolitanian 3 (late variant)

PLATE LXXV

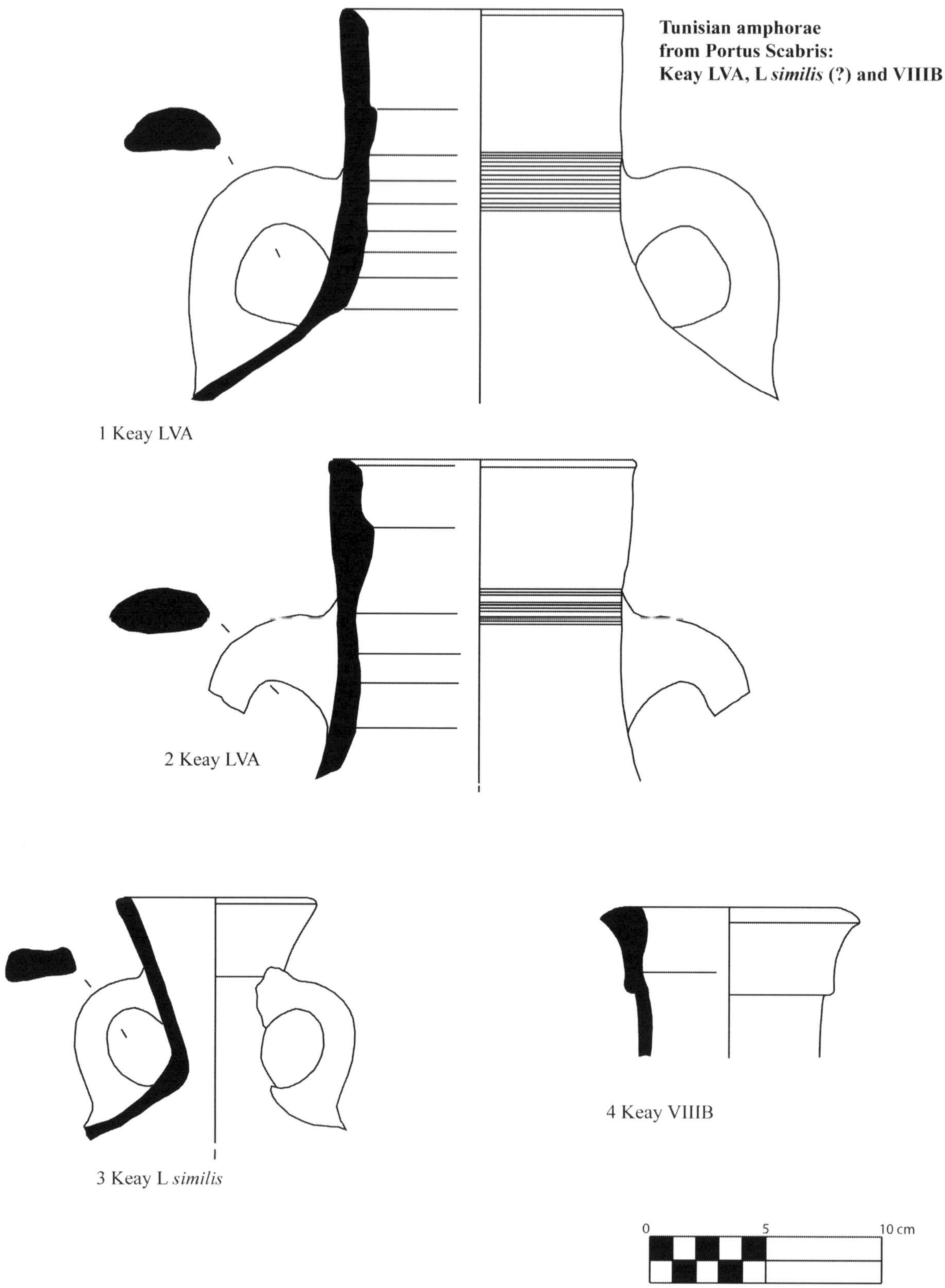
Tunisian amphorae
from Portus Scabris:
Keay LVA, L *similis* (?) and VIIIB
1 Keay LVA
2 Keay LVA
3 Keay L *similis*
4 Keay VIIIB
0
5
10 cm

PLATE LXXVI

Tunisian amphorae
from Portus Scabris:
Keay LXII and
"fondo convesso ombelicato"

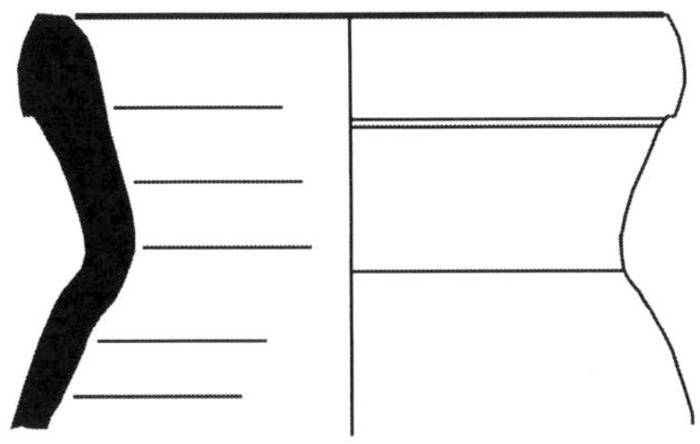

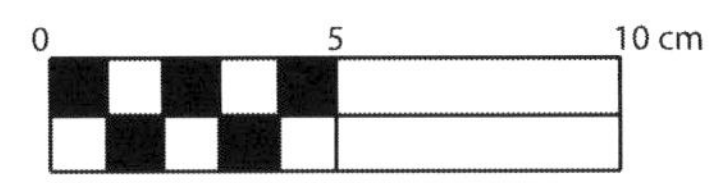

1 Keay LXIIA

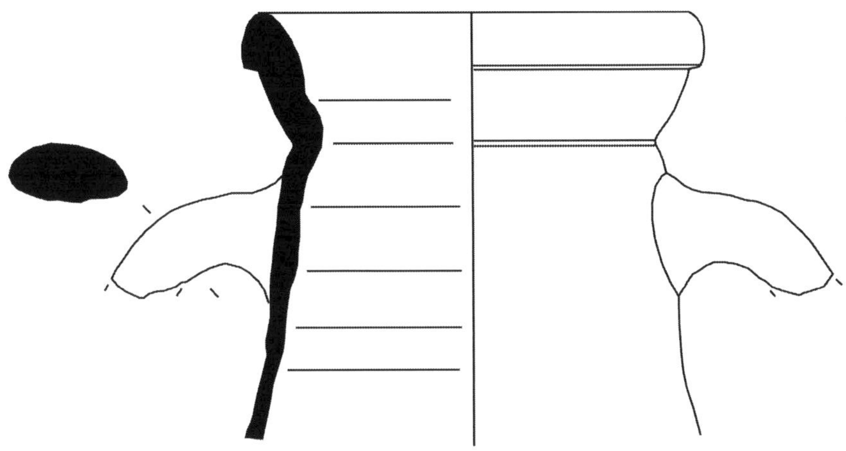

2 Keay LXIIF

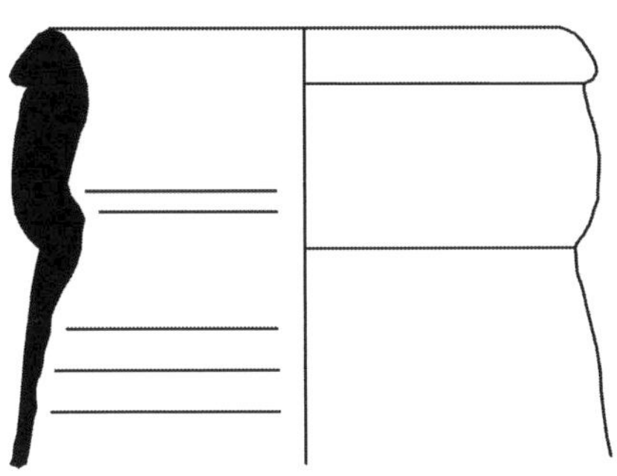

3 Keay LXIIF

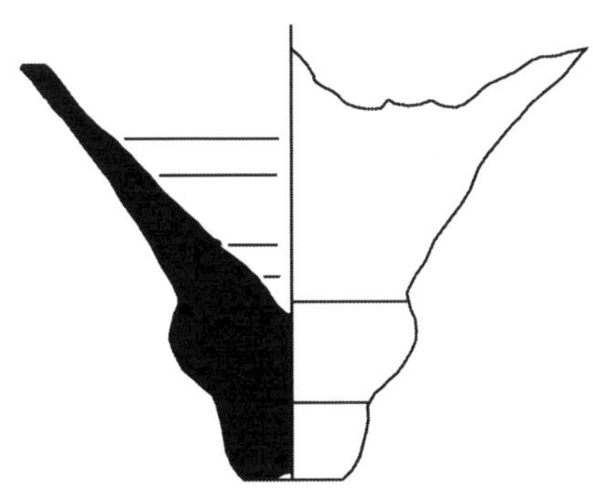

4 Keay LXII

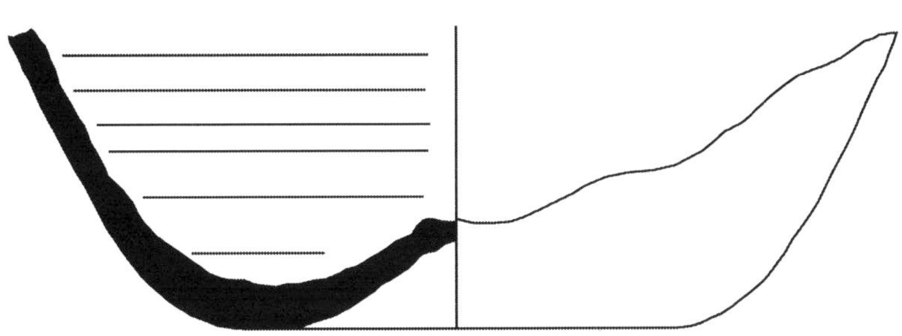

5 "Fondo convesso ombelicato" amphora

PLATE LXXVII

"Empoli" amphorae from the beached shipwreck (Portus Scabris)

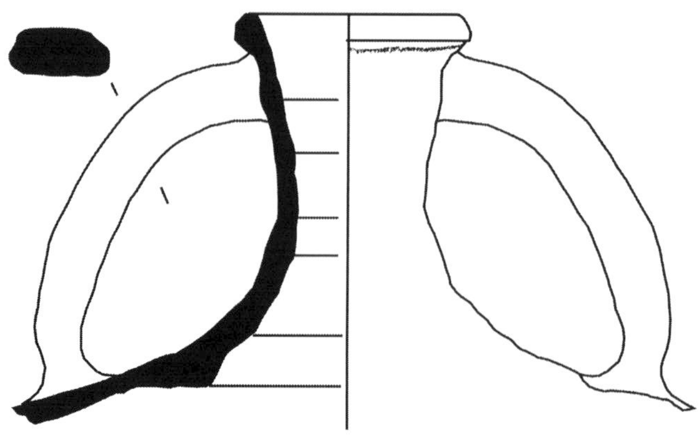

1 Variant 1

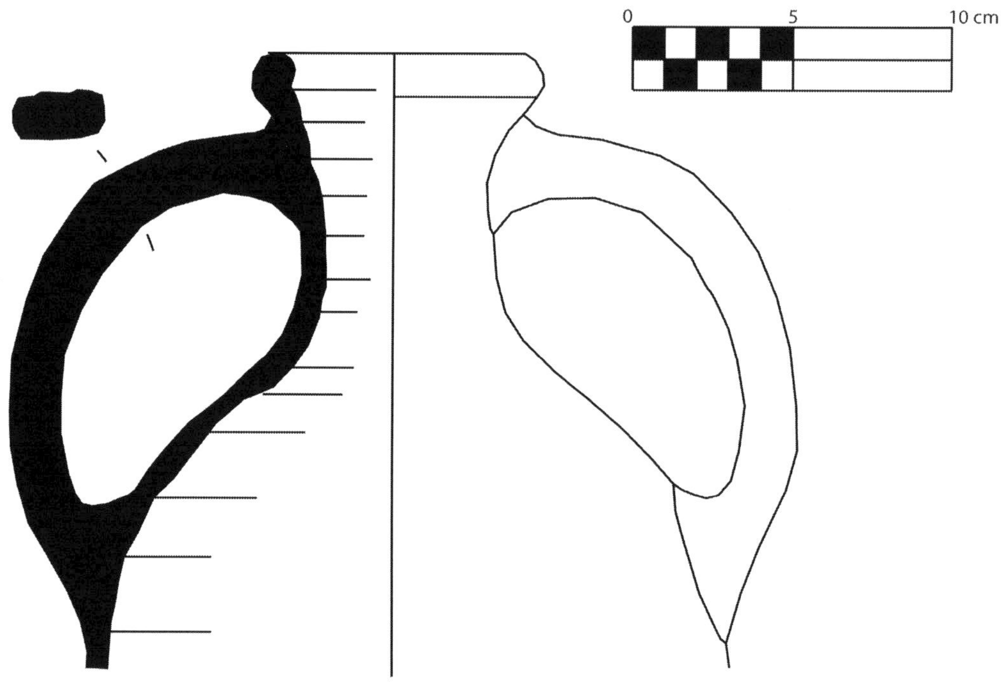

2 Variant 2

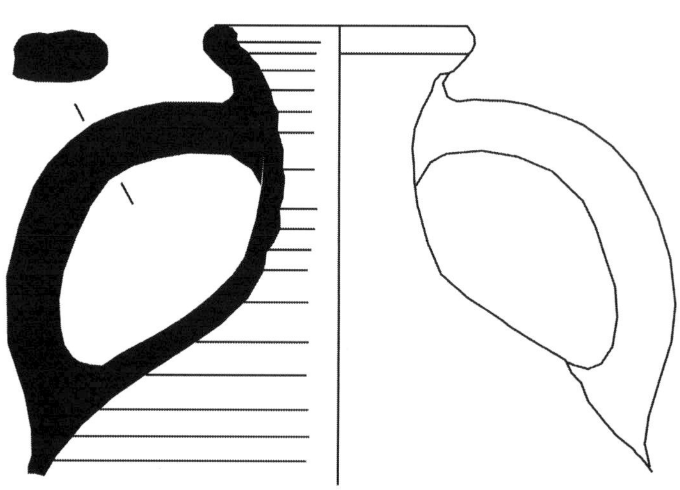

3 Variant 2

PLATE LXXVIII

“Empoli” amphorae from the beached shipwreck (Portus Scabris)

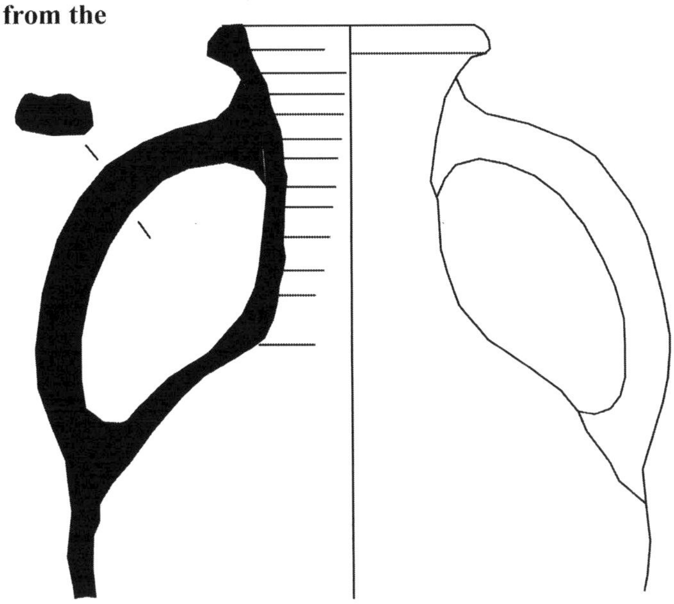

1 Variant 2

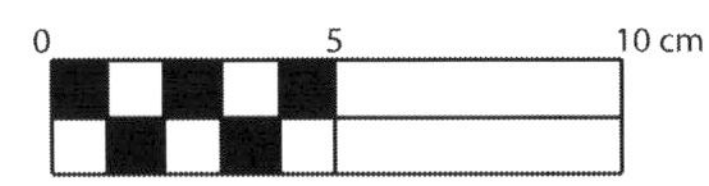

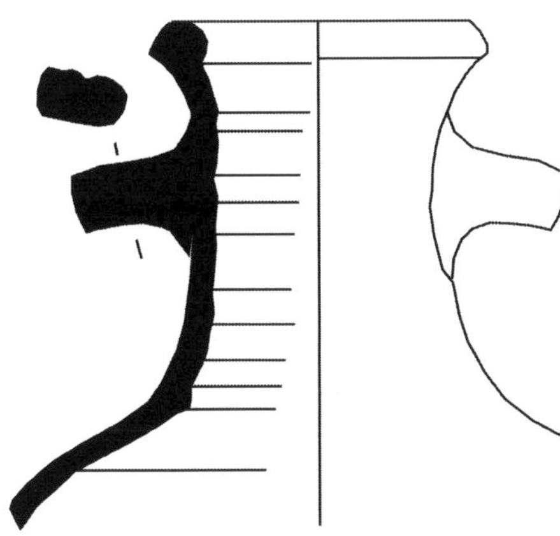

2 Variant 2, bis

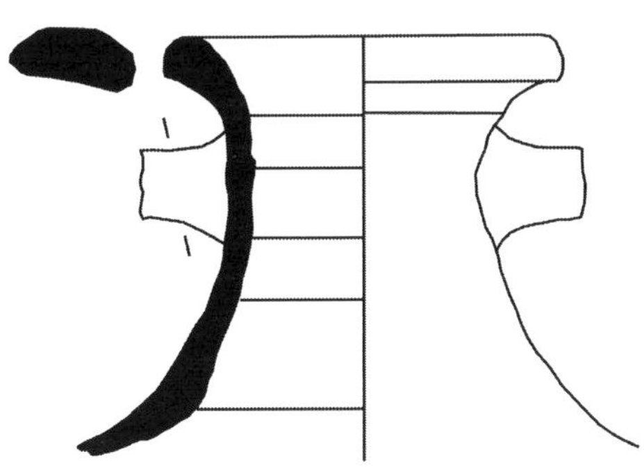

3 Variant 3

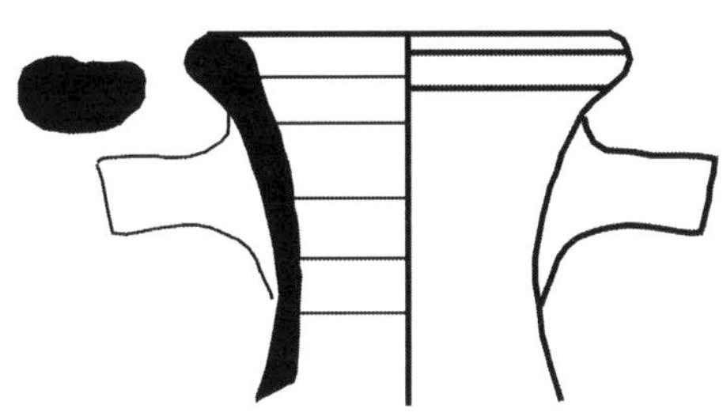

4 Variant 4

PLATE LXXIX

"Empoli" amphorae from the beached shipwreck (Portus Scabris)

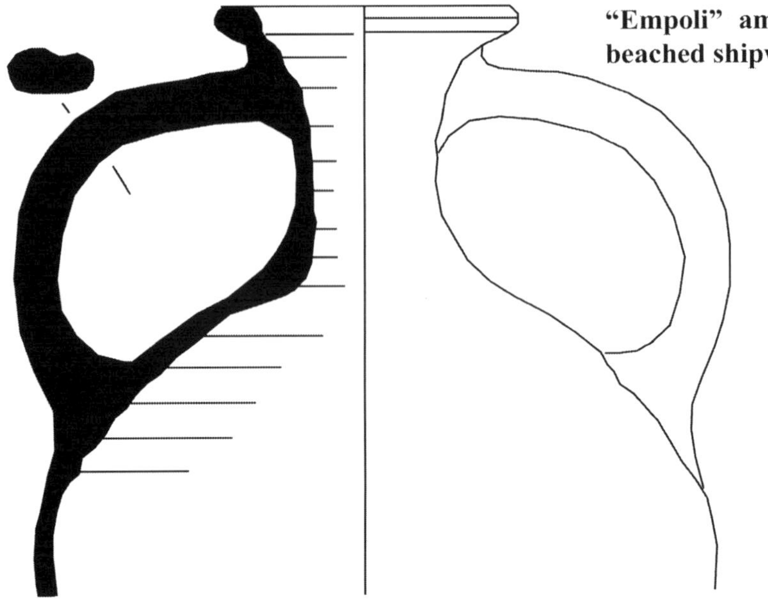

1 Variant 5

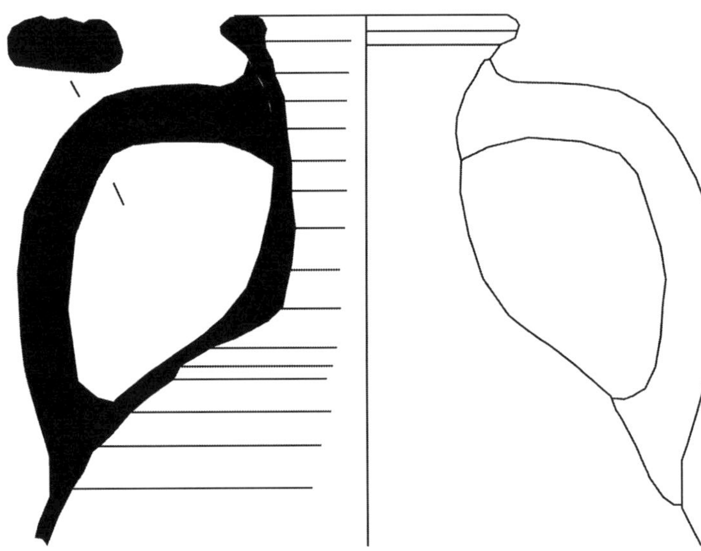

2 Variant 5

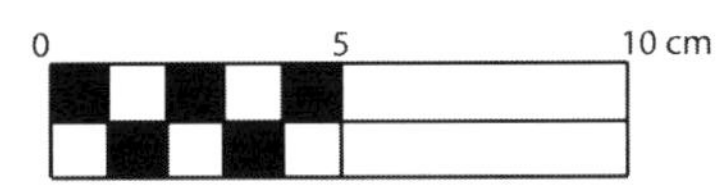

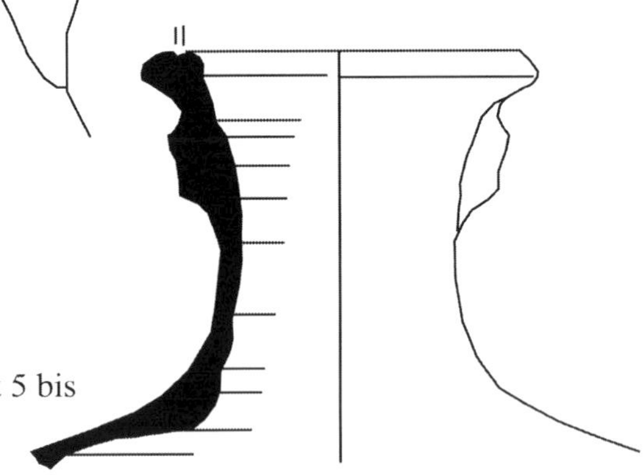

3 Variant 5 bis

PLATE LXXX

"Empoli" amphorae from other sectors of Portus Scabris

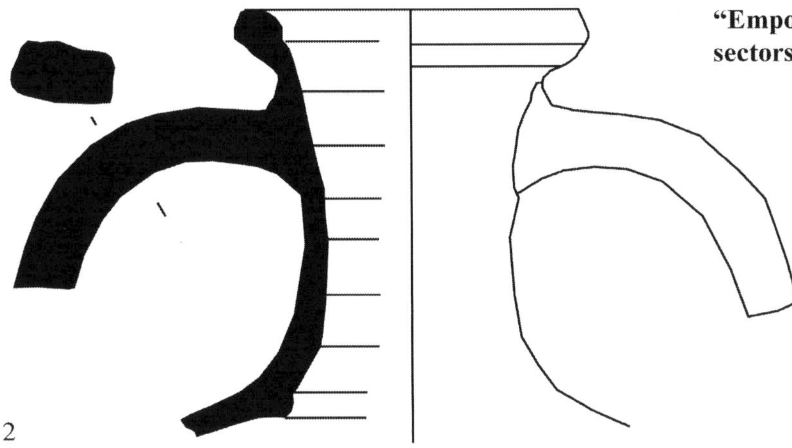

1 Variant 2

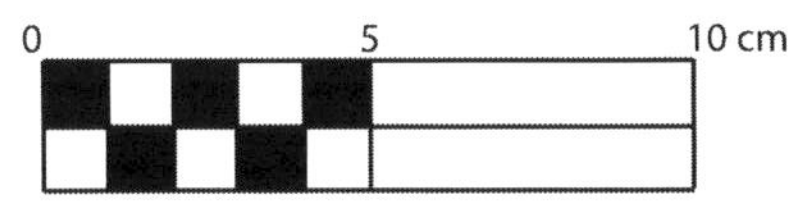

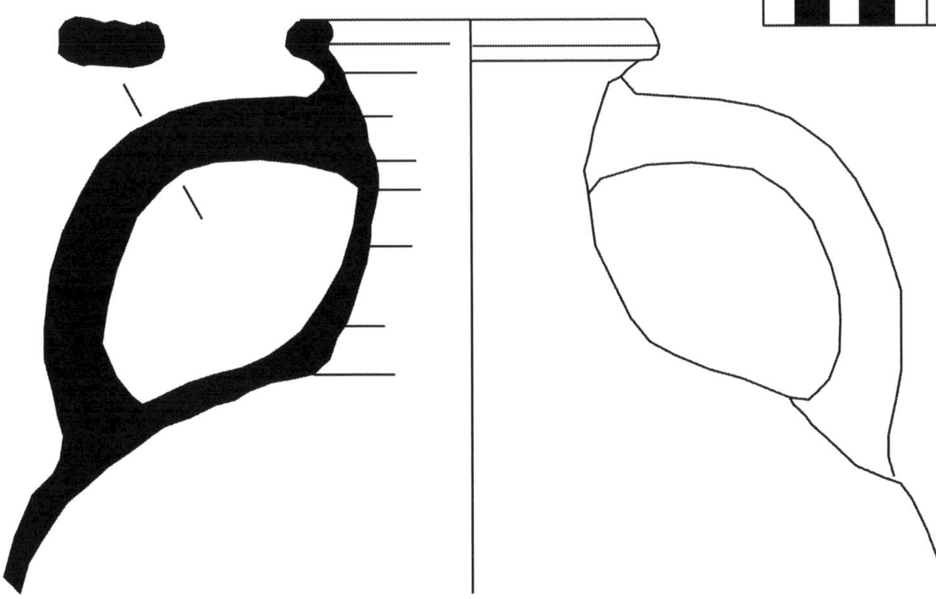

2 Variant 2

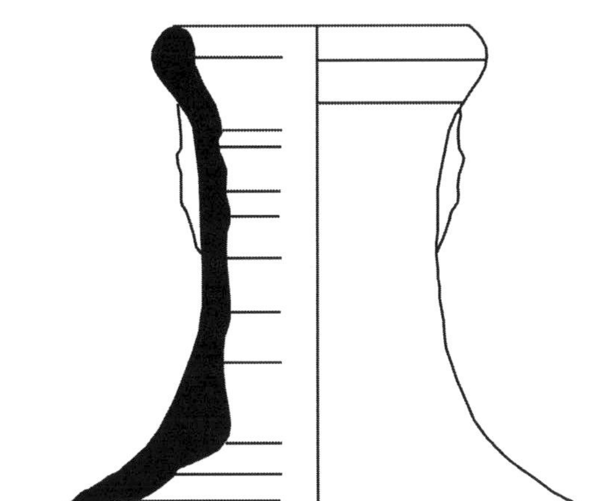

3 Variant 2

PLATE LXXXI

"Empoli" amphorae from other sectors of Portus Scabris

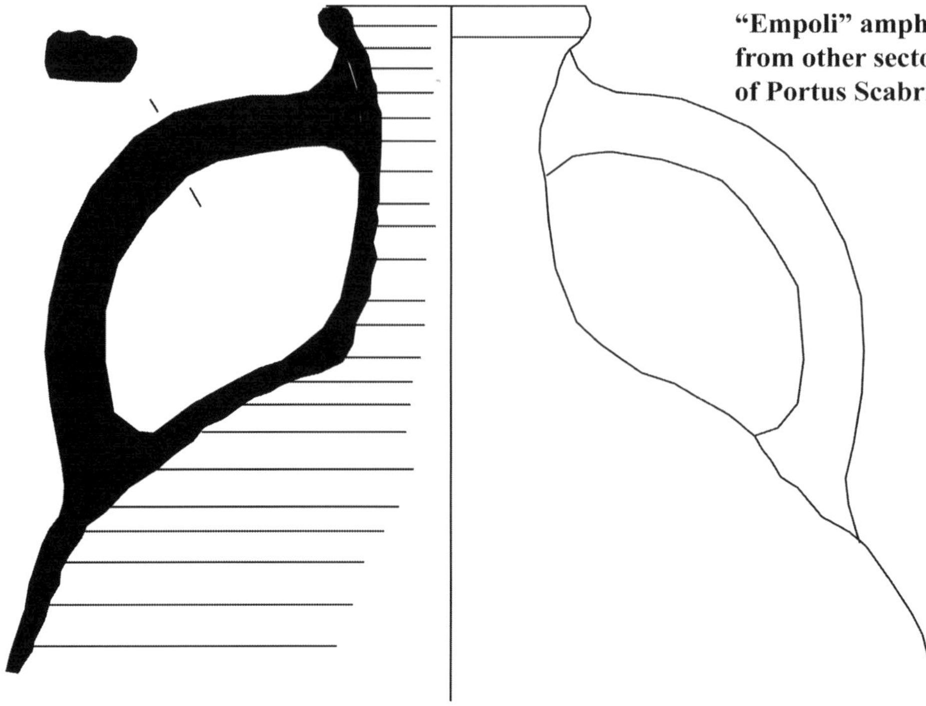

1 Variant 2

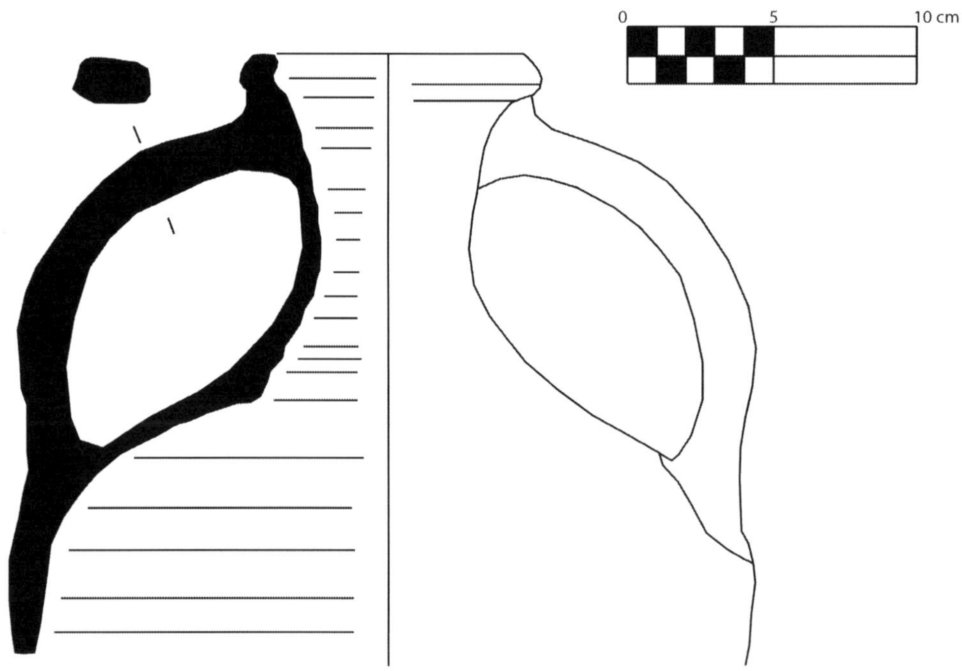

2 Variant 2

PLATE LXXXII

“Empoli” amphorae from other sectors of Portus Scabris

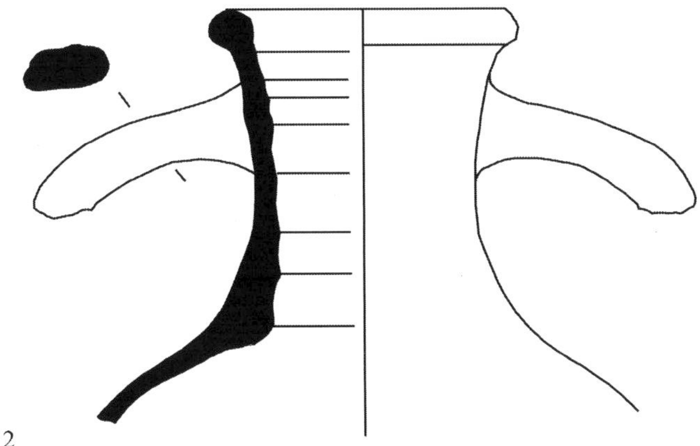

1 Variant 2

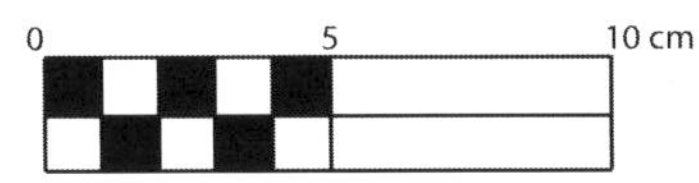

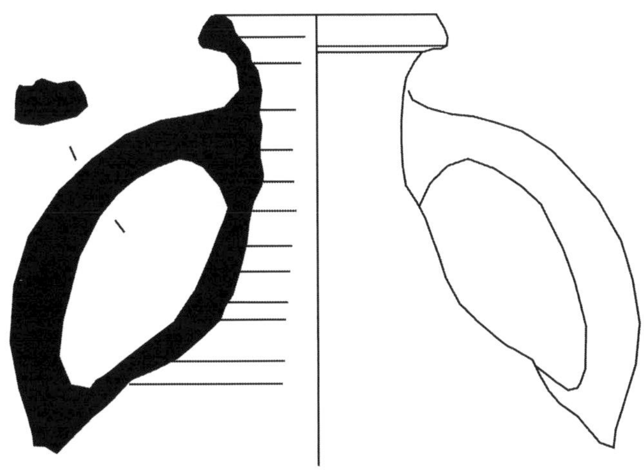

2 Variant 2 similis

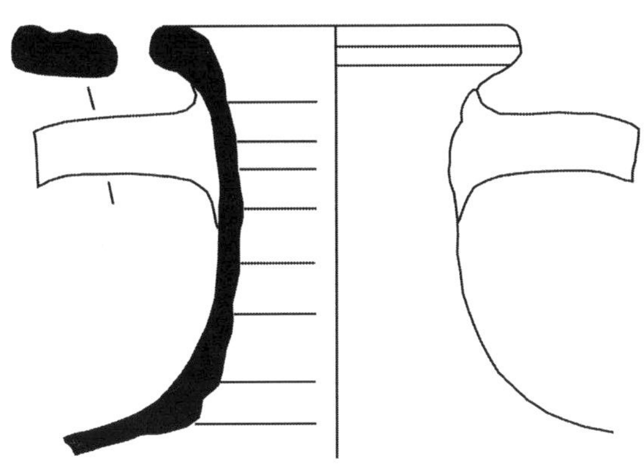

3 Variant 5

PLATE LXXXIII

“Empoli” amphorae from other sectors of Portus Scabris

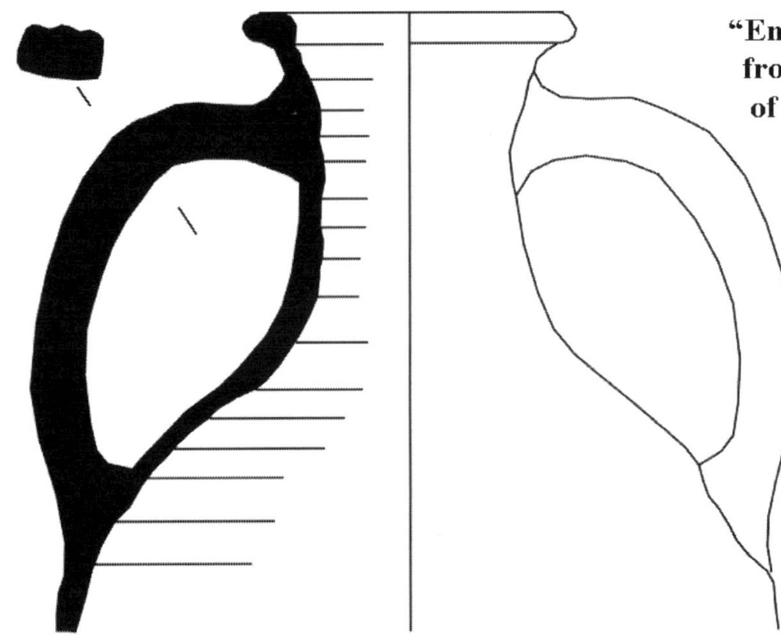

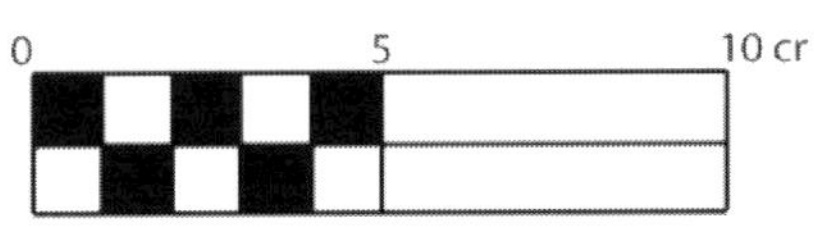

1 Variant 5

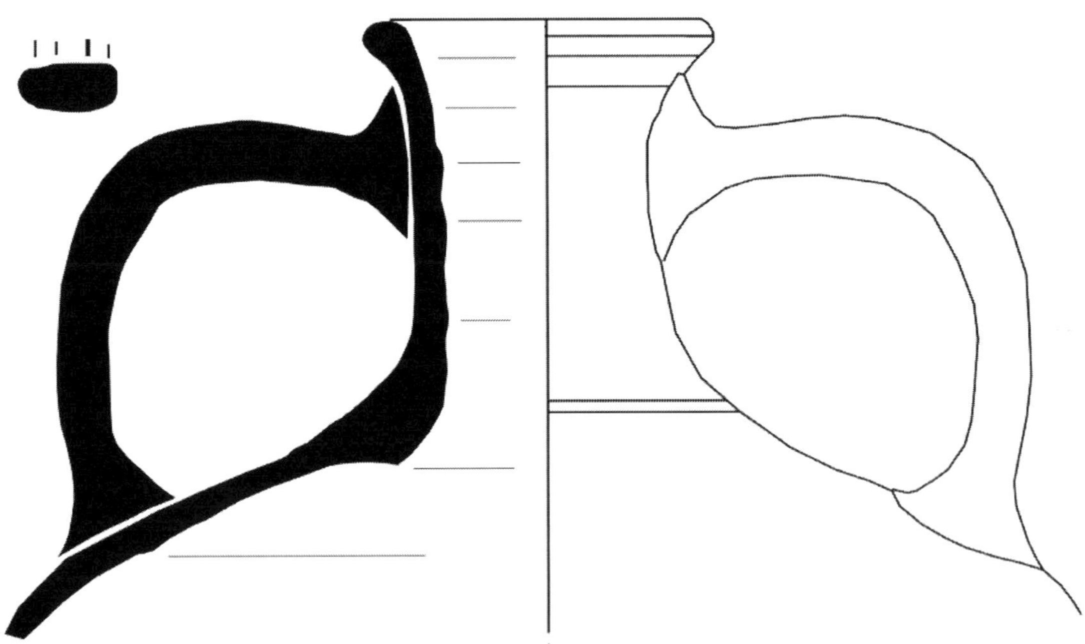

2 Variant 4

PLATE LXXXIV

"Empoli" amphorae from other sectors of Portus Scabris

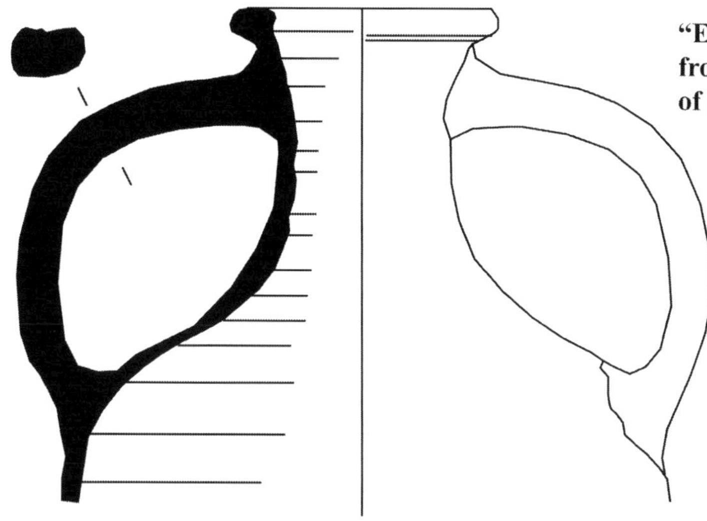

1 Variant 5

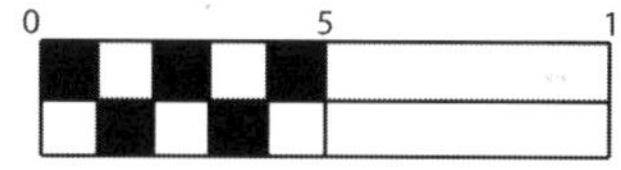

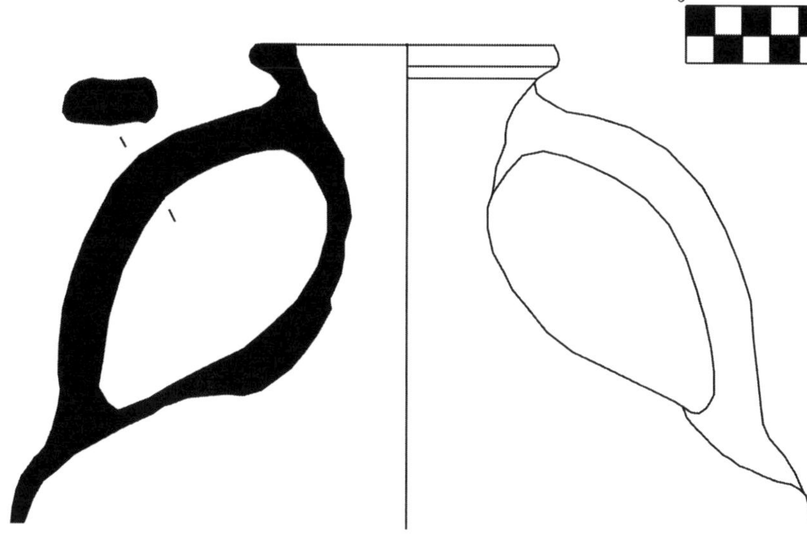

2 Variant 5

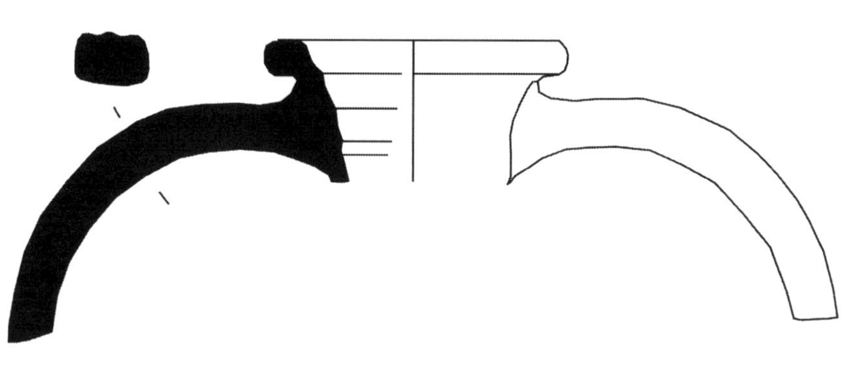

3 Variant 5

PLATE LXXXV

MR1 and Keay LII amphorae from Portus Scabris

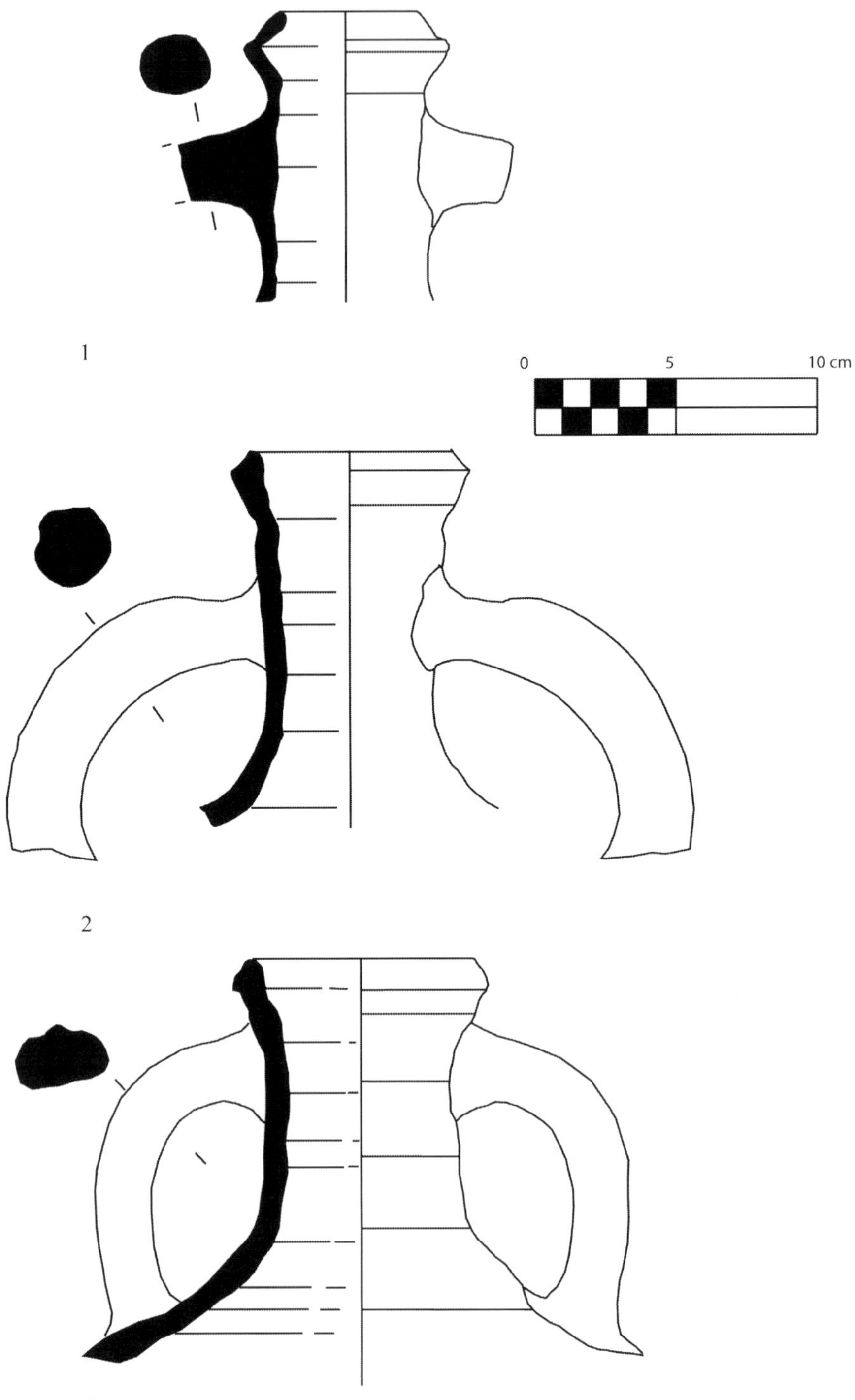

PLATE LXXXVI

Keay LII and late variant of Keay LII from Portus Scabris

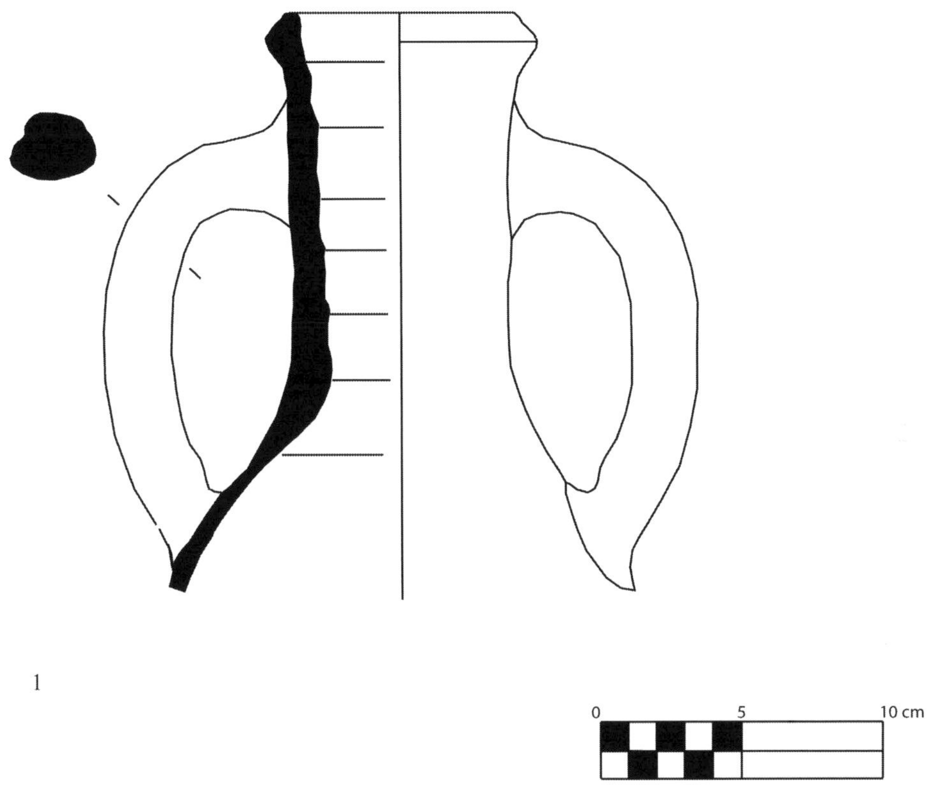

1

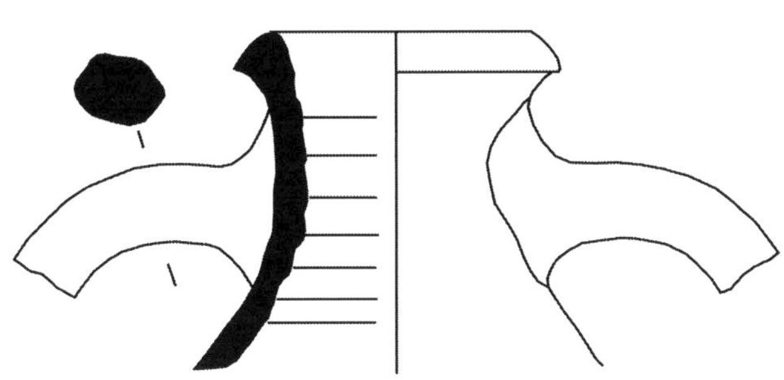

2

PLATE LXXXVII

**Late Dressel 24
and LR 2 amphorae
from Portus Scabris**

1 LR 2A

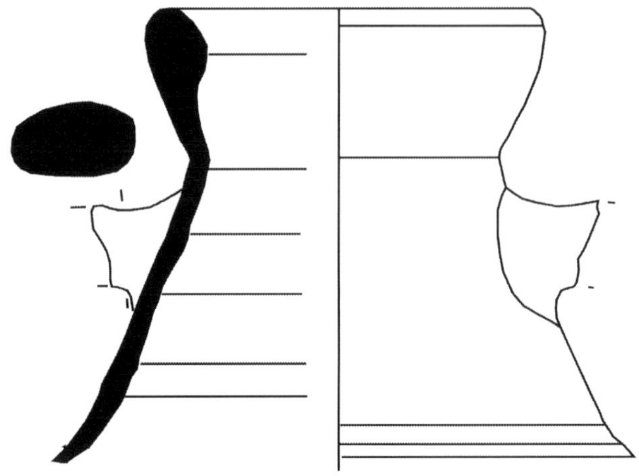

2 Agorà P16074/late Dressel 24 transitional to LR2 (?)

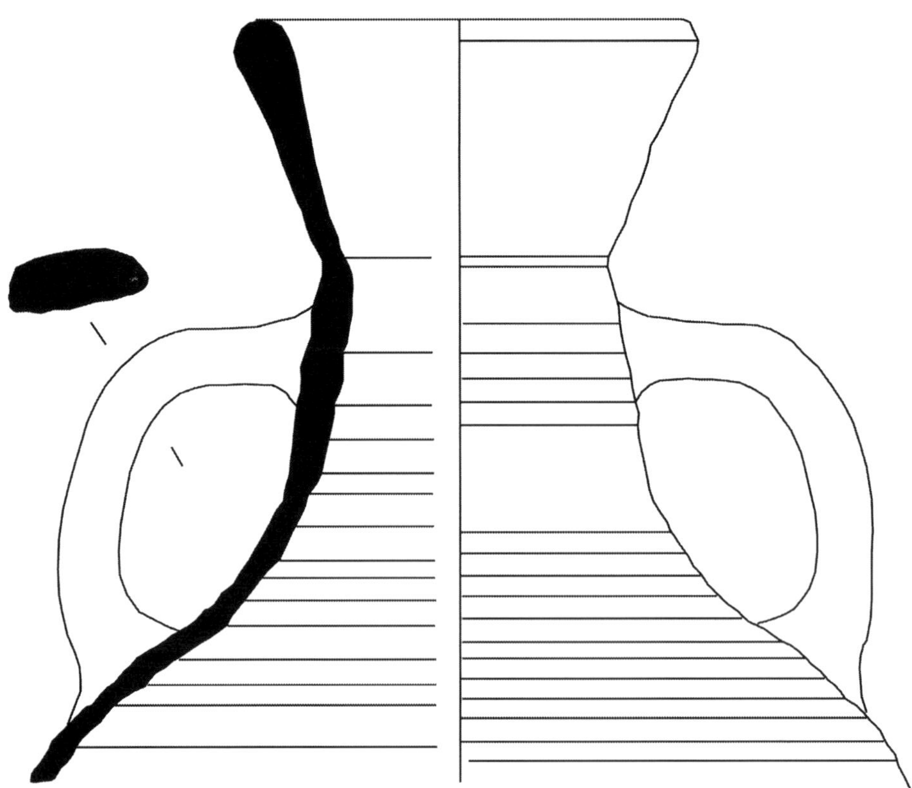

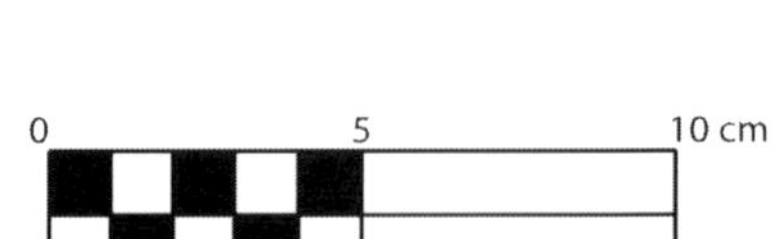

PLATE LXXXVIII

Agorà M273 and Samos Cistern amphorae from Portus Scabris

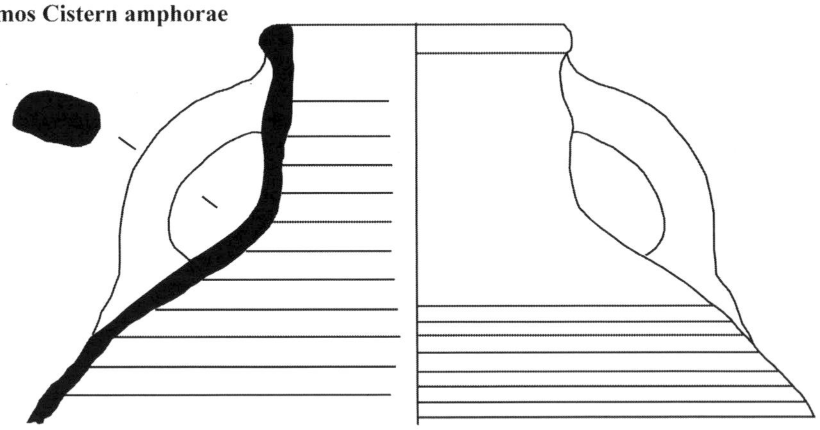

1 Agorà M273

Fabric ANF 112

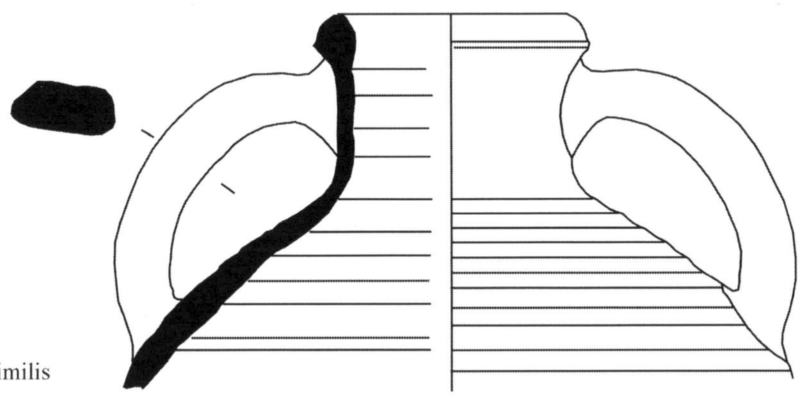

2 Agorà M273 similis

Fabric ANF 121

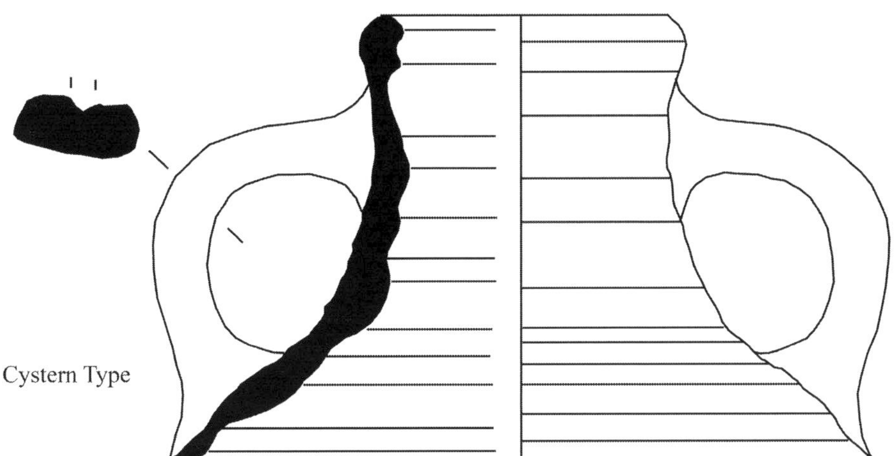

3 Samos Cystern Type

Fabric ANF 119 bis

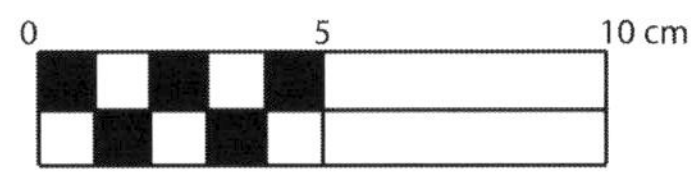

PLATE LXXXIX

LR 5 amphora from Portus Scabris

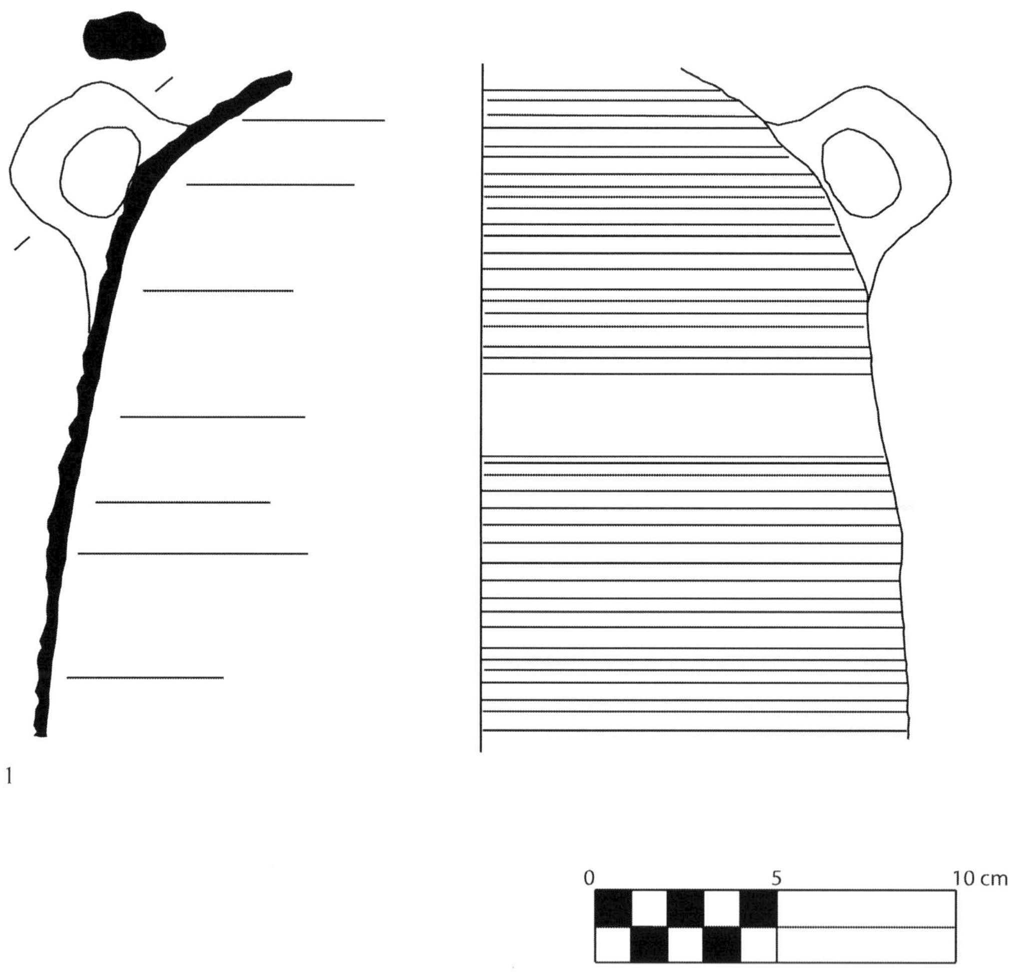

PLATE XC

LR1 A amphorae from Portus Scabris

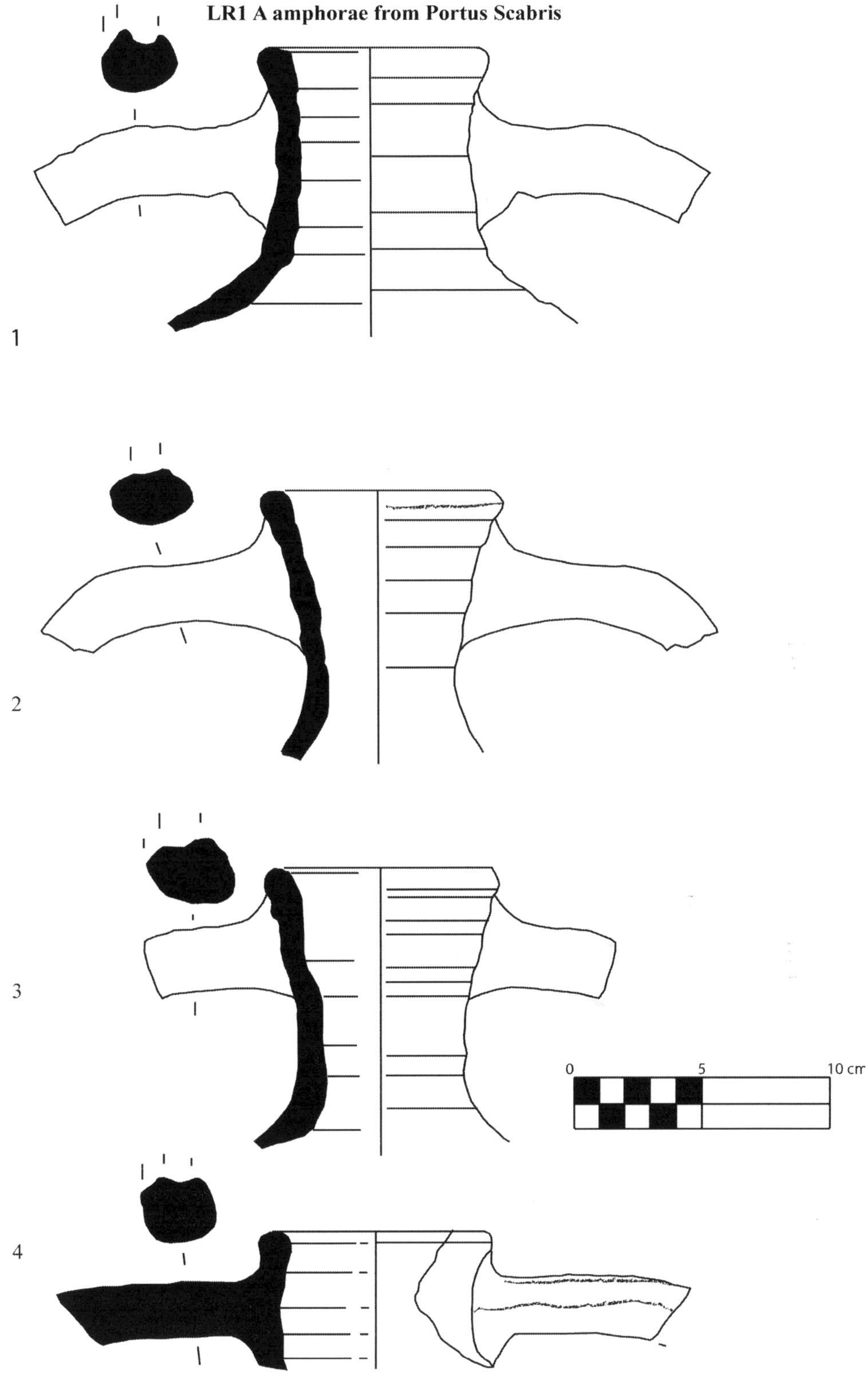

PLATE XCI

LR1B amphorae from Portus Scabris

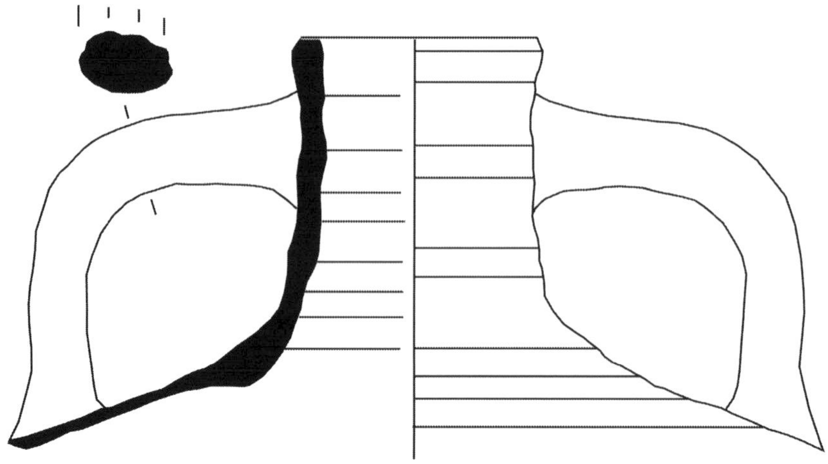

1

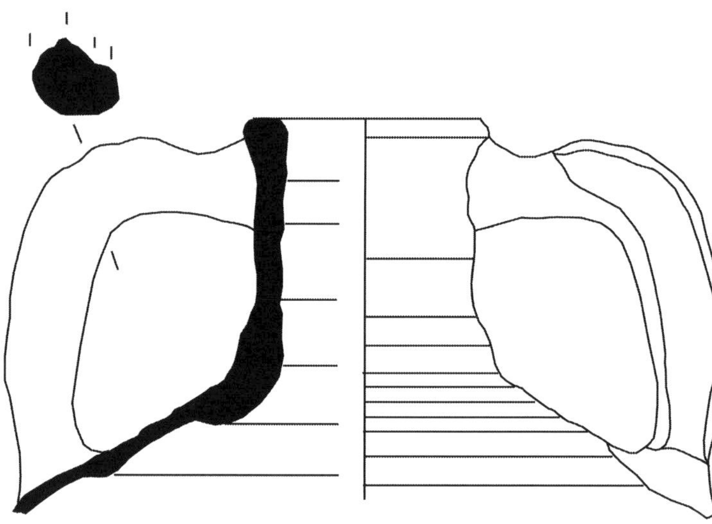

2

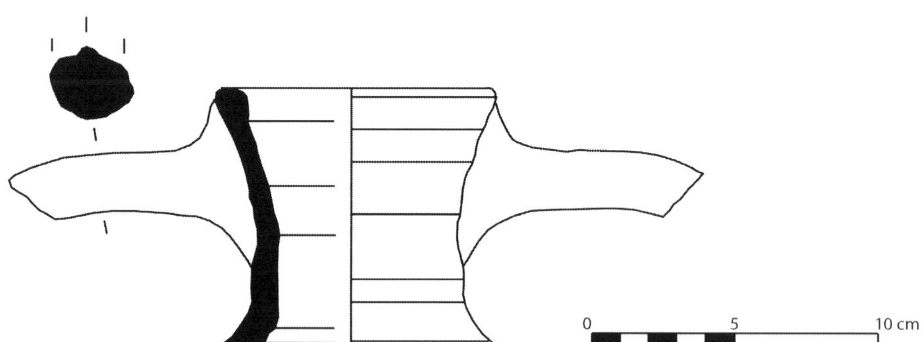

3

PLATE XCII

LR1 B amphorae from Portus Scabris

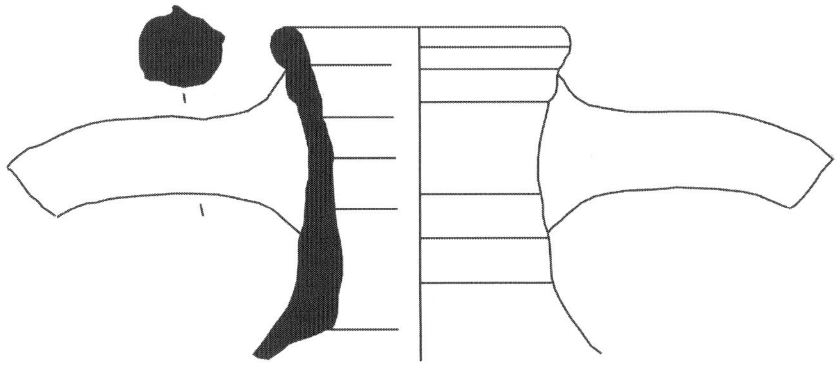

1

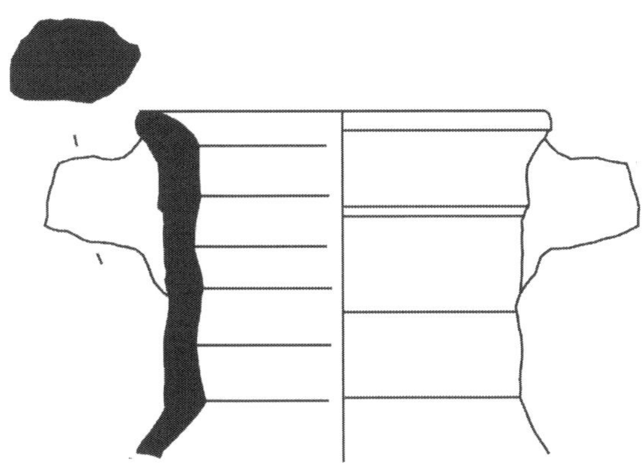

2

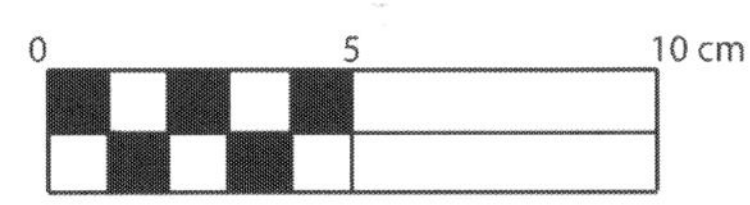

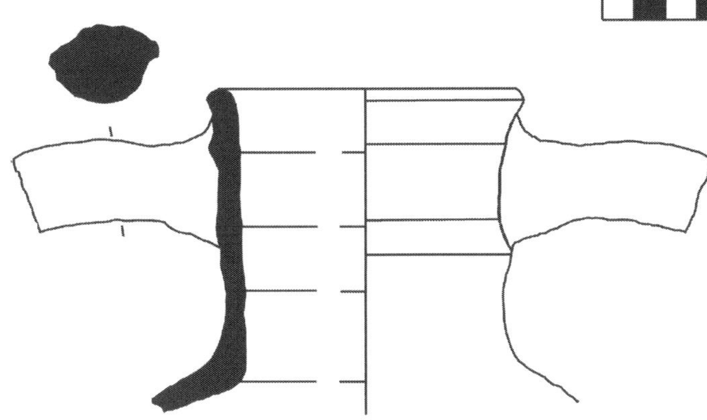

3

PLATE XCIII

Early medieval amphorae from Portus Scabris (various sources)

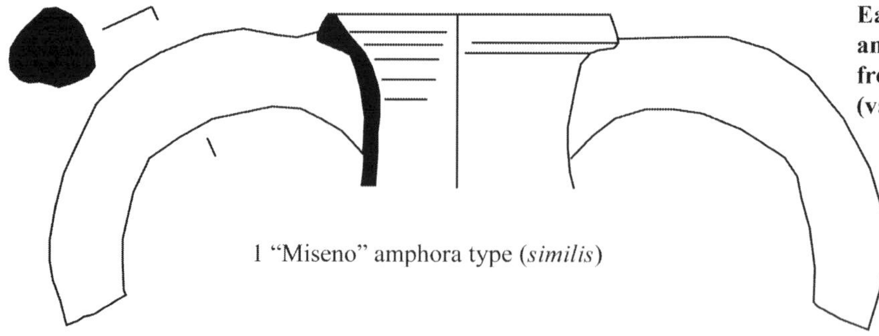

1 “Miseno” amphora type (*similis*)

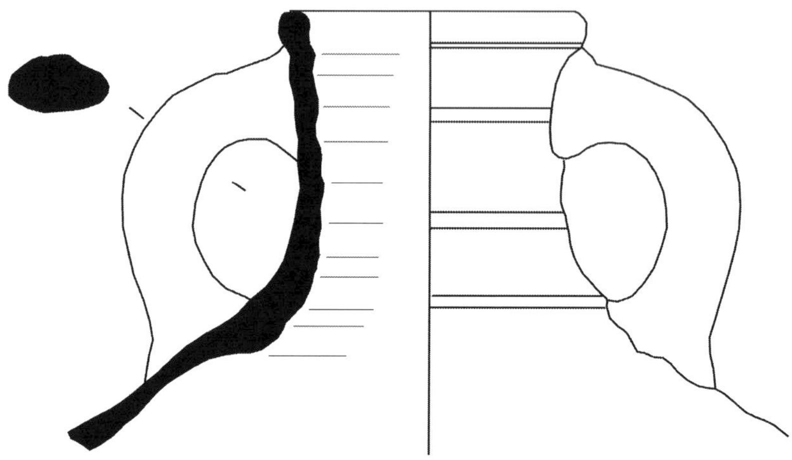

2 Amphora comparable with Saraçhane Type 52

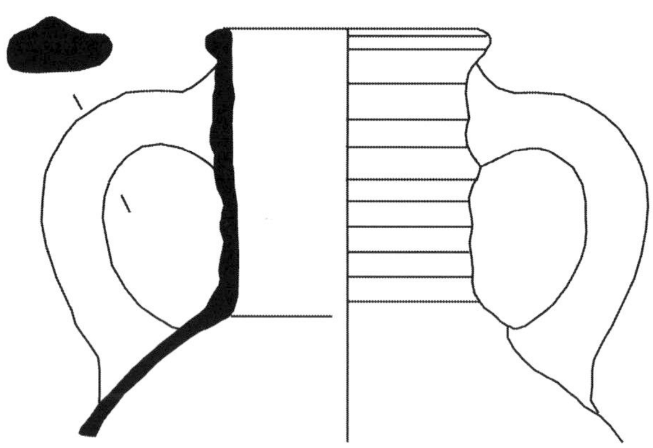

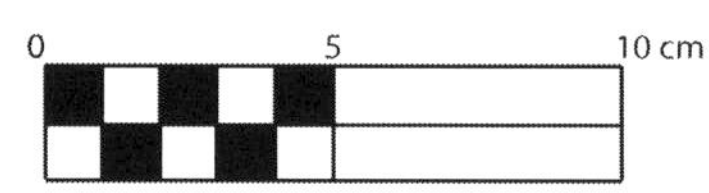

3 Small amphora
comparable with Form P72 from Yassi Ada

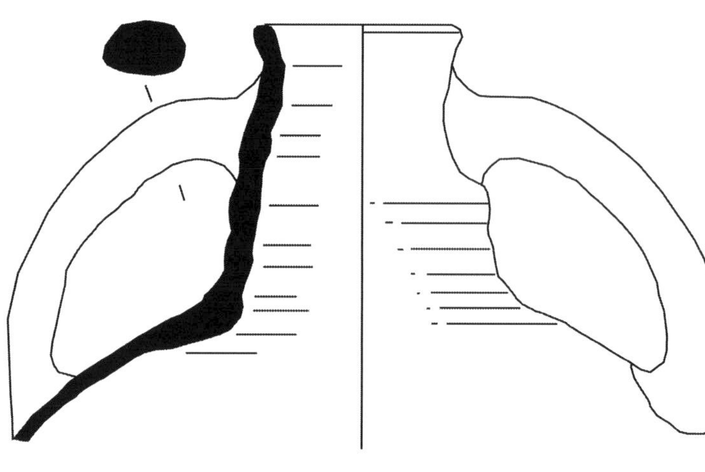

4 Early medieval
globular amphora

PLATE XCIV

Medieval jugs from the territory of Pisa attested at Portus Scabris

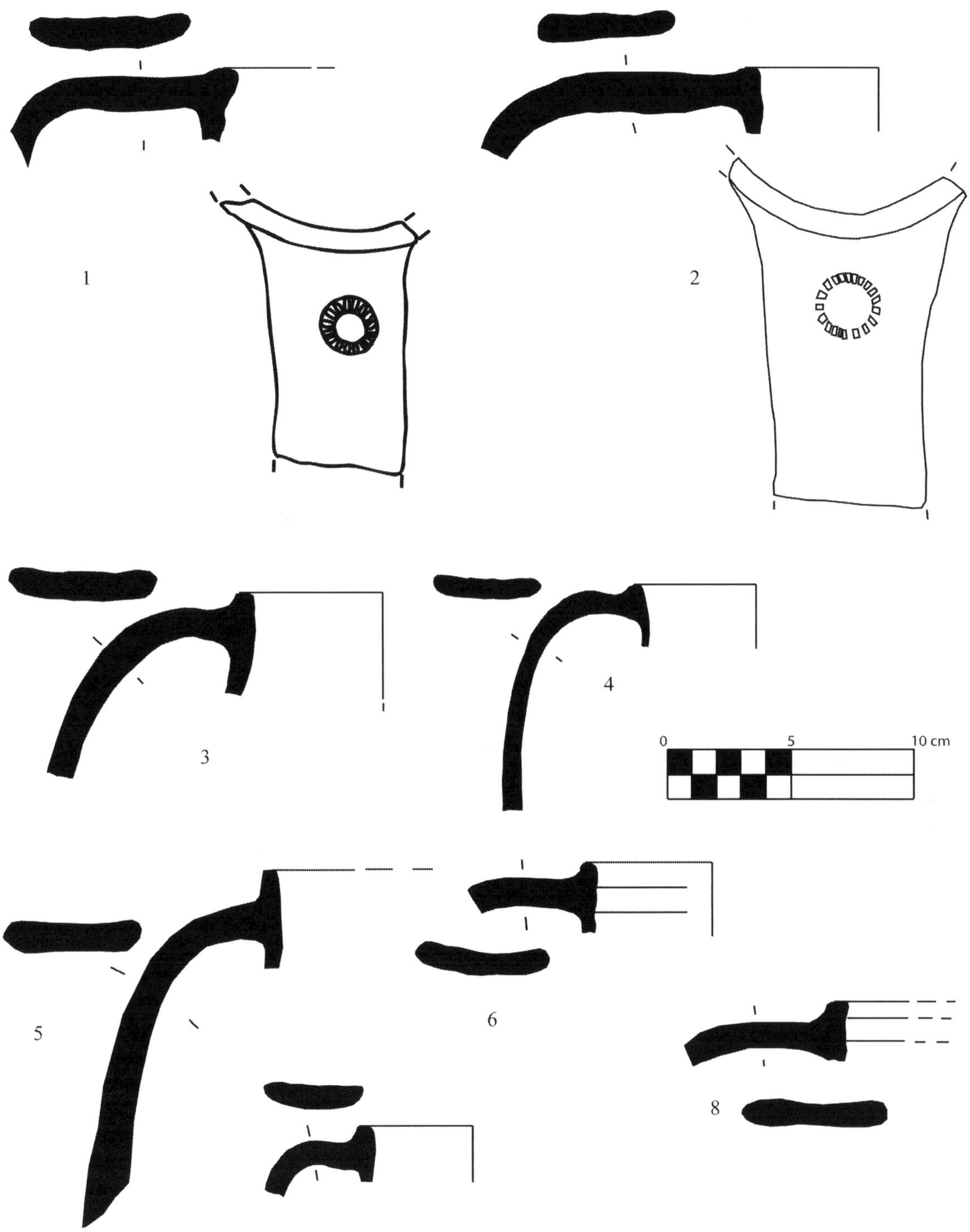

PLATE XCV

Otranto 1 amphora type from Portus Scabris

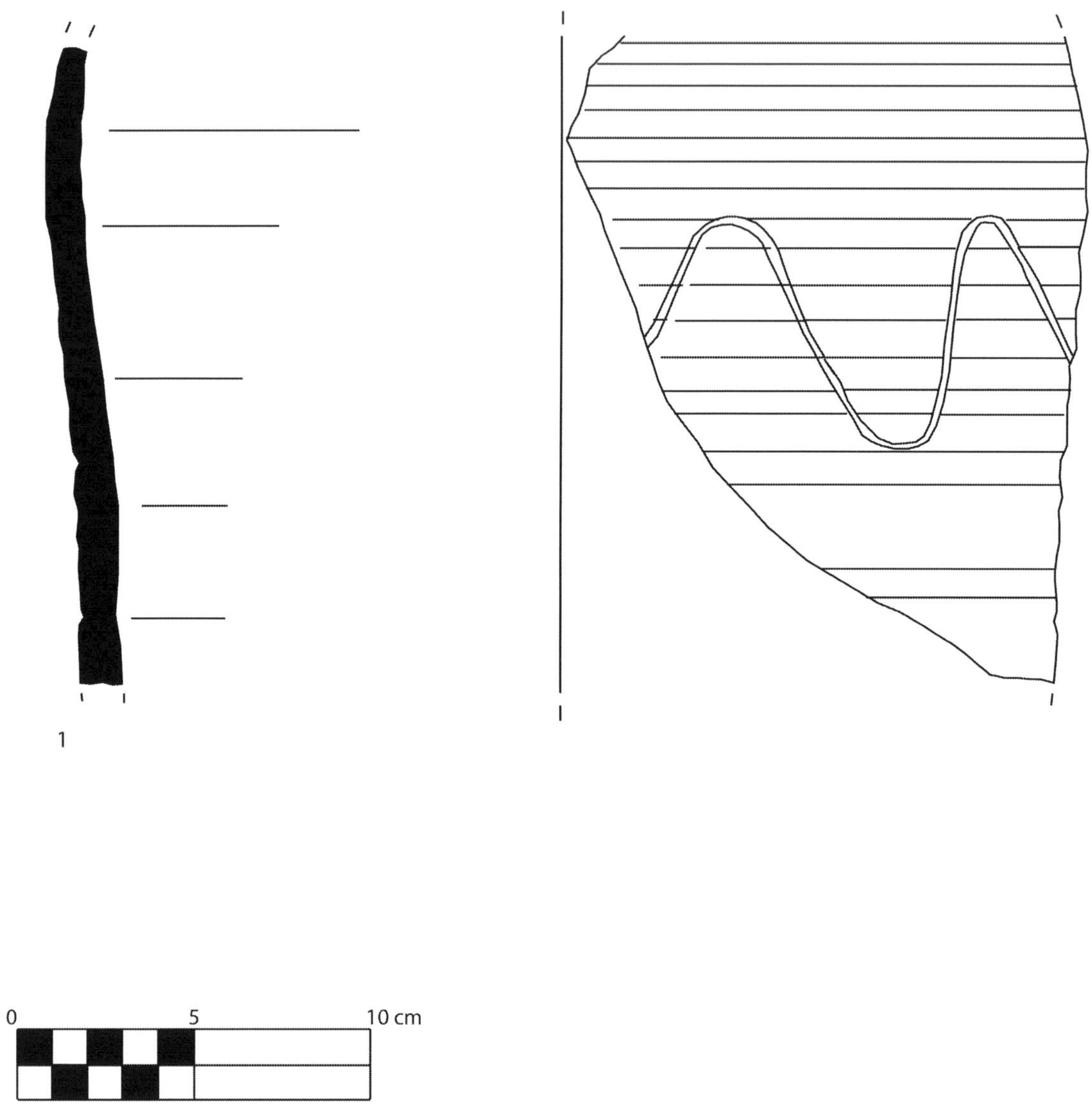

PLATE XCVI

Tunisian amphorae from Site D (Cala del Barbiere-Punta Ala)

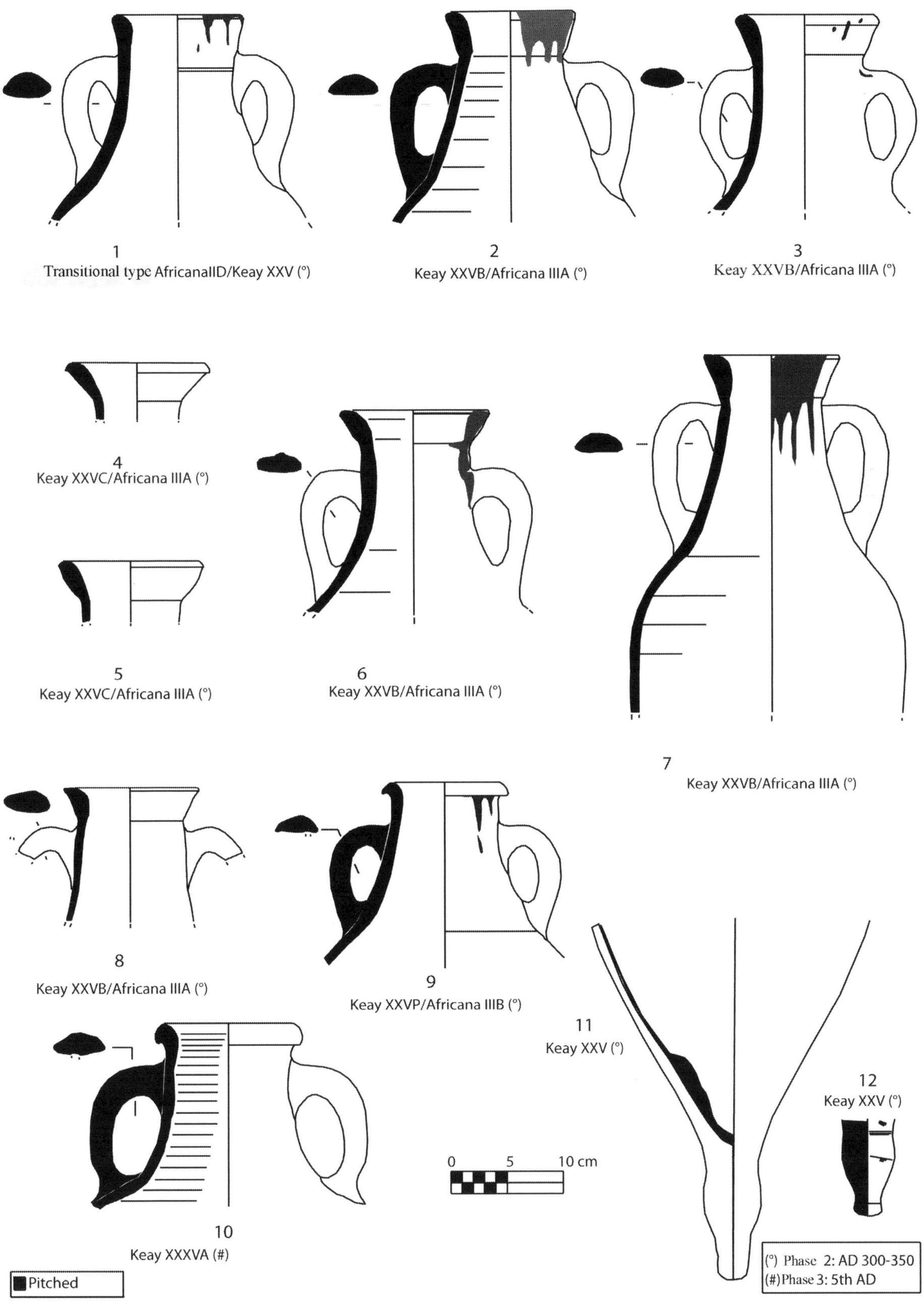

PLATE XCVII

ARS from Site D (Cala del Barbiere-Punta Ala)

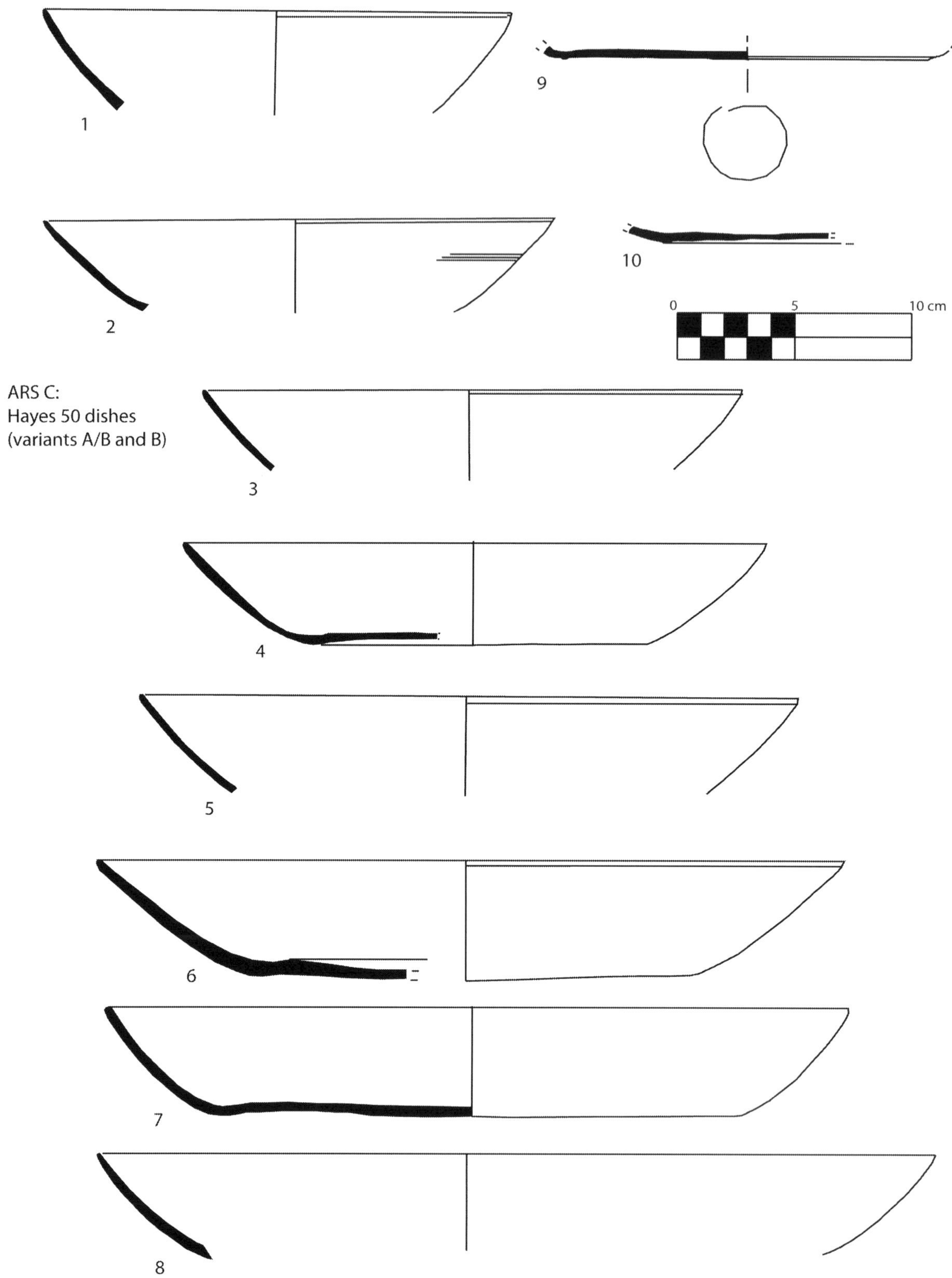

PLATE XCVIII

Tyrrhenian and Tunisian kitchen wares from Site D (Cala del Barbiere-Punta Ala)

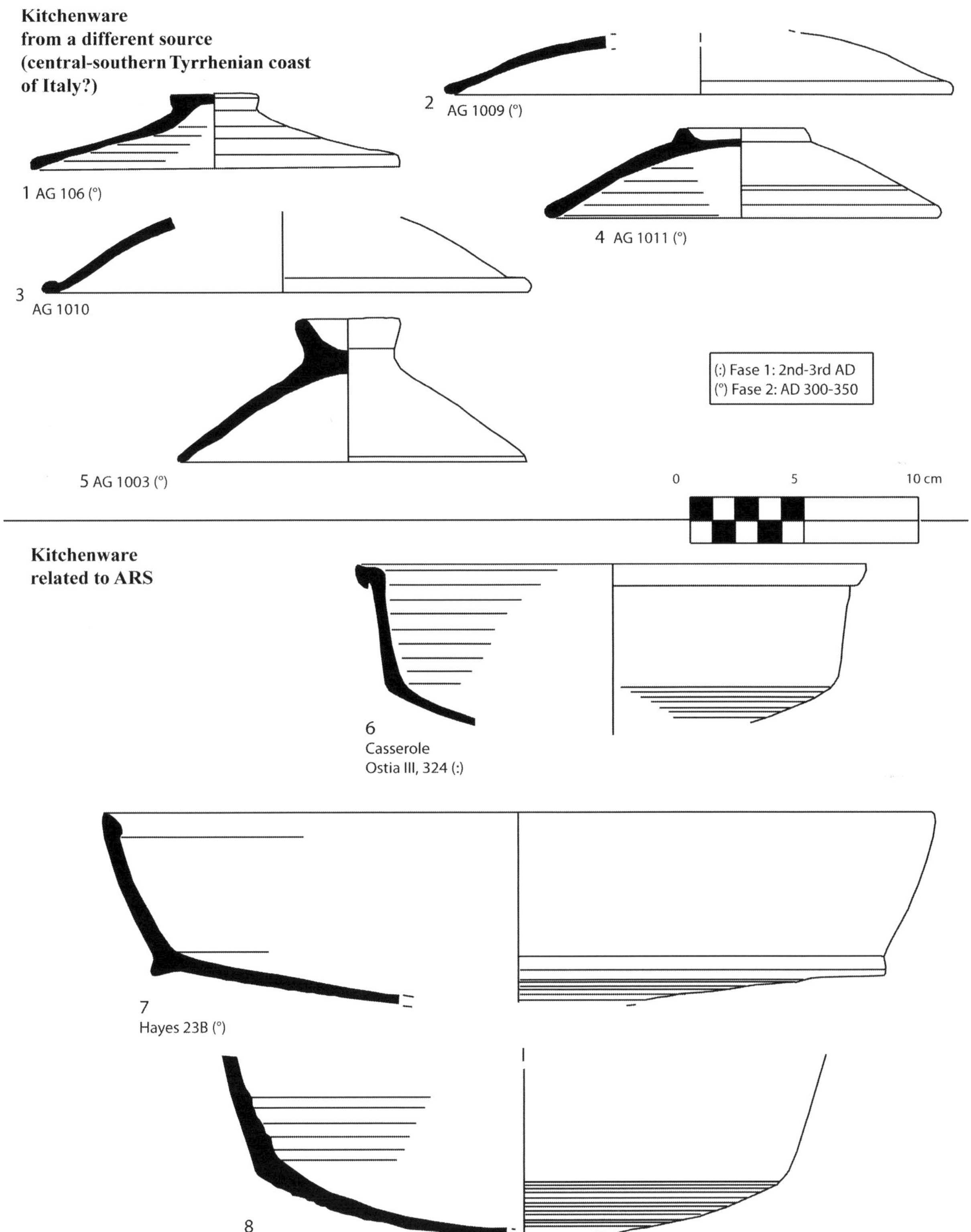

PLATE XCIX

Tunisian and regional kitchen ware from Site D (Cala del Barbiere-Punta Ala)

Kitchenware related to ARS

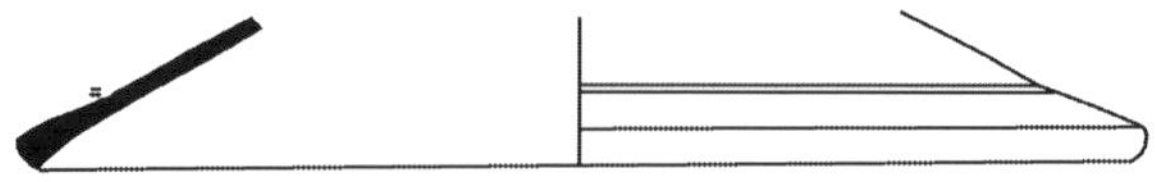

1 Hayes 185 variant/Bonifay culinaire type 9C (:)

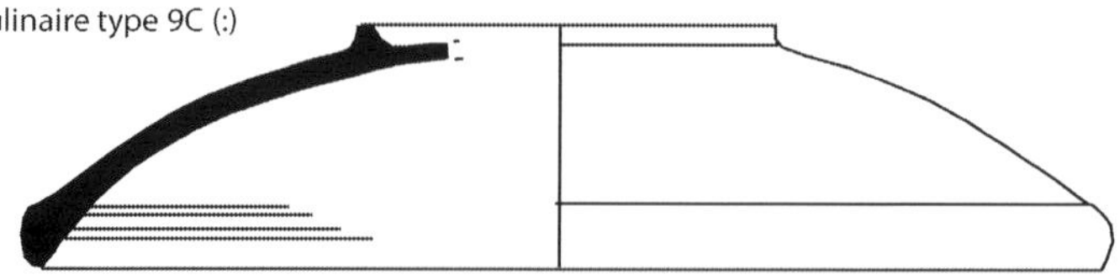

2 Hayes 196 B (:)

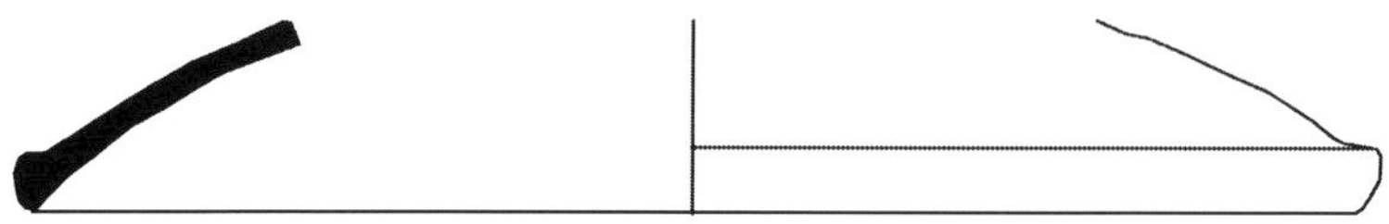

3 Hayes 196 B (:)

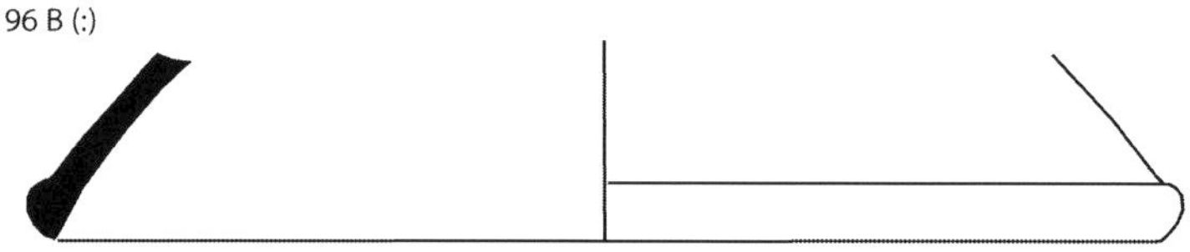

4 Hayes 196 late variant (°)

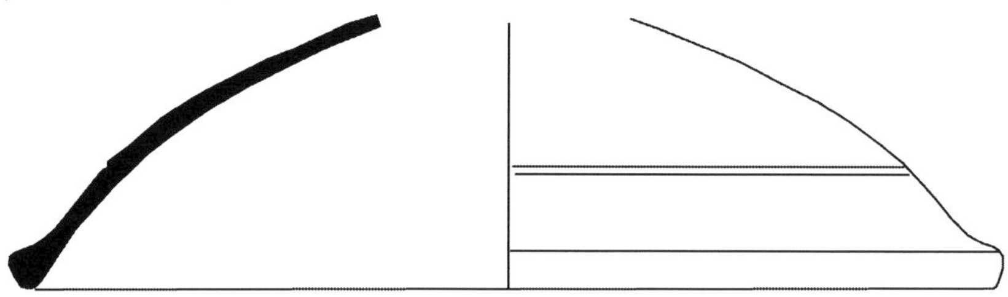

5 Hayes 196 late variant (°)

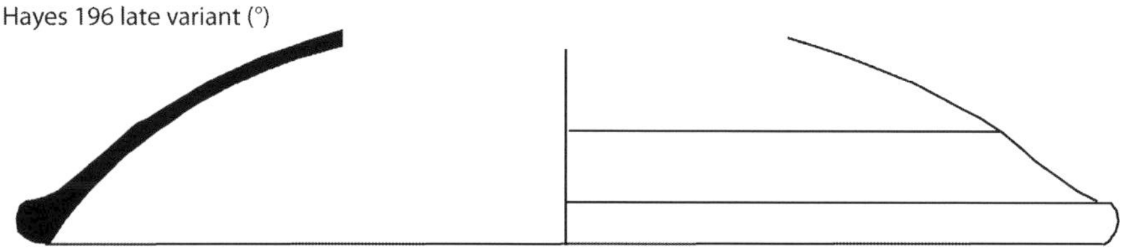

6 Hayes 196 late variant (°)

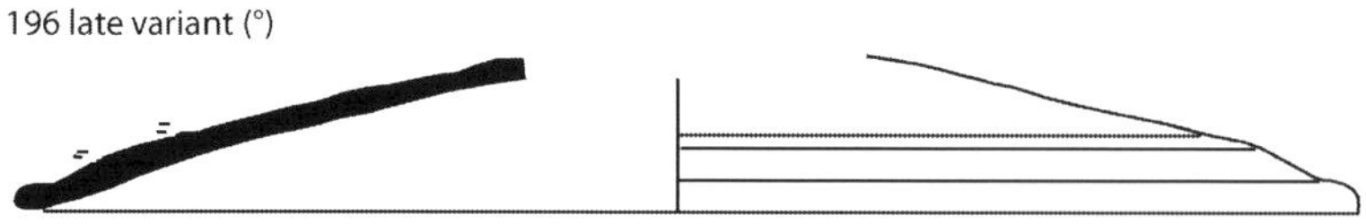

7 Fulford, CW, lids 4.3 (°)

(:) Phase 1: 2nd-3rd AD
(°)Phase2: AD 300-350

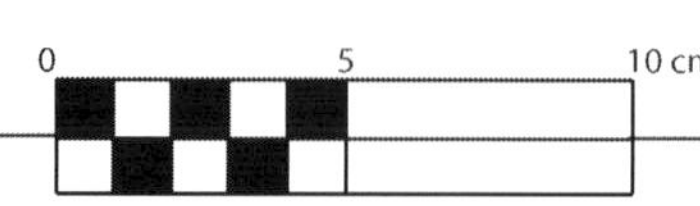

8 AG 1003 (°) ?

Kitchenware from a different source (central-southern Tyrrhenian coast of Italy ?)

PLATE C

Miscellaneous ceramic classes from Site D (Cala del Barbiere-Punta Ala)

Tunisian coarse ware

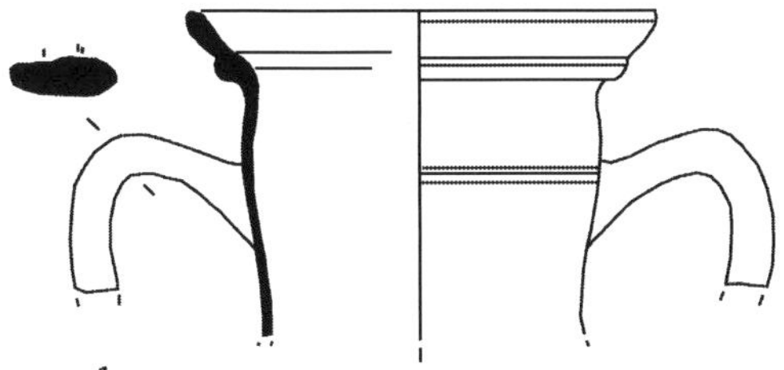

1
Fulford, CW, closed forms 24.1 similis (#)

Ingobbiata di rosso **ware (Tuscan product?)**

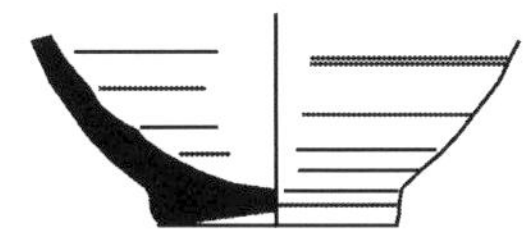

2 Closed form (°)

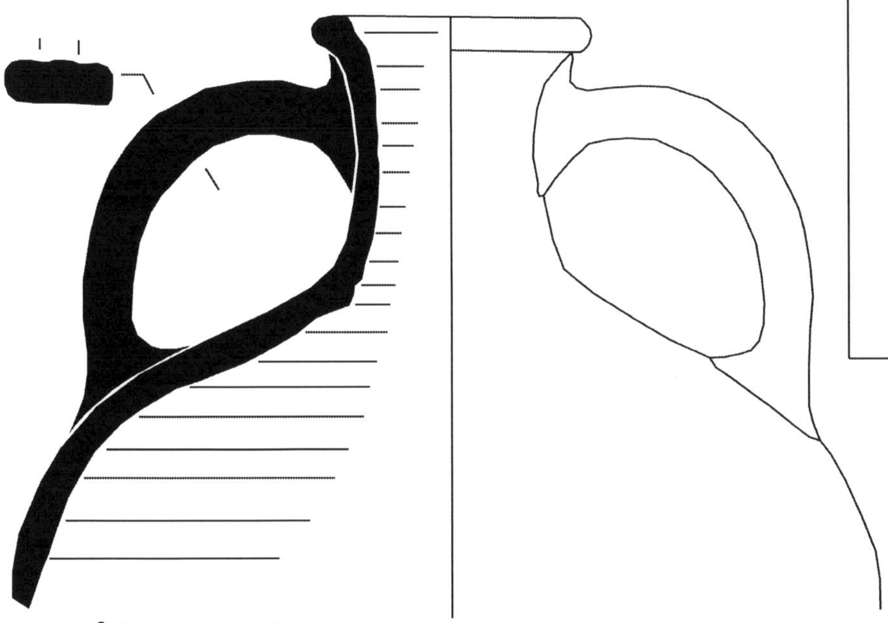

3 Empoli amphora (°)

4 Almagro 51C (°)

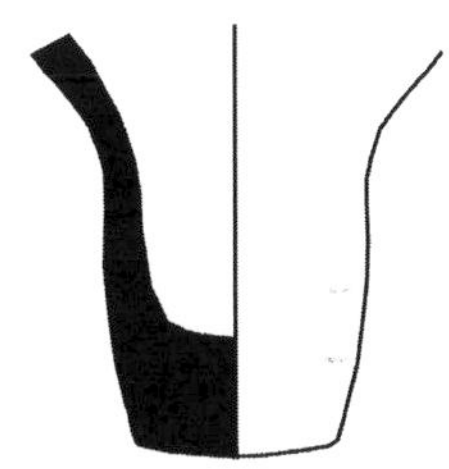

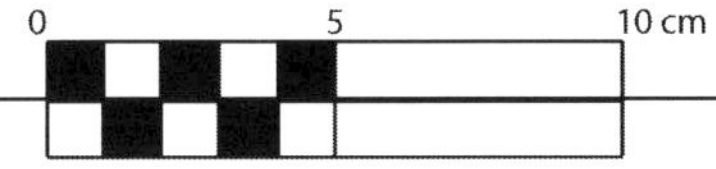

(:) Phase 1: 2nd-3rd AD
(°)Phase 2: AD 300-350
(#)Phase 3: 5th AD

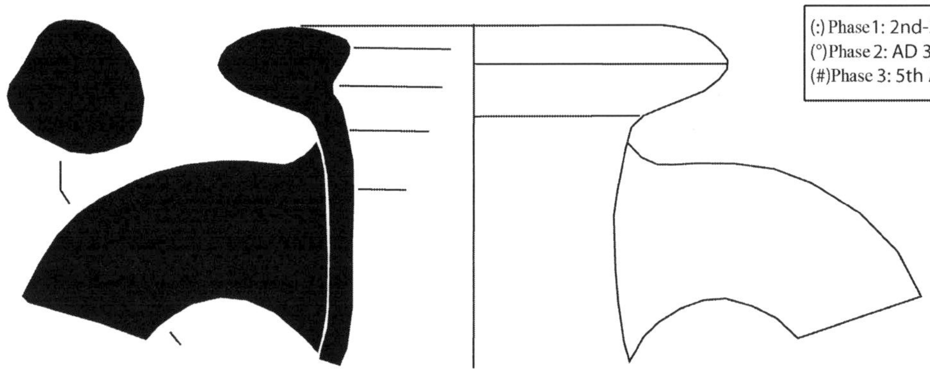

5 Dressel 20 (:)

PLATE CI

6 th century AD sporadic finds from the area of Cala del Barbiere (Punta Ala)

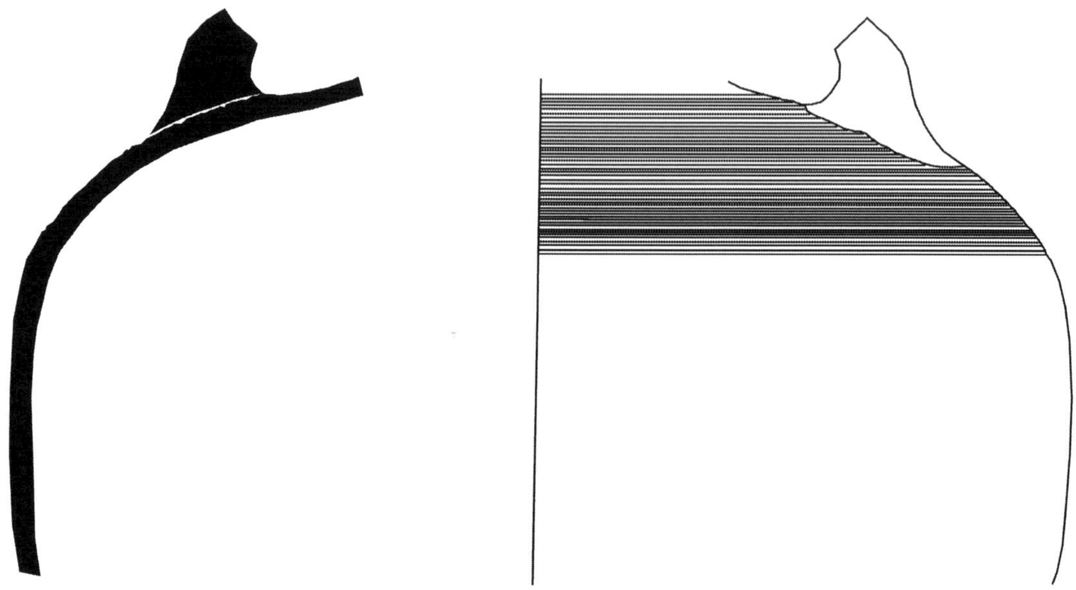

1 LR2 amphora type

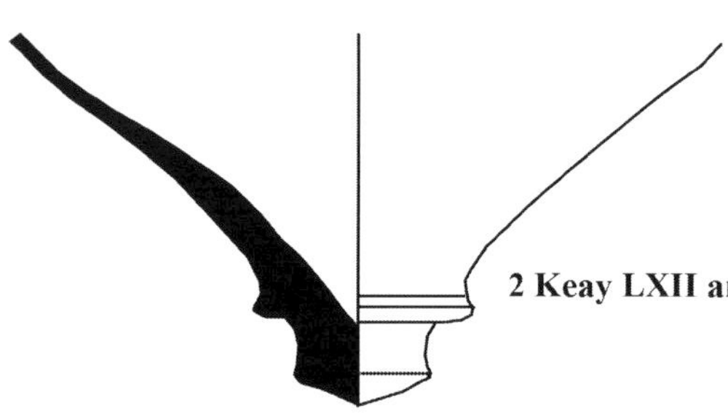

2 Keay LXII amphora

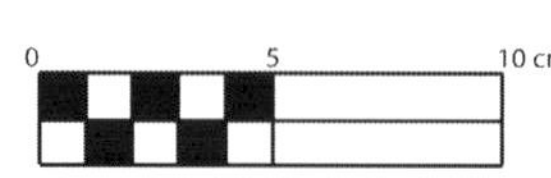

PLATE CII

Early medieval ceramics from Podere Serratone

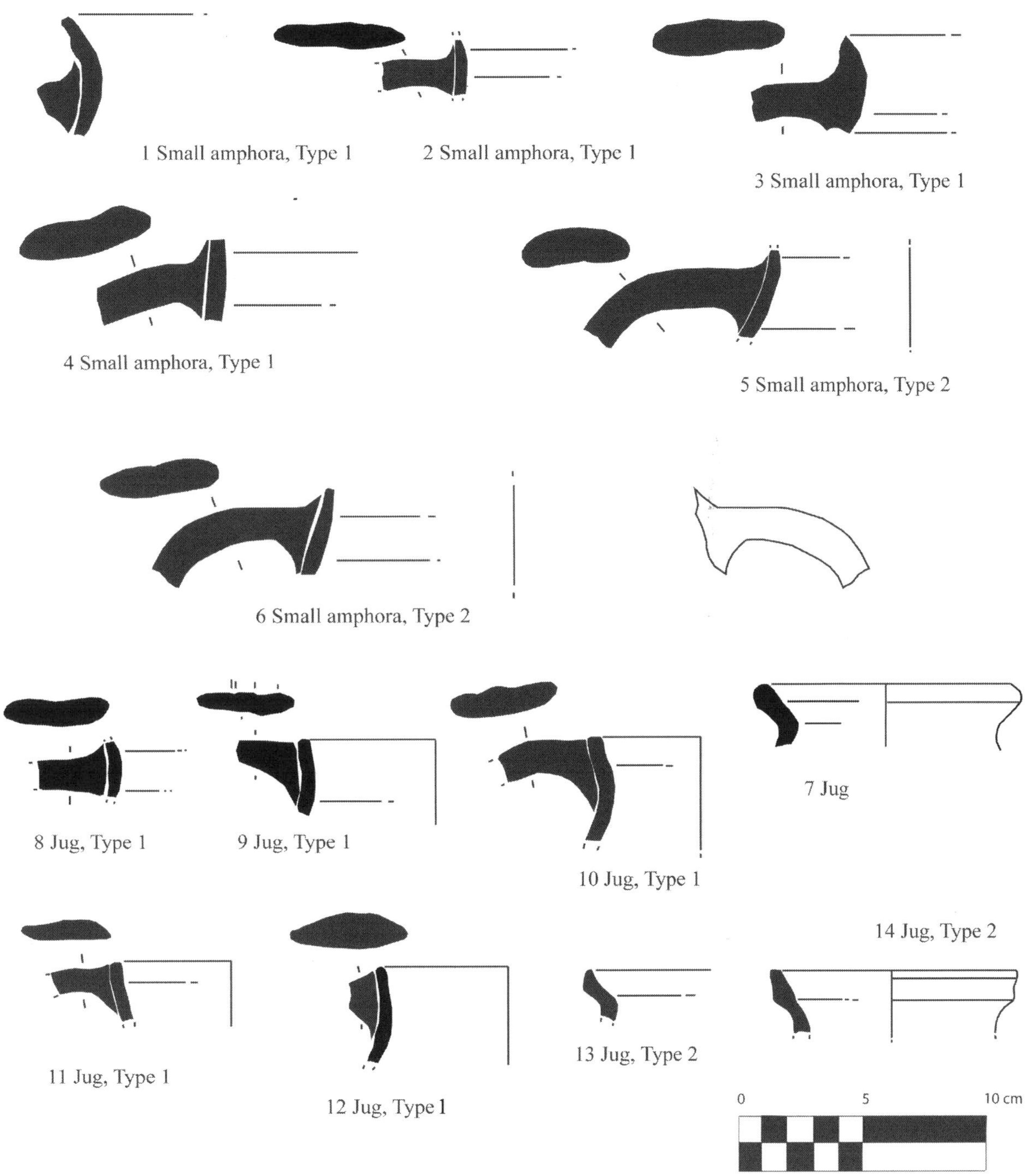

PLATE CIII

Early medieval ceramics from Podere Searratone

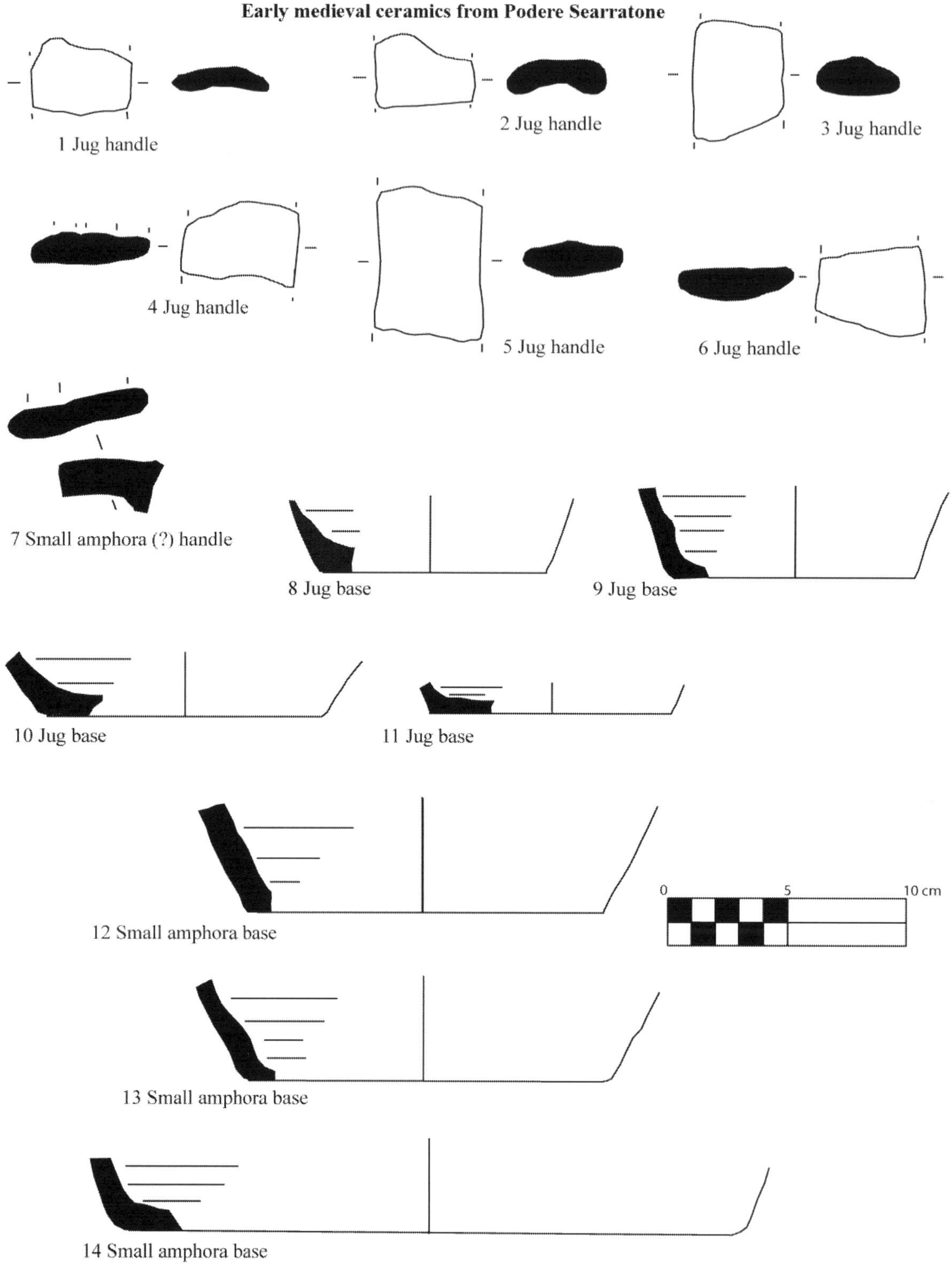

PLATE CIV

Early medieval ceramics from Podere Searratone

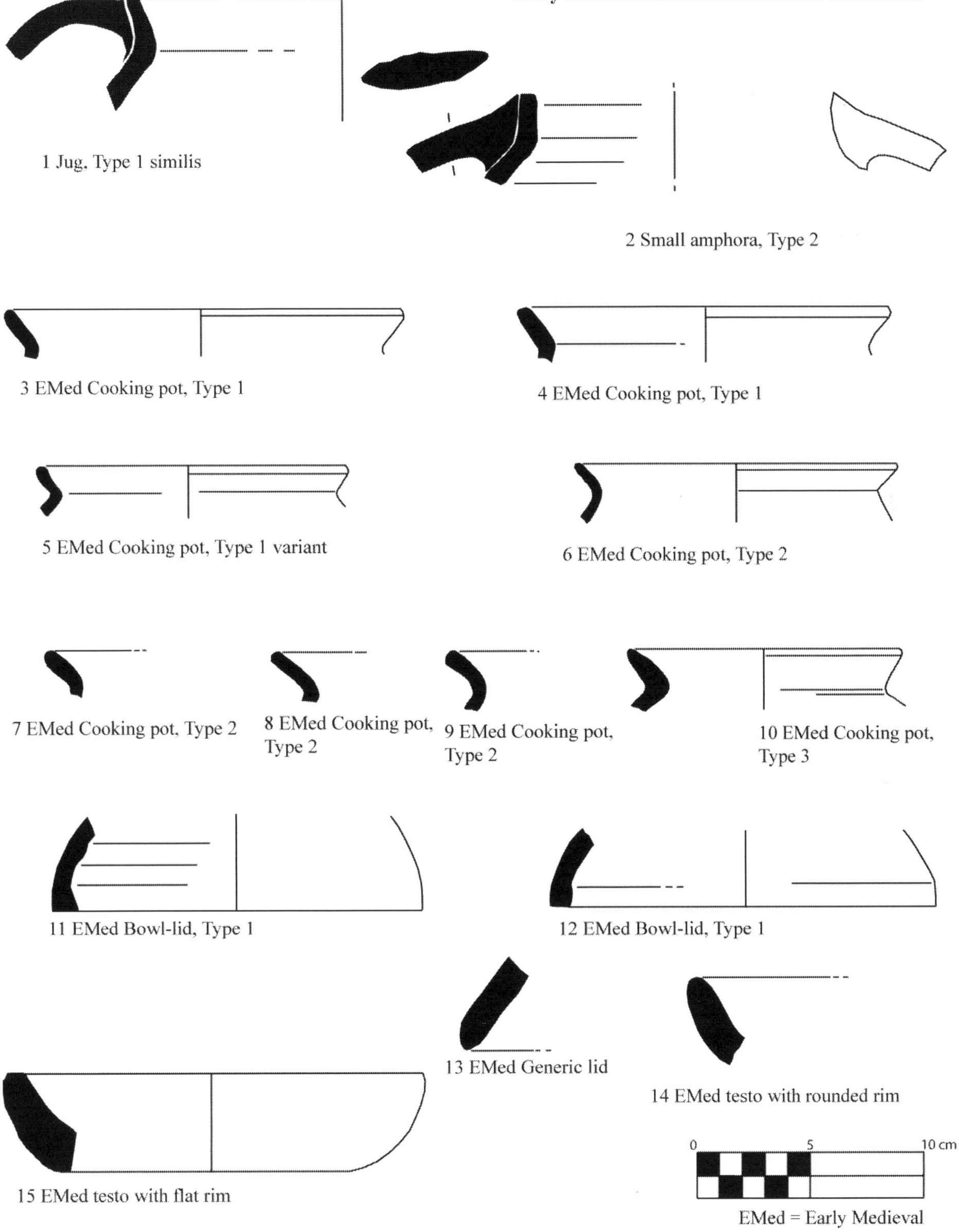

PLATE CV

Early medieval ceramics from Casa Andreoni

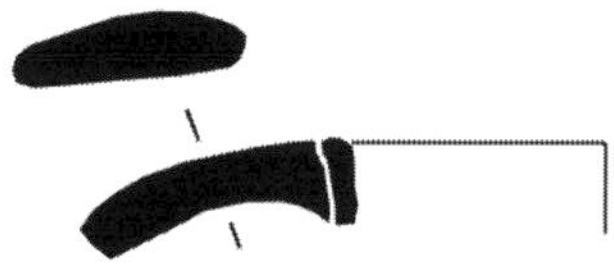

1 EMed Jug, Type 1

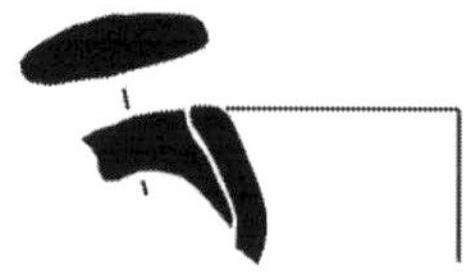

2 EMed Jug, Type 1

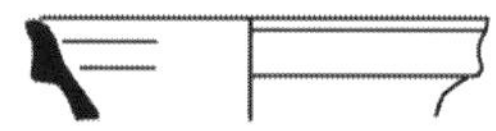

3 EMed Jug, Type 2

4 EMed painted ware

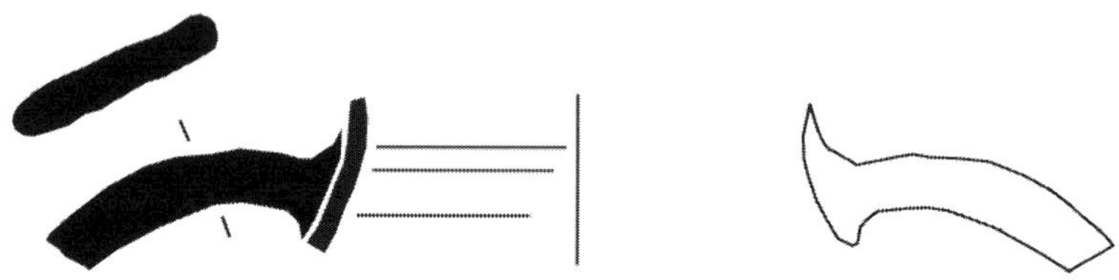

5 EMed small amphora, Type 2

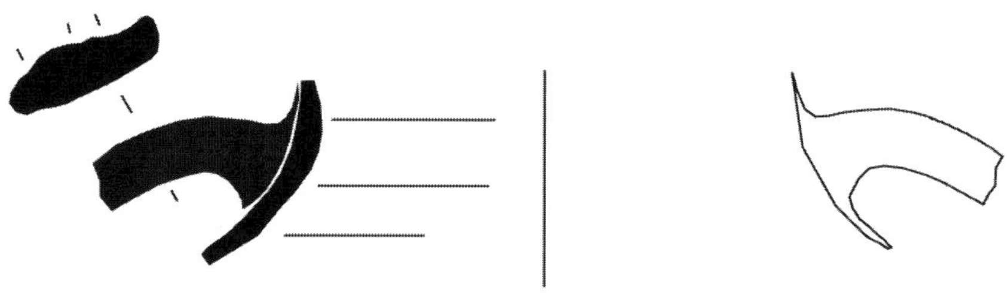

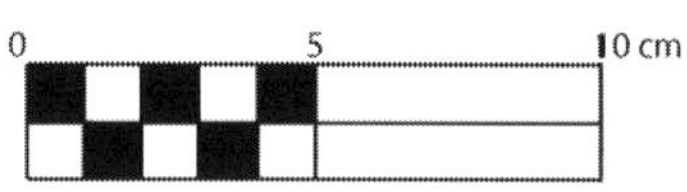

6 EMed small amphora, Type 2

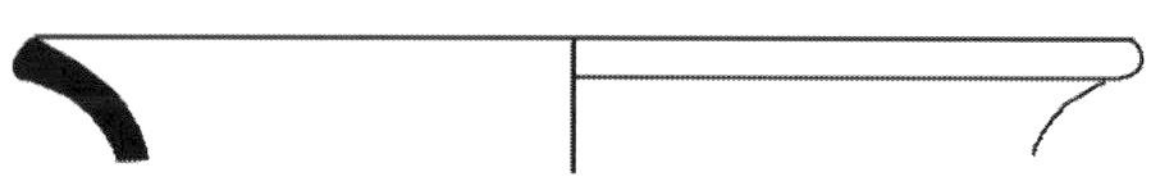

7 EMed large jug, Type 1

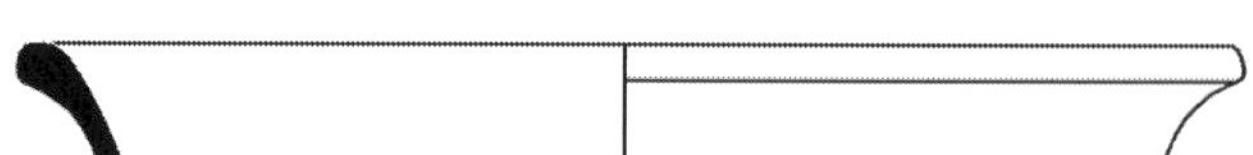

8 EMed large jug, Type 1

PLATE CVI

Early medieval ceramics from Casa Andreoni

1 SU 103. EMed Small amphora, Type 2 (thermoluminescence dosimetry date AD 850±65)

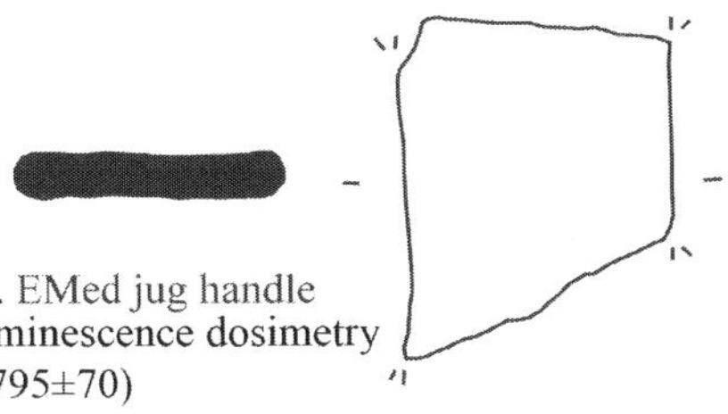

2 SU 103. EMed jug handle (thermoluminescence dosimetry date AD 795±70)

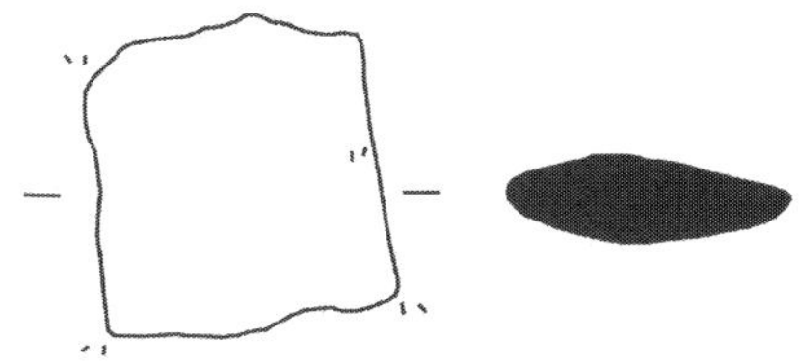

3 SU 103. EMed jug handle

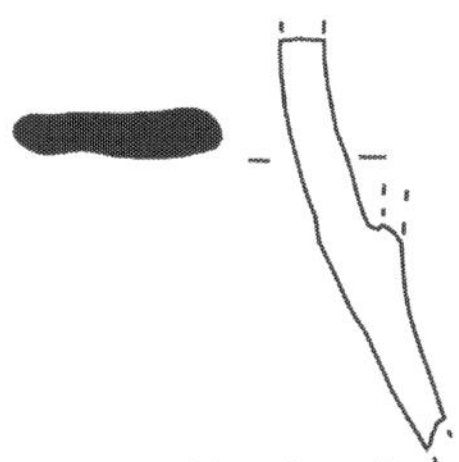

4 SU 103. EMed jug handle (thermoluminescence dosimetry date AD 815±60)

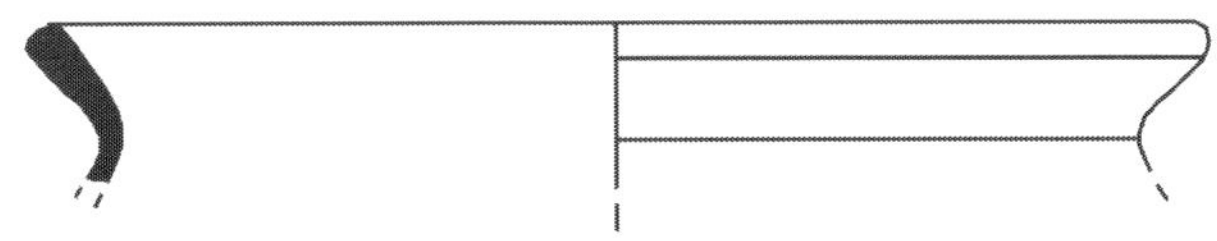

5 SU 103. EMed large jug

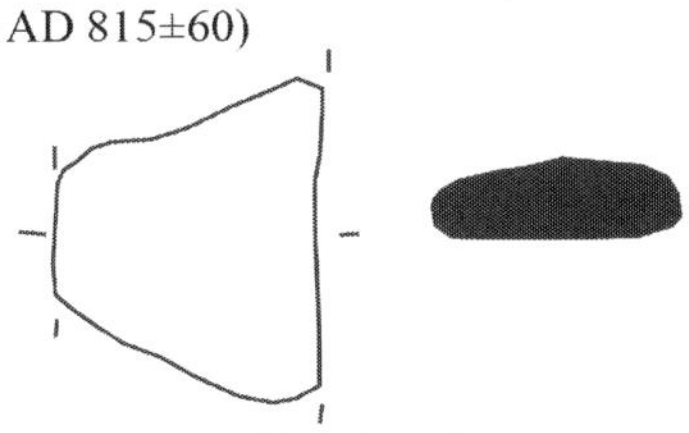

6 SU 101. EMed jug handle

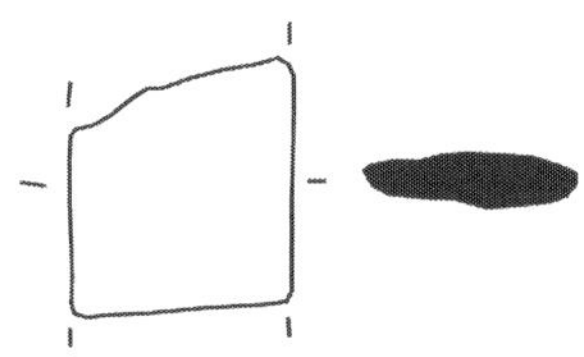

7 SU 101. EMed jug handle

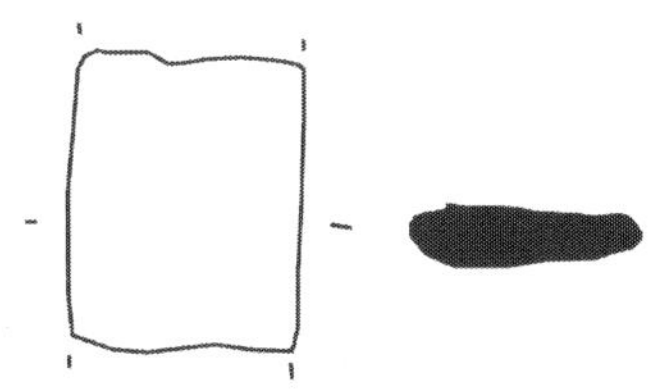

8 SU 101. EMed jug handle

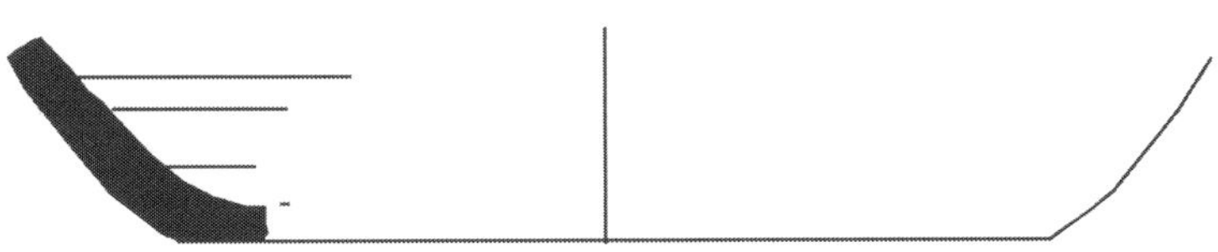

9 SU 101. EMed Small amphora base

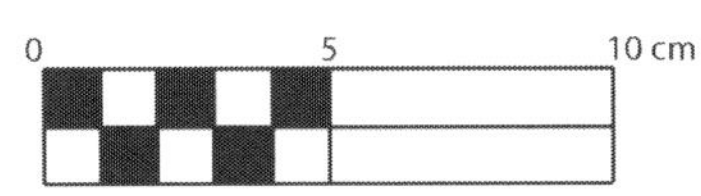

10 SU 101. EMed Small amphora base

EMed = Early Medieval

PLATE CVII

EMed = Early Medieval

Early medieval ceramics from Casa Andreoni

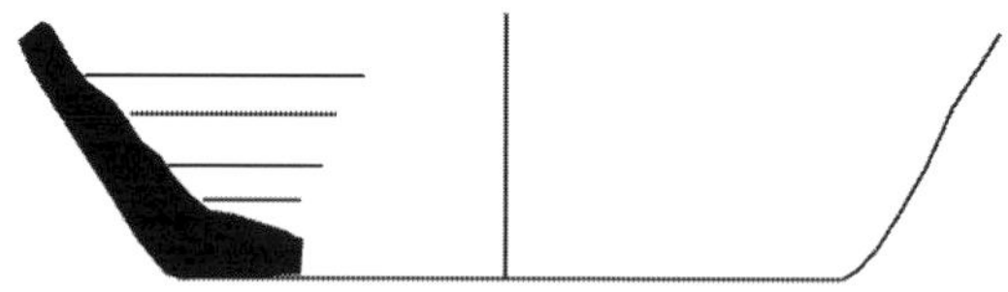

1 SU 103. EMed Small amphora base

2 SU 103. EMed Cooking pot, Type 6

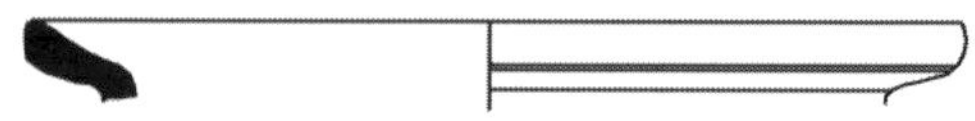

3 SU 103. EMed Cooking pot, Type 6 (variant)

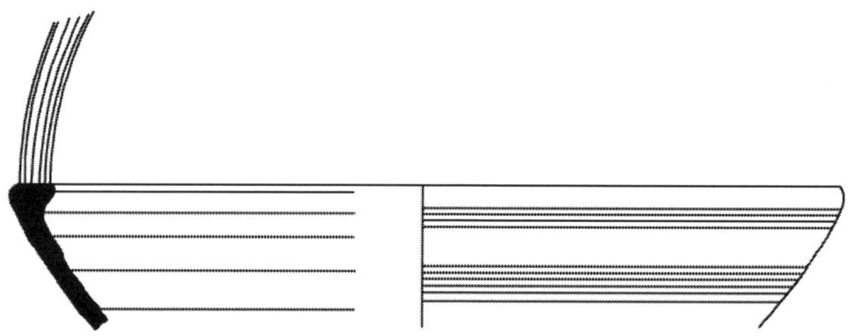

4 SU 103. EMed Bowl-lid, Type 1 (thermoluminescence dosimetry date AD 855±55)

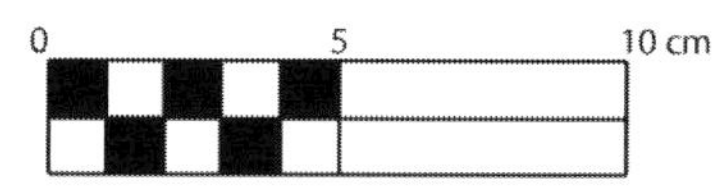

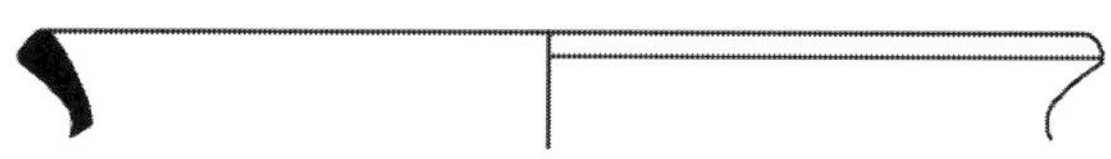

5 SU 103. EMed Cooking pot, Type 1 (variant)

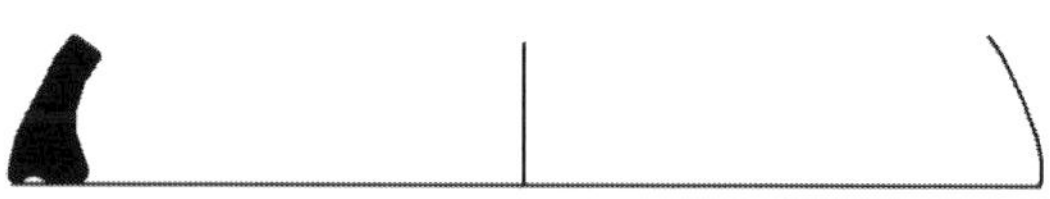

6 SU 101. EMed Bowl-lid

7 SU 101. EMed Jug handle

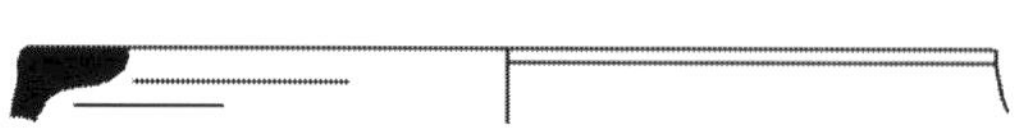

8 SU 605. EMed Basin, Type 1

9 SU 605. EMed Cooking pot, Type 4 (variant)

PLATE CVIII

Early medieval ceramics from Casa Andreoni

1 EMed Cooking pot, Type 4

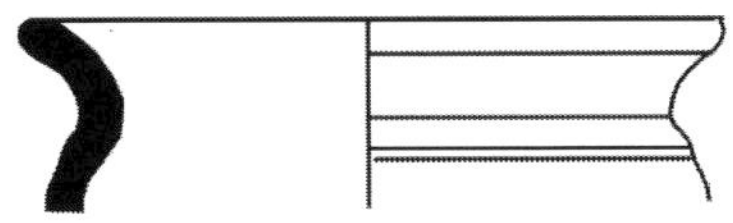

2 EMed Cooking pot, Type 4

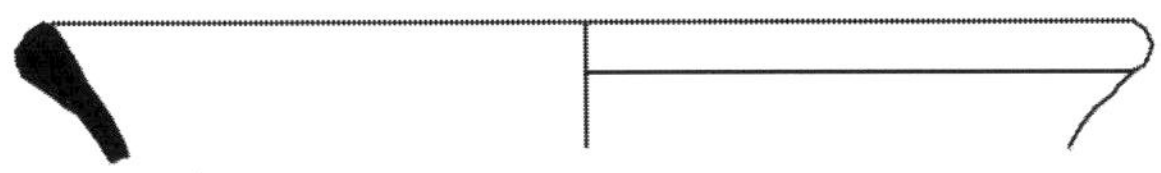

3 EMed Cooking pot, Type 1/Type 4 (variant)

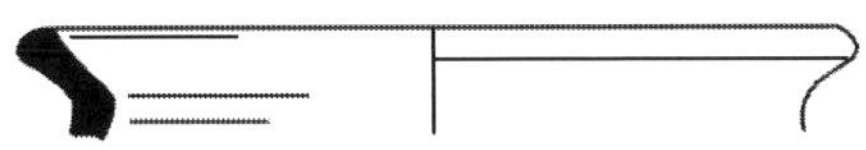

4 EMed Cooking pot, Type 6

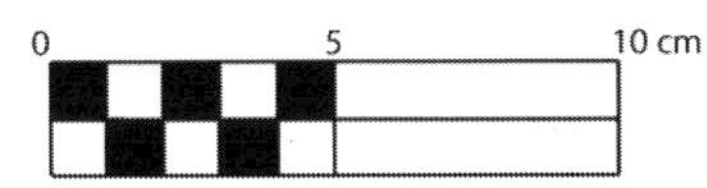

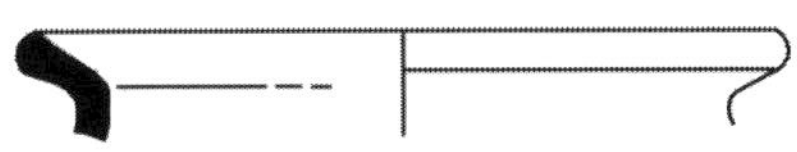

5 EMed Cooking pot, Type 6

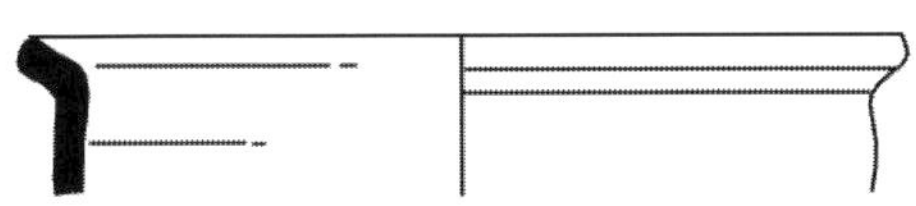

6 EMed Cooking pot, Type 5

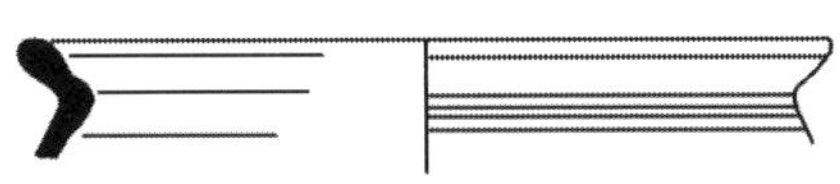

7 EMed Cooking pot, Type 1 variant

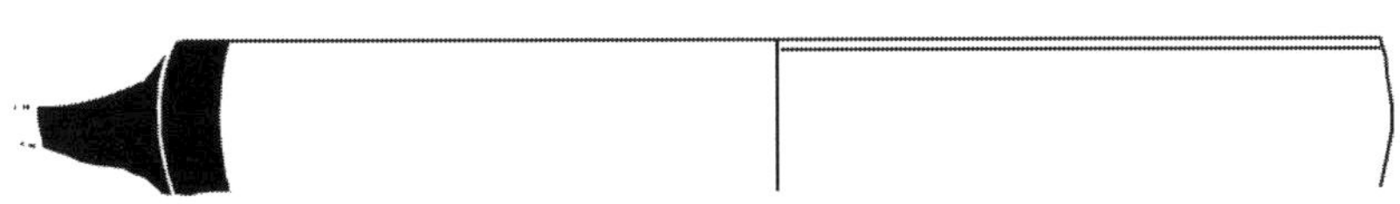

8 EMed handled cooking-pan (tegame)

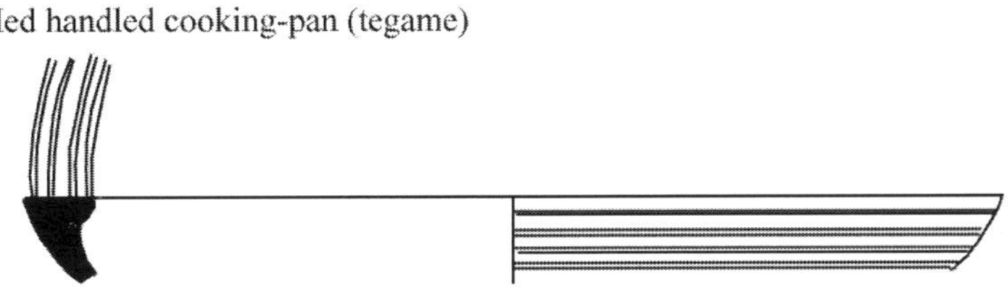

9 EMed bowl-lid, Type 1 (combed variant)

EMed = Early Medieval

PLATE CIX

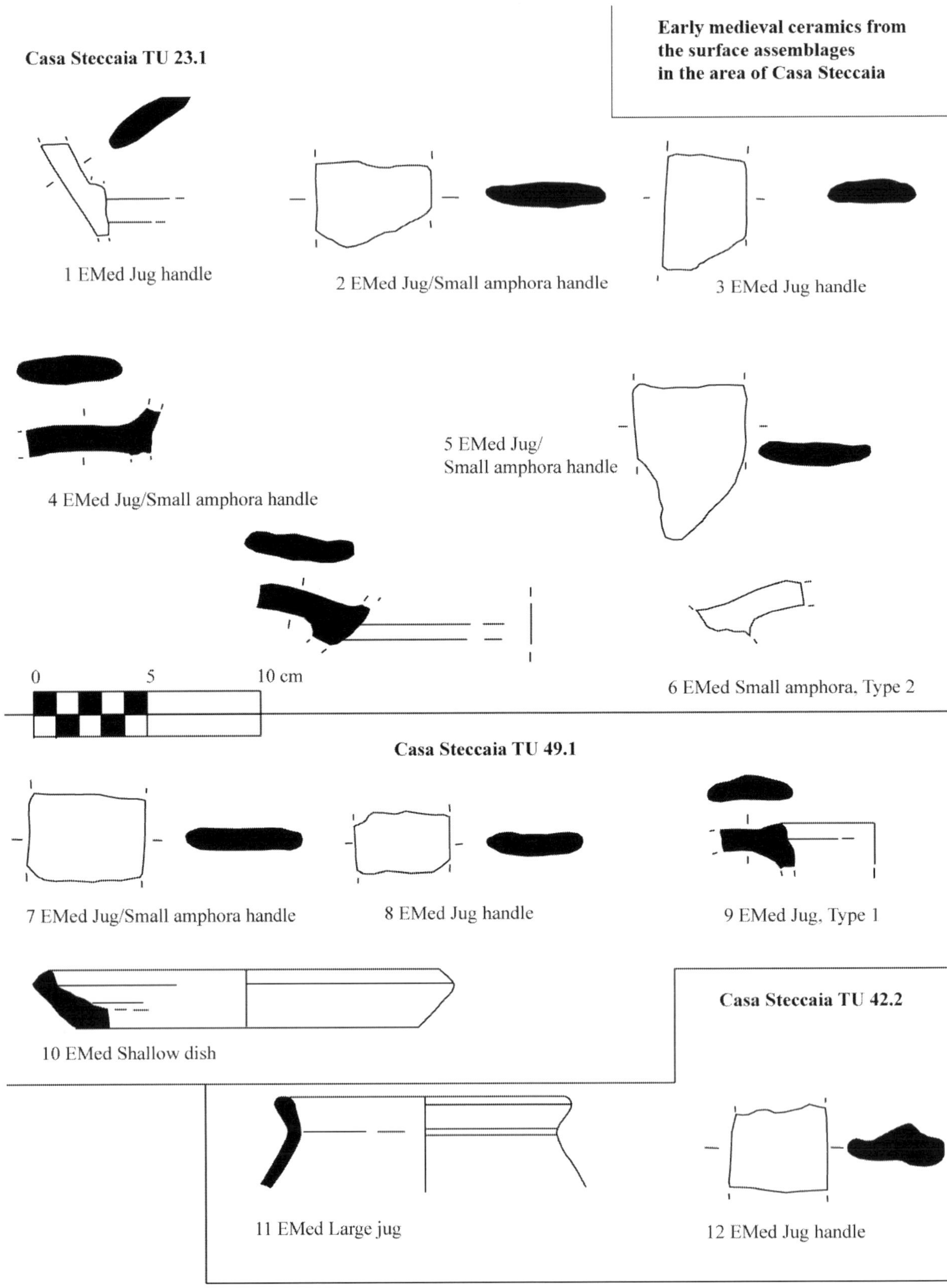

EMed = Early Medieval

PLATE CX

9th and late 9th to 11th AD ceramics from the surface assemblages at *San Martino de plano*

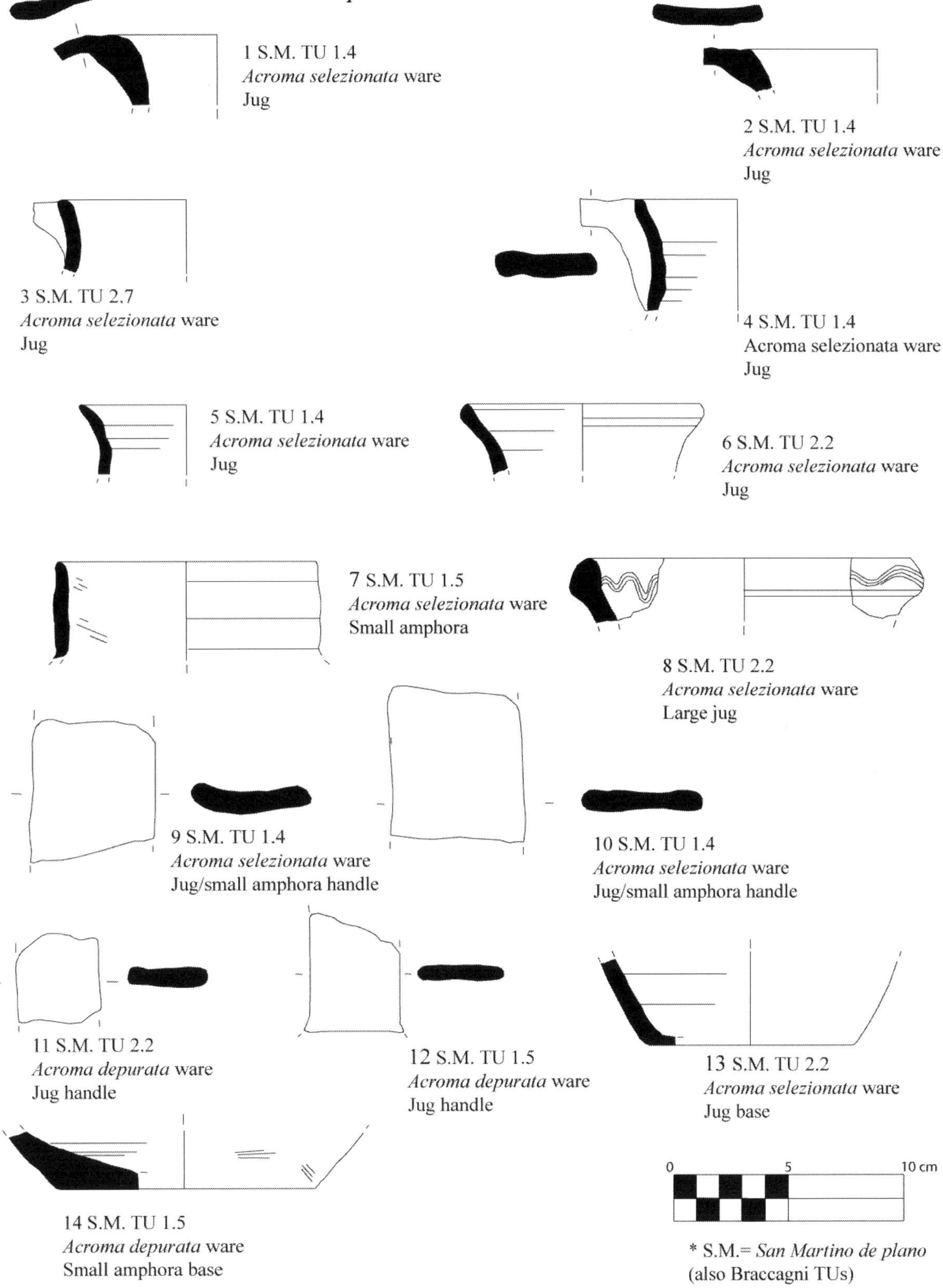

PLATE CXI

9th and late 9th to 11th AD ceramics from the surface assemblages at *San Martino de plano*

* S.M.= *San Martino de plano* (also Braccagni TUs)

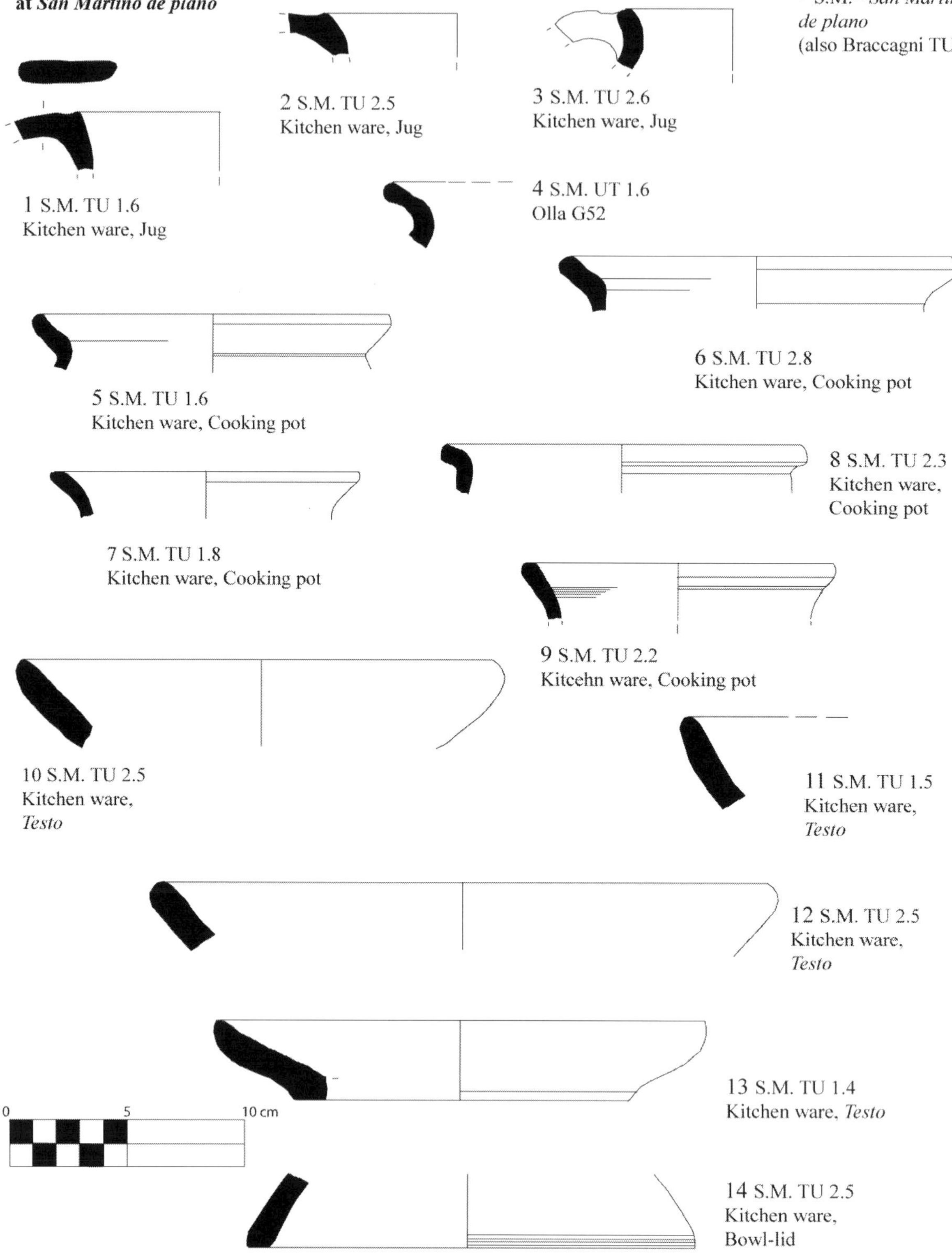

1 S.M. TU 1.6
Kitchen ware, Jug

2 S.M. TU 2.5
Kitchen ware, Jug

3 S.M. TU 2.6
Kitchen ware, Jug

4 S.M. UT 1.6
Olla G52

5 S.M. TU 1.6
Kitchen ware, Cooking pot

6 S.M. TU 2.8
Kitchen ware, Cooking pot

7 S.M. TU 1.8
Kitchen ware, Cooking pot

8 S.M. TU 2.3
Kitchen ware, Cooking pot

9 S.M. TU 2.2
Kitcehn ware, Cooking pot

10 S.M. TU 2.5
Kitchen ware, *Testo*

11 S.M. TU 1.5
Kitchen ware, *Testo*

12 S.M. TU 2.5
Kitchen ware, *Testo*

13 S.M. TU 1.4
Kitchen ware, *Testo*

14 S.M. TU 2.5
Kitchen ware, Bowl-lid

PLATE CXII

Late 8th to 9th AD coarse wares from the rescue excavation at *San Martino de plano*

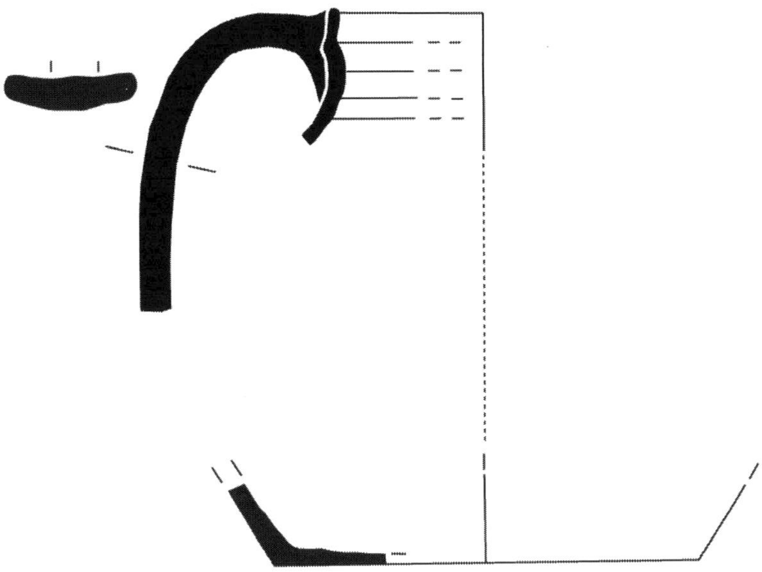

1 SU 4010. Jug, Type 1

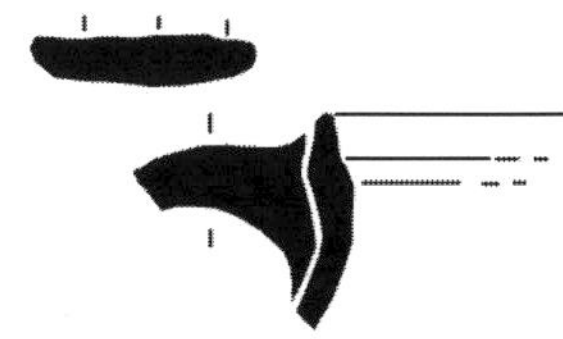

2 SU 4010. Jug, Type 1

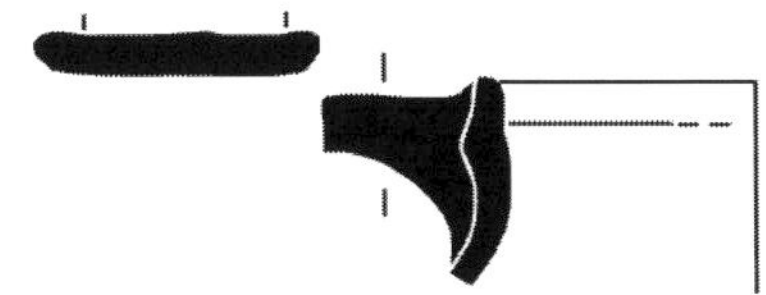

3. SU 4010. Jug, Type 1

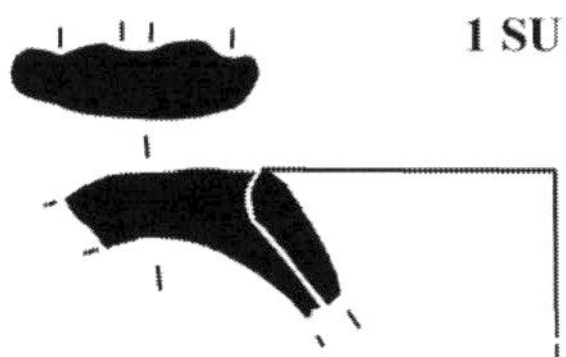

4 SU 4010. Jug, Type 2

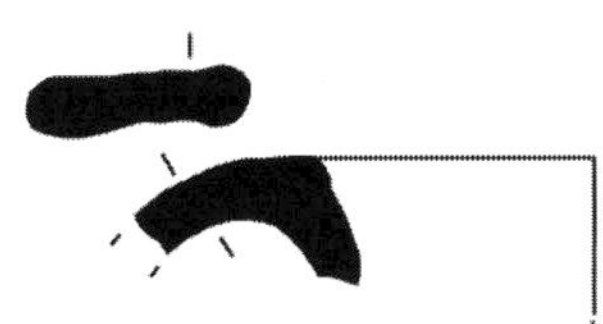

5 SU 4010. Jug, Type 3

6 SU 4010. Jug, Type 4

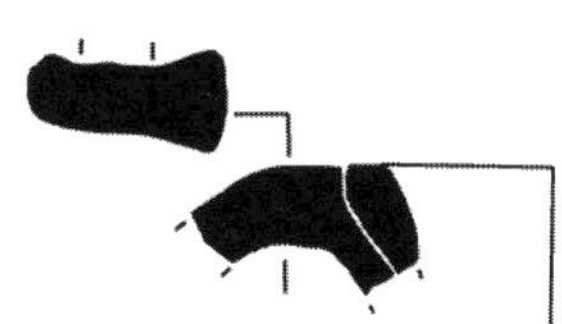

7 SU 4010. Jug, Type 5

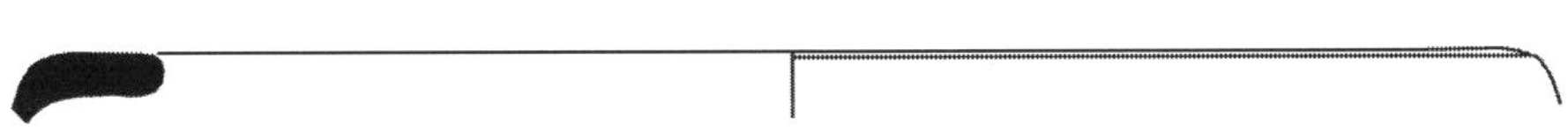

8 SU 4009. Basin with inverted and flattened rim

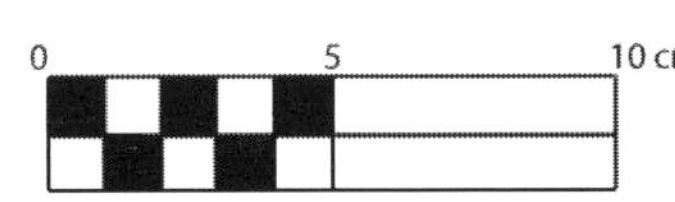

PLATE CXIII

Late 8th to 9th AD coarse wares and late Roman residuals from the rescue excavation at *San Martino de plano*

1 SU 4009. Small amphora

2 SU 4010. Small amphora

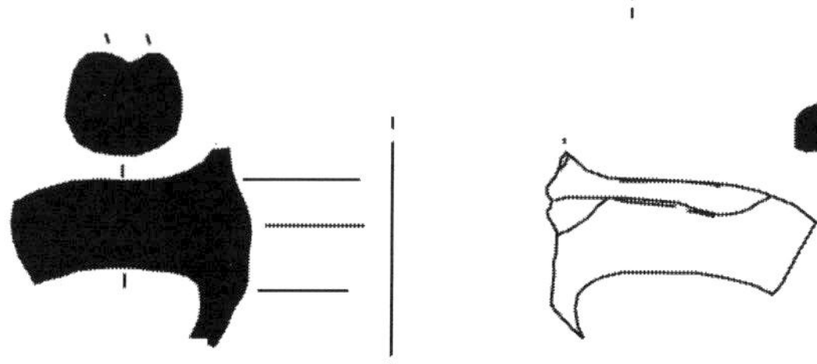

3 SU 4010. Small amphora

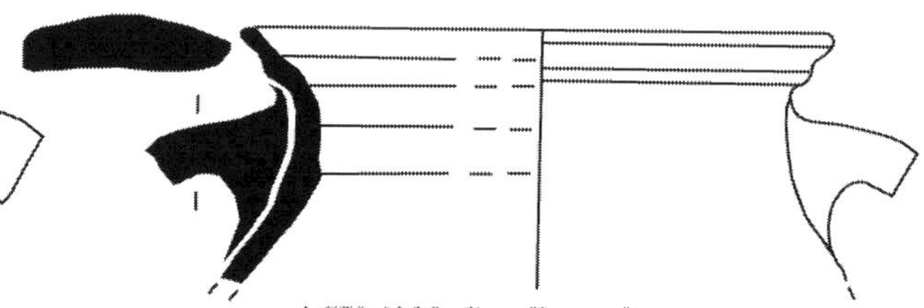

4 SU 4009. Small amphora

9th century AD cooking pots from *San Martino de plano*

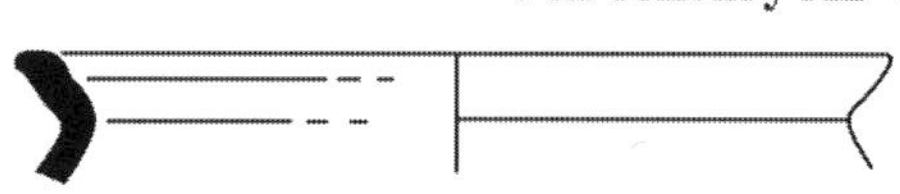

5 SU 4010. Cooking pot

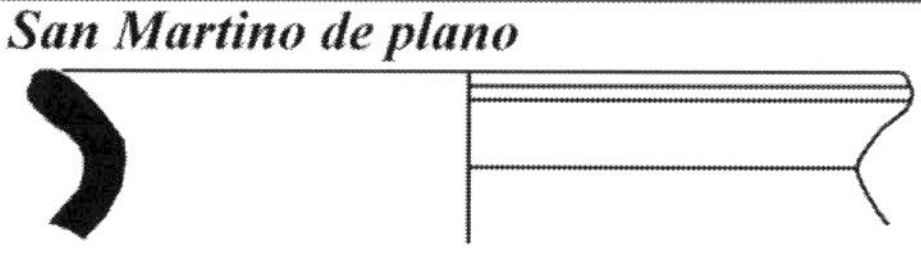

6 SU 4010. Cooking pot

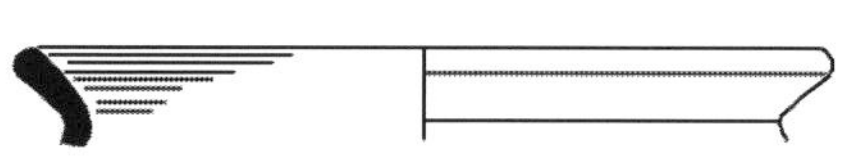

7 SU 4009. Cooking pot

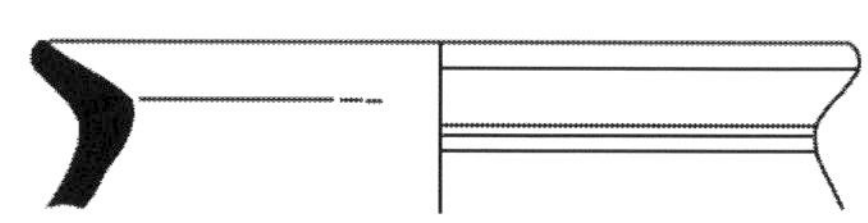

8 SU 4010. Cooking pot

Residual pottery from the 5th-6th centuries AD

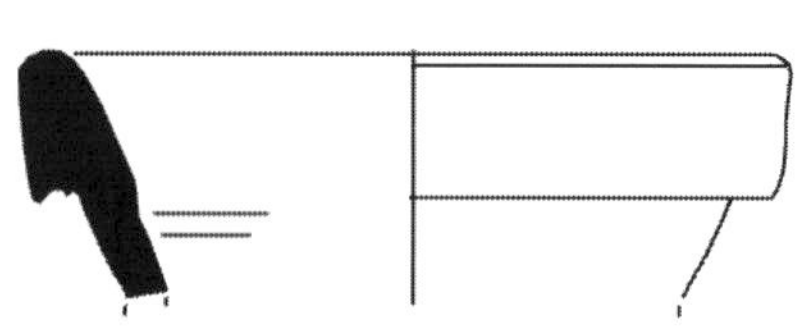

9 SU 4010. Keay LXII amphora

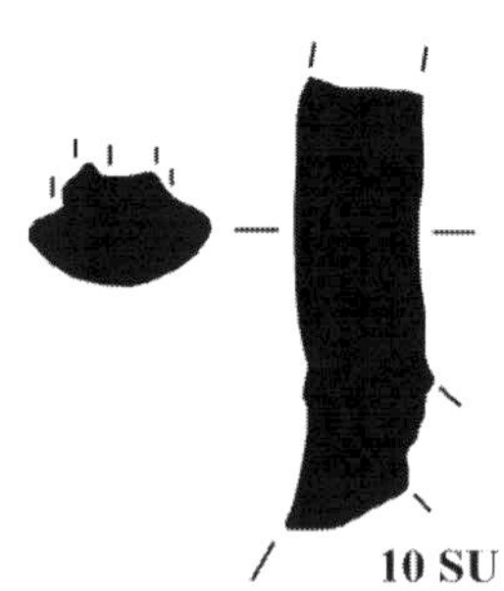

10 SU 4009. LRA1

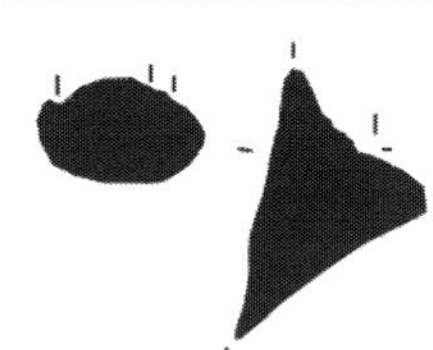

11 SU 4010. LRA 1

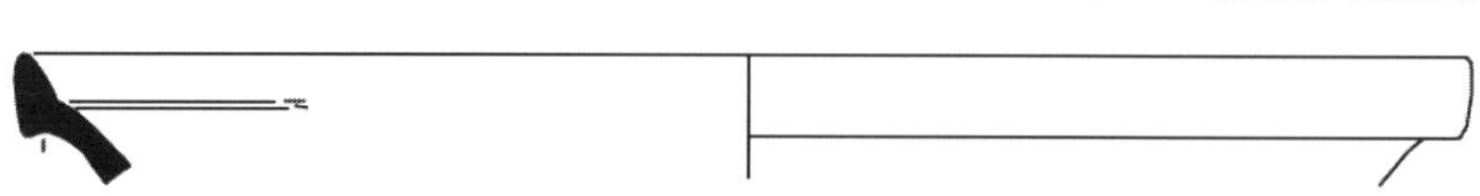

12 SU 4010. Hayes 61B (ARS)

13 SU 4009. Hayes 99 (ARS)

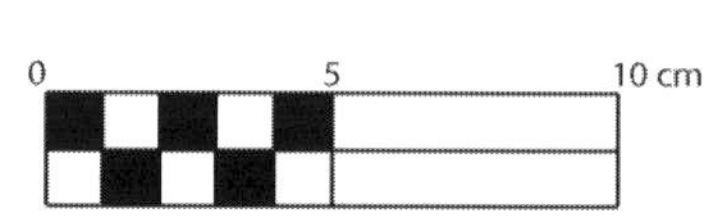

PLATE CXIV